THE PAPERS OF
THOMAS JEFFERSON

BARBARA B. OBERG
GENERAL EDITOR

THE PAPERS OF
Thomas Jefferson

Volume 38
1 July to 12 November 1802

BARBARA B. OBERG, EDITOR

JAMES P. MCCLURE AND ELAINE WEBER PASCU,
SENIOR ASSOCIATE EDITORS

TOM DOWNEY AND MARTHA J. KING,
ASSOCIATE EDITORS

W. BLAND WHITLEY, ASSISTANT EDITOR

LINDA MONACO, EDITORIAL ASSISTANT

JOHN E. LITTLE, RESEARCH ASSOCIATE

PRINCETON AND OXFORD
PRINCETON UNIVERSITY PRESS
2011

DEDICATED TO THE MEMORY OF

ADOLPH S. OCHS

PUBLISHER OF THE NEW YORK TIMES

1896-1935

WHO BY THE EXAMPLE OF A RESPONSIBLE

PRESS ENLARGED AND FORTIFIED

THE JEFFERSONIAN CONCEPT

OF A FREE PRESS

SUPPORTERS

THIS EDITION was made possible by an initial grant of $200,000 from The New York Times Company to Princeton University. Contributions from many foundations and individuals have sustained the endeavor since then. Among these are the Ford Foundation, the Lyn and Norman Lear Foundation, the Lucius N. Littauer Foundation, the Charlotte Palmer Phillips Foundation, the L. J. Skaggs and Mary C. Skaggs Foundation, the John Ben Snow Memorial Trust, Time, Inc., Robert C. Baron, B. Batmanghelidj, David K. E. Bruce, and James Russell Wiggins. In recent years generous ongoing support has come from The New York Times Company Foundation, the Dyson Foundation, the Barkley Fund (through the National Trust for the Humanities), the Florence Gould Foundation, the "Cinco Hermanos Fund," the Andrew W. Mellon Foundation, the Pew Charitable Trusts, and the Packard Humanities Institute (through Founding Fathers Papers, Inc.). Benefactions from a greatly expanded roster of dedicated individuals have underwritten this volume and those still to come: Sara and James Adler, Helen and Peter Bing, Diane and John Cooke, Judy and Carl Ferenbach III, Mary-Love and William Harman, Frederick P. and Mary Buford Hitz, Governor Thomas H. Kean, Ruth and Sidney Lapidus, Lisa and Willem Mesdag, Tim and Lisa Robertson, Ann and Andrew C. Rose, Sara Lee and Axel Schupf, the Sulzberger family through the Hillandale Foundation, Richard W. Thaler, Tad and Sue Thompson, The Wendt Family Charitable Foundation, and Susan and John O. Wynne. For their vision and extraordinary efforts to provide for the future of this edition, we owe special thanks to John S. Dyson, Governor Kean, H. L. Lenfest and the Lenfest Foundation, Rebecca Rimel and the Pew Charitable Trusts, and Jack Rosenthal. In partnership with these individuals and foundations, the National Historical Publications and Records Commission and the National Endowment for the Humanities have been crucial to the editing and publication of *The Papers of Thomas Jefferson*. For their unprecedented generous support we are also indebted to the Princeton History Department and Christopher L. Eisgruber, provost of the university.

FOREWORD

IN EARLY October 1802, Thomas Jefferson returned to the capital after his customary August and September stay at Monticello to avoid the "bilious months" in Washington. While at home, he watched the ongoing construction of the house, settling his account with the stonemason for cutting and laying a floor, making payments for the work of the plasterer, and letting James Dinsmore know that the ornaments for the frieze of the bed chamber had reached Richmond. Jefferson was in regular and substantive communication with his cabinet during these months. The fragile and volatile state of relations with Morocco, Tunis, and Algiers required important decisions to be made that would balance American diplomatic initiatives with some evidence of naval power in the Mediterranean. These critical steps often had to be taken on the basis of incomplete or out-of-date information. Since it took approximately two months for dispatches to reach Washington from North Africa, by the time they arrived the countries might be on a completely different footing. Were relations with Morocco friendly, or had there been a declaration of war? Would the United States allow a shipment of wheat to go to Tripoli? Could Tunis look forward to receiving the warships and gifts that she considered her due? Jefferson, Secretary of State James Madison, Secretary of the Treasury Albert Gallatin, Secretary of War Henry Dearborn, and Robert Smith, the secretary of the navy, struggled to find answers.

Letters they exchanged in August and September sought answers to these questions and struggled to formulate a policy for dealing with the Barbary states. This correspondence also provides a window into the decision-making process followed by the Jefferson administration. In anticipation of the opening session of the Seventh Congress in December 1801, the president had laid out the "mode & degrees of communication" by which he and the heads of departments would proceed. Now, a year later, with Jefferson at Monticello for more than two months and the others away from the capital for short periods of time, letters were the most frequent "mode" of conducting their business. In early August, Jefferson informed his cabinet that the sultan of Morocco had ordered American Consul James Simpson out of the country and seemed to have a "settled design of war against us." The president asked their opinions on what orders he ought to issue to naval commanders in the Mediterranean and whether additional warships should be sent. Madison observed that hostility was a lesser evil than abandoning their rightful ground and that frigates should remain there. Dearborn, after conversing with Smith, suggested appointing a special agent to negotiate. The secretary of the Treasury, lamenting the delays in their correspondence when time was so precious, bluntly observed that the conflict was wasting the nation's resources and peace was a necessity.

The delays in receiving news from North Africa in the capital, and even from Virginia, rendered it difficult to agree upon a course of action. Jefferson went from Monticello to Montpelier for a "personal interview" with his secretary of state to discuss all of the points. The other members of the cabinet consulted with each other in Washington, and in mid-September, with important matters "demanding immediate attention," Smith alerted the president that they "had to *begin* to act" without Jefferson's sanction and confessed they had taken the liberty to "suspend the execution" of his orders countermanding the dispatch of the *John Adams* to the Mediterranean until further communication was received. In the end, Jefferson gave way to the views of Robert Smith, with whom the other heads of department agreed, "'tho not with entire satisfaction." When they had all returned to Washington, Jefferson called a cabinet meeting to discuss the situation. Ironically, their first recorded meeting as a cabinet, in May 1801, considered the same subject. In 1801, he had inquired whether the squadron at Norfolk should be ordered to cruise in the Mediterranean. A year and a half later, he was asking what size naval force ought to remain there over the winter.

In the eighteen months that Jefferson had been in office, requests for government posts had not subsided. He worked most closely with Gallatin on patronage matters, selecting replacements for resignations, deaths, or removals from office. He also consulted with Dearborn and Levi Lincoln, especially for New England. Jefferson was still writing Republican congressmen, governors, and others he trusted for recommendations for the position of bankruptcy commissioner. A request for a post or a recommendation on behalf of a friend or relative often rested upon complaints about the conduct of the incumbent: "delinquency," "incapacity," "intemperance," improper use of government funds, and failure to keep accounts properly. Some requests were routine, but many involved politics (see Appendix 1, List of Appointments). The clamor by Republicans for a larger percentage of federal jobs grew even louder than it had been when Jefferson was elected.

Republicans pointed to specific offices that required the removal of Federalists and the appointment of sound Republicans. Gallatin told Jefferson explicitly, for example, that he did not think the president was "doing enough in Massachts" for Republicans. One of the most delicate cases was that of Samuel R. Gerry, brother of Elbridge Gerry and customs officer at Marblehead, Massachusetts. In 1799, Jefferson shared his political principles with Elbridge Gerry, the former envoy to France, calling him a fellow laborer "in the same cause" and urging him to leave the Federalists behind and join with the Republicans. As president and leader of the Republican party, Jefferson now explained that the "safety of the government" could not be left in the hands of "enemies." He had recently removed several customs officers "most marked for their bitterness and active zeal in slandering and in electioneering." But Gerry's brother, who had periodically failed to render his accounts and those which he did submit contained discrepancies, also had to be replaced. Even when Elbridge Gerry asked whether his brother could not mend his ways and be reappointed, Jefferson could only refuse. He called the removal one of "the most painful and unwilling" duties that he "had to perform."

If appointments were a chore, other tasks Jefferson undertook as president were a pleasure and meshed with his own interests. He arranged for the acquisition of approximately 700 books for the Library of Congress, sending to William Duane in Philadelphia lists of titles to be ordered from Paris and London. The public money for the purchases, Jefferson observed, must be expended with as "rigorous economy as that of an individual." He gave instructions on the most minute of details, specifying "good editions, not pompous ones; neat bindings, but not splendid." John Beckley, the Librarian of Congress, asked whether the past omission of titles in natural history could not be remedied, particularly with the addition of a work by Mark Catesby, "an American."

Despite Jefferson's insistence that his election to the presidency and the achievement of a Republican majority in both houses of Congress signaled the triumph of republicanism, stories of "madness and folly" and "diabolical exertions" by New England Federalists had not disappeared. With the midterm elections in New York, Rhode Island, Connecticut, and New Hampshire already complete, Republicans had seen "considerable advances." Although the New York elections had taken place in the spring, the political situation there was still of concern. The Republican Party was divided between Clintonians, who charged that Aaron Burr conspired with the Federalists to gain the presidency in 1800, and Burr's defenders. Federalists, the Republicans thought, were taking advantage of the Republican "schism." For New Jersey, Pennsylvania, and Delaware, reports on Republican prospects were mixed. Gideon Granger worried about the large number of Federalist newspapers he encountered in circulation as he traveled between Washington and Philadelphia. In contrast, he saw "but one republican Paper." Thomas Leiper wrote that he would be at the meeting of Republicans at the Rising Sun tavern, where he would do what he could to make the Republicans' "Rope of Sand stick to-gether."

"That Louisiana is to be possessed by France is probable," Jefferson stated in August, although the United States lacked "certain information" on Napoleon Bonaparte's intentions. Jefferson concluded that delay would be beneficial to American interests, because if Bonaparte had time to consider the consequences of his actions he would most certainly desist from the measure. The "West Indies business" was a stumbling block for Bonaparte's hopes for French hegemony in the Americas. Although Toussaint-Louverture had surrendered to the French forces, theoretically bringing the island back under French control, their numbers were decimated by the continued resistance of black troops and disease. By October, French General Victoire Leclerc had still not regained control of the island and in November died from the yellow fever.

French forces had also defeated a rebel army on the island of Guadeloupe, and in August and September, New York City's mayor and the governor of South Carolina feared that French ships of war were depositing free blacks expelled from Guadeloupe in that conflict "clandestinely" on U.S. shores. Madison suggested a friendly letter to Louis Andre Pichon, French chargé d'affaires in the United States. Although the president believed the matter was "substantially" within the police powers of the states, he also informed Gallatin that it would be "proper & indeed incumbent on us" to direct custom house officers to be on the alert to detect and prevent the unloading of the ships.

Jefferson counseled his secretary of war that they must impress upon the Indian nations that the new president was as friendly as the former one. The government should establish trading houses and furnish the Indians with "goods enough to supply all their wants," and cheaply enough so the government stores could not be undercut by private traders. Jefferson acknowledged that while in the long run the United States might wish to have more land available for settlement, it was not worth a war or the loss of the affections of the Indians. At the same time, however, he and Dearborn authorized William Henry Harrison, the governor of the Indiana Territory, to obtain title to a large tract of land around Vincennes. On 3 November, Jefferson wrote a long letter to Handsome Lake, addressing the Seneca leader as "brother," applauding his efforts to fight "the abuse of spirituous liquors" and attempting to quiet his uneasiness over recent land cessions. Among issues relating to Native Americans were ongoing efforts by the Jefferson administration to resolve the case of a 1797 murder of some Delaware Indians by three whites, who were now living in Kentucky and evading efforts by federal officials to apprehend them.

Jefferson played a role in the early development of the national capital that was both visionary and practical. He had long had an interest in the planning of towns, particularly in preserving open space and wide streets that would be beautiful and healthy for city dwellers. Such a design would discourage the spread of epidemics like the yellow fever that had raged through Philadelphia. The construction of public buildings in Washington, according to the original plan, would be financed by the sale of lots to private individuals. Purchases failed to live up to expectations, however, and the government was compelled to resort to loans from Virginia and Maryland. In July, a payment of $18,000 interest on the Maryland loans came due, which could be met only by drawing on general Treasury funds. In November, Superintendent Thomas Munroe reported that he had "no monies" in his hands to cover the interest payments. Possibly because of the lack of funds, the response to a petition from a committee of citizens for the erection of a public market to the west of the President's House was to offer the land for free and stipulate that the market house would come from private funds. Cost was also a factor in deciding upon building materials for the new jail. Good white oak was better for every part of the roof, Jefferson was sure, but the choice would depend upon practicality and price. Still, he hoped the walls and roof would be completed before winter.

In the fall of 1802, Jefferson expressed a strong desire to improve his personal financial situation by getting out from under his debts. The task was daunting as he learned that the price his tobacco would bring was low, with no telling what it would be the following year. In August, he had to arrange for urgent repairs to the pump in the President's House, at his own expense because no government funds were provided for it. Around 1 November, John Barnes cautioned him that more "unexpected, unavoidable" demands might confront him. At the end of the year, payments for his workmen and the year's supply of corn came due, coinciding with "the expensive time of a session of Congress." Faced with a multitude of demands upon his income, Jefferson was continuing to buy up parcels of land adjacent to Monticello, sometimes through third parties acting on his behalf.

This activity further strained his resources. In spite of all this, Jefferson was determined to get control over what he owed. He established a payment schedule for his debts to William Short, which was to begin the following March and continue until they were fully discharged. James Lyle gently pressed him for payment, commenting that he knew Jefferson was as anxious to have the matter settled as he was. Facing all these demands, Jefferson calculated and calculated and optimistically concluded that at the end of two years, he would "owe not one farthing on earth."

In July, the matter of the financial "relief" Jefferson had offered to James Callender first in 1797 and 1798 and most recently in May 1801, appeared in the Richmond *Recorder*. By late summer, Jefferson faced charges by Callender even more damaging to his reputation. On 1 September, Callender's first article making public the story of Jefferson's relationship with Sally Hemings appeared in the *Recorder*. Avoiding explicit mention of the explosive subject that Callender unveiled, Jefferson's correspondents used such euphemisms as "the breath of Slander" and the "Slanders which are in circulation" to alert the president to the stories. While Jefferson referred in a letter to Robert Livingston, American minister in Paris, to the "sluices of calumny" in the newspapers, he had often used such language to describe what the Federalist press said about him. On Callender's 1 September charges he remained silent and continued making plans for his daughters to travel to Washington.

When Jefferson became president, he thought that between his trips home and visits by his daughters and grandchildren to Washington, the family would still be together under his roof several months a year. Although he was persistent, his daughters displayed some reluctance. Mary Jefferson Eppes even confided to her father her fear that her older sister would continue to find reasons for delaying the visit. The journey was tedious, and, as Martha Jefferson Randolph pointed out, riding with "a carriage full of small children" was not easy. But the season grew later and the weather colder, with the first "white frost" arriving on the last day of October and the first ice the following day. The impatient father and adoring grandfather was strongly urging Martha and Mary to set a date. Martha assured her father that they were preparing with "all speed" to obey his "summons." Although she was not quite certain when they could set off, she asked him to order from Philadelphia "2 wigs of the colour of the hair enclosed" so that the two women would be fully ready to enter into Washington society on their arrival. In November, she reported another delay, but "of 2 days only."

If Martha felt the impact of the word "obey," her husband felt even more severely that his father-in-law set the rules by which the family lived. Jefferson somewhat impatiently chided his son-in-law for failing to send up-to-date news about Martha's health. Neither had Thomas Mann Randolph set a date or made the travel arrangements for their trip to Washington. Sensing his father-in-law's criticism, Randolph wrote that he felt "extraneous" to the family in which he was joined by marriage and felt "something like shame." Jefferson's towering stature seemed overpowering and, Randolph lamented, he could not "like the proverbially silly bird feel at my ease in the company of the Swans." On 2 November, Jefferson sought to reassure him of his love and respect, and he urged Randolph not to remain in the "shade" into which he had thrown himself. On the same day Jefferson wrote to Martha, urging her again to send details of her travel plans and alerting her that he found no locks of hair included in her letter. He also requested the muffin recipe used at Monticello as his cook in Washington could not "succeed at all in them."

ACKNOWLEDGMENTS

MANY individuals have given the Editors the benefit of their aid in the preparation of this volume, and we offer them our thanks. Those who helped us use manuscript collections, answered research queries, assisted with translations, or advised in other ways are Norman Itzkowitz and William C. Jordan, Princeton University; Russell Hopley for Arabic translations; in the libraries at Princeton, Karin A. Trainer, University Librarian, and Elizabeth Z. Bennett, Colleen M. Burlingham, Stephen Ferguson, Daniel J. Linke, Deborah T. Paparone, AnnaLee Pauls, Ben Primer, and Don C. Skemer; Timothy Connelly of the NHPRC; David Langbart of the National Archives; James H. Hutson, Barbara Bair, Julie Miller, Rosemary Fry Plakas, and the staff at the Manuscript Division of the Library of Congress, especially Jennifer Brathovde, Jeffrey Flannery, Joseph Jackson, Lia Kerwin, Patrick Kerwin, Bruce Kirby, and Lewis Wyman; Peter Drummey and the library staff of the Massachusetts Historical Society, especially Nancy Heywood for providing digital scans; Robert C. Ritchie, Olga Tsapina, and others at the Huntington Library; Anna Berkes and Lucia C. Stanton of the Thomas Jefferson Foundation at Monticello; Nicole Bouche, Regina Rush, and the staff of Special Collections at the University of Virginia Library; Eileen O'Toole and Susan A. Riggs, Swem Library, the College of William and Mary; Sara Bearss and Brent Tarter, Library of Virginia; Dennis Northcott and the staff of the Missouri Historical Society; Martin Levitt, Roy Goodman, Charles B. Greifenstein, and Earl E. Spamer of the American Philosophical Society; the staff of the New York Public Library; the Gilder Lehrman Institute of American History and Jean W. Ashton and Edward O'Reilly of the New-York Historical Society; Charles M. Harris of the Papers of William Thornton, Daniel Preston of the James Monroe Papers at the University of Mary Washington, and our fellow editors at the Thomas Jefferson Retirement Series at Monticello, the Adams Papers at the Massachusetts Historical Society, the Papers of George Washington and the Papers of James Madison at the University of Virginia, and the Papers of Benjamin Franklin at Yale University. For assistance with illustrations we are indebted to Alfred L. Bush of Princeton, Elena Obuhovich of the State Hermitage Museum, St. Petersburg, Russia, Isabelle Mercier of the Musée historique of Lausanne, Switzerland, and Bonnie Coles of the Library of Congress. Stephen Perkins and Jason Bush of dataformat.com provided essential technical support for us with the

ACKNOWLEDGMENTS

XML preparation of these volumes. We thank Alice Calaprice for careful reading and Jan Lilly for her unparalleled mastery of what a Jefferson volume must be. We appreciate especially the support and leadership of Peter J. Dougherty, Director of Princeton University Press. Others at the Press who never fail to give these volumes the benefit of their expertise are Chuck Creesy, Adam Fortgang, Daphne Ireland, Dimitri Karetnikov, Neil Litt, Elizabeth Litz, Clara Platter, Linny Schenck, and Brigitta van Rheinberg.

Beginning with Volume 24 of *The Papers of Thomas Jefferson*, Robert W. Hartle has skillfully and patiently assisted us with transcriptions and translations of French documents. His expertise has been invaluable to us, and we extend our deepest gratitude for his knowledge and dedication.

EDITORIAL METHOD AND APPARATUS

1. RENDERING THE TEXT

Julian P. Boyd eloquently set forth a comprehensive editorial policy in Volume 1 of *The Papers of Thomas Jefferson*. Adopting what he described as a "middle course" for rendering eighteenth-century handwritten materials into print, Boyd set the standards for modern historical editing. His successors, Charles T. Cullen and John Catanzariti, reaffirmed Boyd's high standards. At the same time, they made changes in textual policy and editorial apparatus as they deemed appropriate. For Boyd's policy and subsequent modifications to it, readers are encouraged to consult Vol. 1: xxix-xxxviii; Vol. 22: vii-xi; and Vol. 24: vii-viii.

The revised, more literal textual method, which appeared for the first time in Volume 30, adheres to the following guidelines: Abbreviations will be retained as written. Where the meaning is sufficiently unclear to require editorial intervention, the expansion will be given in the explanatory annotation. Capitalization will follow the usage of the writer. Because the line between uppercase and lowercase letters can be a very fine and fluctuating one, when it is impossible to make an absolute determination of the author's intention, we will adopt modern usage. Jefferson rarely began his sentences with an uppercase letter, and we conform to his usage. Punctuation will be retained as written and double marks of punctuation, such as a period followed by a dash, will be allowed to stand. Misspellings or so-called slips of the pen will be allowed to stand or will be recorded in a subjoined textual note.

English translations or translation summaries will be supplied for foreign-language documents. In some instances, when documents are lengthy and not especially pertinent to Jefferson's concerns or if our edition's typography cannot adequately represent the script of a language, we will provide only a summary in English. In most cases we will print in full the text in its original language and also provide a full English translation. If a contemporary translation that Jefferson made or would have used is extant, we may print it in lieu of a modern translation. Our own translations are designed to provide a basic readable English text for the modern user rather than to preserve all aspects of the original diction and language.

2. TEXTUAL DEVICES

The following devices are employed throughout the work to clarify the presentation of the text.

[. . .]	Text missing and not conjecturable.
[ ]	Number or part of a number missing or illegible.
[roman]	Conjectural reading for missing or illegible matter. A question mark follows when the reading is doubtful.
[*italic*]	Editorial comment inserted in the text.
<*italic*>	Matter deleted in the MS but restored in our text.

3. DESCRIPTIVE SYMBOLS

The following symbols are employed throughout the work to describe the various kinds of manuscript originals. When a series of versions is recorded, the first to be recorded is the version used for the printed text.

Dft	draft (usually a composition or rough draft; later drafts, when identifiable as such, are designated "2d Dft," &c.)
Dupl	duplicate
MS	manuscript (arbitrarily applied to most documents other than letters)
N	note, notes (memoranda, fragments, &c.)
PoC	polygraph copy
PrC	press copy
RC	recipient's copy
SC	stylograph copy
Tripl	triplicate

All manuscripts of the above types are assumed to be in the hand of the author of the document to which the descriptive symbol pertains. If not, that *fact is stated.* On the other hand, the following types of manuscripts are assumed *not* to be in the hand of the author, and exceptions will be noted:

FC	file copy (applied to all contemporary copies retained by the author or his agents)
Lb	letterbook (ordinarily used with FC and Tr to denote texts copied into bound volumes)

Tr   transcript (applied to all contemporary and later copies except file copies; period of transcription, unless clear by implication, will be given when known)

4. LOCATION SYMBOLS

The locations of documents printed in this edition from originals in private hands and from printed sources are recorded in self-explanatory form in the descriptive note following each document. The locations of documents printed from originals held by public and private institutions in the United States are recorded by means of the symbols used in the National Union Catalog in the Library of Congress; an explanation of how these symbols are formed is given in Vol. 1:xl. The symbols DLC and MHi by themselves stand for the collections of Jefferson Papers proper in these repositories; when texts are drawn from other collections held by these two institutions, the names of those collections will be added. Location symbols for documents held by institutions outside the United States are given in a subjoined list.

CSmH	The Huntington Library, San Marino, California
CtY	Yale University, New Haven, Connecticut
DGU	Georgetown University, D.C.
DLC	Library of Congress
DeGH	Hagley Museum and Library, Greenville, Delaware
DeHi	Delaware Historical Society, Wilmington
G-Ar	Georgia State Department of Archives and History, Atlanta
ICHi	Chicago Historical Society
InHi	Indiana Historical Society, Indianapolis
InU	Indiana University, Bloomington
LNHiC	Historic New Orleans Collection
MB	Boston Public Library
MH	Harvard University, Cambridge, Massachusetts
MHi	Massachusetts Historical Society, Boston
MSCL	Springfield City Library, Springfield, Massachusetts
MWA	American Antiquarian Society, Worcester, Massachusetts
MWiW-C	Williams College, Chapin Library, Williamstown, Massachusetts
MdAA	Hall of Records Commission, Annapolis, Maryland
MdHi	Maryland Historical Society, Baltimore

MeB	Bowdoin College, Brunswick, Maine
MiDbEI	Edison Institute, Henry Ford Museum and Greenfield Village Library, Dearborn, Michigan
MoSHi	Missouri Historical Society, St. Louis
NHi	New-York Historical Society, New York City
NN	New York Public Library
NNFoM	Forbes Magazine, New York City
NNMus	Museum of the City of New York
NNPM	Pierpont Morgan Library, New York City
Nc-Ar	North Carolina Office of Archives & History, Raleigh
NcU	University of North Carolina, Chapel Hill
NhPoS	Strawbery Banke, Portsmouth, New Hampshire
NjP	Princeton University
NjPT	Princeton Theological Seminary, Princeton, New Jersey
PHi	Historical Society of Pennsylvania, Philadelphia
PPAmP	American Philosophical Society, Philadelphia
PPCP	College of Physicians, Philadelphia
PPL	Library Company of Philadelphia, Pennsylvania
PPRF	Rosenbach Foundation, Philadelphia
PWacD	David Library of the American Revolution, Washington Crossing, Pennsylvania
TxU	University of Texas, Austin
Vi	Library of Virginia, Richmond
ViFreJM	James Monroe Memorial Foundation, Fredericksburg, Virginia
ViHi	Virginia Historical Society, Richmond
ViU	University of Virginia, Charlottesville
ViW	College of William and Mary, Williamsburg, Virginia

5. NATIONAL ARCHIVES DESIGNATIONS

The National Archives, recognized by the location symbol DNA, with identifications of series (preceded by record group number) as follows:

RG 28		Records of the Post Office Department
	LPG	Letters Sent by the Postmaster General
RG 42		Records of the Office of Public Buildings and Public Parks of the National Capital

	DCLB	District of Columbia Letterbook
	LR	Letters Received
	PC	Proceedings of the Board of Commissioners for the District of Columbia
RG 45	Naval Records Collection of the Office of Naval Records and Library	
	LSO	Letters Sent to Officers
	LSP	Letters Sent to the President
	MLS	Misc. Letters Sent
RG 46	Records of the United States Senate	
	EPEN	Executive Proceedings, Executive Nominations
	EPFR	Executive Proceedings, Foreign Relations
	EPIR	Executive Proceedings, Indian Relations
	EPOR	Executive Proceedings, Other Records
	LPPM	Legislative Proceedings, President's Messages
RG 59	General Records of the Department of State	
	CD	Consular Dispatches
	DD	Diplomatic Dispatches
	GPR	General Pardon Records
	LAR	Letters of Application and Recommendation
	MLR	Miscellaneous Letters Received
	MPTPC	Misc. Permanent and Temporary Presidential Commissions
	NL	Notes from Legations
	PTCC	Permanent and Temporary Consular Commissions
	RD	Resignations and Declinations
RG 75	Records of the Bureau of Indian Affairs	
	LSIA	Letters Sent by the Secretary of War Relating to Indian Affairs
RG 76	Records of Boundary and Claims Commissions and Arbitrations	
RG 94	Records of the Adjutant General's Office	
RG 98	Records of United States Army Commands	
RG 104	Records of the Mint	
	DL	Domestic Letters
	GC	General Correspondence

RG 107		Records of the Office of the Secretary of War
	LRUS	Letters Received by the Secretary of War, Unregistered Series
	LSMA	Letters Sent by the Secretary of War Relating to Military Affairs
	LSP	Letters Sent to the President
	MLS	Misc. Letters Sent
	RLRMS	Register of Letters Received, Main Series
RG 125		Records of the Office of the Judge Advocate General (Navy)
	GCMCI	Transcripts of Proceedings of General Courts-Martial and Courts of Inquiry
RG 233		Records of the United States House of Representatives
	PMRSL	Petitions, Memorials, Resolutions of State Legislatures
	PM	President's Messages

6. OTHER SYMBOLS AND ABBREVIATIONS

The following symbols and abbreviations are commonly employed in the annotation throughout the work.

Second Series   The topical series to be published as part of this edition, comprising those materials which are best suited to a topical rather than a chronological arrangement (see Vol. 1: xv-xvi)

TJ   Thomas Jefferson

TJ Editorial Files   Photoduplicates and other editorial materials in the office of The Papers of Thomas Jefferson, Princeton University Library

TJ Papers   Jefferson Papers (applied to a collection of manuscripts when the precise location of an undated, misdated, or otherwise problematic document must be furnished, and always preceded by the symbol for the institutional repository; thus "DLC: TJ Papers, 4:628-9" represents a document in the Library of Congress, Jefferson Papers, volume 4, pages 628 and 629. Citations to volumes and folio numbers of the Jefferson Papers at the Library of Congress refer to the collection as it was arranged at the time the first microfilm edition was made in 1944-45. Access to the microfilm edition of the collection as it was rearranged under the Library's Presidential Papers Program is provided by the Index to the Thomas Jefferson Papers [Washington, D.C., 1976])

RG   Record Group (used in designating the location of documents in the National Archives)

SJL   Jefferson's "Summary Journal of Letters" written and received for the period 11 Nov. 1783 to 25 June 1826 (in DLC: TJ Papers). This register, kept in Jefferson's hand, has been checked against the TJ Editorial Files. It is to be assumed that all outgoing letters are recorded in SJL unless there is a note to the contrary. When the date of receipt of an incoming letter is recorded in SJL, it is incorporated in the notes. Information and discrepancies revealed in SJL but not found in the letter itself are also noted. Missing letters recorded in SJL are, where possible, accounted for in the notes to documents mentioning them or in related documents. A more detailed discussion of this register and its use in this edition appears in Vol. 6: vii-x

SJPL   "Summary Journal of Public Letters," an incomplete list of letters and documents written by TJ from 16 Apr. 1784 to 31 Dec. 1793, with brief summaries, in an amanuensis's hand. This is supplemented by six pages in TJ's hand, compiled at a later date, listing private and confidential memorandums and notes as well as official reports and communications by and to him as Secretary of State, 11 Oct. 1789 to 31 Dec. 1793 (in DLC: TJ Papers, Epistolary Record, 514-59 and 209-11, respectively; see Vol. 22: ix-x). Since nearly all documents in the amanuensis's list are registered in SJL, while few in TJ's list are so recorded, it is to be assumed that all references to SJPL are to the list in TJ's hand unless there is a statement to the contrary

V   Ecu

ƒ   Florin

£   Pound sterling or livre, depending upon context (in doubtful cases, a clarifying note will be given)

s   Shilling or sou (also expressed as /)

d   Penny or denier

₶   Livre Tournois

℔   Per (occasionally used for pro, pre)

7. SHORT TITLES

The following list includes short titles of works cited frequently in this edition. Since it is impossible to anticipate all the works to be cited in abbreviated form, the list is revised from volume to volume.

Franklin, *Papers*   Leonard W. Labaree and others, eds., *The Papers of Benjamin Franklin*, New Haven, 1959-   , 39 vols.

Gallatin, *Papers*   Carl E. Prince and Helene E. Fineman, eds., *The Papers of Albert Gallatin*, microfilm edition in 46 reels, Philadelphia, 1969, and Supplement, Barbara B. Oberg, ed., reels 47-51, Wilmington, Del., 1985

Garner, *Black's Law Dictionary*   Bryan A. Garner, ed., *Black's Law Dictionary*, 8th ed., St. Paul, Minn., 2004

Grainger, *Amiens Truce*   John D. Grainger, *The Amiens Truce: Britain and Bonaparte, 1801-1803*, Rochester, N.Y., 2004

Hartley, *Alexander I*   Janet M. Hartley, *Alexander I*, London, 1994

HAW   Henry A. Washington, ed., *The Writings of Thomas Jefferson*, New York, 1853-54, 9 vols.

Heitman, *Dictionary*   Francis B. Heitman, comp., *Historical Register and Dictionary of the United States Army*, Washington, D.C., 1903, 2 vols.

Heitman, *Register*   Francis B. Heitman, *Historical Register of Officers of the Continental Army during the War of the Revolution, April, 1775, to December, 1793*, new ed., Washington, D.C., 1914

Higginbotham, *Pennsylvania Politics*   Sanford W. Higginbotham, *The Keystone in the Democratic Arch: Pennsylvania Politics 1800-1816*, Harrisburg, 1952

JEP   *Journal of the Executive Proceedings of the Senate of the United States . . . to the Termination of the Nineteenth Congress*, Washington, D.C., 1828, 3 vols.

JHR   *Journal of the House of Representatives of the United States*, Washington, D.C., 1826, 9 vols.

JS   *Journal of the Senate of the United States*, Washington, D.C., 1820-21, 5 vols.

King, *Life*   Charles R. King, ed., *The Life and Correspondence of Rufus King: Comprising His Letters, Private and Official, His Public Documents and His Speeches*, New York, 1894-1900, 6 vols.

Kline, *Burr*   Mary-Jo Kline, ed., *Political Correspondence and Public Papers of Aaron Burr*, Princeton, 1983, 2 vols.

L & B   Andrew A. Lipscomb and Albert E. Bergh, eds., *The Writings of Thomas Jefferson*, Washington, D.C., 1903-04, 20 vols.

LCB   Douglas L. Wilson, ed., *Jefferson's Literary Commonplace*

Book, Princeton, 1989, *The Papers of Thomas Jefferson*, Second Series

Latrobe, *Correspondence*   John C. Van Horne and Lee W. Formwalt, eds., *The Correspondence and Miscellaneous Papers of Benjamin Henry Latrobe*, New Haven, 1984-88, 3 vols.

Leonard, *General Assembly*   Cynthia Miller Leonard, comp., *The General Assembly of Virginia, July 30, 1619-January 11, 1978: A Bicentennial Register of Members*, Richmond, 1978

List of Patents   *A List of Patents granted by the United States from April 10, 1790, to December 31, 1836*, Washington, D.C., 1872

Madison, *Papers*   William T. Hutchinson, Robert A. Rutland, J. C. A. Stagg, and others, eds., *The Papers of James Madison*, Chicago and Charlottesville, 1962-   , 33 vols.

    Sec. of State Ser., 1986-   , 9 vols.

    Pres. Ser., 1984-   , 6 vols.

    Ret. Ser., 2009-   , 1 vol.

Malone, *Jefferson*   Dumas Malone, *Jefferson and His Time*, Boston, 1948-81, 6 vols.

Marshall, *Papers*   Herbert A. Johnson, Charles T. Cullen, Charles F. Hobson, and others, eds., *The Papers of John Marshall*, Chapel Hill, 1974-2006, 12 vols.

Mattern and Shulman, *Dolley Madison*   David B. Mattern and Holly C. Shulman, eds., *The Selected Letters of Dolley Payne Madison*, Charlottesville, 2003

MB   James A. Bear, Jr., and Lucia C. Stanton, eds., *Jefferson's Memorandum Books: Accounts, with Legal Records and Miscellany, 1767-1826*, Princeton, 1997, *The Papers of Thomas Jefferson*, Second Series

Miller, *Treaties*   Hunter Miller, ed., *Treaties and Other International Acts of the United States of America*, Washington, D.C., 1931-48, 8 vols.

NDBW   Dudley W. Knox, ed., *Naval Documents Related to the United States Wars with the Barbary Powers*, Washington, D.C., 1939-44, 6 vols. and *Register of Officer Personnel and Ships' Data, 1801-1807*, Washington, D.C., 1945

NDQW   Dudley W. Knox, ed., *Naval Documents Related to the Quasi-War between the United States and France, Naval Operations*, Washington, D.C., 1935-38, 7 vols. (cited by years)

Nichols, *Architectural Drawings*   Frederick Doveton Nichols, *Thomas Jefferson's Architectural Drawings, Compiled and with Commentary and a Check List*, Charlottesville, 1978

Notes, ed. Peden   *Thomas Jefferson, Notes on the State of Virginia*, ed. William Peden, Chapel Hill, 1955

OED   J. A. Simpson and E. S. C. Weiner, eds., *The Oxford English Dictionary*, Oxford, 1989, 20 vols.

Owens, *Jefferson's Hammer*   Robert M. Owens, *Mr. Jefferson's Hammer: William Henry Harrison and the Origins of American Indian Policy*, Norman, Okla., 2007

Pa. Arch.   Samuel Hazard and others, eds., *Pennsylvania Archives. Selected and Arranged from Original Documents in the Office of the Secretary of the Commonwealth*, Harrisburg, 1852-1935, 119 vols.

Papenfuse, *Maryland Legislature*   Edward C. Papenfuse, Alan F. Day, David W. Jordan, and Gregory A. Stiverson, eds., *A Biographical Dictionary of the Maryland Legislature, 1635-1789*, Baltimore, 1979-85, 2 vols.

Parry, *Consolidated Treaty Series*   Clive Parry, ed., *The Consolidated Treaty Series*, Dobbs Ferry, N.Y., 1969-81, 231 vols.

Pasley, *Tyranny of Printers*   Jeffrey L. Pasley, *"The Tyranny of Printers": Newspaper Politics in the Early American Republic*, Charlottesville, 2001

Peale, *Papers*   Lillian B. Miller and others, eds., *The Selected Papers of Charles Willson Peale and His Family*, New Haven, 1983-2000, 5 vols. in 6

PMHB   *Pennsylvania Magazine of History and Biography*, 1877-

Preston, *Catalogue*   Daniel Preston, *A Comprehensive Catalogue of the Correspondence and Papers of James Monroe*, Westport, Conn., 2001, 2 vols.

Prince, *Federalists*   Carl E. Prince, *The Federalists and the Origins of the U.S. Civil Service*, New York, 1977

PW   Wilbur S. Howell, ed., *Jefferson's Parliamentary Writings*, Princeton, 1988, *The Papers of Thomas Jefferson*, Second Series

RCHS   *Records of the Columbia Historical Society*, 1895-1989

Rowe, *McKean*   G. S. Rowe, *Thomas McKean, The Shaping of an American Republicanism*, Boulder, Colo., 1978

RS   J. Jefferson Looney and others, eds., *The Papers of Thomas Jefferson: Retirement Series*, Princeton, 2004-   , 7 vols.

Saricks, *Du Pont*   Ambrose Saricks, *Pierre Samuel Du Pont de Nemours*, Lawrence, Kans., 1965

S.C. Biographical Directory, House of Representatives   J. S. R.

Faunt, Walter B. Edgar, N. Louise Bailey, and others, eds., *Biographical Directory of the South Carolina House of Representatives*, Columbia, S.C., 1974-92, 5 vols.

Seale, *The President's House*   William Seale, *The President's House*, Washington, D.C., 1986, 2 vols.

Shaw-Shoemaker   Ralph R. Shaw and Richard H. Shoemaker, comps., *American Bibliography: A Preliminary Checklist for 1801-1819*, New York, 1958-63, 22 vols.

Smith, *St. Clair Papers*   William Henry Smith, ed., *The St. Clair Papers, The Life and Public Services of Arthur St. Clair*, Cincinnati, 1882, 2 vols.

Sowerby   E. Millicent Sowerby, comp., *Catalogue of the Library of Thomas Jefferson*, Washington, D.C., 1952-59, 5 vols.

Stanton, *Free Some Day*   Lucia Stanton, *Free Some Day: The African-American Families of Monticello*, Charlottesville, 2000

Stein, *Worlds*   Susan R. Stein, *The Worlds of Thomas Jefferson at Monticello*, New York, 1993

Stets, *Postmasters*   Robert J. Stets, *Postmasters & Postoffices of the United States 1782-1811*, Lake Oswego, Ore., 1994

Sturtevant, *Handbook*   William C. Sturtevant, gen. ed., *Handbook of North American Indians*, Washington, D.C., 1978- , 14 vols.

Syrett, *Hamilton*   Harold C. Syrett and others, eds., *The Papers of Alexander Hamilton*, New York, 1961-87, 27 vols.

Terr. Papers   Clarence E. Carter and John Porter Bloom, eds., *The Territorial Papers of the United States*, Washington, D.C., 1934-75, 28 vols.

TJR   Thomas Jefferson Randolph, ed., *Memoir, Correspondence, and Miscellanies, from the Papers of Thomas Jefferson*, Charlottesville, 1829, 4 vols.

Tulard, *Dictionnaire Napoléon*   Jean Tulard, *Dictionnaire Napoléon*, Paris, 1987

U.S. Statutes at Large   Richard Peters, ed., *The Public Statutes at Large of the United States . . . 1789 to March 3, 1845*, Boston, 1855-56, 8 vols.

VMHB   *Virginia Magazine of History and Biography*, 1893-

Washington, *Papers*   W. W. Abbot, Dorothy Twohig, Philander D. Chase, Theodore J. Crackel, Edward C. Lengel, and others, eds., *The Papers of George Washington*, Charlottesville, 1983- , 56 vols.

  Col. Ser., 1983-95, 10 vols.

  Pres. Ser., 1987- , 16 vols.

  Ret. Ser., 1998-99, 4 vols.

  Rev. War Ser., 1985- , 20 vols.

WMQ *William and Mary Quarterly*, 1892-

Woods, *Albemarle* Edgar Woods, *Albemarle County in Virginia*, Charlottesville, 1901

CONTENTS

·◦{ **1802** }◦·

CONTENTS

CONTENTS

CONTENTS

CONTENTS

CONTENTS

CONTENTS

CONTENTS

CONTENTS

CONTENTS

CONTENTS

CONTENTS

CONTENTS

CONTENTS

CONTENTS

CONTENTS

APPENDICES

ILLUSTRATIONS

Following page 314

THOMAS MANN RANDOLPH

The artist who made this undated portrait of Thomas Mann Randolph, Jefferson's son-in-law, has not been identified, and nothing is known about the original painting. Illustrated here is a photographic print made sometime in the past from a glass negative. Twentieth-century copies of the painting are owned by the University of Virginia (on loan to the Thomas Jefferson Foundation) and the State Art Collection in Richmond. The copies are 13¾ inches by 10½ inches and 12 inches by 9 inches in size, respectively—dimensions that may reflect the approximate size of the original painting. In the fall of 1802, Randolph, who had married Jefferson's older daughter, Martha, in 1790, confessed to his father-in-law his feelings of inadequacy at being part of Jefferson's family. "I am so essentially & widely different from all within it," Randolph mourned. Jefferson tried to reassure the younger man: "I hold the virtues of your heart and the powers of your understanding in a far more exalted view than you place them in" (Randolph to TJ, 29 Oct. 1802; TJ to Randolph, 2 Nov.).
Courtesy of the Virginia Historical Society.

DRAFT LETTER TO THE SULTAN OF MOROCCO

At Monticello on 5 Aug., Jefferson composed a letter to Mawlay Sulayman, the ruler of Morocco. A polite and straightforward communication written at the urging of James Simpson, the American consul in Morocco, the note asked the sultan to accept 100 wheeled cannon mounts—which Sulayman badly wanted—and requested "hospitality and friendly assistance" for the American naval squadron in its operations against Tripoli. Jefferson left the document unsigned, in the expectation that James Madison might revise it, after which a clerk in Washington was to copy the text onto a blank sheet that already had the president's signature at the bottom. Before that could happen, however, news came that a confrontation between Simpson and Sulayman over a supply of wheat intended for Tripoli had escalated weeks earlier. Relations with Morocco were perhaps "no longer on a footing of amity," as Madison wrote on 14 Aug. Jefferson met with Madison on 20-21 Aug. and drafted a new letter. The revision used the paragraphs of the original version, but became primarily an argument for the right of the United States to stop the wheat from going to Tripoli. The new letter, however, like its predecessor, was never sent, for soon after Jefferson completed the revision, he received word that Morocco had declared war.

Pictured here is the first version of the letter, with Jefferson's later revisions to incorporate it into the second draft. The circular seal visible in the upper right corner and the five-digit number in the lower left are stamps of the Library of Congress. The two states of the letter are printed in this volume at 5 and 21 Aug.
Courtesy of the Library of Congress.

ILLUSTRATIONS

MOROCCO, ALGIERS, AND TUNIS

This volume includes correspondence with the heads of state of Morocco, Algiers, and Tunis: in August, Jefferson made his two attempts to compose a letter to Mawlay Sulayman of Morocco; in September, Hammuda Pasha, the bey of Tunis, wrote concerning his expectation of the gift of a warship; and in October, Mustafa Baba, the dey of Algiers, wrote to protest the choice of a consul for his country and to tout his role as an intermediary with Tripoli. This detail of a map published in 1798 by the English cartographer James Rennell depicts those three countries. Morocco is on the left, the westernmost of the Barbary Coast states, with coastline on the Atlantic as well as along the Mediterranean Sea. Its northern part is labeled on the map as Fez (and for all the detail he included, Rennell omitted the city of Tangier at the western end of the Strait of Gibraltar). To the east of Morocco along the Mediterranean littoral stretches Algiers, and east of it, where the coast makes a sharp turn southward, is Tunis. Rennell's full map, on a sheet approximately $15\frac{3}{4}$ inches high by $27\frac{1}{2}$ inches wide, includes all of Africa north of the equator. He called it "A Map, shewing the Progress of Discovery & Improvement, in the Geography of North Africa." Rennell had firsthand experience in India, but not in Africa, and he compiled from other travelers' accounts his information about the interior of the African continent. In 1792, he was made an honorary member of the African Association (DNB).
Courtesy of the Library of Congress.

LETTER OF MUSTAFA BABA, DEY OF ALGIERS

On 17 Oct. 1802, the dey of Algiers addressed a communication to his "dear friends, the rulers of America." Mustafa Baba, also called Mustafa Pasha, reported that he had obtained the release of mariners from an American merchant brig, the *Franklin*, from imprisonment in Tripoli. He also expressed dismay at the appointment of James Leander Cathcart to replace Richard O'Brien, who had asked to resign as United States consul to Algiers. Two copies of the dey's letter, written in Arabic by his scribes and stamped with his official seal, arrived in the United States: one now in the consular records of the State Department in the National Archives, and the other, pictured here, retained by Jefferson in his personal papers. The document in the illustration is approximately $9\frac{1}{2}$ inches by $12\frac{1}{2}$ inches. No one in the State Department, and no one else available to the president in 1802, could put the dey's missive into English. Jefferson learned what Mustafa had to say only through translations from O'Brien, which the president did not see until May 1803. He answered the letter on 16 July of that year, thanking the Algerian ruler for helping to free the seamen and naming Tobias Lear, rather than Cathcart, as the new consul.
Courtesy of the Massachusetts Historical Society.

THE BOSTON

Jean Jérôme Baugean, a French artist born in Marseilles in 1764, made this engraving of the United States frigate *Boston* in the Mediterranean Sea. Baugean, who drew and engraved many pictures of ships of various nations, published two collections of maritime images. He showed vessels in different settings, sometimes—as in this print of the *Boston*—at anchor with their sails unfurled to air out. Baugean made at least one other picture of the frigate (John Harland, *Ships & Seamanship: The Maritime Prints of J J Baugean* [London, 2000], 6, 40, 53, 63, 90).

The *Boston*, one of the small American frigates built during the maritime conflict with France, was launched in 1799 and carried 28 guns. It was the *Boston* that defeated the *Berceau* off Guadeloupe in October 1800 and took the heavily damaged French corvette to Boston Harbor as a prize. In 1801, Jefferson agreed to allow Robert R. Livingston and Philippe de Létombe, the former French envoy to the United States, to travel to Europe aboard the frigate as it sailed to join the Mediterranean squadron. The vessel's main cabin was modified to accommodate Livingston's entourage on that voyage. The *Boston* appears several times in the present volume, as Jefferson and the cabinet consider whether to keep the frigate in the Mediterranean or bring it home to be laid up at the navy yard in Washington; as they decide to replace its mercurial commander, Daniel McNeill; and as a spurious account, replete with false details, of an engagement between the *Boston* and a Tunisian flotilla makes the rounds of American newspapers (NDBW, *Register*, 68; Vol. 34:546n, 548n, 597n; Vol. 35:125, 187, 188n, 216-17, 292n).

Courtesy of the Department of the Navy / Naval Historical Center and the Naval Historical Foundation.

FRÉDÉRIC CÉSAR DE LA HARPE

In October 1802, Joseph Priestley and Thomas Cooper wrote to Jefferson from Northumberland, Pennsylvania, enclosing long extracts of correspondence from John Hurford Stone, a radical English expatriate living in Paris. Stone believed that Emperor Alexander of Russia would become the engine of change in Europe and restore a momentum for progress that had been lost when Bonaparte rose to power in France. Stone pinned that hope on the new Russian ruler because Alexander, in his youth, had received a thorough grounding in progressive political theory and Enlightenment social thought from his radical Swiss tutor, Frédéric César de La Harpe. When Alexander succeeded to the throne in 1801, he invited his former teacher back to St. Petersburg for a visit of several months' duration. Stone was convinced that Alexander, under the influence of La Harpe and other advisers, would end serfdom, reduce the power of the aristocracy, and change the way Russia was governed. Cooper was more cautious, confiding to Jefferson that he viewed Russia's prospects under Alexander with "fearful hope" (see his letter at 25 Oct., and Priestley's at the 29th).

La Harpe was born at Rolle, in the Swiss region of Vaud, in 1754. He studied at the Academy of Geneva and received a doctor of laws degree from the University of Tübingen at the age of 20. After practicing law for a few years and discarding a plan to emigrate to the United States, he spent a year traveling in Italy as the chaperone of two young Russian aristocrats. That brought him to the attention of Catherine the Great, who persuaded him to move to St. Petersburg to tutor her grandson Alexander and his younger brother. During the first years of the French Revolution, La Harpe, an advocate of the rights of man and an opponent of absolutism, schooled the young grand dukes in his political philosophy. He also kept a strong interest in Swiss affairs, writing public letters to attack the rule of Bern over Vaud. In the late 1790s, after he left Russia, he had a primary role in the creation of the Helvetic Republic that unified Switzerland under the sponsorship of France (Jean Charles Biaudet and Françoise Nicod, eds., *Correspondance de Frédéric-César de La Harpe et Alexandre Ier*, 3 vols. [Neuchâtel, 1978], 1:10-29; R. R. Palmer, *The Age of the Democratic Revolution: A Political History of Europe and America, 1760–1800*, 2 vols. [Princeton, 1959-64], 2:404-5, 408-11, 418).

This portrait, in oil on canvas, is approximately $28\frac{1}{2}$ inches by $32\frac{3}{4}$ inches. It was made in 1803 by the French artist Jacques Augustin Catherine Pajou, a native of Paris who had studied at the French royal academy of painting (Philippe Nusbaumer, *Jacques-Augustin-Catherine Pajou, 1766-1828: Peintre d'histoire et de portrait* [Le Pecq-sur-Seine, France, 1997], 1-2).

Courtesy of the Musée historique de Lausanne, Switzerland.

PORTRAIT OF ALEXANDER I

This undated portrait by an unidentified artist may depict the Russian monarch early in his reign, when John Hurford Stone felt certain that Alexander, under the influence of his "thoroughly republican education" from Frédéric César de La Harpe, would draw on Enlightenment ideals to transform his nation. The young emperor had "great admiration" for Jefferson, Stone understood from La Harpe, and was "earnestly occupied in forming the Mechanism of a free Government" (see the enclosures to Thomas Cooper's and Joseph Priestley's letters at 25 and 29 Oct.). The promise that radicals such as Stone saw in the czar's early, limited considerations of reform was not ultimately fulfilled. This portrait is in oil on canvas, approximately $24\frac{3}{4}$ inches by 32 inches. Photograph by Vladimir Terebenin, Leonard Kheifets, and Yuri Molodkovets, copyright the State Hermitage Museum.

Courtesy of the State Hermitage Museum, St. Petersburg, Russia.

MAP OF THE SOUTHERN FRONTIER

Amos Doolittle of New Haven, Connecticut, engraved this "Map of Georgia, also the Two Floridas," for a 1796 edition of Jedidiah Morse's *American Universal Geography*. Much of the geographical information for the engraving probably came from Joseph Purcell, who had made surveys in the region some years earlier. The map shows the southernmost part of the United States, from the Mississippi River on the west to Georgia on the east. The Spanish provinces of West and East Florida stretch across the lower part of the map. The southern boundary of the United States, which separated its territory from the Floridas, appears in the engraving, but its exact course had not yet been surveyed when the map was made. Doolittle depicted the expanse of country stretching west of the Georgia frontiers to the Mississippi River—what later became the states of Mississippi and Alabama, plus western Georgia—as occupied by the Creeks, the Muskogees (or Lower Creeks), the Chickasaws, and the Choctaws. The Cherokees also had lands in the northern part of the region. Mississippi Territory did not exist when Doolittle made the map, but he did show Natchez on the Mississippi River. Down-

[1]

river was New Orleans, in Spanish territory, and far up the Mississippi, in the upper left corner of the map, is Chickasaw Bluffs, in the vicinity of the modern city of Memphis. This map is approximately $7\frac{1}{2}$ inches by $12\frac{1}{4}$ inches in size (James Clements Wheat and Christian F. Brun, *Maps and Charts Published in America before 1800: A Bibliography* [New Haven, 1969], 133; Jedidiah Morse, *The American Universal Geography, or, a View of the Present State of All the Empires, Kingdoms, States, and Republics in the Known World, and of the United States of America in Particular*, 3d ed., 2 vols. [Boston, 1796], 1: facing 693; Ralph H. Brown, "The American Geographies of Jedidiah Morse," *Annals of the Association of American Geographers*, 31 [1941], 187; A. F. Harley, "Bernard Romans's Map of Florida Engraved by Paul Revere, and Other Early Maps in the Library of the Florida Historical Society," *Florida Historical Society Quarterly*, 9 [1930], 55-6; Dearborn to TJ, 22 Aug. 1802).

Doolittle is best known for his copperplate engravings of the battles of Lexington and Concord in 1775. He produced a variety of printed items, including book illustrations, political cartoons, diplomas, music, bank notes, tickets, and Masonic materials. Plates by Doolittle appeared in two editions of the *American Universal Geography* and earlier in Morse's *Geography Made Easy*. Doolittle also engraved maps for atlases published by Mathew Carey (ANB; Donald C. O'Brien, *Amos Doolittle: Engraver of the New Republic* [New Castle, Del., 2008], 21-9).

Courtesy of Hargrett Rare Book and Manuscript Library, University of Georgia Libraries.

Volume 38

1 July to 12 November 1802

JEFFERSON CHRONOLOGY

1743 · 1826

1743   Born at Shadwell, 13 Apr. (New Style).
1760   Entered the College of William and Mary.
1762   "quitted college."
1762-1767   Self-education and preparation for law.
1769-1774   Albemarle delegate to House of Burgesses.
1772   Married Martha Wayles Skelton, 1 Jan.
1775-1776   In Continental Congress.
1776   Drafted Declaration of Independence.
1776-1779   In Virginia House of Delegates.
1779   Submitted Bill for Establishing Religious Freedom.
1779-1781   Governor of Virginia.
1782   His wife died, 6 Sep.
1783-1784   In Continental Congress.
1784-1789   In France as Minister Plenipotentiary to negotiate commercial treaties and as Minister Plenipotentiary resident at Versailles.
1790-1793   Secretary of State of the United States.
1797-1801   Vice President of the United States.
1801-1809   President of the United States.
1814-1826   Established the University of Virginia.
1826   Died at Monticello, 4 July.

VOLUME 38

1 July to 12 November 1802

5 July   James Thomson Callender publishes evidence of financial support from Jefferson in the Richmond *Recorder*.
16 July   Forwards lists of books to be purchased for Congress to William Duane, George W. Erving, and William Short.
21 July   Leaves Washington for Monticello, arriving 25 July.
5 Aug.   *Conseil d'État* approves decree making Napoleon Bonaparte consul for life.
ca. 5 Aug.   Drafts letter of peace and amity to Mawlay Sulayman, sultan of Morocco.
16 Aug.   Receives erroneous report of alleged engagement between frigate *Boston* and Tunisian squadron.
20-21 Aug.   Visits Madison at Montpelier to discuss Mediterranean affairs.
22 Aug.   Receives news of expulsion of American consul from Tangier and declaration of war by sultan of Morocco.
1 Sep.   Allegations of relationship with Sally Hemings published in the Richmond *Recorder*.
15 Sep.   Meeting at Rising Sun tavern exposes divisions among Philadelphia Republicans.
1 Oct.   Leaves Monticello for Washington, arriving 4 Oct.
16 Oct.   Receives news that peace is restored with Morocco.
18 Oct.   Intendant Juan Ventura Morales closes port of deposit at New Orleans.
28 Oct.   James McGurk hanged in Washington, D.C.
1 Nov.   Ohio constitutional convention convenes at Chillicothe.
3 Nov.   Writes Seneca chief Handsome Lake, endorsing his revitalization program.

To William Bache

DEAR DOCTOR   Washington July 1. 1802.

Your's of June 19. was not recieved till the 28th. I immediately consulted with mr Gallatin and we concluded that it would be best that you should proceed immediately, or as early as you can, to New Orleans, where you will be able by your advice to assist mr Clarke in making such arrangements for the season, as it's advancing state and our limited funds will permit. you consequently recieve letters by this post from the Secretary of the Treasury, one addressed to yourself, and the other to mr Clarke, with authority to draw on the treasury for a quarter's salary (250. D.) in advance. the reasons for silence being now at an end you are free to mention the subject as you shall think proper. I am afraid it is but too probable the French will become masters of Louisiana. I presume they will render it a more agreeable residence; altho' it would have been safer for our peace that it should not change masters. Accept my best wishes for a safe & pleasant journey with assurances of my great esteem & friendship, and be so good as to present me respectfully to mrs Bache.   TH: JEFFERSON

P.S. will you be so good as to notify me in the moment of your actual departure?

RC (facsimile in Adam A. Weschler & Son, Washington, D.C., Catalogue for May 22-24, 1970, Item 411); addressed: "Doctr. William Bache at Franklin near Charlottesville"; franked and postmarked. PrC (DLC).

For Bache's appointment as the physician for the projected marine hospital at NEW ORLEANS, see his letter to TJ of 19 June. For the 3 May 1802 act to provide assistance to sick and disabled seamen, including river boatmen at New Orleans, see Vol. 36:632n.

LETTERS BY THIS POST: in a letter to Bache dated 2 July, Gallatin stated that Bache's pay as physician at New Orleans had been fixed by TJ at $1,000 per year. The salary would begin on 12 July, on the assumption that Bache would depart for Louisiana by that day. Bache could draw on Gallatin for his salary for the first quarter, with the remaining quarterly payments to come from Daniel Clark. Gallatin also wrote to Clark, the United States consul at New Orleans, enclosing that letter in the one to Bache. The act for the relief of ailing seamen, Gallatin explained to Clark, allowed an expenditure of no more than $3,000 at New Orleans. As that amount was considered insufficient for the construction of a hospital, Gallatin authorized Clark to pay Bache's salary and to disburse funds, within the limits of the appropriation, for the occasional and temporary relief of the medical needs of sailors and boatmen (Gallatin, *Papers*, 47:559, 560-2).

To Charles Bulfinch

SIR   Washington July 1. 1802.

The bearer hereof, mr Mills, a native of South Carolina, has passed some years at this place as a Student in architecture. he is now setting out on a journey through the states to see what is worth seeing in that line in each state. he will visit Boston with the same view, and knowing your taste for the art, I take the liberty of recommending him to your notice, and of asking for him whatever information on the subject may be useful to his views while in Boston. Accept assurances of my esteem & respect.   TH: JEFFERSON

RC (photostat in MH); at foot of text: "Mr. Bulfinch." PrC (DLC); endorsed by TJ in ink on verso. Recorded in SJL with notation "by mr Mills."

TJ met architect Charles Bulfinch (1763-1844) in Paris in 1786, during Bulfinch's grand architectural tour of Europe. Largely self-taught, Bulfinch returned to his native Boston in 1787 and spent the next three decades designing some of that city's most prominent architectural works, including the Massachusetts State House and several elegant residences for Boston attorney Harrison Gray Otis. Elected to the city's board of selectmen in 1791, he served as its chairman from 1799 to 1817. In 1818, he was appointed architect of the U.S. Capitol in Washington, in which capacity he over-saw completion of the Senate and House wings and redesigned the building's central dome and rotunda. He returned to Boston in 1830 and shortly thereafter retired from active practice (ANB; Vol. 10:211; Vol. 15:484-5).

Robert MILLS had been studying ARCHITECTURE in Washington under the tutelage of James Hoban. TJ continued to assist Mills with his education and career, granting the young South Carolinian access to his library and introducing him to Benjamin Henry Latrobe, with whom Mills later worked as an assistant for several years (ANB; Rhodri Windsor Liscombe, *Altogether American: Robert Mills, Architect and Engineer, 1781-1855* [Oxford, 1994], 10-15; Latrobe to TJ, 2 Oct. 1803; Mills to TJ, 3 Oct. 1806).

To Mary Jefferson Eppes

MY DEAR MARIA   Washington July 1. 1802.

Mr. Eppes's letter of May 11. is the last news I have heard of you. I wrote to him June 13. your sister has been disappointed in her visit here by the measles breaking out in her family. it is therefore put off to October. I propose to leave this on the 21st. inst. and shall be at Monticello on the 24th. or 27th. according to the route I take; where I shall hope to find you on my arrival; I should very much apprehend that were you to continue at the Hundred till then, yourself, mr Eppes or the little one might be prevented by the diseases incident to the advancing season, from going up at all. it will therefore give me great pleasure to hear of your leaving the Hundred as soon as mr Eppes's affairs will permit. mr Trist and Doctr. Bache will both set out within a few days for the Missisipi with a view to remove their families thither in the fall: so we shall lose those two late accessions to our neighborhood. however in the Summer season our complaint is not the want of society; and in the winter there can be little even among neighbors. Dabney Carr was married on Monday (28th.) and set out yesterday (30th.) with his new wife for Albemarle where he will join his mother now keeping house at Dunlora, till he can fix himself in Charlottesville which will be soon. Sam Carr returns decidedly to live at Dunlora. the marriage of the other sister to Dabney seems to have effected this. Peter and his wife are expected here daily on their way to Baltimore. from this Sketch you may judge of the state of our neighborhood when we shall meet there it will be infinitely joyful to me to be with you there, after the l[ong se]paration we have had for years. I count from one meeting to another as we do between port & port at sea: and I long for the moment with the same earnestness. present me affectionately to mr Eppes and let me hear from you immediately. be assured yourself of my tender and unchangeable affections.   TH: JEFFERSON

RC (DLC); torn; addressed: "Mrs. Maria Eppes at Bermuda Hundred near City point"; franked and postmarked.

I WROTE TO HIM: TJ's letter to John Wayles Eppes, recorded in SJL at 13 June, has not been found.

For the planned journey of Hore Browse TRIST to the Mississippi Territory, see Vol. 36:389.

DUNLORA: the Carr family estate in Albemarle County, located just south of the fork of the Rivanna River (Bryan Clark Green and others, *Lost Virginia: Vanished Architecture of the Old Dominion* [Charlottesville, 2001], 59; K. Edward Lay, *The Architecture of Jefferson Country: Charlottesville and Albemarle County* [Charlottesville, 2000], 126; Vol. 30:406).

From Albert Gallatin, with Jefferson's Notes

Dear Sir   [1 July 1802]

You omitted mentioning the Post office where to direct the Letter to Dr. Bache. I have filled the blank of the commencement of his salary on 12th instt. allowing him a week after receiving your letter to prepare.

Enclosed is a recommendation for "Surveyor of the customs for the district of East River in Virginia." None has been received for the office of collector; but if the surveyor shall be appointed, he may be directed to do the duties of collector until one shall be appointed. The place designated "East river Warehouse" is the proper spot where to fix the port of entry & delivery for the district. An act for that purpose is enclosed for your signature.

For the collector of the[1] port of Marietta, the only recommendation I have is from Mr Fearing also enclosed, but the first on the list was mentioned by Mr Worthington as the[2] best choice; his name Griffen Greene—he received the coolest recommendation from Mr Fearing.

Have any appointments been made, or recommendations received for the offices of Surveyor of customs at Tombstone in the district of Edenton, N. Cara., and at Slade's creek in the dist. of Washington same state?[3] Those two offices, that of Marietta, & those of East River commence this day under the act of last Session approved May 1st. entituled "An Act to provide for the establishment of certain districts &a."

A commission has been sent to John Rowan as surveyor of the port of *Windsor* in N. Carolina. His predecessor's name was William Benson: I never heard of his death or resignation, nor that it was intended to remove him. May not a mistake have taken place & the port intended, be that of *Winton* in same state whose surveyor Lawrence Mooney was represented to have been absent five years?

Your's respectfully   Albert Gallatin

[*Notes by TJ:*]
Mooney returned & was continued
Benson was Surveyor of Edenton
Rowan was recommended by mr Stone in
    the place of a Surveyor of Windsor whom he
    does not name, but says he is dead.
I find in the Roll of officers no such port as Windsor in N.C.

[6]

RC (DLC); undated; with notes by TJ adjacent to Gallatin's closing and signature and in the left margin (see note 3); at foot of text: "The President of the United States"; endorsed by TJ as received from the Treasury Department on 1 July and so recorded in SJL. Enclosure: undated list of three names—Griffin Greene, David Putnam, and Mathew Backus—written on a scrap of paper, perhaps in Paul Fearing's hand, and connected by a brace, with a notation in Gallatin's hand, "Recommended as Collector Marietta by Mr Fearing" (MS in DNA: RG 59, LAR, 4:0730-1; endorsed by Gallatin on verso: "Recommendation Marietta"; endorsed by TJ: "Greene Griffin to be Collector of Marietta recommended by mr Fearing approved by Worthington"). Other enclosures not found.

For Gallatin's LETTER TO William BACHE, see TJ to Bache, 1 July.

William White was evidently the person recommended as surveyor of customs for the new district of EAST RIVER IN VIRGINIA. He received the appointment (*Gazette of the United States*, 12 July 1802; Appendix I). PROPER SPOT: the 1802 act, which established the new district in Virginia, stipulated that the president "designate a proper place" to serve as the port of entry and delivery (U.S. Statutes at Large, 2:181).

Paul FEARING, a Federalist, served as the delegate from the Northwest Territory to the Seventh Congress and led the fight against Ohio statehood. In January 1802, Gideon Granger appointed his friend Griffin GREENE, who became a Re-

publican party organizer, postmaster at Marietta in place of David Putnam, a Federalist. Gallatin immediately informed Rufus Putnam, surveyor general at Marietta, of Greene's appointment as collector (*Biog. Dir. Cong.*; Stets, *Postmasters*, 211; Brown, "Frontier Politics," 436; Donald J. Ratcliffe, *Party Spirit in a Frontier Republic: Democratic Politics in Ohio, 1793-1821* [Columbus, Ohio, 1998], 54; Gallatin, *Papers*, 7:290, 408).

ACT OF LAST SESSION: see Memorandum from Albert Gallatin and Notes on the Establishment of New Revenue Districts, printed at 1 May.

For the appointment of JOHN ROWAN, see Memorandums to Albert Gallatin, 10 June 1802. In May, while Gallatin was in New York, the Treasury Department received a letter from Senator David Stone to the Treasury secretary, which reported the death of the surveyor at Windsor, North Carolina, and recommended Rowan. The department evidently sent the letter directly to the president (same).

For the return of Laurence MOONEY after a long absence, see Memorandum from Albert Gallatin, [before 24 Apr. 1802], and Gallatin to TJ, 24 Apr. The port of Windsor was in the district of Edenton. In the 1802 ROLL OF OFFICERS, the surveyors were listed by districts only (ASP, *Miscellaneous*, 1:260-1, 277; JEP, 1:43).

[1] Preceding three words interlined.
[2] Canceled: "only."
[3] TJ wrote in the left margin "James Clarke Survr" and "<*Jasper Selden*> Selden Jasper Survr."

To John Steele

Th: Jefferson requests the favour of *Mr. Steele* to dine with him *on Saturday next the 3rd Inst*—at half after three.
Thursday July 1st. 1802.
The favour of an answer is asked.

RC (Nc-Ar); printed form, with blanks filled by Meriwether Lewis reproduced in italics; addressed by Lewis: "Mr. Steele."

From John Steele

Sir, Washington July 1st. 1802

I am extremely gratified, and obliged by your favor of yesterday. It has determined me to postpone my journey to Carolina until the last week of this month, which is the more agreeable to me, as my absence will then correspond with the general arrangements of the Executive.

If my private affairs can possibly be made to admit of it, a sense of gratitude for what I consider equivalent to a new appointment will induce me to return:—but whether in or out of Office, I pray you to be assured, that I shall always consider it a flattering distinction to be honored with your confidence, and that it will be my study and my pride to merit the favorable opinion which you have had the goodness to express of me.

I have the honor to be, Sir With the highest consideration Your most Obedient Servt. JNO. STEELE

RC (DLC); at foot of text: "Thomas Jefferson Esqr. President of the United States"; endorsed by TJ as received 1 July and so recorded in SJL. FC (NcU: John Steele Papers).

TJ's FAVOR OF YESTERDAY expressed his satisfaction with Steele's conduct as comptroller and his wish that he continue in office.

From William Tatham

Sir, London July 1st. 1802.

By inclosing to you authentic documents concerning the late inestimable discovery of the *Life-Boat*, which has been introduced into full practice, in saving the crews of vessels wrecked amidst the most tremendous Breakers of this coast, I acquit myself of a duty to my fellow Citizens and to my country. I flatter myself this contrivance will be found of great use on the Jersey coast, such places as the Hatteras shoals &c; and I can have no doubt of its general utility in venturing out upon the Lakes, where a fixed point of land, resisting every wind that agitates a circumscribed surface of water, must necessarily raise the waves to a most aweful surge.

Knowing, Sir, as You do for many years, the nature of my objects and perseverance, I beg leave to refer you to Doctr. Dangerfield: from whom, I trust, you will learn that my integrity is yet unshaken by the contemptible smiles or frowns of foreign intrigue; and that I shall, ultimately, prove to you something more than an unprofitable servant of society.

I have the honor to be, with due consideration, & sincere regard, Your obt H St   WM TATHAM.

RC (DLC); at foot of text: "Thomas Jefferson, President of the United States of America &c. &c. &c."; endorsed by TJ as received 31 Oct. and so recorded in SJL. Enclosures: see below.

William Tatham, a topographer and writer who was once shipwrecked on the coast of New Jersey, had last corresponded with TJ in 1791, since which time he had pursued his varied interests in Virginia, Tennessee, Spain, and England. He returned to the United States for good in 1805 (G. Melvin Herndon, *William Tatham and the Culture of Tobacco* [Coral Gables, Fla., 1969]; WMQ, 2d ser., 16 [1936], 162-3; Vol. 22:xxxviii, 44, 79-85).

The AUTHENTIC DOCUMENTS derived from the report by a special committee of the British House of Commons tasked with determining the relative success of a lifeboat designed by the English ship-builder Henry Greathead. In June 1802, Parliament awarded Greathead £1200 for his invention. TJ forwarded the documents, which eventually were deposited at the State Department, to Samuel Harrison Smith, who printed the first paragraph of Tatham's letter and an abridged version of the report in the *National Intelligencer* on 26 and 29 Nov. 1802 (DNB; TJ to Smith, 16 Nov. 1802).

FOREIGN INTRIGUE: during his time in Tennessee Tatham had come into contact with individuals connected to the conspiracy of William Blount. He later offered intelligence related to the conspiracy to Rufus King, then the American minister in London (William Tatham to Rufus King, 20 June and 30 Aug. 1797, both RCs in DNA: RG 59, MLR; William H. Masterson, *William Blount* [Baton Rouge, 1954], 302-10, 318; Vol. 29:472-4n).

From Henry Dearborn

War Department
SIR,   2d. July 1802

I have the honor to propose for your approbation John F. Heilaman of the State of Vermont and William C. Smith of Pennsylvania to be Surgeon's Mates in the Army.

I have the honor &ca.   H. DEARBORN

FC (Lb in DNA: RG 107, LSP).

On the same date as the letter printed above, Dearborn informed John F. HEILAMAN and William C. SMITH that the president had appointed them surgeon's mates in the army. The Senate approved the appointments in January and March 1803, respectively (FC in Lb in DNA: RG 107, LSMA; JEP, 1:434, 440, 441, 446).

To Mary Jefferson Eppes

My dear Maria   Washington July 2. 1802.

My letter of yesterday had hardly got out of my hand, when yours of June 21st. and mr Eppes's of the 25th. were delivered. I learn with extreme concern the state of your health & that of the child, and am happy to hear you have got from the Hundred, to Eppington, the air of which will aid your convalescence, and will enable you to delay your journey to Monticello till you have recovered strength to make the journey safe. with respect to the measles they began in mr Randolph's family about the middle of June; and will probably be a month getting through the family; so that you had better, when you go, pass on direct to Monticello, not calling at Edgehill. I will immediately write to your sister, & inform her I have advised you to this. I have not heard yet of the disease having got to Monticello, but the intercourse with Edgehill being hourly, it cannot have failed to have gone there immediately; and as there are no young children there but Bet's & Sally's, and the disease is communicable before a person knows they have it, I have no doubt those children have past through it. the children of the plantation being a mile & a half off, can easily be guarded against. I will write to Monticello and direct that should the nail boys or any others have it, they be removed to the plantation instantly on your arrival. indeed none of them but Bet's sons stay on the mountain: and they will be doubtless through it. I think therefore you may be there in perfect security. it had gone through the neighborhood chiefly when I was there in May; so that it has probably disappeared. you should make enquiry on the road before you go into any house, as the disease is now universal through the state & all the states. present my most friendly attachments to mr & mrs Eppes. tell the latter I have had her spectacles these 6. months waiting for a direct conveyance. my best affections to mr Eppes if with you & the family, and tender & constant love to yourself.

                                                TH: JEFFERSON

P.S. I have always forgotten to answer your apologies about Critta, which were very unnecessary. I am happy she has been with you & useful to you. at Monticello there could be nothing for her to do; so that her being with you is exactly as desireable to me as she can be useful to you.

RC (ViU); postscript written in left margin; addressed: "Mrs. Maria Eppes at Eppington near Colesville"; franked and postmarked.

Mary Jefferson Eppes described the STATE OF her HEALTH in her letter to TJ of 21 June.

BET'S & SALLY'S: Betty Brown's young

children were Edwin (b. 1793), Robert (b. 1799), and Mary Colbert (b. 1801). Her sister Sally Hemings had a son William Beverley Hemings (b. 1798) and a daughter Harriet (b. 1801) (Annette Gordon-Reed, *The Hemingses of Monticello: An American Family* [New York, 2008], 535, 550, Hemings Family Tree, 1 & 2).

Beginning in 1795, TJ was employing several NAIL BOYS, young blacks usually between the ages of 10 and 16, in his nailery. By 1800, 16 worked there (Vol. 28:304-5, 341, 405-6; Vol. 31:502).

For the SPECTACLES TJ ordered for Elizabeth Wayles Eppes, see Mary Jefferson Eppes to TJ, 21 Apr. 1802.

To Albert Gallatin

TH:J. TO MR GALLATIN   July 2. 1802.

Doctr. Bache's Address is 'William Bache at Franklin near Charlottesville'

the letter should be put into the Post office before 5. P.M. to-day

William White to be Surveyor for the district of East river.   approved.

Griffin Greene to be collector of the port of Marietta.   approved.

James Clarke to be Surveyor of customs at Tombstone, district of Edenton N.C. recommended by mr Stone.

Selden Jasper was recommended to be Surveyor at the port of Slade's creek, by mr Stanley to mr Stone, who handed it to me with the note that no other of the gentlemen from the state then here, knew any thing of mr Jasper. if no inconvenience would ensue it might be better to write for other recommendation as that of Stanley is very suspicious. of this mr Gallatin must judge.

John Rowan's appointment to the port of Windsor was in conformity with a letter from mr Stone to mr Gallatin (in my possession) informing him the collector (whom he does not name) had lately died, & recommending John Rowan.   TH: JEFFERSON

If mr Gallatin will add the proper titles, or descriptions of office, they may be forwarded to the Secy. of State's office for commissions.

RC (NHi: Gallatin Papers); endorsed by Gallatin. PrC (DLC); lacks postscript. Not recorded in SJL.

For the recommendation of James West Clark (CLARKE) by David Stone, see the enclosure described at Stone to TJ, 1 May 1802. For the endorsement of SELDEN JASPER by Federalist congressman John Stanly, see same. Clark's

parental home, Elmwood, was located on Salmon Creek, the site of Tombstone, the newly designated port. A 1797 graduate of the College of New Jersey, Clark began serving in the North Carolina General Assembly in 1802. He later served one term in Congress and from 1829 to 1831 served as chief clerk of the Navy Department, while his friend John Branch was secretary of the navy. Clark declined the appointment as surveyor (William S. Powell, ed., *Dictionary of North Carolina Biography*, 6 vols. [Chapel Hill, 1979- 96], 1:375; Vol. 37:394-5; Gallatin to TJ, 23 Oct. 1802).

From Albert Gallatin

[2 July 1802]

Will the President enquire from Gen. Dearborn whether Mr Lee is proper to succeed Mr Gerry, as Collector at Marblehead, and whether he has any objection to the commanding officer at Massac being made Collector.—Chribs the present collector is infamous & must be removed but the place is so unhealthy that no other person will go and live there. A similar necessity has existed in the case of Cap. Taylor appointed Surveyor at Beacon Island N.Ca.   A. G.

RC (DLC); addressed: "The President of the United States"; endorsed by TJ as received from the Treasury Department on 2 July and "Gerry Chribbs Taylor" and so recorded in SJL.

William R. LEE of Marblehead had expressed interest in the collectorship at Salem, Massachusetts, in place of the Federalist Joseph Hiller, who was delinquent in his accounts. Jacob Crowninshield wrote TJ in December 1801 warning against Lee's appointment and

recommending John Gibaut, a Salem resident instead (Vol. 35:352; Vol. 36:116-20). For the delinquent accounts of Republican Samuel R. GERRY, see Vol. 36:195-6 and Vol. 37:634-5.

COMMANDING OFFICER AT MASSAC: Daniel Bissell. For his military career, see Washington, *Papers, Pres. Ser.*, 10:240n. Bissell replaced William Chribbs, who had held the collectorship since December 1801 (Vol. 33:678; Vol. 37:634-5; Appendix I). For the appointment of James TAYLOR in 1799, see Vol. 33:164-5.

From Philip Key

ESTEEMED SIR   Chaptico 2d July 1802

A report has prevailed that I had applied to you soon after you was elected President for the office Mr Kelty held in Baltimore

As no such application was ever made by me nor did I ever request any person to solicit you for any place of trust or proffit—I must beg the favor of you to contradict the report by a written certificate which you will please enclose me

I am driven to the necessity of making this application—because an investigation may soon take place that may unfold the infamy—of some men who endeavour to make all around them think that republicanism is nothing more than a wicked & ridiculous clamour.

With sentiments of respect & esteem I am Sir your Ob Svt

PHILIP KEY

RC (DLC); endorsed by TJ as received 4 July and so recorded in SJL.

Philip Key (1750-1820), a planter and lawyer from St. Mary's County, Maryland, had served as a representative in the Second Congress, where he had been aligned with James Madison and other republicans, and as speaker of the Maryland House of Delegates (Papenfuse, *Maryland Legislature*, 2:508-9; Norman K. Risjord, *Chesapeake Politics, 1781-1800* [New York, 1978], 397-8).

The OFFICE to which Key believed he had been connected was that of supervisor of internal revenue for Maryland, a position that John Kilty had held since 1795 (ASP, *Miscellaneous*, 1:283; Washington, *Papers, Pres. Ser.*, 13:439-40; Papenfuse, *Maryland Legislature*, 2:510).

To Martha Jefferson Randolph

MY DEAR MARTHA   Washington July 2. 1802.

I yesterday recieved letters from mr Eppes & Maria. she has been for a considerable time very unwell, with low but constant fevers, and the child very unwell also. mrs Eppes had gone there and staid with her till she was well enough to be removed to Eppington, where the air & the bark had already produced a favorable effect. she wishes to proceed to Monticello as soon as she is strong enough, but is in dreadful apprehensions from the measles. not having heard from you she was uninformed whether it was in your family. I have this day informed her it is there, and advised her when she goes, to pass directly on to Monticello; and that I would ask the favor of mr Randolph & yourself to take measures for having the mountain clear of it by the 15th. of this month, by which time she may possibly arrive there, or by the 20th. at farthest. after that date should any one on the mountain have it they must remove. Squire's house would be a good place for the nail boys, should they have it, and Betty Hemings's for Bet's or Sally's children. there are no other children on the mountain. I shall be at home from the 25th. to the 28th. my affectionate esteem to mr Randolph and tenderest love to yourself.

TH: JEFFERSON

RC (NNPM); at foot of text: "Mrs. Randolph."

LETTERS: John Wayles Eppes to TJ, 25 June 1802, which enclosed Mary Jefferson Eppes to TJ, 21 June 1802.

TJ had learned two weeks earlier from Martha that members of her household were suffering from MEASLES (Vol. 37:618-19).

From Thomas Whitney

Sir   philadelphia July 2d. 1802
The brass work which I repaird no doubt you have received. the charge 1. D 50 C I have been paid. An Artificial horizon such as you mention cannot be had in this City. But a more simple kind have been in use some time which I believe answer every purpose of the Other ones full as well, can be obtained. they consist of a piece of parrallel glass, floated on Quiksilver in a Small Box, which without the Quiksilver (which is put away into a small Bottle when not in use) would not cost above 3. D 50 C. these kind of horizons can be used with a Sextant in Lat. 40. from the 28th of August to the 16th of Aprill and in more Southern or Northern Latitudes, proportionably a Shorter or Longer part of the year. the Observation is made by bringing the Image of the Sun seen by reflection in the Sextant into contact with the Sun seen by reflection in the artificial horizon. half the distance allowing for the Suns Diameter &c is the Altitude thereof. The size of this horizon is generally about three inches and Circular. the largest piece of parrallel glass I have is square and about $2\frac{1}{4}$. Inches by $1\frac{1}{2}$ Inch which will answer the purpose being large enough to contain the Suns Image.

waiting your order I am with much respect yours

THOS. WHITNEY

RC (MHi); endorsed by TJ as received 3 July and so recorded in SJL.

The BRASS piece that Whitney repaired was from a Hadley's reflecting quadrant, a device similar to a sextant. TJ had recently purchased the instrument (TJ to Robert Patterson, 22 Mch.).

The ARTIFICIAL HORIZON was to allow TJ to use the quadrant when the true horizon was not visible. SUCH AS YOU MENTION: see TJ to Whitney, 13 June.

From Thomas Newton, Jr.

Sir   Norfolk July 3. 1802
Doctor Butler a particular acquaintance of mine has for the benifit of his health resolved to spend a few months at the Springs. On his return he wishes to pay his respects to you; Knowing his intention and wish, it is with pleasure I introduce this worthy man to you.—your goodness will pardon this trespass

Wishing you health and much felicity I remain with esteem and regard Yrs. &c   THO NEWTON JR

RC (DLC); at head of text: "Tho: Jefferson Esqre"; endorsed by TJ as received 6 Aug. 1803 and so recorded in SJL with notation "by Dr. Butler."

To Alexander White

DEAR SIR   Washington July 5. 1802.

In your present situation it will probably be practicable for you to furnish me with tolerably exact information relative to the ice-caves in your neighborhood, as I imagine there must be persons in Winchester who can say whether the ice exists there through the summer, whether it is generated in summer &c. I will thank you to communicate to me such information as you can readily get. I expect we shall leave this place in a fortnight so as to avoid passing the last days of July here.

Your favor of June 10. was duly recieved: our recollections of fact correspond nearly. my intention was to use the justification (which was a solid one) as far as the 4000. D. laid out for so useful a purpose; but not actually to draw the balance from the treasury, but to let it stand in account to the credit of the City with the US. it is now quite immaterial, the affairs of the city devolving in fact on the US.

mr Hobens has set up an extraordinary claim to mr Munroe. it is that he continues in his office at 300. guineas a year until the buildings shall be finished, and independent of any body & every body. this he founds on a written appointment of the Commissioners, or perhaps an entry in their journals, which expressing no definite time of continuance, Luther Martin (as Hoben says) deems[1] determinable only by the finishing of the buildings. I believe the writing says he is to continue till they are finished. he claims damages too for what he suffers in his reputation as an architect by their not being finished. I relate these things from mr Monroe, not having seen mr Hobens myself, but he delivered Monroe a written copy of his appointment to shew me. Accept assurances of my esteem & respect.

TH: JEFFERSON

RC (PPRF); addressed: "Alexander White esq. Winchester"; franked; postmarked 6 July. PrC (DLC); endorsed by TJ in ink on verso.

ICE-CAVES: located along North River in Hampshire County, West Virginia, Ice Mountain is known for the refrigeration effect generated within the talus at its base, which vents cold air throughout the year. During winter, the circulation of water and cold air within the talus produces ice, portions of which survive well into the summer months. TJ learned of this phenomenon in 1796 from English agriculturalist William Strickland, who had been informed of its existence by White on a visit to Winchester while touring the area in 1795 (Earl L. Core, "The Botany of Ice Mountain, West Virginia," *Castanea: The Journal of the Southern Appalachian Botanical Club*, 33 [1968], 345-8; Vol. 28:372n; Vol. 29:116-19, 320, 321; Vol. 30:455; White to TJ, 20 Sep. 1802).

In a 26 June letter, James Hoban (HOBENS) was informed by Thomas MUNROE that his salary as superintendent of public buildings for the District of Columbia had ceased as of 1 June with the abolishment of the board of commissioners. "This communication might be deemed unnecessary," wrote Munroe, "it is, however made to prevent the possibility of misunderstanding on the subject." Hoban was first hired by the District of Columbia COMMISSIONERS in 1792 to oversee construction of the President's House at an annual salary of 300 guineas per year. His duties were later expanded to oversee construction of the Capitol in 1798. At their meeting of 24 June 1801, the commissioners agreed to continue Hoban's annual salary of 300 guineas from 1 Jan. 1801 upon his consenting to perform the duties of inspector and superintendent of public works "so long as his Services shall be required." Hoban, who was present at the meeting, agreed to the terms (Dft in DNA: RG 42, LR; ANB; DNA: RG 42, PC; Vol. 24:159n; Vol. 26:462-3).

LUTHER MARTIN was the Federalist attorney general of Maryland and fierce critic of TJ (Vol. 29:408-10, 452-5).

[1] TJ here canceled "it irrevocable until."

From John Beckley

Tuesday Morning
6th. July 1802.—

J:Beckley, with respectful compliments to Mr: Jefferson, and encloses a statement of the balance unexpended of the appropriation for books. He also sends by the servant, one copy of the Journal of H Reps:—for each Session from May 1797, to the last Session, both inclusive; And if Mr: R— comes to the City, he will, with great pleasure, afford him a full use of the Newspaper files, and other printed documents in the Library, and the office.

J:B—begs to submit to Mr: Jefferson, whether in the further catalogue of books, the past omission of the interesting works on natural history by Buffon and Catesby, the last an American, may not be supplied?

RC (CSmH); endorsed by TJ as received 6 July and "library." Enclosure not found, but see below.

As of 30 Sep. 1802, the BALANCE UNEXPENDED from the sum appropriated for books was $2,703.05 (*Letter from the Secretary of the Treasury, Accompanying a Report and Estimates of Appropriation for the Service of the Year 1803; Also an Account of the Receipts and Expenditures at the Treasury of the United States, for One Year Preceding the First Day of October, 1802* [Washington, D.C., 1802], 2d report, p. 21; Vol. 37:228n).

MR: R—: Caesar A. Rodney (see Rodney to TJ, 16 May; TJ to Rodney, 14 June 1802).

WORKS ON NATURAL HISTORY: probably Georges Buffon's *Histoire Naturelle des Oiseaux* and *Histoire Naturelle, générale et particulière* and Mark Catesby's *Natural History of Carolina, Florida,* and the Bahama Islands (see Sowerby, Nos. 1021, 1024, 1027).

From Carlos IV, King of Spain

De Madrid á seis de Julio
MIS GRANDES Y BUENOS AMIGOS.   de mil ochocientos y dos.
Hallandose ajustados los Tratados Matrimoniales de nuestro muy amado hijo Dn. Fernando, Principe de Asturias, con la Infanta de Napoles Da. Maria Antonia, y de nuestra dilectisima hija Da. Maria Isabél con el Principe Heredero de aquel Reyno Dn. Francisco Genaro; y habiendose efectuado en este dia los desposorios de nuestra precitada hija Da. Maria Isabel; hemos creido deberos participar un acontecimiento que nos es tan agradable, no dudando tomaréis en nuestra satisfaccion igual interés al que tomamos en todas vuestras ventajas y prosperidades, deseando tener favorables ocasiones de poder contribuir á ellas.

Vuestro buen amigo   CARLOS.

EDITORS' TRANSLATION

MY GREAT AND GOOD FRIENDS.   Madrid, 6 July 1802
Finding the agreements to be settled for the marriage of our very beloved son Don Fernando, Prince of Asturias, with the Princess of Naples Doña Maria Antonietta, and of our most dearly loved daughter Doña María Isabel with the crown prince of that kingdom, Don Francesco Gennaro, and the betrothal of our aforenamed daughter Doña María Isabel having been carried out on this day; considering ourselves obliged to announce an event that to us is very agreeable, we do not doubt that you take in our satisfaction an interest equal to that which we take in all your gains and prosperities, hoping to have favorable occasions to be able to contribute to them.

Your good friend,   CARLOS.

RC (DNA: RG 59, Ceremonial Letters); in a clerk's hand, signed by Carlos; countersigned at foot of text by Pedro Cevallos; addressed: "A mis Grandes y Buenos Amigos los Estados Unidos de America"; endorsed for the State Department. Dupl (same); entirely in the same clerk's hand with notation certifying the accuracy of the copy ("Concuerda con el Original").

Carlos IV (1748-1819) became king of Spain in 1788. He engaged himself little in policy matters, and the early years of his reign were marked by the views and personalities of two chief ministers from his father's day, the Conde de Floridablanca, who strongly opposed the democratizing elements of the French Revolution, and the Conde de Aranda, who was more ambivalent. Spain's relationship with France became the overwhelming policy issue of Carlos's rule. The two countries went to war after Louis XVI was executed in 1793. Manuel Godoy, who ousted Aranda from power and became the key figure in the Spanish court, brought the war to an end in 1795, and a year later Spain and France formed an offensive and defensive alliance that put Spain in opposition to Great Britain, led to the invasion of Portugal, and made the Spanish monarchy subject to manipulation by France. Dissatisfaction within Spain over that relationship and Godoy's power prompted a seizure of the throne by Carlos's son Fernando in 1808, which gave Napoleon the opportunity to set both kings aside and name his brother Joseph the ruler of Spain. Carlos spent the rest of his life in exile in France and Italy. During his rule, his government introduced some religious reforms, and Alejandro Malaspina made his significant 1789-94 voyage of exploration. Carlos accumulated debts, however, and did little to help his nation meet challenges presented by extended political disruption in Europe. His reign was known for the unequal relationship with France, the influence of Godoy at the sacrifice of national interests, and scandals surrounding the queen, María Luisa, particularly in her relationship with Godoy (Germán Bleiberg, ed., *Diccionario de Historia de España*, 2d ed., 3 vols. [Madrid, 1968-69], 1:706-9; Robert W. Kern and Meredith D. Dodge, eds., *Historical Dictionary of Modern Spain, 1700-1988* [New York, 1990], 36-7, 118-19, 214,

251; Angel Smith, *Historical Dictionary of Spain*, 2d ed. [Lanham, Md., 2009], 137; Vol. 23:266; Vol. 24:669-70; Vol. 25:141, 142n, 191, 194n; Vol. 26:225-6).

TRATADOS MATRIMONIALES: the weddings, which took place in Barcelona on 4 Oct. 1802, were between two closely related branches of the Bourbon family. Reports from Spain indicated that what Charles Pinckney called an exchange of princesses occupied much of the Spanish court's attention during the summer of 1802 and was enormously expensive. An entourage of thousands of people was expected to accompany the monarchs to Barcelona (Teófanes Egido, *Carlos IV* [Madrid, 2001], 271; Madison, *Papers, Sec. of State Ser.*, 3:387, 417, 472-3, 525-6, 552). Carlos's oldest surviving son, FERNANDO, and his betrothed, Maria Antonietta (called María Antonia in Spanish), both turned 18 in 1802. Maria Antonietta's father, Ferdinand, the king of Naples and the Two Sicilies, was Carlos's brother. Fernando's sister María Isabel turned 13 in 1802. There were rumors that Godoy was her biological father. Francesco, her intended husband, born in 1777, was Maria Antonietta's brother. This was his second marriage. His first wife, an archduchess of Austria, died in November 1801 (Bleiberg, *Diccionario*, 1:706, 709; 2:77, 905, 911-12; Giuseppe Coniglio, *I Borboni di Napoli* [Milan, 1995], 213, 233-36, 252; Vol. 35:725n).

To Peter Carr

DEAR SIR   Washington July 6. 1802.

Yesterday a man arrived here with your carriage and a pair of horses, employed by mr Hollins, to come this far. the horses are low in flesh, but dreadfully gaited, owing as is said to the collars being too large for them. the horses are taken care of in my stable and will need some days to [...] and get their sores well. in the meantime I will have their collars rectified. Sam Carr happened to be with us the day they arrived, and said he had a very trusty servant now taking care of a stud horse, & that if he could get his place supplied, he would send him on with the carriage. for fear he may not be able to spare him, we are looking out for a trusty person here; so that between us, you may expect your carriage at Charlottesville from the 11th. to the 15th. instant. I propose to leave this place about the 21st. should you reach it before that time or should any thing detain me here longer, I shall hope that mrs Carr & yourself will take a bed here, and repose your horses a while. S. Carr talks of going to Albemarle the latter part of the month. we have nothing new but what is in the papers. you will see by them that republican Buonaparte is making himself Consul for life, as he did for 10. years by a sham vote of the people. the next step will be to make them vote the succession to his heirs lineal or collateral. present my affectionate respects to mrs Carr, & if this finds you at Warren, to mr & mrs Nicholas; and accept yourself assurances of my esteem & attachment.   TH: JEFFERSON

PrC (DLC); faint; at foot of text: "Peter Carr"; endorsed by TJ in ink on verso.

MR HOLLINS: most likely Baltimore merchant John Hollins, who, like Carr and Wilson Cary Nicholas, had married into that city's powerful Smith family (RS, 2:197-8; Vol. 32:17-18).

Early in July, news began to arrive of a French plebiscite to declare Napoleon Bonaparte CONSUL FOR LIFE. TJ's framing of the issue was similar to the account that appeared in the *New-York Evening Post*, 3 July 1802, which assumed the vote as a foregone conclusion and argued that "but one step more remains to be taken, which is, to perpetuate the Sovereignty in the family of Bonaparte." See also Charles Pinckney to TJ, 24 May 1802.

From John Redman Coxe

DEAR SIR   Philadelphia July 6th 1802

I hasten to forward to you the first copy of my treatise on the Vaccine, which has come to hand. Whilst I request your acceptance of it, I must apologise for the inaccuracies you will doubtless meet with in it. My time has been much occupied in the Dispensary since I put it to Press; I should perhaps have acted more prudently to have delayed it longer; but as I hoped it might prove beneficial to the extension of the disease, I considered it a duty to render the result of my experience public as early as possible. Through the kindness of several respectable practitioners, I have been enabled to add some valuable Communications; and I have most sincerely to thank you, for your kind permission to introduce your important observations; They must certainly tend to promote the speedy progress of Vaccination, wherever they are read. For this as well as for the Infection transmitted by You, I must ever be your Debtor.

As to the Engraving which accompanies the Work, You will find a vast difference between it & the original of Dr. Jenner's; Yet I hope its presence will be serviceable; Nor do I think it a bad specimen of American improvement, considering the novelty of the Subject. The Painting I find the most difficult to execute properly;—Some are superior to others, as the Person improved as she advanced.

I hope in a few days to transmit You a copy on superior paper; and will thank you when You receive it, to deposit for me the present Volume in the Secretary of States Office, as the Law points out.—As I do not expect the Work will be published before the next Week, I thought I owed it to your kindness to transmit you a Copy immediately.

Excuse my interruption;—and be assured Sir of the best wishes for your prosperity, from your much obliged, & very humble Servant

JOHN REDMAN COXE

RC (DLC); endorsed by TJ as received 8 July and so recorded in SJL. Enclosure: an advance copy of Coxe's *Practical Observations on Vaccination: Or Inoculation for the Cow-Pock* (Philadelphia, 1802); Sowerby, No. 953.

Coxe was elected in January 1802 an attending physician of the DISPENSARY, which provided medical treatment for poor people in Philadelphia (ANB; *An Account of the Philadelphia Dispensary, Instituted for the Medical Relief of the Poor,*

April 12, 1786 [Philadelphia, 1802]; Shaw-Shoemaker, No. 2894).

TJ had given Coxe PERMISSION to publish a letter he had written to John Vaughan in which he reported the results of his vaccination efforts at Monticello, a request he had previously denied to Vaughan (Vol. 35:572-3; Vol. 37:364-5). In addition to the letter, Coxe included in his treatise an ENGRAVING that illustrated "a comparative View of the various Stages of the Vaccine and Small-Pox" (Coxe, *Practical Observations*, title page; Shaw-Shoemaker, No. 2095).

From Albert Gallatin

Treasury Department
SIR,   July 6th. 1802

I had the honor to communicate to you, last December, that Mr. Gerry, Collector of Marblehead, having, notwithstanding repeated applications, delayed to render his accounts; and a variation appearing for two years back between the balance of specie in his hand, as stated in his weekly returns, and that ascertained by his quarterly accounts, so far as these had been obtained, it was found necessary to institute an enquiry into the true situation of his office. Although from the result, it appeared probable that a deficiency had existed for a number of years, and that the delays in rendering his accounts, had been intended for the purpose of concealing it, yet as the fact could not be positively ascertained till after settlement of his accounts, as Mr. Gerry's surety who is amply sufficient, requested, on being apprized of those circumstances, that some further time should be granted for that purpose; and as it is difficult to institute a suit on a supposed delinquency, arising from an unsettled account; it appeared most eligible to suspend further proceedings untill the end of last quarter.

I am sorry to be under the necessity of stating, that the indulgence has not produced the expected effect, and that although it is not improbable that a part of the deficiency has since been repaid, Mr. Gerry has during the present year, rendered his accounts for only one quarter ending 30th. March 1801. Under those circumstances, it does not appear consistent with the public service, to remain any longer in that state of uncertainty, and a removal of Mr. Gerry, is, in the opinion of the Secretary, indispensably necessary.

It is also proper to inform you that the appointment of   Chribbs, collector of Massac, though it rested on respectable recommendations, was an unfortunate one; it having been ascertained that his general character renders him unworthy of the trust. Major Swan, Paymaster General, has communicated circumstances on that point, which are decisive; the only difficulty, is that of finding a successor, there being no settlement in the vicinity of Massac, and the spot being considered as unhealthy.

As the case will not, however, admit of delay, it is submitted whether, considering the particular situation of that port, it may not be proper to appoint, with the approbation of the Secretary of war, the commanding officer of the troops stationed there, who is represented to be a suitable character. Under similar circumstances, Captain Taylor of the army, has for some years been the Officer of customs at Beacon Island, in North-Carolina.—

I have the honor to be, with the highest respect Sir, Your Obedt. Servant.   ALBERT GALLATIN

RC (DLC); in a clerk's hand, signed by Gallatin; addressed: "The President of the United States"; endorsed by TJ as received from the Treasury Department on 6 July and "Gerry Chribbs" and so recorded in SJL.

COMMUNICATE TO YOU: Gallatin to TJ, 24 Dec. 1801. Elbridge Gerry served as his brother Samuel R. GERRY'S SURETY (see Vol. 36:196n).

William CHRIBBS received RECOMMENDATIONS from William C. C. Claiborne and others (Vol. 35:392).

COMMANDING OFFICER: Daniel Bissell (see Gallatin to TJ, 2 July).

Memorandum from Albert Gallatin, with Jefferson's Instructions

Will the President be pleased to examine the question? It is becoming important and must be decided at Detroit. Indeed there is some danger in suspending the decision at Michillimakinac the post which forms the entrance of the communication by Michigan & Ouisconsing to Mississipi

1. Shall Portages be construed to mean only *land carriages* from a part of the boundary to another part of the same as at Niagara? This appears to me the true & ultimately will prove the only safe construction.

2. Does the Treaty by Portages mean to include any communication by land or water leading in a straight direction from the Lakes to the Mississipi. This will exclude the Wabash, & possibly the Illinois river communication [...] include the usual route by Fox & Ouisconsing rivers.

3. Is it best only to exclude as not being Portages, those communications which cannot be [...] by any construction, (those leading by Wabash & other rivers [...] Ohio)—and to suspend covering the whole ground which the 1st definition contemplates. Under this idea the annexed sketch was drawn; but the propriety of tolerating any inland navigation & transportation as a portage is doubted—

Respectfully submitted by   ALBERT GALLATIN
                                        July 6th 1802

[*Instructions by TJ:*]
As the discussion of these questions, should any arise with Great Britain, will devolve on the Secretary of state, will he be pleased to consider & give his opinion on them?   TH: JEFFERSON
                                        July 7. 1802.

MS (DLC: Albert Gallatin Papers); torn; in Gallatin's hand, with directions by TJ at foot of text; addressed: "The President of the United States."

The Treasury secretary's QUESTION concerned the interpretation of Article 3 of the Jay Treaty, which dealt with commerce between the United States and Canada and stipulated that duties were not owed on goods that were merely "carried over any of the Portages, or carrying Places on either side, for the purpose of being immediately reimbarked" for further transport. The exemption from duties extended only to goods "carried in the usual and direct Road across the Portage," with no attempt to sell or exchange them. The article granted the right to establish regulations to prevent fraud (Miller, *Treaties*, 2:246-8).

MUST BE DECIDED AT DETROIT: on 1 Aug. 1801, Matthew Ernest, the customs collector at that port, informed Comptroller John Steele that British traders wanted to designate as a portage a route from

Detroit to the Mississippi River, which led from "the Lake to Fort Wayne and from thence across land into the Wabash river, and down that into the Ohio." On 15 Sep., Steele informed the collector that he agreed that the traders had a right to carry their goods free of duty on the route. By the time Steele presented this issue to Gallatin in December 1801, he had revised his position, noting that only those near the U.S.-Canadian border could have been contemplated by the treaty. He thought it desirable to exclude from duty-free status several routes, including "the two which led from Fort Wayne by different branches of the Wabash into the Ohio (as being too nearly connected with our settlements)." He advocated the change, however, only if it could be accomplished "without affording reasonable cause of complaint to British subjects whose interests and convenience may be affected by the regulation" (*Terr. Papers*, 7:31, 33, 35-6).

MICHILLIMAKINAC: the collection district on the straits connecting Lake Huron and Lake Michigan. OUISCONSING: that is, Wisconsin.

The ANNEXED SKETCH has not been found, but it may have been a draft of the letter Gallatin sent to the comptroller on 7 July. Gallatin noted that the exemption from duty did not extend to goods transported by residents of one country, "through *rivers* which are exclusively within the territory of the other country." Exemptions could not be claimed for goods transported on one river and then carried to another. The only goods exempt from duties were those coming from Canada "to land portages, similar to that at Niagara, extending from a landing place on the navigable waters, which form the common Boundary" to a place of embarkation on the same waters. The claims of British merchants at Detroit to carry goods, "without paying duties, through the Miami of the lakes, or other waters emptying into lakes Erie or Michigan, and thence across by land to the Wabash or other rivers, emptying in the Ohio" could not be supported under any construction of the Treaty and was "too dangerous to be tolerated." Those goods were "exclusively intended for the consumption of the Indians living within the Territory of the United States" and for American settlements on the Ohio and were therefore subject to duties. Although the same circumstances existed at Michilimakinac, Gallatin deemed it impractical to enforce the collection of duties in the district at that time (*Terr. Papers*, 7:58-60).

DEVOLVE ON THE SECRETARY OF STATE: on 8 July, Daniel Sheldon, at the Treasury Department, forwarded to Madison both Gallatin's "observations" to the president and his 7 July letter to the comptroller. In correspondence with Rufus King on 20 July, Madison enclosed a copy of Gallatin's 7 July letter, noting that it conveyed "the sentiments of the President on that subject." Madison wrote King that the meaning of portages or carrying places should be limited to cases where the waters forming a boundary between the two countries became unnavigable and a transit by land was necessary to re-enter common waters where they were again navigable. Any other interpretation meant a loss of revenue for the United States and gave an advantage to Canadian traders who did not have to pay duties in conveying goods "to the Indians beyond the Mississippi"; the goods of the American traders using the same channels were "loaded with american duties." Madison expected King to correct any misrepresentations communicated to the British government by Canadian traders and to prepare the government for regulations on portages to produce "a conformity with the true meaning of the Treaty" (Madison, *Papers, Sec. of State Ser.*, 3:389-90, 404-5).

To David Hall

Washington July 6. 1802.

I recieved in due time your favors of May 31. and June 9. the former covering an Address from a Democratic republican meeting at Dover, the latter one from the grand and general juries of the circuit court of the US. held at Dover both of them praying a removal of Allen Mc.lane from the office of Collector of the customs at Wilmington.

When I first came into the administration, complaints were exhibited against Colo. Mc.lane, and an enquiry immediately directed to be made into his conduct. every opportunity, which could be desired, was given on both sides to the producing of testimony, and on a very full investigation he was finally acquitted. he had a right to consider that acquittal as a bar to every thing anterior; and certainly according to sound principles it must be so considered. I am persuaded that the Republican citizens who have concurred in these addresses would be as incapable of wishing me to do any thing which should bring a just censure on the administration, as I should be from yielding to such a wish. we have no interests nor passions different from those of our fellow citizens. we have the same object, the success of representative government. nor are we acting for ourselves alone, but for the whole human race. the event of our experiment is to shew whether man can be trusted with self government. the eyes of suffering[1] humanity are fixed on us with anxiety as their only hope, and on such a theatre & for such a cause we must suppress all smaller passions & local considerations. the leaders of federalism say that man cannot be trusted with his own government. we must do no act which shall replace them in the direction of the experiment. we must not, by any departure from principle, dishearten the mass of our fellow citizens who have confided to us this interesting cause. if, since the date of the acquittal, Colo. Mc.lane has done any new act inconsistent with his duty as an officer, or as an agent of the administration this would be legitimate ground for new enquiry, into which I should consider myself as free to enter. no particular fact of this kind is charged in the addresses; but only that he is disagreeable to the citizens of the place.[2] this would be among the proper considerations on the appointment of an officer, and ought, before appointment, to have weight. but after many years possession of an office, and an exact discharge of it's duties, a removal[3] for this reason would not be approved by those beyond the pale of his unpopularity.

Our opponents are so disposed to make a malignant use of whatever comes from me, to torture every word into meanings never meant, in order to veil their own passions and principles, that I must ask the favor of you to communicate verbally the sentiments of this letter to those who forwarded their addresses through you not permitting the letter or any copy to go out of your own hands. I pray you to accept assurances of my high consideration & respect.

TH: JEFFERSON

RC (DeHi); addressed: "Governor Hall Wilmington Delaware"; franked; postmarked 8 July. PrC (DLC).

For the addresses PRAYING A REMOVAL of Allen McLane from office, see Delaware Democratic Republicans to TJ,

printed at 24 Mch. and 5 June, respectively.

[1] TJ here canceled "man."
[2] Preceding three words interlined in place of "generally."
[3] Word interlined in place of "discharge."

To Thomas Leiper

DEAR SIR   Washington July 6. 1802.

Your favors of June 3. were duly recieved. I made the last year but little tobacco, and my overseer informed me it was not good. it was deemed generally an unfavorable year both for the quality and quantity of tobacco made. in consideration of the quality I have lodged mine at Richmond with a view of selling it there; and had authorised my correspondent to take 6. D. @ 90. days for it. I have lately a letter from him in which he tells me he can get 5. D. cash, but not 6. D. credit. I have made up my mind to let it lie there till I can get 6. D. for it: consequently it is at your service there at that price, & taking it according to it's Lynchburg weights. but it is not, as I expect of the fine quality of some of the crops you have bought of me. mr Randolph makes little or no tobacco. mr Madison told me he had at Richmond either ten thousand weight or ten hogsheads of very superior quality for which he would take what I offer mine at.

You complain that the newspapers named you a Commissioner of bankruptcy, which exposed you to mortification. if I am to answer for what the newspapers hazard, I shall have a heavy reckoning indeed. the depravity of the taste of our countrymen, who will encourage papers altho' full of lies, & many because they are full of lies, leaves no remedy for that evil. the fact is that in advising with some of the members of Congress, and some others, at different times, as to commissioners, your name was sometimes mentioned, & I believe by myself. but the general impression was that you would not accept it, and therefore that it was better to look out at once for those who would.

finally I availed myself of a confidential person going to Philadelphia, who on consultation there presented me the list which he said would be approved. the[1] reason for which you were not named was far from being unfavorable to you. certainly on my part there was no want of confidence in your fitness, nor any want of inclination to do what would have been acceptable to you had it been thought so. I shall certainly not be charged with any leaning towards federalism. it is a plant I shall not nourish by favors! I shall do that sect rigorous justice on all occasions, but not strengthen it's hands. I put an end to the persecutions they were carrying on against the republicans when I came into office, but I set on foot none against them. they still hold nine tenths of the offices of the US. and cry out as if they had nothing, because they have not the other tenth also.

Accept assurances of my esteem and best wishes.

TH: JEFFERSON

a list of the tobacco I now have at Richmd
made at Poplar Forest in 1801.

No.	359.	150	1515
	360.	150	1631
	941	140	1410
	945.	145	1551
	1152	140	1578
	1153	140	1686
	1154	133	1562.
	1155.	133	1569
	1194	140	1796
	1195	140	1559
	1200	140	1568
	1201.	140	1154
			18,466

RC (NN: Arents Collection); addressed: "Thomas Lieper esq. Philadelphia"; franked and postmarked. PrC (MHi); endorsed by TJ in ink on verso.

YOUR FAVORS: Leiper wrote two letters to TJ on 23 June, the first inquiring about TJ's tobacco, and the second protesting the publication of his name among a list of commissioners of bankruptcy for Philadelphia. The CONFIDENTIAL PERSON was probably Albert Gallatin. See note to Memorandums to Albert Gallatin, 10 June 1802.

[1] TJ here canceled "person."

From Levi Lincoln

SIR   Washington July 6—1802

I have the honor to enclose a letter which I recd some time since respecting the continuence of Mr Smith as a marshal of the district of Pennsylvania—

In looking into the act, to amend the judicial system, which passed the last Session, and compareing it with those, with which it connects, I do not find the reappointment of the marshals, which you mean to continue, absolutely, necessary; but as there must be some act of the executive expressive of its continuing the officer, a reappointment may be the best mode of doing it, with a notification to the discontinued one of it, and of his discontinuence. This mode, of reappointment appears to me, the most eligible one, as it will be less likely to admit of any mistake, respecting the taking of new bonds, which appear to me to be indispensable—The existing bonds of a continued Marshal, altho they may bind him under the operation of law, it being his own act, to extend his jurisdiction, & of course his responsibility & hazard; Yet, I conceive, they cannot bind his sureties, to indemnify for any injuries, which may result from the increased Jurisdiction, which the law has given to their principals. The power of the legeslature not extending to such a retrospective effect—

I am Sir most respectfully your obedt Sert   LEVI LINCOLN

RC (DLC); at head of text: "President of the United States"; endorsed by TJ as received 6 July and "Marshals" and so recorded in SJL. Enclosure not found.

John SMITH was the marshal of one of the two districts allotted to PENNSYLVANIA by the Judiciary Act of 1801. The 8 Mch. 1802 repeal of that act removed the additional districts that had been created under the 1801 law, making Pennsylvania once again a single judicial district. The 29 Apr. act TO AMEND THE JUDICIAL SYSTEM empowered the president to "discontinue" marshals from districts that had ceased to exist, making no mention of any ACT OF THE EXECUTIVE required for marshals "who shall be continued in office" (U.S. Statutes at Large, 2:132, 164; Vol. 33:246-7; Vol. 37:85-6).

Memorandum on Appointments

Lyttleton W. Tazewell ⎫
Richard Evers Lee.   ⎬ of Norfolk. Commrs. of bankruptcy
Moses Myers.   ⎪   Virginia
Thomas Blanchard   ⎭

Thomas Ward of Newark
Phineas Manning of N. Brunswick
John Cobb. of Morris.
Isaiah Shinn of Woodstown — do. for New Jersey.
Abraham Brown of Burlington
Anthony F. Taylor of Bordenton

———

Jonathan Loring Austin.
Thomas Dawes junr.
Samual Brown
Joseph Blake — of Boston
Samuel Allen Otis
Thos. Edwards
Josiah Smith
Ralph Cross — of Newbury
Joseph Markwan — port.
Joshua Carter

Joscph Mc.lcllan
Joseph Boyd
Salmon Chase — of Portland
William Widgery

do. for Massachusets.

qu. if those of Portland shd. not be named for Maine which I believe is a separate district.

Thomas Stuart of Tennissee[1] to be Attorney of Tennisee

TH: JEFFERSON
July 6. 1802.

PrC (DLC). Not recorded in SJL.

TJ may have sent this list of appointments directly to the State Department for the issuance of commissions. Previously, however, the president sent the lists to the Treasury Department with the request that Gallatin forward the nominations to the Department of State (see Memorandums to Albert Gallatin, 10 June 1802).

Governor Monroe provided TJ with the candidates for bankruptcy commissioners at NORFOLK and Governor Bloomfield provided those nominated FOR NEW JERSEY (see James Monroe to T.J, 29 June, and Joseph Bloomfield to TJ, 30 June).

FOR MASSACHUSETS: Levi Lincoln and Henry Dearborn were preparing a list of bankruptcy commissioners for TJ in late

June (Lincoln to TJ, 28 June). Before TJ prepared this memorandum, he received an undated list in Dearborn's hand, with the 14 nominees for Boston, Newburyport, and Portland, as they appear above. Dearborn also listed, between the candidates for Boston and Newburyport, five nominees—Nathan Dane, William Lee, Jacob Crowninshield, William Burley, and Isaac Story—for Salem, Marblehead, and Beverly. On the list, TJ interlined "Isaac Story" in place of "William Lee" (MS in DNA: RG 59, LAR; undated; in Dearborn's hand, with emendation by TJ; at head of text: "Commissioners"; endorsed by TJ: "Massachusets Commrs. bkrptcy. Genl. Dearb. mr Lincoln"). The State Department issued commissions for the Boston, Newburyport, and Portland nominees on 6 July and for Burley, Crowninshield, Dane, and Story two days later. MARKWAN: that is Marquand. The commissions for THOSE OF PORT-LAND were designated for the district of Maine (list of commissions in Lb in DNA: RG 59, MPTPC; *National Intelligencer*, 16 July 1802; Benjamin W. Labaree, *Patriots and Partisans: The Merchants of Newburyport, 1764-1815* [Cambridge, Mass., 1962], 215; Vol. 37: Appendix II, Lists 1 and 2). The State Department sent out letters with the commissions for all of the Massachusetts appointees on 12 July (Madison, *Papers, Sec. of State Ser.*, 3:416, 432, 449). On 22 July, Samuel Brown wrote Madison, noting that "existing engagements" prevented him from accepting the commission (RC in DNA: RG 59, RD; endorsed by TJ: "declines commr. bkrptcy"). Other Massachusetts appointees informed the secretary of state that they were returning the commissions, including Carter, Crowninshield, Dane, and McLellan on 21, 22, 24 July and August 1802, respectively. Advanced age and loss of eyesight kept McLellan from accepting the appointment (RCs in DNA: RG 59, LAR, all endorsed by TJ; Madison, *Papers, Sec. of State Ser.*, 3:412, 416, 423, 449). On 28 July, Otis informed Madison that he would like to delay his decision until Congress was in session. If he were again elected clerk of the Senate, he would request permission to hold both offices and if he could not, he would decline the commission. If he were not reelected, the commission would keep him from "being wholly out of employ" (RC in DNA: RG 59, LAR, endorsed by TJ: "Otis Saml. A. to mr Madison Comms. bkrptcy"; Tr in DLC, dated 14 July, at head of text: "Copy"; Madison, *Papers, Sec. of State Ser.*, 3:436-7). On 27 July, Burley wrote Madison declining his commission and recommending Daniel Kilham in his place (same, 432). Dane's name was rendered as "Danna" on TJ's lists and in the State Department records. When Dane, a Federalist who had served in the Continental Congress, returned his commission, he expressed doubt that he was the person intended (list of commissions in Lb in DNA: RG 59, MPTPC; Madison, *Papers, Sec. of State Ser.*, 3:423; Vol. 37: Appendix II, Lists 1 and 2; Vol. 38: Appendix I). For the appointment of Joseph Story in place of Isaac Story, see TJ to Dearborn and TJ to Isaac Story, both at 5 Aug. 1802.

For the recommendation of THOMAS STUART as the U.S. attorney for Tennessee, see Andrew Jackson to TJ, 16 June.

[1] Preceding two words interlined.

From William Bache

DEAR SIR   Franklin July 7th. 1802

It was not till after mondays post had departed that I received your kind communication of the first instant. Arrangments were immediately commenced for complying with the desire of my proceeding as soon as possible, tho I fear that it will not eventually be as soon as proper. I must first dispose of my personal property and arrange the payment of some debts without which I cannot feel easy to leave this place—These affairs will retain me till sometime in the next month; but of this I assure you that I will be unremitting in my endeavours to be off as soon as possible. I wish your advice as to the route to be taken at this season of the year. will it not be risking my family too much to descend the Missisipi in september. If so what port had we best sail from.

As the appropriation is but small will it not be prudent to economise by procuring such medicines, as will be most in demand such as bark &ca, in the U.S. as I understand they are dear at New Orleans—Mrs Bache joins me in sentiments of gratitude & friendship—

WILLIAM BACHE

RC (DLC); endorsed by TJ as received 11 July and so recorded in SJL.

From Albert Gallatin

[7 July 1802]

An endorsement on the enclosed letter somewhat similar to that sketched, will be sufficient authority to justify the payment of interest to Maryland.

Respectfully submitted by   ALBERT GALLATIN

RC (DLC); undated; addressed: "The President of the United States"; endorsed by TJ as received from the Treasury Department on 7 July and "repaimt to Maryland" and so recorded in SJL. Enclosure: see below.

The ENCLOSED LETTER with TJ's endorsement has not been found, but it gave the Treasury Department authority to pay the $18,000 in interest due on the $200,000 Maryland loan, as TJ informs Governor John F. Mercer in a letter of this date. The endorsement SKETCHED by Gallatin is printed below.

ENCLOSURE

Gallatin's Draft of Authorization for Payment on Maryland Loan

A sale of the city lots[1] pledged for the repayment of the within mentioned loan, cannot, in my opinion be made at present, without an unwarrantable sacrifice of the property. The Secretary of the Treasury will direct the interest now due to be paid out of the Treasury in conformity to the provisions of the act entitled "an Act to abolish the Board of Commissioners in the city of Washington, and for other purposes"   Signed T.J.

MS (DLC); undated; entirely in Gallatin's hand.

PROVISIONS OF THE ACT: Section 5 of the legislation called for the president to decide if money for the repayment of interest and installments on the Maryland loan should be paid directly from the U.S. Treasury or from the sale of lots (U.S. Statutes at Large, 2:175-6).

[1] Gallatin first wrote "The sale of lots" before altering the beginning of the sentence to read as above.

From Albert Gallatin

DEAR SIR   [7 July 1802]

Is it not best to do whatever is wanting at once. I have not yet answered Latimer's letter & will not until I hear from you. But I think it is best not to answer him & to act. On that ground it seems to me that the best way would be at same time with the New England appointments to make

Muhlenberg	Collect. Philada.
T. Coxe	Supervr. Pennsylva.
& Mr Page	Collectr. Petersburgh.

I cannot help thinking that you are not doing enough in Massachts. & that intending to strike it should be done with effect & so as not to disgust our friends. Lee for Salem & either Asa Andrews (Collect. of Ipswich a converted federalist[1]) or John Leach of Boston for Marblehead—would do. Tyng's successor will not be considered at home,[2] though highly respectable, as a decided friend—Gerry goes & to give Lee his place is no gain. Add to that that Lee aims at & deserves something better & that it will be peculiarly grating to his feelings to take Gerry's place. Perhaps he may decline & that will put the whole business in an awkward situation—Excuse the freedom of these remarks, but I feel great reliance on their solidity.   At all events commissions should be left for Muhlenberg & Coxe.

With sincere respect & attachment Your obt. Servt.

ALBERT GALLATIN

I wish Capn. Lewis to write to me in New York as Secy. of the Treasy. directing where & in whose hands the library money is to be placed

RC (DLC); undated, but see TJ to Gallatin, 9 July; at foot of text: "The President"; with names and places written by TJ in the left margin adjacent to appearance in the text, including "Latimer," "Muhlenbg Coxe Page," "Lee. Salem," "Asa Andrews John Leach } Marblehead," "Dalton. Tyng," and "Gerry"; endorsed by TJ as received from the Treasury Department on 8 July and "Latimer. Ting. Hiller. Gerry. Muhlenbg. Coxe. Page" and so recorded in SJL.

George LATIMER'S LETTER has not been found, but on 4 July Alexander J. Dallas wrote from Philadelphia that the collector intended to send his resignation by post the next day and that Latimer thought the public interest would be promoted by deferring acceptance of his offer until the close of the month. When the final decision to remove Latimer was made is not clear, but on 4 June Latimer noted to Dallas that reports of his probable removal from office were circulating. If he had to leave office, Latimer preferred to resign so that he might not lose his share of the commissions, which was given in cases of death or resignation, but not removal. He thought resigning would also "prevent clamour." After consultation with Gallatin, Dallas informed Latimer that "an early change" in his office was "contemplated" and that he should go ahead with the "beneficial arrangement" (Gallatin, *Papers*, 7:175, 286, 298). For Dallas's earlier defense of Latimer as collector, see Vol. 36:182n. For the appointment of Peter Muhlenberg to the collectorship at Philadelphia and Tench Coxe to the vacancy caused by Muhlenberg's promotion, see Coxe to TJ, [before 2 Apr. 1802]. Muhlenberg received his commission on 31 July and on 2 Aug. took office (Gallatin, *Papers*, 7:402).

John PAGE received TJ's offer of the collectorship at Petersburg on 17 Mch., but did not accept the position until 1 June (see Vol. 36:613-14; Vol. 37:124-5, 169, 525-6).

Appointed collector in May 1796, ASA ANDREWS, a Harvard graduate and attorney, remained in office at Ipswich until dismissed by President Jackson in 1829 (*New England Historical and Genealogi-*

cal Register, 10 [1856], 192; JEP, 1:212-13). TYNG'S SUCCESSOR: TJ's note in the margin—"Dalton. Tyng"—indicates that he had decided upon Tristram Dalton to replace Dudley A. Tyng, a Harvard-educated lawyer and justice of the peace who was appointed collector at Newburyport in 1795. Dalton declined the appointment (see note above and Dalton to TJ, 19 Aug.; John J. Currier, *History of Newburyport, Mass., 1764-1909*, 2 vols. [Newburyport, Mass., 1906-09], 2:267-8). TJ categorized Tyng's removal as one of those made to give some participation in office to Republicans and to "disarm" those who were using their office "to oppose the order of things established" (Vol. 33:672; Vol. 38: Appendix I).

LIBRARY MONEY: see TJ to Gallatin, 9 July (second letter).

[1] Preceding three words interlined.
[2] Preceding two words interlined.

To Cyrus Griffin

DEAR SIR   Washington July 7. 1802.

As soon as the act was passed transferring to the Executive the duty of naming Commissioners of bankruptcy, measures were taken by enquiries from the members of Congress, and in some instances from the Governors to have a proper selection made. you are sensible of the opinion which has prevailed that the Judiciary of the US. as a body have lent their influence to the promotion of a certain set of political principles disapproved, as is believed, by the great majority of our citizens. while I accuse no one of the body of giving into this practice, I am happy in the opportunity of expressly acquitting yourself of it, according to the best information I have recieved. and I do it that you may be assured that the praetermetting the commissioners who had been occasionally named by the judges in the state of Virginia has not been from any doubt of undue bias, but in pursuit of a general line of enquiry, to wit from the members & Governors of the states. the list was made out for Richmond & Petersburg before the reciept of your letter, and that for Norfolk, tho' the commissions are but lately signed, had been ready some time. not a single person of those named in your letter was known to me personally, so that their omission can be no imputation on them. I pray you to consider this as written for your private information, and to accept assurances of my high consideration & respect.   TH: JEFFERSON

PrC (DLC); at foot of text: "The honble Judge Griffin."

PRAETERMETTING: from the Latin verb "praetermettere," to overlook or to omit.

For the appointment of commissioners in PETERSBURG, see Vol. 37: Appendix I. For Norfolk, see James Monroe to TJ, 29 June.

YOUR LETTER: Griffin to TJ, 6 June.

From Thomas Jenkins

SIR,   Hudson July 7th. 1802—

The bearer hereof Mr. Isaac Dayton has lately been employed as one of the Collectors of the Internal Taxes under Samuel Osgood Esqr late Supervisor for the District of New York, which Office expired on the 30th. June last, in Consequence of the Judicious repeal of the Excise Laws during the last Session of Congress—Should it be deemed expedient and Consistent with sound Policy to remove the present Officers employed in Hudson for the Collection of the Imposts, I hereby recommend Mr. Dayton as a suitable Person to fill the Office now enjoyed by John C. Ten Broeck Esqr. and Shubael Worth Esqr. as a suitable Character to fill Office at present occupied by Henry Malcolm Esqr—I am of opinion that the two Characters I have recommended will meet the entire approbation of a Majority of the Mercantile and most Respectable Men of our City, and as such I beg leave to recommend them to your Consideration—

I am Sir Respectfully Your most Obt. Servt.

                                              THOS. JENKINS

RC (DNA: RG 59, LAR); at head of text: "Thomas Jefferson Esqr President of the United States"; endorsed by TJ as received 15 July and "Isaac Dayton to be Surveyor of Hudson v. Tenbroeck" and so recorded in SJL with a brace connecting this letter to ones from Dewitt Clinton and Samuel Osgood (see below).

Thomas Jenkins (c. 1741-1808) took the leading role in the development of the town of Hudson, New York, at Claverack Landing on the Hudson River in the 1780s by an association of proprietors from New England seaports. Jenkins, a Quaker, was born on Nantucket and was a prosperous merchant in Providence,

Rhode Island, before moving to Hudson. There Jenkins headed a firm that engaged in overseas commerce and whaling. He owned real estate and was involved in rope manufacturing, whale oil processing, and candlemaking. In 1797, his taxable estate was far larger than that of any other resident of Hudson. Jenkins held the offices of alderman and town supervisor from 1788 to 1791. The state Council of Appointment made him the mayor of Hudson beginning in 1793. In the spring of 1804, he participated in local Republican meetings that supported the nomination of Morgan Lewis rather than Aaron Burr as governor of New York. One of Jenkins's sons was Elisha Jenkins, who in 1802 was the comptroller of the state of New York (Stephen B. Miller, *Historical Sketches of Hudson* [Hudson, N.Y., 1862], 6-8, 16, 18, 27-8, 30, 35-6, 113-15; Hudson *Bee*, 7 Sep. 1802, 13 Mch., 10 Apr. 1804, 13 Sep. 1808; Syrett, *Hamilton*, 15:665-6; Vol. 37:539-40).

ISAAC DAYTON had succeeded John C. TEN BROECK as the collector of internal revenues at Hudson after Ten Broeck was removed from that office for "delinquency" a few months before the dismantling of the excise collection system on 30 June, as provided by the 6 Apr. act to repeal internal taxes. Ten Broeck still held two customs positions, as surveyor and port inspector. He was a member of one of the families of Dutch origin that resided in the Claverack area before the proprietors of Hudson began their venture in the 1780s. Although some of those families opposed the proprietary association, the Ten Broecks cooperated with the newcomers and made a place for themselves in the town's governance. SHUBAEL WORTH, a Hudson merchant, was one of the original proprietors of Hudson. The Dayton family was also part of the proprietary association, and like Worth played an active role in a Republican group allied with Charles Holt, publisher of the *Bee*. HENRY MALCOLM was the collector of customs at Hudson (Miller, *Historical Sketches of Hudson*, 6, 7, 9, 10, 19, 23, 28, 34, 43, 64-5, 69, 115-16; ASP, *Miscellaneous*, 1:270, 281; U.S. Statutes at Large, 2:148; JEP, 1:447; Dayton to TJ, 19 Oct. 1802).

On the same day that TJ received the letter printed above, he received communications from DeWitt Clinton at Newtown and Samuel Osgood in New York City, both written on 10 July. Those letters have not been found, but they apparently related to the same subject as Jenkins's letter, for TJ connected the three entries in SJL by a brace with the notation "Isaac Dayton to be collector of Hudson vice Tenbroeck." Clinton likely forwarded a recommendation addressed to him by Ambrose Spencer. Writing at Hudson on 8 July, Spencer called on Clinton's "good offices with the President of the United States" in support of Dayton's quest for "the Offices now held here under the government of the United States" by Ten Broeck. Ten Broeck, Spencer averred, was guilty of "delinquencies as an Officer," misconduct, and "violation of Duty." Spencer also recommended that Worth replace Malcolm, who as a physician was "often called away" from his customs post and should be dismissed "on various accounts" (in DNA: RG 59, LAR).

From Francis Mentges

SIR/   Philadelphia 7th July 1802

I am still without the consolation of Knowing that the statement & requests, which I had the Honor of transmitting to you ℗ Mail on the 2d of June last, have been judged worthy of your favorable attention & interference—indeed, I am without even the satisfaction of Knowing that they have come to your Hand

I cannot permit my self to doubt, Sir, your Candor, your love of justice and your goodness, if I much longer continue in my present destitution of employment, I shall be compelled to make sacrifices *of lands*, which are truly painful and which ought to be reserved for the last resort of my very latest years, when the power of being useful should have finaly submitted to the stroke of old age, I hope and I trust that an early answer will not be found quite incompatible with your numerous engagements, and that by relieving me from many distressing apprehensions no injury will accrue to the public Service, I have the Honor to be—

Sir/ your Ob Humble Servt— F MENTGES

RC (DLC); at foot of text: "The President of the United States"; endorsed by TJ as received 8 July and so recorded in SJL.

In his letter of the 2D OF JUNE LAST, Mentges requested a settlement of his claim on the War Department and a new appointment.

To John F. Mercer

DEAR SIR Washington July 7. 1802.

Altho' your letter, which this acknoleges, was written so long ago as the 5th. Ult. I have not in the mean time been inattentive to it's contents.

By the act of Congress of May 1. which I now inclose, you will percieve that the interest of the 200,000. D. borrowed by the Commissioners of Washington on the guaranty of Congress, is directed to be paid by a sale of the lots, which have never yet been sold; with a proviso that if a sufficient number cannot be sold without an unwarrantable sacrifice of the property, paiment shall be made out of the treasury. time was necessary for this experiment. it has been tried, and a sale found impracticable for prices warranted. by a due regard to the ultimate security of the US. the Secretary of the Treasury is therefore now occupied in remitting this interest according to your desire.

With respect to the 50,000. D. borrowed by the Commissioners, not under guaranty of the US. Congress has authorised the paiment of principal and interest on the 1st. day of November next: for which purpose the lots liable to be resold, are to be re-sold for whatever they will bring, to the amount of the debt; and, if there be a deficiency, it is to be paid[1] out of the Treasury of the US. a list of such lots is accordingly made out, and they are advertised for sale; and the line of conduct will be observed which the law has prescribed.

Accept assurances of my sincere friendship & high consideration.

TH: JEFFERSON

RC (facsimile in Christie's Catalogue, New York City, May 2000, No. 67); endorsed. PrC (DLC), in ink at foot of text: "Governour Mercer." Enclosure: "An Act to abolish the Board of Commissioners in the City of Washington; and for other purposes," 1 May 1802, Sections 5 and 6, of which, outlined the process for the repayment of the Maryland loans (U.S. Statutes at Large, 2:175-6).

YOUR LETTER: TJ responded earlier to Mercer's communication of 5 June in a private letter to the governor dated 23 June.

For the actions taken by the Treasury secretary in REMITTING the INTEREST, see Gallatin to TJ of this date (first letter and enclosure).

As superintendent of the city of Washington, Thomas Munroe compiled the list of lots which were being ADVERTISED FOR SALE in the Washington newspapers (see TJ to Munroe, 16 June 1802).

[1] TJ first wrote "that it be paid" before altering the text to read as above.

From James Monroe

DEAR SIR   Richmond July 7. 1802

I enclose you some columns of a paper here edited by Mr. Callendar. It was whispered sometime since that the federalists knew he was possessed of some letters from you, and were endeavouring to bring them before the publick. In several of his preceding papers he glancd at the subject, but at length enters more directly on it. Perhaps it will be best that nothing shod. be said in reply by any one.[1] Of this you will be the best judge. It may be of use to state to me the periods when the sums he mentions were advanc'd, & the circumstances wh. lead to it. Any light you think proper to communicate relative to the affr., will be used without compromitting any one, in the mode you deem most eligible. If any reply is proper he may be drawn to state facts correctly, by a person knowing them, without it appearing that you gave a hint.

sincerely I am yr. friend & servt   JAS. MONROE

I communicated to Mr. Madison lately that by the last law the office of marshall in this place, or indeed State was abolished. Major Scott who is a man of great merit, feels uneasy in his situation; in whose place it was impossible to put a more deserving man.

I enclose you a letter from a captn. Leach with whom I was acquainted in France, who has repeatedly written me to mention him to my friends in the admn., and who I have mentioned to Mr. Madison, who has I am well satisfied paid the attention to the subject that was proper. I considered him an honest, intelligent man a sound republican.[2] You will perceive what he now seeks. I do not know that he is such a person as it wod. be proper to place in such an office in so important a town. Unless he was supported by the principal republicans there it wod. be improper to bring him forward, as I have heretofore told him. I enclose his letter to you, only because I am writing you, & have not time to write Mr. Madison who has I think correct information of his pretentions.

RC (DNA: RG 59, MLR); endorsed by TJ as received 10 July and so recorded in SJL. Enclosures: (1) Probably James Thomson Callender's "Letter VII" to the public, printed in the Richmond *Recorder*, 5 July 1802, which details the encouragement and financial support that TJ had provided for Callender's writings, particularly the publication of *The Prospect Before Us* in 1800; Callender claims that in the spring of 1798, TJ described him to Philadelphia merchant Thomas Leiper as "the best writer of newspaper paragraphs that he had ever seen either in America, or in Europe"; after receiving the first pages of the *Prospect*, Callender states Jefferson "returned not merely a letter of thanks, but, to my great surprise, he said that he had directed Mr. George Jefferson of Richmond to pay me *fifty dollars*"; when the first part of the second volume of the *Prospect* went to press, Jefferson sent Callender another $50; "These hundred dollars attest, beyond a thousand letters of compliment," asserts Callender, "how seriously the president was satisfied with the contents of the book, and how anxiously he felt himself interested in its success." (2) John Leach to Monroe, Boston, 7 June 1802, seeking Monroe's assistance in securing an appointment as a commissioner of bankruptcy; Leach's only friend from Massachusetts in Congress is William Eustis, from whom he learns that he stands well with the cabinet secretaries and that Levi Lincoln will nominate the commissioners of bankruptcy for his state; Edward Bangs of Worcester has also promised his assistance; Leach believes that more "Commercial Men" need to be made commissioners in Boston and he reminds Monroe of his commercial knowledge acquired as a ship captain; Leach finds himself an "outcast" among his former acquaintances due to his extended residence abroad; "*I have been too long in France a meer Jacobin*—enough to Damn, an Angel in this place"; Leach remains hopeful, however, "of receiving the friendly aid of those whose Political principles are Consonant with my own" (RC in DNA: RG 59, LAR; endorsed by TJ: "see Monroe's letter of July 7. 1802. to be Commr. bkrpts in Boston").

A PAPER HERE EDITED: James Thomson Callender began editing the Richmond *Recorder; Or, Lady's and Gentleman's Miscellany* in February 1802, employing his new forum to vent his wrath upon political leaders on both sides, especially the newly incumbent Republicans. He also used the paper to skewer the aristocratic pretensions of the Virginia gentry, in particular their penchant for gambling, dueling, and miscegenation. TJ found himself the subject of many columns in the *Recorder* throughout the latter half of 1802 and early 1803, which not only embarrassed the president and his party, but also affected TJ's reputation during his lifetime and beyond. These include the first public allegations of TJ's relationship with Sally Hemings, his improper advances toward the wife of John Walker, and his attempt to repay a prewar debt to Gabriel Jones in depreciated currency (Richmond *Recorder*, 1, 22 Sep., 13, 27 Oct., 17 Nov., 8 Dec. 1802; Durey, *Callender*, 148-63; Pasley, *Tyranny of Printers*, 260; Malone, *Jefferson*, 1:153-5, 447-51; 4:206-23; Vol. 2:260-1; Vol. 29:536-7; Vol. 37:435-7).

SOME LETTERS FROM YOU: TJ to Callender, 6 Sep. and 6 Oct. 1799 (Vol. 31:179-82, 200-2). Callender printed both of these letters in full in the *Recorder* on 6 Oct. 1802, with an invitation for readers to view the originals at the office of the *Virginia Gazette* in Richmond. When TJ broke off his relationship with Callender in May 1801, the journalist threatened that he "was in possession of things which he could & would make use of in a certain case." Although TJ declared that Callender "knows nothing of me which I am not willing to declare to the world," Monroe had nevertheless advised him to get back all of his letters written to Callender "however unimportant they are" (Vol. 34:205, 229-30). A third letter, dated 11 Oct. 1798, is the only other known correspondence from TJ to Callender (Vol. 30:558-9). For TJ's recollection of the content of letters, see TJ to Monroe, 15 and 17 July 1802.

HE GLANCD AT THE SUBJECT: by the summer of 1802, Callender was embroiled in a newspaper war with his former employer Meriwether Jones, editor of the Richmond *Examiner*. To counter Callender's written assaults on his character and personal conduct, Jones attempted to denigrate Callender's writing ability, especially the columns he contributed to the *Examiner* in 1799 and 1800. Although the newspaper's circulation and influence had soared during Callender's tenure, the 2 June 1802 edition of the *Examiner* excoriated the "indelicacy, vulgarity and abuse" of Callender's writings and asserted that they had "injured" the *Examiner*. Responding in the *Recorder* in "Letter VI," Callender claimed that far from being told that he was injuring the newspaper, "Jones was constantly encouraging me to write as much as possible." To inspire Callender further, Jones had told him that in the summer of 1799 TJ himself called the *Examiner* "the best conducted newspaper in America" and that James Madison described Callender as wielding "the strongest pen" in the nation. "It is possible that some people may think Mr. Jefferson almost as able as Mr. Jones, to determine upon the talents and accomplishments, of the editor of a newspaper," chided Callender at the close of his letter, and promised to continue with a fresh "series of remarks" in his next installment (Durey, *Callender*, 114-15, 121, 148-57; *New-York Evening Post*, 6 July 1802; *New-York Herald*, 14 July 1802; James Thomson Callender, *The Conduct of Meriwether Jones, In a Series of Letters, Addressed To The Public* [Richmond, 1802], 45-64).

THE SUMS HE MENTIONS: the two $50 payments from TJ alluded to by Callender in the *Recorder* were made in September 1799 and October 1800 (MB, 2:1005, 1028; Vol. 31:179-80; Vol. 32:235).

Joseph SCOTT was appointed marshal of the eastern district of Virginia in 1801. By the Judiciary Act of 1802, Virginia was among the states that were consolidated into single judicial districts, for which the president was authorized to discontinue supernumerary officers. TJ retained Scott as marshal for the state and signed his commission on 8 July 1802 (Madison, *Papers, Sec. of State Ser.*, 3:359-60; Vol. 33:673, 675; Levi Lincoln to TJ, 6 July 1802; TJ to Scott, 1 Aug. 1802).

Mariner John LEACH had written TJ from Ghent in 1794 with a passport request. Monroe had previously recommended him for a consular appointment at Dunkirk. In a 12 Apr. 1802 letter to James MADISON, Monroe described Leach as "an honest deserving man" and recommended him "without reluctance." Leach did not receive a consular appointment, nor was he among the bankruptcy commissioners appointed for Massachusetts (Madison, *Papers, Sec. of State Ser.*, 3:122-3; Vol. 28:103-4; Vol. 33:666).

[1] Preceding three words interlined.
[2] Preceding three words interlined.

From Henry Dearborn

SIR   July 8th. 1802

Will you be pleased to note such of the books & Instruments in Majr. Williams,s list herewith enclosed, as may with propriety be purchased for the School at West point.

with respectfull considerations I am Sir Your Obedt Servt

H. DEARBORN

RC (DLC); at foot of text: "The President of the United States"; endorsed by TJ as received from the War Department on 8 July and "books for the school at West point" and so recorded in SJL. Enclosure not found, but see below.

TJ apparently made his reply directly on Jonathan Williams's enclosed list of BOOKS & INSTRUMENTS, then returned it to Dearborn. In a letter to Williams of 9 July, Dearborn wrote, "You will observe the notes made by the President on the Margin of your list," and authorized him to purchase "such Books and Instruments as may be obtained and the Bill will be paid" (FC in Lb in DNA: RG 107, LSMA).

Also on 8 July, Dearborn sent TJ a letter recommending the promotion of Williams to lieutenant colonel, Decius Wadsworth to major, and George Washington Varnum to first lieutenant, all in the Corps of Engineers (FC in Lb in DNA: RG 107, LSP; not recorded in SJL). Later that same day, Dearborn informed the three officers that the president had approved their appointments (FCs in Lb in DNA: RG 107, LSMA).

From Matthew Adgate

Canaan Columbia County
SIR   State of New York July 9 1802

A fellow Citizen, unknown to you, and bearing a Solitary name, in the Republic of Letters, having drawn, an Epitome of the Creator, in his three fold being:—also, man his Creature, in his likeness, to his Creator:—attempting thirein a discription of the Soul:—together with the scriptures of Truth, as the word of God, unfolding man to himself, in placing the Soul, in its Goverment over the Body of flesh; to lead man back to his god:—and also in this Epitome drawn the picture of man, as co equel in Nature; made so by his God:—and then drawn, a Natural Rule of Goverment for this creature man, in his social state of accountability to God, and man; as practiced at the first:—and now again taking place in mans world over man; whereby unlawfull dominion, and power.—is giving place in our federated state:—thereby restoring true dignity to man, in his Probation world:—concluding the whole by some observations on the Two witnesses so particulerly mentioned in Johns Apocalipse; as Referring to our day, our Acts, and Deeds: and our equel Rights.—

I wish Sir to lay this Epitome at your Door:—that if the greater concerns of the Nation over which you preside:—or your own domestic claims: will at any leasure hour permit: it might pass under your Philosophical eye:—not persuming to ask the Boon, of a reply, to this or that; yet should you think its contents, worthy patronage:— as calculated in our equal day of helping man better to know, his God; himself, and Brother man: I shall readily wish the same to arrest the attention of equel man: that the same common principle of Nature in man: and Natures world, might be better learnt, by every Grade in our Sociel world: —

without further consuming your time, I Subscribe[1] myself your fellow Labourer (in a Low grade of Life) in the field of Social equel man. — MATTHEW ADGATE

RC (DLC); at foot of text: "His Exellency Thomas Jefferson"; endorsed by TJ as received 19 July and so recorded in SJL. Enclosure: probably *A Northern Light; or New Index to the Bible: In Which the Doctrine of the Holy Trinity Is Explained, and the Evidence Thereof Taken from Nature and the Scriptures, Man Himself Being the Great & Leading Truth Thereto* (Troy, N.Y., 1800; Evans, No. 36775), which has been attributed to Adgate.

Matthew Adgate (1737-1818) was born in Norwich, Connecticut, but eventually settled in the part of Albany County, New York, that later became Columbia County. He became politically prominent during the American Revolution and represented Albany County in the convention that drafted New York's state constitution in 1777. Elected one of Columbia County's delegates to the convention called to ratify the Federal Constitution, he assumed an active role in the antifederalist coalition and voted against ratification. He also served several terms in the state assembly and as a judge of the court of common pleas for Columbia County. He later moved to Clinton County, where in 1818 he published *A Digest, or, Plain Facts Stated: In Which the Gospel and Law Are Compared in Some of Their Most Important Parts* . . . (Plattsburgh *Republican*, 7 Mch. 1818; Merrill Jensen, John P. Kaminski, Gaspare J. Saladino, and others, eds., *Documentary History of the Ratification of the Constitution*, 21 vols. to date [Madison, Wis., 1976-   ], 22:1671, 1676).

[1] MS: "Subscriber."

From Henry Dearborn

War Department
9th July 1802

The Secretary of War has the honor to submit to the President of the U States (for his approbation) the following list of promotions
Regiment of Artillerists
Captain George Ingersoll to be Major Vice Wadsworth transferred
1st. Lieutt. Peter Tallman to be Captain Vice Ingersoll promoted
2nd. Regiment of Infantry
1st. Lieut. Thomas Swaine to be Captain Vice Vance Resigned
2nd. Lieut. Edward P. Gaines to be 1st. Lieut. Vice Erwine Resigned
2nd. Lieut. Robert G. Barde to be 1st. Lieut. Vice Swaine promoted
Ensign George T Ross to be 2nd Lieutenant Vice Gaines promoted
Ensign Henry B Brevoort to be 2d. Lieut Vice Barde promoted

FC (Lb in DNA: RG 107, LSP).

To Albert Gallatin

Dear Sir   Washington July 9. 1802.

On recieving yesterday your favor, left here, I consulted with the Secretaries of State & War. we are all of opinion decidedly that mr Latimer's letter ought not to be left unanswered: but that he should be told that it not being intended that he should continue in office an application had been made on his behalf for permission to resign, that to this the Executive had no objection; that his letter, predicated on the ground of the proposition of his resignation having originated with the Executive, is not founded in fact, nor can be admitted to have any effect in their proceedings. if he writes an absolute resignation; well: if not the removal will take it's effect.   we have concluded on a review of the proceedings & opinions of the day before your departure to modify them thus.

Newbury port Dalton vice Ting

Salem. Lee vice Hiller.

Marblehead. Henry Warren vice Gerry.

Commissions accordingly, as well as in the case of Latimer &c will be signed within a day or two.—Capt Lewis will write to you to-day on the subject of bills on London & Paris in favor of Erving & Short for 1000. D. each for the books. nothing new has happened since your departure. accept my best wishes & affectionate respect.

Th: Jefferson

RC (NHi: Gallatin Papers); addressed: "Albert Gallatin Secretary of the treasury now at New York"; franked and postmarked; endorsed: "that Latimer must be put out of office." PrC (DLC). Recorded in SJL with notation "removals &c."

YOUR FAVOR: see Gallatin to TJ, 7 July (second letter). Gallatin also wrote his wife, Hannah, whom he was joining in New York City, a letter from Washington on 7 July. He evidently departed for New York on 8 July (Henry Adams, *The Life of Albert Gallatin* [Philadelphia, 1879; repr. New York, 1943], 304).

For the recommendation of HENRY WARREN for the collectorship at Plymouth, see Josiah Smith to TJ, 7 June 1802. TJ also listed "Dalton vice Tyng Newbury port"; "Lee vice Hiller Salem"; and "Henry Warren vice Gerry Marblehead" on a scrap of paper (MS in DLC: TJ Papers, 124:21451; undated; entirely in TJ's hand).

CAPT LEWIS WILL WRITE TO YOU: a letter in Meriwether Lewis's hand has not been found, but a draft in TJ's hand with formal instructions for bills on London and Paris is printed immediately below.

To Albert Gallatin

SIR   [ca. 9 July 1802]

The committee appointed to carry into execution the act concerning the library of Congress having desired me to act for them in the purchase and paiment of the books, I am to request you to furnish me with a bill on London for 1000. D. payable to George W. Erving or order and another on Amsterdam for 1000. D. payable to William Short esq. or order, to enable them to pay for the books which are to be ordered from those places respectively. I am Sir &c.

Dft (MoSHi: Jefferson Papers); un-dated, but see TJ to Gallatin, printed above at this date.

For the congressional COMMITTEE appointed to oversee purchases for the LIBRARY OF CONGRESS, see TJ to Abraham Baldwin, 14 Apr. 1802.

From Samuel Smith

SIR/   Balt. 9 July 1802

Permit me to introduce my young friend Mr. Abraham Ogden formerly of New York where he had his Commercial Education—Mr. Ogden has established a House of Commerce at Marseilles, & meant to have been an applicant for the Consulate at that Port, but on being informed that Mr. Cathalan would (if practicable) be Continued he expressed his approbation & Spoke in terms highly respectful of that Gentleman,—in that he differed from Mr. Cushing, of Mr. Cushing Mr. Cathalan does not write very favorably—Should Mr. Cathalan not keep the office, permit me in the warmest Manner to recommend Mr. Ogden & believe me to be with truth—

your friend & Servt.   S. SMITH

RC (DNA: RG 59, LAR); endorsed by TJ as received 13 July and "Ogden to be Consul at Mars." and so recorded in SJL.

ABRAHAM OGDEN was a partner in the firm Ogden, Schwartz & Co. of MAR-

SEILLES (Madison, *Papers, Sec. of State Ser.*, 8:80; Stephen Cathalan, Jr., to TJ, 22 Sep. 1804). Isaac CUSHING had previously been recommended to TJ for appointment as commercial agent at the French port (Vol. 37:306-8).

From James Carroll,
with Jefferson's Note

[on or before 10 July 1802]

The Petition of James Carroll of the City of
Washington, Blacksmith;
Most humbly Sheweth,

That at a Circuit Court of the District of Columbia, begun and held
in the City of Washington, on the fourth Monday of June last, your
Petitioner was fined at the suit of the United States in the sum of
Twenty dollars and costs of suit; for an assault and battery on the
body of John Veach, a black man, and in the sum of Twenty dollars
and costs of suit; for an assault and battery on the body of Daniel
McGinnis, a black man; for non payment whereof, he is now
confined in Washington County prison.

That the motive which urged him to these breaches of the Law,
arose from those black men's having previously beat and abused his
employer John Galloway a white man, with whom your Petitioner
then wrought at his trade.

That his reputation has not been sullied by any other charges, than
those for which he is fined, and he trusts that the certificate hereto annexed, attested by persons who have a knowledge of him, and his hu-
mility and affliction, will induce the exercise of the prerogative of
Mercy in his favor

He therefore most humbly implores you to remit the fines aforesaid; and thereby enable him to apply his labor to the discharge of the
costs accruing thereon.

and he as in duty bound will pray &c

[*Note by TJ:*]
rejected on the representation of J.T.M.

RC (DLC); undated; in an unidentified hand; at head of text: "To the President of the United States"; with a subjoined undated certificate, signed by
William Rhodes and 42 others, stating
that Carroll is "a sober, honest and industrious man," that the facts as stated in his
petition are accurate, and that Carroll is
"a proper object" for having his fines remitted; with TJ's note on verso below endorsement; endorsed by TJ as received
10 July 1802 and so recorded in SJL with
notation "imprisoned on fine. petn."

TJ had previously remitted fines incurred by DANIEL MCGINNIS for his non-
appearance at the December 1801 term of
the U.S. circuit court for the District of
Columbia. He had been called to testify in
the assault case against Carroll (Vol.
37:195-6).

Carroll petitioned TJ again in June
1803, requesting a remission of his fines
and costs. TJ responded by ordering a remission of the fines only (Carroll to TJ,
[16 June 1803]).

From Henry R. Graham

HONORD SIR   Fort Stoddert 10th July. 1802

I shall not attempt to apologize for addressing you the motives by which I am actuated sufficiently relieve my mind from any sence of impropriety in applying to the principal of a free nation in the cause of Injured Worth. and will I am confident plead my excuse with him,—

Among those who have fallen victims to the system heretofore established is a Gentleman in the neighbourhood of Washington Ky. by the name of Wm. Hy. Beaumont by birth an Englishman altho a long time in the United States. and one of the few of that nation whoz republican principals have been uniform, he formerly edited a News-paper in the back part of Pennsylvania from whence I understand he was obliged to retrie[t] owing to the persiqution he met with from a junto headed by Judge Addison whoz systim it waz to repress every Republican Press, in Kentucky he also edited a paper, but the implacable resentment of his persecutors purs[uing him] and money being scarse in the state, and having a large family to support, at the end of two years, He found himself unable to continue the publication, and disposed of his right in it to satisfy his creditors—To support his family he has since attempted to institute an academy on a different plan from the generality of schools in the state, but the country was not ripe for such an undertaking, and he waz obliged to terminate it with considerable loss. He is now struggleing in Poverty and though calculated to become a useful member of society and desirous of Provideing by his honest endeavours for a deserving family, He finds himself unable to get into any business that will afford them bread, from Principal I believe him opposed to making any applycation that might relieve him but it strikez me that his case is a hard one and should be known, I can look on him in no other light, but as a Martyr to Republicanism.

His edducation has been a good one. He has been ever thought a man of talents, and his character will stand the test of enquiry

I presume from the place of Mr. Beaumonts former residence he cannot be unknown to Mr. Gallatin and the members of Congress from the western country

I have presumed Sir to state this case to you, Hopeing that in some future arrangements which may be deemed necessary to mak this poor man be thought of. It may not now be amiss, briefly to inform you who I am that have thus taken the liberty of introduce to you anoth. but I [will] hope, if I have been guilty of a presumption in endeavouring to render a service (perhaps the last that I shall ever have in my power) to a much respected Friend, you will forgive me— Either to Mr. S. T. Mason Mr. Rd. Brent or Mr. Jn. Fowler I refer you for any information you may Honor me by wishing for. relative to myself let it suffice for me to say that I waz born in Virginia and have the Honor to bear a commission in the Army of the United States (tho. but a second Lieutenant) Should you confer on me a single line in return, it shall ever be gratefully remembered by Sir Most Respectfully Your Obediant Servant   H. R. GRAHAM

RC (DNA: RG 59, LAR); torn; at foot of text: "His Excellency Thomas Jefferson President, US City of Washn."; endorsed by TJ as received 12 Sep. and so recorded in SJL.

Henry Richard Graham (d. 1819) was commissioned a second lieutenant in the Third Infantry in Feb. 1801. He ended his military career as a captain in the First Rifle regiment in 1815, shortly after the Senate rejected his promotion to major (Heitman, *Dictionary*, 1:467-8).

William Henry BEAUMONT worked as a clerk for Hugh Henry Brackenridge and campaigned for Albert Gallatin in addition to establishing his first NEWSPAPER, the *Western Telegraphe* of Washington, Pennsylvania. In 1797, Beaumont and a partner moved to KENTUCKY and for two years operated the *Mirror* in Washington and the *Palladium* in Frankfort, during which time they also printed Kentucky's resolutions opposing the Alien and Sedition Acts (Hugh H. Brackenridge, *Incidents of the Insurrection in the Western Parts of Pennsylvania, in the Year 1794* [Philadelphia, 1795], 92-7; Brigham, *American Newspapers*, 2:1375; Gallatin, *Papers*, 3:528, 695; Vol. 30:555).

From Dennis Griffith

SIR   Elk Ridge Landing July 10th 1802

I had not the pleasure of receiving your complimentary note of the 9th ultimo with its enclosure untill yesterday: please to accept my Thanks for the attention you was pleased to favor me with. If the communication I made should ultimately prove useful, I shall be very glad indeed,—it is in safe hands; & the sorrow I shall feel from its not answering my expectations, will be mitigated by the motive that produced it, & doubly so, by the reflection, that our enlighten'd men shew a disposition to encourage effort, however feeble, by their polite attention to the authors of such communications.

Previous to the receipt of your favor I had written a few lines on the subject of a Botanical Establishment by our General Government, but reflecting on the critical grounds upon which we at present stand, and the propriety & necessity, perhaps, of applying for a time, all our resources to the extinction of our national debt, I had resolved to suppress the intrusion I had intended upon your useful time; considering also that a postponement of the begining might ultimately be the means of bringing such an establishment to greater perfection & at an earlier period than if attempted at this time—but as I hope it is probable that you may remain a long time at the head of our affairs, I thought it might not be improper to mention it as a memento: I find that you will not attend to it the less, from its proceeding from an obscure citizen.

Our country abounds with esculent & medicinal plants, & some excellent dyes. The aborigines knew members of them from necessity & experience in their respective Characters. Why should *we* not improve? Rags & paper are made from vegetable substances, and we may hope, I think, at least, that we may by judicious investigation find some of our native plants fit for the manufacture of that useful thing called paper, & perhaps some others—permit me to add that I have no sinister object in view in this suggestion, for in all the sincerity of truth I here declare that I beleive myself incapable of filling any appointment that might be made under such an establishment—

I am with sincere & due respect, your Obt. fellow Citizen

D GRIFFITH

RC (DLC); endorsed by TJ as received 16 July and so recorded in SJL.

The NOTE from TJ has not been found and is not recorded in SJL. It no doubt accompanied the American Philosophical Society's acknowledgment of the receipt of Griffith's COMMUNICATION, which was a letter to TJ of 8 Oct. 1801 speculat-ing about the possibility of using the positions of stars to find longitude. That letter was read at a meeting of the APS on 7 May 1802. The meeting referred the matter to Robert Patterson and Benjamin Latrobe, who by 18 June apparently indicated that the subject did not require further attention (Vol. 35:411-12; Vol. 37:431-5).

From William Kilty and James M. Marshall, with Jefferson's Note

Alexandria July 10th 1802

The Undersigned Judges of the Circuit Court of the District of Columbia, respectfully recommend to the President of the United States a Remission of the Fine of Thirty Dollars imposed on Michael Carrigo as appears by the above Transcript of the Proceedings against him—

This recommendation is not grounded on the merits of the Prisoner or any[1] hardship of the Sentence in relation to the Crime of which he was Convicted—but on the following Circumstances—

We are credibly informed that the said Michael Carrigo is unable to pay the said Fine or any part of it and that he has not any relation friend or Acquaintance from whom he might expect assistance for that purpose—That he is nearly destitute of Cloathing and is from that circumstance, from long confinement and from disease, become an Object wretched to himself, Loathsome to others and shocking to Humanity—

We further represent that on a remission of the Fine it might be within the power of the Court to rescind the Order for the Committment which appears in the Proceedings, or to make an Order for the release of the Prisoner, so that the Inconveniencies which we have stated might be removed, and the United States might also be freed from the useless expence of maintaining him in Prison, from which there appears to be no other method of liberating him than the one which we have proposed.   W KILTY
                                                        J MARSHALL

[*Note by TJ:*]
a remission of the fine to be made out   TH: JEFFERSON
                                              July 11. 1802.

MS (DNA: RG 59, GPR); in a clerk's hand, signed by Kilty and Marshall; written at foot of transcript of court's proceedings (see below); with TJ's note below signatures. Enclosed in George Deneale to TJ, 10 July 1802, stating that "I am directed by the Court now sitting in this County, to forward you the inclosed record" (RC in DLC; address clipped: "[. . .]ent of the United States Washington"; endorsed by TJ as received 11 July and so recorded in SJL but with notation "Carrol's case"; also endorsed by TJ: "Carrigo, Michael. Deneale's letter inclosing recommendn of judges for remission of fine of").

The above recommendation was written on a transcript of the U.S. circuit court's proceedings against MICHAEL CARRIGO during its January 1802 session at Alexandria. On 21 Oct. 1801, Carrigo, "with force and arms," had stolen $8\frac{7}{8}$ yards of blue cloth worth $11 from Edward Redman. Found guilty, Carrigo was fined $30 and ordered to receive 30 lash-

es at the public whipping post. The court also committed him to the public jail at Alexandria until his fine was paid (Tr in DNA: RG 59, GPR; attested by George Deneale). Deneale was clerk of the U.S. circuit court in Alexandria County (Madison, *Papers, Sec. of State Ser.*, 3:179).

Daniel C. Brent on 11 July sent TJ another recommendation in the Carrigo case. He stated: "I herewith send a petition from the Court respecting Michael Carrigo who is now confined in Goal at Alexandria—I am requested by the Court to obtain an answer before they rise which is expected to take place on Tuesday" (RC in DLC; endorsed by TJ as received 11 July and so recorded in SJL but with notation "Carrol's case"; enclosure not found). For Carroll's case, see James Carroll to TJ, 10 July.

On 12 July, TJ ordered a remission of Carrigo's fine (FC in Lb in DNA: RG 59, GPR).

[1] MS: "any any."

From Robert Lawson

DEAR SIR,   Richmond July 10th. 1802.

Your friendly, your sympathetic Letter, I had the honor of recieving of the date of June 22nd. 1801.   The benevolent donation of 50 dollars plac'd by your correspondent in the hands of Major Duval, pay'd as far as [...], my board and some necessary cloathing. I was attacked at the time with a severe flux, which I did not get over for upwards of six months: nor was this the only complaint in that time, and since; for exclusive of my long and constant companion the Rheumatism, I have had many acute ones beside to afflict me.

This must be tedious: and I therefore beg you, Sir, to pardon my imperfect account, as being too painfull for me to detail.

My greatest wish, and my repeated applications, have been for some months past, to be remov'd from this place, and to return to Kentucky: But I find from the few who have principally contributed *here* to my support, they cannot raise the whole sum essentially necessary for the purpose, upon the most economical scale of calculation, without benevolent aid. It is known to my feelings how reluctantly I am constraind to sollicit this aid of any one. The situation of my Case, if really known, would plead [...] [...]uation with the liberal of mind at least.

I took the liberty about two months since to write you on this subject, beging yours, and Mr. Madisons benevolence under the circumstances of my situation. I was told the Letter was put in the Post office; but not having heard of; or receiv'd any answer, I am convinc'd it did not come into your hands.

From your known long intimacy and [...]ship, with Mr. Madison, I trust you will be so good as to shew him this. And whatever aid is transmit'd to Govr. Munroe for my use, shall undoubtedly have my humble and [gratef]ull thanks, as the only tribute I can offer; and I am conscious it will be applied to its proper object. But, Sir, as I am so situated as to wish to have an answer as soon as you can make it convenient, so I intreat you to pardon my intimation of it; as a removal from this place is actually necessary as soon as possible, as there are not the means of defraying so extravagant a board, with the most indifferent of accommodation, exclusive of necessary Cloaths.

There is another subject of more delicacy to me, I do not hesitate to decl[are] [...] I introduce it, I know an apology is necessary.

Captn. Samuel Eddins a worthy, a distinguished Officer in the late war,—distinguish'd by a regular, a discreet uniform discharge of duty under various trials from the earliest commencement to the close of it—informs me that he has offer'd his Services, and begs the appointment, if in your Judgment proper, as the Keeper of the light House at Point Comfort in this State.

It has been declared in my hearing frequently, by those who have long known him, as I have done, that from his intimate knowledge of that part of the country, the Bay, Capes &c. no one would probably discharge the duties of the office with more fidelity.

I beg you to accept of my most sincere wishes for your individual Happiness, and the Prosperity of the National Government; and remaining with Gratefull Respect and Esteem

I am—Dear Sir Your much oblig'd Servt   Ro: LAWSON

RC (ViW); torn; addressed: "His Excellency Thomas Jefferson President. by post to Washington City"; with notation on cover sheet: "NB. I will thank the Gentleman who conducts the Genl. post office to forward this Letter without delay. July 10th. 1802 Ro: Lawson"; franked; postmarked 12 July; endorsed by TJ as received 15 July and so recorded in SJL.

YOUR SYMPATHETIC LETTER: TJ wrote to Lawson on 22 June 1801 and for TJ's BENEVOLENT DONATION through William DuVal, see Lawson to TJ, 31 May 1802.

MY SUPPORT: on 19 Oct. 1801, the Virginia Society of the Cincinnati made a charitable payment of $50 for Lawson, who was one of its original members. It later resolved to contribute a $200 annual allowance for him (Edgar Erskine Hume, *Papers of the Society of the Cincinnati in the State of Virginia 1783-1824* [Richmond, 1938], 7, 50, 55, 253).

THE LETTER: that of 31 May.

For the AID transmitted to the governor for Lawson, see TJ to James Monroe, 20 July.

EDDINS: see Vol. 35:112.

From Louis André Pichon

10th. july 1802

Mr. Pichon with his best respects to the President of the United States has the honor to thank him for his note correcting the information of the extraordinary Philadelphia Gazette supposed to have arrived by last thursday's mail. Mr. P. communicated the information in the evening only to Mr Madison & Mr Smith (harrison) both of whom will have had like Mr P. an opportunity by the paper of last night, to correct it.   P.

RC (DLC); endorsed by TJ as received 10 July.

TJ's NOTE has not been found and is not recorded in SJL.

From Martha Jefferson Randolph

My children have escaped the measles most wonderfully and unaccountably for so strongly were we all prepossessed with the idea of it's being impossible that from the moment of it's appearing upon the plantation I rather courted than avoided the infection and the children have been on a regimen for 4 or 5 weeks in the constant expectation of breaking out. Ann has been twice declared full of it once by Doctor Bache and another time by the whole family but it went in as sudenly as it came out and has left much uneasiness upon my mynd for fear of her being subject to something like Mrs Kingkade's I think the smoothness of her skin is affected by it and it shews, upon her heating herself immediately. Cornelia has been very low The sickness which I mentioned to you in my last was but the beginning of a very long and teasing complaint of which however she is getting the better she is still very pale and much emaciated but has recovered her appetite and spirits and I hope will be perfectly well before you return we are entirely free from the measles here now those of our people who had it have recovered and Mr Walton's family living on the same plantation every individual of which had it are all recovered the intercourse between them and us thro the servants was daily yet it has stopped and there is not at this moment one instance of it here. at Monticello the last time I heard from there 3 of the nail boys had it and other's were complaining but whether with the measles or not I could not learn I will send over to Lilly immediately to let him know your orders upon the subject I regret extremely my children having missed it the season was so favorable and it was so mild generally that no time or circumstance for the future can ever be as favorable again, besides having had the anxiety for nothing. I delayed writing to Maria untill I could give her a favorable account, for I know she has had great apprehensions on that score for a long time past adieu my dear Papa I do not know if I gave you a list of the things most wanting in the house I do not exactly recollect what they were but sheets, towels counterpanes and tea china were I think foremost on the list your linen has not arrived or it would have been made up before your return the children all join in love and anxious prayer that nothing may retard your wished for return and believe me with tenderest affections yours   M RANDOLPH

Peter Hemmings is entirely well

RC (ViU: Edgehill-Randolph Papers); addressed: "Thomas Jefferson President of the united States Washington"; franked; postmarked Milton, 12 July; endorsed by TJ as received 15 July and so recorded in SJL.

MRS. KINGKADE: possibly a member of the Kinkead family, longtime residents of Albemarle County (Woods, *Albemarle*, 246-7).

For Martha Jefferson Randolph's LAST, see TJ to Randolph, 18 June 1802. For TJ's ORDERS, see TJ to Randolph, 2 July.

From Henry Dearborn

SIR   [12 July 1802]

Mr. Dalton having declined the office of Collector for Newburyport, it may be somewhat difficult to deside on a successor to Mr. Ting. I am at a loss in determining which of the following Gentlemen to recommend, each of them deserve notic & are I presume[1] capable of performing the duties of the Office,

Genl. Ralph Cross   } of Newbury
Joseph Marquan   } Port—
Genl. William Lyman[2]
Henry Warren[3]

Warren was proposed for Marblehead in the place of Garey, but the emoluments are not sufficient, I fear, to induce him to accept.— Lyman is very poor, and perfectly competant to the office. Marquan is now poor & considers himself intitled to notice. Cross is said to be a good man, but I have no personal aquaintence with him. if as deserving a character could be found in the Town as else where, it might be adviseable to give him the preference, but Lymans uniform zeal, and his standing in society, combined with his pecuniary situation, together with his having been run down by the Fedl. party, seems to constitute a considerable claim on the Government, and under all circumstancies, I think it would be as well to give him the appointment.

with respectfull consideration I am Sir Your Huml Servt,

H. DEARBORN

RC (DLC); undated; at foot of text: "The President of the United States"; endorsed by TJ as received 12 July and so recorded in SJL with notation "Collectors for Mass."; also endorsed by TJ: "Lyman. Warren. Marqwan. Cross. for Collectors."

RALPH CROSS and Joseph Marquand (MARQUAN) were both commissioners of bankruptcy for Newburyport. Cross received an interim appointment to the Newburyport collectorship in August 1802, which was approved by the Senate in January 1803. Following Cross's death in 1811, Marquand succeeded to the post (JEP, 1:432, 2:188; Vol. 37: Appendix II, List 2; TJ to Albert Gallatin, 14 Aug. 1802).

TJ had been attempting to secure a suitable appointment for WILLIAM LYMAN for the past year. He directed a commission be prepared for Lyman as collector at Newburyport, but the general departed for Europe before it was delivered, necessitating the appointment of

Cross in his place. TJ in 1804 appointed Lyman U.S. consul at London (JEP, 1:476; Vol. 34:547, 661-2; Vol. 35:511; Vol. 36:525n; TJ to Albert Gallatin, 20 July; Gallatin to TJ, 9 Aug.).

[1] Preceding two words interlined.
[2] TJ wrote in pencil adjacent to Lyman's name, "Newbury port."
[3] TJ wrote in pencil adjacent to Warren's name, "Marblehead."

To Thomas Newton

DEAR SIR   Washington July 12. 1802

The Secretary at War, Genl. Dearborne, having occasion to visit Norfolk, I cannot omit the occasion of making him known to you. you will find that his public appointment is no more than a just testimonial of his private worth: and I always suppose in bringing two good men together, I render a service to both.

I have to acknolege the reciept of your favor of June 1. it is probable I shall avail myself of your information on the subject of wine, when I shall be returned from Monticello, to which place I shall set out in ten days to pass there the bilious months of Aug. & September. I am happy to find a probability of being supplied with a wine of so superior a quality. I am desirous to get ahead of my consumption of it, so as to have it of good age, but as yet it is not convenient.

Accept assurances of my great esteem & respect

TH: JEFFERSON

PrC (DLC); at foot of text: "Colo. Newton."; endorsed by TJ in ink on verso.

Henry Dearborn visited NORFOLK later that month possibly to inspect a battery that had replaced an earlier fortification

for the city's port (Norfolk *Commercial Register*, 18 Aug. 1802; ASP, *Military Affairs*, 1:158).

Newton had informed TJ of "some fine Brazil" WINE in his possession (Vol. 37:524-5n).

To Albert Gallatin

DEAR SIR   Washington July 13. 1802.

Govr. Hall & mr Rodney, whom you met at Baltimore, passed a day or two here. they are satisfied as to Mc.lane if he does not take an active part in elections. it would be well he should be particularly prudent, & bona fide neutral, except to vote himself as he pleases.— they remonstrated on our having appointed all Philadelphians to report on the works in the Delaware. I told them I thought there would be no difficulty in adding some persons from their state. they preferred rather a separate examination and report on the part of their state. as it is impossible we can be too well informed before we engage in great expences, and rival enquiries may bring forth what a separate one might hide, I should think it not amiss to direct this. it will also give us more time.

Mr. Dalton has declined accepting. Genl. Lyman, Cross & Markwan are suggested to our choice. the first has revolutionary services, & proofs of public confidence in his favor; the two latter have residence in the town. the latter would therefore have a local preference, the former a general one. Genl. Dearborne is gone to Norfolk; mr Madison & mr Smith are here. I continue my purpose of leaving this on the 21st. Accept assurances of my affectionate esteem & high respect.   TH: JEFFERSON

P.S. I promised mr Rodney you would speak with him on your return. it will be almost indispensable.

RC (NHi: Gallatin Papers); addressed by Meriwether Lewis: "Albert Gallatin esquire. Secretary of the Treasury. now at New York"; franked and postmarked. PrC (DLC). Recorded in SJL with notation "Delaware works."

When he traveled to New York, Gallatin often stopped AT BALTIMORE, where he visited Joseph H. Nicholson and family (Henry Adams, *The Life of Albert Gallatin* [Philadelphia, 1879; repr. New York, 1943], 303).

WORKS IN THE DELAWARE: for the appropriation of $30,000 to repair and erect public piers on the Delaware River, see Memorandum on Delaware River Piers, 26 June 1802.

To Gibson & Jefferson

MESSRS. GIBSON & JEFFERSON   Washington July 13. 1802.

Two days ago the Schooner Dolphin, Sprogell, sailed from hence having on board

9. boxes marked T. Jefferson No. 1. to 9.

1. Trunk. No. 10.

a basket

4. barrels T.I. No. 7. 12. 13. 14.

one box

12. barrels fish for myself

3. barrels do. for Sam. Carr. with other articles in the same bill for him. as by the three bills of lading inclosed you will see. they are on

arrival to be forwarded *by water* to Milton to the care of Watson & Higginbotham.

Your favor of July 3. was recieved four days ago. I shall take immediate care to cover the balance therein stated as well as further expences which may occur without delay. I expect to leave this place for Monticello on the 21st. inst. Accept my best wishes & respects.

TH: JEFFERSON

P.S. I will thank you to forward to Monticello with the above articles 2. doz. bottles of Syrop of punch, if to be had.

PrC (MHi); at foot of text: "Messrs. Gibson & Jefferson"; endorsed by TJ in ink on verso. Enclosures not found.

Gibson & Jefferson's FAVOR of 3 July, recorded in SJL as received from Richmond on the 8th, has not been found. On 20 July, TJ directed John Barnes to remit $200 to Gibson & Jefferson (MB, 2:1078).

To Rufus King

DEAR SIR   Washington July 13. 1802.

The course of things in the neighboring islands of the West Indies appears to have given a considerable impulse to the minds of the slaves in different parts of the US. a great disposition to insurgency has manifested itself among them, which, in one instance, in the state of Virginia broke out into actual insurrection. this was easily suppressed:[1] but many of those concerned, (between 20. & 30. I believe) fell victims to the law. so extensive an execution could not but excite sensibility in the public mind, and beget a[2] regret that the laws had not provided, for such cases, some alternative, combining more mildness with equal efficacy. the legislature of the state, at a subsequent meeting, took the subject into consideration, and have communicated to me through the Governor of the state, their wish that some place could be provided, out of the limits of the US. to which slaves guilty of insurgency might be transported; and they have particularly looked to Africa as offering the most desirable receptacle. we might, for this purpose, enter into negociations with the natives, on some part of the coast, to obtain[3] a settlement, and, by establishing an African company, combine with it commercial operations, which might not only reimburse expences but procure profit also. but there being already such an establishment on that coast by the English Sierra Leone company, made for the express purpose of colonising civilized blacks to that country, it would seem better, by incorporating our emigrants with theirs, to make one strong, rather than two weak colonies. this would be the more desireable, because the blacks settled at Sierra Leone, having chiefly gone from these states, would often recieve, among those we should send, their acquaintances and relations. the object of this letter therefore is to ask the favor of you to enter into conference with such persons private & public as would be necessary to give us permission to send thither[4] the persons under contemplation. it is material to observe that they are not felons, or common malefactors, but persons guilty of what the safety of society, under actual circumstances,[5] obliges us to treat as a crime, but which their feelings may[6] represent in a far different shape. they are such as will be a valuable acquisition to the settlement already existing there, and well calculated to cooperate in the plan[7] of civilisation.

As the expence of so distant a transportation would be very heavy, & might weigh unfavorably in deciding between the modes of punishment, it is very desirable that it should be[8] lessened as much as is practicable. if the regulations of the place would permit these emigrants to dispose of themselves, as the Germans & others do who come to this country poor,[9] by giving their labour for a certain term to some one who will pay their passage; and if the master of the vessel could be permitted to carry articles of commerce from this country & take back others from that which might yield him a mercantile profit sufficient to cover the expences of the voyage, a serious difficulty would be removed.[10] I will ask your attention therefore to arrangements necessary for this purpose.

The consequences of permitting emancipations to become extensive, unless a condition of emigration be annexed to them, furnish also matter of solicitude to the legislature of Virginia, as you will percieve by their resolution inclosed to you. Altho provision for the settlement of emancipated negroes might perhaps be obtainable nearer home than Africa, yet it is desirable that we should be free to expatriate this description of people also to the colony of Sierra Leone, if considerations respecting either themselves or us should render it more expedient. I will pray you therefore to get the same permission extended to the reception of these as well as those first mentioned. nor will these be a selection of bad subjects; the emancipations for the most part being either of the whole slaves of the master, or of such individuals as have particularly deserved well. the latter is most frequent.

The request of the legislature of Virginia having produced to me this occasion of addressing you, I avail myself of it to assure you of my perfect satisfaction with the manner in which you have conducted the several matters confided to you by us;[11] and to express my hope that through your agency we may be able to remove every thing inauspicious to a cordial friendship between[12] this country & the one in which you are stationed: a friendship dictated by too many considerations not to be felt by the wise & the dispassionate of both nations. it is therefore with the sincerest pleasure I have observed on the part[13] of the British government various manifestations of just and friendly disposition towards us. we wish[14] to cultivate peace & friendship with all nations, believing that course most conducive to the welfare of our own.[15] it is natural that these friendships should bear some proportion[16] to the common interests of the parties. the interesting relations between Great Britain and the US. are certainly of the first order; & as such are estimated, & will be faithfully cultivated by us. these sentiments have been communicated to you from time to time[17] in the official correspondence of the Secretary of state: but I have thought it might not be unacceptable to be assured that they perfectly concur with my own personal convictions,[18] both in relation to yourself and the country in which you are.　　　I pray you to accept assurances of my high consideration & respect.

Th: Jefferson

PrC (DLC); at foot of text: "Rufus King. M.P. of the US. at London." Dft (DLC). Enclosure: Resolution of the Virginia General Assembly, approved by the House of Delegates and the Senate on 16 and 23 Jan. 1802, respectively, calling on the governor to correspond with the president of the United States about finding a location where "free negroes or mulattoes, and such negroes or mulattoes as may be emancipated may be sent or choose to remove as a place of asylum" (Vol. 35:721n; Vol. 36:576-7n).

BETWEEN 20. & 30. I BELIEVE: 26 people were hanged in Virginia for complicity in the planned slave insurrection of 1800. "Where to arrest the hand of the Executioner," James Monroe, as governor, mused to TJ at the time, "is a question of great importance" (Vol. 32:145). COMMUNICATED TO ME THROUGH THE GOVERNOR: Monroe on 15 June 1801 wrote to TJ concerning a resolution of the Virginia House of Delegates of December 1800 that asked the governor to communicate with the president about obtaining land where "persons obnoxious to the laws or dangerous to the peace of society may be removed." A resolution adopted by the legislature in January 1802 named AFRICA and South America as potential locations (Vol. 34:345-7; Vol. 35:721n; Vol. 36:577n).

In a letter to Monroe of 3 June, TJ had suggested the SIERRA LEONE colony on the western shore of Africa as a potential destination for "black insurgents" and perhaps also for the colonization of "freed negroes and persons of colour." TJ proposed to take the matter up with King. Monroe gave his thoughts on the matter in a reply dated 11 June.

[1] In Dft TJ first wrote "this was suppressed in a single day" before altering the passage to read as above.

[2] Here in Dft TJ canceled "sincere."

[3] Here in Dft TJ canceled "or establish."

[4] Here in Dft TJ canceled "our ins."

[5] Preceding three words interlined in Dft.

[6] Word interlined in Dft in place of "must."

[7] Word interlined in Dft in place of "object."

[8] Remainder of sentence interlined in Dft in place of "obviated in some way."

[9] Word interlined in Dft.

[10] Preceding six words interlined in Dft in place of "our expence might be lessened if not entirely removed," which was interlined in place of "the arrangement would to us be extremely desirable, and as such."

[11] Preceding two words interlined in Dft in place of "since I came to the admn."

[12] Remainder of clause (to colon) interlined in Dft in place of "the two nations."

[13] Preceding three words interlined in Dft in place of "in every act."

[14] Here in Dft TJ canceled "with sincerity."

[15] Sentence interlined in Dft in place of a passage, ultimately canceled, that TJ first wrote, with modifications, as: "these seeds are not sown in barren ground. I have too high an opinion of the understanding of those at the helm of British affairs to suppose they form opinions of the dispositions of this admn from the trash in the public papers. I am sure they have more respect for our understanding than to <suppose> believe, with those papers, that we are Gallomen or Anglomen, or any thing but Americans & the friends of our friends. peace & friendship with all other nations is essentially our system; and." In place of everything beginning with "suppose they form opinions" he interlined, with intermediate modifications, "suppose they judge of the dispositions of this admn. from the miserable trash of the public papers: and <I am sure> I trust they have more respect for ours than to suppose us actuated by blind partialities in our foreign relations. The <interests> welfare of our own country <are> is of course the first [...] with us. we believe this will be best promoted by peace and friendship with all nations."

[16] Word interlined in Dft in place of "relation."

[17] In Dft TJ first wrote "have been fully communicated to you" before altering the passage to read as above.

[18] Remainder of sentence interlined in Dft.

From Alexander White

DEAR SIR   Woodville 13th. July 1802

I am favoured with yours of 5th. instant. In the course of the summer or autumn I intend to visit the Cavities of Ice, and to make more particular observations than heretofore. Should I in the mean time obtain information which may deserve attention I will communicate it. I am much surprised at Hobans conduct—; his agreement with the late Commissioners, as entered in their Journal, ought perhaps to have been more explicit, but I believe it does not express that he should continue in pay till the buildings should be finished a stipulation which I should have considered so improper, would hardly have escaped my recollection, but we need not depend on memory, the writing will speak for itself.   Some years ago both my Colleagues were desirous of getting Hoban out of the way; and amazing exertions were made to find something in his conduct which would justify them in dismissing him. I believe he would then have disputed their right, but I did not understand, either on that occasion, or on a subsequent one, which I am about to mention that he expected to receive his salary after the works should cease—

Towards the close of the year 1800 it was proposed to notify him, that his services would not be required after a certain day, upon a supposition that there would be nothing further done towards carrying on the building till Congress should take [...] therein. He made no objection to this in conversation with me, but the shortness of the notice—the time was then prolonged; and a letter written to him amounting to a discontinuance, and there the matter rested till after you came into office, and ordered the works to be proceeded on—After which we continued his salary by an order, implying, according to my remembrance, that it had been discontinued, but the Minutes will shew how far I am accurate I made no note of this transaction—

Our Harvest is productive beyond example, and the weather generally favourable, though we have at times been interrupted by showers, which promote vegetation in a great degree, but have not been sufficient to affect the Springs or Wells—

I wish you all the pleasure, during your retirement, which domestic life affords, and remain with sentiments of real regard

Dear Sir Your Ob Sv   ALEXR WHITE

RC (DLC); with one word illegible; at foot of text: "Thos Jefferson Esquire P: U."; endorsed by TJ as received 16 July and so recorded in SJL. Dft (PPRF).

A LETTER WRITTEN TO HIM: on 30 Oct. 1800, the District of Columbia Commissioners wrote James Hoban and informed him that his salary would be continued until 1 Jan. 1801 (DNA: RG 42, DCLB).

From Isaac Cox Barnet

SIR,   Bordeaux July 14th 1802.

Persuaded that my removal from the Agency of this Port was owing to some circumstance connected with the general system of your administration—and not to your personal indisposition towards me.—Conscious that my fidelity and Zeal in the service of my Country during more than five years, still give me a claim on Executive patronage—I have once more presumed to address you on the subject.

You have been made acquainted Sir, with my small pecuniary resources—and that I have a large family to provide for.—

You have been informed of the opinion of the french Authorities & Citizens of Brest & Bordeaux—with regard to me—

I am proud to say it is favourable—more happy if, from the information you have yourself collected—you have found me deserving your own.—for whilst it would honour me, it would also attach the suffrage of my fellow Citizens generally. I am jealous of one and both. But to this sentiment is connected the preservation of a right equally dear to me, and which I am desirous of enjoying as far as is compatible with my residence abroad.—It is that of a Citizen of the United States—which you only can maintain for me Sir; and if I have merited the approbation of the Government—my claim upon you is as strong as that of a child for a Father's blessing.—

I have lost many months in anxious expectation of an Appointment—and have not received even one Consolotary line on the subject. This state of inactivity, if longer prolonged, would bring ruin and distress upon my family. I have therefore determined to remain no longer "l'oiseau sur la branche"—but to fix myself at Bordeaux—where I am encouraged to hope for a share of the business of my american friends.—

A commission as *vice*-commercial Agent here, would exempt me from personal taxes—procure me certain *politico*-local advantages—give me a commercial "relief" in my own Country—secure to my children their rights of Citizenship and to my self, those of our Trade (such as holding a registered Vessel &c)—I therefore humbly ask of you, Sir, the Appointment of vice-commercial Agent at Bordeaux. It would in no wise interfere with Mr: Lee, when present and I conceive myself authorized to solicit it upon the precedentt of Havre, where there has always been a vice-Consul 'till now.—

If it were objected by Mr. Lee or his friends, that such a sub-appointment might add weight to the competition and militate against his commercial establishment—I must beg leave respectfully to observe, that it would be no consideration in the decision of a Government *against it*—but on the contrary, would be a strong one in its favour.

Other Governments have in this Port consuls & *vice*-consuls and precedents may be taken from our own constitution and from the organization of our own supreme magistracies—at least I presume they might be so applied.—

The places of Marseilles & Nantes being not yet filled—and Mr. Dobell continuing his residence in this place so long (though a Mr. l'Hospital, his secretary, represents him at Havre) may I not still hope, Sir, that either by non-acceptance or resignation, it may please you to prefer me to one of them.—and as I cannot return to Brest, and my Agent there, Mr. Aubrée, being on the point of leaving it—I beg Sir, your acceptance of my resignation of that Consulate—

I am most respectfully, Sir, Your most obedient and very devoted Servant   I, COX BARNET

RC (DNA: RG 59, LAR); at head of text: "Duplicate"; addressed: "Thomas Jefferson Esquire President of the United States"; endorsed by TJ as received 6 Oct. and so recorded in SJL.

REMOVAL FROM THE AGENCY OF THIS PORT: TJ considered John Adams's appointment of Barnet as commercial agent at Bordeaux, France, to be a midnight appointment. TJ gave the post to William Lee. Seeking another appointment, Barnet, who informed TJ of his PECUNIARY situation in a long letter of 10 Sep. 1801, solicited endorsements from merchants and FRENCH AUTHORITIES. When he wrote the letter above, Barnet did not know that TJ had taken steps to put an end to his ANXIOUS EXPECTATION by naming him, in June 1802, commercial agent at Antwerp (Vol. 33:173n; Vol. 35:247-53; Vol. 37: Appendix I).

L'OISEAU SUR LA BRANCHE: the expression, the literal translation of which is "the bird on the branch," refers to someone in unsettled circumstances.

Originally from Philadelphia, Peter DOBELL was establishing himself as a merchant at Bordeaux when, in the spring of 1801, TJ responded to a recommendation from Caspar Wistar by appointing Dobell the U.S. commercial agent at Le Havre. The person named L'HOSPITAL, who signed himself as the chancellor of the consular office, acted in Dobell's absence. Dobell resigned his position later in 1802 (Madison, *Papers, Sec. of State Ser.*, 3:469, 472; 4:100; Vol. 33:556, 557n, 666).

RESIGNATION OF THAT CONSULATE: George Washington had appointed Barnet the U.S. consul at Brest early in 1797. Adams, when he named Barnet the commercial agent at Bordeaux in February 1801, nominated George Rundle for the post at Brest. Rundle did not receive his commission because his appointment, like Barnet's for Bordeaux, was an end-of-term Adams nomination that TJ did not carry through. That had left Barnet, officially, as commercial agent at Brest. Demand for consular services at that port was so slight, Barnet informed Madison in a letter of 30 June 1802, the office "produced nothing" (JEP, 1:226, 381; Madison, *Papers, Sec. of State Ser.*, 3:352; Vol. 33:173n; Vol. 35:249-50, 252n).

From John Wayles Eppes

DEAR SIR,   B. Hundred July 14. 1802

I left Maria yesterday. She is now in a fair way for regaining her health. She rides every day on horse back & has recovered her strength entirely. But for the dread of the measles I would carry her immediately to the Green-Springs as the cold bath would probably benefit a pain in her back from which she has frequently experienced inconvenience from the time of her miscarriage at Eppington—And indeed to that unfortunate accident I attribute her ill health for the last two years.

We have concluded to postpone our trip to Monticello until you arrive there. You know how large a portion of our happiness depends on the safety of our child, & as in your affection we count on equal caution with our own, we can trust to you for giving us information of the earliest period at which we may join you without exposing him to the danger of the measles—He is now in a neighbourhood where that complaint has not appeared & by the aid of a healthy nurse is recovering very rapidly.

Calculating on your setting out for Monticello on the 20th. I shall direct my next letter to that place—Accept for your health the best wishes of yours

affectionately   JNO: W: EPPES

RC (ViU: Edgehill-Randolph Papers); endorsed by TJ as received 20 July and so recorded in SJL.

MY NEXT LETTER: Eppes to TJ, 18 July, recorded in SJL as received 25 July, has not been found.

From Cornelius McDermott Roe

TO THE PRESIDENT,
OF THE UNITED STATES,   [on or before 14 July 1802]
the Humble, Petition of Cornelius McDermott Roe, showeth That your Petitioner, is unable to work at his trade as he is afflicted with a sore Leg, those two years. past,—and the presant times, presses hard upon him, to suport his famely,—in one case in particular, Which is Depending, between him and the former Commissioners, of the City Washington, that your Petitioner, has a Consederable Ballance Due to him, for work Done at the Presidents. House, in the year 95, and allways hoping, to Receive it or sum part there of whin justice, would take the case into Consederation,—And as the whole of the affears of the City, comes under your care, and protection, and not Doubting in the Least that no king of oppresion to a poor-man, should be Done to your knowlidg,—your Petitioner is called upon by the superentendant, of the City, to pay for sum Bricks. he stands. Charged with un the Books, in his hands. which Acct, the Commissioners, have called for a settlement, in Agust 1800 and your Petitioner, gave his Acct, in[1] Bare of that cleam at the same time, where-in is a Consederable Ballance Due, to your Petitioner,—the Commissioners, being two great a power for your Petitioner, to contend or forse them to pay him what was Due to him and his having, resolved if posible, to avoid Law-suts, your Petitioner carracter, is hear with enclosed, in this Petition, hoping you will take his case into consederation and order him, sum relife in the case, and your Petitioner, will for ever pray for your happiness

RC (DLC); undated; endorsed by TJ as received 14 July and "Petition" and so recorded in SJL.

Irish stonemason Cornelius McDermott Roe (d. 1807) emigrated to the United States as an indentured servant, arriving in Alexandria in 1784. His services were immediately acquired by George Washington, who employed McDermott Roe at Mount Vernon as a mason, bricklayer, and laborer until about 1788. He thereafter moved to Washington, D.C., where he acquired several city lots and received contracts to undertake masonry work on the Capitol and President's House in 1794 and 1795. His work was deemed faulty, however, and he was subsequently sued by the District of Columbia commissioners for the cost of repairing the Capitol's foundations (Nathan W. Murphy, "Cornelius McDermott Roe: Indentured Servant to George Washington," *National Genealogical Society Quarterly*, 95 [2007], 135-46; Bob Arnebeck, *Through a Fiery Trial: Building Washington, 1790-1800* [Lanham, Md., 1991], 206, 212, 217-19, 301-2, 571).

[1] MS: "in in."

To John Ponsonby

SIR   Washington July 14. 1802.

I am to thank you for the specimens of waterproof cotton and cloth which you were so good as to send me. the former was new to me. I had before recieved as much of the cloth as made me a great coat, which I have so fully tried as to be satisfied it is water proof except at the seams. I shall be glad when such supplies come over as will enable us to get our common clothes of them: & should suppose they would sell very readily. the silk must be valuable for summer great coats. perhaps the best thing would be for the company to send a person to perform the operation here. I had also recieved some of the water proof paper, & recommended to the Secretary at war to import a quantity for cartridges.   Accept my respects & best wishes.

TH: JEFFERSON

RC (CtY); at foot of text: "Mr. Ponsonby." PrC (ViW); endorsed by TJ in ink on verso.

For the SPECIMENS OF WATERPROOF COTTON AND CLOTH that Ponsonby sent TJ from Ackermann, Suardy, & Co. of London, see Vol. 37:668-9n.

From William G. Stewart

SIR   Philada. July 14th. 1802

Presuming on your freindship to my Father now at your Estate— and on my having been in the Service of the United States, on board the United States Frigate Philadelphia in her previous Cruize when Commanded by Captn Decatur & in her late Cruize Under Captn. Barron, under whom I served as masters mate—I have to beg of you your friendly influence in my behalf for the purpose of obtaining the Warrant of a Midshipman.

If, a Recommendation of my Character, or of my Conduct during my Service be necessary, I beg leave to refer you to Captain Barron now at the City of Washington or to our Late Commander Captain Decatur, now in this City—Should you be pleased to grant this I Shall allways hold it in gratefull Remembrance meantime believe me your Excellencys

Most Obedt and very Humble Servant

WILLIAM G. STEWART

RC (DNA: RG 59, LAR); at head of text: "His Excellency Thomas Jefferson President of the United States"; endorsed by TJ as received 26 July and so recorded in SJL; also endorsed by TJ: "to be Midshipman."

William G. Stewart was the son of Monticello blacksmith William Stewart.

TJ brought Stewart's application to the attention of Robert Smith, describing him as "a young man of correct conduct" who possessed "an extraordinary mechanical genius." Stewart received his midshipman's warrant in November 1802 and was assigned to the brig *Argus* (NDBW, *Register*, 53; TJ to Robert Smith, 22 Oct. 1802).

To Caleb Strong

SIR   Washington July 14. 1802.

I recieved two days ago your favor of the 6th. inst. on the subject of certain military articles delivered or proposed to be delivered to the US. and immediately referred it to the Secretary at war. from him you will recieve a letter written on the supposition that these articles have never been the subject of a contract between the US. and the state of Massachusets. yet it is possible such a contract may have been made, altho' no evidence of it is found in the War office. should any such evidence exist, which you can be so good as to procure us, the matter will be taken up on that ground, and the contracts of the government of the US. be faithfully carried into execution.

I have also asked the attention of the Secretary of the Navy to that part of your letter which mentions that some of the cannon of the fort were delivered for one of our vessels of war. he will immediately inform himself on the subject, and you may rest assured that whatever is just will be done, & without delay. perhaps your offices might aid us with further specific information of the transaction so far as the department of the Navy is concerned.

I write in this imperfect state of information, because within a few days we shall take our usual recess for the months of August and September, to avoid passing them on the tide waters.

I pray you to accept assurances of my high consideration & respect.

TH: JEFFERSON

PrC (DLC); at foot of text: "Governor Strong."

Caleb Strong (1746-1819) was a Harvard graduate and former United States senator from Massachusetts. He had also represented his state in the Constitutional convention at Philadelphia in 1787. A moderate Federalist, Strong was elected governor of Massachusetts in 1800 and remained in the office until 1807, when he was defeated by the Republican James Sullivan (ANB).

FAVOR OF THE 6TH. INST.: a letter from Strong dated 6 July, recorded in SJL as received from Boston on 12 July, has not been found. The letter pertained to payments sought by Massachusetts for ordnance and military stores supplied to the United States in June 1798, when the state ceded Castle Island in Boston harbor to the United States for the purpose of erecting fortifications and other military facilities. The state placed a value of $41,679.78 on these items. A 23 June 1802 resolution of the Massachusetts legislature directed the governor to forward the proceedings on the subject to the president and to request payment of the money claimed with interest (*Resolves of the General Court of the Commonwealth of Massachusetts...Begun and Held at Boston, in the County of Suffolk, on Wednesday the Twenty-Sixth Day of May, Anno Domini—MDCCCII* [Boston, 1802], 25).

In a LETTER to Strong dated 13 July, Henry Dearborn observed that by the act of cession of June 1798, the ordnance and military stores attached to Castle Island were reserved to the state of Massachusetts and remained state property. An in-ventory and valuation of these articles was made when the United States took possession of the island, but this was not considered a CONTRACT that bound the U.S. to purchase them all. As the secretary of war interpreted the agreement, only items that were not ultimately returned to Massachusetts should be paid for "at a reasonable price." Dearborn deemed the value claimed by the state was far too high and instead suggested that one or more "judicious disinterested persons" from outside of Massachusetts be appointed to reappraise the articles in question (FC in Lb in DNA: RG 107, MLS).

The SECRETARY OF THE NAVY, Robert Smith, wrote Strong on 18 July regarding CANNON and shot taken from the Castle Island fortifications for use by the frigate *Constitution*. Smith noted that the articles were requested by the then secretary of war, James McHenry, in a letter to the governor of Massachusetts dated 30 May 1798, which stipulated that the items would be returned or replaced when no longer needed. In December 1801, Smith directed the navy agent at Boston, Samuel Brown, to return the cannon and shot to the proper state officer. Brown responded, however, that the Massachusetts quartermaster general was unwilling to receive them and sought instead to compel the United States to pay cash for the items. Smith trusted that his letter would convince Strong that the transaction in question was a loan, not a purchase, and that the governor would instruct the proper state authority to receive the cannon and shot (Tr in DLC; enclosed in Smith to TJ, 9 Apr. 1803).

To John Trumbull

DEAR SIR   Washington July 14. 1802.

I have duly recieved your favor of Mar. 10. explaining the motives of the Commissioners for disapproving the conjunction of office which had been proposed in the case of mr Erving. but they needed no explanation. when gentlemen, selected for their integrity, are acting under a public trust, their characters and consciences are sufficient securities that what they do, is done on pure motives. I had the less reason in this case to refuse credit to their sense of official duty, as some of them were known to me personally, and possess my confidence. we had been led to this union of offices by the circumstance of their having been united in the predecessor of mr Erving, and by a desire to extend into every department an economy which we have practised & are practising as the best means of preventing that accumulation of burthens on the public which leads to revolutionary storm.   how that is to end, which has been generated in the neighboring kingdom (for so we may now again call it) some further chapters of it's history will I suppose explain: for I do not expect we are yet at the last chapter. it would seem that our people alone furnish materials for a republic. so thoroughly are their minds imbued with the principle of obedience to the will of the majority, that a majority of one even in the choice of their chief magistrate produces as absolute an acquiesence as an unanimous vote. the unbridled license too of our newspapers serve as chimnies to carry off the smoke. ill humors, instead of being pent up, find vent through them, & leave the party at ease.   Accept assurances of my constant esteem & high consideration.   TH: JEFFERSON

PrC (DLC); at foot of text: "John Trumbull esquire."

TJ had received Trumbull's FAVOR, written at London, on 30 May.

NEIGHBORING KINGDOM: France.

In a letter written not long after TJ's inauguration, Benjamin Rush likened newspapers to chimneys that CARRY OFF THE SMOKE of "party rage" (Vol. 33:262).

To Caspar Wistar

DEAR SIR   Washington July 14. 1802.

Your favor of the 10th. of Apr. in answer to mine of Mar. 22. satisfied me perfectly as to Doctr. Barnwell whom therefore I then concluded to appoint to the hospital of N. Orleans, if established. but learning afterwards that Doctr. Bache had determined to remove to the Missisipi, I could have no hesitation to offer the place to him, as eminently qualified for it. I did so, and he has accepted & will probably depart early in the next month. considering the season & length of the journey, I wish mrs Bache [would] consent to defer her going till autumn.

Mr. Peale informs me that one frontal bone is recieved. one or two others will probably be forwarded. all of them I learn have horns. after you shall have considered them I shall be glad to learn your conclusion on this animal. that he was an elephant some resemblances in his structure argue. that he was not might be inferred from his superior volume, from the climate he inhabited, the form of his teeth, and perhaps from the bone recently recieved if it be not more difficult to ascribe it to the animal we have than to some other of whose existence we have no proof, and who must of course be a creature of imagination.   I expect to leave this place within a week for Monticello where I shall pass the months of Aug. & Sep. not deeming them safe on tidewater. I count therefore on seeing Dr. & mrs Bache there. Accept assurances of my great esteem & respect.

Th: Jefferson

PrC (DLC); blurred; at foot of text: "Dr. Wistar."

MRS BACHE: William Bache's wife, Catharine Wistar Bache, was Wistar's sister (Vol. 30:509).

MR. PEALE INFORMS ME: Charles Willson Peale's letter to TJ of 10 June reported the arrival in Philadelphia of an eagerly awaited BONE from Kentucky.

After he examined the partial skull, Peale confirmed, as others had suggested, that it belonged to a type of bison. In letters to Peale and TJ, however, Samuel Brown, who had not seen the fossil but spoke with people who had, raised questions about the animal and expressed a hope that Wistar or Benjamin Smith Barton might study the specimen (Vol. 37:351-2, 489-90, 550-2, 581-2).

From Jacob Bouldin

Sir   City of Baltimore July 15th 1802

May I beg leave to lay before you, the Heads of Some draughts, for your Examination, & Opinion thereon? as I am diffident of my own abilities—and fear to venture them into the world, before they have undergone the scrutiny of a competent Judge. Therefore,—and because I believe the Agricult'ral, & Mechanical Interests; as well, as the Internal & External navigation of the Union, may be benefitted thereby.—I am induced to make this request. Hoping, & believing, that your Excellency will indulge me therein: and likewise with your advice how to act most benefically for the union.

Should I be so far indulged.—when, & where, will it be most convenient to your Excellency, to examine them? when this shall be the case, I have the presumption be think,[1] you will excuse me for thus impertuning you.

I am, with the most perfect respect, Sir, your most obedient, and very humble servant   JACOB BOULDIN

Should your Excellency oblige me with a line upon this Subject, please to inclose, under Cover, "to Mr Jehu Bouldin" Surveyor for this City.   as above   JB

RC (MHi); addressed: "His Excellency Thomas Jefferson, Esquire President of the united States Washington"; postmarked 17 July; franked; endorsed by TJ as received 19 July and so recorded in SJL.

Jacob Bouldin, a resident of Baltimore, petitioned the U.S. House of Representatives in December 1805, stating that he was "the author of many valuable discoveries" and asking for an appropriation of funds to allow for the testing of his ideas by the executive branch. The House referred the matter to the Committee of Commerce and Manufactures and took no further action. Bouldin's petition declared that his inventions included a method for creating a machine "for taking courses, distances, ascents, descents, and true altitudes"; a method to improve inland navigation; a way of making salt "without the aid of fuel"; a plan for a cul-

tivating machine; a water system and a method of preventing and combatting fires; means of building ships that would not spring leaks; and an apparatus for saving lives at sea. Bouldin had previously been part owner of a water-powered grist mill. In 1807, apparently following some period of confinement for debt, he petitioned a Maryland court for classification as an insolvent debtor under the state's insolvency laws (JHR, 5:189; Baltimore Daily Intelligencer, 28 May 1794; Baltimore Federal Gazette, 9 May, 1 Aug. 1807).

JEHU BOULDIN was city surveyor of Baltimore for several years (James Robinson, The Baltimore Directory, for 1804 [Baltimore, 1804], 111; William Fry, The Baltimore Directory, for 1810 [Baltimore, 1810], 35; Baltimore Patriot & Mercantile Advertiser, 11 Feb. 1818).

[1] Thus in MS.

To John Redman Coxe

Washington July 15. 1802.

Th: Jefferson presents his respectful salutations to Doctr. Coxe, and his thanks for the communication of the volume on vaccination. he has deposited it in the Secretary of state's office as desired, and doubts not it will contribute much to the public satisfaction as to this salutary discovery, and to their information as to the manner of treating it. he prays him to accept his respects & best wishes.

RC (PPCP: Gilbert Collection); addressed: "Doctr. John Redman Coxe Philadelphia"; franked and postmarked. PrC (DLC); endorsed by TJ in ink on verso.

COMMUNICATION: Coxe to TJ, 6 July 1802.

From Cyrus Griffin

DEAR SIR— Williamsburg July 15th. 1802—

I am honoured by your obliging and very friendly letter of July the 7th.

Please to accept my hearty and sincere thanks for the good opinion expressed towards me, and be assured that I have never exerted even my small influence in the promotion of principles thus decidedly condemned by the great majority of our Citizens. Perhaps the affair of Callender might be considered as militating against this declaration; but really certain parts of the *Prospect* were so very exceptionable when applied to almost any chief Magistrate, no sort of proof to support those paragraphs of that Publication, Council having declined to argue the unconstitutionality of the sedition law before the Judges, and although a Court is bound not to assume a jurisdiction, yet in my opinion they are not to reject a law as unconstitutional unless that point by argument shall be substantiated; and after the verdict of a Jury who consider'd both the law & the fact; I did think that a small fine, and a short confinement could not be construed in any way as contradictory to the purest principles of a Republic, where laws and a decency of deportment are essentially necessary to its preservation.

Except two of the gentlemen, I was totally unacquainted with the political tenets of the Commissioners mentioned in a former letter; and those two directly opposed to each other, yet the utmost harmony has always prevailed when engaged upon the duties of their appointment. To be selected by the President would have been highly gratifying to those Individuals; but they do not consider their omission as meaning to convey the slightest imputation upon them.

I found it very difficult to obtain proper Characters who would act, in Richmond, Petersburg, or Norfolk. The line of enquiry, you have been pleased to adopt, is certainly the most eligible for procuring the best information. I do not entertain the smallest doubt that the Gentlemen commissioned will give entire satisfaction, and make particular exertions to merit the honour of their appointments.

Permit me, dear Sir, to express for you personally the most heartfelt esteem; and for your official situation as conducted, a very profound and sincere respect.   CYRUS GRIFFIN.

RC (DLC); endorsed by TJ as received 20 July and so recorded in SJL.

At the sedition trial of James Thomson CALLENDER, held in June 1800, Griffin, the federal district judge for Virginia, sat as assistant judge and concurred in the controversial rulings of Samuel Chase. Callender's COUNCIL, prominent Virginia Republicans George Hay, Philip Norborne Nicholas, and William Wirt, did ARGUE THE UNCONSTITUTIONALITY of the Sedition Act, but Chase squashed the challenge. Callender was assessed a FINE of $200 and sentenced to 9 months in jail (DHSC, 3:435; ANB, s.v. "Griffin, Cyrus"; James Morton Smith, *Freedom's Fetters: The Alien and Sedition Laws and American Civil Liberties* [Ithaca, N.Y., 1956], 353n; Vol. 31:588-90).

FORMER LETTER: Griffin to TJ, 6 June 1802.

To David Humphreys

DEAR SIR   Washington July 15. 1802.

I have to acknolege the reciept of your favor of June 28. and sincerely congratulate you on your safe return to your native country. you will doubtless be sensible of an inconcievable change in manners and opinions since you left it; tho' less perhaps in Connecticut than some other places. After eleven years absence I imagine you will find it more difficult to return from European to American habits than the first change was from American to European. it happens too that the state to which you return as well as the adjoining one of Massachusets, is still under the paroxysm of party feelings, which the other states have worked through more quickly. indeed we are no where as yet entirely clear of the wave of agitation which reached us from Europe in the year 1798. but I trust that the follies & violences, first of one nation then of another, will shortly have cured us all of European attachments & antipathies, and leave us under a conviction that we have no business to take part in them.   I know of nothing which should hinder you from moving in whatever direction the health of mrs Humphreys may require. our affairs with Spain have probably been fully communciated by your letters; and as to the interesting one of Louisiana, I imagine Spain has not acted, nor acts from her own will. the decisions of Paris are what we must prepare to meet. we shall certainly be glad to see you whenever you shall think this place worthy of a visit. the autumn will be pleasanter for the road, but perhaps, after the meeting of Congress, more agreeable as to what is to be seen here. in the mean time accept assurances of my constant esteem & high consideration.   TH: JEFFERSON

PrC (DLC); at foot of text: "Colo. Humphreys."

To Joseph Marie Lequinio
de Kerblay

SIR   Washington July 15. 1802.

Your favor of June 20. has been duly recieved and I present you my congratulations on your safe arrival in these states, as well as my thanks for the civilities expressed in your letter. your character and dispositions, as well as your station, will, I trust, make you an efficacious and useful [instrument in] cementing the friendship & interests of our two countries. I should have been happy to have had the pleasure of seeing you here, as I shall at any future time when you may wish to make a visit to this place. we endeavor on this and all other occasions to avoid establishing any etiquette which may interfere with the convenience or the inclinations of those concerned. I am glad to find you have made proficiency in our language; as you will rarely, in society here, meet with persons who speak yours familiarly. the language of the country is indispensable to the knolege of what is going on in it, and to the perfect understanding of the characters & sentiments of it's citizens. wishing you may find your residence here as agreeable as you may have expected, I pray you to accept assurances of my high consideration & respect.   TH: JEFFERSON

PrC (DLC); blurred; at foot of text: "M. Lequinio Kerblay."

From Joseph Marie Lequinio
de Kerblay

MONSIEUR LE PRÉSIDENT   Newport le 15 juillet an 1802

J'ai reçu l'Exequatur que vous avez bien voulu Donner à ma Commission d'agent des rélations Commerciales de france, et que le citoyen pichon notre Commissaire général m'a fait passer; je vous prie d'En agréer mes remercimens et d'être persuade que je mettrai tous mes soins à justifier votre approbation. je me Croirais vraiment heureux de mériter et d'obtenir quelques Droits à votre estime.

Voudriez vous permettre, Monsieur le président, Que j'aie l'onneur de vous offrir un exemplaire d'un Ouvrage que j'ai publié, il n'y a qu'un petit nombre d'années, sur un département de la france assez Curieux sous Divers aspects. Cet ouvrage A bien des Defauts, et je ne vous l'offre pas Comme une choze digne de vous, mais Comme une marque du Desir que j'aurais d'être Connu de vous et de vous rendre

Certain de ma haute Considération pour votre personne, ainsi que de mon profond respect **LEQUINIO KERBLAY**

EDITORS' TRANSLATION

MISTER PRESIDENT, Newport, 15 July 1802

I received the exequatur that you kindly accorded me as agent for commercial relations of France, and that Citizen Pichon, our commissary general, transmitted to me. Please receive my thanks and know that I will take great care to deserve your approval. I would consider myself truly happy to merit and earn the right to your esteem.

Please allow me, Mister President, the honor of offering you a copy of a work that I published, only a few years ago, about a French *département* that is rather curious in many respects. The work has many weaknesses and I do not present it as an object worthy of you but as a sign of my desire for you to know me and to understand my high esteem, as well as my deep respect, for you. **LEQUINIO KERBLAY**

RC (MoSHi: Jefferson Papers); on printed letterhead stationery of the Republic of France with the heading "Relations commerciales de France" and identifying Lequinio de Kerblay as vice commissary for commercial relations of France at Newport, Rhode Island; at head of text: "à Monsieur de jefferson président des États unis d'amérique"; endorsed by TJ as received 12 Aug. and so recorded in SJL.

OUVRAGE: Lequinio de Kerblay's two-volume *Voyage dans le Jura* or *Voyage pittoresque et physico-économique, dans le Jura* (Sowerby, No. 3881). Editions of the work were published in Paris in 1800 and 1801. There was a delay in forwarding the book; see Lequinio de Kerblay to TJ, 31 July.

To Francis Mentges

SIR Washington July 15. 1802.

I have duly recieved your favor of the 7th. and have taken care that it shall be communicated to the Secretary at war, within whose province it is to consider of the best means of promoting the public interest within his department, and of the agents whom it is best to employ. the duty is a very painful one, which devolves on the Executive, of naming those on whom the reductions are to fall which have been prescribed by the law. we trust to the liberality of those on whom the lot falls, to consider the agency of the Executive as a general not personal thing, and that they will meet it, as they would any other of the numerous casualties to which we are exposed in our passage through life. Accept my respects and best wishes. **TH: JEFFERSON**

RC (PPL: Arthur Loeb Collection); addressed: "Colo. J. Mintges Philadelphia"; franked and postmarked; endorsed. PrC (DLC).

To James Monroe

Washington July 15. 1802.

Your favor of the 7th. has been duly recieved. I am really mortified at the base ingratitude of Callender. it presents human nature in a hideous form: it gives me concern because I percieve that relief, which was afforded him on mere motives of charity, may be viewed under the aspect of employing him as a writer. When the Political progress of Britain first appeared in this country, it was in a periodical publication called the bee, where I saw it. I was speaking of it in terms of strong approbation to a friend in Philadelphia, when he asked me if I knew that the author was then in the city, a fugitive from prosecution on account of that work, and in want of employ for his subsistence. this was the first[1] of my learning that Callendar was author of the work; I considered him as a man of science fled from persecution, & assured my friend of my readiness to do whatever could serve him. it was long after this before I saw him: probably not till 1798. he had in the mean time written a 2d. part of the Political progress much inferior to the first, and his history of the US. in 1798. I think I was applied to by mr Lieper to contribute to his relief. I did so. in 1799, I think S. T. Mason applied for him. I contributed again. he had by this time paid me two or three personal visits. when he fled in a panic from Philadelphia to Genl. Mason's, he wrote to me that he was a fugitive, in want of employ, wished to know if he could get into a counting house, or a school in my neighborhood, or in that of Richmond; that he had materials for a volume, & if he could get as much money as would buy the paper, the profit of the sale would be all his own. I availed myself of this pretext to cover a mere charity, by desiring him to consider me a subscriber for as many copies of his book as the money inclosed (50. D.) amounted to; but to send me two copies only, as the others might lie till called for but I discouraged his coming into my neighborhood.[2] his first writings here had fallen far short of his original Political progress, and the scurrilities of his subsequent ones began evidently to do mischief. as to myself no man wished more to see his pen stopped: but I considered him still as a proper object of benevolence. the succeeding year he again wanted money to buy paper for another volume. I made his letter, as before, the occasion of giving him another 50. D. he considers these as proofs of my approbation of his writings, when they were mere charities, yielded under a strong conviction that he was injuring us by his writings.[3] it is known to many that the sums given to him were such and even smaller than I was in the habit of giving to others in distress, of the federal as well as republican party, without attention to political principles. soon after I was elected to the government, Callender came on here, wishing to be made postmaster at Richmond. I knew him to be totally unfit for it: and however ready I was to aid him with my own charities (and I then gave him 50. D.) I did not think the public offices confided to me to give away as charities. he took it in mortal offence, & from that moment has been hauling off to his former enemies the federalists. besides the letter I wrote him in answer to the one from Genl. Mason's, I wrote him another containing answers to two questions he addressed to me. 1. whether mr Jay recieved salary as Chief justice & envoy at the same time; & 2. something relative to the expences of an embassy to Constantinople. I think these were the only letters I ever wrote him in answer to volumes he was perpetually writing to me.—this is the true state of what has passed between him and me. I do not know that it can be used without committing me in controversy as it were with one too little respected by the public to merit that notice. I leave to your judgment what use can be made of these facts. perhaps it will be better judged of when we see what use the tories will endeavor to make of their new friend.—I shall leave this on the 21st. & be at Monticello probably the 24th. or within 2. or 3. days of that; and shall hope ere long to see you there. accept assurances of my affectionate attachment.

TH: JEFFERSON

RC (NN); endorsed by Monroe. PrC (DLC); in ink at foot of first page: "Monroe Govr."

THE POLITICAL PROGRESS OF BRITAIN by James Thomson Callender first appeared in 1792 as a series of anonymous letters published in THE BEE, a weekly periodical published in Edinburgh by James Anderson. Callender briefly worked for Anderson as an assistant editor on the publication in 1790. TJ and Anderson corresponded regarding the *Bee* in the early 1790s, with Anderson sending copies of the first eleven volumes to TJ (Durey, *Callender*, 28-9; DNB, s.v. "James Anderson (1739-1808)"; Vol. 16:391-2; Vol. 18:111-12; Vol. 24:139-40, 564-5).

Prior to the payments of $50 described in the 5 July issue of the *Recorder*, TJ had demonstrated his READINESS TO DO WHATEVER COULD SERVE Callender with a series of payments to the author made in 1797 and 1798. On 20 June 1797, TJ paid Callender $15.14 for copies of his *History of the United States for 1796*. Several months later, on 8 Oct., TJ asked John Barnes to remit to Callender $20 for "pamphlets" for himself and "some of my neighbors." TJ made four payments to Callender in December 1797: a payment of $16 on 12 Dec.; one of $4.33 on 14 Dec. for "pamphlets"; one of $1.25 on 17 Dec. for a copy of Callender's *History* for James Hopkins, for which TJ noted that he overpaid $.75; and one of $5 on 23 Dec. for "books & pamphlets." On 9 Feb. 1798, TJ paid Thomas Leiper (LIEPER) $5 on Callender's behalf for five copies of his *Sketches of the History of America*, then gave Leiper an additional $16 for Callender on 23 Mch. A final payment to Callender of $3 for "books" was made on 23 May 1798 (MB, 2:963, 971, 975-6, 979-80, 984; Vol. 29:536-7, 544; Vol. 30:188-9).

Senator Stevens Thomson MASON of

Virginia gave Callender refuge at his Loudoun County plantation, Raspberry Plain, after the writer had FLED IN A PANIC FROM PHILADELPHIA shortly before the passage of the Sedition Act in July 1798 (Vol. 30:521-3). Responding to Callender's 22 Sep. 1798 request from Raspberry Plain for employment or financial aid, TJ wrote from Monticello on 11 Oct. that he had authorized Mason to draw on George Jefferson for $50, which TJ hoped might provide Callender with "some aid for the moment" (Vol. 30:558-61). In the letter above, TJ conflates this exchange with his letter to Callender of 6 Sep. 1799, in which he authorized Jefferson to pay Callender $50 for copies of his forthcoming work, *The Prospect Before Us* (Vol. 31:179-181; TJ to Monroe, 17 July 1802)

CALLENDER CAME ON HERE: Callender came to Washington in late May 1801, with TJ using the opportunity to offer a final $50 payment to the journalist through the conduit of his private secretary, Meriwether Lewis. TJ intended the money as a contribution toward repaying Callender's sedition fine. He revoked the offer, however, following the writer's dec-laration that he deemed the payment "hushmoney" rather than charity (Vol. 34:185-6, 205).

ANSWERS TO TWO QUESTIONS: in his 29 Sep. 1799 letter to TJ, Callender had asked for information on the cost of a proposed diplomatic mission to Constantinople in 1786 and on the mode for choosing presidential electors by the individual states in 1796. He also enclosed sixteen draft pages of the *Prospect*. TJ replied on 6 Oct., answering Callender's queries to the best of his recollection and also thanking him for the pages. To protect his letter from "the curiosity of the post offices," TJ sent it unsigned and under cover to George Jefferson. When Callender published this letter in its entirety in the 6 Oct. 1802 edition of the Richmond *Recorder*, he printed the following extract in capital letters: "I thank you for the proof sheets you enclosed me. such papers cannot fail to produce the best effect" (Vol. 31:194-5, 200-2).

[1] TJ here canceled "time."
[2] Preceding eight words interlined.
[3] TJ here canceled: "[but still] I thought him [an object of charity]."

To John Beckley

July 16. 1802

Th: Jefferson with his compliments to mr Beckley informs him that he has this day given orders for the books for Congress according to the catalogue approved by the committee, that they will compose about 700. volumes of different sizes, and will probably require 4. presses of 4 feet width & the common height, or what will be equivalent to that if wider or narrower; which is mentioned for his government in providing presses.

Should mr Beckley make a visit to the Augusta springs, as his best route is by Charlottesville Th: Jefferson will be very happy to recieve him at Monticello and enjoy his company there as long as it may suit him to stay.

The route is to cross at Georgetown, & to go by Fairfax C. H. Songster's, Brown's tavern, Slaterun church, Elkrun church, Stevensburg, Downey's ford, Orange court house, to mr Madison's 93. miles, & then 27. miles to Monticello by the way of Milton which is the best road.

PrC (DLC); endorsed by TJ in ink on verso.

ORDERS FOR THE BOOKS: see TJ's letters to William Duane, George Erving, and William Short, all of 16 July.

The CATALOGUE for the Library of Congress must have been APPROVED BY THE COMMITTEE sometime between 14 April, when TJ sent a list of recommended books to the committee chairman Abraham Baldwin, and 16 July, when TJ began directing orders for book purchases (Vol. 37:227-33).

The portable bookcases or PRESSES were probably constructed of pine and were likely stained or painted. The books previously stored separately by the House and the Senate would be combined with the recently purchased books and "numbered, labelled and set up in portable cases with handles to them, for the purpose of easy removal, with wire-netting doors, and locks" (*Annals*, 12:1292; Anne-Imelda Radice, "The Original Library of Congress: The History [1800-1814] of the Library of Congress in the United States Capitol," in John Y. Cole, ed., *The Library of Congress: A Documentary History* [Bethesda, Md., 1987], 6-7; William Dawson Johnston, *History of the Library of Congress, Volume 1: 1800-1864* [Washington, D.C., 1904], 25, 27).

VISIT TO THE AUGUSTA SPRINGS: beleagured by debt, illness, and responsibilities for a large extended family, Beckley traveled to Martinsburg and Berkeley Springs, Virginia, for nine weeks beginning in September with hopes to restore his health (James Conaway, *America's Library: The Story of the Library of Congress* [New Haven, 2000], 15; Edmund Berkeley and Dorothy Smith Berkeley, *John Beckley: Zealous Partisan in a Nation Divided* [Philadelphia, 1973], 185-6, 188, 246-7).

To William Duane

SIR   Washington July 16. 1802.

I now inclose you catalogues of the books which are to be imported for Congress and which you desired to have placed under your procurement. I have written to mr Short at Paris and mr Erving at London to superintend the purchase in order that the books & their prices may be such as they approve, and I have inclosed them copies of the catalogues; so that your correspondent will have to obtain their approbation in all his proceedings & from them he will recieve his pay, the Secretary of the treasury having ordered money into their hands for the purpose. I inclose you an extract from the letters to them, which will enable you to give proper instructions to your correspondent, & will supply to yourself all further information necessary. to the foot of the catalogues I have subjoined a note which being presented to those gentlemen will authorise their proceeding, and together with my letter to them will serve as duplicates to each other. I have earnestly to recommend dispatch in this transaction, as too much of the season has already slipped away, and it is desireable that the books should be recieved before the meeting of Congress or as soon after as possible. Accept my respects & best wishes.

TH: JEFFERSON

PrC (MoSHi: Jefferson Papers); at foot of text: "Mr. Duane"; endorsed by TJ in ink on verso.

YOUR PROCUREMENT: Duane offered his services and stated his qualifications for importing books from Europe for the Library of Congress in a letter of 10 May 1801 (Vol. 34:72).

See TJ's letters of this day to William SHORT and George W. ERVING regarding book purchases at Paris and London respectively.

SECRETARY OF THE TREASURY HAVING ORDERED MONEY: see TJ to Gallatin, 9 and 16 July and Gallatin to TJ, 17 Aug.

ENCLOSURES

I

List of Books for the Library of Congress

Paris

History.
Annales Romaines par Macquer. 12mo
Essai historique et Chronologique de l'Abbé Berlié. 2.v. 12mo.
Abregé Chronologique de l'histoire ancienne avant Jesus Christ par LaCombe. 12mo.
Abregé Chronologique de l'histoire des Juifs. 12mo.
Abregé Chronologique de l'histoire des Empereurs Romains par Richer. 2.v. 12mo.
Dictionnaire de Moreri. 10.v. fol.
Dictionnaire historique et bibliographique par Lavocat. 4.v. 12mo.
Dictionnaire historique par un societé de gens de lettres. 9.v. 8vo.
Dictionnaire de diplomatique par Dom. de Vaynes 2.v. 8vo.
Abregé Chronologique de l'histoire universelle par Hornot. 12mo.
Tablettes Chronologiques de l'histoire universelle de Fresnoy. 2.v. 8mo.
Tableau chronologique de l'histoire de l'Europe de 476. à 1648. 8vo.
Abregé chronologique de l'histoire d'Espagne & de Portugal. 2.v. 12mo.
Abregé chronologique de l'histoire de France par Henault. 2.v. 12mo.
Abregé chronologique de l'histoire et du droit publique l'Allemagne par Pfeffel. 2.v. 12mo.
Abregé Chronologique de l'histoire du Nord par La Combe. 2.v. 12mo.
Abregé Chronologique de l'histoire de Pologne par l'Abbé Coyer. 2.v. 12mo.
Law of Nature & Nations.
Puffendorf. Devoirs de l'homme et du citoyen. 2.v. 12mo.
Wolff. Droit de la nature et des gens. Lat. Fr. 6.v. 12mo.
Vattel. Questions de droit naturel. 12mo.
Recueil de discours par Barbeyrac. 2.v. 12mo.
Wicquefort de l'Ambassadeur. 2.v. 4to.
Le ministre public par du Franquesnay 12mo.
L'art de negocier par Pecquet. 12mo.
Maniere de negocier par Callieres. 2.v. 12mo.
Mably. Droit public de l'Europe. 3.v. 12mo.

Negociations du President Jeannin. 2.v. 12mo.
Ambassades de la Boderie en Angleterre. 5.v. 12mo.
Negociations du comte d'Estrades a Londres 9.v. 12mo.
Lettres et negociations de J. de Witt. 5.v. 12mo.
Histoire de la traité de Westphalie par D'Avaux. 6.v. 12mo.
Dumont. Corps universel diplomatique. 8.v. fol.
Muratori.
Memoires sur les droits de France et de l'Angleterre en Amerique. 4.v. 4to.
Code de l'humanité par Felice. 13.v. 4to.
Robinet. Dictionnaire morale, politique et diplomatique. 31.v. 4to.
Maritime law.
Il Consolato del mare.
Shardii leges navales Rhodiorum et selectae Rhodiorum.
Us et Coustumes de la mer par Clairac. 4to.
Heineccii scriptores de jure maritimo.
Valin. (his works on Maritime law, titles not known)
Law.
Houard sur les coutumes Anglo-Normans. 4.v. 4to.
Institution du droit François par Argou. 2.v. 12mo.
Commentaire sur l'Ordonnance de la Marine. 2.v. 12mo.
Political.
Arithmetique lineaire de Playfair. 4to. printed in Paris about 1787.
Table des vivans de Susmich.
Geography.
Atlas portatif de Grenet et Bonne. 4to.
the Atlasses of Danville & Delisle.
Encyclopedie de Diderot et Dalembert. folio.
Scapulae lexicon Graecum. folio London edition.
Hederici lexicon. 4to.
Calepinus XI linguarum. fol.
Dictionnaire de l'academie Francaise. 2.v. 4to. bound in 1.
Dictionnaire Etymologique de la langue française de Menage. 2.v. fol.[1]
the Spanish dictionary of their academy.
Diccionario della Crusca
Dictionnaire Espagn. François, et Latin par Sejournant 2.v. 4to.
Dictionnaire Ital. et Francois d'Alberti 2.v. 4to.[2]

Mr. Duane is employed to purchase the preceding books in Paris under the controul & approbation of Wm. Short esq. who is desired to pay for them out of the monies remitted to him for that purpose, & according to the advice forwarded him by   TH: JEFFERSON
                                                      Washington July 19. 1802

MS (MoSHi: Jefferson Papers); entirely in TJ's hand. PrC (DLC: TJ Papers, 232:41552); undated; lacks TJ's final sentence, signature, and date. Enclosed in TJ to William Short, 16 July.

[1] Entry interlined.

[2] TJ canceled his last entry, "Johnson's [Eng.] dict. 2. vols. 4to. such [...] publd. Dublin 1775," which he included as the last entry on his London list (see Enclosure No. 2).

II

List of Books for
the Library of Congress

London

History

Bossuet's universal history. 2.v. 12mo.

Newton's chronology. 4to.

Collier's historical dictionary. 4.v. fol.

Wood's Athenae Oxonienses

The American & British Chronicle of war & Politics, 1773-1783. Lond. 1783. by E.I.S. 8vo.

Puffendorf's introduction to the history of the Universe

Salmon's chronological abridgment of the history of England, in English if to be had. otherwise the French edition 2.v. 12mo.

the Historical register from it's commencement

the Annual register from it's commencement.

Law of Nature & nations

Beller's delineation of Universal law. 4to.

Cumberland's law of nature. 4to.

Grotii mare liberum. in English if to be had. otherwise Latin.

Ward's foundation & history of the law of nations. 8vo.

Zouch de judicio. inter gentes, et de jure faciali.

Bynkershoeck opera. 6.v. 4to.

Rymer's foedera.

Maritime law

Lee's treatise on captures. 8vo.

Vinnius's commentary on the laws of Rhodes.

Schomberg on the maritime laws of Rhodes. 8vo.

Robinson's Admiralty reports. 8vo.

Law.

Lord Kaim's general principles of Equity. the 2d. edition in folio.

Abridgment of cases in Equity. 8vo.

Fitzherbert's abridgment.

Broke's abridgment

Bracton. 4to.

Rolle's abridgment. fol.

Bacon's abridgment. 7.v. 8vo.

Comyns's Digest. 6.v. 8vo.

Spelmanni Glossarium. fol.

Cuningham's Law Dictionary.

Rastal's collection of statutes.

Pickering's collection of statutes. 8vo.

Staundfort's Pleas of the crown. 4to.

Hale's Pleas of the crown. 2.v. 8vo.

Hawkins's Pleas of the crown. 8vo.

Malynes's Lex mercatoria. 2.v. fol.

Calvini lexicon juridicum. fol.
Corpus juris civilis Gothofredi. 2.v. fol.
Frederician code 2.v. 8vo.
Octavo editions of the lawbooks to be preferred in all cases where an
    Octavo edition has been printed
Parliamentary.
    Brady on government. fol.
    Petty's constitution & laws of England. 8vo.
    Sommers's rights of king & people. 12mo.
    Bacon on the government of England.
    Smith's republic of England.
    Burgh's political disquisitions.
    Stuart's historical dissertation on the English constitution. 8vo.
    Spelman's works. fol.
    Selden's works.
    Thurloe's state papers
    Elsynge ⎱ parliamentary works. titles not known.
    Scobell ⎰
    Arcana parliamentaria.
    Hollis's remains. 8vo.
    Orders of the H. of Commons. 12mo.
    Pettus's constitution of parliament. 8vo.
    Brown's privilegia Parliamentaria. 8vo.
    Petit's antient rights of the Commons of England. 8vo.
    Hale's jurisdiction of parliaments. 8vo.
    Dewes's journal.
    Ryley's placita parliamentaria. fol.
    Prynne's Parliamentary writs. 4to.
    Hakewell's Modus tenendi Parliamentum.
    Petyt's Jus Parliamentarium. fol.
    the Case of the Aylesbury election.
    Bohun's debates.
    the Case of Ashby & White. 8vo.
    Townshend's historical collections. fol.
Political.
    Wallace on the numbers of mankind. 8vo.
    Arbuthnot on antient coins & measures.
Geography.
    Busching's geography 6.v. 4to.
    Ainsworth's dictionary Lat. Eng. 2.v. 4to.
    Sewel's Dutch & English dictionary 2.v. 4to.
    Bartholomew's Danish dictionary
    Swedish & Eng. dictionary. ⎱ the best
    German & Eng. dictionary. ⎰
    Lye's Junius's Etymoligicon by Owen. 2.v. fol.
    Skinner's Etymologicon. fol.
    Johnson's English dict. 2. vols. 4to. (such an edn. was publd. Dublin
        1775.)

Mr. Duane is employed to purchase the preceding books in London under the controul & approbation of George W. Erving Consul of the US. who is desired to pay for them out of the monies remitted to him for that purpose & according to the advice forwarded him by

Th: Jefferson
Washington July 19. 1802.

MS (MoSHi: Jefferson Papers); entirely in TJ's hand. PrC (DLC: TJ Papers, 232:41551); undated; lacks final sentence, signature, and date. Enclosed in TJ to George W. Erving, 16 July.

III

To William Short and George W. Erving

Extract from the letters written to mr Short & mr Erving.

'mr Duane is employed this year to make the importation, partly from Paris, partly from London, & to execute the details. but as I am anxious to have it established that the public money must be laid out with as rigorous economy as that of an individual, the proceedings of mr Duane's correspondent are made subject, by my agreement with him, to your superintendence and controul. if his correspondent will not furnish any particular book as cheap as it is to be got elsewhere, I wish it to be got elsewhere. we wish for good editions, not pompous ones; neat bindings, but not splendid. 8vo. and 12.mo. editions to be preferred to folios & 4tos. in all cases where to be had equally good. the purchase to be made with as little delay as possible, that the books may arrive here before the meeting of Congress if possible. they should be packed in trunks, covered with oilcloth, to preserve them from damp.'

PrC (MoSHi: Jefferson Papers).

To Mary Jefferson Eppes

My dear Maria   Washington July 16. 1802

Your sister informs me she has lately given you information of the health of the family. it seems her children have escaped the measles tho some of the negroes have had it. the following is an extract from her letter dated July 10. 'we are entirely free from the measles here now. those of our people who had it have recovered. at Monticello the last time I heard from there three of the nail boys had it & others were complaining, but whether with the measles or not I could not learn. I will send over to Lilly immediately to let him know your orders on the subject.' these orders were to remove every person from the mountain who had or should have the measles. I have no doubt you may proceed with the utmost security. I shall be there before you, to wit on Saturday the 24th. and will take care to have a clear stage, if any body should still have it: but there can be no doubt it will have gone through all who were to have it before that date. I am satisfied Francis will have more to hope from the change of air, than to fear from the measles. and as to yourself, it is of great importance to get up into the country as soon as you are able, the liability to bilious diseases being exactly in proportion to the distance from the sea. I leave this on the 24th. and shall be in great hopes of recieving yourself and mr Eppes there immediately. I recieved two days ago his letter of the 8th. in which he gives me a poor account of your health, tho' he says you are recruiting. make very short stages, be off always by day light and have your day's journey over by ten. in this way it is probable you may find the moderate exercise of the journey of service to yourself & Francis. nothing is more frequent than to see a child reestablished by a journey. present my sincerest affections to the family at Eppington, and to mr Eppes. tell him the tory newspapers are all attacking his publication, and urging it as a proof that Virginia has for object to change the constitution of the US. and to make it too impotent to curb the larger states. accept yourself assurances of my constant & tenderest love. TH: JEFFERSON

RC (NjP); at foot of text: "Mrs. Maria Eppes."

HIS PUBLICATION: upon learning of William Branch Giles's plan to retire from Congress at the end of the next session, John Wayles Eppes wrote an address to the people of Powhatan, Amelia, Chesterfield, and Goochland counties offering his services as a representative for his district. He urged Republicans to work for amendments to the Constitution that would reduce the length of terms for senators to that of representatives and "render the President ineligible after a certain period, until a term of years shall have intervened." Judges would be appointed by Congress for a fixed period of years and would not be permitted to hold any other office during their judgeship (Richmond *Virginia Argus*, 30 June 1802). Criticism of the proposed amendments appeared in such newspapers as the Baltimore *Republican, or Anti-Democrat*, 12 July, and the Boston *Mercury and New-England Palladium*, 13 July.

To George W. Erving

DEAR SIR   Washington July 16. 1802.

Congress have appropriated a sum of money to the procuring books for their use. about one half of it was laid out in London the last year, but at such prices as forbid an application to the same bookseller. mr Duane is employed this year to make the importation, partly from Paris, partly from London, & to execute the details. but, as I am anxious to have it known that the public money must be laid out with as rigorous economy as that of an individual, the proceedings of mr Duane's correspondent at London are made subject, by my agreement with him, to your superintendance and controul. I have flattered myself you would execute this trust for us: and therefore take the liberty of inclosing you a copy of the catalogue furnished to mr Duane, and shall inclose herein a bill of exchange for about a thousand dollars, which being not yet delivered to me, I cannot particularly describe. if mr Duane's correspondent will not furnish any particular book as cheap as it is to be got elsewhere, I wish it to be got elsewhere. we wish for good editions, not pompous ones; neat bindings, but not splendid: 8vo. and 12mo. editions to be preferred to folios and 4tos. in all cases where to be had equally good. the purchase to be made with as little delay as possible, that the books may arrive here before the meeting of Congress if possible. they should be packed in trunks, covered with oilcloth, to preserve them from damps. under this general view of what will be satisfactory here, I am persuaded I have done what is best for the public in placing this matter under your care; hoping at the same time that, the execution of the details being otherwise provided for, it will not give you great trouble. Accept assurances of my great esteem & respect.

TH: JEFFERSON

PrC (MoSHi: Jefferson Papers); at foot of text: "George W. Erving esq."; endorsed by TJ in ink on verso. Enclosure: see Enclosure No. 2 at TJ to William Duane, 16 July. Enclosed in TJ to Gallatin, 16 July.

To Albert Gallatin

DEAR SIR   Washington July 16. 1802.

The bills of exchange for mr Short and mr Erving not being come to hand, I take the liberty of leaving under your cover the letters I have written to them, in which I must request you to insert the bills seal the letters & forward them, without losing the time which would be requisite for returning them to me. the season is already so far advanced as to render it doubtful whether they can be here before the meeting of Congress. accept assurances of my affectionate esteem and respect   TH: JEFFERSON

PrC (MoSHi: Jefferson Papers); at foot of text: "The Secretary of the treasury"; endorsed by TJ in ink on verso. Enclosures: (1) TJ to William Short, 16 July, and enclosure. (2) TJ to George W. Erving, 16 July, and enclosure.

From John Isaac Hawkins

SIR,   Philadelphia July 16th. 1802

I recd your Piano Forte on the 3d inst.—being then about to leave Philada. on a journey, I Postponed informing you till I returned.

The instrument is very much injured by wet, the Captain of the Schooner says it was kept perfectly dry while under his care, it must therefore have been exposed in coming down the river to Richmond.

Having suspended the manufacturing of instruments till my return from Europe, I would propose to you to take a Piano I have on hand, in exchange, it is the best I ever made, & one I can recommend, its price is 300 dollars. if you take it I will allow you the same for yours which you gave, viz. 250 dollars. this however I by no means wish to press, and I would rather furnish you with a Claviol but I shall not in all Probability be able to do it in less than a year.

Of the construction of the Claviol you will be able to judge by the annexed sketch; it is considered highly by all who hear it. a single note on it is much stronger, than the correspondent note on a Violin or Violoncello; so much so, that a full Chord taken by both hands is judged to be as Powerful as 12 or 15 Violins & basses. The loud sound at a distance is similar to that of a full band, in which the hearer imagines he can distinguish Clarinetts, Violins, Horns, Basses, & indeed almost every kind of musical instrument; but near, it resembles the Organ. The Piano of it is extremely soft & sweet, & has been pronounced equal to the harmonica. The Cresendo & diminuendo is Perfect.

There are some imperfections in the machinery of the Claviol which is finished, in consequence of various alterations it has undergone, that would render it almost useless to anyone but myself, I cannot therefore offer it for sale.

As I expect again to leave town in a few days shall be glad you will inform me immediately whether I shall send you the Piano Forte or not, in a line addressed to the Care of Mr. Peale at the Museum.

I am Sir yr Obt Sevt.   JOHN I. HAWKINS

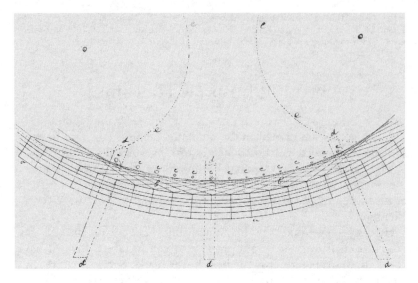

a.a.a.   part of a hoop on the inside of which horse hair […] is stretched so as to form an elastic surface.

c.c.c.   gut strings at rest almost touching the horse hair.

d.d.   &c. slider moved by finger keys to draw the strings against the hair

The hoop is made to revolve by the foot, & the string by pressure on the finger key is brought[1] against the hair, which is rosined. the tone is loud or soft according to the degree of pressure.

as. the hoop could have no axis it is[2] supported on 3 wheels, parts of 2 of them are represented at e.e.e.

SIR/

I had intended to be more particular in my description but to send by this post, I must close immediately, shall take an opportunity soon to add to this: & also describe several little contrivances to save domestic labor & add to our conveniencies. being assured you take pleasure in hearing of useful improvements. yr. Obt Sevt.

JOHN I. HAWKINS

RC (DLC); torn; endorsed by TJ as received 20 July and so recorded in SJL.

TJ had shipped his daughter's out-of-tune PIANO-FORTE to Hawkins for repair; see TJ to Hawkins, 13 Apr., and Hawkins to TJ, 21 Apr. 1802.

FURNISH YOU WITH A CLAVIOL: the claviol, a *sostenete* piano, contained a mechanism to prolong tones. While other inventors had devised methods to keep a piano string vibrating after a note was struck, Hawkins's solution permitted hammers to strike a string repeatedly when a key was depressed (Peale, *Papers*, v. 2, pt. 1:448). TJ suggested that he might accept a claviol if Hawkins would dispose of his piano-forte; see TJ to Hawkins, 17 June 1802. For Hawkins's departure for London and reports that he would send claviols to TJ and Charles Willson Peale, see *Mechanics' Magazine*, 43 (1845), 122-5.

[1] Preceding six words interlined.
[2] MS: "is is."

From John F. Mercer

DEAR SIR   Annapolis July 16th. 1802.

Your favr. of the 7th. never reach'd me 'till yesterday Evening,— the one preceding it came regularly to hand & I have to acknowledge the receipt of the $18,000, by our Treasury, which you advise me woud be paid;—this Sum will answer fully our present purposes, & under such circumstances I cannot but regret the sacrifice & consequent derangement of the Interests of the City, that the reimbursement of the $50,000 will necessarily occasion.—

I have been flatter'd, from public report, with the hope of seeing yourself & Mr. Madison *here*, before this;—I confided in the information,—knowing that you both observe an inviolate fidelity to your engagements, I did not fear that you woud plead the Act of limitation, against a promise of last year & I have considerd it as only postpond.—

You will give me some intimation of the time when I may expect you, as I had designd to visit Baltimore early in August, whence I shoud proceed to Virginia & I did not intend to be seated here again untill late in September:—These arrangements can easily be accommodated to your convenience & I know you will confide in my assurances that I promise myself few gratifications beyond the pleasure of receiving you in any house of which I may be master.—

Mrs. Mercer will not be satisfied unless the Ladies of your families accompany you.—With sincere & affectionate esteem & respect I am Dr Sir yr. Ob St.   JOHN F: MERCER

RC (DLC): endorsed by TJ as received 19 July and so recorded in SJL.

ONE PRECEDING: TJ to Mercer, 23 June.

PROMISE OF LAST YEAR: Vol. 35:499, 529-30.

To William Short

DEAR SIR   Washington July 16. 1802.

Congress have appropriated a sum of money to the procuring books for their use. about one half of it was laid out the last year, but at prices which could not be approved. mr Duane is employed this year to make the importation, partly from Paris, partly from London, and to execute the details. but, as I am anxious to shew that the public money must be laid out with as rigorous economy as that of an individual, the proceedings of mr Duane's correspondent at Paris are made subject, by my agreement with him, to your superintendance and controul. I have flattered myself you would execute this trust for us: and therefore take the liberty of inclosing you a copy of the catalogue furnished to mr Duane, and shall inclose herein a bill of exchange for about 1000. D. which being not yet delivered to me, I cannot particularly describe. if mr Duane's correspondent will not furnish any particular book as cheap as it is to be got elsewhere, I wish it to be got elsewhere. we wish for good editions, but not pompous ones; neat bindings but not splendid. 8vo. and 12mo. editions to be preferred to folios & 4tos. in all cases where to be had equally good. the purchase to be made with as little delay as possible that the books may arrive here before the meeting of Congress if possible. they should be packed in trunks, covered with oilcloth, to preserve them from damp. under this general view of what will be satisfactory here, I am persuaded I have done what is best for the public in placing this matter under your care; hoping at the same time that, the execution of the details being otherwise provided for, it will not give you great trouble. Accept assurances of my constant & affectionate esteem.   TH: JEFFERSON

RC (NHi: Robert R. Livingston Papers); at foot of text: "William Short." PrC (MoSHi: Jefferson Papers); endorsed by TJ in ink on verso. Enclosure: see Enclosure No. 1 at TJ to William Duane, 16 July. Enclosed in TJ to Albert Gallatin, 16 July.

From Mary Jefferson Eppes

Eppington July 17th [1802]

Mr Eppes thinks we had best remain here My Dear Papa till we hear further from you about the measles, I must therefore beg you will write as soon as you can conveniently after arriving at Monticello, you know not how anxious I am to see you, after having so long look'd forward to this period with so much pleasure, to be disappointed at the very moment which was to reunite us after so long an absence requires a greater degree of[1] fortitude than I have to bear it &, your stay at Home will be so short that it makes me doubly anxious to be with you,[2] if my little sons health was not in the precarious state it is I should not fear the disorder so much on his account but he suffers so much & is so ill with every tooth that comes out that I should dread any additional complaint. we had proposed going by the green springs as we went up but the danger of finding the measles there[3] has made us give up that journey. your last letter to Mr Eppes my dear Papa must be deferr'd answering till the happy moment which brings us together, yet suffer me to tell you how much I feel it, your kindness knows no bounds nor is it the first time that it has gone so far as to pain the heart entirely yours, you have allready disfurnish'd yourself too much for us Dearest Papa suffer me to remind you of it & do not take it amiss if with grateful hearts we should not accept this present offer, it will I hope have this good effect on Mr Eppes to make him exert himself to begin a building of some sort at Pantops, he knows I should be satisfied with any for a while & would chearfully agree to any rules of economy when there that would enable him to continue independent & clear of debt, it must before long take place certainly, he is himself becoming very sensible of the many inconveniences attending the life we lead & which are increasing on us the longer we continue it. Adieu My dear Papa this day week I expected to have met you & to have forgotten in the delight of meeting you the pain I have felt in being so long separated from you for I experience more at each separation how little the heart can ever[4] become accustom'd to them! Adieu believe me yours with the tenderest love   M EPPES

RC (MHi); partially dated; endorsed by TJ as received 25 July and so recorded in SJL.

TJ's LAST LETTER to John Wayles Eppes, recorded in SJL at 13 June, has not been found.

[1] Preceding five words interlined in place of canceled text.

[2] Preceding four words interlined.

[3] Canceled: "will."

[4] Eppes first wrote "that the heart can never" before altering the passage to read as above.

From Albert Gallatin

DEAR SIR   New York 17th July 1802

On receipt of your letter I wrote to Mr Latimer & now enclose a copy of my letter & his answer: you will find that he now makes an absolute resignation. I write him by this day's mail that his letter will immediately be transmitted to the President; and will wait your further instructions for a final answer. I suppose there can be no objection to agreeing that his resignation should be considered as taking place the last of this month; and, in that case the signing of commissions should be suspended a few days. They may, however be left, on your leaving the city, with Mr Madison, who, if he shall also leave it before my return, may deliver them to Mr Steele with instructions when to forward them. Will you be pleased, on that subject, to write me a short official note authorizing the Supervisor of the district of Pennsylvania to act as Collector of the internal revenues for the city & County of Philadelphia. It is for the purpose of enabling T. Coxe to hold both. The same had been done at New York in favor of Mr Fish, & is continued for Mr Osgood. I will thank you to return to me Mr Latimer's two letters & the rough draught of mine to him, as I suppose they must be left of record in the office. A blank commission for the surveyor of Slade's Creek, and if you shall have no objection a blank commission for the Collector of Oswego & for the surveyor of   in the same district, may be left under cover to me. I will easily find recommendations here for the two last, which have been suffered to remain vacant, but from information lately received, it is necessary to fill; the whole consumption of heavy articles on black river & thence along Lake Ontario to Sodus being supplied by the way of Canada.

Gov. Hall & Mr Rodney were mistaken in supposing that we had appointed Philadelphians to examine the Delaware. Application was made to M'pherson, naval officer at Philada., and to A. M'Clene, Collector at Wilmington to communicate information. The first applied to the Chamber of commerce in Philada. & these appointed the Pilots & others who made the examination alluded to by Messrs. Hall & Rodney. A. M'Clene knew the river himself & sent information without appointing any persons to examine the river. The examination by the Philadelphians was at their own nomination & at their own expence: only they went in the revenue cutter. But I will write to the Governor of Delaware and request him to collect & transmit information on the subject.

I am sorry that Mr Dalton declines accepting. I suspect that the people of Newbury port may be somewhat clanish, & that a townsman will be considered as an essential qualification.

My health was much impaired when I left Washington; and though better is not perfectly restored. I hope, however, to be in Washington on 2d of August.

With sincere attachment & respect I have the honor to be Your obedt. Servt.   ALBERT GALLATIN

RC (DLC); addressed: "Thomas Jefferson President of the United States City of Washington"; franked and post-marked; endorsed by TJ as received from the Treasury Department on 19 July and so recorded in SJL. Enclosures not found.

YOUR LETTER: TJ to Gallatin, 9 July. I WRITE HIM BY THIS DAY'S MAIL: in his brief correspondence with George Latimer of this date, Gallatin acknowledged the Philadelphia collector's letter of 15 July and promised to transmit it "by this day's mail to the President" (Gallatin, *Papers*, 7:346).

The 1799 act "to regulate the collection of duties on imports and tonnage" established a collection district at OSWEGO,

New York. The district extended from the St. Lawrence to the Genesee River and included "all the shores and waters of Lake Ontario, and the rivers and waters connected therewith," lying within the jurisdiction of the United States. The law authorized the appointment of a collector at Oswego and up to three surveyors, to reside at places within the district as authorized by the president (U.S. Statutes at Large, 1:627, 631). SODUS, a bay and town on Lake Ontario between Oswego and Rochester, was described in 1804 as the best harbor on the south side of the lake. Joel Burt, the first collector at Oswego, was not appointed until 1803 (ASP, *Miscellaneous*, 1:270; JEP, 1:447; Jedidiah Morse, *The American Gazetteer*, 2d ed. [Charlestown, Mass., 1804]).

To Nathaniel Macon

DEAR SIR   Washington July 17. 1802

Your favor of June 17. came duly to hand. it gives me great pleasure to learn that the proceedings of the last session of Congress gives satisfaction in your quarter. it is impossible they should not do it in every quarter where they are not determined not to be satisfied, or kept uninformed of them. the special feasts & rejoicings on the 1st of July, and the toasts of the 4th. of July, as they have been recieved from different quarters prove that all republicans are pleased with them. the result of the elections in New York, Rhodeisland Connecticut & N. Hampshire proves considerable advances in the Republican interest. in Massachusets we do not see it at this distance, but I consider Strong's speech as a decisive proof that he sees it. you will have seen symptoms of a schism in N.Y. between Burr & the Clintonians. it is I believe undoubted that the latter embraces the whole republican interest of that state; the interest of the former is only what is created by the resources of his own mind. the 4th. of July has exhibited evidences of a general [fir]mness on this schism. You will well remember, because you were made to feel as we all were, the contributions levied on us to support the presses suffering under the Sedition law in 98. 99. to pay the fines of Callender, Holt,

Baldwin, Brown, Lyon &c. Callender, who came on here immediately on my election, to get the Postmaster's place at Richmond, for which I knew him unqualified, was so mortified with his disappointment, that he began to haul over immediately to federalism, and is now an open enemy. he is publishing my contributions to him (saying nothing of those by others, or for others), and the tory papers are endeavoring to make me considered as the patron & father of the Prospect before us, and so to impute to me all the scurrilities of that work against Genl. Washington, mr Adams & others.—the affair of Louisiana is still hanging over us. if the French[1] have not yet sent off their troops to take possession of it, I cannot but think our representations, while they show our anxiety for the friendship of that country, will yet convince them of the inevitable consequences of that measure to both France & Spain. however, Buonaparte's wisdom may fall short of our calculation in this instance, as it has in another. when we view the course which things have taken in Europe, in what light ought we to regard the important stage on which we are made to act? we are in truth the sole trustees for the whole race of man now on the globe. on our experiment depends the great question Can man govern himself? in this view it becomes doubly our duty to suppress all local & personal views, and to consider but the one great object of proving that a government may be so free as to leave every man in the unrestrained exercise of all his rights, while it has energy enough to protect him from every wrong.—I shall go the last week of this month to Monticello to avoid passing the months of Aug. and September on the tide waters. and this we propose to establish as a permanent regulation, that Aug. & Sep. shall be a season of recess for the executive, & the only one. it was our practice in Genl. Washington's time, & it is a reasonable one, as well on considerations of health, as that a total abandonment of our private affairs cannot be expected.   I have in contemplation to propose to Congress the building a dry dock here on the principle of a lock, which has never yet been applied to dry docks, because I believe there is not a place in the world, but this spot, where it can be practised. this we owe to the copious streams of running water here, at great heights above the tide; as for instance the Tyber, the Eastern branch, Rock creek, & the Potomac itself. for 150,000. dollars we can make a dry dock which shall place our 12 frigates dry, under a roof, not to cost us afterwards one dollar [a] year except for a centinel. we can at present, by lightening her, bring a 74. here, and as it will be long before we shall have a ship larger than a 74. those of the first size are not now an object of consideration, and consequently we need only say at present that this is the place at which[2] every vessel not larger than a 74. is to be laid up in time of peace. but by no great deal of work with a Mud scoop, the two bars in the Potomac can be made to admit first rates to pass them, when lightened as far as may be done. and Ca[nals?] would bring them over at present. we ought then to look to this as the great & sole repository of the Navy of the US. it derives it's exclusive fitness from the command of running water, depth & softness of it's bed, freedom from worms inaccessibility to an enemy being under the eye of the government[3] central position, and some other considerations not to be descanted on. it ought also to be our only building yard; because if we want ships built elsewhere, experience in England has proved that ships of war are *as well* & cheaper built in private than in public yards. we ought then to own but this single yard, and here to concentrate all our naval works & institutions. in time of war, our ships will come here only for considerable repairs. for smaller ones they may go into private yards in the seaport towns, and be protected by open batteries on the bank, formed by their own guns. indeed such open batteries ought to be provided in every sea-port for it's own protection, as well as to offer an asylum on every part of our coasts to our vessels pursued by an enemy. forts and shipyards are mere contrivances to sink the first expences, and entail everlasting expence afterwards. with a dry dock here in which our ships, kept dry & under cover, will be as sound at the beginning of a 2d. war as they were at the end of a 1st. the agricultural & sea-coast interests might compromise, by building a ship annually, and laying her by. Accept assurances of my affectionate esteem & respect.

Th: Jefferson

Sketch of a dry dock

the vessel floats with the common high tide into the lower bason, which is just big enough to hold a single one. the gate is then shut, and the water of the Tyber let into the Upper bason till both basons are full. the vessel then floats into the Upper one, the gate is opened, the water discharged, & she is left dry on the bottom of the bason.

PrC (DLC); faint and blurred; at foot of first page: "Mr. Macon."

The REJOICINGS ON THE 1ST OF JULY celebrated the abolition of the internal taxes, which went into effect on 30 June (U.S. Statutes at Large, 2:148-50; Trenton *True American,* 5 July 1802; *Kline's Carlisle Weekly Gazette,* 7 July 1802; Richmond *Virginia Argus,* 7 July 1802).

Governor Caleb STRONG'S SPEECH before the Massachusetts legislature on 1 June included remarks condemning "the prevalence of party spirit" and calls for reconciliation and harmony. "It is impossible that all should be of one opinion," the governor declared, "and if the cur-rent opinion is different from ours, we may endeavour, by calm discussion, without artifice or calumny, to correct the supposed error" (*Resolves of the General Court of the Commonwealth of Massachusetts...Begun and Held at Boston, in the County of Suffolk, on Wednesday the Twenty-Sixth Day of May, Anno Domini—MDCCCII* [Boston, 1802], 7).

For TJ's plan for a DRY DOCK for the navy in Washington, D.C., see Thomas Tingey to TJ, 28 June 1802.

[1] Word interlined.
[2] TJ here canceled "our whole."
[3] Preceding seven words interlined.

To James Monroe

DEAR SIR   Washington July 17. 1802.

After writing you on the 15th. I turned to my letter file to see what letters I had written to Callender & found them to have been of the dates of 1798. Oct. 11. & 1799. Sep. 6. & Oct. 6. but on looking for the letters they were not in their places nor to be found. on recollection I believe I sent them to you a year or two ago. if you have them, I shall be glad to recieve them at Monticello where I shall be on this day sennight. I inclose you a paper which shews the Tories mean to pervert these charities to Callender as much as they can. they will probably first represent me as the patron & support of the Prospect before us, & other things of Callenders, & then picking out all the scurrilities of the Author against Genl. Washington, mr Adams & others, impute them to me. I, as well as most other republicans who were in the way of doing it, contributed what I could afford to the support of the republican papers & printers, paid sums of money for the Bee, the Albany register, &c. when they were staggering under the Sedition law, contributed to the fines of Callender himself, of Holt, Brown & others suffering under that law, I discharged, when I came into office, such as were under the persecution of our enemies, without instituting any prosecutions in retaliation. they may therefore, with the same justice, impute to me, or to every republican contributor, every thing which was ever published in those papers or by those persons.—I must correct a fact in mine of the 15th. I find

I did not inclose the 50. D. to Callender himself while at Genl. Mason's, but authorised the Genl. to draw on my correspondt. at Richmond and to give the money to Callender. so the other 50. D of which he speaks were by order on my correspondt. at Richmond. Accept assurances of my affectionate esteem & respect.

TH: JEFFERSON

RC (MiDbEI); at foot of text: "Govr. Monroe." PrC (DLC). Enclosure not found.

From William Irvine

U.S. Arsenal near Philadelphia

SIR/   18th July 1802

When at Washington I took the liberty to recommend Robert Porter Esqr. of Philadelphia to your notice as one of the Commissioners of Bankruptcy for the District of Pennsylvania—Circumstances probably were not favorable at that time to his appointment—as there is now a vacancy by the death of John W. Vancleve, I again solicit your attention to the pretensions of Mr. Porter for that office, which I look upon equal, if not superior in many respects, to some of those who were lately appointed, if I did not I assure you I would not give you this trouble—

Mr. Porter is a Lawyer in considerable repute, he was prevailed on by the Republicans of Philadelphia to suffer himself to be elected a Representative of the State Legislature, which as they sit at Lancaster must have been against his private interest—He & all his connexions, who are numerous & respectable, are warmly attached to the Republican interest—If you will be pleased to take the trouble of inquiring I flatter myself you will find I have not overrated his character or pretensions—

With high respect I am Sir Your Most obedient Servant

WM. IRVINE

RC (DNA: RG 59, LAR); at foot of text: "Thomas Jefferson Esqr President of the United States"; endorsed by TJ as received 20 July and "Porter to be Commr. bkrptcy" and so recorded in SJL.

Irvine, superintendent of military stores at Philadelphia, wrote this letter on the day of John W. Vancleve's death (*Philadelphia Repository, and Weekly Register*, 24 July 1802; Vol. 33:180n). I TOOK THE LIBERTY: Robert Porter appears on TJ's list of candidates for bankruptcy commissioners for Pennsylvania with "Genl. Irwin" identified as the person who recommended him (see Vol. 37: Appendix II, List 1).

THOSE WHO WERE LATELY APPOINT-ED: Joseph Clay, Alexander J. Dallas, Mahlon Dickerson, John Sergeant, Thomas Cumpston, and Vancleve (Memorandums to Albert Gallatin, 10 June 1802).

On 21 July, Mahlon Dickerson wrote Meriwether Lewis regarding the vacancy caused by Vancleve's death. He did not know if TJ would fill the vacancy, because originally the president had intended to appoint only four commissioners for Pennsylvania, the number under the "old establishment." Understanding that several Philadelphians had already sent recommendations, however, Dickerson requested that Lewis recommend Peter S. Du Ponceau to the president "as a very suitable character" to fill the office. Dickerson noted: "he is justly admired for his talents & great learning, & I believe no one at our bar has been more uniformly a republican than he." He also mentioned that he had just read "A view of the political conduct of Aaron Burr," and if the fever outbreak continued in Philadelphia, Dickerson planned to visit New York, where he could investigate some "facts" revealed in the pamphlet that appeared "very mysterious." He was informed that Burr "means to treat all these attacks upon his character with silent contempt; that he will not deign to vindicate his conduct" (RC in DNA: RG 59, LAR; addressed: "Capt Merewether Lewis City of Washington"; forwarded by the postmaster at Washington on 27 July to "Monticello, near Milton Va."; endorsed by TJ: "Dickerson Mahlone to Capt Lewis Duponceau to be Commr. bkrptcy"). TJ obtained a copy of the pamphlet attributed to James Cheetham entitled *A View of the Political Conduct of Aaron Burr, Esq. Vice-President of the United States*, published in New York in 1802 (see Sowerby, No. 3443). For Cheetham's account of Burr's intrigues with New York Federalists during the election of 1800, see Vol. 36:83-8.

From George Logan

DEAR SIR   Stenton July 18th 1802

one of the offices of Commissioner of Bankruptcy having become vacant by the death of Mr: Van cleve, I beg your attention to Robert Porter as a proper character to fill that office—Mr: Porter is the Person in whose favor General Irwin spoke to you some time since for the same appointment; he is at present in the Assembly of Pennsylvania & is well esteemed by his fellow Citizens—

With sentiments of Respect I am your Friend   GEO: LOGAN

RC (DNA: RG 59, LAR); at foot of text: "Thos: Jefferson President of the U States"; endorsed by TJ as received 25 July and "Porter Robt. to be Commr. bkrptcy" and so recorded in SJL, where it is connected by a brace with two other letters received on that date recommending Porter.

GENERAL IRWIN SPOKE TO YOU: see William Irvine to TJ, immediately above.

From Benjamin Nones

SIR,   Philadelphia 18 July 1802

I have already had the Honor to address you in two former Instances.

The Death of Mr. Van Cleve of this City, who is said to have died of the Epidemic, at present unfortunately prevailing here, it is presumed will occasion a vacancy in the Board of Commissioners of Bankruptcy.

I hope your Excellency will excuse the liberty I take of again addressing you, and thus offering my Application for an Appointment to fill the same.

Permit me to refer you to my former Letters and the Recommendations therein contain'd, which I hope will be deemed fully satisfactory, as likewise for the motives which have more particularly induced me to make my Applications to your Excellency.

With Sentiments of the Highest Respect and Esteem, I have the Honor to be Your Excellency's Mo: ob: hb: Servt.

BENJ NONES

RC (DNA: RG 59, LAR); endorsed by TJ as received 20 July and "to be Commr. bkrptcy" and so recorded in SJL.

TWO FORMER INSTANCES: Nones to TJ, 18 Mch. and 11 Nov. 1801.

EPIDEMIC: Philadelphia was experiencing an outbreak of yellow fever, which was largely confined to the vicinity of the Vine Street wharf. On 22 July, the city board of health declared that the fever had "entirely subsided" (*Gazette of the United States*, 17, 20, and 22 July 1802; William Currie and Isaac Cathrall, *Facts and Observations, Relative to the Origin, Progress and Nature of the Fever, which Prevailed in Certain Parts of the City and Districts of Philadelphia, In the Summer and Autumn of the Present Year, (1802)* [Philadelphia, 1802]).

From Charles Willson Peale

DEAR SIR   Museum July 18th. 1802.

When I wrote last, the 10th. Ult., the head of a Common Ox then before me was so imperfect as to lead me into an error about the width of the horns—since I have procured a head from a Butcher, who did not brake the Scull, which cleaned and free'd from the horns, I find the measurement from pith to pith of the Horns is   Inches. I also observe that the difference of form between this head and that from Kentucky is very considerable—and although in the same species of Animal we find a variety of size & some diviations in the forms, yet seldom so great a difference as to make it necessary to constitute a new Character by which they may be known. Whether the Buffalo species differ materially from the Common in the form of that part of the head which joins the atlass, or first neck bone, I do not know. The angle of the top of the head to the part joining the neck is acute in common Cattle, and that of this Kentucky head obtuse & very different, as is best expressed by the enclosed drawings.

The sketches I sent before, was merely to give you some Idea of this head, and done in a hurry, a better choise of the view might have been made, or an additional drawing to shew a greater proportion of the upper part of the head.

My Eldest Son (Raphaelle) intends shortly to go into the western country in search for Bones—He will explore the neighbourhood where this piece of head was found, with a hope of getting the other Bones—As his object is get all the fosil Bones he can, he will have a chance of obtaining the Skeleton which has Grinders with a flat surface, and more corrispondant to Elephants than the Skeletons I have put togather. If he succeeds in either it will be a fortunate undertaking—at any rate, he may make such a collection of Bones, that among them some may be valuable to me, and he will also get Fish of the western Waters, which will be extending an important branch of this Institution.

His first Intention was to visit the Northern Fisheries, to get the Bones of a Whale, this I knew would be a dirty, fateaguing, & expensive undertaking—By my advice he changed it for Kentucky, which I conceive will give him many advantages—among others the opportunity of painting some portraits in miniature which will help to defray his expences. If any Garrisson is near to the places he wishes to explore, the expence of labour may be lessened, if the Soldiers are permited to work for him, and, the publick service may not be injured thereby.

When my Son Titian proposed to travel on a like errand, General Wilkinson promised to aid him, and a few days before Titian was taken with his last illness, he urged me to let him go up the north River to albany, and from thence westward—

I expect the fever will spread, and the Inhabitants of Philada. suffer much distress. It is generally believed that it was brought from St. Domingue, however the season will foster it. This is generally the time of its visitations, when great numbers of Insects are passing into the worm state, with innumerable generation of minute flies &c and the air so contaminated, that meat cannot easily be preserved sweet.

If the fear of this disorder would lead the People to reflect and to adopt a more rational mode of living, than is generally followed by our Countrymen, then instead of a scourge, this visitation would be a blessing.

I was flattered with hopes of seeing you, rapted in wonder, contemplating my great Skeleton—but hearing that you shortly intended southward, I have hastened to send you these rough sketches, and did also intend, for some time past, to have written a description, with drawings, of Mr. Hawkins enginous inventions of movements of his claviol, he is doing it better than I could. The powers of this instrument are wonderful—and I hope he will meet with the reward his ingenuity deserves when he can cross the Ocean.

I am with due respect, your friend C W PEALE

RC (DLC); at foot of text: "Mr. Jefferson"; endorsed by TJ as received 20 July and so recorded in SJL. Dft (Lb in PPAmP: Peale-Sellers Papers).

SKETCHES I SENT BEFORE: see Peale's letter to TJ of 10 June.

Peale's son RAPHAELLE did not make the anticipated journey to the west (Peale, *Papers*, v. 2, pt. 1:448n).

NEIGHBOURHOOD WHERE THIS PIECE OF HEAD WAS FOUND: the bison skull that had reached Philadelphia a few weeks earlier had been found in Kentucky, a few miles from the Ohio River. Big Bone Lick was the best known, but not the only, source of fossils in that region. Scientists had been interested in the area for several decades, but no one had yet mounted a large-scale, systematic search for bones. In 1798, when TJ and other members of a committee of the American Philosophical Society called for the acquisition of more skeletal remains of mammoths and "other unknown animals," they directed particular attention to "the Great Bone Lick on the Ohio" (printed circular, 7 May 1798, in DLC: Thornton Papers; Robert Silverberg, *Mammoths, Mastodons and Man* [New York, 1970], 57-60; Paul Semonin, *American Monster: How the Nation's First Prehistoric Creature Became a Sym-*

bol of National Identity [New York, 2000], 7-9, 84-7, 91-4; Vol. 30:159n; John Brown of Boone County, Kentucky, to TJ, 28 Apr. 1802).

From his excavations in the Hudson Valley, Peale was familiar with mastodons, which had molar teeth with knobby chewing surfaces. Such molars were very different from the GRINDERS of mammoths, which had flat surfaces that resembled the teeth of ELEPHANTS. Bones and teeth of both mammoths and mastodons had been found in North America, but the distinctions between the animals were not well understood until Georges Cuvier classified and named them in 1806 (Silverberg, *Mammoths, Mastodons and Man*, 61-9, 79-81; George Turner, "Memoir on the Extraneous Fossils, denominated Mammoth Bones," APS, *Transactions*, 4 [1799], 512-13).

HIS LAST ILLNESS: Titian Ramsay Peale, the first of two sons of Charles Willson Peale to have that name, died of yellow fever in 1798, not long after his eighteenth birthday (Charles Coleman Sellers, *Charles Willson Peale*, 2 vols. [Philadelphia, 1947], 1:214; 2:105-6).

CONTEMPLATING MY GREAT SKELETON: the mastodon skeleton on display in Peale's museum in Philadelphia (Vol. 36:265-6n).

I

Diagram: Skull of an Ox

View of the back part of the Scull of the common Ox.

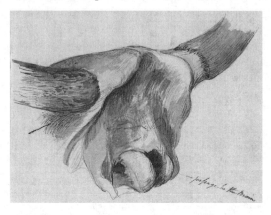

MS (DLC: TJ Papers, 124:21492); in Peale's hand, with a line and notation indicating "passage to the Brain."

II

Diagram: Fossil Skull from Kentucky

View of Bone from Kentucky, presented the
American Philosophical Society.

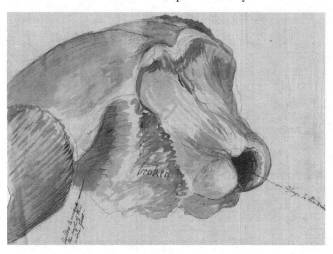

MS (DLC: TJ Papers, 124:21493); in Peale's hand, with a line and notation on the lower left side of the diagram indicating "Hollow to recieve the Angle of the under Jaw," a line and notation on the lower right indicating "Passage to the Brain," and a label across a portion of the diagram, "broken."

III

Diagram: Angles of Skulls and Necks

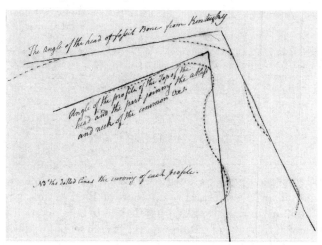

MS (DLC: TJ Papers, 124:21494); in Peale's hand; his label on the larger angle in the diagram is "The Angle of the head of fossil Bone from Kentucky"; his label on the smaller angle is "Angle of the profile of the Top of the head and the part joining the *atlass* and neck of the common Ox"; his label near the bottom of the diagram is "NB The dotted lines the curving of each profile."

From Mathew Carey and Others

SIR.   Philadelphia July 19th. 1802.

Having received information of the death of John W. Vancleve, Commissioner of Bankruptcy for the district of Pennsylvania, We beg leave to recommend Robert Porter of this place, to your attention as a suitable person to fill the vacancy. Mr. Porter was a First-Lieutenant in the army of the United States, in the revolutionary War—After the establishment of our Independence, he applied himself to the study of the law and hath practised with reputation for several years as an Attorney and Counsellor. In the last Session of the General Assembly of this State, he was a Representative for the City of Philadelphia.—We can assure you that he is a Gentleman of talents, integrity, and uniform attachment to republican principles.

We are Sir with the highest respect & consideration your most obedt. hble Servants

MATHEW CAREY
JNO PORTER
JNO GOODMAN JR
J SIMONDS
ROBT. PATTON
R. PATTERSON
SAM CLARKE

RC (DNA: RG 59, LAR); at foot of text: "To Thomas Jefferson Esq. President of the United States"; endorsed by TJ as received 25 July and "Porter Robt. to be Commr. bkrptcy" and so recorded in SJL, where it is connected by a brace with two other letters received on that date recommending Porter.

From Tench Coxe

SIR   Philada. July 19. 1802

I am requested on the part of Robert Porter, Esqre, to mention his name to you for the vacant Commission of Bankruptcy. I have the honor therefore to represent that gentleman to be a practicing Attorney at Law of this city, of good property & character, and [with?] the habits of Business. He was a Lieutenant of Artillery at the close of the Revolutionary war, & a native of Pennsylvania, & the Son of Genl. Porter, who was lately at Washington as a Cincinnati Delegate. Mr. Porter, Junr. is an officer of that Society. He maintained his principles in the trial of 1798, and was run in that year with myself and others by the republican interest to represent this city in the state legislature of which he is at this time a member—As far as my opinion or knowledge of Mr. Porter goes, I wish to be understood, Sir, to consider him as a safe appointment, but I do not mean to depreciate other Applicants, being entirely unacquainted with their Names. I beg you will excuse this freedom which is taken, and of my usual Course for the reasons assigned.

I have the honor to be Sir, yr. respectful humble Servant

TENCH COXE

RC (DNA: RG 59, LAR); faint; at foot of text: "The President"; endorsed by TJ as received 25 July and "Rob. Porter to be Commr. bkrptcy" and so recorded in SJL, where it is connected by a brace with two other letters received on that date recommending Porter.

SON OF GENL. PORTER: Andrew Porter became major-general of the militia in

Montgomery and Bucks counties in 1801, after the resignation of Peter Muhlenberg. On 4 July 1801, the CINCINNATI Society of the State of Pennsylvania elected Andrew Porter, William Irvine, and Muhlenberg delegates to the general meeting of the society for the ensuing year. OFFICER OF THAT SOCIETY: Robert Porter served as secretary and Irvine as president (Washington, *Papers, Pres. Ser.*, 3:534; James Robinson, *The Philadelphia Directory, City and County Register, for 1802* [Philadelphia, 1801], xxiv; *Philadelphia Gazette*, 6 July 1801; *Gazette of the United States*, 31 July 1801, 1 July 1802).

From George Davis

SIR   Philadelphia July 19. 1802.

From the late death of my friend J. W. Vancleve Esq. I take the liberty of introducing myself to your attention for the purpose of filling the Office of a Commissioner of Bankrupts now become vacant in this district—I have the honor of being well known and on terms of acquaintance say friendship[1] with the five surviving Gentlemen, added to which my early attention when I was first placed out to pursue the Law, was directed particularly to that department of the Sollicitors practice in England, where I served a regular Clerkship, and for many years afterwards acted in the profession as an Attorney at Law with reputation—I am and have been long a Citizen of the United States, have been resident in Philadelphia upwards of Eighteen Years—ten of which were industriously and honorably spent in the Superintendance of the Office of the prothonotary of the Supreme Court of this State—Since which I have followed mercantile Affairs, confining my self chiefly to the importation and sale of Law Books. I beg Sir you will be pleased to pardon the freedom I have assumed by these Communications, and that your goodness will permit me to look towards the grant I sollicit.

I have the honor to be most respectfully Sir Your Obedt. hble Servt

GEO DAVIS

I have made free to inclose you a late Law Catalogue, and shall be extremely thankful for your Commands.

G D.

RC (DNA: RG 59, LAR); at foot of text: "His Excellency Thos. Jefferson Esqr."; endorsed by TJ as received 20 July and "to be Commr. bkrptcy" and so recorded in SJL. Enclosure: *Bibliotheca Legum Angliae. Davis's Law Catalogue for 1802...1803, of Latest English and Irish Editions* (Philadelphia, 1802; Shaw-Shoemaker, No. 2118).

Davis may have been an assistant clerk to Edward Burd, who served a long tenure as PROTHONOTARY of the Supreme Court of Pennsylvania during the time of Davis's residence in Philadelphia. Davis operated a law bookstore on High Street in Philadelphia and served for many years as secretary of the city's Society of the Sons of St. George (John Hill Martin, *Martin's Bench and Bar of Philadelphia* [Philadelphia, 1883], 26; *Gazette of the United States,* 15 Dec. 1795; James Robinson, *The Philadelphia Directory, City and County Register, for 1802* [Philadelphia, 1801], xxvii).

[1] Preceding two words interlined.

From H. O. Hebert

DEAR SIR/   Philadelphia 19 July 1802

In the Month of April last, I did myself the Honor of waiting on you, with an Engraving of an "Air pump Vapour Bath" as used in England—Your Politeness on that occasion I shall never forget.

I now take the Liberty of introducing myself, a second Time to your notice, for the Purpose of informing you, that I have this Day received from Mr Whitney, a Machine complete in all its Parts, & fit for immediate Operation—

Dr. Bulles who will do me the Faver to present this Letter, will at the same time convey to you Two Plates of the Machine—which I hope you will do me the Honor to accept—May I presume to hope also that you will extend to my Invention in its Introduction, that Patronage, which you have ever done to all useful Inventions & Improvements, & for which your character stands so iminently & deservedly conspicuous—

The Principle of the "Air Pump Vapour Bath," is to convey Steam or Vapour to diseased Limbs & take off the Pressure of the Atmosphere—It is also calculated to be of the greatest Service by changing the Action of the diseased Parts. And I have no Doubt but, that it will rank among the first of modern Improvements in Medecine—& under the Superintendance of professional Men, prove a powerful Means not only of alleviating, but frequently curing, many Diseases which have hitherto been considered as incurable—I am with the greatest Esteem & Respect

Dear Sir Your mo Obed & very Hble Serv.

H:O: HEBERT
York Street in South Third

RC (MHi); addressed: "To his Excellency The President of the United States ⅌ favor of Dr Bulles"; endorsed by TJ as received 31 July and so recorded in SJL.

Englishman Hildebrand Oakes Hebert arrived in the United States on 1 Apr. 1802 to market the "Air Pump Vapour Bath" for treating body parts afflicted with gout, inflamation, and other maladies. The device was invented by Nathan Smith of Brighthelmstone, England, who appointed Hebert his agent to obtain a patent and promote the device in America. Bearing a letter of introduction from Dr. Edward Stevens, Hebert met with TJ in Washington in late April. Settling in Philadelphia, he published a pamphlet on the invention later in 1802, then unsuccessfully petitioned Congress for a patent in January 1803. Later that same year, he relocated to Baltimore, where he continued to advertise the health benefits of the vapor bath. City directories first listed him as a physician, but later as an accountant. His residence in Baltimore continued until at least 1820, when he de-

clared bankruptcy (Hebert to the Senate and the House of Representatives, 24 Dec. 1802, in DNA: RG 233, PMRSL; *Hebert's Air Pump Vapour Bath* [Philadelphia, 1802], Shaw-Shoemaker, No. 2391; JHR, 4:285-6; *Philadelphia Gazette*, 8 Sep., 30 Nov. 1802; Baltimore *Federal Gazette*, 27 May 1803; *Baltimore Patriot*, 18 Mch. 1818, 20 May 1820; James Robinson, *Baltimore Directory for 1804* [Baltimore, 1804], 49; William Fry, *Baltimore Directory for 1810* [Baltimore, 1810], 91; *Baltimore Directory for 1817-18* [Baltimore, 1817], 86; Vol. 37:234-5).

From David Jackson, Jr.

HONORED SIR   Philada. July 19th. 1802

By the decease of the late worthy Mr Vancleve, a vacancy takes place in the board of Commissioners of Bankruptcy, an appointment to which vacancy if not already made would confer a perpetual obligation upon me—

I have communicated this my application to no person, highly disapproving the practice of many in procuring names recommendatory of their appointment—

I am personally known to a large proportion of our leading republican friends, also well known to the present commissioners of Bankruptcy, particularly Mr. Sergeant, who was a fellow collegian of mine. I am settled with a wife & family around me, in the pursuit of a mercantile occupation for a livelihood, and were I to suggest my intentions to my friends Governor McKean, or Mr Charles Thomson, who is an uncle of mine by marriage, I have no doubt, but that I could have procured every recommendation I could wish; but respected Sir, I wish my Integrity & Character to be my sole recommendation

ever your friend   DAVID JACKSON
                                    Son of the late Dr David Jackson.

RC (DNA: RG 59, LAR); endorsed by TJ as received 25 July and "to be Commr. bkrptcy Phila" and so recorded in SJL.

David Jackson, Jr. (d. 1808) was the eldest son of Dr. David Jackson, with whom TJ had regularly conducted financial transactions and sometimes purchased medicines. His mother was proba-

bly Jane Mather Jackson, of Chester, Pennsylvania, whom his father married in 1770, the widow of his brother Dr. Paul Jackson. After her death, David Jackson married Susanna Kemper, with whom he had nine children. David Jackson, Jr., graduated from the University of Pennsylvania in 1794 and received a graduate degree nine years later. In 1800, he married Rebecca Clarkson and entered the family apothecary business as a wholesale and retail druggist with his own store. After the death of his father in 1801, his stepmother formed a partnership with Dr. Samuel Betton to carry on the business. The Betton & Jackson partnership dissolved in 1803, when David Jackson announced to his friends and customers and to those "of his late father" that business would be conducted at Arch and Fourth streets, the site of his father's establishment, "in conjunction with his father's widow," under the firm of David and S. Jackson. Governor McKean appointed Jackson to Philadelphia's Board of Health in 1804. In 1807, he was elected a director of the Philadelphia Bank (John Hill Martin, *Chester (and Its Vicinity,) Delaware County, in Pennsylvania; with Genealogical Sketches of Some Old Families* [Philadelphia, 1877], 129-30; W. J. Maxwell, comp., *General Alumni Catalogue of the University of Pennsylvania: 1917* [Philadelphia, 1917], 24; DAB, 9:538-9; *Pa. Arch.*, 2d ser., 9:575; *Philadelphia Gazette*, 16 Apr. 1800; *Poulson's American Daily Advertiser*, 25 Sep., 30 Oct. 1801; 15 July 1803; 11 July, 18 Nov. 1808; Philadelphia *Aurora*, 20 Apr. 1804; *United States' Gazette*, 26 Apr. 1806; 10 Feb. 1807; MB, 2:935, 986, 1016; Vol. 32:405n, 415-16; Vol. 34:375n, 581, 582n; Vol. 36:216n, 482, 693).

FELLOW COLLEGIAN OF MINE: John Sergeant studied at the University of Pennsylvania before attending the College of New Jersey at Princeton, from which he graduated in 1795 (*Biog. Dir. Cong.*). UNCLE OF MINE BY MARRIAGE: Charles Thomson's first wife Ruth Mather was the sister of Jane Mather Jackson (DAB; Martin, *Chester*, 129-30).

Memorandum to James Madison

Henry Warren, (of Mass), to be Collector of Marblehead v. Samuel R. Gerry.

William Lyman of Massachusetts to be Collector of Newbury port. vice Dudley A. Tyng.

William R. Lee of Massachuts. to be collector of Salem & Beverly vice Joseph Hiller

Peter Muhlenberg of Pensylvania to be Collector of   vice George Latimer.

John Page of Virginia to be Collector of Petersburg v. William Heth.

Tenche Coxe of Pensylvania to be Supervisor of Pensylvania v. Peter Muhlenberg

Perhaps it may be better to inclose blank commissions to mr Gallatin in all the above cases, to be filled up & sent out by him all together, on his return.

TH: JEFFERSON
July 19. 1802.

PrC (DLC). Not recorded in SJL.

To William Short

DEAR SIR Washington July 19. 1802.

Your's of April 3. came to hand June 13. my last to you was of Apr. 19. when I wrote so fully in answer to your several favors, that I should not have had occasion to write now but by way of supplement as to the particular article of the purchase of stock for you, not then finished. as soon as the peace had produced the whole of it's effect on our stock by depressing it, and it was percieved to be looking up again, mr Barnes instantly directed his correspondent in N. York to purchase 4000. D. of the 3. percents if possible, & if not, then of the 6s. partly by search after that particular stock (the 3s.) which is rarely at market, partly by fallacious expectations of better chances, he did not purchase till about May or June, by which time they had sensibly risen. still however, after adding the interest then immediately due, it makes according to their calculations a gain of about 1. per cent more than the loss of interest which the whole of the delay had occasioned. the original certificates of the rest of your stock being all in my hands, I shall take care to recieve those also of the 4000. lately bought of 6. per cents, no threes being to be had. The latter, when to be found, are understood to be at $66\frac{1}{2}$ per cent. I explained in my last the nature of this stock, and should be glad to learn from yourself to what point of their possible rise, you would prefer them to other stock at their ordinary prices. I will take care by attending hereafter to the quarterly reciepts of your interest, that mr Barnes shall lay them out immediately, or be led by no expectations whatever to go beyond the reciept of the next quarter before they are laid out. circumstances of momentary high price may sometimes justify a short delay.—I took the liberty of asking your superintendance of the purchase of some books for Congress which is committed to mr Duane. I inclosed you the catalogue, & the Secy. of the Treasury was to insert a bill of exchange & forward the letter. I set out in two days to pass Aug. & September at Monticello. Accept assurances of my constant affection. TH: JEFFERSON

RC (DLC: Short Papers); at foot of text: "W. Short"; endorsed by Short with notation "sent to care of Delepres & Co Paris & returned by them to America."

I TOOK THE LIBERTY: TJ to Short, 16 July.

From Samuel Stephens

Dublin 19 of 7 mo 1802

I have had thoughts for some time of sending thee the inclosed phamplet, as a token of my regard, but I am discouraged from the fallicy of Man I have through Life endeavourd to suddy not only myself, but likewise man both in private and public Life, some who I conceived a high opinion of I have found when they have got to a certain pinicle or height, they suddenly stopd there, they like whats called glory, but when they find they have to return to the common mass, and relinquish all their power they often have recourse to indirect mains, to retain it. I think amongst the rest we have a resent instance of it on this side the Atlantic, and that is a Man who I had formed the greatest opinion of as a public Character. I suspect thou'll understand me and what I main, and my wish for thee is that thou may be preserved from all false glory, that thou may steadily persue a reform and renovation, that thy days may be long, and spent in the glorious cause of humanity, that thou may instruct the Ignorant, and teach mankind what true liberty and happiness is, and if thou persues that path, thy name shall be handed down to posterity, more glorious than the Conqueror of Europe, but I trust and hope its not the praise or popularity of Man thou art seeking, that it is the evidence of good Conscience, which will not only carry thee through this Life but shall Land thee safe in the next, may that be thy happy exsperiance saith thy Friend

SAML STEPHENS
Skinner Row

I also send thee a few phamplets wrote by an intimate friend of mine. its the last one I was most desireous thou should see, and as that spakes of the former ones I thought that perhaps thou might have no objection to see and read them at a leasure Hour

I Love true republicans, few understand what it is, they blend aristrocraxcy through it

RC (MoSHi: Jefferson Papers); addressed: "Thos. Jefferson Pr: of the U: States of America"; endorsed by TJ as received 5 Feb. 1803 and so recorded in SJL. Enclosures not found.

Samuel Stephens was a hatter who had broken with Dublin's Quaker community over his Unitarian beliefs, which he promoted in his pamphlet, *An Address to the People Called Quakers: and Others, on the Fallen and Degenerate State of Man* (Dublin, 1802). He later represented his guild on Dublin's Common Council (*Wilson's Dublin Directory for the Year 1798* [Dublin, 1798], 101; *Monthly Repository of Theology and General Literature*, 9 [1814], 127-9; *Anti-Jacobin Review and True Churchman's Magazine and Protestant Advocate*, 55 [1819], 591).

To John Barnes

DEAR SIR   July 20. 1802.

The bearer comes for the *11. D.* small change. I find I have occasion for 30. D. more than I had calculated which therefore I must ask of you by the bearer. bills of any kind will do.

Your's affectionately   TH: JEFFERSON

RC (ViU: Edgehill-Randolph Papers); endorsed by Barnes: "℔ Dougherty."

To Jacob Bouldin

SIR   Washington July 20. 1802.

Your favor of the 15th. came to hand last night, & tomorrow I leave this to pass at Monticello the two bilious months of August & September. I shall not be here again till the 1st. of October. besides the delay this would occasion to your submitting your draughts to my inspection, I ought candidly to mention, that my duties occupying my whole time & calling for more if I had it, I am obliged to deny myself the pleasure of mathematical & other speculations which are not immediately connected with my duty. it is not probable therefore that I should have time to consider the drawings you speak of with attention enough to form a judgment of them. as you do not mention their nature, I am not able to say whether they are in a line on which I should be able to give an opinion. Accept my respects & best wishes   TH: JEFFERSON

PrC (MHi); at foot of text: "Mr. Jacob Bouldin. Baltimore"; endorsed by TJ in ink on verso.

Statement of Account with Thomas Carpenter

Washington—

Thomas Jefferson Esq.

1802

June 14th. To Thomas Carpenter—		Dr.—
To Making a Coat &c of Superfine Cloth with Silk Sleeve Lynings, Velvet Collar & Steele Butts.	}	$ 23.—
To Making a Waistcoat & materials		3.—

2 yds Silk Nankeen @ 11/3 & 18 pearl Buttons 25/	4 —
Making Breeches & materials	2.75
2½ yds Silk Nankeen @ 9/6	3.17
14 small 3 Coat Pearl Buttons	1 —
To a pr of Breeches as above	6.92
To 4 suits of livery (as pr Bill of May —difference in materials 1 Doll per suit)—@ 26$ }	104.—
July 3 To a Nankeen Jacket for John	4.25
20 Making a Coat & materials	4.50
5½ yds Blue Bombazette—@ 7/6	5.50
To a pr of Nankeen Breeches compleat	3.50
	$ 165,59

Servts. 104
4.25
108.25
myself 57.34
165.59

MS (ViU: Edgehill-Randolph Papers); in Carpenter's hand, words and figures in italics added by TJ; addressed: "Mr Jefferson"; endorsed by TJ.

The BILL OF MAY concerning suits of livery has not been found.

JOHN: John Freeman. On 15 July 1802, Dr. William Baker of Prince Georges County, Maryland, appointed his friend Samuel Carr to act as his lawful attorney in his absence and to "sell make over and transfer" his servant John, "(now hired to the President)" for a term not exceeding eleven years or to hire him for two or three years. On 17 July, Carr noted on the verso that on that day he had hired out John to TJ for two years "at the rate of eight dollars per month" (MS in MHi; in Baker's hand and signed by him;

endorsed by TJ "Baker Dr. William"). TJ first hired Freeman from Baker in 1801 (MB, 2:1043, 1053; Vol. 34:208n, 489).

BLUE BOMBAZETTE: bombazet was a smooth cloth, without a shiny finish, made from worsted woolen yarn in a plain or twill weave (Florence M. Montgomery, *Textiles in America, 1650-1870* [New York, 1984], 172; Phyllis G. Tortora, ed., Robert S. Merkel, consulting ed., *Fairchild's Dictionary of Textiles*, 7th ed. [New York, 1996], 64).

On 2 Nov. 1802, TJ ordered John Barnes to pay Carpenter $165 on his account (MS in ViU, in TJ's hand and signed by him, signed by Carpenter acknowledging payment on 3 Nov., endorsed by Barnes; MB, 2:1085).

To James Dinsmore

DEAR SIR   Washington July 20. 1802.

Your's of the 12th. did not get to hand till last night. the ornaments for the frize of the chamber left this on the 10th. and are probably at Richmond by this time. but I shall be at home on Sunday, as early as they will arrive. from what you mention of the rotting of the sleepers of the Bow part of the Parlour, & the ends of the other, I presume that wall was close & that they have dry rotted for want of air. I wish therefore you may have thought to leave holes in the wall, or, which will do better, that you would now have a door made in it, large enough to let a person enter. I will have a wire door made for it which will let in air & keep out rats. Accept my best wishes.

Th: Jefferson

RC (ICHi); at foot of text: "Mr. James Dinsmore."

Dinsmore's letter OF THE 12TH, recorded in SJL as received 19 July, has not been found.

TJ based the ORNAMENTS of the bedchamber frieze at Monticello on a design from the Temple of Fortuna Virilis in Rome (Stein, *Worlds*, 107, 110).

To Albert Gallatin

DEAR SIR   Washington July 20. 1802.

I recieved last night your's of the 17th. and tomorrow I set out for Monticello, so must be brief. Commissions were yesterday directed to be made out with blank dates as follows.

Lee	Collector	Salem
Lyman	do.	Newbury port
Warren	do.	Marblehead.
Muhlenberg	do.	Philadelphia.
Page	do.	Petersburg.
Coxe	Supervisor	Pensva

on desiring mr Madison this morning to have them dated Aug. 1. and kept here till your arrival Aug. 2. he expressed his apprehension they were already gone off under cover to you.—I inclose you the authority you asked for Coxe to act as Collector of Internal duties also. I likewise inclose the resignations of William Goforth as a Commissioner in Symes's case, and Foster's resignation of the place of Register of the land office Marietta. Capt Lewis recommends for the former place a Doctor John Selman of Cincinati whom he represents as a very sensible man, of a correct character, & a good republican. he is not a lawyer. I mention him to you only in case you can get none of better pretensions. for the other place you must be so good as to look out.—those three towns in Massachusets very possibly might have wished for a townsman. but that degree of restriction is impracticable and inadmissible. there are difficulties enough already in the way of getting good men.—blanks are left, so that you can use them for Oswego, & Slade's creek. I hope your health will be improved by the journey; and that on your return here you will retire into the hills, & by no means pass the months of August & September here. Accept assurances of my highest esteem & confidence.

TH: JEFFERSON

RC (NHi: Gallatin Papers); at foot of text: "Mr. Gallatin"; endorsed by Gallatin. PrC (DLC). Enclosures: Authorization for Tench Coxe, printed below. Other enclosures not found.

William GOFORTH had served as a commissioner for settling claims on the Miami Purchase lands of John Cleves Symmes since the fall of 1801. FOSTER'S RESIGNATION: appointed to office in May 1800, Peregrine Foster, brother of Senators Theodore and Dwight Foster, was the first register of lands at the newly es-

tablished land office at Marietta. John Sellman (SELMAN) joined James Findlay, receiver of public monies at Cincinnati, and John Reily on the Symmes commission. Sellman had served as a surgeon's mate in the army on the frontier with Meriwether Lewis (*Terr. Papers*, 3:97; JEP, 1:433, 437; ASP, *Public Lands*, 1:112-13; Bruce H. Mann, *Republic of Debtors: Bankruptcy in the Age of American Independence* [Cambridge, Mass., 2002], 129-30; Sellman to Gabriel Duvall, 4 Oct. 1807, in DNA: RG 59, LAR; Vol. 35:392n; Vol. 36:301-2n, 405n, 486n).

ENCLOSURE

Authorization for Tench Coxe

Should the Secretary of the Treasury find it adviseable The Supervisor of the district of Pensylvania is hereby authorised to act as Collector of the internal revenues for the city and county of Pensylvania. Given under my hand at Washington this 20th. day of July 1802.   TH: JEFFERSON

MS (DLC); in TJ's hand; with Gallatin's instructions to the commissioner of the revenue written below TJ's signature and forwarded (see below). PrC (DLC).

COUNTY OF PENSYLVANIA: that is, Philadelphia.
On 25 July, Gallatin wrote William Miller requesting that he inform Tench

Coxe that the president had authorized him "to continue to exercise the office of collector of the internal revenues" after he commenced his new office on 1 Aug. (RC in DLC; written on same sheet as TJ's authorization above; addressed by Gallatin: "The Commissioner of the revenue"; endorsed).

To James Monroe

DEAR SIR   Washington July 20. 1802.

I recieved lately a letter from Genl. Lawson solliciting a charity which he desired me to send through your hands. I had yielded last year to an application of the same nature from him and although I think his habits & conduct render him less entitled to it than many others on whom it might be bestowed, yet (pour la derniere fois) I inclose for him 30. Dollars which I must ask you to apply to his use as you may think most serviceable for him. I set out tomorrow morning & shall be at Monticello on Sunday. Accept assurances of my affectionate esteem.

TH: JEFFERSON

PrC (DLC); at foot of text: "Govr. Monroe"; endorsed by TJ in ink on verso.

LETTER FROM GENL. LAWSON: Robert Lawson to TJ, 10 July. TJ responded through Monroe to Lawson's previous APPLICATION for aid (Vol. 34:398-9).

POUR LA DERNIERE FOIS: for the last time.

On 20 July, TJ recorded in his financial account book that a payment of 30. DOLLARS in charity for Lawson had been enclosed to Monroe (MB, 2:1078).

To Ellen Wayles Randolph

Washington
MY VERY DEAR ELLEN   Tuesday. July 20. 1802.
    I will catch you in bed on Sunday or Monday morning.
    Your's affectionately   TH: JEFFERSON

PrC (MHi); at foot of text: "Miss Eleonor Randolph"; endorsed by TJ in ink on verso.

From Jonathan Smith

SIR,   Bank Pennsylvania July 20th 1802
    I have the honor to enclose you a post note of this Bank in your favor No. 1133 dated this day at ten days for Three hundred and sixty dollars, being the amount of the dividend for six Months ending the 30th of June last, on Twenty shares of the stock of the Bank of Pennsylvania standing in the name of Genl. Thaddeus Kosciusko.—
    With great respect, I am Sir, Your most Obt Servt.

JONA SMITH

RC (MHi); at foot of text: "Thomas Jefferson Esqr. President of the United States"; endorsed by TJ as received 29 July and so recorded in SJL; also endorsed by TJ: "Kosziusko."

Jonathan Smith (ca. 1767-1839) was cashier of the Bank of Pennsylvania, a position he had held since December 1796. Previously he had worked in the Bank of

the United States. When the Second Bank of the United States opened in 1816, Smith became the new institution's cashier. He left that position by early 1820. He founded the Pennsylvania Fire Insurance Company and became its president, remaining in that office until his death (*Claypoole's American Daily Advertiser*, 24 Dec. 1796; Philadelphia *Weekly Aurora*, 11 Nov. 1816; Philadelphia *North*

American, 21, 22 Nov. 1839; Ralph C. H. Catterall, *The Second Bank of the United States* [Chicago, 1903], 78).

IN THE NAME OF GENL. THADDEUS KOSCIUSKO: in November 1801, under his power of attorney from Tadeusz Kosciuszko, TJ gave Smith the authority to collect the dividends on Kosciuszko's stock in the bank (Vol. 36:126n).

In Washington on 20 July, TJ wrote the following order to Smith: "Sir Be pleased to pay to the order of John Barnes three hundred & sixty dollars, being for the amount of Genl. Thaddeus Kosciuzko's last six months dividend payable the 17th. inst. for value recieved." Barnes wrote on the verso "Be pleased to pay the within" to the order of Edward Penington (RC in MSCL; at foot of text: "To John Smith esq. Cashier of the bank of Pensylvania"; signed by Penington on verso below Barnes's order).

From Josiah Tattnall, Jr.

SIR   Louisville Georgia 20 July 1802

The peculiar and distressing situation of a number of valuable Citizens, who were by the running of the dividing line between the Indians and this State in 1798, left out of the ordinary jurisdictional limits, induces me to solicit that the benevolent attention of the Chief Magistrate of the Union may be directed to their relief

It appears that a Colo. Wafford and about five hundred other white Inhabitants were considered as having settled beyond the line and consequently on ground the property of the Cherokee nation of Indians, altho' at the time of making their establishment it was the general belief they were within the limits—These persons therefore had not the least idea of either violating the Indian right or the law of the United States, but on the contrary were much astonished to find the line of demarkation such as was delineated—Since that period they have conducted themselves very orderly & have preserved harmony with the Indian Tribes, who at this time are unwilling to compel them to retire and leave their Crops buildings &c; altho' I had given orders to several Colonels on our Frontier to aid the officer of the United States in carrying into execution the orders of the Secretary of War to that effect

Thus circumstanced Sir the case of these unfortunate but valuable Citizens about to be deprived of their plantations and the earning of several years of hard labour, claims of me the justice of representing the facts to you and to Solicit in their behalf that a Treaty may be directed to be held with the Cherokees for the extinguishment of their claim to as much of the land as is pointed out in their petition addressed to you Sir as President of the United States and which I have the honor to inclose. The spot of Territory in question is small and is comprehended in the Articles of Agreement and Cession lately executed by the Commissioners on the part of the United States and those of Georgia as intended to be purchased of the Indians, and I am pursuaded from the information I have lately received that they would agree to the sale of it provided it appeared to be the wish of the General Government

The three officers I had directed to assist the Federal Officer in accomplishing the removal above alluded to, were, Colonels Carnes, Easly & Harris of the Counties of Franklin, Clark & Jackson of this State, who from their readiness to Execute my order have gained the confidence & friendship of the Indians—I beg leave therefore to remark that these Gentlemen would be suitable persons to act in conjunction with Genls. Wilkinson & Pickens whom I apprehend would be selected as Commissioners for that purpose

I feel confident Sir you will excuse the Liberty I have taken of addressing you in favor of these our suffering fellow Citizens, well Knowing the desire you possess of extending the fostering Arm of Government to the relief of those who are entitled to it in every part of the Republic.

I have the honor to be Sir with sincere respect & esteem
Yr Obt. hble Servt.

JOSIAH TATTNALL JUNR.
Governor of Georgia

Tr (DNA: RG 75, Records of the Cherokee Indian Agency in Tennessee); at foot of text: "Thos Jefferson Esqr. President of the United States." FC (Lb in G-Ar). Recorded in SJL as received 16 Aug. with notation "W." Enclosure not found.

Located just west of the Cherokee boundary in northern Georgia between the Oconee River and Currahee Mountain, the Wofford (WAFFORD) settlement came to TJ's attention within days of taking office in March 1801, when he was presented with a petition from Colonel William Wofford seeking an adjustment of the Indian boundary line so that his community would be located within the limits of the United States. Cherokee leaders, however, rebuffed efforts to purchase the tract, and instead demanded the removal of Wofford and his neighbors from their lands. Negotiations continued sporadically for years until a treaty was signed at Tellico, Tennessee, on 24 Oct. 1804, in which the Cherokee agreed to cede a nearly 100 square mile tract that included the Wofford settlement in exchange for a payment of $5,000 and an annuity of $1,000. For uncertain reasons, however, the treaty was misplaced and not submitted to the Senate for ratification until 1824. Queried by Secretary of War John C. Calhoun for information on the authenticity and background of the treaty, TJ replied that it was genuine and had his approbation, but could find no evidence that he ever laid it before the Senate. "I take to myself my share in this omission," TJ wrote Calhoun, "and can only say in excuse, 'homo sum'" (Carl Flowers, Jr., "The Wofford Settlement on the Georgia Frontier," *Georgia Historical Quarterly*, 61 [1977], 258-67; William G. McLoughlin, *Cherokee Renascence in the New Republic* [Princeton, 1986], 78-91; ASP, *Indian Affairs*, 1:651, 657, 2:506-11; Vol. 33:220; TJ to Henry Dearborn, 16 Aug. 1802, 15 Feb. 1803; TJ to Calhoun, 25 Apr. 1824).

For the ARTICLES OF AGREEMENT AND CESSION of 24 Apr. 1802 between the

United States and Georgia, which called for the extinguishment of Indian land titles in the state, see Vol. 37:243-5.

COLONELS CARNES, EASLY & HARRIS: possibly jurist and former Congressman Thomas P. Carnes of Franklin County, land speculator and entrepreneur Daniel Easley of Clarke County, and state repre- sentative Buckner Harris of Jackson County (*Biog. Dir. Cong.*; Frances Taliaferro Thomas, *A Portrait of Historic Athens & Clarke County* [Athens, Ga., 1992], 10-14; G. J. N. Wilson, *The Early History of Jackson County, Georgia*, 2d ed. [Atlanta, 1914], 330; McLoughlin, *Cherokee Renascence*, 137-8).

From William Wirt

DEAR SIR. Richmond July 20. 1802

I have just received yours of the 13th. and can only assure you of my constant attention to your interest. I cannot think, with patience, of your having that repose, to which you are so ju[stly] entitled, interrupted, in this way—and yet, rather [incon]sistently, I am sincerely pleased at having an opportunity of being, any way, useful to you: for I am, in very truth, devotedly yours WM. WIRT

RC (DLC); torn, with words in brackets supplied from Tr; at foot of text: "Thomas Jefferson esqr. Monticello"; endorsed by TJ as received 31 July. Tr (MdHi: William Wirt Papers).

No letter OF THE 13TH to Wirt is recorded in SJL. One of 15 May is recorded there, but has not been found. A letter from Wirt to TJ, dated 14 June and recorded in SJL as received 17 June, has also not been found.

From George Jefferson

DEAR SIR Richmond 21st. July 1802

I have to day received another dividend of 3 ℗ Cent on Mr. Short's James River shares, being $:198.—it is placed to the credit of Mr. Barnes, who shall be advised of it by tomorrows post.

Your things from Washington have arrived, and shall be forwarded by the first boats.

I am Dear Sir Your Very humble servt. GEO. JEFFERSON

RC (MHi); at foot of text: "Thomas Jefferson esqr."; endorsed by TJ as received 26 July and so recorded in SJL.

For William SHORT'S investment in the James River Company, see also Vol. 35:137.

THINGS: TJ to Gibson & Jefferson, 13 July 1802.

From J. P. G. Muhlenberg

SIR   Philadelphia July 21st. 1802.

A Vacancy having taken place, in the Comission of Bankruptcy for this State, by the death of Mr. Vancleve—The friends of Robert Porter Esqr. are sollicitous to recomend him To The President, as a Person fit to fill the Vacancy—On this occasion I beg leave to state To The President, that Mr. Porter is an Attorney of considerable repute, and until lately has had his full share of practice—Last year, the Republican Comittee, appointed to Superintend the Election, prest Mr. Porter to stand a Candidate for a Seat in the State Legislature—He consented with reluctance, believing his absence for so long a time, would have a tendency to lessen his practice—He consented at last— was Elected, & servd during the Session—The dimunition of his practice, since that period, is one of the inducements with his friends to recomend him to The Presidents consideration.

I have the Honor to be with the highest Respect Sir Your Most Obedt   P. MUHLENBERG

RC (DNA: RG 59, LAR); at foot of text: "The President of The United States"; endorsed by TJ as received 29 July from "Philip" Muhlenberg and so recorded in SJL; also endorsed by TJ: "Robert Porter to be Commr. bkrpts."

From John Vaughan

DR SIR,   Philad: 21 July 1802

An uncertainty having arisen, whether the adress of Mr Brown was correct, I have taken the liberty to trouble you, with this, letter of thanks from the Society to Mr Brown for the Interesting bone lately Sent—If some of our Members, would now furnish an account of the Mamoth & of this new Acquisition, our 6th Volume might immediately go to press.—& I fear that from the Sons Skeleton, we may be anticipated—It is under this impression, & from a knowledge of the warm interest you take in the reputation of the Society & our Country, that I take the liberty of Suggesting, that a letter from yourself to Dr Wistar, as arising from your own sense of its importance, might accelerate the performance, of what he has I believe had some time in preparation—The Comparative Anatomy he will probably Confine himself to—if he does—possibly Dr Barton might be induced to take up the Natural History &c & M Peale would recite, where found &— & means of acquirement.—When the Torpedo was discovered three or four Different members presented papers to the Royal Society—

Knowing you will pardon the Trouble I give, in favor of the Motives, I remain

with the greatest respect Dr Sir Your obt. Servant.

JN VAUGHAN

RC (DLC); at foot of text: "Thomas Jefferson Prest. of United States"; endorsed by TJ as received 29 July and so recorded in SJL. Enclosure: American Philosophical Society to John Brown of Boone County, Kentucky, not found, acknowledging the receipt on 18 June of the fossil sent by Brown; see APS, *Proceedings*, 22, pt. 3 [1884], 325; Brown to TJ, 28 Apr.; TJ to John Brown (the senator), 14 Aug.

MAMOTH: that is, the mastodon remains excavated by Charles Willson Peale in New York State. The NEW ACQUISITION was the prehistoric bison skull from Kentucky (TJ to Caspar Wistar, 14 July; Peale to TJ, 18 July).

Committees of the American Philosophical Society were attempting to move forward with publication of the society's *Transactions*. The fifth volume had gone to the printer several months earlier. Despite Vaughan's supposition that the next installment MIGHT IMMEDIATELY GO TO PRESS, the first part of the sixth volume of *Transactions* was not set into type until 1804 (APS, *Proceedings*, 22, pt. 3 [1884], 319, 320, 322, 324, 357).

THE SONS SKELETON: the mastodon skeleton that Peale's son Rembrandt had exhibited in New York City and intended to show in Europe (TJ to Charles Willson Peale, 5 May). Vaughan's hopes for an interrelated set of papers by Caspar WISTAR, Benjamin Smith BARTON, and the senior Peale regarding the recent fossil discoveries were not realized.

In the 1770s, John Walsh, John Hunter, Jan Ingenhousz, and Henry Cavendish presented separate papers to the Royal Society of London on aspects of the TORPEDO or electric ray, a fish capable of generating an electrical charge. Benjamin Franklin corresponded with two of the investigators and helped to disseminate the results of the research (Royal Society of London, *Philosophical Transactions*, 63 [1773-74], 461-89; 64 [1774], 464-73; 65 [1775], 1-4; 66 [1776], 196-225; Franklin, *Papers*, 19:160-3, 189, 204-6, 233-5, 286-8, 295; 20:257-67, 433; 21:148, 150, 217).

From James Madison

DEAR SIR   Washington July 22. 1802.

On consultation with the Secretary of the Navy, it has been concluded that the public service will be favored by sending the ship the General Greene, with the provisions & gun-carriages destined for the Mediterranean, instead of chartering a private vessel for the occasion. It has occurred also that as the period at which an annual remittance to Algiers will become due, will arrive before the ship will get to that place, it may be found proper that another thirty thousand dollars should be sent as an experimental measure for avoiding the stipulated & expensive tribute of Stores. Should the substitute be accepted, it will be a saving to the U. States. Should it be rejected, time will be gained for the other remittance. I have written to Mr. Gallatin on the subject, and requested him to make preparation for having the money ready in case your approbation should be signified to him. You will recollect no doubt that if a letter from you to the Emperor of Morocco, should be decided on, as a companion to the Gun carriages, it must be forwarded in time for the sailing of the Ship. May I ask the favor of you to leave it open for the perusal of Mr. Sampson, that it may serve as an explanation & instruction to him in the case. The ship will probably sail from this place[1] in about 20 days from this date.

I observe in the papers that one of the Commissrs. of Bankruptcy for Philada. has been taken off by the fever. I have not heard lately from Mr. Wagner, but think it not improbable that the vacancy will attract the attention of himself & his friends, and that it may be properly bestowed on him, if no particular claim to it be in the way.

With the most respectful attachment I remain Dr. Sir Yrs.

JAMES MADISON

RC (DLC); endorsed by TJ as received 25 July from the State Department and "Barbary affairs" and so recorded in SJL.

PROVISIONS and other supplies for American naval forces operating in the Mediterranean typically were transported in private vessels chartered by navy agents in the United States for the occasion. They were thereafter deposited at Gibraltar and placed under the charge of the American consul, John Gavino, for distribution (NDBW, 1:485, 499-500, 511-12, 548-9, 629, 639-40; 2:59, 191-2, 197, 254, 276).

GUN-CARRIAGES: James Simpson, the United States consul to Morocco, had agreed to arrange in Lisbon for the construction of one hundred carriages for cannons for the sultan (or emperor) of Morocco, Mawlay Sulayman. Simpson's understanding was that the sultan would pay for the gun carriages, but late in 1801, Sulayman let it be known that he wanted the United States to make him a present of the equipment. As Simpson pointed out to the Moroccans, the 1786 treaty "of Peace and Friendship" between the two countries, signed during the reign of Sulayman's father, Sidi Muhammad ibn Abd Allah, contained no stipulation regarding presents or payments from the United States to Morocco. The consul reported to Madison, however, that Sulayman was demanding presents and diplomatic overtures from European nations, had ordered the consul of the Batavian Republic to leave Morocco for failing to meet those expectations, and threatened to do the same with Simpson. Sulayman, Simpson believed, hoped to find an excuse to abandon the treaty of 1786 and make a new arrangement with the United States. Although the treaty did not require annuities, the United States had made a payment to Sulayman in 1795 as an inducement to confirm his father's treaty and gave him presents when Simpson presented his credentials as consul in 1798. Simpson advised Madison that if the United States determined to make a present of the gun carriages, "I would with due submission, beg leave to recommend a Letter being sent by the President to the Emperor on the occasion," particularly as "no direct Communication whatever, has been made to His Majesty on the part of the United States" since 1795. In a reply to Simpson in April 1802, Madison noted that the Moroccan ruler's dissatisfaction was "unexpected" and could have dangerous consequences. Madison asked the consul to assure Sulayman of TJ's regard for him. Due to the sultan's evident "anxiety," Madison informed Simpson, the president had determined that the United States would indeed make a present of the gun carriages, which would be "sent from the United States as soon as they can be compleated, and an opportunity can be provided." The gesture, Madison noted, was to be "a means of conciliating" the sultan "as much as possible for the present, without countenancing expectations in future." TJ might accompany the gift with "a friendly letter to the Emperor," Madison noted, "but on this point it may not be necessary to say any thing." Before Simpson received those instructions from Madison, he wrote more dispatches indicating that the sultan still seemed to be looking for a reason to abrogate the treaty and that Sulayman might send wheat to Tripoli despite American and Swedish protestations. Some of those communications from him arrived at the State Department on 19 July (Simpson to Madison, 8 Jan., 20 Feb., 19 Mch., 13 May 1802, in DNA: RG 59, CD; Madison, *Papers, Sec. of State Ser.*, 2:378-9; 3:141; NDBW, 1:251, 509; Miller, *Treaties*, 2:185-227).

For background on the ANNUAL REMITTANCE TO ALGIERS by the United States, see Vol. 34:115 and Vol. 36:667n. TJ and Madison hoped that the dey, Mustafa Baba, would accept annual payments of $30,000 in lieu of the maritime stores stipulated by the 1795 treaty between the countries (Madison, *Papers, Sec. of State Ser.*, 3:430-1).

In his letter to GALLATIN on 22 July, Madison informed the secretary of the Treasury of the plan to send the provisions for the Mediterranean squadron, the gun carriages for Morocco, and the annuity payment for Algiers, which would come due on 5 Sep., by the *General Greene*. Madison suggested that Gallatin begin to get THE MONEY READY for the annuity payment pending TJ's approval. Madison expected the frigate, after it sailed from Washington, to stop at Norfolk to take on the provisions (same, 414).

MR. SAMPSON: James Simpson.

[1] Preceding three words interlined.

From Thomas Newton

DR SIR   Norfolk July 22—1802

Your favor by Genl. Dearborne I received & thank you for the introduction of him, his stay here is so short a time, that we cannot have the pleasure of shewing what our Country affords & at present our trade is very dull, it being the season when our vessels are all out. I shall be ever glad to see any of your freinds, & hope when they come this way you will let me know them. whenever you should wish to have wine, from this, I shall be happy to send it you. my correspondent in Madeira, has informd me that he has superior to any that has yet been shipped, I intend to direct a pipe or two for trial, tho I think what he has sent, is very fine. with my best wishes for yr. health & happiness

I am respectfully Yr. Obt Servt   THOS NEWTON

RC (DLC); endorsed by TJ as received 12 Aug. and so recorded in SJL.

FAVOR: TJ to Newton, 12 July 1802.

From "A Republican"

SIR   Philada July 23d 1802

It is a recd. opinion in this City that Mr. John L Leib is to have an appointment of Commissioner of Bankruptcy in the place of Mr. Vancleve decd. I hope Sir that this is not the case; the Writer of this article has been an uniform Republican he is neither in search of places of Honor or profit, but purely governed by the warmth of his wishes that all appointments made by you may be such as will reflect Honor not discredit upon your Administration he has been led to address you upon the Subject. The private Character of Mr. Jno L Leib is notoriously bad. His public Character and Conduct I consider equally so—during the reign of *Terror* Mr. Leib was found in the Ranks of Federalists *only* and it was not untill a complete change had taken place in the minds of the people that Mr. Leib was known as a republican. The Man who now addresses you has heard him revile your Character upon two Occasions and if necessary he can bring forward Evidences who were present—To wind up the Conduct of Mr. Leib he thought proper to choose a Wife of a notoriously infamous Character from a Common Bawdy House. I consider the Character of his Brother as equally infamous If your Excellency has Doubts I beg you will make the Enquiry necessary—Pardon the liberty I have taken—beleive me Sir that an Appointment of this kind would meet the decided disapprobation of the warmest Republicans of the City and County of Philada—

I am your real Friend   A REPUBLICAN

RC (DNA: RG 59, LAR); endorsed by TJ as received 31 July and "against John L. Lieb" and so recorded in SJL.

Attorney JOHN L. LEIB and his brother Dr. Michael Leib were members of the Democratic Society of Pennsylvania in the 1790s. REIGN OF TERROR: Mahlon Dickerson recalled in 1829 that John L. Leib had been "among the most active politicians who brought about the change that placed Mr. Jefferson in the presidential chair, and gave a check to aristocracy at that time." On 3 Feb. 1802, Leib, Dickerson, Matthew Lawler, and Mathew Carey were maligned in the *Gazette of the United States* for drawing up the Philadelphia memorial, which supported the repeal of the Judiciary Act of 1801. It was laid before the House of Representatives on 18 Feb. 1802. Michael Leib, a member of Congress at the time, was closely allied with William Duane (Philip S. Foner, ed., *The Democratic-Republican Societies, 1790-1800* [Westport, Conn., 1976], 439-40; Harold D. Moser and others, eds., *The Papers of Andrew Jackson*, 8 vols. [Knoxville, 1980-   ], 7:349-50; *Philadelphia Gazette*, 23 Dec. 1801; PMHB, 17 [1893], 465-6; *Annals*, 11:568; Vol. 33:543; Vol. 36:71). CHOOSE A WIFE: John L. Leib married Margaret Conner of Philadelphia. During the War of 1812, Leib moved his family to Michigan Territory (Clarence M. Burton and others, eds., *The City of Detroit Michigan, 1701-1922*, 5 vols. [Detroit, 1922], 2:1148, 1385-6).

On 19 July, John L. Leib wrote Meriwether Lewis, requesting that he mention Samson Levy to the president as a "suitable Successor" to John W. Vancleve. He noted that his brother had previously recommended Levy and that his friend would fill the office "with honor to himself & usefulness to the publick" (RC in DNA: RG 59, LAR; endorsed by TJ: "Levy Sampson to be Commr. bkrptcy"). See Michael Leib to TJ, 28 Apr., for the earlier recommendation. At that time, TJ recorded Levy's name on his list of candidates for bankruptcy commissioner (Vol. 37: Appendix II, List 1). Later in 1802, TJ received another letter endorsing Levy. On 13 Oct., Moses Levy wrote his friend Alexander J. Dallas in support of his brother as bankruptcy commissioner. His legal acquirements qualified him for the office, Moses Levy observed, and "his Integrity will guard him against any improper Conduct." He declared that Dallas's "favorable representation" to the president would be considered as an act of kindness to a friend (RC in DNA: RG 59, LAR; endorsed by TJ: "Levy Sampson to be Commr. bkrptcy v. Vancleve"). Dallas forwarded another application. On 16 Sep., Joseph B. McKean wrote him soliciting the position for his brother-in-law Andrew Pettit, because, McKean noted, Dallas was finding it inconvenient to have to attend "so constantly" as commissioner of bankruptcy that he wished the vacancy occasioned by the death of Vancleve would be filled. McKean observed that the Philadelphia commissioners were already acquainted with Pettit (RC in same, endorsed by TJ: "Pettit Andrew to be Commr bkrptcy vice Vancleve" and "J. B. Mc.Kean's letter to mr Dallas"; Rowe, *McKean*, 266). For Thomas McKean's support of Pettit for the position, see Vol. 37:591-2. TJ did not fill the vacancy until October 1803, when he appointed Blair McClenachan to the office (list of commissions in Lb in DNA: RG 59, MPTPC).

From Daniel D'Oyley

SIR   Charleston S:C: 24th: July 1802

The inclosed discourse which I request you to do me the honour of accepting was delivered on the last anniversary of the glorious declaration of Independence—as it affords a corroborating testimony of the goodness of Mr. Furman's heart I am well pleased for from the belief with which he was of late impressed he conscientiously opposed the advancement of the Republican party dreading I suppose the destruction in case of their success of what he is devoted to and most explicitly and candidly acknowledges in his thirteenth page is more generally diffused and better supported at present than at any former period—there is an unusual spirit of rationality throughout the piece & it was delivered with a pious respect to the occasion—his invitations and acknowledgements appeared to be the result of conviction and were sincerely and devoutly made—would to God any thing short of submission could change the minds of the leading Federalists here—their works border on desperation, they avow an indifference to all reconciliation and declare they care not how wide the breach is extended—there are two points under which they are at-

tempting to rally and the Government though I know most unde-
servedly are made to bear the blame of both—I fear to enter into particulars—but I beg you to beleive that I am with sincerity and great
attachment true in the profession and practice of the Republican
principles on which our Government was instituted and established,
and undiviating in the most profound respect and venerable affection
I subscribe myself

  Sir Your most Obdt. hble Sevt: DANIEL D'OYLEY

RC (DLC); endorsed by TJ as received
12 Aug. and so recorded in SJL. Enclosure: see below.

Daniel D'Oyley (ca. 1761-1820) of
Charleston was a cousin and political ally
of Charles Pinckney. From 1799 to 1804,
he served as state treasurer of the lower
division of South Carolina. Republicans
in the state, especially Pinckney, repeatedly urged D'Oyley's appointment as
collector at Charleston, but without success. Although the president considered
D'Oyley "a most respectable republican,"
contradictory information about the political situation in South Carolina led TJ
to delay removals there. Questions also
arose about D'Oyley's character, with
Pierce Butler describing him as "a republican from selfish & interested principles."
By the fall of 1802, TJ came to feel that
D'Oyley's desire for office and constant
calls for removals bore "a very dubious aspect." Pinckney later sued his cousin for
mishandling his financial affairs, while in
1807 the South Carolina legislature found
D'Oyley guilty of misconduct while serving as treasurer and disqualified him from
holding public office for five years (S.C.
Biographical Directory, House of Representatives, 3:192-3; Marty D. Matthews,

Forgotten Founder: The Life and Times
of Charles Pinckney [Columbia, S.C.,
2004], 115-21; Vol. 32:348, 349n; Vol.
33:331, 513; Vol. 34:187, 221; Vol. 35:13-
14n, 32, 53; TJ to Thomas Sumter, Sr.,
22 Oct. 1802).

INCLOSED DISCOURSE: Richard Fur-
man's America's Deliverance and Duty. A
Sermon. Preached at the Baptist Church in
Charleston, South-Carolina, on the Fourth
Day of July, 1802, before the State Society
of the Cincinnati, the American Revolution Society; and the Congregation Which
Usually Attends Divine Service in the Said
Church published in Charleston in 1802.
Furman, pastor of the Baptist church in
Charleston and a leading religious figure
in South Carolina, declared in his oration
that victory in the American Revolution
was brought about by God and that the
nation continued to benefit from divine
sanction. As such, he emphasized the nation's obligation to secure and improve
upon the blessings of republican government, including a strenuous attention to
religion and religious freedom, strict adherence to the Constitution, suppression
of party spirit, respect for public authority, and the election of wise and virtuous
national leaders (ANB; Sowerby, No.
1667).

From Albert Gallatin

DEAR SIR   New York July 24th 1802
 I received yesterday your's of the 20th, and will attend to the dates
of the several commissions. I have written to the Dept. of State in
order that they should transmit to you for your signature commissions for the port of Massac, (vice Chribs the horse thief) and to fill

the vacancies caused by the resignations of Foster & Goforth; also two commissions of inspector of the revenue (for signing certificates accompanying spirits transported coastways & inland) for the new collector of Marblehead & for the new supervisor of Pennsylvania. I think you may at once fill that for Commissioner in Symmes case, vice Goforth, with John Selman's name. From Cincinnati I do not expect any better recommendation than that of Capn. Lewis.

T. Coxe wrote to me yesterday that he had been waited upon by the democratic committee of Philada., to announce to him that he was selected as candidate to fill the place of Member of Congress vice W. Jones who cannot serve after next session; but that, on account of the narrowness of his income, he meant to decline; & gave me that information, in order that an idea that he was to be the candidate might not interfere with his official restoration.

Israel Whelen has given me private intimation that, after the next winter he could not hold the office of purveyor of public supplies. I am sorry for it, as he has been the only useful agent in Philada., to procure for the Treasury remittances in Holland. The office is 2000 dollars, & I suppose T. Coxe will want it.

My health is much better & I intend leaving this place so as to arrive in Washington the last day of this month. Whilst here I have succeeded in contracting for 700,000 Guilders more on Holland—I want about one million more before 1st Septer. & am in hopes to obtain them before the end of this month. The exchange continues, and, it is generally expected, will continue unfavorable.

John Vancleve one of the Commissrs. of Bankruptcy for Philada. is dead. Several applications have been made, though not from very sound quarters. I think five are enough & that the vacancy need not be filled.

I am with attachment and respect Your obedt. Servt.

ALBERT GALLATIN

I have evidence of E. Livingston recovering the amount of bonds put in suit, & not paying the same to the Collector. If possible, I will try to probe the thing, but feel very uneasy about the consequences. He knows that all his friends here think the office of dist. atty. incompatible with that of Mayor, & that they will make it so by law at the next meeting of the State legislature; and I have no doubt he keeps it only for the sake of using the public money. His character, in money matters, is blasted; and it must be observed that dist. attornies give no security

RC (DLC); addressed: "Thomas Jefferson President of the United States at Monticello"; also addressed, probably by the Washington, D.C. post office: "Monticello near Milton, Virga."; franked; postmarked Washington, D.C., 28 July; endorsed by TJ as received from the Treasury Department on 31 July and so recorded in SJL.

PRIVATE INTIMATION: on 19 July, Israel Whelen wrote Gallatin that he had incurred financial liabilities, which would require him to leave office. Gallatin later noted that Whelen was "totally ruined" through the "French Speculations" of his son-in-law and former partner, Joseph I. Miller. When Whelen officially resigned on 1 Aug. 1803, Tench Coxe assumed the office (Gallatin, *Papers*, 7:357-8; Madison, *Papers, Sec. of State Ser.*, 5:168, 495, 507n).

The EXCHANGE rate for the purchase of bills on Holland for the payment of the Dutch debt had increased from 40 cents per guilder in November 1801 to 41 cents in June 1802. During his May trip to Philadelphia and New York, Gallatin learned that trade between the U.S. and Holland had decreased; he feared the purchase of four million guilders in the coming months "would indubitably raise, considerably, the rate of exchange" (Gallatin, *Papers*, 7:185, 205; ASP, *Finance*, 2:9; Vol. 35:738n).

COMMISSRS. OF BANKRUPTCY FOR

PHILADA: on 19 July, Clement Biddle wrote Gallatin recommending Charles Biddle for the position, noting that the Treasury secretary could consult their mutual friends Alexander J. Dallas and Aaron Burr for the character of the young attorney (Gallatin, *Papers*, 7:353).

In June 1803, a Treasury Department PROBE of the accounts of the New York district attorney's office revealed a significant shortfall in payments to the U.S. Treasury, later fixed at $44,000, which Edward Livingston promised to pay through the sale of his estate. In July, TJ and the Cabinet decided to remove him for "malversation." Nathan Sanford replaced him as U.S. attorney in mid-August. At the same time, Livingston, who had served as MAYOR of New York since 24 Aug. 1801, offered his resignation to the New York Council of Appointment, but he remained in office until the council elected DeWitt Clinton as his successor on 7 Oct. 1803. Livingston left for New Orleans in December 1803, determined to restore his name and credit (Richard A. Harrison, *Princetonians, 1776-1783: A Biographical Dictionary* [Princeton, 1981], 331-42; New York *Mercantile Advertiser*, 15 Aug. 1801; 15 Oct. 1803; New York *American Citizen and General Advertiser*, 25 Aug. 1801; New York *Morning Chronicle*, 19 Aug. 1803; *New-York Evening Post*, 11 Oct. 1803; Albert Gallatin to TJ, 16 June, 11 Aug. 1803; Notes on a Cabinet Meeting, 16 July 1803).

From Levi Lincoln

SIR   Worcester July 24—1802—

I met my family in health, after a journey of dispatch, and of course, some fatigue. At Hartford, the only place in which I made any stop, The republicans appeared to be very firm, spirited, & full of confidence—They say, the opposition is incensed, strugling, and yielding. That, in may, there was a convocation of the Clergy in that place, at which Mr Morse was present, and that the sunday, next after there were guarded and qualified prayers, for the President & the Genl. Govt., in all their churches. It is a strange religion, which makes an act of piety to God, depend on the vote of man—and religious supplications, & social expressions of Gratitude to Heaven, in which all are supposed to join, be regulated by the pride, or the interest of political priests. The change is undoubtedly from policey, not from a conviction of error, or a cordial reformation.

In, Worcester, and its neighbourhood, I met a spirit some what moderated, or perhaps, only retired or suspended, but which had raged through the winter & Spring with unexampled fury; From the public papers, or private letters, I had formed no idea of the degree of madness and folly to which individuals had indulged themselves— They were constantly receiving letters from Washington, or pretending they were, making the most alarming communications & confirming the most groundless reports. And I am told the federal members, on their return, countenanced, or confirmed these reports generally—The endeavour to convince the people, that they are ruined, unless they can arrest the progress of the present order of things, is unceasing—no meanness is too little, or wickedness too great, for the purpose. Such has been their impudence, their violence, and their abuse, in public, & private; in their printed invectives, and personal denunciations, as to intimidate, & place the republicans, in some degree, in a state of abeyance from duty. Truth has been every where, in this Government, either overwhelmed by falshood & the grossest misrepresentations, or considerably checked, in her progress—Our friends complain very much, of having been neglected and abandoned to the effects of the impositions practiced by the federalist at the seat of Govt. during the last Session of Congress—I think myself, had the republican members there been, as assiduous in communicating truth, as their enemies were, falshoods, it would have produced more spirit & exertions with their constitutents; and that our elections would have been different—For altho few, if any were gained to the federal side, by the torrents of slander & misrepresentations which run thro the country previous to the elections, many were perplexed, brought to hesitate & rendered inactive—

As yet, I have had but little opportunity of seeing the temper of people myself, or of hearing from the various posts of this Govt—Old South called on me, he is of the opinion, that things will yet get right in Boston—that its error was the mere effect of fraud, & force—Eustis is more diffident. Mr Dallas, who has just left me, on his way from thence, to Philadelphia, heard various opinions on the subject— John Quincy Adams is made the most prominent character for federal promotion. They even borrow popularity from his father, as little as he may have to spare, to bestow it on the son—

The appointment, of Commissioners, gives general satisfaction to the republicans—Their enemies, a gogg'd by selecting Otis & Dawes—It is of the last importance that one general, firm, and spirited effort, be made to inform the public mind, & to remove the false impressions, which have been made—Falshood & violence is still the system, of the leaders of the opposition, they will lose their followers, the moment they can be made to understand the principles & the measures of the past & the present Administration. They now oppose, to avoid, the consequences, naturally resulting from the old order of things, & to secure the very objects which will be, the effects of the new measures. They are republicans, in their sentiments, & habits—They reason right on their principles; were these corrected, they would act right—The misfortune is, they have had impressed on them errors of fact—Detect these, and all will be well—There is a probability of persuading Bangs, to run agt. Hastings, he will be more likely to succeed, than any other man in the district—He is in trouble on account, of some groundless reports he has been spreading—I beleive he will not be able to extricate himself—

I have the honor to be most respectfully your obt Sert

LEVI LINCOLN

RC (DLC); addressed: "To Thomas Jefferson—President of U.S. City of Washington"; endorsed by TJ as received 5 Aug. and so recorded in SJL.

CONVOCATION OF THE CLERGY: Republicans speculated that Timothy Dwight, the president of Yale College, was responsible for the gathering in Hartford, Connecticut, during May. Since before the presidential election of 1800, Dwight and his close ally from Massachusetts, Jedidiah MORSE, had been among the most vocal of TJ's critics, depicting him as an extreme threat to religious orthodoxy and to social and political order. Morse and Dwight had founded the *Palladium* to disseminate their views, and in one of his "Farmer" essays, Lincoln struck out against that publication and the New England clergymen who were behind it. Several Connecticut politicians were thought to have been in consultation with the ministers during the May meeting, the conference in Hartford taking place at the same time as elections in the state. Reporting the rumored outcome of the convocation, the *American Mercury*, using a favorite Republican epithet for Dwight, called him "the Pope of Connecticut" and said that he had "issued a Bull, prohibiting the preaching of politics until further orders, except on special emergencies. The reason which his Holiness assigned for this order," the newspaper continued, "was that many of his Clergy had more political zeal than discretion, and preached and prayed so extravagantly, that they injured the cause which they designed to support" (New York *American Citizen and General Advertiser*, 20 May; Hartford *American Mercury*, 15 July; *Massachusetts Spy, or Worcester Gazette*, 28 July; Joseph W. Phillips, *Jedidiah Morse and New England Congregationalism* [New Brunswick, N.J., 1983], 91-101; Richard J. Moss, *The Life of Jedidiah Morse: A Station of Peculiar Exposure* [Knoxville, 1995], 55-6, 81-3; John R. Fitzmier, *New England's Moral Legislator: Timothy Dwight, 1752-1817* [Bloomington, Ind., 1998], 61-2, 132, 149; Charles E. Cuningham, *Timothy Dwight, 1752-1817: A Biography* [New York, 1942], 342; Vol. 34:516, 517n; Vol. 35:146-7, 306n).

Using the pseudonym OLD SOUTH, Benjamin Austin, Jr., of Boston wrote a long series of essays in the *Independent Chronicle* advocating the Republican cause and attacking John Adams and the Essex Junto (ANB; Benjamin Austin, Jr., *Constitutional Republicanism, in Opposition to Fallacious Federalism; as Published Occasionally in the Independent Chronicle, Under the Signature of Old-South* [Boston, 1803]; TJ to Austin, 28 June 1803).

In the election in the fall of 1802, Ed-ward BANGS, one of Lincoln's political associates in western Massachusetts, challenged Seth HASTINGS, who held Lincoln's old seat in the U.S. House of Representatives. Hastings defeated Bangs by a wide margin to retain the seat for the Eighth Congress (Boston *Columbian Centinel*, 6 Nov. 1802; *Biog. Dir. Cong.*; Paul Goodman, *The Democratic-Republicans of Massachusetts: Politics in a Young Republic* [Cambridge, Mass., 1964], 225n; Vol. 35:306n).

From Charles Minifie

HOND. & RESPECTED SIR,   Boston July 24 1802

Having been favour'd on the 5th. Inst. with a sight of the Model for the contemplated Naval Dock in the Eastern-Branch (which tis said is to get a supply of water from a Spring on the Border of the City Plan) and not having been assured of any certainty that its elevation is completely sufficient for the purpose; I humbly trust that your known general Goodness will pardon this liberty, which has no end in view but a wish for the general Good, whilst I beg leave to offer an Idea for consideration in case the Spring should be insufficient or that a different Mode for supplying the Dock may on examination be deem'd more eligible. In the process of enquiry into the different means of Supply permit me Sir to state a few Ideas on furnishing it by a Fire Engine. For example—I would suppose an Aqueduct to be cut from the Tide back to the side of the Dock—that a lifting force be effected by the Fire-Engine constructed on a limitted & cheap Plan for throwing the water over the side into the Dock in order to float the Ships up to the Platform, where they should take the Stocks, at such times as should be required—then to be let off leaving them in their proper Births—Altho' this would require no great expence of Coals it would I humbly conceive be worthy of deliberation to compare the constant working the Engine by day for other purposes to which Water Force might be applied— for instance, working Saw-Mills for the Navy Yard—Machinery for Anchor & other Forge Hammers—Copper flatting Mill— Grindstones, and polishing wheels for Armoury—Lathes, & such like other aids as would infallibly diminish the expence of Manual Labour and be of course a great saving to the Nation.—As a beneficial addition I would also submit the Idea of working the Fire Engine by means of an Oven whereby the expence of Fuel should be nearly if not quite done away.—I mean to Coke or Char the Coals (& the smallest Coals skreen'd from the large will answer equally well or better than both mixed) so that the Coke will be worth as much, or more, for the drying Malt & Blast-Foundries than the Coals cost. This I state from Fact as the general practice in the Sea-Brine Works as well as the refining the Rock Salt: in these I've heretofore been concern'd, therefore I state a Certainty in the process that 20 Bushels of small Coals turn out 22 Bus of Coke which in England fetches a better Price ℔ Bushel than the Coals—and would doubtless do so in this Country as a cheaper & safer fuel for Malt & Corn Kilns—Brass Foundries—drying Tobacco &c &c as it burns without smoke and is the strongest & safest Fire from any kind of Fuel whatever. To return to the Spring—Should it be preferr'd I would suggest the Idea of ascertaining its probable Source by confining the Water in two large Casks, one on another, in order to determine the elevation it may command so as to lessen the expence in digging for a Brick Tunnel or laying down large Free Pipes thro' which the water may be convey'd to the Navy Yard—the experiment is easily made by making the lower Cask tight with Clay & Stones next the Ground, & also the Joint of the upper Cask.—The excellence of the water from said Spring for watering Ships going to Sea—the conveying it for common Uses—and in case of Fire, together with its being applied to the Saw-Mill &c &c (as stated if ℔ fire Engine) are unquestionably great recommendations to the Spring-Supply for the Navy Yard—and undoubtedly call for a comparitive statement of the respective Expence in the different modes—by the Spring—& by the Fire Engine.—The latter I presume might be ascertained to demonstration—& so it may probably be said of supply by the Spring—But Sir is there not a possible interruption conjecturable in considering that in process of Time—the digging of Wells may not strike the Spring & divert the Supply to the total overthrow of the Benefits calculated on?

My leaving the City on the 6th. Instant & having been engaged in Business on my way to this Place claim the Apology & account for my thus addressing You from hence.

Should any Benefit to the Public Good arise from any communication in this Letter I shall feel happy in its effect—But although the *whole* may, from Your acknowledged Superiority in Judgment be found only troubling You to read I shall nevertheless rely on Your taking the Writer's *Will* into consideration apart from *any* other Motive than a Good Intention.

I am Sir with sentiments of sincere Esteem & regard your, perhaps unknown, very obed hble Servant   CHAS. MINIFIE

My future residence will be I expect in the City—I can give lines & directions for fixing the Coking Principle to an Engine & will Pro-bono-publico hold myself bound to give any Aid on such Considerations only.

Yrs. &c   CM

RC (DLC); addressed: "Thomas Jefferson Esqr. President of the United States at Washington City"; franked; postmarked 25 July; endorsed by TJ as received 31 July and so recorded in SJL.

English immigrant Charles Minifie studied law with one brother before leaving to learn manufacturing from another. He operated a soap and candle works in Philadelphia during the 1790s, then put the business up for sale in 1801. He subsequently located in Washington, where he participated in a variety of public and private ventures, including service on the city council and as a director of the Eastern Branch Bridge Company. During TJ's second term, Minifie wrote several times seeking the president's assistance with his claim regarding payment for materials supplied to the navy in 1802. TJ could offer no help with the claim, but did appoint Minifie a justice of the peace for Washington in 1808 (*Philadelphia Gazette*, 8 Nov. 1794; *Poulson's American*

Daily Advertiser, 28 May 1801; JEP, 2:85; RCHS, 33-34 [1932], 270; Daniel Carroll, Daniel Brent, and Charles Minifie to TJ, 24 May 1803; Minifie to TJ, 21 Jan. 1806, 9 Mch., 17 Oct. 1807).

The MODEL of the dry dock referred to above may have been built by Wilson Bryan. In his financial memorandum books under 20 July 1802, TJ recorded an order on John Barnes in favor of Bryan "for a model (abt. 20) and for blinds and book presses &c. in the whole 69.94" (MB, 2:1078). However, Bryan's invoice to TJ of that same date, totaling $69.94, makes no mention of a model in its list of charges (MS in CSmH, with TJ's order on Barnes for payment at foot of account). The $20 payment for the "model" may not have been made until the following year. TJ wrote an order on Barnes for $20 in favor of Bryan on 15 July 1803, but did not specify the reason for the payment (MS in ViU: Edgehill-Randolph Papers).

From Robert Smith

SIR   Navy department 24 July 1802

I have the honor to request your Signature to the Commission herewith enclosed for Lieut Philomon C: Wederstrandt:

This Gentleman has been heretofore Commissioned, but as his Commission was filled up on a blank, originally intended for a Warrant, he is desirous to have it exchanged.

With the utmost respect I have the honor to be Sir Your mo. obt. Servt.   RT SMITH

RC (DLC); in a clerk's hand, signed by Smith; at foot of text: "The President"; endorsed by TJ as received from the Navy Department on 31 July and "Wederstrand's commn." and so recorded in SJL. FC (Lb in DNA: RG 45, LSP).

Philemon Charles WEDERSTRANDT of Maryland served as a midshipman and as a lieutenant during the Quasi-War with France. He was retained as a lieutenant under the Peace Establishment Act of 1801 and was eventually promoted to the rank of master commandant in 1807 (NDQW, Dec. 1800-Dec. 1801, 356; NDBW, *Register*, 58).

From Thomas Underwood, Jr.

SIR   Richmond 25th. July 1802

I hold it to be a duty which every real friend to society owes his Country to give information of, and expose to publick view the misconduct of all and every officer under the government who will not pay due attention to its interest. You will therefore pardon me when I tell you that the Loan officer of Virginia Mr. John Hopkins, is authorised by Law to keep two Clerks; it is found by Mr. Hopkins that one is sufficient to transact all the business in that department and he (Mr. Hopkins) without adhereing to the interest of his Country suffers one Clerk who transacts the whole business to receive the Salary allowed by Law for two; and altho saving of one salary to the publick is but a small consideration yet the Salutory scheme of oeconomy so valuable to our repubican Goverment can not be carried into full effect unless things of this kind be noticed. With a wish to be serviceable to my County,

    I am Sir. Yr. Mo. Ob.   THOMAS UNDERWOOD JR.

RC (MoSHi: Jefferson Papers); endorsed by TJ as received 31 July and so recorded in SJL.

Thomas Underwood had been a lieutenant in the corps of artillerists and engineers from 1795 to 1799 before becoming a lieutenant of the public guard for the Richmond arsenal. In 1804, he secured an appointment as a superintendent of the public tobacco warehouse in Richmond (Heitman, *Dictionary*, 1:978; CVSP, 8:484; 9:298, 381).

JOHN HOPKINS, a prominent Richmond businessman and a Federalist, had served a long tenure as commissioner of loans for Virginia (David Hackett Fischer, *The Revolution of American Conservatism: The Federalist Party in the Era of Jeffersonian Democracy* [New York, 1965], 375; JEP, 1:57; Vol. 32:374). TJ relayed Underwood's report to Albert Gallatin in a letter of 3 Aug. On 17 Aug., Gallatin enclosed a note from Joseph Nourse, dated 11 Aug., that listed the names of the two clerks that Hopkins reported employing. Hopkins remained commissioner until 1804, when he was replaced by Meriwether Jones (JEP, 1:464-5).

From Robert Gourlay

SIR.

Virginia Coffee House
London July 26th. 1802—

I was favor'd with yours of 30th. March, & have Communicated the Contents to Mr. Jenings, who begs me to forward you his best respects.— I have lately had a letter from Philip L. Grymes Esqr. respecting the Guardianship of Windham & Sisters.— I hope soon to see his Bills on me for the amount of their Cash in my hands, about £600 Stg.—

I am Sir—Yours most respectfully,   R. GOURLAY—

Dupl (MHi); at head of text: "His Excellency—Thomas Jefferson—President, United States" and "(Copy)"; endorsed by TJ as received 5 Oct. and so recorded in SJL.

Philip Ludwell Grymes assumed the GUARDIANSHIP of his nephew and nieces Charles Wyndham Grymes, Mary Grymes, and Ariana Grymes after TJ declined legal responsibility for them (Vol. 34:611; Vol. 37:147).

To John Isaac Hawkins

SIR

Monticello July 26. 1802.

I recieved your favor of the 16th. just as I was leaving Washington, & could not therefore answer it until my arrival here. I am obliged to you for your description of the Claviol, and shall certainly prefer ceding to you my piano forte, and taking in exchange at the proper difference in [price], a Claviol as soon as you can furnish one, which you think will be a year first. I suppose it probable, if you go to England, you will be able to get them made there of better materials, better workmanship & cheaper than here. as to mine you will have it made there or here as you please. I sincerely wish you the success which you so well deserve, and tender you my esteem

TH: JEFFERSON

PrC (MHi); faint; at foot of text: "Mr. John I. Hawkins"; endorsed by TJ in ink on verso.

To George Jefferson

DEAR SIR

Washington July 26 1802

On the 21st inst mr Barnes was to remit you 200. D. to be placed to my credit [the funds?] I hope came safely to hand. yours of the

[21st] [...] probable mr Barnes will [...] the 198. D. mr Barnes [...] me for an equal sum in Washington. [this] [...] (formerly [a friend] to you) [...] from Philadelphia [...] I hope is arrived and on it's way with the other things. [...] I [desired in] a letter from Philadelphia [...] [2 days] [...] be forwarded by you with the other articles. [...] [that favor] [...] also repeat the request of [...] my own use, if now [...] the 5. Dollars you [...] Accept my affectionate esteem

Th: Jefferson

P.S. I will pray you also to send me 5 barrels of R.I. inspected lime, best quality

PrC (MHi); faint; postscript added by TJ in ink; at foot of text: "Mr George Jefferson"; endorsed by TJ in ink on verso.

From James Monroe

Dear Sir   Richmond July 26. 1802

On my return lately from Albemarle I found yr. favors of the 15. 17. & 20th. wh. were unopened according to orders I had left in such cases. An attack from Callendar is a harmless thing unsupported by any document from yrself. From such letters as you wrote him I do not think any thing is to be hoped to him or the federalists. If the printers wod. say nothing in reply to the attacks of that party the true ground might ultimately be taken on a view of what was said by the adversary: but that is not to be expected especially at a distance. To contend that it was simply a charity to a man in distress, wod. put them on the proof that it was more, or was given on stronger motives, and wod. admit by implication that if it had any other object in view, such object was an improper one. I shall give such hints as to prevent any thing whatever being done at present, or if any thing is, to give as far as in my power the true direction to the affair. I have been long solicited to make a visit to Norfolk, & have repeatedly promised a complyance, till I find a longer declension wod. excite some chagrine with my friends. To decline it at this moment wod. subject me to the imputation of doing it from fear of the yellow fever, altho none exists there that we know of. I therefore set out for that place in the morning, to return with the least possible delay. I shall hasten to Albemarle on my return here where I hope to arrive in abt. ten or twelve days, at the latest by the 10th. of Augt. I wish you health & happiness being sincerely yr. friend & servt   Jas. Monroe

Major Scott has yet recd. no information whether he is to be continued in service or dismissed. His dilemma is the cause of much pain to him & tryumph to the federalists. He is a most deserving man, of great sensibility, who has as much weight here as any republican cod. possibly have.

RC (DNA: RG 59, MLR); endorsed by TJ as received 31 July and so recorded in SJL.

From "N"

SIR   Philadelphia July 26th. 1802

Permit me to use the freedom of expostulating with you concerning a measure, which, we learn here, you are about to adopt. Believing your ignorance of its oppressive consequences to be the only source, in which it could have originated, I respectfully submit to your consideration such of them as my information enables me to suggest,—and I indulge the hope they shall produce in you such a determination and conduct, as any man of humane feelings would be proud to display on similar occasions. That you may the more clearly comprehend, and sensibly feel the drift and force of the statement I am about to make, I shall for a moment suppose you to be in the precise circumstances of him, who is destined to be the subject of all the distress, which the measure in contemplation is calculated to inflict; and shall lastly address your feelings before you are relieved from the torturing embarrassment of your supposed condition.

Suppose, then, that accident, choice or necessity had driven you early in life to the profession of arms, and that the same motive, which urged you to begin, obliged you to continue the pursuit far into the decline of life; that, after you had retired, your fellow Citizens, sensible of your patriotic services, and your private worth, rewarded both with an appointment of emolument, which it was their wish you should enjoy without molestation during good behaviour. Suppose, further, that you had acquired a family of five children chiefly females, who were educated in tenderness, and in elegance, and were now grown to maturity without any reasonable prospects of comfortable support, but what they expect to derive from public gratitude displayed in continuing to you the enjoyment of your establishment, and that your President, perhaps a stranger to your amiable virtues and ignorant of your straitened circumstances; overlooks all

[132]

the moving considerations, which your situation affords and sacrifices you and all your personal merits, your former toils, and the future distress of your helpless female family to some small advantage in prospect from the substitution of an individual Republican for an individual Federalist,—a mere name for a name, without even a pretence of promoting in the smallest degree the public welfare by the change, would you not feel anguish of the most poignant kind, and would you not want a turn to designate the measure of his cruelty, who could inflict so much distress for so small a gratification?

Permit me now to ask whether you have Daughters yourself, and, if you have, would you not feel the most keen distress, if placed in circumstances here described? To see a worthy man and his amiable family overwhelmed, and devoted to distress is a scene, which no parent can regard with indifference, and which every feeling man must view with horror, when they can trace the cause, not to the sufferer himself but to a compliance with the unreasonable demands of importunate and party spirited men.

I am not acquainted with General McPherson, nor with any of his connections, nor can I assign any reason for the obtrusion of this Letter upon you, than that "Nil humanium alienium a mi puto"

N.

RC (DLC); endorsed by TJ as received from "Anon." on 8 Aug. and "Mc.pherson" and so recorded in SJL.

MEASURE . . . YOU ARE ABOUT TO ADOPT: perhaps the removal of George Latimer as collector at Philadelphia led to the concern that William McPherson, another Federalist at the custom house, would also be replaced. McPherson's EMOLUMENT as naval officer at Philadelphia was about $3,500 per year. When changes in the Philadelphia custom house were advocated in 1801, Republican congressman William Jones and Alexander J. Dallas argued in favor of retaining McPherson. A Washington appointee,

first as surveyor for the port of Philadelphia in 1789 and then as naval officer in 1793, McPherson remained in office throughout TJ's presidency. In 1803, however, the administration again considered changes at Philadelphia, including the removal of McPherson (JEP, 1:25, 143; Vol. 34:428; Vol. 35:102n; Vol. 36:182; Albert Gallatin to TJ, 21 June 1803).

"NIL HUMANUM ALIENUM A ME PUTO": an allusion to the quotation from Roman playwright Terence, "homo sum: humani nil a me alienum puto," loosely translated as, "I am a man; I consider nothing that is human alien to me."

From Thomas McLean

Most Honored Citizen   Frederick County July 27th. 1802

My commerce with literary characters is so limited that I did not know of the existance of a Philosophical society at this time in any part of the United states,† else my first step would have been to enquire how I could convey to them the contents of my letter of May 2nd.: but this I would have done, without the most remote idea that my right to a patent was thereby forfeited; but if it should, I would prefer a transmittal of it to the society, because I am not in circumstance to use it. If I knew at what time to write, and in what manner to direct I would communicate a few things to the society which might be useful, such as the theory and principles of Optical glasses and Telescopes which might be of use in constructing the grand Telescope contemplated at Washington City. In Nicholsons Philosophy and the American addition of the Encyclopedia their Optics appear to me correct as far as the theory is therein ixplained, but that it remains unfinished because, they have not demonstrated that by the diameters of the reflectors and glasses and their focal distances, a Telescope may be constructed to any assigned degree of perfection—Example, a newspaper being placed at one mile distant required a Telescope that will represent it exactly at the distance of three feet: this is what I have not found in their Optics. If your attention to the general good forbids you to send me another line, I cannot complain, but if you can, it will be another cordial to one who has ever been desirous of your promotion and happiness.—   Thomas McLean

† until I recieved your favour of June 9th.

RC (DLC); addressed: "His Excellency Thomas Jefferson President of the United states"; franked; endorsed by TJ. Recorded in SJL as received 5 Aug.

GRAND TELESCOPE CONTEMPLATED AT WASHINGTON: despite calls for the construction of an observatory, first at Philadelphia and subsequently at Washington, those plans did not come to fruition until the 1830s and 1840s (John C. Greene, *American Science in the Age of Jefferson* [Ames, Iowa, 1984], 129, 138, 154).

NICHOLSONS PHILOSOPHY: William Nicholson, *Introduction to Natural Phi-*

losophy, a commonly cited text on natural science; see Vol. 23:364; Vol. 30:594; Vol. 31:68; Vol. 32:180.

Often referred to as the AMERICAN encyclopedia, Thomas Dobson's *Encyclopaedia; or, A Dictionary of Arts, Sciences, and Miscellaneous Literature*, which originally consisted of 18 volumes published at Philadelphia in 1798, was a revision of the third edition of the *Encyclopaedia Britannica* (Robert D. Arner, *Dobson's Encyclopaedia: The Publisher, Text, and Publication of America's First Britannica, 1789-1803* [Philadelphia, 1991], x, 4, 30; Sowerby, No. 4891; Vol. 29:440, 441n).

To Albert Gallatin

DEAR SIR   Monticello July 28. 1802.

The Secretary of state, in a letter of the 22d. instant proposes to me, that as the General Greene will sail about the 10th. of next month with some articles for the Emperor of Marocco, and provisions for our vessels in the Mediterranean, and the period for another annual remittance to Algiers is approaching, we should send another 30,000. D. as an experimental measure for avoiding the stipulated & expensive tribute of stores. should this be accepted, it will be a great saving to the US. As the measure appears to me advantageous to the public, I entirely approve of it, and have therefore to ask the favor of you to take such measures as may be necessary, in conjunction with the Secretary of State, for remitting that sum to Algiers by the conveyance abovementioned. Accept assurances of my great esteem & respect.   TH: JEFFERSON

RC (NHi: Gallatin Papers); addressed: "The Secretary of the Treasury Washington"; postmarked Milton, 30 July; endorsed. PrC (DLC). Recorded in SJL with notation "30. M. D. Algiers."

From Tadeusz Kosciuszko

SIR   [on or after 28 July 1802]

Inclosed I have the honnor to send to you from Mr Pougens. Permit me Sir to recomend to you his desires, you know his merit and his talents. Accept my best wishes and be convinced of my sincier friendship and respect   T KOSCIUSZKO

RC (MB); undated, but supplied from enclosure; at foot of text: "rue de Province No 43"; endorsed by TJ as received 5 Oct. and so recorded in SJL. Enclosure: Charles Pougens to Kosciuszko, 28 July 1802, in French, written at Paris, regarding his hope of receiving a commission from TJ to supply books for libraries and depositories in the United States; he is encouraged by William Duane's having informed Victor Collot of his success selling foreign books in Philadelphia; Pougens wants to set an example for other Paris booksellers; he encloses a notice of his bookselling business, a summary of his planned *bibliothèque française*, and his plan for a new French dictionary (RC in DLC; in a clerk's hand on printed letterhead, signed by Pougens; endorsed by TJ: "Pougens to Genl. Kosciuzko"; enclosures not found).

HIS DESIRES: for Pougens's ambition to supply books to libraries in the United States, see Vol. 30:481, 482n.

From Isaac Story

MOST RESPECTED SIRE,   Marblehead July 28. 1802.

I am as fluent, & ready at language, as any of my Neighbors; but at present I am at a loss in what manner to express the gratitude, with which my breast is filled, for your great kindness & condescension towards me. You have conferred a piece of undeserved honor upon me, by granting me a Commission simply upon my own application, without being accompanied with any recommendatory Letters. I feel myself entirely devoted to you, & have the vanity to think, that you will not have a more faithful servant in all the united States.

I was brought up from a child in the paths of integrity & virtue, & my Conscience bears witness, that I have never swerved therefrom.—

I shall endeavor to defend & establish your Character, support your interest & honor at all times, & in all places and in all possible ways exhibit specimens of my gratitude.

accept the homage of my most profound respects

ISAAC STORY

P.S. Were I not affraid of taking advantage of your indulgence, I could express a wish, that in case Mr. Otis, or any other Gentleman in Boston should decline a Commission of Bankruptcy, the vacancy might be left open to give me an opportunity of returning to Boston, the place of my nativity, & where four of my children are settled

RC (DNA: RG 59, LAR); endorsed by TJ as received 5 Aug. and so recorded in SJL.

MY OWN APPLICATION: in his 8 May 1802 letter to TJ, Story had requested an appointment as a bankruptcy commissioner. TJ granted him a commission on 8 July (Vol. 37: Appendix II, List 2).

Chiles Terrell's Nailery Account

Mr Chiles Terrell   An Account with Ths. Jefferson: Cr
1802

June 22d—	42. ℔	VI d nails:	@ 12¼d	£ 2- 3- 9
	20.	X d Do.	@ 11½d	0-19- 2
	20.	XX d. Do.	@ 10 […]	0-[17]-6
July 22d.	7.	VI d.—Do.	@ 12½	0- 7- 3½
	20.	IV d. Do	@ 15 d	1- 5-
	1.	Cut Sprigs	@ 11 d.	0- 1- 3
				£ 5-13-11½

28th   13. ℔ X d nails   @ 11½   0-12- 5½
                                                       6- 5- 7[1]
                              old balance   - 1- 6
                                                    £ 6- 7- 1

Received the Above for Thomas Jefferson   JAS. DINSMORE

MS (ViU: Watson Papers); blurred; in James Dinsmore's hand; endorsed by Dinsmore: "a/c of Nails Chiles Terrell with Jefferson."

From a prominent Albemarle County family, Chiles Terrell married Margaret Douglas Meriwether, widow of Nicholas Meriwether, and settled on part of the Meriwether grant, about 10 miles northeast of Monticello. There he established an estate that came to be known as Music Hall (Edward C. Mead, *Historic Homes of the South-West Mountains Virginia* [Philadelphia, 1899], 153-4; Woods, *Albemarle*, 326; MB, 2:972).

For Dinsmore's management of the nailery, see Vol. 34:407.

[1] That is, 5, making Dinsmore's subsequent calculation off by two pence.

From William Thornton

SIR   Washington 28th: July 1802—

The Secretary of State received the enclosed this morng. which he desired me to forward to the President.—

I found on my arrival at Mount Vernon, that I was precluded from the pleasure I anticipated in purchasing for you the Terrestrial Globe, which formerly belonged to General Washington; & which you wished to possess, as a Relick.—It was considered as belonging to the Library, &, consequently, the Property of Judge Washington, but the Legatees made him pay dearly for another Globe, which he considered himself in Duty bound not to part with. I mean the Head of the Testator; & this, after I had informed them, that as many Heads of him as there were Heads in the Army he commanded could be had for two or three Guineas each. The Judge did not know this, but declared he would give what any other Gentleman would give. Upon this a young man was advised (as I heard him afterwards acknowledge) to bid 250 Dollars, and the Judge was accordingly obliged to give that Sum.—I was sorry that the Heirs of such a man should have acted so unworthily—But it was unknown to some of them. The Legatees then retired to a chamber & *cast Lots for his Garments*! There was something in the whole Scene, & in the general Proceedings that shocked me. But it was a Scene, which, although devoid of feeling, *was not without Interest.—*

Accept, Sir, my sincerest good wishes & highest Consideration.—

WILLIAM THORNTON

[137]

RC (DLC); at foot of text: "President of the United States"; endorsed by TJ as received 31 July and so recorded in SJL. Enclosure not identified.

Martha Washington's will, probated on 21 June 1802, a month after her death, stipulated that the contents of her estate, with the exception of a few specific bequests, should be sold as soon after her death as possible. The executors advertised a public sale to be held at MOUNT VERNON beginning on 20 July (John C. Fitzpatrick, ed., *The Last Will and Testament of George Washington and Schedule of his Property* [n.p., 1960], 59, 62; *Washington Federalist*, 2 July 1802).

TERRESTRIAL GLOBE: George Washington purchased several globes over the course of his life (Washington, *Papers, Pres. Ser.*, 3:479; 4:149-50; Eugene E. Prussing, *The Estate of George Washington, Deceased* [Boston, 1927], 416-17, 433).

JUDGE WASHINGTON: the first president bequeathed his library and papers to his nephew, Bushrod Washington, one of his executors as well as an associate justice of the Supreme Court. Upon Martha Washington's death, Mount Vernon, which he had left to her in a life tenancy, became part of this nephew's legacy (Fitzpatrick, ed., *Last Will and Testament of George Washington*, xiii, 1, 14, 19).

George Washington's LEGATEES, some of whom were direct descendants of the Custis family and others who were Washington relations, continued to dispute possession of the general's personal effects and whether they belonged with the house inheritance or were free to be sold at auction. Samuel L. Mitchill reported that Washington had not disposed of his clothing by will so the twenty-three "Claimants parcelled out his Wardrobe into as many Bundles, and then drew lots for the Choice!" (Samuel L. Mitchill to Catharine Mitchill, 22 Dec. 1802 in NNMus).

CAST LOTS FOR HIS GARMENTS: for the allusion to Roman soldiers vying for Jesus's clothing at the time of his crucifixion, see John 19:23-4.

From Henry Dearborn

SIR   Washington July 29th: 1802

I have the honour of enclosing a letter from Govr. Harrison, and one which accompanied it, by which it appears that measures have been taken by the british traders or others, for the purpose of inducing the Indians generally, to suspect the sincerity and good faith of Our Government, and for encouraging a hostile disposition towards this country, but in general, there is but little confidence to be placed in stories which are in circulation among the indians.—Govr. Harrison had not received my letters, which when received will satisfy all his queries & authorise him to take all necessary measures relative to boundaries, as well as for holding a conference with the Chiefs of the several Nations on whatever subjects may be proper to discuss.—I shall write him by the next post, requesting him to make every exartion in his power for convincing the Indians, of the real friendly dispositions of Our Government towards them, and for removing the impressions which may have been made by the falshoods & misrepresentation, put in circulation among them,—and in the mean time, to ascertain by every means in his power, the origin & progress of the stories refered to in his letter, together with the extent of any defection which may appear to have taken place with any of the Indian Nations, and their ultimate views & intentions. I also enclose a scetch or copy of the Treaty concluded on, with the Creeks, the Treaty in form, has not yet arrived.

with the most respectfull concideration I am Sir Your Humbe. Servt.—   H. DEARBORN

RC (DLC); at foot of text: "The President of the United States"; endorsed by TJ as received 31 July from the War Department and so recorded in SJL. Enclosures not found.

According to Dearborn's reply to it, the LETTER from William Henry HARRISON, the governor of Indiana Territory, concerned "the apparent hostile disposition of the Indians, and the falshoods and misrepresentations which have been put in circulation" among them. One of those false reports was "respecting sales of land made by Little Turtle" (Dearborn to Harrison, 29 July, in DNA: RG 75, LSIA). The correspondence from Dearborn that Harrison had NOT RECEIVED yet included three detailed letters dated 17 June, a briefer communication of the 18th, and another letter on 3 July. In one of the letters of the 17th, Dearborn, who had consulted with the attorney general, asked Harrison "to exert every means in your power" to apprehend fugitives charged with murdering Indians. Another letter of that date empowered Harrison to complete the laying out of two tracts that were ceded to the United States by the 1795 treaty of Greenville. Little Turtle and "two or three other Chiefs should be present and be consulted on the manner of fixing the boundaries." Dearborn instructed Harrison to ensure that the tracts included navigable portions of the Miami and Wabash rivers, a mill seat, and "as large a share of the most valuable lands for cultivation as circumstances will admit." Harrison's role as agent of the United States in this transaction was, Dearborn indicated, at the request of

the president. In the third letter of the 17th, Dearborn requested that Harrison "sound the Piankishaws, and Kickapoos on the subject of their sale to the company (usually styled the Illinois and Wabash company) in the year 1795, and to know whether they consider that sale as valid," as well as "whether they would consent to the United States' assuming the right, which by their sale they intended to vest in the company on receiving an adequate compensation." If the Indians were not inclined to agree to the latter provision, Harrison should "explain to them the limits of the Territory granted by them to the French Government at Vincennes" and take steps to have that tract surveyed for the United States, ensuring that the tract was as large as the terms of the cession from the Indians to the French would allow. Should evidence indicate that some Delaware Indians had occupied a part of that land at the time the cession was made to the French, then "we might from motives of humanity allow them to remain in possession on condition of Good behaviour." Dearborn deemed it "very desirable" that the government acquire sole rights to a tract on the Ohio and Mississippi rivers between the mouth of the Wabash and the lower Kaskaskias settlements. "Further information will be necessary," Dearborn added, "relative to the extent of the claims of the White Inhabitants at the mouth of the Illinois and Kaskaskias." Dearborn's note of the 18th set Harrison's compensation as agent of the U.S. at three dollars a day plus expenses. On 3 July, responding to four letters from Harrison received on 24 June, Dearborn urged him, at the president's request, to continue to try to apprehend people accused of the murder of Indians, to furnish information regarding the potential lease of a salt spring on Native American land that Dearborn had written to Harrison about in February, to arrange for presents for chiefs with whom Harrison expected to negotiate in August, and to try to induce the Piankashaws, the Kickapoos, and the Kaskaskias to contribute portions of their annuities to make up, with U.S. funds as necessary, a $500 annuity for the Sac Indians. Dearborn also acknowledged Harrison's appointment of Benjamin Parke as an agent to investigate threats to the Kaskaskia Indians from some of the Potawatomi tribe (Dearborn to Harrison, 17, 18 June, 3 July, in DNA: RG 75, LSIA; Harrison to Dearborn, 26 Feb., 27 May, 1, 3 June, recorded in DNA: RG 107, RLRMS; *Terr. Papers*, 7:53-6; Owens, *Jefferson's Hammer*, 62-3, 71, 80, 93, 262-3n; Vol. 36:525n).

I SHALL WRITE HIM: on 29 July, Dearborn wrote Harrison that there "can be no doubt but some evil minded person or persons have been attempting to deceive and mislead the Indians by fals representations relative to the views and intentions of our Government towards them." The letters that Dearborn had already sent would give Harrison "full information" upon which to act, and "every exertion in your power should be made to counteract the views and intentions of those who have been endeavouring to encourage hostile dispositions among the Indians, by the most explicit assurances of the real friendship and good will of the Government towards the Indian Nations generally, within the jurisdiction of the U. States." Harrison should attempt to trace the origins of the rumors that had made the Indians uneasy. The report of land sales by Little Turtle "is without the least foundation; there has been no such thing in contemplation, nor any proposition made on the part of Government or by the Little Turtle or any other Person for purchasing any land in that Quarter." The government, Dearborn noted, was establishing trading houses at Detroit and Fort Wayne, was "disposed to afford the Indians every aid in its power," and was ready "to consider them as friends and Brothers." Should all measures "for cultivating friendship and harmony with our Indian neighbours" prove fruitless, however—if "a few artful and designing men" subverted the government's intentions "and the Indians are to be made the dupes of their wicked and mischevious Acts," with war as the result—then "the Indians must not in future expect any favour from the U. States" (DNA: RG 75, LSIA).

SCETCH OR COPY OF THE TREATY: on 16 July, Dearborn received a letter dated 17 June from James Wilkinson, Benjamin Hawkins, and Andrew Pickens, who wrote from near the Oconee River to announce that on the previous day they had concluded a treaty with the Creek Indians. The agreement, which involved the purchase by the United States of a large tract of land, was intended to resolve a claim by the state of Georgia for territory ceded to the Creeks by an earlier treaty. The commissioners informed the secretary of war that they would send the signed treaty and details of the negotiation to Washington. TJ submitted the treaty to the Senate for ratification in December (ASP, *Indian Affairs*, 1:668-9, 680; DNA: RG 107, RLRMS; Vol. 36:191-2n).

To John Barnes

DEAR SIR   Monticello July 30. 1802.

Mr. Smith has sent under cover to me the inclosed post-note for three hundred & sixty dollars, Genl. Kosciusko's dividend, which, as I have no account opened with him, I inclose you. mr Jefferson writes me he has received Canal dividend for mr Short 198. D. which he credits you for. should you want it you will of course draw for it, otherwise it is not improbable I may have occasion for some money in Richmond before I leave this.—I arrived here without accident on the 25th. my groceries have arrived at Richmond, but not yet here. I will thank you to send off the box left at Washington by the first possible conveyance, as it's contents are considerably wanted. Accept assurances of my affectionate esteem.   TH: JEFFERSON

PrC (CSmH); at foot of text: "Mr. Barnes"; endorsed by TJ in ink on verso. Enclosure: for the "post-note," see Jonathan Smith to TJ, 20 July.

From John Barnes

SIR   George Town—30th. July 1802—

Messrs. G & J., acknowledges recpt of $198 on Mr Short a/c, Canal Co. a/c as well $200. I remitted them on your a/c: Mrs Jackson also. for—[...]0 & $45. which closes Doct Wardlaw's a/c with her late Husband, except £2.1.5. for Int: expresses Her Thanks to Doct Wardlaw for his punctuality &c. your Case of Window Blinds & Books &c. with a Box, with me, Containing 1 doz & 3 bottles Claret. are waiting a conveyance from hence—or Alexandria to Richd.

all is peaceable, at Washington—but not so it seems at New York. see yesterdays Federalist: Brutus No. 3. so full, of pointed Declamation. I cannot forbear noticing—that part, respecting G.C—I am inclined to suspect—its fabrication—is from a quarter directly opposed, to that, which he professes to support: or rather, to mislead the public opinion in general—to disunite the Real friends—(not the B—s)—of Goverment—to divert if possible, the pointed shafts—lately published—against the many and most extrm descriptions long since premeditated & still practiced—against the real Welfare, peace & happiness of the Union—Still—I *trust* & *Hope*, G.C. is not the Character therein described,—to me, it appears, to be impossible?—

I am but a Novice in Political Matters—Still, I may presume to pass, my private Opinion on Certain Characters—If not from real experiences—my feelings force me, to conclude—they are not* Worthy of Confidence—it is indeed a Melancholy picture of Human Weaknesses—

* I wish not to be Understood—that I know, of any Person in your Confidence—*unworthy of it*—for if I did—I should most assuredly, make you fully acquainted therewith.

In case I should be absent from hence from the Middle to last of Augt.—pray recollect, if any thing needful to be done here, in Course of a fortnight—mean while I shall do myself the Honr. to transmit you your July a/c—

I am Sir, most Respectfully—Your Obedt: & very hb Servt:

JOHN BARNES

RC (ViU: Edgehill-Randolph Papers); addressed: "The President U States at Monticello—Virginia"; franked; postmarked 3 Aug.; endorsed by TJ as received 5 Aug. and so recorded in SJL.

G & J: Gibson & Jefferson.

For William WARDLAW'S account with the late Dr. David Jackson and his widow, Susanna Jackson, see TJ to Wardlaw, 11 June 1802. On 20 July, TJ ordered Barnes to pay Mrs. Jackson $45 on Wardlaw's account (MB, 2:1078).

YESTERDAYS FEDERALIST: the 28 July edition of the *Washington Federalist* included "Extracts from Brutus, No. 3," which were taken from the third in a series of letters favorable to Aaron Burr and his faction that appeared in the New York *Daily Advertiser*, a Federalist newspaper. In his third letter, "Brutus" warned TJ of the "treachery of the fawning foes that surround him," who were Republicans from selfish motives only. This was most evident in New York, claimed the author, where TJ had unknowingly confided in men "who, until his elevation to the presidential chair, have uniformly been his enemies." Most notorious among these was Governor George Clinton, who, according to "Brutus," previously considered TJ "a nerveless political trimmer, unfit for the office they intended him, incompetent totally to the discharge of its numerous and important duties" (Kline, *Burr*, 2:726-7).

THE B—S: the Burrites.

From John Redman Coxe

DEAR SIR/   Philada. July 30th 1802

I take the liberty of forwarding to you a Copy of my treatise on Vaccination, which, with many thanks for your very polite attention to my repeated requests, I beg your acceptance of; I sincerely wish it were more worthy of your notice; yet doubtless, though it contains many errors, I hope it may serve as a Pioneer in opening the Way for more valuable communications from our own Countrymen.

With sincere wishes for your health & prosperity—I am, Dear Sir Yrs. respectfully   JOHN REDMAN COXE

RC (DLC); at foot of text: "His Exy. Ths. Jefferson"; endorsed by TJ as received 5 Aug. and so recorded in SJL. Enclosure: Coxe, *Practical Observations on Vaccination: or Inoculation for the Cow-Pock* (Philadelphia, 1802; Sowerby, No. 953).

From Elijah Griffiths

DEAR SIR,   Philadelphia July 30—1802

Mr William Dewees, a practitioner at our Bar, has been advised by his friends to apply for the appointment of Commissioner of Bankruptcy. I have long known this gentleman; his principles & practice has been in unison with the friends of Elective Goverment; his connections are respectable; & his character as a professional man, Stands unimpeached.

Should Mr Dewees be approved of, it will gratify a number of your friends here, who are satisfied the trust will be discharged with ability & integrity; it will be particularly pleasing to the citizens of the county of Philadelphia, where he proposes to reside; & I take the liberty of adding, it will very much oblige your friend & Huml. Sert.

                                                         E. GRIFFITHS

RC (DNA: RG 59, LAR); at foot of text: "Thomas Jefferson Esqr. President of the United States"; endorsed by TJ as received 5 Aug. and "Dewees Wm. to be Commr. bkrptcy" and so recorded in SJL.

TJ saw two other recommendations in favor of WILLIAM DEWEES, a member of the Philadelphia bar since 1799 (John H. Martin, *Martin's Bench and Bar of Philadelphia* [Philadelphia, 1883], 263). Benjamin R. Morgan wrote Madison on 29 July, noting that the Dewees family had "long been establish'd" in Philadelphia and that Dewees, a reputable attorney, was moving to the county of Philadelphia, where the late John W. Vancleve had resided (RC in DNA: RG 59, LAR; endorsed by TJ: "Dewees Wm. to be Commr. bkrptcy"). In a letter to Madison, dated 16 Aug., John Dawson recommended Dewees as "a gentleman of character and of reputation in his profession as a lawyer" (RC in same; endorsed by TJ: "Dewees Wm. to be Commr. bankrupts vice Vancleve").

To James Madison

DEAR SIR   Monticello July 30. 1802.

Your's of July 22. came to hand on the 25th. the day of my arrival here. I think the proposition to tender another 30,000. D. to Algiers a very judicious one, and have therefore written to mr Gallatin to take measures in conjunction with yourself to make the remittance by the General Greene. I have not yet written to the emperor of Marocco; because when one has nothing to write about it is difficult to find the end to begin at. I will sketch something before next post, and inclose it for your alteration with a blank sheet signed, over which they may write the letter.

You are now I presume in the middle of your journey & must have had a good deal of rain. this will be directed to await in Orange for your return. present me respectfully to the ladies, & be assured of my affectionate esteem.   TH: JEFFERSON

P.S. not knowing whether the inclosed letters have past through your hands I forward them to you instead of returning them to the office from whence I recieved them.

RC (DNA: RG 59, MLR); at foot of text: "The Secretary of State." PrC (DLC). Enclosures not identified.

WRITTEN TO MR GALLATIN: TJ to Gallatin, 28 July.

From James Madison

DEAR SIR   Washington July 30. 1802

I inclose several letters for you put into my hands by Mr. Pichon, with some communications of his own, which are proper to be forwarded along with them. I inclose also a letter from Mr Jones at Gaudaloupe, and two others declining commissions of Bankruptcy.

My departure from this place, suspended for a day by preparations for the Mediterranean business stated in my last, has since been prevented by the lameness of a horse which obliges me to leave him behind & to purchase another. Having been thus long detained, & understanding that Mr Gallatin will be here to night or tomorrow, I am induced to submit to a little further delay for the chance of seeing him. By sunday at farthest I hope to be on the road, and in about 10 days from that date to be at home.

Nothing has occurred at this place since you left it which deserves mention.

With the most respectful attachment I remain yours

JAMES MADISON

RC (DLC); at foot of text: "The President of the U. States"; endorsed by TJ as received 31 July from the State Department and so recorded in SJL. Enclosures: (1) Louis André Pichon to Madison, 28 July, acknowledging receipt of news of the case of the *Peggy* and regretting the delay in TJ's decision, which seemed contrary to earlier U.S. restitution cases; also promising to rectify the mistake in the minister of marine's instructions on precautions against yellow fever (Madison, *Papers, Sec. of State Ser.*, 3:437-8). (2) Pichon to Madison, 28 July, enclosing a letter from the French foreign minister Talleyrand to Pichon, 26 Mch., announcing the signing of the definitive peace treaty between Great Britain and France and sending a copy of the treaty to be shared with TJ (same, 3:438). (3) Pichon to Madison, 29 July, enclosing letters for TJ from the Institut National de France and an extract of a dispatch from Pichon to Talleyrand, 18 July, on the workings of the United States press, to be shown to the president (same,

3:439-40). (4) Edward Jones to Madison, 8 July, forwarding his dispatch of 10 May; he reports the lifting of the nearly 30-day prohibition on the export of all produce, excepting rum and molasses; all exports are now allowed upon the payment of designated duties; necessary provisions and lumber may be imported duty free; in a month, Jones anticipates returning to the U.S. from Guadeloupe, recently "restored to perfect tranquility" (same, 3:389). For other enclosures, see below.

TWO OTHERS DECLINING COMMISSIONS OF BANKRUPTCY: possibly two letters written from Norfolk to Madison both acknowledging the secretary of state's 12 July letters enclosing commissions for the district of Virginia. On 22 July, Littleton Tazewell informed Madison that he considered the duties of the office "incompatible with other avocations more important to myself" (RC in DNA: RG 59, RD; endorsed by TJ: "Tazewell Littleton to mr Madison declines commr. bkrptcy"). Moses Myers also wrote to Madison on 26 July, declining his commission and claiming he was "not well calculated to fulfill the duties" of the appointment (RC in DNA: RG 59, LAR; endorsed by TJ: "Myers Moses. Norfolk to mr Madison declines Commr. bkrptcy").

From Henry Dearborn

SIR   Washington July 31t, 1802

I herewith enclose a letter from Mr. Crowninshield of Salem Massachusetts, by which it appears that a mistake has been made in the appointment of Isaac Storey, if the Son could be appointed, it would cure the evil, and in addition to Dane & Burley, would be sufficient for all the business in that quarter, I have shewn this letter to Mr. Madison, & he advised me to write to you on the subject and to propose the immediate appointment of Joseph Story.

with sentiments of respect I am Sir Your Huml Servt

H. DEARBORN

RC (DLC); at foot of text: "The President of the United State"; endorsed by TJ as received from the War Department on 5 Aug. and so recorded in SJL. Enclosure not found.

From Henry Dearborn

SIR   Washington July 31st, 1802

I herewith enclose Genl. Sumter and Col Senfs. letters on the subject of the proposed establishment of an Arsenal & Armoury.—it may be adviseable to make the purchase of a suitable quantity of land as soon as may be,—as a considerable quantity of wood will be necessary for the annual consumption of the works & workmen, and the having a command of timber and other materials for building, would be a desirable object, I take the liberty of suggesting the propriety of making a purchase of the tract mentioned by Genl. Sumpter containing from three, to five hundred Acres at six dollars pr. acre;—the difference between Col Senfs & Genl. Sumpters statements relative to the probable price of the land, is not easy for me to account for, but I presume that Sumpter must be considered as possessing the best information on that part of the business;—in the act entitled an Act for the erecting & repairing of Arsenals & Magazines & for other purposes, pass'd on the second of April 1794, it is among other things enacted, that none of the said Arsenals be erected until purchase of the land necessary for their accommodation be made, with the consent of the Legislature of the State in which the same is intended to be erected.—the resolution of the Legislature of the State of South Carolina, on the subject is herewith enclosed,—there can be no doubt as to the authority for making the necessary purchase,—what quantity of land shall be purchased seems to be the only question necessary to decide at present. when the establishment was contemplated at Harpers ferry, a considerable tract of land appears to have been thought necessary and was accordingly purchased.

with the most respectfull consideration I am Sir Your Huml Sevt.

H. DEARBORN

RC (DLC); addressed: "The President of the United States"; endorsed by TJ as received from the War Department on 5 Aug. and so recorded in SJL. Enclosure: Copy of "An Act to Enable the United States to Purchase a Quantity of Land, in this State, Not Exceeding Two Thousand Acres, for Arsenals and Magazines," passed by the South Carolina General Assembly on 12 Dec. 1795 (*Acts and Resolutions of the General Assembly, of the State of South-Carolina, From December, 1795, to December, 1797, Inclusive* [Charleston, 1798], 9-10). Other enclosures not found.

ESTABLISHMENT OF AN ARSENAL & ARMOURY: plans for a federal arsenal and armory in the southern states had been under consideration since the 1790s. At Dearborn's urging, TJ had reintroduced the topic in his message to Congress of 2 Feb. 1802. The preferred location was at Rocky Mount, on the Catawba River in South Carolina, a site first recommended by George Washington in 1798. Writing to Senator Thomas Sumter on 5 June 1802, Dearborn informed him that it was "the intention of the President" to commence work at Rocky Mount, and requested that Sumter and state engineer John Christian Senf select the site and purchase the land and water rights necessary for the establishment. After TJ approved their recommendations, Dearborn informed Sumter on 9 Aug. that the president favored his proposal to acquire a 300 to 500 acre tract, and requested Sumter to make the purchase and have a survey made. Later renamed Mount Dearborn, the Rocky Mount location proved to be a poor choice. The federal arsenal would be plagued by years of delay and controversy before finally being abandoned and retroceded to the state in the 1820s (Arthur P. Wade, "Mount Dearborn: The National Armory at Rocky Mount, South Carolina, 1802-1829," *South Carolina Historical Magazine*, 81 [1980], 207-31, 316-41; Dearborn to Sumter, 5 June, 9 Aug. 1802 in DNA: RG 107, MLS; Vol. 36:125, 499; TJ to Dearborn, 6 Aug. 1802).

ACT FOR THE ERECTING & REPAIRING OF ARSENALS & MAGAZINES: see U.S. Statutes at Large, 1:352. The act authorized the president to establish three or four "arsenals with magazines" at such locations "as will best accomodate the different parts of the United States."

From Joseph Marie Lequinio de Kerblay

SIR   Newport le 31 July an 1802

On my return from Boston I find the most agreable favour of yours of july 15, entirely full of the very generous expressions in my respect.

had my mind and my heart power enough to reacting in any extensive way upon american and french countries, certainly the friendship's sacred ties contracted between them from your election at presidency should be more and more strained, and never Broken; my such wishing, as sincere as steady, is only my might in that matter. — But your high wisdom, skill, philosophical tinking, and particular Confidence that you have so rightly conquered from the american people, with french government's and first Consul's endeavours will make, I hope, ours Both Nations long time friends and in this point hapy. theze my thougts, I pray, please you admitt for well ascertained et the most delightful my heart's feelings; and be sure of my taking whatever opportunity that can be offered to prove its, and justify as well as I may your good opinion in what does concern me.

you are good enough, Sir, as to mention me pleasure of yours *when I may wish to make a visit to your place*; viz. Washington town; so particular and well situated a city that can't increase but beautiful, and by the single strenth of straitly united states must rapidly grow populous and stately, Deserve, no Doubt, visit of any curious and well tasted man to be payed to; but, (let your modest behaviour pardonn me) I am much more desirous to see and admire nearly a great Man whose unknown desinterested Wisdom make hapy so meny people in new World, as his skilful pen has, mani years ago, illustrated his Country in the Old; wishing such enjoyement I dare expect it from time and some, unforeseen, but very Blessed Circumstance. —

more and more you do keep your generous behaviour in telling, you *are glad to find I have made proficiency in your language.* — Such proficiencies, Sir, are very little; but getting, of Course, your words for an encouragement, I have taken the boldness of writing in

English; please your Bounty yeld my endeavours the requisite indulgence properly undeserved by my ill, uncorrect, and uncorrected
writing.—

two weeks ago the Captain Eveleth, from alexandria, then here, returned to, by the *mont-hope ship* Bounded for that your neighbouring
city; I Committed him a packet directed to you containing two Volumes work[1] of mine, *voyage dans le jura.* the said captain promised
me to get it rendered to you, as well as to Mr: Bushord Washington
at Westmoreland in state of virginia, another packet that I have
afford from the general lafayette; but on my return from Boston, I
have found the two packets remained back, and likely forgotten in the
tavern what was the said Captain living in Before sailing.—such mis-
adventure disapointed me much more for sake of the general lafayette
packet's than for the another. it should indeed have Been, very little
loss for you, and perhaps usefulness for me, to have not sent it.—nevertheless, Sir, Better informed in post office of your enjoying freedom
from taxe for whatever packets, I have Committed to the mail, as they
were, my two volumes, which I pray you to receive with your usual
goodness.—

on the another packet's account, in first time I did not dare to take
the same liberty; but now reflecting upon your great acquaintance
and friendship with general la fayette, and on the great difficulty to
find another opportunity to send it at it's Direction, I Determine to
Committ it to the mail in the same manner, under your adress. I Beg
pardon for that Boldness, and to first reason for my excuse, I Do add
the extremely inciting Civilities of your letter, an argument to which
you do not have Answer.

Be your excellence pleased, Sir, to accept of my humble, sincere an
hearty respects.— LEQUINIO KERBLAY

RC (MoSHi: Jefferson Papers); on
same letterhead stationery as Lequinio de
Kerblay's letter of 15 July; at head of text:
"to his Excellency Mr. th. jefferson president of the united states of america"; endorsed by TJ as received 12 Aug. and so
recorded in SJL.

COMMITTED HIM A PACKET: see
Lequinio de Kerblay to TJ, 15 July. For
the packet for Bushrod Washington from
LAFAYETTE, see TJ to Washington, 13
Aug.

[1] MS: "wok."

From Lucy Ludwell Paradise

DEAR SIR July: 31st. 1802

I take the liberty to trouble your Excellency with a few lines to
enquire after the health of your Excellency and Amiable Daughters.

It is by writing only that we can know if our friends are well and happy. Mr William Smith who was our Minister at Portugal came here a few Months and stayed a short time and I am told he is gone to Holland.

The Russian Ambassador his Excellency Count de Woronzow and the Revd. Mr Smirnove Chaplin of Legation who I think your Excellency remembers have behaved to Me ever Since I have been a Widow with the greatest attention and politeness. I wish My Relations and My Country Men would do the Same and Protect Me now and years to Come. I have nothing to live upon in this Country but my Income from my dear fathers Estates he left in Virginia. A Short letter from your Excellency desiring My Nephew William Ludwell Lee Esqr and Mr Ambler and Mr P Harris to exert themselves to fix me in a good Steward who would follow my orders and Send Me My Remittances and Tobaccoes regularly during My life. *This indeed would be the Greatest favour Your Excellency* could confer upon[1] Me who am

With the Greatest Respect Your Excellencies Most Obedient Humble Servant and Respectful Friend

LUCY LUDWELL PARADISE

My direction is Mrs. Lucy Ludwell Paradise No 29 Howland Street Fitzroy Square London It will confer an honour upon me by sending me an Answer[2]

RC (MHi); at foot of text: "His Excellency Thoms Jefferson Presedend of the United States of North America"; endorsed by TJ as received 17 Nov. and so recorded in SJL.

Upon release from his diplomatic duties in Portugal in 1801, WILLIAM SMITH and his brother traveled throughout western Europe, spending the spring of 1802 in London. In July, the brothers traveled to Holland together but parted company in Amsterdam (George C. Rogers, Jr., *Evolution of a Federalist: William Loughton Smith of Charleston (1758-1812)* [Columbia, S.C., 1962], 337, 339, 340).

Semyon Romanovich WORONZOW, the younger brother of Princess Ekaterina Romanovna Dashkova, was Russian minister at London for 16 years prior to becoming ambassador in 1801. A promoter of amicable Anglo-Russian ties through-out his long service in London, Woronzow arranged that Lucy Paradise's husband, John Paradise, receive a pension from Catherine II for his efforts to prevent England from declaring war on Russia in support of Turkey in 1791 (Nina N. Bashkina and others, eds., *The United States and Russia: The Beginning of Relations, 1765-1815* [Washington, D.C., 1980], 1136, 1139; Gleb Struve, "John Paradise—Friend of Doctor Johnson, American Citizen and Russian Agent," VMHB, 57 [1949], 362-4, 367, 372).

In 1780, Yakov Smirnov (SMIRNOVE) came to London, where he resided for the next 60 years, serving as chaplain of the Russian Embassy Church until 1837 and occasionally filling a diplomatic role. Lucy Paradise referred to him as her "priest" and she and her husband, who was born into the Greek Orthodox Church, regularly attended the legation chapel where he officiated. John Paradise left Smirnov a bequest of £100 (A. G. Cross, "Yakov Smirnov: A Russian Priest of Many Parts," *Oxford Slavonic Papers*, new ser., 8 [1975], 37, 41; Archibald Bolling Shepperson, *John Paradise and Lucy Ludwell of London and Williamsburg* [Richmond, 1942], 438; VMHB, 57 [1949], 363, 364-5, 367; Lucy Ludwell Paradise to TJ, 27 Aug. 1805).

MY DEAR FATHERS ESTATES: Philip Ludwell III of Green Spring, near Williamsburg, left his estates to be divided equally among his three daughters upon his death in 1767 (Shepperson, *John Paradise and Lucy Ludwell*, 33-5).

WILLIAM LUDWELL LEE appointed William Coleman as new STEWARD for his aunt after the death of William Wilkinson in 1800 (Vol. 32:238, 526).

¹ MS: "up."
² Written at head of text.

To Daniel Brent

Monticello Aug 1. 1802.

Th: Jefferson returns the inclosed commission, with his signature, to the Secretary of state's office. he presumes it is to be delivered to mr Gallatin. a commission is wanting for John Selman of the North Western territory, as Commissioner on the subject of Symmes's lands in the room of Goforth resigned.—he begs leave to observe too that mr Scott's commission as Marshal of Virginia, signed July 8. but dated July 1. had not been received by him on the 26th. of July and that the business of the office is at a stand

RC (DNA: RG 59, MLR); addressed: "The Chief clerk of the Secretary of state's office Washington"; franked; postmarked Milton, 6 Aug.; endorsed by Brent as received 9 Aug. PrC (DLC). Enclosure not found.

To Henry Dearborn

DEAR SIR   Monticello Aug. 1. 1802.

Your favor of the 29th. came to hand yesterday, and I now return the papers it inclosed. I am in hopes the measures you have taken will enable Govr. Harrison to satisfy the Indians. I believe there is nothing new in the present circulation of lies among them. I have always understood that they are peculiarly inundated with lies at all times. that vice is practised pretty freely by themselves; but the traders and other whites among them use lies as the ordinary machinery for bending them to their purposes.

I inclose you another commission from Alexandria. whether these resignations (of which I have before sent you several) [are] from federalists chiefly or schismatic republicans I know not. they shew that there is more passion than patriotism on that side of the river. if you will be so good as to enquire for the best substitutes & send me commissions for them they shall be signed. Accept assurances of my sincere & respectful attachment　　　　　Th: Jefferson

P.S. [it would] be well to know beforehand whether the individuals will accept commissions. this I think a good rule in gen[eral cas]es.

PrC (DLC); faint; at foot of text: "The Secretary at War." Enclosures not found, but see below.

Between 20 July and 5 Aug. 1802, TJ recorded in SJL the receipt of at least nine RESIGNATIONS from officers in the District of Columbia militia, none of which have been found. These include George Wise, Charles McKnight, Alexander Kerr, Josiah Faxon, John Johnston, John Stewart, Ferdinand Marsteller, Thomas Addison, and Robert Stewart (see Appendix IV). For a list of militia officers appointed by TJ, see the Alexandria *Times; and District of Columbia Daily Advertiser*, 20 July and the Georgetown *Olio*, 22 July.

From William Jones

Dear Sir　　　　　　　　　　　　Philada. 1st. Augt. 1802

I would reluctantly intrude upon your attention and particularly on the subject of appointments, aware that the numerous applications and recommendations may have a tendency rather to embarrass than lead to a correct choice. I hope however the liberty I have occasionally taken may be viewed with indulgence.

I beg leave Sir on this occasion to recommend to your notice Mr Robert Porter of this City as a suitable person to fill the vacancy occasioned by the death of Jno W Vancleve Esqr. one of the Commissioners of Bankruptcy.

Mr Porter is a member of our State legislature and of the Bar of this State, was a revolutionary officer and is the son of General Andrew Porter who was also a meritorious revolutionary officer and they have both faithfully adhered to the principles thereby established.

I am Sir with the highest regard yours most respectfully

Wm Jones

RC (DNA: RG 59, LAR); at foot of text: "The President of the United States"; endorsed by TJ as received 8 Aug. and "Porter to be Commr. bkrptcy" and so recorded in SJL.

To Joseph Scott

SIR   Monticello Aug. 1. 1802

I learn with great surprise by a letter of the 26th of July from the Governor, that your commission as Marshal of Virginia was not recieved at that date. it was signed by me on the 8th. of July, is recorded in the Secretary of state's office, and I presume was forwarded immediately. the members of the administration did not yield to the opinion that your powers in the Eastern district were suspended by the new law. on an examination of that we were clearly of opinion it had only left it to the Executive to discontinue according to the power they would have had without the law. in the present case however I pray you so far to give credence to this letter as to act under the assurance that you are legally marshal of the state under a commission recorded. you can qualify without producing the commission, but I have this day written to the Chief clerk of the Secretary of state's office to have the transmission of the original commission enquired into & supplied if it has failed. I pray you to accept my respects & best wishes   TH: JEFFERSON

PrC (DLC); at foot of text: "Joseph Scott. esq."; endorsed by TJ in ink on verso.

Joseph Scott (1743-1810), a resident of Amelia County, Virginia, enlisted as a second lieutenant in the 1st Virginia Regiment of Foot in September 1775. Promoted to captain two years later, he was injured and captured by the British at the Battle of Germantown in October 1777. He was later released on parole and served in the Continental Army through the end of the war, mustering out as a brevet major. He returned to Amelia County and attracted many well-placed friends with what an unusually fulsome obituary described as a "hospitable and generous" character and a willingness to do "not only what justice, but the most delicate sense of honor required." Scott was confirmed by the Senate to a permanent commission as marshal of the district of Virginia in January 1803 and remained in the position until his death (Richmond *Enquirer*, 8 Dec. 1810; Heitman, *Register*, 486; M. Lee Minnis, *The First Virginia Regiment of Foot, 1775-1783* [Willow Bend, Md., 1998], 360-1; JEP, 1:433, 437).

NEW LAW: see James Monroe to TJ, 7 July 1802.

On 9 Aug., Scott reported back to TJ that his ORIGINAL COMMISSION "bearing date the 8th July 1802 appointing me Marshal for the Virginia District, came to my hands the 27th Ulto, and on the Same day I wrote to the Secretary of State—acknowledging the rect thereof" (RC in DLC; endorsed by TJ as received 26 Aug. and so recorded in SJL).

From Matthew C. Groves

D<small>R</small>. S<small>IR</small>   Boston August 2nd 1802

the purport of this letter is to inform your excellency, that the Subscriber sails from this port in a day or two for Alexandria, for the purpose of takeing out a patent for a machine for the purpose of discovering the longitude at sea—I wish I may be so happy as to see your excellency at the New City. I rest assured that after a little Conversation your excellency woud be persuaded of the great probabillity of my succeeding in this business; and if I am right, of which I rest positively assur'd, the next object nearest my heart wou'd be, to bring it forward under the auspicious of the president of the united States. to gain this favour woud be Contrary to my own wishes, unless the principle was founded upon so broad a bottom, as to support itself while god is pleas'd to uphold the Course of Nature.

I shall not trouble your excellency concerning my sufferings while engagd. in this pursuit, one Circumstance excepted, which I feel bound in duty to clear up—

Viz when I was carried to the town of Andover, the Massachusetts bedlam, in Eighty Nine, after some days, my scatterd Ideas began Again to Collect to one Center. in stooping to wash my face, I coud not again raise myself erect, the prodigious weight in my head was such, that I was under Necessity of Supporting my head with both my hands, in order to raise myself up again. from this circumstance, I Concluded that the brains of madmen were either hard or heavy; In three or four days this oppression went off: In other after attemps similar to the former in pursuit of this favourite object, when at any time without Sleep for five or six days and nights, whenever I found this [litious?] oppression Collect upon my head. my god Sir what must be done in so terrible a Crisis, the terror of bedlam became so visibly terrible to me, without any prospect if Confind there again, of ever being liberated: my situation I Conceald upon these occations, and of two evils I chose the least, by Counteracting one evil with another. I had recourse to laudlum sometimes this wou'd help me, and when it did not, I had recourse without any particular choice, to every thing upon those temperary occations which had any tendency to stupify, and what yet made me peculiarly unfortunate in this situation, was the irritation upon my nerves was such that I cou'd not stop one moment in one place. I had to walk while my limbs wou'd perform their office—When I was obliged to give up my long services in the town for twenty four years. Cou'd not protect me from being thought intemperate, by such as were not acquainted with my painfull situation—I presume Sir, shou'd I not be so happy as to see your excellency, that Mr. Maddison will meet a man who wears but little marks of intemperance. No more Dr. Sir but remain with sincerity and Esteem your Excellency's Humble Servant

MATTHEW C. GROVES

P.S. the few here Sir, to whom my situation is known, believe me to be engaged in fruitless pursuit; the people in this place have so little Idea of things of this Nature, that seven out of eight of them woud never know I really believe, that there ever was such a body as the sun, if they were not scorch'd with his rays; In Washington I flatter myself I shall be treated with more delicacy—I remain as above—

M. C. GROVES

RC (DLC); blurred; addressed: "Thomas Jefferson Esqr. President of the united States of America"; franked and postmarked; endorsed by TJ as received 12 Aug. and so recorded in SJL.

A former mariner in the West Indies trade, Matthew C. Groves (ca. 1746-1811) operated a mercantile business in Boston specializing in the sale of china and other ceramic wares. He was also an amateur astronomer, who wrote TJ several times during his presidency seeking patronage and support for his method of calculating longitude at sea by observing the eclipses of Jupiter's moons. Traveling to Washington in October 1802, Groves met with TJ, who forwarded his proposals to Robert Patterson and the American Philosophical Society. Neither Patterson nor TJ found any merit in Groves's theories, however, although TJ did give the astronomer $10 in charity before he re-turned to Boston. Groves continued to promote his ideas on calculating longitude at home and abroad, and also continued to seek TJ's patronage. Responding to another of Groves's lengthy communications in 1808, TJ again expressed doubts over Groves's theories and politely suggested that his limited resources would be "better applied to the comfort of your family" (Bedini, *Statesman of Science*, 324-5; *The Boston Directory* [Boston, 1800], 52; Boston *Massachusetts Mercury*, 13 Oct. 1797; *Philadelphia Repository, and Weekly Register*, 10 Sep. 1803; Boston *Independent Chronicle*, 8 Aug. 1811; MB, 2:1084; Vol. 34:687-9; TJ to Robert Patterson, 16 Oct. 1802; Patterson to TJ, 1 Nov. 1802; Groves to TJ, 26 Sep. 1804; TJ to Groves, 19 Oct. 1808).

Groves received a PATENT on 3 Sep. 1802 for an "Astronomical quadrant" (*List of Patents*, 29).

From John Barnes

SIR   George Town 3d Augst: 1802

Previous to the receipt of your favr 30th. which I had the Honr. of receiving by Yesterdays Mail—I had Notice from Mr Penington (to whom your late draft on Mr Smith had been remitted to.) of Mr Smiths transmitting you their Bank post Note, which you now inclosed me—and by this Mail returned Mr Smith—of course Mr Penington will receive paymt. for your late draft.—

with reference to the $198. I can have no immediate Use for it, and have accordingly credited Mr Short and debited your a/c; therefor and it rests, with Messrs: Gibson & Jefferson subject to your order. If no good Opporty. offers for Richmond soon, here is a Vessel expected to sail in abt. 10 days—by whom your Case & Box will be conveyed.

I also Annex your July a/c Appt Ball. $5651.60—still. pointing to an increase of monthly disbursemts. *310.10* $5341.50. former Mo.— I hope and trust however, the present Mos a/c will reduce it considerably—and withal induce me—not to apply for the present Mos. Compensation—if I can possibly—do without it.

I am Sir, your most Respectfull Obedt. Hbl Servant.

JOHN BARNES

Tuesday Eveng.
I have this moment recd. your Magazine to be handed Mr March.

RC (ViU: Edgehill-Randolph Papers); at foot of text: "President UStates at Monticello"; endorsed by TJ as received 5 Aug. and so recorded in SJL. Enclosure not found.

MR MARCH: Georgetown bookbinder John March.

From Daniel Carroll Brent

SIR   Washington, Augt. 3d. 1802

Enclosed is a copy of a Letter from Mr. Hadfield which I think proper to communicate to you and to request your directions on the subject.

As I understood it to be a direction from you to me, that the grates should be fixed in Iron frames, I have contracted for them so to be done, and contrary to the opinion and wishes of Mr. Hadfield, who insists upon his Plan as the best. The article respecting the Iron work of the Windows, is thus expressed—"All the windows in the ground story except in the goalers Room, to have double grates of eight cross Bars each—four upright & four horizontal—All the windows above, except the goalers Room, to have only one cross grate of eight Bars— the windows of the goaler's Room above and below, to have only four upright Bars in each—all the horizontal bars to be one inch and one inch & a quarter thick, and the upright Bars three Inches broad, and three quarters of an Inch thick, to be punched through so as to receive the horizontal Bars—all the Bars to be fixed in an Iron frame, each going through, and well rivetted—the frame to be sunk into the

Stone it's whole thickness—the frame is to be three Inches broad, and three quarters of an Inch thick"

I am not attached to this mode, and am ready to adopt any that may be thought better; but I do not think myself at liberty to make a change without your directions—this change, if deemed proper, will not delay the work—with respect to the Doors, I shall have them iron sheeted, agreeably to your former Instructions. As to the Roof, I should prefer the substatial parts of good white oak—The Rafters and Lathing I think may with safety be of good pine or yellow Poplar—the Roof of course, will be much lighter, and I think, will last as long—We shall commence to lay the foundation on about Monday next. the granite which the undertakers have already got down from the falls, I am told, is of a very excellent quality.

I am, with sentiments of high respect, Sir, Yr. Mo: Obt Servt.

DANIEL C. BRENT

RC (DLC); at foot of text: "President of the United States"; endorsed by TJ as received 5 Aug. and so recorded in SJL. Enclosure not found.

For the involvement of George HADFIELD and TJ in the design of the new jail in Washington, D.C., see Vol. 37:665-6, 694-6.

To Albert Gallatin

DEAR SIR   Monticello Aug. 3. 1802.

Your's of July 24. from New York was recieved on the 31st. this will probably find you at Washington. I immediately wrote to the Secretary of state's office for a commission for Selman vice Goforth in Symmes's case, and shall be ready to sign those for Massac, Marblehead & Pensylvania, as also for a successor to Foster, when presented. I suppose, all circumstances considered, that Wheelan's office when resigned, would be well filled by T. Coxe, and that he ought to have it. I have recieved as strong recommendations as can possibly exist in favor of Robert Porter vice Vancleve. my own sense of Lieper's qualifications & rights make him a competitor. to which it is best to give it, or to neither, may be a subject of consideration when I return, as nothing can suffer in the mean time. whenever the light house at Point Comfort is ready for a keeper, I have irresistable recommendations of a Capt Samuel Eddins. your information respecting E.L. fills me with concern. as soon as it is ascertained, we must take measures to produce a reimbursement and, if necessary, a resignation. some private intimation will probably be the best mode. I recieve information that Hopkins Commr. of loans in Richmd. being allowed by law

2. clerks and having scarceley occasion for one, in fact employs but one, & gives him the salary of two. will you have this enquired into, and exact restitution of the double salary illegally given. you may remember I once troubled you to authenticate officially some extracts of letters relative to the 9000. D. of which E. Randolph claims to be debtor to mr Short instead of the US. I now recieve information from the Attorney employed that *extracts* of letters cannot be given in evidence, that an official copy of the whole letter must be produced. I see at once the propriety of the rule, but unluckily the information comes to me here, while the list of the papers referred to is at Washington, so that it is out of my power to specify the papers necessary. Colo. Minor (our lawyer) happens to mention two as essentially necessary, that is to say mr Short's letters of the 12th. & 30th. of August 1794. on which he says mr Randolph rests principally his claim of that credit. will you be so good as to have these two letters copied from your office authenticated & forwarded to me. Minor says the cause will be tried at the next session of the court. I am happy to hear your health is better, but shall still have more confidence in it if I hear you have retired into the country for these two months. Accept assurances of my affectionate attachment & high respect.

TH: JEFFERSON

P.S. What are the subjects on which the next session of Congress is to be employed. it is not too early to think of it. I know but of two. 1. the militia law. 2. the reformation of the civil list recommended to them at the last meeting but not taken up thro' want of time & preparation. that preparation must be made by us.—an accurate statement of the original amount and subsequent augmentations or diminutions of the public debt, to be continued annually, is an article on which we have conferred before. a similar statement of the annual expences of the government for a certain period back, & to be repeated annually, is another wholsome necessity we should impose on ourselves & our successors. our court calendar should be compleated.

RC (NHi: Gallatin Papers); at foot of first page: "Mr. Gallatin"; endorsed. PrC (DLC).

SECRETARY OF STATE'S OFFICE: TJ to Daniel Brent, 1 Aug.

E.L.: Edward Livingston.

I RECIEVE INFORMATION: see Thomas Underwood, Jr., to TJ, 25 July. For the results of the inquiry, see Gallatin to TJ, 17 Aug.

For TJ's employment of John MINOR as the attorney to protect William Short's interests in the U.S. suit against Edmund Randolph, see TJ to Minor, 10 Mch. 1802. In January 1802, Gallatin sent TJ documents pertaining to the Randolph case (Vol. 36:343-4, 440). In AUGUST 1794, Short had learned that Randolph, as secretary of state, was sending $9,000 to Madrid for him in conjunction with his appointment as minister resident to

Spain. Short complained that the rate of exchange was too unfavorable to receive the money in Spain. He asked Randolph to credit it to him in the United States, requesting "that you would be so good as to pay it to Mr. Jefferson, desiring him to vest it for me in some of the public funds bearing interest—or that you would be so good as to have it done yourself" (Short to secretary of state, 12 and 30 Aug. 1794, both in DLC: William Short Papers; George Green Shackelford, *Jefferson's Adoptive Son: The Life of William Short, 1759-1848* [Lexington, Ky., 1993], 103-4).

REFORMATION OF THE CIVIL LIST: noting that the "great mass of public offices is established by law, and therefore, by law alone can be abolished," TJ urged Congress, in his first annual message, to submit all offices to the "test of public utility." As promised, TJ sent Congress, in February 1802, "a Roll of the persons having office or employment under the US." in 1800. All of the positions discontinued by TJ after he took office were highlighted and printed in italics (Vol. 36:60-1, 210-12, 592-3).

From James Lyle

DEAR SIR   Manchester August 3d. 1802

I have not had the pleasure of hearing from you, since you enclosed me the order on Messrs. Gibson & Jefferson for £300—which was paid the 8th of April 1801. this with £29–12–from Mr. Clark your Attorney in Bedford is all I have received since I sent you a statement of the different payments, by that you would observe that a balance of principal on the fourth bond of £99,2,8¾ remained. I hope you have examined that state, and that the mode met your approbation. Our Company are continually pressing me in the most earnest manner for remittances; I know you are as anxious to have the debt wholly paid off, as we are to receive it, therefore I shall say nothing on the subject farther than that. I expect soon to hear from you. Christopher Clark the Attorney in Bedford promised to send me a state of the bonds put into his hands by you, it have not yet come to hand when it does I will forward you a copy of it. I am with the greatest Regard

Dear Sir Your Mo hul Servt   JAMES LYLE

RC (MHi); at head of text: "His Excellency Thomas Jefferson"; endorsed by TJ as received 6 Aug.

Lyle's STATEMENT of TJ's bonded debt with Henderson, McCaul & Company has not been found but was enclosed in his letter to TJ of 18 Aug. 1800. There had been no recorded communications between the two since TJ had paid $1000, calculated above as £300, toward his BALANCE with the firm (Vol. 32:107, 458-9). During the previous decade TJ hired CHRISTOPHER CLARK to collect payments on several bonds he had issued to people who owed him money and to remit any collections to Lyle (Vol. 28:108-9).

From John Bird

SIR,   New Castle 4th. Augt. 1802

I had the Honor to write you on the 10th. ultimo—Stateing my application for the Office of Collector of the Customs for the District of Delaware, in case a vacancy should happen, by the removal, or resignation of the present officer—: To which be pleased to refer.

In that Letter I took the Liberty to recommend your Excellency to Governor Hall, and C: A: Rodney Esquire, for information, with respect to who, and what I am.   But, as I am apprehensive that those Gentlemen left Washington, before my Letter arrived, I now Sir, take the Liberty to refer you to the Inclosed Document from Archd: Alexander, Esquire, and to Geo. Read, Esqr.—who will also write you on the same Subject in a few days—which I hope may prove satisfactory.

If however, I should not succeed in obtaining this appointment; and some other Person should be more fortunate than myself—Notwithstanding something like chagrin may be the consequence, yet I shall be content, and not speak evil of presidential favours.

There is yet another office, which I am informed will be vacant ere long—to wit "Commissioner of Loans"—If I should fail in the first—I shall have no objection, if thought Competint, to supply the Vacancy which will happen in the latter.

I have the Honor, to be with much consideration and respect, Your Obt. and Very Hbl Servant   JNO; BIRD

RC (DNA: RG 59, LAR); at head of text: "Thomas Jefferson, Esquire, Prest. of the U:S."; endorsed by TJ as received 16 Aug. and so recorded in SJL; also endorsed by TJ: "to be Collector at Wilmington." Enclosure: Archibald Alexander to TJ, 4 Aug. 1802 (recorded in SJL as received 16 Aug. and "Newcastle" but not found).

John Bird (d. 1810) was a New Castle ship chandler who served as a Delaware state senator in 1800 and 1802. He was expelled in January 1801 for involvement in "certain navy contracts," which disqualified him from office holding according to a stipulation in the state constitution. He reclaimed his seat from Robert Maxwell the following year and won reelection without objection. In 1804, he became a member of the Delaware house of representatives and continued in office until his sudden death following the failure of his firm, Riddle and Bird (John A. Munroe, "A Parson in Politics: The Expulsion of John C. Brush from the Delaware General Assembly in 1801," *Delaware History*, 23 [1989], 300-1; Henry C. Conrad, *History of the State of Delaware,* 3 vols. [Wilmington, Del., 1908], 1:264, 272, 273; Delaware Federal Writers' Project, *New Castle on the Delaware*, 3d ed. [Wilmington, Del., 1950], 85, 89).

WRITE YOU: Bird to TJ, 10 July, recorded in SJL as received on the 14th with the notation "Newcastle. To be collector vice McLane," has not been found.

John Stockton, who was appointed in 1795, served as COMMISSIONER OF

LOANS for Delaware for more than 20 years (JEP, 1:189; Report of the Committee of Claims on the Petition of John Stockton, 17 Feb. 1818 [Washington, D.C., 1818; Shaw-Shoemaker, No. 46203]).

From George Jefferson

DEAR SIR, Richmond 4th. Augt. 1802

I some days since forwarded by Mr. Mooney, your things from Washington, the Iron & Steel from Philadelphia, & the syrup of punch; together with some articles for D. Carr.

The lime & linen shall be forwarded by the next boat, if to be had; the latter however I am satisfied, cannot. The Rudimens Rudiments I send by the post-rider.

Mr. Eppes is, I expect, by this with you—if he is not, have the goodness to forward him the inclosed.

I am Dr. Sir Your Very humble servant GEO. JEFFERSON

RC (MHi); at foot of text: "Thos. Jefferson esqr."; endorsed by TJ as received 6 Aug. Enclosure not found.

On 24 Aug., TJ recorded a payment to Richard MOONEY for delivering groceries and other supplies (MB, 2:1079).

To Henry Dearborn

DEAR SIR Monticello Aug. 5. 1802.

Your two favors of July. 31. came to hand yesterday. I have no hesitation in approving of the purchase recommended by Genl. Sumpter, but I retain the papers a post longer to make myself acquainted with them. indeed the volume of my mail is such that subjects which require any consideration cannot be dispatched during the single evening & morning of the post's stay. hence I shall generally on subjects requiring consideration, delay my answer one post.

I am mortified with the affair of Story. his letters to me have been far from announcing a crazy man. they exhibit great ingenuity and learning; yet I am sensible that is compatible with unfitness for ordinary business. I have recieved a letter of thanks from him on the appointment. an expression in the letter gives me a little hold on the subject, and I have written an answer which I inclose open for your perusal. it is an awkward measure to be forced on one, but if you think, as I do, that this is a less evil than to let the thing go uncorrected, be so good as to stick [a little wafer] in it, and put it into the post-office.—I shall not be easy till I hear that yourself & family are removed into the country. they [are] most remarkably sickly on the tidewaters of this country. do not let any false sense of security lull [...] continue on [them?]. Accept assurances of my affectionate esteem & high respect.   TH: JEFFERSON

PrC (DLC); faint; at foot of text: "The Secretary at War." Enclosure: TJ to Isaac Story, 5 Aug. 1802.

To George Jefferson

DEAR SIR   Monticello Aug. 5. 1802.

Yesterday arrived our packages sent up by the boats. I find that during my stay here we shall want another supply of a couple of [hogsh.] more of syrup of punch, which therefore it will be as well to get at [once and] forward when practicible as the boat-navigation is precarious.

By yesterday's post [I learnt] that mr Short arrived on the 28th. at Norfolk, & is to proceed via Baltimore to Washington to see me. whence he will probably come by Richmond to this place. he will probably want money for his expences. the 198. D. of his [which] [...] with you to mr Barnes's account, and any balance of mine place at his service; and should he want beyond that & you can advance it with convenience, I will instantly have it remitted from Washington. Accept assurances of my affectionate attachment.

                                                    TH: JEFFERSON

P.S. be so good as to deliver the inclosed to mr Short on his arrival at Richmond.

PrC (MHi); faint; at foot of text: "Mr. G. Jefferson"; endorsed by TJ in ink on verso. Enclosure not found, but see TJ to William Short, 12 Aug.

YESTERDAY'S POST: William Short to TJ, 28 July, recorded in SJL as received 5 Aug. but not found.

To Isaac Story

SIR   Monticello Aug. 5. 1802.

I recieved last night your favor of July 28 acknoleging the reciept of a commission under the bankrupt law. you mention in that your wish to remove to Boston, and I hardly suppose the commission above mentioned sufficient to prevent that. I indulge this supposition [the rather as you] will learn, with the less dissatisfaction[1] that the name of your son Joseph is that which was desired to be [inserted in] the commission. he was represented to me as a lawyer of eminence and a man of virtue & respectability, [&] as we have confined these appointments entirely to lawyers & merchants, I have assumed you would be as much gratified by his appointment as your own, and under that presumption destined the [place] for him. I judged [as a parent?] of the dispositions of a parent. the error of name however will not be corrected until I have the pleasure of a line from yourself, as I would [but] wish that your consent & desire [should] dictate the correction to prevent every unpleasant inference [on the] [...]. I pray you [Sir?] accept assurances of my high consideration & respect

TH: JEFFERSON

PrC (DNA: RG 59, LAR); faint; at foot of text: "The revd Isaac Story"; endorsed by TJ in ink on verso. Enclosed in TJ to Henry Dearborn, 5 Aug.

[1] Preceding four words interlined.

To Mawlay Sulayman, Sultan of Morocco

GREAT AND GOOD FRIEND   [5 Aug. 1802]

It became known to us, not long since, that it would be agreeable to you that the US. should procure to be made for you one hundred gun carriages at your expence. we have lost no time since this intimation in preparing and sending them to you by a ship of our own; and we feel it more conformable with our dispositions towards your majesty to ask your acceptance of them as a mark of the esteem and respect we bear you, and of the desire we entertain of cultivating that peace and friendly intercourse, which, while it is acceptable to us with all nations, is particularly desired with your majesty.

A war, as unjust as it was unprovoked, having been declared against us by Tripoli, we sent some armed vessels into the Mediterranean for the protection of our commerce in that sea. We gave it in particular charge to our officers to respect your majesty's flag and subjects, and to omit no opportunity of cultivating a good understanding with you: and we trust that should circumstances render it necessary for our vessels to enter your majesty's harbors, or to have communications with them, they will experience that hospitality and friendly assistance which we would practise towards your majesty's vessels and subjects in our own ports or elsewhere whenever we could be useful to them. I pray god to have you, very great & good friend in his holy keeping. Done in the US. of America this   day of August 1802.

FC (DLC: TJ Papers, 125:21646); undated, but recorded in SJL under 5 Aug.; entirely in TJ's hand; at foot of text: "The Emperor of Marocco. rough draught"; at head of text in a clerk's hand: "Copd."; for later alterations by TJ, see his letter to Sulayman of 21 Aug. PrC (DLC: TJ Papers, 125:21553); lacking the later alterations. Enclosed in TJ to Madison, 6 Aug.

As sultan, Mawlay Sulayman (1766-1822) was the religious leader of Morocco as well as head of state. A younger son of the sultan Sidi Muhammad Ibn Abd Allah, Sulayman had not been first in line for the throne, and his education, which entailed years of study with tutors, focused on religious topics. In 1792, when a coalition of military and tribal leaders proclaimed him sultan, he was initially reluctant. His brother, Mawlay al-Yazid, had in a reign of only two years disrupted the stability that marked their father's long rule. Al-Yazid purged the bureaucracy of most of its experienced administrators, and Sulayman, in order to build and maintain the centralized state he desired, had to recruit people from outside the government, including merchants and slaves, to fill important posts. He faced recurring challenges from brothers, cousins, and other relatives while he labored to impose his authority over remote tribes and provinces. In 1799-1800, an epidemic of bubonic plague, the deadliest that the country had suffered in several centuries, killed between one quarter and one half of the population—including powerful opponents of Sulayman's regime, but also key officials of his government. For some time, Moroccan sultans had generally curtailed corsairing, a policy that Sulayman continued. A fear that the country's location on the Strait of Gibraltar made Morocco a target for invasion by France or Spain led him to cultivate good relations with Great Britain. Maintaining a weak navy, he tended to avoid confrontation with other countries except when he thought he could win better treaties. After he ordered attacks on American ships in 1803, a swift reprisal by the U.S. squadron forced him to submit to peace terms. He eventually dissolved his navy. During the last years of Sulayman's life, his rule was weakened by famine, plague, defeats in battle against rebels, and political upheaval. *Mawlay* was an honorific title that meant "my lord" and, like *sidi*, signified descent from the Prophet Muhammad (Mohamed El Mansour, *Morocco in the Reign of Mawlay Sulayman* [Wisbech, Eng., 1990], xiii, xiv, 16-23, 88-100, 104, 107-14, 133-5, 184-202, 218; Mohamed El Mansour, "The Anachronism of Maritime Jihad: The U.S.-Morocco Conflict of 1802-1803," in Jerome B. Bookin-Weiner and Mohamed El Mansour, eds., *The Atlantic Connection: 200 Years of Moroccan-American Relations, 1786-1986* [Rabat, Morocco, 1990], 49-55; Madison, *Papers, Sec. of State Ser.*, 2:378; 3:222).

PARTICULAR CHARGE TO OUR OFFICERS: instructions sent to Commodore Richard Dale in May 1801 included reminders on how to treat the "Vessels, Citizens & Subjects" of nations at peace with the United States. Dale was told to "bear in mind, that we are at Peace & wish to continue in Peace with all Nations," and that the commander of an American squadron should be "as much distinguished for his attention & adherence to all the rights of humanity & hospitality, as by his firmness in support of the honor of his country." In additional orders sent in Feb. 1802, Dale was also told to refrain from capturing or recapturing Tripolitan vessels in waters under the jurisdiction of other nations, "in order that their peace & sovereignty may remain unviolated." Any conduct that brought the United States "into collision" with any other power would be scrutinized "scrupulously and without indulgence" by the Navy Department. Richard V. Morris received similar instructions in March 1802 before departing with his squadron for the Mediterranean (NDBW, 1:468; 2:60, 92; Vol. 34:115n).

To John Barnes

DEAR SIR   Monticello Aug. 6. 1802

Your favors of July 30. and Aug. 3. came to hand yesterday, and on the same day arrived here our boxes, casks &c. shipped from Washington before my departure; all in good order except the tea box containing coffee, sugar &c. which had burst open and lost some of it's coffee; also my Indian busts, which by rough tumbling about, had got broken into many pieces. I learnt by yesterday's post mr Short's arrival at Norfolk on the 28th. he was to proceed the next day to Baltimore by water, then to Washington to see me, thence he will probably come here by the way of Richmond. I believe he will want money for his expences, and have written to mr Jefferson to supply him at Richmd. at Washington you will of course take care of him, and lay every thing I have a right to at his command. should his wants go beyond our immediate resources, I would raise them at the bank on my own note on recieving such information from you. accept my affectionate respects.   TH: JEFFERSON

PrC (CSmH); at foot of text: "Mr. John Barnes"; endorsed by TJ in ink on verso.

For background on the INDIAN BUSTS sent to TJ from Tennessee, via New Orleans and Norfolk, see Vol. 31:195-6; Vol. 34:598-9; Vol. 35:454n.

To Daniel Carroll Brent

DEAR SIR   Monticello Aug. 6. 1802

Your favor of the 3d. came to hand yesterday. whether it be best to insert the bars of the jail windows into an iron frame, or directly & separately into the stone [work], you can, on consultation with so many good judges on [the subject] form a much better judgment than I can, that I must forbear giving any opinion on it. that good white oak is better for every part of the roof than either pine or poplar, I have no doubt: yet it must depend on the practicability of getting it, & it's price how far it may be best to substitute pine or poplar in unimportant parts. I do not think a floor of boards below the pavement necessary to prevent damp. the earth under a house of size is as dry as plank would be; and especially if the water falling on the roof is conveyed by pipes clear of the building. I hope the completion of the jail walls & roof before cold weather will be pushed to effect. Accept assurances of my esteem & respect.

TH: JEFFERSON

PrC (DLC); faint; at foot of text: "Colo. D. C. Brent"; endorsed by TJ in ink on verso.

To Henry Dearborn

DEAR SIR   Monticello Aug. 6. 1802

On further view and consideration of the papers from Genl. Sumpter, and Colo. Senf I continue of opinion that we ought to purchase the lands spoken of by them, about 4, or 500. acres, and further would approve of a purchase of any quantity within the limits of the act of assembly (2000 acres) considering that they must [be moderate in their] price as yet and that much will be wanting for timber & fuel. the purchases should be adjacent to one another. Accept my affectionate esteem   TH: JEFFERSON

PrC (DLC); faint; at foot of text: "The Secretary at War." Recorded in SJL with notation "arsenal in S.C."

From William Henry Harrison

SIR   Vincennes 6th. Augt. 1802

When I had the honour to see you in Philadelphia in the Spring of the year 1800 you were pleased to recommend to me a plan for a Town which you supposed would exempt its inhabitants in a great degree from those dreadful pestilences which have become so common in the large cities of the United States. As the laws of this Territory have given to the Governor the power to designate the seats of Justice for the Counties, and as the choice of the Citizens of Clark County was fixed upon a spot where there had been no town laid out, I had an opportunity at once of gratifying them—of paying respect to your recommendation, and of conforming to my own inclinations— The proprietor of the land having acceded to my proposals a Town has been laid out with each alternate square to remain vacant forever (excepting one Range of squares upon the River)—and I have taken the liberty to call it Jeffersonville—The beauty of the spot on which the Town is laid out, the advantages of the situation (being just above the Rapids of the Ohio) and the excellence of the plan, makes it highly probable that it will at some period not very remote become a place of considerable consequence—At the sale of the lots a few days ago several of them were struck off at 200 Dollars. It is in contemplation to cut a canal round the Rapids on this side—a project which it is said can be very easily executed and which will be highly beneficial to the Town. Indeed I have very little doubt of its flourishing. It is my ardent wish that it may become worthy of the name it bears, and that the Humane & benevolent views which dictated the plan may be reallised—

If Sir it should again happen that in the wide Range which you suffer your thoughts to take for the benefit of Mankind—the accomplishment of any of your wishes can in the smallest degree be aided by me—I beg you to beleive that your commands shall be executed to the utmost extent of my small talent.

I have the Honour to be with sincere attachment Sir your most Hum Sevt.   WILLM. HENRY HARRISON

P.S. I have done myself the Honour to enclose a plan of the Town of Jeffersonville and one which shews its situation with Regard to Louisville & Clarksville.

RC (DLC); at foot of text: "Thomas Jefferson President of the United States"; with postscript on separate sheet; endorsed by TJ as received 29 Aug. and so recorded in SJL. Enclosures not found, but see below.

A PLAN FOR A TOWN: TJ had promoted a checkerboard plan for the layout of American towns since at least 1799, in which each alternate square would remain unoccupied and left in a natural state. He touted the scheme as an effective barrier against yellow fever, which TJ believed was caused by the dense construction of cities in the warm, cloudless environment of the United States. In his checkerboard plan, each square of houses would be surrounded by four open squares, thereby creating a rural atmosphere that would be "insusceptible of the miasmata which produce yellow fever." Besides Harrison, TJ had also discussed this idea with Benjamin Rush, William C. C. Claiborne, and C. F. C. Volney. In

1804, he recommended the checkerboard plan to Claiborne for the enlargement of New Orleans, but it was not put into effect. In 1821, the legislature of Mississippi adopted TJ's checkerboard plan for its new state capital, Jackson, although most of the open squares were subsequently occupied (John W. Reps, *The Making of Urban America: A History of City Planning in the United States* [Princeton, 1965], 314-22; Vol. 31:183-4; TJ to Claiborne, 7 and 17 July 1804; TJ to Volney, 8 Feb. 1805).

The new town of JEFFERSONVILLE was laid out on a 150-acre plot on the north bank of the Ohio River opposite Louisville, Kentucky. The plan was a modified version of the checkerboard layout, in which the squares fronting the river would all be occupied, while the interior squares would adopt TJ's alternating system. More significantly, a diagonal grid of streets was imposed upon the checkerboard plan, intersecting in the open squares and thereby dividing each into four triangles. The unconventional street layout also clipped corners from the exterior lots of the occupied squares and cut off the interior lots from street frontage. The diagonal street plan did not appeal to TJ, who deemed it less convenient than running streets parallel to the squares. Harrison was aware of TJ's preference, but explained that "the proprietor was so parsimonious that he would not suffer it to be laid out in that manner." Residents of Jeffersonville likewise found the unorthodox town plan inconvenient, and in 1816 secured permission from the Indiana legislature to change it. All of the land north of Market Street was subsequently consolidated and laid out into new lots, obliterating the original checkerboard plan (Reps, *Making of Urban America*, 317-21; Carl E. Kramer, *This Place We Call Home: A History of Clark County, Indiana* [Bloomington, Ind., 2007], 40-2; TJ to Harrison, 27 Feb. 1803; Harrison to TJ, 29 Oct. 1803).

To James Madison

DEAR SIR   Monticello Aug. 6. 1802.
I now return you the letters of mr Pichon, and of Jones; also those of Van Polanen & Thos. Sumter. the letter to be written to Van Polanen should be so friendly as to remove all doubt from the Batavian government that our suppression of that mission proceeds from any other motive than of domestic arrangement & economy.[1]—I inclose you a draught of a letter to the emperor of Marocco, which make what it should be and send to your office to be written over the blank I have signed. a letter from mr Short, dated Norfolk July 29. gives me reason to expect him here hourly. present my respects to the ladies, & accept assurances of my constant & affectionate esteem & respect.

TH: JEFFERSON

RC (DNA: RG 59, MLR); at foot of text: "The Secretary of State." PrC (DLC). Enclosures: see enclosures listed at Madison to TJ, 30 July, and see below.

Roger Gerard VAN POLANEN, minister to the United States from the Batavian Republic, had written to Madison from Philadelphia on 30 July to announce that his government had recalled him. Noting that his removal was the result of the decision by the United States to close its diplomatic mission to the Dutch republic, Van Polanen expressed hope that "the cordial sentiments of mutual good-will between the two Nations" would remain strong. Madison wrote to Van Polanen on 13 Aug., conveying the president's assurance of the "cordial dispositions" of the

United States (Madison, *Papers, Sec. of State Ser.*, 1:481n; 3:445-6, 475-6; Vol. 34:130-1n, 208-9).

Thomas SUMTER, Jr., had written a brief letter to Madison from Paris on 18 May, requesting permission to resign his position as secretary to Robert R. Livingston. In September, Daniel Brent sent TJ a copy of Sumter's letter (Tr in DLC; Madison, *Papers, Sec. of State Ser.*, 3:228, 555).

LETTER TO THE EMPEROR: Jefferson to Mawlay Sulayman, Sultan of Morocco, 5 Aug.

The letter from William SHORT was actually dated 28 July; see TJ to Short, 12 Aug.

[1] MS: "eonomy."

From Newburyport, Massachusetts, Citizens

Sir   Newburyport August 6th 1802

Convinced as we are, that we have no power to control the dismissions or appointments to the subordinate offices of Government, yet we feel a right, and it becomes a duty, when measures are pursued, that tend to lessen our confidence in that Government which we have hitherto gloried in supporting, respectfully to give our Judgment and to express our opinions of their tendency.

In exercising this right, we are forcibly induced to express our astonishment, at the reported dismissal of Dudley Atkins Tyng Esqr. from the office of Collector of this port. He has conducted the business of this office more than seven years, and in that time we are authorized to say, that the United States have never met with the smallest loss in the collection by, or payment from him, of the duties payable in his department: whilst he has vigilantly secured the Interests of the Public, his capability, integrity and urbanity, have insured him the decided approbation and esteem, of every person who has had any transactions in his office, and which we, as his fellow citizens, independent of party politics, are proud to bear this public testimony of: nor can we refrain from remarking, that in retaining or appointing to the subordinate offices of his department, he has never been guided by any other consideration than that the men he appointed were honest and were capable of performing their duties.

Impressed with these sentiments, we cannot but suppose that his dismission has been occasioned by the most gross and daring misrepresentations; as we are not yet ready to believe, that the views of the administration are governed by motives as pernicious in their tendency as they are contracted in their policy: We therefore respectfully request you to reconsider the reported dismission, with that candour and impartiality that you have publicly pledged yourself to maintain: and we still shall hope that a man may be retained in office, who is so universally respected by his fellow citizens, and all who know him, as is Mr Tyng.

we are Sir with due respect Your most Obedient huml Servants

RC (DLC); in a clerk's hand, signed by William Coombs and 269 others; certified and signed by Ebenezer Stocker, "President of the Newbury Port. Marine Insce. Compy" in Newburyport on 11 Aug., stating "that of seventeen thousand tons of shipping, belonging to and owned in, the District of Newburyport, the owners of four thousand tons, are absent, living in distant Towns: & That the subscribers to the Inclosed Memorial are owners of about twelve thousand tons";

also certified and signed by Newbury-port assessors Samuel Cutler, Stephen Howard, and Joshua Greenleaf on 11 Aug., stating "that the subscribers, to the Memorial annexed; are possessed, agreeably to the rate of valuation, of taxable Estates in said Town; of nearly Two thirds of the Whole amount of property taxed"; at head of text: "To the President of the United States"; endorsed by TJ as received 19 Aug. and so recorded in SJL with notation "Newbury port. merchts against Tyng's removal"; also endorsed by TJ: "remonstrance on removal of Ting."

REPORTED DISMISSAL: on 30 July, the *National Intelligencer* carried the news of the appointment of William Lyman as collector at Newburyport in place of Dudley A. Tyng. The news arrived in Newburyport on 5 Aug. and the *Newburyport*

Herald proclaimed it the next day, noting sarcastically that the "*mild conciliating tolerant* Jefferson, aided by his *immaculate* minions" had removed Tyng and appointed in his place "a Mr. Lyman of *no one knows where*, and of a character—*no one knows what*; except that report says, he belongs to the County of Hampshire, and was a noted ring leader of Shay's insurrection." The editor exclaimed that while the people of Newburyport had no control over presidential appointments, they had "the right of judging of their merit and making their judgment known."

Never reinstated as collector, Tyng became reporter of decisions for the Massachusetts Supreme Court (John J. Currier, *History of Newburyport, Mass., 1764-1909*, 2 vols. [Newburyport, 1906-09], 2:267-8).

From Henry Dearborn

SIR,   War Department August 7th. 1802

The necessity of an early answer to the inclosed letters from Governor Harrison induced me to send him one prior to my consulting you on the subject, a copy of Which I herewith transmit, and on a further consideration of the subject I have taken measures for forwarding by a Gentleman who sets out this day for Kentucky, some Medals, and fifteen hundred dollars in silver—the money to be received in Kentucky and forwarded by a suitable person to Governor Harrison by the fifth of September at farthest—our situation with the Indians in that quarter appears to be such as requires prompt attention, And as the meeting of the Chiefs is to take place at Vincennes on the first of Septemr. there was no time to loose, I therefore have taken measures without much time for reflection, but hope they will not be considered improper—I will thank you Sir, for your opinion respecting any farther measures, which you may deem useful in relation to this subject—

I am with sentiments of Esteem your Obedt. Servt.

H. DEARBORN

RC (DLC); in a clerk's hand, signed by Dearborn; at foot of text: "The President of the United States"; endorsed by TJ as received from the War Department on 12 Aug. and "Govr. Harrison's lre concerning Indian affairs" and so recorded in

SJL. FC (Lb in DNA: RG 107, LSP). Enclosures: (1) William Henry Harrison to Dearborn, three letters written at Vincennes, one of 14 July and two of the 16th, all regarding Indian affairs, received together at the War Department on 5 Aug. but not found (recorded in DNA: RG 107, RLRMS). (2) Dearborn to Harrison, 5 Aug., answering Harrison's letters of 14 and 16 July "by the first mail" without waiting for consultation with the president; regarding the bounds of the tract at Vincennes ceded by the Indians to France by an earlier treaty, prudence "forbids our extending our claim to any such length as may increase any unfavourable impressions already made on the minds of the Indians"; Harrison should handle that issue "in such manner as your own judgement shall dictate, under existing circumstances"; Harrison is authorized to spend $1,000 to $2,000 for gifts for the chiefs at his conference with them, should the medals and clothes sent for the purpose not arrive in time; trading houses are being established at Fort Wayne and Detroit, "but their being continued or not will depend on the friendly conduct of the Indians"; Dearborn will send along "any particular Instructions" he receives from TJ on these matters; meanwhile "you will please to continue your exertions for quieting the minds of the Indians; you will be fully authorised in expressing the strongest assurances of the real friendly disposition of the President towards his red children, and that he intends by all the means in his power to render them as happy as possible" (FC in Lb in DNA:RG 75, LSIA).

Having no large MEDALS on hand in Washington, Dearborn sent 15 smaller ones and arranged for larger medals to be sent from Philadelphia "for some of the principal Chiefs who have not received any from the United States." The SILVER was for Harrison's use in buying clothing and other articles as gifts. Dearborn gave Daniel Vertner, a War Department provisions contractor from Washington, Kentucky, the medals and a draft for $1,500 on the supervisor of the revenue for Kentucky. After arriving in Kentucky, Vertner was to draw the funds in silver, then send the money and the medals to Harrison "by some sober trusty person," ensuring that everything got to Harrison by 5 Sep. Dearborn stated that the War Department would pay Vertner's expenses and something "for your own trouble" (Dearborn to Harrison, 6 Aug., in same; Dearborn to Vertner, 6 Aug., in DNA: RG 107, MLS; Vertner to Dearborn, 11 Mch., 12 Nov. 1802, recorded in DNA: RG 107, RLRMS).

MEETING OF THE CHIEFS: Harrison's intended conference with Indian leaders concerning land titles. Harrison expected to meet with representatives of the Wea, Potawatomi, Eel River, Piankashaw, and Kickapoo groups after the distribution of their annuities in August (Owens, *Jefferson's Hammer*, 63; note to Dearborn to TJ, 29 July).

From Albert Gallatin

SIR   Treasury Department 7th August 1802

I have the honor to submit to your consideration the "regulations concerning the Mississipi trade" prepared in pursuance of the act of Congress of the 1st of May last. They were, at my request, digested by the Comptroller under whose immediate superintendence the customs are placed, and have been made, so far as practicable, conformable in their details with the general regulations of that establishment. On examination, I have approved the whole with one single exception, which will be easily distinguished, three lines and half being erased.

Of the principles there are but two on which any hesitation took place; the one, which was introduced on my suggestion, & contained in the 4th regulation prevents the extension of the priviledges (exemption of duty) to *foreign* goods imported from the Mississipi to the Atlantic ports. These can only be lead or spanish cotton which being first imported from Spanish Louisiana to Natchez and having there paid the duties should be re-exported to any such atlantic port. It is highly improbable that such re-exportation should take place, and if, in order to ensure an exemption of a double payment of duty to such as may take place, the present regulations were extended to that case, it would open a door to innumerable frauds by the importation of every species of Spanish produce from N. Orleans to the atlantic ports as having paid already duties at Natches.

The other is that of the 5th regulation which precludes coasting vessels employed in that trade from carrying any foreign goods whatever. The Comptroller apprehended much danger to the revenue from their admission to such trade, and, although I doubt whether that regulation may not substantially exclude coasting vessels altogether from that trade, yet, as they have been heretofore excluded & cannot complain of the proposed arrangement, the proposition is submitted with the others to your consideration.

The regulations when approved by you, will, with such alterations as you may direct, be transmitted to the several collectors of customs, and immediately carried into effect.

I have the honor to be with the highest respect Sir Your most obedt. Servt.   ALBERT GALLATIN

RC (DLC); at foot of text: "The President of the United States"; endorsed by TJ as received from the Treasury Department on Aug. 12 and "regulns commerce Missisipi" and so recorded in SJL. Enclosure not found.

Section 6 of the ACT OF CONGRESS of 1 May 1802 that established new revenue districts called for goods carried by U.S. vessels in the coastal trade "between the Atlantic ports of the United States, and the districts of the United States on the river Mississippi" who landed at New Or-

leans to be exempt from duties, provided the same goods would not be "subject to duty, or liable to seizure, if transported from one district of the United States, on the sea-coast, to another." The act called upon the Treasury secretary, with the approbation of the president, to draw up regulations to enable the custom collectors to carry out the congressional mandate and, at the same time, to prevent "frauds on the revenue" (U.S. Statutes at Large, 2:182).

MY REQUEST: on 21 July, Gallatin wrote Steele that he found drawing up regulations for the New Orleans trade more difficult than he had thought, especially regarding "the exemption of duty on foreign goods *landed* at New Orleans." A certificate confirming the collection of duties at the originating Atlantic port would suffice for vessels going to the Mississippi Territory. But if cargoes were landed and unloaded at New Orleans, the U.S. consul at the port must provide a certificate affirming the identity of the goods "to secure the exemption from duty." The consul at New Orleans would also be called upon to determine whether transported cotton was grown in Spanish Louisiana or the United States. Gallatin asked Steele to "throw together all your ideas" for the regulations, "which you understand much better than I do" (Henry M. Wagstaff, ed., *The Papers of John Steele*, 2 vols. [Raleigh, N.C., 1924], 1:295-7).

The final regulations concerning the Mississippi trade—six sections in all, dated 26 Aug. 1802, and sent as a circular to the custom collectors on the 27th—

probably differed only slightly from the draft Gallatin enclosed in this letter. Vessels descending the Mississippi were to present a manifest to the collector at Fort Adams specifying the cargo. If the cargo consisted of articles grown, produced, or manufactured in the United States to be transported by way of New Orleans to any U.S. port, a certificate would be issued exempting the cargo from duty. The 4TH REGULATION stated that articles produced outside of the U.S. and liable to duties were not entitled "to the benefits of these regulations." The 5TH REGULATION stated: "Coasting vessels employed in this trade are to be restricted to the transportation of articles of the growth, produce or manufacture of the United States" (Gallatin, *Papers*, 7:508-9). After his correspondence with TJ, Gallatin expanded the designation of "consul" to "consul, vice-consul, or other authorized agent of the United States" at New Orleans (TJ to Gallatin, 14 Aug.; Gallatin to TJ, 19 Aug. 1802).

From Étienne Lemaire

MR.   Washington Sity du 7 aoux 1802

J'e prend, la Liberté, E Lhonneur de Vous Sualuer toute Votre Respectable, famille, J'espair que la presente Resûe, vouve trouve En Bonne Sentez Monsieur je vous, previens que la pompe de l'a Maison a Bien besoint d'etre Reparé Vûe, que les J'our qu'ils, plêut Beâucoupe les aêut Se trouve Renplie d'e vâsse, je vous prie monsieur de vouloir E Crir a Mr. m'onerot, il n'e veûx, Rien, fair fair Sant, vôs, ordre, ainsit mr. Come Sest ûne, Chôsse bien Esensiel, J'e vous, prie de vouloir, Bien vous En Rapeller,—J'e fait venir 21½ Corde de Bois, demême 400 Boisôt De Charbon de ter, de la Même personne, qui, En a fourni, avant, Ses mr. Barnes qu'il Me la Envoyé je pence que voila l'a proviseont pr. les feûx Bien, Conplette pr. toute l'anné il, m'est arivé de philadelphia, 6. Caisse de Sirot de ponge Qui est Bien bon,

Monsieur je l'honneur de vous, Souaiter une heureus E parfaite Sentez,—J'e fini aveque, toute l'atachement possible Je Sui vôttre tres unble E tre obeisent Serviteur,   E F. LEMAIRE

SIR.   Washington City, 7 Aug. 1802

I take the liberty and honor of greeting your eminent family. I hope this letter finds you in good health. I inform you, Sir, that the pump at the house is in urgent need of repair, since on days when it rains a lot, the sewers fill with mud. Please, Sir, could you write to Mr. Munroe; he does not want to have anything done without your orders and this is essential. I beg you please remember to do it. I ordered $21\frac{1}{2}$ cords of wood as well as 400 bushels of coal from the same person who furnished them before. Mr. Barnes recommended him to me. I think the heating provisions are now complete for the entire year. I received from Philadelphia six cases of syrup of punch which is very good indeed.

Sir, I have the honor of wishing you a happy and perfect health. I conclude with all possible fidelity. I am your very humble and obedient servant.

E. F. LEMAIRE

RC (MHi); endorsed by TJ as received 12 Aug. and so recorded in SJL.

From Gideon Granger

DEAR SIR.   Washington August 8th. 1802

Messrs. Bull and Dodd have notified me of their declining to accept the appointment of Commissioners. this has most certainly originated in the fixed determination of their friends in the City to persevere in their Attempts to obtain the removal of the Commissioner of Loans, and Postmaster. It exhibits a spirit in some measure assuming and really not very pleasing—I have not heared whether Mr. Nichols has concluded to serve, or has declined. I could wish that the vacancies might remain at present, and untill I shall write from Connecticut. It is my determination to retire from this City in a fortnight unless You should wish me to remain here. my Contracts are closed, and I think advantageously tho, by no means with such reductions, as in the large contracts in the War departmt: The State of my Office is such that the public Service will suffer no Injury from my absence. The Contest between the Clintonians and the Burrites runs very high in New York. I think it daily assumes a more serious Aspect. The Inclosed Letter I received from a friend by the last mail. Some parts of it, particularly what respects the Spanish Grants, appeared to me of Sufficient Importance to warrant my Submitting it to your perusal.

I am Sir With great Esteem and Respect—Yours

GIDN GRANGER

RC (DLC); at foot of text: "The President"; endorsed by TJ as received 12 Aug. and so recorded in SJL. Enclosure: Thomas Fenton to Granger, Natchez, 27 June 1802, reporting that in his exploration and mapping of the lands of Mississippi Territory "to which the Indian title has been extinguished," he finds "that one half of the Land granted by the Spanish Government has been done since the Ratification of the Treaty with that Nation—the difficulty is those Grants have been Antedated"; when considering candidates for surveyor general it will be necessary "to prevent Certain Characters from being appointed who are absolutely Interested in those antidated grants"; Fenton recommends Seth Pease as being "as suitable a Person for the office of Surveyor General as any to be found in the states"; Presley Nevill of Pittsburgh is also suitable for the office (RC in DNA: RG 59, LAR, endorsed by TJ: "Pease to be Surveyor genl. of Missisipi"; *Terr. Papers*, 5:154-5).

TJ followed Granger's recommendations in the appointment of bankruptcy commissioners for Connecticut. Both Jonathan BULL and John DODD wrote the secretary of state on 19 July from Hartford declining their commissions. Bull noted that by accepting the appointment he would give the opposition reason to take the state judicial offices he held away from him. He also noted: "It is the opinion of my Friends here that the cause in which we are engaged will not be advanced by my acceptance, but the reverse." Dodd informed Madison that "duty to my self and in my opinion to the Public require me to decline accepting the appointment." William Imlay, who began serving as COMMISSIONER OF LOANS for Connecticut in 1780 and was continued in office by President Washington in 1789, retained the position until his death in 1807. TJ then appointed Bull to the office. Dodd replaced Ezekiel Williams as POSTMASTER at Hartford in January 1803. I HAVE NOT HEARED: on 27 July, John Nicoll wrote Madison that he would not be able to serve as bankruptcy commissioner at New Haven because he was "frequently absent from the State" (RCs in DNA: RG 59, LAR; Madison, *Papers, Sec. of State Ser.*, 3:400, 403, 433; Washington, *Papers, Pres. Ser.*, 3:368; Stets, *Postmasters*, 99; JEP, 2:56; Vol. 34:42-3; Vol. 37: Appendix II, Lists 1 and 2). Elisha Hyde declined his appointment as bankruptcy commissioner as well. Writing the secretary of state on 24 Aug. from Norwich, Connecticut, Hyde noted that many of his Republican friends urged him to retain his seat in the state legislature instead of serving as a commissioner. There were, he observed, "too many" in the state government who felt "very uncandid towards the present Administration." He would have "an opportunity to be more active in favour of the present measures of the General Government" as a legislator (RC in DNA: RG 59, RD; endorsed by TJ: "Hyde Elisha. Connecticut declines Commn. bkrptcy").

To Thomas Munroe

DEAR SIR   Monticello. Aug. 8. 1802.

The inclosed letter to mr Mason, & that from mr Stoddert will explain themselves. be so good as to peruse & deliver them to mr Mason, and consult with him on their contents. whatever he and you think may be lawfully done, which may be an indulgence to mr Stoddert and not injure the public, I would wish you to do without delaying to consult me. Accept my best wishes & respects.

TH: JEFFERSON

PrC (DLC); at foot of text: "Mr. Monroe"; endorsed by TJ in ink on verso. Enclosures: (1) TJ to John Thomson Mason, 8 Aug. 1802 (recorded in SJL but not found). (2) Benjamin Stoddert to TJ, 8 Aug. 1802 (recorded in SJL as received from Georgetown on 8 Aug. but not found).

The missing enclosures related to efforts by Benjamin STODDERT to delay the forced sale of his lots in Washington, D.C. As part of the act abolishing the board of commissioners for the city, the superintendent of Washington was directed to dispose of all city lots sold prior to 6 May 1796, but which remained unpaid for, by 1 Nov. 1802. Proceeds were to be applied toward repayment of the $50,000 loan from the state of Maryland. In June, Munroe began advertising the public sale of a sizable number of city lots to take place on 30 Aug. Writing Munroe on 28 Aug., Stoddert forwarded a list of 96 lots that he wished "to be preserved & not offered at Public sale, until 20 October, before which time I hope to pay for them." After consulting with Mason, Munroe agreed to the postponement (U.S. Statutes at Large, 2:176; *Washington Federalist*, 9 Aug. 1802; Stoddert to Munroe, 28 Aug. 1802, in DNA: RG 42, LR; TJ to Munroe, 10 Sep. 1802). For background on Stoddert's landholdings in Washington and his previous efforts to delay their sale, see Vol. 35:97-100, 113, 175-6.

To Henry Dearborn

DEAR SIR   Monticello Aug. 9. 1802

I inclose you some more resignations of militia commissions. I think we should do well in all cases to know that a commission will be accepted, before [...].

We have recieved information that the emperor of Marocco, having asked passports for two vessels loaded with wheat to go to Tripoli while blockaded by us, and being refused, has ordered away our Consul: this demand of his is so palpably against reason & the usage of nations as to bespeak a settled design of war against us, or a general determination to make common cause with any of the Barbary powers at war with us. I had just written him a friendly letter to accompany 100. gun carriages asked by him of the former administration. but the state of things is so changed that it will not be proper now to send these. we expect the Boston to return shortly. there will then remain there the Chesapeake, Constellation & Adams; of which we had thought of recalling one, as two were deemed sufficient for Tripoli. it is now a question whether we should not leave the three there, & whether we should send [another? and a] very important question is What is the nature of the orders which should be given to the commanders of our vessels in the Mediterranean with respect to Marocco? as circumstances look towards war, I have asked the opinions of the heads of departments on the preceding questions, and will beg the favor of yours by the return of post, as the Genl. Greene [will] probably be detained to carry our orders.

Accept assurances of my affectionate esteem & respect.

TH: JEFFERSON

P. S. will you be so good as to ask [. . .] of Simpson's & Morris's letters at the Navy [office]?

PrC (DLC); faint; at foot of text: "The Secretary at War."

WE HAVE RECIEVED INFORMATION: for the dispatches received from James Simpson and Richard V. Morris, see TJ to Madison, 9 Aug.

WHEAT TO GO TO TRIPOLI: early in 1802, a Tripolitan ambassador in Morocco had requested and received a gift of wheat from Mawlay Sulayman, who also granted permission to load the cargo in Moroccan ports. Reporting these events in his dispatches from Tangier, James Simpson at first doubted that vessels could be chartered for Tripoli while that place was under blockade. The sultan, however, persisted in the plan. In May, Simpson reported that the sultan had ordered a Moroccan schooner to load wheat for Tripoli, and that a British brig had been chartered in Gibraltar for the same purpose. The motives behind the sultan's generosity toward Tripoli were unclear to Simpson, who could not decide whether it was an act of charity toward fellow Muslims or "an aid in their present Contest" and an attempt by the sultan to "get quit" of the 1786 treaty with the United States. Later in the same month, Simpson and the Swedish consul, Peter Wyk, received word from the sultan's chief minister, Muhammad Ibn Abd al-Salam al-Salawi, that if the wheat were permitted to ship with the departing Tripolitan ambassador as the property of the sultan, "it

will be very well." If not, Simpson and Wyk were to "do what is regular, and as is established by the Treaties of Peace" between their countries and Morocco. The 1786 treaty contained no provision for such a case, however, and Simpson reiterated his lack of authority to grant the requested passports. On 13 June, the governor of Tangier, Abd al-Rahman Ashash, informed Simpson that the sultan had directed the vessels carrying wheat to Tunis instead of Tripoli, much to Simpson's relief. Writing James Madison the following day, the consul praised the sultan's change of mind, "as by that means we get rid of what threatened to be a very unpleasant piece of busyness." At the governor's request, Simpson wrote the emperor to explain "the powerfull motives why I could not sanction Vessels going to Tripoly," but that he was ready to grant "the usual Certificates" for Tunis (Madison, *Papers, Sec. of State Ser.*, 2:379, 481; 3:50, 221-2, 278, 307; NDBW, 2:66, 149; Mohamed El Mansour, *Morocco in the Reign of Mawlay Sulayman* [Wisbech, Eng., 1990], 12, 19-20, 50).

FRIENDLY LETTER: TJ to Mawlay Sulayman, Sultan of Morocco, [5 Aug.].

WE EXPECT THE BOSTON: on 13 July, Robert Smith had sent orders recalling Captain Daniel McNeill and the frigate *Boston* to Washington, where the vessel was to be placed in ordinary (NDBW, 2:201).

To Albert Gallatin

DEAR SIR   Monticello Aug. 9. 1802.

We have recieved information that the emperor of Marocco having asked, & been refused, passports for two vessels loaded with wheat to go to Tripoli, while blockaded by us, has ordered away our Consul. this demand of his is so palpably against reason & the usage of nations, as to bespeak a settled design of war against us, or a general determination to make common cause with any of the Barbary powers at war with us. I had just written him a friendly letter to accompany 100. gun carriages asked by him of the former administration. but the state of things is so changed that it will not be proper now to send these. we expect the Boston to return shortly. there will then remain there the Chesapeake, Constellation & Adams, of which we had thought of recalling one, as two were deemed sufficient for Tripoli. it is now a question whether we should not leave the three there, and whether we should send another? and a very important question is What is the nature of the orders which should be given to the Commanders of our vessels in the Mediterranean with respect to Marocco? as circumstances look towards war, I have asked the opinions of the heads of departments on the preceding questions, and will beg the favor of yours by return of post, the Genl. Greene being probably detained to carry our orders. if you will take the trouble of calling at the Navy office, you can see the letters of Simpson & Morris on this occasion. Accept assurances of my affectionate esteem & respect. TH: JEFFERSON

RC (NHi: Gallatin Papers); addressed: "Albert Gallatin Secretary of the Treasury Washington"; endorsed. PrC (DLC).

From Albert Gallatin

SIR   Treasury Department 9th August 1802

I have the honor to enclose a letter from the Commissioner of the revenue together with one from the Collector of New London, and unite in recommending Joseph Griffin as a suitable person to keep the light house on Faulkner's island.

I have the honor to be with the highest respect Sir Your most obdt. Servt.   ALBERT GALLATIN

RC (DLC); at foot of text: "The President of the United States"; endorsed by TJ as received from the Treasury Department on 12 Aug. and "Light house Faulkner's island" and so recorded in SJL. Enclosures not found.

COLLECTOR OF NEW LONDON: Jedediah Huntington. For the construction of the lighthouse on Falkner's Island and recommendations for another candidate as lighthouse keeper, see Vol. 35:91-2, 492. Joseph Griffing (GRIFFIN) served as lighthouse keeper from 1802 to 1808 (Harlan Hamilton, *Lights & Legends: A Historical Guide to Lighthouses of Long Island Sound, Fishers Island Sound and Block Island Sound* [Stamford, Conn., 1987], 116).

From Albert Gallatin

DEAR SIR   Washington 9th August 1802

I arrived here last week, and found much business to do, but principally mere details with which I will not trouble you.

A second report has come to hand in relation to the Delaware piers recommending Reedy Island, in lieu of Marcus hook: finding three persons to have been appointed by a law of the State of Delaware superintendents to erect piers at New-castle, I wrote to them for information in relation to that spot, and when[1] that shall have been received will forward the whole to you.

The Collector of Norfolk, instead of sending the detailed estimate of the repairs necessary for the hospital, transmitted one consisting only of four items & amounting to near 11,000 dollars. I wrote him again for details; but finding one of the items for six hundred dollars to be for that wing which is now occupied by the seamen, & which, by the representation of the collector, and Gen. Dearborn's statement, was so leaky that the sick were shifted from place to place whenever it rained, I thought those repairs might be immediately authorized without waiting for your official approbation which I knew under those circumstances, would not be refused.

I have written to you two official letters, one relating to the appointment of a light house keeper, the other enclosing a set of regulations for the Mississipi trade. These I wish you would be good enough to examine as soon as convenient and to return with your approbation or alterations, as I only wait for their return to dispatch a circular, after which I will take an excursion to the hills.

I enclose the recommendation for Slade's Creek, the only one which I have received, &, for your recollection, enclose also your letter to me of the 2d ulto. as it relates to Jasper. I think Tooley may be appointed.

General Dearborn has written to you that Lyman is gone to Europe, and has I suppose recommended Cross in his place for Newbury-port, and he has also, I presume, written that Warren will not accept Marblehead. For this last place W. R. Lee recommends Joseph Wilson; his letter I enclose. There are blank commissions left at the Secretary of State's office which will be filled for both places as you may direct. I stopt just in time the commissions for Lyman & Warren & the Comptroller's letters of dismission to Tyng & Gerry. Smith had, however, published in his papers the intended appointments—but that will not prevent the dismissed officers from continuing to act till the successors shall have been appointed. Crowningshield writes from

Salem that Lee is an improper appointment—is that well grounded? or mere clanish prejudice? If the first, it is really extremely wrong in our friends to give such erroneous information, for who could be more strongly recommended than Lee? But Crowningshield recommends John Gibaut, who to me, by an old personal friend, a clergyman in Salem had also been very strongly recommended, but on hearing the manner in which Lee was spoken of, did not even mention Gibaut's name. He would certainly have been better for Salem. Cr. now recommends him for Gloucester (the only port in Essex left untouched) instead of Tuck whom he represents as worse than Tyng. I suppose Gen. Dearborne has written all this & have mentioned it only in order to say that under present information, and for the purpose of pacifying Salem I would not think it wrong to appoint Wilson—Cross—& Gibault in lieu of —— Tyng—Gerry[2]—Tuck for —— Newburyport—Marblehead—Gloucester. Lee has got his Salem commission. Had I seen Crown.'s letter I would also have stopt it, (as Lee was willing to take Marblehead,) till you had had the whole subject once more before you.

Appearances are strong at New York—the schism disgusts many republicans, is fomented by the federalists—Wood's pamphlet has done & will do no inconsiderable injury.   Every thing seems placid in Pennsylvania, though the party makes a tolerably ingenious argument out of M.'s appt. I apprehend we have lost some ground in New Jersey: it is said we have gained in Delaware. I doubt it.

With affection and respect Your obedt. Servt.

ALBERT GALLATIN

RC (DLC); with emendations by TJ (see note 2 below); addressed: "Thomas Jefferson President of the United States"; endorsed by TJ as received from the Treasury Department on 12 Aug. and "appointments" and so recorded in SJL. Enclosures: (1) TJ to Gallatin, 2 July 1802. (2) Perhaps William R. Lee to Henry Dearborn, 16 July 1802, recommending Joshua Orne, a moderate Federalist, as collector at Marblehead, or Joseph Wilson, "who is in my opinion equal to the trust, his character good, his politicks republican"; offering also to accept for himself the collectorship at Marblehead if the position at Salem does not become vacant; and warning that under no circumstance should "our ex parson" (Isaac Story) receive an appointment from the administration, noting that he

differs in politics, uses "ungarded expressions, respecting the President," and is "of a character in whome no confidence can be placed" (RC in NHi: Gallatin Papers, endorsed by Dearborn: "Joseph Wilson collector for Marblehead," endorsed by Gallatin: "to Gen. Dearborn"; Vol. 35:517n; Dearborn to TJ, 3 Sep. 1802). Other enclosures not found.

THREE PERSONS: the supplementary act for the erection of piers in New Castle passed by the Delaware general assembly on 1 Feb. 1802 named Archibald Alexander, James Riddle, and James McCallmont as commissioners to superintend the work (*Laws of the State of Delaware; Passed at a Session of the General Assembly, Which was Begun and Held at Dover, on Tuesday, the 5th day of January, and*

Ended on Friday, the 5th Day of February, in the Year of our Lord One Thousand Eight Hundred and Two [Dover, Del., 1802], 223-8).

On 6 Aug., Gallatin wrote William Davies, COLLECTOR OF NORFOLK, and authorized the expenditure of $600 to repair the east wing of Gosport Hospital. Gallatin also requested a more detailed estimate, including the cost of "repairing the roof of the whole building, and such other repairs as may be essentially necessary" (Gallatin, *Papers*, 7:425). For an earlier report by Davies on conditions at the Norfolk hospital, see Vol. 34:681-2. DEARBORN'S STATEMENT has not been found, but see TJ to Thomas Newton, 12 July, for the secretary of war's trip to Norfolk.

TWO OFFICIAL LETTERS: see the preceding letter of this date and Gallatin to TJ, 7 Aug.

The recommendation for surveyor at SLADE'S CREEK, North Carolina, has not been found, but it was evidently for Henry Tuley (TOOLEY), who received the appointment (David Stone to TJ, 1 May 1802).

DEARBORN HAS WRITTEN TO YOU: see his letter to TJ at 10 Aug.

MORE STRONGLY RECOMMENDED: William Heath, Levi Lincoln, and James Sullivan were among those who endorsed William R. Lee (Vol. 35:315-16,

498, 686). CROWNINGSHIELD RECOMMENDS: see Jacob Crowninshield to TJ, 15 Dec. 1801, for his earlier recommendation of John Gibaut instead of Lee at Salem. OLD PERSONAL FRIEND: William Bentley. The Salem clergyman wrote Gallatin on 7 Jan. 1802, recommending Gibaut, his former pupil at Harvard. Noting Gibaut's abilities in mathematics, accounts, and all branches of natural history, Bentley declared: "He has the most extensive commercial knowledge of any man I know." He valued Gibaut, now his neighbor and friend, "for his virtues, his talents, & his republicanism" (Gallatin, *Papers*, 6:427). Recommended by the leading Essex County Federalists, William TUCK had served as collector at Gloucester since 1795 (Prince, *Federalists*, 30; JEP, 1:180-1).

John WOOD'S PAMPHLET, *A Correct Statement of the Various Sources from which The History of the Administration of John Adams was Compiled* was published in New York in late July (see Vol. 36:478n). M.'S APPT.: Muhlenberg's appointment as collector at Philadelphia (Gallatin to TJ, [7 July], second letter).

[1] MS: "what."

[2] TJ here interlined in pencil "Cross" above "Tyng" and "Wilson" above "Gerry" (see TJ's second letter to Gallatin at 14 Aug.).

From Elbridge Gerry

MY DEAR SIR   Cambridge 9th August 1802

Being apprized, by the gazettes, that Major Warren is appointed Collector, in the room of my brother S M Gerry, I cannot conceal from you, the high sensations of pleasure & pain, which have been the result, in my mind, of this event; & at the same time the conviction, that you have considered it as an indispensable measure.

Major Warren is a very worthy character, & a branch of a family with which I have long been in the habits of the most intimate friendship. General Warren & his sons have high claims on the gratitude of their country, have for this reason, for a number of years, been persecuted by faction, & are justly entitled to the rewards of their services & sufferings. the promotion therefore of Major Warren, abstractedly

considered, was very grateful to my feelings. but the affliction was inexpressible, which resulted from a veiw of Mr Gerry's case. inured to
adversity, I should certainly have suffered in silence, the pains of fra-
ternal sympathy, the jeers of implacable & triumphant enemies, & pecuniary losses which will fall heavy on my numerous young family,
rather than to have imparted to any friend, my inevitable grief; had
I not been informed from undoubted authority, that altho Major
Warren earnestly wishes to accept the proffer'd honor, he cannot do
it without a sacrifice of property to the smallness of the emolument,
an exchange of his most intimate friends for new connections, &
an abandonment of his important & increasing political influence in
the county of Plymouth: & that for these & other reasons, he will
be obliged to decline the appointment. thus circumstanced, I am
impelled by a sense of indispensable duty, to present, to your veiw
the case of that depressed, honest, but unfortunate officer Mr G.; to
enquire, whether in case Major Warren declines, a new nomination
may not be prevented by the fulfillment, on the part of my brother, of
certain stipulations, & what these are? & to assure you that nothing
in my power shall be wanting, to aid him, in being reinstated in the
favor of an administration; to the support of which, I am urged by
every consideration of a public & private nature.

On the 7th & 14th of December last, I wrote to Judge Lincoln, &
communicating fully to him, my ideas of this affair, requested him to
impart them to the Secretary of the Treasury. I have never received
an answer to either of those letters, or any information on the subject;
except from Doctor Eustis, to whom they were enclosed; who, several weeks after his return from Congress, stated to me that the letters were received, & gave me too much reason to beleive, that his
own conduct on the occasion was by no means friendly. this is an
enigma, which I should be very glad to have explained.

Permit me, dear Sir to communicate the purport of the letters referred to . . . . after premising, that during the revolutionary war, Mr
Gerry had lost all his property, by the capture of seven or eight vessels in which he was concerned, & that after the war he had purchased some fishing vessels, mortgaged his estate for the payment of
them, & being unsuccessful, was obliged to sell them & apply the
proceeds to the payment of his debts; which left him in arrears about
14, or 1500 dollars: I stated, *that* in the summer of 1790, the merchants of Marblehead, unanimously recommended him to the President, & *that* he was appointed, in preferrence to another candidate,
who had the support of Mr Hamilton & his party: his character being
that, of an industrious, honest, benevolent but unfortunate man. *That*

the distressed state of Marblehead made the office wretched; *that* he himself had but an inadequate idea of it; & *that* till within a few days, previous to the date of my letters, I knew nothing of the subject. *that* at that period, he informed me, of the dissatisfaction of the secretary of the Treasury, in regard to his accounts, & of an agent, sent to inspect them. *that* a short time afterwards, the agent informed me, that Mr Gerry had made no quarterly returns for the year, or weekly returns for the quarter, & that from an estimate, not accurate, he was 3,831 dollars in arrears. *that* chagrin'd & astonished at the information, I repaired to Mhead, & hastily concluded, that Mr Gerry had adventured at sea, & lost this property. *that* expressing this sentiment to him, & reproaching him for his conduct, he heard me patiently, but with marks of the deepest distress. *that* in answer he declared, that he was an unfortunate, but honest man: that every one who knew him, & God himself, could witness to the fact. *that* his books & files might be examined & scrutinized, *that* he had never squandered a farthing of the public money, in gambling, speculation, or commerce of any kind, *that* he had been always temperate, industrious, œconomical, & moral, & *that* neither he or his wife could be charged with a vice of any kind. *that* when he accepted the office, having five children from seven to eighteen years old, & being indebted about 14, or 1500 dollars, he dismissed his servants & had lived without any to that period. *that* he had kept, neither horse or chaise, had entertained no company, had sought no kind of amusements, & during eleven years of his being in office, he had barely existed. *that* his creditors reduced him to the sad alternative, of paying his debts, or relinquishing the office: *that* the latter must have involved his family in misery, & he submitted to the former from necessity; not in the least doubting, that the government would allow him more than a bare subsistence, & that the surplus would soon offset his debts. *that* he employed a clerk three years, gave him one hundred & twenty dollars, with the fees of weighing & gauging, & then dismissed him; because he was unable to pay him. *that* he had since done all the business of the office himself, except when sick, or pushed by business, & then he was obliged to pay two dollars a day. *that* after dismissing his clerk he discovered a deficiency of fifteen hundred dollars & could never account for it. *that* his eldest daughter being married & his sons at sea, his family was now reduced to himself, wife, & youngest daughter, & *that* if permitted to wade thro his difficulties, he had now a prospect of emerging from them; but *that*, if he was to be deprived of his office, after all his sufferings, he had but one request to make, that a pistol may be placed to his head & another to his wife's, & an end be put to their wretched existence. *that* this declaration from a virtuous & unfortunate brother, struck me dumb, & with deep regret, for having unduly reproached him.

that I enquired of him the amount of his annual expences; *that* he in answer said, he had kept an account of them, but he had never footed it, being always enveloped in the business of his office; *that* when requested by me, he had cast up his expences for the three first years & ascertained their amount, and was convinced, that the fifteen hundred dollars, which he could not account for before, must have been expended in his family: for his emoluments from the 20th of august 1790 to the same date 1793 were then discovered to have been but 1007 $ 80—or 335 dollars $ 93 cents a year. *that* his office was burthened with the extra business of seventy sail of fishermen; the allowance for which, was but ninety cents a year for each. *that* by a statement of his emoluments from the 20th of August 1790 to the 31st of december 1800, being ten years four months & eleven days, they amounted to but 6137 $ 56 averaging 595 dollars & 26 cents a year. *that* on examining his family expences they averaged from eight to nine hundred dollars a year. *that* on enquiring what property he had, he stated, that he had only his furniture, which he owned when he began the office, & that he would dispose of it, if requisite, to discharge a part of his debt. *that* in my enquiry, into the cause of his not having stated his case to the former secretaries of the treasury, he replyed, that they knew it perfectly well, & if they had not a disposition to releive him, he could not create it: that poverty he had braved, but was unequal to beggary. *that* on enquiry, why he had not stated to the secretaries the amount of his arrears, he said that when the merchants to whom he owed money, had stopped it out of their bonds, & the amount of the debts he was thus compelled to pay, was added to the 1500 dollars which he could not before this time account for, he was depressed & terrifyed; lest his misfortunes should by a party spirit be imputed to him as a fault: that he determined to cancel this debt, by the most rigid œconomy: but that herein he was defeated by the high prices of the necessaries of life, & the poverty of his office: & *that* in every extremity, his accounts would prove, he had conducted with integrity. that in aid of his office, he was promised the agency of building the fort, & an allowance on tonnage & hospital money; but these promises were delusive. that his political conduct was narrowly watched, he was obliged to give up the Chronicle, & threatned with the loss of office, merely for having in his house a french Jacobin picture, & he considered himself as a victim of party spirit, & as having been intentionally neglected.

[183]

That from the commencement of his office, he had credited the bonds due, *as cash*, & had always supposed it agreable to rule, untill he received the instructions of Mr Gallatin to the contrary: but that these should in future be strictly observed.

That he had complied with the earnest request of the merchants, in not demanding so much of their bonds, as would be cancelled by their debentures, & fishery bounties: this indulgence however had been attended with no loss to the public, having been confined to merchants of undoubted credit.

That in the cases of two who failed, he had anticipated the event, had applied to the district attorney for an attachment of their property before the bonds became due, & finding this impracticable, had put them in suit, on the day they became due—had recovered judgment, extended an execution, & committed the merchants to prison; who afterwards swore out, & were dismissed by certificates, shewn to him, from Mr Woolcot. *that* these bonds were nevertheless, not passed to his credit. I also stated from my own knowledge, That this officer had devoted his whole time to the office, had attended it morning noon & in the evening from the commencement of his appointment to that period, not even allowing himself sufficient time for exercise. that his health was greatly injured thereby, & chronic disorders were the consequence. to these facts, stated simply as they were delivered, & added some remarks.

I think the general testimony of the inhabitants of Marblehead, can be adduced if requisite, to prove, that Mr Gerry lived in a very humble style indeed, for a collecter of the United States: & that humble as it was, it could not be supported for six, or under eight or nine hundred dollars a year. this being established, & it being an uncontrovertible fact, that he devoted to the office his whole time, without the possibility of increasing his assiduity, his delinquency in not bringing up his accounts, cannot as I conceive be charged to him as a fault: because that object could only be attained by the hire of a clerk, & by an application of the public money to pay his wages; & he justly considered a delay of his accounts a less evil, than an increase of his defalcations. had he Sir not been indebted to the public, & not without property of his own, there would have been no apology for the backwardness of his accounts: but as he commenced the office without property, & the emolument of it was so small as to immerse him, every year deeper in debt, I conceive, but I may be mistaken, that insisting in such a case on punctuality, would be insisting on a measure not physically practicable: & sure I am, that the present government requires but a thorough knowledge of the greivance, to redress it. the fact is Sir, & it ought not to be concealed, that the establishments of the collectors, made under the former administration, were in many cases partial, & in others oppressive . . . fifteen to twenty thousand dollars a year for the services of one collector, & six hundred dollars for those of another collector, equally indefatigable, can never in my opinion be reasonable or just. Congress have rectified the error as it respected excesses, & I doubt not they will as it relates to any deficiencies. had I been in time apprized of Mr Gerry's situation, I should have urged him to have communicated it to Congress without delay, & all the unpleasant consequences which have resulted from the radical error pointed out would have probably been prevented: for a competent salary or income[1] would have enabled him to have subsisted his family decently & hired a clerk, & then by his humble style of living, he in a few years might have saved an offset to his debts.

I am not informed whether he has been blamed or not, for the indulgence granted to the merchants in not collecting so much of their bonds as might be cancelled by draw backs & fishery bounties: but It is presumed not; because his object being merely to accomodate trade & unattended with loss to the public, could not I presume be veiwed in an objectionable light, unless persued subsequent to a prohibition; & as to the losses which resulted from the two bankruptcies, he fully discharged his duty, if he can establish the facts which he has stated in regard to them, & of which I have not the least doubt. indeed by endeavoring to put the bonds in suit, before they became due, he performed a work of supererrogation.

He will at first blush appear to be more culpable, for concealing the ballance due from him to the public, than he really was. he had commenced his office with the practice of entering bonds due, whether received or not, as cash; & this practice of course swelled the ballance of his cash account, beyond it's true amount, & was not corrected by the former administrations of the treasury. the subsequent debt, which he contracted in the manner herein truly stated, was thus unascertained by the former Secretaries, & he was anxious it should remain so, in hopes of an increase of his emoluments, by a decrease of his family & of the prices of necessaries of life, & an increase of his revenue—the terror he was in from the time of his discovering this debt was great; for unfortunately he confined his distress to his own bosom, not imparting it till the arrival of the agent to any person, not even his wife or myself. the debt of 1500 dollars which he missed, was unknowingly & unexpectedly contracted, by his not seperating his emolument every quarter from the public money. had this been done he could not have failed to have discovered the excess, the first quarter. but if he had, a question will arise, how was he to subsist? he had no credit or resources, other than those of his office, which were inadequate to his subsistence; the department of the treasury, which in the first instance had reported to Congress a system for rewarding the revenue officers, without documents to equalize it, were to my certain knowledge, when these could be obtained, to have reported them & have corrected the inequalities: but they neglected this, for reasons to me unknown, & have thus carried on a shameful system of favoritism towards some officers, & of oppression towards others: & I beleive on scrutinizing the subject, it will appear that very few, if any officers, not guilty or suspected of the crime of republicanism, were victims of this unjust system. I do not wish to extenuate the culpability of my brothers conduct, in any respect; if he has under all circumstances merited censure, infamy, or death, let him suffer it; but if his hard fate has been that of a persecuted,[2] oppressed & neglected, but at the same time of a virtuous diligent & honest officer, I only request my dear Sir, that his conduct may not be veiwed abstractedly, but in relation to that of his persecutors & oppressors: & I think that his offences must appear to be venial. the system which you have established for conducting the fiscal operations I admire & think them excellent. the gentleman under whom you have placed their administration, I have not the pleasure of being acquainted with, but being acquainted with his general character & conduct, have no hesitation to declare, that if abilities, probity, industry, & a sacred regard to impartial justice are recommendation to the office, I know not the person in America who could supply his place. he is a foreigner, it is true, & so was Mr Hamilton; & the latter moreover was a descendant of a british officer. indeed during the revolutionary war, Congress passed a resolution, which I drew myself, inviting Doctor Price to be our financier. he considered it as a high honor, & declined it on account of age & inability to cross the atlantic. I cannot be suspected therefore of a wish, it is hoped, of continuing in office a friend, at the expence of embarrassing your system. but the office at Mhead I think cannot be duly executed without a clerk, & the emolument has not rendered the hire of one practicable. besides my dear Sir, why should a collector, be subject not only to the responsibility of character but of bonds for the faithful execution of his office, with a revenue of 600 dollars, & the clerks of Collectors in the neighboring ports receive, as some of them actually have done, 1500 dollars a year, without any responsibility, or danger of public disgrace by dismissal? to aid & assist my brother, under his penurious establishments & the extravagant rates of necessary articles of life,[3] I have given him his house & office rent, & the improvement of my land on Mhead, & have imparted property to his sons, when qualified to pursue their fortunes at sea; otherwise his defalcations must inevitably have been greater. I observed the sparing hand of the former treasury secretaries towards him, & easily conceived the cause; but could not submit to solicit even justice for a brother, of those gentlemen . . . . after ten or twelve years of hard service & close living, he is two thousand dollars more in debt, than when he entered the office—It is to be regretted, that in answer to my letters, I had not been informed of the probability of his dismissal, & of the practicability or impracticability of avoiding it: because the silence adopted on the occasion, induced me to suppose, that the government, informed of all the circumstances attending this case, would not come to a sudden decission, & that on the return of Judge Lincoln, I should be minutely informed on the subject. being earnestly solicitous that he should bring up his accounts, & then prefer to Congress a petition for redress, stating candidly & explicitly the favorable & unfavorable circumstances of the case, I have repeatedly been to Mhead, & found Mr Gerry always occupied in his office & exerting himself to accomplish that object: but the business of the office, he informed me, had greatly increased by the repeal of the internal taxes & an unusual number of clearances during the spring; & that he could not at that time procure a proper person to assist him, & after June he should have not much other business to attend to . . . but the period for accomplishing his wishes arrived too late.

If there is yet a possibility of saving this officer, I hope the conditions will be as favorable, as the case will admit, & I will send a clerk from this neighbourhood at my own expence, if one cannot still be procured there, to compleat his accounts: but if his doom is irrevocable, he must submit to his fate; the pains of which, I think, will not be of long duration.

Having finished my remarks on this very painful subject, permit me to observe, that I have for a long time thot it expedient, to place on your files a more minute & authentic relation of my mission to france, than is contained in a cursory letter which I wrote you by Judge Lincoln: if this meets your full approbation. I have expected & hoped that pickerings dismissal, Hamilton's strictures on Mr Adams &c &c would have rendered a statement of facts necessary on my part, & have given me an opportunity of exposing the numerous mis-representations & falsehoods, which have been propagated in regard to myself, & been altogether on my part unnoticed.

I wish also to give some general hints in regard to public concerns. your election has had the effect expected, of reuniting the Adamites & Hamiltonians; & I am informed they are more acrimonious than before. a new sect will probably spring up, in consequence of the republican scisms, but it will not be very extensive. under these circumstances, it will be incumbent on the republicans, to be vigilant, firm, & persevering: for if the federalists should regain their ground, which God forbid, the condition of republicans would be more intollerable than ever. I bid you adeiu, my dear Sir, & remain with the highest esteem, & most respectful attachment your sincere friend

E GERRY

RC (DLC): at foot of text: "His Excellency Mr Jefferson President of the UStates"; ellipses in original; endorsed by TJ as received 22 Aug. and so recorded in SJL. Enclosed in Tristram Dalton to TJ, 19 Aug.

APPRIZED, BY THE GAZETTES: on 5 Aug., the *Boston Gazette* reprinted a list of "Appointments by the President" that had first appeared in the *Washington Federalist* of 30 July. According to the list, Henry WARREN was replacing Samuel Russell Gerry as the collector of customs at Marblehead.

GENERAL WARREN: James Warren.

For Gerry's attempts to communicate through Levi LINCOLN and William EUSTIS in December 1801, see Vol. 36:195-6, 205.

When the collectorship at Marblehead became vacant by the death of the incumbent IN THE SUMMER OF 1790, Elbridge Gerry wrote to George Washington and John Adams in support of his brother. He may also have sent Washington a testimonial from more than fifty MERCHANTS OF MARBLEHEAD. Besides Samuel Gerry, at least three people either sought the position or were suggested for it (Washington, *Papers, Pres. Ser.*, 5:172n; 6:78, 87-8, 123-5; Syrett, *Hamilton*, 6:498).

AGENT: in November 1801, Gallatin ordered an investigation of the Marblehead custom house, under the supervision

of Benjamin Lincoln (Vol. 35:587n; Vol. 36:196n).

Samuel R. Gerry's WIFE was the former Sarah Thompson (Linda Grant De Pauw and others, eds., *Documentary History of the First Federal Congress of the United States of America*, 17 vols. to date [Baltimore, 1972-], 2:504).

BUILDING THE FORT: that is, the fortifications on Castle Island to protect Boston harbor (Vol. 34:81-2, 85n).

GIVE UP THE CHRONICLE: the staunchly partisan *Independent Chronicle* was the voice of prominent Massachusetts Republicans, who often met at the newspaper's offices. In 1798-99, its editor, who at that time was Thomas Adams, was prosecuted for seditious libel (Pasley, *Tyranny of Printers*, 107-8; James Morton Smith, *Freedom's Fetters: The Alien and Sedition Laws and American Civil Liberties* [Ithaca, N.Y., 1956], 247-57).

CONGRESS HAVE RECTIFIED THE ERROR: beginning 30 June 1802, by an act of 30 Apr., the annual emoluments of a collector of customs, excluding fines, forfeitures, and penalties and after the deduction of necessary expenditures, could not exceed $5,000. The limit for naval officers was $3,500, and for surveyors of customs, $3,000 (U.S. Statutes at Large, 2:172-3).

GENTLEMAN UNDER WHOM YOU HAVE PLACED THEIR ADMINISTRATION: Albert Gallatin.

By a RESOLUTION of 8 Oct. 1778, the Continental Congress extended an offer of American citizenship to Richard Price and asked for his "assistance in regulating their finances." Price declined the invitation (Worthington C. Ford and others, eds., *Journals of the Continental Congress, 1774-1789*, 34 vols. [Washington, D.C., 1904-37], 12:984-5; Franklin, *Papers*, 28:200-1; Robert J. Taylor and others, eds., *Papers of John Adams*, 15 vols. to date [Cambridge, Mass., 1977-   ], 7:361-2).

Gerry discussed his MISSION TO FRANCE in a letter of 15 Jan. 1801, concluding the account in a second letter dated five days later. He asked Levi Lincoln to carry the communications (Vol. 32:465-9, 489-95).

[1] Preceding two words interlined.
[2] MS: "perscuted."
[3] Preceding eight words and ampersand interlined.

To James Madison

DEAR SIR   Monticello Aug. 9. 1802.

The inclosed letter from mr Simpson our Consul in Marocco was forwarded to me from your office by yesterday's post. the demand of the emperor of Marocco is so palpably against reason & the usage of nations that we may consider it as a proof either that he is determined to go to war with us at all events, or that he will always make common cause with the Barbary powers when we are at war with any of them. his having ordered our Consul away is at any rate a preliminary of so much meaning, that the draught of the letter I had forwarded you for him, as well as the sending him the gun carriages, are no longer adapted to the state of things. on this subject I should be glad of your opinion, as also of what nature should be the orders now to be given to our officers in the Mediterranean.

The Boston frigate is expected to return: there will then remain in the Mediterranean the Chesapeake, Morris, the Adams, Campbell, & the Constitution Murray; one of which perhaps would have been recalled, as two are thought sufficient for the war with Tripoli, especially while Sweden cooperates. in the present state of things would it not be adviseable to let the three remain? or does it seem necessary to send another?

I inclose you a letter from Richard Law dated New London. I suppose he may be the District judge & should be answered.[1] the proper notification of the Commrs. of bankruptcy to the judges seems to be[2] their commission exhibited by themselves to the court, as is done in the case of a Marshal, the only other officer of a court appointed by us.

Accept assurances of my constant & affectionate esteem.

TH: JEFFERSON

P.S. a letter from Capt. Morris informs us he had gone over to Tangier, but had not yet had any communication with the government: but that he should absolutely refuse the passports.

RC (DNA: RG 59, MLR); at foot of text: "The Secretary of State." PrC (DLC). Recorded in SJL with notation "Marocco business" with "do." at letters of this date to Navy, War, and Treasury Departments. Enclosures: (1) James Simpson to James Madison, Tangier, 17 June 1802, informing the secretary "with great concern" that the information received by himself and the Swedish consul "on Sunday last," respecting Mawlay Sulayman's decision to send his wheat vessels to Tunis rather than Tripoli, was either "extremely fallacious" on the part of the governor of Tangier or that the sultan "must have very speedily repented" his declaration; this morning the governor told Simpson that he had received new instructions from the sultan, "with Orders to demand from me Passports for those Vessels to go direct to Tripoly and in case of refusal that I was to quit the Country, adding that the Letter was written in such strong terms, as must prevent his consenting to any mitigation"; after "a very long conference" with the governor, Simpson was permitted time to write Commodore Morris at Gibraltar, "which I am now about to do fully, on his answer will depend my remaining in this Country, or being compelled to retire from it" (see below); since a Portuguese brig is about to depart for Gibraltar, Simpson will not enlarge further on the matter but assures the secretary that "nothing possible for me to accomplish, for good of the Public Service on this occasion, shall be neglected" (DNA: RG 59, CD; Madison, *Papers, Sec. of State Ser.*, 3:319-20). (2) Richard Law to TJ, 29 July 1802 (recorded in SJL as received from New London on 8 Aug. but not found).

THE CONSTITUTION: here, and in his letter to Robert Smith of the same date printed below, TJ mistakenly wrote the *Constitution*, which was in ordinary at Boston at this time, instead of the *Constellation* (NDBW, *Register*, 70-1). TJ identified the vessel correctly in his letters

to Henry Dearborn and Albert Gallatin of this date, printed above.

WHILE SWEDEN COOPERATES: Sweden, like the United States, was at war with Tripoli. In 1801, after the Swedish government refused to ratify a treaty that would have stopped hostilities but required substantial payments to Tripoli, Swedish warships arrived in the Mediterranean with instructions to work in conjunction with the U.S. squadron. Swedish and American naval commanders agreed to provide convoy protection to both countries' merchant ships and cooperated in blockading Tripoli. Through John Quincy Adams, before he left his post as U.S. minister to Prussia, Sweden renewed a suggestion that the United States join with Denmark and Sweden in a formal alliance in the Mediterranean. During John Adams's presidency the United States had received a similar overture, which Adams rejected because the United States was not then at war with any of the Barbary states and had treaties of amity with all of them. Although TJ and Madison continued to shun an official alliance, in April 1802, when Madison gave James L. Cathcart instructions for negotiating with Tripoli, he took note of the "good disposition which Sweden has shewn to unite her measures with those of the U States, for controuling the predatory habits of the Barbary powers." Madison asked Cathcart to continue cooperating informally with the Swedes (Madison, *Papers, Sec. of State Ser.*, 1:4-5, 348-9, 370; 2:83-4, 97; 3:136; NDBW, 1:599, 603, 605, 610-11, 620, 627, 637; 2:28, 41, 52-3, 163; Michael Kitzen, "Money bags or Cannon Balls: The Origins of the Tripolitan War, 1795-1801," *Journal of the Early Republic*, 16 [1996], 617, 619; Ray W. Irwin, *The Diplomatic Relations of the United States with the Barbary Powers, 1776-1816* [Chapel Hill, 1931], 122; Vol. 36:667).

LETTER FROM CAPT. MORRIS: on 20 June 1802, Commodore Richard V. Morris wrote the secretary of the navy that he had arrived off Tangier, but had not been on shore or received new communications from James Simpson. He would send any information by the first available conveyance, and in the meantime awaited the arrival of the frigate *Adams* with instructions from the secretary. Until then, Morris avows that "I certainly shall not consent to granting the passports required by the Emperor of Morocco." Morris also enclosed copies of Simpson's letter to him of 17 June and his reply of ca. 19 June. Simpson's communication informed the commodore of the sultan's renewed passport demands for the wheat vessels intended for Tripoli and his threat to expel Simpson if the request were not granted. He also told Morris that the sultan planned on sending "a Captain and crew with his passport" for a Tripolitan ship "that lies at Gibraltar, which would be navigated under his flag." The governor of Tangier agreed to suspend the sultan's orders until Simpson could write Morris and receive his answer. Simpson believed that granting the passports would inflict "far less national injury" than a refusal would have on American commerce in the region. Although Morocco had "not a single cruiser to send to sea," Simpson feared increased insurance premiums and pointed out that several American vessels were currently at Mogador, with more expected. Simpson attempted to explain to

the governor the consequences of carrying out the sultan's orders, but to no effect. "Thus situated," Simpson felt that "it is better to grant the passports than to come to a rupture with this country." There was not "the least shadow of hope" that he would be allowed to remain if the sultan's request was not granted. In response, Morris wrote that although he regretted Simpson's situation and the effect his expulsion would have on American trade, he could not consent to granting the passports. The "unreasonableness" of the sultan's demands "instantly points out the conduct we are to pursue," Morris replied. "Surely, the United States would not blockade a port, at considerable expence," he added, "if the government contemplated their officers would permit supplies to be furnished the ports in that situation by neighboring powers, and thus defeat the intent of the blockade." The secretary of the navy, however, had promised Morris instructions on this point by the *Adams*, which is "momently expected," and Morris urged Simpson to negotiate a suspension of the sultan's orders until the frigate arrived (NDBW, 2:181-3).

[1] TJ here canceled "I suppose."
[2] Preceding three words interlined in place of "is."

From Samuel Morse

DEAR SIR,   Savannah, 9th. Augt 1802.

I have the pleasure to inclose you a copy of an oration delivered on the 3d of July, the day chosen by the citizens of this place for the commemoration of our independence. This oration is the very hasty production of a young friend of mine, who is now aid to gen. Jackson. I pursuade myself that you will receive some pleasure in the evidence he gives of the firmness of his republicanism, though, taking the impressions in a different sense, he disagrees with you on the subject of the unanimity of national sentiment.

I think I do not decieve myself in believing you take some little interest in my welfare, and that when I inform you I have been severely ill and am not yet recovered, it will not be obtruding information in which you have *no* interest. Our press not having yet arrived from Philadelphia, the paper is not yet commenced; to what the disappointment is owing I cannot divine, but hope it will soon be removed.

My weakness prevents my extending this letter to some subjects on which reflections have arisen but when blessed with renewed health, any information in my power will be *fully* communicated.

With the sincerest affection & respect Yours   SAML MORSE

RC (MHi); at foot of text: "Th: Jefferson Esq. President"; endorsed by TJ as received 26 Aug. and so recorded in SJL. Enclosure: Thomas U. P. Charlton, *Oration in Commemoration of American Independence; Delivered at the Exchange, in the City of Savannah, July 3d, 1802* (Savannah, 1802; Sowerby, No. 4682).

VERY HASTY PRODUCTION OF A YOUNG FRIEND OF MINE: Thomas U. P. Charlton dedicated his Independence Day oration, written "on the spur of the occasion" and "in the course of a few hours," to the Republicans of Chatham County, Georgia. He challenged TJ's idea of coalition as expressed in the first inaugural address and

deemed it the "meek and conciliatory language of a great and benevolent Statesman." Instead, Charlton urged Democratic-Republicanism to rely on its own strength (*Oration*, preface, 9-10, 12; Vol. 33:479).

PAPER IS NOT YET COMMENCED: Morse, who had suffered from measles earlier in the year, formed a printing partnership with James Lyon and published the first issue of the Savannah *Georgia Republican & State Intelligencer* on 21 Aug. 1802. TJ paid Morse $6 on 6 June 1802 for a year's subscription and continued to subscribe until 1809 (MB, 2:1074; Vol. 32:34; Vol. 36:655).

From John Page

MY DEAR FRIEND   Roswell Augt. 9th. 1802

A Shock of Vertigo, one of a series of its Attacks which I have sustained since the middle of Apl deterred me from declaring to you that I would be ready to execute your Commands at Petersburg about the 15th. Instt. I waited a few days in hopes of having no return of that dreadful Disorder, & of being better qualified to comply with my Promise. but on Saturday 30th. July I was again violently attacked with little intermission till Wednesday Morng. God only knows now whether I shall ever be able to act as Collector or not, so miserably am I shattered both in Body & Mind. Accept Sir this Apology for not sooner offering to act. & with it my Resignation of the Office, which by the News-papers I find you have honored me with, as from the nature of my Disorder & my experience of its Effects in 1774 & part of 1775 it utterly disqualifies me for paying that Attention to Calculations Accounts & minute Examination of various Copies of important

Papers, & the appearance of various kinds of Coins & bank Notes, which is indispensably necessary to the due Execution of the duties of Office as well as to the preservation of the officer's Reputation & his, & his Securities, Estates. At a great risk of a shock I write this. Accept my best thanks & believe me truely yours—

JOHN PAGE

RC (DLC); endorsed by TJ as received 26 Aug. and so recorded in SJL.

YOU HAVE HONORED ME: during the first week of August newspapers began to announce Page's appointment as collector of customs in Petersburg. Other reports at about the same time identified him as a likely successor to James Monroe as governor of Virginia (Baltimore *Republican or, Anti-Democrat*, 2 Aug. 1802; Richmond *Virginia Argus*, 21 July 1802).

To Robert Smith

DEAR SIR   Monticello Aug. 9. 1802.

I recieved yesterday the inclosed copies of letters from Simpson & Commodore Morris forwarded from your office. the demand of the emperor of Marocco is so palpably against reason and the usage of nations, that it bespeaks either a determination to go to war with us at all events, or that he will always make common cause with any of the Barbary powers who may be at war with us. his having ordered away our Consul is a preliminary of so much meaning, that the letter I had written him and the sending him the gun carriages, are no longer adapted to the state of things. I have therefore suggested to the Secretary of state the stopping them, which I would wish you to do till you hear further from us. in the mean time I will ask your opinion of what nature should be the orders now to be given to our officers in the Mediterranean? and whether we should leave there all the three frigates, Chesapeake, Constitution & Adams? you know we supposed two sufficient for Tripoli? you will judge, should the Genl. Greene be ready, whether she should not be detained till we decide on the orders to be given. Accept assurances of my affectionate esteem & respect.   TH: JEFFERSON

RC (MdHi); at foot of text: "The Secretary of the Navy." PrC (DLC). Enclosures: (1) James Simpson to Madison, 17 June (Enclosure No. 1, listed at TJ to Madison, 9 Aug.). (2) Richard V. Morris to secretary of the navy, 20 June, with enclosures (see TJ to Madison, 9 Aug.).

From Samuel Smith

SIR/   Baltimore 9 June [i.e. August] 1802

Capt. Norman (a respectable Man of this City) has arrived here from Trieste, he has just informed me, that on his passage he Came thro: the Phare of Messina, & landed at the City, that he was informed that a Courier had passed thro: (the Day preceding) from Syracuse with an Account that a Neapolitan frigate was Chased by a Tunisian Squadron, that Capt. McNeill ran between and Cut off the Chase, on which the Tunisian Commodore fired into the Boston. the Fire was immediately returned—a general Action ensued, in which two of the Tunisians were Sunk, two dismasted, and three ran away—The Neopolitan gave no Aid—The Account Stated that the Boston was greatly injured & many of her Officers & Men killed—The imprudence of that Mad Man will I fear have brought a Severe Enemy upon us— # the Tunisians will pay themselves from our Merchant Men—Capt Norman left Messina the 2d. June & arrived at Gibraltar the 19th. he there Saw Capt. Morris, who informed him of what was passing between him & the Emperor of Morocco, on which subject He brought Letters to the Secy—The Emperor had two Ships lately launched & built by Spanish Workmen, the one pierced for 36 Guns & the other for 22, but not mounted. they were loading with Wheat & for them he had resumed his former Demand for passports, as well as the Demand to take possession of the Tripolitan Ship at Gibraltar with his Men, both which were refused by our & the Swedish Consuls—in Consequence both were ordered from the Empire & the Swedish Consul had Actually arrived at Gibraltar—our Consul remained until he Could hear from the Commodore, with whom Capt. Norman had stretched over to Tangiers—I regret excessively that the Commodore had not had the power to permit the Trading ships to pass—The Emperor will be so dangerous that No ship will Venture to go to the Mediterranean—Morris desired Capt. N. to tell me that without Small Vessels there was no Safety for our Ships for that Frigates Could not Cruize in the Gut—he must either Cruize out to Sea or within the Mediterranean—He told Capt. Norman to tell me that War with the Emperor was Certain and that a reinforcement was absolutely necessary—that he meant to send for Lt. Sterett by first oppy.

I observe that the Essex has been ordered to Washington. I am sorry for it—She will be wanted. I pray that the orders for the Boston

---

the Vice Consul at Messina believed the Acct.

to come there may be Changed—It will Create more Uneasiness than Can easily be Conceived & will greatly prejudice the next Elections— besides from every Appearance she will Soon be wanted to return & can be manned much easier at Boston than at Washington—I pray you to believe that this Opinion is given from my great Anxiety for your Administration and that I am in truth

your friend & Serv   S. SMITH

RC (DLC); addressed: "T. Jefferson, Esqr. President of the United States"; endorsed by TJ as received 16 Aug. and so recorded in SJL with notation "[June for] Aug. 9."

Captain James NORMAN of the brig *Hope* arrived at Baltimore on 3 Aug. (Madison, *Papers, Sec. of State Ser.,* 1:380; Baltimore *Federal Gazette,* 3 Aug. 1802). Additional reports of the alleged engagement between a TUNISIAN SQUADRON and Captain Daniel MCNEILL of the frigate *Boston* also appeared in the Boston *Columbian Centinel* on 7 Aug., the *New-York Evening Post* on 9 Aug., and the Norfolk *Commercial Register* on 16 Aug. No official confirmation of the engagement ever came to Washington, however, and American consuls in the Mediterranean could neither verify the account nor discover its source. Writing James Madison on 25 Jan. 1803, James Leander Cathcart emphatically declared, "Nothing of the kind ever happen'd" (Madison, *Papers, Sec. of State Ser.,* 3:507n, 592; 4:282).

PHARE: a strait or channel lit by a lighthouse, frequently used in reference to the Strait of Messina (OED).

TWO SHIPS LATELY LAUNCHED: in dispatches sent from Tangier during the spring and summer of 1802, American consul James Simpson reported the launch of two frigates at Rabat on 2 May, each pierced for 26 guns, as well as the preparation of two galleys at Tetuán. Simpson added, however, that it would be "some time" before any of these vessels would be ready for sea (Madison, *Papers, Sec. of State Ser.,* 3:50, 222, 279, 343).

TRIPOLITAN SHIP AT GIBRALTAR: early in 1802, in conjunction with his de-

mand for passports for the wheat shipments to Tripoli, Mawlay Sulayman had also requested a passport for a Tripolitan warship at Gibraltar, which had been blockaded there by American frigates since July 1801. James Simpson deflected this initial request in February 1802 by informing the sultan that he was not authorized to issue the requested passport, but would forward the matter to Commodore Richard Dale. The following month, Dale replied that he could not issue a passport for the vessels without the approval of the president. The sultan renewed his demand in June, with Simpson replying again that he had no authority to issue the passport but hoped to receive instructions on the matter soon (Madison, *Papers, Sec. of State Ser.,* 2:481; 3:50, 51n, 278; NDBW, 2:77, 80; Vol. 35:219).

THE GUT: that is, the Gut, or Strait, of Gibraltar (OED).

The frigate ESSEX returned to New York from the Mediterranean on 23 July and was immediately ordered to proceed to Washington. The order caused consternation among the ship's crew, who had already exceeded their 12-month enlistment and had expected to be discharged at New York. Expressing their displeasure to Captain William Bainbridge, the crew were given the choice of "doing their duty, or to be carried in irons" to Washington. Eighteen members chose the latter option. After receiving provisions at New York, the *Essex* departed for Washington on 29 July. Arriving on 9 Aug., the ship was placed in ordinary (NDBW, 2:118, 210, 225-6).

ORDERS FOR THE BOSTON: see TJ to Henry Dearborn, 9 Aug.

To Benjamin Stoddert

SIR   Monticello Aug. 9. 1802.

Your favor of the 8th. is duly recieved. not having here a copy of the act of Congress for the resale of the lots, it is out of my power to decide [how far that act] [...] discretionary power over the sale. but I have by this post written to mr J. T. Mason, our ordinary counsel in the city affairs, to consider & advise mr Monroe as to the extent of our discretionary power over the sale of the lots, and then on a consultation with mr Monroe if it should be their opinion that a compliance with your desire will be legal, & not injurious to the public, then to yield the indulgence without the further delay of [consulting with me:] and I have expressed to mr Monroe as well as to [him] that I consider individual accomodation as a duty whenever it is legal, and of no detriment to the public. I sincerely wish the indulgence may be found to be within these limits as no man feels more sensibly than I do the task of carrying into execution laws which bring on private distress. Accept my good wishes & respects.

                                                    TH: JEFFERSON

PrC (DLC); faint; at foot of text: "Benjamin Stoddert esq."; endorsed by TJ in ink on verso.

FAVOR OF THE 8TH: see Thomas Munroe to TJ, 8 Aug.

From John Barnes

SIR   George Town 10th Augt. 1802

I am again honored with your favr. 6th. Announcing Mr Shorts arrival at Norfolk, 28 Ulto. expected to embark the next day for Baltimore, in his way to Washington and Richmond.—my particular inquiries have not been successfull. I rather presume, his having learned your absence from Washington—have since determined him, to alter his rout via Hampton & Williamsburg &c. or, should he pass thru Washington—every Attention my Finances & Services can possibly Afford him shall be offer'd—and every other satisfactory document presented him, respecting his Public Stock & a/c in my Possession—of which (—in Case, I have not the Honr. of meeting with him—) you can inform him (—if not, the particulars with you—) it may be proper for me to Minute here, viz "His a/c to 22d. June last—as transmitted to him (but probably not recd when He left Paris—)—

Then Balance in his favr. $154.94 only: since when,
viz 1st July By Quarterly Int.   458.55 and, on the
3d. Augt. via G&J Canal divd.   <u> 98.</u>
                                 $711.49 less

Negocbls. &c—comprizes the whole of his a/c to the present time.
By schr. Tryal, from Philada. a few days since were recd (but by
whom shipped, I could not learn ℔ the Capt)
viz. two Boxes Merchandize one Keg of China ⎫ as ℔ freight
six Boxes Liquers & one Spear—   ⎭ List $4.12½
these are in possession of Mr LeMaire, to whom I sent particular directions—in Case Mr Short should call to see the House, to apprize
me immediately,—your Case,—and two Boxes ℔ Schr Dolphin I expect will leave this in 2-3 days. I am waiting advises from Mr Hopkins in answer to mine of the 6th. Inst.—at all events, I shall not *now*
leave this, before I learn from you, whether or not, Mr Short stands
in need of an immediate supply of Cash, and in what mode best
suited, to remit him—

I have to beg, you will present, my humble respects to Mr Short
and accept with unfeigned Esteem those of

Sir your most Obedient   JOHN BARNES

RC (ViU: Edgehill-Randolph Papers); at foot of text: "The President US: Monti-cello"; endorsed by TJ as received 12 Aug. and so recorded in SJL.

From Elias Boudinot

DEAR SIR   Rosehill August 10. 1802

Knowing your fondness for Agriculture, and every thing connected with it, tho' in a collateral respect, I take the liberty of
troubling you, amidst the arduous affairs of government, with the
following fact—If it is new to you, your curiosity will be gratified; if
not, the information you will be able to give me, as to the native soil
of this production, will lay me under peculiar obligations—

In the fall of 1800, I was presented, at second hand, with a few
quarts of an extraordinary wheat, from a distant Country; but
from whom it came or from what country, have wholly slipped my
Memory.

At seed time, when cleaning it for sowing, I discovered four uncommon grains, which I was wholly unacquainted with, the legs &
beard (which I afterwards found belonged to them) being entirely
broken off by the friction with the wheat—I put them up carefully till

the spring, and then planted them in a good soil—At Harvest, they turned out to be a species of Oats of a peculiar Nature—When ripe, I was collecting them from the Straw by hand—Having picked 14 or 15 I laid them on the grass, till I gathered more; but in 10 minutes they disappeared, and could not be found—I gathered a number more & put them in the center of a Salver with a perforated rim, and carefully placed it over night, where it could not be disturbed—The next morning, I found every grain at the rim of the Salver, with its head thro' the holes of the Rim—I then dipped one in Water, and laid it on paper, when it not only plainly discovered a power of loco-motion, but sprang about half an Inch. On trying others I was con-vinced that providence had endued them with this power to propa-gate themselves. On carefully examining them with a magnifying Glass, there appeared a spiral line round the upper part of the leg, which I presume is the cause of their motion—I have called them, an-imated Oats, for indeed they are the nearest line between Vegetation and animation, that I know of.

Many Gentlemen, both natives & Foreigners, have seen them dur-ing the past year, but no one could inform me of their native Country.

This last spring, I sowed more of them, and have just gathered a new crop. They are so great a curiosity to me & my acquaintances, that I have ventured to trouble you, with a small Box containing a few of them for your examination—If I should be mistaken and they should not be new to you, I hope you will charge it to my ignorance of natural history, and excuse the liberty I have taken, from a desire of gratifying your love of Agriculture—

By taking one of them by the end of his long legs, and dipping him under water about the second of a minute, and laying it on a sheet of Paper, you will soon percieve its operation—They should be carefully dryed in the Sun, or Air—and when whet again they will repeat the Motion—Some of them may fail, on account of their not being thor-oughly ripe—They are most brisk in damp weather—

I have the honor to be with great respect D Sir Your obedt Hble Servt   ELIAS BOUDINOT

RC (DLC); addressed: "The President of the United States Washington"; also on address sheet in Boudinot's hand, "private" and "with a small box"; franked and postmarked; endorsed by TJ as re-ceived 16 Aug. and so recorded in SJL.

Often referred to as ANIMATED OATS, *Avena sterilis* is an oat grass that exhibits "curious movements of the spikelets, caused by the twisting of the awns under the influence of moisture or dryness" (*Webster's New International Dictionary of the English Language* [Springfield, Mass., 1953], 106).

From Daniel Brent

Dep: of State, August 10th 1802.

Daniel Brent respectfully informs the President that a duplicate Commission was sent some time ago to Mr Scott, and that he acknowledged the receipt of it on the 27th of last month. He begs leave also to inform the President that a Commission for Mr Selman is made out, and sent to the Treasury Department;—one of the Blanks already signed by the President and Secretary of State having answered the purpose.

RC (DLC): endorsed by TJ as received from the State Department on 12 Aug. and so recorded in SJL.

From Henry Dearborn

SIR   Washington August 10th. 1802

Genl. Lyman having sailed for Europe & it being uncertain when he will return, I know of no character who I could recommend to fill the place now held by Ting who would probably be more deserving and would give better satisfaction than Genl. Ralf Cross of Newbury port—I inclose part of a letter from Mr. Crowninshield, for the purpose of shewing his opinion on the propriety of removing Mr. Tuck, the Collector at Cape Ann, and puting Mr. Gibaut in his place.—Mr. Crowninshield & Mr. Dane both having declined acting as Commissioners in cases of Bankrupcies it will be necessary to appoint one other in addition to young Mr. Story. You will observe Mr. Crowninshields recommendation of Prentice & Killam, Prentice being a member of the Legislature, it may be proper to prefer Killam.— I have this day forwarded your letter to Story.—I think it would be as well to appoint his son whether the old Gentleman consents or not.—the person proposed by Mr. Gallatin to be Collector of Marblehead who is so highly recommended by Col. Lee, I should presume may be appointed with a reasonable expectation of his being a suitable character.—

with sentiments of respectfull consideration I am Sir Your Hume Sevt   H. DEARBORN

P.S. Sir please to accept my thanks for your friendly admonition respecting my early removal from this place.—I hope to be able to git away in eight or ten days.—   H.D

RC (DLC); at foot of text: "The President of the United States"; with postscript written on a separate sheet; endorsed by TJ as received from the War Department on 12 Aug. and "Lyman, Ting, Cross &c" and so recorded in SJL. Enclosure not found.

PRENTICE & KILLAM: that is, Joshua Prentiss, representative from Marble-head, and Daniel Kilham of Wenham. TJ appointed Kilham a bankruptcy commissioner on 27 Aug. (Vol. 37:430-1, 707; Memorandum on Appointments, 6 July 1802; TJ to Madison, 27 Aug.).

YOUR LETTER TO STORY: TJ to Isaac Story, 5 Aug.

PERSON PROPOSED BY MR. GALLATIN: Joseph Wilson (Gallatin to TJ, 9 Aug.).

From William Jarvis

SIR   Lisbon 10th Aug: 1802

Ever attentive to your commands I have been enquireing for the Oeiras Wine, but cannot find any here to be depended on as genuine, there being several times more sold under that name than is made on the Estate. Presumeing Sir that none but the first quality would suit you, I supposd it would be more agreeable to wait a few weeks longer untill I could get the best from the Country, than to have such sent as I could obtain in this place.

With the most profound Veneration & Respect I am Sir Your Most Hble Servant   WILLIAM JARVIS

RC (DLC); at foot of text: "His Excellency Thomas Jefferson"; endorsed by TJ as received 9 Oct. and so recorded in SJL.

William Jarvis (1770-1859) was born into a prominent Boston family and educated at schools in Bordentown, New Jersey, and Philadelphia. Embarking on a mercantile career, he apprenticed in Norfolk and Portsmouth, Virginia, before establishing his own firm in Boston. Despite an early business failure, he managed to conduct several successful transatlantic trading ventures, gaining particular expertise in Portugal. Personally known to Henry Dearborn, Jarvis applied to the Secretary of War in August and October 1801, as well as to James Madison, to become the American consul in Lisbon and was confirmed in the position in February 1802. He remained consul until 1811, also operating a commission house there. After Bonaparte's armies invaded the Iberian peninsula,

Jarvis took advantage of the disordered situation and acquired about 3,500 merino sheep, a breed that the Spanish government had previously guarded against export. In addition to distributing small numbers of sheep throughout the United States, including a handful that he gave to TJ, Jarvis established a substantial sheep-raising operation on a farm he purchased in Weathersfield, Vermont. He remained there for the rest of his life, pioneering the American cultivation of merino wool, which soon emerged as the dominant agricultural activity in Vermont, and becoming a staunch advocate of protective tariffs and of the National Republican and Whig Parties that championed them (Jarvis to Henry Dearborn, 22 Aug. and 1 Oct. 1801, RC in DNA: RG 59, LAR, endorsed by TJ: "to be Consul at Lisbon"; Jarvis to James Madison, 22 Aug. 1801, RC in same; JEP, 1:406-7; DAB; Randolph A. Roth, *The Democratic Dilemma: Religion, Reform, and the Social Order in the Con-*

necticut *River Valley of Vermont, 1791-*
1850 [Cambridge, 1987], 165, 173-4, 177,
248; John J. Duffy, Samuel B. Hand,
and Ralph H. Orth, eds., *The Vermont*
Encyclopedia [Hanover, N.H., 2003],
170; RS, 2:166).

OEIRAS WINE was a dry variety named
after the ESTATE near Lisbon on which
it was produced (John Hailman, *Thomas*
Jefferson on Wine [Jackson, Miss.,
2006], 276; MB, 2:1097).

From Dr. Samuel Kennedy

Hardwick Township, Sussex County,
& state of Newjersey

HOND. SIR/   Aug. 10th 1802

from the commencement of our Revolution I was amongst the
warmest Advocates for Independence; viewing an entire seperation
from great Brittain absolutely necessary for our political salvation
& anxiously waited for that event—.—ever since the declaration of
independence, I looked forward with pleasing expectation that you
would fill the presidential Chair—being fully convinced that a Gentleman of your well known abilities & philanthropic principles, an extensive knowledge and high esteem for the just Rights & Liberties
of mankind; consistent with good order & Government, as well as
Amor. patriæ, would, in the estimation of every true republican, federal Citizen, fill it with safety to the people & with honour respect, &
applause to yourself—therefore I do sincerely congratulate my fellow
Citizens that you fill the Chair—heartily despising the illiberal &
wanton abuse you have recd., both by tongue & press, from those self
stiled friends of order & good government.—& rejoice that your exalted & philosophic sentiments raises you above all their venom—
envy is its own destroyer—as a small mite or token of my esteem &
respect for true republican principles, a steady adherence to the spirit
of our constitution & the rights of mankind both civil & religious—I
named my son born the 18th. July last Thomas Jefferson—not from
ostentation, or any expected emolument either to myself or son, but
to testify to my fellow Citizens my approbation of the man whose
name my son will have the honour to bear—that the Allmighty Ruler
of the Universe may long, long preserve your life; for the happiness
of the Union—is the earnest prayer of Hond. Sir, with unfeigned
respect your sincere, tho' unknown, friend & fellow Citizen

DOCR. SAML. KENNEDY
one of the Judges in &
for the County of Sussex

[201]

RC (MWA); endorsed by TJ as received 22 Aug. and so recorded in SJL.

Samuel Kennedy (ca. 1740-1804), the son of the Scottish-born theologian and doctor by the same name, was a prominent physician who resided in Johnsonburg, New Jersey. A member of the state assembly in 1780, he was also appointed a county judge in 1800 and was the father of many children, including TJ's namesake, whom he had with his second wife, Anna Shaeffer Kennedy (Casper Schaeffer, *Memoirs and Reminiscences Together with Sketches of the Early History of Sussex County, New Jersey* [Hackensack, N.J., 1907], 52-4; James P. Snell, comp., *History of Sussex and Warren Counties, New Jersey* [Philadelphia, 1881], 159, 161).

From William Lee

Agency of the United States

SIR Bordeaux August 10th 1802

I take the liberty to enclose the Moniteur of the 6th inst containing the new Organization and have the honour to remain

with much respect your humble servant WILLIAM LEE

RC (DLC); endorsed by TJ as received 5 Oct. and so recorded in SJL. Enclosure: *Gazette Nationale ou le Moniteur Universel*, 18 Thermidor Year 10 (6 Aug. 1802), containing the text of the *sénatus-consulte organique* of 16 Thermidor (see below).

NEW ORGANIZATION: on 3 Aug., the *Sénat* of France certified the results of the national plebiscite. The official count included more than 3.5 million votes in favor of granting Bonaparte life tenure as first consul and fewer than 8,400 votes in opposition. Bonaparte had already supervised the drafting of a new frame of government, which became the constitution of the Year 10. The *Conseil d'État* received it on 4 Aug. in the form of a *séna-tus-consulte*, or senate decree, which the *Conseil* approved the next day. In addition to making Bonaparte first consul for life, the instrument gave him the power to choose his successor. The *Corps Législatif* lost potency and the role of the *Sénat*, which Bonaparte would be able to control, increased. The constitution created a system of electoral assemblies at the canton level, but they had no direct role in choosing members of the governing bodies. The constitutional changes gave Bonaparte the means to rule France unencumbered by elections or an independent legislature (Thierry Lentz, *Le Grand Consulat, 1799-1804* [Paris, 1999], 341-6; Tulard, *Dictionnaire Napoléon*, 498-501).

From James Monroe

Augt. 10. 1802.

Jas. Monroe's best respects to Mr. Jefferson. He has the pleasure to send him a letter from Mr. Short with two pamphlets. He is very sorry he has it not in his power to call on him at present. An injury which he recd. in his leg a few days before he left Richmd., wh. is much increased by inflamation in coming up, confines him to his room. He hopes however that a few days repose will relieve him from so painful an embarrassment.

RC (DLC); endorsed by TJ as received 10 Aug. and so recorded in SJL. Enclosures not found.

The letter from William SHORT to TJ was probably one of 6 Aug., recorded in SJL as received from Richmond on the 10th, but not found.

IN COMING UP: Monroe had traveled from Richmond to Albemarle County, where he intended to sell some property near Charlottesville (Preston, *Catalogue*, 1:131).

From Edmund Custis

DR SIR,   Baltimore 11th Augt. 1802

On hearing of the death of Mr. Dandrige Consul at Auxcayes, in St. Domingo & finding bussiness extreamly dull here, Am induced to Solicit an appointment to succeed him, having been long Accustom'd to that Climate

I am Dr Sir Very Respectfully your Mo. Obt. Servt

EDMUND CUSTIS

RC (DNA: RG 59, LAR); addressed: "Thos. Jefferson, Esquire President of the U. States"; franked and postmarked; endorsed by TJ as received 16 Aug. and so recorded in SJL; also endorsed by TJ: "to be Consul at Auxcayes."

Bartholomew Dandridge (DANDRIGE), Jr., died at Cayes, Saint-Domingue, on 17 July. TJ had named him commercial agent at Port Républicain (Port-au-Prince) in November 1801 (Baltimore *Democratic Republican*, 10 Aug. 1802; Vol. 33:677, 678; Vol. 35:312-3). For a previous attempt by Custis to SOLICIT AN APPOINTMENT, see Custis to TJ, 15 Mch. 1801.

From George Jefferson

DEAR SIR   Richmond 11th. Augt. 1802

I yesterday sent you by direction of Messrs. Watson & Higganbotham 20 Bushels of Coal—I likewise forwarded by R. Mooney 2 dozn. syrup of punch. there is no Rhode Island lime to be had here. there is some from Philadelphia, which *the owners* say is good. I cannot yet procure any such linen as you require.

Mr. Short is gone to Washington, of which I suppose you will have heard by the Governor.

I am Dear Sir Your Very humble servt.   GEO. JEFFERSON

RC (MHi); at foot of text: "Thos. Jefferson esqr."; endorsed by TJ as received 27 Aug. but recorded in SJL as received 26 Aug.

From James Madison

DEAR SIR   Orange Aug. 11. 1802

I reached home just before dark this evening, after the most fatiguing journey I ever encountered, having made the tour I proposed over the mountains, and met with every difficulty which bad roads & bad weather could inflict. As this must be at the Court House early in the morning, I have only time to inclose you some despatches from Mr. Livingston which I recd. the night before I left Washington, and decyphered on the journey, with some others which I found here on my arrival[1] & have but slightly run over. The inclosed patent may be sent[2] with your signature to the office without returning thro' my hands. Your favor of the 30th. Ult: I also found here on my arrival.

Yrs with respectful attachment   JAMES MADISON

RC (DLC); at foot of text: "The President of the U States"; endorsed by TJ as received from the State Department on 12 Aug. and so recorded in SJL. Enclosures: probably (1) Robert R. Livingston to Madison, 27 Mch., regarding complaints by the French government against Daniel McNeill, French involvement in the West Indies, duties on exports in foreign vessels, and U.S. arms to Saint-Domingue (Madison, *Papers, Sec. of State Ser.*, 3:76-9; Pierre Samuel Du Pont de Nemours to TJ, 12 May). (2) Livingston to Madison, 10 May, regarding French debt repayment, the French invasion of Saint-Domingue, and assassination plots against the first consul (Madison, *Papers, Sec. of State Ser.*, 3:204-6). (3) Livingston to Madison, 10 May, regarding Napoleon's life tenure as first consul, Italian troops embarking for Saint-Domingue, and Jean Baptiste Bernadotte's supposed command of a French occupation force to Louisiana (same, 207). (4) Livingston to Madison, 12 May, regarding Napoleon's life tenure as first consul and the issue of succession, the resignation of Thomas Sumter, Jr., and Livingston's desire to name a secretary of legation (same, 219-20);

Daniel Brent, in September 1802, sent TJ a two-sentence extract on Livingston's desire to name a secretary of legation (Tr in DLC; Madison, *Papers, Sec. of State Ser.*, 3:220, 555). (5) Livingston to Madison, 20 May 1802, regarding U.S. claims against France, armaments for Louisiana, Napoleon's life tenure as first consul, Livingston's fitness for his office as minister, and renewal of the slave trade (same, 229-33). (6) Patent not identified, but see note to Matthew C. Groves to TJ, 2 Aug. 1802, for one of nine patents issued between 17 Aug. and 24 Sep. (*List of Patents*, 29).

FATIGUING JOURNEY: probably a family trip to Harewood, near Charles Town, Virginia, to visit Lucy Payne Washington, Dolley Madison's sister. While also commenting on the "fatigues" of the journey, Dolley Madison noted that she spent three happy days with her sister (Mattern and Shulman, *Dolley Madison*, 50-1, 414; Ralph Ketcham, *James Madison: A Biography* [New York, 1971], 381).

[1] Remainder of sentence interlined.
[2] MS: "may sent."

To William Short

Dear Sir   Monticello Aug. 12. 1802.

Your letter of July 28. from Norfolk reached me here on the 5th. inst. I immediately wrote to mr Barnes at Washington & mr Jefferson at Richmond to furnish you with any sums of money you might want, and to the latter I inclosed a letter to yourself recommending to you to get from the tide waters as soon as you could, in consideration of the season, and pressed your coming and making this your head quarters for the months of Aug. and September during which I shall be here. by your letter of the 6th. from Richmond I percieve you would leave that place before mine of the same day could get there; and tho the present goes by the first post for Washington, yet the rapidity of your motions and the uncertainty in what direction they will next be may perhaps disappoint this also of it's aim. under the contrary possibility however, I hazard it to repeat my invitations to you to make this place your home while I am here, persuaded you will find none more healthy, none so convenient for your affairs and certainly none where you will be so cordially welcome:[1] and particularly to press your not remaining any time on the tidewaters, between this & frost, after having been so long unacclimated to them. I shall reserve matters of business & of news for our personal interview, and in the hope that that will be speedy, I will only repeat here assurances of my constant & affectionate esteem & respect.   Th: Jefferson

RC (DLC: Short Papers); addressed: "William Short esq. to the care of mr John Barnes Georgetown. Columbia"; franked; endorsed by Short as received at Georgetown about 15 Aug.

immediately wrote: TJ to George Jefferson, 5 Aug., and to John Barnes, 6 Aug.

inclosed a letter: according to SJL, TJ wrote to Short on 5 Aug. That letter has not been found. For the one from Short of 6 Aug. from richmond, see James Monroe to TJ, 10 Aug.

[1] Preceding ten words interlined.

From Joseph Yznardi, Sr.

Exmo. Señor   Cadiz. 12 de Agosto de 1802

Muy Señor mio, y de mi Estimasion

He llegado a este Pais Algo endeble pero Conosco el beneficio de mi Salud despues de desenbarcado, y no pierdo momento en Manifestar á V.E lo Inmenso de mi gratitud teniendo presente los Infinitos favores, y distinciones qe se digno Consederme durante mi permanencia

{ 205 }

en los Estados Unidos y desseo dar pruebas de mi reconocimiento, no dudando me Continuará en su Amistad

Escribo a el Secretario de Estado Sobre los Deveres de mi enpleo, que Serviré con la Fidelidad propia de mi Celo, á pesar de la Justa quexa qe debo tener de lo poco qe se me ha protijido en la Injusta Solicitud de Josef Isrrael que recuerdo á V.E afin de qe se termine, pues, poco me ha preguntado por el Govierno Sobre ello y tanbien, en el particular del Insulto del Bergantin Español Cavo de Hornos, y sus Marineros, de lo qe Nada he dicho ni puedo decir porqe el Rey con sus Ministros pasan á Barcelona oy para el Casamiento del Principe é Infanta

se ablos con probavilidad qe buena parte quiere Coronar como Rey en el Ducado de Saboya al principe de la Paz, que yo no dudaría porqe este Cavallero es el todo poderoso, en este Reyno

asta la buelta de la Corte no paso á Madrid con Cuyo Motibo tengo escrito á Mr Pinckney dandole Memorias de V.E, y de sus Conocidos qe me lo encargarón

parese se tratava del Nonbramiento de Comisionados para el Arreglo de Presas hechas en la Guerra en Cuya Junta si puedo Servir de Algo, Manifestaré la rectitud de mi Opinion y Conosimientos positibos

Los Moros han hecho otra pressa americana Segun lo Comunico oy al Secretario de Estado, y el Comercio Americano, en estas Mares se halla, sin Ninguna proteccion, y temo Mucho Salgan del Mediteraneo los Corsarios, qe no abria Subsedido, si mi Plan se Ubiece Admitido aumentando fuercas Mayores

Espero qe V.E me encargará lo qe ce le ofresca de este Pais, y qe me favoresca de tienpo en tienpo, con la permanencia de su Salud, y Mras Ruego á Dios se la guarde Muchos anos.

Exmo. Señor BLM de V.E su obedte Servidor

JOSEF YZNARDY

MOST EXCELLENT SIR   Cadiz, 12 Aug. 1802

Dear Sir and with my respect,

I arrived in this country in a somewhat weakened state, but I recognize an improvement in my health after disembarking, and I will not waste a moment in manifesting to Your Excellency my immense gratitude, bearing in mind your infinite favors and the distinctions that you deigned to grant me during my stay in the United States; and I wish to give proof of my appreciation, not doubting that you will continue your friendship.

I wrote to the secretary of state about the duties of my post, which I will fulfill with the loyalty characteristic of my diligence, in spite of the rightful complaint that I should have for the scant protection I have received in the unfair lawsuit of Joseph Israel, of which I remind Your Excellency so that it may end, since little has been asked of me regarding it by the government; and also about the issue of the affront of the Spanish brig *Cabo de Hornos* and its sailors, about which I have said nothing and cannot say anything because the king and his ministers will go to Barcelona today to celebrate the marriages of the prince and the princess.

It is said that probably a good number of people want to crown the prince of the peace as king in the duchy of Savoy, which I would not doubt because this gentleman is all-powerful in this kingdom.

I will not go to Madrid until the return of the court, about which I have written to Mr. Pinckney, giving him Your Excellency's regards and that of his acquaintants who have asked me to do so.

It appears that the naming of commissioners for settling prize captures made during the war has been dealt with, at which meeting, if I can be of some service, I will show the rectitude of my opinion and my helpful knowledge.

The Moors have made another American prize, according to what was communicated today to the secretary of state, and American trade in these seas finds itself without protection; and I much fear that the corsairs will leave the Mediterranean, which would not have happened if my plan of increasing forces had been accepted.

I hope that Your Excellency will request of me whatever this country has to offer, and that you will favor me from time to time with your continued good health, and further I pray to God to preserve it for many years.

Most Excellent Sir, your obedient servant kisses Your Excellency's hand.

JOSEF YZNARDY

RC (DLC); at foot of text: "Exmo. Sr. Dn Thomas Jefferson"; endorsed by TJ as received 20 Oct. and so recorded in SJL.

HE LLEGADO A ESTE PAIS: Yznardi traveled on a Spanish ship that left Philadelphia early in June and arrived at Cadiz on 20 July. Ships arriving from the United States were held in quarantine for a period before their passengers could disembark (*Philadelphia Gazette*, 3 June; NDBW, 2:208).

ESCRIBO A EL SECRETARIO DE ESTADO: Yznardi had written to Madison on 10 Aug. (Madison, *Papers, Sec. of State Ser.*, 3:472-3).

INJUSTA SOLICITUD DE JOSEF ISRAEL: Yznardi persistently sought the government's aid against a lawsuit by shipmaster Joseph Israel. The conflict between Israel and Yznardi began during Yznardi's time as acting consul at Cadiz

in the 1790s (Vol. 36:6n and Yznardi to TJ, 16 Mch., 22 Apr. 1802).

BERGANTIN ESPAÑOL: for the incident involving the *Cabo de Hornos*, see "Yankey Doodle" to TJ, 14 Apr.; Madison to TJ, 11 May; and TJ to Madison, 14 May 1802.

Manuel Godoy had the title PRINCIPE DE LA PAZ—prince of the peace—and was the dominant figure at the Spanish royal court (Charles Pinckney to TJ, 24 May 1802; note to Carlos IV to TJ, 6 July).

COMISIONADOS PARA EL ARREGLO DE PRESAS: Charles Pinckney's instructions as minister to Spain asked him to seek the creation of some mechanism such as a "joint tribunal," similar to the bilateral commissions established to resolve claims under the U.S.-Spanish treaty of 1795 and Articles 6 and 7 of the Jay Treaty, to deal with "spoliations committed on our trade, for which Spain is held responsible." In the spring of 1802, Pinckney reported that the Spanish government was amenable to the formation of a commission. After negotiating the form the commission should take, Pinckney and Pedro Cevallos signed a convention on 11 Aug. for the establishment of a panel that would meet at Madrid for a term of eighteen months to review evidence, decide which claims to allow, and determine the amounts to be paid. The agreement provided for a five-member board, with two commissioners appointed by the Spanish government, two by the United States, and the fifth member of the commission chosen by the other four. The convention was to take effect upon ratification by both countries, which did not occur until 1818 (Miller, *Treaties*, 2:250-2, 335-6, 492-7; Madison, *Papers, Sec. of State Ser.*, 1:274; 2:441-2; 3:31, 32n, 142-3, 146n, 483-7).

PRESSA AMERICANA: on 17 June, while en route from Marseilles to the West Indies, the Philadelphia brig *Franklin* was taken by a squadron of Tripolitan corsairs off Cape Palos, Spain. A second American brig, the *Rose*, traveling in company with the *Franklin*, evaded capture. The Tripolitans carried their prize to Algiers on 26 June, but were ordered away by the dey two days later. The *Franklin* and its cargo were subsequently taken to Tunis and sold, while the captain, Andrew Morris, and his crew taken in chains to Tripoli, arriving on 19 July. The British chargé at Tripoli secured the release of

three of the crew as British subjects, and two other foreign members were also released, leaving Morris and his remaining crew prisoners. Their captivity, however, would be brief. At the urging of American consul Richard O'Brien, the dey of Algiers wrote the bey of Tripoli in early July and requested the release of the American prisoners. The bey complied, and Morris and his remaining crew were released on 21 Sep. (NDBW, 2:176-8, 187, 194, 204-5, 208, 212, 259, 281-2, 288-9; Madison, *Papers, Sec. of State Ser.*, 3:307; ASP, *Foreign Relations*, 2:463-4; Mustafa Baba, Dey of Algiers, to TJ, 17 Oct. 1802; Annual Message to Congress, 15 Dec. 1802).

LO COMUNICO OY AL SECRETARIO DE ESTADO: news of the capture of the *Franklin* had arrived at Cadiz while Yznardi was quarantined. On 13 Aug., Yznardi forwarded to the State Department more recent information being circulated by U.S. consuls in the Mediterranean, including a letter from O'Brien, dated Algiers, 26 June, in which O'Brien speculated that ships he had seen at a distance were a Tripolitan corsair with a second captured American brig. O'Brien also reported the arrival of the *Franklin* at Algiers, a rumor that there were six Tripolitan corsairs at sea, and indications that American and Swedish warships were blockading Tripoli (NDBW, 2:187, 208; Madison, *Papers, Sec. of State Ser.*, 3:391, 477-8).

To Henry Dearborn

DEAR SIR   Monticello Aug. 13. 1802.

I inclose you more militia resignations, as also a petition of Benjamin Dame of Newington praying the discharge of his son under age enlisted in the army. this being a matter of right, and not of discretion in us, which he might effect by a Habeas Corpus, I hold it a duty that he be discharged. if I recollect rightly we did the same in a similar case on some former occasion. Accept assurances of my affectionate respect   TH: JEFFERSON

PrC (DLC); at foot of text: "The Secretary at War." Recorded in SJL with no-

tation "Dame's petn." Enclosures: Benjamin Dame to TJ, 30 July 1802 (recorded in SJL as received from Newington on 12 Aug. with notation "W," but not found). Other enclosures not identified.

On 17 Aug., Dearborn ordered Lieutenant Colonel Thomas H. Cushing of the First Regiment of Infantry to discharge Private John DAME from the United States Army, "provided he is not twenty one years of age" (DNA: RG 107, LSMA; JEP, 1:413).

For a SIMILAR CASE, which involved the discharge of underage soldier Bartholomew Burrus, see TJ to Dearborn, 27 June 1801.

To Henry Dearborn

DEAR SIR   Monticello Aug. 13. 1802.

Your's of the 7th. with the inclosed papers came to my hand only last night. I now return the papers with an entire approbation of your letter to Govr. Harrison & proceedings. the white people who are among the Indians, having designs of their own to answer, & no principle to restrain them, make great use of lies to effect their purposes, and fabricate them from time to time according to the circumstances which arise. that they should avail themselves of the circumstance of a new President coming into office, to form new falsehoods was to be expected. I am in hopes there is nothing [...] the degree of uneasiness which is produced from this source. it is our [business] however to counteract them by impressing on their minds that the new President is as friendly to them, and will as sincerely patronize their rights as any former one; and to press our rights derived from their cession of lands to the French only so far as will not indispose them towards us. however we may wish in time to extend our possessions, the doing it at this time in that quarter cannot be worth a war, nor the loss of the affections of the Indians. Govr. Harrison seems to think the lands [below] the French grant between the Kaskaskia, Missisipi & Ohio, may be easily obtained. I should certainly concieve it the most important to be [obtained] inasmuch as settlements adjacent to the Ohio & Missisipi would consolidate with [those south] of Ohio, & therefore be stronger than an insulated settlement [...] on the Wabash on it's higher parts. if, getting what we can by friendly persuasions & by donations in money or goods, we can avoid a formal relinquishment of claim on the other side of the Wabash, it would be better; because that claim might serve hereafter as introductory to new purchases. but [it seems] absolutely necessary, after giving Governor Harrison our general ideas to leave matters [...] to his discretion, to be pressed or yielded according to the aspect of things at the treaty, of which we cannot judge. the cheapest & most effectual instrument we can use for preserving the friendship of the Indians: is the establishment of trading houses among them. if we could furnish goods enough to supply all their wants, and sell them goods so cheap that no private trader could enter into competition with us, we should thus get rid of those traders who are the principal fomenters of the uneasiness of the Indians: and by being so essentially useful to the Indians we should of course become objects of affection to them. there is perhaps no method more irresistable of obtaining lands from them than by letting them get in debt, which when too heavy to be paid, they are always willing to lop off by a cession of lands.—last night's mail being very voluminous I shall not be able to answer your letter covering Crowninsheild's till the next post. Accept assurances of constant & sincere affection & respect.　　　Th: Jefferson

PrC (DLC); faint; at foot of first page in ink: "The Secretary at War." Recorded in SJL with notation "Indian Affairs." Enclosures: see enclosures listed at Dearborn to TJ, 7 Aug.

LETTER COVERING CROWNINSHEILD'S: Dearborn to TJ, 10 Aug.

To Albert Gallatin

Monticello Aug. 13. 1802.
Th: Jefferson presents his friendly salutations to mr Gallatin and returns him the papers relative to the lighthouse at Faulkner's island with his [approbation] of Joseph Griffin as keeper of it. the extraordinary voluminousness & late arrival of his last night's mail puts it out of his power to answer mr Gallatin's other letter of the 9th. and that of the 7th. till the next post.

PrC (DLC); faint. Recorded in SJL with notation "appmts." Enclosures not found.

To Étienne Lemaire

Dear Sir　　　　　　　　　　　Monticello Aug. 13. 1802.
Mr. Monro has no funds in his hands which the law allows to be applied to any object about the President's house: consequently all necessary repairs must now be made at my expence. that of the pump being necessary, you will be so good as to have it repaired and mr Barnes will pay the bill. I recieved your letter of the 7th. last night only. I am in hopes the family with you is all well, as you say nothing

to the contrary; and particularly that you are so yourself. Accept my best wishes and assurances of my attachment.

TH: JEFFERSON

PrC (MHi); at foot of text: "Mr. Lemaire"; endorsed by TJ in ink on verso.

To James Madison

TH:J. TO MR MADISON   Monticello Aug. 12. [i.e. 13] 1802.

The post having made it night before his arrival yesterday and my mail extraordinarily voluminous, I have been able to read & now return you the inclosed papers only. mr Livingston's shall come by the next mail. I do not like this mistake of Capt Mc.Niel's, and fear it will be very embarrassing. other dispatches oblige me to close here with assurances of my affectionate esteem & respect.

PrC (DLC); date assigned from Madison to TJ, 14 Aug. and SJL. Recorded in SJL as a letter to the State Department of 13 Aug. Enclosures not identified.

From Thomas Munroe

SIR,   Washington 13th. August 1802

Mr King the late Surveyor of the City, and his Son Robert having this morning informed me that they shall on Sunday next sail for England in a vessel lying at Alexandria—and that several persons have applied to them within the last day or two to lay off lots & give levels, and other necessary information relative to buildings, which it will not be in their power to do before their departure—And as some inconvenience may arise from the want (even for a short time) of a person to perform these particular duties I have deemed it proper to communicate the circumstances for your directions on the subject.—

Mr. King, the younger, tells me there are upwards of seventy houses now building, or about to be commenced in the City, if so many applications will be made by the builders for information similar to that heretofore given by him under his Appointment from the Commissioners to regulate the lines and levels of Lots, and to carry into effect the general regulations for building declared by the President on the 17th October 1791.—

I fear the State of the Surveying Department, generally, is more irregular and confused, and will require much more attention and labour to adjust & compleat it than has been supposed.—Some inconvenience has lately been experienced & complained of from the want of a Surveyor properly qualified to attend the Office—Several of the Lots advertised for sale on[1] the 30th Instant I find have not been calculated, and their contents in square feet ascertained, nor have the divisions of all the squares been perfected—. I think we cannot do well without a Surveyor at the sale—Various cases have occurred at all past sales which required the services of one. If there be any documents or materials which may be deemed useful in correcting the plate for a permanent plan of the City they can be more conveniently collected during the present, & two next months, than at a later period in case you should honor me with any directions on the subject.—

　With sentiments of the highest respect I have the honor to be Sir Yr mo Ob Servt　　　　　　　　　　　　　　　THOMAS MUNROE

RC (DLC); endorsed by TJ as received 16 Aug. and so recorded in SJL. Dft (DNA: RG 42, LR).

Robert KING, Sr., recently made an unsuccessful attempt to extend his employment as SURVEYOR, which included requests for a salary increase and continued employment for HIS SON ROBERT (King to TJ, 5 June 1802; TJ to King, 7 June 1802).

The GENERAL REGULATIONS FOR BUILDING in the federal district proclaimed by George Washington on 17 Oct. 1791 included a provision that all buildings on streets "shall be parallel thereto." Before constructing any such building, application was to be made to "the person or persons appointed by the Commissioners to superintend the buildings within the City, who will ascertain the lines of the walls to correspond with those regulations" (Washington, *Papers, Pres. Ser.*, 9:97-9).

SALE ON THE 30TH INSTANT: see TJ to Munroe, 8 Aug.

[1] Remainder of sentence interlined.

To Bushrod Washington

Monticello Aug. 13. 1802.

　Th: Jefferson presents his respectful salutations to Judge Washington and incloses him a package which came to Th:J. in a very voluminous mail. opening the letters hastily & without always reading the superscription, he had opened this and read some lines in M. de la Fayette's letter before he discovered it not to be meant for him. looking at the corner & finding his mistake he instantly re-incloses it with an assurance on his honor that he did not see a word beyond the 4th. or 5th lines in la Fayette's letter and not one in the others. he hopes Judge Washington will accept his apology & his regret for this accident

PrC (MoSHi: Jefferson Papers); endorsed by TJ in ink on verso. Enclosure not found.

For transmission of the PACKAGE intended for Bushrod Washington, see Joseph Marie Lequinio de Kerblay to TJ, 31 July. Washington had been compiling a history of the American Revolution and relied heavily on Lafayette's correspondence with George Washington (Lafayette to James McHenry, 22 Nov. 1801, in NHi: Gilder Lehrman Collection at the Gilder Lehrman Institute of American History).

From Luisa and Aurora Bellini

ECCELLENZA   Firenze 14 Agosto 1802

Non abbiamo sperimentata strada più sicura ℘ far pervenire Le Lettere a Williamsburg nella Virginia in mano di Carlo Bellini, che indirizzandole a Vstra. Elza. In fatti d'una scrittale ℘ La di Lei direzione se n'ebbe risposta. D'altre tre posteriori dirette forse ℘ diverso canale non se n'ha avuto riscontro alcuno. Ricorriamo nuovamente alla di Lei bontà pregandola a voler usare ogni premura ℘ far pervenir L'acclusa al detto Carlo Bellini, e supplicandola a volere Lei medesimo contemporaneamente informasi appieno di ciò, che ne sia, e renderci consolate con una sua gentilissima notificandoci se viva ancora, o se morto (il che non sia) abbia lasciate nissune disposizioni; giacché dalla sua Vita, o dalle disposizioni di ciò, che gli apparteneva a nostro favore, in caso di morte dipende il nostro sostegno in questi nostri anni senili.

Qualora si rappresenti due Sorelle abbandonate da tutti, e molto avanzate in età avrà un motivo sufficiente ℘ scusarci della Libertà, che ci prendiamo, e dell'incommodo, che Le arrechiamo, protestandole che Le saremo perpetuamente obbligate. Intanto ci permetta che abbiamo L'onore di dichiararci

Di Vtra. Enza. Devme. Obligme. Serve   LUISA, ED AURORA
                                          Sorelle Bellini

EDITORS' TRANSLATION

YOUR EXCELLENCY   Florence, 14 Aug. 1802

In our experience, there has been no safer way to have letters reach Carlo Bellini in Williamsburg, Virginia, than by addressing them to Your Excellency. Indeed, one that we sent to your direction was answered; three other later ones, addressed perhaps through a different channel, have gone unanswered. We appeal again to your goodness and pray that you exercise all the possible care to have the enclosed letter reach the aforementioned Carlo Bellini. We also pray that you fully inquire at the same time about what has happened to him and that you most kindly console us with a letter of yours notifying us if he is still alive, or if—having passed away (may that not be so)—he has left any testament, since on his living or, in case of death, on his bequeathing to us of what belonged to him, depends our sustenance in this old age.

If you imagine two sisters who have been forsaken by all and have advanced well into old age, you will have sufficient reason to forgive us for the liberty we take and for the inconvenience we cause you as we pledge that we will forever be obliged to you. In the meanwhile, allow us to have the honor of declaring us the most devout and obliged servants of

Your Excellency. LUISA AND AURORA
Sisters of Bellini

RC (DLC); addressed: "The Right Honble Thomas Jefferson The President of Philadelphia North America"; endorsed by TJ as received 21 Mch. 1803 and so recorded in SJL. Enclosure not found.

CARLO BELLINI, the ailing widowed professor of modern languages at the College of William and Mary, stopped teach-ing in 1803 and died in poverty in Williamsburg the following June. His last letter to TJ was 16 Mch. 1801 (ANB; Vol. 31:86; Vol. 33:306-7). For TJ's efforts to remit the claim on Bellini's effects to his sisters, see Thomas Appleton to TJ, 22 Mch. 1805, with enclosed memorial on behalf of the Bellini sisters. See also RS, 4:185.

To John Brown

DEAR SIR   Monticello Aug. 14. 1802.

The inclosed letter of thanks from the Philosophical society has been sent me to forward to you.

We have been unfortunately delayed in our Hospital establishment at New Orleans by different accidents: and I just now learn that mr Daniel Clarke, who is to be the Superintendent, is lately returned from New Orleans to Philadelphia; in which case he will have left the place just before our letters and instructions could have reached it. I have this day written to the Secretary of the Treasury to get him take measures here for establishing the hospital in his absence by some persons there in whom he can confide, and Doctr. Bache (grandson of Dr. Franklin) appointed Surgeon, will proceed the moment he knows that arrangements are ordered to be made. in the mean time our suffering boatmen will have nearly lost the benefit intended them this season.   We have no certain information yet of the definitive resolution of France as to Louisiana. delay however is favorable to us, as it gives us time to be heard, and to speak with urgency on the subject. if France takes time to think before she acts, it appears to me impossible she should not desist from this measure. there is in that country (& especially among the military) considerable ferment.

the attempt on Buonaparte's life in April was a serious one. fortune however seems to take care of him. mr Short is just arrived from France, but has not yet reached this place. Accept assurances of my affectionate esteem & respect   TH: JEFFERSON

P.S. I absent myself from the tidewaters during these two months (Aug. & Sep.) and most of the other members of the administration do the same. the lower part of Virginia is peculiarly sickly at present.

PrC (DLC); at foot of text: "John Brown esq." Enclosure: American Philosophical Society to John Brown of Boone County, Kentucky (see John Vaughan to TJ, 21 July).

Daniel Clark (CLARKE) was in New York in mid-August, expecting to travel to England on personal business (Madison, *Papers, Sec. of State Ser.*, 3:487).

ATTEMPT ON BUONAPARTE'S LIFE: early in May, Joseph Fouché, the French minister of police, thwarted two plots against the first consul by officers of the army. Robert R. Livingston discussed one of the attempts in two letters to Madison of 10 May that were among the dispatches that Madison forwarded to TJ on 11 Aug. There were also a few reports in American newspapers in July and August, reprinting news from London and Paris, that mentioned one of the failed designs to kill the first consul. Because Fouché knew of the plans before they could be carried out, Bonaparte's life was not in danger and the minister of police did not consider the schemes SERIOUS threats to the regime. Army generals implicated in the plots were demoted or exiled away from Paris. The conspiracies exhibited the discontent of a number of military officers, particularly in reaction to Bonaparte's rapprochement with the Catholic Church and his evident abandonment of revolutionary principles. Livingston thought that ill feeling in the officer corps was "pretty extensive." In June, Fouché and other officials suppressed a conspiracy by officers who attempted to initiate a widespread revolt of the army (Thierry Lentz, *Le Grand Consulat, 1799-1804* [Paris, 1999], 347-51; Madison, *Papers, Sec. of State Ser.*, 3:205, 206n, 207; Charleston *Carolina Gazette*, 15 July; *Washington Federalist*, 11 Aug.; Vol. 35:194n).

SICKLY: TJ may have referred to measles in particular. The disease had been a problem not just in Virginia, but in Washington, Philadelphia, New York, and elsewhere, and was "uncommonly mortal." In mid-August, measles still lingered at Norfolk, where it had been present for several weeks and was responsible for the deaths of some children. Yellow fever had not yet reached Norfolk, but, as a preventive measure, in August the municipal government instituted a quarantine on ships arriving from Philadelphia, Baltimore, the West Indies, and the Bahama Islands. In a similar step, James Monroe appointed a superintendent for a quarantine at Richmond. Yellow fever did enter Virginia later in the season, causing several hundred fatalities at Norfolk by early autumn, and Fredericksburg also took quarantine measures (*Philadelphia Gazette*, 18 Aug.; CVSP, 9:316, 317; Preston, *Catalogue*, 1:130-1; Wyndham B. Blanton, *Medicine in Virginia in the Nineteenth Century* [Richmond, 1933], 225, 237).

To Henry Dearborn

DEAR SIR   Monticello Aug. 14. 1802.

Having had occasion to write more fully to mr Gallatin on the appointments for the customs in Massachusets as well as other places, I beg leave to refer you to that letter which I have asked him to communicate to you, & that you & he will decide definitively what is to be done. I therefore now reinclose the sheet of capt. Crowninsheild's letter recieved from you. it does not contain any thing relative to Prentis and Killam as you supposed, but, on the opinion you express, I would wish the latter to be appointed a Commr. of bankrupts vice Crowninsheild & Danna, and if you think the objection of Prentis's being a member of the legislature not insuperable, let him have the other vacancy. leaving this to your judgment, I will pray you, if you so determine, to direct commissions to be filled up at the Secy. of State's office & to be forwarded to me. as there will then be three to act, we can await an answer from old mr Story, as my letter gave him reason to expect, that the change might be his voluntary act. should he not voluntarily relinquish, I must revoke his commission: taking shame to myself for having given it, on the faith of well written letters, without any other knolege of personal character. Accept assurances of my constant & affectionate esteem & respect.

TH: JEFFERSON

PrC (DLC); at foot of text: "The Secretary at War." Recorded in SJL with notation "appmts." Enclosure not found (see Dearborn to TJ, 10 Aug.).

WRITE MORE FULLY: see TJ's second letter to Gallatin of this date. THREE TO ACT: TJ probably had not learned of William Burley's decision to decline his commission (Memorandum on Appointments, 6 July).

MY LETTER: TJ to Isaac Story, 5 Aug. For Story's WELL WRITTEN LETTERS, see Vol. 35:515-17; Vol. 36:357-9; Vol. 37:430-1; and Story to TJ, 28 July.

To Albert Gallatin

DEAR SIR   Monticello Aug. 14. 1802

I have duly considered the regulations concerning the Missisipi trade inclosed in your letter of the 7th. and should have signed them, but that a single fact, perhaps unknown to you, renders them impracticable without some alteration. neither Spain nor France allows any foreign nation to keep a consul in their colonies in time of peace. in consequence of this our Consul at N. Orleans has had his functions suspended by the Governor, and peremptorily inhibited from the use of them. I think it even doubtful whether they would permit us to have there even an informal agent to exercise any public duty. we are endeavoring by negociation to have N. Orleans considered as so peculiarly situated with respect to us, as to require an exemption from their general rule, but even if we obtain it, time will be requisite, and in the mean while some other provision should be made.[1] it would be well if possible to make such provisions as could be executed at Fort Adams, and render the touching at New Orleans as indifferent as at any other foreign port. if this be impossible we may try the substitution of an informal agent at N. Orleans, but still some provision should be made for the case of his being disallowed. when you shall have made the necessary alterations, I shall be ready to sign them.

With respect to the 5th. section, taking from coasting vessels employed in this trade the privilege of carrying any foreign articles, if yourself & mr Steele concurred in this, I should be content with it. but if you were of a different opinion, I should join you on the general principle of never imposing a restriction which can be done without.

The newspapers tell us mr Clarke is returned to N. York or Philadelphia. this will delay Dr. Bache's departure till we can inform him what he is to do there. I am in hopes mr Clarke will be able to arrange the details of the plan here, and to give such orders at N. Orleans as will begin the establishment, and provide the field for Dr. Bache to act on. will you be so good as to engage him to do this, and to give the necessary information to Dr. Bache. we have been unfortunate in the delays of this institution. Accept my constant & affectionate esteem.

Th: Jefferson

RC (NHi: Gallatin Papers); at foot of text: "The Secretary of the Treasury"; endorsed by Gallatin as answered on 19 Aug. PrC (DLC). Recorded in SJL with notation "reguIns Missi."

OUR CONSUL AT N. ORLEANS: adhering to the policy set by the Spanish government in 1799, Manuel de Salcedo, the Spanish governor of Louisiana from 1801 to 1803, refused to recognize Daniel Clark, the recently appointed U.S. consul at New Orleans. In May 1802, Salcedo also warned William E. Hulings, the U.S. vice consul at the port since 1798, to abstain from all public functions (Madison,

Papers, Sec. of State Ser., 1:139; 3:147, 197-8, 330-1, 489).

In June 1801, the secretary of state instructed Charles Pinckney to negotiate with the Spanish government at Madrid to have New Orleans exempted FROM THEIR GENERAL RULE. Madison argued that a U.S. consul was necessary at the port "to take care of the American rights and interests" and to provide papers authenticating the cargoes shipped on American accounts. On 20 May 1802, Pinckney reported that he had been unable to gain Spanish consent to a consul or agent at New Orleans. A few days later, Pinckney wrote of his plans to make another attempt to persuade the Spanish government, using all of the arguments and suggestions he could assemble in favor of the U.S. claim. Madison wrote, on 26 July, that he hoped Pinckney would succeed in his second representation and Spain would yield (Madison, *Papers, Sec. of State Ser.*, 1:277; 3:235, 250, 428).

NEWSPAPERS TELL US: on 24 July, the *Philadelphia Gazette & Daily Advertiser* reported that Clark was among the passengers on the schooner *Eliza* who landed at Wilmington, Delaware. On 28 July, the *New-York Gazette & General Advertiser* noted that the schooner had arrived at Philadelphia. ENGAGE HIM TO DO THIS: Gallatin wrote Clark at New York on 5 Aug. For Clark's reply, see the enclosure at Gallatin's first letter to TJ, on 19 Aug.

[1] Preceding three words interlined in place of "will be required."

To Albert Gallatin

DEAR SIR   Monticello Aug. 14. 1802

In your letter of the 9th. inst. you propose the following arrangement,

Wilson vice Tyng Newbury port ⎱ which I imagine ⎰ Cross vice Tyng Newbury port
Cross vice Gerry Marblehead   ⎰ should be thus ⎱ Wilson vice Gerry Marblehead
Gibault vice Tuck. Gloucester   Gibault vice Tuck. Gloucester.

I suppose this because it is consonant with Lee's letter inclosed by you, with Genl. Dearborne's letter, and with what I recollect of former conferences, wherein Cross was placed in competition with Lyman for Newbury port. as Tyng and Gerry are to go out, this arrangement is approved. with respect to Gibault vice Tuck, my only hesitation arises from the proposition being new, and proceeding too, as far as I see, from a single person, capt Crowninsheild. I have been taught to have great confidence in him, yet we all know how frequent it is for the best persons to be warped as to personal character by views peculiar to themselves, & not agreeing with the general opinion. of this he furnishes an instance in his opinion of Lee, whose recommendations are from many of the first characters in Massachusets, and are so strong that could they be doubted, all confidence in any degree of recommendation must be given up. I think too that Genl. Dearborne & mr Lincoln both concurred in considering Lee as entitled to our first favors. still, if Genl. Dearborne and yourself, (for I suppose mr Smith not to be with you) are satisfied that Tuck ought to be removed, on the ground of active opposition to the present government, that is to say, if the fact be that he is actively opposed, I approve of that change also, and think, if it is to take place, it had better be at the same time with the others. will you be so good as to communicate this to Genl. Dearborne, as I am pressed in time by other business?   the appointment of Henry Tooley to be Surveyor at Slade's creek is approved.

Accept assurances of my great esteem & respect.

Th: Jefferson

RC (NHi: Gallatin Papers); at foot of text: "The Secretary of the Treasury"; endorsed. PrC (DLC). Recorded in SJL with notation "appmts."

Lee's letter inclosed by you: see Enclosure No. 2, listed at Gallatin to TJ, 9 Aug. (second letter).

Dearborne's letter: Henry Dearborn to TJ, 10 Aug.

To Joseph Marie Lequinio de Kerblay

Monticello Aug. 14. 1802.

Th: Jefferson presents his thanks to M. Lequinio Kerblay for the book he has been so kind as to send him. his occupations rarely permit him to read any thing beyond the size of a pamphlet; but he will certainly avail himself of his first vacant moments to give a reading to a work from which he is certain of deriving amusement and information. he prays M. Lequinio to accept his salutations & assurances of his high consideration & respect.

PrC (MHi); endorsed by TJ in ink on verso.

From James Madison

Dear Sir   Orange Aug. 14. 1802

I red. last evening your two favors of the 9 & 13th. Before I left Washington I wrote to Simpson approving his refusal of passports in the cases required by the Emperor, and understood that the instructions from the Navy Dept. to Comodore Morris were founded on the same principle. It is to be inferred therefore that we are no longer on a footing of amity with Morocco: and I had accordingly retained your letter, and concurred in the provisional step taken for stopping the Gun carriages. As it is possible however that things may take a more favorable turn in that quarter, I have desired Mr. Brent to forward, with the quickest[1] attention, whatever accounts may arrive, and also to let me know the day, as soon as it can be done, on which the General Greene is to sail. Should it be found that peace with Morocco

[219]

cannot be preserved or restored without the concession demanded by him, my opinion decides that hostility is a less evil than so degrading an abandonment of the ground rightfully taken by us. As a consequence of this opinion, I concur in that which your quere intimates, that neither of the frigates in the Mediterranean in a condition to remain ought to be recalled. I should prefer if circumstances admitted, that the force there ought rather to be increased, and with the greater reason as the blunder of McNeil may endanger the footing on which we stand with Tunis. May it not be proper, as soon as authentic information of this occurrence comes to hand, that something of a healing nature should be said from the Govt. to the Bey, in addition to the explanations which will no doubt be made from the naval commander.

The letter from Law the District Judge of Connecticut, was preceded by one to me from a Comissr. of Bankruptcy at Boston, representing the objection of Davis the D. Judge there, to proceed without such a notification as is proposed by Law. Viewing as you do the Commission itself, as the most authentic of all notifications, I did not give any answer, presuming that the scruples of the Judge would yield to further reflection. The letter from Law shall be answered to the effect which you suggest.

Among the papers now inclosed are applications from the Mechts. of Boston & Philada. for an interposition in behalf of their vessels &c detained in Spanish America. This is a delicate subject, and must be so handled as well for their interest as for the honor & dignity of the Govt. I suppose they may be told that Spain does not object to a Board for deciding on our complaints & that Mr. P. will endeavor to give it latitude eno' for all just cases. The sending a public ship, as suggested by Fitzsimmons seems to have no National object, and to be of an injurious tendency.

Yrs. with respectful attachment   JAMES MADISON

RC (DLC); at foot of text: "The President of the U. States"; endorsed by TJ as received from the State Department on 16 Aug. and so recorded in SJL. Enclosures: (1) Stephen Higginson, Sr., and others to Madison, 23 July, not found (see Madison, *Papers, Sec. of State Ser.*, 3:549, 550n). (2) Thomas FitzSimons to Madison, 6 [Aug.], not found (see same, 548-9). (3) Elias Boudinot to Madison, Philadelphia, 6 Aug., asking the secretary to convey his concerns to the president

that the "malignant fever" spreading through Philadelphia would soon force a temporary closure of the mint; the disease has come within 500 yards of the establishment, which has "greatly alarmed" the employees and left Boudinot "little hope" of his being able to keep them at their work; Boudinot encloses a "rough copy of the Orders I shall issue in case my fears are verified, that if any alteration should be agreeable to Government, it may be made"; the Mint currently has a large supply of gold and silver bullion on hand, which, Boudinot reports, "cannot be worked up under four or five weeks" (same, 459-60). (4) John Dawson to Madison, Fredericksburg, 8 Aug., suggesting the need to appoint commissioners of bankruptcy at Fredericksburg to relieve the "great inconveniences" suffered by the lawyers and merchants of that place from the want of such officers; Dawson recommends John Minor, Hugh Mercer, Benjamin Day, Stephen Winchester, and Thomas Goodwin as "proper persons, should it be determined to appoint" (DNA: RG 59, LAR; endorsed by TJ: "Dawson John to Mr. Madison Commrs. bkrptcy Fredsbg").

Writing to James SIMPSON on 27 July, Madison expressed his approval of the actions taken by the consul in response to the demands by Mawlay Sulayman, complimenting Simpson for pursuing "a plain course of duty, in which you justly counted on the approbation of the President" (Madison, *Papers, Sec. of State Ser.*, 3:431-2; see Samuel Smith to TJ, 9 Aug.).

Regarding the INSTRUCTIONS to Richard V. Morris, see Robert Smith to TJ, 16 Aug.

RETAINED YOUR LETTER: TJ to Mawlay Sulayman, Sultan of Morocco, [5 Aug.], enclosed in TJ's to Madison of 6 Aug.

LETTER FROM LAW SHALL BE ANSWERED: writing to Richard Law on 14 Aug., Madison acknowledged receipt of Law's letter to TJ of 29 July (see TJ to Madison, 9 Aug.) and stated that the

president considered sufficient notification by bankruptcy commissioners of their appointment "to be the exhibition of their commissions, as in the case of Marshals," whose appointment required no additional documentation (Madison, *Papers, Sec. of State Ser.*, 3:479).

APPLICATIONS FROM THE MECHTS.: Thomas FitzSimons, who was the president of the Philadelphia Chamber of Commerce, and Stephen Higginson, Sr., with a committee of Boston merchants, had written to Madison about "injuries suffered by American Merchants in Spanish Colonies." Although Americans in Buenos Aires blamed the viceroy of La Plata for interference with their business, the fundamental issue was a decision by the Spanish government to prohibit trade by neutrals in ports throughout SPANISH AMERICA. Carlos Martínez de Irujo announced the policy in communications to Madison in the spring of 1802. Ships that violated the restriction faced seizure and confiscation. Madison received several entreaties on the subject. The merchants, according to Madison's reply to the Boston and Philadelphia committees on 6 Sep., wanted some "interposition" of the U.S. with the government of Spain and suggested that "a public vessel" be sent to the Spanish colonies "with an Agent authorized to demand a more prompt justice from the local authorities" (Madison, *Papers, Sec. of State Ser.*, 3:75, 86-8, 111-12, 281-4, 548-50; Vol. 35:425).

MR. P.: Charles Pinckney.

[1] MS: "quckest."

To Josiah Smith

DEAR SIR   Monticello Aug. 14. 1802.

Your favor of July 19. finds me here, where I mean to pass the two bilious months of Aug. & Sep. withdrawn from the tidewaters. we have extended the appointments of Commissioners of bankruptcy, only to the great Commercial towns; and therefore in most of the states there are only one set. in Massachusets we have appointed at

Boston, Marblehead, Newbury port & Portland, these towns, tho' of the 2d order being considerable. in other places, distant from principal towns, it will be necessary, should a bankruptcy happen, to make application to the Executive for a special appointment, which will hardly any where take more than three weeks to write for & obtain. were we to appoint all over the face of every state, the number would be infinite and the appointments useless 99. times in an hundred.

We hear nothing certain yet from France on the subject of Louisiana. delay however is favorable to us, as it gives us time to be heard. I am not without some hope she may see that the possession of that country would not advance her interests. Accept assurances of my great esteem & respect. TH: JEFFERSON

RC (MWiW-C); addressed: "The honble Josiah Smith Member of Congress for Massachusets to be retained at the post office Boston until called for"; franked. PrC (DLC).

YOUR FAVOR: Smith's letter of 19 July, recorded in SJL as received from Pembroke on 12 Aug., has not been found. For Smith's revelation that he did not write the letter, see Smith to TJ, 8 Sep. In a letter to Smith of 24 Sep., TJ reported the names of those recommended as bankruptcy commissioners by the unknown correspondent.

From Henry Dearborn

SIR   Washington August 15th. 1802

A rumor had been in circulation in this neighborhood for several days, that you were so sick as to have five or six physicions constantly about you, I had not been able to trace the report any further than to Mr. Stoddard, the reciet of your last letters has relieved our anxiety. Your letters of the 9th. & 13th. with their enclosiers have been duly received.—The Secretary of the Navy has this day informed me that the New York was to be sent to the Mediterranian insted of the Genl. Green and that she was to be sent as a fighting Ship, but would carry the Gun carriages, which would be of very little inconvenience, and if on arriving at Gibralter it should be found to be improper to deliver them to the Emperor of Morocco they might be disposed of without much loss. I have conversed with Mr. Smith on the subject of our Mediterranian relations generally, the result of which was, that we should suggest to you the propriety of appointing some suitable person as a special Agent to the Barbary States generally to superintend such negociations as may be attempted with any of those powers, and in the mean time to Associate Commodore Morris with Mr. Cathcart in any overtures for peace with Tripoly which may have been contemplated.—in a conversation with Capn. Bainbridge he informed me that Mr. Cathcart is very unpopular at Algiers on account of his having been a prisoner there as a person in a very subbordinate capacity. they speak of him as a person of no consequence.—

as the term for which the crew of the Boston ingaged has already or must very soon expire I should be of oppinion that she ought to return soon, and that the other Ships including the New York, should remain until the result of any negociations which are to be attempted is known.—

The Additional orders to be given to Commodore Morris in consequence of what may be apprehended from Moroco or Tunis should in my opinion be couched in some general expressions, such as, You will protect the commerce of the United States by all the means in your power[1] against any of the Barbary powers who shall declare war upon the United States or actually commence war upon the Citizans of the United States.—or—you will protect the commerce of the United States by all the means in your power, against any of the Barbary powers who shall openly declare war, or actually commence war, upon the United States.

I take the liberty Sir of enclosing a letter lately received from Mr. Bowdoin.

with respectfull consideration I am Sir Your Huml Servt.

H. Dearborn

RC (DLC); at foot of text: "The President of the United States"; endorsed by TJ as received from the War Department on 19 Aug. and "Barbary affairs" and so recorded in SJL. Enclosure not found.

James Leander CATHCART was a prisoner in ALGIERS from 1785, when he was captured as an 18-year-old seaman aboard an American merchant schooner, until 1796. Under the patronage of the minister of marine, who became the dey of Algiers during Cathcart's captivity, Cathcart held various clerical positions in the bureaucracy, owned property, and became a secretary to the dey. He was, however, technically a slave, having been sold into bondage along with other members of the schooner's crew soon after their capture. The dey with whom Cathcart had a close relationship, Ali Hassan, died in 1798 (DAB; Robert J. Allison, *The Crescent Obscured: The United States and the Muslim World, 1776-1815* [New York, 1995], 114-15; Vol. 33:364n).

For the ADDITIONAL ORDERS to Richard V. Morris, see Robert Smith to TJ, 27 Aug. (first letter).

[1] Preceding seven words interlined.

To Daniel D'Oyley

Monticello Aug. 15. 1802.

Th: Jefferson returns his thanks to mr D'Oyley for the sermon of mr Furman forwarded to him. temper and even truth, on the subject of his character, have been so seldom found in the ecclesiastical gentlemen, as to furnish strong proof of a sound conscience and temperate way of thinking in any individual of that order who exhibits an instance of them. the restoration of the rights of conscience to two thirds of the citizens of Virginia in the beginning of the revolution, has merited to those who had agency in it, the everlasting hostility of such of the clergy as have a hankering after the union of church & state. the right of political opinion is as sacred as that of religious, and altho' a man's political opinions ought to have influence in confiding political trusts, they should no more affect the state of society than his religious opinions. he prays mr Doyley to accept his salutations & assurances of his high respect.

PrC (DLC).   THANKS TO MR D'OYLEY: D'Oyley to
                                   TJ, 24 July.

To Gideon Granger

DEAR SIR   Monticello Aug. 15. 1802

Your favor of the 8th. was recieved on the 12th. the letter of mr Fenton therein inclosed, relating only to the uncreated office of Surveyor Genl. I retain if you will permit me, because it suggests some necessary insertions when such an office shall be created. mr Nichols, as well as Messrs. Bull & Dodd has declined serving as Commr. under the bankrupt act. [this leaves] but two at Hartford. still it is better to await your recommendations from the spot; because if a bankruptcy arises in the mean while a Commr. from the nearest of the other towns which have any, can be called in, or a new recommendation can come on in time. with respect to your visit to Connecticut, you are the best judge whether the public service could suffer by it, and my entire confidence in your discretion & public spirit render me perfectly easy in leaving it to yourself. if no ill can arise to your office, a prudent attention to your health, not yet acclimated to Washington, would certainly dictate it as a measure of pre[science?] & self preservation. I always expected the New York schism would produce a boisterous struggle. I am sorry to see the freedoms taken to implicate in it some characters. the manner in which Dr. Eustis and mr Bishop have been spoken of is neither just nor judicious. the difficulty will be for the republicans to avoid permitting personal [...] them from principle, and to play into the hands of the tories. this can hardly be hoped. I shall be glad to learn from you the state of [their politics?] and in the New-England states on your return. Accept assurances of my affectionate esteem & respect.   TH: JEFFERSON

PrC (DLC); faint; in ink at foot of text: "Gideon Granger."

LEAVING BUT TWO AT HARTFORD: Hezekiah Huntington and Joseph Hart (Vol. 37: Appendix II, List 2).

In a pamphlet published in July 1802, James Cheetham charged that Dr. William EUSTIS was following the opinion of his friend, the vice president, when he spoke and voted against the repeal of the Judiciary Act of 1801. Cheetham accused the Massachusetts congressman of attempting to divide the Republican vote. During the presidential campaign, Cheetham noted that Burr had spurred

Abraham BISHOP to travel to Lancaster to influence the Pennsylvania legislature to cast all of the state's electoral votes for TJ and Burr. According to the plan, New Jersey Federalist electors would give their votes to Burr once they had no hope for the success of their own candidates and make him president of the United States ([James Cheetham], *A View of the Political Conduct of Aaron Burr, Esq. Vice-President of the United States* [New York, 1802], 43-4, 103-5; JHR, 4:119-20). For the pamphlet and newspaper charges implicating Bishop with Burr intrigues and his response, see Kline, *Burr*, 2:728-9.

From John Barnes

SIR   George Town 16th. Augst. 1802

The Accident which deprived you (for the Present) The pleasure of Mr Shorts Company last week Conveyed him to my simple abode, made me exceedingly happy—that it suited so well—his almost exhausted frame—after so tedious & fatiguing persuit of his Brother.

Moreover he had leisure to look over the particulars of his funds—my a/c. &c. &c. copies of which I instantly furnished him with—Apparently—quite satisfactory—with Offers—inforced by your letter of the 6th. to supply him with whatever he might have Occasion for, which will not I apprehend be of any Considerable Amot.—it has however Obliged me to Apply for your last Mos. Compensation sooner than I intended—

I have to regret, our fridays Mail (as formerly) do not convey letters from hence—direct to Charlottesville of course, the exchange is only Once a Week—Mr Short seems yet undetermined, as to Berkley Springs—anxious I presume to Commune with you, he seems rather inclined to shape his Course direct for Monticello:—

nothing of Moment transpires at Washington, To Mr LeMair I have paid Wages a/c to 4th Inst: $141. & for Wood $99.43—

with great Regard & Esteem I am Sir your most Obedt. Servt:

JOHN BARNES

RC (ViU: Edgehill-Randolph Papers); at foot of text: "The President UStates at Monticello"; endorsed by TJ as received 19 Aug. and so recorded in SJL.

HIS BROTHER: Peyton Short.

Also known as Bath, Berkeley (BERK-LEY) Springs in Berkeley County, Virginia (now Morgan County, West Virginia) was a popular health retreat known for its warm springs and mineral waters (Washington, *Papers, Pres. Ser.*, 13:170).

To Henry Dearborn

DEAR SIR   Monticello Aug. 16. 1802.

The inclosed letter from Govr. Tatnall and petition from the inhabitants over the Cherokee boundary, on a subject which Colo. Wafford had before presented to us, renders it necessary to advert again to it. I think we have had some information from our Commissioners of the unsuccessful endeavors they used, according to our instructions, to obtain indulgence for these settlers, but I do not recollect it distinctly enough to act on. it would seem that the settlers have had private negociations with the Cherokees, and thence concieve an expectation that they would consent to a correction of the boundary so as to include these settlements. it remains for us to consider what proceedings can be instituted to obtain this at an expence not too disproportioned to the object. for I can hardly presume it would justify that of proposing a formal collection of the nation & a special treaty with that for this object. Accept assurances of my affectionate esteem & respect.   TH: JEFFERSON

PrC (DLC); at foot of text: "The Secretary at War." Recorded in SJL with notation "Tatnal's lre on Wafford's case." Enclosures: Josiah Tattnall, Jr., to TJ, 20 July. Other enclosure not found.

BEFORE PRESENTED TO US: see Vol. 33:220.

From Pierre Samuel Du Pont
de Nemours

J'ai trouvé ici des préventions très défavorables contre votre Nation, et l'habitude d'attribuer par *indivis* à votre Gouvernement les choses dont la France a réellement à se plaindre de la part de celui de Mr Adams et de ses Ministres.

J'ai représenté que c'êtait précisément tomber dans la même erreur que si l'on reprochait au Premier Consul les fautes du Directoire.

J'ai trouvé les Commandans et les Administrateurs de la Louisiane nommés. Cependant je ne désespere point qu'en stipulant qu'un Commerce libre et exempt de droits y sera ouvert aux Français, vous ne puissiez obtenir ce que vous désirez à cet égard.

Le Chancelier Livingston vous rendra compte de la négociation. Il a fait de très bons Mémoires qu'il a bien voulu me communiquer.

Il daigne croire que je lui suis et lui serai de quelque utilité auprès du Gouvernement.

Je vous supplie de l'être à notre cher *La Fayette* dont la fortune est dans un état déplorable.

Je vous ai montré qu'il a consumé *cent cinquante mille dollars* au service des Etats Unis.

Une jeune homme, comme Mr. *Randolph* par exemple, s'immortaliserait en proposant de le secourir par un don de *soixante mille dollars.*—Et ils ne sortiraient pas de l'amérique; car il en doit plus de *cinquante mille* à des Americains.

Je continue de vous demander vos bontés, et surtout le raffinage de votre Salpêtre pour mes Enfans.

Il n'est peut-être pas impossible que vous fassiez aussi pour moi une chose qui me serait agréable.

Beaucoup de Français sont interessés dans les *Stocks* américains.— Ils sont actuellement obligés de recevoir leurs rentes et leurs remboursemens à Amsterdam, et cela leur coute des Fraix.

Si votre Trésorerie voulait s'entendre avec ma Maison de Banque pour effectuer à Paris les payement *de ceux qui le préfereraient,* je ne vous demanderais aucune Commission. Je ne prendrais à vos Créanciers que la même qu'ils payent à Amsterdam. Ils gâgneraient les Fraix du change d'Amsterdam à Paris. Et il en résulterait un concours de plus pour l'achat de vos *Stocks* qui en eleverait le prix au profit des Citoyens des Etats unis qui auraient à en vendre aux Français.

Voudriez vous bien en conférer avec mon Fils Victor et Mr Gallatin.

J'ai souvent à faire passer des fonds aux Etats unis. Ce serait une double économie qu'ils s'y trouvassent tout portés, parceque votre Trésorerie les remettrait à mon Fils en raison de l'acquittement que je ferais à Paris de vos rentes et de vos remboursemens.

Quand je retournerai aux Etats unis, et je ne le pourrai que dans quelques années, je laisserai ma Maison de Paris à des Associés de toute solidité.

Salut et Respect.   DU PONT (DE NEMOURS)

EDITORS' TRANSLATION

MISTER PRESIDENT   Paris 16 Aug. 1802

I found very unfavorable prejudices here against your nation, and a tendency to attribute to your administration things that France should really have complained about with the Adams administration. I made the point that this was precisely to fall in the same trap as to blame the first consul for the errors of the Directory.

I found that the military and civil officers for Louisiana have been named. I do not despair, however, that, by opening a duty free trade area to the French there, you may obtain what you desire on that account.

Chancellor Livingston will report on the state of the negotiations. He produced excellent documents which he kindly shared with me. He deigns to believe that I am and will be of some use to him in dealing with the Government.

I beseech you to come to the aid of our dear Lafayette, whose fortune is in a deplorable state. I showed you that he spent *one hundred fifty thousand dollars* in the service of the United States. A young man, like Mr. Randolph for instance, would win immortality by proposing to help him with a gift of sixty thousand dollars. And his money would not leave America, since Lafayette owes over fifty thousand dollars to Americans.

I continue to ask for your kindness, and especially in securing saltpeter refining contracts for my sons.

It might also be possible for you to do something for me that would be helpful. Many of the French have invested in American stocks. They must currently receive their income and reimbursements via Amsterdam, and face costly expenses. If your Treasury could allow those clients who wish to do so to go through my bank to handle remittances, I would not charge any additional commissions. I would only charge creditors what they pay in Amsterdam, and they would save the exchange fees from Amsterdam to Paris. As a result, competition would grow, and the price of your stocks would rise for the benefit of those American citizens who sell them to the French. Would you kindly confer about this with my son Victor and Mr. Gallatin?

I often have to transfer funds to the United States. We could obtain double savings if the funds were already there, because your Treasury could remit them to my son as a counterpart for the income and reimbursements I would pay for you in Paris.

When I return to the United States, and this will only be possible in a few years, I shall leave my Paris office in good hands with trustworthy associates.

Hail and respect.   DU PONT (DE NEMOURS)

RC (DLC); at head of text: "a Son Excellence Thomas Jefferson Président des Etats unis"; endorsed by TJ as received 24 Oct. and so recorded in SJL. Enclosure: Circular from Du Pont de Nemours Père et Fils et Compagnie, Paris, 5 Thermidor Year 10 [3 Aug. 1802], announcing that they have moved their commercial and banking house from New York to Paris; their business in the United States will now be in the hands of Victor du Pont; they will with pleasure handle all sorts of collections and commercial business, and they hope to continue their relations with their clients (MS in DLC; printed; signed by Du Pont, who added salutation "Monsieur"; endorsed by TJ as dated 16 Thermidor 1802 received 24 Oct.; recorded in SJL as a letter without date received 24 Oct. with notation "a circular of business").

LES COMMANDANS ET LES ADMINISTRATEURS DE LA LOUISIANE: Bonaparte had chosen Claude Victor Perrin, a career army officer who went by the single name Victor, to be the commander of the military force that was in preparation to occupy Louisiana. Robert R. Livingston reported Victor's selection in a letter to Madison on 16 Aug. In September, Bonaparte's government issued decrees concerning the government of the new colony. Pierre Clément Laussat was to be the *préfet*, or chief civil administrator (E. Wilson Lyon, *Louisiana in French Diplomacy, 1759-1804* [Norman, Okla., 1974], 131, 134; Madison, *Papers, Sec. of State Ser.*, 3:492; Tulard, *Dictionnaire Napoléon*, 1041, 1717).

RAFFINAGE DE VOTRE SALPÊTRE: see Du Pont de Nemours to TJ, 12 May 1802.

MAISON DE BANQUE: on 23 Oct., the day before TJ received this letter, the New York firm run by Du Pont's son Victor began to advertise the sale of bills of exchange on London and Amsterdam (New York *Mercantile Advertiser*, 23 Oct., 12 Nov. 1802).

From Albert Gallatin

DEAR SIR   Treasury Dept. 16th Augt. 1802

I received this morning your letter of the 9th instt. on the subject of Morocco & the Barbary powers. The arrangement of the mail between this & Monticello is not favorable, since this answer to your's of the 9th cannot leave Washington before to morrow evening 17th. This I regret, as time on such occasion is precious. I will write, on the supposition that you have received the account of the engagement of the Boston with the Tunisian flotilla, which, although we have not yet received any confirmation, carries, unfortunately strong marks of its being true.

Our object must clearly be to put a speedy end to a contest, which unavailingly wastes our resources, and which we cannot, for any considerable time, pursue with vigor without relinquishing the accomplishment of the great & beneficial objects we have in view. The most ample powers & orders if practicable to make peace, and a sufficient force to protect and at least have time to withdraw our Mediterranean trade, appear to me necessary. In respect to peace, taking it for granted that the instructions for Tripoli are sufficient, there remain Morocco & Tunis. However contrary to the usage of civilized nations the pretensions of Morocco may be, we cannot decide whether they are considered as unreasonable by a nation not within the pale of civilization, and the conduct of Morocco has certainly been far from unfriendly since our treaty with that country. That treaty has been till now faithfully adhered to by the Emperor; he has shown no disposition to favor Algiers during our negotiations with that regency, and he even evinced forbearance during his blockade of a rebellious port. Hence I am not without hopes that he may still be smoothed, and I would at all events send the gun carriages which had been promised, in order that our negotiator may be able to give them if they shall be useful in bringing on a friendly arrangement; nor do I see any objection to sending the intended letter properly modified to accord with the present circumstances. And if Simpson can be fully trusted with a negotiation of that kind, I would also, out of the general mediterranean appropriation, send 20 or 30 thousand dollars which may be wanted either there or at Tunis to assist in accommodating differences. As to Tunis, I would not hesitate to promise an indemnity if M'neil shall have been the aggressor: on that supposition it is due in justice to them as much as it would to any other nation under similar circumstances; and to refuse it would be an inducement to Algiers to make a common cause; since there would be no security to any of the Barbary *powers*, whilst we had a frigate left in the Mediterranean, if we shall countenance an interference of that kind.

As to the force necessary there, I feel no hesitation. The Secretary of the Navy had consulted me before I received your letter, and I advised that Capn. Morris should be immediately instructed to retain the Boston in case hostilities should have commenced either with Tunis or Morocco, and that the Gen. Greene should be sent with her full complement of men instead of going half-manned. Mr Smith has since informed me that that frigate, which was originally a merchant vessel being a bad fighting vessel, he had substituted the New-York to her. That change, of which I am no judge, was, I take for granted, necessary;—the difference of expense between the two vessels is at the rate of 25000 dollars a year. If there is war with Morocco, no less than four frigates are necessary vizt two at Tripoly, one at least in the vicinity of the gut to convoy our vessels in and out, and one off Sallee to protect principally our Madeira & other island trade, if not to blockade effectually that port. I do not know whether Morocco has any other ports from which cruizing vessels (not boats) can sail on

the Atlantic. If Tunis is also at war, five frigates will hardly be sufficient, as three frigates could not keep in constant blockade the ports
of that regency & Tripoli. If we had two small ships instead of one of
our large frigates, they could, I think be more advantageously disposed; but we have no option, and it is clear that we cannot do less
than to provide the five frigates under present circumstances, which
will be effected, if the Boston is kept & the New-York sent; but I
much apprehend that if we have to encounter Tunis, Tripoli, & Morocco, we will be compelled to give up the Mediterranean trade & be
satisfied with defending the gut. Under that impression, I sincerely
wish you could reconcile it to yourself to empower our negotiators to
give, if necessary for peace, an annuity to Tripoli. I consider it no
greater disgrace to pay them than Algiers; and indeed we share the
dishonor of paying those barbarians with so many nations as powerful and interested as ourselves, that, in our present situation, I consider it a mere matter of calculation whether the purchase of peace is
not cheaper than the expense of a war which shall not even give us
the free use of the Mediterranean trade. It is also worth considering,
that the capture of some of our merchant men would, at all events, ultimately compel us to pay much more for their redemption than the
value of an annual tribute. Eight years hence we shall, I trust, be able
to assume a different tone; but our exertions at present consume the
seeds of our greatness & retard to an indefinite time the epoch of our
strength. As our present differences with Morocco have taken rise in
the war with Tripoli, it is probable that peace with this power would
terminate the hostilities with the Emperor. Might not that man's
pride be flattered with an intimation either that his offices would not
be rejected, if he chose to act as mediator, or that a wish to preserve
harmony with him contributes in accelerating our endeavours to
make a reasonable peace with Tripoli.

The application of the force in the Mediterranean towards Tunis &
Morocco, in case of hostilities existing between either of those powers & ourselves, appears to me a matter of course. The executive cannot declare war; but if war is made, whether declared by Congress or
by the enemy, the conduct must be the same, to protect our vessels, &
to fight take & destroy the armed vessels of that enemy. The only case
which admits of doubt is whether, in case of such war actually existing, we should confine our hostilities to their armed vessels, or extend
them by capture or blockade to their trade. The policy of adopting
either course must depend on the power we may have to injure that
commerce. How far are they commercial, & liable to be affected by
an attack upon that commerce? Something may also depend on the

personal disposition of the sovereigns of the two countries. If there is hope of peace by a conciliating conduct, perhaps it might be better, whilst we offer it to show our favorable disposition by only doing what is strictly self defence, fighting their cruisers. I presume that, in that particular respect, some discretion must be left to our commanding officer.

Whatever shall be done, I think that no delay ought to take place; the New York will, it is said, be ready to sail in ten days, say a fortnight. She should not be detained, & the instructions should be sent by her.

I do not know that any thing else occurs to my mind; you will, I hope, excuse the incorrectness of these hastily digested ideas. I have only to add that our Mediterranean appropriation, is on account of the 24,000 dollars sent by the Adams to Cathcart, & of the heavy drafts made by Eaton, reduced to 44,000 dollars. The 30,000 dollars destined for Algiers will be taken from another appropn. made specifically for that object. The naval appropriation will be sufficient to fit the New York; but we will be embarrassed if the Boston shall return before the meeting of Congress. That is, I believe, owing to miscalculations in the estimate of repairs, which especially for the Constitution have cost much more than had been estimated.

I remain with sincere attachment & respect Your obedt. Servt.

ALBERT GALLATIN

I had forgotten to say that Mr Smith suggested the idea of joining Morris to Cathcart for the negotiation with Tripoli. That would have been desirable, in order to provide against accidents, & in the instructions which may be sent to treat with Morocco & conditionally with Tunis, it would not be amiss that two persons should be named either of whom might act.

RC (DLC); addressed: "Thomas Jefferson President of the United States at Monticello Milton *Virginia*"; endorsed by TJ as received from the Treasury Department on 19 Aug. and "Barbary affairs" and so recorded in SJL.

HIS BLOCKADE: during the Moroccan civil war of the mid-1790s, Mawlay Sulayman blockaded the ports of Dar al-Bayda (Casablanca), Tit (near El Jadida), Safi, and Agadir in order to halt wheat exports that funded the rebellion in his southern coastal provinces. The

trade had been encouraged by European merchants residing in these ports, whom Sulayman later expelled and ordered to Mogador (Essaouira) (Mohamed El Mansour, *Morocco in the Reign of Mawlay Sulayman* [Wisbech, Eng., 1990], 56, 93-4, 97; Daniel J. Schroeter, *The Sultan's Jew: Morocco and the Sephardi World* [Stanford, Calif., 2002], 31, 197).

In May 1802, James Madison informed James Leander CATHCART that $24,000 was to be placed at Leghorn subject to his orders. The sum, wrote

Madison, was meant for Cathcart's "admission as Consul to the Dey of algiers" (Madison, *Papers, Sec. of State Ser.*, 3:202).

In October 1801, the frigate CONSTITUTION commenced an extensive overhaul at the navy yard in Boston, including repairs to the deck, hull, yards, galleries, and rigging. In June 1802, however, Robert Smith halted work on recoppering the hull, citing the limited funds remaining for the repair of navy vessels. To save expenses, the secretary instead ordered that the ship be laid up in ordinary (Tyrone G. Martin, *A Most Fortunate Ship: A Narrative History of Old Ironsides*, rev. ed. [Annapolis, 1997], 65-6; NDBW, 2:43, 131, 176, 179).

To James Madison

DEAR SIR   Monticello Aug. 16. 1802.

I now return all the papers recieved from you by this post, except those relative to our affairs at Buenos Ayres.

Mr. Boudinot's provisional measures for taking care of the Mint on shutting it up appear entirely proper. the 5th. alone seems imperfect, as I do not see why a positive conclusion should not have been formed as to the care of the bullion, the most important part of the charge. I presume the bank of the US. would have recieved that as well as the papers, keys &c. however it is too late to say any thing on that subject, and I have no doubt that effectual care has in the end been taken.

With respect to Commissioners of bankruptcy at Fredericksburg, you are sensible that if we were to name Commissioners over the whole face of every state in the Union, these nominations would be infinite, & 99 in 100. of them useless. to draw some line therefore was necessary. we have accordingly confined our nominations to the greater commercial towns only. I am sensible however that bankruptcies may happen in small towns and even in the country, and that some regulation should be provided to which resort may be had more conveniently than to that of referring the case to the commissioners of the large cities who may be distant. what would you think of writing a circular instruction to the district attornies of the US. to notify us when any case arises too distant for the established commrs. to take up, sending us at the same time a recommendation of proper persons to act in that case, whom, or such others as may be preferred, may be commissioned to act in that special case? he should inform the judges of this instruction so that they will apply to him to procure commissioners in any case before them. the delay of this will be trifling. or will you propose any thing you may like better? Accept assurances of my affectionate esteem & respect.   TH: JEFFERSON

RC (DLC: Madison Papers). PrC (DLC); in ink at foot of text: "The Secretary of State." Recorded in SJL with notation "Mint. Commrs. bkrptcy."

PAPERS RECEIVED FROM YOU BY THIS POST: see Madison to TJ, 14 Aug.

To Thomas Munroe

SIR   Monticello Aug. 16. 1802.

Your's of the 13th. is this moment recieved, informing me of the vacancy in the office of Surveyor of the city, by the departure of the late Surveyor, & of the necessity of an immediate appointment. according therefore to what had been proposed, on that event's taking place, I presume it is proper to appoint mr Nicholas King to that place. I believe this appointment was heretofore made *by the Commrs.* with the approbation of the President, but that the appointment had only their signature. if so, your's is now to supply that, and consequently you will give the formal authority to mr Nicholas King to act. should I be mistaken in this, and should a commission signed by the President be requisite, then let such an one be forwarded to me for signature, and desire him to act in the mean time under the authority of this letter, that nothing may suffer. Accept my best wishes & respects.   TH: JEFFERSON

PrC (DLC); at foot of text: "Mr. Thomas Munroe"; endorsed by TJ in ink on verso. Tr (MHi: Adams Papers). Tr enclosed in Roger C. Weightman to John Quincy Adams, 23 May 1827.

To Craven Peyton

DEAR SIR   Monticello Aug. 16. 1802.

The certificate for 1000. acres of land in the name of John Peyton which you inclosed me shall be forwarded to the war office by this day's post. without some authentic designation however of the person to whom the patent is to be granted it will of course come out in the name of John Peyton. I mention this, that if you wish it otherwise, you may furnish me with the supplementary papers requisite. accept my best wishes & respects.   TH: JEFFERSON

RC (ViU); addressed: "Mr. Craven Peyton."

YOU INCLOSED ME: a letter from Craven Peyton to TJ of 16 Aug., recorded in SJL as received the same day, has not been found.

FORWARDED TO THE WAR OFFICE: on 16 Aug., TJ requested that Dearborn "put the inclosed paper into the proper channel to be acted on, it being the case of a friend whom Th:J. wishes to serve without knowing to whom the certificate should be committed immediately" (PrC in DLC; recorded in SJL with notation "Craven Peyton's certif.").

From Robert Smith

SIR, Navy Dep. Aug. 16. 1802

Your favor of the 9h. I had the pleasure of receiving yesterday. The disposition manifested by the Emperor of Morocco is evidently hostile and evinces a determination to go to War with us unless we abanden the expedition against Tripoli. And the unhappy affair of Capt McNeill with the squadron of Tunis cannot but have involved us with that power. This state of things demanding immediate attention and prompt proceedings, we regretted your absence and lamented that we had to *begin* to act without the guidance and sanction of your advice.

On Friday last we in consultation conceived it adviseable to avail ourselves of an opportunity of a Vessel going the Sunday following (yesterday) to the Mediterranean from Baltimore to send to Commodore Morris a letter recommending to him to pursue such a Course of Conduct as would most effectually tend to produce a State of peace, and authorising him at the same time to retain the Boston in Case of war with either Morocco or Tunis. In this letter I have informed him that $30,000 would be sent to him for the Dey of Algiers and 100 Gun-Carriages for the Emperor of Morocco and also perhaps some money to be employed with these and the other Barbary powers for the purposes of peace. In this letter I also informed him that the frigate New-York would in the Course of two Weeks be dispatched to his aid, and would convey to him the Gun Carriages and the money. We are, Sir, still of the opinion that the Gun Carriages ought to be sent to be deposited at Gibralter and to be used as circumstances may render expedient and that your letter also ought to be committed to the discretion of Commodore Morris to be used if necessary. We are also still of the opinion that the New-York ought to be sent instead of the General Greene, because the Genl Greene is not at all calculated for a fighting frigate. From her peculiar Construction a large portion of her guns could not be used in action. Her appearance instead of being formidable to the Enemy, would rather serve to give them Confidence. She is besides so bad a Sailer that she Could not afford the necessary protection. And the difference of the expence between the one & the other is below consideration. I have therefore transferred the Officers and Men from the Genl Greene to the New-York and have put her under the Command of Capt James Barron who is here. She will be ready to go hence in ten days from this time.

The orders to be given to the Officers in the Mediterranean, in my apprehension, ought to authorise them to defend the American Commerce not only against the Corsairs of Tripoli but also against those of Morocco, Tunis or any other Barbary power that may have *declared* war against us and in such case to proceed against every such Corsair in the same manner as they have been authorised with respect to Tripoli.

Ought not additional instructions to be sent to Mr Cathcart to enable him to negotiate a peace with Tunis and to some person or persons to adjust our difference with Morocco. Mr Cathcart from certain *prejudices* may and I am informed, is odious to some of the Deys. He may be dead or unable from various Causes to attend to this business. From these and other Considerations, I am inclined to think it would be well to associate with him Commodore Morris, and that the authority ought to be joint and several. It would be a subject of much regret, if a final adjustment of our differences with the Barbary powers could not be effected because we had not a person near them duly authorised.

I expect, Sir, that we shall equip and send to Sea the New-York with a promptness that will astonish and Confound the enemies of the Eastern Branch. This I am very anxious to do.

Be pleased to accept the assurances of high regard and esteem with which I am Sir, Your Obedt Sert   Rt Smith

Would it not be adviseable to forward your Communications to us by Express?   RS.

RC (DLC); endorsed by TJ as received from the Navy Department on 19 Aug. and "Barbary affairs" and so recorded in SJL.

SEND TO COMMODORE MORRIS A LETTER: Smith's instructions to Commodore Richard V. Morris, dated 13 Aug. 1802, were carried from Baltimore in the brigantine *Nancy*. In addition to the gun carriages for Morocco and the $30,000 for Algiers, Smith informed Morris that the frigate *New York* would also carry "about twenty thousand or thirty thousand dollars to be applied in your discretion to the conciliating of the Emperor of Morocco and the Deys of Tripoli and Tunis" (NDBW, 2:232; Smith to John Stricker, 13 Aug. 1802, in DNA: RG 45, MLS).

For TJ's previous ORDERS to navy officers WITH RESPECT TO TRIPOLI, see Circular to Naval Commanders, 18 Feb. 1802. This circular authorized commanders "to subdue, seize, and make prize" of any vessel belonging to the bey of Tripoli or his subjects.

ENEMIES OF THE EASTERN BRANCH: that is, critics of the navy yard at Washington, located on the Anacostia River (or Eastern Branch) near its confluence with the Potomac River (Vol. 33:278, 545; Vol. 34:30; Vol. 36:62-3).

From Augustus B. Woodward

Washington, August 16. 1802.

Nothing will satisfy the unhappy James Mc.Girk, who is sentenced to be executed on the twenty eighth of this month, but that I should go to Monticello, to intercede with the President for his life. Oppressive and inconvenient as it is to me at this time, I suppose I must comply. I am the rather prompted to it, as I persuade myself that when his case is *fully* understood by the President, he will consider it as almost unavoidably necessary to make him an object of mercy. Some facts which exist in his case, and which were entirely unknown at his trial or sentence, seem to entitle him to pardon. He has addressed a number of letters to the President, written in prison, which I have hitherto suppressed as they might have been deemed intrusive. I shall bring these to submit to the President, with the papers and petitions which accompany his prayer for pardon. I shall probably arrive within a day or two of this letter, which is committed to the post. AUGUSTUS B. WOODWARD.

RC (DLC); endorsed by TJ as received 19 Aug. and so recorded in SJL.

SENTENCED TO BE EXECUTED: for James McGurk's case, see his first petition for pardon, printed at 19 Apr. 1802. In April the circuit court of the District of Columbia found McGurk guilty of murdering his wife and sentenced him to death. In its July term, the court set the date of execution (*Washington Federalist*, 14 Apr., 27 Aug.; Georgetown *Olio*, 5 Aug.).

If Woodward showed TJ documents that McGurk had WRITTEN IN PRISON since his appeal for clemency in April, TJ did not retain them. No communication from the condemned man to the president between April and October 1802 has been found or is recorded in SJL.

From Augustus B. Woodward
and Others

TO THOMAS JEFFERSON PRESIDENT OF
THE UNITED STATES OF AMERICA.   [ca. 16 Aug. 1802]

The undersigned, compassionating the unhappy situation of James Mac Gurk, now confined in the jail of the County of Washington, in the District of Columbia, and sentenced to be executed on the twenty eighth day of August, 1802, and conceiving that his severe and rigid confinement for one year in the said jail, loaded with irons, a confinement protracted on account of the legal embarrassments which arose relative to his execution between the executive and judicial authorities of the District of Columbia, has been in itself in a great degree a punishment of the offence of which he has been found guilty, too moderate indeed if the murder of which he has been convicted were premeditated and intentional, but in some measure not so greatly disproportionate to the offence if it were the effect of his unfortunate temper and habits without any formed design, beg leave with the highest consideration and respect to approach the President of the United States, to whom has been wisely entrusted the exclusive and absolute power to pardon offences against the United States, and to interpose their humble but earnest solicitations to obtain from him the boon of life to the miserable and repentant offender.   AUGUSTUS B. WOODWARD

RC (DNA: RG 59, GPR); undated, but see preceding document; in Woodward's hand; signed by Woodward and 94 others, with 55 additional names written in one unidentified hand; endorsed by TJ as received 20 Aug. and "Mc.Girk's case. Petition" and so recorded in SJL; also endorsed by TJ: "reprieve to Oct. 28."

THE UNDERSIGNED: the first signers of this petition in James McGurk's behalf were, in addition to Woodward, the Irish-born architect James Hoban; the Washington property developer Pierce Purcell, who was Hoban's partner in some real estate ventures; and John Kearney, who like Hoban was an architect and real estate developer from Ireland. Other signers included Charles Jones and Alexander McCormick, who were leaders in the establishment of a masonic lodge in Washington in 1804, and the surveyor and mapmaker James Reed Dermott. Hoban, Kearney, Jones, and McCormick were candidates in city council elections at various times in the early nineteenth century. A number of the signers of the memorial printed above had Irish surnames (RCHS, 3 [1900], 202, 281; 5 [1902], 87; 6 [1903], 161; 7 [1904], 78, 80, 135; 33-34 [1932], 268, 270; National Intelligencer, 13 Apr. 1804, 31 May, 3 June 1805; DAB, 9:91-2; Vol. 33:204-5).

LEGAL EMBARRASSMENTS: see TJ's request for the opinions of Levi Lincoln and John Thomson Mason on the question of the warrant for McGurk's execution, 11 Apr. 1802, and Lincoln's and Mason's replies of 12 Apr.

From William Firby

Brookhaven, Suffolk County,
SIR/   Long-Island. Augt. 17th 1802

Encouraged by that Philanthropy of disposition for which you are so eminently distinguished among the human race, I presume to lay before you a few particulars, which, tho' they only relate to myself in the first place, yet you may possibly think not beneath your serious attention, as the object to which they are finally and ultimately directed, is the relieving the Miseries and Distresses of a considerable part of our fellow-creatures. Sir, not to be too tedious, I am an English Republican, from Yorkshire, whom the Despotic disposition of Mr. Pitts administration in the year 1797, inspired with a resolution to seek for Liberty in America: the greatest part of the time since my arrival here, I have acted in the Capacity of Schoolmaster, tho' bred a Farmer and Mechanic; and having for many years past been inclined to the study of Physic in my leisure hours, I have at length happily discovered a remedy for every kind of Scorbutic disorders, let the degree of Inveteracy be ever so great, and the time of its continuance have been ever so long. That you may not think I am wilfully violating the Truth in saying thus much, I will give you a brief detail of some cases which I have had in hand since I came into America, with the times of their being undertaken, in which my Endeavours have been blest with the happiest success.

Case 1st. January, 1799. Christn. Dunn of Throgs Neck, West Chester, a Yorkshire man, Neighbour to me, a scorbutic disorder in his face, so inveterate that his face was nearly all in one incrusted scab cured in 5 or 6 Weeks. Case 2d. April, 1799. James Dunn Junr. brother to the above, a scorbutic Ulcer on his Leg, brought from England 7 or 8 years before, incurable by the faculty there; cured in one Month.

Case 3d. May 17th. 1800. William Baker of Patchogue, Brookhaven Township, Suffolk County, Long-Island, a Scorbutic Ulcer on his Leg, 4 Inches long by $3\frac{1}{2}$ broad, deep, malignant and fetid; discharged incurable from the Faculty at New York 18 or 19 years before, and given up by many of the Faculty upon L. Island since; cured in about 12 Months. Case 4th December 21st. 1801, Samuel Green Son of the Revd Zachariah Green; Minister of the Presbyterian Church in Sataucket, Suffolk County, aged 11 or 12 years, the most inveterate scorbutic Case I ever saw: fully of running ulcers from the crown of his head to the soles of his feet, of 4 or 5 years continuance; [...] Lazarus; given up by the Drs Comstock and Punderson; not expected by his parents to live many days, yet perfectly cured in 10 or 11 weeks, and had the Meazles in the mean time. Case 5th March 19th. 1802, Samuel Satterley of Satauket, an inflamatory scorbutic humor in his face, now well. Case 6th. March 31st. 1802, Henry Newton of Middle Island, a scorbutic ulcerated Leg of 8 or 9 years standing, cured in 3 Months. Case 7th May 14th. 1802. Isaac Newton, Middle Island, brother to the above, a scorbutic ulcerated Leg, having 12 or 14 Ulcers thereon, of 9 or 10 years standing, now well.

These Sir are the Cases I have had in hand, and which are well known to every person in the respective neighbourhoods where they occurred.

Now Sir, not having studied, and been instructed in the College at Edinburgh under the great Cullen, nor had a Licence therefrom, I am sensible that in all this business I have acted without any legal power or Commission, and possibly thereby incurred the displeasure of the laws of America; in which case, on being notified thereof, I am willing to stay my hand or, if you Sir, and the Government at the head of which you have the honor to preside, think fit to grant me a Licence to continue the exercise of my abilities for the benefit of the afflicted, I am ready to accept it with thankfulness, as it will not only gratify my own feelings, but likewise the ardent wishes of those to whom I have had the happiness of administring relief; and as this dreadful Malady the Scurvy, is a Disease which has hitherto generally baffled the skill of the most eminent Physicians in every Country, should it be thought likely to be of more extensive advantage to the Community at large, I am willing to make a full and perfect discovery of the remedy, upon receiving a pecuniary Compensation adequate to the [...] of such Discovery. If Sir you have any doubts whether I am a shameless Impostor, you may be perfectly satisfied of the truth of what I have here advanced, by applying to the Revd Mr Green, or to either of the Judges Strong and Woodhull in Satauket, two Characters with whom I presume you are acquainted. If you think my proposals deserving your serious Consideration, I shall think myself honoured by receiving your Commands, and giving you any further Communication on the subject that you may wish for. Please Sir to direct to me, to the care of Major Jonas Hawkins, Stony-Brook, Satauket Long-Island.

I am Sir, with the most profound respect, Your most Obedient Humble Servant   WILLIAM FIRBY

RC (DNA: RG 59, LAR); torn; addressed: "Thos. Jefferson Esq. President of the United States of America, Washington, State of Virginia"; franked; endorsed by TJ as received 26 Aug. and so recorded in SJL; also endorsed by TJ: "office."

William Firby was granted a certificate to practice medicine by a special act of the New York state legislature, which cited the sponsorship of several citizens of Suffolk County, "he having performed a number of extraordinary cures in the said county, principally of the scorbutic kind." The unusual licensing raised the eyebrows of a New York-based professional journal, which argued that it "savours

very much of obtaining the doctorate by *popular* mandate." Firby practiced medicine in New York City for a few years, advertising his cures for scurvy, leprosy, and venereal disease (*Laws of the State of New York*, 6 vols. [Albany, 1804], 3:639; *Medical Repository of Original Essays and Intelligence*, 4 [1806], 197; New York *Republican Watch-Tower*, 29 Sep. 1804; *Longworth's American Almanac, New York Register, and City Directory* [New York, 1807], 180).

Selah STRONG and Abraham WOODHULL served at different times as judges of the court of common pleas for Suffolk County (*New-York Packet*, 26 Aug. 1788; New York *Spectator*, 3 Feb. 1802).

From Albert Gallatin

Dear Sir   Tr. Dept. Augt. 17th 1802
    I enclose herewith the following papers
                                    ————

Recommendation for Commisrs. of Bankruptcy at Poukepsie in support of those formerly made by Bailey & Van Cortland

Certificate of Mr Nourse showing that Mr Hopkins has *charged* for two clerks according to law. Whether he has employed only one, your informant should substantiate if it be true.

Letters relative to the incapacity of Claud Thomson collector of Brunswick Georgia. As the most speedy way of obtaining a recommendation I have written to P. Butler who is now at Philada., & having a large estate in that vicinity, is better acquaintted than Jackson, who besides that, would not answer under several weeks.

Copies of letters on subject of improper & unauthorized advances made by our Consuls, a subject which deserves consideration & immediate remedy.

Sundry letters from Portsmouth recommending for the office of surveyor, & for those of Master & mate of the revenue cutter. To the last there is, nor can be any objection. For the office of surveyor, Geo. Wentworth is recommended by John Langdon & Joseph Whipple, and Samuel Penhallow junr. by Mr Gardiner & sundry other republicans. I called on Gen. Dearborn for his opinion: he is in favor of Wentworth, an old & very deserving character, already employed in a subordinate office in the customs & very poor: he says, however, that Penhallow, who is a young lawyer & also a republican, would probably be the most active officer. If you shall prefer Wentworth, I can write to Mr Gardiner, that the recommendation in his favor had been received previous to the other's; which is true.

Recommendation in fav. of — Woods for register land office vice Foster, by Meigs the only republican of note at Marietta.

The weekly return of Warrants paid last week
                                    ————

The letter to Erving for books, for use of Congress is gone: no bill on Paris having been obtained that for Mr Short had been detained, & you have doubtless heard of his arrival here. To whom is the money to be sent? If Duane has not written to his correspondent in France, it might do to send the 1000 dollars destined for that place, to Mr Erving, as I apprehend your London catalogue alone will amount to 2000 dollars.—No letters from Mr Short of the dates you mention can be found at present in the office. I suspect that Mr Jones the principal clerk who is absent on account of his health, & who had the extracts transcribed which you requested, has not returned them to the proper file; we have ransacked every corner in vain.

You have heard that Mr Page absolutely refuses the office of collector at Petersburgh. He has written two decisive letters to Mr Tucker, one received this day. This is unfortunate, and it is necessary that some immediate decision should take place.   A nearly unanimous petition in favor of Tyng may be expected from Newbury port; the nonappointment of a resident has made the removal extremely unpopular; but Lee's appointment works better than had been apprehended by Crowningshield. Hiller on the 6th Augt. saw the appointment announced in the National intelligencer of the 30th July, & on the same day sent his resignation which is also enclosed.

This makes up the whole of what I have to communicate: last night I wrote in relation to the Barbary business which is of more importance than all the rest. This city continues healthy and the weather is much more moderate than it was last year.

With sincere respect & esteem I remain your obedt. and affectionate Servt.   ALBERT GALLATIN

Have you heard that Sumpter & Mr Livingston have disagreed, and that the first is on his return? T. Coxe writes that from the most undoubted authority he knows that France will take possession of Louisiana as soon as her West Indies business is arranged.

RC (DLC); addressed: "Thomas Jefferson President of the United States at Monticello Milton Virginia"; endorsed by TJ as received from the Treasury Department on 19 Aug. and "miscellans. affairs" and so recorded in SJL. Enclosures: (1) Smith Thompson, Brockholst Livingston, and Edward Livingston to James Madison and Albert Gallatin, Poughkeepsie, 4 Aug. 1802, requesting that the president appoint bankruptcy commissioners at Poughkeepsie, being midway between New York City and Albany, where commissioners have already been appointed, but the two cities are 160 miles apart and too far away to accommodate the flourishing towns along the Hudson River, particularly in Dutchess County; recommending Aaron Stockholm, "formerly a merchant and now one of our most respectable Farmers," Samuel Hawkins, and James Tallmadge, Jr., lawyers, as candidates, all being competent, with a reputable standing in the community, and noted for their republican principles (RC in DNA: RG 59, LAR, 10:0627-9, in an unidentified hand, signed by all, endorsed by Gallatin: "Recommendation for Comrs. of Bankruptcy at Poukeepsie—Note Hawkins & Tallmadge had been recommended by Bailey & Van Cortland," endorsed by TJ: "Thompson & Livingston to Mr. Gallatin } Commrs. bkrptcy at Poughkeepsie"; Madison, Papers, Sec. of State Ser., 3:454). (2) Certificate by Joseph Nourse, Register's Office, Treasury Department, 11 Aug. 1802, listing Thomas

Taylor and William Dandridge as the two clerks employed during 1801 and the first two quarters of 1802 by John Hopkins, commissioner of loans for Virginia, each at the rate of $500 per year (MS in MoSHi: Jefferson Papers; in a clerk's hand, signed and dated by Nourse; endorsed by TJ: "Hopkins's case. Nourse's certificate"). (3) Gallatin to Madison, 16 Aug. 1802, questioning the legality of the expenditures incurred by U.S. consuls for the relief of seamen after 1799, when the laws of 1798 and 1799, authorizing reimbursements for "reasonable expenditures," expired and the permanent law of 14 Apr. 1792, limiting the allowance for distressed seamen to 12 cents per day again went into effect; a number of bills drawn by the consuls and commercial agents on the State Department should not have been paid and the balances they claim "cannot be admitted"; noting that the expenditures of William Lee at Bordeaux were much larger than could be expected or allowed "under any possible circumstances"; and enclosing Richard Harrison to Gallatin, 11 Aug., requesting the "sentiments" of the secretary of state on reimbursements for the relief of seamen before the consular accounts were settled and annexing a list of the accounts of the U.S. consuls and agents received at the auditor's office from the State Department (Madison, *Papers, Sec. of State Ser.*, 3:489-90; Gallatin, *Papers*, 7:450-1). (4) John Langdon to Gallatin, Portsmouth, New Hampshire, 4 Aug. 1802, reporting the death of Samuel Adams, surveyor of customs at the port, and recommending George Wentworth, now employed at the custom house, as a person proper and well qualified for the position (RC in DNA: RG 59, LAR). (5) Langdon to Gallatin, Portsmouth, 6 Aug. 1802, recommending Hopley Yeaton as a proper person to take command of the revenue cutter being built at Portsmouth, describing him as a good officer, honest, "and always a good Republican," who, as the vigilant commander of the first revenue cutter, "was most shamefully dismissed, by the late President, at the same time that Joseph Whipple and William Gardner were, and for the same reason" (RC in same; en-

dorsed by TJ: "Langdon John to mr Gallatin } Yeaton Hopley. command revenue cutter"). (6) Joseph Whipple, Collector's Office, Portsmouth, 4 Aug. 1802, informing the Treasury secretary of the death of Adams and recommending Wentworth, an employee at the custom house noted for attention and fidelity to his work and "attachment to the government"; also recommending Hopley Yeaton as master and Benjamin Gunnison as first mate of the revenue cutter, "which will be ready for Service in 6 or 7 weeks," both of whom were faithful, active officers on the previous cutter (RC in same; endorsed by TJ: "Whipple to mr Gallatin } Wentworth George to be Surveyor of district of Portsmouth vice Adams dead Yeaton Hopley to be Master Gunnison Benjamin 1st. mate } revenue cutter"). (7) William Gardner to Gallatin, Portsmouth, 6 Aug. 1802, noting the death of Adams and recommending Samuel Penhallow, Jr., as surveyor, a gentleman who is well known to him as being "very capable—of strict integrity and a firm Republican"; and enclosing a petition in Penhallow's favor, dated 6 Aug., signed by Gardner and at least 15 others, including John Pickering, district judge (RC in same; endorsed by TJ: "Gardner Wm. to Mr Gallatin } Penhallow Saml. to be Surveyor of Portsmoth vice Adams. dead"). Other enclosures not found.

For the recommendation FORMERLY MADE by New York congressmen Theodorus Bailey and Philip Van Cortlandt, see their letter to TJ of 3 May 1802.

YOUR INFORMANT: see Thomas Underwood, Jr., to TJ, 25 July.

John Adams appointed CLAUD THOMSON collector at Brunswick, Georgia, in December 1800. Gallatin wrote Pierce BUTLER on 12 Aug. that Thomson was "from intemperance, so far impaired in his understanding, as not to be capable of fulfilling his official duties." Requesting recommendations for a replacement, Gallatin called for a person who was not connected with trade and would accept the office, which offered a permanent salary of $200 and inconsiderable fees and commissions (Gallatin, *Papers*, 47:575; JEP,

1:357). Butler had previously advised the Treasury secretary. On 7 May, he wrote Gallatin from Georgia urging him not to remove Randolph McGillis, the collector at Saint Mary's. He described the collector, appointed by Adams in January 1800, as "of fair Character" and generally esteemed. Butler observed that it would not be easy to supply his place (RC in DNA: RG 59, LAR, endorsed by TJ: "Butler Pierce to mr Gallatin. Mc.Gilles collector of St. Mary's not to be removed"; JEP, 1:332-3).

ADVANCES MADE BY OUR CONSULS: in April 1802, Robert R. Livingston informed Madison that action was necessary to provide relief from the expenses incurred by U.S. officials charged with the care of U.S. seamen. He thought ship owners and captains should be held responsible for the crews they brought to foreign ports. William Lee described the distressing situation of American seamen at Bordeaux under his charge. In early 1802, he provided provisions and arranged passages back to the United States for more than 150 stranded seamen (Madison, *Papers, Sec. of State Ser.*, 2:414, 479; 3:157-8, 416-17).

MASTER & MATE OF THE REVENUE CUTTER: Hopley Yeaton and Benjamin Gunnison were recommended for the new cutter being built at Portsmouth, New Hampshire (see Enclosures No. 5 and 6, above). In August 1801, Yeaton had petitioned to be restored as captain of the Portsmouth cutter (Vol. 35:654-5). For the 1801 consideration of George WENTWORTH as naval officer at Portsmouth, New Hampshire, see Vol. 33:219. TJ recorded Wentworth's appointment as inspector and surveyor of the revenue at the port on 25 Aug. 1802 (Appendix I).

The recommendation of Joseph Wood (WOODS) by Return Jonathan MEIGS, Jr., has not been found, but on 3 Aug., Griffin Greene wrote Gideon Granger that Meigs had written the Treasury secretary on that day in Wood's behalf. Greene added his own recommendation, noting that Wood was of good character, "a Man of industry, & method" and a sound Republican whose appointment would please other Republicans at Marietta (Gallatin, *Papers*, 7:409).

TJ's letters to George W. ERVING, William SHORT, William DUANE, and Gallatin on book orders for the Library of Congress are printed at 16 July. LONDON CATALOGUE: Enclosure No. 2, at TJ to Duane, 16 July.

TJ had REQUESTED transcriptions of 1794 letters from William Short to Secretary of State Edmund Randolph (see TJ to Gallatin, 3 Aug.).

PETITION IN FAVOR OF TYNG: see Newburyport, Massachusetts, Citizens to TJ, 6 Aug.

From Étienne Lemaire

MONSIEUR   Washington Sity aoux du 17 1802
Jespair que la presente Resûe vous trouvaira En bonne Senté, je resûe, vôtre, honorable lettre le 16—datée du 13 ausitôt, Je me sui, Enpraicé, d'avoir l'honneur di repondre. Monsieur Je fait venir, le pompié pour examiner la pompe de la maison, il, ma promit de la mettre En bonne ordre,—Monsieur, le paûvre, petit Enfant asnet est Mor le 14. du Courant, mais je vous asur que le Bon dieux, lui a, Rendue, un grand Service ainsi qua Sa mer, vûe qui l'aurait Eté infirme, toute Sa vie. Monsieur toute la, famille Son joint a moi pr. vous fair Mille, remerciment, il, se porte toute, tres, bien—

Monsieur Je fini avecque, toute latachement possible. Je Sui, votre, tres afectionné Serviteur,   E LEMAIRE

SIR   Washington City, 17 Aug. 1802

I hope this mail finds you in good health. I received on the 16th your honorable letter, dated the 13th, and hasten to have the honor of replying. Sir, I brought in the pump man to examine the pump at the house. He promised to get it back in working order. Sir, the poor little child Asnet died on the 14th of this month, but I assure you that the good Lord rendered a great service to him and to his mother, since he would have been infirm all his life. My family joins me in sending you a thousand thanks, Sir. They are all well.

I conclude, Sir, with all possible fidelity. I am your very devoted Servant.

E LEMAIRE

RC (MHi); endorsed by TJ as received 22 Aug. and so recorded in SJL.

To James Madison

DEAR SIR   Monticello Aug. 17. 1802.

I now return you the papers forwarded by the merchants of Philadelphia and Boston on the subject of the wrongs they complain of at Buenos Ayres. I observe that they have not gone into a developement of the subject. two or three cases are opened with some degree of detail; as to the rest we have only a list of the ships for which our interference is claimed. but in cases where a hair's breadth of difference makes the thing right or wrong, full details are requisite. I think we ought to be informed what was the extent and what was to constitute the termination of the indulgences granted to Neutrals under which these vessels have ventured there: as also the specific circumstances under which every vessel went.[1] Spain had a right, according to the practice established, to give to those indulgences what duration she thought proper, only not withdrawing them so suddenly and on such short notice as to make the indulgence a trap to catch our vessels. reasonable[2] time should be allowed them to settle their affairs. on this last ground only can we urge any claim against Spain. we should therefore have a precise statement of the case of every vessel, and strike off from the list all those which cannot be brought within the limits of the indulgences, urging, under the authority of the government, only such cases as are founded in right. there seems to have been a great breach of faith by individuals, Spanish subjects: for these their courts should be open to us: or perhaps these cases could be got before the Commrs. proposed by mr Pinckney in the Algesiras depredations. I hazard these reflections that you may consider whether a detailed statement of cases should not be called for from the merchants, lest we should be committing ourselves in behalf of mere interloping & contraband adventures. Accept assurances of my constant affection & respect.   TH: JEFFERSON

RC (DNA: RG 59, MLR); at foot of text: "The Secretary of State." PrC (DLC). Enclosures: see Madison to TJ, 14 Aug.

For the bilateral board of commissioners PROPOSED to Spain by Charles PINCKNEY, see Joseph Yznardi, Sr., to TJ, 12 Aug.

ALGESIRAS DEPREDATIONS: the cap-

ture of American vessels in 1801, under pretext of a Spanish blockade of Gibraltar, by ships operating from the port of Algeciras on the Mediterranean (Madison, *Papers, Sec. of State Ser.*, 2:199-203; Vol. 35:406, 407n, 425, 488, 507, 545, 593-5, 660-1).

[1] TJ here canceled "we should."
[2] Word interlined.

From Marblehead, Massachusetts, Inhabitants

To the President
of the United States   Marblehead Augt. 17th. 1802

We the Subscribers, Merchants, & other Inhabitants of Marblehead, have noticed, with no small concern, the information, contained in the public prints of the intended removal from office, of Samuel R. Gerry esqr. Collector of this port. And altho' we have no disposition improperly to interfere in any of the acts of your administration, and are persuaded that, in this instance in particular, you have been influenced by a sense of apparent duty nevertheless, we cannot forbear, on so interesting an occasion, respectfully to communicate to you our feelings and some statement of facts. We do this, not without hoping, that if Major Warren should not accept the appointment, we may be so happy as to prevent a second nomination. — Suffer us therefore to remark, that when the impost under the present Constitution was adopted, the revenue offices being established without rule, thro' want of correct documents to ascertain the imports & exports of the several districts, it was presumed that resulting inequalities in the emoluments of offices, would be adjusted as soon as they could be ascertained. This however, has never yet been done, as it respects Mr. Gerry, for it appears that his annual income, from the time of his entering into office, to Decr. 1800. *on some years* has not amounted to the sum of Three hundred dollars, and *on an average*, has been something less than six hundred.

The business of office, greatly increased by 70 sail of fishing vessels, for each of which he has received but 90 cents ℔ annum, has been more than one man could transact. The emoluments, with the strictest econemy, having been inadequate to the support of his family, this officer has been obliged to dismiss his clerk, in consequence of which his official business has fallen in arrears. This we conceive to be *one* source of dissatisfaction on the part of government—

With respect to that, which is probably the *principal* source, vizt. a delinquency in the settlement of accounts—we would humbly observe, that this in our opinion, is not so much his *fault* as his *misfortune*. We can state, that he has been indefatigable in attention to the duties of the office; that he has lived in a stile by no means expensive; that he has kept no servant, horse, or vehicle of any kind; that he has entertained but little company; that he has sought no amusements; and by neglecting exercise has nearly fallen a victim to the office.— The inhanced price of the necessaries of life, in every place, & in this place in particular, will also be considered.—The fact is, that after 12 years of hard and faithful public service, he is more in debt than when he entered the office, & has now the gloomy prospect of being a disgraced and ruined man—far worse off than an unfortunate Merchant, who by an act of bankruptcy, is sure, on delivering up his property, to be discharged from his creditors—while others, who, to say the least, have not made greater exertions than he, have been able to live in a handsome stile, to employ clerks, and to make fortunes after all.— Such we believe to be the real circumstances of the case. They are such as have not failed to call forth our sympathy & compassion—and we are content to submit the matter to your wise consideration—most cheerfully can we testify to the diligent & obliging manner in which Mr *Gerry* has discharged the duties of his office—The uprightness and benevolence of his character have engaged our continual esteem and good wishes—and it is our sincere and earnest desire, that, with credit to himself, and with due security to the Government, he may be enabled to regain their confidence, and be restored to his former situation. We shall ever esteem him an upright, benevolent, and industrious, tho unfortunate officer—

With every sentiment of esteem and respect—we are Sir Your obedient Humble Servants

P.S. The Subscribers beg leave to apologize for the soiled & mutilated appearance of this memorial. while they regret that, in its passage thro' numerous hands greater care has not been used to preserve it undefaced, they venture to submit it, just as it is, to the indulgent eye of the President, as they think it important to avoid any further delay—

RC (DLC); in an unidentified hand, with more than 160 signatures attached; postscript written on verso of a sheet of signatures. Recorded in SJL as received on 29 Aug. with notation "merchts. petn in case of Gerry."

PUBLIC PRINTS: see Elbridge Gerry to TJ, 9 Aug. 1802.

To Robert Smith

DEAR SIR   Monticello Aug. 17. 1802.

I inclose you a letter from a mr Isaac Mansfield as attorney for the representative of James Mugford, who was killed in an action on board a vessel which he commanded whereby, under the then existing regulations, his widow became entitled to a bounty. I inclose it to you because, if entitled by the existing laws, the [inquiries] first come to your office for it's sanction before it could be presented at the treasury. if there be no laws auth[oriz]ing the claim I presume the application should be through the member of his district to Congress. I will ask the favor of you to give to mr Mansfield the answer which on examination of the case you shall deem proper. Accept assurances of my affectionate esteem & respect.   TH: JEFFERSON

PrC (DLC); faint; at foot of text: "The Secretary of the Navy." Recorded in SJL with notation "Mansfield & Mugford's case." Enclosure: Isaac Mansfield to TJ, 2 Aug. 1802 (recorded in SJL as received from Marblehead on 16 Aug. with notation "N" but not found).

ISAAC MANSFIELD, a Harvard graduate and former minister, was a lawyer from Marblehead (Washington, *Papers, Pres. Ser.*, 11:130-1).

On 17 May 1776, JAMES MUGFORD of Marblehead, commander of the armed schooner *Franklin*, captured a British transport near Boston that contained a valuable cargo of military stores. Two days later, he was killed repelling a British attack on his vessel. In January 1797, Mugford's WIDOW, Sarah, and her current husband, Arnold Martin, unsuccessfully petitioned Congress for the prize money and BOUNTY due Mugford for his naval service, basing their claim on a resolution of the Continental Congress of 28 Nov. 1775 that granted the widow or children of navy commanders killed in action a bounty of $400 (Washington, *Papers, Rev. War Ser.*, 4:329-30, 347-8; JHR, 2:645, 659; Worthington C. Ford and others, eds., *Journals of the Continental Congress, 1774-1789*, 34 vols. [Washington, D.C., 1904-37], 3:386).

From Robert Smith

                                           Navy department
SIR: 17 August 1802.

Captain James Barron and some other Officers of the Navy who have been heretofore commissioned but whose Commissions for the want of proper blanks being then ready were filled up on such as were originally intended for Warrants, are solicitous for the sake of appearance, to have them exchanged; I have therefore the honor to request your signature to the 15 blank Commissions transmitted herewith, which I will cause to be filled up and distributed to such of the above mentioned Officers as may be entitled to them. I also enclose a Warrant for Wallace Wormley Midshipman & William Sweeney Gunner lately appointed, and 15 blank Warrants, which on receiving your signature I will have filled up & issued to such Gunners Boatswains and other Officers as may be entitled to them.—

With much respect, I have the honor to be, yr mo ob servt,

RT SMITH

RC (DLC); in a clerk's hand, signed by Smith; at foot of text: "The President.— Monticello"; endorsed by TJ as received from the Navy Department on 19 Aug. and "Commns. & Warrants" and so recorded in SJL. FC (Lb in DNA: RG 45, LSP). Enclosures not found.

From Adams & Rhoades

Chronicle Office

SIR   Boston August 18 1802

The inclosed Copies of a Correspondence, are most respectfully submitted by

Your most obedient & very humble Servants

ADAMS & RHOADES

RC (DLC: Rare Book and Special Collections Division); at foot of text: "The President of the United States." Enclosure: see below.

Abijah Adams (1754-1816) of Boston, worked for his younger brother Thomas Adams as clerk and bookkeeper for the Boston *Independent Chronicle*, the chief organ of Jeffersonian support in New England. In 1799 both brothers were charged with seditious libel although Thomas died before his own case came to trial. Abijah was convicted and served 30 days in jail prior to assuming control in 1800 as senior editor of the semiweekly newspaper with Ebenezer Rhoades (Brigham, *American Newspapers*, 1:307-8, 2:1367, 1472; DAB).

COPIES OF A CORRESPONDENCE:

Adams & Rhoades enclosed a pamphlet recently printed for them entitled *Four Letters: Being an Interesting Correspondence between Those Eminently Distinguished Characters, John Adams, Late President of the United States; and Samuel Adams, Late Governor of Massachusetts. On the Important Subject of Government* (Boston, 1802; Sowerby, No. 3287). The letters, written in 1790, included two by John Adams of 12 Sep. and 18 Oct. and the responses by Samuel Adams of 4 Oct. and 20 Nov. (The last of these is dated 25 Nov. 1790 in Harry Alonzo Cushing, ed., *The Writings of Samuel Adams*, 4 vols. [New York, 1904-08], 4:344). Evidence indicates that TJ had access to the communications before their publication in pamphlet form, with Dr. Charles Jarvis transmitting them to him in 1801 or early

1802. TJ's undated endorsement of Meriwether Lewis's transcription of the correspondence reads: "Letters between John Adams and Samuel Adams. the originals were communicated by S. Adams to Doctr. Jarvis of Boston, who copied them & communicated the copy to Th:J. from which this copy is taken" (Trs in DLC; in Lewis's hand). On 24 Apr. 1801, Samuel Adams introduced Jarvis to TJ, noting that the doctor, "a man of much information," was among his "small circle of intimate friends." Adams "heartily" wished that "an epistolary correspondence" would develop between Jarvis and TJ (Vol. 32:348, 349n; Vol. 33:638-9).

From Andrew Jackson

SIR   Nashville August 18th. 1802

A late attempt at a monopoly of Salt in this Western Country—occasions me to trouble you with this letter—To counteract the banefull effects of this monopoly a company has formed with a determination to lower the price of this necessary of life—This will be effected provided they can procure a lick either by purchase or on Lease, that will answer the purpose the company has in View—but it is to be lamented, that all the Valuable licks that have been discovered within our boundery, are either in the hands [of] the monopolisers or those that combind with them in raising the price of salt—one of immense worth, within the Indian boundery near to the wabash river, would answer the purpose provided a lease could be procured for it from the Indians—This lick, would aford abundant supply for all the western world on lower terms, perhaps than at any yet known off—and the rent would yield to the Indians an annual Supply of this necessary of life—and tend much to the benefit of the publick—I am not informed whether the Indian agent is possessed with powers to lease such property for the Indians—or whether the Executive is cloathed with such authority to cause it to be done (if the interest of the Indians require it) without Legislative sanction—If the President is invested with the power, and the thing tend both to the benefit of the indians and the western citizens—would the President at the Expense of the company appoint an agent, to procure a lease from the Indians, for and on behalf of the company—If a lease can be obtained, the company (who I represent) wishes it to include five thousand acres—for which they are willing to pay to the Indians anual rent in Salt, to give bond and Security not to Tresspass on the Indian boundery beyond those limits, and come under obligations not to sell to the citizens at a higher than a certain stipulated price, which shall be as low as it can be made for, to sink the expence in the profits—keeping in View the different places of delivery and deposit—the real object of the company, is to counteract the attempt not to monopolise this article—to benefit our country and not self agrandizement—Indian property has been leased by an agent under the direction of the Secretary at war—I will name one case—The Ferry at South west Point—which brings to the Indians a handsome anual stipend—The lick Spoke off, in its present situation is unproductive to the Indians, and will continue so to be, untill it is [placed in] a state of cultivation, when the anual profits [will give] them an anual supply of that necessary they so [much] stand in need off, and will benefit the whole western world—Its local situation not more than Eight miles from the ohio, still nearer to the wabash—will supply all the western world with half the expence in portage that it can be done from any lick I know of—

Will you Sir when disengaged from objects of greater national concern, be good enough to answer this letter, and inform whether such power (to lease) is invested in the Executive, or the Indian agent—If the Executive, whether it is an object of such publick utility, as would induce you to exercise the power—If the President is not cloathed with the power, could the Legislative by law give the power of doing the thing, without the expence of a general treaty—

Publick good being the only object the writer has in View, the president will excuse the freedom he has taken—with the highest sentiments of Esteem & respect, I am Sir

yr mo, ob, Serv,   ANDREW JACKSON

RC (DLC); torn; addressed: "Thomas Jefferson President of the United States of america Federal City"; franked; postmarked Jonesborough, 19 Aug.; endorsed by TJ as received 9 Sep. and so recorded in SJL.

MONOPOLY: one company controlled production at Bullitt's Lick, Kentucky, the largest salt works in the western United States, and at other salt works in the vicinity. In 1802, after stockpiling salt in its warehouses, the firm stopped production at Bullitt's Lick to drive the price of salt sharply upward (John A. Jakle, "Salt on the Ohio Valley Frontier, 1770-1820," *Annals of the Association of American Geographers*, 59 [1969], 697-700; Robert E. McDowell, "Bullitt's Lick: The Related Saltworks and Settlements," *Filson Club History Quarterly*, 30 [1956], 259-60).

COMPANY HAS FORMED: Jackson, his friend George Michael Deaderick, and Deaderick's banking and mercantile partner, Howell Tatum, were seeking to invest in salt manufacturing (Harold D. Moser and others, eds., *The Papers of Andrew Jackson*, 8 vols. [Knoxville, 1980-], 1:222n, 271n, 307, 310-13, 349).

Black Hoof, on his visit to Washington in February 1802, had called attention to a salt spring on INDIAN lands near the Ohio River several miles below the mouth of the WABASH. Henry Dearborn asked William Henry Harrison to look into arranging a lease for the Indians' benefit. Harrison recommended instead that the United States obtain title to the locale, which he believed was the best source of salt between the Allegheny Mountains and the Mississippi River. In September, when Harrison met with Potawatomis and other Indians concerning the Vincennes tract, he obtained perpetual rights for the United States to the salt from the spring, along with title to a plot of surrounding land four miles square. Harrison did not consider Black Hoof's Shawnees to have any claim to the spring, and they were not represented at the conference in September. Soon, Harrison led an effort to have control over the Saline, as the salt spring was called, given to the legislature of Indiana Territory, but the initial response from Congress was unfavorable. Jackson and his associates lobbied for the privilege of extracting salt from the site. In May 1803, Jackson wrote to his wife: "I can only say and when I do say it, it is only for your eye alone, that we will I believe get the Wabash Saline. If we do, my hope is that it will place me above the frowns or smiles of fortune." Jackson tried with limited success to focus TJ's attention on the topic during a conversation they had in Washington later that year (same, 307, 317, 331, 361, 399; Esarey, *William Henry Harrison*, 1:47, 56-7, 65, 75; Vol. 36:517, 524, 525; note to Dearborn to TJ, 29 July).

The site of a FERRY over the Clinch River at Southwest Point, Tennessee, was rented from the Cherokees (Vol. 34:315).

From James Madison

DEAR SIR   Orange Aug. 18. 1802

Your favor of the 16th. came duly to hand with the papers to which it referred. I now forward others recd. by the last mail.

I have signified to Mr. Sumpter that his resignation was acquiesced in, and have used a language calculated to satisfy him that he retains the good opinion of the Executive. What is to be said to Mr. Livingston on his requests that he may appt. a private Secretary, and fill provisionally consular vacancies? Considering the disposition of a Secretary of Legation, acting as private Secy. to view himself on the more important side, and of the Minister to view & use him on the other, it is to be apprehended, that there may be difficulty in finding a successor to Mr. Sumter who will not be likely to be infected with the same dissatisfaction. I am not aware that the other proposition of Mr. L. is founded in any reason claiming equal attention.

Yours with respectful attachment   JAMES MADISON

RC (DLC); at foot of text: "The President of the U. States"; endorsed by TJ as received from the State Department at Orange on 19 Aug. and "Sumpter" and so recorded in SJL with notation "Sumpter's resignn." Enclosures not identified.

Madison's letter to Thomas Sumter, Jr., on the subject of Sumter's RESIGNATION from his position as Robert R. Livingston's secretary has not been found (Madison, *Papers, Sec. of State Ser.*, 3:498n).

CONSULAR VACANCIES: in a letter to Madison of 20 May, Livingston had written that he thought it would be "convenient & proper" to make Fulwar Skipwith, the U.S. commercial agent at Paris, the general commercial agent for France. "The power of the Minister," Livingston declared, "ought to extend to filling up vacancys & appointing to places where the commercial agents may be found necessary till the presidents pleasure is known" (same, 233).

From Isaac Story

MOST RESPECTED SIRE,   Marblehead Augst. 18. 1802

I have just received a line from you, informing me that the Commission, which I received, was designed for Joseph Story Esqr. of Salem.

I have never yet acted under it, & *never shall*, unless I should receive *further* authority from you. He is not my son, but my Nephew.—

I am very desirous of receiving some Commission from you in the civil department, as I have left the clerical. As I have the strongest assurance that Mr. Lyman, who was appointed Collector for Newbury-Port, is out on a Voyage to Europe, I suppose another will be appointed. And should you see fit to confer that honor upon me, I shall be equally pleased as with the other Commission, & it will lay a lasting debt of gratitude on my heart. And I presume that I can procure letters of recommendation from the honbl. Elbridge Gerry Esqr, & the Honbl. Doctr. Eustis.

accept the homage of my most profound respect

ISAAC STORY

RC (DNA: RG 59, LAR); endorsed by TJ as received 29 Aug. and so recorded in SJL.

A LINE FROM YOU: TJ to Story, 5 Aug.

From Tristram Dalton

SIR   City of Washington 19th August 1802

Last evening I had the pleasure to receive from my long valued Friend E Gerry Esqr, a Letter, accompanied by One for Yourself, which he requests me to enclose and forward to Monticello under *my own* Cover. This I now have the Honor to do, and embrace the opportunity to pray You to be assured that

I am, with the highest Respect, Sir, Your obliged, and most obed. hble. Servt   TRISTRAM DALTON

RC (MHi); at foot of text: "Thomas Jefferson Esq President of the United States"; endorsed by TJ as received 22 Aug. and so recorded in SJL. Enclosure: Elbridge Gerry to TJ, 9 Aug.

Tristram Dalton (1738-1817), a native of Newburyport, Massachusetts, graduated from Harvard College, became a merchant, and entered politics. He served as a U.S. senator from 1789 to 1791 and treasurer of the Mint from 1792 to 1794. He moved to the Federal City, where he speculated in city lots and became a director of the Washington branch of the Bank of the United States.

In March 1801, John Adams appointed him a commissioner of the District of Columbia, a position that Dalton held until the board ceased its operations on 1 June 1802. Adams also named Dalton a justice of the peace, but he was among the appointees who did not receive their commissions after TJ became president. In June 1802, TJ nominated Dalton as a bankruptcy commissioner, but he declined the office. He also turned down the customs collectorship at Newburyport. He later returned to New England, where during Madison's presidency he accepted an appointment as surveyor of customs at Boston (*Biog. Dir. Cong.*; Washington, *Papers, Pres. Ser.*, 7:459n; JEP, 1:121-2, 156; Vol. 23:482n; Vol. 33:481n; Vol. 35:46-7n; Vol. 36:314; Vol. 37:523, 698, 709; TJ to Gallatin, 9, 13 July 1802).

From Albert Gallatin

DEAR SIR   Treas. Dep. 19th Augt. 1802

I once more return the proposed regulations concerning the Mississipi trade. Nothing can be substituted to the agency of the Consul or Vice Consul at New Orleans: that agency constitutes the essence of the regulations & was always contemplated whilst the bill was framed & discussed: the identity of the article cannot otherways be proven than at the port where the vessel takes her cargo, or breaks bulk. Under the general laws, we have heretofore made use of the collector at Fort Adams, & wanted this special authority, only because that mode was found inefficient.   It seems to me that so long as we have a Consul at N. Orleans, although he may not be recognized there as such, we may attach what authenticity we please to his certificates; and it will become the interest of exporters of domestic produce to apply for them. May not, this modification answer, vizt. instead of "Consul" say "Consul, Vice-consul, or other authorized agent residing at New Orleans"; this is proposed only in order that Spain may not be obliged to take notice of our regulations & forbid the Consul to act.

As soon as I heard that Mr Clarke had arrived, I wrote to him & enclosed a copy of the letter which had been written him on the subject of the Marine hospital. His answer is enclosed; if Doctr. Bache will make out a list of medicines, I will have the order executed & the box shipped for N. Orleans, but I cannot select the medicines which are wanted for that place, and he is the best judge; a small assortment at first will do. You see by Mr Clarke's letter that the Spanish Govt. will assent to the establishment of the hospital, and, unless strongly cautioned, how much more expensive than the funds will admit, he would make it. Mr Clarke seems also to think that Dr. Bache's departure need not be delayed, and that Mr Huling will do in his (Clarke's) absence.

With sincere respect & attachment Your obedt. Servt.

ALBERT GALLATIN

RC (DLC); at foot of text: "The President of the United States"; endorsed by TJ as received from the Treasury Department on 22 Aug. and "Missipi reguIns" and so recorded in SJL.

PROPOSED REGULATIONS: see Gallatin to TJ, 7 Aug. President Adams, in January 1800, appointed John F. Carmichael COLLECTOR for Mississippi Territory at

Loftus Heights, the site of Fort Adams (JEP, 1:333).

In his letter to Daniel Clark of 5 Aug. (not found), Gallatin ENCLOSED A COPY of one addressed to him at New Orleans, which informed the consul of legislation passed for the relief of sick seamen at the port (see note to TJ to William Bache, 1 July).

ENCLOSURE

Daniel Clark to Albert Gallatin

SIR,   New York, 16th: August. 1802

I have had the honor of receiving your Letter of the 5th: inst. with its enclosure of the 2nd. ultimo.[1]—It gives me particular pleasure to learn that measures have been taken to relieve the distresses of our seamen in New-Orleans; but the provision is by no means adequate to the end, & the sum appropriated would for many years to come be absorbed in the Erection of a Building fit to receive and accomodate the numbers that in Sickly seasons will apply for admittance.—The Spanish Government will, without difficulty permit the building of an Hospital, but untill the funds are augmented I would recommend your authorizing the hire of such a building as may best suit present purposes, and that this should be done by the Doctor & Consul, or vice Consul to whose judgment jointly I think every thing relative to the application of the funds destined for the support of the Hospital might be intrusted.—By associating the Doctor with the Consul or vice Consul it may prevent misunderstandings or reflections which otherwise it might not be possible to avoid.—The Expenses of providing for, and attending on the Sick, especially in times of dangerous fevers are excessive.—I have paid for Seamen who have been but ill attended three dollars a day, independent of Doctors Bills, and I am persuaded that the Physician appointed by the President will immediately on his arrival in New Orleans, see how inadequate the funds are for the purpose, and will join in a representation to endeavour to have them augmented.—The major part of the expense incurred will be between the months of July & November, and as the danger is then more imminent, and the number of Patients greater than at any other time, or during the remainder of the year, it might be adviseable to authorize the Consul or vice Consul to expend in the sickly season, if it should be necessary, the whole of the present appropriation: at other times sickness is comparatively but little known among the Seamen & the Captains not having a Doctors bill to pay may be easily induced to pay a great part of the other Expense.—I should thank you to be informed whether the Physicians salary makes a part of the $3000 appropriated, and if medicines are purchased in the United States, which will be necessary in order to save expense, whether their Cost will likewise have to be deducted from it. The Physician best knows what medicines suit a Southern Climate, and I recommend his taking out a small assortment with him; on his arrival he will be better able to Judge of what may be wanting, and can order a supply as occasion may call for it.—The Physician, with the consent of the Consul or vice Consul, might be authorized to order from any Druggist in the U.S. the articles wanted, or contract with any Merchant to Supply them at fixed prices, as orders sent to public Deposits are not always speedily complied with, and the Sick would be exposed to suffer by delay.—A set of Surgical Instruments for amputation and apparatus for setting fractured limbs, the Physician should provide himself with before leaving home: every thing else may be procured in the way I have already pointed out.—Molasses, Sugar, Rice & wine for the Hospital are always to be had in Orleans, and these things may be left out of any supply he may bring with him.—As I shall be absent from New-Orleans four or five months, I would thank you to address your Letters to me or to the Vice Consul in my absence, whose well Known Zeal in the service of his fellow Citizens authorizes me to assure you that nothing will be left undone by him which can contribute to their assistance.—

I shall write to him on the subject, and flatter myself the Physician will find in him a friend whose experience and advice will be very useful on his arrival in the Country.—I shall give directions to Mr. Hulings respecting the payment of the Physician's Salary & Expenses, and should any difficulty Occur in Negotiating Bills, will advise you of the method I think most proper to pursue for remitting the amount of the Expenditures.—

I have the honor &ca &ca   (signed) DANIEL CLARK

Tr (DLC); in a clerk's hand; at head of text: "Copy"; at foot of text: "Hon. Albert Gallatin Secy of the Treasury"; endorsed by Gallatin: "D. Clark's letter copy." Tr (LNHiC: Clark-Gallatin Papers).

THANK YOU TO BE INFORMED: according to the 3 May 1802 act for the relief of sick and disabled seamen, all expenditures, including the physician's salary, "convenient accommodations," and supplies, were to come from the $3,000 appropriation for New Orleans (U.S. Statutes at Large, 2:192).

[1] MS: "utimo."

From Albert Gallatin

Treasury Department August 19th. 1802.

The Secretary of the Treasury, respectfully represents to the President of the United States, that Joshua Head, collector of customs for the port of Waldoborough (Massachusetts) has failed in rendering his quarterly accounts, none later than those for the quarter ending on the 30th september, last, having been received: nor has he, from that time, rendered any weekly, or other return, whatever, of the monies received and paid by him. A letter, a copy of which is hereunto annexed, was, on the 21st. June last, written to him on that subject, to which no answer has been received. Under those circumstances, it becomes the duty of the Secretary of the Treasury, to submit to the President, the propriety of removing that officer from his employment.

Respectfully submitted by his very obdt. Servant

ALBERT GALLATIN

RC (DLC); in a clerk's hand, signed by Gallatin; at foot of text: "The President of the United States"; endorsed by TJ as received from the Treasury Department on 22 Aug. and so recorded in SJL with notation "Head Collr. Waldoboro"; also endorsed by TJ: "Joshua Head. Collector of Waldoborough (Mass) for delinquency." Enclosure: Gallatin to Joshua Head, 21 June 1802 (see note to Memorandum from the Treasury Department, 20 June 1802).

President Adams appointed JOSHUA HEAD collector at Waldoborough in March 1799. On his lists, TJ noted that Head was removed for being "delinquent" (JEP, 1:321; Vol. 33:673; Appendix I).

From Bushrod Washington

SIR   Mount Vernon Augt 19. 1802

I had the honor to recieve your note of the 13th. inst. with the enclosures from Genl La fayette, and I pray you to accept my thanks for your politeness in recieving & forwarding them to me.

I regret that the mistake to which you allude should have given you a moment's concern. It was extremely natural under the circumstances which attended the rect. of the package, and is one for which I have more than once had to apologize.

I have the honor to be Sir Yr Mo. ob. Servt.

BUSHROD WASHINGTON

RC (DLC); endorsed by TJ as received 22 Aug. and so recorded in SJL.

From John Barnes

George Town 20th Augt. 1802

I now find Sir, that the post to Charlottesville & Milton goes for Certain, twice aweek, Tuesdays & fridays. of course, I embrace this mail—

Mr Short left Town, this morning for Berkley Springs expecting to meet his Brother there—from thence—I presume in the course of 10 or 12 days direct for Monticello—I pressed upon him $400. with his other occasional Bills carriage &c—[100]—which he says will be more than sufft. for his prest. wants, untill he persues his expected rout to New York, &c—The remnant of my prest. Bank, is little more than $1000. which I shall husband with all possible Care, as no *real* resources can be drawn before Octr. my Sepr receival, being ingaged to take up the $2000. a Bank. [Middle said Int.] by Mr. Hopkins late advices—I dispair of his accomplishing my business untill his return—from conveying his two Children to a School at Brunswick—N.Jersey, so that I shall decline my intended Journey, to Richmond—at lest save the extra expences, and Content my self with doing—in short—worse than nothing—for these three tedious months to come—I called on Mr L. Maire for a few minutes Yesterday. he produced to me your Letter respecting the Pump. I desired him to advise with Doctr Thornton, who probably would engage the pump maker—to repair it faithfully, and on reasonable terms, and I would pay the Account

with great Respect I am Sir your Obed: hb Sevt.

JOHN BARNES

RC (ViU: Edgehill-Randolph Papers); at foot of text: "The President U States at Monticello"; endorsed by TJ as received 26 Aug. and so recorded in SJL.

YOUR LETTER RESPECTING THE PUMP: TJ to Étienne Lemaire, 13 Aug.

To Henry Dearborn

DEAR SIR   Monticello Aug. 20. 1802.

Your favor of the 15th is recieved and I now return mr Bowdoin's letter forwarded in it. his doctrine is unquestionably sound. I have enjoyed uninterrupted good health, the story of the five physicians notwithstanding. by this post I recieve the opinions of the Secretaries of the Treasury & navy as well as yours on the subject of our Barbary affairs. I had before asked & recieved that of the Secretary of state: but as his opinion does not go to all the points arising out of the others, and explanations by letter would lose us one if not two posts, I propose immediately on closing my mail by the post of this day, to set out to his house, so that definitive answers will go by the next post which will arrive at Washington on Tuesday the 24th at 8 P.M. the following is the arrangement of our posts.

Friday and Tuesday at 7. P.M. leaves Washington
Sunday & Thursday at noon arrives at Milton.
Monday & Friday at 1. P.M. leaves Milton.
Tuesday & Saturday at 8. P.M. arrives at Washington
Accept assurances of my affectionate attachment & respect.

TH: JEFFERSON

PrC (DLC); at foot of text: "The Secretary at War."

SET OUT TO HIS HOUSE: Madison's letter to TJ of 25 Aug., which refers to TJ having been "here," confirms that TJ did go to Montpelier to confer with the secretary of state. TJ wrote letters at Monticello on the 20th and the 22d. If he left Monticello after finishing his correspondence on the 20th, he probably stayed that night at Madison's house and left for home on the 21st. He evidently stopped for the night of 21-22 Aug. at Castle Hill, Francis Walker's residence about 14 miles northeast of Monticello, where on the 22d he left $1.50 in "vales," or tips to the household staff (MB, 2:937, 1079).

To Albert Gallatin

DEAR SIR   Monticello Aug. 20. 1802.

Your favors of the 16th. & 17th. were recieved the last night. the contents of the latter shall now be distinctly noted.

Commrs. of bankruptcy at Poughkeepsie. I have proposed a general arrangement to the Secretary of state which may save the necessity of appointments over the whole face of every state, 99. out of 100. of which would be never called on to act, and would yet give opportunities of indulging favoritism by enlarging the field of selection. the answer not yet recieved.

Mr. Nourse's certificate retained for investigation.

the Successor to Claud Thomson collector of Brunswick Georgia. I will sign the commission when recieved from you. the papers are returned.

letters respecting unauthorised advances by our Consuls, retained, & shall be returned after a conference with mr Madison, by next post.

Surveyor of Portsmouth. I observe Penhallow's recommendation is the effect of sollicitation, as is evident by so many signatures to one formula. Langdon's & Whipples opinions in favr. of Wentworth, the facts they mention, Genl. Dearborne's preference of him, & yours as I infer, induce me to prefer him also. I am therefore ready to sign the commission. I retain the recommendations.

Wood's commission as Register of the land office at Marietta I have signed & will carry on to be signed by mr Madison & forwarded. I retain the recommendation.

Hiller's resignation returned.

Mr. Short will be here in three days: I will consult with him about the books to be bought in Paris.

On mr Jones's return I will thank you to think again of the letters in the case of mr Short & E. Randolph.

I have not heard from mr Page, and should much wonder at his declining the appointment at Petersburg. should he do so, there can be no question as to the substitute. Dr. Shore's appointment would be more *locally* popular, & very much so generally. he has every right to it.

I have recieved the address of *two thirds* of the merchants of Newbury port on the subject of Tyng's removal, & praying a reconsideration. it is impudently malignant. I shall not notice it.

That Louisiana is to be possessed by France is probable. that any man in America has undoubted authority that it will be so I do not think.

The last post brings me the opinions of the Secretaries at War & of the Navy, as well as your's on our Barbary affairs. I had before asked & recieved that of the Secretary of State. but as his did not go to all the points arising out of the others, and explanations by letter might lose us a post or two, I shall immediately on closing my mail for this day's post set out to mr Madison's, so that the next post shall carry definitive arrangements to Washington where it will arrive on Tuesday (24th.) at 8. P.M. the movements of our post do not seem to be understood with you. they are as follow.

Fridays and Tuesday's at 7. P.M. leaves Washington

Sundays & Thursdays at noon arrives at Milton.

Mondays & Fridays at 1. P.M. leaves Milton

Tuesdays & Saturdays at 8. P.M. arrives at Washington.

Accept assurances of my affectionate esteem & respect.

Th: Jefferson

RC (NHi: Gallatin Papers); at foot of first page: "The Secretary of the Treasury"; endorsed. PrC (DLC). Recorded in SJL with notation "miscellans. affairs."

GENERAL ARRANGEMENT: see TJ to Madison, 16 Aug.

TJ recorded John SHORE'S APPOINTMENT as collector at Petersburg on his list of appointments at 6 Sep. 1802. Shore continued in office until his death in 1811 (Vol. 35:278n; Appendix I).

For the OPINIONS OF THE SECRETARIES on the Barbary affairs, see Henry Dearborn to TJ, 15 Aug., and Robert Smith and Gallatin to TJ, both at 16 Aug. TJ received all three letters on the 19th. THAT OF THE SECRETARY OF STATE: Madison to TJ, 14 Aug.

From Albert Gallatin

I have received your letter of the 14th instt., in which you justly correct my transposition of Newbury-port & Marblehead. General Dearborn approves of Tuck's removal; but as there is no inconvenience in waiting a week longer, & we have been rather unfortunate in selecting individuals who could not or would not accept I have concluded to wait for your answer to this letter before I would send any of the three commissions to those Essex ports. I have made a report in the case of Head; if you approve a commission will be filled with the name of such person as Gen. Dearborn will recommend, it being in his own vicinity, and all those commissions may then go together.   There is another case which does not admit of delay; it is the collectorship of Petersburgh. Heath has received his letter of dismission, & Mr Page not accepting, we have no collector; nor is it very clear how far the surveyor, of whom I know nothing, can act if Heath has ceased his functions.

Since my last you will have heard that Morocco has declared war. By the letters which Robt. Smith has shown me, it appears that their force consists first and principally of row boats which, I understand, never go out of sight of the coast—secondly of half gallies at Tetuan which as well as Tangier is within the straights—thirdly of Frigates at Rhabat the modern name of Sallee & on the Atlantic. This seems to require three frigates; one to convoy our vessels through the gut, by alternately sailing from Cadiz to Malaga; which will be sufficient protection against the boats; one to blockade Tetuan, without which the half gallies will sail through the mediterranean beyond Malaga; and a third to block up Rhabat alias Sallee. I do not know that the Moors have any other port on the Mediterranean but Tangier & Tetuan; but I am confident they have some other on the Atlantic, perhaps none north, but at least one south of Sallee, the same which the Emperor kept blockaded, but the name of which I forget—(Magadore I believe). I mention this to show the necessity of peace: we never had calculated on a war with Morocco which affects not only our Mediterranean but also our Madeira and Atlantic trade. If Tunis has made war, our situation will be still worse; yet as they are a commercial people there is less danger. On reading the Morocco treaty I find that Captives are not to be treated as slaves, that an exchange is provided for, & that the balance is to be paid by the losing party at 100 dollars per head; the whole is arranged like the rules by which gamesters agree to play; and it is presumable that the Emperor wants money. This, however, must be attended to in the instructions to our officers; we must try to make prisoners; if we win, his majesty may be disposed to cease playing. If you attend to the latter part of the 3d article of the same treaty, you will, I think find the reason which he may alledge in support of his pretensions. Yet, the doctrine of blockades, (which is not made an exception in that treaty to the general rule laid down in the 3d article) is not unknown to the Emperor, since he has practised upon it: perhaps, however, their understanding was only that no foreign nation had a right to assist rebels.

I can add nothing but to repeat my wishes for peace, & express my anxiety that no delay may take place in the measures adopted at the present moment. Had the instructions to Cathcart arrived before Morocco had declared war, we should be at present at peace with both.

With respect and attachment Your obedt. servt.

ALBERT GALLATIN

I wish much to be out of this city at this time; but will wait until the result of your determination in that business is ascertained—

RC (DLC); at foot of text: "The President of the United States"; endorsed by TJ as received from the Treasury Department on 22 Aug. and so recorded in SJL with notation "Marocco. Heth, Page."

MAGADORE: Mogador.

According to the contemporary English translation of Article 16 of the 1786 TREATY between Morocco and the United States, in the event of war between the two nations, "Prisoners are not to be made Slaves, but to be exchanged one for another, Captain for Captain, Officer for Officer and one private Man for another," with any "defficiency" in the exchange to be compensated by payment of $100 "for each Person wanting." Prisoners were to be exchanged within twelve months of their capture (Miller, *Treaties*, 2:215).

HE MAY ALLEDGE IN SUPPORT OF HIS PRETENSIONS: Article 3 stated that should one of the parties to the treaty be at war with another nation, it could not detain its enemy's goods if they were aboard vessels belonging to the other party to the treaty. As Gallatin observed, there was no EXCEPTION in the article to allow the United States, through its blockade of Tripoli, to stop the wheat that Mawlay Sulayman wanted to send to that country (same, 213).

From David Higginbotham

DEAR SIR   Milton August 20th. 1802

The bearer hereof Mr. Isham Henderson of Milton, being desirous to obtain the loan of such books as may be usefull in the study of Law, not being in Circumstances to purchase them, I beg leave to recommend him to your favour as a young man of integrity and good deportment having no doubt but that should you be pleased to favour his request, he will take special care of the books with which you may intrust him

I am Dear Sir Your Mo Ob: DAVID HIGGINBOTHAM

RC (ViU); endorsed by TJ: "Henderson Isham. lent him 4th. Blacstone Ruffhead: Jacob's L. Dict" and "June 7. 08. wrote to C. Peyton to recover it."

David Higginbotham (1775-1853), an Albemarle County merchant, had been the factor for Brown, Rives & Co. and had recently established a trading house in Milton with John Watson. He later emerged as one of TJ's larger creditors and in 1813 purchased William Short's Indian Camp property in a triangular arrangement that transferred TJ's obligations from Higginbotham to Short. Higginbotham renamed the property "Morven" and upon his death left an estate worth more than $100,000, including 56 slaves (William Montgomery Sweeney, "Higginbotham Family of Virginia," WMQ, 1st ser., 27 [1918], 124; MB, 2:944, 988; RS, 4:154; Vol. 30:29; Vol. 35:28).

ISHAM HENDERSON, a son of Bennett Henderson and one of the sibling heirs who in March 1801 had indirectly conveyed part of the Henderson property in Milton to TJ, eventually moved to Kentucky, where he was a successful lawyer and politician (Woods, *Albemarle*, 226-8; Lewis Collins and Richard H. Collins, *History of Kentucky*, 2 vols. [Covington, Ky., 1878], 2:339; Z. F. Smith, "Dueling, and Some Noted Duels in Kentucky," *Register of the Kentucky Historical Society*, 8 [1910], 84; Vol. 35:xlvi-iii, 342-4, 455n).

From James Madison

DEAR SIR   Aug. 20. 1802

The inclosed letters will shew the object of the Bearer Mr. Baker. From his conversation, I find that, placing Bourdeaux & Gibralter out of view, he wishes to be appd. as Consul, to Minorca, where he says a Consul will be admitted, now that it is again under the Spanish Government, and where he observes a consul may be of use to the U. States, particularly during our bickerings with the Barbary powers. I find from his conversation also that he is a native of Minorca, whilst under British Govt, but that he has been in the U. States about six years & is an American Citizen. Nothing has passed between us that can influence his expectations or calculations, of the result of his pursuit.

Always with affectionate respects yrs.   JAMES MADISON

RC (DLC); endorsed by TJ as received from the State Department at Orange on 21 Aug. and "John Martin Baker to be consul [...]" (torn) but recorded in SJL as received 20 Aug. Enclosures (see Madison, *Papers, Sec. of State Ser.*, 3:447-8, 451): (1) Frederick Weissenfels to Edward Livingston, New York, 28 July 1802, asking Livingston to recommend John Martin Baker, who is Weissenfels's son-in-law, to be vice consul at Bordeaux or Gibraltar; Baker is "master" of the English, Spanish, French, and Italian languages, has "a General Knowledge" of commercial matters, and is of good character, which allows Weissenfels to "Vouch for his abilitys, Honor and Fidelity" (RC in DLC); see Enclosure No. 3. (2) Certificate, New York, 30 July, attesting to Baker's knowledge of languages, good character, and commercial ability (RC in same; in Baker's hand, signed by Weissenfels, William Tredwell, and John Casenave); see Enclosure No. 4. (3) Livingston to Madison, New York, 31 July 1802, enclosing Weissenfels's letter (Enclosure No. 1); Livingston knew Baker at Philadelphia about four years ago, when Baker worked as clerk for a gentleman who had "very extensive concerns"; Livingston understands that Baker performed well in that job, has been engaged in "respectable" pursuits since that time, "is well acquainted with several of the Modern languages," and "might be useful in the Office he solicits" (RC in same). (4) Aaron Burr to Madison, New York, 2 Aug. 1802, enclosing the certificate (Enclosure No. 2) at Weissenfels's request; having served with Colonel Weissenfels during the Revolutionary War, Burr asserts that he was "a brave & Valuable officer, a man of integrity & honor"; Burr is not personally acquainted with Baker, but from his "knowledge of two of the persons attesting in his favor, I cannot doubt of the truth of their Certificate" (RC in same). (5) Weissenfels to Madison, New York, 3 Aug. 1802, recommending the bearer, Baker, "Whose object to your City is, to obtain an appointment from our Governement, in the Consular department" (RC in same).

Great Britain held the Mediterranean island of MINORCA for a number of years before 1756, again from 1763 to 1782, and from 1798 until 1802, when the island returned to Spanish control under the peace of Amiens along with most other Spanish possessions taken by the British in the 1790s. The port of Mahón (Maó), which the British developed in the eighteenth century as a naval base, was on the island (Miquel Àngel Casasnovas Camps, *Història de Menorca* [Mallorca, 2005], 312, 322-5, 356-61; Grainger, *Amiens Truce*, 33, 41; Parry, *Consolidated Treaty Series*, 56:292; Vol. 34:646).

HIS EXPECTATIONS: Baker wrote to Madison from New York on 28 Nov. 1802 to say that the islands of Majorca and Ibiza should be included in the consulate for Minorca and that he and his family were "ready to embark" (RC in DNA: RG 59, LAR; endorsed by TJ as a letter from Baker to Madison and "to be Consul of Majorca Minorca Yvica"). Baker again wrote to the secretary of state from New York on 4 Jan. 1803, indicating that a ship would be leaving for the Mediterranean in three weeks and that Baker hoped to take advantage of that opportunity, "being particularly pressed through Mrs. Baker's present situation" (RC in same; endorsed by TJ as from Baker to Madison and "to be Consul at Minorca"). TJ nominated Baker to be consul for Minorca, Majorca, and Ibiza early in February 1803 and signed a commission for him on 1 Mch. (commission in Lb in DNA: RG 59, PTCC; TJ to the Senate, 2 Feb. 1803).

To Robert Smith

DEAR SIR   Monticello Aug. 20. 1802.

Your favors of the 16th & 17th were recieved last night; but neither the commissions or Warrants mentioned in the last to be forwarded have come. I suppose they have been put into the post office after the hour and will [be on] by the next post. I recieve by this your opinion & those of the Secretaries of the Treasury & War on our Barbary affairs. I had before asked & received that of mr Madison: but as his opinion does not go to all the points which arise in the others I shall, immediately on making up my dispatches for the post of this day, set out for his house, as a personal interview will enable us to answer finally by the next post, which will arrive at Washington on Tuesday at 8 P.M. whereas doing the business by letter would lose one if not two posts. the [returns] of our post seem not understood at Washington. they are as follows.

Friday & Tuesday at 7. P.M. leaves Washington

Sunday & Thursday at Noon. arrives at Milton.

Monday & Friday at 1. P.M. leaves Milton

Tuesday & Saturday at 8. P.M. arrives at Washington.

The misfortune is the departure of the post from Washington at 7. P.M. and the Milton post arriving there an hour after. for the letters to come to me & [...] [be answered] the arrangement is perfect; but not for my writing to Washington & [recieving an] answer by return of post. Accept my affectionate good wishes & respect

TH: JEFFERSON

PrC (DLC); faint; at foot of text: "The Secretary of the Navy."

From Robert Smith

SIR,   Navy Dept: Augt. 20. 1802

From the dispatches herewith sent you will perceive the state of our affairs in the Mediterranean. I am seriously apprehensive that Commodore Morris may not have considered himself authorised to retain the Boston and that, if he has retained her, he will not, with the addition of the New York, be able to protect our Citizens. The Enemys Coast is so extended that the dangers are great. And the taking of one Merchant Vessel would cost us more than would maintain two frigates. But considerations more powerful incline me to think that a further reinforcement of at least one frigate ought to be sent to Morris. I possess the funds to send her out. It was my intention to have explained myself at large upon this subject. But I have by continued interruptions, been prevented. The mail is just closing. My object in sending out this additional force is to prevent a Continuance of the War—that is to avail ourselves of the impression thereby produced in order to Obtain a favorable peace. Such a peace under the influence of such a force could be effected in the course of *this* year. With a less force the War may Continue for years which would be playing a hazardous game. The John Adams or the Congress could be equipped for Sea in two Weeks

The New York will be ready to depart next Week—The Gun Carriages will not be sent

With great respect & Esteem I am, Sir, Your Ob Ser

RT SMITH

RC (DLC); at foot of text: "The President"; endorsed by TJ as received from the Navy Department on 22 Aug. and "Marocco" and so recorded in SJL. Enclosures: (1) James Simpson to James Madison, Gibraltar, 26 June 1802, informing the secretary of state with regret that the governor of Tangier has compelled him to leave that place after receiving "positive orders" from the sultan of Morocco on 22 June, "accompanied with advice of his having declared War against the United States"; Simpson and Commodore Richard V. Morris have tried unsuccessfully to delay the expulsion of the American consul, hoping to convince the sultan of the impossibility of their allowing shipments of wheat to be sent to Tripoli; "But same Evening a Soldier arrived with the Emperours second Order for my quitting the Country immediately, *in a state of War*," Simpson reports, "that is the best translation can be given of the Arabic Word used on the occasion"; making his declaration at a public audience on 19 June, the sultan directed that "the utmost expedition should be used" to prepare his cruisers for sea; Simpson is puzzled over the sultan's decision to declare war over such a "trivial" matter; he will delay writing the sultan until the arrival of dispatches by the frigate *Adams*, "that I may not fall into the error of giving His Majesty room to hope for more, than I may be authorised by you to do"; Simpson will remain at Gibraltar and gather "information of what may happen in Barbary, respecting their sending out armed Boats, which is my chief fear"; the frigates at Rabat and the half galleys at Tetuán will not be ready for some time; Simpson trusts that his property remaining in Tangier is safe, due to his friendly relationship with the governor; he has entrusted his house and garden to the Spanish consul; Simpson also transmits the two other enclosures (RC in DNA: RG 59, CD; Madison, *Papers, Sec. of State Ser.*, 3:342-3, 507; NDBW, 2:185-7). (2) Simpson to Madison, 17 June 1802 (see Enclosure No. 1 at TJ to Madison, 9 Aug.). (3) Simpson's circular to U.S. consuls and commercial agents at the chief ports of Europe, Gibraltar, 25 June, informing the officials that he has been forced to leave Tangier, Morocco having declared war against the United States; requesting that all means be used to inform U.S. citizens and advise "all Masters of our Merchant Vessels to be very carefull to avoid the Moors Cruizers, especialy in & near the Straits of Gibraltar, where it is highly probable they will have many small armed Boats" (Tr in DNA: RG 59, CD; NDBW, 2:183-4).

From Isaac Story

MOST RESPECTED SIRE,   Boston Augst. 20th. 1802

When I received your Commission, I was fully sensible; that I should retain the exercise of it; during your pleasure, & no longer.

When therefore I received your letter on the 18th. of this month, desiring my resignation, as the Commission was designed for another *Story*, I immediatly sat down, & penned my resignation, as was in duty bound.

But I couched it in such terms as to leave an opening to be re instated, if it should be agreeable to your Excellency. I did not know, when you found that Joseph Story was not my son, & that Mr. Dane had declined accepting the Commission of Bankruptcy, as has been publickly announced, you might alter your determination. Though not brought up a Lawyer or Merchant, I have considerable acquaintance with both Law & Merchandize; & I think that I thoroughly understand the Bankrupt law.—

It is unfortunate for me, that my letter of Thanks should produce the destruction of my Commission. A grateful mind always appeared to me to be a great ornament to human nature. *But if ye suffer for well-doing*, says the Apostle, *happy are ye*. I hope it will operate for my benefit. If I am an Enthusiast in any thing, it is in the governing providence of God, for I am firmly persuaded that all things shall work together for good to the virtuous & grateful.

I afterwards applied for some civil employment, for though above want, I am not above business. A state of Indolence is disagreeable to my active mind. And understanding that there was a vacancy at Newbury-Port, I applied for the Collector's place; and accordingly waited upon the honble. Elbridge Gerry Esqr. yesterday for his recommendation. His answer was, that if it depended upon his fiat, I should have the office that moment, in the room of Colo. Lyman*; but he was so wounded by the situation of his brother, he could not think of writing to Government on any other Subject, until he had ascertained, whether he had lost his influence, or not. I also called at the house of the Honble. William Eustis Esqr., but found him gone out of Town.

I can not but cherish a hope, that I shall be remembered, when a suitable opening presents, if I fail of this appointment.—

Please to accept the homage of my most profound respects

ISAAC STORY

* who was supposed gone to Europe

RC (DNA: RG 59, LAR); addressed: "His Excellency Thomas Jefferson Esqr President of the united States Washington, or Monticello"; franked and postmarked; endorsed by TJ as received 29 Aug. and so recorded in SJL; also endorsed by Henry Dearborn: "to be returned to the President."

THE APOSTLE: 1 Peter 3:14-17.

Stay of Execution

Whereas sentence of death hath been passed by the Circuit Court of the District of Columbia for the County of Washington on James McGirk, convicted of murder in due form of law, which sentence was ordered to be carried into execution on the twenty eighth day of the present month of August, and whereas reasonable cause hath been suggested why such execution should be stayed; Now therefore be it known that I Thomas Jefferson, President of the United States, do hereby reprieve the said James McGirk until the twenty eighth day of October next, to which day the execution of the said sentence is accordingly adjourned.

Done under my hand & the seal of the United States, this twenty first day of August one thousand eight hundred two.

TH: JEFFERSON

FC (Lb in DNA: RG 59, GPR); in Daniel Brent's hand; at head of text: "Respite" and "Papers on file"; at foot of text: "By the President. James Madison Secy of State."

DO HEREBY REPRIEVE: TJ was at Madison's residence in Orange County on the day he signed this order of temporary reprieve (see TJ to Dearborn, 20 Aug.). When the stay of execution reached Washington, a rumor began that TJ had granted James McGurk a pardon. Even after the correction of that report, TJ's opponents attacked him for issuing the reprieve. "What then has influenced the mind of our gracious chief magistrate," asked the *Washington Federalist*. "Is it an innate respect, a natural regard for every thing that is base and unprincipled?" (*Washington Federalist*, 27 Aug.).

To Mawlay Sulayman, Sultan of Morocco

GREAT AND GOOD FRIEND   Aug. 21. 1802.

A war, as unjust as it was unprovoked,[1] having been declared against us by the Bey of[2] Tripoli, we sent some armed vessels into the Mediterranean for the protection of our commerce in that sea. We gave it in particular charge to our officers to respect your majesty's flag and subjects, and to omit no opportunity of cultivating a good understanding with you: and we trusted[3] that should circumstances render it necessary for our vessels to enter your majesty's harbors, or to have communications with them, they would[4] experience that hospitality and friendly assistance which we would practise towards your[5] vessels and subjects in our own ports or elsewhere whenever we could be useful to them.

We learnt then with great concern[6] that your M's sensibility excited by the sufferings of Tripoli of a nature indeed to make us forget the wrongs which had produced them, had induced you to propose a relief not admitted by the ordinary rules of war:[7] and that a refusal which was regular on the part of our officers, had drawn on our Consul marks[8] of YM's displeasure.

If the views of Y.M. were confined to the single instance of relief which was the subject of that application, certainly our great esteem & respect for you would have led us to give as we[9] now give that proof of the value we set on your friendship; & we do it under a full confidence that your justice could not have contemplated a permanent relinquishmt on our part of the rights which nature has given us, of reducing an unjust enemy to reason by an infliction of all those evils which a state of war authorises.[10]

As an additional[11] proof of the confidence we repose in Y.M.'s justice, we also declare that if in the further exercise of your benevlce & frndshp towards Tripoli, you should think proper to interpose your powerful influence with that Bey to induce him to return again to the paths of justice towds us, we require no other price for the restoration[12] of peace, considering as we do[13] the just pursuits of industry as more beneficial to a nation than the most successful war.

We had been given to understand[14] some time since[15] that it would be agreeable to you that the US. should at your expence[16] procure to be made for you one hundred gun carriages. we have lost no time[17] in preparing and sending them to you by a ship of our own; and we feel it more conformable with our dispositions towards your majesty to ask your acceptance of them as a mark of the esteem and respect we bear you, and of the desire we entertain of cultivating that peace and friendly intercourse, which, while it is acceptable to us with all nations, is particularly desired with your majesty.

I pray god[18] to have you, very great & good friend in his holy keeping. Done in the US. of America this _____ day of August 1802.

Dft (DLC: TJ Papers, 125:21646-7); entirely in TJ's hand; dateline at foot of text on fol. 21647; text consists of two components, the first one (fol. 21646) being the FC of TJ to Sulayman, [5 Aug.], with emendations, to form the first, fifth, and sixth paragraphs of the letter printed above according to notations "§. 1," "§. 3," and "§. 4" (see notes 1, 14, and 18 below); the second component (fol. 21647) comprising additional text, heavily emended, to form the second, third, and fourth paragraphs of the letter with notation "§. 2" for sequence (see note 6 below), written on a clipped address sheet, probably from Samuel Smith to TJ, 9 Aug., containing a partial address to TJ at Monticello and a Baltimore postmark of 10 Aug. Not recorded in SJL.

EXCITED BY THE SUFFERINGS OF TRIPOLI: "Frequent representations on the distress of the people in Tripoly for

Grain, I know have been made to Muley Soliman," James Simpson wrote to Madison on 13 May; "whether his well known Charitable disposition towards all Mussulmen in want, may have induced him to endeavour at sending these supplys of Wheat (for he gives it gratis) or if it be done as an *aid* in their present Contest, it is impossible for me to say" (Madison, *Papers, Sec. of State Ser.*, 3:222).

THIS   DAY OF AUGUST: according to Madison to TJ, 25 Aug., TJ left this letter at Montpelier when he visited on 20-21 Aug. (see TJ to Dearborn, 20 Aug.). The version that he left with Madison has not been found. Madison wrote on 25 Aug. that he erased a paragraph before forwarding the letter to Washington, and that deletion does not appear on the draft printed above. On 21 Aug., TJ and Madison were unaware that news had arrived in Washington of a declaration of war by Mawlay Sulayman. After receiving that information on the evening of 22 Aug., TJ informed Madison that "of course" the letter to the sultan could not go forward. Robert Smith and Albert Gallatin anticipated that decision and instructed Daniel Brent not to send the letter (Madison, *Papers, Sec. of State Ser.*, 3:508, 517; Enclosure No. 1 described at Robert Smith to TJ, 20 Aug.; TJ to Madison, 23 Aug.; TJ to Smith, 23 Aug.).

¹ In margin: "§. 1." This paragraph is from the FC of the 5 Aug. letter (fol. 21646). TJ interlined the salutation above this paragraph.

² Preceding three words interlined.

³ Final two letters of word inserted.

⁴ Word interlined in place of "will."

⁵ TJ here canceled "majesty's."

⁶ TJ first wrote "It is with great concern we have learnt" before altering the passage to read as above. This paragraph and the two paragraphs that follow it are from TJ's Dft of new text for this version of the letter (fol. 21647). In margin: "§. 2."

⁷ The preceding passage replaced a heavily reworked passage that included the clause "of the injustice of which they are the consequence" replaced by "produced by the necessary consequences of their own injustice" followed by "had desired to extend to them a relief which the laws of war would not regularly admit."

⁸ Word interlined in place of "proofs."

⁹ Preceding six words interlined in place of "yielded to the." TJ also here canceled "given you & would."

¹⁰ TJ first wrote "set on your friendship; & we regret it was not done, convinced that Y.M. knows too well the rights of an injured nation to reduce their enemy to reason by—   Y.M's justice had not contemplated a permanent dispensation on our part with the rights which the laws of war give us, of reducing an unjust enemy <*by distress to*> to reason by inflicting on him all those evils which a state of war authorises" before altering the passage to read as above. TJ continued, but canceled: "and [. . .] [neutral] friend."

¹¹ Preceding three words interlined in place of "And in further."

¹² Word interlined in place of "reestablmt."

¹³ TJ first wrote "preferring as we <*always*> ever do that" before altering the passage to read as above.

¹⁴ Preceding three words interlined in place of "notified." At beginning of paragraph: "§. 3." This paragraph was the opening paragraph of the 5 Aug. letter. TJ canceled the salutation of the earlier letter.

¹⁵ Preceding nine words interlined in place of "It became known to us not long since."

¹⁶ Three words interlined here and canceled at end of sentence (see 5 Aug. letter).

¹⁷ TJ here canceled "since this intimation."

¹⁸ Before "I," TJ made a bracket to mark the new paragraph break (see 5 Aug. letter), and he interlined "§. 4."

From Richard Claiborne

Sir   Washington City, 22. Augt. 1802

The success of my experiments has been such as to induce me to
publish my invention, as you will see in the newspapers. I conceive
that I have made a considerable improvement as to the Flaps in sim-
plifying them, and in increasing their effect by accelerating the power
applied. I have besides, invented a method of working the setting
poles, to be operated in conjunction with the paddles, or separately as
occasion may require. These remain however to be tried, but I have
no doubt of their success; and I expect they will be proved shortly.
Thus then I may venture to hope for a complete system of inland navigation, as far as my humble abilities can go. I am endeavoring to get
a steam engine brought forward, where the great advantage lies. My
knowledge of your favorable disposition towards the arts I trust will
be an apology for my intruding this information on you.

Now, Sir, permit me once more, to submit my application to you
for some situation of public service, when ever an occasion may offer.
My present circumstances require it—yet I would by no means excite
your benevolence, but in compatibility with the public interest. Nor
would I be intrusive in frequent repetitions—only that I feel it my
duty to revive the intimation amidst your various concerns. Delicacy
would forbid my pointing at any particular situation, except that the
one my mind leads me to, might not strike your attention. It is the
"Commissioner of Loans" for the state of Virginia, whenever that
office may become vacant, and it should be kept up.

The present Commissioner told me, last winter, that he expected it
would be the last dividend he should make—and Mr. Giles informed
me that the office would, in more than probability, be continued
under a new arrangement that the suceeding Congress might adopt.
But, Sir, as this is a remote subject, I will rest on any intermediate appointment that may offer. I left Mr. Beckley's department the lst. of
July last, to give way to a previous promise he had made, but I have
no doubt of his approbation and sanction.

I am, Sir, With the highest personal and political respect—Your
most obedient, and most humble servant—   R Claiborne

RC (DLC); addressed: "The President
of the United States"; franked; postmarked 24 Aug.; endorsed by TJ as received 26 Aug. and so recorded in SJL;
also endorsed by TJ: "office."

Richard Claiborne and TJ corresponded often during the Revolution when TJ
was governor of Virginia and Claiborne
was deputy quartermaster for the state,
and later when TJ was living in Paris and
Claiborne in London. TJ had last written
Claiborne in 1795, after Claiborne's return to the United States (Vol. 28:273-

4). A letter from Claiborne, dated 1 Jan. 1801, has not been found but was recorded in SJL as received 22 Apr. 1801 with the notations "Mononga. glades" and "Off."

Having been an associate of steamboat pioneer James Rumsey, Claiborne worked for many years to perfect his INVENTION of a mechanical boat propulsion system. He advertised his design, which was eventually termed the "hinge or duck-foot paddle," as adaptable to manual, horse, or steam power, and touted the "constant effect" created by its "double or successive stroke." At an unknown time, but almost certainly before the letter above, TJ participated in a demonstration of the invention when he and members of

his cabinet, including Henry Dearborn who operated the device, crossed and recrossed the Anacostia River on a boat powered by Claiborne's system. In October, TJ gave $50 to Claiborne. Although Claiborne never profited from his invention, he continued to refine it and in 1818 was granted a monopoly by the Louisiana state legislature (*Washington Universal Gazette*, 16 Sep. 1802; Curtis Carroll Davis, "'A National Property': Richard Claiborne's Tobacco Treatise for Poland," WMQ, 3d ser., 21 (1964), 94-6, 111-17; MB, 2:1083; Claiborne to TJ, 12 Dec. 1802).

COMMISSIONER OF LOANS: John Hopkins (see Thomas Underwood, Jr., to TJ, 25 July 1802).

From Henry Dearborn

SIR   Washington August 22d. 1802

I have been honoured with your letters of the 14th, & 16th, an ill state of health for a few days, prevented an earlier answer, in a letter lately received from Mr. Crowninshield he mentions a Mr. William Cleveland of Salem who he conciders as well qualified in all respects for a Commissioner of Bankruptcies, and who is a sound Republican I have therefore taken the liberty of having a commission made out for him & for Killam,—Mr. Gallatin shew me your letter respecting the arrangement in the Customs which we concidered necessary to be carried into effect immediately including the case of Tuck of Cape Ann—I herewith enclose a paper relative to the Choctaw bounderies &c received from Genl. Wilkinson, which appears to be an important document, it may be proper to give additional instructions to Wilkinson on the subject, but I concieve that we cannot materially alter the principels proposed in the former instruction rilative to the Chocktaw bounderies, which were, that he should ascertain the best terms on which the Indians would agree to establish the lines formerly agreed to between them & the British Government, and report the same, for the concideration of Congress. from the enclosed statement it appears that the Indians actualy received the stipulated sums from the British Govt, for all the Cessions made, and of course ought not to demand any farther concideration, but it never the less may be adviseable to make them a present, if by that means we can establish the lines as deliniated in the enclosed paper, and if such necessary present should not amount to more than one or two thousand dollars it may be a question whether we can with propriety authorise Genl. Wilkinson to stipulate for the payment of such sum, on having the lines ascertained & remarked. I will thank you Sir for any remarks you may think proper to make to me on the subject, I shall write to Genl. Wilkinson by the way of Natchez as soon as I receive your opinnion on the subject—I do not see that any thing can at present be done on the subject of the Petition &c enclosed with Govr. Tatnals letter.

I shall set out on a trip into the Country to morrow morning, but shall be back in a few days, I intend taking a stand somewhere in the Country within eight or ten miles of the City for a few weeks, but shall be at the Office once a week.

with respectful concideration I am Sir Your Hume Servt,

H, DEARBORN

P,S, having received the Senecas, I enclose them for your perusal,— the one made at Connadaeque, appears evidently to have been dictated by Chapin who is very angry at being removed,—the Talk of Cornplanter & others is good evidence of the artfull part which Chapin must have taken in procuring such a Talk at Connadaeque, I shall let him know that his conduct required a thicker cloak than he has given it, to prevent its being well understood.

H. DEARBORN

RC (DLC); endorsed by TJ as received from the War Department on 26 Aug. and "Indn. affrs." and "Commrs. bkrptcy Salem" and so recorded in SJL. Enclosure: Statement of Joseph Purcell regarding the boundary of Choctaw lands surveyed in 1779, not found, but recorded in DNA: RG 107, RLRMS as received by the War Department from James Wilkinson at Savannah, Georgia, on 19 Aug. Other enclosures not found.

TJ signed commissions for WILLIAM CLEVELAND and Daniel Kilham as bankruptcy commissioners for Salem, Massachusetts, on 27 Aug. 1802 (list of commissions in Lb in DNA: RG 59, MPTPC; TJ to Dearborn, 27 Aug.).

YOUR LETTER: TJ to Gallatin, 14 Aug. (second letter).

CHOCTAW BOUNDERIES: in the 1760s and 1770s, the Choctaws had agreed to the delineation of a boundary between their lands and British settlements. By December 1801, when Wilkinson, Benjamin Hawkins, and Andrew Pickens negotiated a treaty with the Choctaws, the location of that line was largely forgotten. According to an article of the 1801 treaty, however, "the old line of demarcation, theretofore established by and between the officers of his Britannic Majesty and the Choctaw nation," would be the border between Mississippi Territory and the Choctaws' lands. For Dearborn's FORMER INSTRUCTION to Wilkinson concerning preliminary steps for having the boundary marked again, see TJ to Samuel Smith, 24 June. Wilkinson had gotten access to the detailed field notes of Purcell, the surveyor and mapmaker who had marked the Choctaw boundary line for Great Britain in 1779 (ASP, *Indian Affairs*, 1:658-9, 661-2; Louis De Vorsey, Jr., *The Indian Boundary in the Southern Colonies, 1763-1775* [Chapel Hill, 1966], 208, 210, 225-7; *Terr. Papers*, 5:175, 213, 237, 331; Wilkinson to Dearborn, 6, 9 Aug., recorded in DNA: RG 107, RLRMS).

GOVR. TATNALS LETTER: Josiah Tattnall, Jr., to TJ, 20 July; see TJ to Dearborn, 16 Aug.

Chiefs of the SENECAS, Onondagas, and Cayugas who were on their way to Albany attended a public meeting at the courthouse in Canandaigua, New York, on 3 Aug. The gathering was in response to the arrest of a Seneca man, called Stiff-Armed George, who had fatally stabbed a white man during a melee near Buffalo Creek. Red Jacket, the primary speaker for the Senecas' national council and a leader of the Senecas at Buffalo Creek, made the principal address at Canandaigua and asked that his remarks be conveyed to the president. The speech appeared in newspapers by 12 Aug. and received wide circulation thereafter. Declaring that the Senecas had no treaty with the state of New York that covered punishments for killings and that whites were not punished for the deaths of Indians, Red Jacket protested the state's intention to prosecute Stiff-Armed George for murder. Red Jacket hoped that the president would intervene to allow the Senecas to deal with the offender, for Seneca punishment, unlike the state's law, would take the man's intoxication at the time of the incident into account and would not execute him for an act done in the heat of a moment. In his address at Canandaigua, Red Jacket made several references to the recent replacement of Israel CHAPIN with Callender Irvine as the U.S. government's agent to the Six Nations tribes. Chapin lived at Canandaigua, and Seneca leaders conferred with him about Stiff-Armed George's case. Chapin mediated between the Senecas and local authorities, arranging for the chiefs to see Stiff-Armed George and for him to be returned to the sheriff's custody after their visit. Irvine, whom the Senecas did not know, had not yet taken up his post, and Red Jacket in his speech depicted a situation in which the Indians, without Chapin as agent, had "no Guardian" and no means by which problems with the United States could be resolved. The president, Red Jacket asserted, "is called a Great Man, possessing great power—he may do what he pleases." Alluding to Chapin's removal, the orator said that TJ

"may turn men out of office; men who held their offices long before he held his." Chapin had lost his job, Red Jacket asserted, "because he differs from the President in his sentiments on government matters." Some Republican newspapers decried the address at Canandaigua as a "fabrication," the work of "some intriguing busy body" falsely presented as "a real *bona fide* speech of Red Jacket." Federalist editors, in response, endorsed the oration as a genuine expression of its speaker's sentiments. Red Jacket brought up Stiff-Armed George's case again when Seneca chiefs met with Governor George Clinton at Albany on 18-20 Aug. to negotiate land sales. As George's trial by a state court was pending in February 1803, Dearborn wrote Clinton to say that it was "the desire of the President of the United States that I should suggest to your Excellency's consideration the propriety of taking such measures as your own judgement may dictate for procuring a pardon, in case of conviction, of the Seneca Indian." Dearborn explained that the head of Stiff-Armed George's family had been "killed a few years since in time of peace by white men," and no one had been convicted of that crime even though the Senecas believed there was sufficient evidence against at least one individual. "The Indians complain loudly of the partiality in our Courts in cases of this kind," Dearborn wrote, "and we cannot but admit that their complaints are too well founded." A pardon in George's case "would undoubtedly have a good effect on the minds of the Indian Nations generally." The court found Stiff-Armed George guilty, after which Clinton, who had also received a letter from Brockholst Livingston in favor of clemency, pardoned him (Granville Ganter, ed., *The Collected Speeches of Sagoyewatha, or Red Jacket* [Syracuse, N.Y., 2006], 118-28; Dearborn to Irvine, 14 Aug. 1802, to Chapin, same date, and to Clinton, 14 Feb. 1803, in DNA: RG 75, LSIA; Chapin to Dearborn, 25 July, 1 Aug., recorded in DNA: RG 107, RLRMS; ASP, *Indian Affairs*, 1:667-8; *Albany Centinel*, 20 Aug.; New York *Daily Advertiser*, 27 Aug.; *Windham Herald*, 23 Sep. 1802; Hudson, N.Y., *Bee*, 28 Sep.; *Providence Phoenix*, 28

Sep.; *Green Mountain Patriot,* 6 Oct. 1802; Christopher Densmore, *Red Jacket: Iroquois Diplomat and Orator* [Syracuse, N.Y., 1999], 61-2; Vol 37:31, 32-3, 35, 36n, 39n.

The accounts that circulated of the meeting at Canandaigua did not mention CORNPLANTER, who was in opposition to Red Jacket, his nephew, on several significant issues of Seneca politics. Dearborn was perhaps disposed to find fault with the Senecas in general, and with Red Jacket in particular, in August 1802, due to an incident earlier in the year when Red Jacket and two other Senecas broke

into a storehouse, removed merchandise that had been seized for customs violations, and returned the goods to their owner. Dearborn deemed the episode a "glaring outrage" on U.S. authority and a "very disagreeable business." Through Chapin, Red Jacket and the others apologized and averred that they had not understood the government's laws (Dearborn to Chapin, 14 June, in DNA: RG 75, LSIA; Densmore, *Red Jacket,* 60; Thomas S. Abler, *Cornplanter: Chief Warrior of the Allegany Senecas* [Syracuse, N.Y., 2007], 150-1; Vol. 37:33).

To Robert Smith

DEAR SIR   Monticello Aug. 22. 1802.

I have just returned from Mr. Madison's, where I have had conferences with him on the subject of our Barbary affairs & on consideration of the opinions of yourself & the Secretaries of the Treasury & War. there is an entire concurrence of opinion among us in every material point. the amount of these opinions is, and consequently the decision on them as follows.

The hundred guncarriages, and the letter to the Emperor of Marocco, which I have modified to the new circumstances, are to be sent, to be delivered if, in the judgment of Commodore Morris, it shall be deemed consonant with the state of things which shall be then existing. in the letter to the Emperor, without committing ourselves to his mediation, I have suggested the use of his influence with Tripoli to produce a peace, of which we ask no price. I mention also my regret that the special relief he wished to send was not permitted to pass, merely from our regard for his friendship, & our confidence that he did not mean to ask an indefinite right of supplying them. but it is not thought consistent with the interest or the spirit of our nation (sufficiently manifested) after a war so far successful against Tripoli, to finish by paying them a tribute. besides the dishonor, & premature abandonment of the ground our predecessors left us in possession of, it would oblige us immediately to pay a tribute to Tunis & Marocco. Cathcart's powers go fully to the conclusion of this peace. he is by new instructions fully impressed with our desire to have peace, and to consider Commodore Morris as his Counsellor on the subject; and that his own judgment, sanctioned by the approbation of

Commodore Morris, will satisfy us in whatever he does. we have thought it best to give the Commodore a due weight & controul in the negotiation with all the three powers in this way, rather than by joining him in commission, because the public service at sea might suffer were he taken off to participate in these negociations, and because it is thought not safe that he should quit his ship & put himself in the power of the Barbarians. in the principal case he would have to go to Marocco or Fez, both of them distant from the ocean. the sending of 20,000. Dollars is approved, to be delivered to the Commodore, to be employed by Simpson at Marocco & Eaton at Tunis in procuring a reestablishment of harmony. it's disbursement to be superintended as much as possible by him, and paid on their draughts approved by him.

Mr. Eaton will be instructed by the Secretary of state to represent to the Bey of Tunis our regret at the rumor which has reached us of an action between a frigate of ours & some cruisers of his: that we are not informed which party was the aggressor: that if his officer was, we are satisfied it was not by his orders, & are willing to leave the proceedings in consequence of it in his own hands entirely; that if ours was the aggressor, he shall be proceeded against according to the laws of our country, and that every reparation shall be made to him which justice & honor shall call for. the substituting the New York for the General Greene is entirely approved, as is also the retaining the Boston there till further orders if necessary, and if it can be done without too much violating the desires of the crew. I should think it would be well to endeavour to re-engage them till the 1st. of November, or any other term you think more adviseable, even by the offer of a proportionable bounty if it be necessary and within the authorities given us by the law. and I refer to you to consider and decide whether a discretionary instruction should not be given to Capt. Morris to arrest Capt. Mc.Niel if his conduct in the Tunisian affair calls for it, & to send him home for trial, substituting such other commander for the Boston as you shall think proper. and should the arrest be deemed improper, then I submit it to yourself to consider & determine whether, Mc.Niel being deranged, it would not be expedient now to substitute his successor in the ship. the instructions to the officers should be to protect our commerce, against the *armed vessels* of any Barbary power who may either declare or wage war on it. I pray you to communicate this letter to the Secretaries of the Treasury & War, to give to Commodore Morris all the instructions it requires (the Secretary of state doing the same to the Consuls) and particularly that he make full communications to each consul of all matters respecting our affairs with the power he resides with. Accept assurances of my great consideration & respect.   TH: JEFFERSON

PrC (DLC); at foot of first page: "The Secretary of the Navy."

CATHCART'S POWERS: in instructions dated 18 Apr. 1802, Madison informed James L. Cathcart that TJ had decided "the time is come when negotiations may advantageously take place" with Tripoli. Authorizing Cathcart to undertake those negotiations, Madison instructed the consul that he was "in the most peremtory manner to stifle every pretension or expectation that the United States will on their side make the smallest contribution" to Tripoli as a condition of peace. In the NEW INSTRUCTIONS of 22 Aug., the secretary of state observed that problems with Morocco and Tunis might complicate negotiations with Tripoli. "To provide for any contingency to yourself which might produce disappointment or delay," Madison informed Cathcart, "Commodore Morris will be instructed, should the negotiation not be over, to carry it on himself if necessary; and as he will be in a manner the center of information, and will have a certain relation to all the measures connected with our Medi-

terranean affairs, the President thinks it proper, that the proceedings which may remain for the fulfilment of your instructions, should be concerted with him and receive his sanction" (Madison, *Papers, Sec. of State Ser.,* 3:135-6, 504).

Writing to William EATON on 22 Aug., Madison said that any "explanations and apologies" relating to the reported clash between the *Boston* and Tunisian vessels must be left to Eaton's discretion. Unacquainted with "any of the circumstances of the encounter," Madison wrote, nor "even certain that it has taken place," he and TJ could not be precise in their instructions to Eaton (same, 506).

MC.NIEL BEING DERANGED: here, and in Smith's reply to TJ of 27 Aug., the word "deranged" is used to describe a person removed from office, and not as a synonym for insanity (OED). For Daniel McNeill's recall, see TJ to Henry Dearborn, 9 Aug., and Smith to TJ, 16 and 27 Aug.

GIVE TO COMMODORE MORRIS ALL THE INSTRUCTIONS: see Smith to TJ, 27 Aug. 1802 (first letter).

To Albert Gallatin

DEAR SIR   Monticello Aug. 23. 1802.

Your three letters of Aug. 19. 19. & 20. are recieved. I now return you the Missisipi regulations signed. I should think the modification you propose of inserting 'Vice-consul or *other authorised agent*' a necessary one. it appears proper to remove Head of Waldoborough, as his failure after such warning to render his accounts is a sure symptom that he is using the public money: and I shall be ready to sign a commission for any body recommended by Genl. Dearborne. I have never heard a word from mr Page of his non-acceptance, nor I imagine have you, as you do not say so. the fact is too much to be apprehended from his letters to Dr. Tucker mentioned by you. should he decline I believe there can be no competition with Doctr. John Shore for the office, for whom therefore a commission may be made out. there has been a time when he would have accepted it, and I am in hopes he will now.[1]

I had written yesterday to mr Smith, after a conference with mr Madison on the measures to be pursued with respect to the Barbary powers, on the state of things as supposed to exist at the date of your letter of Aug. 16. the receipt of another letter from him after mine of yesterday had gone to the post office informs me of the declaration of war by the Emperor of Marocco. I have this day written a second letter to mr Smith, making the alterations in the former which are rendered necessary by this circumstance, and particularly approving of his proposition to send another frigate in addition to the New York. but for particulars I must refer you to those letters which I have asked him to communicate to yourself & Genl. Dearborne. I wish much to hear that you have left the Federal city, as I think the danger of remaining there great, in this season. nothing else would prevent my going there now, as the transaction of the public business here is infinitely more laborious, than it would be there, and leaves it in my power to be of little use to my private matters. Accept assurances of my affectionate esteem & respect.   TH: JEFFERSON

RC (NHi: Gallatin Papers); at foot of text: "The Secretary of the Treasury"; endorsed. PrC (DLC). Recorded in SJL with notation "Missi regulns. Barbary."

ANOTHER LETTER FROM HIM: see Robert Smith to TJ, 20 Aug. For the PARTICULARS to be communicated, see TJ to Robert Smith, 23 Aug.

[1] Sentence interlined.

From John F. Gaullier

Laucks tavern Winchester

SIR   august 23d 1802

The Great are the image of God, they loves to be pray'd to—importunity, I have had the honor to Writte to you last may, but Suppose you have not receive my letter, as be Silence, you would not add comtempt And a refusal! to an unfortunat who after God have but you Sir for refuge, o! do not froun at what you will call my impudence, my Situation is my excuse, I Shall not trouble you With a repetion of it, I have a respite from my creditors till the fifteen of September, if in that time your Goodness forSoek me, I am lost…I have told you that two hundred dollars were my dettes, I have made one hundred, but for Save my life I canot make up the other, I know that if the President was to relieve all unfortunats, it would be hard on him, but Give me the means to earn this little Sum, and my exactness to return it will equal my wants. I Shall be here till the first of october, do not disdaing to let me know what I have to hope, I promiss my word of honor, that no mortal, even my Wife Shall know nothing of yr. condecension.

With the utmost respect I have the honor to be Sir Your most humble and devoted Servant   JOHN F. GAULLIER

RC (DNA: RG 59, LAR); ellipses in original; endorsed by TJ as received 3 Sep. and so recorded in SJL.

Gaullier's letter of 15 MAY, recorded in SJL as received 1 June, has not been found.

From Gideon Granger

DR: SIR   Washington Augt. 23d. 1802.
Yours of the 15th. was duly received. I have no use for Mr: Fenton's Letter. On Thursday next, If my health permits, I shall leave this for Connecticut. For the last Ten days I have been confined with the Dysentery. It has reduced me somewhat. my return to the Seat of Government will be as early as shall appear safe. In the National Intelligencer of friday last. The dismissals in the post Office departmt. are stated and considered at some length. The approaching elections induced the publication. The only thing I fear is a new swarm of Applications from Our friends. The department in my opinion, (a few cases excepted) is in a hopeful Situation. The changes are as rapid as the prompt execution of the duties & the safety of the Departmt: will admit. I have appointed about 250 Postmasters Independt. of the Offices on the New post roads amounting to 129. so there will be 379. new Officers. The Inclosed is from a respectable Merchant and Mr: Tracey is a respected worthy Man.

I am Sir with great Esteem Yours   GIDN GRANGER

RC (DLC); at foot of text: "The President"; endorsed by TJ as received 26 Aug. and so recorded in SJL; also endorsed by TJ: "Frederick Tracy to be Consul at Cape Francois." Enclosure: Simeon Thomas to Gideon Granger, Norwich, 18 Aug. 1802, recommending Captain Frederick Tracy as consul at Cap-Français, where he has established a firm and carries on business; a staunch Republican, he is "a Man of great information, strict integrity" and "more than common abilities," who is "well versed in the French language"; the U.S. merchants at the port need a consular official "to make Protests give Certificates for goods landed there for drawbacks &c"; the person Tobias Lear left in charge is neither "friendly to the Present Administration" nor well qualified for the office (RC in same).

FRIDAY LAST: the article entitled "Calumny refuted" and signed "A Friend to Truth" appeared in the *National Intelligencer* on 20 Aug. The writer noted that of the 1,095 postmasters in office when Granger became postmaster general, it was difficult to find a single officer who was friendly to the government and included in their midst were some of the "most bitter opponents of the administration." They were entrusted with the whole correspondence of the country. Granger had dismissed 45 postmasters since taking office, including one for insanity; one to restore a former postmaster to the office from which he had been unfairly dismissed; one for being under the age of 18; one for the "flagrant abuse of government and charging the executive with treason"; two for being Tories during the Revolutionary War and continuing their regard for British supremacy; two for negligence; three for "farming" out their offices; five for misconduct; five for maintaining offices in locations inconvenient for the public; eight for being printers and editors of newspapers; and finally sixteen to give participation in offices to some of the friends of the administration. The writer defended the actions of the postmaster general in six particular cases, including the dismissal of Augustine Davis, the newspaper publisher. Instead of the persecutor and tyrant depicted in the Federalist press, Granger was a vigilant officer who sought to improve the department "entrusted to his charge." SOME LENGTH: the article extended over four full and two partial columns. Granger feared a NEW SWARM OF APPLICATIONS because the article concluded that the "friends of the administration" did not yet hold the proportion of offices justice demanded.

OFFICES ON THE NEW POST ROADS: the 3 May 1802 act "to alter and establish certain Post Roads; and for the more secure carriage of the Mail of the United States" discontinued a few postal routes but added many more in every state and the Northwest Territory. In New Jersey, for instance, postal service was established and postmasters appointed at 16 new sites (U.S. Statutes at Large, 2:189-92; Stets, *Postmasters*, 166-71).

From Robert King, Sr.

On board the Richmond, in the
SIR. Potomac River—August 23rd. 1802.

Altho unknown to you I take the liberty of inclosing my Ideas on inland Navigation. If the subject be worthy attention you can best bring it forward to the consideration of the Citizens. As a National concern, it may at a future day afford a Revenue to Government without oppressing individuals; diffuse wealth and population through the Western Country and tend to the prosperity of the United States. If these hints should in the smallest degree tend to so desireable an end, I shall be amply repaid.

Yours respectfully R KING

RC (ViW: Tucker-Coleman Collection); at head of text: "Thomas Jefferson Esqr."; endorsed by TJ as received 5 Oct. and so recorded in SJL; also endorsed by TJ, perhaps at a later date: "see Canals, among papers arranged according to Subjects."

ALTHO UNKNOWN TO YOU: King had recently corresponded with TJ about his work in the District of Columbia's surveyor's office. See Robert King, Sr., to TJ, 5 June 1802, and TJ's response of 7 June.

Plan for System of Inland Navigation

[*23 Aug. 1802*]. Circumstances inducing him to leave the United States, King thinks it proper to commit to writing, his ideas on the subject of inland navigation, particularly the most proper situations and routes for canals. In Europe, the rise of manufactories has been the principal inducement to building canals. Where establishments are not near rivers, merchants have resorted to canals for the transport of bulky articles. The facility of this mode of conveyance, its safety, and its freedom from obstructions, other than frost, have given it a manifest advantage over river navigation, which, being subject to floods or scarcity of water, can occasion serious delays. It is more convenient and less expensive in many cases to make canals along the sides of navigable rivers than to remove impediments from those rivers. The United States should learn from Europe's experience as to the "incompetency" of rivers above tidewater and direct their energies towards connecting the states by canals. Such canals should commence at tidewater, where river navigation begins to be inconvenient, then rise by locks to such height as to pass by the headwaters of lesser rivers and along the highest land upon which level pools could be maintained, thus providing connections between the principal rivers near the points of their origin. From there, canals might descend to tidewater again, between any other principal rivers whose sources are in that area. Canals might then extend into almost every part of the United States. King perceives many advantages to this system. Canals would be the shortest that the terrain permits. Those constructed beside or near rivers must either use expensive aqueducts to carry them over streams or runs that flow into the rivers, or wind around said runs, thus increasing the distance and expense. Canals upon the heights will frequently be circuitous but less so than those that follow rivers. Aqueduct bridges will not be necessary, and small runs of water that develop above the level of the canal can be "Moled" under the canal. The warping and filling up with silt from heavy rains is avoided. Distance from navigable rivers will prevent any interference with river navigations, and the facility with which vessels travel along the canals will give them the advantage. One might ask what will supply these canals with sufficient water. King answers that the highest mountains generally abound with springs, and that having designed a canal to pass along the lowest convenient part of a ridge, an engineer could collect water from springs of the land rising above. Also, reservoirs might be formed for carrying rain water. A series of these canals, connecting the principal rivers at the summit of the country and promoting trade, would "unite the general interests of the Inhabitants, and prove an indissoluble bond of Union." Such canals would prove less expensive to maintain than carriage roads. Furthermore, at high ground, the soil is generally stronger and more "clayey," thereby mitigating the many problems faced by canals at lower levels, where sides consisting of "made earth" are liable to leak and give way to water pressure. King now offers two potential examples. On the Virginia side of the Potomac, a canal might begin below Mason's Island, rise by locks and pass the headwaters of the Occoquan, Thornton, Rapidan, and Rivanna Rivers, cross the mountains at the most convenient gaps, and then descend by the waters of the Kanawha or Guyandotte Rivers to the Ohio. Or it might pursue higher ground by the Holston River and enter the state of Kentucky. Such a canal deserves national support. Toll revenues would exceed the interest on the money advanced, and the canal would shift the trade of Kentucky from New Orleans to the District of Columbia. It would improve the bonds between the western and Atlantic states. Canal branches might also extend into Tennessee and other southern states. Another canal might be carried from Tyber Creek past the headwaters of the Monocacy and other streams flowing into the Potomac, across the Ohio, and then into the Northwest. The size and dimensions of these canals will be important. Some engineers prefer large canals, from 30 to 80 feet in width with a depth in proportion. The largest are proper for cutting through an isthmus, such as that between the Mediterranean and Red Seas. In inland navigations, canal widths seldom exceed 40 feet. Advocates for these larger canals tout the economies of scale yielded by large vessels, which will also have the benefit of excluding small, less responsible operators. Large canals inspire ideas of the greatness of the project while, by contrast, a small canal seems "a common ditch." To avoid the latter impression, engineers will recommend larger canals so as to acquire reputation at the expense and risk of their employers. King points out the many disadvantages of pursuing large canals. First, the greater difficulty in cutting through and barrowing the earth increases costs. Large canals also require broader and deeper lock gates, which increase lock expenses. Such canals, which are often fordable, will need aqueducts and communication bridges. They make some smaller trades impractical, as the boats carry more cargo than a single client might have occasion to transport, thus forcing boats either to detain cargo or proceed with part of a load. Large canals are subject to greater waste of water through increased pressure on the canal, greater surface evaporation, and increased need to let out water for cleansing. Small canals have the following advantages. They cost less while bringing the same tolls, occasion fewer of the delays resulting from boats waiting for cargo, and require less expensive boats, making it more convenient for smaller proprietors to provide water carriage.

MS (DLC: TJ Papers, 137:23722-5); Editors' summary; 8 p.; undated; endorsed by TJ: "Canals. R. King's paper. see his letter."

To James Madison

Dear Sir   Monticello Aug. 23. 1802.

Yesterday's post brought me, as I suppose it did you, information of the Emperor of Marocco's declaration of war against us, and of the capture of a merchant vessel of ours (the Franklin, Morris) off cape Palos, by a Tripoline as is said in a New York letter, but a Marocquin as I am in hopes from the place, & the improbability of a Tripoline being there. the letter to the Emperor, & the gun carriages are of course to be stopped, and I have approved a proposition from mr

Smith to send another frigate, which he says can be ready in two weeks, in addition to the New York. these with those already there, & the Swedes, are surely sufficient for the enemies at present opposed to us. these are the only alterations made in the arrangements we had agreed on. I have desired mr Smith to recommend a liberal attention in our officers to the interests of Sweden in the Mediterranean, and if peace with Marocco does not take place this year, I should think it proper that we should undertake the forming a permanent league of the powers at war, or who may from time to time get into war with any of the Barbary powers. Accept assurances of my constant & affectionate esteem.

Th: Jefferson

RC (NjPT); at foot of text: "The Secretary of State." PrC (DLC).

For Mawlay Sulayman's DECLARATION OF WAR against the United States, see Robert Smith to TJ, 20 Aug. 1802. A widely circulated initial report of the capture of the brig FRANKLIN came from the ship *Protector*, which arrived in NEW YORK from Cadiz on 18 Aug. (New York *Commercial Advertiser*, 18 Aug. 1802; New York *Daily Advertiser*, 19 Aug. 1802; New York *Mercantile Advertiser*, 19 Aug. 1802).

From Margaret Page

Rosewell. August 23d. 1802

On me, Sir, has devolved the painful Task of informing you of the continued Indisposition of Mr. Page; an Indisposition, doubly afflicting, as it incapacitates him from profiting by your friendship in fulfilling the Duties of the Office to which you have had the goodness to appoint him.

The first attack of his Complaint, he experienced in the Month of April, a severe one—which was followed by several others—at different intervals—less alarming; but on the last of July they became so violent as to render him extremely Ill—and this was the Cause of his not writing to inform you of his readiness to repair to Petersburg,—for with great difficulty, and not without injury, he wrote you a few lines descriptive of his Situation, on the 9th of this Month—at which period, and since, the Vertiginous Symptoms have continued, with great Nervous debility, so as to render him incapable of reading, or writing, or even taking the necessary exercise.

This Complaint, from which he suffered greatly in the years 1774 and —75, he informs me was *even then*, greatly increased by any application to Accounts, Reading, or Writing; and his Physician being of Opinion it would now prove inimical to the restoration, or continuation of his Health, should the present alarming Symptoms disappear; from a full conviction of his inability to execute the Duties of a Collector, he is compelled to resign his Commission, which he has only this Day received, it having been, by mistake sent to the Post Office at Petersburg.

With his resignation, accept, dear Sir, the warmest sentiments of Gratitude, and Personal attachment, which early friendship and a perfect knowlege of your Character can inspire—and having been, in the first Instance, the Occasion, tho' not the Cause, of Mr. Page's application to you, permit *me*, respected Sir, to express the deep Sensibility with which I shall ever retain an indelible remembrance of that Act of Friendship which might have proved so beneficial to my Children.

With the most perfect respect, esteem, and gratitude I am, Sir, your obedient Servant   MARGARET PAGE

RC (DLC); endorsed by TJ as received 3 Sep. and so recorded in SJL. Enclosed in John Page to TJ, 25 Aug.

Margaret Lowther Page (1760-1835), daughter of William Lowther of Scotland, was a native of New York and the second wife of Virginia congressman and governor John Page of Rosewell, whom she married in 1790. They resided in Williamsburg and Rosewell and had eight children, including one born earlier in the summer of 1802. She and her husband wrote and exchanged poems with other members of a Williamsburg literary circle that included St. George Tucker. She collaborated with her husband on the joint publication of a privately printed work, *Dodsley*, and her own poems, elegies, and riddles appeared in Mathew Carey's *American Museum*, the *New-York Magazine; or Literary Repository*, and the Philadelphia *Port Folio* (Daphne Hamm O'Brien, "From plantation to Parnassus: Poets and poetry in Williamsburg, Virginia, 1750-1800" [Ph.D. diss., University of North Carolina, Chapel Hill, 1993], 43, 120, 140, 160-1, 164, 169); T. B. McCord, Jr., "John Page of Rosewell: Reason, Religion, and Republican Government from the Perspective of a Virginia Planter, 1743-1808" [Ph.D. diss., American University, 1990], 3, 1122-3; *Daily National Intelligencer*, 30 Oct. 1835; ANB, s.v. "Page, John"; John Page to TJ, 1 June).

To Robert Smith

DEAR SIR   Monticello Aug 23. 1802.

I had yesterday written & committed to the post office a letter in answer to yours of the 16th. on the measures to be pursued with respect to our Barbary affairs. this was grounded on the supposition that we might still be at peace with Marocco. your's of the 20th. was recieved yesterday evening, and informs me of the declaration of War by the Emperor of Marocco. it was not very unexpected. for as I mentioned to you in a former letter, the demand was so much out of the course of the acknowleged right of nations in case of blockaded places as to shew he was determined on war & was making a pretext. the change of the circumstance of possible peace for certain war, renders it necessary to retain my letter to the Emperor of Marocco, and also the gun carriages, and instead of them to send an additional frigate. this, even if the Boston returns, will I presume be sufficient, if Tunis remains at peace, as we may hope from the very satisfied state in which our presents had recently placed that Bey. mr Simpson, by his connections & acquaintance with those around the Emperor, will be able probably to find out what was his real reason & object in declaring war, without the smallest pretense of having recieved any injury from us. if it was a [mere] [mias?] of humor, the money sent for the purposes mentioned in my letter, may enable him to smooth his ill humor, to open conferences of peace, & to agree to a suspension of hostilities till we can give regular powers for treating. this course of proceeding is certainly within their usage. if his object was to obtain new presents, or a regular tribute, he will come round in the [...] also: but if the war has been commenced on a superstitious idea that he ought not to let Musselmen suffer unaided (as has [been suggested]) peace with him will be more difficult until we have it with Tripoli. to this last object Cathcart must bend his views. you will judge which of the frigates it is best to send, and you are sensible of the importance of dispatch. nothing should be spared to make the Emperor feel our vigor, & particularly to destroy his [two] new vessels either in harbor, or on their coming out. Accept assurances of my affectionate esteem & respect.   TH: JEFFERSON

P.S. I re-inclose the papers sent me. we should be very liberal to our attentions to the interests of Sweden in the Mediterranean. if Marocco does not quickly [come] [...] [we ought to undertake to form] the nations at war with those powers into a [league to be as permanent as] [...]

PrC (DLC); faint; with postscript written in left margin; at foot of text: "The Secretary of the Navy."

A FORMER LETTER: TJ to Smith, 9 Aug. 1802.

For the PRESENTS of arms, naval stores, and luxury items recently sent to the BEY of Tunis, see TJ to the Senate and the House of Representatives, 1 Mch. 1802.

From Albert Gallatin

DEAR SIR   Washington Aug. 24. 1802

I duly received your letter of the 20th & will attend to its contents. I have not had less business to do since I have been in office, & have nothing to communicate. Your answer to my last, & your determination in respect to Barbary I am waiting for, with some anxiety, as, although I am yet well, the weather is intensely hot & bilious complaints begin to appear. Gen. Dearborn left the city this morning; he had been unwell for several days; my first clerk is expected daily; the next is sick & unable to attend; & so is Miller the comr. of the revenue; the Auditor was complaining & is gone. I intend going at once to New York for my family & to be here the latter end of September. Will you be good enough to direct your letters to me there. Whilst there, I will think of whatever, within the Treasury department, may be necessary for the meeting of Congress, whether for information or to occupy their deliberations. I presume that they will have little or nothing to do, and think the less for the present the better. Mr Page certainly declines; but Heath, on retiring, has appointed a deputy who can legally act until a successor takes possession. I know not Dr. Shore's christian name, and it is of some importance to ascertain whether he means to accept.

I am with attachment & respect Your obedt. Servt.

ALBERT GALLATIN

RC (DLC); endorsed by TJ as received from the Treasury Department on 26 Aug. and "Page. Heath. Shore" and so recorded in SJL.

YOUR ANSWER: see TJ to Gallatin, 23 Aug. For the Treasury secretary's LAST letter on the BARBARY affair, see Gallatin to TJ, 20 Aug.

MY FIRST CLERK: Edward Jones recovered from his illness and returned to Washington by 13 Sep. NEXT IS SICK: Daniel Sheldon continued unwell and left to visit his family in Connecticut as soon as Jones resumed his duties (Gallatin, *Papers*, 7:510, 534, 537, 587; Cunningham, *Process of Government*, 328).

On 13 Sep., the Norfolk *Commercial Register* carried the news that John PAGE had declined the appointment as collector at Petersburg. Four days later it noted John Shore's appointment.

From Gideon Granger

DEAR SIR   General Post Office August 24th 1802

I have just received a Letter from Judge Robertson of Bennington In which he assures me that from the best observation he could make, republican principles acquire additional Strength in that State, and the elections are expected to be favorable. At the same time he remarks that the federalists are making the most Violent Exertions and that the dispute between Burr & Clinton has done us a Sensible Injury. The Postmaster at Wilmington who is a well informd. Man, thinks the election of Mr. Rodney certain if the Republicans unite in one Ticket—how that may be appears in some degree uncertain—I leave this next day after tomorrow and take this opportunity of once more expressing my Esteem & Attachmt   GIDN: GRANGER.

RC (DLC); at foot of text: "The President"; endorsed by TJ as received 26 Aug. and so recorded in SJL.

JUDGE ROBERTSON: perhaps Jonathan Robinson, a Republican who served as chief judge of the Vermont supreme court from 1801 to 1807, when he was elected to the U.S. Senate. He was the younger brother of Moses Robinson, whom TJ visited at Bennington during his "Northern Journey" in 1791 (*Biog. Dir. Cong.*; Bennington *Vermont Gazette*, 10 May 1802; Vol. 33:125, 131n, 423-4; Vol. 34:602; Vol. 35:684-6).

Granger appointed Joseph Bringhurst POSTMASTER AT WILMINGTON, Delaware, in early 1802 (Stets, *Postmasters*, 106).

To John Milledge

DEAR SIR   Aug. 24. 1802.

I heard but an hour ago of your being in Charlottesville with mrs Milledge, & being prevented going there myself, take this method of expressing my hope we shall have the pleasure of seeing you here. it would give me great satisfaction if you could make this your headquarters, and at all events I hope we shall see you before you determine otherwise. can not mrs Milledge & yourself come up tomorrow? we shall be very happy to see you & present you both personally with assurances of my great esteem & respect   TH: JEFFERSON

RC (Rosa Milledge Pattillo, Atlanta, Georgia, 1971); at foot of text: "Colo. Milledge Charlottesville." Not recorded in SJL.

PLEASURE OF SEEING YOU: Milledge had previously visited Edgehill in May 1802 (Vol. 37:384, 398).

From Thomas Munroe

SIR,   Washington 24th August 1802

I have the honor of enclosing a Letter which I yesterday received from Mr Nicholas King.—

The Commissioners have always heretofore appointed the Surveyors by Letter, or by entry in the minutes of their proceedings, but in case Mr Kings proposition respecting Salary shall be acceded to, a short

Letter of appointment from the President would, I have reason to believe, be more agreeable to him than if it were otherwise conferred, and if there be no objections to his being gratified it will be quite as agreeable to me as any other mode of appointment.—

I have the honor to be with the most respectful consideration Sir Yr Obt Servt   THOMAS MUNROE

RC (DLC); at foot of text: "President of the United States"; endorsed by TJ as received 26 Aug. and so recorded in SJL. Dft (DNA: RG 42, LR). Tr (MHi: Adams Papers). Enclosure: Nicholas King to Munroe, 23 Aug. 1802, making observations on "that part of the Presidents Letter you shewed me" and explaining his current situation and engagements; for the past two years, King has declined leaving Washington or accepting other work so that he could be on hand to provide his surveying services "if required on the dissolution of the Board of Commissioners by Congress," at which time he expected a permanent plan of the city to be made, the commissioners' accounts closed, the gradation of the streets completed, and a "general revision of what had been done in the Offices entered upon"; when the dissolution finally took place, however, King believes that the state of city affairs was misrepresented to Congress and the president, and "Whatever service it was believed could be rendered by my going into that employ, might have been overstated"; to support himself and his family, King accepted an appointment in the Treasury Department as clerk to the register of lands for the Northwest Territory at an annual salary of $800; he has also earned an additional $200 to $300 annually "by Mapping, and such other employment in the mornings, and evenings, as I have heretofore had"; King will cheerfully accept an appointment by the president as city surveyor "with such a compensation, as that I shall be no loser by the change"; King plans to retain his current clerkship until 1 Oct., and in the interim will attend to laying off city lots "and such other most immediately necessary duties, as may prevent any material injury to the City arising until the end of the Quarter, or the President's determination is known"; in a postscript, King adds that if he quits his current office, it would be proper to provide notice so that the "public service may not suffer" (RC in DLC; endorsed by TJ). Tr enclosed in Roger C. Weightman to John Quincy Adams, 23 May 1827.

From John Gemmil

Staunton 25th Augt. 1802

It was, Sir, my desire & intention to deliver the enclosed with my own hand, But, by a fall from my carriage, in returning from the sweet Spring I received a sprain in my ankle which disables me from walking a step, & renders the jolting of the carriage, in a high degree, painful. To avoid the South mountain I must, therefore, pursue the valley route by Winchester to New Haven. Not knowing but the letter from Governour Mc.Kean may contain more than an introduction of myself I esteem it my duty to forward it. And I take the liberty of expressing my regret that my accident should preclude from an interview & some personal acquaintance with the President of the

United States, one who, with the highest veneration and most affectionate esteem for your character; connects the most fervent desire for a long continuance of your excellent administration, & for your happiness here and hereafter.   JOHN GEMMIL

RC (MHi); at foot of text: "The President, U.S—"; endorsed by TJ as received 10 Sep. and so recorded in SJL.

John Gemmil (1759-1814) was born in Mifflin County, Pennsylvania, and earned a bachelor's degree from the University of Pennsylvania. After being ordained a Presbyterian minister, he served as pastor of a church in Chester County near Philadelphia. In 1798, he took charge of a Presbyterian church in New Haven, Connecticut. Initially popular, he later fell into disfavor, perhaps over his pro-Republican activities, and was dismissed in November 1802. Returning to Pennsylvania, he achieved some renown for an open letter to Thomas Paine that appeared in newspapers throughout the country and was later included in the 1803 pamphlet, *Paine versus Religion; or, Christianity Triumphant. Containing the Interesting Letters of Sam. Adams, Tho. Paine, and John Gemmil* (Shaw-Shoemaker, No. 4809). He later was principal of the West Chester Academy and represented Chester and Delaware Counties in the state senate (University of Pennsylvania, *Biographical Catalogue of the Matriculates of the College* [Philadelphia, 1894], 25; Leonard Bacon, *Thirteen Historical Discourses, on the Completion of Two Hundred Years, from the Beginning of the First Church in New Haven* [New Haven, 1839], 279; *New-York Evening Post*, 13 Mch. 1802; *Poulson's American Daily Advertiser*, 24 Dec. 1814).

ENCLOSURE

From Thomas McKean

DEAR SIR,   Philadelphia. May 8th. 1802.

Permit me to introduce to your notice the Reverend Mr; John Gimmel of Hartford in Connecticut, who is on a tour to the warm springs in Virginia for health. You will find him worthy of your Excellency's acquaintance; he is the Minister of the Presbyterian church in Hartford, and known to me as a Gentleman of liberality in religious and political principles, and possessing a good heart and well informed mind. Few Gentlemen in Connecticut are to be found, who are capable & willing to communicate the state of religion and politics in that country in the manner he can: he knows the springs of all the movements of the political characters in that State.

I have learned, that you have set out for Monticelli on Tuesday last, where Mr; Gimmel intends to wait upon you.

Accept of the best wishes of Your Excellency's Most obedient humble servant   THOS M:KEAN

RC (MHi); at foot of text: "His Excellency Thomas Jefferson Esquire"; endorsed by TJ as received 10 Sep. and so recorded in SJL with notation "by mr Gemmil."

From James Madison

DEAR SIR   Aug. 25. 1802

Yours of the 23d. has been duly recd. Mr. Brent had informed me that copies of the letters from the Mediterranean had been sent to you by Mr. Smith, and therefore I did not send the originals by express. The declaration of a rupture by the Empr. of Morocco, put me at a loss what to say to Simson on the subject of the Gun carriages, and how to decide as to the letter you left with me. As the event however was anticipated when you were here, as a necessary consequence, of Morris's concurrence in the refusal of Simson, and of the instructions sent from the Navy Dept. by the Adams, I concluded that the Gun carriages ought still to go, subject to the discretionary & conciliatory use of Morris & Simson, and have written to Simson on that supposition. I was the more inclined to this opinion, by the anxiety & the ideas of the Secretary of the Treasy. Reasoning in a similar manner, I sent on to Mr. Brent your letter to the E. of M. with an erasure of the last paragraph, & some little alteration besides, & a request that the Secretaries present would decide what ought to be done; and have in my letter to Simson given him like discretion over it, as I gave him with respect to the Gun carriages. In pursuance now of your decision agst. sending either, I shall write by the next mail to have a postscript added by Mr. Brent signifying the change that has taken place. Nothing appears in the communications to me, relative to the affair between the Boston & the Tuniscain cruisers. In my letters to Cathcart Eaton OBrien & Simson, I have spoken of it as report believed here, and have fashioned my instructions accordingly particularly those to Eaton. I find from Gaveno's letters to me, that the capture of the American vessel, was ascribed to a Pirate, and not to a cruiser of Tripoli or Morocco.

With most respectful attachment I remain Yrs.

JAMES MADISON

RC (DLC); at foot of text: "The President of the U. States"; endorsed by TJ as received from the State Department on 29 Aug. and "Barbary" and so recorded in SJL.

LETTER YOU LEFT WITH ME: TJ to Mawlay Sulayman, Sultan of Morocco, 21 Aug.

MORRIS'S CONCURRENCE: see Enclosure No. 1 described at Robert Smith's letter of 20 Aug.

HAVE WRITTEN TO SIMSON: Madison wrote to James Simpson on 22 Aug., stating that in spite of "hostile declarations" from Morocco, the gun carriages and the president's letter to the sultan would still be sent on the *New York* as "conciliatory tokens of the esteem and good will of the U: States." Madison left it to Simpson and Richard V. Morris to determine whether those items should be delivered: "How far it may be best, in case use can be made of them at all, to tender the Carriages, or send the letter or both, or to communicate only on your receipt of them, must be decided according to circumstances of which yourself & Commodore Morris can best judge." Madison expected Simpson to consult with Morris whenever it was practical to do so, instructing the consul "to continue your endeavors, as far as circumstances will justify to convey to the Emperor the regret of the U. States, at his unexpected and unprovoked conduct, and their disposition to renew the friendship which has been unhappily interrupted." The United States, Madison affirmed, would respond to any hostile acts "by opposing force to force." Madison also decided to send Simpson the dispatch he had prepared on 27 July, "altho' written with reference to a state of things different from that presented in the last communications" (Madison, *Papers, Sec. of State Ser.*, 3:507-8).

SENT ON TO MR. BRENT: on 23 Aug., Madison sent Daniel Brent TJ's letter to the sultan and the dispatches to Simpson and the other consuls, but Madison's cover letter with instructions to Brent has not been found (same, 517).

The surviving Dft of TJ's letter to Mawlay Sulayman shows no ALTERATION by Madison. The paragraph that he erased from the version of the letter he sent to Brent was evidently the one relating to the gun carriages, beginning "We had been given to understand" (TJ to Sulayman, 21 Aug.).

DECIDE WHAT OUGHT TO BE DONE: on 31 Aug., Brent added a postscript to Madison's letter to Simpson of the 22d, stating that the "Heads of Departments, who were at the seat of Government" when Madison's packet arrived, having "discretionary powers from the President to stop the letter referred to for the Emperor of Morocco, and the Gun Carriages, if the state of things should in their judgment, render such a step advisable, have determined that it would not be proper to send either." The letter and the gun mounts "are both accordingly witheld." Brent appended a similar postscript, referring only to the gun carriages, to Madison's letter of 22 Aug. to James Leander Cathcart (Madison, *Papers, Sec. of State Ser.*, 3:505, 508).

For Madison's letter of 22 Aug. to William EATON, see TJ to Smith of that date. The letter to Richard O'Brien has not been found (Madison, *Papers, Sec. of State Ser.*, 3:516).

GAVENO'S LETTERS: John Gavino had sent several dispatches from Gibraltar during the second half of June. One of 29 June reported that the *Franklin* had been captured by a galliot with three lateen sails, and that a similar vessel that had attempted to take a Swedish schooner was presumed to have been a pirate ship. Gavino later forwarded information from O'Brien indicating that the captors of the *Franklin* were from Tripoli and that two Tripolitan corsairs, each of which was a three-sailed galliot, had stopped at Algiers earlier in June en route to the coast of Spain with the intention of targeting American and Swedish merchant vessels (same, 309, 328, 347-8, 349, 388-9).

From John Page

Rosewell Augt. 25th. 1802

The inclosed my dear Sir accept as from me.

The Commission of Colr. of Petersbg. I this day return to the Comptroller's office. pardon & pity me. I can only add that

I am most affectionately yours   J. PAGE

RC (DLC); endorsed by TJ as received 3 Sep. and so recorded in SJL. Enclosure: Margaret Page to TJ, 23 Aug.

From Caesar A. Rodney

HONORED & DEAR SIR   Wilmington Augt. 25. 1802

I regretted that the Secretary of the Treasury was obliged to pass thro' this place without making any stay, in order to make the arrangement relative to the fixing piers within this state, proposed by Col. Hall, and which you were kind enough to approve of. Doctr. Alexander however, shewed me the other day, a communication from Mr. Gallatin on this subject as it related to New Castle, satisfactory to them. Many of our Citizens supposing that this place has claims on the same subject, I beg you will direct Mr. Gallatin to authorise the Corporation, to have a report made, of their harbour Creek &c. and of such place as may be deemed suitable for piers, together with a plan or draught of the same. The style of the corporation is the Burgesses & Assistants of the Borough of Wilmington.

Electioneering goes on with great zeal & spirit on the Republican side. I trust the old adage, *magna est veritas et prevalebit*, will be proved correct, by the result. Yours most Sincerely

C. A. RODNEY.

RC (DLC); endorsed by TJ as received 5 Sep. and so recorded in SJL.

TJ requested that the SECRETARY OF THE TREASURY meet with Rodney and David Hall to discuss the Delaware PIERS on his return trip to Washington from New York (TJ to Gallatin, 13 July).

COMMUNICATION FROM MR. GALLATIN: see Gallatin to TJ, 9 Aug.

DIRECT MR. GALLATIN: see TJ to Gallatin, 8 Sep.

MAGNA EST VERITAS ET PREVALEBIT: that is, "truth is mighty and shall prevail."

From Thomas Leiper

                                Crum Creek, Snuff Mills (near Chester)
DEAR SIR   Aug. 26th. 1802

The Yellow Fever which is a sore evil in every sense of the word and your making up your mind not to sell your Tobacco for less than six Dollars pr Cent and I making up my mind not to give it especially as you inform me it is not of the first quality is the sole cause whey you have not had an answer from me sooner to your of the 6th. Ultimo—My last letter from Richmond is dated the 10th. the price of Tobacco' then were from 25/ to 28/ pr Ct. Virginia Currency and at no period have I heard of Tobacco' being higher than Five Dollars and One Third for the Crop of 1801 and this was a sale made at a considerable credit—The best Tobacco' I have seen from Richmond were purchased for 27/ V. Cy. and I think I can purchase them for six Dollars now as the last purchase I made of 14,000 [...] of Jacob Sperry & Co I purchased at that price—But their is no telling what the price of Tobacco will be next year as W C Nicholas informs me he intends to plant no more and I should suppose a Gentleman of his standing would have a great number to follow his example—But sufficient to the day is the evil there of for the higher Tobacco is the less I shall make by my business for I have never been able to make my snuff [marck] up with the price of Tobacco'—

When self is the Subject Sterne says their is no end to it but believe me I now write with a view of making you more correct in future—I did complain of the news papers for my name being mentioned as a Commissioner of Bankruptcy but I should have gone one point further and complained of you as being the cause of it—Did you not inform your secretary Mr. Lewis that I was to be one—this information Mr. J L Leib give me as comming from him—Mr. Duane did write the same thing to his son with a view of his mentioning it to me which he did—Mr. Patton at the Post office said the thing was certain to the Tory & strong Federalist Mr. Poyntal who mentioned it to me—You may rely on it you have let yourself down and me too to the great comfort and consolation of every Tory in the State—Now the Question is asked me did you write the President you would not serve? if I speak at all I must speak the truth I said no—This is a very extraordinary thing the answer is that the President should take off[1] your name and[2] put on Cumston's without all the circumstances are known[3] the thing is extraordinary and even with them to be plain with you I think it is rather a left-handed piece of business but for your sake I have been full with them for I find at this time it is absolutely necessary our President should be immaculate—I have always told them who came to find fault with you respecting this business that Captain Jones interested himself in favor of Mr. Cumston and wanted me to sign a recommendation to you in his favor and I had no doubt but that Mr. Dallas and a number of others had done it but the best story of all I have to relait comes from Mr. Duane who left it at my House in my absence that he was present when the names were fixed on and a person present said I would not serve This by the bye is not true and when that person speaks again doubt him for I always said when spoak to on the subject it was time enough to give my opinion when I received my Commission which I think would rather convey an Idea I would serve but on this subject no man had ever any other opinion and I have made up my mind they shall not—But Sir I always finished Cumston's business by saying that if

Captain Jones our member of Congress and Mr. Dallas Attorney of the district recommended any man it was impossible for you to get over it you must appoint him and I now can add I have it from the best Authority that the President of the U States relied on a Confidential friend comming to Philda. and if I am asked I shall suppose to be Mr. Gallatin and I will carry the Point further that Mr. Dallas and him settled the Whole business and that you are not to blame in any part of it—Dallas to us once was a Host but his usefullness is not so great as they have been—He signed a memorial to Congress and put his name under Joseph Hopkinson's how emmencely little it appeared to us we had never seen it on so disrespectfull a View—He give a ball to General Dayton's daughter the night after the general arrived from Washington. had he done it the night before his enemies could have never had it to say it was intended for the General— His daughter went on a visit to the General's daughter he and Mrs. Dallas follow They go to York and resolve to visit Boston at the very time the Aurora publishes Burr's going there to hold a Caucas This is all small wise but you may rely on it it hurts his standing with many people especially as he neglected his law business which to my certain knowledge he promised to attend to—Your confidential friend we blame here for keeping so many of John Adams friends in office I see you make them nine tenth. the quicker and faster you reduce the number the better—Gallatin's name is up he is to pay the national Debt in 15 or twenty years. I could find you men with the funds you possess do the business in seven or eight—what do you make of your surpluss money You give it to the Bank of the United States for them to Discount on for the benefit of whom George the 3d and his subjects for they hold $\frac{3}{4}$ of the Stock—They will divid this year 8 pr Ct. and they will also divid a surpluss fund of 4 this makes Twelve—look at Sir not like a Virginian who is against all Banks. but turn this advantage from the Stock Holders to the benefit of the U States discount on your own money Whigs will then be able to Borrow as it now stands they cannot procure a shilling if a Tory wants it—

Mr. Samuel Carswell Mercht. of our City spent the day with me yesterday he is well known to Mr. Gallatin and to shew you how he stands he is One of Governor Mc.Kean's late appointed Aldermen— He informs me that Cumston was a British soldier and served against us last War—He says he had his information from Mrs. John Wilson—she is good Authority I am certain Jones and Dallas never heard this I can say I never 'till yesterday and I still hope it is not true—When you was made President we expected to have a grand

Republican Goverment that you would out with every man who had been for John Adams and his measures—but by your own account $\frac{9}{10}$ of them are in still in—This in my opinion is not a correct measure—what you have done lately pleases—but do it all at once for their is as much said in New Papers at one as there would be at Two or Three Hundred—When You make your appointments have in View to old Con[tinental?] Officers and men who have suffered by the War and take [the] Poorest of them first—You can have a list of them from every state from men who want no office but take care in turning out men who have served well in the War and are poor that very poverty perhaps was the cause they acted as they did—I have in my eye at this very time our General Macpherson—had some other person had the command of his Blue's I do not think things would have settled down so smooth as they did—Being on opposite side I have a right to know I am with the Greatest respect and esteem Yr Most Obed't

THOMAS LEIPER

RC (DLC); torn at seal; words partially obscured by tape; addressed: "Thomas Jefferson President of the United States" and "Private"; franked; postmarked: "Chester Pa. August 27 1802"; endorsed by TJ as received 2 Sep. and so recorded in SJL. Enclosed in TJ to Madison, 3 Sep.

I DID COMPLAIN: see Leiper to TJ, 23 June (second letter). For the recommendation by Congressman JONES in favor of Thomas CUMPSTON, see Vol. 37:382.

DALLAS AND HIM SETTLED THE WHOLE BUSINESS: for the lists of candidates for Pennsylvania bankruptcy commissioners prepared by Alexander J. Dallas and Gallatin, see Vol. 37:578.

Dallas, Joseph B. McKean, Peter S. Du Ponceau, and Joseph Hopkinson were among the 37 members of the Philadelphia bar who signed the MEMORIAL laid before the U.S. Senate by James

Ross on 2 Feb. 1802. They opposed the repeal of the Judiciary Act of 1801, noting the "superiority of the present system over that which existed" before the passage of the 1801 act. The abolition of the new circuit court system would "probably be attended with great public inconvenience." On 3 Feb., Dallas wrote the vice president detailing the reasons for his opposition to the repeal (*Gazette of the United States*, 30 Jan., 5 Feb. 1802; JS, 3:175-6; Kline, *Burr*, 2:666-8).

For Gallatin's plan to pay the NATIONAL DEBT, see Vol. 36:102-4.

OUR GENERAL MACPHERSON: for an anonymous defense of the naval officer at the Philadelphia custom house, see "N." to TJ, 26 July.

[1] MS: "of."
[2] MS: "a."
[3] MS: "know."

From Henry Preble

SIR   Havre August 26th. 1802

Having established myself at this Port; and finding that Mr. Peter Dobell who was some time since appointed Commercial Agent of the US. at Havre, intends to resign that office, I beg leave to solicit the same when vacant; it would be particularly valuable to me, as I shall most probably pass great part of the remainder of my life at this Place.

I have thought it needless to trouble you with the solicitations of my friends in Europe & America in my favor; for as it relates to my character, I flatter myself there are many recommendations in favor of it, now in the Department of State at Washington; and I trust my abilities are fully equal to fill the office of Commercial Agent of the US. at Havre, with honour to my Country, & justice to my fellow citizens.

I earnestly beg Sir, you will pardon this intrusion on your valuable time.

With the highest consideration and respect—I have the honor to be Sir Your Obt hume Servt   HENRY PREBLE

RC (DNA: RG 59, LAR); at head of text: "His Ex Thomas Jefferson President of the U.S. of America"; endorsed by TJ as received 20 Oct. and so recorded in SJL; also endorsed by TJ: "to be Consul at Havre."

RECOMMENDATIONS: Preble had tried without success to acquire a consular appointment at Cadiz or a French port (Vol. 32:162; Vol. 34:58; Vol. 35:493-5; Vol. 36:483).

From Joshua Wingate, Jr.

SIR,   War Department August 26. 1802

The Secretary of War being absent, I have the Honor to request that if the enclosed nominations for Officers of the Militia of the District of Columbia, should meet with your approbation, that you would sign the Blank Commissions herewith enclosed, and forward them to Mr. Madison, to be by him countersigned and transmitted to this Office—

I have the honor to be very respectfully your Obedt. Servt.—

JOSHUA WINGATE JUNR.

RC (DLC); at foot of text: "The President of the United States"; endorsed by TJ as received from Wingate at the War Department on 29 Aug. and "Militia Commissions" and so recorded in SJL. FC (Lb in DNA: RG 107, LSP). Enclosures not found, but see below.

Joshua Wingate (1773-1843) grew up in Essex County, Massachusetts, and graduated from Harvard in 1795. He married Henry Dearborn's daughter Julia and lived in Maine, where his father had become a successful merchant. After serving as chief clerk for his father-in-law at the War Department, he was named the postmaster at Portland in 1804. Two years later TJ appointed him the collector for Bath, Maine. In addition to his duties as collector, Wingate served as a brigadier general in Maine's militia and represented Bath at Maine's constitutional convention in 1819. After resigning as collector in favor of a brother in 1820, he lived in Portland, engaged in politics, including an unsuccessful run for governor, and served as president of the board of directors of the Portland branch of the Bank of the United States (*National Intelligencer*, 15 Nov. 1843; "Letter from General Henry Dearborn to his Son, Henry A. S. Dearborn," *Magazine of History*, 8 [1908], 55; Emma Huntington Nason, *Old Hallowell on the Kennebec* [Augusta, Me., 1909], 130-1; Stets, *Postmasters*, 131; JEP, 2:20-1; Vol. 36:200).

The NOMINATIONS likely consisted of replacements for several officers who resigned in July (TJ to Henry Dearborn, 1 Aug. 1802). On 17 Aug., Francis Peyton sent a list of nominees for the militia's second legion to Henry Dearborn. Peyton assured Dearborn that he was recommending "no person who is unwilling to accept the appointment" (RC in DNA: RG 59, LAR, torn, endorsed by TJ: "Peyton Francis to [Genl.] Dearborne. Militia Commissions"). Wingate had previously been appointed brigade major and inspector of the militia (Alexandria *Times; and District of Columbia Daily Advertiser*, 23 July 1802).

From Jacob Bouldin

SIR   City of Baltimore 27th August 1802

On the 24th Ulto I received the letter which you did me the honor to write me from Washington dated the 20th. in reply to mine of the 15th. of the same: And Wherein you mention your intention to pass at Monticello, this, & the ensuing Month.

I, therefore, take the liberty to forward to you, at that place, the inclosed. Though perhaps I ought to apologize for Obtruding myself upon you a second time. But when I consider the Occasion, and believing, as I do, that I ought to lay the same before you & before I make it public. I am incouraged to hope your Excellency will not only excuse the freedom taken, but will devote a few hours towards examining into the principles upon which those intended improvements are founded—their Applications—probable effects &c: And that you will so far Condescend as to give your sentiments thereon.

You will be pleased to pardon prolixity in the explainations &c— Aware of your mind being Engrossed by the Various, and important, concerns of the union.—they were meant, as well, as Memento's, as explainations. by sir,

your Most Obedient, & very humble Servant

JACOB BOULDIN

NB. I have invented Sundry other kinds of Machinery—which I expect will be of some service in the Union. perticular a Boreing Machine, to be Worked by Water—Will bore 80 feet, & with expedition.[1] And a Boat, upon[2] an extensive scale, for internal Navigation: and which I hope, & beleive, will be found a strong bonding-link between the Western & Atlantic States—and an extensive, & sure, nursery for seamen. But those lay under different predicaments from the above. I am. as above   JB.

RC (MHi); endorsed by TJ as received 5 Sep. and so recorded in SJL. Enclosure not found.

¹ MS: "epedition."
² Bouldin here canceled "a large."

To Stephen R. Bradley

DEAR SIR   Monticello Aug. 27. 1802.

I am afraid some want of sufficient explanation has prevented my recieving recommendations of proper persons as Commissioners of bankruptcy for your state. I had thro' a particular channel desired that the favor might be asked of yourself & judge Smith to recommend; & understood it would be done on your return home. a recent circumstance however makes me doubt whether you had so understood it. I have therefore now to ask the favor of you, as I also do of Judge Smith to name three or four persons, lawyers or merchants, of republican principles, convenient for the exercise of the office at the place where the federal court holds it's session in your state, and whose understanding and integrity qualify them for the office. to avoid the infinite number of nominations which would be necessary to spread these officers over the whole face of every state, most of which would be useless, we instruct the attorney of the district to apply to the Secretary of state whenever any case arises too distant for the general commissioners, & to recommend others for the special case. Accept assurances of my great esteem & respect.

TH: JEFFERSON

RC (ViU); at foot of text: "The honble Genl. Bradley Vermont." PrC (DLC).

Born in Connecticut, Stephen R. Bradley (1754-1830) received an undergraduate degree from Yale in 1775 and a master's degree in 1778, after which he began reading law with Tapping Reeve at Litchfield. At the same time, he served intermittently in the state militia and was aide-de-camp to General David Wooster at the Battle of Danbury when the general was killed in 1777. Bradley moved to Westminster, Vermont, in 1779, where he practiced law. Judge Moses Robinson promptly appointed him clerk of the superior court. Bradley represented Westminster in the Vermont General Assembly, served on the 1789 commission that settled the boundary dispute between New York and Vermont, and promoted the 1791 state convention, which led to Vermont's admission to the Union. Bradley and Moses Robinson became Vermont's first U.S. senators in 1791. Elijah Paine, a Federalist, defeated Bradley for reelection in 1795, but when Paine resigned in 1801, Bradley, a Jeffersonian Republican, was again appointed. He served in the U.S. Senate from December 1801 to March 1813, after which he retired, first to Westminster and then across the Connecticut River to Walpole, New Hampshire. A founding trustee of Middlebury College, Bradley continued to be active in its affairs during his retirement (ANB; *Biog. Dir. Cong.*; Dorr Bradley Carpenter, ed., *Stephen R. Bradley: Letters of a Revolutionary War Patriot and Vermont Senator* [Jefferson, N.C., 2009], 23-31, 140-2; *Acts and Laws Passed by the Legislature of the State of Vermont* [Windsor, Vt., 1801], 131-4; Vol. 28:203; Vol. 36:100-1).

RECENT CIRCUMSTANCE: on this date, TJ saw the letter that Israel Smith addressed to Madison on 16 Aug. from Rut-

land, Vermont. Having not yet heard that the president had appointed bankruptcy commissioners for his state, Smith recommended Samuel Prentiss, a young attorney, and a "man of good morals and good habits," who was "very capable of discharging the duties of a Commissioner" (RC in DNA: RG 59, LAR, endorsed by TJ: "Israel Smith to James Madison } Commrs. bkrptcy Vermont"; TJ to Madison, 27 Aug.).

WE INSTRUCT THE ATTORNEY OF THE DISTRICT: for TJ's discussion of this procedure, see TJ to Madison, 6 Sep.

To Henry Dearborn

DEAR SIR   Monticello Aug. 27. 1802.

Your's of the 22d. was recieved last night, and I now return the papers it inclosed. the exact statement of the boundary of cession by the Choctaws to the British is indeed important. I know not the character of Purcell [...] writer, but the minuteness of the details call for credit. I think the [spirit] of our former instructions is to be observed, but as they looked only generally [to] the [...] boundary between the Choctaws & us, without designating it, [it] seems open to whatever designation is the right one. as they have [...] consented to this boundary, their consciousness of it's obligation [on them] as well as the same motives of expediency, will induce their consent: after [...] the only question will be whether we pay them[1] more or [...] for it. I am for holding to the boundary rather than to the sum to be paid. when we consider the importance of making the Missisipi territory [as] strong as possible, & the daily increasing reluctance of the Indians to cede lands, we should hold tenaciously whatever they have once [given] us hold of. I should therefore be for recommendg. to Genl. Wilkinson [to] ascertain & obtain the best terms on which we can get their [consent?] to the running of this boundary, but rather leaving every thing open [...] unfinished than to irritate the Indians on one side or cede our [...] on the other.—I have read Chapin's speech through the mouth [of Red] Jacket. so much of it as relates to the punishment of the murder [...] but his [...] to the [...] [of what we have] [...] nor rely [...] any confidence on my memory, I must refer to [...] to originals [...] [you may think right,] which I shall [...]dy to confirm. if I recollect rightly, Chapin was removed because

[299]

he [did] not reside [conveniently to the Indians.] if so, Red Jacket should be [told so] and that [...] a pretense of Chapin's that he was removed for a difference of politics.—I have signed two commissions to be filled up with the names of Wm Cleveland &   Killam. I am glad to learn you have removed [in to] hilly country. Accept assurances of my sincere & respectful esteem & respect

TH: JEFFERSON

PrC (DLC); faint; at foot of text: "The Secretary at War." Recorded in SJL with notation "Indn. affrs."

On 7 Sep., Dearborn wrote to James WILKINSON to convey "the opinion of the President" that Wilkinson should be given discretion to resolve the boundary issues with the Choctaws and the Creeks. Wilkinson, who could call on the assistance of Benjamin Hawkins, was to allow no compensation to the Choctaws for agreeing to the running of the old British boundary except "the usual presents." If the Choctaws did want something more, Wilkinson should "ascertain their lowest terms" and, "if the sum should be small," attempt to gain consent for the running of the line while making clear that any pay-

ment would be subject to the approval of Congress and the president (Lb in DNA: RG 75, LSIA). See TJ to the Senate, 7 Jan. 1803.

IF I RECOLLECT: "From your conversation when last at this place," Dearborn wrote to Israel Chapin on 7 July, "I presume that you will be pleased with being releived from the duties of Indian Agent; had your residence been at a more convenient distance from the principal settlements of the Indians the duties would have been performed with more convenience to yourself and perhaps with more extensive usefulness to the Indians" (same).

[1] TJ here canceled "fully for."

To Albert Gallatin

DEAR SIR   Monticello Aug. 27. 1802.

Your's of the 24th. came to hand last night. the rapidity with which the post moves between Washington & New York will render our communications probably quicker while you are there than if you had retired into the country.

Mine of the 23d. gave you the Christian name of Doctr. Shore, to wit *John*. a further conversation with the Governor leaves no doubt of the propriety of the appointment. there is a General Jones of the same place, equally worthy, equally republican & efficacious in the maintenance of good principles: but embarrassed in his affairs, and therefore less secure as the depository of the public money. tho' in the same politics, they are personally hostile to each other. both have been formerly willing to recieve this office, and I know of no reason to doubt their being so now. having recieved only yesterday mr Page's resignation (tho' dated the 9th. inst.) the commission for mr Shore may be made out. for this you will be pleased to make the usual application to the proper office, and have it forwarded to me for signature unless they have blanks already signed.—you have heard the general suspicion that the Federalist agents of our government among the Indians have inspired them with distrust & jealousy of the dispositions of the present administration to them. a late speech of Red jacket fixes the fact as to Chapin, who thro' his mouth has spoken a high toned party speech.—Accept assurances of my affectionate esteem & respect.   TH: JEFFERSON

RC (NHi: Gallatin Papers); addressed: "Albert Gallatin Secretary of the Treasury New York"; endorsed. PrC (DLC). Recorded in SJL with notation "miscells."

GENERAL Joseph JONES became postmaster at Petersburg in January 1804. He succeeded John Shore as collector in 1811 (Stets, *Postmasters*, 267; JEP, 2:192).

From Albert Gallatin

DEAR SIR   Treasury Depart. 27th Augt. 1802
I leave the office under the care of Mr Nourse, and if I can stand the journey will set off for New York this day, but feel much indisposed.

Please to let me know whether you approve the recommendations of Messrs. Langdon & Whipple for officers of the revenue cutter, and in that case to send me their names with which I may fill blank commissions. I have presumed to get a commission for the surveyor of Albany recommended by Govr. Clinton.

Whenever you shall have decided on a successor to Colo. Heath, & for one to Mr Reynolds, you may inform Mr Madison of it, who will direct his clerk Mr Brent, in whose hands he has left signed blank commissions, to fill the same.

Please to direct to this place, until you shall further hear from me. If I am absent, the letters will be forwarded to New York.

I am with respect & attachment Your obedt. & affectionate Servt.
                                                    ALBERT GALLATIN

RC (DLC); endorsed by TJ as received from the Treasury Department on 29 Aug. and so recorded in SJL with notation "Appointmts."

John Langdon and Joseph Whipple recommended Hopley Yeaton and Benjamin Gunnison as officers for the new revenue cutter at Portsmouth (see Enclo

sures No. 5 and No. 6 listed at Gallatin to TJ, 17 Aug. 1802).

SURVEYOR OF ALBANY: Governor George Clinton's recommendation has not been found, but Abraham Bloodgood received the appointment (Vol. 33:670; Appendix I).

For the death of William REYNOLDS, see TJ to Monroe, 3 Sep.

To James Madison

DEAR SIR   Monticello Aug. 27. 1802.

I inclose you a letter from W. Hampton & Fontaine Maury on the subject of apprehensions that the negroes taken from Guadaloupe will be pushed in on us. it came to me under the superscription of mr Brent, so may not have been seen by you. would it not be proper to make it the subject of a friendly letter to M. Pichon. perhaps Govr. Clinton should also recieve some mark of our attention to the subject.

I received under the same cover a letter from Israel Smith to you on the subject of Commrs. of bankruptcy for Vermont. I had been expecting a General recommendation from him & Bradley. I therefore make this the occasion of reminding them of it.

Of the blank commissions of bankruptcy which came to me with your signature, I signed & send two to mr Brent to be filled with the names of Wm. Cleveland &   Killam of Salem. the rest you will recieve herewith.   I have no further news from the Mediterranean.   Genl. Dearborn has been unwell & quitted Washington. Gallatin not well and gone to New York. his 2d. clerk sick, Miller also, and Harrison unwell and gone away. there seems to be much sickness begun there.   mr Short left Washington on Saturday last, & comes here by the way of the Berkley springs. Pichon does not come.   Accept assurances of my affectionate esteem & respect.   TH: JEFFERSON

RC (DLC: Madison Papers); at foot of text: "The Secretary of State." PrC (DLC). Recorded in SJL with notation "miscells." Enclosure: Wade Hampton and Fontaine Maury to Madison, New York, 21 Aug., concerning three French ships of war that arrived in New York with "a number of renegado negroes" from Guadeloupe aboard; three additional French naval vessels transporting more people are "momently expected," and the total number of blacks from Guadeloupe carried by the six ships is estimated at about 1,500; the French apparently intended "to sell, or otherwise dispose" of the deportees at Cartagena in South America, but Spanish authorities prevented them from doing so; the French squadron is awaiting further instructions from the West Indies; "from the best information we can collect after having been at much pains to procure it," Hampton and Maury write, "we have little doubt" but that the French "will attempt to disperse" the blacks from Guadaloupe "clandestinely along the Southern coast" of the United States; the French have already "in many instances" attempted to sell some of the captives in New York City "in open violation of the laws"; 60 of the people from the ships have fallen ill and gone to the marine hospital, "to which number, daily additions may well be expected"; while "this information may not in every respect be correct," Hampton and Maury "believe it nearly so, and from the extreme agitation which exists in the public mind, we have deemed it expedient to give it to you, with a view, that you make such use of it as you think proper to guard against a measure which if carried into effect may considerably endanger the peace and tranquility of the Southern States" (Tr in NHi: Gallatin Papers, endorsed by Brent; Madison, *Papers, Sec. of State Ser.*, 3:503-4).

NEGROES TAKEN FROM GUADALOUPE: in 1802, a French expeditionary force defeated a rebel army and brought Guadeloupe back under French control. The French then expelled several thousand blacks and people of mixed race. Some rumors held that the deportees would be sent to work in the mines of Spanish America. According to one estimate, the French navy deposited about 2,000 of the exiles on the coast of Florida and eventually took about 1,000 others to Brest, France. French officials imposed harsh restrictions on people of color remaining in Guadeloupe, and Bonaparte's government decreed the restoration of slavery there and in Saint-Domingue (Laurent Dubois, *A Colony of Citizens: Revolution & Slave Emancipation in the French Caribbean, 1787-1804* [Chapel Hill, 2004], 404-7, 411-12; Josette Fallope, *Esclaves et Citoyens: Les noirs a la Guadeloupe au XIXe siècle dans les processus de résistance et d'intégration (1802-1910)* [Basse-Terre, Guadeloupe, 1992], 50-2; Tulard, *Dictionnaire Napoléon*, 847; New York *Commercial Advertiser*, 6 Aug.; *Federal Gazette & Baltimore Daily Advertiser*, 6 Aug.; *Philadelphia Gazette & Daily Advertiser*, 9 Aug.; Keene *New-Hampshire Sentinel*, 14 Aug.; Richmond *Virginia Argus*, 18 Aug.).

For the communication FROM ISRAEL SMITH, see TJ's letters to him and to Stephen R. Bradley on this day.

For the SICKNESS among Treasury employees, see Gallatin to TJ, 24 Aug.

PICHON DOES NOT COME: see Louis André Pichon to TJ, 9 Sep.

To Israel Smith

DEAR SIR   Monticello Aug. 27. 1802

I am afraid some want of sufficient explanation has prevented my recieving recommendations of proper persons as Commrs. of bankrupts for your state. I had thro' a particular channel desired that the favor might be asked of yourself & General Bradley to recommend, and understood it would be done on your return home. by your letter to mr Madison of the 16th. inst recommending Samuel Prentiss only, I apprehend you had not so understood the thing. I have therefore now to ask the favor of you, as I also do of Genl. Bradly to name three or four[1] persons, lawyers or merchants of understanding & integrity[2] of republican principles convenient for the exercise of the office at the place where the federal court holds it's session in your state. to avoid the infinite number of nominations which would be necessary to spread these officers over the whole face of every state, most of which would be useless, we instruct the Attorney of the district to apply to the Secretary of state whenever any case arises too distant for the general commissioners & to recommend others for the special case. Accept assurances of my great esteem & respect.

TH: JEFFERSON

PrC (DLC); at foot of text: "The honble Judge Israel Smith Rutland."

Born in Suffield, Connecticut, Israel Smith (1759-1810) moved to Bennington County, Vermont, with his parents, Daniel and Anna Kent Smith. He graduated from Yale in 1781 and returned to

Bennington to study law with his brother Noah, another Yale graduate. He was admitted to the Vermont bar in 1783 and served several terms in the state general assembly. In 1789, Smith and Stephen R. Bradley were appointed to the commission to settle the boundary dispute between Vermont and New York and, in 1791, both attended the state constitutional convention, which led to statehood. Later that year, Smith was elected to Congress, where he served in the House of Representatives from October 1791 to March 1797. His alliance with the Jeffersonian Republicans in the House, as they unsuccessfully opposed appropriations for the Jay Treaty, led to his defeat for re-election. He served briefly as chief justice of the state supreme court, but was removed when the Federalists regained

control of the state government in 1798. Smith was defeated in his gubernatorial bid against Isaac Tichenor in 1800, but returned to Congress, serving in the House from 1801 to 1803, and in the Senate until 1807, when he became governor of Vermont. One of the founding trustees or fellows of Middlebury College in 1800, Smith continued his interest in education as governor (ANB; *Biog. Dir. Cong.*; Dexter, *Yale*, 4:201-2; *Acts and Laws Passed by the Legislature of the State of Vermont* [Windsor, Vt., 1801], 131-4).

YOUR LETTER: see TJ to Stephen R. Bradley of this date.

¹ Preceding two words interlined.
² Preceding three words and ampersand interlined.

From Robert Smith

SIR,   Navy Dept. Augt. 27. 1802

Agreeably to your letter of instructions of the 23d I have put in Commission the additional frigate. I have selected the John Adams because she is the smallest and of course the Cheapest and she will, besides, answer all the purposes of the largest frigate. Dispatch is of the Utmost importance. Notwithstanding the oppressively hot weather we have been progressing with the New York with an expedition that will not be credited to the Eastward. She will to a certainty haul off from the Wharf and drop down out of the Eastern Branch on Sunday next¹ completely equipped. She will then have to receive a great variety of small articles and will perhaps be delayed until Tuesday. She now has on board her complement of men and her guns. Some of the Officers have not yet joined her owing to the difficulty of conveying letters to them. The John Adams will be supplied with equal dispatch. To relieve your mind with respect to funds, it is proper to state to you that the *aggregate* of the appropriations will carry me through even if the Boston should return and be paid off within the year. My clerks being all much engaged I have to send to you the first draught of my letter to Morris. Some time since I authorised Commodore Morris to send Capt. McNeill home and to appoint a certain Lieutenant to the Command of the Boston. I did not consider it necessary to state in this order any ground for the proceeding. Such a Committment was not necessary. It was sufficient for us to know that he had been deranged. And we can now, if necessary, take as broad a ground as we please. But his Offences are many as an officer. Duplicates will be sent.

The idea of a league suggested in the Marginal Note of your letter of the 23d. entirely accords with my opinion and I am Confident it could be accomplished by a Gentleman of talents and address. Would not Mr Short be well qualified for such a negotiation?

Some of the officers attached to the John Adams are already on board of her and with the Seamen of the Ships in Ordinary are making great progress. Her Officers will be all here in the course of a few days.

Accept assurances of my high respect and Esteem

RT SMITH

On *friday next* the John Adams will be in such forwardness that I shall be able to state to you with certainty the day she will be completely equipped for Sea. It will be some day of the second Week—

R. S.

RC (DLC); endorsed by TJ as received from the Navy Department on 29 Aug. and "Barbary affairs. ships" and so recorded in SJL. Enclosure: probably a draft of Smith's instructions to Commodore Richard V. Morris, ca. 27 Aug. 1802, enclosing copies of State Department dispatches for Morris's perusal and informing him that he is to have "a superintending agency" in the peace negotiations with the Barbary powers; in this charge Morris is to cooperate with consul James Leander Cathcart to bring about "an honorable accommodation" with Tripoli, Morocco, and any other Barbary power at war with the United States; William Eaton is not to be considered "an authorized agent of the Government" in these negotiations; Smith also mentions Daniel McNeill's reported engagement with a Tunisian squadron on or about 1 June; "This Report, I am willing to persuade myself, is not correct," writes Smith, but if true, the aggressor in the action deserves punishment; the administration trusts that if Tunis was at fault, it was not by order of the bey and that proceedings in consequence thereof should be left to Tunisian hands; if McNeill was the aggressor, however, "he will be pro-ceeded against according to the Laws of our Country and every reparation will be made which Justice and Honor shall require"; the $30,000 for the dey of Algiers and the $20,000 for the other Barbary powers should be employed as per the secretary of state's instructions; since Morocco has declared war on the United States and other Barbary powers might be induced to do the same, "it is the Command of the President and you are hereby instructed to protect our Commerce by all the means in your Power against the armed Vessels of any Barbary State that may either declare or wage War against us"; the frigates *New York* and *John Adams* are being dispatched to reinforce Morris's squadron and, "considering the varying aspects of our affairs in the Mediterranean," Smith leaves the deployment of American naval forces in the region to Morris's discretion, although he trusts that the commodore will employ at least one frigate in convoying merchant vessels through the gut of Gibraltar between Cadiz and Malaga; the gun carriages and letter from the president for the emperor of Morocco are now being withheld; Morris is to cooperate with Sweden and with "every other nation at

War with those Barbary Powers that may have declared or waged war against us," while avoiding anything that might "have a tendency to bring us in collision with any friendly State" (NDBW, 2:257-8).

In his 13 Aug. instructions to COMMODORE MORRIS, Smith ordered the removal of Daniel MCNEILL as commander of the frigate *Boston* and that command of the ship be given to LIEUTENANT Charles Stewart of the frigate *Constellation* or to Lieutenant Isaac Hull of the frigate *Adams* (NDBW, 2:232; Smith to TJ, 16 Aug.). McNeill's OFFENCES as commander of the *Boston* from 1801 to 1802 included running the ship aground in New York harbor, stranding several of his officers at Malaga, lying to health officials at Toulon in order to avoid quarantine, then abruptly leaving the port with a party of French officers and the chaplain of the frigate *President* still on board. He later enticed members of a Neapolitan military band to desert and join his ship as musicians. Such conduct earned McNeill the disapprobation of Commodore Richard Dale and Robert R. Livingston, and culminated in his dismissal from the service in October 1802 (Christopher McKee, *A Gentlemanly and Honorable Profession: The Creation of the U.S. Naval Officer Corps, 1794-1815* [Annapolis, Md., 1991], 191-3; NDBW, 2:27-8, 44-5, 232-3, 307; Madison, *Papers, Sec. of State Ser.*, 3:76-9; Vol. 35:446-7).

[1] Remainder of sentence interlined.

From Robert Smith

SIR   Navy department 27th Augst. 1802.

Being apprehensive that the blank Commissions & Warrants mentioned in my Letter to you of the 17th instant, to have been transmitted to receive your signature, and which appear to have been Mis-sent, may not be recovered in time to accomodate Capt. Barron &. some other officers attached to the New York, I now do myself the honor to enclose twelve blanks of each, additional, & have to request that you will be pleased to sign & return them by next Monday's Mail—If the former have been recovered & you should have sent them on, you can retain those now transmitted or return them at your leisure.

I have the honor to be with the utmost respect Sir Your mo obt Servt   RT. SMITH

RC (DLC); in a clerk's hand, signed by Smith; at foot of text: "The President"; endorsed by TJ as received from the Navy Department on 29 Aug. and "blank commns" and so recorded in SJL. FC (Lb in DNA: RG 45, LSP). Enclosures not found.

To Elbridge Gerry

DEAR SIR   Monticello Aug. 28. 1802.

You very justly suppose, in your's of the 9th. inst. that the act of duty which removed your brother from office, was one of the most painful and unwilling which I have had to perform. very soon after our administration was formed, the situation of his accounts was placed under the notice of the Secretary of the treasury, and consequently communicated to me. he was written to. the failure to render accounts periodically, the disagreement among those he did render, gave reason to believe he was imprudently indulging himself in the use of the public money. what were the circumstances which led him to this, was not an enquiry permitted to us. if the perquisites of his office were insufficient to support him, it was a case for the legislature, not for us to remedy. our duty was to see their will carried into execution. we could only give a little more or less time for the rectification of his proceedings, according to our hope of it's being effected. besides monitory letters which were unanswered, friends were relied on to give the necessary warning. the derangement of his accounts being known to you, and the deficiency, tho' ultimately to fall on you as his security, not being paid up, on which he would have been continued, was evidence to me that you probably thought that if he were relieved by such a sacrifice on your part, he would relapse again, and that therefore you had made up your mind to let legal consequences take their course. it became then an indispensable duty to put an end to indulgences, which after being extended from quarter to quarter for near 18. months, gave no hope but of further deficiency. however afflicting this act of duty might be to you, I knew you would see in it a proof of that justice which was the foundation of your esteem & confidence in the administration. mr Warren having declined accepting the place, another was appointed before the reciept of your letter. altho' the performance of the same office in other cases was cutting down the foes instead of the friends of republican government, yet like the office of the hangman, it has excited the most revolting sensations. the safety of the government absolutely required that it's direction in it's higher departments should be taken into friendly hands. it's safety did not even admit that the whole of it's immense patronage, should be left at the command of it's enemies, to be exercised secretly or openly to reestablish the tyrannical and delapidating system of the preceding administration, and their deleterious principles of government. rigorous justice too required that as they had filled every office with their friends to the avowed exclusion of republicans, that the latter should be admitted to a participation of office, by the removal of some of the former. this was done to the extent of about 20. only out of some thousands, and no more was intended. but instead of their acknoleging it's moderation, it has been a ground for their more active enmity. after a twelvemonth's trial[1] I have at length been induced to remove three or four more of those most marked for their bitterness and active zeal in slandering and in electioneering; whether we shall proceed any further will depend on themselves. those who are quiet, and take no part against that order of things which the public will has established, will be safe. those who continue to clamour against it, to slander & oppose it, shall not be armed with it's wealth & power for it's own destruction. the late removals have been intended mearly as monitory. but such officers as shall afterwards continue to bid us defiance shall as certainly be removed as the case shall become known. a neutral conduct is all I ever desired: and this the public have a right to expect. our information from every quarter is that republican principles spread more and more. indeed the body of the people[2] may be considered as consolidated into one mass from the Delaware Southwardly and Westwardly. New Jersey is divided, and in New York a schism may render inefficacious what the great majority would be equal to. in your corner alone priestcraft & law craft are still able to throw dust into the eyes of the people. but, as the Indian says, they are clearing the dust out of their eyes there also. the republican portion will at length rise, & the sediment of monarchism be left as lees at the bottom. Accept assurances of my affectionate esteem & high consideration.

Th: Jefferson

RC (NjP); at foot of first page: "Elbridge Gerry esq."; endorsed. PrC (DLC). Enclosed in TJ to Granger, 29 Aug. 1802 (see Granger to TJ, 5 Sep.).

COMMUNICATED TO ME: in late June 1801, Gallatin sent TJ a list of delinquent collectors, which included Samuel R. Gerry. On 18 Aug. 1801, the Treasury secretary informed TJ that Gerry still had not rendered his accounts for 1800 and that he had written him a "pressing letter" (Vol. 34:280-1n; Vol. 35:108-9).

For Elbridge Gerry's role as SECURITY for his brother, see Vol. 36:195-6. END TO INDULGENCES: see Gallatin to TJ, 6 July 1802.

In an 1802 list, TJ entered 24 cases of removals made before Congress adjourned to give PARTICIPATION OF OFFICE to Republicans (Vol. 33:668-70).

AS THE INDIAN SAYS: in Native American diplomacy, a metaphorical wiping of dust from the eyes was a prelude to understanding. At a conference with Delaware Indians in 1756, Conrad Weiser of Pennsylvania asked his listeners "to wipe the dust from your Eyes and clear your Ears, so that you may look clear & freely at your Brethren and to distinguish what the Governor of Pennsylvania in Council shall say to you from the Singing of the Birds." In an earlier letter to Gerry, in May 1797, TJ referred to Federalists throwing "dust into the eyes of our own citizens" (Samuel Hazard, ed., Minutes of the Provincial Council of Pennsylvania, 10 vols. [Philadelphia, 1851-52], 7:309; Lawrence C. Wroth, "The Indian Treaty as Literature," Yale Review, 17 [1928], 757; Vol. 29:363).

[1] Preceding four words interlined.

[2] Preceding five words interlined in place of "it."

To Craven Peyton

DEAR SIR: Monticello Aug. 28, 1802

Being unacquainted with the rules of proceeding in the land office of the U.S. I am unable to say whether they will admit a patent to be made out for yourself, rather than the heir at law. I suspect it must be for the latter; leaving you to make good your claim in opposition to him in a court of law, but this is conjecture only. Perhaps if not inconvenient for you to come by, you might in conversation give me a more accurate view of the case. Accept my best wishes

TH: JEFFERSON

Tr (Mrs. E. M. Amick, Washington, D.C., 1956). Not recorded in SJL.

To Elias Boudinot

Monticello Aug. 29. 1802

Th: Jefferson presents his compliments to mr Boudinot, and his thanks for the grains inclosed him, which have been safely recieved. tho' not entirely unknown here, it has been so rare as not to afford an opportunity of investigating it's botanical appellation. it has been once raised in the neighborhood by the name of the *live-oat*: yet it may be doubted whether it be an oat at all. he prays him to accept his respects.

PrC (MHi); endorsed by TJ in ink on verso.

From William Deblois

SIR Havre Augt. 29th: 1802

I am induced to this freedom by the desire of Thomas Paine Esqr. who is shortly to embark from hence for America; He very deservedly merits my friendship and esteem, and from his observations on his long tryed acquaintance with you, I am induced to entertain a hope you will look with an indulgent eye, on the liberty I now take, and when you know the cause I wish it may plead a further excuse; That of releieving a Wife and large familly, for by a train of unavoidable misfortunes my finances are at a low ebb.—Peter Dobell Esqr: for whom I now act, in his absense as Agent, is about to resign the Consularship of this place, and I have to solicit your Excellencey in nominating myself to that Office—I am an American by birth, and 'ere this trust my name is not wholly unknown to you—I have resided nearly five years in France, and know well the people I am among. should it please your Excellencey to grant my request, be assured it will be my endeavour to merit that Honor, and never abuse the trust reposed in me—

Accept Sir, my sincere wishes that you may long live, to be at the head of a free and enlighten'd people, and believe me to be with sentiments of the highest respect and esteem—

Your Obedient & very hble: Servt.   WM: DEBLOIS.—

Dupl (DNA: RG 59, LAR); at head of text: "His Excellencey Thomas Jefferson esqr. President of the United States"; at foot of text: "(Copy) Orriginal by Thos. Paine Esqr"; endorsed by TJ as received 22 Oct. and "to be Consul at Havre" and so recorded in SJL. RC (same); endorsed by TJ as received 20 Dec. and "to be Consul at Havre" and so recorded in SJL.

Before his time in Le Havre, William Deblois (ca. 1758-1811) was a Boston-based ship captain and merchant. Neither TJ nor James Madison seems to have considered Deblois for the position of commercial agent or vice-consul of the French port. He returned to Boston and after being declared a bankrupt in 1803

worked for the remainder of his life as a ship captain (Madison, *Papers, Sec. of State Ser.*, 4:426; Boston *Continental Journal*, 26 Feb. 1784; New York *Morning Chronicle*, 15 Oct. 1803; Boston *Columbian Centinel*, 26 Oct. 1811).

Deblois enclosed his solicitation in a letter of 31 Aug. to THOMAS PAINE, who had experienced difficulty in finding a ship captain willing to give him passage to the United States and had turned to Deblois for help. Deblois asked Paine that if TJ had not already chosen a replacement for PETER DOBELL, to "use your influence that I may remain as I now am—Consul pro tempo" (RC in DNA: RG 59, LAR; *Gazette of the United States*, 6 Nov. 1802).

To Gideon Granger

DEAR SIR   Monticello Aug. 29. 1802

Not knowing whether the postmasters from hence to & at Boston are all true, I inclose the within to you and ask the favor of your cover to the postmaster or any other person you can confide in at Boston to deliver it. Your favors of Aug. 23. & 24. are recieved. pray forward me by post one of mr Bishop's new pamphlets, & let it stand in account between us till we meet. I see with sincere grief that the schism at New York is setting good republicans by the ears, and is attacking characters which no body doubts. it is not for me to meddle in this matter; but there can be no harm in wishing for forbearance. if the mortification arising from our division could be increased, it would be by the triumph and chucklings & fomentations of the Federalists. Accept assurances of my great esteem & respect

TH: JEFFERSON

PrC (DLC); at foot of text: "Gideon Granger esq." Enclosure: TJ to Elbridge Gerry, 28 Aug. 1802.

Jonathan Hastings was the POSTMAS-TER at Boston (Stets, *Postmasters*, 145).

BISHOP'S NEW PAMPHLETS: on 20 Aug., the *National Intelligencer* printed a few extracts from the pamphlet recently published at Hartford, Connecticut, enti-tled *Proofs of a Conspiracy, Against Christianity, and the Government of the United States; Exhibited in Several Views of the Union of Church and State in New-England*, by Abraham Bishop (see Sowerby, No. 3277). In the concluding numbers of his 166-page work, Bishop contrasted the policies of the Adams ad-ministration with those of the first year of the Jefferson administration. He derived his report on the achievements of the re-cent session of Congress from the *Nation-al Intelligencer*. He noted that the main force of federalism, concentrated in Mas-sachusetts, New Hampshire, and Con-necticut, "would instantly have perished" under the new administration "were it not for the nursing care of the political clergy" who ridiculed republican princi-ples. With their vision of right, Bishop contended, "we are not to wonder at their abuse of the president, their abhorrence of Mr. Gallatin, their zeal for taxation and their vengeance against republicans." Bishop concluded: "The political clergy are the worst enemies of the church. The federal leaders are the worst enemies of our revolution, and both are enemies to the common people" (Bishop, *Proofs of a Conspiracy*, 148-66).

From James Madison

DEAR SIR [on or before 29 Aug. 1802]

Yours of the 27. came duly to hand. I had recd. the letter from W. Hampton & F. Maury. I had proposed to observe to them, that the case fell wholly within the State laws, & that it was probable the sev-eral Governors would be led to attend to it by the correspondence be-tween the Mayor of N.Y. & the French consul & Admiral. It had occurred also that it might not be amiss for the President to intimate to the Secy. of the Treasury, a circular letter from that Dept. to the Officers of the Customs, calling on their vigilance as a co-operation with the State authorities in inforcing the laws agst. the smugling of slaves. As a further measure a letter may be written to Mr. Pichon as you suggest, and whatever else you think proper from me shall also be attended to.

I inclose several land patents which you will please to send, with your sanction, to Mr. Brent; also a letter from Govr McKean & another from James Yard; to which is added a letter from a Mr. Cochran, which gives some ideas & facts which will repay the pe-rusal. I need not observe that the answer to his inquiry will transfer his hopes of patronage from the Genl Govt. to the State Govts.

What is decided on the subject of our Tobo. by Leiper, and what are to be the price & paymts. if he is to have it?

Yrs. always with respect & attachment JAMES MADISON

RC (DLC); undated; at foot of text: "The President of the U. States"; endorsed by TJ as received from the State Department on 29 Aug. and so recorded in SJL with notation "French negroes." Enclosure: Thomas McKean to Madison, 16 Aug., explaining the delay in the investigation of the fracas that occurred in Philadelphia in April between ship carpenters and the crew of the Spanish brig *Cabo de Hornos*; McKean has "good reason" to believe that Carlos Martínez de Irujo "is now persuaded no indignity to his Sovereign or wrong to his Subjects was contemplated or committed," and McKean attributes the "whole misunderstanding" to the "zeal" of the Spanish consul general, Valentín Tadeo Echavarri de Foronda (Madison, *Papers, Sec. of State Ser.*, 3:493; "Yankey Doodle" to TJ, 14 Apr.; Madison to TJ, 11 May). Other enclosures not found.

PROPOSED TO OBSERVE TO THEM: Madison did not reply to the communication from Wade Hampton and Fontaine Maury. Instead, when he had occasion to write Hampton for another purpose on 8 Nov., he acknowledged receipt of their letter (Madison, *Papers, Sec. of State Ser.*, 4:103).

Newspapers had printed an exchange of CORRESPONDENCE on 14-15 Aug. involving Edward Livingston, the MAYOR of New York City; Louis Arcambal, who was acting as FRENCH commissary for

commercial affairs there; and Charles Nicolas La Caille, the commandant of the French ships that had stopped at New York. Livingston wrote to Archambal about the "great number of negroes (slaves or prisoners) confined on board" the ships. He asked for assurance from the commander of the squadron that "none of those people shall under any pretence be permitted to land." The mayor continued: "I hope too it will not be deemed an indiscretion, on a point so interesting to our police to ask whether the force on board is fully adequate to prevent any risque of insurrection or escape." Arcambal passed Livingston's concerns along to La Caille, who replied that the people being transported on his ships were peaceful. He added that "this country does not seem calculated to inspire them with any ideas of revolt." The commandant, who had given strict orders that no "man of colour" from the ships was to have "any communication with the land," declared that he had "more than sufficient" force aboard his ships to keep everything "in good order." As a reassuring gesture, La Caille sent one frigate back to the harbor's quarantine area. In a letter of thanks to Arcambal, Livingston referred to the people held on board the French ships as "the slaves" (New York *Commercial Advertiser*, 17 Aug.; Madison, *Papers, Sec. of State Ser.*, 2:219-20; 3:525n, 599).

See TJ to Gallatin, 30 Aug., for the proposed CIRCULAR LETTER.

To Willem H. van Hasselt

SIR   Monticello Aug. 29. 1802.

Your favor of June 20. was recieved only on the 23d. inst. there was certainly nothing in my former letter which was meant to give you offence, nor can I, on a review of it, find any thing more in it than the caution of a stranger writing to a stranger. the sample of silk is recieved & shall be forwarded to some manufacturer of that article in Philadelphia or wherever else I can hear of one: for I doubt whether there be in the United States any such thing as a manufacture of silk unless in some private family as a matter of curiosity. having no correspondent in France in the botanical line, I will avail myself of the presence of a friend who is here and going to France, to obtain the particular Mulberry tree (Murier-Rose) which you deem necessary for the success of this article. but it is but candid to observe to you at the same time that my other occupations so little permit the attentions of detail which might be necessary to ensure the obtaining it, that it would be well to procure some gentleman in South Carolina or Georgia, who has the means of a foreign correspondence & the leisure necessary to follow it up until obtained. Accept my best wishes for the success of your enterprise, & assurances of my respect.   TH: JEFFERSON

PrC (DLC); at foot of text: "W. H. Van Hasselt esq."

MY FORMER LETTER: TJ to van Hasselt, 27 Aug. 1797 (Vol. 29:518-19).

From Henry Warren

SIR   Plymouth August 29. 1802

A few weeks since I received an intimation from General Dearborn that you had determined to appoint me Collector for the Port of Marblehead: since which it has been publicly announced in the papers.   Be pleased to suffer me at this moment, to express to you my grateful sentiments for your notice & attention—and the extreme regret I feel at declining the acceptance of any appointment with which you might think proper to honor me.—In my reply to Genl. Dearborn, which I presume was considered as declining this appointment, I detailed the reasons which operated on my mind: I hope he communicated them to you;—in which case you will do me the justice to believe that I shrink not from your service—nor voluntarily retire from your notice—but that I am driven to this determination by circumstances of indispensable duty & necessity.—

Permit me, Sir, still to solicit your favor, & to be borne on your recollection in any future arrangements you may think proper to make. If, as is generally expected, the Marshal of Massachusetts district, or the Collector of the Port of Plymouth should be removed, you will pardon me for suggesting my wishes to succeed either of them. I flatter myself that my qualifications to sustain such an office are not inferior to the present possessors—my claims to the emoluments of them—without presumption, are greater: and I should hope so to execute the duties as neither to disgrace your nomination,—or injure the public interest: certainly I should not defame the Administration, or revile the first Magistrate.—

Accept, Sir, my humble assurances of every effort to support your Administration and my profound respect for your person & character. —

I have the honor to be, Sir. Your grateful & very hum: Servt.

HENRY WARREN

RC (DNA: RG 59, LAR); at foot of text: "Thomas Jefferson Esq. Prest. of US."; endorsed by TJ: "to be Collector of Plymouth or Marshal of Mass." Recorded in SJL as received 9 Sep. with notation "office."

Henry Warren (1764-1828), the fourth son of Massachusetts Republicans Mercy Otis Warren and James Warren, married Mary Winslow in 1791 and they had nine children. According to Benjamin Lincoln, under whom he served as an aide-de-camp during Shays's Rebellion, Warren possessed a "good mercantile ed-ucation." He briefly served as clerk when Lincoln was customs collector at Boston. Although unsuccessful in 1789 as an applicant for the collectorship of Plymouth and Duxborough, Warren later received TJ's appointment and ultimately held the post from 1803 until his removal in 1820 (Washington, *Papers, Pres. Ser.*, 3:104-5, 5:509-10; Rosemarie Zagarri, *A Woman's Dilemma: Mercy Otis Warren and the American Revolution* [Wheeling, Ill., 1995], 23, 156; JEP, 1:453, 455; Boston *Commercial Gazette*, 7 Aug. 1820; Warren to TJ, 10 Nov. 1802).

To Henry Dearborn

DEAR SIR   Monticello Aug. 30. 1802.

I inclose for your consideration & to take order, a petition from the inhabitants of Cahokia, a letter from I. Darneille on behalf of those of Pioria, and a letter inclosing them from Govr. Harrison. the Poutawatamies have killed two Americans on their farms about 5. leagues above Cahokia; and altho' the inhabitants of that place call it a declaration of war, yet from the amount of the aid they ask, it would seem as if they, as well as Govr. Harrison in his letter, viewed it rather as a breach of the peace than an act of war. the dispositions however shewn by this tribe for some time past give it a very serious aspect. the fact should be first ascertained, and the murderers peremptorily demanded, and a firm declaration made to them that unless delivered up or put to death by themselves, we shall deem it war and send a force into their country, as will be done also on any repetition of these enormities. they should be made sensible that we will do them every act of justice & friendship while they remain friends, but that if they once force us to draw the sword, exemplary vengeance will be taken. in fact, should they force us to war, it is to be considered whether we should ever cease it till the tribe be driven beyond the Missisipi as an example. these first ideas are submitted for your consideration. the whole business I presume must be committed very much to the discretion of Govr. Harrison. Can the troops they ask be furnished

Thomas Mann Randolph

Recop.

Great and good friend

§.3. It had been given to understand to us some time since, that it would be agree-able to you that the U.S. should procure to be made for you at your expense one hundred gun carriages at your expense. we have lost no time in preparing and sending them to you by a ship of our own: and we feel it more conformable with our dispositions towards your majesty to ask your acceptance of them as a mark of the esteem and respect we bear you, and of the desire we enter-tain of cultivating that peace and friendly intercourse, which, while it is acceptable to us with all nations, is particularly desired with your majesty.

§.4. Great and good friend.

A war, as unjust as it was unprovoked, having been declared against us by the Bey of Tripoli, we sent some armed vessels into the Medi-terranean for the protection of our commerce in that sea: we gave it in particular charge to our officers to respect your majes-ty's flag and subjects, and to omit no opportunity of cultivating a good understanding with you: and we trust that should circumstances ren-der it necessary for our vessels to enter your majesty's harbors, or to have communications with them, they would experience that hospitality and friendly assistance which we would practise towards your vessels and subjects in our own ports or elsewhere wherever we could be useful to them. I pray god to have you, very great & good friend in his holy keeping. Done in the U.S. of America this   day of August 1802.

21646

The Emperor of Morocco. rough draught.

Draft Letter to the Sultan of Morocco

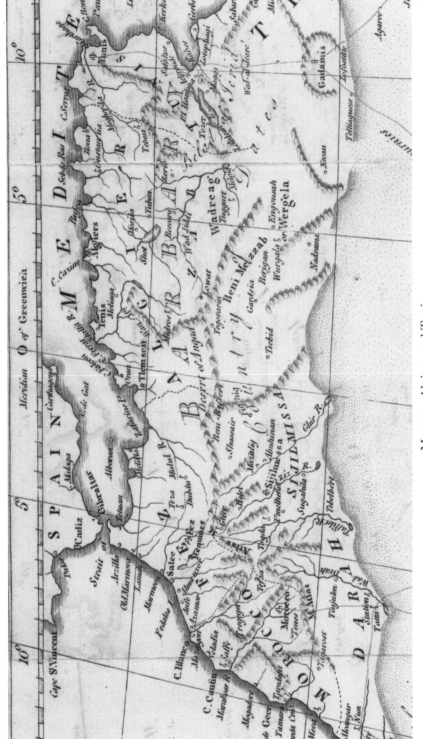

Morocco, Algiers, and Tunis

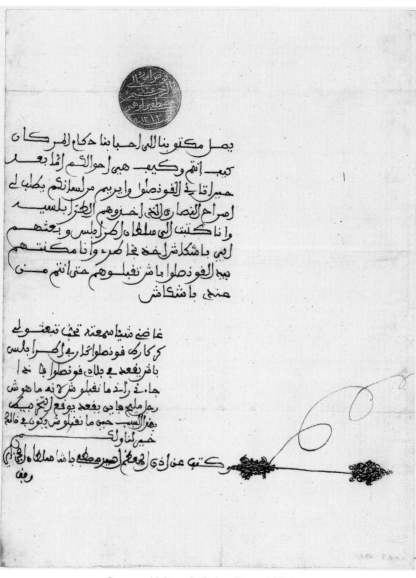

يصل مكتوبنا الى احبابنا حكام المركان
كيب انتم وكيف هي احوالكم اما بعد
حيراقا نا فى القونصلوا وايريم مرلساز نكم يطلب لنا
اصراح النصارا الخ خصروهم الطرابلس يه
وانا كتبت الى سلطا الكرابلس وبعثهم
لابى باشكا شرا خذ خا صره وانا مكنتهم
بيه القونصلوا باشر نفيلوهم حتى انتم منى
عنى باشكا ش

غا ضى شيا مه عنه تحب نبعتوله
كم كاركه قونصلوا احدار يه الكرابلس
باشر يفعد بيلاد قونصلوا فا نحا
جا.... راند ما نفبلو شر لا نه ما هو ش
ره مليح وا بن يفعد بوقع ارنخ بيهـ
دفز السب حبن ما نفبلو ش يكون به ذالخ
خبر لنا ولك
كتب عنا ذى اله عظم اصير مه طه با شا ملطا ه الخ ارا
وفيه

Letter of Mustafa Baba, Dey of Algiers

The *Boston*

Frédéric César de La Harpe

Portrait of Alexander I

Map of the Southern Frontier

them? will it be a proper disposition of them? if we are forced to strike a blow what militia could be taken to our aid? can we so separate the Poutawatamies for punishment as to avoid the danger of other tribes involving themselves & us in a more general war? while such preliminary measures are taking as our present information orders proper, we should be making these enquiries in the event of more serious operations becoming necessary. every thing satisfies me that the Traders are the people who disturb our peace with the Indians, & that we can exclude them peaceably no otherwise than by an extension of our trade & underselling them. in the mean time the agents might withdraw their licenses from such individuals as are most mischievous. while we are taking measures of satisfaction against the Poutawatamies, we should repeat assurances of friendship to the other tribes.

Mr. Clarke gives us information that the Spanish Governor of N. Orleans has given mortal offence to the great Chickasaw chief at the head of the Spanish interests & of opposition to us in that tribe: and that he resigned a pension of 500. d. & came away declaring he would now become an American. I will desire the Secretary of state to have an extract from the letter sent you, as it will be proper we should avail ourselves of the incident to cultivate the friendship of that chief.

I send you two letters from mr Story for perusal, & to be returned. Accept my affectionate esteem & respect.   TH: JEFFERSON

PrC (DLC); at foot of first page: "The Secretary at War." Enclosures: (1) Petition of inhabitants of Cahokia, date unknown, not found, recorded in SJL as "Cahokias. inhab. of. Petition" received 29 Aug. (2) Isaac Darneille to TJ, 27 July, not found, recorded in SJL as received from Cahokia on 29 Aug. (3) William Henry Harrison to TJ, 8 Aug., not found, recorded in SJL as received from Vincennes on 29 Aug. (4) Isaac Story to TJ, 18 Aug. (5) Story to TJ, 20 Aug.

KILLED TWO AMERICANS: Alexander Dennis and John Vanmeter were clearing land on the east side of the Mississippi River above St. Louis when they were killed by a group of Potawatomi Indians. A chief named Turkey Foot, who was defiantly opposed to accommodation with the United States, led the attackers. The killers were never DELIVERED UP to U.S.

authorities (R. David Edmunds, *The Potawatomis: Keepers of the Fire* [Norman, Okla., 1978], 154-5; Vol. 36:276). William Henry Harrison reported the killing of the two men in a letter to Dearborn of 22 July, which arrived at the War Department on 12 Aug. but has not been found (DNA: RG 107, RLRMS).

MR. CLARKE GIVES US INFORMATION: after the American Revolution, the Chickasaws were divided on questions of diplomacy, with one group favoring the United States and another group preferring Spain. The pro-Spanish faction, initially very influential, lost much of its power by the late 1790s. After pro-American chiefs, in the treaty of October 1801, gave the United States permission to open a road through Chickasaw territory, Ugulayacabe, or Wolf's Friend, a leader of the Spanish-allied Chickasaws, went to New Orleans for aid in opposing the road. As Daniel Clark informed Madison in a letter written at New York on 16 Aug., Ugula-yacabe was taken aback when Governor Manuel de Salcedo, "in a fit of impatience," treated the Chickasaw badly "& scarce listened to him." In response to that snub, Ugulayacabe renounced a $500 annual stipend that the Spanish had paid him since the mid-1790s—"saying that as he was to become an American he would do so in earnest." The chief's new preference for the United States "ought perhaps to be encouraged at this juncture," advised Clark. "The ignorance, incapacity, & dotage of the old Spanish Governor have thus effected a Breach with those Indians whom his Predecessors have so long courted & which his successor will make the greatest efforts to repair." Almost a decade earlier, when TJ was secretary of state, Spanish officials had complained that William Blount, as governor of the territory south of the Ohio River, tried to turn Ugulayacabe from the

Spanish to the American side. Several years after that, Ugulayacabe journeyed to Philadelphia and met President John Adams; TJ was home at Monticello when the chief made that visit to the capital in October 1798 (Madison, *Papers, Sec. of State Ser.*, 3:488, 489n; Duane Champagne, *Social Order and Political Change: Constitutional Governments among the Cherokee, the Choctaw, the Chickasaw, and the Creek* [Stanford, Calif., 1992], 79; James R. Atkinson, *Splendid Land, Splendid People: The Chickasaw Indians to Removal* [Tuscaloosa, Ala., 2004], 124-5, 127-8, 173, 178, 181-2; Arrell M. Gibson, *The Chickasaws* [Norman, Okla., 1971], 80-90; Vol. 26:119n, 263, 265-6; Vol. 30:437n, 603n; Vol. 35:518n).

On Madison's instructions, Daniel Brent sent Dearborn the EXTRACT from Clark's letter (Madison, *Papers, Sec. of State Ser.*, 3:555).

From John Drayton

                                          South Carolina
SIR   Charleston August 30th: 1802:

I have the honor of herewith transmitting you, a certified copy of a Talk, lately received from the head men of the Upper Cherokee indians. The purport, I flatter myself will be gratifying to you: and I have written them, that I will promptly transmit any matters, which you may think proper to communicate to them through me, on the subject.

With high respect and consideration I have the honor to be Sir Yr. most obt. svt.

                                          JOHN DRAYTON

RC (DLC); at foot of text: "Thomas Jefferson Eqe President of the United States of America"; endorsed by TJ as received 12 Sep. and so recorded in SJL. Enclosure not found.

The Cherokees most directly affected by, and most concerned about, encroachments by settlers from Georgia lived in the UPPER Towns, located in western North Carolina, eastern Tennessee, and northern Georgia. Cherokee leaders who

spoke for the nation as a whole tended to be from the Lower Towns, which were along the Tennessee River. The Glass, who was from the Lower Towns, brought up the problem of the settlements during his visit to Washington in the summer of 1801, but continuing dissatisfaction in the Upper Towns helped undermine the U.S. commissioners' attempt to negotiate with the Cherokees later that year (William G. McLoughlin, *Cherokee Renascence in the New Republic* [Princeton,

1986], 28, 30, 58-61, 78-83; Thomas Foster, ed., *The Collected Works of Benjamin Hawkins, 1796-1810* [Tuscaloosa, Ala., 2003], 369-84; Vol. 34:506; Vol. 35:196n, 308).

To Albert Gallatin

DEAR SIR   Monticello Aug. 30. 1802.

Your's of the 27th. was recieved yesterday. mine of the 20th. had informed you that I approved of mr Wentworth on the recommendations of Messrs. Langdon & Whipple, & that of the 24th. gave you the name of John Shore as successor to Heath; but I write by this post to mr Madison to order his commission to be filled up & forwarded. I must take time to enquire of a good successor for Reynolds. the commission for Bloodgood for Albany is approved. the application for it left to yourself as you are on the spot. I inclose for your perusal a petition from the merchants of Marblehead in favor of Gerry. before recieving it I had written to his brother that a second appointment had rendered it impossible to do any thing; which is my view of the case. return the petition if you please. I inclose you a letter from Maury & Hampton giving reason to apprehend an attempt at smuggling some French negroes into our country. although this will of course be met by the several state authorities, yet I think it would be proper & indeed incumbent on us, that you should write a circular letter to the custom house officers to be on the alert to detect & prevent such an attempt to smuggle in these unfortunate creatures. —I sincerely lament your stay at Washington, & fear that even if you have been able to leave it it is only to carry the seeds of serious illness elsewhere. long experience & observation have taught me to fly the tidewaters in August & September. no other considerations would keep me from Washington in the present state of affairs. but I know that to go there to transact them, would shortly put it out of my power to transact them at all. I hope my bodings of your situation will prove false, & that this tho directed as you desire to Washington will find you at New York in health. accept my affectionate esteem & respect.   TH: JEFFERSON

RC (NHi: Gallatin Papers); at foot of text: "The Secretary of the Treasury"; endorsed. PrC (DLC). Recorded in SJL with notation "various." Enclosures: (1) Marblehead, Massachusetts, Inhabitants to TJ, 17 Aug. 1802. (2) Wade Hampton and Fontaine Maury to Madison, 21 Aug. 1802 (see enclosure described at TJ to Madison, 27 Aug.).

I HAD WRITTEN TO HIS BROTHER: TJ to Elbridge Gerry, 28 Aug.

Gallatin may have issued a CIRCULAR LETTER, but it has not been found. On 8 Nov., Madison wrote Wade Hampton that the Treasury Department had ordered the custom house officers "to cooperate with the vigilance of the State authorities, in preventing the threatened evil" (Madison, *Papers, Sec. of State Ser.,* 4:103-4).

To James Madison

DEAR SIR   Monticello Aug. 30. 1802.

Your two favors of the 25th. & blank were recieved yesterday; and all the papers forwarded me are returned by this post. I must pray you to direct an extract from so much of mr Clarke's letter as relates to the dissatisfaction of the Chickasaw chief with the Spanish governor, to be taken & sent to Genl. Dearborn to whom I have written on the subject. mr Clarke's letter cuts out a considerable job for us, but the several matters are so important that I think a detailed instruction should be sent[1] to mr Pinckney. indeed I wish we could once get the European powers to give to their diplomatic representatives here such provisional authorities as would enable them to controul the conduct of their governors in whatever relates to us. we are too far from Europe to dance across the ocean for attendance at their levees whenever these[2] pigmy kings in their colonies think proper to injure or insult us. be so good as to order a commission from your office for John Shore of Virginia as successor to Heath at Petersburg. the stile of the office must be obtained from the treasury: also a Commission for Abraham Bloodgood for Albany, for which mr Gallatin will apply.—on the suggestion in the newspapers that Simpson is recalled to Marocco, I have suggested to mr Smith, *if it be known certainly before the John Adams sails*, to consider whether we ought not to retain her. tho' armed by Congress to employ the frigates largely, it was in confidence we would not do it lightly. I wish you to consider whether it would not be useful, by a circular to the clerks of the federal courts, to call for a docket of the cases decided in the last twelvemonth, say from July 1. 1801. to July 1. 1802. to be laid before Congress. it will be satisfactory to them, & to all men to see how little is to be done by the federal judiciary, and will effectually crush the clamour still raised on the suppression of the new judges. I think it a proper document to be furnished annually, as it may enable us to make further simplifications of that corps. I have written to mr Gallatin respecting the Guadaloupe negroes. Accept assurances of my affectionate friendship.   TH: JEFFERSON

P.S. I before mentioned to you what I had written to Lieper on the subject of our tobo. I have recd no answer. the same letter said something of his disappointment of office. I suspect it has not pleased him. I own I have thought something of his silence, were it only on account of the use Callender is making of his name.

RC (DLC: Madison Papers); at foot of text: "The Secretary of State"; lacks postscript. PrC (DLC); postscript on second sheet; endorsed by TJ in ink on verso. Recorded in SJL with notation "various."

See 29 Aug. for Madison's letter of BLANK date, and see TJ to Dearborn, 30 Aug., for the repudiation of Spain by the CHICKASAW leader Ugulayacabe.

CONSIDERABLE JOB FOR US: Daniel Clark's letter to Madison of 16 Aug., in addition to reporting Ugulayacabe's new affection for the United States, stated that in Louisiana "all the People of Property" were alarmed and "indignant" at the report that Spain was ceding the colony to France. Many people in the region hoped that the United States might get possession of Louisiana, Clark asserted, and only a little encouragement would "induce the leading Characters to take the Government into their own hands & put themselves under the Protection of the U.S. & form an integral part of it." Clark indicated that he was forwarding a "Memorial"—not now extant—that "leading & influential men" in Louisiana wanted TJ to see. Clark asked Madison not to allow "this Paper to get to Light," for the matter was "of a delicate nature and might commit the Lives & fortunes of Hundreds." These people "perceive & tremble at their destiny in the Hands of France," Clark declared. Clark also mentioned that he could be of "no service" to the United States at New Orleans as long as Spanish authorities refused to recognize him as consul (Madison, *Papers, Sec. of State Ser.*, 3:487-8).

The merchant ship *Protector* had provided a widely reprinted account of Barbary affairs, including a report that, following a blockade of Tangier by Richard V. Morris with the frigate *Chesapeake*, the sultan of Morocco was allowing James SIMPSON to return and had granted a term of six months to reconcile the differences between the nations. The account was largely confirmed by subsequent dispatches from the Mediterranean. Writing to the secretary of state from Gibraltar on 3 July, Simpson reported that he had received a letter dated 30 June from Abd al-Rahman Ashash informing him of Mawlay Sulayman's decision to permit Simpson to "remain" in Morocco for an additional six months and that he was free to return to his house in Tangier. "Had this order arrived in time to prevent my expulsion," wrote Simpson, "all would have been well." But since the sultan had declared war on the United States and expelled the American consul, Simpson believed that "something beyond this letter from a Governour will be highly necessary." The governor's letter did not explain why the term for Simpson's return was limited to six months. Simpson felt he should not return until the sultan had made some public declaration of "his Peace & Friendship with the United States as heretofore." Before making any decision, however, Simpson wished to consult with Morris, who was at sea. Simpson added that the United States now had an opportunity "for coming to an Explanation" with Sulayman regarding presents, a subject that the sultan's ministers "have been at a loss how to enter upon." It would be highly desirable if Morris could display the American naval squadron off Moroccan ports, Simpson advised, for nothing would carry more weight than "shewing the Moors that a Naval force is at hand, to act against them in case of need." Writing again from Gibraltar on 16 July, Simpson informed the secretary of state that he would defer his decision to return to Tangier until the arrival of the frigate *Adams* with the secretary's instructions. Simpson's dispatches of 3 and 16 July arrived in Washington on 1 Sep. and were forwarded to Madison by Daniel Brent on 3 Sep., with additional copies sent directly to TJ at Monticello (NDBW, 2:190-1, 205-6; Madison, *Papers, Sec. of State Ser.*, 3:369-70n, 538-9; New York *Commercial Advertiser*, 18 Aug. 1802; Alexandria *Columbian Advertiser*, 23 Aug. 1802; *Washington Federalist*, 25 Aug. 1802; Georgetown *Olio*, 26 Aug. 1802; Robert Smith to TJ, 1 Sep. 1802; TJ to Smith, 6 Sep. 1802).

SUGGESTED TO MR SMITH: see TJ to Robert Smith, 30 Aug.

WRITTEN TO MR GALLATIN: TJ to Gallatin, 30 Aug.

[1] MS: "sent to be."
[2] TJ here canceled "petty."

From Louis Sébastien Mercier

CITOYEN-COLLEGUE

12 fructidor an X de La Republique
[i.e. 30 Aug. 1802]

honoré de L'amitié de Thomas Payne, permettéz que Je sois ici L'interprete du corps litteraire qui voit avec joye sur la liste de ses membres Le nom d'un de ces hommes éminement chers aux lettres et à la liberté. c'est donc un hommage merité et volontaire que nous nous sommes empressés à vous rendre. nous avons acquitté la dette de plus d'une Nation et nous nous sommes ainsi honorés nous mêmes aux yeux de L'Europe et de La Postérité—Madame Bonneville que nous connoissons sous les rapports de L'Estime et de L'amitié en quittant L'Europe S'est separée de personnes qui la cherissoient. Nous vous prions de vouloir bien remplacer les amis qu'elle a perdus. C'est à vous seul, tres honnoré Collegue, qu'il appartient d'affoiblir aujourdhui nos regrets et de nous consoler de sa separation

MERCIER.

EDITORS' TRANSLATION

CITIZEN COLLEAGUE

12 Fructidor Year 10 of the Republic
[30 Aug. 1802]

Honored by the friendship of Thomas Paine, I ask that you permit me to speak on behalf of the literary society that joyfully acknowledges on its membership list the name of a man who is eminently dear to letters and to liberty. It is thus a willing and deserved honor that we were eager to bestow on you. We have fulfilled the debt of more than one nation, and in so doing have brought honor upon ourselves in the eyes of Europe and posterity. Madame Bonneville, for whom we have both esteem and friendship, has left behind in Europe people who cherished her. We beg you to replace the friends she has lost. You alone, most honored colleague, can assuage the loss we feel today and console us for this separation.

MERCIER

RC (DLC); addressed: "à Thomas Jefferson, President des Etats unis et de L'Institut-national de france"; English date supplied; endorsed by TJ. Tr

[320]

(DLC). Tr (NHi: Gallatin Papers); endorsed. Recorded in SJL as received 6 Dec. 1802.

Louis Sébastien Mercier (1740-1814) was once one of the best-known writers in France. He penned, among other works, dramas, novels, literary criticism, social and political commentary, satire, and essays. Early in his career he taught rhetoric at Bordeaux, and he was later a professor of history. He admired Diderot and made Rousseau's writings available to a wider audience, but alienated Voltaire, Robespierre, and Bonaparte. In the 1780s, the government banned publication of Mercier's *Tableau de Paris*, a multivolume collection of anecdotes and observations of his native city. The author moved to Switzerland for several years of self-imposed exile and had his works printed outside France. TJ sent Madison a copy of the *Tableau* from Paris in the summer of 1787, describing it as "truly a picture of private manners in Paris, but presented on the dark side and a little darkened moreover. But there is so much truth in it's ground work that it will be well worth your reading. You will then know Paris," TJ continued, "(and probably the other large cities of Europe) as well as if you had been here years." Mercier returned to France and served in the National Convention during the Revolution. After imprisonment in the Reign of Terror, he sat on the Council of Five Hundred. Among his writings were a satire of France cloaked as a utopian description of the year 2440; a series of allegorical tales, the *Songes philosophiques*; and the *Néologie*, a lexicon of new words and meanings. TJ owned, in addition to the *Tableau de Paris*, some volumes of Mercier's historical dramas, a set of reflections from the author's residence in Switzerland, and *L'An 2440*, the futurist treatise (*Biographie universelle*, 28:12-16; H. Temple Patterson, *Poetic Genesis: Sébastien Mercier into Victor Hugo* [Geneva, 1960], 35-49; Robert Darnton, *The Literary Underground of the Old Regime* [Cambridge, Mass., 1982], 26, 64, 140-1; Richard Becherer, "The Revolutionary Look of Louis Sebastien Mercier's *Tableau de Paris*," *Journal of Architectural Educa-*tion, 42 [1989], 3-14; Tulard, *Dictionnaire Napoléon*, 1165; Sowerby, Nos. 173, 174, 1351, 1352, 3890, 4593; Vol. 11:663).

DU CORPS LITTERAIRE: Mercier in 1795 was named one of the founding members of the class of moral and political sciences of the National Institute. In December 1801, TJ was elected as the first *associé étranger* of that class (Amable Charles, Comte de Franqueville, *Le premier siècle de l'Institut de France, 25 Octobre 1795-25 Octobre 1895*, 2 vols. [Paris, 1895-96], 1:78-9; Vol. 36:208-9).

Marguerite (Margaret) Brazier de BONNEVILLE was the wife of the French writer and publisher Nicolas de Bonneville, who had printed several of Thomas Paine's tracts. Paine also lived with the Bonnevilles in Paris beginning in 1797. After Nicolas de Bonneville, a longtime promoter of republican ideals, made a comparison between Bonaparte and Oliver Cromwell, the police closed down his newspaper and kept him under surveillance. Paine's return to the United States presented an opportunity for Marguerite and the Bonnevilles' three young sons to leave France. Paine arrived at Baltimore on 30 Oct. 1802. Marguerite de Bonneville and her sons landed at Norfolk by mid-November. Paine, who was then in Washington, undertook to pay the cost of her passage and advised her to go to Bordentown, New Jersey, where he expected to be in several weeks' time. He also offered to deliver the letter, printed above, that she had brought for the president from her husband's friend Mercier. Over the next several years Marguerite received some financial assistance from Paine, although he refused to pay all her expenses. Paine in his will bequeathed most of his assets to the Bonnevilles and named Marguerite one of the executors of his modest estate. In a derogatory biography published soon after Paine's death in 1809, James Cheetham declared that the old pamphleteer and Marguerite de Bonneville had been lovers. One of Marguerite's sons, according to Cheetham, had "the features, countenance, and temper of Paine." After a well-publicized trial, a New York court found Cheetham guilty of libel and fined him $150 for his statements about Madame de Bonneville's relationship with Paine. Marguerite de Bonneville corresponded with TJ in 1809, seeking an appointment for her son Benjamin to the U.S. Military Academy, and in 1813, about TJ's correspondence in Paine's papers (*Dictionnaire*, 6:1036-7; *Biographie universelle*, 5:38; Philip S. Foner, ed., *The Complete Writings of Thomas Paine*, 2 vols. [New York, 1945], 2:1430-1, 1499-1500; James Cheetham, *The Life of Thomas Paine* [New York, 1809], 226-8, 234-8; *Speech of Counsellor Sampson on the Trial of James Cheetham, for Libelling Madame Bonneville, in his Life of Thomas Paine; with a Short Sketch of the Trial* [New York, 1810], 4-6; John Keane, *Tom Paine: A Political Life* [London, 1995], 354, 433, 435, 437-8, 451-2, 494, 512, 521-2, 532-3; Madison, *Papers, Sec. of State Ser.*, 4:151-2; ANB, s.v. "Bonneville, Benjamin Louis Eulalie de"; Vol. 32:192n; Paine to TJ, [on or before 3 Nov. 1802]; TJ to Mercier, 6 Feb. 1803; Marguerite de Bonneville to TJ, 22 Jan. 1809, 13 Mch. 1813, in DLC).

To Robert Smith

DEAR SIR   Monticello Aug. 30. 1802.

Your's of the 27th. was recieved yesterday. the host of commissions had come to hand and been signed & sent back by the last post. those now recieved are therefore returned: as are also the instructions to Commodore Morris with the suggestion of a small alteration or two. I doubt too whether it might not be proper to say something on the conditions of peace with Tripoli & Marocco; to wit that as to neither is any tribute to be yielded, and as to Marocco only the ordinary presents may be given, such for instance as we gave on the former treaty: I do not recollect what they were, and therefore submit the amount to your enquiry & consideration: but as to Tripoli I should think it against our interests & our honor to stipulate one dollar; and that *we* should not render our nation tributary to any new power. should the newspaper accounts prove true that Simpson is recalled to Marocco & 6. months given for explanations, you will consider whether the sending the John Adams would not be unnecessary, and an improper use of the confidence reposed in us by Congress, that tho' they gave us extensive authority to arm, yet they trusted we would employ it no further than should be absolutely necessary.   I am much pleased with the expedition with which these vessels are prepared: it does great credit to the diligence of Capt. Tingey & the officers, and will fully justify our preference of Washington as a naval deposit. compared with the time taken at New York to send off the Boston, the advocates for Northern positions must be silenced. I pray you to express to Capt. Tingey and the officers my extreme satisfaction at finding that at the hour of call, every thing is in the readiness it ought to be.

you are right in the recall of Mc.Niel on general ground. Accept my best wishes and respects.   TH: JEFFERSON

PrC (DLC); at foot of text: "The Secretary of the Navy." Recorded in SJL with notation "Barbary."

From John Barnes

SIR   George Town 31st. Augst. 1802.

Not having been favd: with any of yours since the 6th. Ulto. I am quite uneasy—lest some untoward accident hath deprived me that satisfaction augmented by recent publications &c. fabricated—by the breath of Slander—so prevalant, basely scandalous, & disgracefull to society.

from a review of last Mos a/c, it does not much exceed $600.—a few such would be gratifying indeed:—a state thereof shall be handed you ℔ next mail—as Mr Pechon does not meet Mr Short at Bath (expecting to set out for New York.) the latter Gentn. will of course in a few days I expect leave the springs for Monticello—to which place I shall address his future letters (if any.) in my Care—

with high respect and Esteem—I am Sir, Your most Obedt. Hble Sevt: JOHN BARNES

Since the above—
I have found leisure to inclose, this Mos. particular & genl. a/c appx. Balance $4267.91½. EE—   J BARNES

RC (ViU: Edgehill-Randolph Papers); at foot of text: "The President UStates Monticello"; endorsed by TJ as received 2 Sep. and so recorded in SJL. Enclosure not found.

RECENT PUBLICATIONS: Barnes presumably refers to James Thomson Callender's recent articles in the Richmond *Recorder*. On 1 Sep., the newspaper printed Callender's first account of TJ's relationship with Sally Hemings:

"It is well known that the man, *whom it delighteth the people to honor*, keeps, and for many years past has kept, as his concubine, one of his own slaves. Her name is SALLY. The name of her eldest son is TOM. His features are said to bear a striking although sable resemblance to those of the president himself. The boy is ten or twelve years of age. His mother went to France in the same vessel with Mr. Jefferson and his two daughters. The delicacy of this arrangement must strike every person of common sensibility. What a sublime pattern for an American ambassador to place before the eyes of two young ladies!

"If the reader does not feel himself *disposed to pause* we beg leave to proceed. Some years ago, this story had once or twice been hinted at in *Rind's Federalist*. At that time, we believed the surmise to be an absolute calumny. One reason for thinking so was this. A vast body of people wished to debar Mr. Jefferson from the presidency. *The establishment of this* SINGLE FACT would have rendered his election impossible. We reasoned thus; that if the allegation had been true, it was sure to have been ascertained and advertised by his enemies, in every corner of the continent. The suppression of so decisive an enquiry serves to shew that the common sense of the federal party was overruled by divine providence. It was the predestination of the supreme being that they should be turned out; that they should be expelled from office by the *popularity* of a character, which, at that instant, was lying fettered and gagged, consumed and extinguished at their feet!

"We do not wish to give wanton offence to many very good kind of people. Concerning a certain sort of connections, we have already stated that, "of boys and batchelors, we have said nothing, and *we have nothing to say*." They will be pleased, therefore, to stand out of the way. When the king of Prussia was upon the point of fighting the great and decisive battle of Lissa, he assembled his principal officers, and, under the penalty of his utmost contempt, exhorted them to bravery. In the midst of this address, an old veteran dissolved into tears. "My dear general," said Frederic, "*I did not refer to* YOU." Some of our acquaintances are, upon the same principle, requested to believe that we do not, in this allusion, refer to *them*. We have formerly stated that *supereminent pretensions to chastity are always suspicious*. This hint was sufficiently plain to shew that the Recorder does not desire to set up a manufacture of wry faces. The writer of this essay does not bear the stamp of a Scots presbyterian parson of the last century. But still, we all know that some things may be overlooked, which can hardly be excused, and which it is impracticable either to praise, or even to vindicate. Such is human nature, and such is human life. One of our correspondents very justly observes that "there is nobody, of whom something disagreeable may not be said."

"By this wench Sally, our president has had several children. There is not an individual in the neighbourhood of Charlottesville who does not believe the story; and not a few who know it.

"If Duane sees this account, he will not prate any more about the treaty between Mr. Adams and Toussaint. Behold the favorite, the first born of republicanism! the pinnacle of all that is good and great! in the open consummation of an act which tends to subvert the policy, the happiness, and even the existence of this country!

"'Tis supposed that, at the time when Mr. Jefferson wrote so smartly concerning negroes, when he endeavoured so much to *belittle* the African race, he had no expectation that the chief magistrate of the United States was to be the ringleader in shewing that his opinion was erroneous; or, that he should chuse an African stock whereupon he was to engraft his own descendants.

"Duane and Cheetham are not worth asking whether this is a lie or not? But censor Smith is requested to declare whether the statement is a FEDERAL MISREPRESENTATION? Mute! Mute! Mute! Yes very mute! will all those republican printers of political biographical information be upon this point. Whether they stir, or not, they must feel themselves like a horse in a quick-sand. They will plunge deeper and deeper, until no assistance can save them.

"The writer of this piece has been arraigned as capable of *selling himself* to a British ambassador. The impeachment was made by a printer, who is in the confidence of Mr. Jefferson. The president had the utmost reason to believe that the charge was an utter fiction. This charge was met in a decisive stile. We, at once, selected and appealed to the testimony, or belief, of *five persons*, who were intimately acquainted with the situation of Callender, at the period of the pretended project of sale. These were Mr. Israel Israel, Dr. James Reynolds, Mr. John Beckley, Mr. John Smith, federal marshal of Pennsylvania, and Mr. Mathew Carey, bookseller, whose name has been heard of in every county and corner of the United States. This appeal harmonised with the feelings of innocence and defiance. If the friends of Mr. Jefferson are convinced of *his* innocence, *they* will make an appeal of the same sort. If they rest in silence, or if they content themselves with resting upon a *general denial*, they cannot hope for credit. The allegation is of a nature too *black* to be suffered to remain in suspense.

We should be glad to hear of its refutation. We give it to the world under the firmest belief that such a refutation *never can be made*. The AFRICAN VENUS is said to officiate, as housekeeper at Monticello. When Mr. Jefferson has read this article, he will find leisure to estimate how much has been lost or gained by so many unprovoked attacks upon J. T. CALLENDER."

The *Recorder* printed additional commentary on TJ and Hemings throughout the fall of 1802, although little new information was added to the story. On 15 Sep., a satirical advertisement for a series of prints suggested that TJ and Hemings had five children together. One week later, on 22 Sep., Callender corrected his statement that Hemings had traveled to France with Jefferson, clarifying that she instead came afterwards with TJ's daughter Mary. Descriptions of Hemings in the *Recorder* became progressively cruder and more virulent in tone, especially regarding her alleged promiscuity.

Later columns depicted Hemings as "a slut as common as the pavement," dubbed her alleged eldest child "President Tom," and called her other children "the president's mahogany coloured propagation." The newspaper also reprinted satires, poetry, and denials of the liaison from other newspapers, as well as Callender's repeated taunts for critics to refute his allegations. No direct comment by TJ on Callender's writings regarding his relationship with Hemings has been found (Richmond *Recorder*, 15, 22, 29 Sep., 20 Oct., 10, 17 Nov., 8 Dec. 1802; ANB, s.v. "Hemings, Sally"; Durey, *Callender*, 157-63; Annette Gordon-Reed, *Thomas Jefferson and Sally Hemings: An American Controversy* [Charlottesville, 1997], 59-77; Joshua D. Rothman, "James Callender and Social Knowledge of Interracial Sex in Antebellum Virginia," in Jan Ellen Lewis and Peter S. Onuf, eds., *Sally Hemings & Thomas Jefferson: History, Memory, and Civic Culture* [Charlottesville, 1999], 87-113).

From James Monroe

Augt. 31. 1802.

Jas. Monroe's best respects to Mr. Jefferson. as he sits out to Richmond to morrow or next day, & will probably not see him before his departure, he will thank Mr Jefferson for information on the following subjects. The state of Maryld. has set up a claim to the territory lying within this State no. the so. Branch of Potowk., on the principle that the so. branch is her true boundary. She proposes to submit the question to arbitrators. Was not that point settled by the King in Council, in a controversy between Lds. Fairfx & Baltimore? Was not the settement of the jurisdiction of the Chesppeake & Potowk. understood to be an adjustment of all interfering claims between the 2. States? This latter took place abt. the year 1785. between George Mason & Mr. Stone.

The line between this State & Tenissee is to be settled this fall. J.M. has obtnd. from F. Walker a copy of the survey of his father. Is any other document necessary on our part? Walker's line is established with No. Carolina, but presumeably after the seperation of Tenessee from that State.

J.M. presumes that Mr. Jefferson has taken the course intimated in his last letter relative to our Slaves of causing the directors of the African compy. to be sounded thro' our minister in London, as to our being permitted to colonize them there. This subject however is not so material at present. J.M. may return in the course of next week; he certainly will return in time to see Mr. Jefferson before he sits out for Washington when he will have the pleasure of confering with him on that interesting subject.

RC (DLC); addressed: "Mr. Jefferson. Monticello"; endorsed by TJ as received 31 Aug. and so recorded in SJL.

At the end of 1801, John F. Mercer had communicated to Monroe Maryland's appointment of three commissioners to negotiate the state's outstanding territorial CLAIM with Virginia. The General Assembly of Virginia responded in January 1802 with a resolution empowering Monroe to appoint commissioners who would help resolve the far western boundary between the two states. At issue was Maryland's contention that the states' north-south boundary should extend along the south, or longer, BRANCH of the Potomac River, a logical interpretation of the original colonial charter granted by Charles I to Cecelius Calvert, the second Lord Baltimore, which bounded the colony along the south bank of the Potomac to the then unknown location of "the first fountain." This boundary, however, became confused by the Northern Neck proprietary, a grant of the land lying between the Rappahannock and Potomac Rivers inherited by the Lords Fairfax but under the jurisdiction of Virginia. In the 1740s, George II had approved a survey of the proprietary that placed a boundary marker near the headwaters of the Potomac's northern branch. Maryland had not been a party to this survey and never accepted it, but first the French and Indian War and then the Revolution had prevented a timely ADJUSTMENT of the boundary. The Compact of 1785 between the two states, brokered by commissions that included

Virginia's GEORGE MASON and Maryland's Thomas STONE, focused on navigation rights in the Chesapeake and Potomac, not on the boundary issues (CVSP, 9:262; Acts Passed at a General Assembly of the Commonwealth of Virginia: Begun and Held at the Capitol, in the City of Richmond, on Monday, the Seventh Day of December, One Thousand Eight Hundred and One [Richmond, 1802], 53, Shaw-Shoemaker, No. 3470; Louis N. Whealton, "The Maryland and Virginia Boundary Controversy, 1668-1894" [Ph.D. diss., Johns Hopkins University, 1897], 5-6, 19-23; Robert A. Rutland, ed., Papers of George Mason 1725-1792, 3 vols. [Chapel Hill, 1970], 2:812-23).

On 28 Aug., Monroe received information from Francis WALKER. In 1779, Walker's father, Dr. Thomas Walker, made surveys for the boundary between western Virginia and the part of North Carolina that became the state of Tennessee. Walker's line and one laid down by commissioners for North Carolina both failed to follow the line of latitude specified by North Carolina's colonial charter. In 1803, the legislatures of Virginia and Tennessee accepted a compromise line that split the difference between the two earlier surveys (Stanley J. Folmsbee, Robert E. Corlew, and Enoch L. Mitchell, History of Tennessee, 4 vols. [New York, 1960], 1:1-2; Preston, Catalogue, 1:132; Vol. 22:448-9n; Vol. 28:63-4).

LAST LETTER RELATIVE TO OUR SLAVES: TJ to Monroe, 3 June.

To Thomas Munroe

SIR   Monticello Aug. 31. 1802.

I have delayed some days answering your favor of the 24th. instant on the subject of Mr Nicholas King's appointment to be Surveyor of the City, because possessing no papers nor means of information on the subject here, and not having it in my memory, I feel some difficulty. I have some idea that that officer has not been heretofore salaried, but has depended on perquisites paid by those who employ him. The act of Congress having directed that all money received for lots should go into the Treasury of the U.S. and making no exception as to salaries, you know the fixing the salary of your office (not provided by law) excited a doubt which was overcome only by the necessity of the case and the presumption that the law having established the office intended its salary should be fixed by the President as those of the former Commissioners were. But for me to undertake to give salary to an office existing before on perquisites alone, presents difficulties to my mind. At the same time I place real importance in acquiring Mr King's talents, and information for the use of the City. As he is so kind as to say that he will, out of his present office hours, attend to the necessary duties, so as to prevent any material injury to the City, I must pray that the matter may rest on this footing three or four weeks longer when my return to the City will enable me to have it finally settled. Accept my best wishes & respects

TH: JEFFERSON

Tr (MHi: Adams Papers); at foot of text: "Thomas Munroe Superintendent of Washington." Recorded in SJL. Enclosed in Roger C. Weightman to John Quincy Adams, 23 May 1827.

From Robert Smith

SIR   Navy department 31 Augt. 1802

On making out Capt. Barron's orders I find that we are without your signature to any of the printed instructions to the commanders of our armed vessels, I have therefore the honor to enclose twelve copies, & to ask that you will be pleased to Sign & return them by the next Mail—

Capt. Barron is hauling out of the Eastern Branch, & will have dropped down to Hampton Road before these instructions can return, but as he will have to recruit some men & take in some stores at

Norfolk they may probably overtake him there—If not, they must be sent by the John Adams which will follow in a few days, and in the mean time Capt. Barron will not be without authority for acting under the general instructions of the Department and the orders of Commodore Morris

I have the honor to be with the utmost respect Sir Your most obt Servt. RT SMITH

The Commissions & Warrants have been receive'd.

RC (DLC); in a clerk's hand, signed by Smith; at foot of text: "The President"; endorsed by TJ as received from the Navy Department on 2 Sep. and "printed instrns to officers of Navy" and so record-ed in SJL. FC (Lb in DNA: RG 45, LSP, dated 30 Aug. 1802). Enclosures: twelve printed copies of TJ's Circular to Naval Commanders, 18 Feb. 1802 (NDBW, 2:260; Vol. 36:605).

From Robert Smith

SIR   Navy Dep. Aug: 31. 1802

In addition to the Instructions to Commodore Morris copy of which had been transmitted to you by the last Mail, I have found it necessary to send to him further powers of which the enclosed is a Copy. From the best information I have been able to obtain through various channels these Gun Boats will be indispensibly necessary.

Accept the assurances of my high respect— RT SMITH

RC (DLC); endorsed by TJ as received from the Navy Department on 2 Sep. and so recorded in SJL with notation "gunboats Marocco"; also endorsed by TJ: "Gunboats." FC (Lb in DNA: RG 45, LSP). Enclosure: Smith to Commodore Richard V. Morris, 31 Aug. 1802, authorizing Morris to purchase gunboats from Spain or Great Britain if he finds that "the species of warfare" practiced by Morocco would make their acquisition "essentially necessary for the protection of our Merchantmen in the Straits of Gibraltar during calms"; before procuring any gunboats, however, Morris is to consider whether the season is too far advanced; "The Christian powers of Europe do not, I believe, use these Gun boats but in the Summer, and their practice ought to be a guide to us" (Tr in DLC; unsigned, in a clerk's hand).

BY THE LAST MAIL: Smith to TJ, 27 Aug. 1802 (first letter).

Survey and Plat for Land Purchased from Richard Overton

[on or after 31 Aug. 1802]

1802. Aug. 31. courses run by mr Fitch.

Beginning in the road in the Thoro'fare at the crossing from Monticello to Montalto, and running on the West side of a fence which runs on the level of the Thoro'fare.

N. 12. W. 12. po.
N. 57. W. 6.
N. 33. W. 4.
N. 21. W. 10.
N. 23 W. 8. 52
N. 28. W. 8. 80
N. 15. W. 10. 40
N. 2. E. 7. 20
N. 28$\frac{3}{4}$ W. 5. 60 to a pine
   side line within the fence

so far is within the old patent lands of Th: J.

N. 18. W. 11. 60
N. 2. W. 6. 64
N. 17. W. 5.
N. 9$\frac{1}{2}$ W. 8. 40
N. 12$\frac{1}{2}$ W. 9. 60
N. 7$\frac{1}{2}$ E. 7. 32
N. 23$\frac{1}{4}$ E. 7. 36 to a gum sapling near the road to the Secretary's ford, consequently in the former line, East $\frac{4}{10}$ po. into the road; then up the road, keeping within it
S. 6. W. 8. 92
S. 23$\frac{1}{4}$ E. 6. 36
S. 65. E. 4. 80
S. 25. E. 4. 96
S. 48$\frac{1}{2}$ E. 5. 36 to intersection of the lower roundabout
S. 13$\frac{1}{4}$ E. 4. 88
S. 18. E. 4.
S. 24$\frac{1}{2}$ W. 7. 12
S. 5$\frac{1}{2}$ E. 2. 12 to the supposed crossing of the S. 37. W. line
S. 37. W. 15 08 to the fence
S. $\frac{4}{10}$ po. to the sideline pine tree above mentioned

---

Then beginning at the gum-sapling and running down & in the road to the lower corner of the land bought of N. Lewis, merely to connect the two plats together.

N. 14. E. 9. 52

N. 54½ E. 4

N. 32. W. 7. 20

N. 3. W. 2. 40 to intersection with the Spring roundabout

sa. co. 5. 28 to Western post of the gate.

N. 30½ E. 6. 80

N. 64 E 11. 64 to pointers, the lower corner of the land bot of N. L.

N. 29. E. 12. po.

N. 50. E. 19. 52

N. 28. E. 11. 60

N. 25 W. 8.

N. 20½ E. 17. 20

N. 37½ E. 18. to the open land

N. 21. W. 9. 60

N. 77. E. 22.

N. 30½ E. 8.

N. 8½ E. 12. 44

N. 4½ E. 18 to the river at an Ash, white oak & maple marked as pointers, just above a remarkeable hole, then down river

S. 72½ E. 6. 80

S. 60. E. 7.

S. 85½ E. 5.

N. 74 E. 2. 60 to the antient corner on the river.

then to close the work the 2. lines S. 13 W. 86. 4 po. & S. 63. W. 72¼

po. run by N. Lewis, were taken without actually running them.

the result by mr Fitch's

plat was in the upper piece 2¾ acres

in the lower   22½ (of which 1. acre is for the

24¼ margin outside of the road)

MS (CSmH); survey notes and plat (see facing page) entirely in TJ's hand; plat undated; see Nichols, *Architectural Drawings*, No. 517. MS (ViU: Edgehill-Randolph Papers); survey notes only; in Gideon Fitz's hand, with some variations from TJ's version.

MR FITCH: that is, Gideon Fitz, a young carpenter whose education TJ was supervising. Fitz went on to a successful career as a surveyor (MB, 2:1082; RS, 1:215; Vol. 37:654n).

TJ purchased land from Nicholas Meriwether LEWIS in 1799. The plot lay between the two parcels TJ was now purchasing from Overton, as reflected in the survey (Vol. 31:140-3).

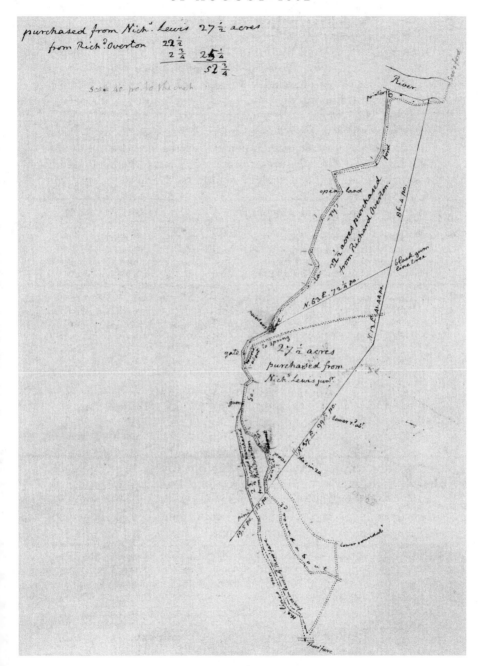

From James Madison

DEAR SIR   Sep. 1. 1802

The mail not having returned from Milton when my messenger left the Court House on monday evening, & it having been inconvenient to send thither at any time since, I can not now acknowledge any favor which may have come from you since my last. Among the letters inclosed is one from Higginson seconding the application from Philada. for your patronage to a demand on the vice Govt of the La plata provinces. The measure as proposed seems to be inadmissible on several grounds; but I shall be glad to have your sanction if you think it proper, to a refusal.

Yours with respectful attachment   JAMES MADISON

RC (DLC); at foot of text: "The President of the U. States"; endorsed by TJ as received from the State Department at Orange Court House on 2 Sep. and "La Plata" and so recorded in SJL. Enclosure: Stephen Higginson, Sr., and others to Madison, 11 Aug., not found (see Madison, *Papers, Sec. of State Ser.*, 3:530n). Other enclosures not identified.

APPLICATION FROM PHILADA.: see Madison to TJ, 14 Aug.

VICE GOVT: Joaquín del Pino was viceroy of the Spanish viceroyalty of Río de LA PLATA, which had its capital at Buenos Aires (Susan Migden Socolow, *The Bureaucrats of Buenos Aires, 1769-1810: Amor al Real Servicio* [Durham, N.C., 1987], 2, 13-14).

From James Monroe

                                                          Sepr. 1. 1802.

Jas. Monroe's best respects to Mr. Jefferson. If he has a moment of leisure, he will thank him for a few words on the subject of a note he left at Monticello yesterday, in addition to wh. he begs to trouble him with the inclosed. If the accommodation wh. it proposes can be given, it will essentially forward the arming of the militia of the State. He will be happy to bear Mr. Jefferson's commands to Richmond, whither he sits out tomorrow morning.

RC (DLC); address sheet torn; addressed: "[Thomas Jefferso]n [Presi]dent of the UStates"; endorsed by TJ as received 1 Sep. and so recorded in SJL. Enclosures not found, but see TJ to Monroe, 2 Sep. 1802 (second letter).

From Elihu Palmer

Constant Street No. 71

SIR New York Sep 1 1802.

I send you a Copy of the Second Edition of my Principles of Nature. I beg that you would accept of it as a mark of that profound Respect which I entertain for premient talents and Virtue Your Elivation by the Voice of the People to the Chief Magistracy of the United States is an Event consoling to the feelings of every true[1] Republican and you will Permit me to pertake of the General Joy upon this occation. I know that the Book which I send you contains nothing new to you and furnishes only an evideance of sincere attachment to you and the Principles for which you have contended

Health & Respect ELIHU PALMER

RC (DLC); in an unidentified hand, but see below; at foot of text: "Thomas Jefferson Presidant of the United States"; endorsed by TJ as received 19 Dec. and so recorded in SJL.

Elihu Palmer (1764-1806), originally of Canterbury, Connecticut, graduated from Dartmouth College in 1787. After reading in divinity in Pittsfield, Massachusetts, he assumed a Presbyterian pulpit on Long Island. In Philadelphia, he joined the Baptists who later dismissed him in 1791 for his heretical denial of the divinity of Christ and other heterodox views. Abandoning Christianity altogether, he relocated to western Pennsylvania, where he read law. In 1793, he gained admission to the Philadelphia bar just as the yellow fever epidemic fatally struck his wife and left him totally blind. Palmer spent some time in Augusta, Georgia, where he promoted deism. In 1794, he founded a deistic society, the New York Theistical Society. He wrote several addresses and articles and initiated the publication of two deist journals, the Philadelphia *Temple of Reason* and the New York *Prospect; or, View of the Moral World* (Roderick S. French, "Elihu Palmer, Radical Deist, Radical Republican: A Reconsideration of American Free Thought," *Studies in Eighteenth-Century Culture*, 8 [1979], 90-91; Kerry S. Wal-

ters, *The American Deists: Voices of Reason and Dissent in the Early Republic* [Lawrence, Kans., 1992], 240-2, 306; Nathalie Caron, "Introduction to the Life and Work of a Militant American Deist: Elihu Palmer [1764-1806]," *Annales du Monde Anglophone*, 9 [1999], 35-45; DAB).

SECOND EDITION: Palmer's magnum opus, *Principles of Nature; or, a Development of the Moral Causes of Happiness and Misery among the Human Species*, which he dictated to his second wife, was first published in New York in 1801 and appeared in a revised edition with five new chapters in 1802 (Sowerby, No. 1290). The publication became the textbook of the New York Theistical Society and copies of the volume were reputedly sent by the Society to TJ and Thomas Paine (Kline, *Burr*, 2:727-8; John Wood, *A Full Exposition of the Clintonian Faction, and the Society of the Columbian Illuminati* [Newark, N.J., 1802], 32, 41, Sowerby, No. 3280; Kerry S. Walters, *Elihu Palmer's "Principles of Nature": Text and Commentary* [Wolfeboro, N.H., 1990], 14-15, 28-9, 71; *Washington Federalist*, 1 Oct. 1802; John Fellows, comp., *Posthumous Pieces by Elihu Palmer* [London, 1824], 9).

[1] Word interlined.

From Robert Smith

SIR,   Washington Sep. 1. 1802.

The instructions to Commodore Morris having been sealed and delivered to Capt Barron the day before I had the satisfaction of receiving your favor of the 30th Ult. and the Captain being at this time on board of his Ship proceeding down the River, I have not considered the alterations suggested of sufficient moment to justify the delaying of the Ship. If you should conceive it necessary to send any additional instructions respecting the conditions of peace with Tripoli and Morocco or on any other subject[1] the Sailing of the John Adams[2] will afford you a good oppertunity. The question of Tribute is attended with difficulties. If we appear in the Mediterranean in the view of the Barbary powers in great force so as to induce them to class us with the great Nations of Europe, they may be disposed to make peace with us as with them—that is—with a secret understanding, that whatever we may give them shall be in the Character, not of a Tribute, but of a voluntary present.

The Declaration of War by the Emperor of Morocco has not been revoked and therefor Simpson has remained at Gibralter. From his letter of the 16 July to the Secretary of State which will be forwarded to you by this Mail, it appears that the Emperor of Morocco had granted a permission to Simpson to *remain*. This was given under the idea that he had not left his dominions and further under the expectation probably that the Adams would bring Simpson an authority to grant the passports required—I am satisfied that nothing but a dread of us will produce a peace with the Morocco, or will incline the Dey of Algiers to accept the 30,000 Dol. A formidable force displayed at this time will make a favorable impression, will repress every disposition hostile to us and will thus save us great trouble and much expence. It will acquire to us a character that will hereafter protect us against all such aggressors.

Capt Barron & his Officers have made exertions that do them great honor. I am yet to be satisfied that Capt Tingey is entitled to any Credit—I found the Ship in a situation very different from what had been represented to you as well as myself.

Accept assurances of my great respect—   RT SMITH

RC (DLC); endorsed by TJ as received from the Navy Department on 12 Sep. and "Barbary" and so recorded in SJL.

HIS SHIP: James Barron commanded the frigate *New York*.

For James Simpson's letter of 16 JULY

TO THE SECRETARY OF STATE, see TJ to
James Madison, 30 Aug.

[1] Preceding five words interlined.
[2] Preceding two words interlined in place of "New York."

From Frederic Herlitz

DEAR SIR!   Petersburg 2th Septbe 1802.

The first lines which run out of my pen, are pardon of taking the liberty to trouble you with a few lines. I will give you at first a description of my birth and situation, I was born at Newyork in a very respectable family, but my parents being reduced, were obliged to send me to Germany to one of their acquaintance, for my education, where I staid nearly 17 years and as soon as I had finished my apprentice ship, which I served to a very respectable merchant in Hamburg, returned to America, by my arrival was surprised of the death of my Father and Grandfather, my mother is still alive, but by the death of my father being disabled to do any thing for me, and by being so long absent, lost my mother Language most intirely, for that reason had to get my living in many different kind of ways, sometimes, by sea and sometimes by land, but I always made it my only study to gain ground in the English language; and I think I am so far advanced, that I may look out for a better situation, than my present one. I am perfect master of the german language, and if I had an opportunity to spend a few months in France, would also make me perfect in that language, as the foundation to it is already laid.

Since my arrival in America, I have seen a great deal of the United States, and the more I see of them, the better I like them. I am bold to say that it is one of the happiest countrys in the world, the Government is mild, and willing to assist the helpless, with horror I look back on the Tyranny, which still reigns in Europe, where every mouth is filled with curses against the Government but on the contrary here in this happy land, I hear nothing but the blessings for the Government & its President, therefore having heard so much of your Goodness, I take the liberty to see if you could not also in a way to be one of your happy Citizens, I am at present twentie-two years of age, and am willing to undertake any kind of[1] business, civil or military, or any commission in the navy would thankfully received,

Having no friends, nor acquaintance in America, I thought it would be the best way to address myself at once to you if any thing should fall out, you think me able to undertake I hope that you will think of me, as for my character I can name you several respectable gentlemen who will answer for it, I recommend myelf to your favour, and with the assurance of whatever is in my power is devoted for your service, I am with greatest

Esteem your most obedient humble Servant

FREDERIC HERLITZ

I shall stay here a few weeks longer, and then go on to Boston where I shall remain, if you favour me with an answer in that time be pleased to direct Frederic Herlitz

to the care of Daniel Strobel esqr

to be left with Mr. John Bell Petersburg

if not be pleased to direct to Boston to the care of Mr. Carter

RC (DNA: RG 59, LAR); addressed: "Thomas Jefferson esqr President of the United States of America City of Washington"; franked; endorsed by TJ as received from Frederic "Hulitz" on 9 Sep. and so recorded in SJL.

RESPECTABLE FAMILY: Herlitz's father was likely the Frederick Herlitz whose New York mercantile firm Herlitz and Blackwell was dissolved in 1781 (New York *Royal Gazette*, 5 Dec. 1781). His grandfather was probably Joseph Hallett, a New York merchant who had served during the Revolution on New York's Committee of Safety (William J. Van Schreeven and others, eds., *Revolutionary Virginia: The Road to Independence*, 7 vols. [Charlottesville, 1973-83], 6:52; *Collections of the New-York Historical Society for the Year 1906* [New York, 1907], 173-4).

[1] MS: "kind of kind of."

To James Monroe

DEAR SIR   Monticello Sep. 2. 1802.

I should have rode to your house yesterday to speak with you on the subject of your note of the preceding day, but that it rendered it doubtful whether you would not be gone to Richmond.

The claim of Maryland to the South branch is under the words of her charter which granted to the meridian '*primi* fontis fluminis de Potomac,' the word primus, there meaning *principal* or most remote source,[1] as it is impossible to give it any other reasonable construction. this was at first uncertain, but it has been since fixed 1. by the uninterrupted exercise of jurisdiction of Maryland & Virginia to the North branch: 2. by a judicial decision between Lords Baltimore & Fairfax founded on an actual survey of the two streams, and fully reported in one of the Chancery reporters, Vezey, I believe, or Wilson.

3. by the possibility that in early times the N. branch had the most water & even now may have.[2] 4. by the convention since the revolution settling their boundary, [I do not think I have ever seen this, but presume Colo. Mason has worded it with attention] 5. by occupation & limitation of time: for tho' acts of limitation are generally by the civil power. yet there is also among nations, founded in reason and practice, a right rendered indefeasible by long possession. I have understood that the late George Mason had collected materials & made notes for the justification of the right of Virginia. they must be valuable if they can be got. it is a great subject, and ought to be put into the hands of an able lawyer & diplomatist: and no gratification or excitement spared to engage his utmost industry. the Constitution of the US. gives them a right to provide for the decision of such a case, but they have made no provision. the proposition of Maryland therefore, to arbitrate, tho' it appears candid, is cunning: because it proposes to us to authorize a power to dismember our state, where no such power exists. perhaps it might be prudent to agree to enter into a discussion with Maryland on the grounds of their claim, in which I am persuaded[3] the world may be made to see that reason is entirely with us. after such a demonstration we may more justifiably refuse to submit our right to a decision which cannot be divested of party & state prejudice; and it would be much more difficult to procure from the legislature the establishment of a judicature, which would in fact have power to cut up states as they pleased; for there could always be found pretences of some sort, and this judicature would be the judges of them.

With respect to the Tennessee line, it depends exactly on the same question as that settled with N. Carolina, towit, the location of the line of latitude 36.° 30.' which needs nothing but a good instrument & good observer. I think that Tennessee has applied to the US. for a settlement[4] of the same line as it respects them, and also Kentucky. I imagine we had better make a common business of it. I do not recollect what measures have been taken by the US. towards settling it; but will enquire on my return.

I have written to mr King on the subject of our blacks, and hope to have his answer in time to communicate to you for the next session of the legislature: but will certainly send you a copy of my letter.

As I shall not leave this for three weeks yet, I shall certainly see you here, and converse more fully on the subjects of this letter. Accept my friendly and respectful salutations. Th: Jefferson

RC (NN); brackets in original; addressed: "Governor Monroe Richmond"; franked; postmarked Milton, 3 Sep.; endorsed by Monroe. PrC (DLC).

PRIMI FONTIS FLUMINIS DE PO-TOMAC: from Maryland's colonial charter in its original Latin, meaning "the first fountain of the river Potomac" (William Kilty, *Laws of Maryland*, 2 vols. [Annapolis, Md., 1799-1800], 1:iv-v).

TJ's discussion of the JUDICIAL DECISION conflates two unrelated rulings. In 1745 the Privy Council's Committee on Plantation Affairs established the western boundary of the Northern Neck Proprietary and ordered a line surveyed from the headwaters of the southern branch of the Rappahannock River to the headwaters of the Potomac's northern branch (Douglas Southall Freeman, *George Washington*, 7 vols. [New York, 1948-57], 1:507-9; Stanley Phillips Smith, "The Northern Neck's Role in American Legal History," VMHB, 77 [1969], 285-6). In 1750, the Lord Chancellor of Great Britain rebuffed some territorial claims of Lord BALTIMORE in Penn v. Baltimore, a case that was included in the chancery reports of Francis VEZEY (Sowerby, No. 1756). TJ believed that the latter case, although not connected to the boundary dispute between Maryland and Virginia, helped establish Maryland's far western boundary along a meridian from the headwaters of the northern branch to the Mason and Dixon line, thereby ratifying Virginia's claim (TJ to Bishop James Madison, 19 June 1803).

CONVENTION: the Compact of 1785 between Maryland and Virginia (see Monroe to TJ, 31 Aug. 1802).

WRITTEN TO MR KING: TJ to Rufus King, 13 July.

[1] Preceding three words interlined in place of an illegibly canceled word.

[2] TJ interlined clause number "3." and renumbered the succeeding clauses.

[3] TJ here canceled "[it will]."

[4] TJ here canceled "[...] their territory &."

To James Monroe

DEAR SIR   Sep. 2. 1802.

I now return mr Clarke's & Shee's letters inclosed in your's of yesterday. mr Clarke's object is to save 6. cents a stock. this is proper for him as an economical manager. but you & I must see of what other aspects it is susceptible. the US. have gun stocks *for sale*. they are to suspend the sale & lend them to the state of Virginia, that she may return them in kind afterwards with a saving to herself of 6. cents a piece. in this the US. will have trouble, double accounts, delivery & receipt, suspension of sale, & no benefit: this is what will be said in the volumes of slander to be added to the hue & cry against Virginia & against us. this is not the view which I should take; but that in the present disfavor of Virginia, she should ask no favor; she should not for a small savings have her name or conduct dragged before the public, but pursue her own path in silence, dignity & self-sufficiency. if the stocks are of real importance, she had better *buy* them of the US. on the terms on which individuals would buy, with her cash in hand. but if this matter appears differently to you, I will do in it what you shall on consideration desire. Accept my affectionate esteem & respect   TH: JEFFERSON

RC (NN); at foot of text: "Governor Monroe"; endorsed by Monroe. PrC (DLC).

CLARKE'S & SHEE'S LETTERS: John Clarke was superintendent of the Virginia Manufactory of Arms near Richmond. John Shee of Philadelphia served as a procurement agent for the factory, supplying the works with gun stocks, iron, leather, tools, and other necessary materials (Giles Cromwell, *The Virginia Manufactory of Arms* [Charlottesville, 1975], 11-12, 32, 35, 183, 187; Vol. 35:663n).

From Daniel Dinsdale Thompson

New York No 90 William Street
SIR   Septr 2nd, 1802.

A series of complicated distresses having necessitated me to leave my native country (England) & friends & to repair to Jamaica— which proving injurious to my health & repugnant to every Sentiment of humanity I quited with an intention of passing the remainder of my existence in America.   Adversity with insatiate vengeance hath persued me hither—the Gentleman to whom I brought a Letter of recommendation (which I still possess) having left America (previous to my arrival) for the country I had deserted.   Altogether friendless & unknown I know not to whom to apply for employment, & being incapable of labor no resource but a petition to you Sir, is left me: although personally unknown to me you are become familiar to my ear by the urbanity benevolence & liberality of your character.   Under this exalted impression I have presumed to address you Sir, & to solicit some employment, service or occupation however low (being able to give respectable references as to character & conduct both in England & Jamaica) within your extensive Government whereby I may obtain the means of Subsistence.

The Department for which I suppose myself best qualified is some outdoor situation in the Customs (the place of my nativity being a maritime town wherein I have passd the [great] part of my life) but any Situation however trivial affording a maintenance you may have the humanity to bestow will be received with Sensations of inexpressible gratitude.

[339]

The business which I followd in England was that of a Grocer & Tea dealer—in Jamaica I was a Bookkeeper on a Sugar Estate. I have also some knowledge of Corn, Meal, & Grain my father being a Dealer in that line.

I have not enterd into the detail of my misfortunes (great Part of which I can substantiate by Documents & which originated in the treachery of a person in whom I placed implicit confidence) through fear of trespassing on your time but will obey with alacrity should you be interested in the Disclosure.

Your attention to my almost peculiar distressing situation (the solicitude of which can scarcely be conceived by those who were never reduced to the verge of Penury a few Dollars being all my finances which are decreasing with the most alarming rapidity) will for ever insure the most grateful sensations & devoted Service of

Sir your distressd most respectful & obedient Servant

DANL. DINSDALE THOMPSON

A wretch forlorn—a wanderer & unknown
And void of hope except from you alone
To you whose ample pow'r can joy dispense
Calm the rackt soul & brighten every sense
To you this futile essay of his grief
He sends—oh grant the implored relief

Mr. John Turnbull whose house is the above number in William Street hath permitted me to date my Letter from thence

RC (DNA: RG 59, LAR); torn; addressed: "His Excellency The President of the United States of America"; endorsed by TJ as received 9 Sep. and so recorded in SJL.

In October 1801, Daniel D. Thompson applied to Alexander Hamilton for assistance in finding a job. Thompson had worked for 16 months in Jamaica as a bookkeeper and, at the time of his writing, had been unemployed in New York City for 9 weeks. In 1803, he served as Hamilton's representative in transactions between Aaron Burr and Louis Le Guen (Syrett, *Hamilton*, 25:423).

To Henry Dearborn

DEAR SIR   Monticello Sep. 3. 1802.

I inclose you a letter recieved from Governor Strong on the subject of the military articles furnished us with the fort. considering that our predecessors may have engaged more fully than we suppose, and that in all cases where a state is urgent, the General government ought to exercise towards it the liberality & indulgence of a parent, I should be for yielding whatsoever was not too unreasonable. I am not sufficiently possessed of the particulars to know if there be any thing of that character in this case. but I am entirely disposed to let the state governments know the General one only by it's kindnesses & fostering cares of them. as this letter concerns the Naval department in a smaller degree I must ask a communication of it to mr Smith. Accept my friendly salutations & respect.

TH: JEFFERSON

PrC (DLC); at foot of text: "The Secretary at War." Recorded in SJL with notation "Govr. Strong." Enclosure: Caleb Strong to TJ, 23 Aug. 1802 (recorded in SJL as received from Boston on 2 Sep. with notation "W," but not found).

For earlier correspondence with Caleb STRONG on the subject of MILITARY ARTICLES supplied by Massachusetts to the United States, see TJ to Strong, 14 July 1802.

THE FORT: Fort Independence, on Castle Island in Boston harbor (Justin Winsor, *The Memorial History of Boston, Including Suffolk County, Massachusetts, 1630-1880*, 4 vols. [Boston, 1880-81], 3:305-6; Vol. 36:43).

Dearborn replied to Strong on 10 Sep., acknowledging receipt of the governor's letter of 23 Aug. as forwarded by TJ. Dearborn reiterated his opinion that the value placed on the items by Massachusetts was far too high and repeated his earlier proposal to have a disinterested third party examine and appraise the articles in question, recommending either Colonel Ebenezer Stevens or Colonel Henry Burbeck as suitable candidates. Dearborn also enclosed a sketch of prices paid by the United States for arms and ammunition in the past as evidence of the unreasonableness of the price now claimed, "especially when it is considered that the cannon &c at Castle Island were old and many of them, exclusive of those which had been materially damaged, had not been recently inspected and proven" (FC in Lb in DNA: RG 107, MLS; Vol. 35:238n).

From Henry Dearborn

SIR,   War Department September 3d. 1802

Yesterday on my return from the Highlands I was honored with your favors of the 27th. and 30th. Ulto. with the enclosures accompanying them—I have written to Governor Harrison, on the subject of the several communications from him and others, A copy of which I herewith enclose you—If any thing farther is necessary to be said to him on the subject, or if any part of what I have written should not meet your approbation, I will thank you Sir for your directions— I conceived it of importance that the outlines at least, of what might be considered necessary to communicate to the Governor should be forwarded as soon as possible, which is my apology for not submitting it to your inspection previous to its being forwarded to the

Governor—It appears evident that one or more companies will be necessary on the waters of the Illinois, but I doubt whether the necessary orders can be received in time to remove a company from Detroit before the season will be too far advanced—I am of opinion that a company may be Spared from Boston and one from Philadelphia if necessary, there being two compys. at each of those places—Enclosed you will receive a letter from Governor Clinton, One from Mr. Taylor and a Treaty with the Senecas, by which they have ceeded the strip of land on Niagara River, including what is called Black rock, the proposed site for a Military Post, and also a letter from Paul Busti Agent of the Holland Company, accompanyed with a Treaty with the Senecas—The exparson appears very accommodating, and there can I presume be no risk in agreeing to notice his request for some appointment, when he shall produce the recommendations of the Gentlemen he mentions; but at all events *if sincere in his professions*, he will acquiesce in whatever may happen—

I have the honor to be with respectful consideration Your Hume. Servt.

H. DEARBORN

RC (DLC); in a clerk's hand, signed by Dearborn; at foot of text: "The President of the United States"; endorsed by TJ as received from the War Department on 5 Sep. and so recorded in SJL with notation "Poutewattms.—Senecas—treaties N.Y."; also endorsed by TJ:
"murders by Poutewattamies
    by a Seneca Indn.
Treaty between Senecas & N.York
            do. & Holland land co.
fort at Black rock." FC (Lb in DNA: RG 107, LSP). Enclosures: (1) Dearborn to William Henry Harrison, 3 Sep., stating that "although the Government of the U. States would not willingly appeal to arms except from necessity" and after "every other means of redress" had failed, the "unjustifiable act of violence" by the Potawatomis "demands immediate satisfaction"; the Potawatomis must "without delay" hand the murderers over to Harrison "or punish them with death, (and promptly)"; if they fail to do this, the Potawatomis will have violated their treaty with the United States and "measures will be taken for obtaining such redress as justice and policy shall dic-

tate"; the Potawatomis' annuities for the present year should not be paid until they comply; should they "prefer war to peace" they can "never expect to have peace again upon any other condition than that of their Nations quiting the Territory of the U. States, for no confidence will again be placed in a Nation which will be guilty of such base conduct after the experience they have had of the friendship and liberality of the Government of the U. States towards them"; Harrison should use all means in his power "to convince the Chiefs of the other nations, of the impropriety of the conduct of the Pottawattamas, and of the necessity of their using their influnce for bringing their deluded neighbours to a just sense of their duty"; Dearborn states also that traders who have done anything "to disturb the peace and harmony, which has subsisted between the white people and the Indians," should have their licenses revoked, and traders should not be allowed "to supply the Indians with spiritous liquors, on any pretext whatever"; it is too late in the season to send new troops to Cahokia, but the company of soldiers at

Kaskaskia can be moved closer to the mouth of the Illinois River if Harrison thinks it would be helpful to do so; Dearborn believes that more troops will be required in that region; it might be "improper" to post troops within the "immediate vicinity" of the Potawatomis until it is known if they are actually at war with the U.S.; a post at Peoria or on the eastern shore of Lake Michigan, or both, may be required, along with one at the mouth of the Illinois River, and one or more companies may have to be taken from the seaboard to garrison those new posts; meanwhile Harrison should use his "best endeavours for keeping the Indians and the Citizens quiet" and should assure Isaac Darneille and the people who sent the petition from Cahokia that the president has seen their appeals for aid "and that measures will be taken for the more effectual protection of that part of our frontier" (Lb in DNA: RG 75, LSIA). (2) George Clinton to Dearborn, 21 Aug., from Albany, reporting that he "yesterday effected the purchase of the Lands on the Niagara River including Black Rock from the Seneca Nation of Indians," and he is ready to cede a portion of the land to the United States for the establishment of a military post; encloses an act of the New York legislature on this subject (see Enclosure No. 3, below); Clinton's personal involvement in the negotiation helped reconcile the Senecas to the use of the land for a military post; regarding the case of the Seneca man arrested for murder, Clinton informed the chiefs that under state law an accused murderer cannot be released on bail and can only be pardoned by the legislature; Clinton promised them that the prisoner will be treated well, and if the court finds him guilty during the legislative recess, Clinton will have the man's execution postponed until the legislature meets and can consider granting a pardon; Clinton explained to the Senecas the "propriety" of reaching this understanding about the murder case prior to "the completion of the Treaty for the purchase of the Lands, lest their deliberations might be influenced by expectations that I could not realize"; he encloses (not found) some documents he received from western New York relative to the murder and the "Turbulent conduct of the Indians" (RC in DNA: RG 46, EPIR, 7th Cong., 2d sess.; in a clerk's hand, signed by Clinton). (3) Act of the legislature of the state of New York, 19 Mch. 1802, authorizing the governor or his agents to hold a treaty with the Seneca Indians to extinguish their claim to a one-mile-wide strip of land along the Niagara River including Black Rock and "so much land adjoining as shall be sufficient for establishing a Military Post"; further authorizing the governor to convey the land to the United States, provided that the United States pays the expense of holding the treaty negotiation or such part of it as the governor "shall judge reasonable" and provided that the people of the state retain access to the land for portage, a road, and a ferry; authorizing the governor also to purchase reservation lands of the Cayuga and Onondaga nations; and authorizing grants of land to Jasper Parrish and Horatio Jones, within the tract along the Niagara, of no more than one square mile each (Tr in same, enclosed in Enclosure No. 2). (4) John Tayler to Dearborn, Albany, 23 Aug., transmitting the treaty for the sale of the land on the Niagara River with assurance "that the business was conducted with the greatest fairness and Cordiality" (RC in same; endorsed by Dearborn: "to be transmitted to the President"). (5) Treaty agreed to at Albany on 20 Aug. by Tayler, Clinton, and "sachems, chiefs and warriors" of the Seneca Indians, who give up their claim to a one-mile-wide strip of land along the river; the Senecas retain their right to camp on the river for fishing and to travel on ferries free of toll; the state of New York pays the Senecas $200 now and will pay an additional $5,300 in money and $500 value in "chintz, callico, and other goods suitable for their women"; plots will be set aside for Parrish and Jones (printed copy in same). (6) Paul Busti, general agent of the Holland Land Company, to Dearborn, from Philadelphia, 9 Aug., concerning an exchange of land tracts between the company and the Senecas, who have long been unhappy with the location of a parcel of land granted to them in 1797; Joseph Ellicott, for the company, took advantage of Tayler's presence at Buffalo Creek as U.S. commissioner for other negotiations to conclude an agreement with the Senecas; as the terms of a deed of cession from Massachusetts to New York require that a superintendent from the former state must be present for any purchase from the Indians, and a law of the state of New York forbids the disposition of lands "without the authority and Consent of the Legislature," Ellicott's transaction would appear to have "no binding force" without the approval of the two states' legislatures; the Holland Land Company prefers to avoid the expense of a new negotiation with the Senecas, and it is important "to every other person who may be Interested in the Success of future Negociations with these Indians" to prevent any "loss of Confidence" in transactions that are "solemnly made under the authority of the General Government" through its commissioner; Busti suggests that the government consider "the propriety of Submitting this Instrument" to the two legislatures "for their approbation" (RC in same; endorsed by Dearborn: "to be transmitted to the President"). (7) Indenture, 30 June, between "sachems, chiefs and warriors" of the Seneca nation and the Holland Land Company (Wilhem Willink and others, all of Amsterdam), the result of a treaty held at Buffalo Creek; Ellicott representing the company as agent and attorney, Tayler representing the United States; the Senecas exchanging two tracts, located in lands reserved by them in 1797, for a tract owned by the company (printed copy in same). Enclosures Nos. 2-7 enclosed in TJ to the Senate, 27 Dec., transmitting Oneida and Seneca treaties.

In November 1801, Red Jacket, as chief speaker for the Senecas, had expressed a willingness to sell the STRIP OF LAND along the Niagara River that included the site called BLACK ROCK. TJ in March 1802 named John Tayler as the commissioner for the United States in the talks between the Senecas and the State of New York. Opposition to the sale by a number of Senecas, including Handsome Lake, undermined a first attempt by New York commissioners to negotiate the transaction. Only after "several councils" among the Senecas, according to Red Jacket, could talks resume. This time Clinton held the conference at Albany and took a direct role (ASP, *Indian Affairs*, 1:663, 666; Granville Ganter, ed., *The Collected Speeches of Sagoyewatha, or Red Jacket* [Syracuse, N.Y., 2006], 123-8; Vol. 36:633-4).

EXPARSON: Isaac Story (see Enclosure No. 2 listed at Gallatin to TJ, 9 Aug., and TJ to Dearborn, 30 Aug.).

To James Madison

DEAR SIR   Monticello Sep. 3. 1802.

Yours of the 1st. was received yesterday. I now return the letters of Higginson, Davis &c. praying that a public vessel may be sent to demand their vessels of the Viceroy of La Plata, indemnity for the detention, & a full performance of existing contracts with the Spanish merchants of La Plata. it would certainly be the first instance of such a demand made by any government from a subordinate. certainly we have never sent a ship on such an errand. I cannot also but repeat the observations made in mine of the 17th. that among the papers sent you by the merchants there were but two or three cases so specified as that we could form any judgment about them, & even for these some very material information was wanting to shew that they went under license, all commerce with a Spanish colony being primâ facie contraband. as to the other cases they named only the ships & masters, which cannot but excite some doubts of contraband. I see no reason for departing from the regular course and committing our peace with Spain by a vapouring demand of what, for any thing which has been shewn, may turn out to have been smuggling adventures. the merchants must pursue their own measures in the first place, and for such cases as they shall shew to have been contrary to right, we must aid them with our interposition with the Spanish government. in the mean time mr Pinckney should be desired to look into the cases should they go there, satisfy himself of those which are right, ask redress for them, abandoning those evidently illicit: except indeed so far as sudden changes of their regulations may have entrapped a bonâ fide trader.

I send you an answer from Lieper recieved yesterday. I suppose he meant the answer to my proposition as an answer to your's also, altho' the cases differed in a material circumstance. Accept my affectionate esteem & respect.   TH: JEFFERSON

RC (DLC: Madison Papers); at foot of text: "The Secretary of State"; endorsed by Madison. PrC (DLC). Recorded in SJL with notation "La Plata."

The DAVIS who joined Stephen Higginson, Sr., and others in seeking redress of problems encountered by merchants in Spanish America was probably Thomas Davis, the president of the Boston Marine Insurance Company (Madison, *Papers, Sec. of State Ser.*, 4:109).

In a letter of 25 Oct. that concerned the joint Spanish-U.S. claims commission, Madison notified Charles PINCKNEY that he could expect "an extensive application from Merchants in Boston and Philadelphia." Madison advised the merchants to sort their cases into categories to help Pinckney determine how to present the claims to the Spanish government. Madison asked Pinckney to assist the merchants if they wanted to send agents to Spain or to Spanish colonies to resolve claims. On 10 Nov., Madison forwarded to Pinckney a request from Boston insurers and merchants for information on "the reasons for detaining at Rio La Plata sundry vessels and cargoes" (same, 56, 109).

ANSWER FROM LIEPER: Thomas Leiper to TJ, 26 Aug.

From James Madison

Dear Sir   Sep. 3. 1802

I have duly recd. yours of the 30th. Ulto. with the several papers to which it refers. I have directed the commissions for Shore & Bloodgood to be made out, and have sent the extract from Clark's letter as you required to Genl. Dearborn. He had however been made acquainted with it by Mr. Brent, before the letter was forwarded to me. May it not be as well to let the call for the Dockets be a rule of Congress, as there is no specific appropriation for the expence, and a regular call by the Ex. might not be regarded as within any contingent fund? to this consideration it may be added that the Ex. have no power over the Clerks of the Courts, & that some of them might refuse to comply from a dislike to the object. When the object was not known, there was a manifest repugnance in some instances. Your final determination in the case shall be pursued. I have thought also that it might be as well to postpone till the reassembling at Washington any general regulation with regard to the appointment of Commissioners of Bankruptcy; but shall in this case also cheerfully conform to your pleasure.

Mr. Brent informs me that he has sent you copies of Eaton's letter of May 25-27. & Cathalan's of June 10. It does not seem necessary that the communications[1] of the former should be made the subject of further instructions till we receive further accts. from other sources. Thornton you will see is renewing the subject of the Snow Windsor, May he not be told that the remedy lies with the Courts, and not with the Ex. The absence of the Vessel can no more be a bar to it, than the sale was. It seems proper however that the irregularity in sending the vessel out without the legal clearance should be prosecuted. The law is I believe defective on this point. The Correspondent referred to in Steel's letter is, I take it, Mr. Brown the Kentucky Senator.

Yours with respectful attachment   James Madison

RC (DLC); at foot of text: "The President of the U. States"; endorsed by TJ as received 5 Sep. and "Dockets—Commrs. bkrptcy Barbary affairs. Thornton & snow Windsor.—Steele" and so recorded in SJL. Enclosures: (1) Edward Thornton to Madison, 27 Aug., complaining that the snow *Windsor* remained at Boston for several months despite the U.S. government's orders that the vessel leave the port; that the vessel was sold to a private individual and subsequently passed into other hands due to a bankruptcy; the sale of the vessel and its failure to depart promptly are violations of the treaty of amity between the United States and Great Britain; the *Windsor* was converted from a snow to a ship and has departed for the East Indies "without any regular papers from the Custom House" (Madison, *Papers, Sec. of State Ser.*, 3:523-4). (2) John Steele of Natchez to Madison, 20 June, concerning the "stain" that his removal from the office of secretary of the Mississippi Territory places on his reputation; he has learned that his removal was due to a report that he opposes William C. C. Claiborne; "I assure myself," he writes, "that such is your love of Justice that you will take pleasure in expressing to the President of the United States my desire, that my Accuser may be made known to me, and that I may be indulged in attempting to shew the accusation is not founded in fact" (same, 3:326-8).

WHEN THE OBJECT WAS NOT KNOWN: in 1801 and early 1802, Madison and TJ compiled information about activity in U.S. circuit courts (Vol. 35:658n; Vol. 36:66, 638-40, 654-5, 658).

MR. BRENT INFORMS ME: in a letter to Madison on 31 Aug., Daniel Brent noted that he had sent TJ copies and extracts from correspondence of William Eaton and Stephen Cathalan, Jr. (Madison, *Papers, Sec. of State Ser.*, 3:529). EATON'S LETTER to Madison, begun at Tunis on 25 May, reported that Eaton had been summoned to the palace for a meeting with Yusuf Sahib-at-Taba, the master of the seal and prime minister, who conveyed an offer from Hammuda, the bey of Tunis, to serve as mediator between the United States and Tripoli. Eaton stated that he was "not vested with powers to negociate" terms to end the war, but was confident that Tripoli would need to "make suitable retractions for the insult offered our flag, and reasonable indemnities for the expense resulting from it." When the prime minister argued persistently that the United States should give the bey of Tripoli "a small voluntary present" because it was customary to do so and because such an offering would cost the United States less than the expenses of continuing the war and protecting American shipping, Eaton replied that the United States "never supposed our commerce in this sea more secure than at present." Tripoli, he declared, "has forfieted her title of *Friend*" and should not expect presents. According to Eaton's report of the conversation, he told the Tunisian official that Americans "have no inducements whatever to *desire* a war with any nation on earth," but if Tripoli insisted on "dishonorable" terms for peace, "four or five years of warfare with that State, will be but a pastime to our young warriors." Eaton's dispatch was enclosed in one to Madison from Cathalan at Marseilles (same, 258-61, 300; Kenneth J. Perkins, *Historical Dictionary of Tunisia* [Metuchen, N.J., 1989], 119).

COMMUNICATIONS OF THE FORMER: in his letter to Madison, Eaton also stated: "I am partial to my original plan of restoring the rightful Bashaw." Since March 1802, Eaton had been promoting a plan to displace Yusuf Qaramanli as bey of Tripoli in favor of Yusuf's brother Ahmad. Eaton enlisted the aid of James L. Cathcart and Yusuf Sahib-at-Taba, and, meeting with Ahmad in Tunis, discouraged him from returning to Tripoli and falling under his brother's control. Eaton endeavored to keep Ahmad within the reach of the U.S. Navy and informed Cathcart on 21 May: "Lieutenant Sterret assures me that seven days ago the Bashaw Ciddi Mohammed"—that is, Ahmad—"was at Malta waiting the arrival of our Squadron—Captain McNeill signifies to me by letter of the 17th Inst, that this is by arrangement between them." In September, Daniel Brent sent TJ an extract from Eaton's letter to Cathcart that contained those statements about Ahmad and this news: "It is favorable to us here that the Captures of Tunisian merchant-men Complained of, have all been done by the Swedes—This Circumstance relieves me from incalculable perplexities with this Govt." (RC in DLC, unsigned, in Brent's hand, at head of text: "Extract of a letter from Wm Eaton to James Leander Cathcart, dated May 21st 1802," endorsed by TJ as received from the State Department on 19 Sep. and "extract Eaton's lre," not recorded in SJL; Madison, *Papers, Sec. of State Ser.*, 3:5n, 45, 260, 519; NDBW, 2:97, 111-12, 239).

The WINDSOR had been an issue between Great Britain and the United States since the summer of 1801, after French and other prisoners took control of the vessel during a storm and brought it into Boston harbor. On 3 Sep. 1801, Gallatin had instructed Benjamin Lincoln to see that the ship left the jurisdiction of the United States even though TJ and his advisers did not believe they were obliged to expel the vessel. Following protests by British chargé Edward Thornton in April and June 1802, Gallatin informed Madison that the vessel was in the possession of Stephen Higginson's company. As the sale was prohibited under the provisions of the Jay Treaty, the "present pretended owners will therefore receive neither clearance or any Kind of Papers from the Custom house Officers, in their own name," Gallatin wrote. Madison declared to Thornton on 3 July that any remaining issues were "between those who owned and those who seized the vessel," and "it is considered by the President that the Government of the United States is not obliged farther to interfere." After receiving Thornton's letter of 27 Aug., Madison asked Gallatin about Thornton's new concerns. In December, Madison passed along to Thornton information and depositions that Gallatin collected in response to that query. The documents, Madison explained, showed that the delay in the ship's departure was due to repairs, and that the original owners had failed to take action to forestall the disposition of the vessel. Earlier, Thornton had admitted privately to his government that there was little chance of winning any "pecuniary compensation" from the United States, and he believed that pressing the matter of "the culpable negligence, if not the intentional misconduct" of the customs officials at Boston would give TJ a reason to remove more Federalists from office (Madison, *Papers, Sec. of State Ser.*, 3:115-16, 351-2, 358, 361-2, 524n, 551n; 4:16, 104n, 174-5; Vol. 35:37-9, 79, 81, 110, 124-5, 159n).

Madison was correct in surmising that a person whom John Steele called "my Friend (who I presume is known to you)" was Senator John BROWN, who had met with TJ and Madison about Steele's situation (Madison, *Papers, Sec. of State Ser.*, 3:326-7; Vol. 36:389).

[1] Word abbreviated in MS, "commications."

To Stevens Thomson Mason

DEAR SIR   Monticello Sep. 3. 1802.

I have taken time to press on Colo. Monroe your purpose of resigning & the importance of his filling the vacancy. but he has firmly made up his mind to return to the business of the law, has bought a place near Richmond, and will go into no public business. in this state of things the Commonwealth must not be deserted. you must [...] look abroad and see who [could] be sent to the Senate. I hope therefore you will reconsider your purpose. be assured that all is not yet re[newed]. the lies and misrepresentations of the federalists have prevented the [im]pression of a great deal of the good we have done, & given it the [...] of ill in effect or in design: and their lies are so little contradicted that they have effect. add to this that the session of Congress after the next (when we hope to have $\frac{2}{3}$ in the Senate) will be the most important one we have seen or shall see for some time. I think if the republicans will hold on a little longer till the effect of our measures and their object is [generally felt] & acknoleged we shall never more be in danger, but for the present be assured the fermentation is not allayed. I hope therefore you will consent to be elected again.—I shall be at Washington the last of this month. Accept assurances of my affectionate esteem & respect.

TH: JEFFERSON

PrC (DLC); faint; at foot of text: "Genl S. T. Mason."

YOUR PURPOSE OF RESIGNING: during his most recent journey from Washington to Monticello, TJ visited Mason on 22 July at Raspberry Plain, his home in Loudoun County. After additional coaxing by TJ, Mason allowed himself to be reelected to the United States Senate in December 1802 (MB, 2:1078; TJ to John Wayles Eppes, 11 Dec. 1802; Eppes to TJ, 23 Dec. 1802).

To James Monroe

Monticello
TH: JEFFERSON TO GOVERNOR MONROE.   Sep. 3. 1802.

Reynolds, collector of York, is dead, and Wm. Carey of that place is recommended very strongly by mr Shields. tho' I have great confidence in mr Shields's recommendation, yet as the best men some times see characters thro' the false medium of friendship I pray you to make what enquiry you can in Richmond & communicate it to me. Accept assurances of my constant & affectionate esteem & respect.

TH: JEFFERSON

PrC (DLC); at foot of text: "Governor Monroe."

William REYNOLDS had served as collector and inspector of the revenue at Yorktown, Virginia, since 1794 (JEP, 1:165). On 2 Sep., TJ received a letter from Samuel Sheild, dated 25 Aug., rec- ommending William Carey to succeed Reynolds (recorded in SJL as received from York County and "Wm Carey to be Collector York" but not found). On the same date, TJ received a 26 Aug. letter from Carey applying for the position (recorded in SJL but not found; see Appendix III).

To Robert Smith

Dear Sir   Monticello Sep. 3. 1802.

Your two favors of Aug. 31. are recieved. the printed instructions are signed & accompany this. I presume the instruction as to the procuring gunboats is right, tho' I can judge here from reason only and not information. we ought to rely also in the discretion of our officers so far as that they will not commit our men in these small vessels to an unequal or even equal fight. we ought above all things to avoid letting them ever get the better of us in an action. the gun boats and gallies of the Mediterranean are formidable. still as our officers ought to make but a prudent & safe use of them, we must presume they will do so, in which case they will be useful. I still place some confidence in the newspaper information that on Morris's blockading Tangier, Simpson was recalled & 6. months allowed; and am clear, if that proves true that the John Adams ought to be detained. Tripoli has made overtures of peace thro' the mediation of Tunis, as you can see by a letter from Consul Eaton in the Secy. of State's office. I should be against giving them a single dollar even as a present, for if we made peace, we must still keep a frigate or two there, which is sufficient to secure our trade against them even in war.   I have recieved a letter from Governor Strong on the subject of their cannon &c. which concerning the War department principally, I inclose to Genl. Dearborne, and must ask the favor of you to be referred to him for a sight of it. I think, where a state is pressing, we should yield in cases not very unreasonable, and treat them with the indulgence and liberality[1] of a parent. Accept my friendly salutations & respect

Th: Jefferson

PrC (DLC); at foot of text: "The Secretary of the Navy." Recorded in SJL as a letter to the Navy Department with notation "Gunboats. Govr Strong."

LETTER FROM CONSUL EATON: see James Madison to TJ, 3 Sep. 1802.

LETTER FROM GOVERNOR STRONG: see enclosure listed at TJ to Henry Dearborn, 3 Sep. 1802.

[1] Preceding two words interlined.

From William Killen

Dover Kent County and State
of Delaware Sep. 4th. 1802.

HONOURED SIR.

I Shall not trouble you with any apology for the abrupt and uncourtly manner in which I presume to introduce myself to your notice; as I can hardly suppose you have; at any time heretofore heard my name mentioned. Hence, Sir, I feel myself constained to indulge a little to egotism, (however unpolite) that you may be thereby better enabled to determine in what point of view you ought to consider, the sentiments express'd in the present letter, I have the honour to address to you; after you will have condescended to give it even a cursory perusal.

I Am now verging towards the close of the Eightieth year of my age,—Sixty two years [wh'e] of, lacking a few months, I have been resident in that part of America now called the State of Delaware; and my knowledge of the world is almost wholly bounded by the limits of this small state—never had the advantage of an academical or classical education; nor an intimate acquaintance, or frequent conversation with any man celebrated for his erudition, or knowledge of science—have been almost a recluse for some years past; and since the era of our independence, have never solicited an appointment to any office under the united states, or any individual state, in the union.

Having given you, Sir, this brief sketch of my biography, little interesting to you or the public; I think it incumbent upon me, to mention to you, the motive inducing me to address these lines to you; altho' I use the pen with pain and difficulty, and [...] first time to express my sentiments upon any political subject, or of men concerned in the administration of our general[1] government, or in that of any individual state

The motive alluded to is; the impressive sense I entetain, in unison I believe, with that felt by a respectable, and every day encreasing number of the citizens, even[2] of the little, tory state of Delaware; of your virtues as a man, your accomplishments as a man of the most noble and useful sciences; and what is still more important to society, your patriotism and unremitting endeavors, evinced by every act of your God-like administration, of our general government, to preserve the peace, and promote the happiness of the citizens, of the united states. On the contrary; your virtues as well public as private,

[351]

have a quite different effect upon the minds of certain miscreant enemies, to God and man, and every happy civil institution, dispersed
through out the union. They (your virtues) inflame the rage and
malice of these persons against you, Sir, to intoxication and madness; evidenced by their libellous writings, and their speeches deliver'd on the floor of Congress; in defiance of all regard to decency or
decorum. And why? the answer is obvious. Because every act of your
administration encreases the number of your friends, which, I hope
and believe form a great majority of the community, and will I trust
defeat the³ exorbitant ambition of offices, of power, and wealth, so
conspicous in every movement, of your political enemies.

I now feel myself disposed, Sir, to make a transition from farther an-
imadverting on the diabilical malice of your enemies, to add a few
words, to what I have already said, concerning your conduct as chief
magistrate of the united states; and to do justice to your political
character, I cannot express my opinion thereof, in words more expressive and energetic, than by barely stating that your administration of our general government forms a perfect contrast, to that of
your immediate predecessor Mr. John Adams, of *pious memory*, (for
he is said to be politically defunct) who is reported to have exclaim'd,
with great emphasis; "The finger of God points to war," And that
upon seeing a number of boys, armed in their way, with black cock-
ades in their hats, he cried aloud, with the like emotion—"To arms,
to arms, my young friends!" These were times, I suppose, when Mr.
Adams was big with the expectation and hope of having his brow
adorned, at no very distant period, with a diadem, by the instrumen-
tallity of a numerous standing army, and a formidable navy to the
utter annihilation of everything dear and estimable to the freemen of
the united states. It is also said in several publications, that have
lately come to my hands; that he has repeatedly declared; that the
people of the united states could never be happy, until their chief
magistrate and senate were made hereditary; and that he has already
found out, or created, four noble families in Boston, or Massachusets;
of whom his Grace the Duke of Braintree, holds the [high] rank;
altho' we are told his father was a shoemaker, and that he himself followed the same mechanical business for a livelyhood; for some time
in his younger years; which if true, *this alone*; would not degrade him
in my estimation. I Am, Honoured Sir, with the most perfect esteem,
love and veneration of your virtues

Your most obedient and most Humble Servant

WILLIAM KILLEN

RC (DLC); words obscured from bleeding of ink; endorsed by TJ as received 13 Oct. and so recorded in SJL. Enclosed in Caesar A. Rodney to TJ, 6 Oct. 1802.

William Killen (1722-1805), born in Ireland, immigrated to the United States at the age of 15 and settled in Dover, Delaware, where he became resident tutor to the young John Dickinson. A surveyor for Kent County, he later studied and practiced law and became active in local politics. In 1777, he served as chief justice of Delaware and remained in that office until the Constitution of 1792 reorganized the state courts. Respected by his peers of both parties, he obtained the appointment as Delaware's first chancellor, a position he held from October 1793 to December 1801 (J. Thomas Scharf, *The History of Delaware, 1609-1888*, 2 vols. [Philadelphia, 1888], 1:218, 224, 547-8; Ignatius C. Grubb, "The Colonial and State Judiciary of Delaware," *Papers of the Historical Society of Delaware*, 17 [1897], 32, 34, 51; Wilmington *Mirror of the Times & General Advertiser*, 16 Oct. 1805; Vol. 34:613).

[1] Word interlined.
[2] Word interlined.
[3] Preceding five words interlined.

Survey and Plat for Land Purchased from Benjamin Brown and Thomas Wells, Jr.

[on or after 4 Sep. 1802]

Mr. Fitch's Notes Sep. 4. 1802.

Beginning 7. C. 40. S $15.$ *po.* 60^1 above the Road at a Hickory & two Chesnuts pointers in the old Line thence

po			C	L	
18.	S 60	W—	9—		pointers in a Bottom
79.	S 50—	W—	39—	25	Chesnut Oak
10. 20	S 37½	W—	5—	5—	Chesnut tree
10.	S 43—	W—	5—		Spanish Oak
47. 20	S 60—	W—	23—	30	pointers
19.40 ⎫ 10. ⎭	S 25—	W—	9—	35	to Mr. Well's line then 5 C.² more same Course
20.	S —	—	10—		Branch then up the same
6.40	S 37—	E—	3—	10	Gum tree in the fork of the Branch. then on the s. fork
	S 16—	W—	2—	25	*= 5 po.*
	S—	—	3—	37	*= 7.48*
	S 41—	E—	4—		*6. po. to the gum at which the level line ended, then sa. co. 2. po. further.*
	S 43—	E—	4—	—	*8.*
	S 49—	E—	8—	—	*16.*
	S 61½	E—	4—	—	*8.*
	S 49—	E—	5		*10.*
	S 26½	E—	3—	40	*7.60*
	S 64½	E	5—	21	*10.84*
S. 34¼ E.	S 67—	E—	7—	5	* *14.20*
43. poles	S 56—	E—	5—	18	*10.72*
	S 64—	E—	3—	=6.	<Chesnut Oak>
po.	S 59—	E—	4—	—	*8.*
20	S. 31—	W—	10—		this Course is across the Mountain to the Branch again. *
	S 20—	E—	5—	40	to the spring = *11.60*
S. 36½ E	S 28¼	E—	3—	15	*= 6.60*
26.48 po. by	S 9—	E—	8—	35	*= 17.40*
protraction	N 81½	E	5	10	to the Old Cor. Chesnut on the
not marked				po	top of the Mountain
	N 4½	W—			

[354]

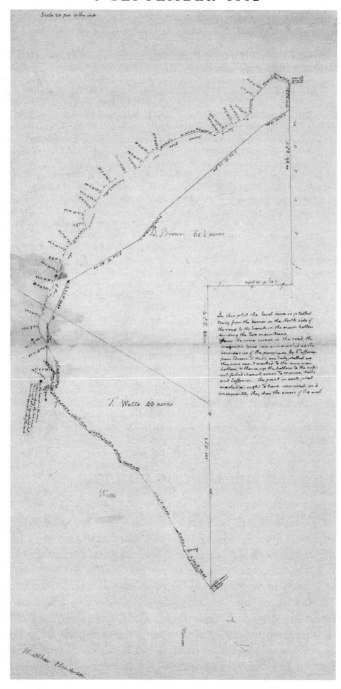

MS (ViU: Edgehill-Randolph Papers); survey notes only; in Gideon Fitz's hand, with words and numbers in italics and braces in TJ's hand. MS (CSmH); plat; undated; entirely in TJ's hand; see Nichols, *Architectural Drawings*, No. 518.

As he did for his planned purchase of land from Richard Overton, four days previous to this, TJ used Gideon Fitz's (FITCH'S) survey notes to inform the drawing of a plat for land he was in the process of buying from two of his neighbors, Benjamin Brown and Thomas Wells, Jr. (see Promissory Note to Thomas Wells, Jr., 6 Sep.; Deed for Purchase of Land from Benjamin Brown, 9 Sep.). Rather than completely copying and revising the notes, as he had done for the previous survey, TJ mainly added notations that substituted poles, his preferred unit of measurement, for Fitz's use of chains and links. The measurements, beginning with "S. 60 W 18. po.," conform to the flatter of the two lines on the plat that run from the top right, down to the left, where they intersect. The measurements continue for the line that descends rightward to the bottom of the plat, from "S 41 E 6. po." to "S. 36½ E 26.48." Fitz had apparently included in his survey notes, measurements that did not conform to TJ's preferred line, and TJ subsumed these measurements under

his own, which he denoted with braces. The note to the right of the plat reads: "In this plat the level line is platted truly from the corner on the North side of the road to the branch in the main hollow dividing the two mountains. from the same corner on the road, the magnetic lines run and marked as the boundaries of the purchase by T. Jefferson from Brown & Wells are truly platted as they were run & marked to the same main hollow, & thence up the hollow to the antient forked chesnut, corner to Monroe, Wells and Jefferson. the point in each plat marked (a) ought to have coincided, and consequently they shew the errors of the work." Beside the asterisk, he wrote, "on the branch in the main hollow dividing the two mountains, and at a remarkable hollow in the opposite side of the bank." TJ drew an additional plat of the property on which he described the other of the two parallel lines: "a line beginning at Overton's Brown's and Jefferson's corner on the North side of the public road and running level to the valley between the two mountains dividing the lands of Wells and Jefferson" (MS in CSmH; undated; entirely in TJ's hand; see Nichols, *Architectural Drawings*, No. 519).

[1] Preceding two numbers and abbreviation interlined by TJ.

[2] Above the preceding number and initial, TJ wrote "10. po."

From Gideon Granger

DEAR SIR   Suffield Septr: 5th. 1802.

Yours of the 29th. Ulto: was received by the mail yesterday. The Inclosed Letter for Mr: Gerry I have forwarded under cover to Doctor Eustis. I feel perfectly satisfied of his Integrity, and under existing circumstances I tho't the mark of confidence might not be all together useless. I have forwarded by this mail one of Mr: Bishop's pamphlets. In my tour from Washington to Philadelphia I took the back road, Through Montgomery, Fredirek York, Lancaster, &c.—I found on the road a very general circulation of federal papers. They were to be seen at most of the Public houses while on the whole rout—say 190 miles, through the best farming Country, I saw but one republican Paper. This was not alltogether pleasing to One who believes that public Opinion will in a great measure be governed by that Vehicle of Intelligence. At Philadelphia I found the federalists of the City preparing to regain the representation of the City—but the Republicans were active and confident. In passing through New Jersey as opportunities presented I inquired & in evry instance I found them active and apparently next to certain of Success—In New York I breakfasted with Col. Burr—It is his opinion that the Republicans of New Jersey will carry the Elections—Not a word passed respecting what had happened in New York. I was prepared to converse, but not to open the conversation on that Subject. Luckily I met with DeWitt Clinton & had a lengthy conversation—he avers the Substantial facts charged in the Pamphlet can be proved. he says the State is perfectly Safe. he thinks the City is so too. from him I learned that Udna Hay felt certain of success in the Vermont Election.

At New haven I spent a day with Edwards & Bishop—They do not appear to believe the Charges agt: Col. Burr but say that being once proved he will be abandoned by All. In Connecticut the Republicans are making evry exertion without expecting success. The Attorney Genl.s family is visited with Sickness & misfortune. You will soon be visited by some principal People from New York & pardon me, Sir, for the liberty I take in reccommending caution & circumspection while in their company. The visit to me appears inexplicable. I am not alone in this opinion—

Your Sincere friend

GIDN GRANGER

RC (DLC); at foot of text: "The President"; endorsed by TJ as received 12 Sep. and so recorded in SJL.

BISHOP'S PAMPHLETS: see TJ to Granger, 29 Aug. 1802.

The New York PAMPHLET was *A View of the Political Conduct of Aaron Burr, Esq. Vice-President of the United States*, attributed to James Cheetham (see note to William Irvine to TJ, 18 July, and TJ to Granger, 15 Aug. 1802).

Udny HAY, Republican candidate in Vermont's northwestern district in the race for a seat in the Eighth Congress, was defeated by Martin Chittenden. Hay won election to the Vermont General Assembly in 1802 (Randolph, Vt., *Wanderer*, 18 Sep. 1802; *Biog. Dir. Cong.*; *Journal of the General Assembly of the State of Vermont, at Their Session, Begun and Holden at Burlington, in the County of Chittenden, the Fourteenth Day of October, A.D. One Thousand Eight Hundred and Two* [Bennington, 1802], 5).

YOU WILL SOON BE VISITED: on 9 Sep. (first letter), Gallatin informed TJ that Edward Livingston had gone to Virginia, but he did not indicate that the New York district attorney planned to visit Monticello.

To Henry Dearborn

DEAR SIR   Monticello Sep. 6. 1802.

I recieved yesterday yours of the 3d. and now return the papers it covered. the treaty between New York & the Senecas I suppose is to be laid before the Senate on their meeting as well as the deed of exchange between the Senecas and the Holland land company. our approbation being the only function which belongs to us, we should go out of our line in laying the latter before the legislatures whose acts are still necessary to validate the proceeding as stated by mr Busti. this is in fact a private contract, and those interested are alone to pursue the measures necessary to effect it. we have done our part. I do not recollect that the actual erection of a fort at Black rock has been a subject of consultation among us, altho' Govr. Clinton seems to urge it as if it had been settled. I am in hopes he will take such measures with respect to the murderer as will soothe rather than irritate the Indians. we should only see that they ascribe our indulgence to friendship and not to fear. your letter to Govr. Harrison is entirely approved: and it is left to yourself altogether to make such alterations in the position of the troops as you think necessary. Accept my friendly salutations & respect.   TH: JEFFERSON

PrC (DLC); at foot of text: "The Secretary at War." Recorded in SJL as a letter to the War Department with notation "Indn. affairs."

TJ conveyed the Seneca treaties to the SENATE in a message dated 27 Dec. 1802.

LEGISLATURES WHOSE ACTS ARE STILL NECESSARY: see Enclosure No. 6 listed at Dearborn to TJ, 3 Sep.

YOUR LETTER TO GOVR. HARRISON: the first enclosure described at Dearborn's letter of 3 Sep.

To James Madison

DEAR SIR   Monticello Sep. 6. 1802.

Your's of the 3d. came to hand yesterday. I am content that the questions relative to Commissioners of bankruptcy and dockets should remain until we meet: altho' I think there are reasons of weight for not leaving the latter for Congress to do, for that would be abandoning it. the repeal of that law has been unquestionably pleasing to the people generally; and having led Congress to it, we owe to them to produce the facts which will support what they have done. it would rally the public opinion again to what is right, should that any where have been shaken by the volumes of misrepresentation which have been published, and shew we are not to be dismayed by any thing of that kind. perhaps our directions may better go to the district attornies to procure the dockets. they have a right as individuals to demand them. I believe we need ask only the *cases determined* during the year. this would be very short indeed.—I do not sufficiently recollect the particulars of the Snow Windsor to be exact on that subject. but I know that I had not a doubt as to the justice of what we concluded before, nor do I see any thing in mr Thornton's letter to create a doubt. we did our duty in ordering the vessel away. the delays which followed were such as the vigilance of no government can prevent: and the treaty at length placed her at liberty. if delays are to be paid for by a government, what have we not to demand from Great Britain? I think with you we should shew our sincerity by prosecuting for the departure of the vessel without a clearance, as far as the laws justify.—I have written to mr Smith to stop the John Adams. the war being returned to it's former state against Tripoli only, we should reduce our force to what had been concluded on as to that power, as soon as we learn the state of things with Tunis. in the mean time the New York will go on.—mr Steele's labours to shew he is agreeable to the Govr. shew pretty clearly the reverse, independent of the Governor's own evidence. Accept my affectionate esteem & respect.

Th: Jefferson

RC (DLC: Madison Papers); at foot of text: "The Secretary of State." PrC (DLC). Recorded in SJL as a letter to the State Department with notation "dockets. Commns. bkrptcy. Windsor. Barbary."

THAT LAW: the Judiciary Act of 1801. For Edward THORNTON'S LETTER to Madison, see Madison to TJ, 3 Sep.

WRITTEN TO MR SMITH: TJ to Robert Smith, 6 Sep.

THE GOVR.: William C. C. Claiborne.

Promissory Note to Thomas Wells, Jr.

6 Sep. 1802

I promise to pay to Thomas Wells junr. or order forty pounds current money of Virginia on or before the 1st. day of the ensuing month of October. Witness my hand this 6th. day of September 1802.

Th: Jefferson

MS (ViU: Edgehill-Randolph Papers); entirely in TJ's hand; endorsed by John Barnes: "Thomas Wells Junr 19 Oct. 1802 $133.33."

Thomas Wells, Jr., resided in Albe-

marle County and was an officer in the county militia. In September 1802, TJ purchased from Wells and others several small parcels of land adjoining Monticello, consisting of a $61\frac{1}{4}$-acre tract from Benjamin Brown on 9 Sep. for £85.15

Virginia currency ($285.83), a 40-acre tract from Wells on 15 Sep. for £40 Virginia currency ($133.33), and two tracts totaling 25¼ acres from Richard Overton for $346.67 (Woods, *Albemarle*, 372; Albemarle County District Court Deed Book No. 1:165-7; Albemarle County Deed Book No. 14:16-17; MB, 2:1082-3, 1090; TJ to Craven Peyton, 2 Nov. 1802).

A series of endorsements on the verso indicate that the above note to Wells passed through several hands before being presented for payment. On 5 Oct., the note was successively assigned to Frederick Harris, John T. Hawkins, and Opie Norris. The final assignment was made by Norris to P. Hoffman. On the recto, below TJ's signature, Georgetown merchant Elisha Riggs signed acknowledging receipt of $133.33 for Wells on 19 Oct. (RCHS, 33-34 [1932], 149-50; 44-45 [1942-43], 134-5).

To Robert Smith

DEAR SIR   Monticello Sep. 6. 1802.

We have now authentic information from mr Simpson that the Governor of Tangiers has by letter informed him of the Emperor of Marocco's permission to him to return for six months. this is a clear enough expression of his object, which is presents, and peace. on these we have time to consider. but this change in the state of things renders it proper that we should change our purpose of sending out the John Adams. the war being returned to it's former state, with Tripoli only, we should return to our former plan & force there. the approach of winter too renders it really dangerous to have so many frigates in the Mediterranean. you know our conclusion, confirmed by the opinion of Dale was to leave two frigates only in that sea. however until we hear further as to Tunis, I propose no new orders except as to the John Adams. the New York of course is gone or going. it would not do to offer the gun carriages at present and until a firm peace be reestablished by new negociations. it will depend on these whether those carriages will now be desired by the emperor: and probably by that time other opportunities of sending them, if necessary, will occur.[1] I suppose therefore we need not change our last determination of not sending them. this I submit to your consideration. Accept my affectionate salutations and esteem.

TH: JEFFERSON

RC (ViU: Coolidge Deposit); closing text and signature clipped (see note 1); at foot of text: "The Secretary of the Navy." PrC (DLC). Recorded in SJL as a letter to the Navy Department with notation "Barbary."

AUTHENTIC INFORMATION FROM MR SIMPSON: see TJ to James Madison, 30 Aug. 1802.

[1] Remaining text and signature supplied from PrC.

From John Barnes

SIR   George Town 7th Sept 1802

Your much esteemed favr. 3d. recd Yesterday was very Acceptable—not hearing from Mr Short since the 24th. ulto. and having recd five several letters to his address. via Boston, N York, & Richmond I must presume they will very soon reach him at Monticello, to which place, I shall address them (if not Otherwise directed) by next friday's Mail. I have also two letters for Mr Peyton Short, but where to address them, I know not.

I have paid Mr LeMaire $141. Mos. Wages a/c to the 4th Inst. as well Mr Dougherty—32.50 for Oats, straw, Chariot & Horses a/c—the Carriage tax Collector, called on me, respecting yrs—I requested him to leave it untill your return, as I knew not, what they consisted of.[1]

On the 13th. I expect to obtain a Wart. for $2,500 to close the half years Compensation, and therewith take up your Bank engagemts. (I had flattered myself for the last time)—but unforeseen events, must be guarded against, and provided for. Still I hope some favorable event, may yet intervene to forego that Alternative but whatever you may judge needfull shall on my part be Attended too—permiting me, to ward off, the *evil day*, to the extent of my feeble resources.—

I am Sir, most Respectfully, your very Obedt: Hble Servt.

JOHN BARNES

RC (ViU: Edgehill-Randolph Papers); at foot of text: "The President UStates at Monticello"; endorsed by TJ as received 9 Sep. and so recorded in SJL.

YOUR MUCH ESTEEMED FAVR. 3D.: TJ's letter to Barnes of 3 Sep. 1802 is recorded in SJL but has not been found.

[1] MS: "off."

From Daniel Brent

Dep: of State Sepr 7th 1802.

Daniel Brent respectfully informs the President that the Secy of War has intimated, a Commission for Joseph Story, as a Commr of Bankruptcy in Massachusetts, is wanted—A Blank Commission for the President & Secy of State's signatures is accordingly herewith sent.   Danl Brent begs leave further to signify to the President, that a Parcel of Blank Commissions of the same kind were forwarded to him from this office some time ago for his signature, and that they are not yet returned.

RC (DLC); endorsed by TJ as received from the State Department on 9 Sep. and "blank commns. bkrptcy" and so recorded in SJL; also endorsed by TJ: "Commn. for Storer." Enclosure not found.

COMMISSION FOR JOSEPH STORY: on his list of appointments, TJ entered Story's designation as bankruptcy commissioner at 10 Sep. (see Appendix 1). For the Secretary of War's efforts to have Joseph Story appointed in place of Isaac Story, see Dearborn to TJ, 31 July and 10 Aug. 1802. According to SJL, on 31 Aug. TJ wrote Dearborn regarding "Storer's commn bkrptcy," but the letter has not been found.

From David Brown

SIR,   Philadelphia, September 7, 1802

From the encouragement that literature has invariably received from you, I am encouraged to solicit the honor of your name to the inclosed Proposals—not doubting, but what a people daily increasing in learning (if given) will follow the example,—as being made by the Guardian of their country.

I have the honor to be, Sir, your excellency's most obedient, and most humble servant,   DAVID BROWN.

RC (MHi); at foot of text: "To the hon. T. Jefferson President of U.S. Sept. 7, 1802"; endorsed by TJ as received 16 Sep. and so recorded in SJL. Enclosures not found, but see below.

The author of the above letter may have been the same David Brown of Philadelphia who, in June 1802, began advertising a proposal to publish by subscription a five-volume set of John Wesley's *A Compendium of Natural Philosophy*. The printer pledged to publish a volume every three months at a cost of $1.40 per volume, with a list of subscribers to appear in the final volume. Work would commence once the project met with "sufficient encouragement" (Savannah *Georgia Gazette*, 24 June 1802; Newark, N.J., *Centinel of Freedom*, 14 Sep. 1802).

From George Read, Jr.

                               State of Delaware
SIR   New Castle September 7. 1802

The application of Mr. Bird, for the collector's office in this District, in case of a Vacancy in that office, being made known to me, and he, expressing a wish that his character should be duly appreciated by correct information being conveyed to you on the occasion—I beg leave to recommend Mr. Bird to your notice as a Gentleman of unexceptionable private character, well versed in Mercantile affairs and an accurate accountant—He is at present a member of the Senate of the State of Delaware for New Castle County—a democratic republican in principle, he is decided & unequivocal in the expression of his approbation of the measures of the present administration.

From my knowledge of Mr. Bird's attention talents and integrity, I believe him to be perfectly qualified to discharge all the duties attached to the office of collector of this District; and I have no doubt but that his appointment to fill the office would receive the sanction of public opinion:—I hope, Sir, Mr. Bird's reference to me for information, will be a sufficient apology for thus frankly mentioning my sentiments on this subject.

I have the honor to be Sir with great respect Your most Obedient Servant   G. READ

RC (DNA: RG 59, LAR); at foot of text: "The President of the United States"; endorsed by TJ as received 16 Sep. and so recorded in SJL; also endorsed by TJ: "John Bird to be Collector Wilmington."

APPLICATION OF MR. BIRD: see John Bird to TJ, 4 Aug. A letter from Bird to TJ of 8 Sep., recorded in SJL as received from New Castle on the 16th, has not been found.

To Jacob Bouldin

SIR   Monticello Sep. 8. 1802.

I have duly recieved your favor of Aug. 27. and given to the paper inclosed and now returned such a cursory perusal as my scanty time would permit: but so incessant are the calls for my attention to objects more immediately within the line of my official duties that I am forced to deny myself the satisfaction of looking into matters of literature & science, altho' they would be much more agreeable to me, and of course of giving any opinion on things which I cannot take time to understand. the law, by opening a patent office, seems to have contemplated that as the most expedient means of encouraging useful inventions. wishing you in your researches every success which can be beneficial to yourself & useful to the public, I pray you to accept my salutations & respects.   TH: JEFFERSON

PrC (MHi); at foot of text: "Mr. Jacob Bouldin. Baltimore"; endorsed by TJ in ink on verso. Recorded in SJL as a letter of 9 Sep.

From Henry Dearborn

SIR,   War Department September 8. 1802

I herewith enclose a letter from Mr. Livingston, Mayor of the City of New York, an extract from which has been transmitted to the Secretary of State, conceiving that the subject generally came more immediately under the direction of his Department—I have doubts whether we can with propriety interfere any farther in guarding those people than affording protection to the Hospital and I am not certain that any other Guard is contemplated by Mr. Livingston, but from an expression in his letter he indicates that he wishes a guard posted in such a manner as to prevent desertions from the Ships—I conceive that some arrangments between the Commanding Officer of the Shipping, Mr. Pichon and the Secretary of State should precede any act of this Department relative to Guards, and as the Secretary of State has been applied to on the subject, I have thought proper to decline any definite answer to Mr. Livingston, until I received your directions—

I have the honor to be with esteem your Hume. Servt.

H. DEARBORN

RC (DLC); in a clerk's hand, signed by Dearborn; at foot of text: "The President of the United States"; endorsed by TJ as received from the War Department on 12 Sep. and "French squadron at N.Y." and so recorded in SJL. FC (Lb in DNA: RG 107, LSP). Enclosure: Edward Livingston to Dearborn, 1 Sep., stating that the French ships holding between 1,100 and 1,200 "black prisoners" are at the "quarantine ground," where the sick and wounded have been received into the state hospital; the hospital cannot accept those patients "without totally abandoning the principal object of the institution, which was to provide for the numerous emigrants on board of private ships at this season daily arriving"; Livingston believes that either "the General Government" or Louis André Pichon should arrange for the accommodation of the people from the French ships, "the more particularly as their stay is indefinite, and the season will augment the number of the sick"; as the president has the power to use U.S. troops to enforce quarantine laws, "and as numbers of these blacks are daily escaping from the hospital and the Ships," Livingston asks that "a proper

guard" be dispatched from the garrison at New York "to prevent their taking refuge in our Country" (in Daniel Brent to Madison, 7 Sep., in Madison, *Papers, Sec. of State Ser.*, 3:556).

SECRETARY OF STATE HAS BEEN APPLIED TO: Dearborn did not write to Madison directly. A letter from Daniel Brent on 7 Sep. informed Madison of Livingston's requests. "Mr Pichon intends," Brent wrote, "if he can effect it, to send the Ships and Negroes to France" (same, 3:555-6).

THOUGHT PROPER TO DECLINE: Brent was apparently mistaken when he informed Madison on 7 Sep. that Dearborn had issued an order for guards from the garrison at New York City. Acknowledging Livingston's letter on the 8th, Dearborn told the mayor that he was passing his concerns along to the secretary of state and the president, and that if TJ should decide "in favor of a guard conformably to your request, the necessary orders will be immediately given" (in DNA: RG 107, MLS; Madison, *Papers, Sec. of State Ser.*, 3:556).

To Albert Gallatin

DEAR SIR   Monticello Sep. 8. 1802.

I have recieved from Delaware another application on the subject of the piers &c to be erected in their river. it is on behalf of Wilmington which prays to have it's claim for these things taken into consideration with others, and for this purpose that the corporation be authorised to have a report made of their harbour, creek &c. the style of the corporation is 'the Burgesses & assistants of the borough of Wilmington.' I suppose it proper to hear all claims on this subject and adopt what is best. the date of the letter to me is of Aug. 25. and as you have passed through Wilmington since, possibly you may have recieved the same application, and taken order in it.

On recieving authentic information that the Emperor of Marocco had recalled our Consul, and allowed 6. months for explanation, I have countermanded the sailing of the John Adams. information from Tunis gives us to believe that that power was in perfect good dispositions towards us. we hear nothing authentic of the affair of the Boston, but hope if true, it will not occasion a breach. Tunis is solliciting a peace for Tripoli, by authority from it's Bey: so that I trust all will be smoothed in that quarter. a little money must be given to Marocco. Accept my friendly salutations & respect.

TH: JEFFERSON

RC (NHi: Gallatin Papers); addressed: "Albert Gallatin Secretary of the Treasury Washington"; franked; postmarked Milton, 10 Sep.; endorsed. PrC (DLC). Recorded in SJL as a letter to the Treasury Department of 9 Sep. with notation "Wilmington piers. Barbary."

ANOTHER APPLICATION: see Caesar A. Rodney to TJ, 25 Aug. 1802.

AUTHENTIC INFORMATION: see TJ to Madison, 30 Aug. 1802.

From Hammuda Pasha, Bey of Tunis

MONSIEUR LE PRÉSIDENT   A Tunis Le 8e: Septembre 1802.

J'ai vu arriver et j'ai reçu successivement avec beaucoup de plaisir et avec une égale satisfaction tous les Articles de Munitions de guerre et Navales ainsi que les superbes bijouts, que votre gouvernement m'a fait passer pour ma Regence et pour Moi, en exécution de nos Capitulations pour L'affermissement et la consolidation de la bonne harmonie et L'Alliance qui Dieu merci ont été établies et subsistent actuellement entre Nous.

Tandis que je me plais à vous donner cette assurance bien sincere de mon plein contentement, Je ne dois pas Vous dissimuler que je ne me vois pas cependant traité avec la même distinction et avec les mêmes égards que Vous avez eu pour vos autres Amis, et puisque J'en suis egalement un, Je vous avoue avec franchise, comme Je L'ai declaré à Mr. Eaton votre Consul, qu'il m'aurait été infiniment agréable que Vous m'eussiez aussi fait don d'un Batiment de guerre

Mr. Eaton n'ayant pas trouvé convenable de se charger de vous faire lui même cette demande de ma part, Je me suis decidé à Vous temoigner directement par la presente, qu'il me serait très agréable que Vous m'envoyassiez une bonne Fregate de trente six pieces de Cannon, ce qui ajouterait à la haute estime que J'ai pour votre Nation et cimenterait de plus en plus les Liens de notre Amitié, que de mon Coté Je conserverai permanente et imperturbable

Convaincu d'avance comme Je le suis, Monsieur le President, que cette demande prise en considération obtiendra le plein effet que J'en attends, Je Vous renouvelle L'assurance de mon estime la plus distinguée, et Je prie Dieu tout puissant de Vous avoir in sa sainte garde

HAMUDA PACHA BEY
Prince des Princes de Tunis
La Ville la bien gardée, le
Sejour du Bonheur

EDITORS' TRANSLATION

MISTER PRESIDENT   Tunis 8 Sep. 1802
I have seen arrive and then received with much pleasure and equal satisfaction all the military and naval stores as well as the superb jewels that your government has sent for my regency and for me, following up on our agreements to strengthen and consolidate the harmony and alliance which, thank God, have been established and continue between us.

While I am pleased to give you this very sincere assurance of my full contentment, I must not hide from you that I nevertheless do not see myself treated with the same distinction and respect as your other friends. Since I too am a friend, I must frankly admit, as I told your consul, Mr. Eaton, that I would have been infinitely pleased if you had also given me a warship.

Since Mr. Eaton did not judge fitting to communicate this request, I have resolved to express directly through this letter that I would be pleased if you could send me a good 36-gun frigate. This would add to the high esteem I have for your nation and strengthen ever more the ties of our friendship which, on my side, I will preserve as firm and inviolable.

Convinced in advance, Mister President, that this request will be taken into consideration and obtain the desired effect, I renew the assurance of my most distinguished esteem and pray that almighty God may have you in his holy keeping.

HAMMUDA PASHA, BEY
Prince of Princes of Tunis,
the City Well Guarded,
the Abode of Happiness

RC (DNA: RG 59, CD, Tunis); in a clerk's hand, with Hammuda's seal; at head of text: "Le Pacha Bey de Tunis au President de la Republique des Etats Unis d'Amérique." Dupl (same); in William Eaton's hand; in code; at head of text: "Duplicate copy by translation"; with an addition by Eaton, 9 Oct., in code, advising that a surprise attack by 800 men during the winter or spring could destroy Tunis's naval arsenal and larger warships (Madison, *Papers, Sec. of State Ser.*, 4:8n); postscript to that note, in clear text: "It must sooner or later come to this, except something more impressive be done in the east"; endorsed by Jacob Wagner: "Recd. in W. Eaton's 9 Oct. 1802." Tripl (same); in Eaton's hand; in code; at head of text: "Triplicate copy by translation"; with same addition in code and postscript in clear text; endorsed. Tr (DNA: RG 59, CD, Tripoli); in Eaton's hand; in French; at head of text: "Copie litteralle"; lacks the phrase "et avec une égale satisfaction" in the opening sentence; endorsed by Eaton: "Copy"; endorsed by James L. Cathcart: "Recd. by me at Leghorn Septr. 30th. 1802—Cathcart"; endorsed by Wagner; enclosed in Cathcart to Madison, 8 Oct. (Madison, *Papers, Sec. of State Ser.*, 4:3-4). Tr (CSmH); in Wagner's hand and with his signed attestation; in French; at head of text: "Copy." Tr (same); in Eaton's hand; in English; at head of text: "Translation"; endorsed. Recorded in SJL as received 21 Mch. 1803.

ARTICLES DE MUNITIONS DE GUERRE ET NAVALES AINSI QUE LES SUPERBES BIJOUTS: the United States had sent Hammuda personal items mounted with diamonds and a supply of naval stores, cannons, and lumber (Vol. 36:667-8n). MR. EATON N'AYANT PAS TROUVÉ CONVENABLE: the bey wanted William Eaton to make the request for a warship, but the consul, believing that Hammuda and his ministers would hold him responsible for the satisfaction of any demands they made through him, refused. Should he agree to make the request, Eaton explained to Madison, the Tunisians would "raise an assumpsit on this compliance." When the bey, having determined to write directly to the United States government, expected the consul to draft "*a form* of the letter," Eaton again refused. The Tunisians, he reported, insisted that "the Prince of America" must bestow a frigate on Hammuda as an "expression of *friendship*" comparable to tokens of good will from the United States to Algiers. The demand for the ship, however, was in Eaton's opinion simply "a pretext" for breaking the peace between Tunis and the United States: Hammuda had a "penetrating and subtile" mind, Eaton wrote to Madison, and was not "stupid enough" to think that the United States would yield to his demand for a 36-gun warship. Yusuf Sahib-at-Taba, attempting to point out the possible consequences of Eaton's "neglect of duty," acknowledged that there could be a "rupture" between the two countries. The prime minister, whose demeanor the consul described as "irritated," signaled that his government's patience was growing thin and that its "forbearance" toward the United States might end. Yusuf Sahib-at-Taba told Eaton that Tunis wanted to communicate with the U.S. government "in the English language that we may be understood," but in the end, the bey's letter, produced without Eaton's assistance, was in French (Eaton to Madison, 12 Sep., in DNA: RG 59, CD; Madison, *Papers, Sec. of State Ser.*, 3:574-8).

LES LIENS DE NOTRE AMITIÉ: Eaton did agree to provide a conveyance for the bey's letter. Earlier he had used an armed ship that he owned, the *Gloria*, for what he considered to be official business in the

Mediterranean, until Captain Alexander Murray put an end to the practice as a "needless expence." Anticipating that the bey's advisers would expect him to dispatch the *Gloria* to the United States with the letter, Eaton rid himself of the ship, sending it to Leghorn to be sold. He did, however, give the document to the *Gloria*'s captain, Joseph Bounds of Baltimore. After making arrangements for the disposal of the ship, Bounds was to avail himself of "the first safe passage" to the United States and deliver Hammuda's letter in Washington—"for which you will receive compensation from the Government," Eaton promised. Bounds left Tunis with the letter on 14 Sep. Eaton sent the coded duplicate and triplicate of the bey's letter to the U.S. in October. In a dispatch to Madison dated 22 Oct., the consul repeated his suggestion, which he had included with the coded versions of Hammuda's letter, that the United States make a preemptive attack on the Tunisian navy (Madison, *Papers, Sec. of State Ser.,* 3:98, 99n, 577; 4:6, 51; NDBW, 2:145, 240, 273, 304).

To George Jefferson

DEAR SIR   Monticello Sep. 8. 1802.

You some time ago wrote me word you could get 5. Dollars cash[1] for my last year's crop, of which I sent you the weights. I now inclose you the manifest to be sold if that price can be [met?].

I shall have occasion to draw on you in favor of our sheriffs for about 600. Dollars payable about the last days of this month, that they may be entitled to the allowance from the treasury. if my tobo. [is?] sold, it will of course [put you in cash]. if not, I must remit it from Washington, which cannot be till the 6th. of October. in case of the tobo. not being sold could you advance the [600.] D. for the [space] of 6. or 8. days? it will be a [singular accommodation?] to me, and I will ask the favor of an immediate answer that my mind may be at ease. Accept my affectionate salutations & esteem.

TH: JEFFERSON

PrC (MHi); faint; at foot of text: "Mr. George Jefferson"; endorsed by TJ in ink on verso. Recorded in SJL as a letter of 9 Sep. Enclosure not found.

In a letter of 16 June 1802, George Jefferson had informed TJ that he should expect no better than $5 CASH per 100 pounds of his 1801 crop of tobacco, the WEIGHTS of which TJ had sent on 12 June.

TJ recorded several tax payments to Virginia SHERIFFS on 16 and 25 Sep. and enumerated these and other transactions in a subsequent letter (MB, 2:1080-1; TJ to George Jefferson, 5 Oct. 1802).

[1] Word interlined.

From George Jefferson

DEAR SIR   Richmond 8th. Septr. 1802

Having been requested by Mr. D. Carr to procure copies of some papers for you out of the office of the High Court of Chancery, I made immediate application for them, but was informed that they could not possibly be had sooner than tomorrow night. I directed them to be made out, and will look out for some private opportunity by which to send them; as, from Mr. C's letter, I suppose that next post might probably be too late—should I however not sooner meet with an opportunity, they shall be then forwarded: as I imagine it is uncertain on what day of the Court the suit will come on. The Settees from Phila., & a Case & two small boxes from Geo. Town,[1] have arrived, & shall be forwarded by the first safe opportunity.

I am Dear Sir Your Very humble servt.   GEO. JEFFERSON

RC (MHi); at foot of text: "Thos. Jefferson esqr."; endorsed by TJ as received 11 Sep. and so recorded in SJL.

Dabney CARR was one of the attorneys hired by TJ to prosecute a suit over his Pouncey's tract land. In 1804, the Superior Court of CHANCERY in Richmond ruled in TJ's favor (MB, 2:1003, 1106; Vol. 32:419n).

TJ had previously ordered through Thomas Claxton six SETTEES made in Philadelphia (Vol. 35:152-3, 204-5).

[1] Preceding two words, abbreviation, and comma interlined.

From Josiah Smith

DEAR SIR   Pembroke the 8th of September 1802

I Received a Few days Since from the Boston Post office a Letter from you Dated the fourteenth of August with Surprise I Learnt therefrom you had Received a Letter from me dated the 19th of July Last Pased Respecting Commissioners of Bankruptcy[1] you May Rest assured I never wrote the Letter you mentioned & that the writer of Said Letter was Unathorized by me & is Unknown to me & I Supose it was Intended as an Imposition upon you or me or Perhaps upon Both   I have a wish the Said Letter may be Preserved that I may See the Contents & hand writing if I Should have health to arrive at the Seat of Government in Decbr. next I am Dear Sir with Esteem & affection your Friend

& Humble Servt.   JOSIAH SMITH

PS I Shall in a Few days write a duplicate Least this Should Miscarry & to Prevent Impositions   JS

RC (MoSHi: Jefferson Papers); endorsed by TJ as received 23 Sep. and so
recorded in SJL.

[1] Smith here canceled "Dear Sir."

From Carlos IV, King of Spain

Igualada, Spain, 9 Sep. 1802. Having received the news that the
betrothal of his son Fernando, the prince of Asturias, and Maria Antonietta of the Two Sicilies was celebrated at Naples on 25 Aug., and
knowing from experience how much interest the United States takes
in the affairs of his family, he is confident that the United States will
share his satisfaction on this pleasing occasion.

RC (DNA: RG 59, Ceremonial Let-
ters); 1 p.; in Spanish, in a clerk's hand,
signed by Carlos and countersigned by
Pedro Cevallos; addressed: "A mis
grandes y buenos amigos los Estados
Unidos de America"; sealed; endorsed for
the State Department as received 28 Jan.
1803.

TJ answered this communication in a
brief, formal letter dated 29 Jan. 1803.
Acknowledging the receipt of the king's
news "with the greatest satisfaction," TJ
stated: "As the United States cherish a
sincere and cordial friendship for your
Majesty, an event like the present, which
adds so much to your happinesss, has not
failed to inspire us with sentiments corresponding with the occasion. Accept our
congratulations and our wishes, that
your Majesty may be blessed in the
virtues of your Royal family and the prosperity of the Nation under your charge."
TJ's letter to Carlos of 29 Jan. was similar
in structure and presentation to the one of
15 Oct. printed in this volume (FC in Lb
in DNA: RG 59, Credences; in a clerk's
hand; not recorded in SJL).

Deed for Land Purchased from
Benjamin Brown

This Indenture made on the 9th day of September One thousand
Eight Hundred and two Between Benjamin Brown of the one part
and Thomas Jefferson, of the other part, both of the County of Albemarle Witnessith, that the said Benjamin, In consideration of the
sum of[1] Eighty five pounds fifteen Shillings Virginia Currency to
him paid by the said Thomas hath Given, granted, bargained and
sold unto the said Thomas a certain parcel of Land in the County of
Albemarle aforesaid on the Mountain called the High Mountain
containing by Estimation Sixty one and one quarter acres, more or
less, Contained within the following Bounds to Wit, Begining at a
Hickory and two Chesnuts now marked as pointers in the former dividing line Between the said Benjamin and Thomas seven Chains &

Forty Links from where they cornered with Richard Overton on the public road, And runing thence S. 60° W. 9 Chains to pointers near-ly in a bottom, S. 50° W. 39½ Chains to a Chesnut Oak. S. 37½° W. 5 ch. 5 links to a Chesnut, S. 43° W. 5 chains to a Spanish Oak S. 60° W. 23 ch. 30 Links to pointers S. 25° W. 9 chains 35 Links to the dividing line Between the Sd. Benjamin and Thomas Wells, Thence up the mountain along the sd: dividing line to where it cor-nered in a side line of the said Thomas Jefferson, thence along the dividing lines Between the Sd. Benjamin and Thomas Jefferson to the Begining. Together with the Appurtenances: And also that the said Benjamin in consideration of the further sum of Ten pounds Virginia Currency to him paid by the said Thomas And to the end that the said Thomas and his Heirs and Assigns Owners of his Lands at and adjacent to the seat called Monticello may forever have a free way and out Let from the said Lands Westwardly, even if the public road now passing from the Thorough fare Between Monti-cello and the High Mountain towards Charlottesville, And forming with Moores Creek the Northern Boundary of the Lands of the said Benjamin should ever be discontinued by Public Authority, Hath Given Granted, bargained, and sold to the said Thomas, a margin of Land of One pole and a half in Breadth along the said boundary of the said Benjamin from the point where the sd. Benjamin & Thomas corner with Richard Overton on the public road aforesaid to Where the said road enters or may enter into the road from Charlottesville across Moor's Creek going Southwestwardly along the upper side of the mountain towards Hardware: To have and to hold the said Mar-gin of Land, And to use the same without stoppage or Hindrance, Whensoever the said public road may be suppressed to him the sd. Thomas Jefferson his Heirs and Assigns owners of his Land as aforesaid. And the said Benjamin his Heirs, Executors, And Admrs the said parcel of Lands first above conveyed, And also the sd. sec-ond parcel or Margin lastly conveyed, to the sd. Thomas and his Heirs will forever warrant and Defend. In Witness Whereof the said Benjamin hath hereto put his hand & seal on the day and year above mentioned.   BENJN. BROWN

Signed sealed, and Delivered in ⎱
presence of   ⎰
TIPTON LEWIS
JOHN T. HAWKINS
THOMAS WELLS JUNR.
THOMAS C. FLETCHER

At a Superior Court directed by Law to be holden in Charlottesville for the District composed of the Counties of Albemarle, Louisa, Fluvanna and Amherst the 15th day of September 1802. The above Indenture was produced into Court, and acknowledged by Benjamin Brown party thereto and ordered to be recorded.TESTE

JOHN CARR CDCC

Tr (Albemarle County District Court Deed Book No. 1:166-7); entirely in a clerk's hand.

Benjamin Brown (d. 1851) was a lawyer who owned Mooresbrook, a plantation on and along Montalto. He later also represented the Mutual Assurance Society, from whom TJ purchased insurance (Woods, *Albemarle*, 154; Merrow Egerton Sorley, *Lewis of Warner Hall: The History of a Family* [Baltimore, 1979], 674; RS, 1:320).

For TJ's consolidation of the land bordering Monticello on HIGH MOUNTAIN, or Montalto, see also Promissory Note to Thomas Wells, Jr., 6 Sep., and the indenture of Wells on 15 Sep. TJ had likely been contemplating the purchase of Brown's land since at least March 1802. A letter from TJ to Brown, recorded in SJL as sent 7 Mch., has not been found, nor has a response of 11 Mch. from Brown, recorded in SJL as received 17 Mch. At an unknown time, TJ copied a plat of Brown's 372 acre property, which Brown had commissioned along with William Champe Carter (MS in CSmH; entirely in TJ's hand; copy of survey by Hardin Davis, 18 July 1801; see Nichols, *Architectural Drawings*, No. 514).

TJ entered this deed into the DISTRICT court for Albemarle, Louisa, Amherst, and Fluvanna Counties, rather than the Albemarle County Court, which generally handled this kind of business. The district courts had been created in 1788 to alleviate the delays that hindered prosecution of criminal cases in the Virginia county courts (William Waller Hening, *The Statutes at Large; Being a Collection of All the Laws of Virginia*, 13 vols. [Richmond, 1809-23], 12:532-3).

[1] "Five" canceled here.

From Albert Gallatin

DEAR SIR   New York 9th Septer. 1802

I have been here four days, and have felt the effects of my late stay in Washington: I am now recovered, but lament that the situation of that place should be an impediment to that constant superintendence, which is so essentially necessary in the Treasury department. On the 20th instt., I intend leaving this place with my family, and expect to be at the seat of Government before the end of the month.

In my own department, I have nothing of any importance to communicate. The commissions to Cross & to Wilson for Newburyport & Marblehead have been forwarded. Mr Brent of the Dept. of State has been instructed to forward that to John Shore for Petersburgh. That for Gibault vice Tuck for Gloucester I have enclosed in a private letter to Capt. Crowninshield with a request that he should make positive enquiries as to the propriety of the appointment & removal, &

the certainty of Gibault accepting, & in case of any impediment, that he should return the new commission to me to be cancelled, & keep the matter, in that case, in silence. I have yet no information for Oswego & Brunswick (Georgia), & wait for your instructions in relation to Yorktown (Virginia)—When I transmitted the recommendation for Wentworth as surveyor of Portsmouth (New Hampshire), I also sent letters from Messrs. Whipple & Langdon making recommendations for Master & Mate of the revenue cutter there. The cutter is ready, and the commissions, which are ready signed & in my possession, should be transmitted. Will you be pleased to signify your approbation, & to send me the names & christian names of the two persons recommended, as I have preserved no copy?

I was sorry to find that you had approved the sending of another frigate (the John Adams), as I did not believe that it was necessary, & the appropriations for that object were exhausted. In recommending the sending the New York, I went as far as those appropriations would permit, and did not know that application had been made to you for another, until after it was done & the mail closed.

Edward Livingston has not yet rendered his account of bonds put in suit & is gone to Virginia. I continue very uneasy to that account.

I wrote to Colo. Lee the new collector of Salem who had recommended Wilson as successor of Gerry & whose name (Wilson's) appears to the petition in favor of Gerry, that his removal was indispensible. The petition is returned.

I enclose a letter from Colo. Hay of Vermont, but have informed his friends here that the French would not admit any Consul in their West Indian Colonies.

I am with great respect & attachment Your obedt. Servt.

ALBERT GALLATIN

RC (DLC); addressed: "Thomas Jefferson President of the United States"; endorsed by TJ as received from the Treasury Department on 16 Sep. and so recorded in SJL with notation "various"; also endorsed by TJ: "the several commns. master & mate of revenue cutter Portsmth. the John Adams Edwd. Livingston Udney Hay." Enclosure: Udny Hay to Albert Gallatin, Underhill, Vermont, 17 Aug. 1802, recommending his nephew Alexander Hay as U.S. consul at Martinique, where he has lived for about three years and wishes to remain; his nephew, educated in Great Britain, came to the United States in 1792; he speaks French and is "active, diligent and accurate in business"; his appointment would support Gallatin's wish to "patronise merit" and also promote the public good (RC in DNA: RG 59, LAR; endorsed by TJ: "Hay Udney to mr Gallatin. Alex. Hay to be Consul Martinqe").

See Enclosures No. 5 and 6 listed at Gallatin to TJ, 17 Aug., for the recommendations of Hopley Yeaton as MASTER and Benjamin Gunnison as MATE OF THE REVENUE CUTTER at Portsmouth, New Hampshire.

APPROPRIATIONS FOR THAT OBJECT WERE EXHAUSTED: in the 1803 appropriation for the navy, almost $200,000 was allocated to cover the deficiencies of 1802, including the pay, provisions, and other expenditures for the Mediterranean squadron (Gallatin to TJ, 18 Jan. 1803).

PETITION IS RETURNED: see TJ to Gallatin, 30 Aug.

HIS FRIENDS HERE: Udny Hay wrote that he was also contacting Governor George Clinton on his nephew's behalf (see enclosure described above).

From Albert Gallatin

DEAR SIR   New York Septem. 9th 1802

Since I closed my letter of this day, Mr Madison has enclosed to me the within recommendation for the office of collector of York town Virginia.

With sincere respect Your obedt. & affecte. Servt.

ALBERT GALLATIN

RC (DLC); at foot of text: "Thomas Jefferson President U.S."; endorsed by TJ as received from the Treasury Department on 16 Sep. and "Cary to be Collector York vice Reynolds" and so recorded in SJL. Enclosure: Samuel Sheild to James Madison, York County, Virginia, 25 Aug. 1802, recommending William Carey as collector at Yorktown, who fortunately will accept the office; being one of the oldest inhabitants of the town, Carey is "quite easy in his Circumstances, of strict Integrity," and punctual in the discharge of all business he undertakes; although "Antirepublicanism" is still prevalent in York County, Carey is a moderate who uniformly voted for Sheild as a candidate for the Virginia Assembly "even in the most trying Times" (RC in same).

William Carey received the appointment of COLLECTOR at Yorktown, but he immediately resigned (Madison, *Papers, Sec. of State Ser.*, 3:518; Gallatin to TJ, 5 Oct. 1802).

From James Madison

DEAR SIR   [on or before 9 Sep. 1802]

Yours of the 6th. instant was duly brought by the last mail.

I inclose under cover to Mr. Brent, the answers to the Merchts. of Boston & Philada; which if approved you will be so good as to seal & send on to him. I inclose also a letter from Mr. Brent to me, for the sake of the explanation it gives relative to the consulate at Nante. If Mr. Grant should not go, it is to be recollected that the vacancy there has been thought of for Mr. Patterson whose appointment to l'Orient interferes with the situation of Mr. Vail.

Docr. Thornton & his family are with us; and I believe mean to pay their respects to Monticello before their return. We shall ride up at the same time, if my absence from home should not be forbidden by circumstances which I am endeavoring to deprive of that tendency. With respectful attachment I remain Yours

JAMES MADISON

RC (DLC); undated; at foot of text: "The President of the U. States"; endorsed by TJ as a letter from the State Department received from Orange on 9 Sep. and "merchts. Boston & Phila—Consulate Nantes—Sumpter," and so recorded in SJL; also endorsed by TJ: "Dr. Thornton." Enclosures: (1) Madison to Stephen Higginson, Sr., and other members of the committee of merchants of Boston, 6 Sep., noting that the president "feels every disposition to patronize the commercial rights of his fellow Citizens" but "sees very strong objections" to the suggestion that the United States should send a ship to make demands of Spanish colonial authorities, especially without more information about "the sanctions under which" the trading voyages to South America were made; regarding the other suggested course of action, representation to the Spanish government at Madrid, Madison states that Charles Pinckney already has instructions to bring claims before a board of commissioners; Madison advises the merchants with grievances to send "a particular statement to Mr. Pinckney of their respective cases accompanied with whatever documents in support of them may be attainable"; he recommends that the statement show "how far" the claims "rest, on general regulations or special licences from competent authorities; how far on licences reasonably presumed to be competent, though in strictness not so; how far on sudden & ensnaring repeals of general regulations, or discontinuances of special indulgences; how far on the calculation from existing circumstances, that the ordinary Colonial policy of Spain would be relaxed; and how far on fraudulent proceedings of Spanish subjects"; the claimants may also need to provide documentation "that satisfaction has been sought in vain from the regular Tribunals" in the Spanish colonies; Madison asks for a copy of the finished statement

for use in preparing further instructions to Pinckney and in asking the Spanish minister to the United States to intercede with the viceroyalty of Río de la Plata (Madison, *Papers, Sec. of State Ser.*, 3:549-50). (2) Madison to Thomas Fitz-Simons, 6 Sep., a brief letter to cover a copy of Enclosure No. 1 (same, 548-9). (3) Daniel Brent to Madison, 3 Sep., which among other subjects refers to letters to Madison from Elkanah Watson and Jeremiah Van Rensselaer pressing the appointment of Simon Lynch as commercial agent at Nantes; Brent has information that Thomas Gantt, the appointee for that position, "has not yet been in France, and that he has no intention of going thither"; Brent writes that "under these Circumstances" it appears "that some other person should be appointed without delay"; understanding that TJ "has been already Applied to on this subject" (see TJ to Madison, 10 Sep.), Brent has written to Watson advising him of Madison's absence from Washington (Madison, *Papers, Sec. of State Ser.*, 3:538-40).

MR. GRANT: Thomas T. Gantt, who had received the appointment as commercial agent at Nantes in 1801, wrote to Madison from Georgetown early in October 1802 to resign from the position. TJ named William PATTERSON, who had the support of Robert R. Livingston, to the post (Gantt to Madison, 5 Oct., RC in DNA: RG 59, RD, endorsed by TJ "Gantt declines consulship of Nantes"; Madison, *Papers, Sec. of State Ser.*, 3:539n; Vol. 35:371, 664; TJ to the Senate, 2 Feb. 1803).

After TJ appointed Patterson as commercial agent at L'ORIENT, France, in 1801, Livingston was distressed that his advocacy of Patterson had resulted in the displacement of Aaron VAIL. Vail had sought the consulship at L'Orient since at least 1791, when he approached TJ about the matter. About 1793, he began to perform the duties of acting consul in the port, not with a presidential commission, but under an appointment from the consul at Bordeaux. Livingston traveled through L'Orient in the fall of 1801 and pronounced Vail "a firm republican" who had the respect of the merchants in the port. Livingston continued to remind Madison about Vail, until, finally, the opportunity to move Patterson to Nantes allowed TJ to make Vail the commercial agent at L'Orient (Madison, *Papers, Sec. of State Ser.*, 2:238, 265-6, 391, 467; 3:444, 468-9; Vol. 22:272;

Vol. 33:672, 677; TJ to the Senate, 14 Feb. 1803).

FORBIDDEN BY CIRCUMSTANCES: Madison was plagued by ongoing concerns in chancery court over Kentucky lands he and his late brother Ambrose once owned. Authentication of the deeds may have required his presence in county court. In September, Madison also prepared legal paperwork for the exchange of property resulting from an informal addenda to the will of his father that was challenged by other members of his family (Madison, *Papers, Sec. of State Ser.*, 2:124-6, 197, 268; 3:109, 529-30, 588-9).

From Louis André Pichon and Émilie Brongniart Pichon

Georgetown le 9 Septembre 1802

Mr. et Me Pichon ont l'honneur de presenter leurs respects à Monsieur le Président des Etats Unis et prennent la liberté de lui témoigner tout le regret qu'ils éprouvent de ne pouvoir profiter des obligeantes invitations que Mr. le Président a eu la bonté de leur faire de faire une excursion à Monticello. Mr Pichon étant impérieusement appellé à New York par la présence des frégates françaises qui y sont mouillées, ne peut Pour cette saison se diriger de ce coté des Etats Unis: sans cet incident il aurait au moins seul, été rendre ses hommages à Mr. le Président.

EDITORS' TRANSLATION

Georgetown 9 Sep. 1802

Monsieur and Madame Pichon are honored to present their respects to the president of the United States and to assure him of all their regret at not being able to benefit from the president's kind invitation to take an excursion to Monticello. Mr. Pichon, having been urgently called to New York by the presence of the French frigates docked there, cannot travel to that part of the United States during this season. Without that incident, he would have come, even if alone, to pay homage to the president.

RC (DLC); endorsed by TJ as a letter of 1 Sep. received 7 Sep.; recorded in SJL as a letter of 1 Sep. received 9 Sep.

Alexandrine Émilie Brongniart Pichon (b. 1780), whom Lafayette described as

"a Very Amiable Young Lady," married Louis André Pichon in December 1800. The youngest child of Louise d'Egremont Brongniart and the architect and designer Alexandre Théodore Brongniart, Émilie grew up in an intellectual and creative circle in Paris that included the chemist Antoine François de Fourcroy, who was a relative, and several artists. Jean Antoine Houdon made busts of Émilie's two older siblings when they were children. Another sculptor, Jean Louis Couasnon, modeled a bust of Émilie, or "Ziguette" as she was called in the family, at the age of four. Élisabeth Vigée-Lebrun painted a lively portrait of her at the age of eight, and when Émilie was fifteen, a portrait by François Gérard enthralled critics at the Salon of 1795. Émilie developed her own artistic skills under the tutelage of Jacques Louis David, who gave her access to his studio to copy some of his works, and the sculptor Denis Antoine Chaudet. She knew Latin, studied music, and attended public lectures. According to a family tradition, she turned down a marriage proposal from her brother's friend, Georges Cuvier. She was about nine years younger than Pichon, who proposed marriage to her a few weeks before he expected to depart for the United States as *commissaire général*. A week after their wedding and two days before they left for the United States, Talleyrand hosted a dinner for the couple and the bride's family. Of Émilie, Lafayette wrote to Alexander Hamilton: "I Have foretold Her she would Be very well Liked in America." The Pichons took up residence in a house in Georgetown, and Émilie became good friends with Dolley Madison and Margaret Bayard Smith. She had a son during her residence in the United States, but the child died in 1804. She and Pichon had three other children, the oldest of which was born in 1805, soon after the Pichons returned to France. In 1830, Émilie became a *baronne* (baroness) when the restored French monarchy bestowed a title of nobility on her husband (Jacques Silvestre de Sacy,

Alexandre-Théodore Brongniart, 1739-1813, Sa Vie—Son Œuvre [Paris, 1940], 62n, 90-6, 100-4, 112-13, 124; Louis de Launay, *Une grande famille de savants: Les Brongniart* [Paris, 1940], 22, 86; Michèle Beaulieu, "Le Buste d'Émilie Brongniart par J.-L. Couasnon," *La Revue du Louvre*, 24 [1974], 105-8; *Alexandre-Théodore Brongniart, 1739-1813: Architecture et décor: Musée Carnavalet, 22 Avril-13 Juillet 1986* [Paris, 1986], 22-3; Tony Halliday, *Facing the Public: Portraiture in the Aftermath of the French Revolution* [Manchester, Eng., 1999], 4, 49, 52-5; Margaret Bayard Smith, *The First Forty Years of Washington Society*, ed. Gaillard Hunt [New York, 1906], 34, 44, 213-18; Mattern and Shulman, *Dolley Madison*, 46, 53, 59, 68, 71, 75; Jacques Henri-Robert, *Dictionnaire des diplomates de Napoléon: Histoire et dictionnaire du corps diplomatique consulaire et impérial* [Paris, 1990], 286-7; Syrett, *Hamilton*, 25:336; Albert H. Bowman, "Pichon, the United States, and Louisiana," *Diplomatic History*, 1 [1977], 259; Madison, *Papers, Sec. of State Ser.*, 8:238, 483; Vol. 32:430).

According to a letter from Daniel Brent to Madison, Louis André Pichon knew by 3 Sep. that he would have to go to New York and would not be able to make his planned EXCURSION into Virginia. On 7 Sep., Brent understood that Pichon had left for New York that morning, and on the 14th Brent reported that the French chargé was "still at New York." If Brent's information was correct, Pichon may have misdated the letter printed above or was not actually at Georgetown when he wrote it. TJ misread the date that Pichon put on the letter, and perhaps for that reason had a faulty recollection of the day on which he received it (Madison, *Papers, Sec. of State Ser.*, 3:539, 555, 580).

From Isaac Cox Barnet

SIR,   Bordeaux September 10th. 1802.

I received with lively sensibility, the honourable mark of confidence and good opinion you have been pleased to confer upon me by appointing me to the Commercial Agency of Antwerp.—

It was the more impressive from my having received no previous notice from any person and I esteem it the more flattering from a hope that my past conduct has merited your approbation and been the principal agent in restoring me to a situation where I may again be useful to my Country—a situation which, from present prospects, is the most disirable for a commercial establishment and in which, Sir, under the auspices of your fostering Administration, I may hope to acquire the means of supporting my family, whilst my only ambition will be to merit your continued patronage.—

I am using all diligence to repair to my Post—and am proud today that I go with the kind wishes of the people of Bordeaux who have ever honoud me with their good opinion.—If, Sir, I am so fortunate as to sec[ure] yours and gain that of my fellow Citizens [...]—my political happiness will be compleat when [I can?] acquire that also of the people of my new residence. Accept Sir, the [effu?]sions of a grateful heart, and the assurances of my [...] respect & dévouement.

I. Cox Barnet

RC (DLC); torn; at foot of text: "Thomas Jefferson Esquire"; endorsed by TJ as received 11 Nov. and so recorded in SJL.

MARK OF CONFIDENCE: TJ signed Barnet's commission as commercial agent to Antwerp on 18 June 1802 (FC in DNA: RG 59, PTCC).

To Daniel Brent

Sep. 10. 1802.

Th: Jefferson presents his compliments to mr Daniel Brent and informs him that the blanks for commrs. of bankruptcy were signed, & by the return of the same post, were forwarded either to mr Madison or mr Brent, he rather believes the former. that for Storey is signed & returned by this post to mr Madison for his signature. the post of the 20th. inst. is the last one by which any thing should be forwarded to me here.

PrC (DLC).

To Christopher Clark

Sir   Monticello Sep. 10. 1802.

About 9. or 10. years ago I put into the hands of mr Lyle of Manchester some bonds toward paiment of a debt I owed, part of which I understand he remitted to you for collection. my attention being lately called to this subject, it appears so far as respects your portion of the collection to stand thus.

bonds delivd to mr Clarke

payable 1793.	Dec. 14.	[Milliner] Miller & Miller	121-7-6
		[Perrow] Clarke & Clarke	[20]-10-0
		Branch & [three] Minors	40-[12]-6
		Clarke & Clarke	[55-15]-0
		Hawkins, Perrow & Dillon	41-16-0
			280-1-0

[pay]able 1794.	Dec. 14.	[Milliner] & Millers £[120]-7-6	
		[do. to Th:J & by] [...] 72-8-[8]	4[8]-18-10
		[Perrow] Clarke & Clarke	20-10-0
		Branch & three Minors	[40-12-6]
			110-1-4

Credits by mr Lyle as paid by mr Clarke

1794.	Oct. [20?]	£48-[13?]-10
1795.	[March 30?]	49-0-0
	Oct. 5	120-0-0
1797.	May 15.	89-1-3
1798.	May 15	[...]

As these bonds bore interest from the periods above stated, and where suits were brought, costs would be recovered, I suppose they must yield their principal and interest without any other deduction than your commision, unless there was any insolvency. calculating the two sums of £280-[1-0 with intt. from] 1793. Dec. 14. [...] and 110-[1-4] with int. from 1794. Dec. 14 and giving credits by the paiments above stated, at their [...] dates, I should conclude, after deducting your commission on those paiments that there must be between 50. & 60. £ with interest from 1798 [May?] 18. [still] uncollected. [but what] losses or other accidents may have diminished this balance I cannot judge. the object of this letter is to ask the favor of you to inf[orm me] of the state of the collection, and whether & when any further [remittance be] expected from it & the business be finally closed. [...] remaining [...] to be paid to mr Lyle, altho the information is asked for myself to guide [...] [with him]. Accept assurances of my esteem & respect. Th: Jefferson

PrC (MHi); faint; arranged by TJ with the credits column to the right of the column with bonds delivered to Clark; at foot of text: "Mr. Christopher Clarke"; endorsed by TJ in ink on verso.

MY ATTENTION BEING LATELY CALLED:

James Lyle to TJ, 3 Aug. 1802. A probable response from Clark, recorded in SJL as a letter of 28 Oct. 1802 received 7 Nov., has not been found.

Correctly deducting £72.8.8 from £120.7.6 would have actually left a sum of £47.18.10, payable by Milliner and the

MILLERS as of 14 Dec. 1794. In a letter of that day to James Lyle, agent of one of his major creditors, TJ had calculated the sum as £49.18.10 (Vol. 28:218).

To James Madison

DEAR SIR   Monticello Sep. 10. 1802.

Yours by yesterday's post is recieved. the letter to Higginson & others is entirely approved, and is sealed & forwarded to mr Brent. the Consulate at Nantes must be disposed of according to our former arrangement. I do not know whether the mr Lynch recommended is the one who was living at Nantes when I was in France, or his son. of that one there is something not favourable resting in my mind, altho' I cannot recollect the particulars. but Patterson's claims are certainly superior.—I recd. from mr Brent extracts from the letters of Chancr. Livingston & Sumpter concerning the resignation of the latter. I presume he does not wait for a formal permission. but suppose it had better be sent. I inclose you a commission of bankruptcy for your signature. it is to correct an error of having given a former one to a person of the same surname, for which this is now substituted. mr Brent reminds me of a parcel of blanks he sent for signature. I remember signing them, & sending them either to yourself or him.

We shall be very happy to see yourself, family, & Dr. & mrs Thornton here. the Govr. is up at present; goes down on Thursday (16th.) and returns on Tuesday (21st.) when you get to the forks of the road at Will Becks's, the other side of Milton, a turn of the road forces you to the river at Milton, & when there it is better to cross there & come round along the public road on this side the river, my private one being hardly wide enough & safe for a carriage, altho' my waggons & carts do pass it. this adds a couple of miles to the length of the journey. with my best respects to the ladies accept assurances of my constant & affectionate friendship.   TH: JEFFERSON

P.S. I notify[1] the offices at Washington that the post which leaves that place on the 24th. inst. is the last by which any thing should be forwarded to me here.

RC (DLC: Madison Papers); at foot of text: "The Secretary of State." PrC (DLC). Enclosure: Commission for Joseph Story, not found (see Daniel Brent to TJ, 7 Sep.).

YOURS BY YESTERDAY'S POST: Madison to TJ, [on or before 9 Sep. 1802].

For appeals to TJ to appoint Simon LYNCH to the position at Nantes, see Vol. 37:526-7, 538, 539.

Daniel Brent had sent TJ EXTRACTS of two letters addressed to Madison, one from Robert R. Livingston on 12 May and one from Thomas Sumter, Jr., on 18 May. As Brent explained to Madison on 7 Sep.: "I fear that you will be a good deal puzzled in the reading of the press Copies of Mr Livingstons letters, from their faintness. I forward an extract to the President from that part of one of them which relates to Mr Sumpter, and an entire Copy of Mr Sumpter's own letter, herewith sent to you" (Madison, *Papers, Sec. of State Ser.*, 3:555, 556n; TJ to Madison,

6 Aug.; Madison to TJ, 11 Aug., Enclosure No. 4).

MR BRENT REMINDS ME: see TJ to Brent, 10 Sep.

THE GOVR.: James Monroe.

WILL BECKS'S: William Beck appeared in TJ's financial records for providing a variety of goods and services beginning in 1768 (MB, 1:30n, 70, 145, 150-1, 201, 292, 293, 378, 515, 532; 2:1005, 1049, 1050).

[1] TJ first wrote "I have notified" before altering the passage to read as above.

To Thomas Munroe

DEAR SIR   Monticello Sep. 10. 1802.

The inclosed letter from Doctr. Thornton informs me that mr Mason & yourself had concluded that it would be no injury to the public to postpone for a time the sale of mr Stoddert's lots, and that you had postponed it till the 25th. of Oct. and he asks the same indulgence for himself. the same reason pleading for this as in the other case, I think it right that the same indulgence should be given to Dr. Thornton, & therefore recommend the postponement of the sale of his lots to the 25th. of Oct. also; and the rather as the late sales I understand have not only been ruinous to the individuals, but have left some danger of loss to the public. Accept my best wishes and respects.   TH: JEFFERSON

PrC (DLC); at foot of text: "Mr. Thomas Munroe"; endorsed by TJ in ink on verso. Enclosure: William Thornton to TJ, 8 Sep. 1802 (recorded in SJL as

received from Orange on 9 Sep., but not found).

SALE OF MR STODDERT'S LOTS: see TJ to Munroe, 8 Aug. 1802.

To William Thornton

DEAR SIR   Monticello Sep. 10. 1802.

Your favor of the 8th. was recieved yesterday. by that I learn that on my letter to mr Munroe, referring to himself and mr Mason to consider whether the sale of mr Stoddert's lots might be postponed for some time without injury to the public, they had been of opinion it could, and had accordingly postponed it to the 25th. of Oct. the same reasons being in favor of the indulgence you ask. I have no hesitation at yielding it, and shall be very happy if the delay can serve you while it neither injures the public nor disobeys the law by which I am bound. I accordingly write by this day's post to mr Munroe to postpone the sale of your lots to the 25th. of October also, which letter he will recieve tomorrow evening.

Mrs. Thornton & yourself having approached so near us (for we think little of 30 miles here) I hope will give us the pleasure of seeing you here. and the rather as mr Madison & family had [given?] us the hope of a visit. my daughters, who are with me, will receive mrs Thornton with great pleasure. an early breakfast at mr Madison's will enable you to be here by half after three, our dinner hour, to which the [cook?] adds a considerable margin some times. mr Madison's fine prospect will have taken off considerably from the novelty of ours but the same thing under a varied aspect sometimes is pleasing. in the hope of seeing you here in a few days I pray you to accept assurances of my esteem & respect.   TH: JEFFERSON

PrC (MHi); faint and blurred; at foot of text: "Doctr William Thornton"; endorsed by TJ in ink on verso.

YOUR FAVOR: Thornton to TJ, 8 Sep. has not been found but is recorded in SJL at 9 Sep. with notation "Orange."

MY LETTER TO MR MUNROE: TJ to Thomas Munroe, 8 Aug.

MR MADISON'S FINE PROSPECT: in her diary entry for 5 Sep. 1802, Anna Maria Thornton described Montpelier, as situated in "a wild & romantic Country" and "commanding an extensive view of the blue ridge, which by constant variation in the appearance of the clouds, and consequently of the mountains, form a very agreeable and varied object, sometimes appearing very distant, sometimes much separated and distinct and often like rolling waves" (MS in DLC: Anna Maria Brodeau Thornton Papers).

From James Madison

DEAR SIR   Sepr. 11. 1802

Yours of the 10th. is duly recd. I answered by duplicates Mr. Sumter's resignation as soon as it had been submitted to you. Mr. Livingston's request that he may appt. a successor has not yet been answered. It is probable he will expect to know your determination in the first letter that may be written to him. The blanks of which Mr. Brent reminded you, came to me from you some time ago, and were sent on to him with my signature.

You will receive herewith two letters from Mr Livingston of May 28, & June 8th. and one from Mr. King of June 20th. I am glad to find that Otto is to share in the negociations concerning Louisiana, because it is probable he may retain the original policy of France on that subject, and because his destination to this country gives him an interest in a policy that will be welcome to us. The arrival of Dupont also will be very apropos. The reasoning of Mr. L. to the Spanish Minister, has a certain degree of force, but if not managed cautiously may commit us in other points of view.

We can not yet fix the day of our visit to Monticello. Yours as ever

JAMES MADISON

RC (DLC); endorsed by TJ as received from the State Department on 12 Sep. and "Livingston's & Kings's dispatches" and so recorded in SJL.

LETTERS FROM MR LIVINGSTON: in a dispatch addressed to Madison on 28 May, Robert R. Livingston reported his supposition that the French expedition to take possession of Louisiana had been delayed by disagreement between France and Spain about whether the Floridas were to be included in the cession of Louisiana. Believing that under those circumstances the best course of action for the United States was to "alarm" Spain and provide information that could be useful to the Spanish government in opposing the claims of France, Livingston on 28 May wrote to José Nicolas de Azara, Spain's minister to France. Livingston suggested to Azara that Spanish possession of the Floridas was required by Pinckney's treaty, under which Spain was to control Indian tribes in the region, to allow only Spanish subjects and U.S. citizens to navigate the Mississippi except by special convention, and to guarantee U.S. citizens the right to deposit merchandise at New Orleans and export it free of duty. In a dispatch to Madison of 8 June, Livingston enclosed Azara's answer, which stated the Spanish diplomat's opinion that the Floridas were not part of the territory ceded to France. Livingston also reported that when he pressed Talleyrand for information about the Louisiana transfer, Talleyrand said that Louis Guillaume Otto, who was intended to be the next French minister to the United States, would soon be in Paris and would be able to discuss the Louisiana issue with Livingston (Madison, *Papers, Sec. of State Ser.*, 3:264-6, 289-91).

Writing to Madison on 20 June, Rufus KING reported that he was prepared to complete the exchange of ratifications for the convention with Great Britain to settle claims covered by Article 6 of the Jay Treaty, and that the commission handling claims under Article 7 was proceeding with its work. King also reported that the British had postponed taking any action on their countervailing duties until they could be more certain of the intentions of Congress regarding the discriminating duties of the U.S. (same, 328-9; TJ to the Senate, 29 Mch. 1802; Edward Livingston to TJ, 2 Apr.).

From Daniel Rapine

SIR   Washington City Septr. 11th. 1802

On account of the indisposition, & by particular desire of Mr. Claxton, I take the liberty of informing you, that the Sofas with their equipment, made for you in Philada., were shipped from there, consigned to Messrs. Gibson & Jefferson, Richmond, about the first of last month—This information is given you in order that you may make the necessary arrangement with your friends at Richmond to have them safely conveyed to you, if that has not already been done

I am, Sir, Your most obt. Servt.　　　　　　DANL. RAPINE

RC (DLC); endorsed by TJ as received 16 Sep. and by Rapine "for Claxton" and so recorded in SJL.

From William Thornton

DEAR SIR　　　　　　　　　　　　Orange County Septr. 11th. 1802—

I have the honor of receiving your Letter of yesterday. I am exceedingly obliged not only by the friendly Disposition evinced, but still more so by the kind attention shewn in transmitting so soon your Directions to the Superintendant.

We return our respectful acknowledgments for the very polite Invitation we have received to visit Monticello.—We flatter ourselves with great Enjoyment in accompanying our Friends to pay our respects to you & the Ladies of your Family. The Secretary of State, whose Movements are dependent on very remote Causes will regulate our Excursions; &, I think, from the general predisposition, our visit will not long be delayed.—

We join in respectful Compliments to your Family.—

Be pleased, dear Sir, to accept the assurances of my highest Consideration.—　　　　　　　　　　WILLIAM THORNTON

RC (MHi); at foot of text: "President of the United States"; endorsed by TJ as received 12 Sep. and so recorded in SJL.

YOUR DIRECTIONS: sometime in the summer or early fall of 1802, William Thornton, functioning as a clerk within the state department, assumed the title of superintendent of the newly formed patent office (Cunningham, *Process of Government*, 92; Madison, *Papers, Sec. of State Ser.*, 3:356).

ACCOMPANYING OUR FRIENDS: Anna Maria Thornton wrote to Dolley Madison on 24 Aug. that despite delays, the Thorntons and Ann Brodeau were eager to turn their backs on the "dull tho' Great City" of Washington and "greet with Joy, our beloved Friends beyond the mountains." From Montpelier, they planned to join Bishop James Madison and William Short in a visit to Monticello (Mattern and Shulman, *Dolley Madison*, 50-1; Madison to TJ, 15 Sep.).

From John Drayton

SIR　　　　　　　　　So. Carolina Charleston Septr. 12th: 1802.

By letters in my possession from Colonel Wade Hampton of this State at New York, I am informed, that notwithstanding all the

French Commodore's promises to the Mayor of New York, it can be proven the French Negro incendiary prisoners on board the French Vessels, are about to be landed clandestinely on the coasts of the Southern States of our Union.

The situation of Carolina, the feelings of her inhabitants jealously alive at all times to matters which may in the least affect the Negro property they possess, and my own public duty, imperiously required, my taking immediate steps on the occasion. I accordingly wrote a letter on the subject to the French Agent at this place Citizen Chancognie; a copy of which, with his answer, are inclosed. I have also, issued Orders to the Military of this State, to oppose their landing by force of Arms: and have also sent out two scout Pilot boats, to give as early information as possible, respecting any attempt of the Kind which may be made on our coasts. I have also written on the subject, to the Governors of No. Carolina, & Georgia.

I consider it my duty, to transmit you this information: not doubting, but you will take such steps in the premises, as the information you receive, and the interests & safety of the Southern States a respectable part of the American Union, shall require.

With high respect & consideration I have the honor to subscribe myself Sir Yr. Mo. obt. S.   JOHN DRAYTON.

NB. In one of the letters written by Col. Hampton on the above subject, mention is made, that two sloops were put into a sudden state of preparation at Newark, having an unusual quantity of provisions & water put on board; & platforms erected in their holds—They sailed: & in the evening were along side of the French frigates in New York harbour, & have not been heard of since—☞ One of our pilots informed me yesterday, that one of them, had passed our bar, bound for the river St. Marys.

RC (DLC); above postscript: "Thomas Jefferson Esqe President of the United States of America"; endorsed by TJ as received 5 Oct. and so recorded in SJL. Enclosures: (1) Drayton to Simon Jude Chancognie, Charleston, 9 Sep., informing him that from letters "of respectable authority" Drayton has learned "that the incendiary negroes and people of colour Prisoners on board of the french Squadron at New-York, and also on board another french Squadron destined to some part of these United States, are to be landed in some part of this Union"; Drayton, "unwilling to charge to your Nation, a step so full of mischief to ourselves," trusts that the information may be incorrect; however, because his position requires him "to be vigilant in these matters," he has "given orders, that should any attempt of the kind be made in this State, all persons concerned, aiding or assisting in the same, are to be repelled by force of arms"; he informs Chancognie of this decision so "you may have it in your power to avert if possible, any unpleasant circumstances, which may arise, betrixt republican and friendly Nations" (Tr in DLC; in a clerk's hand). (2) Chancognie to Drayton, Charleston, 22

Fructidor Year 10 (9 Sep. 1802); acknowledging Drayton's letter, he states that American newspapers are his only source of information about the arrival of French ships in New York with prisoners from Guadeloupe; he does not know the ultimate destination of the ships, but he cannot think that the intent of the expedition is to repeat in this country the disastrous events of France's colonies; the circumstances that forced the ships to put into ports of the United States have given the enemies of France an opportunity to slander his country; but French naval officers and government officials would not betray the confidence of an allied nation or pervert the good mutual understanding that has been so well restored between two republics (Tr in same; in French; in a clerk's hand).

In July 1801, Louis André Pichon appointed Simon Jude CHANCOGNIE as his agent and sent him to Charleston to put the affairs of the vacant French consulate there in order. Chancognie had previously been a clerk in the French legation in Philadelphia under Philippe de Létombe (Madison, *Papers, Sec. of State Ser.*, 1:450-1).

To James Lyle

DEAR SIR   Monticello Sep. 12. 1802.

Your's of Aug. 3. has been some time at hand, tho' it is but lately I [have] been able to look into the subject. I had always for my own satisfaction kept by me a statement of my bonds to your company, of the paiments made on them, and the bonds delivered you for collection to be applied to the paiment of mine. as these bonds bore interest, I considered them as equivalent to a like sum of my own bonds and therefore set them off against it in the manner stated in the 1st. & 2d. page of the inclosed paper. this differs from your's only as the latter [credits?] the actual paiments only, which I acknolege is right, because I stand responsible for any [losses?] in the collection. but when that collection is compleated, our statements [will] coincide in their result. I observe, for instance, that at the date of the [...] [credit] of 1790. May 18.[1] in your statement, [you make £85-19-7] [...] on the 3d. bond whereas mine makes it overpaid at that time. this difference proceeds from 2. sources 1st. I do not see a credit for John Bolling's bond £[52-19-8 currency] and interest. 2d. on examining mr Clarke's paiments I find that his [collection] cannot have been compleated, as will [appear] by a statement I have made in the lower half of the 2d. page [of his inclosed paper], by which it would appear that between £50. & £60 are still [uncollected]. I have written to him on this subject; and [these two articles, when set to right] will bring [our] calculations together, and [shew] that the 5th. bond [is paid or very nearly so. there will then be?] [...] 6 [...] of this debt [...] from my mother, and on the [unmentioned?] account of [...] to [these] I am unwilling to name specific days [...], because [...] [brought on me?]

by the very heavy outfit of my present office [...] not [...] [finally yet through?], they will be so shortly: and [the paiments to you shall commence, & when begun] the whole will be paid off [...] [I will] [...] in the course of the next & following year; at the end of which I shall owe not one farthing on earth. I pray you to accept assurances of my constant friendship and respect.   TH: JEFFERSON

PrC (MHi); faint; at foot of text: "Mr James Lyle"; endorsed by TJ in ink on verso. Enclosure not found.

I HAVE WRITTEN TO HIM: TJ to Christopher Clark, 10 Sep.

[1] Interlined: "of 1790. May 18."

From Joseph Pannill

Natchez Missisippi Territory.
September—12th. 1802

SIR

From the slight acquaintance I had with your Excellency, at the city of Washington, in June last, I take the liberty of soliciting from you the appointment of Surveyor of this Territory.—

Should you think proper, or be pleased to bestow the same upon me, your Excellency may depend upon a faithful discharge of the duties of the office, and that I shall act in all respects agreeable to my instructions. The occupation I have been long and constantly engaged in, both before and since the War, and had once the honor of being appointed Surveyor General of the state of Georgia—

I am Sir, With the greatest respect Your obt. Servant.—

JOSEPH PANNILL

RC (DNA: RG 59, LAR); at foot of text: "His Excellency Thomas Jefferson Esqr. President of the Unites States"; endorsed by TJ as received 30 Nov. and "to be Surveyor Missipi terry." and so recorded in SJL.

Joseph Pannill (d. ca. 1811) was a former Continental army officer and surveyor from Georgia. He acquired land grants in Mississippi and relocated to the region around 1795. In 1802, the territorial legislature named Pannill one of the initial trustees of Jefferson College (Heitman, *Register*, 424; *Georgia Historical Quarterly*, 38 [1954], 346, 348; JHR, 4:283; *Statutes of the Mississippi Territory* [Natchez, 1816], 310; J. Estelle Stewart King, *Mississippi Court Records, 1799-1835* [Baltimore, 1969], 16).

From Stephen R. Bradley

SIR   Westminster Sept. 13th. 1802

I have the honour to acknowledge the receipt of your letter of the 27th. of August, yesterday, and can assure you it was the first intimation, that you[1] expected from me a recommendation of proper persons, as Commissioners of bankruptcy in this State—had it before come to my knowledge, I certainly should have embraced the earliest oppertunity of giving you all the assistance in my power. You will permit me to observe that this state has a range of Mountains runing north and south through almost the whole length of the same, that most of the Inhabitants are settled on the east and west side of the State, and but very little commerce or intercourse across the mountains that the Legislature hold their Sessions alternately on each side as do also the courts of the United States. I should deem it most expedient to appoint four on each side that is four in the district in which Judge *Smith* lives & four in the district in which I live, I mention four that in case of Death, or other causes that might incapacitate one, there might be a sufficient number in the district without having to cross the mountains. Under a conviction of the expediency I will take the Liberty of recommending four living on the eastern Side of the mountains, expecting Judge Smith will recommend proper characters on the western side—And will name *Mark Richards* and *Reuben Atwater* of Westminster *James Elliot* of Brattleborough and *Oliver Gallop* of Hartland—The first is a Very respectable Merchant the three last mentioned are Lawyers, they are all Men of known probity, abilities, and firmly attached to Republican principles,[2] and would no doubt if appointed discharge the duties with faithfulness, required of *them*.

I cannot but remark before I close this letter that last week the Election took place throughout this State for Members of the Legislature—Nothing can equal the diabolical exertions made by the Feds., the lies, falshoods, and spurious productions, they have published, would disgrace the pen of an Infernal, and all we flatter ourselves to no purpose, from the returns received we are Induced to believe the Legislature at their ensueing Session Next Month will be more republican than they were last Year—

I am Sir With Sentiments of the highest respect, Your Most Obedt Humble Servt   STEPHEN R BRADLEY

RC (DNA: RG 59, LAR); at foot of text: "The President of the United States"; endorsed by TJ as received 23 Sep. and "commrs bankruptcy. Windsor" and so recorded in SJL. Dft (ViU).

JUDGE SMITH WILL RECOMMEND: on 13 Sep., Israel Smith wrote the secretary of state recommending Darius Chipman and Richard Skinner, reputable lawyers at Rutland and Manchester, respectively, and Samuel Prentiss as bankruptcy commissioners for the district on the western side of Vermont (RC in same; endorsed by TJ: "Israel Smith to mr Madison. Commrs. of bankruptcy Rutland"). Smith had recommended Prentiss in an earlier letter to Madison (see TJ to

Bradley, 27 Aug.). Smith noted, however, that TJ's letter of 27 Aug. was the "first intimation" that the president sought his recommendations. For the appointment of Smith's three and Bradley's four candidates, see Memorandum to James Madison, printed at 18 Oct. 1802.

ELECTION TOOK PLACE: the choice of a U.S. senator during the October 1802 session of the Vermont Assembly indicated the extent of the Republican victory in the fall election. On 19 Oct., the House elected Israel Smith by a 102 to 75 vote over the Federalist candidate. In the council, 9 out of 13 votes were cast for Smith (Bennington *Vermont Gazette*, 25 Oct. 1802; *Journal of the General Assembly of the State of Vermont, at Their Session, Begun and Holden at Burlington, in the County of Chittenden, the Fourteenth Day of October, A.D. One Thousand Eight Hundred and Two* [Bennington, Vt., 1802], 47-8).

[1] In Dft, Bradley here wrote "*the President of the United States.*"
[2] Dft lacks remainder of sentence.

To Henry Dearborn

DEAR SIR   Monticello Sep. 13. 1802.

Your favor of the 8th. was recieved yesterday. I cannot [but consider?] the case of the French negroes at New York as substantially within the police of the state: and that [cases] of that kind will not be as well provided against by the General government as by the government of the place. our relations with it are only incidental, to wit, as it comes within the laws of contraband or quarantine. on the former ground I desired the secretary of the treasury some time ago to give circular instructions to all the custom house officers to be on the alert, & to see that none of the negroes were smuggled in. as a case of quarantine I leave it to your discretion to order a part of the troops as required for the hospital or any other particular spot where there is reason to apprehend a breach of the Quarantine law will be attempted. I write this day to the Secretary of state to make a friendly communication of this measure to mr Pichon. I have inclosed him mr Livington's letter to be returned to you.[1]

I inclose you a talk from the Cherokees to the Govr. of South Carolina from whom I recieved it last night. considering that we have no point to carry with them, with or without their consent, I should be for availing ourselves of this opening to do them the kindness they ask, and to send them a friendly & soothing speech. you can think of this by the time of my return, which is not distant. in this view I will desire that after the mail which leaves Washington the 24th. inst. nothing may be forwarded to me at this place.

On recieving authentic information, from mr Simpson that the Emperor of Marocco has permitted him to return and allowed 6. months for explanation I recommended to mr Smith the stopping of the John Adams; we shall have 5. frigates in the [Mediterranean] [...], which if Tunis continues peaceful as I have no doubt she will, will be 2. or 3. too many. Tripoli is asking [...]. our finances do not permit us to expend money for the vague [impression] which a shew of our whole force may make. we are told in the papers that Algiers is making war on Spain who has 40. or 50. ships of the line at her door. Accept my affectionate salutations.

TH: JEFFERSON

PrC (DLC); faint; at foot of text: "The Secretary at War." Recorded in SJL as a letter to the War Department with notation "guard N. York. Cherokee talk." Enclosure not found, but see John Drayton to TJ, 30 Aug.

OR QUARENTINE: by an "Act respecting Quarantines and Health Laws" of 25 Feb. 1799, customs collectors, "all other officers of the revenue," revenue cutters, commanders of army garrisons along the coast, "and all such officers of the United States" were, under the direction of the secretary of the Treasury, "to aid in the execution" of state quarantine and health

laws affecting ships in ports (U.S. Statutes at Large, 1:619).

SPAIN and Algiers were not at war, although relations between the two countries were tense. To avoid hostilities, Spain made a tribute payment and allowed Algiers to keep three captured merchant vessels, but Algiers began to make new demands. TJ may have seen reports of a raid in search of provisions by ships from one of the Barbary regencies on the Spanish coast between Cartagena and Alicante (*Rutland Herald*, 23 Aug.; Madison, *Papers, Sec. of State Ser.*, 3:383, 389n; 4:37n, 45-6).

[1] Sentence interlined.

To Albert Gallatin

DEAR SIR   Monticello Sep. 13. 1802.

On learning the death of Wm. Reynolds Collector of York, and that mr Griffin his deputy would not act at all, I made immediate enquiries for a proper successor, and learn that William Carey of the same place is the best person we can appoint. I this day desire mr Madison to order a commission. I have done this because of the urgency of the case, of your distance, & my presence on the spot.

I have always forgotten to ask of you a general idea of the effect of the peace on our revenues so far as we have gone. it is of the utmost importance, if these diminish, to diminish our expences. this may be done in the Naval department. I wish it were possible to increase the impost on any articles affecting the rich chiefly to the amount of the sugar tax, so that we might relinquish that at the next session. but this must depend on our reciepts keeping up. as to the tea & coffee tax, the people do not regard it. the next tax which an increase of revenue should enable us to suppress should be the salt tax. perhaps indeed the production of that article at home is already undermining that tax.

I have desired the offices to forward me nothing to this place after the mail which leaves Washington on the 24th. inst. Accept my affectionate salutations.   TH: JEFFERSON

RC (NHi: Gallatin Papers); addressed: "Albert Gallatin Secretary of the treasury at New York"; franked; postmarked Milton; endorsed. PrC (DLC). Recorded in SJL as a letter to the Treasury Department with notation "Cary—revenue—tax on sugar."

According to the Treasury Department statement on duties and drawbacks dated 5 Jan. 1802, the SUGAR TAX or the duty collected on sugar imports amounted to $2,818,258 in 1800, but after the payment of drawbacks totaling $1,576,062 on sugar re-exported the amount was decreased to $1,242,196. In 1800, the revenues from the duty on SALT totaled $682,197, after the payment of drawbacks. The repeal of internal taxes in April 1802 reduced revenues by at least $650,000. During the debate over repeal, which extended from 15 to 22 Mch. in the House, the Federalists introduced amendments to eliminate import duties, or external taxes, on brown sugar, salt, coffee, and bohea tea, items consumed by all, instead of the excise or internal tax on carriages, auction sales, and refined sugars, that benefited only the rich (ASP, *Finance*, 1:702-3, 727-8; *Annals*, 11:1015-74; U.S. Statutes at Large, 2:148-50).

To James Madison

DEAR SIR   Monticello Sep. 13. 1802.

I now return you the papers which came in your letter of the 11th. I am not satisfied that the ground taken by Chancellor Livingston is advantageous. for the French government & the Spanish have only to grant him all he asks (and they will in justice & policy do that at once) and his mouth must be shut: because after-sought objections would come from him to great disadvantage. whereas the true & solid objection remains in full force, after they shall have the merit of granting all he asks.

Judge Law's letter can be nothing more than an effort to save himself from the appearance of retreating. The Commrs. will surely exhibit their appointments to him, in the expectation of being called into action. if they do not the District attorney (according to what I propose) will on the application of the judge ask appointments from us.

I inclose you a letter from the Mayor of New York, who asks a guard or guards from us to prevent the French blacks from escaping into the country. if a guard to their hospital would suffice, that could be admitted under the provisions of the Quarentine law: and Genl. Dearborne (with whom I concur) seems disposed to this. I think therefore to leave to his discretion to order the guard. but I think it would be well that you should write a friendly explanation of the measure to mr Pichon, to whom it might otherwise wear an unfriendly aspect. I cannot but view this case as still lying substantially within the police of the states, and that we have only small & incidental relations with it; viz. as within the cases of contraband or smuggling. Colo. Monroe has in contemplation to carry his family down on Thursday, not to return. mr Short & Bp. Madison arrived here yesterday. we shall hope to see you here before Monroe goes, as I think an interview with him would not be unuseful. Will you be pleased to order a commission for Wm. Carey to be collector of York vice Wm. Reynolds dead? Accept my affectionate salutations TH: JEFFERSON

P.S. return Livingston's letter to the War office

RC (DLC: Madison Papers); at foot of text: " The Secretary of State." PrC (DLC). Recorded in SJL as a letter to the State Department with notation "sundries." Enclosure: Edward Livingston to Henry Dearborn, 1 Sep. (see Dearborn to TJ, 8 Sep., and TJ to Dearborn, 13 Sep.).

JUDGE LAW'S LETTER: Madison had evidently passed along a letter from Richard Law that has not been found. "I will communicate the names of the Comms. of Bankruptcy in Connecticut to Judge Law by this day's mail," Daniel Brent wrote to Madison on 7 Sep. "I forward a letter herewith, just reced. from him" (Madison, *Papers, Sec. of State Ser.*, 3:556). For an earlier letter from Law to TJ, see TJ to Madison, 9 Aug.

ON THURSDAY: that is, 16 Sep.; the 13th was a Monday.

AN INTERVIEW WITH HIM WOULD NOT BE UNUSEFUL: it was perhaps on one of the occasions when TJ and Monroe were both in Albemarle County in August and September that TJ received from Monroe an untitled, undated essay that began "The acquisition of Louisiana by the French govt. seems to have excited much alarm in the UStates." Monroe probably wrote the comments with the intent of publishing them in a newspaper, for two similar pieces by him, also on the subject of Louisiana, appeared anonymously in the Richmond *Examiner* on 5 and 12 May 1802. In the essay that came into TJ's possession, Monroe argued against any potential alliance of the United States and Great Britain to counter the retrocession of Louisiana to France (MS in DLC: TJ Papers, 126:21776-9, entirely in Monroe's hand; Dft in ViFreJM; Daniel Preston and others, eds., *The Papers of James Monroe*, 4 vols. to date [Santa Barbara, Calif., 2003-   ], 4:589-91, 593-5, 599-601).

From John Barnes

SIR   Geo: Town. 14th. Sepr 1802.

Your two esteemed favrs: 7th & 10th: I recd Yesterday. with reference to Brown & Relf, I find my friend Mr. J. Richards paid them abt. 9th: May 1801. eight dolls: thro. me on your a/c, as by my Entry,

& to your debit, the 13th of which, I shall write them for further explanation in order to its adjustmt:—your Minute of a/c to 4th Sep. agrees exactly with mine, to this day—having Yesterday Negociated, with the Treasury, a Warrant in your favr. for $2,500, as well, taken up your $2000 at Bank, reduces your a/c. to the sum mentioned $1767.91½—

To this Balance, I could with *pleasure Bow*, for two—or even four Mos. rather than have recourse to that painfull Alternative—more especialy in your Absence—and withal so soon after—the late one—

do thou, I pray you Sir, permit me to Accomodate you. I can—under no great inconveniency furnish you with the sum required at Richmond as you may direct—without Applying, as you are pleased to propose, which even admiting the trial, would I presume (—under present circumstances—) be informal, to their Bank regulations—Suffer me then to avoid these Mortifying incidents & to wait at lest, untill your return, your little supplies at Washington are easily Accomodated.—If then thro: Accident, you should not receive this, in time, to favr. me with Answer, by return of the Mail, say 20th. Inst. I purpose taking the liberty & risque upon myself, of transmiting Messrs: Gibson & Jefferson said $1200, subject to your Order.—

I have to intreat your excuse for any seeming inadvertencies (not intentionally advanced)—

but, with unfeigned regard, Esteem, & Respect, wherewith—I am Sir, your most Obedt. Servt.— JOHN BARNES

RC (ViU: Edgehill-Randolph Papers); at foot of text: "President UStates, at Monticello"; endorsed by TJ as received 16 Sep. and so recorded in SJL.

TWO ESTEEMED FAVRS: TJ's letter to Barnes of 7 Sep. 1802 is recorded in SJL, but has not been found. The letter from TJ of 10 Sep. mentioned above probably refers to a letter to Barnes recorded in SJL at 9 Sep., but which likewise has not been found.

Andrew BROWN, Jr., and Samuel RELF published the *Philadelphia Gazette* from July 1799 to September 1801, when Relf became the newspaper's sole publisher (MB, 2:1012; Brigham, *American Newspapers*, 2:911). For the payment of $8 to them by John RICHARDS in May 1801, see Barnes's sketch of TJ's account, 14 May 1801 (Vol. 36:690).

PAINFULL ALTERNATIVE: presumably another bank loan.

SUM REQUIRED AT RICHMOND: see TJ to George Jefferson, 5 Oct. 1802.

From Gideon Granger

DEAR SIR.   Suffield Sept: 14. 1802
In a packet which will go by this days mail, I have forwarded a copy
of Mr. Wolcots late pamphlet and Two Letters which were forwarded to me evidently with a view of Submitting the same to your
perusal, which I think it my duty to do without remark. I understand
we have completely triumphed in Rhode Island. The news from
Vermt. continues favorable—The Slanders which are in circulation
agt. you exceed every thing you can possibly conceive of. I have had
a Swelling in My Throat which came to a head yesterday & I hope
soon to be in Health.

    Your Affectionate friend   GIDN: GRANGER

RC (DLC); at foot of text: "The President"; endorsed by TJ as received 23
Sep. and so recorded in SJL.

LATE PAMPHLET: Oliver Wolcott's *An
Address, to the People of the United States,
on the Subject of the Report of a Committee
of the House of Representatives, Appointed
to "Examine and Report, Whether Monies
Drawn from the Treasury, Have Been
Faithfully Applied to the Objects for which
They Were Appropriated, and Whether the
Same Have Been Regularly Accounted
for." Which Report was Presented on the
29th of April, 1802* (Hartford, 1802;
Sowerby, No. 3285). The pamphlet,
dated 12 July 1802, defended the
previous administration against the accusations made in the 29 Apr. 1802 congressional report, that discussed inappro-
priate expenditures and misapplication of
public monies. John Steele, the comptroller, also criticized the findings (see Steele

to TJ, 28 June 1802). Wolcott sent
Alexander Hamilton a copy of the pamphlet, noting that it furnished several useful truths "to those who wish to comment
upon the conduct of our present administration" (Syrett, *Hamilton*, 26:44-5). For
the call for the investigation, see Vol.
36:212n. The congressional report is
printed in ASP, *Finance*, 1:752-821.

    The TWO LETTERS which Granger for-
warded have not been identified.

    In the election held on 7 Sep., voters in
RHODE ISLAND chose Republicans Nehemiah Knight and Joseph Stanton, Jr.,
to represent the state in the Eighth Congress. The Republican newspapers noted
that, except for the merchants of Providence, the Rhode Island voters were
"firm and numerous in favor of Republicanism" (*Biog. Dir. Cong.*; Boston *Mercury and New-England Palladium*, 10 Sep.
1802; Newport *Rhode-Island Republican*,
9 Oct. 1802).

From Robert Smith

SIR,   Navy Dept. Sep. 14. 1802
    I have received your favor of the 6th. containing your instructions
to me not to send out the John Adams.
    As the crew of this Ship are all engaged and the usual two months
pay advanced them and as of course there will be no additional expence incurred during these two months I have taken the liberty to

suspend the execution of your orders until I shall have the satisfaction of being favored with another letter expressing your determination. This letter I may receive from you on Saturday next. In the mean time we may know to a *certainty* the disposition of the Emperor of Morocco and of the other Barbary Powers. This great advantage we may have by the delay and without any additional expence. And it is from this consideration only that I have not carried into immediate execution your opinion.

It does not appear to me that the state of things with respect to Morocco has been changed by the letter of the Governor of Tangiers to Simpson. War having been formally declared by the Emperor and there having been no revocation of it by him, can we consider it revoked? Was it so considered even by Simpson? — It was, evidently, not so considered by the Emperor himself; because his warlike preparations at Tetuan, Larache and Sallee were not discontinued, but were progressing and at Tetuan with great activity.

The permission of the Emperor to Simpson was not to *return*, but to *remain*. It must have been given under the idea that Simpson had not then left Tangiers and it was probably given under the expectation that the Adams (then daily expected) would bring, as Simpson had repeatedly assured the Governor, instructions to grant the required passports. — Why did not Simpson accept the invitation to return? Because we were, as he conceived, in a State of War with Morocco as the Declaration of War had not been revoked.

With respect to the new negotiations with the Emperor mentioned in your last letter it is my opinion that he will not negotiate a peace but, under the influence of *presents* or of *fear*. *Presents* of such magnitude are not contemplated. And *fear* cannot be excited but by a respectable squadron promptly displayed in the view of his ports.

There is besides strong ground to apprehend that the Dey of Algiers will not be inclined to receive the 30,000 Dollars and that he will be much disposed to reject Cathcart. A formidable force in the neighbourhood of Algiers would probably have the affect of restraining such evil dispositions.

Our anxieties moreover about Tunis have not been Officially or in any form removed.

So far from considering that Tripoli is to be our only Enemy, I am rather inclined to believe that nothing but a formidable squadron will prevent all the Barbary powers waging war against us. A superior force in the Mediterranean will ensure us an early peace and will enable us to dictate the terms that will be the most honorable and beneficial to us. A feeble force, on the Contrary, will subject us to the necessity of purchasing a peace upon the same terms that have from time to time been imposed upon the small powers of Europe.[1]

It may not be improper to inform you, that the John Adams has been equipped with such dispatch that she will be ready to weigh anchor on Friday next. She will however be detained for your further orders.

Be pleased to accept the assurance of the great respect and esteem with which, I am Sir,

Your Ob. Servt.   RT. SMITH

RC (DLC); at foot of text: "The President"; endorsed by TJ as received from the Navy Department on 16 Dec. and "the John Adams" and so recorded in SJL, but as received 16 Sep. Dft (MdHi).

WARLIKE PREPARATIONS: for Mawlay Sulayman's efforts to refit his naval forces at Tetuán and Salé, see Samuel Smith to TJ, 9 Aug., and Robert Smith to TJ, 20 Aug. In his 3 July dispatch to the secretary of state, James Simpson reported

that the sultan had also ordered the preparation of a "neglected" frigate at Larache, but added his opinion that "I think it is scarce possible she can be made fit for Sea" (NDBW, 2:191).

[1] In Dft, Smith here began a new paragraph and then canceled it: "These desultory remarks I submit with great deference to your judgment, and with alacrity I will attend to your Ultimate determination."

Deed for Land Purchased from Thomas Wells, Jr.

This Indenture made on the 15th day of September 1802 between Thomas Wells Junr. of the one part and Thomas Jefferson of the other part, both of the County of Albemarle Witnessith, that the said Thomas Wells In consideration of the sum of Forty pounds Current Money of Virginia to him paid by the said Tho. Jefferson hath given granted, Bargained and sold unto the said Thomas Jefferson a certain Tract or parcel of Land in the said County of Albemarle containing by estimation Forty acres more or less and bounded as followith, to Wit, Begining at an antient forked Chesnut in the Gap between the High Mountain and the one next adjoining it, being already a corner to the Lands of the said parties And of James Monroe And runing thence along the dividing line of the said parties on the north side of the said High Mountain One Hundred and five poles to where the Lands of the said Thomas Wells and Benjamin Browne cornered in a side line of the said Thomas Jefferson Thence down the said Mountain along the dividing line between the said Thomas

Wells and Benjn Browne to where it is now to corner with the Lands purchased by the said Thomas Jefferson of the said Benjamin Browne, and with the remaining Lands of the said Thomas Wells & Benjamin to Wit in a marked line runing S. 25° W. thence along the said marked line Ten poles Thence South Twenty poles to a Branch in the main valley dividing the said High Mountain And the one next adjoining it. Thence up the said Branch and main valley according to their course to the head Spring of the said Branch, Which branch and valley may be traced by the following Magnetic courses, to Wit, S. 37° E. $6\frac{4}{10}$ poles S. 16° W. 5 poles. South $7\frac{48}{100}$ poles S. 41° E. 8 po. S. 43° E. 8 po. S. 49° E. 16 po. S. $61\frac{1}{2}$° E. 8 po. S. 49° E. 10 poles S. $26\frac{1}{2}$° E. $7\frac{6}{10}$ po. S. $64\frac{1}{2}$° E. $10\frac{84}{100}$ po. S. $34\frac{1}{2}$° E. 13 po. S. 20° E. $11\frac{6}{10}$ po. to the said Spring: Thence up the said valley S. $36\frac{1}{2}$° E. $26\frac{48}{100}$ po. to the Begining at the forked Chesnut, Which Last mentioned course being found by protraction, the Trees thereon, were not marked: To have and to hold the said parcel of Land with its appurtenances to him the said Thomas Jefferson and his Heirs. And the said Thomas Wells his Heirs, Executors and Administrators the said parcel of Land with its appurtenances to him the said Thomas Jefferson and his Heirs will forever Warrant and Defend. In Witness Whereof the said Thomas Wells hath hereto set his hand and seal on the day and Year above Written, to Wit on the   day of September One thousand Eight Hundred and two.

THOMAS WELLS JUNR.

Signed, sealed and Delivered in }
presence of
BENJM. BROWN }
RN. LINDSAY }
MICH. WOODS }
At a Superior Court directed by Law to be holden in Charlottesville for the District composed of the Counties of Albemarle, Louisa, Fluvanna and Amherst the 15th day of September 1802. This Indenture was produced into Court and acknowledged by Thomas Wells Junr. party thereto and ordered to be recorded.   Teste

JOHN CARR CDCC

Tr (Albemarle County District Court Deed Book No. 1:165-6); entirely in a clerk's hand.

Perhaps to aid in the preparation of this INDENTURE, TJ copied, on an unknown date, a survey that Wells had ordered for his $496\frac{1}{2}$ acre property earlier in the year (MS in CSmH; entirely in TJ's hand; copy of survey by William Woods, 29 Mch. 1802; see Nichols, *Architectural Drawings*, No. 516).

Witnesses to the delivery of the deed most likely included Reuben LINDSAY, an old friend of TJ, or Lindsay's nephew of the same name who lived just below Milton, and Micajah woods, who later served as an Albemarle deputy sheriff (Woods, *Albemarle*, 257, 354; mb, 1:292; 2:1231).

From G. Louis de Golz

Newburyport—Massachusetts
Sir! the 15th: Septembr: 1802.

Pardon my boldness in sending this letter as an humble suitor in my behalf, to entreat Your kind and benevolent Patronage and protection in my present distressing situation, having been deprived of my property by the late desolation dd: 5 Febry: a.c., of Cape François, where unluckily I then happened to be with my property consisting of Merchandises consumed by the flames. Now an unfortunate foreigner, placed in a distant Country, where every one is Suspicious of my character, activity &c: borne down by distress, Want, and despair of Success or application, and deprived even of the Small money of defraying the expences of a Voyage to my Native Country to Swisserland, or any other Part of Europe, where my Character, and abilities are already known, and where of Course, I should find some eligible employment, by which means I then might Repair my losses, or at least prevent the dreadful idea of inevitable destruction. Thus, my situation being exceedingly distressing, I presume to crave Your leave to lay at Your feet, my best tribute of duty and thankfulness, for any employment and application of my best services; I will readily accept of any employment, however small the income, as of a clerk or any thing else. I would only wish for an opportunity, when I might be able to develope my real activity, and abilities connected with the most sober Character.

Honoured Sir! Pardon my importunity in presenting You, tho' against the rules of delicacy and decorum, the enclosed analytical Sketch or description of my Circumstances and situation—

Whatever Your pleasure shall be, I entirely submit to Your discretion, and shall rest satisfied with Your disposition of my services. Let me hear soon good news, which may releive and rejoice me; let me be removed hence wheresoever You please, and give me liberty to importune You, to lay Your Command upon me, that I might have soon occasion for paying You my best tribute of duty and Gratitude.

Sir! Your most humble Servant   G. Louis de Golz

P:S. My direction or rather that of letters for me is to Mr: *Ralph Cross*—Collector of the District of Newburyport.

RC (DNA: RG 59, LAR); endorsed by TJ as received 23 Sep. and "Office" and so recorded in SJL. Enclosure: "An Analytical Sketch of the Circumstances of G. Louis de Golz," stating that de Golz was born in 1774 near Lake Constance in the Swiss canton of Schaffhausen, where lay the ashes of his parents; his mother "sacrificed every thing for the best education of her only Son," which permitted de Golz to cultivate his interest in "all the European languages," as well as "all the sciences, belles lettres, technical arts, Agriculture &c: in order to form a Systematical idea of Cosmography"; in accordance with his mother's wishes, however, de Golz studied law "and the other respective Sciences" at Basel and Leipzig before removing to Vienna, following the prevailing "false opinion" that only Joseph von Sonnenfels could successfully instruct young men in "the Sciences of Finance, Diplomacy, &c"; following the death of his mother, de Golz found that his inheritance would not answer his wants; he turned to mercantile pursuits on advice received from Count von Hertzberg, the Prussian minister of finance; he served as a clerk in Hamburg for six years, conducting mercantile correspondence in several languages and traveling on business to many European countries, which further enhanced his knowledge of European languages, manners, and customs; after 18 months at a Paris counting house, de Golz went to London, where he was employed in claiming the naval prizes of neutral merchants at the Court of Admiralty; peace ended this employment and de Golz subsequently invested all his property in "Merchandize proper for the West Indian Markets"; he left London after the preliminary treaty of peace was signed and traveled by way of Charleston, South Carolina, to Havana, Cuba, where he sold his goods "with a very flattering advantage"; returning to Charleston, he then went "with a fresh Speculation" to Saint-Domingue, where the French fleet appeared on 5 Feb. 1802, a few days after his own arrival; the presence of the French "induced the Negroes to set fire to all the houses &c: at Cape-François, where all my Merchandises and goods were distroyed, and I but with difficulty could save myself from destruction" (MS in same).

For the LATE DESOLATION of Cap-Français, see Vol. 36:598-600; Vol. 37:574-7.

From George Jefferson

DEAR SIR   Richmond 15th. Septr. 1802

I am duly favor'd with yours of the 8th., and shall endeavour to dispose of your Tobo. to the best advantage. I have not yet been offered more than 5 dollars, but shall not now be satisfied with that, as it is in rather more demand than it was when I last wrote to you on the subject.

Whether it is sold or not however, you are at liberty to draw for the sum you require.

In consequence of the River being so low I sent you some days ago with some things of Mr. Randolph's, and by a waggoner of his acquaintance, the two *small* boxes which arrived from Geo. Town and one which was since recd. from Philadelphia, and which I hope will arrive safe with you.

I am Dear Sir Your Very humble servt.   GEO. JEFFERSON

RC (MHi); at foot of text: "Thos. Jefferson"; endorsed by TJ as received 17 Sep. and so recorded in SJL.

From James Madison

DEAR SIR   Sepr. 15. 1802

I have duly recd. yours of the 13th. I had been apprised of the application by the Mayor of N.Y. for a guard. Considering as you do, that the federal Govt. have only an incidental connection with the case of the French Negroes, I have waited for more particular information concerning them, before writing to Pichon, who I learnt from Mr. Brent, and also from himself, was exerting himself to get them away. His plan was to ship them to France, but he was at a loss for the means. I had my fears that if prematurely pressed on the subject, it might lead to applications for aid. The mail of tomorrow, I hope will bring me from Mr. Brent an answer to some enquiries which will assist in framing a proper letter to him.

I am sorry to learn that Col. Monroe is so soon to leave Albemarle with his family. I had assured myself that I should see him on our visit to his neighbourhood, as your letter intimated that he would not leave it till tuesday next. We propose to be with you, accompanied by Dr. Thornton his lady & her mother, on saturday evening, and still hope, that the oppy. may not be lost. It will add to the satisfaction, to find Bishop Madison as well as Mr. Short at Monticello. I shall direct a comission to be made out for Mr. Cary to take the place of Mr. Reynolds.

Yours as ever   JAMES MADISON

RC (DLC); at foot of text: "The President of the U. States."; endorsed by TJ as received from the State Department at Orange on 16 Sep. and "guards for N.Y." and so recorded in SJL.

I HAD BEEN APPRISED: Daniel Brent had sent Madison, on 7 Sep., a copy of Edward Livingston's letter to Dearborn of 1 Sep. (Madison, *Papers, Sec. of State Ser.*, 3:556).

AND ALSO FROM HIMSELF: the communication from Louis André Pichon has not been found. Brent's letter of 7 Sep. informed Madison that "Mr Pichon intends, if he can effect it, to send the Ships and Negroes to France." Pichon wrote to Madison from Frankfort, Pennsylvania, on 25 Sep., after his visit to New York. He assured Madison that the "prisonniers de couleur" would be transported to France. The French chargé instructed Louis Arcambal to collect information about any of the involuntary émigrés who escaped before the ships left the harbor (Madison, *Papers, Sec. of State Ser.*, 3:555, 598-9).

WE PROPOSE TO BE WITH YOU: the Madisons, Thorntons, and Mrs. Ann Brodeau departed from Montpelier on the morning of 18 Sep. for a week-long stay at Monticello. Accompanied for 12 miles along the way by Bishop James Madison and his son, they arrived after dark because of bad roads and warm weather. According to Anna Maria Thornton's diary, an approaching storm and the dangerous terrain prompted all of the party except for Mrs. Brodeau to walk the final three-quarters of a mile, with lightning illuminating their way and a violent thunderstorm commencing shortly after their arrival. Mrs. Thornton recorded her expectation of seeing Monticello as an "unfinished house" and her first impressions of "being much struck with the uncommon appearance & which the general gloom that prevailed contributed much to increase." She described a place that had been "so frequently pulled down and rebuilt, that in many parts without sides it looks like a house going to decay" from the time it was built. Monticello had "a whimsical and a droll appearance" and she concluded there was "something grand and awful in the situation but far from convenient or in my opinion agreeable—it is a place you wou'd rather look at now and then than live at" (MS in DLC: Anna Maria Brodeau Thornton Papers; Irving Brant, *James Madison: Secretary of State 1800-1809* [Indianapolis, 1953], 44).

From Anthony Haswell

RESPECTED SIR,   Bennington, Septr. 16th. 1802.

Emboldened by your acknowledged courtesy, at the request of a distressed neighbour, I trouble you with the present address.—

While Major H. Buell was recruiting in this quarter a young man in his 19th year, greatly against the will of his parents enlisted into Captain M'Clary's company, and soon after marched off for Pittsburgh.—The young man's name is Jeremiah[1] Battels, he enlisted in December 1799, and is now about 21 years of age.—

Being his father's greatest dependance, (who is somewhat in years, and scarcely able to manage his little place) the old gentleman has solicited me to write to obtain his discharge, presuming that as the new law forbids such enlistments, redress of a grievance long endured under a different system, may possibly be attainable.—

Indefatigable exertions have been made by the opposition to procure a federal representation in our approaching session of the state legislature, but from my present returns I conceive they have failed— The districting of our state for the choice of federal representatives, the choice of a senator for the Western District, and some other important businesses, render the existence of a republican house highly desirable.—

With grateful millions, Sir, I sensate the advantages of your auspicious administration, and sincerely pray the sovereign arbiter, to award you length of days and happy accompaniments, equal to the arduousness of your toils and the purity of your intentions.—

Enclosed herewith I send a compilation, made from an obscure manuscript of only three sheets;[2] my boldness in doing which you will excuse, and permit me

With heart felt esteem, and the respect of a sincere republican, to subscribe Your fellow citizen ANTHONY HASWELL.

P.S. My much respected neighbor Moses Robinson is chosen our representative for the town of Bennington, in the ensuing legislature.

RC (DLC); endorsed by TJ as received 5 Oct. and so recorded in SJL. Enclosure: probably Anthony Haswell, *Memoirs and Adventures of Captain Matthew Phelps; Formerly of Harwington in Connecticut, Now Resident in Newhaven in Vermont* (Bennington, Vt., 1802; Sowerby, No. 518).

YOUR ACKNOWLEDGED COURTESY: see Vol. 35:265.

CAPTAIN Andrew M'CLARY, a member of the North Carolina line during the Revolutionary War, also fought with Anthony Wayne in the later Indian wars.

Honorably discharged in 1802, he accepted a clerkship in the War Department (Hiram Carleton, ed., *Genealogical and Family History of the State of Vermont,* 2 vols. [New York, 1903], 2:18; Virgil D. White, *Genealogical Abstracts of Revolutionary War Pension Files,* 4 vols. [Waynesboro, Tenn., 1990-92], 2:2247).

MOSES ROBINSON served his only term in the Vermont General Assembly in 1802 (*Biog. Dir. Cong.*).

[1] Interlined in place of "William."
[2] Preceeding four words interlined.

To Henry Dearborn

DEAR SIR   Monticello Sep. 17. 1802.

The permission of the Emperor of Marocco to our Consul to remain for six months for the purpose of explanations, which is their way of declaring a state of peace having materially changed the state of things in the Mediterranean, I had recommended to mr Smith to stop the sailing of the John Adams. I now recieve a letter from him pressing her sailing. I had thought the thing so obvious as not to have asked opinions. however I shall now be glad of advice on the subject & will ask the favor of your opinion by return of post, which, altho' I must write to mr Smith on the subject before I can recieve it, will yet be in time for an ultimate determination.[1] Accept my friendly salutations.   TH: JEFFERSON

PrC (DLC); at foot of text: "The Secretary at War." Recorded in SJL as a letter to the War Department with notation "the John Adams."

A LETTER FROM HIM: Robert Smith to TJ, 14 Sep.

[1] TJ here canceled: "should you recieve this in the [even]ing of tomorrow, another post which."

To Albert Gallatin

DEAR SIR   Monticello Sep. 17. 1802.

Your's of the 9th. came to hand yesterday only so that it has missed a post somewhere. I thought that in my letter of Aug. 20. answering your's of Aug. 17. that I had answered every point distinctly; but I find on recurring to it that the recommendations of messrs. Langdon & Whipple for Hopley Yeaton to be master and Benjamin Gunnison 1st. mate of the revenue cutter in Newhampshire, tho' intended to have been approved were omitted. I now approve of them.

Mine of the 8th. will have informed you that I had countermanded the sailing of the John Adams on an invitation of the Emperor of Marocco to Simpson to remain. but I have yesterday recieved a letter from mr R. Smith strongly dissuading that countermand and pressing for her departure. I do not answer finally by this post, because mr Madison is to be with me tomorrow & we will consider the subject on your's & mr Smith's letters. I had thought the thing so plain on general grounds, that I had asked no advice on it. but I have now written to Genl. Dearborn for his opinion. I confess I see no argument for 6. frigates which does not go to 12.

I shall be at Washington on the last day of this, or 1st. of the next month. Accept my affectionate salutations & respect.

TH: JEFFERSON

RC (NHi: Gallatin Papers); addressed: "Albert Gallatin Secretary of the Treasury Washington"; franked; postmarked Milton; endorsed. PrC (DLC). Recorded in SJL as a letter to the Treasury Department with notation "do." for "the John Adams" and "master &c of revenue cutter."

DISSUADING THAT COUNTERMAND: Robert Smith to TJ, 14 Sep.

WRITTEN TO GENL. DEARBORN: see the preceding letter.

To James Madison

DEAR SIR   Monticello Sep. 17. 1802.

I recieved yesterday your's of the 15th. in the hope of seeing you here tomorrow I return no papers. I will pray you not to fail in your visit. I have recd. a letter from mr R. Smith disapproving of the countermand of the John Adams for reasons detailed; & one from mr Gallatin disapproving of the original order for her sailing. (he had not then, Sep. 9. heard of the countermand) the vessel now awaits our decision, which I have delayed till the next post, in order to consult with you on the subject. this renders it interesting that you should preserve your purpose of coming tomorrow, when I shall be happy to recieve your's & Dr. Thornton's families & friends. Bp. Madison is gone. Colo. Monroe was to go off yesterday; but I have not heard whether his family is gone or not. if not, he will be back on Tuesday. but I rather expect they are gone. Dr. Bache has broken up house-keeping, ready for his departure. accept my affectionate salutations.

TH: JEFFERSON

PrC (DLC); at foot of text: "The Secretary of State." Recorded in SJL as a letter to the State Department with notation "do." for "the John Adams."

SMITH DISAPPROVING: Robert Smith to TJ, 14 Sep.

From Thomas Munroe

SIR,   Washington 17th. September 1802

The Sale of Lots which commenced on Monday the 30th. ulto. was continued from day to day during that week, and was adjourned on Saturday the 4th. Instant 'till monday the 13th Instant, and has since been continued daily.—About 100 Lots were sold the first week, & four only have been sold this week—the whole Amount of sales is about $9,500.—After the third or fourth day of sale competition amongst the purchasers almost ceased, the best and the largest lots (which were first called up) having been by that time nearly all sold.—

One or two persons have since offered from five to fifteen, & in one instance twenty, dollars ℔ Lot for many Lots w'ch owe the public from one to two hundred Dollars, but thinking so great a sacrafice at so early a period of the sale would be unjustifiable I have hitherto declined selling at such very low prices, knowing the lots will at any other time during the sale bring at least as much, if not more—by so doing I have in several instances got ten times the Amount of the rejected bids for the same Lots, by afterwards setting them up at something near the sums due on them, whenever I have observed as many persons attending the sale as to render competition probable.— Altho' in some instances the sales which have been made will, I fear, be very injurious to individuals, it is generally said here that the prices have been much higher than was expected, but however great the sacrifices may have been considered there are the strongest reasons to expect they must be much greater before all the Lots advertised can be sold.—I have offerred to sell as low as a quarter of a Cent ℔ square foot, or $30 ℔ Lot, yet have not made a single sale, or recd.

a single bid today or the two preceeding days, nor do I expect to make any more sales until it is made known that the Lots will be sold for whatever may be bid for them, but the probable consequence thereof, I think, will be that as we have no distant purchasers; and there being so little money or demand for Lots amongst the people here, the few who have money will purchase as many of the best lots as they want at, from five to ten Dollars each; which will fall very far short of producing the $50,000 due to the State of Maryland, even if the worst Lots should sell at that price also—.

I shall keep the sale open from day to day and continue to do the best I can until I may be honored by your instructions on the subject which I beg leave, Sir, respectfully to solicit.

I presume it will be proper to give a week or ten days previous notice (in case nothing better can be done) that on, and after a certain day any sum which may be offerred for a Lot will be received as a bid—The Bank of Columbia has threatened me with an execution for the $2,500 due on the Commissioners note endorsed by me. I supposed that the money arising from the present sales was applicable to the payment of that note but Mr Mason appears to be of a contrary opinion—I take the liberty of enclosing the Law & Mr. Ms. Opinion for your perusal in case your leisure will admit of it.—

I have the Honor to be with the highest respect Sir Yr mo Ob. Servt.   THOMAS MUNROE

RC (DLC); addressed: "President of the United States"; endorsed by TJ as received 19 Sep. and so recorded in SJL. Enclosures: (1) probably a copy of "An Act to abolish the Board of Commissioners in the City of Washington; and for other purposes," enacted by Congress on 1 May 1802 (U.S. Statutes at Large, 2:175-8). (2) John Thomson Mason to Munroe, 7 Sep. 1802, observing that by the wording of Section 4 of the act abolishing the board of commissioners for the city of Washington, it appears that only funds received by Munroe as superintendent when the law passed can be applied toward paying the debt due to the Bank of Columbia, since the debt was contracted by the commissioners and no special provision for its payment exists elsewhere in the law; "That is the gramatical construction of the clause," Mason writes, "But that could not be the meaning of Congress, for you only came into existence after the passage of the law, and could therefore have received no monies when it passed"; a slight rewording of the clause would have given Munroe power to use funds from the sale of lots, but the provision at the end of Section 6 stands "very much in the way" by directing that all monies from the sale be applied toward the Maryland loan and the interest due thereon, and only allows the Treasury to pay the remaining deficiency once the proceeds of the sale have been applied; "Upon the whole," Mason concludes, "I would advise you to postpone the application of any part of this money until you obtain the directions of the President" (RC in DLC; endorsed by TJ: "opn on paiment of monies").

For notes drawn by the District of Columbia commissioners on the BANK OF COLUMBIA, see ASP, *Miscellaneous*, 1:228; Vol. 36:166-7; Vol. 37:586-7.

To Robert Smith

DEAR SIR   Monticello Sep. 17. 1802.

The object of the present is merely to acknolege the reciept of yours of the 14th. and to mention that I have recieved a letter from mr Gallatin disapproving of the first order for the sailing of the John Adams, on general grounds & also on the special ground that the appropriations for that object were exhausted: further that mr Madison will be with me tomorrow, and that I will then take the subject into consideration and give you the result by the post which leaves this the 20th. you will recieve it the 21st. in the mean time I would recommend that[1] the vessel should not be moved from her present birth. Accept assurances of my affectionate esteem & respect.

TH: JEFFERSON

PrC (DLC); at foot of text: "The Secretary of the Navy." Recorded in SJL as a letter to the Navy Department with notation "the John Adams."

A LETTER FROM MR GALLATIN: Gallatin to TJ, 9 Sep. (first letter).

[1] TJ here canceled "the preparations be suspended."

From Caleb P. Wayne

SIR,   Philadelphia, September 17. 1802.

Enclosed you will receive Proposals for publishing by Subscription, a History of the late General George Washington; your presenting it to any of your friends, will greatly oblige me, and should you think proper to sanction it with your own name, it will be duly appreciated

By Sir, Your most obedient Servant,   C. P. WAYNE

RC (DLC); printed, with date and signature in Wayne's hand; endorsed by TJ as received 23 Sep. and "subscribed 1. copy." Enclosure not found, but see below.

Caleb P. Wayne (1776-1849) published the short-lived Boston *Federal Gazette* in 1798 before moving to Philadelphia and assuming control from 28 May 1800 to November 1801, of the *Gazette of the United States*. After more than two years of negotiations, in September 1802, he reached agreement with Bushrod Wash-

ington, the trustee of George Washington's papers, on the terms for publication of a multi-volume work on the *Life of George Washington* to be written by John Marshall in five octavo volumes, with the first to be published in January 1803 (Brigham, *American Newspapers*, 1:295, 2:913; Marshall, *Papers*, 6:220-1; *Alexandria Advertiser*, 6 Sep. 1802; *Gazette of the United States*, 22 Sep. 1802; New York *Daily Advertiser*, 25 Sep. 1802).

SANCTION IT WITH YOUR OWN NAME: TJ subscribed to one copy of Marshall's work and made corrections and marginal annotations to it. He had previously proposed that Joel Barlow write a Republican history to counter Marshall's Federalist interpretation (Sowerby, No. 496; Vol. 37:401).

From Thomas Leiper

DEAR SIR   Crum Creek Snuff Mills Septr. 19th. 1802

The Plan with the opposition is to divid and I am affraid they have in some measure effected their purpose but how can it be otherwise when our Principle men are at Daggers Drawn Logan & Lieb who certainly at this time should unite are saying very hard things of each other and supposing what they say on both sides is true it answers no other purpose but to destroy the usefulness of both and where it will end time can only tell this I am clear in as the Sun at noon day they are injuring the republican cause—The meetting at the Rising Sun on the 21st. has nothing in View but to[1] turn Lieb out of the Ticket for member of Congress for altho they add members of Assembly this is a very secondery matter—Lieb's name being fixed by the Committees of the District renders this meetting a very improper measure and if the point is carried we shall all be in the wind—

The Germans in Pennsylvania are a very powerful Body and their incress are more rapid than any other people and they will stick to-gether—Muhlenburg & Leib are some where about the Head of them and they have no political Ideas abstracted from each other and it appears to me that Lieb is first in command—Logan cannot be a stranger to this and if it is true that Logan is at the botham of this business it says very little for him as a Politician—I spoak to Leib on this subject and informed him it was very improper for him and Logan to have any misunderstanding at this time—He informed me without any ifs or ands that Logan was making a Business of destroying his and G Muhlenbergs standing and informed me further that Logan meant to be Governor and that he would traduce the character of every one who stood in his way—This is certainly looking a long way a Head for I think Mc.Kean has a fee simple in that office for ten years to come—I intend to be at the Rising Sun next Tuesday and do what I can to make our Rope of Sand stick to-gether—Let me not be misunderstood our Rotten Rope extends no further than the City and county of Philadelphia and the county of Delaware the other parts of the State stand fast to their original principles—I was always of the opinion you should turn out of office to make room for the Old Soldier and others who may have been reduced by the war. but I have another reason for turning out to make room for some men of whom I am affraid their habits of Republicanism will not be steady without an office—This I look upon as one of our greatest misfortunes and the evil cannot be corrected but by a change in office notwithstanding any thing Madison or Gallatin may say to the contrary— Dallas & Cox are at outs but they may come in at their leisure their difference cannot hurt us but I was very much surprized at the appointing of a Committee It was mention'd if Cox was appointed Dallas would not serve—the same thing was said of Logan if Leib was appointed, but I appointed both—Logan declined serving—This information I thought it my duty to put you in possession of I am Your most obedient Sert   THOMAS LEIPER

RC (DLC); endorsed by TJ as received 23 Sep. and so recorded in SJL.

In one of the earliest open breaks within the Republican coalition in Philadelphia, a group of Republicans opposed to Michael Leib organized a meeting at the RISING SUN tavern outside of Philadelphia on 15 Sep. There they warned of rifts arising from the nominations of that "improper character" for Congress and of some of the Republicans running for the state legislature. They also called for a general county meeting to be held on the 21st. The movement was probably instigated by United States senator George LOGAN, who had unsuccessfully attempt-

ed to block Leib's nomination during the summer (Philadelphia *Aurora*, 17 Sep. 1802; Higginbotham, *Pennsylvania Politics*, 43-5; Frederick B. Tolles, *George Logan of Philadelphia* [New York, 1953], 233-4).

At a 6 Sep. meeting of supporters of Thomas McKean's reelection as governor, Leiper sat in the chair and supervised the selection of a Republican correspondence COMMITTEE. Leiper served on the committee, along with Alexander J. DALLAS, Leib, and several other Philadelphia Republicans (Higginbotham, *Pennsylvania Politics*, 45-6).

[1] MS: "t."

From John Callender

SIR/   Boston Septr. 20th. 1802.

Previous to the amendment of the bankrupt act, I held an appointment under the judge of this District as a commissioner of bankrupts—by which I was enabled to support myself & family—the loss of this office in consequence of the new arrangement has been a serious misfortune to me—as it was the principle source of my subsistence—I observe that one or two of the gentlemen appointed here do not accept, & are not employed in the duties of this office—I therefore take the liberty most earnestly to request of the president, that he would be pleased to appoint me as commissioner aforesaid—The president is respectfully referred to Mr Morton for any information which he may wish concerning the character & capacity of this applicant. I am sir with sentiments of respect your most obedient and very hble servt

RC (DNA: RG 59, LAR); at head of text: "Thomas Jefferson Esqr. President of the United States"; endorsed by TJ as received 10 Nov. and so recorded in SJL with notation "for emploiment." Enclosed in Perez Morton to Levi Lincoln, 4 Oct. and Lincoln to TJ, 29 Oct. 1802.

John Callender (1772-1833) of Boston, was a 1790 graduate of Harvard College, a lieutenant in the Boston Light Infantry in 1798, a member of the state legislature, secretary of the Massachusetts Society of the Cincinnati, and a clerk of the Supreme Judicial Court (James Spear Loring, *The Hundred Boston Orators Appointed by the Municipal Authorities and Other Public Bodies, From 1770 to 1852*, 2d ed. [Boston, 1853], 257-8).

From Henry Dearborn

SIR   War Department Septr. 20th, 1802

I have this morning been honoured with your letter of the 17th. on receit of your former letter in which you mentioned the subject of the sailing of the John Adams, I had a conversation with the Secretary of the Navy relative to the propriety of the sailing of any other force to the Mediterranian, the John Adams being then almost ready for Sea, with her crew on board, it was then our mutual opinion that it would be adviseable to send her down to Hampton road, and there to wait until some further information should be received from the Mediterranian, by which the real intentions of the Emperor of Morocco could be with more certainty ascertained, and that her ultimate destination should depend on what by such information should appear to be the real state of things relative to Morocco,—the men having received their two months advance, and nearly the whole of the expence necessary for the equipment of the Ship having been incurred, her going down the river & waiting for further information, which Mr. Smith presumes will undoubtedly be received within a few days, would not materially increase the public expence. Mr. Smith appears to place very little confidence in the pacific disposition of the Emperor, and urges Mr. Simpsons declining to return to Morocco in evidence of his opinion—

with the most respectfull consideration I am Sir Your Huml Sevt.

H. DEARBORN

RC (DLC); at foot of text: "The President of the United States"; endorsed by TJ as received from the War Department on 23 Sep. and "the John Adams" and so recorded in SJL.

From George Divers

Dr. Sir Dr. Sir   Farmington 20th Sepr. 1802

I have received a letter from Mr. Thomas Mitchell the Father of the young Gentleman who is the bearer of this, requesting that I would introduce his son to you, He wishes an appointment as a midshipman on board one of the frigates bound to the Medeteranian,

I am well acquainted with his Father and Uncle Wm. Mitchell of Richmond, but the Young Gentleman is unknown to me; He appears a spritly young fellow & I doubt not if there be a Vacancy but that he would fill it very well, & indeed I feel a wish if that should be the case he should get the appointment. with respect

    I am yr. friend & Serva   George Divers

RC (DNA: RG 59, LAR); endorsed by TJ as received 22 Sep. and "Francis Mitchell to be Midshipman" and so recorded in SJL.

From 26 Mch. 1794 to 12 Sep. 1800, TJ recorded in SJL exchanging seven letters with Divers, his old friend and fellow Albemarle County resident. None of those letters, each of which was written while TJ was staying at Monticello, has been found (MB, 2:913, 920, 973, 994, 1001, 1027; Vol. 24:663; Vol. 25:3-4).

For Francis Mitchell, the YOUNG GENTLEMAN, see TJ to Mitchell, 21 Nov. 1802.

To Albert Gallatin

Dear Sir   Monticello Sep. 20. 1802.

In my last I informed you I should have an opportunity of getting mr Madison's opinion on the expediency of the sailing of the John Adams. I have done so, communicating to him your's & mr Smith's letters on the subject. the latter having informed us that two months pay were already advanced to the men, & her stores provided, the[1] consideration of a defective appropriation was already got over, & we were committed in it: and the remaining expences of the voyage were thought so small as to be overweighed by the advantages which may result from her going. to this opinion I have acceded, tho' not with entire satisfaction I confess. perhaps I build too much on the expectation of a state of peace with Marocco & Tunis. perhaps I see too strongly the embarrasment of the defective appropriation. would it be possible to put the extra advances on the footing of a debt incurred, the arrearages of which might be covered by a future appropriation? should the John Adams find us at peace with all the Barbary powers except Tripoli, I have referred to mr Smith to recall all the frigates except two, before winter, or to let the question lie till we get together. I expect to set out for Washington this day sennight, & to be there on the last day of the month; but I may be 1. 2. or 3. days later. mr Madison will not be there so soon. Accept my affectionate salutations.   TH: JEFFERSON

RC (NHi: Gallatin Papers); addressed: "Albert Gallatin Secretary of the Treasury Washington"; endorsed. PrC (DLC). Recorded in SJL as a letter to the Treasury Department with notation "do." for "the John Adams."

MY LAST: 17 Sep.

YOUR'S & MR SMITH'S LETTERS: that is, Gallatin's first letter of 9 Sep. and Robert Smith's of the 14th.

[1] TJ here canceled "question."

To Thomas Munroe

DEAR SIR   Monticello Sep. 20. 1802.
   Your favor of the 17th is recieved. I think that while there is a prospect of getting better prices by postponing the sale of the lots, the public interest requires they should be postponed. to what time I leave to your own judgment, observing only that the law has fixed a limit beyond which we cannot postpone.
   With respect to the paiment of your note to the Columbia bank I am in hopes no inconvenience may arise by my deferring to [...] up an opinion [on] it till I return. I shall leave this place this day sennight & be in Washington the fourth day. Accept my best wishes & salutations   TH: JEFFERSON

PrC (DLC); faint; at foot of text: "Mr. Thomas Munroe."

LAW HAS FIXED A LIMIT: the 1 May

1802 act of Congress required that the sale of lots in Washington take place prior to 1 Nov. 1802 (U.S. Statutes at Large, 2:176).

From Nathaniel Niles

                                          West Fairlee (Vermont)
SIR   Septr. 20. 1802
   Permit me, with an honest confidence in your disposition to gratify every individual as far as your duty and the public good will allow, to solicit a favour at your hand, for Mr. William Watson an aged gentleman at Plymouth, Massachusetts, who at the commencement of our revolutionary troubles, seperated himself from the body of his relatives and particular friends (which was large and respectable) and attached himself inviolably to the cause of our country, and by doing so, sacraficed, as I have been informd, much of his property. He has

indeed ranged himself on the side of the federal party, from the begining of Mr. Adams's presidency; but every part of his political conduct has been marked with moderation. He has at present almost no
means of support, except a very small income as judge of a county
court, & that arising from his office in the custom house. The favour
I ask, is that he may not be removed from that [office], unless the
public good shall unquestiona[bly de]mand it.

[...] of his friends have been affraid, he would be displaced. To
these I have uniformly and freely given it as my opinion that he is in
no danger under your administration. This opinion is founded in the
belief that his continuance in office will be much more friendly to
your great object than his removal could be. My only apology for
troubling you with this is that the solicitude of his other friends may
be quieted. Yet, Sir, affection and respect for this Gentleman may
have misled me. He is Father to Mrs. Niles.

The cruelties inflicted on you Sir, in the news papers, sometimes
almost prompt a wish that the sedition law were still in full force, and
duely executed; but the [next] cool thought condemns it as inconsistent with the spirit of our Government.

I have the honour to be Sir with the most profound respect Your
obedient Humble Servant   NATHL NILES

RC (DNA: RG 59, LAR); torn; endorsed by TJ as received 5 Oct. and so
recorded in SJL; also endorsed by TJ:
"Watson of Plymouth not to be removed."

For the removal of WILLIAM WATSON,
collector at Plymouth, see Vol. 34:531-4
and Vol. 35:223n.

MRS. NILES: Elizabeth Marston Watson, the daughter of William Watson,
who became the second wife of Nathaniel
Niles in 1787 (Vol. 32:582).

To Robert Smith

DEAR SIR   Monticello Sep. 20. 1802.

I have had an opportunity of consulting with mr Madison and
of considering with his assistance the question whether the John
Adams should proceed. I had before been favored with a letter from
mr Gallatin which with yours furnished material considerations on
the subject. the defect of specific appropriation presented the greatest difficulty: but that seems already incurred by the advance of
the two months wages, and the additional expences of her mission
are not likely to increase it much. considering the smallness of
expence now to be incurred, the conclusion is that that will be overweighed by the advantages which may arise from her proceeding;

which therefore you will be pleased to consider as approved, & to order her to proceed with as little delay as possible. I have considerable expectations that Marocco and Tunis will both be found in a state of peace with us. should this be the case, and no good[1] cause of apprehension exist more than is now known to us, I refer to your consideration to order home such a proportion of the force there as shall not be necessary against Tripoli. we formerly considered 2. frigates as sufficient for that power, and I have seen no reason to change the opinion. I confess I should feel very great anxieties for their safety against the winter, were they to remain there till that season. if you think the question What force shall be left there? of sufficient difficulty to delay it's final decision till the 10th. or 12th. of the ensuing month, when we shall be all together, it might be deferred till then, after which we shall doubtless have opportunities of forwarding the orders, tho' the John Adams will be gone.—the favorable[2] information I had recieved of the expedition with which the New York had been fitted out, induced the wish in my letter of Aug. 30. to express my satisfaction: but if I misunderstood the persons to whom we were indebted for it, I hope you suppressed the notice I took of it. Accept assurances of my affectionate esteem and respect.   TH: JEFFERSON

RC (ViU: Coolidge Deposit); addressed: "Robert Smith Secretary of the Navy Washington." PrC (DLC). Recorded in SJL as a letter to the Navy Department with notation "the John Adams."

[1] Word interlined.
[2] Word interlined.

From Samuel Stephens

Dublin 20 of 9 mo. 1802

I wrote and sent thee a few phamplets of a Religious nature about two Month since. I now send thee one of a differant sort believing from thy situation it will not be unacceptable to thee, as I consider it such as will convey to thee some information whereby thou can judge a little of the situation of things amongst us, A matter which I exspect may be the more deserving of thy attention considering the great emmagration from this to America, and to know some what the cause thereof, a variety of circumstances contribute towards it, and what is hinted at there is one of them. it does not seem my present business to enlarge on it therefore shall conclude thy Friend and wellwisher   SAML STEPHENS

RC (MoSHi: Jefferson Papers); endorsed by TJ as received 5 Feb. 1803 and so recorded in SJL. Enclosure not found.

¹ WROTE: Stephens to TJ, 19 July 1802.

From Alexander White

DEAR SIR   Woodville 20th. Septemr. 1802

Agreeably to my expectations expressed in a former letter, I, on the 9th. instant, visited the ice caves, or as they are called by the People of the Neighbourhood *the cold holes*
I found the face of nature much changed since I saw them before—the hill at the foot of which these holes are, appears to be a pile of stones, a large space of it immediately above the holes, is perfectly bare, not a particle of earth either on the surface or in the interstices of the stones, as far as I could discover—The hill from the cavities upwards, perhaps 10 or 12 poles, is covered with earth bearing some shrubs and scrubby timber—the cavities extended into this earthy part; in one of which, when I saw the place the last week of May 1795, was a cake of ice I believe nearly 20 inches long, more than half as wide on an average, and from one to two inches thick; it was so far within the cavity that I could scarcely reach it. I saw many smaller pieces at various distances from the openings of the Cavities

To my very great regret I now found the earth which formed the Covers or upper parts of the principal Cavities, removed, so as to leave the stones which formed the backs and sides, bare, and stones piled in front, which I suppose have been removed by People searching for ice. I saw no ice, but some of the Neighbours reviewed the information I formerly received; that the ice remains all summer and disappears during the winter snows; they said ice could now be found by those who knew how to search for it.
When I saw this place before, there was a strong current of wind proceeding from the mouth of each Cavity, cold (to my feeling at least) beyond anything I had ever experienced. I did not now observe any wind as I approached, but putting my hand near the stones which formed the back of one of the Cavities I percieved a very cold air issuing from the interstices, but bearing no comparison to what I formerly felt; Whether this difference was owing to the state of the atmosphere, it being now very calm, or whether the removal of the earth which confined the vent of the air to a small compass, might have that effect or contribute to it, I know not.
I obtained no new information to enable me to determine whether

the ice is generated in summer. The fact which was formerly stated to me, and now repeated, that there is ice in summer, and none during the winter snows, seems hard to be accounted for on any other principle, than that ice is generated by the action of the wind passing through some substance in the interior of the mountain, but what substance in nature can produce that effect, from such a cause, is the difficulty with me. I have now given you all the information I have been able to obtain respecting this Phenomenon which seems scarcely to have been noticed previous to my seeing it in 1795. I had myself never heard of it till a year or two before, though I had lived within 30 miles of it from my birth and had passed within two miles of it more than one hundred times—

Whether the subject deserves further investigation is not for me to say; the face of the earth is greatly changed from its natural state, and the exterior appearances lessened, but the operating cause must still remain

I am Dear Sir Your most Ob Ser   ALEX WHITE

RC (DLC); at foot of text: "Thos. Jefferson President of the U. States"; endorsed by TJ as received 26 Sep. and so recorded in SJL.

A FORMER LETTER: White to TJ, 13 July 1802.

From John Barnes

SIR   George Town 21st. Septr 1802.

I am duly Hond: with your favr: 17th.—in answer, to mine, of the 14th.—in Conformity I have Noticed Mr Claxton—to furnish me with his two a/cs: in order to discharge them—before your expected return. and shall make the necessary remittance to Richmond abt. 8th. Octr.

Mr LeMaire, is much indisposed. (but not dangerous.) Bile, & foul Stomack. accompanied with a Violent fever.—Doctr. Gant attends him Constantly—as well Julian—who is quite the good Nurse—sets by him, day & night. nothing will be wanting towards his recovery. but like most patients He is fretfull & fearfull.—

Most Respectfull I am Sir, Yr Obedt: H St   JOHN BARNES

I have no letters for Mr Short. but my best respects (you will be pleased.) awaits him—

RC (ViU: Edgehill-Randolph Papers); postscript on verso; at foot of text: "The President UStates"; endorsed by TJ as received 23 Sep. and so recorded in SJL.

YOUR FAVR: TJ's letter to Barnes of 17 Sep. is recorded in SJL, but has not been found. The letter apparently directed Barnes to pay Thomas Claxton for the sofas and cushions he recently acquired for TJ in Philadelphia. See George Jefferson to TJ, 8 Sep. and Daniel Rapine to TJ, 11 Sep.

From Albert Gallatin

DEAR SIR   New York Septer. 21st 1802

I intend leaving this city this evening & expect to meet you at Washington the last of this month. As I take my family along, we will travel but slowly.

I should suppose that your intention to countermand the sailing of the Adams came too late: both ships indeed, were prepared for sea in a much shorter time than could have been expected.

Your letter informing of the favorable aspect in the Mediterranean gave me true satisfaction: it will enable us to diminish our naval expenditures, but to what extent must be left to a future discussion & will rest on the prospect of our revenue. Of this, it is very difficult to form, as yet, a correct idea: it has diminished, and, in my opinion, will experience a greater decrease next year: but our data are not sufficient to draw positive inferences. Before the meeting of Congress, we will have a comparative view of imports & exports for the year ending 30th of this month, which will give us on the whole the best account we can prepare. I can ascertain with precision how much the importation has diminished; but although we can have also an account of exports for the same period, the greater part of these arises from the importations of the preceeding year; & the difficulty lies in judging of the quantity of the importations destined for exportation & which will be exported generally next year. Upon the whole, all I can yet say is that we cannot think for this year of giving up any taxes, and that we must reduce our expence (naval, military & foreign) to the estimates we had made and on which rested the propriety of the repeal of the internal taxes.

Mr Christie, late member of Congress for Maryland, has just arrived from London & brought dispatches from Mr King which he put in the post office—also the ratification of the Convention. Mr King told him he intended asking to be recalled next year.

I enclose a letter from Mr Symmes—How shall we ascertain the true conduct of Govr. St. Clair? Nothing of the decision in his case has been communicated to the parties. This will not be considered by them as perfectly just.

My health is not yet perfectly good. I hope travelling & then winter will restore it; but I cannot do as much work in the same time as I did last fall. Hoping to have soon the pleasure of seeing you, I remain with sincere respect & attachment

Your obedt. Servt.   ALBERT GALLATIN

Mr. Burr has communicated to me a letter which he writes to Govr. Bloomfield in which he makes an explicit denial of the charges & assertions of his having either intrigued with the federal party or in any other way attempting, during the late election or balloting, to counter act your election. That transaction, I mean the attack on Mr B. by Cheetham, has deeply injured the republican cause in this State.

RC (DLC); at foot of text: "Thomas Jefferson President U.S."; endorsed by TJ as received from the Treasury Department on 26 Sep. and so recorded in SJL. Enclosures: (1) John Cleves Symmes to Gallatin, New Germanton, New Jersey, 30 Aug. 1802, requesting that the Treasury secretary transmit the enclosed papers (see Enclosures Nos. 2 and 3) to the president (Gallatin, *Papers*, 7:514). (2) Daniel Symmes to John Cleves Symmes, Cincinnati, 5 Aug. 1802, informing his uncle that to the "mortification and astonishment" of the local Republicans, Governor St. Clair on his return to the Northwest Territory in July set "every tool and machine at work to distract and intimidate the people from going into a State Government"; Republicanism is progressing rapidly and there is certain support for a Republican ticket unless defeated by the ambiguity of the election law; Symmes requests that his uncle obtain the opinion of the attorney general or secretary of state on whether Congress intended the counties to vote in their own districts as "in case of members of the Legislature under the Supplemental act; or whether at the Court-house as the law before stood"; Republican interests will suffer if they are not permitted to vote in districts (same, 7:515). (3) The 31 July 1802 issue of the Cincinnati *Western Spy*, which includes the first of a series of essays by former congressional delegate William McMillan as "Frank Stubblefield" to the people of Hamilton County, with queries about the method of electing delegates to the convention considering statehood under the 30 Apr. 1802 enabling act (same, 7:516; Brown, "Frontier Politics," 271; U.S. Statutes at Large, 2:173-5).

YOUR LETTER: TJ to Gallatin, 8 Sep. TJ brought up the subject of revenues and taxes in his 13 Sep. letter to Gallatin. For the ESTIMATES of expenditures for 1802, see Vol. 35:631-3; Vol. 36:48-9.

The 20 Sep. issue of the New York *Commercial Advertiser* carried news of the arrival of Gabriel CHRISTIE in New York after a 38 day passage from London. PUT IN THE POST OFFICE: the State Department acknowledged receipt of the dispatches on 1 Oct. (Madison, *Papers, Sec. of State Ser.*, 3:605). The diplomatic correspondence included a 16 July letter from Rufus King informing the secretary of state that ratifications of the 1802 CONVENTION were exchanged with Lord Hawkesbury on 15 July and that Christie was delivering an original copy of the British ratification and a certificate of exchange to the State Department. For the convention negotiated by King, see TJ to the Senate, 29 Mch. 1802. The Senate ratified the convention on 26 Apr. ASKING TO BE RECALLED: King wrote Madison on 5 Aug. requesting that the president accept his resignation as minister to Great Britain effective April 1803 (King, *Life*, 4:148, 154-5; Madison, *Papers, Sec. of State Ser.*, 3:398, 457-8; JEP, 1:421-2).

On 20 Mch. 1802, shortly after his arrival in London, Christie wrote Madison soliciting the appointment of his son Charles as consul at Madeira. He requested that Madison speak to the president on his behalf (RC in DNA: RG 59, LAR, endorsed by TJ: "Gabriel Christie to mr Madison his son to be Consul at Madeira"; Madison, *Papers, Sec. of State Ser.*, 3:52-3). For other correspondence with the State Department on the appointment for his son, see same, 3:128-9, 605; 4:26, 239-40. On 23 July, Robert Smith informed Madison that he had received "intimations" from a friend that led him to think that the son was not qualified "for the appointment of Consul." Smith added: "This may be a subject of some delicacy. But to such unpleasant situations we are frequently exposed" (RC in same; endorsed by TJ: "Christie as Consul. R. Smith to mr Madison"). Charles Christie did not receive the consulship.

The vice president's letter to his friend Joseph BLOOMFIELD of 21 Sep. is printed in Kline, *Burr*, 2:739. Burr was responding to the New Jersey governor's letter of 17 Sep. in which Bloomfield requested a refutation of the charge in James Cheetham's publications that Burr had "combined with the Federal party to defeat the election of Mr. JEFFERSON." Burr authorized Bloomfield to publish his denial "if you shall think proper." Both letters were printed in the newspapers. At the same time, Cheetham began submitting a series of letters to the press, which were published as a pamphlet in early 1803 entitled, *Nine Letters on the Subject of Aaron Burr's Political Defection* (same, 2:737-8).

From John Mercer

DEAR SIR   New-York. Septr. 21st. 1802.

Mr. Richard S. Hackley, an estimable Man and respectable Merchant of this City, has expressed his wish to receive the appointment of Consul at Nantes, should the vacancy continued by the Non-acceptance of Mr. Gantt, be not supplied at this Time: and should the Information communicated respecting him, render him in your Estimation worthy of the office—With this view, he has requested me to trespass so far upon your valuable Time, as to introduce his Name to your attention—This I do with much pleasure, as there are few Individuals with whom I am more intimately acquainted, and none of whose excellent moral and political Character I can speak with more Certainty, than of Mr. Hackleys. This Gentleman is a Native of Fredericksburg in Virginia—was bred from his earliest youth to the Business of a Merchant and has prosecuted it in this City for the last three years, during which Time, his Conduct as far as I can learn, has been without Reproach—His Age is thirty two years.

I have the honour to be, with every Sentiment of Respect, your Obedient Servant   JOHN MERCER

RC (DNA: RG 59, LAR); endorsed by TJ as received 26 Sep. and so recorded in SJL; also endorsed by TJ: "Hackley Richd S. to be Consul at Nantes."

John Mercer (1772-1817) of Fredericksburg, Virginia, was a son of General Hugh Mercer, who died in the American Revolution in 1777. Educated as an attorney, Mercer represented Spotsylvania County in the House of Delegates from 1797 to 1803, and from 1816 to 1817. In 1803, he traveled to France to serve as James Monroe's unofficial private secretary during the Louisiana negotiations, and was subsequently named a commissioner to settle American debt claims on France. Returning to the United States in late 1805, Mercer declined TJ's offer in 1806 of a judicial appointment in the Orleans Territory, citing his long retirement from the law and his poor health. His infrequent correspondence with the pres-

ident generally consisted of letters recommending his Fredericksburg acquaintances for office (John T. Goolrick, *The Life of General Hugh Mercer* [New York, 1906], 106; Leonard, *General Assembly*, 209, 213, 217, 221, 225, 229, 287; Madison, *Papers, Sec. of State Ser.*, 4:522-3, 5:5-6, 69-70; *Daily National Intelligencer*, 5 Nov. 1817; Vol. 36:615; Mercer to TJ, 13 Dec. 1805, 20 June 1806; TJ to Mercer, 10 June 1806).

RICHARD S. HACKLEY received an appointment as consul at Sanlúcar de Barrameda in 1806 (JEP, 2:45).

From John Jones Waldo

SIR   Boston Septr 21st 1802

By the recommendation of Messrs Livingston, Barlow & Skipwith, I presume to address you upon the Subject of the Consulship of Marseilles now become vacant in Consequence of the French Government refusing to accredit French Citizens as Commercial Agents for Foreign powers—I rest my pretensions upon the testimony of those Gentlemen, as I can Say but little in my own favor except that I have been the victim of my attachment to the French revolution, having made a large Contract with the French Minister in this Country in the Year 1795, which is unpaid to this day—

Should you Sir do me the Honor to appoint me to that Office I shall exert my utmost to merit your & my Country's approbation & Shall ever Strenuously Support that Government whose interests I should Represent: I herewith inclose two letters from Messrs Barlow & Skipwith & remain with Sentiments of respect Your Mt Obedt Servt

JOHN J. WALDO

RC (DNA: RG 59, LAR); endorsed by TJ as received 5 Oct. and "to be Consul at Marseilles" and so recorded in SJL. Enclosures: (1) Joel Barlow to TJ, 29 July, recorded in SJL as received from Paris on 5 Oct., but not found. (2) Fulwar Skipwith to TJ, 30 July, from Paris, stating: "The bearer Mr. Jno. Jones Waldo of Massachusettes is the Gentleman in whose favor Mr. Livingston and myself solicited some time ago the Commercial Agency at Marseilles in consequence of this Government refusing to accredit Mr.

Cathalan in that character for reason of his being a french Citizen. Mr. Waldo being on the point of embarking for the U. States, and in the intention of presenting himself to you, I take the liberty of recommending him to your notice as a person of the most amiable mind, of unblemished character, and as a merchant of regular and solid acquirements. And should you deem it fit to confer on him an appointment to any commercial Agency whatever, I beg to add my firm persuasion of his conduct being such as to afford the

Public and you intire Satisfaction. I have the honor to remain with constant respect and attatchment, Sir, Your Mo Ob Servant" (RC in DNA: RG 59, LAR; endorsed by TJ as received 5 Oct. and so recorded in SJL).

John Jones Waldo (ca. 1769-1803) graduated from Harvard College in 1787, in the same class as John Quincy Adams and William Cranch. He became involved in transatlantic shipping, initially between Boston and Bristol. In February 1801, John Adams named him commercial agent at Nantes. The Senate confirmed the appointment, but TJ withheld Waldo's commission, treating the case as one of Adams's late-term nominations that must be "considered as Null." In February 1803, Waldo's financial situation came before the bankruptcy commissioners in Boston. He was bankrupt at the time of his death in Bordeaux in December of that year (Boston *Independent Chronicle*, 19 July 1787, 24 Mch. 1803; *Boston Gazette*, 16 Nov. 1789, 14 Feb. 1803, 29 Mch. 1804; Boston *Columbian Centinel*, 28 May 1791, 9 June 1792, 4 June 1803; Boston *New-England Palladium*, 3 June 1803; Boston *Democrat*, 25 Jan. 1804; JEP, 1:381, 385; Vol. 33:173n, 671, 672, 677).

Robert R. LIVINGSTON, writing to Madison on 31 Dec. 1801, and Fulwar SKIPWITH, in a letter to TJ in October of that year, both mentioned Waldo's desire for a commercial agency in France (Madison, *Papers, Sec. of State Ser.*, 2:360; Vol. 35:526-7). Waldo had also solicited support from Thomas Sumter, Jr., and Levi Lincoln, who had "a family connection" to Waldo through his wife, Martha Waldo Lincoln (ANB; Vol. 36:575).

From Ephraim Kirby

SIR   Litchfield Septemr. 22nd. 1802

Being recently elected a member of the Legislature of Connecticut, and feeling unwilling to disappoint the wishes and expectations of my constituents, I have to solicit a discharge from the office of Supervisor of the Revenue. The business of this office is so far advanced toward a conclusion, that I apprehend the public can experience no essential inconvenience from my discharge at the present time. It will be important that I should know your pleasure on this subject by the 11th. of October.

I embrace this opportunity to express my gratitude for the honor you have done me, and to assure you of my highest

esteem & respect   EPHM. KIRBY

RC (DLC); at foot of text: "His Excy. Thos. Jefferson President of U. States"; endorsed by TJ as received 5 Oct. and so recorded in SJL; in TJ's hand, above inside address: "the suppression of the office is approved. Th:J Oct. 5. 1802."

TJ appointed Kirby SUPERVISOR OF THE REVENUE for Connecticut in July 1801 (Vol. 35:599n).

From Thomas Leiper

DEAR SIR   Crum Creek, Snuff Mills, Septr. 22d. 1802

I wrote you on the 17th. to which I refer—The business of the Rising Sun is over and settled very much to my satisfaction but I impute it very much to Mr. Dallas and Captain Jones being there—The Citizens on both sides were very full of Fire—Colonel Ferguson had a sett of Resolutions had they been proposed would have divided the Whigs in the County—it is very True C Ferguson said he did not like them and was of the opinion they contained too much pepper & agreed that Mr. Dallas should manufacture some thing for the Day which he did and they were proposed by the Colonel to the Chair and adopted by the Meetting—As we from the city were on the Middle Ground our Arguments were plean. Gentlemen do not divid us— Grice, Groves, Donaldson & others who signed the Call of the Meetting are as well Braved as any in the County, but notwithstanding it is my opinion the meetting had Federalism at bottam but these men did not know it—The Aurora man says he is in possession of Documents to prove it but we beged him he would not use them being of the opinion it would not answer any good purpose We have his promise he would not unless their was a necessity or something turn up to make it necessary—I inquired for Doctr. Logan and was informed he was gone to the Jersey—The Doctr. has rendered us many services but I do think he was very remiss in not being at the Rising Sun yesterday But Dallas and Jones saw the necessity of being there and it was well for the Republican Cause they were—Dallas is manufacturing an Address to the people it will be out on Saturday I like every part of it excepting the part speaking of the Executive—they have divided the Honours & Proffits of the Goverment with whom I shall ask and the answer from every honest man will be with their enemies—I have been Robbed in this county at Law some Two Thousand Dollars & I have no doubt but they could find Juries & Judges that would find me guilty of High Treason—Once a Tory always a Tory and they never will forgive a Whig—you may as well think of reclaiming a Wolf—Charles the 2d rewarded his Fathers enemies— The Whigs brought William the 3d In and the Tories kept him In. Practices like unto those in my opinion helped to upsett Washington & Adams for they never considered that every man had a Vote—I am most respectfully Dear Sir Yr. Most Obedt. St.

THOMAS LEIPER

[421]

RC (DLC); endorsed by TJ as received 26 Sep. and so recorded in SJL.

17TH: that is, the 19th.

At the RISING SUN tavern meeting of 21 Sep., supporters of the earlier Republican nominations overwhelmed those advocating a different slate of Republican candidates for Congress and the state legislature. The meeting issued a formal declaration in favor of the previously agreed-upon selections, while suppressing a denunciation of the Republicans who had called the meeting. William Duane, presumably the AURORA MAN to whom Leiper referred, had denounced the Ris-

ing Sun movement as Federalist-inspired but in the wake of the second meeting smoothed over any differences, praising the challengers' willingness to cast their lot with the majority and regretting "that any cause should have arisen for our animadversions upon their proceedings before" (Philadelphia *Aurora*, 22 Sep. 1802; Higginbotham, *Pennsylvania Politics*, 44; Leiper to TJ, 19 Sep.).

The ADDRESS of the Republican correspondence committee to the "Republicans of Pennsylvania" appeared in the *Aurora* of 27 Sep. and was also printed in pamphlet form (see Shaw-Shoemaker, No. 2134).

From John Barnes

SIR   George Town 24th. Septr 1802

Nothing of moment transpires at Washington, since 21st: when I had the pleasure of Answering your favr. 17th.—Mr LeMaire, tho weak, is recruiting fast,—by the time of your expected & welcome return will, I hope be perfectly reinstated in his health.

respecting late rumours—the rising of the Negroes here: I judge it proper to inform, (lest you may have heard some imperfect Accts.)—

It has subsided,—a few nightly patrols—and other necessary precautions, have guarded against any fatal consequences, which might otherwise have insued—. the most probable conjectures are—that the idle, and worthless, of both: Whites & Blacks,—whose sole business is *plunder*—would, at a fit opporty. have set fire, to some distant, Building while, they plundered others, in the confused state of the Town—for, I cannot think it probable—or possible, that any regular system, of combination, & subordination could be formed, by these scattered, distressed, objects both, of pity, and contempt.

with the highest Respect—I am Sir, your most Obed. H Servt:

JOHN BARNES

RC (ViU: Edgehill-Randolph Papers); at foot of text: "The President, U, States at Monticello"; endorsed by TJ as received 30 Sep. and so recorded in SJL.

Writing James Madison on 21 Sep., State Department clerk Daniel Brent reported on the rumored RISING OF THE

NEGROES in Georgetown that took place on 19 Sep.: "You will probably hear of the alarm which prevailed in Geo. Town on Sunday night, last, from the discovery of a supposed design on the part of the Negroes there to burn down the town, and of the very serious measures that were taken to prevent the execution of this design—

in arming the Militia, and keeping them all night on guard. It gives me pleasure to inform you, after a full examination has been had into all the Circumstances of the supposed plot, that there appears now to have been no cause for serious alarm—tho' a few worthless fellows have been committed to prison under appearances of rather a suspicious cast, but not implicating such extensive, or any immediate, mischief, and Mr J. T. Mason has actually sold the reputed leader of the Party to some Georgia men, under the same appearances. The alarm, I believe, has entirely ceased" (Madison, *Papers, Sec. of State Ser.*, 3:596).

To Henry Dearborn

DEAR SIR   Monticello Sep. 24. 1802.

Your favor of the 20th. is recieved. on consultation with mr Madison who came here the day after mine of the 17th. to you, he appeared so clearly to concur with mr Smith in sending the John Adams, towards which the present state of her preparation had considerable influence, that I thought it better to conclude on her departure, and so wrote to mr Smith by the post of the 20th. I had intended to have been at Washington on the last day of the present month, but several days of rain have so retarded my operations here, that I shall be 2. or 3. days later in my arrival there. Accept my affectionate salutations.

TH: JEFFERSON

PrC (DLC); at foot of text: "The Secretary at War." Recorded in SJL as a letter to the War Department with notation "the John Adams."

To George Jefferson

DEAR SIR   Monticello Sep. 24. 1802.

I some days ago drew an order on you for 79.69 D in favor of Burgess Griffin for my taxes in Bedford; but fearing it may not get to his hands in time to deliver to his sheriff William Trigg[1] before his departure, I pray you to pay him on demand with or without the order. but I believe the true sum should have been 76.92 but of this he can inform you.

On the 21st. inst. I drew on you in favor of Randolph Jefferson for 60. D. Our sheriffs have not yet called on me: but I suppose my draughts in their favor will amount to about 600. D. I have a letter yesterday from mr Barnes in which he informs me he shall be able to replace all [...] 8th. of [the next] month.   on the 20th. of August I drew on you in favor of John B. Magruder for 104.54 payable at I forget how many days sight, but enough I know to enable mr

Barnes's remittance to anticipate it. I leave this on the 28th. or 29th. for Washington. Accept my affectionate salutations

TH: JEFFERSON

PrC (MHi); faint; at foot of text: "Mr. George Jefferson"; endorsed by TJ in ink on verso.

A letter to BURGESS GRIFFIN, recorded in SJL as sent 16 Sep., has not been found, but TJ did note the tax payment in

his account book at the same date (MB, 2:1080). For TJ's accounts with several Virginia SHERIFFS, see TJ to George Jefferson, 5 Oct. 1802.

[1] Name interlined.

To Josiah Smith

DEAR SIR   Monticello Sep. 24. 1802.
　Your favor of the 8th. is recieved. that of July 19. under your name is preserved & shall be forwarded to you by post if desired. it recommended Wm. Goodwin of Plymouth, Capt. Robert Ells of Hanover, capt. Joseph Hunt or Hurst of Marshfield, Danl. Snow of Bridgewater to be commissioners of bankruptcy for Plymouth County, or perhaps for that & Barnstable. mr Madison tells me he received a letter from you on the subject of an address to me. perhaps this might be from the same hand, which I observe differs from that of yours of the 8th. Accept my friendly & respectful salutations.

TH: JEFFERSON

RC (George S. Heyer, Jr., New Haven, Connecticut, 1960); at foot of text: "Josiah Smith esq." PrC (MoSHi: Jefferson Papers); endorsed by TJ in ink on verso. Tr (MWA: William Bentley Papers).

Federalist William GOODWIN served as revenue inspector and postmaster at Plymouth, Massachusetts. Robert Ellis (ELLS) became postmaster at Hanover

and JOSEPH HUNT at Marshfield, both in Plymouth County, in March and April 1802, respectively. Republican Daniel SNOW ran for the state senate in 1802 and won election to the Massachusetts House of Representatives in 1803 (Prince, *Federalists*, 41; ASP, *Miscellaneous*, 1:264; Stets, *Postmasters*, 147-9; Boston *Independent Chronicle*, 15 Mch. 1802; *Newburyport Herald*, 13 May 1803).

To Albert Gallatin

DEAR SIR   Monticello Sep. 27. 1802
　Your's of the 21st. came to hand yesterday. the matter of it shall be the subject of conversation when we meet at Washington; to which place I had intended to set out this day, so as to have arrived there on the last day of the month. but unexpected delays in getting my car-

riage ready will detain me here till the last day of the month, if not the 1st. of the ensuing. I shall be with you of a certainty on Sunday or Monday. in the mean time accept my affectionate salutations.

TH: JEFFERSON

RC (NHi: Gallatin Papers); addressed: "Albert Gallatin Secretary of the Treasury Washington"; franked; postmarked "Milton"; endorsed. PrC (DLC).

TJ arrived in Washington on MONDAY, 4 Oct. (MB, 2:1082).

From John Langdon

SR.   Portsmo. Septem 27th. 1802

Permit me to name Capt Hopley Yeaton to command the Revenue Cutter at this port; this gentleman formerly held this Station, and was dismissed for the same reasons and at the same time (by the late President) that Mr. Whipple and Mr. Gardner were he is an able Seaman, an honest man and good old officer—I have mentioned his name to Mr. Gallitin—

I pray you Sr. to accept of my best wishes and believe me with the highest consideration sincerely—

your's &c   JOHN LANGDON

RC (DNA: RG 59, LAR); at foot of text: "the President of the US."; endorsed by TJ as received 5 Oct. and so recorded in SJL with notation "Hopley Yeaton"; also endorsed by TJ: "Yeaton Hopely to command cutt."

I HAVE MENTIONED HIS NAME: see Enclosure No. 5 listed at Albert Gallatin to TJ, 17 Aug. 1802.

To James Madison

DEAR SIR   Monticello Sep. 27. 1802.

Unexpected delays in getting my carriage ready will render it impossible for me to leave this till Thursday or Friday, probably Friday: and as you will be gone or going by that time, and we shall meet so soon at Washington, I shall not have the pleasure of seeing you at your own house, but get on as far as the day will let me. mr Gallatin left N. York on the 21st. and expected to be at Washington before the 30th. my respects to the ladies & affectionate salutations to yourself.

TH: JEFFERSON

RC (DGU); clipped, lacks inside address. PrC (DLC); at foot of text: "The Secretary of State."

From John Allen

SIR Pepperelboro, September 28th 1802

By hard Study, close applycation and long experiance I have found out a Successfull method of cure for that dreadfull disorder that cruel scorge to mankind the yelow fever. In a great number of cases in which I have used it, it has been successfull. I verily believe that it will if applied be Successfull in any part of the world. I am well aware that the disorder has baffled the united knowledge of the most learned of the Faculty: and the Idea that it did so, was a great impediment in my way, to the obtaining the knowledge of my present plan. That which supported me in my studies and recearches was a firm persuasion that a method might be found out whereby the disorder might be successfully combated with medicine.

Thank *God* I have found that method. In upwards of sixty cases in which the attacks was very Severe and in many of them the simtomes were dreadfull I have lost not one patient.—

It may be said why have you not made your plan publick before? The fact was that notwithstanding repeated success, I still doubted. I have been a fare greater unbeliever in that respect than Gedion with his fleece of Wool.

But now being firmly persuaded of its utillity, it only remains, what is the best method of making it publick? I have had thoughts of making it known to some medical society, or to go to some warmer climate and there to ascertain if possible more fully its utillity and success: but my circumstances scarce admit of my going. Again I thought of making the discovery to congress; as it is a national object, let it be a national concern.—Your advice and direction concern'g what method I shall take to mak the plan publick to the world will be very acceptable to

Sir Your most obet. and Very Humbl. Servt.   JOHN ALLEN

RC (DLC); at foot of text: "Thomas Jefferson Esqr President of the united States"; endorsed by TJ as received 8 Oct. and so recorded in SJL.

John Allen (d. 1825), an English physician who began his practice in Saco, Maine, in 1796, was an original member of the Saco Lodge of Free and Accepted Masons in 1802 (W. W. Clayton, *History of York County, Maine. With Illustrations and Biographical Sketches of Its Prominent Men and Pioneers* [Philadelphia, 1880], 158, 168).

FLEECE OF WOOL: an Old Testament allusion to the sign that Gideon twice requested from God that Israel would be saved through him as promised (Judges 6:36-40).

From John Barnes

SIR George Town 28 Sepr. 1802

My last dispatch of the 24th. I perceived the next day had not been forwarded ℔ that Evening's mail—in the supposition of the office keeper that only Tuesdays mail, convey'd letters to Charlottesville—of course, I received them back, supposing your return here would be in a few days.—when yesterdays mail handed me your favr: same date—inclosing E. Lanhams letter on Accot. of Mr Oldhams $80 note—

It was, with some difficulty I could learn the parties & particulars—it seems the suit against Lanham—on Accot. of Mr Oldham, is yet depending: but it also appears that the Court—which by Lanham's letter, was to set next Mo. will not commence untill decr: or Jany—

Mr Morse the attorney, who holds the note, is absent, & not expected to return under a fortnight. of course it can be adjusted without further exps. save the Int.—

I purposely called to see Mr LeMaire on Saturday—he is almost perfectly recovered & Doctr Gantt assures. Sir presuming you will not leave Monticello before the 3d. or 4th Octr. I have ventured to send forward by this mail my former letter & papers as well, mine to Mr Short with inclosures &c.

I am Sir, most Respectfully Your Obed. H Servt.

JOHN BARNES

RC (ViU: Edgehill-Randolph Papers); at foot of text: "The President of the UStates, at Monticello"; endorsed by TJ as received 30 Sep. and so recorded in SJL.

YOUR FAVR: SAME DATE: TJ's letter to Barnes of 24 Sep. is recorded in SJL, but has not been found. Under the same date in his financial memoranda, however, TJ wrote: "Desired J. Barnes to pay Lanham for James Oldham his note with interest & costs amounting to between 90. & 100. D." (MB, 2:1081). For TJ's earlier advice to Oldham regarding the suit against Elisha Lanham, see Vol. 37:654-5.

From Gideon Granger

DR SIR. Suffield Septr. 28. 1802

Our Elections are passed and altho the Tories will have a handsome majority yet their Infamous falshoods notwithstanding we have certainly gained upon them. I have a return from Thirty Nine Towns who return 73 members—we have Thirty nine members—They

34—last may—They had 46—we 27. I have This moment examined an additional list. There are many new names—but I can perceive, among those I know an Increase of Three or four in our favor. I have visited my friends in Hamp: Co. Ms. In that State I think we may calculate upon 7 members of Congress—have an even chance for the eighth—and one not desperate for the Ninth. I shall visit Boston shortly—on my return I will communicate Such Information as I shall acquire.

With great Esteem your friend   GIDN GRANGER

RC (DLC); at foot of text: "The Presidt. of the United States"; endorsed by TJ as received 5 Oct. and so recorded in SJL.

Massachusetts elected seven Republicans and ten Federalists to the Eighth CONGRESS (*Biog. Dir. Cong.*).

From John Harvie

D SIR   Belvedere Sptr 28th 1802

My Old friend Mr William Mitchell one of the most Respectable Merchants in Richmond has Introduced to me this Morning his Nephew Francis Mitchell, for whom he is very desirous of Obtaining the Appointment of a Midshipman on Board the Navy, this is the Young mans Choice for his pursuit in life, I am told he is of Regular Conduct & of an Active Enterprizing Spirit

I Write this under a Raw lingering fever which has prevented me this Fall from paying you my Annual Visit at Monticello, believe me to be Ever with the most Respectful Regard

My Dr Sir yr Ob Servt   JN HARVIE

RC (DNA: RG 59, LAR); endorsed by TJ as received 5 Oct. and so recorded in SJL; also endorsed by TJ: "direct to mr Francis Mitchell at Richmd."

Harvie's most recent letter to TJ, dated 9 Feb. 1802, was recorded in SJL as received 13 Feb. but has not been found.

For another recommendation of FRANCIS MITCHELL, see George Divers to TJ, 20 Sep.

From Nicholas Norris

SIR.   Baltimore Septr. 28th. 1802

The Inclosed is forwarded by me, for your perusal, when done with it, please to transmit it to me, I could say much to you, but I do not wish to be Irksome. Your Friend.   NICHOLAS NORRIS

RC (MoSHi: Jefferson Papers); endorsed by TJ as received 5 Oct. and so recorded in SJL. Enclosure not found, but see TJ to Norris, 14 Oct. 1802.

Baltimore merchant Nicholas Norris (d. 1836) later served the city as a justice of the peace and experimented with silk cultivation at his country residence (Bridgeport, Conn., *Republican Farmer*, 21 July 1830; *Baltimore Gazette and Daily Advertiser*, 10 Sep. 1836; Vol. 34:433n).

Notes on an Agreement with James Walker

Minutts of an agreement entired into with Walker Sep. 28. 1802.

The said Walker being previously engaged to build a mill for mr Scott, that is to be considered as his paramount obligation; but mr Scott not being in a state of readiness, and it being believed that on that account he may have leisure sufficient to do the mill wright's [part] of my large & superintend & direct all the works relative to it, he agreed to undertake mine also.

he is to come over, designate to mr Lilly & mr Hope the spot where my small mill is to be built, so as not to be in the way of the large one, and is to give John Perry a bill of scantling for the saw mill, which mr Walker is to come & build in time for [her] to work thro' the winter.

In the spring he is to designate to mr Lilly & mr Hope the spot for the large mill, which he is to plan exactly conformably to mr Cocke's, except that it is to be 10. feet longer, and to be a tub instead of a [geered] mill: he is at all times when not engaged for mr Scott, to be employed in preparing the millwright's work of this large mill, and to direct mr Hope the Mason, John Perry the Carpenter & mr Stewart the smith how they are to execute their parts of the work.

When employed otherwise than in the millwright's work he is to recieve ten shillings a day: the millwright's work is to be paid at the prices for which he does similar work for mr Cocke.

Committed to writing Sep. 30. 1802. for remembrance.

Th: Jefferson

PrC (MHi); faint; endorsed by TJ in ink on verso: "Walker James. agreemt."

James WALKER, a millwright, installed machinery at Shadwell for TJ's toll and manufacturing mills (MB, 2:1162).

Charles A. SCOTT was a builder of several mills in Buckingham and Fluvanna counties and a ferry operator on the Slate River (MB, 2:1262; RS, 3:371).

Michael HOPE, a stonemason working at Monticello from 1802 to 1805, completed flagging work for TJ in September 1802 (possibly the underground passageway). He also laid stone in two of TJ's Shadwell mills and several out-buildings (MB, 2:1080).

From "A Sybill Leafe"

MR JEFFERSON, [28 Sep. 1802]

America in general, feels itself under great obligations to Mr Paine. But is very unwilling you should Represent its gratitude, at the expence of your own popularity—And the very *Gods*, conjure you, never to meddle with the religious prejudice's of your country—for this reason—because the moment you become a party concerned, you forfeit the merit of A judge—You may think what you please about this schrawl, with one exceiption—which is this, Your Good understanding is not meant to be insulted by it.

A SYBILL LEAFE

RC (DLC); undated, with date supplied from postmark; addressed: "Thomas Jefferson President of the United States at the City of Washington"; franked; postmarked "Bristol," 28 Sep.; endorsed by TJ as received from "Anon." on 5 Oct. 1802 and so recorded in SJL.

For previous letters from the same anonymous author, see Vol. 35:575-6; Vol. 37:458-9.

From George Jefferson

DEAR SIR Richmond 29th. Septr. 1802

I received some few days since on acct. of Mr. Short $:441.62, being the amount recovered of Mayo exclusive of the costs of the suit.

I yesterday made sale of your Tobacco at 5.½$ to Mr. John Richard who was specially commissioned by *Jackson & Wharton* of Philadelphia to purchase it.

I am Dear Sir Your Very humble Servt. GEO. JEFFERSON

RC (MHi); at foot of text: "Thomas Jefferson esqr."; endorsed by TJ as received 5 Oct. and so recorded in SJL; also endorsed by TJ:

"18,353
   5½
 917.65
 91.765
1009.415."

For George Jefferson's efforts to recover the debt owed by John MAYO to William Short, see Vol. 31:501, 519, 532, 540; Vol. 32:81, 93; Vol. 34:198; TJ to Short, 19 Apr. 1802.

Merchants JACKSON & WHARTON had purchased some of TJ's tobacco in Richmond in late 1800, then harshly criticized the crop's quality upon its arrival in Philadelphia (Vol. 32:516, 545-7, 573-4; Vol. 33:7-8, 33-4, 92, 215-16). For TJ's record of this 1802 sale, see MB, 2:1083.

From James Sylvanus McLean

Sir   Lancaster Coy. Septr. 30 1802

During the recess of Congress,[1] when your mind is probably less occupied by the immediate concerns of government, it may perhaps not be disagreable, nor wholly unimportant, occationally to see some of the objects which investigation selects for her hours of retirement—Obscurity May have its use, and retirement is sometimes favourable to investigation; for in remote situations, physical and moral phenomena being divested of adventitious attractions, and presented to the mind in their true colours and real relations, are likely to attract its energies in proportion to their importance: at least, in this medium, many objects almost invisible in a more luminous and diversified scene, are seen so large, as compleatly to conceal some of these which with a little fomentation excite the most ardent popular attention—

Of the first of these, Steam appears to me as one of the largest and most important, and have for several years anxiously expected to hear of its extensive application to the more immediate concerns of life— Could this powerful agent be applied to agriculture?—This is believed to be possible—A great simplefication of steam enginry, so as to render it easily applicable to many purposes hitherto unattempted, is certainly practicable—This I trust would have been effected long ago, had local circumstances permitted; but in this insulated corner, not only the habits and opinions of society are unfavourable, but the entire want of mechanical assistance, and even of the most ordinary emplements of mechanism, renders the entire execution of any such thing impossible—I have been withheld however from making any communication or proposal to this effect, for several years, expecting to be able to carry my ideas into effect, notwithstanding the difficulties arrising from situation: but finding this impossible, without encountering difficulties by very considerable expence of both time and money, and which might not be sufficiently obviated in this situation, even by these means; and strongly impelled by a conviction, strengthened by every day's attention to the subject, that important advantages might easily be derived to society from this source, I have taken the liberty on the authority of fame, to mention the subject to you, with a few observations, with a view of exciting an attention which might easily give reallety to these objects—It would give me much pleasure to involve what I possess (which I trust would be much more than sufficient) on the success of what I propose; and were I so situated as to be able to use this mode of effecting the improvement contemplated, no other would be resorted to—This however only expresses my confidence; but the grounds of this, or the facts on which it is founded, are not so easily explained, and in fact, are not of a nature perhaps, to be clearly & fully elucidated in this manner—

The principal circumstances which circumscribe the use of steam engines in their present construction, are the quantety and weight of the engine; the number of its members; and the quantety of power expended in moving these members, and keeping up a condensing vaccuum—These defects are chiefly owing to the quantety of permanently elastec fluid generated by the distillation carried on in the engine, and are also a little augmented by defective Mechanism—The very large condensing vacuum, and its attached air-pump, are greatly inconvenient, and a considerable expenditure of power is effected by this member of the engine: and when with this, the force required to move the rejecting pump against atmospheric pressure, and that for overcoming the friction of valves and plug-frames, and of all the numerous members moving in close contact, are viewed in agregate, the force remaining to be applied to use, will be found to be scarcely more than half the power generated; and the enginry requiring this great expenditure, very unweildy and complicated—These defects can be removed, it is believed, by a great simplefication of the enginry: by removing, not by adding members, and the condensing area may be brought to a very small comparative size—

The quantety of Carbon in the greese used to lubricate the moving parts of the engine, tho small, has doubtless a very hurtful effect, and ought to be removed—The affinety between metals heated to a certain degree, and Oxygene, being sufficient to draw this latter from its connection with Caloric, restrains the most useful application of steam to a pressure of about twelve pounds to the square inch: in some metals this is rather too much to preserve smoothness—This force however can conveniently be applied, and is as near to atmospheric pressure as convenience & utillety will well admit; because it is better to perform some motions of the enginry by the remaing weight of the atmosphere, than by the same additional power of steam: and when this power is wholly applied to use, except as much as is necessary to keep up a condensing vacuum, and expell the condensed steam and small portion of elastic fluid, on a very small area of real pressure, the effect produced will greatly exceed any thing hitherto exhibited or attempted, and will be effected with fewer members, and these greatly diminished in size, except only that which receives & applies the force generated—

The engine here contemplated, beside various other purposes, will be easily applied to driving heavy land carriages; to the convayance of mails; and perhaps, to pleasurable carriages; which machines, if properly constructed with divided axles and friction wheels, would not only require much less force, but would bear a considerably greater speed without inconvenience or injury, and would be equally as simple in construction, as handsome, and much more manageable—I find this construction of a single chair, with a small alteration so as to require no harness, to be much better than the common awkward and cumbersome mode—Could ploughs be driven by this engine?—And could not one man with this assistance, do the business of twenty?—This is believed to be practicable—It will certainly be attempted under every difficulty of situation, should no better easily be obtained—

I would be highly gratefied to see these things attempted under circumstances favourable to success—And tho, to be the author of so great an utillety, is worthy of ambition; and that the idea of public estimation justly acquired, and the connecting general advantages to individual convenience, are stimuli which strongly actuate my mind, I would chearfully relinquish these minutia, to one whose situation in respect to manufactures & mechanics, might render success easy— Under this impression, I shall be ready at any time, to make such communications on this subject, both chymecal and mechanical, as circumstances will permit, to any person quallefied, and desirous of receiving them: I mean, such an one as would afterwards act on his own convictions; for it should be well understood, that this is not a proposal for assistance in a pecuniary way; this would be unnecessary, could the objects be effected in this situation, by reasonable expenditure—

I shall just observe finally, that this communication, which is believed to be dictated by a desire of extending real utillety, and a conviction that much is derivable from this source, is addressed to the philosopher and philantrophist, not to the president; and is indebted for its direction principally to the sentiment, not advice, of an enlightened friend in an adjoining county—Whether it may have any effect or not, or whatever may be the opinion of the reader, the writer thinks that he is discharging a duty which he ows to society, in making some attempt to realize objects useful to society, which only local circumstances prevents him from effecting alone—Were this a matter affecting an individual only, such communication would be impertinent; but when an object is contemplated by which thousands may be benefited, it is contrary to benevolence and good citizenship, not to make such exertions for its completion, as may be within the reach of the person with whom it exists—With these observations, which are submitted to your attention with diffidence, accept the expression of my most respectful consideration   JAMES SYLV. MCLEAN

RC (DLC); at head of text: "His Excellency Thomas Jefferson"; endorsed by TJ as received 7 Oct. and so recorded in SJL.

A native of York, Pennsylvania, James Sylvanus McLean received a patent in 1796 for an improvement in piano fortes. Although noted for his talents and erudition, McLean was unable to find a settled situation. He lived in several southern states, including South Carolina, where he wrote for a time for the *Charleston Courier*, a connection he severed after the editor attempted to steer McLean from what had been deemed his maniacal pursuit of a scheme to propel boats by steam. In April 1809, a month before spending what was almost certainly an uninvited night at Monticello, he defended himself against accusations that he had passed a forged note to a Charleston doctor. Two years later McLean began boarding in Philadelphia under an assumed name, with the intention of manufacturing soda water there. Instead, he was charged as author of a plot to extort money from Stephen Girard, a wealthy Philadelphia merchant whom McLean apparently blamed for the loss of a substantial fortune. Acquitted due to insanity in March 1812, McLean was described at the trial by his attorney, who concealed the plea from his client, as suffering from "mental wildness and incapacity," a paranoid convinced that a conspiracy existed to block his scientific and entrepreneurial efforts. After the acquittal, reports claimed that McLean, who had included TJ among his tormentors, vowed to move to France and exert his influence over Bonaparte (*List of Patents*, 11; Charleston *City Gazette and Daily Advertiser*, 20 Apr. 1809; *Alexandria Herald*, 24 June 1811, 9 Mch. 1812; *Report of the Trial, of James Sylvanus M'Clean, Alias J. Melville, and William L. Graham, before the Supreme Court of Pennsylvania* [Philadelphia, 1812; Shaw-Shoemaker, No. 26420]; RS, 1:209).

[1] MS: "gongress."

From John Steele

SIR,   Salisbury September 30th. 1802.

After leaving the seat of Government on the 6th. of last month with the permission which you did me the favor to grant to me, I arrived at this place on the 17th. where I found my family in their usual health; but I had been at home only a few days before nearly the whole of them (& Mrs. Steele of the number) were taken down with a fever which prevails very generally among the inhabitants of this part of the country. Scarcely a single family in our neighbourhood can be said to have escaped. Mine continues to be so much indisposed, that I am under the necessity of relinquishing (for the present) the intention of removing them to the seat of Government, and consequently of requesting that you will be pleased to accept my resignation of the office of Comptr. of the Treasury. With my resignation you will I hope also have the goodness to accept an assurance that I am duly sensible of your polite treatment, and that in future it cannot but be a source of pleasing and grateful reflection to me to have been invited by you to continue in the public service.

I have the honor to be, Sir With perfect consideration, Your most obedient & huml serv   JNO. STEELE

A letter to the Secretary of the Treasy. of which the enclosed is a copy, suggests several modes by which the unfinished business of the Office may be compleated.   J. S.

RC (DNA: RG 59, RD); above postscript: "Thomas Jefferson Esqr. President of the United States"; endorsed by TJ as received 17 Oct. and so recorded in SJL. Enclosure: John Steele to Albert Gallatin, 30 Sep. 1802, informing the Treasury secretary that he is submitting his resignation to the president; he outlines three ways by which to complete the unfinished business of the comptroller's office; the first, preferred by Steele, calls for the transfer by post to North Carolina for his signature all "warrants, reports &c.," which were prepared under the signature of David Rawn, the principal clerk, with the department keeping a descriptive list of the documents sent and retaining the vouchers for the accounts but allowing "the statements and remarks of the examining Clerks to accompany the reports"; the second calls for the president to issue a special warrant authorizing the principal clerk "to complete the unfinished business," using, as a model, the form given by the president during Steele's absence in 1797, for the settlement of Edmund Randolph's account; the third calls for Steele to travel immediately to Washington to complete his unfinished business; Steele's compensation will cease from the day the president accepts his resignation (Tr in DNA: RG 59, RD; in Steele's hand; endorsed, in part, by Steele: "For the President of the United States").

Deed for Land Purchased from Richard Overton

[This Indenture made on the   day of September One thousand eight hundred & two Between Richard Overton of the one part and Thomas Jefferson of the other part both of the County of Albemarle Witnessith that the said Richard in consideration of the sum of   to him secured to be paid by the said Thomas hath given, granted, Bargained and sold unto the said Thomas] a certain parcel of land in the sd county of Alb.[1] extending from the Rivanna river up the Mountain called Monticello and bounded as follows to wit

Beginning on the sd Rivanna river at pointers, corner to the lands of the sd Richard & Tho. and running thence[2] on their former boundaries S. 13 W. 86.4 po to a black gum S. 63 W. $72\frac{1}{4}$ po. to pointers on the road leading from Monticello house down to the

Secretary's ford: thence down the said mountain keeping at the distance of one pole Westward from the Western side of the said road to the river at an Ash, White oak & maple marked as pointers, just above a remarkeable hole in the earth, which road may be traced from the sd upper to the lower pointers by the following magnetic[3] courses to wit, N. 29. E. 12 po &c [N. 50° E. $19\frac{52}{100}$ poles N. 28° E. $11\frac{6}{10}$ poles N. 25° W. 8 po: N. $20\frac{1}{2}$° E. $17\frac{2}{10}$ poles N. $37\frac{1}{2}$° E. 18 poles to the Open Land N. 21° W. $9\frac{6}{10}$ poles N. 77° E. 22 poles N. $30\frac{1}{2}$° E. 8 poles N. $8\frac{1}{2}$° E. $12\frac{44}{100}$ poles] to N. $4\frac{1}{2}$ E. 18 po. [to the river at the ash, oak and maple pointers aforesaid] thence from the said pointers down the sd river as it meanders S. $72\frac{1}{2}$ E. 6.80 S. 60. E. 7. po. S. $85\frac{1}{2}$ E. 5. po. N. 74. E. 2.60 to the beginning,[4] which parcel contains by estimation $22\frac{1}{2}$ acres; also one other parcel[5] higher up the mountain adjacent to the same road on the Western side thereof contained within the following lines to wit, Beginning where the N. 37. E. line of the parties crosses the same road, and running along the said line S. 37. W.[6] 15. po to a pine tree marked as a side line in the said line, which tree will be found to be in the level of the gap of the mountain, called the Thoroughfare Where the Public road passes thro' it, and running thence N. 18. W. 11.60 po. &c.— [N. 2° w. $6\frac{64}{100}$ po. N. 17° W. 5 poles N. $9\frac{1}{2}$° W. $8\frac{4}{10}$ poles N. $12\frac{1}{2}$° W. $9\frac{6}{10}$ poles. N. $7\frac{1}{2}$° E. $7\frac{32}{100}$ poles] N. $23\frac{1}{4}$ E. 7.36 po. to a gum Sapling on the Western side of the sd road to the Secretary's ford being in the former boundary of the parties, thence up the sd former boundary to the beginning, which latter parcel contains by estimation $2\frac{3}{4}$ acres: and with the parcel first-described makes $25\frac{1}{4}$ acres, & is[7] the whole of the lands held by the said Richard on the Eastern side of the sd road, from the Secretary's ford up till it gets into the level of the thoroughfare aforesd and then to the Eastward of that level, and a margin of one pole in breadth on the Western side of the sd road & level [To have and to hold the said two parcels of Land with these appurtenances to the said Thomas and his Heirs: And the said Richard his Heirs Executors & Administrators the said parcels of Land with these appurtenances to the said Thomas and his Heirs will forever Warrant and defend. In Witness whereof the said Richard hath hereto set his hand and seal on the day and year above Written,   RICHARD OVERTON]

Dft (ViU: Edgehill-Randolph Papers); undated; incomplete; in TJ's hand, except text in brackets supplied from Tr; endorsed by TJ on verso: "Overton to Jefferson} $25\frac{1}{4}$ as." Tr (Albemarle Coun-ty Deed Book No. 14:16-17); partially dated; entirely in a clerk's hand, including Overton's signature with facsimile seal; attested by John Nicholas as produced by Richard Overton and ordered to be recorded at the "Albemarle September Court 1802."

A letter from TJ to Overton, recorded in SJL as sent 2 Sep., has not been found. TJ paid a SUM of $346.67 for the two parcels (MB, 2:1090).

¹ Preceding four words and two abbreviations interlined.
² TJ interlined the passage that follows from this point through "to the beginning," in place of "up sd river to a remarkeably large hole in the bank, which will be found at the end of a line   from the beginng. then from the <said> river adjacent to the said hole   to a point 1. pole on the outer or <N.W.> Western side of a road formerly opened & made by the sd Thomas & leadg. from the Secretary's ford to his house on the top of the mountain (which road is understood to rise generally 1.

foot on every 9. or 10. feet) then from the sd point along a line parallel with the said road & 1. pole distant from it to the Western termination of the S. 63. W. line which is their present boundary, thence along the said line N. 63. E. $72\frac{1}{4}$ po. to their black gum corner & N. 13. E. 86. 4 po. to the pointers on the river at the beginning."
³ Word interlined.
⁴ Tr: "antient course begun at" in place of "beginning."
⁵ TJ here canceled "near to the former &" and interlined the passage that follows through "side thereof."
⁶ From this point through "level of the," TJ first wrote "till it gets <onto> to a point which is on the exact level of the ground at the" before altering the passage to read as above.
⁷ TJ first wrote "parcel first-mentioned constitutes" before altering the preceding passage to read as above.

From John Appleton

SIR   Calais October 1. 1802
    I take the liberty of sending you a variety of Specimens of Printing, from a celebrated Artist in Paris. He has been rewarded by a Medal from the first Consul & requested me to say, He shall be highly gratified, if these Specimens, will place Him in your estimation, in the list of Artists of Merit.—
    I shall be happy Sir if they are acceptable to you & hope they may stimulate our own Artists to an imitation—
    I have the Honour to be respectfully Your Obedt. Servant
                                   JOHN APPLETON
                                   Coml. Agent. Calais

RC (DLC); at foot of text: "Thomas Jefferson President of the United States of America"; endorsed by TJ as received 19 Feb. 1803 and so recorded in SJL. Enclosures not identified.

John Appleton (1758-1829) was the son of Boston merchant Nathaniel Appleton and the brother of Thomas Appleton, the American consul at Leghorn. He went to Europe in 1780 and became ac-

quainted with several influential Americans, including TJ, who remembered Appleton as "young, handsome and devoted to pleasant pursuits." Establishing himself in business in France, Appleton became the American commercial agent at Calais in 1802. He resigned his post in 1807 and returned to Massachusetts, where he sought unsuccessfully an appointment as navy agent at Boston (Isaac Appleton Jewett, *Memorial of Samuel*

Appleton, of Ipswich, Massachusetts [Boston, 1850], 36; L. H. Butterfield and others, eds., *Adams Family Correspondence*, 9 vols. to date [Cambridge, Mass., 1963-], 3:390n; Madison, *Papers,*

Pres. Ser., 6:4; Vol. 33:678; Vol. 36:488; Appleton to TJ, 10 Aug. 1807, recorded in SJL as received 19 Aug. and "to be Navy Agent Boston," but not found; TJ to Robert Smith, 20 Aug. 1807).

To James Walker

Sir   Monticello Oct. 1. 1802.

On examining more carefully into the work still to be done in the canal, I find there is no prospect of getting the water to the mill seat before the ensuing summer. consequently there is no occasion to do any thing towards the buildings this winter. in March I shall be here, when I shall be able to form a still better judgment, and will inform you of our progress & expectations. Accept my best wishes.

Th: Jefferson

PrC (MHi); at foot of text: "Mr. Walker"; endorsed by TJ in ink on verso as "Walker (Milwright)."

Construction on the CANAL to TJ's toll mill on the Rivanna River, begun in 1776, and intermittent until 1796, was not completed until 1803 (Betts, *Farm Book,* 343).

From John Jeffers

Esteemed and   New York the 2d of the
Respected Friend,   10th Month 1802

It is with reluctance that I lift the pen to make my address to thee upon any ocation, Seeing that thou art a Statesman of the first rank and power in these states; and I an alien and stranger to thee.

I do not intend making any appology to thee, in regard of my uncouth manner of writing to thee, as i am no gramerian; yet i wish to convey my ideas to thee after as agreeable a maner as i am capable of doing.

I trust that a man of thy superior talent will not look upon these lines as an insult, for it is realy the reverse, as thou may discover in the sequal of my unfortunate state; of which i will give thee a few hints without teasing thy mind, only i wish to make this remark to thee, that there has been instances in diffrent ages of the world, of Kings and rulers of Sundry Nations, and of Various titles who has lent an hand to help the unfortunate.

To make thee acquainted with my situation, take it as foloweth, viz. In the year 1795 I brought six children over from Ireland to New

York, my eldest being over two years before, I brought them over free, and they remain so still two is since dead, and the eldest deserted me as they grew up, there is but two that I have any expectation of living with me, and my eldest Son is striving to keep my daughter from me, which is all the nurse i have.

Therefore I request the favour of thee, as a steward under the Supreme governor of heaven and earth, that thou of thy liberality, would be pleased to send for me, and my young Son and daughter, and place us on some agreeable spot of land that we may cultivate it for thee. as thou shalt think meet, in a neighbourhood of well disposed people if there be any such thing to be found.

I have no money, neither have i defrauded any one, i am free, yet, to go where i chuse; there is none can arest me for debt; therefore I cannot become bankrupt; I wish to be in a situation to procure the necessarys of life with out being in debt, which is all i desire.

If thou will be so kind as to take my case into thy serious consideration thou will not think it beneath thy exalted situation to be recorded[1] as a benefactor.

Lest thou should be mistaken of my ideas, I will inform thee viz. If thou would put me on a place with creatures to work it I would be enabled to make such a restitution as thou would require, or what I would prefer, to let me have a place till I would be able to pay for it, and if I could not it would be thy own.

My situation requires a quick change, as I am in New York without any thing to suport me; my son and me could work a small place, that would furnish us with the necessarys of life, and aforde a proportion to my benefactor for giving me an oppertunity of doing it.

I need not trouble thee with a catalouge of my misfortunes, nor the deceitfulness of the humane heart that I have experenced to be the case with many. I do not asume to my self the garb of a sycophant, I do not solicit thee for any favour under a mask. If my dialect be rude, I am sincere. I am an advocate for truth, and freedom from the Shakles of tyrany and opression and that all men should have the liberty to chuse thier mode of worshiping the Thing of heaven, and to chuse thier temporal rulers, men are free agents, they by deceit and wickedness have unmaned thier selves, with only a few ceptions; they wrestle for impossibilities, they wish to have all things at thier will, but they fall short. Man is only like a shadow that passeth, his imaginations turns on the rong axis, there is perhaps but a day or an hour betwen his earthly glory and the grave, there is nothing but strugles and anxieties in human life, time fails me, I do not undertake to teach thee wisdom, because it only comes from God, for the wisdom of this

[439]

world is a false substitute for the wisdom of the creator, the children of men deceive others by being deceived thier Selves.

If thou thinks fit to take notice of such an obscure being as me, be pleased to write an answer to this, with as quik dispatch as is convenient to thee

Direct to Abrm. Bell No 291 Pearl Street New York for John Jeffers

Look to the power that is above

that is the evidence of pure love

P.S. I do not presume to be aquainted with great men but they often have it in thier power to do good, which is a true distinction between vice and virtue

be not offended with my lenthy scrole, I wish to make thee as well aquainted with my meaning as possibe, and if I have offended it is not with a design, therefore I rest confident that thou will excuse me

RC (DLC); addressed: "To the much Esteemed Thomas Jefferson President of the united States of America"; franked; postmarked 4 Oct.; endorsed by TJ as received 6 Oct. and so recorded in SJL.

[1] MS: "to recorded."

From William Norvell

SIR   Post office Lynchbg. Oct. 3d: 1802

Mr Griffen your Manager in Bedford applied here a few days since for a letter & was told by my assistant there was none. but on Saturday last he got the letter. My assistant says it came by the Richmond Mail he suspects, but is not sure. As I have some reason to believe the mistake happend here, it is proper that I should acknowledge it, in order that no blame may attach to Mr Griffen

I have uniformly paid great attention to the duties of the office, and did not entertain any idea of any neglect in my assistant, and I have made use of such chastisement as I am sure will prevent a similar occurance.

As I believe this is the first breach in this office of any kind, I hope I am first in giving the information to you, whose letter was neglected

I have the Honor to be Yr Humb servt   WLL NORVELL

RC (DLC); at foot of text: "Thomas Jefferson Esquire President of U States"; endorsed by TJ as received from "Meenowell" on 8 Oct. and so recorded in SJL.

William Norvell (1770-1823) served as postmaster for Lynchburg from 1798 to 1805. A leader within Lynchburg's business circles, he became president of the town's branch of the Bank of Virginia. He also was placed in charge of distributing arms to militias in Lynchburg and the surrounding area. In 1812, he acted as trustee for a mortgage between TJ and another Lynchburg merchant. An obituary described Norvell as "not *showy* but *solid*—not one who *professed*, but who *practiced* virtue" (*Richmond Enquirer*, 4 Nov. 1823; Stets, *Postmasters*, 263; CVSP, 9:219, 459, 503; RS, 5:61-2).

While at Monticello, TJ wrote four letters to his Poplar Forest MANAGER Burgess Griffin, recorded in SJL at 6 Aug., 5 Sep. (two letters), and 16 Sep. None has been found.

From Pierre Samuel Du Pont de Nemours

MONSIEUR LE PRÉSIDENT   Paris 4 Octobre 1802.

Notre Négociation n'a pas eu autant de succès que je l'aurais désiré. Cependant je suis loin de la croire en aussi mauvaise position qu'elle me semble le paraitre à Mr. le chancelier Livingston, qui s'ennuie de ne recevoir pas de réponses positives par écrit, car les verbales sont bonnes.

Il ne peut y avoir aucun doute que vos Traités avec l'Espagne relativement aux limites des deux Etats, et au Commerce ainsi qu'à la Navigation du Mississipi, ne soient respectés, confirmés, renouvellés.

Il est certain que c'est l'interêt de la France que le Commerce des Etats Unis jouisse de tous ses droits et même de toute faveur à la Nouvelle Orléans; et que les Administrateurs qu'on y envoie sont pénétrés de cette vérité; paraissent disposés à en faire la règle de leur conduite.

Il n'y a aucun doute non plus que si le fait, très peu vraisemblable, que les Anglais eussent êté plus favorisés à St. Domingue que les Américains était vrai, ce ne fût contre les intentions les plus fortement prononcées du Gouvernement de France, qui donne à cet égard comme en tout autre point de commerce la plus absolue préférence aux Américains sur les Anglais.

Quant à la Nouvelle Orléans et aux Florides, il me parait qu'on veut avoir pris possession avant d'entrer en aucune Négociation. Mais, après que ce préalable sera rempli, rien n'annonce le refus de négocier.

S'il me convenait de donner conseil aux deux Puissances à cet égard, attaché comme je le suis à l'une et à l'autre par toutes sortes de devoirs, et croyant avoir bien calculé leurs interets respectifs, je proposerais ce que vous trouverez sur l'autre Page.

Article 1er.

"La France cédera aux Etats Unis la Nouvelle Orléans et les deux Florides, sous la condition que les Français et leurs Bâtimens y pourront exercer le Commerce aussi librement que les Citoyens et les Bâtimens des Etats unis, et sans y payer aucuns droits."

Art. 2.

"Les Etats Unis s'engagent à ne faire participer aucune autre Nation à ces avantages, qui sont une condition spéciale de la cession, et à maintenir sur le Commerce des autres Nations dans cette acquisition nouvelle, qui n'a pu être embrassée par les stipulations d'aucun Traité antérieur, les principes et la perception des Tarifs établis dans les douanes américaines."

Art. 3.

"La France se réserve formellement tous les autres territoires dépendant de la Louisiane et qui sont situés à la Rive droite du Mississipi.

"La Navigation du Fleuve sera libre et commune aux deux Nations."

Art. 4

"Les Etats Unis payeront à la France, pour prix de la cession mentionnée en l'article premier, Six millions de dollars."

Si vous voulez aller jusques là, quelles que puissent être les dispositions actuelles et l'effet des préventions, que je crois mal fondées, qui ont été prises à St. Domingue, où l'on a cru votre Nation plus favorable aux Noirs qu'aux Blancs, je ne desespere pas du succès. Et il vaut certainement mieux que le danger de rejetter votre Peuple, si justement fier de son indépendance, sous les griffes du léopard britannique, et de vous rendre les instrumens de la puissance ou des vengeances de vos anciens oppresseurs qui ne seront jamais pour vous que des amis faux, trompeurs et dédaigneux.

Vous voyez, Monsieur le Président, que je vous parle avec la liberté d'un homme que vous honorez de votre amitié.—Elle m'est infiniment chere. C'est par des services réels que je voudrais en mériter la continuation.

J'ai pensé à celui de faire à Paris les payemens des rentes que les Etats unis peuvent devoir à des Français, comme à un moyen de hausser encore votre crédit et d'annoncer une bienveillance, un esprit de communication et de rapports que je crois propre à favoriser vos négociations.

Mon Fils vous expliquera sur ce point toutes mes idées. Je n'en aurai aucune qui ne tende à l'avantage réciproque des deux Nations; Et ce que je puis y trouver de personnellement agréable ou utile n'est pas une objection pour votre cœur.

Permettez moi de réclamer toutes vos bontés pour *La Fayette* réduit à douze cent dollars de rente, et en devant Soixante et quinze mille, dont Soizante mille dans les Etats unis pour lesquels il en dépensé plus de cent cinquante mille de sa cidevant fortune.

En payant ses dettes, ils ne s'acquitteront pas de la moitié des avances que lui coute leur liberté, et ils ne verseront presque aucun argent que dans leur Pays, sur leurs propres citoyens.

Je vous salue avec un tendre et profond respect

DU PONT (DE NEMOURS)

EDITORS' TRANSLATION

MISTER PRESIDENT, Paris, 4 Oct. 1802

Our negotiations have not been as successful as I would have wished. However, I am far from believing them in as bad a place as Chancellor Livingston appears to think, who is irritated at not receiving positive replies in writing, since the verbal ones are good.

There can be no doubt that your treaties with Spain, concerning the boundaries of the two states, commerce, and navigation on the Mississippi, will be respected, confirmed, and renewed.

It is certainly in France's interest for the commerce of the United States to enjoy every right and even every favor in New Orleans, and for the officials we send there to be convinced of this truth and disposed to act accordingly.

Nor is there any doubt that if it were true (however improbable) that the English were more favored in Saint-Domingue than the Americans, this was contrary to the most strongly articulated intentions of the French government, which, in this as in all other business matters, gives absolute preference to the Americans over the English.

As for New Orleans and the Floridas, there seems to be a desire to take possession before undertaking negotiations. But after this is accomplished, there is no obstacle to our negotiating.

If it were appropriate for me to advise the two powers on this matter, being attached to both by many kinds of duties, and believing that I have carefully weighed their respective interests, I would propose what you will find on the next page.

Article 1

"France will cede New Orleans and the two Floridas to the United States, on condition that the French and their vessels be allowed to conduct their business as freely as the citizens and vessels of the United States, and without paying any duties."

Article 2

"The United States pledges not to allow any other nation to benefit from these advantages, which are a special condition of the cession, and to continue to apply the principles and tariffs established by American customs to the commerce of other nations in this new acquisition—which could not be included in the agreements of any previous treaty."

Article 3

"France explicitly reserves possession of all other territory dependent upon Louisiana, situated on the right bank of the Mississippi. Navigation on the river will be free, and shared by both nations."

Article 4

"The United States will pay France six million dollars for the cession mentioned in Article 1."

If you are willing to go this far, despite the present situation and the effect of the prejudices—which are unfounded in my opinion—engendered by the Saint-Domingue affair, where it was believed that your nation favored blacks over whites, I do not despair of success. And it is certainly better than the danger of casting your people, so justly proud of their independence, back under the claws of the British leopard and making yourselves instruments of the power or vengeance of your former oppressors, who will never be other than false, deceitful, and disdainful friends for you.

You see that I address you, Mister President, with the freedom of a man you honor with your friendship. It is infinitely dear to me. I wish to deserve its continuation through genuine service.

Specifically, I have thought of making payments in Paris to Frenchmen who are owed money by the United States, as a way of enhancing your credit and signaling your good will and the spirit of exchange which I think will be susceptible to favoring your negotiations.

My son will explain all my ideas about this to you. I have none which do not seek the reciprocal advantage of both nations. What I find personally agreeable and useful in them is not an objection in your eyes.

Allow me to impose upon your kindness on behalf of Lafayette, who has been reduced to twelve hundred dollars income and owes seventy-five thousand, including sixty thousand in the United States—a country for which he spent more than a hundred and fifty thousand dollars of his own fortune. By paying his debts, the United States will reimburse less than half the amount its liberty cost him, and will spend almost all the money in its own country, on its own citizens.

I send you my affectionate wishes and deepest regards.

DU PONT (DE NEMOURS)

RC (DLC); at head of text: "a Son Excellence Thomas Jefferson President des Etats Unis"; endorsed by TJ as received 31 Dec. and so recorded in SJL.

From William Barry

5th. Octr. 1802
City of Washington

An application For the Exspultion of Wm. W. Burrows at present Lieutt. Col. Commg. Marines—For His Tyranical Treatmt. to the Non Commisioned Officers and privates that Has been and are In the Service of the U. States—Is seriously and finally Transfer'd to your Excellency In Hopes of being put Into Execution—Whereas on the 15th. August 1802—the said Wm. W. Burrows—Caused to be brot. before Him From an old Grudge on acct. of a Letter wrote to your

Excellency about the 13th. or 14th. Feby. Last with Respect to my not being willing to go out to sea in the Constellation—she being bound for a Long Cruize and my time—being short—a Certain Wm. Barry—a Late Corpl. of Marines, For Endeavouring to Solicit or prevail on a Certain Peregrine White &. Wm. Prine two Private Marins on board the U. States Frigate Essex to Desert there was an application made to me by the aforesaid two Private Marines but I refused to Coincide with them In opinion—it—at Length displeased them—In Consequence thereof they made a Report to the aforesaid Wm. W. Burrows—that I solicited them to Desert—therefore the said Wm. W. Burrows ordered a Court Marshall and from a/cs. gave the Court Directns. to Sentence me one Hundred Lashes the wright side of my Head shaved and drumed out—In Consequence thereof Have thought proper to Come Forward to your Excellency for Refuge and to Know weather we are to be treated in this Manner—

I therefore Conclude Honourable Sir as a Child Petitioning His Father—that you will Have the aforesaid Wm. W. Burrows Banished out of the Service of the U. States. I Remain Honl. Sir, your Servt.

WM BARRY

RC (DLC); addressed: "To His Excellency Thomas Jefferson President of the U. States City of Washington"; endorsed by TJ as received 5 Oct. and so recorded in SJL.

William Barry had previously served as a Marine on the frigate *United States* during the Quasi-War with France. On 15 Sep. 1802, a court-martial held at the Marine barracks in Washington found Barry guilty of endeavoring to persuade two Marine privates from the frigate *Essex* to desert with him. The court sentenced Barry to receive 100 lashes, reduced his rank, and dismissed him from the service, "after having one half of his head shaved" (NDQW, Dec. 1800 to Dec. 1801, 65; Tr in DNA: RG 125, GCMCI).

A LETTER WROTE TO YOUR EXCELLENCY: a letter from Barry dated 1 Feb. 1802 is recorded in SJL as received from Philadelphia on 4 Feb., but has not been found (Vol. 36:683).

From Albert Gallatin

SIR   Treasury Department 5th Octer. 1802

I have the honor to enclose a letter from the collector of Boston, in which he recommends the appointment of an additional mate for the revenue cutter. The present establishment is a master & a mate. From Mr Lincoln recommending the measure, I have no doubt of its propriety and beg leave to submit the same to your consideration.

I have the honor to be very respectfully Sir Your obedt. Servt.

ALBERT GALLATIN

RC (DLC); at foot of text: "The President of the United States"; endorsed by TJ as received from the Treasury Department on 5 Oct. and so recorded in SJL. Enclosure not found.

In July 1803, Gallatin reminded TJ of this communication from Benjamin LINCOLN. He noted that similar applications had been received from other collectors with revenue cutters. Gallatin recommended that a second mate and two "men or boys" be added to crews of the cutters. The president agreed and the Treasury secretary promptly informed the collectors (Gallatin to Benjamin Lincoln and other collectors, 13 July 1803, in Gallatin, *Papers*, 8:534; Gallatin to TJ, 11 July; TJ to Gallatin, 12 July 1803).

From Albert Gallatin

SIR   Treasury Department 5th Octer. 1802

I have the honor to enclose the following papers vizt.

A letter from the collector of New-York announcing that the keeper of the light house at Sandy hook had resigned, and that he had appointed W. P. Schenck as a temperary keeper

Sundry recommendations for the office of light house keeper at Cape Hatteras

The resignation of Mr Carey who had been appointed collector at Yorktown, and a recommendation by Mr J. Page in favor of Mr T. Archer as a proper person to fill that office

A recommendation in favor of Joseph Turner for the collectorship of Brunswick in Georgia, vice Claud Thompson incapacitated from the effects of intemperance.

Whilst at New York, I made some enquiries relative to Mr Schenck, & think his appointment proper: it is difficult in that place to find a suitable character for so small a salary, and it is fortunate that he was willing to accept. I have no personal knowledge or other information in the other cases.

Permit me to refer to a former report in which the propriety of removing the collector of Louisville in Kentucky has been urged. Robert New Esqre. of Kentuckey had been strongly recommended for that office, and the papers transmitted to you.

I have the honor to be with great respect Sir Your obedt. Servt.

ALBERT GALLATIN

RC (DLC); at foot of text: "The President of the United States"; endorsed by TJ as received from the Treasury Department on 6 Oct. and "Collectors of York, Brunswick, Louisville Keepr. lighthouses Sandy Hook & Hatteras, & beacon Shellcastle" and so recorded in SJL. Enclosures: (1) David Gelston to Gallatin, New York, 30 Sep. 1802, announcing the resignation of Matthew Ely as lighthouse keeper at Sandy Hook and recommending the permanent appointment of William P. Schenck, an honest man "capable of performing the duties of the

Office with propriety" (RC in DNA: RG 59, LAR; endorsed by TJ: "Schenck. William P. keeper of lighthouse at Sandy hook vice Matthew Ely resigned. David Gelston's letter to mr Gallatin"). (2) John Page to Gallatin, Rosewell, 4 Oct. 1802, recommending Thomas Archer, a resident of Yorktown and highly respected by Page's friends there, as a proper person to be appointed collector at that port (RC in NHi: Gallatin Papers). Other enclosures not found.

On 8 Oct., Gallatin appointed John Mayo keeper of the beacon at Shell Castle Island, part of the lighthouse establishment at CAPE HATTERAS. Mayo declined the appointment (Gallatin, *Papers*, 8:227).

JOSEPH TURNER became collector at Brunswick, Georgia, in March 1803 (Gallatin to TJ, 14 Mch. 1803). For the Treasury secretary's search for a candidate to replace Claud Thomson, see Gallatin to TJ, 17 Aug. 1802.

SO SMALL A SALARY: the lighthouse keeper at Sandy Hook received $333 in annual compensation (ASP, *Miscellaneous*, 1:306).

COLLECTOR OF LOUISVILLE: for Gallatin's previous effort to have Robert Anderson New replace James McConnell at Louisville, see Gallatin to TJ, 24 Apr. 1802. Although New's name appeared on TJ's 24 Apr. list of candidates for appointments, it was not among those TJ submitted to the Senate on 27 Apr. One of the earlier PAPERS TRANSMITTED to TJ was a letter from Kentucky congressman Thomas T. Davis to Gallatin, 4 Oct. 1801, recommending Robert A. New, son of Virginia congressman Anthony New, as a young man of fair character who had moved to Kentucky and would be an eligible replacement for McConnell (RC in DNA: RG 59, LAR; endorsed by TJ: "New Robert Anderson. to be Collector at Louisville Thos. T. Davis to mr Gallatin").

From Albert Gallatin

SIR   Treasury Department 5th Octer. 1802

I have the honor to enclose a letter from Mr Kirby Supervisor of Connecticut, in which he requests to be discharged from the duties of his office. The Commissioner of the revenue with whom I consulted on the occasion agrees with me that the whole direct tax having been collected in that State, and the amount of outstanding duties being trifling and ascertained, no inconvenience can arise from the office being immediately discontinued. The second section of the Act to repeal the internal taxes authorizes the President of the United States to discontinue any of the offices of supervisor whenever the collection of the internal duties & direct tax shall have been so far completed in any State or District as, in his opinion, to render that measure expedient. The propriety of exercising that authority so far as respects Connecticut is respectfully submitted.

I have the honor to be with great respect Sir Your obedt. Servt.

ALBERT GALLATIN

RC (DLC); at foot of text: "The President of the United States"; endorsed by TJ as received from the Treasury Depart-ment on 5 Oct. and so recorded in SJL. Enclosure: Ephraim Kirby to TJ, 22 Sep. 1802.

For the presidential authority to DIS-CONTINUE the office, see U.S. Statutes at Large, 2:148-9. On 6 Oct., Gallatin informed Ephraim Kirby that considering the "situation of the district," the president thought it was "most consistent with the public interest that the office of Su-pervisor for Connecticut should be discontinued" effective 10 Oct. Kirby would receive information for the closing of the accounts from William Miller, commissioner of the revenue (Gallatin, *Papers,* 7:600).

From Albert Gallatin

DEAR SIR   Tuesday evening [5 Oct. 1802]

On reading the enclosed piece in Poulson's paper, I was induced to answer it, as a similar misrepresentation has already appeared in the Boston centinel; and being on that subject I was led into some discussion of the remission of Callender's fine. My idea was that Smith should obey the request of "a plain citizen," by reprinting his piece, and should add as his own remarks the substance of what I have written dressed in his own way & corrected as he may think fit. Will you be good enough to look at it & to see whether it wants any additions, corrections or curtailing?—I mean as to facts & arguments, not as to style—this Smith must modify.

Your affectionate Servt.   ALBERT GALLATIN

Did you grant any other sedition pardon but that to Callender?

You will perceive that Mr Kirby's letter ought to receive an immediate answer—   A. G.

RC (DLC); partially dated; date written adjacent to signature above postscript; at foot of text: "Mr Jefferson"; endorsed by TJ as received from the Treasury Department on 6 Oct. and "Callender's fine" and so recorded in SJL. Enclosure: "A Plain Citizen" to Levi Lincoln, Philadelphia, 29 Sep. 1802, charging that the attorney general had rendered inconsistent opinions; in the case of the remission of James T. Callender's $200 fine, Lincoln ruled "that a fine paid into the hands of any public and lawful agent (other than the Secretary of the Treasury) was returnable at the pleasure of the President (on his *retrospective* pardon)"; in another case involving citizens of Georgetown, Alexandria, and the city of Washington who applied to the president for the remission of penalties paid to the District of Columbia commissioners,

Lincoln's opinion was "*that money having been once paid into the hands of the public agent was not at the disposal of the President*" (printed in *Poulson's American Daily Advertiser,* 2 Oct. 1802, with the request that it also be printed in the *National Intelligencer*). Other enclosure not found, but see below.

SIMILAR MISREPRESENTATION: on 28 Aug., the Boston *Columbian Centinel* published documents, including Callender's pardon and correspondence between Levi Lincoln and David Meade Randolph, the former U.S. marshal, observing that they indicated that Callender's fine had been paid to the proper officer and was therefore "PROPERTY OF THE PUBLIC" over which the president had no control.

SOME DISCUSSION: Gallatin's draft response to the piece in Poulson's newspaper has not been found, but on 20 Oct. a reprint of the "Plain Citizen" letter along with an essay contradicting its assertions appeared in Samuel H. Smith's *National Intelligencer*. In his rebuttal, Gallatin contended that no citizens of Georgetown, Alexandria, or Washington, D.C. had applied to the president or the Treasury secretary for remission of penalties and consequently the attorney general had given no opinion. Gallatin assumed the author was referring to a case in which the U.S. attorney for the district was consulted to determine whether monies collected by a public agent were meant for the use of the United States or the county commissioners. In the other case, the president had pardoned Callender. In Lincoln's opinion, the pardon "remitted and restored" to Callender "a fine collected by the marshal, but not yet paid into the Treasury." Gallatin noted that even after the publication of the original documents in the case, the Federalist press continued to repeat "that the money was paid from the Treasury to Callender." Fines once paid into the Treasury cannot be remitted by the "mere effect of a pardon," Gallatin noted, because no monies can be drawn from the Treasury without an actual appropriation. Monies are not legally considered as being in the Treasury, however, until paid to the Treasurer and sanctioned by a warrant. Callender's fine had been collected by the marshal, but not paid to the Treasurer. Consequently, it was proper to return the fine. Gallatin argued that the president had acted fully within his powers by issuing the pardon. Having come into office believing the Sedition Act to be unconstitutional, TJ "granted pardons in every case where a conviction had taken place, and where it was not ascertained that the whole of the punishment had been incurred." The Treasury secretary contended that TJ had let the pardons "have their legal effect without any other interference on his part." Gallatin's rebuttal of "A Plain Citizen" was printed in Poulson's paper on 25 Oct. For the remission of Callender's fine, see Vol. 33:46-7, 157-8, 566, 573-5. For Gallatin's earlier response to the controversy over the payment of Callender's fine, see Gallatin, *Papers*, 7:489-93.

To George Jefferson

DEAR SIR   Washington Oct. 5. 1802.

The draughts heretofore[1] made on you, and which now ought to be covered, have been as follows.

Magruder		104.54
Griffin		79.69
R. Jefferson		60.
Yancey		321.09
Taliaferro		309.40
Isaacs		48.81
		923.53
now drawn.	Benj. Brown	285.83
	Thos. Wells	133.33

I now inclose you the first halves of 1200. Doll. branch bank of the US. the other halves shall follow immediately. as some of the first draughts above mentioned have not reached their term of paiment, and it will be some time before the two last get round, I will take a

little more time to provide for them (as I arrived here last night only) as well as for some other paiments I have still to make in Richmond. this on the supposition that the money recieved for mr Short has been drawn or will be wanting for himself. should it be otherwise, and remain in account between yourself & mr Barnes, I will exchange money here for it, and it will more than cover all I shall want there. on this subject you will be so good as to inform me. Accept my affectionate salutations.
TH: JEFFERSON

PrC (MHi); at foot of text: "Mr. George Jefferson." Recorded in SJL with notation "1200."

TJ had purchased meat from David ISAACS (MB, 2:1082). On this day TJ also wrote letters to Benjamin BROWN and Thomas WELLS, Jr., recorded in SJL with the notations "285.83" and "133.33," respectively. Neither note has been found. Wells responded with a letter of 8 Oct., recorded in SJL as received 10 Oct. but not found (see MB, 2:1083; Promissory Note to Thomas Wells, Jr., 6 Sep.).

[1] Word interlined.

From James Lyon

SIR   Wash. City, Oct. 5. 1802.

The obligations under which your benevolence or your friendship have laid me, make it my duty, if vanity fails to prompt me, to omit no opportunity to appear to advantage before you, that you may feel a self approbation for the countenance you have been pleased to give me. Impelled by this sentiment I enclose you the first number of the Georgia Republican, &c. I hope the offering will be acceptable. With much exertion, expence, and I fear, hazard, it has been established. My partner in this enterprize I found destitute. But believing him honest and capable, I produced, with my small funds and some responsibility, the necessary materials to commence the establishment; not, it is true, without hope of remuneration.

The political object of this paper, is to inculcate the principles of Representative democracy, and to defend the present administration against its natural enemies, error and falshood.

With yourself I have no doubt of being allowed the merit of consistency, industry, and perseverence in a good cause; and were there any advantages to my pursuits immediately in your gift, not claimed by superior merit, I am confident a tory printer would hold a poor competition for them. But there either is no merit in my exertions, or there is not a disposition, under some of the departments of the government to reward it: neither avarice nor necessity should force such an expression from me, were the friends of the administration in possession of all their favors. But the tory printer whom I heretofore mentioned, and of whom there seemed to be some missunderstanding, if he does not receive a greater share of patronage, I believe he has full as much as under the former administration. It is matter of exultation with some of the dispensers of these favors, that "their work is not done by a democrat." If I am not mistaken, a single bill of this printer, for work done for the Clerk of the House of Rep. last session, amounts to more than all the *printing* I have done for the public; exclusive of his printing for the Senate, and the Register, Auditor, paymaster Gen. Adjt. Gen. &c. Mr. Gallatin, (to whom I am this day to be obliged for the first order from him for printing) when I mentioned this subject to him, replied that Mr. *Way* came here on purpose to print for the public. The Sec. will not deny that Mr. Adams, likewise came here,—to be President of the United States; and that Mr Wolcott also came here to be Sec. of the Treasury. They both retired before the indignation of the republicans. Whether the full exercise of the principles the predominance of which drove them into retirement, would not compel their adherents and abettors to follow them, is left to be decided by those whose functions embrace the subject; I will however, take the liberty to add, as a case more directly in point, that Mr. Ross came here expressly to print the laws and journals, &c, but that printing has been given to others and Mr. Ross has returned. Begging your indulgence for this *long* letter, I shall only add, (fearing I trespass not only on patience but propriety) that I am with the most profound respect

Your obt. and most Humble Servt.   J. Lyon

RC (DLC); addressed: "The President of the United States"; endorsed by TJ as received 7 Oct. and so recorded in SJL. Enclosure: Savannah *Georgia Republican & State Intelligencer*, 21 Aug. 1802.

MY PARTNER IN THIS ENTERPRIZE: Samuel Morse (Vol. 32:34).

TORY PRINTER: Andrew Way (see Vol. 36:71-3).

Lyon wrote to Albert GALLATIN on 2 May requesting that his partner Richard Dinmore be substituted in his place to report the outstanding tonnage for the Treasury Department. Asserting that Dinmore could discharge these duties

and was not as "well versed" in the art of printing, Lyon hoped to pursue more printing business himself (Gallatin, *Papers*, 7:120-1).

Printer of the House journals during the Adams administration, William ROSS relocated from Philadelphia to Washington in 1801 to continue government printing contracts through the second session of the Sixth Congress. He returned to Philadelphia when Samuel Harrison Smith became House printer (Martin P. Claussen, ed., *The Journal of the House of Representatives*, 5 vols., [Wilmington, Del., 1977], 2:v; Evans, No. 32969; Shaw-Shoemaker, No. 1485).

From Henry Dearborn

SIR   Octobr. 6th. 1802

I have given the necessary direction for the discharge of Jerimiah Bettels mentioned in your note of this day.   H. DEARBORN

RC (DLC); addressed: "The President of the United States"; endorsed by TJ as received from the War Department on 7 Oct. and "Battel's case" and so recorded in SJL.

On 7 Oct., Dearborn ordered Lieutenant Colonel Thomas H. Cushing to

DISCHARGE Jeremiah Battels from the army (DNA: RG 107, LSMA). For the background on Battels's case, see Anthony Haswell to TJ, 16 Sep., and TJ to Haswell, 13 Oct.

YOUR NOTE OF THIS DAY: a letter from TJ to Dearborn dated 6 Oct. has not been found, nor is one recorded in SJL.

To Albert Gallatin

TH:J. TO MR GALLATIN   Oct. 6. 1802.

The inclosed is entirely approved. I recollect one other pardon; to Brown, who was in jail in Boston for a seditious writing under the sedition law. he had long since suffered the term of imprisonment sentenced, and had remained many months over from inability to pay his fine, petitioning mr Adams repeatedly for a discharge, on the ground that he had nothing, & must suffer perpetual imprisonment if he could not be discharged till he should pay the fine. I do not recollect any other pardon; tho' there may have been. this can only be known in the Secretary of State's office.

Th:J. asks the favor of mr Gallatin to peruse the inclosed letters from mr D'Oyley & return them. too[1] he reincloses some formerly recieved from mr Gallatin.

RC (NHi: Gallatin Papers); addressed: "The Secretary of the Treasury"; endorsed. Enclosures: (1) perhaps Daniel D'Oyley to Gallatin, 17 June 1801, requesting information on the laws, constitution, and internal regulations of the Bank of Pennsylvania that would be of use in establishing a bank at Charleston, in which the state had an interest (Gallatin, *Papers*, 5:199). (2) D'Oyley to Gallatin, 29 July 1801 (see Enclosure No. 2, listed at Gallatin to TJ, 17 Aug. 1801). (3) D'Oyley to Gallatin, Charleston, 5 Sep. 1801, describing the intrigues of the Federalists and divisions within the Republican party that led multiple candidates to

seek the U.S. Senate seat vacated by Charles Pinckney; noting that Thomas Sumter, Sr., had indicated that "no pains should be taken" to procure the seat for him, but if the governor saw fit to appoint him he would accept it; describing his efforts to influence Governor John Drayton to nominate Sumter, D'Oyley contends that while the governor was elected by the Republicans and pays some attention to their interests, "his connections by marriage & by blood" are with the opposition; suggesting that if Judge Aedanus Burke, who was dividing the Republican vote, were appointed U.S. district attorney in place of Thomas Parker, he would withdraw from the race and the Republicans would unite around a single candidate (RC in DNA: RG 59, LAR, endorsed by TJ: "Doyley Danl. to mr Gallatin"; Vol. 34:157n; Vol. 35:41-2, 101-2n; Vol. 36:262n). (4) D'Oyley to Gallatin, Charleston, 24 May 1802, describing the low morale of Republicans in South Carolina after receiving no support from Washington for their political sacrifices; the political conciliation experiment has failed; Republicans are not motivated and believe that in the next congressional election "no struggle they can make under existing circumstances" will allow them to prevail (Gallatin, *Papers*, 7:161-2). (5) Perhaps D'Oyley to Gallatin, Charleston, 22 June 1802, informing the Treasury secretary of the intentions of the U.S. Circuit Court judges to meet at Philadelphia on 17 July to prepare for bringing the question of the constitutionality of the repeal of the Judiciary Act of 1801 before the U.S. Supreme Court; D'Oyley fears the consequences and hopes the plan can be "arrested before it is matured" (same, 7:253). (6) D'Oyley to TJ, 24 July 1802. Other letters not found.

INCLOSED IS ENTIRELY APPROVED: see Gallatin to TJ, 5 Oct. (fourth letter). TJ signed David Brown's PARDON on 12 Mch. 1801 (see Vol. 33:251-2). For the president's interest in all of those prosecuted under the Sedition Act, see Vol. 36:258-60.

[1] MS: "to."

From Albert Gallatin

SIR,   Treasury Department October 6th. 1802.

I have the honor to enclose a letter from John Young, a mariner, who being sick within the limits of one of those sea-Ports (Middletown Connecticut) in which no hospital has been erected, nor the expence of any monies arising from the hospital Fund, been authorized. Under those circumstances, relief may be granted in special cases, by order of the President. On that account Young's application is respectfully submitted to your consideration.

I have the honor to be with great respect, Your obedt. Servant

ALBERT GALLATIN

RC (DLC); in a clerk's hand, signed by Gallatin; at foot of text: "The President of the United States"; endorsed by TJ as received from the Treasury Department on 7 Oct. and "John Young's case" and so recorded in SJL. Enclosure not found.

For the 3 May 1802 legislation that established a general fund for the PRESIDENT to use for the benefit of sick and disabled American seamen, see Vol. 36:632n.

To George Jefferson

DEAR SIR   Washington Oct. 6. 1802.

I yesterday inclosed you the first halves of bills of the branch bank of the US. for 1200. D. for purposes then expressed. I now inclose the second halves.   since mine of yesterday your's of Sep. 29. has been put into my hands. I shall still expect information from you whether the 441.62 D be wanting by mr Short there, or is to be transferred to mr Barnes. I am satisfied with the price got for my tobo. the proceeds, deducting your commission, are engaged to Martin Dawson of Milton for Rives & co. of which I shall advise them, and give an order. my daughters proposing to pay me a visit here shortly, I desired them to apply to you for any articles they might want from Richmd which I will pray you to furnish them and carry to my debit. Accept my affectionate salutations.

TH: JEFFERSON

PrC (MHi); at foot of text: "Mr. George Jefferson"; endorsed by TJ in ink on verso.

On 5 Oct., TJ tallied the sale of his 1801 crop of tobacco for $995.30, a total that included the deduction of George Jeffer-

son's COMMISSION. Two days later he recorded an order in favor of Martin Dawson for $1000 (MB, 2:1083). A letter to Dawson recorded in SJL at that date has not been found. A response from Dawson of 10 Oct., recorded in SJL as received 13 Oct., is also missing.

From Thomas Newton

DR SIR   Norfolk. Octr 6—1802

An act of Assembly passed in the year 1761 dividing the County of Norfolk, into three distinct Parishes, the whole being in one, that part which Norfolk Borough lies in, petitiond the Assembly to allow the Vestry, to purchase four lotts in Town to accommodate the Minister, between the years 1761 & .65 which was granted & obtaind the Royall assent on payment of ten guineas as well as I remember, Ld Dunmore in the distruction of our records, deprived us of the Act & we cannot obtain it, if you have it among yr. Collection, I shall be Much obliged to you for a Copy of it. I beg your excuse for this trouble, but rest assured I shall with pleasure make returns—health &c attend you, with the greatest Respect I am Yr. obt

THOS NEWTON

RC (DLC); endorsed by TJ as received 10 Nov. and so recorded in SJL but with notation "Oct. 6 for Nov. 6," but see Newton to TJ, 25 Oct.

The ACT of the Virginia Assembly subdividing the Anglican parish comprised of Norfolk County also mandated the sale

of the original parish's glebe land, with proceeds to be divided between the three new parishes. After the parish that included NORFOLK BOROUGH realized that the town's rapid population growth and the area's poor soil would make the purchase of a new parcel of glebe land impracticable, it gained approval of a law in 1764 authorizing the purchase of up to four lots in town that would provide a commensurate level of financial support for the minister (William Waller Hening, ed., *The Statutes at Large; Being a Collection of All the Laws of Virginia*, 13 vols. [Richmond, 1809-23], 7:416-19; 8:14-16). Newton's interest in the latter act almost certainly derived from an 1802 Virginia law that authorized local overseers of the poor to seize for sale or assume the proceeds of all Anglican property, excepting churches and churchyards, still in the possession of the Protestant Episcopal Church of Virginia. The Church retained any property acquired since 1777 (*Acts Passed at a General Assembly of the Commonwealth of Virginia: Begun and Held at the Capitol, in the City of Richmond, on Monday, the Seventh Day of December, One Thousand Eight Hundred and One* [Richmond, 1802; Shaw-Shoemaker, No. 3470], 8-9; George MacLaren Brydon, *Virginia's Mother Church and the Political Conditions under Which It Grew: The Story of the Anglican Church and the Development of Religion in Virginia, 1727-1814*, 2 vols. [Philadelphia, 1947-52], 2:499-503).

From Caesar A. Rodney

HONORED & DEAR SIR,   Wilmington Octob. 6. 1802.

Since I last wrote to you I have been on the verge of the grave. I was taken ill at Dover on my way to Sussex, early in September (a most unfortunate period) & was confined ten days to my bed. Since I came home, I have had the enclosed pamphlet published which is I understand producing good effects.

Our election took place yesterday throughout the state. In this County there were more votes taken than ever known before & the majority for Democracy larger than at any former election.

> Total number of votes recd.   2,371.
>
> For J: A. Bayard   707
>
> For C: A. Rodney   1,664.

Leaving us a majority of 957 to ballance the Federal majorities of Kent & Sussex. Whether it will or not I think somewhat uncertain. Last year 783 was more than sufficient, but in Kent the Federalists then had but 63. of a majority. This year I fear the result there for reasons with which you are acquainted

I inclose you a letter from the late Chanc: of this State, a venerable old whig. A few lines in reply will be gratifying him to he[ar.]

Octob. 7.

By the mail I have the Kent Polls. As I expected Bayard is 219. ahead. This majority is four times as great as any they have had these eight yrs past. You will be sensible of the reason of this change. This renders the state election doubtful & at all events secures Bayard a safe birth in the Senate.

In Sussex there are 2,346 votes. 700. are polled & I am yet 30. votes ahead there, but they are from favourable hundreds.

Every nerve has been strained by them. Their old paper printed by Smith has been revived & a new one the "Ark" set up, compared with which Callenders & Porcupines are chaste.

Octob. 9. 1802.

The result of our contest is now known. The majorities stand thus,

In new-Castle Coy. for C. A. Rodney   957
In Kent for J. A. Bayard   219   ⎫
In Sussex for J. A. Bayard   723   ⎬ 942
Majo'y. for C. A. Rodney   15

With great esteem & respect Yours most Sincerely

C. A. RODNEY

RC (DLC); clipped at margins. Recorded in SJL as received 13 Oct. Enclosure: William Killen to TJ, 4 Sep. 1802. For other enclosure, see Rodney to TJ, 15 Oct. 1802.

SECURES BAYARD A SAFE BIRTH IN THE SENATE: the Federalists continued to control the Delaware General Assembly after the election of 1802, allowing them to fill the U.S. Senate seat held by Samuel White, a Federalist, whose term was expiring. James A. Bayard decided not to be a candidate, and in January 1803 the general assembly reelected White (Morton Borden, *The Federalism of James A. Bayard* [New York, 1955], 135-6, 141-2; *Journal of the Senate of the State of Delaware, at a Session of the Gen-* *eral Assembly, Commenced and Holden at Dover, on Tuesday the Fourth Day of January, in the Year of our Lord One Thousand Eight Hundred and Three* [Dover, Del., 1803], 12-15; Vol. 35:207-8n).

OLD PAPER: for a time in 1802, William C. Smyth suspended publication of the Wilmington *Monitor; or, Delaware Federalist*, which had been in existence since 1 Feb. 1800. The revival of the newspaper was short-lived, the last extant issue being that of 1 Sep. 1802. NEW ONE: William Black established *The Federal Ark* in Dover, Delaware, in September 1802. Smyth joined Black as publisher of the new paper for a few months in 1803, after it was moved to Wilmington (Brigham, *American Newspapers*, 1:77, 83-5).

From Alexander Addison

SIR   Pittsburgh 7th Octr 1802

I understand that by contract the mail from the eastward ought to come to this post office on the mornings of Tuesday and Friday. It in fact comes in the evenings before between six and seven o'clock. There is a convenience in this as the mail can thus be forwarded in due time to Washington Pa. and return here to the eastward with more ease. There would also be a convenience to men of business if they could receive their letters in the evenings of Monday and

Thursday as in consequence of them they might wish to send letters next morning to Kentucky &c. But the Postmaster here says he has laid down a rule not to give out letters till the mornings of Tuesday and Friday, and says he has a right to make this rule because he is not obliged to receive the mail till then. In this he may be right if the Post offices be established for the convenience of the Postmasters and not of the publick; or if the attendance of the Postmaster is to be regulated by the last moment that the Contractor may delay the mail. But I should think when the mail comes pretty regularly at a certain time before the limitation by contract, it becomes the duty of the Postmaster to attend at that time and with all reasonable diligence after that give out letters within reasonable hours. I see no connection between the duty of a Postmaster and that of a Contractor if a Contractor usually performs his duty within less than the limited time.

The office of Pittsburgh is kept under the same roof and on the same ground story with the shop the parlour and the kitchen of the Postmaster separated from them by a thin partition and communicating with them by an inner door. The kitchen as well as the shop has a street door and the post office door is close by the street door.

I make this statement from no resentment to the Postmaster and submit to you whether the rule he has laid down be such as results from a just comparison of his accommodation with that of the publick, or whether you think different instructions ought to be sent from the Postmaster General.

I have the honour to be Your most obedient Servant

ALEXR ADDISON

RC (DLC); at foot of text: "The President of the United States"; endorsed by TJ as received 17 Oct. and so recorded in SJL.

Born and educated in Scotland, Alexander Addison (1759-1807) immigrated to western Pennsylvania in 1785. Admitted to the bar two years later, he supported the ratification of both the federal constitution of 1787 and the new state constitution of 1790. He was appointed presiding judge of Pennsylvania's fifth judicial district in 1791, in which position he eventually became one of the most influential and most strident Federalists in the state. His voluminous writings, his frequent antidemocratic addresses to grand juries, and his refusal to allow his Republican associate on the bench to speak, made Addison particularly obnoxious to Pennsylvania Republicans, who succeeded in removing him from office in 1803. Informing TJ of Addison's impeachment, Governor Thomas McKean declared that "federalism will fall with him in the six Western counties" (G. S. Rowe, "Alexander Addison: The Disillusionment of a 'Republican Schoolmaster,'" *Western Pennsylvania Historical Magazine*, 62 [July 1979], 221-50; Peter Charles Hoffer and N. E. H. Hull, *Impeachment in America, 1635-1805* [New Haven, 1984], 191-205; Washington, *Papers, Ret. Ser.*, 2:277-8; McKean to TJ, 7 Feb. 1803).

THE POSTMASTER HERE: Hugh Scott became postmaster at Pittsburgh in April 1801 (Stets, *Postmasters*, 224).
A 16 Mch. 1804 letter from Addison to TJ is recorded in SJL as received from Pittsburgh on 29 Mch. with the notation "P.Mast.," but has not been found.

From Henry Dearborn

War Department
SIR,   7th. October. 1802.

The Secretary of War has the honor of proposing to the President of the United States, that, Alexander McComb Jur. of the State of New York, now a second Lieutenant in the 1st. Regiment of Infantry be appointed first Lieutenant in the Corps of Engineers, That Joseph G. Swift of Massachusetts, and Simon Levy of the State of   now serving as Cadets, be appointed second Lieutenants in said Corps of Engineers, that Ephraim Emmory of Massachusetts, be appointed second Lieutenant in the Regiment of Artillerists: and That, Henry Irvine of Pennsylvania, Peyton Gay of Massachusetts, Josiah Taylor of Connecticut, William L. Chew of Maryland, and William Simmons of Virginia, be respectively appointed Ensigns, in the 2nd. Regiment of Infantry, in the Army of the United States.

FC (Lb in DNA: RG 107, LSP). Recorded in SJL as received from the War Department on 7 Oct. with notation "appmt. officers."

To Mary Jefferson Eppes

MY DEAR MARIA   Washington Oct. 7. 1802.

I arrived here on the fourth day of my journey without accident. on the day and day after my arrival I was much indisposed with a general soreness all over, a ringing in the head & deafness. it is wearing off slowly, and was probably produced by travelling very early two mornings in fog.   I have desired mr Jefferson to furnish you with whatever you may call for, on my account; and I insist on your calling freely. it never was my intention that a visit for my gratification should be at your expence. it will be absolutely necessary for me to send fresh horses to meet you, as no horses, after the three first days journey, can encounter the 4th. which is hilly beyond any thing you have ever seen. I shall expect to learn from you soon, the day of your departure, that I may take proper arrangements.

[458]

present me affectionately to mr Eppes, and accept yourself my tenderest love.   TH: JEFFERSON

P.S. mr Eppes's bridle is delivered to Davy Bowles.

RC (ViU).

TJ ARRIVED on 4 Oct. and recorded $22.12 in his financial memoranda of that date as the whole expense for his trip. Before his departure from Monticello on 1 Oct., he gave Mary $18.50 to pay small household expenses (MB, 2:1082).

On 7 Oct., TJ recorded an order on John Barnes for DAVY BOWLES for $43.75 (MB, 2:1083).

To Albert Gallatin

TH:J. TO MR GALLATIN   Oct. 7. 1802.

The application of the bank of Baltimore is of great importance. the consideration is very weighty that it is held by citizens while the stock of the US. bank is held in so great a proportion by foreigners. were the bank of the US. to swallow up the others & monopolize the whole banking business of the US., which the demands we furnish them with tend strongly to favor, we might, on a misunderstanding with a foreign power, be immensely embarrassed by any disaffection in that bank. it is certainly for the public good to keep all the banks competitors for our favors, by a judicious distribution of them, and thus to engage the individuals who belong to them in the support of the reformed order of things, or at least in an acquiescence under it. I suppose that on the condition of participating in the deposits, the banks would be willing to make such communications of their operations & the state of their affairs as might satisfy the Secy. of the Treasury of their stability. it is recommended to mr Gallatin to leave such an opening in his answer to this letter, as to leave us free to do hereafter what shall be adviseable on a broad view of all the banks in the different parts of the Union.

P.S. if your information as to the intemperance of Thompson[1] be not compleatly satisfactory, a mr Sibbald of that state of whom I made some enquiry, says he can procure good information from a person in town

RC (NHi: Gallatin Papers); endorsed. PrC (DLC); pressed on same sheet following the memorandum on appointments, 7 Oct.; lacks salutation, dateline, and postscript.

The Maryland legislature chartered the BANK OF BALTIMORE in December 1795, giving it the right to sell stock at $300 per share to raise up to $1,200,000 in capital. James McHenry promoted the establishment of the bank and his protégé George Salmon became the first president. The charter gave the state of Maryland the right to invest up to $180,000 in the stock of the bank. Henry Payson and Luke Tiernan, recently appointed bankruptcy commissioners, served on the board of directors. During the legislative session that began in November 1802, the Maryland Assembly decided to purchase 220 shares of Bank of Baltimore stock with $66,000 of unappropriated monies in the state Treasury (*Votes and Proceedings of the House of Delegates of the State of Maryland. November Session, One Thousand Eight Hundred and Two* [Annapolis, 1803], 76; *Laws of Maryland, Made and Passed at a Session of Assembly, Begun and Held at the City of Annapolis on Monday the Second of November, in the Year of Our Lord One Thousand Seven Hundred and Ninety-Five* [Annapolis, 1796], chap. 27; *Laws of Maryland, Made and Passed at a Session of Assembly, Begun and Held at the City of Annapolis on Monday the First of November, in the Year of our Lord One Thousand Eight Hundred and Two* [Annapolis, 1803], chap. 58; Washington, *Papers, Pres. Ser.*, 7:341-2; ANB, s.v. "McHenry, James"; Baltimore *Federal Gazette*, 7 Dec. 1802; Vol. 37: Appendix II, Lists 1 and 2).

The Bank of the United States established an office of discount and deposit in Baltimore in 1792 and by 1800 its capital had expanded from $200,000 to $600,000. In January 1798, it was estimated that FOREIGNERS owned 13,000 of the 25,000 shares of the Bank of the United States. The proportion increased in June 1802 when the U.S. sold 2,220 shares to British financier Alexander Baring at $580 per share. In exchange, Baring agreed to have over 3,000,000 guilders available at Amsterdam for the payment of the Dutch debt falling due during the first five months of 1803. Baring agreed to the rate of 41 cents per guilder, which was much better than what Gallatin anticipated if the U.S. had tried to obtain bills on Holland for such a large amount (James O. Wettereau, "New Light on the First Bank of the United States," PMHB, 61 [1937], 269, 277-8; ASP, *Finance*, 2:9, 29; Madison, *Papers, Sec. of State Ser.*, 3:287n). For Gallatin's fear that funds could not be accumulated in Amsterdam without raising the exchange rate, see Vol. 37:157-9. Neither the letter of application from the Bank of Baltimore nor Gallatin's ANSWER has been found. State banks received an increasing proportion of Treasury funds during TJ's years in office, but the deposits were usually in regions where there was no branch of the Bank of the United States (Wettereau, "The Branches of the First Bank of the United States," *Journal of Economic History*, 2 [1942], 86n).

MR SIBBALD: perhaps George Sibbald of Georgia (see TJ to Thomas Mann Randolph, 12 Mch. 1802).

[1] Name interlined in place of "Mc-Connel."

From Albert Gallatin

DEAR SIR   [7 Oct. 1802]

An advertisement for the plan of a marine hospital published in the Boston papers has produced only the within plan. Is it sufficiently perfect to deserve the 50 dollars & ought we to carry it into effect? As to a contract, it must, like those for light houses, be advertised by the Collector at Boston who will transmit to us the proposals. I had had the advertisement for a plan inserted only in the Boston papers, as I thought it would please the people there better to have the hospital built after a plan of one of their own architects. If we now advertise here for a plan, it will delay another month, & we shall not have entered into a contract for that object by the time Congress shall meet. You know that the eastern people made that hospital a sine qua non of generalizing the fund.

With respect your obedt. Servt. ALBERT GALLATIN

RC (DLC); at foot of text: "The President"; endorsed by TJ as received from the Treasury Department on 7 Oct. and "marine hosp. at Boston" and so recorded in SJL. Enclosure not found, but see below.

For the ADVERTISEMENT seeking designs for a marine hospital at Boston, see Vol. 37:649. WITHIN PLAN: Asher Benjamin, author of *The Country Builder's Assistant*, published in Greenfield, Massachusetts in 1797, submitted the design enclosed. A native of Connecticut, Benjamin wrote Gideon Granger, requesting that he intercede with the Treasury secretary. Since leaving Suffield, Benjamin informed Granger, he had designed and built houses in Massachusetts, including Deerfield Academy, and a "Meeting House & 3 other Large Houses" in Windsor, Vermont. On 13 Aug.,

Granger forwarded Benjamin's letter to Gallatin, describing him as "one of the first mechanicks in New England" who, as "a poor boy unaided by friends," through industry and talent, "raised himself to the first rank of his profession." The marine hospital, built on the grounds of the Charlestown Navy Yard, was reportedly modeled after the almshouse designed by Boston architect Charles Bulfinch (ANB, s.v. "Benjamin, Asher" and "Bulfinch, Charles"; Gallatin, *Papers*, 7:457, 846; Florence Thompson Howe, "More about Asher Benjamin," *Journal of the Society of Architectural Historians*, 13 [1954], 16-19).

Massachusetts Republican William Eustis led the debate making the hospital a SINE QUA NON for changes in the distribution of the seamen's fund (*Annals*, 11:1163-4; Vol. 36:632n).

To Albert Gallatin

TH:J. TO MR GALLATIN   [on or after 7 Oct. 1802]

Altho' the plan of the hospital has but moderate merit, yet having no other I suppose we must use it, and, using it, pay for it. I presume therefore we may at once adopt it and call for estimates or undertakers.

RC (NHi: Gallatin Papers); undated, but see Gallatin to TJ, immediately above; written on verso of an address sheet; addressed by TJ: "The Secretary of the Treasury" in place of "The President of the United States" in Gallatin's hand; endorsed: "for the building of an hospital at or near Boston." Not recorded in SJL.

On 11 Oct., Gallatin informed Benjamin Lincoln, collector at Boston, that Asher Benjamin should receive the re-

ward for his PLAN OF THE HOSPITAL, although "not possessed of very great merit." Gallatin enclosed the adopted plan with alterations of the second floor marked in pencil and requested that Lincoln prepare a newspaper advertisement to secure bids for the construction of the two-story brick building with a stone cellar. The edifice was to be completed by 1 Dec. 1803, at the latest, and not to exceed the appropriated sum. Gallatin advised that the contract be drawn "to secure the best materials, good workmanship, and a compliance with the intended Plan." When Lincoln received the proposals, he was to compare and then transmit them to the Treasury Department with his recommendations (Gallatin, *Papers*, 7:625). The advertisement appeared in the 30 Oct. issue of the Boston *Columbian Centinel*. Lincoln detailed the specifications for the hospital. Noting that it was "difficult to give a very minute detail of all the particulars which must be embraced by a full execution of the plan," he invited those interested to study the plans for the building at his office. Contractors were to submit "their terms in writing sealed" to Lincoln by 1 Dec. 1802.

Memorandum on Appointments

Oct. 7. 1802.

William P. Schenck is approved as keeper of the light house[1] at Sandy Hook.

Thomas Archer of Yorktown is approved as Collector at that port in the room of William Carey resigned

Joseph Turner is approved as Collector of Brunswick in Georgia vice Claud Thompson to be removed for intemperance.

Robert Anderson New of Kentucky is approved as Collector of the customs at Louisville in Kentuckey vice James Mc.Connel to be removed for failing to make due returns.   TH: JEFFERSON

PrC (DLC); pressed on same sheet as TJ to Gallatin, 7 Oct. (first letter).

TJ sent this memorandum to Gallatin to acquaint him with the Treasury Department appointments. The Treasury secretary then sent it to the State Department for the preparation of the commissions. For Gallatin's delay of the TURNER appointment, see his letter to TJ of 8 Oct.

[1] Remainder of sentence interlined in place of "New York."

To Martha Jefferson Randolph

MY DEAR MARTHA   Washington Oct. 7. 1802.

I arrived here on the fourth day of our journey without accident. travelling early one or two mornings through fog brought on some degree of indisposition, which I felt strongly on the day & day after my arrival, but it is wearing off slowly. it has been chiefly an excessive soreness all over and a deafness & ringing in the head. I have desired mr Jefferson to procure you whatever you may call for on my account, and I pray you to do it freely. it never was my intention that a journey made for my gratification should bring any expence on you. I must press on you to let me send horses to meet you, as I am convinced that no horses after the three first days journey, can encounter the 4th.

which is hilly beyond any thing you have ever seen below the mountains. I shall expect soon to hear from you. present me affectionately to mr Randolph & kiss the children for me. to yourself my tenderest love.   TH: JEFFERSON

RC (NNPM); at foot of text: "Mrs. Randolph."

From Henry Dearborn

SIR   Octobr. 8th. 1802

On further enquirey & concideration I am induced to repeat my request for the appointment of the officers I had the honour of proposing for your concideration yesterday.—

McComb, Swift & Levy being in the Army and having strong claims on the score of services for promotion, on general principles it would be improper to postpone them.

Irwin, Gay & Chew are said to be active republicans.—

Taylor, Sims & Emmery may be concidered as having no politics, but would probably be fixed by their appointments.

with respectful conciderations I am Sir Your Huml Servt

                                                                       H. DEARBORN

RC (DLC); at foot of text: "The President of the United States"; endorsed by TJ as received from the War Department on 8 Oct. and "appmts" and so recorded in SJL.

APPOINTMENT OF THE OFFICERS: TJ approved Dearborn's nominees on 12 Oct. and submitted their names for Senate approval on 11 Jan. 1803, with the exception of Henry Irvine, who declined his appointment. The Senate consented to the appointments of Alexander Macomb (McComb), Joseph G. Swift, Simon M.

Levy, Josiah Taylor, William L. Chew, and William Simmons on 25 Jan., but rejected the nominations of Ephraim Emery (Emmery) and Peyton Gay on 22 Feb. (JEP, 1:434, 440, 445; Dearborn to Thomas H. Cushing, 12 Oct. 1802 [two letters] and 16 Mch. 1803, in DNA: RG 107, LSMA; William Wingate to TJ, 7 Feb. 1803). Macomb would later serve as commanding general of the U.S. Army from 1828 to 1841, while Swift, the first graduate of the military academy at West Point, became colonel and chief of engineers in 1812 (ANB).

From Albert Gallatin

DEAR SIR   Friday morning [8 Oct. 1802]

I return D'oyley's letters: these connected with that I received in June or July last & communicated to you, leave it doubtful whether he is actuated by personal motives or a sense of the general republican interest. His observations on the conduct of the Bank of the United States at Charleston, corroborated by the several applications of the Banks of Pennsylvania & Baltimore deserve consideration.

If you have any means of obtaining, through Mr Sibbald, further information, not in relation to Claud Thompson's intemperance, but concerning the fitness of the person proposed as his successor by Gen. Jackson, it might be useful; and, for that purpose, I will suspend applying to the Dept. of State for a commission in that case, till next week—

Before I transmit an official communication on the subject of the piers in Delaware, I will state that the repairs of all the existing piers have been contracted for and are nearly completed—that the chamber of commerce & other persons interested in the subject at Philadelphia have now recommended that the money which may be spared should be applied in the first instance to the improvement of Reedy Island or Fort Penn harbour, that ten thousand dollars should be left for New castle, & that they would trust future appropriations if any can be obtained (which, by the bye is not probable) for the piers at Marcus hook, Mud Island & Gloucester point. You will perceive that, by that proposition, the points which they give up are all in Pennsylvania, and that the places which they recommend are all in Delaware. The gentlemen from New castle state the expence there at about 15,000 dollars, of which 3000 have been supplied by a state lottery, leaving 12,000 dollars to be provided for by the public funds. The result of the plan which I feel inclined to recommend is

For all repairs—already contracted for	6,361.20
New piers at Reedy Island alias Fort Penn, the lowest harbour in Delaware	11,638.80
Piers at New castle	12,000.—
Total appropn.	30,000.—

I enclose for your perusal the papers lately received which you may compare with my former report. I will want them again, in order to make a formal report to you, but wish, previously, to know your opinion. As to Wilmington, it has never been thought of; the choice would, if that place shall be taken into consideration, between it & New castle: but it has already a natural harbour, in Christina Creek, secure from the river ice; and any improvements there would go to an actual improvement of a particular harbour & not to the erection of piers against ice; to which must be added that it wants that depth of water, which, on account of the public ships, is the great argument in favor of New castle.

Respectfully Your obedt. Servt.   ALBERT GALLATIN

RC (DLC); partially dated; at foot of text: "The President"; endorsed by TJ as received from the Treasury Department on 8 Oct. and "Piers in Delaware" and so recorded in SJL. Enclosures on Delaware River piers not found.

For D'OYLEY'S LETTERS, see enclosures described at TJ to Gallatin, 6 Oct.

SEVERAL APPLICATIONS: for that of the Bank of Pennsylvania, see Memorandum from Albert Gallatin, printed at 18 June, and TJ to Gallatin, 19 June 1802; for the Bank of Baltimore, see TJ to Gallatin, 7 Oct. (first letter).

GENTLEMEN FROM NEW CASTLE: probably the three commissioners appointed by the state legislature to see that piers were erected at that site (see Gallatin to TJ, 9 Aug.). For the monies from the STATE LOTTERY, see Caesar A. Rodney to TJ, 28 June.

Gallatin's FORMER REPORT has not been found, but TJ may have written his Memorandum on Delaware River Piers, at 26 June 1802, in response to it.

From George Jefferson

DEAR SIR   Richmond 8th. Octr. 1802

I yesterday received your favor of the 5th. inclosing the first halves of 1200$ in B. Notes.

I some days since wrote Mr. Barnes that Mr. Short would have occasion here for the money of his now in my hands.

I am Dear Sir Your Very humble servt.   GEO. JEFFERSON

RC (MHi); at foot of text: "Thos. Jefferson esqr."; endorsed by TJ as received 10 Oct. and so recorded in SJL.

From George E. Cordell

HONOURED SIR.   Leesburg Oct. 9th. 1802.

My self and a Number of This Country's well wishers are highly pleased with what ever you have done since you have been elected Our Chief Magistrate. But more especially with your blessed fortitude. Forbaring to take Notice of the many Scandalous misresentations of your Administration. dear Sir I am nothing more than a Mecanic. but am Acquainted with a multitude of People of the upper, and middle Class, and am Often surprised to hear the Fedl. party complaining about the internal Taxes being loped off. &c two years is not yet passed since I heard the same people complaining of the weight of the Taxes. I have made free with some of the restless souls, and told them to forward the Tax on their Cariages to the Treasury and let them there abide till their Apprehended mission takes place. then I should think them Patriotts indeed.

Frederick county in Maryland have voted in four very Good

men.   last monday I hope all the Other counties in that state and this will follow their example. pray Sir excuse me for making so free with a Gentleman of your importance as to inclose a little paper to Smile at. I am Sir.

with unfained good wishes. your hearty well wisher for the United States sake and my own &c.   GEO. E. CORDELL

RC (DLC); addressed: "His Excellency Thomas Jefferson Esqr. City of Washington"; franked; postmarked 10 Oct.; endorsed by TJ as received 11 Oct. and so recorded in SJL. Enclosure not identified.

George E. Cordell was presumably the same individual who years later advertised the sale of livestock, furniture, and "two good CLOCKS" in order to fulfill "a

desire to remove from Leesburg" and "to discharge all my debts of every description" (Leesburg, Va., *Genius of Liberty*, 15 July 1817).

FOUR VERY GOOD MEN: on the previous day *Bartgis's Republican Gazette* of Frederick, Maryland, reported the election of the Republican slate of candidates to represent the county in Maryland's House of Delegates.

To Albert Gallatin

TH:J. TO MR GALLATIN   Oct. 9. 1802.

E. Randolph has offered to mr Short to give him personal security, such as he will be satisfied with, for the whole sum & interest due to mr Short. mr Short will not accept it, viewing the public as his debtor, but is willing to endeavor to obtain the security, on condition it shall not prejudice his right against the public, considering it as so much saved to the public which may otherwise be desperate. Messrs. Pickering & Wolcott agreed to a similar condition on E.R.'s offering a judgment of which he was the holder, in part of paiment; by which about 7000. D. were secured. I wish to avoid all possible agency in this matter, and therefore refer to yourself to decide whether mr Short shall be authorised to accept the security without prejudice to his rights? it will be necessary for me to recieve your answer this afternoon, as the letter must go by the afternoon's post or he will have left Richmond.

PrC (DLC).

E. RANDOLPH HAS OFFERED TO MR SHORT: see TJ to William Short, 9 Oct. Short still had an unresolved claim for salary that depended on the final settlement of Edmund Randolph's accounts as secretary of state. During the Adams ad-

ministration, Timothy PICKERING and Oliver WOLCOTT acknowledged that the government was liable for the obligation to Short, and invested funds in public securities in trust for him in anticipation of an eventual settlement (Vol. 36:162-3n, 455-7).

From Albert Gallatin

SIR,   Treasury Department October 9th. 1802.

In answer to your note of this morning, stating that Mr. Edmund Randolph had offered to Mr. Short personal security for the sum due to him, which Mr. Short would not accept, unless it was agreed that it should not prejudice his right against the public; I have the honor to observe that not being sufficiently acquainted with the nature of that transaction, and the Comptroller being now absent, I could not assent to any modification differing in its principle from what has heretofore been agreed on.

But I find by a letter of Mr. Wolcott to you dated the 10th. day of May 1800, that he acknowledges it to have been mutually agreed that any sums which might be received by Mr. Short's agent from Mr. Randolph, should not prejudice the claim of Mr. Short against the United States for any balance which might remain unsatisfied.

There can be no objection to extending the agreement which was thus made, in relation to any payments which might arise under the assumpsit of Messrs. Edmund Pendleton & P. Lyons, to any payments which may be made in consequence of the new security offered by Mr. Edmund Randolph, to Mr. Short; and it will be understood that Mr. Short, by accepting that security, will not prejudice his claim against the United States; provided that such acceptance shall not differ, substantially, from the manner in which his agent had accepted Messrs. Pendleton & Lyons assumpsit.

I have the honor to be, very respectfully, Sir, Your obedt. Servt.

ALBERT GALLATIN

RC (DLC: William Short Papers); in a clerk's hand, signed by Gallatin; at foot of text: "Mr. Jefferson." Enclosed in TJ to William Short, 9 Oct.

For information that Gallatin had received from the COMPTROLLER earlier in the year about Edmund Randolph's accounts and William Short's salary claim, see Vol. 36:343-4. The letter from Oliver WOLCOTT replied to a query from TJ, who asked, as Short's AGENT, if Short's claim against the government would be voided by his acceptance of some money that Edmund PENDLETON and Peter LYONS owed Randolph (Vol. 31:497-9, 574).

From George Jefferson

DEAR SIR   Richmond 9th. Octr. 1802.

I have now only to acknowledge the receipt of your favor of the 6th. inclosing the second halves of the 1200$, the first of which came to hand by last post.

I am Dear Sir Your Very humble servt.   GEO. JEFFERSON

RC (MHi); at foot of text: "Thos. Jefferson esqr."; endorsed by TJ as received 12 Oct. and so recorded in SJL.

To William Short

DEAR SIR   Washington Oct. 8. [i.e. 9] 1802.

Your's of the 5th. came to hand yesterday evening after the departure of the post. this can go only this afternoon, & tomorrow is Sunday.

I sincerely regret it is not in my power to furnish any thing in aid of your brother till the epoch I had mentioned to you. the close of the year calls for the paiment of all hired laborers, of my workmen, the year's provision of corn & this during the expensive time of a session of Congress. it was on a view of this, that, seeing my resources till Feb. inclusive would be absorbed, I fixed on March as the beginning of a monthly or quarterly paiment of 500. or 1500 D perhaps 2000. and which shall not then cease till compleated. I think I know mr Ross too well to suspect even that he would think an action preferable to any reasonable instalments which you would undertake or guarantee. he and I have had a bloody contest which has separated us, so that we could not transact any thing together pleasantly. but any stipulations you shall find it convenient to enter into, or orders in favor of your brother, so far as built upon what I have here promised shall be religiously fulfilled. your application needs no apology. my wishes are to know yours & to fulfill them to the utmost of my power.

On the subject of E. Randolph's proposition to give you personal security, altho' I think he cannot do it, yet the chance should not be thrown away. but mr Gallatin must be seen, which shall be in the course of the day, and the result communicated herein, if obtained before the departure of the post. Tho' messrs. Pickering & Wolcott actually purchased but 2000. D. for you, they acknoleged the public liable to interest for the whole.

Your servt had better stay here. he adds nothing sensibly to our family, and will hardly object to the walk while you shall be at mr Barnes's. indeed I think you will find it more agreeable yourself to take a hack & come here generally at the hour of dinner. Accept my affectionate salutations. TH: JEFFERSON

Mr. Gallatin's note is inclosed. the men you accept should be good.

RC (DLC: Short Papers); probably written on 9 Oct. (see below), although recorded in SJL under 8 Oct.; addressed: "William Short esquire Richmond" with notation "to the care of Messrs. Gibson & Jefferson"; franked; postmarked 9 Oct.; endorsed by Short as received at Richmond on 12 Oct. Enclosure: Gallatin to TJ, 9 Oct.

TJ's references to YESTERDAY and TO-MORROW, along with his enclosure of Gallatin's letter of 9 Oct., suggest that he wrote the letter printed above on the 9th rather than on 8 Oct. According to SJL, he received Short's letter of 5 Oct., which has not been found, from Richmond on the 8th. The 9th, moreover, was a Saturday, which fits TJ's assertion that the day following the one on which he wrote would be SUNDAY.

BEGINNING OF A MONTHLY OR QUAR-TERLY PAIMENT: in the spring of 1800, after TJ found that he owed Short a significant sum, he informed Short of his intention to begin paying the money back in 1801 and to clear the debt in two or three years—"this is certain," he declared. Short replied that he did not yet need the money, and he did not want TJ to have to sell property in order to begin paying the debt right away. After Short's arrival in the United States, he and TJ agreed on terms of repayment, probably when Short visited Monticello in September 1802. TJ knew, when he first discovered the shortfall, that the amount he owed was $9,607.97 "exclusive of interest." He did not immediately calculate the interest, which must be "computed from the date of every article"—that is, calculated for each appropriation he had made of Short's funds. Short worked out the interest and found that as of 1 Jan. 1800, principal and interest together amounted to $11,771. According to notes that Short made for himself in the spring of 1803, TJ was to pay him the $11,771, plus six percent annual interest calculated from the beginning of 1800. TJ made his first payment of $500 in March 1803, and finished paying Short back in July 1807 (statement and list of property, 20 Apr. 1803, in DLC: Short Papers; MB, 2:908n, 1206; Vol. 31:503, 508, 510n; Vol. 32:87, 157; TJ to Madison, 13 Sep.; TJ to Short, 3 Mch. 1803).

The BLOODY CONTEST between David Ross and TJ involved disputed business transactions from the 1780s. A decision by arbitrators in January 1802 settled the matter. It was "owing to mr Ross," TJ asserted, that the issue had not been resolved years earlier (Vol. 31:209-10; Vol. 35:375; Vol. 36:369-70).

From Joseph Anderson

Jefferson County

SIR   10th October 1802

Permit me to recommend—John Crozier Merchant and Edward Scott Esqr atty at Law—as proper Charecters for Commissioners of Bankruptcy—for East Tennessee and George M Deaderick Merchant, and Samuel Donaldson Esqr Atty at Law, for West

Tennessee—The two former reside at Knoxville the two latter at Nashville—It hath been Suggested to me by the Atty General, that Several Cases will shortly occur in which *those* Gentlemen will be requird to act—with Sentiments of high Consideration and respect—   JOS: ANDERSON

RC (DNA: RG 59, LAR); endorsed by TJ as received 17 Nov. and "Commrs. bkrptcy" and so recorded in SJL.

John CROZIER, Edward SCOTT, and George M. DEADERICK received bankruptcy commissions dated 28 Mch. 1803. Samuel Donelson, however, was not appointed and the final Tennessee bankruptcy commission instead went to Moses Fisk of Nashville (list of commissions in Lb in DNA: RG 59, MPTPC; Vol. 37:711; Joseph Anderson, William Cocke, and William Dickson to TJ, 6 Jan. 1803).

From John Bond

SIR.   Winchester Octbr. 10th, 1802
   amidst the extensive multitude who have publickly declared their Joy, in your being elected to the first office in our country, in reverence I approach the important undertaking, in contributing to you the internal Consolation I have enjoyed as well as others: the present epoch is undoubtedly pregnant with the most valuable blessings enjoyed by man, and are the productions of American independance. which I hope will never be impaird to our latest Generation, for if men are destin'd by their maker to be free, as they certainly are, for my God whom I serve, pronounces with a loud acclamation, & is the surest pledge of present & future happiness. when I view the day in which we were delivered from british tyranny, I consider it as a seal of Rational happiness stamp'd upon humanity, & to obtain this freedom, I forsook all and rush'd into the field, till tyranny was oblig'd to cease waving one solitary banner over the injured rights of man. thrice happy day, let us ever remember the sacred eminence, and constantly view the establis'd foundation and source of knowledge, and may you still remain at the helm, may you continue to be our attracting guide, and under your administration, freedom of religion, peace, at home and abroad, and may the wise disposer of all natural, & supernatural blessings, protect and save you, from all dangers to which you may be expos'd, and from the insurrection of wicked doers, and may you rise superior—and triumph over all opposition. Till you with all your friends may discover, Justice ruling, equity dwelling amongst us. True benevolence—and peace spreding their balmy

wings, over our land; and of the increase of such a government may
there be no end,—Amen and amen.   J. B.

Sir. excuse me for Troubling your honor with the perusal of my
lines, who am only a poor man, a labourer in the Gospel, called by
name a Republican Methodist. I only request you to Receive these
lines as a pledge or acknowledgement of my Joy, ever remaining
Your most obt. & Hble. Servt.   JOHN BOND

(I require no answer. J. B.)

RC (DLC); at head of text: "Mr. Thomas Jefferson President of the united states of America"; endorsed by TJ as received 30 Nov. but recorded in SJL at 29 Nov.

John Bond, a veteran of the Revolutionary War from Virginia, wrote to TJ again on 4 Feb. 1805, requesting compensation of 100 acres and $100 for his past military services. After congressional claims committees considered his petitions in 1806, he was invited to withdraw his request (JHR, 5:321, 348, 356).

To Daniel Carroll Brent

DEAR SIR   Washington Oct. 10. 1802

On a suggestion that Judges Kelty & Marshall who pronounced
sentence on Mc.Gurk were divided as to the recommending him to
mercy I reprieved him that the opinion of judge Craunch might be
obtained, who had also sat on the trial. I have this day recieved his
opinion against a pardon. this is known to the criminal; and I have
good information that, seeing all other hope cut off, he means to try
every thing to make his escape. I therefore have thought it material to
apprize you of this, and to recommend that no vigilance be spared to
prevent his escape. not knowing the construction of the jail I can suggest nothing as to the position of the guard, but your knolege of
it will enable you so to place it as to render his escape impossible
without connivance. Accept my friendly salutations & assurances of
respect.   TH: JEFFERSON

PrC (DLC); at foot of text: "Colo. D. C. Brent."

OPINION OF JUDGE CRAUNCH: William Cranch wrote to James McGurk's lawyer, Augustus B. Woodward, from Quincy, Massachusetts, on 20 Sep., responding to letters from Woodward and McGurk. Although there was

"no direct Evidence" that McGurk had been motivated by a "deliberate intention to kill his wife," the jurist noted, there was also "no evidence of any circumstance which could justify his striking her at all." Cranch, who thought juries often demonstrated a "great tenderness" in cases involving capital punishment, was surprised that the jury deliberated only a few minutes before finding McGurk guilty, but he considered the verdict to be correct. In McGurk's case, the judge noted, no "adequate punishment, short of death" was available to the court. When the choice was either "an unqualified pardon" or "a just punishment of the offender," Cranch wrote, "whatever I might be disposed to do as a private citizen, I can not, as a judge, recommend the criminal to the mercy of the President. The interests of society, which it is my duty to protect, demand that crimes like these should be severely punished" (in DNA: RG 59, GPR; endorsed by TJ "Mc.Gurk's case" and "Judge Craunch's opinion").

To William Duane

DR SIR   Washington Oct. 10. 1802.

You know the arrangements which were communicated to you early in July for procuring books for Congress from London and Paris. unfortunately, mr Short, to whom the business was confided in Paris, was come away. I have therefore to ask information from you of the steps you have taken as to Paris[1] that I may be able to give proper directions to mr Livingston to do what mr Short had been desired to do in this matter. Accept my best wishes and salutations.

TH: JEFFERSON

PrC (DLC); at foot of text: "Mr. Duane"; endorsed by TJ in ink on verso.

import books for the Library of Congress, see TJ to Duane, 16 July.

For the ARRANGEMENTS TJ made to

[1] Preceding three words interlined.

From George W. Erving

RESPECTED SIR   London Oct: 10th. 1802

I have been honor'd by your letter containing a catalogue of books to be procured for the use of congress, & your instructions as to the œconomy & details of the purchase; & from the Treasurer of the United States I have at the same time received a remittance for this purpose of 226£. 14s. 9d Stg in a Bill payable at 60-days sight, which has been duly accepted; I shall give all possible attention to this business, & cause the order to be executed with as much dispatch as the nature of it will admit of;—The greater part of the Books being of a kind not Easily to be found, must be hunted up & collected from various dealers, which will require some considerable time; this circumstance too will make the prices a little arbitrary; new books have a fixed value, but that of old & curious books is variable & capricious.—

Mr. Duane has sent his order to Mr. Johnston an highly respectable bookseller, & perhaps the one most capable of Executing it satisfactorily; he has given me the best assurances upon this subject & I will take all collateral means of seeing that justice is done to it;—your instructions do not contemplate the probability of the fund remitted being more than sufficient for the purpose of this purchase, but there will be I believe a considerable surplus; I will venture Sir to avail myself of this circumstance to substitute better Editions than those required where they are to be had & are not very Extravagantly dear, & where a book has been completely transplanted by another (as is Cunningham's Law Dictionary by Jacob's) I hope that you will not disapprove of my making a change in the Catalogue.—

I am happy in this as I must be on every occasion which offers me a portion of your confidence & good opinion, & affords me an opportunity of assuring you of the perfect respect & sincere devotion with which I am always Respected Sir

Your very faithful Servt   GEORGE W ERVING

RC (DLC); at head of text: "To Thomas Jefferson"; endorsed by TJ as received 9 Dec. and so recorded in SJL.

YOUR LETTER: TJ to Erving, 16 July. A BOOK HAS BEEN COMPLETELY TRANSPLANTED BY ANOTHER: Timothy Cunningham's two-volume *A New and Complete Law-Dictionary, or, General Abridgment of the Law*, first published in London in 1764-65, was superseded by Giles Jacob's *A New Law Dictionary*, corrected and enlarged in its ninth edition by Owen Ruffhead and John Morgan in 1772. *Jacob's Law Dictionary*, as it was commonly known, continued to be published in several other revised editions and remained popular even 60 years after the original author's death in 1744 (DNB; Sowerby, No. 1814).

From Christopher Gore

SIR,   London 10 October 1802

In consequence of being left by Mr King, in charge with the affairs of the United States, and of his desire, that I should inspect all letters directed to him, I opened that from yourself, under date of the 13th July, & which was receiv'd on the 13. ult.

This, Sir, I must pray you to accept as an apology, for having broken its seal—and if my subsequent conduct shall appear an intrusion, you will do me the justice to impute it to the most respectful motives, combined with an earnest desire to promote the object of the letter,— if, in no other way, at least, in obtaining, & forwarding all such information, as could be procur'd here, and might tend to advance the wise, and humane plan, you have so benevolently contemplated, of opening a path for the emancipation of the Blacks, on such terms, as may prove beneficial to themselves, & not injurious to others—I was the more induced to act in this business, from the belief that Mr King would not be here, to attain any information, in season to reach the U. States, until late in the winter—

Lord Hawkesbury to whom, I thought it proper, first to mention the subject, profess'd a warm desire to do every thing in his power, to promote your views, but at the same time said the affair must rest entirely with the Directors of the Sierra Leone Company, and that he was really fearful, their late experience had been such, as to deter them from the admission of characters like those alluded to—

I then took an opportunity of confering with Mr Thornton, chairman of the court of directors, & stated to him the resolution of the Legislature of Virginia, and your idea of the best mode of carrying the same into effect, with such arguments, so far as I could think of any, in addition to those contained in your letter, to show that the admission of the Blacks from the U States, might, under such regulations as wisdom, & prudence should prescribe, prove an addition of strength, & benefit to their Colony. But the establishment has sufferd much from the maroons, who have been permitted to go there from Jamaica, and the Directors consider that the rise of their Colony has been rather impeded, than advanced by the Blacks from Nova Scotia—They have lately been obliged to apply to Parliament for pecuniary aid, & to ask assistance of troops, to keep in check the restless, and disturbed spirits already there. The military force is not so great, as they wish'd, and they entertain serious apprehensions, if it be sufficient to protect the well disposed, and repress the constant disposition, manifested in many of the Colonists to revolt, & overturn the existing Government—

These reasons appear to have great weight in Mr Thornton's mind, against the policy of admitting such settlers, as would be most likely to come from the U. States—He has, however, come to no determination against the measure, but promises to advise with his friends, & see if any expedient can be devised, by which the dangers to be feared, from acceding to the proposal, may be guarded against—

It is possible, that on Mr King's return, he may be able to suggest such reasons, as shall induce the Directors to lend a favourable ear to the plan—He is intimate with some of the most influential of them, and if aught[1] can be added to the strong motives they profess, and I have no doubt, sincerely, to do every thing acceptable to the exalted character, at whose instance the proposition has been made, it may be expected from the personal influence of this gentleman. Although from the considerations mention'd, which, with others are to be seen in the state of the Colony, as described in the memorial to Parliament, and the report of the Committee, I do not think there is much reason to hope, that an incorporation of the Blacks of the U.States with those at Sierra Leone, can be reconciled, in the minds of the Directors, to the safety, and prosperity of the establishment.

I am indebted, to Mr Thornton, for the papers above referr'd to,* and which, you will find, give an accurate statement of that Colony, the evils most to be guarded against, with the means thought necessary for its security, and the expences of the establishment—As these papers are scarce, and contain information, that may be valuable on this subject, I have taken the liberty to enclose them with this letter—

Should an occasion occur, which may promise advantage to the proposal from any endeavours of mine, you may rely on their being cheerfully, and faithfully exerted to that end—and if further information can be procured, which, in my judgment, may be useful in this interesting business, before the arrival of Mr King, I pray you, Sir, to be assured, that I shall derive great pleasure in forwarding it—

I have the Honour to be, Sir, with perfect Respect, your very obedt servant.   C. GORE

---

* only one yet received. the other, when obtained, shall be sent.

RC (Vi: Executive Papers); at foot of first page: "Thomas Jefferson &c &c &c"; endorsed by TJ as received 9 Dec. and so recorded in SJL. FC (Lb in NHi: Rufus King Papers). Enclosure: Printed report of a House of Commons committee on the petition of the Sierra Leone Company, May 1802, stating that the funds allocated by Parliament to the colony of Sierra Leone have been insufficient to provide the "Degree of Security" required for "the Maintenance of the Settlement," but the continued existence of the colony is justified; the petition of the chairman and directors of the company, appended to the report, recounts the history of the colony, including insurrections within the settlements and attacks by outsiders, and noting, as one obstacle to the colony's progress, the "unfavourable Character" of some of the settlers from Nova Scotia; the directors ask for an increase of the power of the colony's government and maintenance of an adequate military force there

(House of Commons, "Report from the Committee on the Petition of the Court of Directors of the Sierra Leone Company," *Sessional Papers, 1801-2*, 2:339, Reports of Committees, no. 100, printed by order of 25 May 1802). Enclosed in TJ to John Page, 23 Dec. 1803.

IN CHARGE: Rufus King, who was traveling in Europe on leave, had made Gore acting chargé d'affaires in his absence. When George Washington named Gore to the bilateral commission to resolve claims under Article 7 of the Jay Treaty in March 1796, Gore was a 37-year-old Boston lawyer with Federalist political connections, a director of the Boston branch of the Bank of the United States, and the United States attorney for Massachusetts. TJ as secretary of state exchanged several letters with Gore relating to official business that involved the U.S. attorney's office. The last of that correspondence was in 1793 (Madison, *Papers*,

Sec. of State Ser., 3:110, 310-11; JEP, 1:204-5; ANB; Vol. 17:530-3; Vol. 19:629; Vol. 20:564-5; Vol. 22:15-16, 399; Vol. 23:5, 16-17; Vol. 24:219; Vol. 27:13-14, 79-82, 261, 338-40, 416, 427, 456, 523).

A successful banker, philanthropist, and writer on political economy, Henry THORNTON had served as chairman of the Court of Directors of the Sierra Leone Company since 1791 (DNB).

Gore wrote TJ from London on 3 Nov. regarding the PAPERS enclosed with the letter printed above: "Sir Upon examination, I find the report of the Committee of the House of Commons on the petition of the Sierra Leone Company, as inclosed with the letter I did myself the Honour to address you on the 10. ulto. contains every material fact, & document stated, or refered to in their petition, & have therefore concluded it unnecessary to transmit a copy thereof. I have the Honour to be, Sir, with perfect Respect, Your very obedt servant" (RC in DLC, at foot of text: "His Excellency Thomas Jefferson," endorsed by TJ as received 10 Feb. and so recorded in SJL; FC in Lb in NHi: Rufus King Papers). That brief communication was the last correspondence between Gore and TJ.

[1] MS: "ought."

To Robert R. Livingston

DEAR SIR   Washington Oct. 10. 1802.

The departure of Made. Brugnard for France furnishes me a safe conveyance of a letter which I cannot avoid embracing, altho' I have nothing particular for the subject of it. it is well however to be able to inform you, generally, through a safe channel, that we stand compleatly corrected of the error that either the government or the nation of France has any remains of friendship for us. the portion of that country which forms an exception, though respectable in weight, is weak in numbers. on the contrary it appears evident that an unfriendly spirit prevails in the most important individuals of the government towards us. in this state of things we shall so take our distance between the two rival nations as, remaining disengaged till necessity compels us, we may haul finally to the enemy of that which shall make it necessary. we see all the disadvantageous consequences of taking a side, and shall be forced into it only by a more disagreeable alternative; in which event we must countervail the disadvantages by measures which will give us splendour & power, but not as much happiness as our present system. we wish therefore to remain well with France. but we see that no consequences however ruinous to them, can secure us with certainty against the extravagance of her present rulers. I think therefore, that while we do nothing which the first nation on earth would deem crouching, we had better give to all our communications with them a very mild, complaisant, and even friendly complection, but always independant. ask no favors, leave small & irritating things to be conducted by the individuals interested in them, interfere ourselves but in the greatest cases, & then not push them to irritation. no matter at present existing between them & us is important enough to risk a breach of peace; peace being indeed the most important of all things to us, except the preserving an erect & independant attitude. although I know your own judgment leads you to pursue this line identically, yet I thought it just to strengthen it by the concurrence of my own.   you will have seen by our newspapers that with the aid of a lying renegado from republicanism, the federalists have opened all their[1] sluices of calumny. they say we lied them out of power, and openly avow they will do the same by us. but it was not lies or arguments on our part which dethroned them, but their own foolish acts, sedition laws, alien laws, taxes, extravagances & heresies. Porcupine their friend wrote them down. Callendar, their new recruit, will do the same. every decent man among them revolts at his filth: and there cannot be a doubt that were a presidential election to come on this day, they would have but three New England states & about half a dozen votes from Maryland & North Carolina, these two states electing by districts. were all the states to elect by a general ticket, they would have but 3. out of 16. states. and these 3. are coming up slowly. we do indeed consider Jersey & Delaware as rather doubtful. elections which have lately taken place there, but their event not yet known here, will shew the present point of their varying condition.

My letters to you being merely private, I leave all details of business to their official channel. Accept assurances of my constant friendship and high respect.   TH: JEFFERSON

P.S. We have recieved your letter announcing the arrival of M. Dupont.

RC (NNMus); addressed: "Robert R. Livingston esquire M.P. of the US. at Paris"; endorsed by Livingston. PrC (DLC).

DEPARTURE OF MADE. BRUGNARD: see Louise d'Egremont Brongniart to TJ, 11 Oct.

LYING RENEGADO: James T. Callender. Before his departure from the United States early in 1800, William Cobbett, calling himself Peter PORCUPINE, was, for TJ and his political allies, the archetype of an irresponsible and dangerous Federalist newspaperman (Vol. 31:320, 322n; Vol. 33:262, 656).

YOUR LETTER: in a dispatch to Madison dated 30 July, Livingston mentioned that Pierre Samuel Du Pont de Nemours had arrived in Paris (Madison, *Papers, Sec. of State Ser.*, 3:443).

[1] TJ first wrote "the" before altering the word.

From James McGurk

I Beg lave once more to adress yaur Exilency as the Onley and last means that I have for my life in my Latir to you By Mr. wodward I mentioned that Judge keltey and Cranch was willing to have my life Saved But Since there has Been a politicle partey that has Ecused Me with faulls Storeys in the washinton feaderelist I Bleive That Induced the Judges to not Concent to my Pardon I Bleive the Spite the had against you and not me if you had not parened me the would acused you leike Weise But I hope you will not pay any atintion to those Fauls Stareys

The hand of provedince Seems to Bee Concerned in My fate it now lays in your Breast to put a man to Death or not that has Sufired near one year in as grate Punishement as could Bee inflicted to proserve life and Aftir Sufering this to have my life teakin I lave you To Judge if it is hard or not to put me to Death when I have Inforimed you of my last Sentemints if you Put me to Death I will Dye in the wrong

The tiranicle goveriment that I was Raised under Could not Bcc mutch hardir you knaw that I am Flesh and Blood the Same as your Exelincey is and when Wee are in the Grave wee will Bee on a levill And now when God Inviested you with that pawir Superier To melions of your felow Citesins Bee mercifull

if you think I have not Sufired onaf I Beg you to Chuse for my fate your Choise af fore Choises let me quit the united Steats or put me One year in the armey thereaf or inflict on me What punishment you think prapir or let my Blood Bee Spild in the wrong

O Mr Jeffirson I Beg for mercey mercy mercy

Your Exelinceys mast obedient Servint

Unfortunate · JAMES MCGURK

NB) the numbir of fauls acusitions would Bee two Tedious for me to mention that the have fetched Against me the last plan the have teakin is to Drap[1] Letirs for you to get hoping that it might provent you of Dooing any thing for me all theyer plans is graund less and fauls if you wauld think propir I wauld Send to a nuber of good Sitisens that is Near has Been aquent with me Sevvril year in Philadelphia and By thyer tetamony you could Judge what Sort of a membir of Susiety I was

RC (DNA: RG 59, GPR); endorsed by TJ as from "Thos." McGurk, received from jail on 11 Oct., and so recorded in SJL.

MY LATIR TO YOU: presumably one of McGurk's letters that Augustus B. Woodward brought to Monticello in August; see Woodward to TJ, 16 Aug.

FAULLS STOREYS IN THE WASHINTON FEADERELIST: some newspapers, railing at TJ's granting of the stay of execution, tried to associate McGurk with incidents of political intimidation (Vol. 37:284n).

¹ That is, "draw up."

To J. P. G. Muhlenberg

DEAR GENERAL   Washington Oct. 10. 1802.

I must beg you to find the apology for this sollicitation in the nature of the case itself. there is here a mr John Barnes, for a long series of years resident in Philadelphia where he was a teadealer, acted on commission &c. till the government removed here. being agent for some of the contractors which required him to be near the treasury, he removed here with the government, & set up his former business of teadealer. but he finds it will not do here, & his commissions being insufficient to support him he means to return to Philadelphia this winter. he is old (between 60. and 70) but is as active as a boy, always in good health, and the most punctual and assiduous man in business I ever knew. after an acquaintance with him of 40. years, I can pronounce him in point of fidelity as to any trust whatever, worthy of unbounded confidence. there is not a man on earth to whom I would sooner trust money untold. he is an accurate accountant, of a temper incapable of being ruffled, & full of humanity. I give you his whole character because I think you may make good use of him for the public. my long & particular acquaintance with him interests me much in his behalf, and makes me very desirous that he could get some berth of about 1000. D. a year which would secure him from want. if any such should offer itself at any tme within your department, I would deem it a great favor to myself were you to think of him, and I know that I should serve the public by placing with them a most honest & faithful servt. and of unequalled diligence. these considerations must be my apology to you for a liberty which I have never before taken in any case, and shall generally and carefully avoid. my anxieties on behalf of mr Barnes have overcome my unwillingness to intermeddle in applications. it will occasion less impertinence in the public papers, if nothing be said of *my* being the recommender. Accept my friendly salutations and assurances of my esteem & respect.

TH: JEFFERSON

PrC (DLC); at foot of text: "Genl. Muhlenberg"; endorsed by TJ in ink on verso.

WITHIN YOUR DEPARTMENT: Muhlenberg had been appointed collector at Philadelphia in July 1802 (Gallatin to TJ, [7 July 1802]; Appendix i).

From Joseph Parsons

GOOD SIR   City Goal Sunday October 10 1802

Excuse my writing You But I am actuly Confind here for my Doctor bill & find my self unable to pay it at preasent and what Grives me more; with my wife along side of me she as no other home I shall not trawble you with a Long List of my sufferings as I suppose you have seen them in Mr Lions paper from my own hand I am your most humble Servant   JOSEPH PARSONS

RC (DLC); endorsed by TJ as received 11 Oct. and so recorded in SJL.

MR LIONS PAPER: probably the *American Literary Advertiser*, published in Washington by James Lyon and Richard Dinmore since March 1802 (Brigham, *American Newspapers*, 1:98; Vol. 34:405n).

To William Bache

DEAR DOCTOR   Washington Oct. 11. 1802.

I am to pay you £10. for Polly Carr, making, with the balance due yourself 143.33 D   you will of course drop me a line as soon as you shall have fixed a day for your departure, and the money shall be lodged in mr Jefferson's hands before you will be there.   we wish you to be at your destination before the French take possession. if they have sent troops from France on that destination as is said in the newspapers, they will perhaps find employment in St. Domingo which has risen again in general insurrection. present my respectful salutations to mrs Bache and accept yourself assurances of my friendship & respect.   TH: JEFFERSON

RC (Mrs. W. F. Magie, Princeton, New Jersey, 1945); addressed: "Dr. William Bache near Charlottesville"; franked and postmarked.

In his financial memoranda, TJ recorded the amount of the payment to his niece, Mary (POLLY) Carr, as $33.33. In December, he made her a second payment of the same amount, that time through Gabriel Lilly. Together the two payments were "towards hire of her negro" for the year (MB, 2:1085, 1088).

American NEWSPAPERS mentioned that troops had embarked from France during the summer, bound for Louisiana. The news, which originated in Rotterdam and London, was incorrect. The French government did not receive Carlos IV's royal order ceding the territory until 25 Oct. (New York *Commercial Advertiser*, 2, 5 Oct.; E. Wilson Lyon, *Louisiana in French Diplomacy, 1759-1804* [Norman, Okla., 1974], 134).

RISEN AGAIN: a resurgence of resistance by blacks that began in the summer had developed into what General Victoire Emmanuel Leclerc bluntly labeled "a war of colors" in Saint-Domingue. The rebels controlled large portions of the island. With the army units he had brought from Europe almost destroyed by yellow fever, Leclerc had been forced to rely on black soldiers to fight the insurgents. By October, he became so fearful of defections that he ordered the execution of a number of soldiers of color who were still part of his army. In June, he had warned his government that if there were to be an army on the island in the fall, it would have to consist of fresh troops sent from France (Laurent Dubois, *Avengers of the New World: The Story of the Haitian Revolution* [Cambridge, Mass., 2004], 281-92).

From Louise d'Egremont Brongniart

le 11 8bre 1802

Mme Brongniart est extrêmement reconnaissante des souhaits que monsieur Le president a la bonté de former pour le succès de son voyage. Elle s'empressera à son arrivée de remettre elle même à Mr Livingston la lettre de monsieur Le president dont elle se charge avec le plus grand plaisir.

EDITORS' TRANSLATION

11 Oct. 1802

Madame Brongniart is extremely grateful for the president's kind wishes for the success of her journey. She is happy to take care of the president's letter and will hasten to deliver it personally to Mr. Livingston on her arrival.

RC (MHi); endorsed by TJ as received the same day as written and so recorded in SJL.

Louise d'Egremont Brongniart (b. 1744) was the mother of Émilie Brongniart Pichon. At the time of her marriage to Alexandre Théodore Brongniart in 1767, she owned an apothecary shop in Paris. In the spring of 1793, when her husband, unable to obtain architectural commissions in Paris, moved to Bordeaux to design a theater, she remained in Paris with Émilie, their youngest child, keeping up their household and the family's social routines in the metropolis through the Terror and until Théodore returned in 1795. During his absence she lobbied the Convention to exclude him and other artists from a decree against people who had gone to Bordeaux seeking a more moderate political climate. In May 1802, anxious to see Émilie and Louis André Pichon, Madame Brongniart embarked on a visit to the United States. Her husband, who supplemented his architectur-

al income with a government position as inspector general of buildings and with nonarchitectural design work, did not accompany her on the journey. In 1828, Émilie Pichon reported to a friend in the United States that her mother was in good health and living with the Pichons in Paris (Louis de Launay, *Une grande famille de savants: Les Brongniart* [Paris, 1940], 19-20, illus. facing 26; Jacques Silvestre de Sacy, *Alexandre-Théodore Brongniart, 1739-1813, Sa Vie—Son Œuvre* [Paris, 1940], 89-91, 94-6, 106-8, 128, 133-5; *Dictionnaire*, 7:420; *La Revue du Louvre*, 24 [1974], 105; Margaret Bayard Smith, *The First Forty Years of Washington Society*, ed. Gaillard Hunt [New York, 1906], 218).

LA LETTRE: TJ to Robert R. Livingston, 10 Oct. Madame Brongniart also took a letter from Madison to Livingston. She had brought dispatches from Livingston when she traveled to the United States during the spring (Madison, *Papers, Sec. of State Ser.*, 4:204, 278; Livingston to TJ, 4 May 1802).

From Albert Gallatin

DEAR SIR   Octer. 11th 1802

I enclose the resignation of the surveyor of the customs at Smithfield, an out post attached to Norfolk. The office is trifling; yet it may be acceptable to some person there who ought to have it. If you have any correspondent in that vicinity who can give information, it will relieve me from the inconvenience of writing to the Collector Mr Davies.

With respect & attachment Your obedt. Servt.

ALBERT GALLATIN

RC (DLC); at foot of text: "The President"; endorsed by TJ as received from the Treasury Department on 11 Oct. and "Thos. Blow surveyor of Smithfd. resigned" and so recorded in SJL. Enclosure: Thomas Blow to William Davies, Smithfield, 1 Oct. 1802, notifying the collector that he was resigning his commission because he was leaving Smithfield (RC in same).

RESIGNATION: Thomas Blow had served as surveyor and inspector at Smithfield, Virginia, since February 1800. In 1801, he received a $250 salary as surveyor, plus $4 in commissions and fees, but deductions for office expenses reduced his compensation to $198.50 (*Letter from the Secretary of the Treasury, Accompanying a Statement of the Emoluments of the Officers Employed in the Collection of the Customs, for the Year 1801* [Washington, D.C., 1802]). For his income in 1800, see ASP, *Miscellaneous*, 1:274.

From Albert Gallatin

SIR   Treasury Department October 11th. 1802

I have the honor to enclose a letter of the Commissioner of the revenue, enclosing a copy of the resignation of the Supervisor of Delaware.

From the state of the collection of duties in that District, it does not appear necessary that the Office should be continued any longer: but although the acceptance of Mr. Truett's resignation, without filling the vacancy, will produce the effect; yet it seems proper, under the provisions of the Law repealing the internal Taxes, that the discontinuance of the Office should be sanctioned by the President.

I have the honor to be, with great respect, Sir, Your obedt: Servant

ALBERT GALLATIN

RC (DLC); in a clerk's hand, signed by Gallatin; at foot of text: "The President of the United States"; endorsed by TJ as received from the Treasury Department on 12 Oct. and "Discontince. Supervisorship Delaware" and so recorded in SJL. Enclosure not found.

George Truitt became SUPERVISOR of the revenue for the district of DELA-

WARE in July 1797. A Federalist, he was elected governor of the state in October 1807 (JEP, 1:247-8; Robert Sobel and John Raimo, eds., *Biographical Di-* *rectory of the Governors of the United States, 1789-1978*, 4 vols. [Westport, Conn., 1978], 1:215).

Statement of Account with John March

Georgetown

Thomas Jefferson, Esqr

To J: March

1802					
July	8	To Binding Wood's Administration of Adams, 8vo			$ 00.75
"		Binding Philosophie de Kant, 8vo.			00.75
	15	Putting in extra boards 6 vols: 8vo.—State Papers, &c			1.50
"		Do	1 vol: folio	Do	1.00
Octr:	11	½ Binding 5 vols: folio		News-Papers	12.75
"		Do	1 vol: folio	State Papers	3.50
"		Do	1 vol: folio	Journals Legisr: Virginia	2.75
"		Do	1 vol: 4o	Do	1.50
"		Binding	2 vols: 8vo. gilt	Aristoteles	1.75
"		Do	1 vol: 12mo gilt	Leggenda de Giosafat	0.62½
"		Do	2 vols: 18o gilt	Diogene Laerce	1.00
"		Do	1 vol: 18o gilt	Passe Partout Galant	0.50
"		Do	10 vols: 8vo: Morocco	Seneca Philosophers	22.50
"		Do	1 vols: 8vo: Calf	Histoire de Bonapart	1.00
"		Do	1 vol: 8vo	Cooper's Bankrupt Laws	0.75
"		½ Binding	2 vols: 8vo	State Papers	1.50
"		Do	2 vols: 8vo	Monthly Magazine	1.25
"		Do	2 vols: 8vo	Weekly Magazine	1.25
"		Do	6 vols: 8vo	Pamphlets,—Arts, &c.	3.00
"		Do	5 vols: 8vo	Pamphlets,—American	3.12½
"		Do	2 vols: 8vo	Pamphlets,—English & Foreign	1.00
"		Do	5 vols: 8vo	Eulogiums on Washington, &c:	2.50
"		Do	4 vols: 12mo	Swedenborg on the Soul, &c.	1.50
"		24 Cases for Writings, Mill-Board, &c.			8.00
					$ 75.75

MS (MHi); in March's hand; addressed: "For The President"; endorsed by TJ: "March J."

PHILOSOPHIE DE KANT: Charles François Dominique de Villers, *Philosophie de Kant: Ou, Principes fondamentaux de la Philosophie transcendentale* (see Vol. 35:708).

ARISTOTELES: *La Poetica de Aristoteles* *dada a nuestra lengua Castellana*, published in Madrid in 1778 (Sowerby, No. 4693).

LEGGENDA DE GIOSAFAT: *Vita di san Giosafat convertito da Barlaam* by Johannes Damascenus, an eighth-century theologian of the Eastern Church (Sowerby, No. 1552).

DIOGENE LAERCE: Diogenes Laertius, *Diogene Laërce, de la Vie des Philosophes*

(Sowerby, No. 33; MB, 1:16n; Vol. 31:285n).

PASSE PARTOUT GALANT: a collection of anti-clerical satires published in 1710 by an anonymous author, self-described as a "Chevalier de l'Ordre de l'Industrie & de la Gibeciere." TJ included the title under the classification of poetry and romance in his 1783 Catalogue of Books (MS in MHi).

SENECA PHILOSOPHERS: see Vol. 37:156.

HISTOIRE DE BONAPART: Jean Chas, *Tableau Historique et Politique des Opérations militaires et civiles de Bonaparte* (Vol. 36:96n).

COOPER'S BANKRUPT LAWS: Thomas Cooper, *The Bankrupt Law of America, Compared with the Bankrupt Law of England*, printed in Philadelphia in 1801 (Sowerby, No. 1994).

MONTHLY MAGAZINE: *Monthly Magazine and American Review* (Vol. 32:94n).

WEEKLY MAGAZINE: *Weekly Magazine of Original Essays, Fugitive Pieces, and Interesting Intelligence*, printed in Philadelphia in 1798 by James Watters & Co. (Sowerby, No. 4898).

SWEDENBORG ON THE SOUL: Emanuel Swedenborg, *Du Commerce de l'Ame et du Corps* (Sowerby, No. 1365).

To Thomas Newton

DEAR SIR   Washington Oct. 12. 1802.

Thomas Blow, surveyor of the customs at Smithfield, has resigned his office. it is of small value, but yet may be acceptable to some person there. I will thank you if from your own knowledge or from the best information you can collect, you would be so good as to recommend to me the properest person. it would be material to be assured he will accept.   Our last information gives reason to believe that the rupture with Marocco will not take place. Algiers & Tunis remain entirely friendly, so that we are likely to have only Tripoli on our hands who are seeking peace thro' different channels. Accept assurances of my constant friendship & high respect.

TH: JEFFERSON

PrC (DLC); at foot of text: "Colo. Thos. Newton"; endorsed by TJ in ink on verso.

LAST INFORMATION: see TJ to James Madison, 30 Aug.

From Joseph Parsons

Washington City October the 12th 1802

Your Excellency was pleased to condecend to take notice of my unfortunate situation and release me from Prison. I now take this earlyest opportunity to render you my humble and warmest acknoledgments for your humane and generous interference in my favour—That you may live long and enjoy all the blessings this life can bestow will be the constant prayer of your Excellencys;—

Most Obedient & much Obliged Humble Sert.

JOSEPH PARSONS

RC (DLC); endorsed by TJ as received 12 Oct. and so recorded in SJL.

HUMANE AND GENEROUS INTERFERENCE IN MY FAVOUR: on 11 Oct., TJ sent Daniel C. Brent, the marshal for the District of Columbia, an order on John Barnes for $30 in charity for Parsons, which secured his release from jail (MB, 2:1083).

From Francis Peyton

DEAR SIR,   Alexandria 12th. Octo. 1802

Capt. Matthew C. Groves who has made some longitudinal discoveries, for which he has obtained a patent from the U. States, is extremely desirous of submitting them to you, and has asked of me a note of introduction,

I am wholly unacquainted with Mr. Groves, but have received assurances from Colo. Gilpin who has known him upwards of twenty years, that he is a decent and respectable character

I am respectfully Yr. Obe. Servt.   FRANCIS PEYTON

RC (DLC); endorsed by TJ as received 15 Oct. and so recorded in SJL.

From Samuel Richardet

SIR   Philadelphia Octr. the 12. 1802

I take the liberty to address you from having the Honneur of Knowing the President of the U:S: at the time I lived with Theos: Cazenove's Esqr. as is Steward till I want in business, Mr: Petit succeed me at Mr: Cazenovs

my Wife & Daughters have gone to England, been hout of business; my wiches is to devote my self to the manegement of some Gentelman family if your Excellence or aney of your friends ad such imployment will Exert my self to please I am

Sir Your Very *Humble* Servant   SAMUEL RICHARDET

RC (MHi); at head of text: "Your Excellence"; endorsed by TJ as received 16 Oct. and so recorded in SJL.

Samuel Richardet operated the City Tavern and Merchants' Coffee House in Philadelphia from 1796 to 1799. The establishment offered overnight accommodations, meals, beverages, and a reading room supplied with current newspapers from the United States and Europe. Merchants and ship captains used the coffee house as an exchange where they could meet and post information. Médéric Louis Elie Moreau de St. Méry dined there with Talleyrand not long after Richardet became the proprietor. In 1807, Richardet made arrangements to run the Indian Queen tavern, also in Philadelphia (*Gazette of the United States*, 4 Jan. 1797; PMHB, 46 [1922], 75; 47 [1923], 176-7; 128 [2004], 169; Kenneth Roberts and

Anna M. Roberts, trans. and eds., *Moreau de St. Méry's American Journey*, 1793-1798 [Garden City, N.Y., 1947], 214; Vol. 33:360).

STEWARD: Théophile Cazenove lived in Philadelphia from 1790 to 1798. On his arrival in the United States as the business agent of Dutch investors, he carried a letter of introduction to TJ from the Amsterdam banking firm of Van Staphorst & Hubbard (ANB; Vol. 15: 562-3; Vol. 20:331-2).

From Henry Dearborn

SIR [13 Oct. 1802]

I should presume that it might not be amiss to enquire of Genl. Sumpter, W. Hampton, or other known respectable characters in S.C., what wieght & credit is to be given to the representations of Mr. D. and what would be proper to be done for him (if any thing) by the Exect.—he may become a mischevious man, and in the critical situation of that State, however undeserving, it may be proper to take some notice of him. from all that I have seen from him & heard of him, I conclude that he would be very quiet about removals &c. if he could git a snug place for himself. Mr. Gallatin might easily obtain all necessary information, & if it should appear that Mr. D. is neither intitled to notice, or to be feared, he might be permited to continue his complaints through his tedious letters. H. D.

RC (DLC); undated; addressed: "The President of the United States"; endorsed by TJ as received from the War Department on 13 Oct. 1802 and "D'Oyley's letters" and so recorded in SJL.

For the REPRESENTATIONS of Daniel D'Oyley, see TJ to Gallatin, 6 Oct. and Gallatin to TJ, 8 Oct.

To Albert Gallatin

TH:J. TO MR GALLATIN Oct. 13. 1802.

You know my doubts or rather convictions about the unconstitutionality of the act for building piers in the Delaware, and the fears that it will lead to a bottomless expence, & to the greatest abuses. there is however one intention of which the act is susceptible & which will bring it within the constitution; and we ought always to presume that the real intention which is alone consistent with the constitution.

altho the power to regulate commerce does not give a power to build piers, wharfs, open ports, clear the beds of rivers, dig canals, build warehouses, build manufacturing machines, set up manufactories, cultivate the earth, to all of which the power would go, if it went to the first, yet a power to provide and maintain a navy, is a power to provide receptacles for it and places to cover & preserve it. in chusing the places where this money should be laid out, I should be much disposed, as far as contracts will permit, to confine it to such place or places as the ships of war may lie at, and be protected from ice: & I should be for stating this in a message to Congress in order to prevent the effect of the present example. this act has been built on the exercise of the power of building lighthouses as a regulation of commerce. but I well remember the opposition, on this very ground, to the first act for building a lighthouse. the utility of the thing has sanctioned the infraction. but if on that infraction we build a 2d. on that 2d. a 3d &c. any one of the powers in the constitution may be made to comprehend every power of government.—will you read the inclosed letters on the subject of New Orleans, and think what we can do or propose in the case? Accept my affectionate salutations.

RC (NHi: Gallatin Papers); endorsed by Gallatin: "President Delaware piers." PrC (DLC). Recorded in SJL as a letter to the Treasury Department with notation "piers in Delaware." Enclosures: (1) Daniel W. Coxe to James Madison, Philadelphia, 8 Oct., arguing the importance of authorizing the customs collector at Natchez to grant clearances to American ships "loading with *American* Produce at New Orleans, & bound to British European Ports" (Madison, *Papers, Sec. of State Ser.*, 4:1-3). (2) Printed broadside consisting of the British statute of 22 June 1802 repealing several acts relating to the admission of certain articles in neutral vessels by issuing Orders in Council for that purpose, to continue in effect until 1 Jan. 1804; and a letter from Green & Wainewright dated Liverpool, 14 Aug., explaining that the act provided that U.S. produce can only be imported in British vessels or in American ships, built and registered in the United States, with the master and "three-fourths of the Crew at least American" (same, 4:2n; Gallatin, *Papers*, 7:613). (3) Extract of Green & Wainewright to Coxe, Liverpool, 18 Aug. 1802, noting that existing British laws do not allow the importation of American produce from New Orleans, but customs officers think it will be allowed if the produce is transferred from boats from the U.S. settlements to "Ships having regular Clearances from an American Custom House on the Mississippi"; cotton not grown in the U.S. would have to be sent to the British West Indies or any other port where it could be transferred to British vessels; if the plan suggested "is not practicable, the Vessels must touch at a port of the United States for a Clearance & the Crew must be particularly attended to as We have been Witness to several very disagreeable circumstances thro' this point" (same, 7:614; Madison, *Papers, Sec. of State Ser.*, 4:2-3n).

On 17 July 1789, the New York *Daily Advertiser* recorded OPPOSITION to proposed legislation for the establishment and support of lighthouses by South Carolina congressmen Thomas Tudor Tucker and William Loughton Smith. The bill authorized the U.S. government to assume the expenses for building and maintaining lighthouses. The state had only to apply to the Treasury secretary and cede to the federal government the land upon which the lighthouse was to be built. Tucker and Smith argued that the bill was an infringement on the rights of the states and that lighthouses "were not necessarily incidental to the power of commerce." If Congress were given this power, they declared, it "might with equal justice take possession of the mouths of rivers, and seize all such convenient places, as they should deem proper for the regulation of trade." On 7 Aug. 1789, Washington signed the "act for the establishment and support of Lighthouses, Beacons, Buoys, and Public Piers" (U.S. Statutes at Large, 1:53-4; *Biog. Dir. Cong.*).

From Albert Gallatin

SIR,   Treasury Department October 13th. 1802

I have the honor to enclose the report of Richard L. Green, of the repairs necessary to prevent the further decay of that part of the Gosport marine Hospital which is not now used.

The Collector of Norfolk, by whose direction it was prepared, informs that the necessary repairs of that part of the building which is now occupied by the sick Seamen, are nearly completed; and I beg leave to submit the propriety of authorizing the repairs, of which the estimate is now enclosed, as they will cost less than 1500 dollars; and if completed before winter, may prevent, hereafter, a much greater expense.

I have the honor to be, with great respect Sir, Your obedt. Servt.

ALBERT GALLATIN

RC (DLC); in a clerk's hand, signed by Gallatin; at foot of text: "The President of the United States"; endorsed by TJ as received from the Treasury Department on 13 Oct. and "repairs of hospital at Norfolk" and so recorded in SJL. Enclosure not found.

For repairs at the GOSPORT MARINE HOSPITAL, see Gallatin to TJ, 9 Aug. 1802 (second letter). COLLECTOR OF NORFOLK: William Davies.

From Albert Gallatin

SIR,   Treasury Department October 13th. 1802

I have the honor to enclose a second Report of the Chamber of commerce of Philadelphia, and a letter from the Commissioners appointed by the State of Delaware for the purpose of applying certain monies to the erection of piers near New castle; both of which documents relate to the application of the sums appropriated by the law of last Session, for the repairs and erection of piers in the river Delaware.

From these and the former communications on the same subject, it appears that the manner of applying the money which will be generally most agreable to the persons interested in the navigation of the Delaware, will be the erection of the intended piers, at Reedy-Island and at New castle.

I am inclined to believe not only that the selection of those two places is the most advantageous to the commercial Interest of Pennsylvania & Delaware, but that the intended piers will, in both places, afford a protection to the public Ships of the United States, which they cannot now find in any part of the river below Philadelphia

From those considerations, I am induced to submit to your consideration the propriety of authorizing the expenditure of the balance (amounting to, near, 24,000 dollars) of the appropriation which will remain after having completed the repairs, to the erection of the intended new Piers at the two abovementioned Places.

I have the honor to be, with great respect, Sir, Your obedt. Servant

ALBERT GALLATIN

Depth low water at New castle piers 24 feet.
Do.   Do. Do. at Reedy Isld. new do. 23 do.
common Tides rising 7 feet.

RC (DLC); in a clerk's hand, signed by Gallatin; endorsed by TJ as received from Treasury Department on 14 Oct. and "piers in Delaware" and so recorded in SJL. Enclosures not found.

For the COMMISSIONERS APPOINTED by Delaware, see Gallatin to TJ, 8 Oct.

To Anthony Haswell

SIR   Washington Oct. 13. 1802.

Immediately on the reciept of your letter of Sep. 16. stating the enlistment of Jeremiah Battels, an infant, against the will of his father, directions were sent to the proper officer to enquire into the fact and, if true, to discharge him. perhaps however the officer may not be in a situation to obtain evidence, and the order fail from that cause. in such case it is proper the father should know that by applying to a judge for a Habeas corpus, the young man will be brought before the judge, to whom the father may exhibit the proofs, and, if satisfactory, the judge will discharge him on this ground that an infant is incapable of engaging himself to any thing without the consent of his father or guardian. this method of discharge, where it can be conveniently resorted to, is preferable to the other, because it is useful to exhibit examples of the military will controuled & circumscribed by the civil authority. Accept my best wishes & respects.

TH: JEFFERSON

PrC (DLC); at foot of text: "Mr. Anthony Haswell. Bennington."

To Thomas Newton

DEAR SIR   Washington Oct. 13. 1802.

I this moment recieve a letter from John Hyndman Purdie of Smithfield asking the office on which I wrote you yesterday, and another from his father George Purdie. the latter I formerly knew, and he was a man of merit. I know nothing of their politics; yet that article of character is not to be neglected: and if there be a republican who will do, he should be preferred in the state of great inequality which at present exists. I mention this application that this person may be one of the subjects of your enquiry. accept my friendly salutations & respects.   TH: JEFFERSON

PrC (DLC); at foot of text: "Colo. Thos. Newton"; endorsed by TJ in ink on verso.

A letter dated 8 Oct. from JOHN HYND-MAN PURDIE was recorded in SJL as received 13 Oct. with the notation "to be Surveyor Smithfield vice Thos. Blow resigned." TJ also recorded receiving a letter of the same date from George Purdie. Neither letter has been found. The

younger Purdie was a doctor who later represented Isle of Wight County in the Virginia House of Delegates for four terms, while the elder was a merchant who had long been a leading citizen of Smithfield and from whom TJ had recently tried to obtain hams (Ruth L. Woodward and Wesley Frank Craven, *Princetonians, 1784-1790: A Biographical Dictionary* [Princeton, 1991], 516-17; Vol. 34:229).

From Albert Gallatin

DEAR SIR   Oct. 14. 1802

I enclose the report of the persons appointed to survey the sound together with some other papers connected with the same subject, and the rough draught of a letter intended for the Commr. of the revenue, for the purpose of carrying the law into effect—

Respectfully Your obt. Servt.   ALBERT GALLATIN

RC (DLC); at foot of text: "The President"; endorsed by TJ as received from the Treasury Department on 14 Oct. and "lighthouses in Sound" and so recorded in SJL. Enclosures not found.

The 6 Apr. 1802 act for the erection of lighthouses directed that the Treasury secretary appoint "proper and intelligent persons" TO SURVEY Long Island SOUND to determine where lighthouses should be built and buoys placed. In June, Gallatin appointed Captain Nathan Post of Bridgehampton, New York; merchant John Cahoone, of Newport, Rhode Island; and Nicholl Fosdick, of New London, Connecticut, to make the survey and requested that the revenue cutter at New London be placed at their disposal. The men conducted the survey in August. CARRYING THE LAW INTO EFFECT: the law directed the Treasury secretary to purchase the land, build the lighthouses, and appoint lighthouse keepers, using funds from the U.S. Treasury, provided the states ceded jurisdiction over the proposed sites to the United States (U.S. Statutes at Large, 2:150-1; Gallatin, *Papers*, 7:76, 259; 8:197).

From Albert Gallatin

[14 Oct. 1802]

The difficulties attending the New Orleans trade & suggested in the enclosed letters, cannot certainly be obviated without a law, nor probably without a special convention on that subject. By the British navigation acts, american produce cannot be imported into Great Britain from a port *not of the United States* except in British vessels. Missisipi cotton grown within the United States cannot, therefore, be exported from New Orleans except in such vessels. It is proposed in the letter that the custom house officer of Natchez or rather of Loftus heights (the lowest american port on the river) should grant clearances to american vessels bound from New Orleans to English ports. That he certainly has no right to do without a law of Congress. How the Spanish Govt. would view such procedure, which is almost tantamount to considering N. Orleans as an american port cannot be ascertained: and it seems very doubtful whether the British Govt. would consider such clearance as legal & vessels thus cleared as bound from an american port. If they are disposed to do it, they will find no objection to entering into a special convention for that purpose, or to some modification of their Laws. It must, however be observed, that the inconvenience complained of is one of the least attending the New Orleans trade. Considering the course which a vessel bound from that port to Europe must follow, it cannot be any very great inconvenience to touch at some Georgia or S. Carolina port, where, when (as in the supposed case) the cargo will consist solely of american produce, a regular clearance may be obtained which will admit the vessel to enter the British ports—

Respectfully Submitted ALBERT GALLATIN

RC (DLC: Albert Gallatin Papers); undated; at foot of text: "The President"; endorsed by TJ as received from the Treasury Department on 14 Oct. and "Missisipi regulns" and so recorded in SJL. Enclosures: see those described at TJ to Gallatin, 13 Oct.

For the recent implementation of regulations for the Mississippi and NEW ORLEANS TRADE, see the exchanges between Gallatin and TJ on 7, 14 (first letter), and 19 Aug.

MODIFICATION OF THEIR LAWS: on 11 Aug. 1803, the British passed a law allowing American goods to be imported from New Orleans in U.S. vessels (Madison, *Papers, Sec. of State Ser.*, 4:2-3n).

To William Killen

SIR   Washington Oct. 14. 1802.

I recieve with great pleasure the sentiments of approbation which you are so kind as to express of my administration. I claim only the merit of pure and disinterested intentions, in no way warped by any love of power. for the wisdom of our course, whatever it may be, I must ascribe it to those to whom it is due, my wise coadjutors.   the leaders of the federal faction after an ineffectual trial of the force of political lying & misrepresentation, are trying what impression can be made by personal lies and defamation. on me none. the only revenge I shall ever stoop to will be to sink federalism into an abyss from which there shall be no resurrection for it. as to the effect on my fellow citizens, it is a great consolation to me to believe that they consider a life spent in their presence & service, & without reproach either political or moral, as better evidence than the calumnies of a party whose passions and interests impel them strongly to regard neither truth nor decency in their endeavors to obtain victory, and whose conduct shews they act under that impulse.

I congratulate you on the event of your election. there is one phaenomenon in it, the increase of the federal majority in Kent, which I cannot account for, and which has struck me the more as it is the only district in the US. which has exhibited such an increase in the late elections, as far as I have heard of them.   I pray you to accept assurances of my high consideration & respect.

TH: JEFFERSON

PrC (DLC); at foot of text: "William Killen esq."

SENTIMENTS OF APPROBATION: Killen to TJ, 4 Sep.

From J. P. G. Muhlenberg

SIR   Philadelphia Octobr. 14th. 1802.

I am this morning honor'd with your favor of the 10th. inst.—and take the earliest Opportunity to acknowledge it—& to assure The President, that I shall with great pleasure endeavour to obtain a birth for Mr. B. agreeably to his wishes—Men of such a Character, as Mr. B. is stated to bear, are rarely found, & deserve encourage-ment   I could imediately put him into a place of $600. Pr. Ann. in which he would have leisure to attend to other business, until he can be better provided for, which I have reason to believe can be done with propriety during the Winter—

I have the Honor to be with great Respect & sincere Attachment Your Most Obedt   P. MUHLENBERG

RC (MHi); at foot of text: "The President of The U.S."; endorsed by TJ as received 16 Oct. and so recorded in SJL but as a letter of 12 Oct.

To Nicholas Norris

SIR   Washington Oct. 14. 1802

I now return the letter which you were so kind as to inclose me, and am thankful for the opportunity of perusing it, as I am for all the information which individuals are so kind as to give me. the line of conduct of the Executive was not taken up but after very general en-quiry & information from the different parts of the Union, and a very extensive consultation with the prominent characters among the Re-publicans. the monopoly of all[1] the offices of the US. by a particular party exclusively is a conduct in our immediate predecessors which[2] we have ourselves condemned as unjust & tyrannical. we cannot then either in morality or decency imitate it. a fair & proportionate partic-ipation however ought to be aimed at. as to the mode of obtaining this I know there is great difference of opinion; some thinking it should be done at a single stroke; others that it would conduce more to the tranquility of the country to do the thing by degrees, filling with republicans the vacancies occurring by deaths, resignations & delinquencies, and using the power of removal only in the cases of persons who continue to distinguish themselves by a malignant activity & opposition to that republican order of things which it is their duty to cooperate in, or at least to be silent. we have formed our own opinion on a very mature view of the whole subject, and not

[493]

without a just attention to the temper and wishes of every part of the union, reduced as well as we have been able to do it, to a general result. Accept my respectful salutations and best wishes.

TH: JEFFERSON

PrC (DLC); at foot of text: "Nicholas Norris esq. Baltimore."

THE LETTER: see Norris to TJ, 28 Sep.

¹ Word interlined.
² Preceding five words interlined.

From John Barnes

SIR   George Town 15th. Oct. 1802.

I am this Moment favd: with your Mo.ly statements from the present to the 4th: March—will guide me, in arranging, your Necessary paymts. for the present Mo:—nothing will suffer—

And while I can avoid—discounting—*your Note*, I must confess it will be to me—far preferable,—my Only fear is—that even, the generous Allowance for Monthly expenditures, Other, unexpected, & unavoidable Ones, will Attach themselves,—to your particular situation—but untill any of them Appear, and become pressing—I should still hope and wish, to forego, that Alternative.—

with great Respect, I am Sir Your most Obedt. Hb St

JOHN BARNES

Mr. Short is expected in Town this Evening, or to Morrow.

RC (ViU: Edgehill-Randolph Papers); at foot of text: "The President. UStates"; endorsed by TJ as received 15 Oct. and so recorded in SJL.

I AM THIS MOMENT FAVD: a letter from TJ to Barnes dated 15 Oct. is recorded in SJL but has not been found.

From Charles Willing Byrd

                                    Secretary's Office—Cincinnati—North
SIR   Western Territory. 15th of Oct. 1802.

The subject of this Letter will, I trust, plead my apology for the liberty I now take in trespassing on your time.

Governor St Clair has at last committed an act which, unless he should be immediately removed from office, will preclude the possibility of my discharging, any longer, some of the most essential duties that are attached to the office of Secretary of the Territory.

Not contented with the violation of the Act of Congress, which in the absence of the Governor, invests the Secretary with all the powers and injoins upon him all the duties of the first Magistrate, by taking with him from the Territory on one of his visits to his private Estate at Ligonier in Pensylvania the public Seal of the Territory (with a view to prevent me from appointing Republicans to office)— not satisfied with having removed several meritorious Republicans whom I had commissioned during his last absence, and with throwing every obstacle in my way, merely because I enjoy the confidence of the Republican Party who have lately elected me to the Convention,—he withholds from me the Records of my office which he obtained the possession of (some months ago) by deceiving me with a promise of returning them as soon as he should have looked over the statement of my official proceedings during his late visit to the Atlantic States.

The relative situation in which I stand as the second officer in the Government, together with other motives of delicacy and the prospect of our having a State Government in the course of the ensuing Summer, has prevented me heretofore from representing to the General Government some of his manifold misdeeds. Indeed it is with much reluctance that I am constrained to do it on this occasion: but it is a duty of justice which I owe to my office to give you the above statement as I can no longer perform some of the most important duties injoined upon me, unless he should be compelled to return to me the Journals of my office immediately, which he will not do until he is removed.

There is another consideration to which I beg leave to call your attention. The last Session of our Legislature cost the Territory ten thousand dollars; and the Session to be held on the fourth monday in next month promises also to be an expensive one. It is the opinion of all those persons, who are not dependent on the Governor for their continuance in office, that as we are so soon to have a State Government and a State Legislature (which is now fully ascertained by the Returns of the Members chosen to the Convention) that there is no necessity for another Session of the Territorial Assembly. But the People are so thoroughly satisfied that an application to Governor St Clair for the postponement of the Legislature, would prove abortive, that they are discouraged from making it. They have told me that they would petition for his removal from office even at this late hour, in order to save the useless expence of another Session of the Territorial Assembly, if they had not been convinced by experience that their petitions on this subject would not be attended to.

I have the honor to be Sir with very high respect yr—mo—ob—servt—

CHARLES WILLING BYRD

RC (DLC); addressed: "The honble, Thomas Jefferson Esquire President of the United States City of Washington" and "Favored by H Cadbury Esqr."; endorsed by TJ as received 1 Dec. and so recorded in SJL.

For background on the acrimonious relationship between Byrd and Arthur ST CLAIR, see Vol. 37:505-6. During St. Clair's LAST ABSENCE from the Northwest Territory from March to July 1802, Byrd appointed dozens of Republicans to militia and judicial posts, many on the advice of Nathaniel Massie, his brother-in-law and one of the territory's leading Republicans. After returning to the territory, St. Clair obtained the executive journals from Byrd and demanded that the secretary explain why the appointments were made. He further directed Byrd to obtain offices to house the territory's public records, in order that the governor and "every person might have access, and where the business of the Territory might be transacted" (*Terr. Papers*, 3:240-2, 533-5; Brown, "Frontier Politics," 268-9).

ELECTED ME TO THE CONVENTION: Republicans easily carried the October election of delegates to the Ohio constitutional convention, winning 26 of 35 seats and predominating in every part of the territory except the Federalist bastion of Washington County. Byrd was among the ten delegates chosen from Hamilton County (Brown, "Frontier Politics," 270-6; Randolph Chandler Downes, *Frontier Ohio, 1788-1803* [Columbus, 1935], 239-46; Thomas Worthington to TJ, 8 Nov. 1802).

To Carlos IV, King of Spain

GREAT AND GOOD FRIEND,

I have lately received the letter of your Majesty bearing date the 6th day of July last, announcing that contracts of marriage had been adjusted between your much beloved son Don Fernando, Prince of Asturias and the Infanta of Naples Donna Maria Antonia; and between your very dear Daughter Donna Maria Isabel and the hereditary Prince of that Kingdom Don Francis Genaro. From the interest we take as your Majesty very justly supposes in all the events which contribute to your happiness, we pray your Majesty to receive our cordial congratulations on these occasions which we fervently hope may promote both the happiness of your Majesty and of your August family. And while we express our acknowledgments for your friendly interest in our prosperity, we pray God to have you great and good Friend always in his holy keeping.

Written at the City of Washington, the Fifteenth day of October in the year of our Lord one thousand Eight hundred and two; and of the Independence of the United States of America, the Twenty Seventh.

Your Good Friend,   TH: JEFFERSON

FC (Lb in DNA: RG 59, Credences); in a clerk's hand; at head of text: "Thomas Jefferson, President of the United States of America, To His Majesty Don Carlos by the Grace of God King of Castile, of Leon, of Aragon, of the two Sicilies, of Jerusalem, of Navarre, of Granada, of Toledo, of Valencia, of Galicia, of Mallorca, of Seville, of Sardinia, of Cordova, of Corcega, of Murcia, of Jaen, of the Algarves, of Algecira, of Gibraltar, of the Canary Islands, of the East and West Indies, of the Islands and Main Land, of the Ocean—Archduke of Austria, Duke of Burgoña, of Brabant, and of Milan, Count of Apsburg, of Flanders, of Tirol and of Barcelona, Lord of Biscay and of Molina &c"; below signature: "By the President" and "James Madison Secretary of State." Not recorded in SJL.

To James Dinsmore

DEAR SIR   Washington Oct. 15. 1802.

On opening the door leading from the passage into my bookroom, and on the shelves to the left, immediately on entrance, are a parcel of locks which I omitted to give out to mr Perry to be put on the doors he made. there are 3. small[1] Cup-board locks for the 3. lockers in the kitchen.

3. japanned closet locks, for the 3. servants rooms, and a 4th. I think for the North necessary. of the stock locks in the same place, the 2. worst are for the doors of the kitchen & wash-house. the best is for the outer door of the Smoke house. the inner door will not need a lock till I come. one door of the kitchen is to be bolted within. be so good as to deliver them to mr Perry with a request that he put them on immediately. Accept my best wishes.   TH: JEFFERSON

RC (privately owned, Philadelphia, 2002); addressed: "Mr. James Dinsmore Monticello near <Charlottesville> Milton"; franked and postmarked.

[1] Word interlined.

From Caesar A. Rodney

HONORED & DEAR SIR,   Wilmington Octob. 15th. 1802.

Enclosed is the pamphlet which ought to have accompanied my last. I should like to have an opportunity of giving you a history of the electioneering business. It would take a quire of paper to do it, & I must defer it, until I have the pleasure of seeing you. Tho' our majority be small, I trust it is an important victory which the Opposition will sensibly feel. By the Polls it appears that the Fedl. candidate did not keep pace with his ticket in either New Castle or Kent Counties whilst the Republican candidate was ahead of his in all the Counties. Falsehoods calumnies & abuse, the usual weapons in a lost cause, have been lavished upon us all during the contest. Mr. Bayard is held up as a demi-god by their "Ark" & the character of the state is destroyed, in consequence of his losing his election. With great esteem I am Dr. Sir

Yours most Sincerely
C. A. RODNEY

P.S. Permit me to mention the names of Mr. Bonsal who is a bookseller in Baltimore & his partner Mr. Niles who resides here as young men of quaker families whose zeal & uniformity entitle them to notice & attention. They have printed the pamphlet enclosed & a great number of other things during the contest. Mr. Niles with my friend J. Warner signed the certificate relative to H. Latimer which I see printed in Duane's paper of yesterday & which was printed in a hand bill by Mr. Niles who drew up the comments which followed the certificate a few days before the election. It had a wonderful effect.

I mention these facts of those gentlemen as Administration may do them some service without going out of that path of rectitude which I trust will ever mark their course.

RC (DLC); endorsed by TJ as received 16 Oct. and so recorded in SJL. Enclosure: *Authentic Information Relative to the Conduct of the Present & Last Administrations of the United States* by "A Friend to Liberty, Peace & Economy," printed by Bonsal and Niles, with statements of the savings made by TJ and Congress as documented, in part, by the 18 Mch. 1802 letter of New York congressman Theodorus Bailey to his constituents; using committee reports and the journals of the House to compare the Republican and Federalist stands on repeal of internal taxes and redemption of the public debt in 1802 and the passage of the stamp tax, the land tax, the $5,000,000 loan, additional duties on salt, and other legislation from 1797 to 1799, always highlighting James A. Bayard's vote with the Federalists; concluding with a statement of the tax savings the people of Delaware would experience through the repeal of internal taxes and the judiciary act, a total of $11,463.10, and observing that by TJ's "prudent measures" Delaware will save more than the $10,500 annual expense of the state government "by lopping off oppressive taxes and useless offices" (Wilmington, Del., 1802; Shaw-Shoemaker, No. 1792), 3-32.

Vincent BONSAL and Hezekiah NILES had offices in Wilmington, Delaware, and Baltimore. Niles had served an apprenticeship with Benjamin Johnson, a Wilmington printer, bookbinder, and bookseller, and gained the reputation of being "the quickest, most efficient typesetter in America." In 1799, Bonsal and Niles printed the Wilmington *Delaware Gazette*, and from 1799 to 1804 they printed and sold almanacs, including the *Bonsal and Niles' Town and Country Almanac*, in both cities (see Evans, No. 36442; Shaw-Shoemaker, Nos. 313, 880, 1432, 1923, 3853-5, 7379; ANB, s.v. "Niles, Hezekiah"; Cornelius William Stafford, *The Baltimore Directory, for 1803* [Baltimore, 1803], 20-1; Brigham, *American Newspapers*, 1:81). For other publications printed by them, see Vol. 36:220n, 239n.

On 2 Oct., Niles and Wilmington Republican merchant John WARNER signed a certificate claiming that Henry LATIMER, a Delaware senator from 1795 to 1801, had declared in their presence that farmers, mechanics, and laborers in the United States lived too well, consuming roasted meats, coffee, and tea and "that they must be reduced to the same state as the peasants of Ireland, Who Live on Herrings and Potatoes." Latimer continued, "that rather than live under such an administration as Jefferson's He would remove to the dominions of the Empress Kate of Russia." Niles commented that TJ's system of economy in government would "enable the people *to live yet better*, and have more leisure to bestow in contemplating upon, and acting in, public affairs—and *all this* in direct contradiction and defiance of the *principles* of Mr. *Latimer*" and other leaders of the Federalist party (Philadelphia *Aurora*, 12 Oct. 1802; John A. Munroe, *Federalist Delaware, 1775-1815* [New Brunswick, N.J., 1954], 213, 252).

From Caspar Wistar

DEAR SIR   Philada. Oct. 15. 1802.

I beg leave to recommend to you the Bearer, Mr. P. Kuhn Junr., a very amiable & worthy young gentleman who is about establishing a commercial house at Gibralter—He is the Son of a Gentleman of very high character for honour & integrity, who has been long & successfully engaged in the mediterranean trade—as he has been educated in his Father's Compting House, & has acquired a knowledge of Gibralter & its neighbourhood by two voyages, I believe he would perform the duties of Consul to your satisfaction if you should think proper to appoint him—

With most grateful and affectionate recollection of your kind attention, & with sincere wishes for your health & happiness, I am most respectfully Your obliged friend   C. WISTAR JUNR.

RC (DNA: RG 59, LAR); at foot of text: "His Excellency The President of the United States"; endorsed by TJ as received 26 Oct. and "Kuhn. P. junr. to be Consul at Gibraltar" and so recorded in SJL.

For Peter KUHN, Jr., see his letter to TJ of 5 Nov.

From John Barnes

Geo. Town 16th. Oct 1802

I have to thank you Sir—which I most Sincerely do, for your very flattering & honorable introduction of me, to Genl M—with his very polite & immediate Answer

—but, Situated as my Store and Accts are—and probably will be untill spring—(for I have had no Offers—nor purchasers), nor person—in whom to confide in—Such a Charge—I am of Necessity Obliged to decline Accepting so favorable an Offer.—If Sir—you should judge it proper for me, I would either write or wait personally on G M—

I am Sir, most gratefuly, your most Obedt. H St.

JOHN BARNES

RC (ViU: Edgehill-Randolph Papers); at foot of text: "The Presidt: UStates"; endorsed by TJ as received 16 Oct.

GENL M: J. P. G. Muhlenberg. See TJ to Muhlenberg, 10 Oct., and Muhlenberg to TJ, 14 Oct.

From John Barnes

SIR   Geo: Town 16t Oct 1802

Reflecting on your much Esteemed favr. with which you Hond. me this morning—

I am very Apprehensive you have in the warmth of your friendly recommendation far—very far—exceeded the humble abilities I *really* possess—and withal not made the Necessary Allowances, for my Age, & defects which, the want of practice, may be indispensible in the rotine of business there—in which Case, I should be exceedingly Mortified indeed—in Attempting to Obtrude myself, at the expence of discrediting my employer, & Principal—on the Other hand, could I but be made Acquainted with the Particulars, thereof, I could then judge of the Necessary Qualifications—to insure both, or, however reluctantly, to decline the Boon so freely offered—Under these particular circumstances I beg leave to Submit it, to your better Judgment if, it would not be prudent in me to wait on G M. in person, or, to write to him—on the Subject, of my embarrassments.

With the most gratefull Esteem & respect—I am Sir your Obliged & very H St.

JOHN BARNES

RC (ViU: Edgehill-Randolph Papers); addressed: "The President of the United States"; endorsed by TJ as received 17 Oct. and so recorded in SJL.

FAVR. WITH WHICH YOU HOND. ME THIS MORNING: a letter from TJ to Barnes dated 16 Oct. has not been found, nor is one recorded in SJL.

From Albert Gallatin

DEAR SIR   Oct. 16th 1802
I enclose a letter of Capn. Crowningshield recommending the removal
of the Surveyor of Gloucester. The new collector's (Gibaut) letter
making a similar representation was sent to you some days ago.
     with respect & attachment Your obedt. Servt.
                                              ALBERT GALLATIN

The sickness & absence of the principal accounting clerk of this office
(Mr Sheldon) has prevented my transmitting the weekly return of
Warrants.   A. G.

RC (DLC); addressed: "The President
of the United States"; endorsed by TJ as
received from the Treasury Department
on 16 Oct. and "removal of Surveyor of
Gloster." Enclosure not found.

Samuel Whittemore, a Harvard graduate and Federalist, had served as SUR-
VEYOR OF GLOUCESTER since 1789. He
was removed in 1803 (Washington, *Papers, Pres. Ser.*, 5:196n; JEP, 1:9, 12; Vol.
33:673).

From Thomas Jenkins, Ambrose Spencer, and Alexander Coffin

SIR.   Hudson October 16th: 1802
     Without any personal acquaintance we take the liberty to address
you, in relation to two gentleman holding Offices in this City, under
the general government, deriving their appointments thro' the nomination, & liable to be removed by the President of the United
States—
     We are not insensible, that in the exercise of your constitutional
prerogative, there has been a constant regret on your part, to remove
Incumbents, even when justifiable, & demanded by circumstances
in themselves imperious; we have however witnessed in the discharge of your functions, in relation to removals a firmness & decision, commanding our respect & admiration; & we cannot permit
ourselves to doubt a continuance of a disposition which has secured
to you, the approbation of all Republicans possessed of discernment
& intelligence—
     The Officers to whom we have reference are Henry Malcolm Col-
lector of this port, & John C. Ten Broeck Surveyor. In our estimation
(& the opinion is not lightly adopted,) their removal is justifiable and
we think called for on the grounds of political expediency, & an equal

participation in the Honors & Emoluments of Office; both of these Gentlemen have held their offices ever since their creation, & they are both in an eminent degree, hostile to the Administration, & the very principles, for which we are contending—

Their removal however is not sollicited on these grounds alone; Mr. Malcolm is a practising Physician & is frequently called out of the place, hence we assert it as an indisputable fact, that there has arisen & will constantly arise delays & embarrassments to Masters of Vessels & Coasters, which ought not to be tolerated—

Mr. Ten Broeck has evinced in another Office from which he has been removed on that principle solely, a want of punctuality & fidelity highly exceptionable; He has in fact used the public money to a considerable amount & at this moment retains it—We submit therefore whether he has not justly forfeited the public confidence & whether he merits any further countenance from the government—

We forbear to name to you any persons for the Offices, which we wish vacated by the present Incumbents, you will undoubtedly take measures to inform yourself of suitable Characters—

Permit us Sir, to assure you that we have no other objects in view, in this communication, than the good of the Republic & the maintenance of principles to us most sacred—

We are with sentiments of high respect and unalterable esteem Your Excellency's Obedt. Servts—

THOS. JENKINS
AMBROSE SPENCER
ALEXR. COFFIN

RC (DNA: RG 59, LAR); in Spencer's hand, signed by Jenkins, Spencer, and Coffin; at foot of text: "His Excellency Thomas Jefferson Esqr. President of the United States"; endorsed by TJ as received 4 Nov. and "Henry Malcolm Collector of Hudson John C. Tenbroeck Surveyor of do. to be removd" and so recorded in SJL.

Ambrose Spencer (1765-1848), a native of Connecticut and a Harvard graduate, moved to Hudson, New York, in the mid-1780s as a law clerk preparing for the bar. In the 1790s he won election to the state assembly and the state senate, served on the New York Council of Appointments, and forged a political alliance with DeWitt Clinton. In 1804, he became a member of the state supreme court (ANB; Gideon Granger to TJ, 14 May 1802).

Alexander Coffin (1740-1839), like Jenkins, was originally from Nantucket Island and was one of the original proprietors of Hudson. A merchant sea captain, at various times he held local and state political offices. In February 1802, he became postmaster of Hudson on the removal of Cotton Gelston, a Federalist who had held the position since 1790 (Daily National Intelligencer, 22 Jan. 1839; Hudson Balance, and Columbian Repository, 16 Feb. 1802; Stephen B. Miller, Historical Sketches of Hudson [Hudson, N.Y., 1862], 6, 18, 31, 113, 114, 115).

WITHOUT ANY PERSONAL ACQUAINTANCE: TJ and Madison passed through Hudson, and stopped there for breakfast, in May 1791. During that visit, Seth Jenkins, Thomas Jenkins's brother, conversed with TJ about his distillery (MB, 2:819, 823; Vol. 20:559-60).

From Levi Lincoln

SIR   Worcester Octo 16. 1802—

I hope a letter, some time since, directed to you at the seat of Govt. altho it contained no treason, did not fail of reaching you. The spirit, and bitterness of the opposition is as great as ever. The numbers has however, not increased; I think, some what, diminished: Every thing, every calumny, which malice can invent, or baseness propagate, is put in circulation. Respectable people, or at least many of them, who say, and openly effect, to dislike, and to censure aspersions, as infamous & false, yet secretly countenance them. Their sincere, and pointed disapprobation, would soon put and end to them. The object is, to hunt down destroy, and render odious, in the eyes of the people, the administration, and the whole republican character and interest. Some of the opposition leaders say, it must be done, and are stupid enough, to beleive it can, and will be done. Under this impression it is not strange, as truth will not serve them, they should have recourse to falshood and abuse. These topicks I trust are nearly exhausted. It is evident they are losing their effects, with the body of the people. The Exertions on both sides will be great at our approaching election. The Republicans, in general, have hitherto, in my opinion, been too inattentive. They have been too timid and accomodating to their enemies:—to those who never will accommodate, but on the terms, of an unconditional surrender. There can be no reconciliation, consistent, with the present measures, with the preservation of the existing republican system of Government—I once thought otherwise. I hope we shall have six or seven Republicans from this State[1]—

My family has been extremely sick, my house a perfect hospital. For near two months, I have been the constant companion of sick chambers. The attentions, to a sickness requiring the attendence of three physicians[2] repeatedly in the course of the day & four watchers in the night, in some degree impaired my own health. We are getting better, and hope in the fore part of the next month to be able to leave Worcester for Washington—

With the most respectful esteem I have the honor to be Sir your most obedient   LEVI LINCOLN

RC (DLC); at head of text: "The President of the U. States"; endorsed by TJ as received 22 Oct. and so recorded in SJL.

LETTER: Lincoln to TJ, 24 July.
EXTREMELY SICK: severe dysentery caused a number of deaths, particularly among children, in several locales in New England during the summer and fall of 1802 (Boston *Massachusetts Mercury*, 24 Aug.; Worcester *Massachusetts Spy*, 25 Aug.; *Salem Gazette*, 3, 13, 16 Sep.;

Hartford *Connecticut Courant*, 20 Sep.;
Boston Gazette, 30 Sep.; Litchfield *Monitor*, 13 Oct.).

[1] Sentence interlined.
[2] MS: "physians."

To Robert Patterson

DEAR SIR   Washington Oct. 16. 1802.

The inclosed is merely the letter of form communicating the paper it covers to the society. but I promised Capt Groves to write you a private & more particular one. he has proposed a new method of observing the eclipses of Jupiter's satellites at sea. you will percieve that he is not expert at explaining his ideas. he has invented an instrument too for making the observations, but what are it's advantages or disadvantages I have not had time to examine. his proposition can be fully explained by the use of an instrument we already possess, that of Hadley's sextant. instead of the small telescope sometimes fixed to that, substitute one of sufficient power to shew Jupiter's satellites. perhaps a reflector would be more convenient than a refractor of equal power. take your observation, at sea, by drawing the planet & satellites down to or near the horison, in which situation, the body being erect can preserve it's position by humoring the motion of the ship and have a steady view of the immersion or emersion of the Satellite. this seems to be a substitute for the Marine chair, and being a simple, easy & cheap thing, instead of a complicated, expensive & bulky one, several observers may act at the same time, the better to ascertain the instant of immersion. for the true time of the immersion he depends, as the marine chair does, on the time keepers in use. Capt Groves is not a man of science, & does not perfectly know how to estimate the merit of his invention. I told him I believed it would be within the usual course of the proceedings of the society to refer his paper to a committee, who would report their opinion & explain the degree of usefulness of his proposition. this is precisely what he wishes, for being very poor, he is anxious to make from it whatever it is worth. should I have mistaken the usual course of the society in supposing they would give an opinion on the merit of the proposition, then I would ask of you to favor me with a private statement of your view of it, to be communicated to him. to these favors I would sollicit that of dispatch to be added because he means to stay here until he learns the result, which in the very low state of his finances is not convenient to him. Accept my friendly salutations and assurances of high respect.   TH: JEFFERSON

RC (PPAmP); at foot of first page: "Mr. David Patterson." PrC (DLC); TJ corrected Patterson's first name in ink at foot of first page. Enclosures: (1) TJ to Patterson, 16 Oct.: "Dear Sir I inclose you a paper recieved from the hands of Capt Matthew C. Groves of Massachusets, wherein he proposes a more convenient method of observing the eclipses of Jupiter's satellites for the purpose of ascertaining longitude at sea, than he supposes to have been hitherto practised. I communicate it to the society at his request, and tender you the assurances of my great esteem & respect" (PrC in DLC; at foot of text: "Mr. Robert Patterson. one of the V.P. of the A.P.S."). (2) Description by Groves of "a new mode of observing the Eclipses of Jupiter's Satellites &c.," not found; presented to the American Philosophical Society in a meeting on 5 Nov. and referred to Patterson, who gave a report on Groves's paper in a meeting on 18 Nov. (APS, *Proceedings*, 22, pt. 3 [1884], 327, 328).

From Thomas Mann Randolph

DEAR SIR,   Edgehill October 16. 1802.

It has occurred to me that perhaps a special licence for me to pass with my Slaves through South Carolina might be obtained from the Executive of that State upon my giving security that not one of them should remain in it. I have not heard that such an application has been made but I do not see any solid reason why leave should not be granted as the end of the laws restraining the passage is to hinder importation only and that end cannot be at all defeated if a penalty larger than any profit which could be made by sale in the State be taken. What those laws are I have no means of knowing and therefore it may not be possible to obtain what I wish: should it not be I must resolve on the circuitous rout, though from a person just arrived in this neighbourhood from Georgia I learn that the difficulty and cost must be very much greater. That person if I could get permission could carry out my Slaves for me on terms more reasonable than I ever expected; by the ordinary rout: from his estimate they cannot cost me more than 5 or 6 Dollars each including waggon hire for their baggage: he returns next month. you will render me a service of importance by giving me some information early on the subject.— Martha has recovered completely: the children are all well. With true affection.   TH: M. RANDOLPH

RC (MHi); endorsed by TJ as received 20 Oct. and so recorded in SJL.

Randolph feared that his plan, discussed in a letter to TJ of 20 Mch. 1802, to move some of his SLAVES to Georgia to start a cotton plantation was being stymied by a series of South Carolina LAWS banning the importation of slaves into that state. Most recently an 1801 act had imposed a $100 fine on every slave or free black imported from outside the state and empowered sheriffs to seize for sale any slaves found to be in the state illegally (*Acts and Resolutions of the General Assembly of the State of South Carolina. Passed in December, 1801* [Columbia, S.C., 1802; Shaw-Shoemaker, No. 3100], 30-6). The bans, which were never well enforced, ended after 1804, but by then Randolph's interest in Georgia had faded

(Rachel N. Klein, *Unification of a Slave State: The Rise of the Planter Class in the South Carolina Backcountry, 1760-1808* [Chapel Hill, 1990], 127-8, 234-5, 253-5; William H. Gaines, Jr., *Thomas Mann Randolph, Jefferson's Son-in-Law* [Baton Rouge, 1966], 47).

To Robert Smith

DEAR SIR   Washington Oct. 16. 1802.

We have this morning recieved authentic information from mr Simpson that a state of peace is happily restored between us & the emperor of Marocco. information habitually recieved shews there has never been any danger of rupture between us & Tunis or Algiers. in this state of things, and considering the approach of winter, it becomes necessary we should have a general consultation of the heads of departments on the plan we are to pursue in the Mediterranean: and considering the advance of the season & the circumstance that the New York & John Adams are still at Norfolk, even 24. hours of delay becomes important, because if it is necessary for them to go they may carry our orders. under these circumstances I must ask your immediate attendance here for the purpose of consultation.   some other matters also, interesting to the Navy department require immediate attention; particularly the procuring regular estimates &c. on the subject of our dry dock. I pray you to accept assurances of my affectionate esteem & respect.

TH: JEFFERSON

PrC (DLC); at foot of text: "The Secretary of the Navy."

THIS MORNING RECIEVED: on 16 Oct., dispatches written by James Simpson on 12 Aug. and 3 Sep. arrived at the State Department. Although Mawlay Sulayman was pressing a demand for annual gifts from the United States, Simpson had decided to remain in Morocco, raise the flag on the consulate, and notify other consuls that peace had been restored. He made the decision after conferring with Richard V. Morris, who said he could not remain close to the Moroccan coast given

the "very urgent" need for the squadron's ships elsewhere in the Mediterranean. "Your return to your Consular station under the circumstances which led to it, is entirely approved by the President," Madison wrote to Simpson on 21 Oct. "It was proper both as it secured a temporary state of peace at a critical moment, and as it facilitates the use of other means for effecting a permanent reconciliation." Madison also assured the consul that the president approved his conduct in refusing the Moroccans' "claim of periodical presents" (Madison, *Papers, Sec. of State Ser.*, 3:475, 542-5; 4:38).

From Joseph Coppinger

SIR   New York 17th October 1802

You will easily perceive by the style of this letter that a farmer (for such I profess myself to be) is but poorly qualified to address personages in high station, much less the first Magistrate of a great and a rising Nation. Were I thus to address Majesty in the old Country (from whence I am only a few months removed) it would at once be put down to the account of folly, and weakness, and I might expect to fare accordingly. But in this Country of good sense, where the pride of the state lies in promoting the true, and real happiness, of its People, I venture to promise myself a different result. My object in addrg you this letter is to be informed (through one of your Secretarys for I neither wish, nor expect you should take the trouble yourself) how I am to proceed in order to procure a Patent for preserving animal, and vegetable substances, either in their naturel or a cuit state, and this without the aid of Salt by simple and easy operations of preperation and Package After which they will preserve sound and unaltered both in quantity and quality as long as they can be possibly wanted so to do, as food for Man, and beast, and this without danger of waste or loss. In short If my opinion of this simple, and Judicious theory be Just, and I trust on a full, and fair tryal, it will be found so, and that it can be acted on to the extent And variety I suppose it capable of, few objects will be found more worthy of National encouragement, or National reward. In the business of victualing fleets, Armys, and trading ships, its savings, and benifites are not easily estimated, untill first fairly tried. I would have taken out a Patent in England but on enquiery I found I should take out three in order to cover every part of the discovery, the cost of which would amount to nearly what I was worth for which reason I declined In this Country I am informed matters are more wisely ordered and that such Patents are granted to the parties applying free of expence a Judicious encouragement this to the full exertion of genius and talent

If I am to be favoured with an answer to this letter, might I request to be informed what are the conditions required on which Patents are granted to individuals in this Country, and is a Journy to Washington in this case of indispensible necessity I am particular in asking this question as the present state of my family, and finances, would ill accord with such a necessity. Having occasion in the course of a few days to go into the state of Pennsylvania a letter addressed to me at Messrs. James Clibborn & English's Philadelphia will be forwarded—

I have the honour to be with great Respect Sir Your most Obt. & Very Hb. Servt.   JOSEPH COPPINGER

RC (DLC); endorsed by TJ as received 22 Oct. and so recorded in SJL.

Joseph Coppinger, a self-described "practical brewer" and itinerant inventor emigrated from Harbour View, Ireland, to New York around July 1802. As one of six sons born to an Irish gentry family, he used his Irish Catholic connections to his advantage in America, relying on references from his brother William, a bishop in County Cork. Coppinger moved to Pittsburgh later in 1802 and became a partner in the purchase of Point Brewery. After the dissolution of the partnership, Coppinger pursued new projects in several southern states. In 1803, he advertised for a naturalized citizen to file his patent improvements on his behalf, but six years later, having himself become a United States citizen, he obtained five of them in his own name. In an "Address to the People of America" published in 1809, Coppinger praised TJ, the "polar star," for his service to the country and recommended the immediate establishment of a national institute for instructing youth in "all the useful arts, trades, and sciences" necessary for the growth of manufacturing in the United States. In 1815, he solicited

TJ's subscription for the establishment of a national brewing company in Washington, D.C. Coppinger prepared a prospectus for a book entitled *The American Practical Brewer and Tanner*, published in New York in 1815. TJ repeatedly inquired about the status of its publication (Shaw-Shoemaker, No. 34445; John Burke, *A Genealogical and Heraldic History of the Commoners of Great Britain and Ireland*, 4 vols. [London, 1834-38], 2:328; Baltimore *Federal Gazette*, 10 May 1803; ASP, *Miscellaneous*, 2:138; Stanley Baron, *Brewed in America: A History of Beer and Ale in the United States* [Boston, 1962], 132-3, 139-43; Lexington *Kentucky Gazette*, 13 Mch. 1809; Coppinger to James Madison, enclosing list of 14 inventions, 16 Dec. 1810, in DLC: Madison Papers; Louis Du Bourg to John Couper, 8 Nov. 1809, in same; RS, 6:510-11, 533, 597, 647; Coppinger to TJ, 3 Jan. 1803, 6 Apr. and 15 Sep. 1815; TJ to Coppinger, 25 Apr. 1815).

Coppinger received the patent for PRESERVING ANIMAL, AND VEGETABLE SUBSTANCES on 23 Nov. 1809 (*List of Patents*, 77).

To James Monroe

Commissioners of Bankruptcy.

Richmond: George Hay. declined. George Tucker appointed in his
                     place
              Wm. Duval.
              George W. Smith.
              Benjamin Hatcher. declined.
Norfolk   Lytleton W. Tazewell. declined
              Richard Evers Lee.
              Moses Myers. declined
              Thomas Blanchard.

Th: Jefferson to Govr. Monroe.

You will see by the above Statement that we are still in want of one Commr. of bankruptcy at Richmd. or Manchester, and of two at Norfolk. whom shall we appoint?

Washington Oct. 17. 1802

PrC (DLC); endorsed by TJ in ink on verso.

For Monroe's previous recommendations of BANKRUPTCY commissioners for Richmond and Norfolk, see Vol. 37:510-11, 690-1.

From Mustafa Baba, Dey of Algiers

To, Our great friends

The american Government— Equal to October The 17th. *1802*

We Salute and pray for your health and happiness. Your Consul OBrien in your name demanded The favour of us to seek and Obtain, The release from Slavery of your Subjects, in the possession of The Pascha of Tripoli. we wrote and Obtained The Same and gave them to your Consul to send to you as a present, and we pray you to receive the same and be assured of our friendship—

We have been much dissatisfyed to hear That you would think of sending near us The Consul, That you had at Tripoli. whenever he comes we will not receive him. his Character does not Suit us, as we know, wherever he has remained That he has created difficulties and brought On a *war*

And as I will not receive him I am shure it will be well for both nations

Done in our divan at Algiers with The great Seal of Mustapha Pascha

Tr (DLC); in hand of Richard O'Brien; at foot of text: "Certifyd to be The Substance of The deys letter to The Presidt. of the UStates OBrien" and "NB. The dey requests, That Capt Morris will deliver his letter to The President of The UStates"; endorsed by O'Brien: "Letter of Dey of Algiers"; endorsed by TJ as received 19 May 1803 and so recorded in SJL. Tr (DNA: RG 59, CD); in O'Brien's hand; endorsed by Jacob Wagner. Tr (same); in O'Brien's hand. Tr (same); in O'Brien's hand; subjoined to O'Brien to James Leander Cathcart, 10

Feb. 1803. RC (same); in Arabic; with Mustafa's seal at head of text; editors' translation: "May this letter of ours arrive among our dear friends, the rulers of America. How are you and how are your circumstances? As for what follows, there are concerns regarding the consul Wabriim (O'Brien), your envoy who has requested that I free the Christians whom the Tripolitans seized. I wrote to the sultan of Tripoli who sent them promptly. I placed them in the hands of the consul such that you yourselves might receive them from my possession without delay. I am dismayed by something I have heard. You wish to send to me Karkari (Cathcart), the consul who was in Tripoli, that he might remain in our land as consul. If he comes to me, I shall in no way receive him since he is not a good man. It is clear that wherever he spends time he creates a great disturbance. For this reason, our not accepting him is for our and your good. Written with the permission of our master, the blessed sir, Mustafa Pasha, sultan of Algiers"; endorsed by Wagner. Dupl (MHi); in Arabic; same seal and text as RC.

Mustafa Baba (d. 1805) became the dey of Algiers in 1798 and ruled during a period of political, economic, and social instability. A military cadre of foreign janissaries, many of them Anatolian Turks, controlled the selection of the dey and always named someone from their own ranks. They chose Mustafa following the death of his uncle, the dey Ali Hassan. Before he came to power, Mustafa directed the treasury and had ties to Jewish brokers who exercised a powerful role in financial policy and foreign affairs. He made one of those financiers, Naphtali Busnach, his principal adviser. William Eaton, after an audience with the new dey in 1799, left a harsh description of Mustafa as "a huge shaggy beast" seated on a velvet cushion in a dark room "with his hind legs gathered up like a tailor, or a bear." Mustafa's foreign policy often seemed capricious to the Ottoman government and to European countries. In Algiers, he had to contend with rebellion, a guild of sea captains who controlled the corsair fleet, and autonomous provinces. Plots against him failed in 1801 and 1804. In 1805, as popular discontent rose during a famine, a janissary murdered Busnach and set off a wave of violence against Jews. Members of the janissary corps determined to replace Mustafa as dey and killed him as he attempted to flee Algiers. *Baba*, from a Turkish word for "father," was an honorific title like *pasha*. Mustafa was sometimes called Mustafa Pasha (Louis B. Wright and Julia H. MacLeod, *The First Americans in North Africa: William Eaton's Struggle for a Vigorous Policy against the Barbary Pirates, 1799-*

1805 [Princeton, 1945], 31, 187-8; H. D. de Grammont, *Histoire d'Alger: sous la domination Turque (1515-1830)* [Paris, 1887], 354-62; William Spencer, *Algiers in the Age of the Corsairs* [Norman, Okla., 1976], 21-2, 41-2, 59-65, 163-4; P. M. Holt, Ann K. S. Lambton, and Bernard Lewis, eds., *The Cambridge History of Islam*, 2 vols. [Cambridge, 1970], 2A:277-85; Mouloud Gaïd, *L'Algérie sous les Turcs* [Tunis, 1974], 167-71; Philip C. Naylor, *Historical Dictionary of Algeria*, 3d ed. [Lanham, Md., 2006], 298, 391; Robert J. Allison, *The Crescent Obscured: The United States and the Muslim World, 1776-1815* [New York, 1995], 158-9, 172-3; NDBW, 2:198, 200; H. A. R. Gibb and others, eds., *The Encyclopedia of Islam: New Edition*, 11 vols. [Leiden, 1960], 1:838).

DEMANDED THE FAVOUR: O'Brien reported that "at my request in the name of the united States," Mustafa had written to Yusuf Qaramanli of Tripoli asking him to turn over Andrew Morris and the crew of the *Franklin*. O'Brien promised that the U.S. would pay Algiers $5,000 for the release of the captives. After Yusuf sent the American prisoners to Algiers, Mustafa gave the Tripolitan ruler expensive gifts, including wheat and luxury items (O'Brien to Madison, 11 Oct., in DNA: RG 59, CD; Madison, *Papers, Sec. of State Ser.*, 4:16).

YOUR SUBJECTS: Morris and four members of his crew arrived in Algiers on 6 Oct. Mustafa composed his letter to TJ in the expectation that Morris would deliver the document. O'Brien also gave Morris some dispatches to carry. The mariner delivered the papers in Washington on 19 May 1803 (same, 4:16-18, 50; 5:47).

THAT YOU HAD AT TRIPOLI: when O'Brien called on Mustafa on 8 Oct. to thank him for obtaining the release of the captives, the dey objected to the appointment of James L. Cathcart as consul at Algiers and declared his intention to write to the president on the subject (same, 17).

The DIVAN was the Algerian council of state (Spencer, *Algiers in the Age of the Corsairs*, 50-2; Naylor, *Historical Dictionary of Algeria*, 391).

To John Barnes

Oct. 18. 1802.

Th: Jefferson has occasion to send an hundred dollars to Monticello if mr Barnes can furnish him with them. it would suit best in US. bank or branch bank bills of 10. D each, as they are to be paid out in small parcels. the post goes this afternoon.

RC (CSmH).

TJ received the HUNDRED DOLLARS from Barnes the same day and immedi-ately forwarded it to his daughter Martha (MB, 2:1084; TJ to Martha Jefferson Randolph, 18 Oct.).

From William Duane

SIR,   Frankford, Octr. 18, 1802

The bustle attendant on our election affairs here will I hope excuse the delay of three days since the receipt of your letter. Upon the receipt of the Instructions concerning the Books from London and Paris, I immediately addressed the originals to Messrs Johnson in London and Pougens in Paris, with Duplicates of each in my hand writing to Mr Erving and Mr. Short—directing the Booksellers to call on those Gentlemen. I fear the removal of Mr Short may retard the business at Paris; the business in London is in a fair train as I have had a letter from my correspondent there, within the present month. I shall take the first occasion that presents itself to address Mr Pougens again; tho' I have no doubt that from your note, independent of the confidence which he has already manifested in me that the order will be duly executed, even if he should not have thought it advisable to apply to Mr Livingston.

Our elections in Pennsylvania generally are as they ought to be. Some unhappy misunderstandings have secretly existed which alarmed many and portended some injurious consequences. The evil has, however, been in this county & the City completely checked; tho at the expence of a good man's feelings. I mean Dr. Logan. No man esteems him more than I do, but he was the true instigator of the late divisions in the county, and I am afraid it may yet come to an unpleasant issue. I have kept his name out of View, but I had written evidence of his being the cause of the dissention; the consequences if not thwarted might have been fatal throughout the State.

The jealousy among the principal republicans here requires a most vigilant attention. Unfortunately while I am endeavoring to check it,

I am exciting the ill will of men whom I love, merely because I do not suffer myself to be led aside from a great public interest to the views of one or another individual.

The following is an outline of our leading men's dispossitions towards each other—and these five may be said to hold the principal weight

1 Mr. Dallas—	offended with 2, unreservedly opposed to 4,—cold to 3 & 5
2 Dr Logan—	violently hostile to 1; Do. 3 & 5; good understanding with 4
3 Dr Leib—	Hostile to 2;—familiar with 1 & 4; common cause with 5.
4 Mr Cox—	Estranged but willing to be friends with 1; friends with 2; familiar and friendly with 3 and 5
5 Mr Muhlenburg—	Friendly with all—but displeased with 2; and rather distant than familiar with 4

I am sorry to say that no actual cause of *jealousy* exists with foundation between them, but what is *wholly political*. Each of them in one way or another considers his neighbor a rival!—And the loss of any one of them would be to us a very serious evil. The Judiciary business had nearly destroyed Mr. Dallas, the late Address has I think removed a great portion of the odium of that measure. Dr. Logan looks to the governmental chair at the next election; but I fear his attacks upon Mr *Dallas* and Dr *Leib*, will shut him out from every hope of that kind. Indeed No. 1, 3 & 4. are the truly efficient men with us. Dr. Logan without the aid of the rest could do nothing; Mr Muhlenburg by his strength of character & influence among the Germans possess a great weight—and this Leib shares with him; but Mr Dallas and Mr. Coxe who are the most capable men as writers, possess severally a great influence in the city & county—It were much to be wished they could be reconciled; for obvious reasons. The next two years will require all our strength of talents and activity—and Mr Burr I make no doubt is laboring to assail every man's passions who he may conceive of weight, or likely to go into the erection of a third party—

From the rising young men we have not much to expect; Mr Dickerson is the only one who is decidedly republican that displays talents. In the late County discussions he has been silent, knowing the interest wh[ich] his friend Dr Logan took in the affair. Young Mr. Sergeant the Commissioner of Bankrupts, associates wholly with the hostile party and barely says he is a republican; he possesses talents, but they are of no public use, but in his law pursuits; young Richard Bache (Benjns. younger brother) possesses talents but he is yet a student with Mr Dallas; there are about four other young men lawyers who do not display any capacity for public affairs. The Value of such men as Mr Dallas & Mr Coxe, and Mr Dickerson is not to be lightly estimated, considering that all the lawyers at the bar here are men of much weight as members of society & property and as they threaten to bring out unprecedented efforts against the next presidential election.

Sitgreaves will not succeed in Montgomery:—*Conrad* a stupid intriguing mercenary of no sound political principle will be the member—to the exclusion of a man of worth and talents, Mr Boileau. However Conrad cannot do harm.

I had written some time since a very long letter soliciting some hints to enable me to repel the monstrous calumnies of a wretch that deserves Not to be named—I was fearful of sending it directly—and delayed it until I gladly perceived the public resentment was roused against the Calumniator—Should there be any facts which may be used to throw the villainous aspersions into a still more odious light, I should wish to have them—I however propose about the close of this month to go to Washington City to look after my business there, as I find my clerk has been ill and the office wholly unemployed.

The adverse party here now say they mean to give up further contest, and to look on until they find us so effectually divided as to be enabled to step in and decide by joining the party which will enter into their views. This was expressed by *Jacob Shoemaker* an influential Quaker in Philadelphia who acted as one of the Inspectors of the Election.

I am, Sir, with the greatest respect your obliged & faithful Sert

WM DUANE

RC (DLC); torn; endorsed by TJ as received 21 Oct. and so recorded in SJL.

YOUR LETTER: TJ to Duane, 10 Oct. INSTRUCTIONS CONCERNING THE BOOKS FROM LONDON AND PARIS: TJ to Duane, 16 July.

UNHAPPY MISUNDERSTANDINGS: see Thomas Leiper to TJ, 19 and 22 Sep.

For Alexander J. Dallas's opposition to repeal of the JUDICIARY act, see Leiper to TJ, 26 Aug. His ADDRESS to Pennsylvania Republicans appeared in the *Aurora* of 27 Sep.

Samuel SITGREAVES, a Federalist and former congressman, attempted to take advantage of a split in Democratic-Republican ranks in Pennsylvania's second congressional district, which included the counties of MONTGOMERY, Bucks, Northampton, Wayne, and Luzerne. A meeting of Republicans held in Northampton had nominated Frederick CONRAD of Montgomery to be one of the district's three representatives, drawing spirited opposition from Montgomery Republicans who preferred Nathaniel B. BOILEAU and considered Conrad's selection a product of political intrigue and barter. Boileau received over 1,500 votes but did not draw enough support away from Conrad to enable Sitgreaves's election (Philadelphia *Aurora*, 9 and 28 Sep., 16 and 27 Oct.; Higginbotham, *Pennsylvania Politics*, 46-7).

WRETCH: presumably James T. Callender.

To Mary Jefferson Eppes

MY DEAR MARIA   Washington Oct. 18. 1802.

I have been expecting by every post to learn from yourself or your sister when I might send to meet you. I still expect it daily. in the mean time I have sent to mr Randolph, who I understand is to be your conductor, money for the expences of the road, so that that may occasion no delay.   the indisposition mentd in my letter by Davy Bowles turned out to be rheumatic: it confined me to the house some days, but is now nearly gone off. I have been able to ride out daily for a week past. the hour of the post leaves me time to add only assurances of my constant & tender love to you; and to pray you to tender my best affections to mr Eppes when he returns.

TH: JEFFERSON

PrC (CSmH); at foot of text: "Mrs. Eppes"; endorsed by TJ in ink on verso.

MY LETTER BY DAVY BOWLES: TJ to Mary Jefferson Eppes, 7 Oct.

To Nathaniel Macon

DEAR SIR   Washington Oct. 18. 1802.

I think the gentlemen of Congress from your state undertook on their return home to recommend to me proper persons as Commissioners of bankruptcy for the state. not having recieved any recommendation, I take the liberty of asking you to name either from your own knolege, or on such information as you can, four persons who may be proper for that appointment. it would be desireable there should be two lawyers & two merchants; but one of each description at least will be indispensable; and all republicans if to be had. if there be but one set, I presume Newbern is the most central position for them. but perhaps Wilmington & Edenton, may be too distant from it, and may require commissioners of their own. if so, 4 persons for each of the three places will be necessary. Accept assurances of my sincere esteem & respect.   TH: JEFFERSON

RC (O. O. Fisher, Detroit, Michigan, 1950); addressed: "The honble

Nathaniel Macon Speaker of the H. of R. of the US. Warrenton"; franked and postmarked. PrC (DLC); endorsed by TJ in ink on verso. TJ recorded this letter in SJL and connected it by a brace with letters on the same date to Abraham Baldwin, James Jackson, John Milledge, William Cocke, Joseph Anderson, and William Dickson (all of which are missing) with the notation "Commrs. bkrptcy."

For the COMMISSIONERS OF BANK-RUPTCY appointed for North Carolina, see Vol. 37: Appendix II, List 2.

Memorandum to James Madison

Commissioners of bankruptcy Vermont.
√ Saml. Prentiss
√ Darius Chipman
√ Richard Skinner.
√ Mark Richards
√ Reuben Atwater
√ James Elliot
√ Oliver Gallop
Commissions to be made out

TH: JEFFERSON
[...] 1802.

Also a Commission for Robert [Elliott Coc]ockran to be Marshal of S. Carolina vice Charles B. Cockran resigned　　TH:J.

RC (ViU); torn; dated on or before 18 Oct. from list of Commissions in Lb in DNA: RG 59, MPTPC and Madison, *Papers* (see below); addressed: "The Secretary of State." Not recorded in SJL.

COMMISSIONERS OF BANKRUPTCY VERMONT: see Stephen R. Bradley to TJ, 13 Sep., for the recommendations of the seven candidates. Madison wrote the appointees on 18 Oct. and enclosed their commissions. DARIUS CHIPMAN returned his to the secretary of state on 6 Dec. 1802, explaining that if he accepted it he would have to resign a state appointment "of some consequence" because Vermont law forbade holding both federal and state appointments (RC in DNA: RG 59, LAR, endorsed by TJ: "Chipman Darius to mr Madison resigns as Commr. bkrptcy Seymour Horatio of Middlebury recommended by Israel Smith"; Madison, *Papers, Sec. of State Ser.*, 4:31). JAMES ELLIOT resigned his commission after

being elected to Congress. He wrote Madison on 25 Mch. 1803 and recommended Samuel Elliot, his brother, as his successor (RC in DNA: RG 59, LAR; endorsed by TJ: "Elliot James to mr Madison. resigns as Commr. bkrptcy Elliot Samuel to succeed him").
MARSHAL OF S. CAROLINA: when Charles B. Cochran submitted his resignation to Madison on 4 Oct., he recommended his brother for the position. About the same time, Robert E. Cochran wrote Madison requesting the appointment and enclosing a certificate testifying to his ability to carry out the duties of the office (RC in DNA: RG 59, LAR, undated, endorsed by TJ: "Cockran, Robert Elliott. to mr Madison to be Marshal S. Carola v. Charles B. Cockran resigned"; Madison, *Papers, Sec. of State Ser.*, 3:609). For descriptions of Charles B. Cochran as marshal and efforts early in TJ's administration to have him removed, see Vol. 33:331-3, 513, 657-8.

From Joseph Parsons

Washington City October 18th 1802

After the kind interference on your part which occasioned my release from A Loathsome Prison, I vainly flattered myself with the hope that I should have no further ocation to trouble you on the same subject again, but the Injury I sustained by an unjustifyable out-rage, has been far greater than I was aware of, I find myself incapacitated from following my usual employment, of cours am destitute and friendless in A strange part of the Country and no relation or friends nearer than New Hampshire Having lost my Birth, as Yeoman of the Gun Room, on Board of the United States Frigate Jno. Adams, in which was engaged me by Capt. Tingey previous to my imprisonment To whome I appeal for the truth of my ascertion I have also in my possession The Testimony of Mr. S. Smallwood Cleark of the Navey Yard of my Industry Honesty and Soberness while engaged near twelve months in the service of the United States. Also another Testimoney of Mr. Richard Charles whome I Boarded with five months and acquainted with near one year. — But I am unable to persue my usual labourous occupation & am of course unable to provide in the usual Way for myself & family I am therefore compelled to state these circumstances for your considerations in hopes that their may be within your knowledge some small post obtained which will afford some relief, at least for the present, till A return of my health and Strength, — I Well know the important duties, in which your Excellency is daily imployed, will have little time for attention to claims simular to mine, yet I am equally persuaded that you bestow A proportion of your care on all those objects which come under your notice, however trivial in the eyes of most people Under the impression that I shall so soon as your time and convenciency will permit, & receive attention to this. —

I respectfully Remain your Much Obliged Humble Servent

JOSEPH PARSONS

RC (DLC); at head of text: "To His Excellency Thomas Jefferson Esqre. President of the United States"; endorsed by TJ as received 20 Oct. and so recorded in SJL.

KIND INTERFERENCE ON YOUR PART: see Parsons to TJ, 10, 12 Oct.

To Martha Jefferson Randolph

My dear Martha   Washington Oct. 18. 1802.

I have been expecting by every post to learn from you when I might send on to meet you. I still expect it daily. in the mean time I inclose you 100. Dol. for the expences of yourself, Maria & all your party. mr Randolph would do well to exchange the bills for gold & silver which will be more readily [...] on the road. the indisposition I mentioned in my letter by Bowles turned out to be rheumatic. it confined me to the house some days, but is now nearly gone off so that I ride out daily. the hour of the post obliges me to conclude here with my affectionate attachment to mr Randolph & tender love to yourself & the children.   Th: Jefferson

PrC (CSmH); blurred; at foot of text: "Mrs. Randolph"; endorsed by TJ in ink on verso. Enclosure: see TJ to John Barnes of this date.

LETTER BY BOWLES: TJ to Martha Jefferson Randolph, 7 Oct.

To William Short

Oct. 18. 1802.

Th: Jefferson with his friendly salutations to mr Short sends him by his servant the bundle of papers relative to his affairs which Th:J. had kept with him at the seat of government, because they have been written or recieved there. this with the bundle communicated to him at Monticello contains every thing relative to mr Short's affairs which are in the hands of Th:J. in this bundle particularly are the assignment of the decree by E. Randolph to mr Short, a mortgage from Th:J. to mr Short, and all the original certificates of the stock of mr Short which were not delivered at Monticello. of the certificates of stock delivered at Monticello & those now sent in the bundle, Th:J. will thank mr Short for a list by way of Voucher of the delivery in the event of mr Short's death, in which case Th:J. might be called on for proofs of the delivery.—the two last of the letters of Th:J. to mr Short he could not have recieved before he left France.

RC (DLC: Short Papers); endorsed by Short as received at Georgetown on 18 Oct.

While Short was at Georgetown in October and November, he asked Gallatin and Madison if his salary claim against the State Department could be separated from the government's suit against Edmund RANDOLPH and settled on its own merits. He also volunteered to accept the surety that Randolph had offered him, not in expectation that he would receive payment from Randolph, but as a means of securing that part of the government's claim against the former secretary of state. Gallatin and Madison agreed that Short's claim should be paid, and Madison authorized the payment to include not only salary, but also diplomatic outfits, travel expenses, and interest. As part of the payment, in November the Treasury Department transferred to Short 28 shares of eight percent stock, worth a total of $2,800, that had been subscribed at Timothy Pickering's direction in the expectation that it would ultimately go to Short (Gallatin to Short, 28 Oct., Gallatin to Richard Harrison, 10 Nov., and Short's list of stock certificates, 16 Apr. 1803, in DLC: Short Papers; Madison, *Papers, Sec. of State Ser.*, 4:37, 82-3, 86-7, 105-7, 108, 133).

TJ had drawn up a MORTGAGE on his Bedford County lands in 1800 to cover the money he owed Short (Vol. 31:503).

According to a memorandum Short made for his files, the CERTIFICATES that TJ conveyed to him in October 1802 were for "stock which stood in my name on the books at Washington." The value of the certificates was $11,256.63 in three percent stock; $15,324.18 in "old" six percent stock; $6,000 in deferred stock; and $5,700 in eight percent stock. Short gave TJ a receipt for the certificates, at Georgetown on 20 Oct. (list of stock certificates, 16 Apr. 1803, in DLC: Short Papers).

TWO LAST OF THE LETTERS: probably TJ to Short, 16 and 19 July.

Memorandum from the State Department

[on or before 18 Oct. 1802]
Memorandum for the President.

Peter Muhlenberg,	Collector of the Customs for the District of Pennsa. Commn. dated	28 July 1802
William R. Lee,	Collector for Salem & Beverly	31 July —
Daniel Bissell,	Do. for Massac	11 Augt.
Do. Do.	Inspector of the Revenue for Do.	11th
Joseph Farley Jr.	Collector for the District of Waldoborough	} 25 Augt.
Do. Do.	Inspector of the Revenue for Do.	
John Gibaut,	Collector for Gloucester	25 Augt.
George Wentworth,	Inspector of the Revenue for Portsmouth	} 25 Augt.
Do. Do.	Surveyor for the same	
Joseph Wilson,	Collector for the District of Marblehead	} 25 Augt.
Do. Do.	Inspector for the port of Marblehead	
Ralph Cross,	Collector for Newburyport	25 Augt.
Abraham Bloodgood,	Surveyor for the Port of Albany	} 28 Augt.
Do. Do.	Inspector for Do.	
<Tench Coxe Supervisor of the Revenue for the District of Pennsa.>		
John Shore,	Collector for Petersburg	6 Sept.

<*William Carey, Do. for Yorktown Virga. 20 Sept.*>   (declind to accept)[1]

Thomas Archer,	Collector for Yorktown	11 Octr.
Do. Do.	Inspector of the Revenue for Do.	11th.
Robert Anderson	Collector for the District of Louisville	
New,	Dated	11th Octr.
Robert Anderson	Inspector of the Revenue for the port	
New,	of Louisville	11th Octr.

Joseph Wood[2]   Register of the Land office at Marietta—26 Augt.

William Cleveland   ⎤   Commissioners of Bankruptcy for Salem in the

——   Killam   ⎬   District of Massacts.—The two first are dated the

Joseph Story[3]   ⎦   27 Augt. 1802 the latter 13th Sept.

Tench Coxe, Supervisor of the Revenue for the District of Pennsa. July 28. 1802.

John Selman, Commr on Symme's land Claims (permanent) Augt.

Note—Thomas Munroes Commn is dated June 2d. 1802 (permanent).

RC (DLC); undated; in a clerk's hand, with last three entries in Daniel Brent's hand; with two emendations, probably by TJ (see notes below); endorsed by TJ as received from the State Department on 18 Oct. and "Commissions issued 1802 July 28.—Oct. 11."

TJ probably requested the State Department to provide him with a list of the commissions issued while he was away at Monticello. He recorded neither the request nor the receipt of this list in SJL.

TJ probably used this list to aid in compiling his chronological list of appointments (see Appendix 1). One discrepancy with that list is TJ's entry of JOSEPH WOOD at 1 Aug., not the 26th as above.

[1] Closing parenthesis supplied by Editors.

[2] A horizontal stroke was later drawn through this name.

[3] A diagonal stroke was drawn through the preceding three names.

To John Barnes

Th: Jefferson will be obliged to mr Barnes for 20. Dollars in five dollar bills.   Oct. 19. 1802.

RC (ViU: Edgehill-Randolph Papers); addressed: "Mr Barnes"; endorsed by Barnes; endorsed by TJ: "Barnes John."

According to TJ's financial memoran-

da, on 19 Oct. Barnes sent $15 to the president, who also gave $10 in charity on the same day. The following day, TJ made two additional charitable gifts of $5 each (MB, 2:1084).

From William Barry,
with Jefferson's Note

[19 Oct. 1802]

A second application For the Expultion of William W. Burrows as before Stated—Lieutt. Colo. Commg. Marines For His Tyrannical Treatmt to a Certain Wm. Barry, on the 15th. August 1802 It being as before Stated to your Excellency Contrary to the Rules and Regulations Concerning the Marine Corps therefore Hope your Honour will as before Stated Banish the aforesaid Wm. W. Burrows out of the Service of the U. States—which Ought to uv been dun Long ago—if your Excellency [...] [require shall?] Consider it a grievance therefore Hope and pray as before Stated as a Child petitiong to His Father that you will grant the Petitioners Request I Remain Honoured Sir, your Servt. to Commd.   WM. BARRY

[*Note by TJ:*]
he was sentenced by a court Martial duly

RC (DLC); top of sheet clipped; at head of text: "To His Excellency Thos. Jefferson Esqr." Recorded in SJL as a letter of 19 Oct. 1802 received from Washington on 21 Oct. Enclosed in TJ to Robert Smith, 22 Oct.

A SECOND APPLICATION: see Barry to TJ, 5 Oct.

From Isaac Dayton

SIR/   Hudson Octr. 19th. 1802

Having understood that a representation has been or is about, to be forwarded to your Excellency upon the subject of removing the Collector & Surveyor of this port, I take the liberty to remind you of the recommendations now in your hands in my favour. Having been honourd with the appointment of Collector of the internal revenue on the dismission of mr. Ten Broeck from that office for delinquency, & haveing exersised that Office but a few months, I hope it will not be deemed, presumptuous in me, to sollicet the Office of Collector, in case that office be vacated; should only the office of surveyor be vacated, I then ask for that appointment.
I considered it superfluous to trouble your Excellency with any further recommendations.

With the highest respect & esteem for Your Character I am Your Excellency's Obedt. Servt.   ISAAC DAYTON

RC (DNA: RG 59, LAR); at foot of text: "His Excellency Thomas Jefferson Esquire"; endorsed by TJ as received 24 Oct. and "to be Collector & Surveyor of Hudson vice   " and so recorded in SJL.

Isaac Dayton (ca. 1753-1825) resided in Hudson, New York. A native of Rhode Island, he had family connections to Elisha and Thomas Jenkins. In 1810, Dayton was the master of a merchant brig (Hudson *Northern Whig,* 4 Apr. 1809; New York *Columbian,* 12 June 1810; Providence *Rhode-Island American,* 22 Mch. 1825).

REPRESENTATION: Thomas Jenkins, Ambrose Spencer, and Alexander Coffin to TJ, 16 Oct.

For the RECOMMENDATIONS that Dayton took to Washington a few months earlier, see Thomas Jenkins to TJ, 7 July.

In March 1803, TJ removed John C. TEN BROECK as surveyor and inspector of customs at Hudson and appointed Dayton in his place. Dayton had previously succeeded Ten Broeck as collector of internal revenue. Federalists declared that the only reason for Ten Broeck's dismissal from the customs position was politics, the replacement of a Federalist with a Republican. The Hudson *Balance* called Dayton "the most contemptible of beings" and declared that "no man could be more unfit or undeserving, the office of surveyor and inspector." The *Bee* countered by saying that Ten Broeck had deficiencies in his accounts and lost the job "by his own conduct." Dayton, the Republican paper declared, "paid every farthing of his dues" when his internal revenue collectorship ended. In his record of appointments, TJ classified Ten Broeck's

removal among those necessary "for Misconduct or delinquency," and next to Ten Broeck's name he noted "delinqt of old." The Senate approved Dayton's appointment as customs surveyor and inspector of the port on 3 Mch. 1803 (Hudson *Balance, and Columbian Repository,* 22 Mch. 1803; Hudson *Bee,* 29 Mch. 1803; JEP, 1:447; Vol. 33:673; Thomas Jenkins to TJ, 7 July 1802; TJ to the Senate, 1 Mch. 1803).

SHOULD ONLY THE OFFICE OF SURVEYOR BE VACATED: on 12 Nov., Dayton wrote to Samuel Osgood to explain that a prior arrangement, under which Shubael Worth would be recommended for the customs collectorship and Dayton would be recommended for the surveyor's position, had been altered. Worth had "agreed cheerfully to accept the surveyors office, if the President thought fit to grant me the collectors office," Dayton wrote. He stated also that he and Worth had agreed on the change before Dayton visited Washington earlier in the year. Dayton asked Osgood to recommend him now for the collector's position. At the foot of Dayton's letter, Ambrose Spencer added a note to Osgood, also dated 12 Nov., stating that he was present at the conversation in which Worth said that he would "confine his pretensions & application" to the surveyorship. Osgood, who had already written TJ on Dayton's behalf, did not write again, but passed along Dayton's letter with Spencer's note, which came into TJ's hands (RC in DNA: RG 59, LAR, endorsed by TJ: "Dayton Isaac to Saml Osgood to be Collector" and "Worth Shubael to be Surveyor," with the latter endorsement canceled; Thomas Jenkins to TJ, 7 July).

From Albert Gallatin

DEAR SIR   [19 Oct. 1802]

I enclose two recommendations for the office of *inspector* at Smithfield—it should be "*surveyor*".

I also enclose as a favorable specimen of Mr Kilty's official abilities, his report on & analysis of the laws concerning stills; a subject so complex that not one officer of the Treasury understood it well, or had any correct ideas of the proper amendments to be introduced in case the law had continued to exist. I might add to this, every official report he makes to this department: notwithstanding the complexity & difficulties attending the execution of the laws laying internal taxes, he preserved his district in perfect good order. I have mislaid a paper he communicated in relation to the suppression of the inspectors, but recollect that the report I made to you was in a great degree grounded in the opinion Mr. K. had given. His report on the extra-commissions to excise officers will in a few days be acted upon & the results officially communicated to you; as it is shorter than the other paper it is also enclosed.   My *personal* predilections would be for David Stone and Clay; but, although I think them both in many respects superior to Mr Kilty, he is the only person whom I may mention with perfect confidence that he will fulfill the official duties with activity & correctness. The reason why he is the only one is owing to my not having any means of information but what arises from correspondence with the revenue officers in the customs & in the internal taxes dept.—Of all these he is in my opinion the first. The arrangement which I would like best, would be either to have a new additional Auditor, or that Mr Harrison should be removed; for if we had two places to give, we might take talents of different kinds & distribute them properly; but with such an Auditor as Mr Harrison, it is of the highest importance that the other man should be unquestionably what is called a man of business. I wish we had some means of ascertaining the precise rate & species of talents of Clay; he is certainly a good accountant, but with the correctness of his judgment, his method & arrangement in doing business &a. I am totally unacquaintted.

With great respect & attachment Your obedt. Servt.

ALBERT GALLATIN

RC (DLC); undated; at foot of text: "Mr Jefferson"; endorsed by TJ as received from the Treasury Department on 19 Oct. and "Comptroller" and so recorded in SJL. Enclosures not found.

OFFICIAL ABILITIES: John Kilty, considered by Gallatin as a candidate for comptroller of the Treasury, was born in London, England, and received part of his education in France. He had settled in Maryland by 1771, while still a minor, and served with the Maryland forces during the Revolutionary War. In 1795, he became supervisor of the revenue for the district of Maryland, an office he held until late 1803 when he was appointed register of the land office for the Western Shore of Maryland. He wrote an account of the history and practices of the land office entitled *The Land-Holder's Assistant, and Land-Office Guide; Being an Exposition of Original Titles, as Derived from the Proprietary Government, and More*

Recently from the State, of Maryland, published in Baltimore in 1808 (Washington, Papers, Pres. Ser., 13:439-40n; Papenfuse, Maryland Legislature, 2:510;

Kilty, Land-Holder's Assistant, iii-iv, viii). REPORT I MADE TO YOU: see Gallatin's Report on Collection of Internal Revenues, 28 July 1801.

From Michael Leib

SIR,   Philadelphia Octr. 19th. 1802

I am applied to by a young man, Mr. Kuhn, to state to you his desire to be appointed Consul at Gibraltar—He is of a very respectable german family in this City, extensively connected with the german interest, and of sound democratic principles—His father is a merchant in large business, and is among the few here who were not to be intimidated from the maintenance of their principles by federal menaces or bank proscriptions—

Mr. Kuhn has established a mercantile house at Gibraltar, and seems to suppose, that a public function would enable him to transact business with more advantage, and as he is well deserving of it, permit me to recommend him—

Allow me, Sir, to congratulate you on the complete triumph of our cause in this City—We had a hard struggle; but it was crowned with the amplest success—Unusual efforts were made by the tories—They even marshaled their young men, who were made runners of to scour the wards, and be at the outposts—Each individual, on whom they had the smallest reliance, had a note sent him by a committee of vigilance, entreating him to attend the poll and to vote for the federal ticket; and to these unusual efforts were added the usual practise of slandering us in mass and in detail—Being defeated after such a mighty exertion they have fallen into a State of debility, from which, they confess, they cannot nor will not again rise, untill we begin "to cut each other's throats"—

Sitgreaves has not succeeded notwithstanding the divisions among our friends in that district—A letter from a friend of mine in that quarter gives me the agreeable information that the three democratic candidates are elected—So depreciated is federalism in Pennsylvania, that not a federalist will be returned to Congress—

The accounts from Jersey are not of so agreeable a complexion—If they are true, we have retrograded in that State; but as yet we have nothing definitive

You, Sir, are better acquainted with the State of things in the south—We have some apprehensions here that all is not right in that quarter, it would be a relief to us, therefore, to have them dissipated

With sentiments of sincere respect & esteem I am, Sir, Your fellow Citizen
M Leib

RC (DLC); addressed: "Thomas Jefferson Esqr. President of the U.S. Washington" and "Favd. by Mr. Kuhn"; endorsed by TJ as received 26 Oct. and so recorded in SJL, where it is connected by a brace with five other letters received on that date with the notation "Kuhn P. junr. to be Consul at Gibraltar" (see Peter Kuhn, Jr., to TJ, 5 Nov.).

THREE DEMOCRATIC CANDIDATES: Robert Brown, Frederick Conrad, and Isaac Van Horne were elected in Pennsylvania's second Congressional district (Michael J. Dubin, *United States Congressional Elections, 1788-1997: The Official Results of the Elections of the 1st through 105th Congresses* [Jefferson, N.C., 1998], 27).

From Pierre Jean Georges Cabanis

auteuil près paris Le 28 Vendémiaire
Monsieur Le président,   an 11 de La R. f.

je prends La Liberté de vous offrir un exemplaire d'un ouvrage que je viens de publier en france, et dont Le Sujet forme La Base de toutes Les Sciences morales. au milieu des importans objets qui vous occupent, je n'ose espérer que vous puissiez prendre Le tems de Lire deux gros volumes: mais j'espere que vous Recevrez avec Bienveillance, Cet hommage Bien Sincere de mon admiration & de mon Respect. je me flatte aussi que vous n'aurez pas oublié Les personnes qui ont eu Le Bonheur de vous voir chez La très Bonne made helvétius, & Chez Le Digne Docteur franklin. nous avons perdu made helvétius; & Le Cit. La Roche & moi, nous occupons sa maison, Legs d'autant plus touchant de Son amitié, que Ses Cendres reposent dans Son jardin. C'est là, Monsieur Le président, que j'ai eu L'avantage de vous voir quelques fois; C'est là, qu'après votre départ pour L'amérique, nous avons Si Souvent parlé de vous avec Cette vénérable amie. que tous Ces Souvenirs vous fassent Recevoir avec quelque intéret, L'hommage des Sentimens tendres et Respectueux que j'ai toujours eu pour vous, & que votre administration vraiment Républicaine me rend encor plus Chers.
Cabanis

EDITORS' TRANSLATION

Auteuil, near Paris, 28 Vendémiaire Year 11
Mister President,   of the French Republic [i.e. 20 Oct. 1802]

I am taking the liberty of sending you a copy of a work that I have just published in France and whose subject is the foundation of all the moral sciences. Amid the important topics that occupy you, I do not dare hope that you might take time to read two large volumes, but I hope you will accept, with good will, this very sincere sign of my admiration and respect. In addition, I flatter myself in thinking that you have not forgotten those who had the pleasure of seeing you at the homes of dear Madame Helvétius and the worthy Doctor Franklin. We have lost Madame Helvétius; Citizen La Roche and I take care of the house, a legacy of her friendship that is all the more touching because her ashes rest in the garden. That is where I sometimes had the privilege of seeing you, Mister President. That is where this venerable friend and I often talked about you, after your departure for America. May all these memories inspire you to accept with some interest the gift of warm and respectful sentiments that I have always had for you and that your truly republican government renders all the dearer to me.   CABANIS

RC (DLC); at head of text: "À Mr. Thomas jefferson président des états unis d'amérique"; endorsed by TJ (damaged). Recorded in SJL as received 13 May 1803.

Pierre Jean Georges Cabanis (1757-1808), a physician and professor, wrote on medicine, public health, medical education, and philosophy. Writing to Charles Willson Peale on 13 Mch. 1808, TJ described Cabanis as the premier physician in France and the author of that country's best works on medical topics. Before studying medicine, Cabanis was a student poet and secretary to a Polish bishop of noble birth. In the 1780s, he joined the salon of writers and thinkers, including Volney and Condorcet, that Anne Catherine de Ligneville Helvétius sponsored at Auteuil, outside Paris. He responded to the French Revolution with enthusiasm, but fell under suspicion during its most violent period. When Condorcet could not evade execution in 1794, Cabanis helped the mathematician and philosopher arrange his affairs and furnished the poison that Condorcet used to take his own life. The National Institute elected Cabanis a member in December 1795, in the category of moral and political sciences. In 1798, he became a deputy in the Council of Five Hundred. He may have taken part in the planning of the Brumaire coup in 1799, and he certainly promoted the constitutional changes that put Bonaparte into power as first consul. Cabanis promptly became a member of

the *Sénat*. In the Institute, however, he had become affiliated with the *idéologistes* or *idéologues*, and like them he became alienated from Bonaparte's regime beginning in 1802. On 13 July 1803, writing to Cabanis in reply to the letter printed above, TJ recalled the circle of friends that used to gather in the "delicious" village of Auteuil in the period before the French Revolution: "in those days how sanguine we were!" (*Dictionnaire*, 7:752-3; Tulard, *Dictionnaire Napoléon*, 316-17; DSB; Amable Charles, Comte de Franqueville, *Le premier siècle de l'Institut de France, 25 Octobre 1795-25 Octobre 1895*, 2 vols. [Paris, 1895-96], 1:120; Vol. 34:439, 441; Vol. 36:481n).

UN OUVRAGE: Cabanis's *Rapports du physique et du moral de l'homme*, first published in Paris in a two-volume edition in 1802. The book, which was a compilation of a dozen scientific papers that Cabanis wrote in the 1790s, discussed the interrelationship of physiology, environment, and moral philosophy. TJ, impressed by Cabanis's treatment of the problem of mind and body, later commended the book to Thomas Cooper, John Adams, and Lafayette (Sowerby, No. 1246; DSB). See also the second letter of Robert R. Livingston at 28 Oct. and the first one from Lafayette at 1 Nov.

The Abbé Martin Lefebvre de LA ROCHE had lived in a pavilion on the grounds of Madame Helvétius's estate at Auteuil for a number of years (Franklin, *Papers*, 27:590).

From John Drayton

SIR   Charleston Octr: 20th: 1802.

On the 12th: September, I had the honor of writing to you, respecting information received of an intended landing, of the French incendiary negroes, on coasts of the Southern States of this Union; from on board the French frigates, which were at New York.

Since that time, a false alarm has been given on Waccamaw neck, in the North Eastern part of this State; which occasioned the marching of troops towards the sea coast. As this news, will no doubt reach you, & may be mistated, I transmit you herewith a report of the same; as taken from the orderly book of Brigadier General Peter Horry, who commands in that part of the State.

With sentiments of high consideration I have the honor to be Sir Yr. most ob   JOHN DRAYTON

RC (PHi: Daniel Parker Papers); at foot of text: "Thomas Jefferson Esq. President of the United States of America"; endorsed by TJ as received 28 Oct. Enclosure: "Statement from Govr. Drayton S. Carolina, relative to the landing of French Negroes, &c," 20 Oct. 1802, certified by Daniel Huger, private secretary to the governor, that the annexed papers are true copies taken from the orderly book of the Twenty-Fifth Regiment of the Sixth Brigade; according to General Peter Horry's account, during the afternoon of 10 Oct. Captain Paul Michau delivered Horry a report by Sergeant John Brown, which asserted that "people of colour" were landing on Long Bay near the house of Ensign Peter Nicholson; informed by his officers that Sergeant Brown was of good character and that his report could be trusted, Horry issued an alarm and sent orders mobilizing his militia and directing a battalion toward the coast to "oppose with force of arms" the alleged invasion; the next day, while proceeding up Waccamaw neck with his military escort, Horry was informed by Benjamin Allston, Sr., that "the alarm given was a false one"; Horry questioned Captain Joshua Ward, who denied any fault in the matter, about the false alarm; Horry remained adamant that the officer responsible should be punished, deeming it "shameful, to sport with the feelings of so many men now on their march; & to occasion distress to their families"; Horry placed Ward under arrest and then questioned Sergeant Brown, who admitted his error and explained that he received his information from his brother, Sergeant Percival Pawley; after reviewing the communications in the affair, Horry was "now better satisfied" with Ward's conduct and released the officer from arrest; Horry then left Allston's house, gave orders demobilizing his brigade, and returned to Georgetown; Drayton also included copies of several militia communications, including Ward to Horry, 12 Oct., requesting a court of inquiry into his conduct; a summons by Ward to Pawley, dated midnight, 9 Oct., ordering Sergeants Pawley and Brown to call their men and have them "armed & accoutred, & ready to act on the defense"; Ensign Peter Nicholson to Ward, dated "past 9 oClock at night," 9 Oct., reporting that he had taken into custody "a black french Creole, who can not give any account of himself," and given the "general report of danger" from the coast, "I fear has come up to my house, to see what reception he will meet with; while his companions are lying in ambush. He is dressed with a sailor's jacket, & his undercloths are now wet"; Nicholson will keep him under guard, "fearing his Companions if any may attempt a rescue," and sends his re-

[526]

port to Ward by express, "so that no delay may take place & that as much as possible we may be prepared for the worst"; Ward to Horry, 11 Oct., enclosing copies of Nicholson's letter and Ward's summons of 9 Oct., and explaining that he had been following Horry's recent directions to keep his company ready and maintain "a watchful eye on the sea board; apprehending the landing of french negroes from on board frigate"; Ward deemed it unnecessary to forward Nicholson's report, and was therefore surprised to discover that word of the affair had reached Horry at Georgetown and that "a considerable part of your Brigade have, & are about to march to Long Bay"; Ward enclosed copies of Nicholson's report and his own summons to Pawley in order to prove "my reason for calling out my company; & the mode by which, they were summoned"; Ward referred Horry to Sergeant Brown for additional information, who would also deliver to him "the negro taken by Mr. Nicholson, subject to

your future order: whom I expect you will judge of a very suspicious character" (printed in Howard A. Ohline, "Georgetown, South Carolina: Racial Anxieties and Militant Behavior, 1802," *South Carolina Historical Magazine*, 73 [1972], 130-40).

On 20 Oct., in the aftermath of the false alarm over the alleged LANDING, OF THE FRENCH INCENDIARY NEGROES in Georgetown District, South Carolina, Drayton issued orders thanking PETER HORRY and his militia brigade for their "prompt attention to orders received respecting a late threatened danger along the sea-coast." The governor observed that "Safety is best assured by alertness; and alarms serve to render the soldier more vigilant." South Carolina was prepared to defend itself, Drayton concluded, "and watches over the welfare of the people" (*National Intelligencer*, 17 Nov. 1802).

From John Rutledge, Jr.

SIR   New Port October 20th. 1802

Your name having been connected with the subject of this letter, will, I trust, be considered as some apology for the liberty I take in troubling you with it. Two letters dated in August 1801, signed N Geffroy, and addressed to you, have been published in one of the prints of this place, and charged upon me, on account, as it was said, of "the parity of hands": Persons desirous of comparing the hand writing of these letters with mine, were invited to examine the originals at the printing office. Many gentlemen of Carolina long in correspondence with me, & others well acquainted with my hand writing, were here at the time, & profiting of the printers invitation, called to examine these letters, & all of them declared their conviction of the writings not being mine.

As a great deal of the most foul and vulgar abuse had repeatedly been addressed to me in the same paper, many persons here thought I should discover an unbecoming condescension by noticing this ridiculous & anonymous attack; the desire however of checking it, impelled me to a publication, & to declare, on oath, that I had been

[527]

utterly ignorant of the transaction before reading the newspaper announcing it. It was to have been hoped that my solemn denial, supported by the oaths of every person here acquainted with my writing, would have destroyed this calumny: but the Author & Propagator of it, not discouraged by these circumstances, made a tour through this State, & into Massachusetts, and got a number of Persons, who knew nothing of me, who had never seen my writing, and many of whom (I am credibly informed) could neither read nor write, to swear they believed the letters in question were written by me. This contrivance not producing the desired effect, the postmaster, after a lapse of several weeks, was induced to swear that they were delivered by a girl saying she had lived with me, & saying also that I had sent her. His Son, less cautious, swore they were delivered by my Servant. I fortunately procured very ample & respectable countervailing testimony, which completely nullified the depositions of these officious postmasters. As it is probable, Sir, that the Papers of this place may not be received at Washington, I feel it a respect due to you (whose name has been used in this business as authorizing the publication of the letters) no less than to myself, to forward the enclosed documents disproving my having had any agency in the puerile and ridiculous transaction which malice & ignorance have ascribed to me.

Altho' the mere circumstance of my being a federalist would be quite sufficient, in this season of violent party spirit and jealousy, to make many persons believe, without examination, that I am capable of any thing infamous with which I might be charged in our licentious papers, yet, I feel persuaded, Sir, notwithstanding the declarations of your having authorized the publication of the letters signed Geffroy, that your mind is too much elevated above suspicion and credulity to have for a moment supposed me capable of the deception which has been attempted. Indeed, Sir, I should not have troubled you with this letter, nor taken the liberty of soliciting your perusal of the documents it encloses, were it not for the deposition of the postmaster, which is the only thing like proof of my agency in the folly with which I have been charged, and which is calculated to render impressive the calumnious tale where the infamous characters of the postmaster and his deputy are not known.

I have the honor to be Sir Your most obedient and humble Servant

JOHN RUTLEDGE

RC (DLC); endorsed by TJ as received 29 Oct. and so recorded in SJL. Enclosures not found, but see below.

For the TWO LETTERS received by TJ from Nicholas GEFFROY, dated 1 and 7 Aug. 1801, see Vol. 35:3-6. They were printed in the 18 Sep. 1802 edition of the Newport *Rhode-Island Republican*.

AUTHOR & PROPAGATOR OF IT: Christopher Ellery.

Depositions dated 5 Oct. 1802 by Newport POSTMASTER Jacob Richardson and HIS SON, assistant postmaster Jacob Richardson, Jr., appeared in the *Rhode-Island Republican* on 9 Oct. Both men testified that two letters addressed to the president were received by the Newport post office in early August 1801 "by a Girl, who said she lived with Mr. Rutledge," and that the letters appeared to be in Rutledge's hand, but disguised. The men made similar declarations in August 1801 to Christopher Ellery, who forwarded their testimonials to TJ (Vol. 35:156-7). In a 29 Aug. 1801 letter, the elder Richardson informed Washington publisher Samuel Harrison Smith of the mysterious letters to TJ. "I knew the hand writing," Richardson claimed, "& suspected they were anonymous Letters, as they were from one of the Presidents greatest enemies." Richardson also expressed his belief that the South Carolina congressman was "a bad man & I have thought so a long time, & I will never forgive him, for his Scheme of bringing in a third person for President," referring to Rutledge's support for Aaron Burr during the contested election of 1800. Richardson's letter was probably the enclosure mentioned in Smith's letter to TJ of 4 Oct. 1801 (RC in MHi; Robert K. Ratzlaff, "John Rutledge, Jr., South Carolina Federalist, 1766-1819" [Ph.D. diss., University of Kansas, 1975], 187-9; Vol. 35:387).

COUNTERVAILING TESTIMONY: the 19 Oct. edition of the *Newport Mercury*, the Federalist counterpart of the *Rhode-Island Republican*, contained testimonials by Cleland Kinloch of South Carolina and William Moore, Jr., Horace Senter, and Rhody Chappell of Newport, countering claims by the Richardsons that the Geffroy letters had been delivered to the Newport post office by a girl in Rutledge's employ. Rutledge compiled these and other articles from the *Mercury* in his defense into a pamphlet entitled *A Defence Against Calumny; Or, Haman, in the Shape of Christopher Ellery, Esq. Hung Upon His Own Gallows* (Newport, R.I., 1803; Shaw-Shoemaker, No. 4053).

From James Monroe

DEAR SIR   Richmond Octr. 21. 1802

There are two persons in this place who according to the information I have recd., have respectable claims to the office in question. The first of these is Jacob I. Cohen, a Jew but sound in his principles, of fair character & much employed in the business of the corporation. the other is Tarlton W. Pleasants, a brother of the clerk of the h. of Delegates, of equally fair character, and other respectable pretentions. I can give no name for Norfolk at present, but will as soon as I can.   I had some expectation of seing you the beginning of the next week, having proposed meeting Mr. Prevost at that time at the federal city or near it, who is so kind to come, take charge of and conduct my family to New York. But a late distressing event the death of my sister in Caroline will put it out of my power to proceed further than Fredbg., on acct. of the meeting of the council wh. is on friday in the next week. On my return I may be able to give a name for Norfolk. You will of course recollect to transmit me what the state of the affr. will permit relative to a provision of some place abroad to wh. to transport certain offenders.

with great respect & esteem yr. friend & servt

JAS. MONROE

RC (DNA: RG 59, LAR); endorsed by TJ as received 26 Oct. and so recorded in SJL with notation "T. W. Pleasants to be Commr. bkrptcy Richmd."

German immigrant JACOB I. COHEN settled in Richmond after the American Revolution and became one of the city's most prosperous businessmen. TARLTON W. PLEASANTS was the former copublisher of the Petersburg *Virginia Gazette*. His mercantile firm of Anthony & Pleasants had recently declared bankruptcy. Neither Cohen nor Pleasants received a commission from TJ (Myron Berman, *Richmond's Jewry, 1769-1976:*

Shabbat in Shockoe [Charlottesville, 1979], 1-11; Brigham, *American Newspapers*, 2:1134; Richmond *Virginia Argus*, 15 Sep., 9 Oct. 1802).

CLERK OF THE H. OF DELEGATES: James Pleasants (Vol. 36:577n).

John B. PREVOST, a stepson of Aaron Burr, was the former secretary to Monroe as minister to France (Madison, *Papers, Sec. of State Ser.*, 4:23; Vol. 33:309, 420).

MY SISTER: Elizabeth Monroe Buckner, wife of William Buckner of Mill Hill in Caroline County (Madison, *Papers, Pres. Ser.*, 5:361).

Notes on a Cabinet Meeting

1802.

Oct. 21. present the 4. Secretaries. 1. What force shall be left through the winter in the Mediterranean?

2. what negociations, what presents shall be proposed to Marocco?

Answ. 1. the two largest frigates, President & Chesapeake, the time of whose men is out in December, ought to be called home immediately.

the two last frigates, the N. York, and John Adams, which are smallest also, & the men engaged till Aug. next to remain through the winter, even if peace be made with Tripoli.

the Adams, whose times are up in April, to remain thro' the winter, or come away accdg to appearances with Marocco.

Answ. 2. forbid Simpson to stipulate any presents or paimts. at fixed periods. but allow him to go as far as 20,000 D. to obtain a firm establmt of the state of peace with Marocco.

Shall the expences of transporting our abandoned seamen home, by the Consul Lee, be paid by us, and out of what fund?

unanimously that it must be paid, & out of the contingent fund of 20,000. D.

MS (DLC: TJ Papers, 112:19297); entirely in TJ's hand; follows, on same sheet, Notes on a Cabinet Meeting of 18 Jan. 1802.

PRESIDENT & CHESAPEAKE: that is, the *Constellation* and the *Chesapeake*. The *President* had returned to the United States in the spring of 1802 under the command of Richard Dale. "I have it in charge from the President," Robert Smith wrote to Richard V. Morris on 23 Oct., to order the *Constellation* and *Chesapeake* back to the United States "without delay." The enlistments of the crew of the schooner *Enterprize* were to expire on 15 Feb., but Smith hoped that enough officers and crew would elect to extend their service to allow Morris to keep that vessel in the Mediterranean (NDBW, 2:115, 306-7).

ACCDG TO APPEARANCES WITH MAROCCO: Smith instructed Morris to send the *Adams* home if "our differences with Morocco" were resolved (same, 306).

Madison wrote to James SIMPSON on 21 Oct., authorizing the consul to draw funds from Morris. Simpson was not to expend more than $20,000, "nor to go as far as that sum, unless it shall produce a firm peace and an express or tacit relinquishment" of Morocco's demand for "presents at stated periods," which Madison called "another name only, for tribute." Simpson was to be "as sparing of expense" as possible, "both from a regard to œconomy, and to the policy of keeping down the hopes and pretensions of these mercenary powers" (Madison, *Papers, Sec. of State Ser.*, 4:38).

Regarding ABANDONED SEAMEN at Bordeaux, see Gallatin to TJ, 17 Aug.

CONTINGENT FUND: the 1802 appropriations act, passed on 1 May, allocated $20,000 for "defraying the contingent expenses of government" (U.S. Statutes at Large, 2:188).

From William Barton

SIR,   Lancaster, Oct. 22d. 1802.

Mr. Peter Kuhn, junr. having informed me of the object of his present journey to Washington, I pray that I may be permitted to add my testimony to that of some of my most esteemed friends, in his behalf.—

The father of Mr. Kuhn, and myself have been friends from our youth. He has been many years established at Philadelphia, as a prosperous and respectable Merchant; principally engaged in the trade of the Mediterranean coast of Spain. In his political opinions, he has long been distinguished as an uniform and a most decided Republican.—

My removal to this place, more than five years since, has deprived me of an opportunity of much personal acquaintance with Mr. Peter Kuhn, the younger. I find, however, that his private character is very well esteamed, by persons of great worth, among my friends: And my own occasional acquaintance with him, during my residence in Lancaster, has perfectly satisfied me of the rectitude of his political principles; as well as given me a favorable opinion of his general character. —

My brother, the Doctor, passed some time with us, here, on his return from Virginia—We were happy to find him much improved in his health, by the journey. —

With the sincerest wishes for your public and private prosperity, And the highest personal attachment and respect, I have the Honor to be, Dear Sir, Your most obedt. servt.   W. BARTON

RC (DNA: RG 59, LAR); at foot of text: "The President of the United States"; endorsed by TJ as received 26 Oct. and "Kuhn P. junr. to be Consul at Gibraltar" and so recorded in SJL.

Barton's BROTHER, Benjamin Smith Barton, traveled to Virginia in the sum-

mer to observe and collect samples of the local flora. During the trip he visited the president at Monticello (W. L. McAtee, "Journal of Benjamin Smith Barton on a Visit to Virginia, 1802," *Castanea: The Journal of the Southern Appalachian Botanical Club*, 3 [1938], 85-117).

To Thomas Mann Randolph

DEAR SIR   Washington Oct. 22.

Your's of the 16th. is recieved. there is nobody here who can give me any information of the law of S.C. Doctr. Tucker, the only person here from that state, having been too long from it to possess the information you wish. I have written for it to Genl. Sumpter at Statesborough, and think we may have an answer in three weeks from this time, which may be communicated to you by the middle of November. in the mean time should any South Carolinian of information pass through here, I shall not fail to make enquiry & communicate the result.

You say in your letter 'Martha has recovered compleatly.' it is the first notice I have that she has been unwell, your letter being the only scrip I have recieved from Edgehill or Monticello since I left home. I have been in daily expectation of recieving notice of the day on which you would set out for this place, that I might send horses, or horses & carriage to meet you at Strode's. The last day's journey from Brown's by Fairfax courthouse, tho' but of 30. miles is so dreadfully hilly, that no horses in the world, after having drawn for three days, would go through it without everlasting baulking. I would advise you by all means to engage Davy Bowles as far as Strode's or even to Elkrun church, as the road is so difficulte that nobody unacquainted can possibly find it. from Elkrun church the person I should send to meet you may be a safe guide. I must refer you to a former letter for the stages, distances & notes. mr Granger not being here, I am unable to tell you when the Georgia stage will begin to run. if I can in any way aid your views in Georgia, explain it freely, as nothing will gratify me more than to do so. believing that I cannot serve my family more solidly than by clearing the old debts hanging on us, I am straining every nerve to do it; and hope to accomplish it by the time my term of service expires. present my tender love to Martha & the children & accept yourself my affectionate attachment.   TH: JEFFERSON

RC (DLC); at foot of text: "T M Randolph"; endorsed by Randolph as received 10 Nov., but see Randolph to TJ, 29 Oct. PrC (MHi); endorsed by TJ in ink on verso.

WRITTEN FOR IT: TJ to Thomas Sumter, Sr., 22 Oct.

TJ had enclosed information on the STAGES of the journey between Randolph's estate at Edgehill and Washington in a letter of 3 June to Martha Jefferson Randolph.

To Robert Smith

Francis Mitchill of Richmond in Virginia has been recommended for a midshipman's place by Colo. John Harvie of that place and mr George Divers, gentlemen worthy of all confidence[1]. I saw him myself, & found from his own statement that he had proceeded in geometry as far as the 6. first books of Euclid.

William G. Stewart of Philadelphia applies for a place of midshipman. I am personally acquainted with him, but do not know the extent of his education. he is a young man of correct conduct, of an extraordinary mechanical genius good understanding[2], well disposed, and served in the Philadelphia in her previous cruize under Capt Decatur, and in her last cruize under Capt Barron as master's mate.

The Complaint of William Barry is referred to the Secretary of the Navy to enquire whether there has been any thing irregular in the proceedings against him.   TH: JEFFERSON
                                                          Oct. 22. 1802.

PrC (DLC). Recorded in SJL with notation "nominations." Enclosure: William Barry to TJ, 19 Oct.

[1] Preceding five words interlined.
[2] Preceding two words interlined.

To Thomas Sumter, Sr.

DEAR SIR   Washington Oct. 22. 1802.

My son in law Thos. M. Randolph has for some time contemplated the establishment of a cotton plantation in Georgia, and proposes to carry thither this fall some portion of his negroes. he has been informed that a law of S. Carolina against the importation of slaves, has been so construed as to prohibit even a citizen of the US. from an innocent passage thro' the country with his property in that form, and has written to me for information of the fact. but I find nobody here who can give me that information, which is the reason of my troubling you for it. an answer written without delay, will reach me in time for his purpose. he would willingly on entering the state give any security for passing the whole through the state in as few days as the length of road will admit: or to accept of a watch, appointed by the authorities of the state, to attend them through, his object being bona fide to establish them all on a plantation of his own in Georgia.

We are very hard pressed to extend the removals from office considerably in your state. it is against our inclination and we believe that except in the 3. or 4 middle states, removals dissatisfy more republicans than they gratify; and that the slow but effectual method of restoring equilibrium by filling vacancies as they happen, will effect justice in the end with the least disturbance to the tranquility of our country,[1] adding to these removals for delinquency, and for electioneering activity. I pray you to make up an opinion on this question, on the best information you can obtain, & when made up to communicate it to me. I will say to you *confidentially* that mr D'Oyley is the principal urger of this measure, and has carried his remonstrance so far as to express sentiments of very dubious aspect. a friend of his proposed him for the office of Collector of Charleston. the present incumbent is considered as a meritorious & punctual officer, who had indeed been very violent against the late change but promised an honest acquiescence under it, & I have never heard that he has broke his promise. Accept assurances of my affectionate esteem & high respect.   TH: JEFFERSON

PrC (MoSHi: Jefferson Papers); at foot of text: "General Sumpter"; endorsed by TJ in ink on verso.

A FRIEND OF HIS: Charles Pinckney had urged that Daniel D'Oyley be appointed collector at Charleston in place of James Simons (Vol. 33:331-3, 514n; Vol. 34:187). PROMISED AN HONEST ACQUIESCENCE: TJ received and kept a letter written by Simons at Charleston to Comptroller John Steele on 30 Sep. 1802. Noting that the general election was being held in South Carolina on 11 and 12 Oct., the Charleston collector observed: "I deem it proper to state to you as my friend, and I do so on my Sacred honor, that *I have not, nor will not*, take any part whatever, either directly, or indirectly, in it.—I have refused, and shall continue to refuse, all invitations to dine out, until the election is over." By attending to business and spending time with his family, Simons tried to shield himself from "sus- picion and calumny." By this strict con- duct, he confided, he would "put it out of the power of envy itself, to say any thing against me" (RC in DNA: RG 59, LAR; endorsed by TJ: "Simonds to mr Steele").

[1] Remainder of sentence interlined.

To Joseph Coppinger

Sɪʀ   Washington Oct. 23. 1802.

The invention mentioned in your letter of the 17th. inst is certainly of great importance to society. by turning to the act of Congress of Feb. 21. 1793. c. 11. you will have all the information it is in the power of any person to give you. the patent fees can be inclosed to the Treasurer, and the other papers to the Secretary of State, and the business be effectually done without your being at the expence of a journey here. the patent would of course be inclosed to you under such address as you shall desire.   Accept my best wishes & respects.   Tʜ: Jᴇꜰꜰᴇʀsᴏɴ

PrC (DLC); at foot of text: "Mr. Joseph Coppinger"; endorsed by TJ in ink on verso.

Aᴄᴛ ᴏꜰ ᴄᴏɴɢʀᴇss ᴏꜰ ꜰᴇʙ. 21. 1793: the patent law, "An act to promote the

progress of useful Arts; and to repeal the act heretofore made for that purpose," stipulated a $30 filing fee and required United States citizenship of the patentee (U.S. Statutes at Large, 1:318-23).

From J. P. P. Derieux

Mᴏɴsɪᴇᴜʀ   Charlotte ville ce 23. oct. 1802.

Etant actuellement sur mon chemin pour aller M'embarquer, et es- perant que vous etiés encore a Monticello; J'avois pris la liberté de m'y presenter pour avoir L'honneur de vous assurer de mes respects, et vous demander La grace de voulloir bien m'accorder un passe-port pour France, et un certifficat de ma résidence en Virginie depuis 1784. avec celui de mon caractere et des malheurs du feu qui m'ont réduits dans une trés grande indigence avec ma femme et huit en- fants; oserai-je prendre la liberté de vous supplier, Monsieur de voul- loir bien me faire la grace de me les adresser Chés Mr. George Jefferson Mercht a Richmond ou je serai dans peu de Jours.

La dépreciation extraordinaire dans la fortune de Mde. Bellanger, dont j'ai eté plus particulierement informé par mes dernieres lettres de France, presse encore davantage sur ma grande necessité d y aller moi même faire des exertions personnelles sans les quelles il est evident que je ne pourois esperer n'y de faire honneur a mes affaires ici, n'y donner aucune existance a mes enfants. Il m'en coute beaucoup de me séparer de ma famille dans un tems ou sa subsistance est si incertaine, mais les raisonements de Mde. DeRieux ont eté Si persuasifs, quils ont prevalus sur ma grande difficulté a la laisser dans une telle situation, et elle a préferé s'assujettir a touttes les peines de mon absence plutot que de vivre plus longtems dans des incertitudes qui font le malheur de ses jours. Elle est a 4. miles de Lewisburg dans Le County de Green brier avec nos huit Enfants sur une plantation Louée dont mes deux garçons ainés cultivent la terre.

J'ay L'honneur d'etre dans les sentiments du plus profond respect Monsieur Votre trés humble et trés obeissant se[rviteur]

JUSTIN PIERRE PLUMARD DE RIEUX

EDITORS' TRANSLATION

Sir   Charlottesville, 23 Oct. 1802

Being en route to embarkation, and hoping you were still at Monticello, I took the liberty of presenting myself there to have the honor of assuring you of my respect and to request that you grant me a passport for France and an attestation of my residence in Virginia since 1784, as well as of my character and of the misfortunes of fire which have reduced me to the greatest indigence, along with my wife and eight children. May I take the liberty of entreating you, Sir, to do me the favor of addressing it to Mr. George Jefferson, merchant in Richmond, where I shall be in a few days?

The extraordinary depreciation of Madame Bellanger's fortune, of which I have been specifically informed in my most recent letters from France, makes it all the more urgent for me to go in person to undertake the personal efforts without which it is clear that I could never hope to do justice to my business here or provide for my children. It is painful for me to leave my family at a time when their survival is so uncertain, but Madame Derieux's arguments were persuasive enough to overcome my great difficulty in leaving her in such a situation. She preferred to assume all the burdens of my absence rather than continue to live in the uncertainty that causes her daily unhappiness. She is four miles from Lewisburg in Greenbrier County with our eight children on a rented plantation, cultivated by my two eldest sons.

With my deepest respect, Sir, I have the honor of being your very humble and obedient servant.   JUSTIN PIERRE PLUMARD DE RIEUX

RC (DLC); torn; addressed: "Ths. Jefferson Esqr President of the U. States Washington City"; franked; postmarked 25 Oct.; endorsed by TJ as received 27 Oct. and so recorded in SJL.

MALHEURS DU FEU: in 1796, Derieux and his family lost all their possessions when an ordinary they occupied and ran as a "wet store" in Goochland County burned down. Derieux had previously encountered serious financial setbacks, and the fire left him without assets. TJ and others provided aid and set him up on a leased farm in western Virginia, but Derieux continued to struggle to make a living (Vol. 28:58-60, 370-1; Vol. 29:123, 125n, 141; Vol. 30:29; Vol. 31:544).

Derieux's aunt, Madame Plumard de BELLANGER, had died in France. When TJ called on her in 1787, she intended to make some provision for her nephew in her will, but she lost patience with him and stopped sending money in 1795. He received only a modest inheritance from her estate (Vol. 12:125-6; Vol. 19:603; Vol. 28:370-1; Vol. 29:164; Vol. 31:544, 545n; Madison, *Papers, Sec. of State Ser.,* 5:320).

MDE. DERIEUX: Derieux's wife, Maria Margarita Martin Derieux, was Philip Mazzei's stepdaughter (Vol. 31:545).

From "Friend"

SIR   Washington October 23rd 1802.

I am conscious that little attention on ordinary occasions are due to annonomous writers, yet the importance of the subject, aided by a belief that the writers name if known would add little (if any) weight to the Arguments proposed, induced the adoption of the present mode without the fear of incurring Censure, because I am sensible truth will never be disagreeable to you in whatever manner it shall be conveyed—If the subject should be deemed by you unworthy of your further Notice, I retain too exalted a sense of your character to believe any Name, however high on the list of fame would divert you from the Strict line of your duty.—Under these impressions I approach the Threshold of the organ of a Government, founded on the purest principles of Justice, an organ faithfull to the cause of humanity in general and the distressed in particular—I say Sir, I approach You in behalf of James McGurk now under the dreadfull sentence of death, in doing which, let me be permitted to believe that the subject is not one of the least which occupies daily your time and care, let me be permitted to hope that your decision on this important case will be favourable to humanity, finally let me be permitted to hope that the infliction of a sanguinary punishment will be averted.—Your penetration and sound Judgment, has I am persuaded long since taught you to contemn the savage Cruelty of Laws founded during the Ages of Gothic ignorance & barbarity, Laws which in this Age of reason and experience ought to be expunged from the Codes of Civilized nations—The Crime of which this unhappy man is convicted is confessedly of the first Magnitude, Murder, by the Most eminent civilians has long since been defined, to give a definition here, would be both superfluous and Presumptuous—I shall content myself, with merely stating facts, by which with the force of your own Judgment you will readily perceive that his crime has been mistaken.—from the Testimony of every Witness it appears that death was occasioned by a-buse and ill-treatment at various times yet from no one Witness nor from their Testimony Collectively can there be found a single circumstance which would lead to a belief that the death occasioned was intended, in his most unguarded moments, when rage had full and unrestrained controll of his mind, such a Wish or such an intention never escaped him—How widely different is a death thus occasioned from one premeditated and intended, the latter *alone* constitutes the Horrid Crime of Murder, the former assumes both in Law & equity a milder term, and it follows of course a different Punishment.—It is not denied but that punishment severe and exemplary is due to the offense, and it is by no means contended that his ignorance as to the extent and consequences of his cruelty should be plead in Justification.—yet I shall ever hold it absurd to say that his punishment ought to be equal to that inflicted for a Crime committed intentionally and with malice aforethought.—If therefore from any cause Whatever, it has been neglected by those whose duty it is to guard by equal Laws the rights of the Citizen & thereby has placed *him* who commits a Crime by accident, on the same footing with *him* who commits a Crime intentionally, the Organ of the Constitution wisely placed to correct errors of the kind, is doubly bound to prevent the evill, he is bound to interfere for the preservation of the injured rights of the Citizen, and he is equally bound to use his endeavours to cause the enacting of Laws more congenial to reason & Common sense, Laws in which crimes are recognised in their various grades and punishments prescribed adequate to their extent.—

It is not a novell thing to deny the right of any human authority to deprive a fellow creature of Life on any pretence whatever, the folly cruelty and injustice of such a measure, has by many able and wise men been often and fully proven, both from reason & its ablest co-adjutor Religion—nay so powerfull and unanswerable are the arguments in favour of the principle, that the most strenious advocates for sanguinary Punishments, have been obliged to excuse themselves for a continuation of the Horid practice, with alledging, that others are detered from the Commission of similar Offenses, this poor attempt at a Justification, like all others in support of any cause opposed to Humanity & sound reason, will be found futile and untenable.—for let me ask, does the frequent and sanguinary Punishments in Europe, lessen the number or limit the extended catalogue of Crimes? rather let me ask if they are not Multiplyed.—Permit me to claim for a moment your attention to the Penal Code of Pennsylvania, the

Mildness of which, was considered by some of the first characters of that State as the production of a few Visionary Philanthropists, and misguided Legislators, and for some time were treated as such, till at length reason dawned, and what was considered folly and Weakness after being submitted to a fair trial the wisest of her citizens, acknowledged with a Candor that will ever do them honor, their ignorance of human nature, they saw at once, that violent and oppressive Laws had numerous victims, and it was found to be a Melancholly truth, that the more sanguinary the punishments, the more numerous & attrocious were the Crimes.—Murders of the most agravated nature were committed in the streets of their most populous Cities, under the Rigid system—while similar crimes under their present code are scarcely known, and it is a fact which will be recorded to the praise of Pennsylvania in the fair page of faithfull history, that Ten Executions has not taken place in the whole state for Ten Years last past.—Ignorance alone will inquire the cause.—

After having thus far trespassed on your time, I hope you still have patience to travell with me onward to the point. After denying the Policy and proving the injustice and Cruelty of inflicting death for *any* Crime, after admitting the unhappy McGurk deserved punishment, let us see if his Sufferings already are to be disregarded, let us examine them and I am pursuaded little more if any thing is due to society— On the 15th. day of January last the unhappy man was committed to the Jail of this City—. Am I to expose to the World the situation of this place, am I to tell the Chief Magistrate of the United States what a confinement he has endured.—ye Religious, ye humane and benevolent inhabitants of Washington have ye subjected yourselves to the just reproaches of insulted humanity—ye have—the extreeme sufferings of a human being imperiously demand it—the violated rights of humanity require it—the unhappy prisoner is now numbering the 10th. Month of his sufferings and at this moment confined in a Room scarcely seven feet square, loaded with near 60 ℔ of Irons—his Ears assailed every hour of the day, nay momently with the most obscene expressions and horid Imprications & his small appartment where he breaths a little air, covered with filth issuing from an adjoining apartment* (fill'd with Criminals and runaway Slaves) under these disadvantages & under an accumulation of poignant distress, he has to prepare for the great and awfull change, with Death

---

* It is not to be understood by any means that fault is to be attached to the keeper of the prison, his attempts are earnestly directed to every thing that under existing circumstances can make the objects under his care comfortable, his kindness & attention cannot be exceeded—

staring him in the face, its terrors momently increased as with hasty strides it approaches his dreary Cell.—Where is the man who views this picture, the faithfull representation of the original whose heart does not relent, is there a man so callous to the dictates of Humanity, that does not pity,—that does not forgive—Parents Brothers, Kindred and friends, of ever rank and station in life let me call to your recollection, that the victims destined to drink the very dregs of the bitter cup of affliction is as uncertain as death itself; no case ever called more loudly for the exercise of this unerring rule, "—do to others as you would wish others do unto you," than the present.—Were I to address myself in such terms to the ignorant and thoughtless I should receive their well deserved ridicule. but in addressing the Chief Magistrate of the United States I feel a confidence that they will be duly appreciated.—the truths here unfolded and exposed to view will be regarded—the attempt to save a fellow Creature from a Horrid & violent death by the unering rules of Reason & candor, deserves and will receive due attention—no subscription have been asked for, or raised to aid in deceiving the President, no Quibbles have been resorted to in support of this Cause, Justice and humanity Pleads—Under these impressions I have volunteered my humble efforts, they are feeble indeed yet still may aid in prolonging the days of McGurk.—they may afford the means of our beholding him a good Citizen and a reformed man,—Will the Sacrifice on the Alter erected by Ignorance and dedicated to false prejudices obtain more—It will not.—and I am pursuaded should the sufferings of this unhappy man be made known, and sufficiently promulgated there will be found few indeed who would resist the pleasing Satisfaction of eagerly embracing the opportunity of remitting the cruell sentence—To Conclude—Thursday next is the day appointed; the period is fast approaching and before this reaches you another day will be taken from the few that now remains—Let not the clamors of the Idle and disolute. (who had rather witness the dreadfull scene of an Execution than be the bearers of a Pardon) be heard by you, let the Still voice of reason, still retain her influence over your mind, and I feel assured that the issue will be favourable to cause of humanity—

With a well founded hope that you will Pardon me for the trouble I shall give you, I wish you every blessing which it is possible for the good and virtuous to enjoy and with sincerity subscribe myself your,

FRIEND

RC (DNA: RG 59, GPR); at head of text: "To The President of the United States"; endorsed by TJ "Anon." and "Mc.Gurk's case," and so recorded in SJL with 26 Oct. as date of receipt; also endorsed by TJ "Woodward"; with clerk's endorsement for TJ's 21 Aug. stay of execution to 28 Oct.

Deeming it "the wish of every good government to reclaim rather than to destroy," the PENNSYLVANIA legislature reduced the number of capital crimes in 1786, and, by a statute of 1794, divided the crime of murder into two degrees. Under the 1794 law, first degree murder had to involve premeditation or be committed in conjunction with another serious offense, and was the only crime punishable by death. During the nineteenth century, other states followed Pennsylvania's example in reforming their systems of punishment (David Brion Davis, "The Movement to Abolish Capital Punishment in America, 1787-1861," *American Historical Review*, 63 [1957], 23-46; James T. Mitchell and Henry Flanders, comp., *The Statutes at Large of Pennsylvania from 1682 to 1801*, 16 vols., [Harrisburg, Pa., 1896-1911], 12:280-90; 15:174-81).

VOLUNTEERED MY HUMBLE EFFORTS: although the letter printed above is not in Augustus B. Woodward's handwriting, TJ's endorsement associated Woodward with the document. Some of the phrasing used by "Friend" is similar to wording in documents that Woodward composed. For example, Woodward's letter to TJ of 16 Aug., the petition of Woodward and others printed at that date, a letter from Woodward to the editors of the *Washington Federalist*, and "Friend" all described James McGurk as "unhappy." The petition and "Friend" said that McGurk was "loaded" with irons, mentioned "humble" efforts to aid the condemned man, referred to "rigid" penal systems, and argued that McGurk's killing of his wife was not "premeditated and intended" ("Friend") or "premeditated and intentional" (the petition). In the *Washington Federalist*, Woodward advanced an argument against capital punishment that foreshadowed the reasoning of "Friend" in the letter above. In that discussion, Woodward, like "Friend," called the death penalty "sanguinary" and pointed to Pennsylvania as a model of reform. In a second piece for the newspaper, Woodward argued that the president must be able to grant clemency "unbiassed by clamor and dissention," a sentiment echoed by "Friend" at the end of the letter printed above (*Washington Federalist*, 1, 8 Sep.).

From Albert Gallatin

DEAR SIR   Saturday morning [23 Oct. 1802]

I enclose some recommendations for the appointt. of surveyor at Smithfield near Norfolk. I had, some days ago, transmitted to you two others, but, whether they were for any of the persons now mentioned, I do not recollect—

Is it not time to decide what answer shall be given to Mr Steele? I wait to write to him on the subject of closing his official transactions, until I shall have heard in what manner you intend writing to him—

With great respect Your obedt. Servt.   ALBERT GALLATIN

P.S. Mr Steele has written to Mr Rawn his principal clerk that he had resigned; & the fact is now made public—   A. G.

I also enclose letters announcing that — Clarke appd. Survr. at Tombstone N.C. would not accept & recommending Jehu Nichols—

As this gentleman is recommended by Mr Stone in whose district Tombstone lies, & the Collector approves, I do not believe that better recommendations need be expected—

RC (DLC); partially dated; at foot of text: "Mr Jefferson"; endorsed by TJ as received from the Treasury Department on 23 Oct. and "Comptroller. Surveyor & Inspector Tombstone. Surveyor Smithfield" and so recorded in SJL. Enclosures: (1) Samuel Tredwell to John Steele, collector's office at Edenton, 11 Sep. 1802, informing the comptroller that he has received the commission for James Clark as surveyor at Tombstone sent on 15 July; he has written Clark several times but has not received an answer; he understands that Clark has been elected to represent Bertie County in the North Carolina General Assembly; Judge David Stone, upon learning of Clark's candidacy, spoke to Tredwell "of another Gentleman in case Mr Clark did not accept the Appointment" (RC in DNA: RG 59, LAR). (2) Tredwell to Steele, collector's office at Edenton, 13 Oct., learning that Clark declines to serve as surveyor and inspector at Tombstone, he returns the commissions and instead recommends Jehu Nichols, who lives near the place and is spoken of approvingly by Stone "as a fit person to fill the office" (RC in DNA: RG 59, LAR; endorsed by TJ: "Nichols John to be Surveyor & Inspector of the revenue for the port of Tombstone N.C. v. James Clarke decld"). Other enclosures not found.

SOME DAYS AGO: see Gallatin to TJ, 19 Oct.

WHAT ANSWER SHALL BE GIVEN: see John Steele to TJ, 30 Sep., and the enclosed copy of his letter to Gallatin of the same date, received on 14 Oct. by TJ.

John Steele on 14 Oct. wrote David RAWN of his resignation. Rawn, characterized by William Duane as an "Exterminator," received the letter on 23 Oct. and immediately conferred with Gallatin (Henry M. Wagstaff, ed., *The Papers of John Steele*, 2 vols. [Raleigh, N.C., 1924], 1:325-7; Gallatin, *Papers*, 6:354-5).

From Robert Smith

Navy Department
SIR,   23rd. October 1802

I have the honor of Sending to you herewith, for your Consideration a Copy of a letter from me to Captain Tingey, and also a Copy of his report to me upon the Several objects therein Submitted to him.

With great respect I have the honor to be Sir Your most obt Servt.

RT. SMITH

RC (DLC); in a clerk's hand, signed by Smith; at foot of text: "The President"; endorsed by TJ as received from the Navy Department on 25 Oct. and "Tingey's report on Dry dock" and so recorded in SJL. FC (Lb in DNA: RG 45, LSP). Enclosures: (1) Smith to Thomas Tingey, 13 July 1802, explaining that the advantage of having several streams running above the tide in Washington suggests "the practicability of having a dry dock on the principle of a lock," in which to lay up navy vessels so as to maintain them "in a state of perfect preservation" and save the expense of the "constant repairs" necessary when vessels are laid up in water and exposed to the sun; to determine which stream may be most advantageously used and to enable Congress to decide on the expediency of the project, Smith directs Tingey to examine Young's Spring, Tiber Creek, and the Potomac and ascertain the following: the highest point to which the tide has risen at the navy yard, points on Young's Spring and Tiber Creek that are 24 feet above said high water mark, the quantity of water yielded by these streams, and the height of water in the Potomac Canal above the tide water and its distance to the navy yard; Smith requests Tingey to perform these tasks immediately and to report the results to him "for the consideration of the President" (Tr in DLC). (2) Tingey to Smith, 22 Oct. 1802, presenting his report per the secretary's request, which was prepared with the assistance of Nicholas King; Tingey states that Young's Spring, more commonly known as Stoddert's Spring, rises 32 feet 3 inches above the high water mark in the Eastern Branch and discharges 49 cubic yards and 1 foot of water per hour; a canal to carry this water to the navy yard along the bank of the Eastern Branch would of necessity be "so nearly level, as only to allow a current sufficient to overcome slight obstructions, and prevent the water from stagnating"; such a canal would be about $3\frac{1}{8}$ miles in length and two or three lesser springs along the route could be employed to overcome any water lost by absorption along the way; the fall and quantity of water from Tiber Creek was ascertained along its route to the mill belonging to the estate of Notley Young; the water in the race below the mill wheel was 29 feet $5\frac{3}{10}$ inches above the high water mark in Tiber Creek and the Potomac, while the water in the race above the wheel measured 46 feet $7\frac{3}{10}$ inches above the high water mark; the volume of water in the Tiber at this mill was $144\frac{44}{100}$ cubic yards, although measured in a dry season; Tingey suggests two possible routes to convey the water: one around the end of Piney Branch thence to Stoddert's Spring, about $1\frac{3}{4}$ miles, thence joining the waters of the aforementioned canal to the navy yard; the other route would pass around the head of Piney Branch and then run west along the face of "the Hill" and around the Capitol to the navy yard, a distance of about $4\frac{1}{2}$ miles; the height of the water when high enough to navigate between the great and little falls of the Potomac to the locks on the latter measures 31 feet $4\frac{1}{5}$ inches above the high water in the river; a course from the locks at the lower falls to the navy yard would be 8 miles, assuming the use of aqueducts to cross the stream near Foxall's furnace, over Rock Creek, and over the Tiber near the Capitol, making the distances $2\frac{7}{8}$ miles from the locks to Rock Creek and thence $5\frac{1}{8}$ miles through the city to the navy yard; Tingey points out that these measurements were taken during a dry season, and consequently the water in the little falls canal was small, "not so high by two feet, as when the Boats pass along it"; allowing for dry seasons, the height of the canal above high water should not be estimated at more than 29 feet for the purposes of this survey; if the waters of Tiber Creek and Stoddert's Spring are to be used, Tingey recommends creating a large reservoir containing twice the amount of water estimated to be held by the dry docks, so that they may be filled speedily; if such a reservoir were built, it would probably be necessary to purchase Young's mill and some adjacent ground, with Tingey estimating the cost at about $4,000; Tingey has not yet learned Mr. Carroll's price for his land on the Eastern Branch convenient for the dry docks, but suggests instead using land in the navy yard west of the warehouses since it is already public property and would not require stopping up any streets and thereby help thwart possible opposition to the scheme; Tingey does not offer a cost estimate for constructing the canals because Smith possesses "superior data for the purpose than any I am capacitated to give" (Tr in same).

To Samuel Harrison Smith

TH: JEFFERSON TO MR SMITH   Oct. 23. 1802.

The inclosed paper seems intended for the legislative as well as Executive eye; but certainly not to be laid before the former in a regular way. the only irregular one would be in the newspapers. but this must depend on it's merit and your opinion of it. there are a few just ideas in it, but they are as a few grains of wheat in a bushel of chaff. I know not from what quarter it came, there being no postmark on the cover. do with it as you may think of it worth or want of it.

RC (DLC: J. Henley Smith Papers); addressed: "Mr. Samuel H. Smith Pensylvania avenue"; endorsed by Smith. Enclosure not identified.

To John Barnes

Th: Jefferson will be obliged to mr Barnes for thirty dollars either this evening, or by Mr. Lemaire tomorrow morning.—

Sunday. Oct. 24. 1802.

RC (ViU: Edgehill-Randolph Papers); addressed: "Mr. Barnes"; endorsed by Barnes: "℞ J. Dougherty—same Eveng." TJ received THIRTY DOLLARS from Barnes later the same day (MB, 2:1084).

From Benjamin H. Latrobe

SIR,   Philadelphia October 24h. 1802.

I beg leave to transmit to you by my particular friend, and near relation,—Mr Eakin of the War-office the enclosed letter, in which I have taken the liberty to give to you all the information which I possess on the proposed plan of a canal communication between the Delaware & Chesapeake bays. I have done this with a view to suggest the propriety of this subject being taken up by Congress as an important national object;—which is now in the way of being either irretrievably lost, or advantageously accomplished,—& which, I am convinced, that your recommendation would call into the notice it deserves. Mr. Eakin possesses lands in the probable neighborhood of the canal, and with a clear & impartial judgement possesses much information on this subject. On this account, and as a young man of no common merit, I beg leave to recommend him to your polite notice.

I am with true respect Your faithful hble Servnt

B HENRY LATROBE.

RC (DLC); endorsed by TJ as received 20 Nov. and "by Eakin" and so recorded in SJL.

James EAKIN was a cousin of Latrobe's wife, Mary Elizabeth Latrobe, and had a long career as a clerk in the War Department (Latrobe, *Correspondence*, 1:177n).

ENCLOSURE

From Benjamin H. Latrobe

Philadelphia, 27 Mch. 1802. Latrobe takes the liberty to offer ideas on the canal intended to connect the Chesapeake and Delaware Bays. He is assured of the practicability of the project and shall not take up TJ's time proving it. The principal difficulty will be to prevent the jealousies of Baltimore and Philadelphia from resulting in an imperfect or useless work. Baltimore fears that in a few years it will lose its commerce with the western counties of Pennsylvania to Washington, which will accept produce via Conococheague Creek, and to Philadelphia, which by fostering communication with the Susquehanna River can draw produce that now goes to Baltimore. The Susquehanna produce will travel to the Schuylkill River by a canal that must be completed in a few years; by the Philadelphia and Lancaster Turnpike, now nearly extended as far as Columbia; and by the river to Havre de Grace. Baltimore anticipates this natural course of things, and by the reluctance of capital to leave an established arena and by the exertions of its leaders, the city may retain its current trade, but Philadelphia and Havre de Grace will enjoy increasing advantages. The interests of Baltimore with respect to the canal are: to prevent its becoming an easy means of water communication between Philadelphia and the Chesapeake; to prevent its becoming a means of conveying Susquehanna produce to Philadelphia; to prevent its assisting the growth of Havre de Grace; and, if possible, to delay or prevent its construction altogether. Baltimore may accomplish this by locating the canal as far down the Chesapeake as possible and by making it suitable only for barges. A prohibitively expensive shifting of cargoes at each end of the canal would then take place, and the proximity of the Delaware end to the ocean would render the canal useless in times of war without a protecting fleet. The interests of Philadelphia are opposite to those of Baltimore, but Latrobe does not think that the canal will benefit his city as much as its merchants believe. The principal convenience to Philadelphia commerce will arise when the price of produce there, less the canal tolls, exceeds that in Baltimore. *Then*, the Susquehanna produce will go to Philadelphia. His city will also benefit from shorter and safer trips to the Chesapeake. Yet these advantages depend upon making the canal deep enough for sea-faring vessels and cutting it as high up the two bays as possible, at least to Reedy Island on the Delaware end and no lower than Sassafras River on the Chesapeake. Baltimore leaders worry little over the "infant City" of Havre de Grace because of their wealth, the supposed unhealthiness of the place, its lack of convenient wharves, and the difficult navigation of the Susquehanna. But Havre de Grace seems to Latrobe the natural outlet for all produce that passes Columbia. Baltimore merchants already send their ships to Havre to take in produce, and agents for these merchants purchase and store at Havre the cargoes of boats that cannot go further. Havre de Grace has suffered from the impracticability of the Susquehanna. During the last summer, however, Latrobe supervised the clearing of the river below Columbia, and now, "in a modest swell of the river," an ark may travel from Columbia to Havre in seven hours. $50,000 more would render the river navigable in all seasons. His report on this subject has been laid before the Pennsylvania legislature and published in the *Aurora*. Rendering the river navigable upwards will be more difficult but less important, as the value of produce exported from western Pennsylvania counties so far exceeds imported commodities in that region as to make land transport affordable. Havre de Grace has all the advantage of the Susquehanna improvements and on its east side has as deep a harbor as does Baltimore. The canal will first render Havre a store house to Philadelphia, as well as to Baltimore. It will grow rich from the trade of the cities to which it is subservient and "set up for itself." When Havre is thus advanced, the canal will open to her the trade of South Jersey. Her interests, then, coincide with those of Philadelphia and require a deep canal, not below Sassafras. The canal is of immense importance to Delaware in spite of legislation there that retards its execution and taxes its potential profits. Latrobe is sure he need say little that will convince the president of the importance of the canal to the United States. It will unite the most distant states and in war offer safe internal communication. Yet its advantages would be imperfect unless vessels capable of navigating the bays could pass from one end to the other without shifting cargo.

1 June 1802. Latrobe intended to send this letter to TJ in time to have the subject submitted to Congress, but circumstances prevented its completion, and he trusts that TJ will forgive the intrusion during the recess. There are three viable proposals for canal routes and three or four local interests that might affect the outcome with no regard for the public good. The highest of these lines is from the head of Elk River to Christiana Bridge and thence to Wilmington; the second from Bohemia to Drawyer Creek or Appoquiniminck River, the third from Sassafras to Appoquiniminck. Lately a "very amiable and entertaining french Gentleman," Major Varlé, who "is certainly not as well acquainted with the mathematical science and practical engineering, as with Music," has published a map of Delaware. A new route for the canal laid down in this map strikes the Delaware at Hamburg. Latrobe cannot form an opinion as to its practicability, but gentlemen of that area have ridiculed the plan, which, wanting a good harbor on Delaware Bay, exists only to enhance the value of the lands of Varlé's patron. A proposal to cut the canal into the Chester River and thence to Blackbird or Duck Creek would suit the interests of Baltimore but in every other view is inadmissable because of the danger in Delaware Bay, from the enemy and the weather, and because of the circuitous communication with the Susquehanna. Cutting the canal from Elk River to Christiana Bridge would ensure a certain supply of water to the upper levels and an entrance into the Delaware above Reedy Island, which affords a harbor and good shelter to a fleet in case of war. The disadvantages are the risk of soil filling up the water at Frenchtown due to the many rapid streams that flow from the granite ridge, the rough and rocky country through which the canal would pass, and a difficult navigation down the Christina River to the Delaware. He believes that at least two locks at each end will be necessary. The advantages of the route from Bohemia to

Drawyer or Appoquiniminck (the former being a branch of the latter) include good water up the Bohemia River, better and lower ground, and a short cut through the marshes to the Delaware that would save a distance of more than ten miles. The disadvantages are a dubious supply of water to the lower level and an entrance into Delaware Bay below Reedy Island. The line from Sassafras to Appoquiniminck is in most respects "Circumstanced as the last" but has an entrance lower down the Chesapeake and is farther from an upper level water supply. If deemed of great importance that the Delaware Bay entrance of the canal be easily defended, it will be best to cut it from Frenchtown to Wilmington. But on no other account ought this line to be favored, as in Latrobe's view the ground and the distance will make it the most difficult to cut. Bohemia and Sassafras will afford the cheapest and easiest cutting. He now offers his opinion of what should govern the work. The canal should carry eight feet of water, with a lock at each end of not more than eight feet of lift at high tide. If the entrance be made practicable at half tide, the lift on the Delaware at high water should only be five feet. A survey of the middle ground found that its highest elevation is 66 feet, but Latrobe doubts that this elevation extends far. Ravines come up from each bay, and ground low enough to save much digging is available. The stone work required at each end, not the digging, will require the most skill and money. Multiple locks should not be substituted for digging, as the expense in their maintenance and the delays they would cause would prove a persistent loss. He believes that once all the timber is cleared and the earth cut below the strata in which they now lie, the tributaries of the Bohemia, Sassafras, Drawyer, and Appoquiniminck will prove insufficient to maintain the water in the upper level at the necessary height. He proposes, therefore, to cut a shallow canal from the high land about the sources of the Christina to serve as a feeder to the summit level of the grand canal and also as a means of conveying the produce of the country on either side. This canal would have many descending locks and terminate in a large reservoir, but whatever the line chosen for the grand canal, the upper country will have to supply water to the summit level.

24 Oct. 1802. He pleads sickness and other pressing business for the delay in concluding this letter. He hopes the subject itself and his sincere respect for TJ's opinion permit the intrusion upon the president's time. He now lays before TJ the reasons for the canal project's suspension. Under the legislative acts incorporating the canal company, subscriptions were allowed on a fixed day, so that individuals of each of the three states should have an equal chance of influencing the measures of the company. The capital of the company is set at $500,000 in shares of $200 each. By Delaware's legislation one half must be subscribed before the company can be formed. No subscription has yet been obtained in Baltimore, and in Delaware only 210 shares have been purchased. It was supposed that merchants in Philadelphia would quickly fill the subscription book, but only 216 shares have been put down. Although some feared that Baltimorians would fill up the shares and be able to defeat the work or serve only Baltimore's interests, this has not happened, and Latrobe finds that only about 500 shares have been purchased, leaving a deficiency of $150,000. The canal now depends on the federal government's obtaining full control over its execution. If Congress were to authorize the government to "subscribe a commanding number of the deficient shares," the plan could proceed without the influence of local interests and private speculation, which have "ruined almost all attempts at great public Works in America." Delaware has also limited its incorporating act to some time in May 1803, unless its subscription mandate is met. Latrobe does not doubt that the subscription would fill rapidly if either Congress or one of the state legislatures, particularly Pennsylvania's, subscribed largely to the work. But from the Pennsylvania legislature nothing can be expected. He deprecates the choice of representatives in his state and adds that "men of sense seem to be ineligible in the unanimous opinion of the Majority."

RC (DLC: TJ Papers, 121:20961-6; 127:21886-9); Editors' summary; 19 p.; endorsed by TJ as received 20 Nov. and "Delaware Canal" and so recorded in SJL. Printed in full in Latrobe, *Correspondence*, 1:208-19.

Although the Chesapeake and Delaware Canal Company sold enough shares by May 1803 to begin operations, insufficient funds forced it to suspend work in

December 1805. During that period, Latrobe worked as surveyor and then chief engineer for the project and directed construction of a branch canal intended to feed water to the proposed main canal connecting headwaters of the Elk and Christina Rivers (Latrobe, *Correspondence*, 1:315-16; Ralph D. Gray, *The National Waterway: A History of the Chesapeake and Delaware Canal, 1769-1985*, 2d ed. [Urbana, Ill., 1989], 14-22).

From John Oakley

[on or before 24 Oct. 1802]

John Oakley as Justice of the peace for the County of Washington District of Columbia has four Constables to wait on him before Breakfast every day and they having their pockets filled with Warrants Accounts, Blank Supersedeses &c. &c. &c. entertain him so completely throughout the Day that he has not dined 6 times in two Months To Morrow I am engaged in taking Bail from a Colonel for feloniously (so says the deposition) taking a Girl from a General I have pledged myself to Morrow to so many that my Breakfast will resemble a Levee and I shall scarcely extricate myself by Suppertime Ludicrous & improbable as this may appear it is a melancholy fact that I issue & try as many Warrants in a Week as would neatly folded make a smart Octavo—I hope this will be considered as a sufficient apology or I shall be unhappy from the appointment which engrosses all my time—I have enclosed Mr Stoddert's letter to me respecting the Subscription for the River Potomak. I remain with great Respect Your very hble Servt.

JOHN OAKLEY

RC (MoSHi: Jefferson Papers); undated; endorsed by TJ as received 24 Oct. and so recorded in SJL. Enclosure not found.

John Oakley became revenue inspector and collector for the port of Georgetown in October 1801. John Thomson Mason had described him to TJ as a "very honest upright man, of very good understanding, *very eccentrick*" but not a good money manager. Oakley and 14 others received a commission dated 27 Apr. 1802 to serve as justices of the peace for Washington County (FC of commission in Lb in DNA: RG 59, MPTPC; JEP, 1:423; Vol. 33:231n, 670; Vol. 35:190; Vol. 36:314, 320; Vol. 37:181).

SUBSCRIPTION FOR THE RIVER POTOMAK: a shallow channel in the Potomac prevented large vessels from loading at Georgetown. Its merchants feared that mudbanks would ruin navigation to their wharves and give Alexandria a competitive edge. Many Georgetown citizens supported public works for the river, including the use of a dredging or mud machine to clear the silt deposits in the channel below Analostan Island. Former secretary of the navy Benjamin Stoddert dreamed that Georgetown would one day rival Baltimore, Philadelphia, New York, or Boston as a trading center. In July 1802, TJ paid to see the "Mud-scoop work" and, according to his financial memoranda, on 25 Oct. directed John Barnes to pay Oakley $100 for his subscription for deepening the bed of the Potomac River to Georgetown (MB, 2:1077, 1085: Bryan, *National Capital*, 1:496-7; John Lauritz Larson, "A Bridge, a Dam, a River: Liberty and Innovation in the Early Republic," *Journal of the Early Republic*, 7 [1987], 355, 356, 358; TJ to Nathaniel Macon, 17 July 1802).

To John Allen

SIR   Washington Oct. 25. 1802.

The duties of my office calling for all my time, I do not find myself at liberty to indulge in pursuits of the nature of that which is the subject of your letter of September 28. I observe that physicians are as far from being agreed as to what is the yellow fever, as what is it's cure. if the disease which you have so successfully treated be that which all of them would call the yellow fever, and your remedy so certain, I shoud imagine some of the great cities in which it has prevailed & is still prevailing, would be the best scene for exhibiting proofs of your discovery. it's reality, once established, the advantages derived from it's practice would in all probability produce satisfactory recompence. but whether in this or in what other way you can best reap the fruits of your discovery, I am not qualified to judge. I do not think an application to Congress could be useful, because they have already as far as their constitutional powers go, done what they thought best for securing to inventors the benefits of their inventions. Accept my best wishes & respects.   TH: JEFFERSON

PrC (DLC); at foot of text: "Mr. John Allen. Pepperelboro'."

From Jonathan Brunt

SIR,   George-Town, Oct 25, 1802

Last November I addressed a Pamphlet to you, from Schenectady, near Albany, (N.Y.S.) which I hope you received. As I have followed the Printing-Business in America without much success, thro' the minds of the people being somewhat contaminated with *corrupt* speculations; (which is not actuated by a principle of laudable enterprize in *honest Industry*;) I hoped you would not be displeased if I enquired of you, if it would be practicable to get a place as a writer or copyist under your Government.

I am, Sir, your obedt. Servt.   JONATHAN BRUNT, printer

RC (DLC); at head of text: "Hon. Thomas Jefferson"; endorsed by TJ as received 25 Oct. and so recorded in SJL.

Jonathan Brunt (b. 1760), an itinerant printer and bookseller from Beighton, Derby County, England, came to the United States in 1794. His acquaintances feared he was deranged, and they had him committed to New York's City Hospital in December 1797 for 18 weeks. Over the next several years, his family sought his whereabouts and repeatedly attempted to persuade him to return to England. His *Extracts, from Locke's Essay on the Human Understanding and other Writers; containing a Defence of Natural, Judicial, and Constitutional Rights, on the Principles of Morality, Religion, & Equal Justice, against the Private and Public Intrigues of Artificial Society* was printed and sold in Frankfort, Kentucky, in 1804 and included a short account of the publisher's difficulties (Sowerby, No. 3320). Brunt traveled widely, including to Canada and some of the southern states and visited TJ at Monticello on 27 Sep. 1807. Beginning in December 1809, TJ occasionally gave him a few dollars in charity (Brunt, *Few Particulars of the Life of Jonathan Brunt Junior, Printer & Bookseller*, 3d ed. [1797]; Boston *Democrat*, 17 Dec. 1806; MB, 2:1250, 1270, 1306; RS, 1:403n, 4:168; Brunt to TJ, 30 Nov. 1807).

PAMPHLET: probably *Rush's Extracts, Containing the Evidences of Genuine Patriotism, and the Love of Our Country*, printed for Brunt in 1801 by Elihu Phinney in Cooperstown, New York (Shaw-Shoemaker, No. 245).

From Thomas Cooper

DEAR SIR,   Northumberland Octr 25. 1802.

Having finished all that I undertook, as my department of the Wyoming Controversy for Pennsylvania Lands, I have returned hither. Dr Priestley being desirous of communicating to you extracts from Mr Stone's letter, I have copied it for him. Passages respecting himself which he would probably have omitted, I have sent you without scruple; for I take for granted that every thing relating to his literary labours will be interesting privately and publicly, to Mr Jefferson and to the World.

You will observe that the measure of prohibiting in France, the introduction of British Newspapers which Mr Stone thought Buonaparte would not venture upon, has been done. You will be somewhat surprized to, that Dr Priestley's correspondent, considering his veneration for your character, and what he might have known of the simple organization of American governments, should intimate for a moment that the Republicans of France look to England for principles of Liberty! To England where the boldest friends of freedom propose with hesitation as doubtful theories, what America has long regarded and practiced as political axioms established beyond the necessity of farther discussion! To England, where liberty so far as it is known is the mere footstool of Party. The Whigs and the Tories—the Ins and the Outs—the Pittites & the Foxites of that Country are to me equally detestable. All of them equally dread the real Freedom of the Press, but have not the boldness of Buonaparte to lay the ax to the root. They all know how necessary it is for party purposes, and therefore, and therefore only, and to that extent only, does the one party permit, and the other advocate it. That the Whigs and Foxites, are enemies to the genuine principles of liberty appears evident to me from the doctrines on this Subject laid down by Belsham in page 203-205 of his Memoirs of the reign of Geo. 3rd Vol 5. Belsham I consider (tho' Dr. P. thinks otherwise) is a party-writer and book-compiler under the Patronage of Fox Sheridan & what is usually called the Whig Party of that Country; & as laying down their Opinions. Thank God, within these Ten Years another party has arisen, the Party of the People. Truth is with it, and it will prevail.

I am clearly of opinion with Mr. Stone that notwithstanding the political errors of the french Governments, and the horrible vices of their rulers, the Cause of Liberty has gained much in that Country. Those who have observed the quiet and gradual but irresistible effects of extended Knowledge by means of the press, will not be terrified at the temporary storms of political Usurpation. I do not think with Paine that men cannot *unknow* what they have once known; for this *has* happened in England, as well as in France; and even in this Country: but while the press is free, it will prove but a temporary night of Intellect. Locke wd. not have written as he did if the *Vindiciæ contra Tyrannos*, the *Lex Rex*, the Speeches of Falkland, Hampden, Pym &c And the writings of Milton, Sydney and above all of Harrington, had not preceded him: and without him, the morning twilight of 1688 would not have been the harbinger of the day of 1776. I look forward therefore to the ultimate event, with undiminished hope. But we have much yet to learn. We have to learn even in this mildest of Governments, how easy it is to govern too much and how prone the best of rulers, are from the best of principles, to overact their part. Permit me however sincerely to except from this Observation your principles, and your practice. I know that I state your opinions when I say, that wise men have just begun to suspect that the art of Governing, consists in knowing how to govern as little as possible.

I give credit to Mr Stone's character of Alexander of Russia, sufficiently to wish that you were his correspondent if you be not so. But I cannot help regarding Mr Stone, and even M. de la Harpe, as characters too obscure to become in any degree the vehicles of your Correspondence. Much of what Mr Stone has related of Alexander, is also mentioned by Kotzebue in the 3rd. Vol of his acct. of his Imprisonment in Russia 75, 79, 214. Kotzebue mentions La Harpe also as Alexanders Tutor with great respect 181. Alexander is young. I regard him with fearful hope.—

How very gratifying it is to your friends to hear of the high respect paid to your Character among the best of Men throughout the enlightened World! Almost am I persuaded that your principles are now too habitual, and your Character too fixed, for your practice to be warped, or your Conduct to waver. *Almost;* for looking at the Buonoparte's of present and former times, who of us can say he can compleatly trust himself, under every vicissitude of popular favour and popular Ingratitude? My earnest prayer is that you may continue as you have begun: and that Power and prosperity may never tempt you from the honourable path that led you to them; or deprive you of the exquisite Luxury of knowing and feeling, how anxiously you are looked up to, and how sincerely you are beloved by those who love mankind.

I remain with great respect your sincere friend.

THOMAS COOPER

RC (DLC); endorsed by TJ as received 6 Nov. and so recorded in SJL.

WYOMING CONTROVERSY: from March 1801 to August 1804, Cooper served as a Luzerne commissioner to settle the ongoing title disputes between Pennsylvania and Connecticut over territory in the Wyoming Valley. Hoping to avoid further violence over these controversies, Cooper favored conciliation and a judicious legal interpretation, which often seemed sympathetic to the Connecticut claimants. He published his opinions on pending amendments to the compromise act of 1799 as *Observations on the Wyoming Controversy, Respectfully Submitted to the Legislature of Pennsylvania* in Lancaster in March 1802 and gave a copy to William Duane, who printed it in the Philadelphia *Aurora* on 17 Mch. (Shaw-Shoemaker, No. 2087; Dumas Malone, *The Public Life of Thomas Cooper, 1783-1839* [New Haven, 1926], 150-64; Vol. 31:25-6; Vol. 34:300n).

Bonaparte blocked the INTRODUCTION

OF BRITISH NEWSPAPERS by ordering French officials not to enforce parts of a treaty that covered postal exchanges with Britain (Grainger, *Amiens Truce*, 149).

Memoirs of the Reign of George III, by William BELSHAM, first appeared in 1795 as a four-volume edition that described the monarch's reign to 1793. A fifth edition of the work, published in 1801, added two volumes that carried the narrative to 1799. On the pages cited by Cooper, Belsham, a political moderate, discussed the treason trial of some "overheated partizans of reform" who had followed "the novel and extravagant doctrines of Paine" and sought a reform of Parliament upon "visionary, if not pernicious, principles." Because the defendants in the trial had participated in associations that were "infected with the leaven of republicanism," Belsham commended the government's spying on the radicals and putting a stop to their "rash and seditious conduct." The narrative of George's reign was part of a larger series by Belsham, *Memoirs of the House of Brunswic-Lunenburg*, which TJ considered to be a fundamental work on English history (William Belsham, *Memoirs of the Reign of George III*, 5th ed., 6 vols. [London, 1801], 5:203-5; Sowerby, No. 408; DNB; Vol. 30:595).

Thomas PAINE wrote in *The Rights of Man*: "The mind, in discovering truth, acts in the same manner as it acts through the eye in discovering objects; when once any object has been seen, it is impossible to put the mind back to the same condition it was in before it saw it. Those who talk of a counter-revolution in France show how little they understand of man. There does not exist in the compass of language, an arrangement of words to express so much as the means of effecting a counter-revolution. The means must be an obliteration of knowledge; and it has never yet been discovered how to make a man *unknow* his knowledge, or *unthink* his thoughts" (Philip S. Foner, ed., *The Complete Writings of Thomas Paine*, 2 vols. [New York, 1945], 1:320).

For the 16th-century Spanish mystic Saint John of the Cross, the NIGHT OF INTELLECT was a renunciation of knowledge in preparation for union with God.

Writers in the 19th century used the expression to denote situations in which understanding is lacking (Kieran Kavanaugh and Otilio Rodriguez, trans., *The Collected Works of St. John of the Cross* [Garden City, N.Y., 1964], 47-8, 52-3, 201; Charles Lamb, *Elia: 1823* [Oxford, 1991], 8; Duncan Wu, ed., *The Selected Writings of William Hazlitt*, 9 vols. [London, 1998], 6:37; Charles Dickens, *Nicholas Nickleby*, ed. Paul Schlicke [Oxford, 1990], 500).

VINDICIÆ CONTRA TYRANNOS: a French Huguenot treatise first published in 1579, *Vindiciae, contra Tyrannos* argued that religious and political covenants gave sovereignty to the people and made government a social compact. Hubert Languet and Philippe du Plessis Mornay have been most often named as probable authors of the tract, which appeared under a pseudonym. TJ owned a copy of the work (Stephanus Junius Brutus, the Celt, *Vindiciae, Contra Tyrannos: or, Concerning the Legitimate Power of a Prince over the People, and of the People over a Prince*, ed. George Garnett [Cambridge, Eng., 1994], xix-xlv, lv-lxxvi; J. Wayne Baker, "Faces of Federalism: From Bullinger to Jefferson," *Publius*, 30 [2000], 27-30, 37; Sowerby, No. 2324).

LEX REX: Samuel Rutherford, a Puritan theologian, made a case for natural rights, limited government, and resistance to tyranny in *Lex, Rex: The Law and the Prince. A Dispute for the Just Prerogative of King and People*, published in London in 1644 (Peter Judson Richards, "'The Law Written in their Hearts'?: Rutherford and Locke on Nature, Government and Resistance," *Journal of Law and Religion*, 18 [2002-3], 151-89).

In 1784, on the invitation of Empress Catherine of Russia, Frédéric César de LA HARPE had become a tutor to the czarina's grandson Alexander (born in 1777) and his younger brother Constantine. La Harpe, who was 29 years old when he began to instruct Alexander, was a native of the Swiss canton of Vaud and had a law degree from the university at Tübingen. He became the dominant influence in Alexander's education and moral development. Under La Harpe, the young grand duke learned history,

Enlightenment principles, and republican political philosophy. In 1793, the government of Bern demanded that Catherine expel La Harpe from Russia for his advocacy of revolutionary change in Switzerland, but La Harpe remained in St. Petersburg as Alexander's preceptor until the spring of 1795. John Hurford Stone and La Harpe were acquainted (Jean Charles Biaudet and Françoise Nicod, eds., *Correspondance de Frédéric-César de La Harpe et Alexandre Ier*, 3 vols. [Neuchâtel, 1978-80], 1:10-18; Hartley, *Alexander I*, 13-16, 26; J. C. F. Hoefer, *Nouvelle biographie générale depuis les temps les plus reculés jusqu'a nos jours*, 46 vols. [Paris, 1855-66], 28:885-7; Jean Charles Biaudet and others, eds., *Correspondance de Frédéric-César de La Harpe sous la République Helvétique*, 4 vols. [Neuchâtel, 1982-2004], 4:251, 271, 413).

In 1800, officials in Russia arrested the playwright August von KOTZEBUE as he entered the country on a visit. Kotzebue, who had lived in Russia for several years in the 1780s and 1790s, was held in Siberia until Emperor Paul allowed him to go to St. Petersburg. Kotzebue, a native of Weimar, later returned to Germany, but he was in the Russian capital when Paul was assassinated in 1801 and Alexander became emperor. On the pages cited by Cooper in the English translation of the playwright's memoir of his detention, Kotzebue said that Alexander's subjects "gave themselves up to joy" when he became emperor, that the new monarch's actions "tended to encourage and confirm" the people's expectations, that the appearance of a "round hat" in St. Petersburg the day after Paul's death caused excitement as a signal of changes to come, and that Alexander would be "a powerful stimulus" to progressive action by the nobility. Kotzebue called Alexander's former tutor "the estimable La Harpe" (August von Kotzebue, *The Most Remarkable Year in the Life of Augustus von Kotzebue; Containing an Account of his Exile into Siberia, and of the other Extraordinary Events which Happened to Him in Russia*, 3 vols. [London, 1802], 1:11-12, 16, 24-5, 35-6, 87-9; 2:105, 222-9, 237-9; 3:73-5, 79, 181, 214; George S. Williamson, "What Killed August von Kotzebue? The Temptations of Virtue and the Political Theology of German Nationalism, 1789-1819," *Journal of Modern History*, 72 [2000], 890-943).

ENCLOSURE

Extracts from a Letter of John Hurford Stone to Joseph Priestley

[10 Aug. 1802]

"I have just recd. my dr. Sir yr interesting communication by Mrs Fenwick, which only serves to heighten my esteem and admiration for your Presidt. We have now two men in the world to whom we look with mingled respect and anxiety. These two men are placed at opposite points of our globe, but their principles, their Sentiments and Conduct appear to be in exact sympathy with each other: The intermediate space is filled up by chiefs of different descriptions of good and evil, tending in general I think rather toward good, but who will not go far astray, when they have two Sentinels such as Jefferson & Alexander to keep them in order.

It might have appeared extraordinary to you, that I shd. put the Autocrat of the Russians and your President in the same line, had I not given you some intimations in former letters of the Character & dispositions of the former. Since I last wrote to you, M. de la Harpe who educated this young man, is return'd from Petersburgh to Paris near which he resides. It wd. be too long to detail to you all that he tells me respecting his pupil, but a few traits will lead you to fill up the picture. In the course of a whole years conversation with the Emperor (for his intercourse was such with him as to be called so) La Harpe never once heard him pronounce the word *Subjects* or *empire*. Whenever Alexander talked of the Russians he always called them his *Countrymen* his *fellow citizens* (compatriotes, concitoyens) when he talked of Russia it was *sa patrie* whenever he talked of himself it was his *post*, his *place* his *charge*, as if he had been an elected magistrate. The idea of absolute authority was so far from his mind that in the flow of conversation where all was unpremeditated free & open, no expression intimating it, once strayed from his lips. His uneasy moments were, when the forms & ceremonies of Court recalled to his mind his superiority; at these times he wd. not suffer la Harpe to be a witness of what he called the degradation of mankind; no instances of which so much excited his indignation as what occurred at his own Coronation at Moscow, where he was compelled to submit to such humiliating usages, as were thought natural by his predecessors, but which it is probable he will be careful; if he live long enough to spare those who come after him. Their usages were the accustomed ceremonies of Genuflexion, Prostrations and Adorations exhibited at the Coronation of their Autocrats and which appear from the abhorrence with which he speaks of them to have made a very salutary impression on his mind.

But these impressions are connected with no wild or extravagant notions of Liberty: there is no enthusiasm in any of his movements; and when he is resolved on doing some act of enlarged Beneficence, he is careful to disguise it under antient forms, so as to keep out of sight as much as possible the Idea of Innovation. Thus for instance, Classes of Russians who were incapacitated to possess property; he has contrived to admit into the Cast of Proprietors: this is the blow which Henry 7th struck at the feudal System; on his own territorial possessions, he suffers no Slave or Serf to be bought or sold; he has made it understood, that tho' he does not mean to infringe on property of any kind, yet that he is personally under no Obligation to follow the barbarous usages of his unenlightened Ancestry. The hint has been taken, and the Gazettes which used to be filled with Columns of this kind of Serf-traffick, are at present perfectly innocent, since no one wishes to be ranked among the class of barbarous descendants. In a convenient season the Emperor will *obey the impulse given by the People*, and abolish formally an Usage which the *enlightened nation of the Russians has already proscribed*, the people themselves having taken the initiation in this abolition. This young man you see, is almost as Machiavelian in stealing away Despotism from among his Subjects, as others in Europe are in stealing away Liberty from their fellow Citizens. The powerful sentiment that weighs in his mind is Justice. In this principle he remains unshaken: nothing can seduce him from this point. He bears the most filial and affectionate attachment to his Mother; the Dowager Empress solicited some time since a favour for some one. The Emperor referred her to another day. As my mother Madam says he, you may command every thing that your Son can give, but as a Magistrate I am responsible for every action of my life. In granting your demand, I do an act which I cannot justify, and I am sure you will not urge it further. His Valet de Chambre had been with him from a child; he had Friendship and even Affection for him. The Emperor had one day intimation that some General of his Court had given him money for services rendered or to be rendered him with the Emperor. The man being interrogated owned the Transaction: no atonement could be made: both were banished instantly from the Court, with a suitable provision however for the Domestic.

He is become as one wd. naturally suppose, an object of Adoration to the People of Russia; it is this kind of Sentiment he is much solicitous to correct. You know the Ceremony of prostration whenever the Emperor was met even in his Carriage, which Paul exacted very rigorously. Alexander had made it at first understood that these homages were disagreeable to him, but finding them continued he was compelled to issue a decree to force the People to keep themselves erect, & he has so far succeeded, that he walks now in the Streets, or in the public promenades with his wife, witht. undergoing any farther this kind of molestation: wherever he goes, he is unattended by guards, or by any other than a simple domestic behind his Carriage, or on Horseback into the Country.

He is at this moment earnestly occupied in forming the Mechanism of a free Government, by arranging such an administration as shall become the Vehicle, first of instruction, next of introducing the notions of civil liberty. This is a work of great labour and length of time, and requires both courage & perseverance. He is indefatigable in research, & has auxialiaries as earnest and as active as their Principal. In short this Country unknown half a Century back in the System of European Governments, is rising fast to an elevated seat amongst them, & if it continue as it has begun, its influence will become more preponderant than is suitable to the views of some, who equal Alexander at present in Power, but are infinitely below him in wisdom & in goodness.

Of the present rulers of nations, your President ranks the highest in Alexander's esteem and affection. He speaks always of Mr Jefferson with high respect as a Man and with great admiration of his Conduct as an Administrator: and did the bounds of a letter permit me, I cd. convince you that this young Emperor is not unworthy of a return of the same Sentiment from your republican chief. I have just mentioned to you that the Emperor is earnest in his researches to form a good administration. I am persuaded that he wd. be highly gratified in receiving some account of the internal administration of the United States; by which I mean the mere *machinery*, such as the mode of Communication between the President and Ministers—of Ministers with each other—of ministers with their Bureaus of these bureaus with inferior administrations—and by what Channels affairs reach the higher from the lower departments. In such tableau, there is nothing as you will perceive that is political, & if there be no difficulty in procuring it, great service might be rendere'd at little expence. I could ask Joel Barlow, but he I should imagine is not sufficiently instructed in the detail. Yr Ambassador might be better informed, but I never ask any question of Diplomates.

I have kept you long enough you will say in Russia, "let us hear what you have to say of Affairs nearer home." This is a much more difficult and unpleasing task, for surely never did the Revolution under any of its Phases, present us with any thing so truly ludicrous as the present. For these four Months past, we have been retrograding at so furious a rate, that the most lynx-eyed observer has scarcely been able to keep pace with the motion, & heaven only knows when we shall stop. Within these 2 or 3 Days (10th. August 1802) we have made a kind of pause, having stumbled on something like a new Constitution, if such a name can be given to a string of resolutions said to be explanatory of the late Constitution; & by which we understand just so much, as that it is[1] pretty nearly the inverse, and that all power, legislative, executory, judiciary & administrative is committed to the first consul who settles himself in office for life with the power of naming his Successor. This I am persuaded is only a turn of the wheel which will go round again, for nothing so monstrous so absurd and ridiculous can have any duration. This man in whom we had fixed part of our hopes (for we have learnt to fix them totally on no man) is become an object with us less of indignation, which is too elevated a sentiment, than of contempt. He is got so many more degrees below his place than we thought possible, that we know no longer how to estimate him. The Hero has totally disappeared beneath the Prince, and his vanity has got the better of his pride. More anxious of reigning than governing, while he plays the dictator, he is under the direction of (politically speaking) the most abandoned and perverse of Men. The honours which he had acquired from his glory, has let him totally to forget it, & the egregious flattery that has been poured upon him seems to have altered his Judgement. While he ambitioned being the Pericles of France, his ambition might have been tolerated in favour of the real benefits he contributed to introduce, but wanting to become the Augustus, he has sunk beneath the Usurper.

You will readily suppose that these innovations are not regarded by the people with a favourable eye. All thinking men look on them with abhorrence, but as the press is under the severest restriction, there is no mode of communicating the public Sentiment. The only representation that France has of the public voice, is the English Press, and the only power which Buonaparte is at war with at present, and which perplexes him more than the Coalition, is the English Newspapers. He has made remonstrances in vain to the English Government, which refuses to put the press in England under the same restrictions as Buonaparte has imposed on it in France. Finding no redress from this quarter he has entered the field against them in his official Journal, which a few days since amused the Parisians exceedingly, when they read a Manifesto evidently written by himself, and which by its manner and stile of abuse, seemed to have issued from the Cabinet of some doubly irritated Jacobin. I trust this petulance will go no farther than newspaper discussion, and that his madness will not proceed so far as to light up again the flames of War, an event of which I have no great apprehension, since he must know that such an attempt could not fail of being attended with serious consequences to himself. He seems at present omnipotent but this is only seeming: I have lived long enough here not to be deceived by appearances, & the art or mechanism of Revolutions is so well known from the frequent practice that nothing is stable which is built on violence or power. Who could have predicted, a week before the fall of Robespierre, that this sanguinary chief was so near the scaffold. The late directory was overthrown against all expectations. Our present chief requires only a few men to look him steadily in the face, & such an event may happen when we are least aware of it.

In the mean while the great principles of the Revolution are gaining ground every day. Perhaps this Season of extravagance & folly on the part of our Governors, is as necessary for its purpose as other events that have taken place. A season of enormities is that of enquiry, & tho' Buonaparte affects to do all *par* le peuple et *pour* le peuple, the people are by no means the dupe.

They do not as you may suppose behold witht. abhorrence these proceedings; & tho' the Senate have just declared him consul for life on the vote of upwards of three millions, you may be assured that had the slightest scrutiny taken place not a fiftieth part wd. have acceded to this measure. Never was there a juggle so scandalous from the first to the last carried on by any Government, and never was contempt of all forms and decency more openly avowed or exhibited.

It might be presumed from the audacity with which these acts of despotism are pushed forward, that some understanding had taken place between the french Government and foreign powers as guarantees of these Innovations. This, which is the opinion of many who cannot otherwise account for the Phenomena, I have good reason to believe is by no means the case. It is nothing but the delirium of Ambition the drunkenness of Power, such as sometimes seized the Directory after the events of the 18th. fructidor, and from which the awakening will be terrible for him. Whenever this event takes place the struggle if there be any will only be internal; I am confident that no power whatever will interfere; on the contrary there is not one but will take pleasure in seeing this arrogance humbled. He has just now personally insulted the English Government & in the grossest manner: he has I know personally insulted Russia. The alliance of this last with Prussia is become more intimate, & you know the extent of the friendship of Austria toward France. He has insulted the Army where he has the fewest friends. He has degraded every constituent authority in the state; & notwithstanding his public declarations respecting *equality* & the *people*, he scarcely ever dissembles his opinion of such chimæras. You will see by the *Senatus consulte organique* which he has lately published explanatory of the Constitution and which is diametrically opposite to every principle of it, the measure of his regard for the Laws & Liberties of his country. Admitting that the people have named him consul for life, by what authority does he name his Successor? or take the whole power of the State into his own hands? But this is a² theme that would never finish. Let us escape therefore from the ungrateful Subject.

I have weighed a great deal my dear Sir, all that you say respecting yourself. No selfish motive shall ever induce me to wish you to take any step but such as shall contribute to your happiness. We shd. certainly be abundantly gratified in possessing you, nor are the opinions you have formed respecting yr. welcome here at all founded. The chymists whom you oppose look to you with the greatest reverence; nor are you to believe from the lateness of your nomination to the Institute, that there was any Opposition whatever to your admission. You were not named the first because your nomination was secure, and because as member of the former academies, you had a right. It was a struggle for more uncertain Candidates that caused this delay. As to others, there is no friend of Liberty or of Science here who does not think like Mr Jefferson, so that your objections on this head, are all unfounded. Your health it seems is recovering, nor is yr. age such as to preclude such a Voyage. You are now about 68. This is not with studious men the Season of decay, either corporeal or mental. We have a friend here who is now 85 who has just published a Poem in 3 Vol called *Gli Animali parlanti*, a severe satire on the modern governments of Europe, and which rivals for its poetical Beauties Ariosto. He is now publishing 3 other 8vo. vols of poetry, which he has just finished, & which display all the richness of imagination of 40 Years. Your friend Mr Lindsay is recovered from a severe illness; he is older than you. Miss Williams has just received a lively letter from him. I trust therefore your health would be no hindrance, could other obstacles be removed.

I am happy to see that you are publishing your Church history. I shd. very willingly sit down to give you farther accounts of the modern state of Religion in this part of the world, but I propose sending you 4 Vols on that Subject written by our friend the late Bp of Blois M. Gregoire. This work will be the history of religion in France since the Revolution, which I think of translating with notes. The Bp you know is very Catholic & very antipapist, but he is also very liberal. you will find with the annotations we shall make, much information on the parts you wish. He is now in England, where he has been recd. with great honour by the Literati and by the *Jews* of whom he was the official defender here previous to the Revolution. They have evinced their Gratitude by a deputation to present him with their Thanks & a piece of plate worth 100 £.

Your notes on all the books of Scripture cannot fail of being a most valuable work. Mr Russel had already spoken to me about it. The price of printing here is at least 75 per Cent cheaper than in England. If you will send the work when ready we will print it here, and agreeable to the intimations contained in your former letter I will make Mr Russel advance half the expence, and I will undertake the other. He has promised to share with me that of printing the translations of yr works which I am going on with.

I have just received a Deputation from a Body of Christians of rather opposite principles to ours, the Missionary Society in London. These Gentlemen like ourselves are anxious to propagate the Gospel in France, & have proposed to me 6 months since the publication of the new Testament with an introduction of about 250 Pages which they sent me. I return'd it with much erasure and changes, which it seems they have adopted. Their principal is a Mr Bogue of Gosport who superintends an Academy for the education of independent Ministers. The Gentleman who is here & who was a Student under him tells me that yr theological works form at times part of their Lectures. He has given me a very interesting account of the state of Religion in England, and among other things informs me, that the Bishops have agreed to ordain none who do not subscribe to the 39 articles in the sense which they have laid down, which is far from being a liberal one. He assures me also tho' much allowance is to be made for his professional Attachments, that the Secessions from the Church are growing very alarming to the establishment, and if the facts he related to me are true, there may be some reason. As our house twice a week is somewhat of a Tower of Babel, where people of all Tongues and Professions assemble, We had a visit last evening from one of the Royal Chaplains, Dr Glasse who translated you know the Charactacus of Mason into Greek measure. From his acct. also there appears to be division in the house hold. He inform'd me however that your old Antagonist Dr. Horsley was translated last week to another Bishoprick that I *think* of St. Asaph with 6000 £ to the great discontent of his Brethren, but it seems that it was the King's particular pleasure. Horseley's incredulity in Religion he informs me has become proverbial as his profligacy in morals has become notorious.

You will be desirous no doubt of hearing some thing about the State of

Religion here in France. You have seen in the Papers the Concordat both for Catholics and Protestants. They are now by law placed on an equal footing and salaried alike. The protestants feel however the Indignity done to their profession, & have lately held a meeting in Paris & agreed to address the Government on certain points where the interference of the latter seems incompatible with Liberty of Conscience. They have also formed a central Committee of Correspondence with all the protestant churches throughout France. I have very little hopes and few wishes that the Government shd. accede to their Proposals in the first instance, tho' it is not unlikely from the personal Character of the first Consul, who affects great liberality of Sentiment on these points, that he may in some moment of Caprice accede to a revision. It seems that he has declared himself repeatedly in favour of protestant principles, tho' the truth is he knows nothing about either. Happily however the Laws give the greatest latitude to all other religious persuasions, and though the *Catholic Lutheran* and *Calvinist* are bound by certain articles & Conventions, the Socinian, Anabaptist, Independent, Jew, and others may open any churches at their own expence. In some parts of France the Catholics are very Zealous; in others the Protestants are not less so. On the Rhine the two Communions have joined, and in the South the secession from the Catholic church to the protestant has been and continues very great.

I cannot close this long letter without turning once more to temporal matters, and observing that the cause of Liberty has made some progress in England. Mr W. Smith is elected at Norwich in the room of Mr Wyndham, and Sr. Francis Burdett has turn'd out the Court Candidate for Middlesex. This last the more surprizes me as Sr. Francis informed me here at Paris, where he was loitering till within a week of the Dissolution that he had no intention of going into Parliament, & had made no preparation to canvas. It is singular, but we look toward England for Liberty, as till lately we looked toward France; and the present Government in the late Manifesto written by the Consul, talks of the English Government as either impotent to defend itself or willing to disturb the Social order of Europe.

I have other matters &c &c.—

Tr (DLC: TJ Papers, 108:18571-6); undated, but supplied from contents; in Thomas Cooper's hand; at head of text: "Copy of a Letter to Dr Priestley."

John Hurford Stone (1763-1818) met Joseph Priestley in the congregation of religious dissenters led by the radical preacher Richard Price at Hackney in Middlesex. When Talleyrand made a trip to England in 1792, Stone introduced him to Priestley, Charles James Fox, and Richard Brinsley Sheridan. Later that year Stone moved to Paris, where he was a committed supporter of the French Revolution. He engaged in mercantile and manufacturing ventures and opened a printing house called the Imprimerie Anglaise, or English Press, that issued works by Thomas Paine and Joel Barlow, as well as TJ's First Inaugural Address as a pamphlet and as a broadside on silk. Although Stone sometimes omitted the name of his establishment from title pages, letters from Volney to TJ of 21 Mch. and 10 May 1803 identify Stone as the publisher of the English translation of Volney's *Ruines* made by TJ and Barlow. Stone's exile from Great Britain became permanent in 1796, when the British government used his correspondence as evidence in an unsuccessful prosecution of his brother William for high treason. In 1798, William Cobbett and others sought to discredit Priestley by publishing an intercepted letter from Stone that praised the actions of France and alluded with favor to a pending invasion of England. In his *Letters to the Inhabitants of Northumberland*, Priestley sought to explain, rather than deny, the opinions and associations revealed by the intercepted letter. Perhaps the *Letters*, Priestley explained to TJ, would "give some satisfaction to my suspicious neighbours" (DNB; Madeleine B. Stern, "The English Press in Paris and Its Successors, 1793-1852," *Papers of the Bibliographical Society of America*, 74 [1980], 307-59; Jenny Graham, "Joseph Priestley in America," in Isabel Rivers and David L. Wykes, eds., *Joseph Priestley, Scientist, Philosopher, and Theologian* [Oxford, 2008], 225-7; *Copies of Original Letters Recently Written by Persons in Paris to Dr. Priestley in America* [Philadelphia, 1798]; Vol. 31:346; Vol. 33:341-2n; Vol. 34:441-2n).

Priestley's INTERESTING COMMUNICATION to Stone may have been a letter dated only "1802," perhaps written in the spring of the year. In it, Priestley said that the "continuation" of his *General History of the Christian Church* was in press. He praised Cooper, lamented the renewal of war in Saint-Domingue, and indicated that he had sent TJ an extract from an earlier letter from Stone. Priestley also enclosed a copy of a letter he had received from TJ, almost certainly that of 21 Mch. 1801, which TJ apologetically called "a long disquisition on politics." In it, the new president commented at some length, in negative terms, about the recent era of "bigotry in Politics & Religion" in the United States. TJ lauded the Republicans' success in breaking the stalemate of the stalled presidential selection by "peaceable & legitimate" means and expressed his confidence that America was at the beginning of a new age. In his letter to Stone, Priestley declared that if TJ's comments should be made public, "I should forfeit his friendship." Priestley insisted that the letter "may not, on any account, go out of your own hands, or a copy be taken of it, much more that it be not translated and printed." Priestley, however, was so taken with TJ's letter that he also sent a copy to his brother-in-

law in England, and through some channel, other associates of Stone and Priestley also saw it. TJ's letter did find its way into print and caused him some political embarrassment, but not until 1813 (John Towill Rutt, *Life and Correspondence of Joseph Priestley*, 2 vols. [London, 1831-32], 2:474-7; Vol. 33:393-5).

Although Cooper transcribed the name as "Mrs" FENWICK, Priestley expected his letter to reach Stone "by means of Mr. Fenwick, though he will go to England before he sees France." The bearer of the letter may have been Joseph Fenwick, the former American consul at Bordeaux. On 28 Apr., he informed Madison from Philadelphia that he would "embark in the May packet for London," then after about two weeks in England he would go to France to spend a month or two attending to personal business. Fenwick was married, and perhaps Stone received the letter through Mrs. Fenwick (Rutt, *Life and Correspondence*, 476; Madison, *Papers, Sec. of State Ser.*, 3:162; Vol. 33:334-5).

RETURN'D FROM PETERSBURGH: Alexander and La Harpe corresponded after the latter's departure from Russia in 1795. On Alexander's accession to the throne six years later, the new emperor invited his former teacher, who was living near Paris, to visit St. Petersburg. La Harpe spent ten months in Russia on that trip, returning to France in the spring of 1802 (Biaudet and Nicod, eds., *Correspondance de Frédéric-César de La Harpe et Alexandre Ier*, 1:19-29).

SA PATRIE: his native land.

ADMIT INTO THE CAST OF PROPRIETORS: a December 1801 decree allowed purchases of land by classes other than nobles, ending a monopoly on landholding by the Russian nobility (Hartley, *Alexander I*, 46-7).

Alexander's WIFE was Elizabeth Alekseevna, a princess originally from Baden (same, 15).

SOMETHING LIKE A NEW CONSTITUTION: the *sénatus-consulte*, approved 5 Aug., that gave Bonaparte power for life (see William Lee to TJ, 10 Aug.).

Bonaparte had placed restrictions on NEWSPAPERS in Paris, suppressing some publications and keeping the remainder under tight control (Tulard, *Dictionnaire Napoléon*, 1397-8).

ENTERED THE FIELD AGAINST THEM: on 8 Aug., the front page of the *Moniteur* carried Bonaparte's MANIFESTO in the form of an unsigned opinion piece. The article accused the *Times* of London of publishing "invectives" against France, said that disaffected émigré bishops living in England were libeling the church in France, and declared that Britain, in violation of the Amiens treaty, was harboring "brigands" who had tried to undermine order in France and advocated the assassination of the first consul. Questioning a liberty of the press that allowed such treatment of a friendly nation, the author suggested that a country must be responsible for its citizens' conduct toward other states. Rather than continue a long series of episodes in which France and Britain sought to undermine each other, beginning with Richelieu's aid to revolution in England, would it not be better to foster strong commercial relations and deny refuge to criminals? The French government was at present more solidly established than Britain's, the author declared, and the British should not doubt France's ability to respond. Protecting assassins and insurrectionaries, the article concluded, was beneath Britain's generosity, civilization, and honor, and failed to protect "l'ordre social européan" (*Gazette Nationale ou le Moniteur Universel*, 20 Thermidor Year 10). Bonaparte was particularly angry at newspapers published in London by disaffected French émigrés. In August, he lodged a formal protest with the British government, to which Lord Hawkesbury replied that Great Britain "cannot and never will" accede to any demand by a foreign power that could "in the smallest degree" compromise freedom of the press (Grainger, *Amiens Truce*, 146-9; Thierry Lentz, *Le Grand Consulat, 1799-1804* [Paris, 1999], 463).

PAR LE PEUPLE ET POUR LE PEUPLE: by the people and for the people.

INSULTED RUSSIA: at the beginning of his reign, Alexander wanted to ensure the continuation of peace in Europe, reclaim a role for Russia as a mediator of European affairs, and keep his empire independent of both Britain and France. Although Alexander did not entirely trust Bonaparte and Talleyrand, France and Russia signed a treaty of peace in the fall of 1801. In a secret convention, the two nations agreed to coordinate their policies regarding specific places and issues that were important to Russia. They cooperated in 1802 to influence the Diet of the Holy Roman Empire in the reorganization of German states under the Lunéville treaty of 1801. Regarding other areas in which Alexander took an interest, such as Switzerland and the Italian states, Bonaparte informed the Russians of general developments but did not consult them about his policies. In at least one case, that of Sardinia, he let it be known that Russia could expect to play no role (Parry, *Consolidated Treaty Series*, 56:221-5, 231-7; Hartley, *Alexander I*, 60-5; Lentz, *Grand Consulat*, 458-9; Thierry Lentz and others, eds., *Napoléon Bonaparte: Correspondance Général*, 6 vols. to date [Paris, 2004-], 3:979-80, 1074-5, 1129, 1130).

Alexander, without consulting his advisers, had met with King Frederick William III to establish a friendly relationship with PRUSSIA (Hartley, *Alexander I*, 65; Henri Troyat, *Alexander of Russia: Napoleon's Conqueror*, trans. Joan Pinkham [New York, 1982], 77).

AUSTRIA, which lost both territory and influence to France by the Lunéville treaty and by Bonaparte's assertion of control over various states in Europe, had almost precipitated war in July by resisting Bonaparte's arrangement for the disposition of one German bishopric (Grainger, *Amiens Truce*, 21-2, 115-18).

INSULTED THE ARMY: see TJ to John Brown, 14 Aug.

LATENESS OF YOUR NOMINATION: the National INSTITUTE of France elected Priestley a foreign associate in May 1802. He was the seventh person elected as an *associé étranger* and the third scientist to be so honored, following Joseph Banks and the British astronomer royal, Nevil Maskelyne. Priestley had been a foreign associate of the Académie Royale des Sciences, one of the FORMER ACADEMIES that preceded the National Institute (Amable Charles, Comte de Franqueville, *Le premier siècle de l'Institut de France, 25 Octobre 1795-25 Octobre 1895*, 2 vols. [Paris, 1895-96], 2:55-7, 459-61).

GLI ANIMALI PARLANTI: an epic poem in 26 songs of sextuplets, published in Paris in 1802, was written by Italian poet and author Giovanni Battista, who was then 78 years old and died the following year (Giovanni Battista Casti, *Gli Animali Parlanti*, ed. Luciana Pedroia [Rome, 1987], xi, xxviii).

Priestley's close friend, the theologian and Unitarian minister Theophilus Lindsey (LINDSAY), was a reluctant dissenter who first hoped to reform the Church of England from within before breaking with it to preside over the Essex Street Chapel, the first Unitarian congregation. He had a paralytic seizure in the spring of 1801 followed by a severe stroke in December but resumed his work in January 1802. He published some of Priestley's works as well as his own, including *Conversations on the Divine Government* in 1802 (DNB; Thomas Belsham, *Memoirs of the Late Reverend Theophilus Lindsey* [London, 1812], 432-3).

Helen Maria WILLIAMS, a British-born bluestocking and author of abolitionist poetry as well as of eight volumes of *Letters from France*, recounted her travels there beginning in 1790 and continuing through the French Revolution and Reign of Terror. Rumored to have had a close relationship with Stone, who lived with her family during the French Revolution, she counted among her salon friends many other reformers of the day, including Joel Barlow, Frédéric César de La Harpe, and Henri Grégoire (DNB).

CHURCH HISTORY: for Priestley's four-volume *A General History of the Christian Church, from the Fall of the Western Empire to the Present Time*, see Priestley to TJ, printed at 12 June (two letters).

William Russell (RUSSEL), a merchant and reformer from Birmingham and a leader in the local Presbyterian-Unitarian congregation, was a close friend, political ally, and patron of Priestley. Russell's partial inheritance of his father's interest in the Principio iron company in Maryland prompted him to travel to America in 1795, but he later returned to Europe, settling in France from 1802 to 1814 (DNB; Rivers and Wykes, eds., *Joseph Priestley*, 205).

David BOGUE, an Independent minister and missionary promoter trained in Scotland; he taught in schools in England before establishing the Gosport Academy in 1789 to educate young men for the Independent ministry. In 1795, he was one of the founding directors of the Missionary Society, later renamed the London Missionary Society, an interdenominational group intent on propagating the gospel rather than ideas of particular church structure and governance. Never traveling much beyond the Continent himself, Bogue trained the society's prospective overseas missionaries at his Gosport Academy from 1800 until his death. He prepared an *Essay on the Divine Authority of the New Testament* in 1802, which was widely translated and appeared as a preface to a French edition of the New Testament (DNB; John Morison, *The Fathers and Founders of the London Missionary Society. A Jubilee Memorial*, new ed. [London, 1844], 156-217).

George Henry GLASSE, the son of Royal Chaplain Samuel Glasse with whom Stone had him confused, published a Greek translation in 1781 of *Caractacus, A Dramatic Poem: Written on the Model of the Ancient Greek Tragedy,* written by William Mason and published in London and Dublin in 1759 (Walter Crouch, "Dr. Samuel Glasse, Rector of Wanstead, 1786-1812," *Essex Review*, 10 [1901], 141; DNB, 7:1299).

Samuel HORSLEY, an elected fellow of the Royal Society from 1767 to 1784, became an outspoken defender of religious orthodoxy affirming the doctrine of the Trinity and the apostolic succession of the Anglican clergy. He denounced Protestant and Unitarian dissenters, railed against Priestley's *History of the Corruptions of Christianity*, vigorously opposed the slave trade, and became bishop of St. Asaph in June 1802. Known for overindulgence in food and wine and nepotism to his daughter-in-law's family, he ran into debt and died insolvent in 1806 (DNB).

The French government began to develop a policy toward PROTESTANTS several months before the signing of the Concordat with the Catholic Church in July 1801. A law of 8 Apr. 1802 recognized the two major Protestant groups, the LUTHERAN churches, located mainly in Alsace and the Rhine Valley, and the Reformed or CALVINIST congregations found primarily in the south and southwest of France and in scattered pockets elsewhere. The law created a hierarchical organization that aligned more closely to Lutherans' accustomed practice than to the Calvinists'. The new system was based on consistory churches of 6,000 people living in the same *département*, a requirement that could not be met by dispersed Reformed Church congregations. Protestants generally considered the law to be a significant step forward. Bonaparte received praise as a protector of religious diversity, likened to the Persian emperor Cyrus the Great (Tulard, *Dictionnaire Napoléon*, 1415-16).

Britain held a general election for the House of Commons during July, the first general election since 1796. William SMITH and Francis BURDETT, both of whom were denounced by their opponents as radical Jacobins, were members of the previous Parliament, but won seats from larger constituencies in 1802. Smith, a religious dissenter and advocate of reform who was acquainted with Priestley, defeated William Windham, the former secretary at war in William Pitt's government, to take the seat for Norwich. Burdett, a baronet who had called attention to the treatment of political prisoners, took the Middlesex County seat from William Mainwaring. After Mainwaring's supporters, including the London *Times*, accused Burdett of electoral fraud, the election for the Middlesex seat was voided (DNB; London *Times*, 13, 16, 26, 28, 29 July; John Ehrman, *The Younger Pitt: The Consuming Struggle* [London, 1996], 287n, 574).

[1] Word supplied.
[2] Word supplied.

From Albert Gallatin

DEAR SIR   25th Oct. 1802

The certificate in the case of Daniel Cutter, is similar to what has usually been prepared when the expense is to be paid out of the contingent fund. The only form required is that you should annex the word "Approved" to the certificate & return it with your signature to this office—

Respectfully Your obedt. Servt.   ALBERT GALLATIN

RC (DLC); at foot of text: "The President." Recorded in SJL as received from the Treasury Department on 25 Oct. with notation "Cutter for seamen contingt fund." Enclosure not found.

On 26 Oct., Gallatin reminded TJ: "Captn. Cutter waits for the payment of the money allowed for the transportation of seamen from Bordeaux; which cannot be done until your approbation to the certificate transmitted yesterday shall have been received" (RC in DLC; partially dated: "Tuesday"; addressed: "The President of the United States"; endorsed by TJ as received from the Treasury Department on 26 Oct. and "Cutter seamen Contingt. fund" and so recorded in SJL).

From William Jarvis

SIR   Lisbon 25 Octr. 1802

I have the honor to acquaint you that I have shipped on board the Adelaide for Baltimore, John Mun Master, two half pipes Oeiras Wine of the Vintage of 1798, which I address'd to Genl Smith. The House from which I obtained it, is the only one in this City that had any; but I am apprehensive Sir that it will not prove altogether agreeable to your taste, it appearing to me a little too sweet to answer your description, tho time will rectify this fault, it growing drier by age. Whatever may be its defects I assure you Sir that not any better can be had, as neither pain nor price has been spared to procure the first quality

Since the old Marquis Pombal's death it is said the Wines from that Estate have not been so good as in his life time, owing to the Vineyards not being so well attended, nor so much pain taken with the Vintage. But should it meet your approbation it will be a source of infinite pleasure to me—

with the most profound Respect I have the honor to be Sir Your mo: devoted Servt   WILLIAM JARVIS

RC (DLC); at foot of first page: "Thomas Jefferson Esquire"; endorsed by TJ as received 6 Jan. 1803.

The OEIRAS WINE that TJ had requested arrived in Baltimore in January 1803 and was eventually shipped to Monticello (MB, 2:1115; TJ to S. Smith & Buchanan, 12 Jan. 1803).

To Levi Lincoln

DEAR SIR   Washington Oct. 25. 1802.

Your favor of the 16th. is recieved, and that of July 24. had come to hand while I was at Monticello. I sincerely condole with you on the sickly state of your family and hope this will find them reestablished with the approach of the cold season. as yet however we have had no frost at this place, and it is believed the yellow fever still continues in Philadelphia if not in Baltimore. we shall all be happy to see you here whenever the state of your family admits it.   you will have seen by the newspapers, that we have gained ground generally in the elections, that we have lost ground in not a single district of the US. except Kent county in Delaware, where a religious dissension occasioned it. in Jersey the elections are always carried by small majorities, consequently the issue is affected by the smallest accidents. by the paper of the last night we have a majority of 3. in their council & 1. in their house of representatives, another says it is only of 1. in each house; even the latter is sufficient for every purpose. the opinion I originally formed has never been changed; that such of the body of the people as thought themselves federalists, would find that they were in truth republicans, and would come over to us by degrees; but that their leaders had gone too far ever to change. their bitterness increases with their desperation. they are trying slanders now which nothing could prompt but a gall which blinds their judgments as well as their consciences. I shall take no other revenge than by a steady pursuit of economy, and peace, and by the establishment of republican principles in substance and in form, to sink federalism into an abyss from which there shall be no resurrection for it. I still think our original idea as to office is best. that is to depend for the obtaining a just participation, on deaths, resignations, & delinquencies; this will least affect the tranquility of the people, and prevent their giving into the suggestion of our enemies, that ours has been a contest for office, not for principle. this is rather a slow operation, but it is sure, if we pursuit it steadily; which however has not been done with the undeviating resolution which I would wish. to these means of obtaining a just share in the transaction of the public business shall be added one other, to wit, removal for electioneering activity or open & industrious opposition to the principles of the present government legislative & executive. every officer of the government may vote at elections according to his conscience; but we should betray the cause committed to our care, were we to permit the influence of official patronage to be used to overthrow that cause. your present situation will enable you to judge of prominent offenders in your state in the case of the present election. I pray you to seek them, to mark them, to be quite sure of your ground that we may commit no error or wrong, and leave the rest to me. I have been urged to remove mr Whittermore the Surveyor of Gloucester, on grounds of neglect of duty and industrious opposition. yet no facts are so distinctly charged as to make the step sure which we should take in this. will you take the trouble to satisfy yourself on this point. I think it not amiss that it should be known that we are determined to remove officers who are active or open mouthed against the government, by which I mean the legislature as well as the Executive. Accept assurances of my sincere friendship & high respect.

TH: JEFFERSON

RC (MHi: Levi Lincoln Papers); addressed: "Levi Lincoln esquire Atty Genl. of the US. Worcester"; endorsed by Lincoln. PrC (DLC).

RELIGIOUS DISSENSION: charges appeared in the *Federal Ark* that the Methodist Society had been disturbed in their devotions, abused, and assaulted by the Republicans of New Castle. The Republican press countered that the abuse came from the Federalists. While the people of New Castle knew this, "A friend to toleration" feared that the citizens of Kent and Sussex did not realize that "those '*disturbing mobs*' were composed of some of John Adams's good federal *midshipmen!*" The Federalists also charged that James Payne, a leading Methodist on trial at Wilmington, was being "persecuted by the democrats," who anxiously awaited his conviction. The *Mirror of the Times* argued that the principal persons engaged against Payne were Federalists. Indeed Caesar A. Rodney served as a leading counsel for Payne (Wilmington *Mirror of the Times, & General Advertiser*, 22, 25, 29 Sep., 4 Oct. 1802).

SMALL MAJORITIES: some newspapers were reprinting, from the *Aurora* of 22 Oct., a tally that gave Republicans a three-vote majority in the 13 seats of the New Jersey Council and a one-vote margin in the 39-member House of Assembly (Alexandria, Va., *Columbian Advertiser*, New York *Morning Chronicle*, and New York *American Citizen*, all 25 Oct.).

To James Sylvanus McLean

SIR   Washington Oct. 25. 1802.

The duties of my present office calling for the whole of my time and more than the whole, if more there could be, I have been obliged to deny myself the gratification of indulging in speculations of the nature of those in your letter of Sep. 30. speculations which were I free would be peculiarly agreeable to me. that the introduction of so powerful an agent as steam will make a great change in the situation of man I have no doubt. to extend it's application nothing is wanting as you observe, but to simplify the machinery, and make that & the fire apparatus more portable. no law of nature forbids us to hope this, and the ingenuity of man leaves us to despair of nothing within the laws of nature. some effective steps towards this simplification have been lately taken, but nothing which approaches to your object of moving carriages by that agent. that you may succeed in it, I sincerely wish. I should suppose no place in the US. so likely as Philadelphia to furnish artists equal to the execution of the requisite machinery, & persons willing to embark in the enterprize itself, for a just share in it's profits. but of this your acquaintance in that place probably enables you to form a better judgment than I can. to the guidance of your own judgment I must leave it with my best wishes for it's success & for your personal welfare.   TH: JEFFERSON

RC (DLC); addressed: "Mr. James Sylv. Mc.lean Lancaster"; franked and postmarked; endorsed: "Dead letter, returned to the General post office,—from Lancaster Pennsylvania The President U.S."; endorsed by TJ in ink on address sheet. PrC (DLC).

From Thomas Newton

D<small>R</small> S<small>IR</small>   Norfolk 25th Octr. 1802—

I wrote you some days past & inclosed Mr Eassans letter to me, I
have since been informed that he is a good man, from gentlemen from
that County. & they wished him to succeed.

I am happy to hear that our prospects in the Mediteranean brightens,
I have hopes all the European powers will join in stopping the depredations of the States of Barbary. you have not said whether I shall in-
gage any cyder for you this year. I am respectfully

   Yr. Most Ob S   T<small>HOS</small>. N<small>EWTON</small>

I took the liberty of asking you for a copy of a law respecting this
Parish (Eliza River) passed in 1764 allowing them to buy 4 lotts in
lieu of a glebe, we cannot obtain a copy in this place. if you have it I
will thank you for a Copy

RC (DLC); endorsed by TJ as received
17 Nov. and so recorded in SJL.

I WROTE YOU SOME DAYS PAST: one of
two letters Newton wrote to TJ on 21
Oct., neither of which has been found. TJ
recorded the first in SJL as received 26
Oct. and the second as received the following day with the notation "John Easson Surveyor Smithfield." John Eason
had represented Isle of Wight, Surry, and
Prince George Counties in the Virginia
Senate for three terms and was confirmed
as surveyor at Smithfield in January 1803
(Leonard, *General Assembly*, 205, 210,
214; JEP, 1:433, 440).

For the LAW RESPECTING Elizabeth
River Parish, see Newton to TJ, 6 Oct.

To Thomas Claxton

S<small>IR</small>   Washington Oct. 26. 1802.

Observing that the roof of the Representatives chambers has sunk
in the middle, that the walls are cracked in several places and pressing out from the perpendicular, I think it necessary that the cause
should be examined into by good & experienced persons, that we may
know whether they may be safely left in their present state until the
next season, when such steps may be taken as Congress shall in the
mean time authorize, or whether, and what, *immediate* steps are necessary to prevent the injury from going further until the next season.
I would wish Mr. Blagden, mr Herbaugh & mr Hadfield to be called
in, and to recieve their opinions in writing; which therefore I request
you to do, as you have the immediate care of that chamber under your
charge. Accept my best wishes.   T<small>H</small>: J<small>EFFERSON</small>

PrC (DLC); at foot of text: "Mr. Claxton."

ROOF OF THE REPRESENTATIVES
CHAMBERS: beginning with the first ses-

sion of the Seventh Congress, members of the House of Representatives met in the Capitol in a temporary brick structure in the south wing designed by James Hoban and built by William Lovering and William Dyer. From three design options, TJ had approved a plan that would allow some of its features to be used in the permanent structure of the Capitol. The selected elliptical one-story arcade was intended to support columns 30 feet high that would ultimately help support the roof. When the walls of the "Oven," as the hot and stuffy legislative chamber was commonly known, began to buckle under the weight of the roof, builders braced them with heavy timber. TJ's concerns about the architectural soundness of the chamber were not unfounded and the structure was razed entirely in 1804 and rebuilt in favor of Benjamin Henry Latrobe's revised plans for the south wing (Office of the Architect of the Capitol, *The United States Capitol: A Brief Architectural History* [Washington, D.C., 1990], 5, 7; Donald R. Kennon, ed., *The United States Capitol: Designing and Decorating a National Icon* [Athens, Ohio, 2000], 20-1; William Bushong, *Glenn Brown's History of the United States Capitol* [Washington, D.C., 2005], 98, 102-3; Latrobe, *Correspondence*, 1:268-84; Vol. 34:234-5; Benjamin H. Latrobe to TJ, 4 Apr. 1803, and enclosure).

To Albert Gallatin

TH:J. TO MR GALLATIN   Oct. 26. 1802.

Will you be so good as to peruse & return the inclosed? what Dupont says of N. Orleans will require a verbal explanation. he will probably be a very efficient instrument for us in that business, and I should very much wish to render him the personal service he asks as to paiments in Paris, if you find such an arrangement can be made agreeably to what is right & useful for us. it would lessen the amount of bills you have to procure here for Amsterdam.

PrC (DLC). Enclosure: Pierre Samuel Du Pont de Nemours to TJ, 16 Aug. 1802.

From Albert Gallatin

DEAR SIR   [Oct. 26. 1802]

I return Mr Dupont's letter: we do not pay in Europe any part of the interest on our domestic debt which is that alluded to by him as partly held by French stockholders. The Bank of the U.S., for a majority of the foreign stockholders whose attorneys have made that institution their attorney, and the special attorneys of the others remit the quarterly interest to England & Holland where the sd. stockholders have wished it to be paid. If the French Stockholders will make Mr Dupont's house their agents, the business may be transacted by him as he wishes; but we have nothing to do with it: his error arises from his having supposed that the remittances for domestic[1] interest to Holland, were made by Government; it is only the interest & principal[2] of our foreign debt which Govt. remits; & that is exclusively held in Holland.

On the subject of the Comptroller, on which I feel much interested, I have made up my opinion, after a fuller examination of his duties than I had yet bestowed on it, that a certain degree of legal knowledge is the most essential qualification: as it is difficult to find any one man in whom the several requisites are united, it would be preferable to obtain a sound lawyer, or at least a man of perfectly sound judgment & possessed of legal information (who had at least read law) & who had only a general idea of accounts, than a perfect accountant without law knowledge. Not only the general nature of the duties of that office leads me to that conclusion; but it is also expressed with considerable force by the consideration that I am not a lawyer; the law questions which arise in the Treasury (exclusively of those relating to the settlement of accounts) are numerous: during the comptroller's absence, nearly one half of my time is occupied by questions directed to me by collectors & which I would refer to him if he was present, or directed to him & which his clerks refer to me during his absence. If we have a Comptroller who is not a lawyer, it will considerably encrease my labour or rather prevent its being applied in the most proper manner, and the business will not be so well done, as I will be compelled to decide on a much greater number of law questions. The other two important requisites for a Comptroller is that he should possess method and great industry: without the first, the last would be of no avail; and to fill well his duties he cannot be too laborious. Another essential point is that he should write, if not with elegance, at least with precision & great facility; for his correspondence is very extensive & consists principally of decisions, instructions, & explanations. I cannot write even a decent letter without great labour, and that is another reason why I desire that the Comptroller may be able to write himself; for the duties of the two offices are so blended in what relates to the collection of the impost, that a great part of the correspondence with collectors[3] may fall either on the one or the other as may be agreed on between them. But I repeat that legal knowledge and a sound judgment are the most important qualifications. Who will answer that description I do not know. Unless we had a personal knowledge of men, I am afraid of the eastward, both on account of their species of law knowledge on which I could not, generally speaking, place much greater confidence than on my own judgment, and because their style of writing is not as classical & correct as it ought to be. Mr Madison has mentioned judge Duval of whom I never heard any thing but favorable, but whom I do not sufficiently know justly to appreciate his rate. Who was that comptroller of New York whom Dewitt Clinton once proposed for naval officer, intending that Bailey should have his office. He spoke highly of him; but I recollect neither his name nor profession.

I enclose two recommendations for Mr Kuhn; also a letter from Worthington which induces a belief that politics are settling the right way in the north west territory

With sincere respect & attachment Your obedt. Servt.

ALBERT GALLATIN

Impost for last quarter.

———

paymts. in the Treasury—about 3 millions 4 hd. thd. dollars or 200,000, dollars more than in any preceding quarter—see the enclosed

RC (DLC); undated; addressed: "The President"; endorsed by TJ as a letter of 26 Oct. received from the Treasury Department on the same day and "paimt of interest at Paris. comptroller. 3d. quarters rect. of Impost" and so recorded in SJL. Enclosures: (1) Joseph Clay to Albert Gallatin, Philadelphia, 19 Oct. 1802, introducing Peter Kuhn, Jr., as a young man with extensive mercantile and business information and "of sound political principles"; Clay will consider as a "personal favor" any attention Gallatin shows Kuhn as he visits Washington (RC in DNA: RG 59, LAR; endorsed by TJ: "Kuhn Peter. Clay Joseph. to mr Gallatin"). (2) Thomas Worthington to Gallatin, Chilicothe, 15 Oct. 1802, predicting that three-fourths of those elected to the convention for statehood will be Republicans; all five from Ross County are from the party; although Elias Langham, shortly before the election, requested an investigation into Worthington's conduct as register of the land office, Langham "is left out by a great majority" and Worthington is among the five elected; he predicts that the state legislature "will be almost entirely republican" and those sent to Congress and presidential electors "will be decidedly so" (Gallatin, *Papers*, 7:652-3; see *Terr. Papers*, 3:248-51, for

the charges against Worthington). (3) List of 51 ports with receipts for the third quarter ending 30 Sep. 1802 paid into the Treasury by each collector for a total income of $3,397,598.68; Gallatin notes below the total: "The real amt. will exceed this sketch several Hd. dollars" (MS in DLC; in Gallatin's hand; endorsed by Gallatin: "Receipt in Treasury Impost—3d Qr. 1802"). Other enclosure not found.

Gabriel Duvall (DUVAL) was chief justice of the General Court of Maryland (Vol. 33:268n). Robert R. Livingston considered Elisha Jenkins, a businessman, well qualified to serve as naval officer, before he was appointed COMPTROLLER OF NEW YORK by Governor George Clinton in 1801 (George Rogers Howell and Jonathan Tenney, *Bi-Centennial History of Albany. History of the County of Albany, N.Y., from 1609 to 1886* [New York, 1886], 133; Vol. 35:62; Elisha Jenkins to TJ, 4 June 1802). DeWitt Clinton's recommendation has not been found.

[1] Word interlined.
[2] Word and ampersand interlined.
[3] Preceding two words added in margin.

From João, Prince Regent of Portugal

Lisbon, 26 Oct. 1802. He announces that his wife, the princess of Brazil, has this day given birth to a son. He knows that the United States will receive this news as another sign of his constant readiness to cultivate the relations of understanding and friendship between the two countries.

RC (DNA: RG 59, Ceremonial Letters); 2 p.; in Portuguese, in a clerk's hand, signed by João as prince of Brazil and countersigned by João de Almeida de Mello e Castro as secretary of state for foreign affairs and war (see Vol. 35:442n); addressed: "A Os Estados Unidos da America que muito amo e prezo" ("to the United States of America, which I very much love and esteem"); endorsed by Jacob Wagner as received 29 Mch. 1803 and "To be answd."

The baby born at Queluz Palace in Lisbon on 26 Oct. was the seventh child of João and his wife, Carlota Joaquina. They named the child Miguel (José Correia do Souto, *Dicionário de História de Portugal*, 6 vols. [Lisbon, 1985], 4:83, 306).

Notes on Bounds of the Vincennes Tract

[on or after 26 Oct. 1802]

Convention between the Poutawatamies, Eel river Indns. Piankeshaws, Weaws, Kaskaskias & Kickapoos & Govr. Harrison for the US. at Vincennes Sep. 17. 1802.

In considn that the US. relinquish all claim to lands 'in the nbhood of Vincennes except the following described tract' they cede to the US. the following described tract, viz. 'beginning at Point Coupee on the Wabash river, thence running a Westwardly line 4. leagues, thence South Westwardly[1] by a line drawn parallel to the general course of the Wabash river until it will be intersected by a Westwardly line drawn from the confluence of the White river and Wabash river, thence from the point of intersection aforesd along the sd line by the confluence of the White & Wabash rivers in an Easterly direction 24 leagues, thence North *westwardly*[2] by a line drawn parallel to the General course of the sd Wabash river until it will intersect an Easterly line drawn from Point Coupee aforesd on the Wabash river, thence by the line last mentioned to Point Coupee the place of beginning.'

also to transfer & make over to the US 'the right & privilege of making salt for ever at the salt lick on the Saline river near the Ohio river,[3] & also a tract of land 4. miles square including the Salt lick aforesaid.'

MS (DLC: TJ Papers, 126:21749); undated, but see below; entirely in TJ's hand, including one corrective note in margin (see note 2); endorsed by TJ: "Indians. Boundaries established between the US. and Indians around Vincennes."

On 26 Oct., the War Department received a copy of the CONVENTION from which TJ made the notes printed above (William Henry Harrison to War Department, 20, 24 Sep., recorded in DNA: RG 107, RLRMS). The document seen by TJ has not been found, but the text of the convention is in Moses Dawson, *A Historical Narrative of the Civil and Military Services of Major-General William H. Harrison* (Cincinnati, 1824), 27-8, and reprinted in Esarey, *William Henry Harrison*, 1:56-7.

In June, Henry Dearborn had authorized William Henry HARRISON to negotiate the limits of the tract around VINCENNES and to investigate other possible acquisitions of territory by the United States (Dearborn to TJ, 29 July, 7 Aug.). The Vincennes tract, granted by Indians in the region to France in the colonial period, could be claimed by the United States through succession, the grant having passed from France to Great Britain, along with other French lands east of the Mississippi, by the 1763 Treaty of Paris, and similarly from Britain to the United States by the 1783 treaty that ended the Revolutionary War (Parry, *Consolidated Treaty Series*, 42:326; 48:491-2).

TRANSFER & MAKE OVER TO THE US: five Potawatomis, two members of the Eel River tribe, three Piankashaws, three Weas, one Kaskaskia, and two Kickapoos agreed to the convention signed on 17 Sep. In addition to setting bounds of the Vincennes tract, the instrument authorized a group of four chiefs, including Little Turtle, to conclude treaties and agreements for the formal cession to the United States of the Vincennes lands and the saline springs. Little Turtle was present during the negotiation of the convention, not as a party to the transaction, but, with his son-in-law, William Wells, to help Harrison complete the agreement (Dawson, *Historical Narrative*, 27-8; Owens, *Jefferson's Hammer*, 63-6). In his annual message on 15 Dec. 1802, TJ advised Congress that the agreement on the lines of the Vincennes tract meant the "extinction" of Native American titles to a tract 24 leagues wide running about the same distance down the Wabash River.

[1] Dawson, *Historical Narrative*, 27: "southwardly."

[2] In margin, keyed to this word with a "+," TJ wrote "*Eastwardly.*" Dawson, *Historical Narrative*, 28: "northeastwardly."

[3] Preceding four words lacking in Dawson, *Historical Narrative*, 28.

From Connecticut Republicans

SIR   [27 Oct. 1802]

In a government like ours, where the confidence of the people is the best support and reward of political merit, a testimony of this confidence from the republicans of Connecticut will not be unacceptable to the chief executive of our country.

Among the United States, this State affords the solitary fact of republicans, whose voice has on no occasion been allowed a public expression, either in their State legislature, or in the councils of the nation, or in the choice of a President.

Persuaded that a season has arrived when our hopes and fears ought to be equally at rest as respects the enemies of liberty, and that the majority of our fellow citizens are republican, we will not delay the expression of our confidence in your character and administration.

We rejoice that the principles of our revolution triumphed eminently in your election to the highest of offices, the presidency of a free people, and that the arts which were designed to prevent that triumph, at a memorable crisis of public anxiety, were defeated. Your appointments of the distinguished men who preside over the departments, and the legislative measures, adopted under your sanction, tending to the decrease of patronage and expence, have concurred with the general prosperity of the United States to advance the republican cause in this State. Your forbearance, and spirit of conciliation, extended even to this time, towards some powerful opposers of your administration, have persuaded the people of your sincere wish to restore harmony to social intercourse, and ought to have silenced those clamours which were raised against a few early & justifiable discriminations.

We confide fully in your motives and measures, and are sure that the general interests of the union will be the unvarying object of your labours; and whenever these interests can be promoted by an extended exercise of that discretion which the constitution has confided to the President in the choice of officers, even in the subordinate grades of his administration, we shall rejoice that the general interests coincide with our wishes.

You have known, Sir, a part of the abuse and revilings which our political opponents in this State have heaped on your name, your friends, and the cause of liberty. What has not been made public, we hope may be concealed from you and the world; but we are not unmindful of these testimonies of a radical hostility to the principles of our revolution.

In the midst of republican successes on every side of us, we will not complain of delays. Through a continuance of the wise system of measures already begun, when their tendency shall have been fully perceived, we have full confidence that this State will regain a political standing in the union, and that the President will hereafter receive a more official, though it cannot be a more sincere, tribute of attachment and respect.

In the name of the republicans of the State of Connecticut.

Wm. Judd Chairman
Jno T. Peters Clerk.

RC (DLC); undated; in a clerk's hand, signed by Judd; at head of text: "To the President of the United States." Recorded in SJL as received 4 Nov. Enclosure: Notice that a general meeting of Connecticut Republicans held at New Haven, 27 Oct. 1802, with Judd serving as chairman and John T. Peters as clerk, unanimously approved an address to the president of the United States reported by the committee appointed at the last meeting, consisting of Judd, Pierpont Edwards, Joseph Willcox, Asa Spalding, John Welch, and Abraham Bishop, and resolving "That it be signed in our name by the Chairman of this Meeting, and forwarded by him to the President" (MS in same; on a separate sheet; in a clerk's hand, signed by Peters). Enclosed in William Judd to TJ, New Haven, 28 Oct. 1802, stating, "Pursuant to a resolve of the republicans of the State of Connecticut, I have the honor to enclose their Address to you, passed at General Meeting, together with a Copy of their Resolve" (RC in DLC, in a clerk's hand, signed by Judd, endorsed by TJ as received 4 Nov. and "Address of a general meeting of the Republicans of Connecticut at New Haven, Oct. 27. 1802" and so recorded in SJL).

For William Judd, see Vol. 36:109n. John T. Peters, clerk of the meeting, was a member of the state legislature from Hebron (Hartford *Connecticut Courant*, 17 May 1802).

From George Hadfield, Leonard Harbaugh, and George Blagden

SIR   City of Washington October 27 1802

The under signed have examined the construction of the Eliptical Room south of the Capitol agreeable to your wish expressed through Mr Clackston and are of opinion that the signs of instability which have appeared in the building are entirely owing to the Roof which presses the walls outward, but they believe that no immediate bad consequnces can hapen.

They would recommend all the cracks to be stopped up, and if any further marks should appear that the Building is still giving way the walls may be propped up on the out side to insure the Building till after the next session of Congress—

Sir We are Yr. Obt. Servants

GEO HADFIELD
LEONARD HARBAUGH
GEORGE BLAGDEN

RC (DLC); in Hadfield's hand, signed by all; addressed: "The President of the U: N: States." Recorded in SJL as received 28 Oct.

Leonard Harbaugh (d. 1822), a contractor from Baltimore, came to Washington in 1792 at the invitation of the Board of Commissioners to work on the capital city. He built the flawed Rock Creek Bridge, but achieved success building Trinity Church and finishing the Little Falls locks on the Potomac. Named chief engineer for the Potomac Company by 1797, he also oversaw the construction and opening of the Great Falls locks. In 1798 and 1799 he received contracts for the construction of the Treasury and the

War Department buildings (Douglas R. Littlefield, "Eighteenth-Century Plans to Clear the Potomac River: Technology, Expertise, and Labor in a Developing Nation," VMHB, 93 [1985], 315-16; William W. Warner, *At Peace with All Their Neighbors: Catholics and Catholicism in the National Capital 1787-1860* [Washington, D.C., 1994], 22-3, 125-30; Vol. 23:379; Vol. 26:426-7n).

George Blagden (d. 1826), an English-born stonemason who came to the United States sometime before 1794, was super-intendent for stonework and quarries at the Capitol. He was active in Washington civic, business, and church affairs and was killed by the collapse of an embank-ment of the Capitol (Henry Hope Reed, *The United States Capitol: Its Architecture and Decoration* [New York, 2005], 192; Latrobe, *Correspondence*, 1:284n).

YOUR WISH: see TJ to Thomas Claxton, 26 Oct.

From John F. Mercer

Council Chamber Annapolis
DEAR SIR,   October 27. 1802

In the Letter you did me the honor to write me of the 7th of July last, you gave me information that the Interest due on the loan of two hundred thousand Dollars made by the State of Maryland to the Commissioners of the City of Washington and guaranteed by Congress would be immediately paid—The Sum of eighteen thousand Dollars then due on this loan, was soon after actually remitted by the Treasury of the United States, to that of this State, but the succeeding quarter's payment of three thousand Dollars which became due on the first of this Month, still remains unpaid.

It contained also an assurance, that the loan of fifty thousand Dollars with the Interest due thereon and which now amounts to three thousand Dollars would be also paid on the first Monday in November next.

As the Legislature of Maryland convene on that day, to enable the Executive to lay before them a Statement of the public resources, they are anxious that you would direct the Secretary of the Treasury to remit on the 1 of November next, the Sum of fifty six thousand, two hundred and fifty Dollars, which will be due, to Thomas Harwood Treasurer of this State.

With the sincerest affection & Respect I remain your Obed Servant
JOHN F. MERCER

RC (DLC); in a clerk's hand, signed by Mercer; endorsed by TJ as received 29 Oct. but recorded in SJL at 28 Oct. FC (MdAA: Letterbooks of Governor and Council); in same clerk's hand; dated 26 Oct.

On 5 Nov., Governor Mercer reported to the LEGISLATURE OF MARYLAND that the "last loan with the Interest due on the 1st. of November, and all the Interest of the two first loans except for the last quarter have been received into the Treasury.—The Interest due for this quarter, we are informed will be paid in a few days and from the assurances of the President of the United States, we have no doubt of a punctual and liberal compliance with the law" (Mercer to the General Assembly, dated 6 [i.e. 5] Nov. 1802, in MdAA: Letterbooks of Governor and Council; *Votes and Proceedings of the House of Delegates of the State of Maryland, November Session, One Thousand Eight Hundred and Two* [Annapolis, 1803], 5).

From Craven Peyton

DEAR SIR   Stumpisland 27th. Octr 1802

I made it my bussiness to call on Mr. Henderson immediately aftar getting to the state of Kentuckey And as soon as possible to compleat the purchase, the land in the County of Boone which he has conveyed in Trust is more clear of disputes than Any land they hold. as I was informed, its not being divided is the reason of my not being more particular in the discription of it, from what I coud. discovar Hendarson appeared to be in good credit, And much respected. I entared into the purchase with the Widow Henderson without your naming Any particular sum, shoud. the sum given be more than you contemplated, I should be quite willing for you not to take it, as my fervant wish is to give you entire satisfaction. for your own inspection, I have enclosed all the papars. shoud Any alterations be necessary please pint them out, And they shall be executed. respecting the payment £650.0.0 will be required the Tenth of the next month. And shoud. the dower proparty meet your approbation the Money coud continue in your hands untill some time the next year, from yours of the 8th June I am extremely fearfull that this sum may put you[1] to some inconvenience which woud. give me much pain. And have since my arrival endeavoured to make sale & indeed a considerable sacrafice so as to throw the payment to the next year, for your Own Accommodation, but my endeavours have proven inaffectual. please drop me a line by the return mail

I am with great Respt: yr. mst Obet   C PEYTON

RC (ViU); endorsed by TJ as received 31 Oct. and so recorded in SJL.

CALL ON MR. HENDERSON: James L. Henderson acted on behalf of his younger siblings, the Henderson minors who had moved with their mother to Shelby County, Kentucky, the previous fall (Boynton Merrill, Jr., *Jefferson's Nephews: A Frontier Tragedy* [Princeton, 1976], 65, 67; Vol. 35:455n).

PURCHASE WITH THE WIDOW HENDERSON: see Vol. 35:xlvi-xlviii, 342-4n, 362-4.

YOURS OF THE 8TH JUNE: see TJ's first letter to Peyton of that date.

[1] Word interlined.

I
Elizabeth Henderson Deed for Dower
to Craven Peyton

Know all men by these presents that I Elizabeth Henderson of the state of Kentucky have this day bargained and sold to Craven Peyton of the state of Virginia, all my right, title and interest in all the property[1] in the county of Albemarle in said state of Virginia which I possessed[2] as Dower after the death of my husband Bennett Henderson in said county of Albemarle, except the mill, warehouse, and improved lots in the town of Milton; to have & to hold the sd lands and appurtenances to him the sd Craven[3] & his heirs: and the sd Elizabeth, the sd lands and appurtenances to him the sd Craven & his heirs will for ever warrant and defend. in witness whereof the sd Elizabeth have hereunto set her hand & seal this 18th. day of Sep. 1802.

ELIZABETH HENDERSON

Teste
JAMES L. HENDERSON.   CHARLES HENDERSON.
ELIZA. HENDERSON £250.–0–0

Tr (ViU); entirely in TJ's hand, with hand-drawn facsimile seal beside Elizabeth Henderson's signature; on same sheet as Enclosure No. 2; endorsed by TJ: "Elizabeth Henderson to Craven Peyton } Deed for Dower Sep. 18. 02. except Mill, warehouses improvd lots in Milton." Tr (same); in a clerk's hand; lacks sum of money after E. Henderson's signature; includes Isham Henderson and John Gentry as testators; acknowledgement of deed in Shelby County, Kentucky, by James L. Henderson, Isham Henderson, and John Gentry before Mathews Flournoy and Thomas I. Gwin, justices of the peace, 6 June 1804; certified by James Craig, clerk of Shelby County Court, same date; Craig's certificate certified by Isaac Ellis, justice of the peace for the court, same date; attested by John Nicholas, clerk, as deed to be recorded by the "Albemarle July Court 1804"; endorsed: "Henderson to Peyton } Copy Deed Exd."; endorsed by TJ: "Elizabeth Henderson. Dowress. deed to Craven Peyton 1802. Sep. 18. for Dower in all the lands except the Mill Warehouse improved lots in Milton." Tr (Albemarle County Deed Book No. 14:497-8); includes Isham Henderson and Gentry as testators; acknowledgment of deed by James L. Henderson, Isham Henderson, and Gentry before Flournoy and Gwin, 6 June 1804; certified by Craig, same date; Craig's certificate certified by Ellis, same date; certified and ordered to be recorded by Nicholas at the Albemarle Court, July 1804.

[1] 2d and 3d Trs: "real property."
[2] 2d and 3d Trs: "possess."
[3] Here added in 2d and 3d Trs: "Peyton."

II

Craven Peyton's Contract with Elizabeth Henderson

'It is understood that whereas I Elizabeth Henderson have this day sold to Craven Peyton of Virginia my[1] dower in certain property in Albermarle county Virginia, including the house I formerly lived in, and Know ye that whereas I rented the sd house to John Henderson of said state,[2] and that there is nothing to be so construed in my sale of said house to sd Peyton as to damage me, but if sd Henderson agrees to keep sd house, he does, so long as he thinks proper, agreeable to our articles:[3] but sd Peyton is to recieve said rent after this year: sd Peyton to be bound by the articles of agreement between sd Henderson & myself.

I, said Peyton, doth bind myself to the above writing, as witness my hand & seal this 18th. of Sep. 1802.

Teste

James L. Henderson
Charles Henderson

Tr (ViU); entirely in TJ's hand; written on same sheet below Enclosure No. 1; endorsed by TJ: "Craven Peyton to Elizabeth Henderson } Declaration as to dwelling house leased to J. Henderson." Tr (same); entirely in Craven Peyton's hand; lacks signature; endorsed by Peyton: "C. Peyton to E. Henderson"; endorsed by TJ: "Peyton to Henderson."

[1] 2d Tr: "My Own."
[2] 2d Tr: "County & state."
[3] 2d Tr: "Article."

III

James L. Henderson Deed to Craven Peyton

Know all Men by these presents that I James L. Henderson of the state of Kentucky have this day bargained & sold Unto Craven Peyton all the right title & interest of the within named legatees of Bennett Henderson Decd. Viz. Bennett Hill Henderson, Eliza, Frances, Lucy, & Nancy Henderson, to all their Lands in the County of Albemarle in the State of Virginia And its appurtenances there to except a Mill Ware House & Store House in Milton for which Lands I have receaved full payment the Receipt of which I do hereby acknowledge & do bind my self my Heirs Executors & administrators in the sum of Five Thousand Pounds Lawfull Money that the above Named Bennett H., Eliza Frances Lucy And Nancy shall make a good & sufficient right title to the above mentioned Lands & appurtenances immediately aftar Marriage Or becomeing of Lawfull age to him the said Craven Or his Heirs. Or assigns, given under my hand & Seale this

Eighteenth day of September 1802   James L Henderson
Test.   £650.0.0

Ch Henderson
G Tennill
Jas. Barlow

MS (ViU); in Craven Peyton's hand, signed by all; with hand-drawn facsimile seal beside James L. Henderson's signature; endorsed by Peyton: "Conveyance James L. Henderson to Peyton"; on a separate sheet, in a clerk's hand, acknowledgment of deed in Shelby County, Kentucky, by James L. Henderson before Mathews Flournoy and Thomas I. Gwin, justices of the peace, 6 June 1804; on another sheet, a signed and sealed certificate in the hand of James Craig, clerk of Shelby County Court, dated 6 June 1804, verifying the positions of Flournoy and Gwin, with Craig's certificate verified, signed, and sealed by Isaac Ellis, presiding justice of the peace for the court; on verso, John Nicholas, as clerk of the "Albemarle July Court 1804," testified and signed: "This Bill or Bargain & sale from James L. Henderson to Craven Peyton was Produced into Court duly certified from the County of Shelby & State of Kentuckey, and Ordered to be recorded"; endorsed: "James L. Henderson To Craven Peyton } Conveyance"; endorsed by Nicholas: "July 2nd. 1804 Certified & to be recorded"; endorsed by TJ: "James L. Henderson for Bennet H. Eliza, Frances, Lucy & Nancy C. to Craven Peyton. Sep. 18. 1802. £650. except Mill. warehouse & storehouse in Milton." Tr (Albemarle County Deed Book No. 14:520-1); lacks the sum of £650; acknowledgment of deed by James L. Henderson before Flournoy and Gwin, 6 June 1804; certified by Craig, same date; Craig's certificate certified by Ellis, same date; certified and ordered to be recorded by Nicholas at the Albemarle Court, July 1804. Tr (ViU); in William Wertenbaker's hand and signed by him as deputy clerk of the Albemarle County Court; lacks the sum of £650; also in Wertenbaker's hand: "Acknowledged by James L Henderson before two Justices of the peace for the County of Shelby State of Kentucky the 6th day of June 1804 and Recorded in Albemarle County Court at July Court. 1804" and "The foregoing is an extract from the County Court of Albemarle"; endorsed by Wertenbaker: "Henderson to Peyton } Extract Deed"; endorsed by TJ: "Hendersons, Bennet H. Eliza. Frances, Lucy, Nancy to James L. Henderson to Peyton. Deed. 1802. Sep. 18."

To J. P. Derieux

DEAR SIR   Washington Oct. 28. 1802.

I recieved last night your favor of the 23d. and now inclose under cover to mr Jefferson, as you desired, this letter with the certificate requested. I have not named you a citizen of the US. because I do not know the fact, and I doubted whether it would be of service to you. I have to the certificate subjoined a passport, without subscribing in any official capacity, because in that capacity I never sign either passports or certificates. Wishing you a happy voyage, successful pursuit of your affairs and safe return to your family I pray you to accept assurances of esteem and respect.   TH: JEFFERSON

PrC (DLC); at foot of text: "M. De Rieux"; endorsed by TJ in ink on verso. Enclosed in TJ to George Jefferson, 28 Oct.

Certificate and Passport

I hereby certify to[1] all whom it may concern that Justin Peter Plumard de Rieux a native of France, & nephew of Madame Bellanger of St. Germaine with whom I was acquainted, was on my return from Europe in 1789. living in the state of Virginia & has lived therein ever since; and as I have been well informed had lived there some years previous to 1789. during my absence from the state: that he has during the whole time conducted himself as an honest, sober, industrious & good man, greatly esteemed by his neighbors & acquaintances; that he has now a wife in the said state and a numerous family of children, all minors: that he has been unsuccessful in his various endeavors to increase the means of supporting his family & educating his children, & particularly in having his house burnt and nearly every thing in it.

And the said Justin Peter Plumard de Rieux, now proposing to go to France to obtain his portion of the estate of Madame Bellanger & for other purposes of business, it is hereby recommended to all persons to permit the said J. P. P. deRieux to pass & repass freely and without molestation or hindrance wherever his lawful affairs may call him, he conducting himself honestly & peaceably, as foreigners generally are by the laws and customs of this country permitted to pass freely & under their protection in like cases. Given under my hand at Washington the seat of the government of the US. this 28th. day of October 1802.   TH: JEFFERSON

PrC (DLC).   [1] Word supplied.

To George Jefferson

DEAR SIR   Washington Oct. 28. 1802.

At the request of Mr. DeRieux, I inclose you a letter for him, which he will call for in a few days, being about to embark for France. I believe you know his entire inability to repay any aid he may recieve, which I mention lest he might apply to you on the ground of my acquaintance with him. the truth is he has some time since exhausted all the charities I could justifiably extend to him, and can do nothing more for him. Accept my affectionate salutations.

                                          TH: JEFFERSON

PrC (MHi); at foot of text: "Mr. George Jefferson"; endorsed by TJ in ink on verso. Enclosure: TJ to J. P. P. DeRieux, 28 Oct., and enclosure.

TJ last recorded offering AID to DeRieux on 13 Oct. 1799 (MB, 2:1007).

From Robert R. Livingston

DEAR SIR   Paris 28th. October 1802

The enclosed packet marked No 1, was written at the time it is dated—The subject of it is very painful to me, & I have retained it for the reasons mentioned in the enclosed letters No. 1 & 2—by which I trust it will appear how much I sacrificed both of my rights, & my feelings, to prevent this matter from causing you, or the connections of Mr. Sumter any uneasiness—I continued to act with Mr. Sumter presuming that long before this, his resignation would have been accepted, or that he would have changed his conduct with respect to me—but he has all along appeared to consider himself not as my Secretary, but as my coadjutor and when his *constructions* of my instructions dosse not square mine, he refuses expresly to execute my orders—the enclosed statement shews that he has explicitly discharged himself from the duties of the office, by refusing to perform those I have enjoined to him—I shall accordingly employ a secretary to execute them & shall draw for his pay, making the best bargain I can for the United States—But that I may not be again exposed to what I have suffered from the independence of the Secretary upon his principal I must explicitly request that if it continues to be the system of the government to give the Ministers *a secretary of the Legation*, & no private Secretary that my resignation may be accepted. It will appear by Mr. Sumters own statement, that he thinks, he is to be judge when I am to interpose in behalf of a citizen of the United States, & when not, and that he is to determine thro' what channel business is to pass, & when he differs in opinion with me, that he is entitled to refuse to obey my orders—I would observe that the whole duty previous to Mr. Sumter's last refusal for at least two months has not been such as would have occupied one half hour in a day, so that it has not been of the burthen of business that he has had to complain—

I forbear to mingle any other matter with the disagreeable subject of this letter—

I have the honor to be Dear Sir with the most respectful Esteem, Your most Obt Hble Svt   ROBT R LIVINGSTON

This letter & the statement enclosed have been submitted to Mr. Sumters inspection—as well as my former letter on the same subject.

RC (DLC); in a clerk's hand, signed and postscript added by Livingston; at foot of text: "Thomas Jefferson Esqr. President of the U:S:"; endorsed by TJ as received 9 Feb. 1803 and so recorded in SJL. Enclosures: (1) Livingston to TJ, 4 May, and enclosures (Vol. 37:410-16). (2) "Statement of the request made by

Mr. Livingston, of Mr. Sumter, & his refusal to comply therewith," declaring that in August, Livingston "transmitted the inclosed note" to Talleyrand and directed Thomas Sumter, Jr., to subjoin to it the letter of Captain Thomas Newell, "which contained a statement of his case, together with a copy of the decree of the council of prizes and a certificate of the Minister of the Marine, from which it might be infered that the vessel taking Capn. Newlands, had no commission"; Talleyrand replied that "those papers were not in his office"; Livingston "then wrote the enclosed note No. 2" and directed Sumter to make a copy of the original communication and the subjoined papers, to which Sumter replied "that he had no copies of them, & that it was not his business to keep copies of private papers, that they should go to Mr. Skipwith's office"; Livingston requested Sumter to get copies of the papers from James C. Mountflorence, who had been Newell's agent; Sumter refused, "alleging that it is a private case & that by the instructions of the Secretary of State, Mr. Livingston, nor he, had nothing to do with it, & that all applications of this nature must come thro' Mr. Skipwith. Mr. Livingston was accordingly compelled to obtain the papers by personal application to Mr. Mountflorence" (MS in DLC: TJ Papers, 127:21901; undated; in a clerk's hand, final sentence in Livingston's hand); for Newell's claims against Spain and France for the capture of the brig *Fame*, see Madison, *Papers,* *Sec. of State Ser.*, 4:11, 12n. (3) Livingston to Talleyrand, 20 Aug., regarding the claim of Newell, whose ship was captured after the completion of the Convention of 1800 by a vessel pretending to have authority from the French government; Livingston also complaining of delays in settling all such claims by American citizens (Tr in DLC: TJ Papers, 125:21642-3, undated, endorsed by Madison: "Note in Capt. Newals case, which Mr. *Sumter considering* insufficient & one the minr. was not authorized to pursue, *refused* to procure the papers to have annexed when they had been mislaid in Mr. Tallerands office"; Tr in DNA: RG 59, DD, with dateline Paris, 20 Aug., and "Duplicate" added at head of text by Jacob Wagner, endorsed by Wagner, endorsed by TJ: "refd. to Secy. of state. or has it been already acted on? Th:J. May 9, 1803"; Dft in same, in Livingston's hand). (4) Livingston to Talleyrand, 21 Vendémiaire Year 11 (13 Oct. 1802), noting that he has not yet received an answer to his communication of 20 Aug. (Tr in DLC: TJ Papers, 126:21740-1); Talleyrand's reply of 28 Vendémiaire (20 Oct.), stating that he does not have the papers for the case and asking for copies, is in DNA: RG 59, DD. (5) Livingston to Talleyrand, 29 Vendémiaire (21 Oct.), advising that he has directed copies of the papers to be made for Talleyrand and commenting on the case (Tr in DLC: TJ Papers, 126:21858-9).

From Robert R. Livingston

DEAR SIR   Paris 28th. Octr 1802

Nothing very important having occured for some time past I have not thought it necessary to trouble you, particularly as I conclude that you would for a time have quited the seat of government & sought repose from the fatigues of politicks. While the union between France & Russia subsists, the discontents which almost every nation in Europe feels to the extreme loftiness of the first, will be suppressed. but as fear & not affection occasion the suppression, they are ready to break out on the first favourable moment. many think that moment not very distant. Great changes have taken place in the administration, Woronzoff is known to be inclined to Britain, & I find that the change occasions considerable sensation here, not only *among the foreign Ministers but among those of France*. one effect of it has been the preparing to send off Andreosi who has hitherto been retained till lord Witworth arrived, even tho' formal notice had long since been given that he was to go in eight days. Britain is seriously dissatisfied, & indeed has some reason to complain. several of her vessels which put in here (as is said by stress of weather) having been detained, & Mr. Merrys representations treated with neglect. The affairs of Helvetia have also excited great uneasiness in England, where all parties seem to concur in wishing to oppose some barrier to the power of France. The british republicans are disgusted with the changes that have taken place here, while the royalists dread the stability that the government has assumed in the hands of the first consul. The mercantile & manufacturing interests who looked to peace for the renewal of the treaty of commerce from which they derived such advantages are sore at the severity with which their commerce is interdicted here. You will accordingly find by the british papers that both those of the majority, & minority teem with abuse on france & blow aloud the trumpet of discord.

By the treaty of Madrid you recollect that the reigning duke of Parma & placentia was to renounce them in favor of France, in consideration of which his heir was to have the kingdom of Etruria. This he has constantly refused to do, & has lately died without making any renunciation. The Spanish Ambassadeur here has been called upon to compleat the treaty. he replied that he had no powers, & general Bournonville has gone express to Spain to effect this object, the king of Etruria being now duke of parma. Whether he will prefer the crown he now holds to his hereditary dominions, I know not but I think he must submit to what is dictated here or risk the loss of both. *The Mississippi business, tho' all the officers are appointed and the army under orders, has met with a check. The army under orders is obstructed for the moment. events may possibly arise of which we may avail ourselves*. I had two days ago a very interesting conversation with *Joseph Bonaparte*. having put into his hands a copy of the memoir on Louisania which I sent the secretary of State, I took occasion to tell him that the *interest he had taken in settling the differences between our respective countries* had entitled him to our confidence & that I should take the liberty to ask his advise in matters that were like to disturb the harmony that subsisted between our respective republicks. he seemed pleased at the compliment and told me that he would receive with pleasure any communication I could make but as he would not wish to *appear to interfere with the Minister he begged my communication might be informal and unsigned* exactly what I wished because I should act with less danger of committing myself & of course with more freedom. He added you must not however suppose *my power to serve you greater than* it actualy is *my brother is his own* counsellor *but we are good brothers and he hears me with pleasure and as I have access to him at all times* I have an opportunity of *turning his attention to a particular subject* that might otherwise be passed over. I then asked him whether he had read my notes on Louisiana he told me he had & that he had conversed upon the subject *with the first Consul who he found had read them with attention that his brother had told him that he had nothing more at heart than to be upon the best terms with the U.S.* I expressed to him my apprehentions of the jealousies that would naturally be excited from their vicinity & the impossibility of preventing abuses by[1] a military government established at so great a distance from here.

Wishing to know with certainty whether the Floridas were excluded (which however I had pretty well assertained before), I told him that the only causes of difference that might arise between us being the debt and Louisiana I conceived that both might be happily & easily removed by making an exchange with Spain & returning them Louisiana retaing. New Orleans & giving the latter & the floridas for our debt.

He asked me whether We should prefer the Floridas to Louisiana. I told him that there was no comparison in their value but that we had no wish to extend our boundary across the Missisipi or give colour to the doubts that had been entertained of the moderation of our views. That all we sought was our security & not an extention of territory. He replied that he believed *any new cession on the part of Spain would be extremely difficult that Spain had parted with* Trinidad and Louisiana[2] *with great reluctance.* I have however reason to think that Bournonville is instructed to effect this object not however *with a view to my project but* with intention to procure for France some port in the gulph from which they think they may secure their own & anoy the british commerce so that if we should contrary to our hopes *make any bargain with them I fear that East Florida will not be included.* However every thing is yet in air, & I doubt much considering the present state of things in Europe whether *Spain will make any exchange that will give France a command of the gulph.* Tho this is a favorite object with France she may not in the present state of things in Europe think it prudent to press too hard. It is time that she should acquire *some character for moderation*. I find your cypher extreamly difficult & laborious in the practice nor does it appear to me to have any advantage over that introduced into the office of foreign affairs which without being so intricate is equally secure & more easy in the use. I shall therefore pray you to send me by the first safe opportunity one constructed upon that principle, & in the mean time as my letters to you will not pass thru' the office or thru' my office when marked private, I will continue to use that I now have. I shall write on some other subjects to the secretary of state, to whom you will I presume deliver the letters relative to the disagreeable business between Mr Sumter & myself, which I have endeavoured as far as possible to keep from coming to extremities, but which no prudence or attention will prevent, where the secretary thinks he has a supporting interest at home. I have endeavoured agreeably to your advise to avail myself of every aid that I could draw from Mr Dupont whose dispositions towards us are very favourable but who is not, in the present state of things able to aid us so much as he would wish, having no personal interest with the first consul. Mr. King having written to me that he intended to be here (where he now is) and to come by the way of Holland & Switzerland, I postponed my intended visit to Britain & made a short excurtion to Holland having been only absent twenty days from here. I found upon inquiry that our merchants have great cause of complaint in the perception of duties (as I before mentioned to the secretary of State) & still greater from the most scandalous fraud in their private agents. The first of these demands the interposition of our government. I shall pray you to extend your permission to travel to Italy in the course of the next year, if the state of things should admit. I shall take care not to be absent long at a time, & never except in a season of the most perfect leasure. I send by a vessel going to Baltimore a packet containing an interesting work of Mr. Cabanis from the author to you & another to the philosophical society. The first consul is gone to Rouen & is to be back by the 18 brumaire. The British fear that he means to examine the coasts. The prospect of a rupture grows more serious I can tell you with *certainty*[3] that a remonstrance in pretty strong terms has been presented by her minister on the subject of the consuls interference in the Affairs of Helvetia. How it will be received I know not, but I think it would not have been made if it had not been the intention of Britain to seek a quarrel—

I refer you to the secretary of State for information on our particular affairs, tho as this goes by the way of England I am fearful it will not be in my power to send my official dispatches by this conveyance, as I can not, in the present state of things think it *proper, to avail myself of Mr. Sumters aid,* and I have *not yet supplied his place.*[4] I must just mention to you the memoire of Col: De Viene heretofore transmitted to the Secy of State, such is the distress of this poor family, consisting of himself, his wife & three children, that they have been compelled to pawn their clothing & must actualy have starved if I had not advanced about 15 guineas[5] for which I have drawn on the government who will stop it from his pay, which I think they can not refuse to give him. If otherwise they must charge it to my private acct. Genl La fayettes situation demands the aid of our country. His debts amount to about 24000 $ & he[6] has nothing but his wifes farm for his support. He was ready to sacrafice every thing for us & we owe him something effectual. I must pray you to get Mr. Randolph or some other leading member of Congress to patronize him. Our gratitude will do us honor abroad & not be unpopular at home. I have the honor to be dear Sir

with the most respectful essteem your most Obt Hum: Servt

ROBT R. LIVINGSTON

29th. I have this moment made inquiries from one I can depend on— Remonstrances have been made but they are only *verbal.*[7] No answer has been given—Andreosi goes this evening.—The other points of dispute as money, ships detained, &c. it is thought will not occasion a war tho no satisfaction is like to be soon given.

RC (DNA: RG 59, DD); below signature: "Thomas Jefferson Esqr president of the US"; written partially in code (see Ralph E. Weber, *United States Diplomatic Codes and Ciphers, 1775-1938* [Chicago, 1979], 467-77; Vol. 36:208n); with interlinear decipherment in Jacob Wagner's hand reproduced in italics; for italics that signify underlining rather than deciphered code, see notes 3-4 and 7; endorsed by TJ as received 9 Feb. 1803 and so recorded in SJL; endorsed by Wagner with notation "open Cypher." Tr (DNA: RG 46, EPFR, 8th Cong., 1st sess.); consisting of a composite of extracts in two clerks' hands, omitting some text; transmitted to the Senate in October 1803 (see TJ to the Senate, 17 Oct. 1803, and TJ to the Senate and the House of Representatives, 21 Oct. 1803); printed in ASP, *Foreign Relations,* 2:525-6.

The GREAT CHANGES took place in Russia, where in September Emperor Alexander reorganized the government's ministries. Count Aleksandr Romanovich Vorontsov (WORONZOFF) was the new foreign minister. His brother, Count Semen Romanovich Vorontsov, was the Russian minister in London (Hartley, *Alexander I,* 38, 42-3, 63, 65; Madison, *Papers, Sec. of State Ser.,* 4:35n).

TO SEND OFF ANDREOSI: Bonaparte had named Antoine François Andréossy as French minister to Great Britain several months earlier, but Andréossy and his counterpart, Baron Charles Whitworth, the new British minister to France, had not yet taken up their posts (Jacques Henri-Robert, *Dictionnaire des diplomates de Napoléon: Histoire et dictionnaire du corps diplomatique consulaire et impérial* [Paris, 1990], 93-4; Tulard, *Dictionnaire Napoléon*, 93; Vol. 37:481, 484n).

MR. MERRYS REPRESENTATIONS: Anthony Merry was acting as the British minister to France ad interim (Madison, *Papers, Sec. of State Ser.*, 4:205n; Vol. 35:297n).

By a proclamation of 30 Sep., Bonaparte ordered the cantons of Switzerland—HELVETIA—to send deputies for an assembly in Paris. Christopher Gore reported to Madison from London that the British government, viewing Bonaparte's action as "a new evidence of the disposition of France to assume the command of all the Nations of Europe," was determined "to resist the interference of the first Consul in the affairs of Switzerland." Britain stopped reducing the size of its armed forces and halted the return of territories to France under the terms of the Amiens peace (Madison, *Papers, Sec. of State Ser.*, 4:33, 34n, 144, 208).

Under the Treaty of Aranjuez between Spain and France in 1801, the northern Italian duchy of PARMA ceased to exist. The French government put Médéric Louis Élie Moreau de St. Méry, who had left Philadelphia for France in 1798, in charge of the French occupation of Parma and Piacenza (PLACENTIA), but the duke of Parma, Ferdinando Borbone Parma, refused to abdicate. Biding his time until Ferdinando died on 9 Oct. 1802, Bonaparte then made Moreau de St. Méry *adminstrateur général* of the region. Ferdinando was a brother of Queen María Luisa of Spain. By the terms of the Aranjuez treaty, France had made Ferdinando's son Louis, who was also the son-in-law of María Luisa and Carlos IV, king of the new state of ETRURIA (same, 4:111n; Parry, *Consolidated Treaty Series*, 56:45-9; Tulard, *Dictionnaire Napoléon*, 1199-1200; Roberto Lasagni, *Dizionario Biografico dei Parmigiani*, 4 vols. [Parma, 1999], 1:630-4; Douglas Hilt, *The Trou-*

bled Trinity: Godoy and the Spanish Monarchs [Tuscaloosa, Ala., 1987], 113).

José Nicolás de Azara was the SPANISH AMBASSADOR in Paris; see Madison to TJ, 11 Sep.

GENERAL BOURNONVILLE: in September, the Marquis de Beurnonville became the French ambassador to Spain. He had completed a diplomatic mission to Berlin, and previously had attained the rank of lieutenant general in the army (Tulard, *Dictionnaire Napoléon*, 212).

MEMOIR ON LOUISANIA: in August, Livingston wrote a long essay on the question "Whether it will be advantageous to France to take possession of Louisiana." He answered in the negative, arguing that holding Louisiana would drain resources, prove of no economic benefit to France, and push the United States into an alliance with Britain. Livingston recommended "a cession of New Orleans to the United States," with France reserving the right of entry, paying the same duties as American ships, and the right to navigate the Mississippi River. After having 20 copies of the essay printed, he distributed them to Talleyrand and "such hands as I think will best serve our purposes" (Madison, *Papers, Sec. of State Ser.*, 3:468, 470n; ASP, *Foreign Relations*, 2:520-4).

INTEREST HE HAD TAKEN IN SETTLING THE DIFFERENCES: Joseph Bonaparte participated in the negotiation of the Convention of 1800 between the United States and France, and his estate at Môrtefontaine was the site of the ceremony to commemorate the pact's signing (Vol. 32:159n).

APPEAR TO INTERFERE WITH THE MINISTER: that is, with Talleyrand.

The expected DEBT of France to the United States was for spoliation claims under the Convention of 1800 (Vol. 37:418).

Spain had to cede the island of TRINIDAD to Great Britain under the terms of the Amiens treaty, which obliged the British to return most other captured territory to France and its allies (Parry, *Consolidated Treaty Series*, 56:292).

YOUR CYPHER: the transposition cipher designed by Robert Patterson that TJ sent to Livingston in April (Vol. 37:263, 267-77). ONE CONSTRUCTED UPON THAT PRINCIPLE: that is, a code that substituted sequences of digits for syllables and words, similar to the one that Livingston used in this letter.

SHALL WRITE ... TO THE SECRETARY OF STATE: Livingston wrote to Madison on 2 Nov. He discussed the small prospect of France paying the money owed to the United States, the claims of John Rodgers and William Davidson over their detention in Saint-Domingue, Livingston's relations with Talleyrand, and some subjects from the letter printed above (Madison, *Papers, Sec. of State Ser.*, 4:76-82).

See Livingston's other letter of 28 Oct. for the LETTERS RELATIVE TO THE DISAGREEBLE BUSINESS of Livingston's relationship with Thomas Sumter, Jr.

Livingston had advised Madison in July that the Batavian government was allowing the Dutch West India Company to add DUTIES on goods from the United States, even though American merchants were supposed to pay no more in duties than their European counterparts. In his letter to Madison of 2 Nov., Livingston reported that he had found on his recent visit to Holland "that our Merchants had been uniformly defrauded out of much greater Sums by the Dutch mercantile agents that they employ as their Consignees—who have very generally charged the duties upon the war prices when in fact the Government only received them on the average peace prices" (Madison, *Papers, Sec. of State Ser.*, 3:367; 4:79).

Earlier in the year when Livingston asked PERMISSION for a trip to England, Madison replied that TJ consented, leaving "the time and the duration of your absence to your own judgment, assuring himself that both will be in due subordination to the important duties of your station" (same, 3:177).

GONE TO ROUEN: Napoleon and Josephine Bonaparte left Paris on 28 Oct. on an official tour that included Rouen, Le Havre, Dieppe, and other cities. The first consul was away from Paris until mid-November (Thierry Lentz, *Le Grand Consulat, 1799-1804* [Paris, 1999], 454; Madison, *Papers, Sec. of State Ser.*, 4:86n).

The British REMONSTRANCE was, according to Rufus King, "a verbal insinuation" by Anthony Merry to the French government that George III would not view French interference in Switzerland "with indifference" (same, 4:144).

MEMOIRE OF COL: DE VIENE: in July, Livingston forwarded to Madison a memorial addressed to the president and members of Congress by the Marquis de Vienne asking for compensation for his service on behalf of the United States during the American Revolution. Livingston brought the matter up again in a letter to Madison on 2 Nov. "The case of Mr. De Vienne is wholly beyond the compass of the Executive authority," Madison wrote Livingston on 15 Oct. Vienne's claim later came before the House of Representatives (undated memorial in DNA: RG 59, DD; Madison, *Papers, Sec. of State Ser.*, 3:366, 368n; 4:25, 80).

[1] Livingston wrote "in" at the foot of a page and "by" at the start of the next page. Tr: "in."

[2] Word supplied from Tr. MS: "*ui ret an ni*," which is Wagner's correct decipherment of what Livingston wrote in code. Preceding those syllables there is an element that Wagner could not decipher because it does not appear in the code.

[3] Word interlined, not coded, in MS.

[4] Italics in the preceding sentence signify underlining, not code.

[5] Word abbreviated in MS ("guns.").

[6] MS: "his."

[7] Word underlined, not coded, in MS.

From James McGurk

[28 Oct. 1802]

I Beg for my life onley [as] Judge Cranch Coms home I know he has given Some Remarks in writeing But wee Doo not know what way he might Bend if he Was on the Spot I Should think I had afare Chanc for my Life I hope if his Should Bend Judg keltey would Bind

Can not the presedint of the united States grant this Requist to aman That will Bee put to Dath in the wrong without the Presidents mercey I never can bleive But you will if you Can by fare manes Save me till I get ancir from your own han which I Requist By the Bearor as I am now going to the Galos   JAMES MCGURK

RC (DNA: RG 59, GPR); torn; undated, but see below; addressed: "Thomas Jefferson Esqr. Presedent of the unted States"; endorsed by TJ: "Mc.Gurk."

NOW GOING TO THE GALOS: James McGurk was executed on 28 Oct. (*National Intelligencer*, 29 Oct.).

Memorandum to Albert Gallatin

Candidates for the office of Surveyor of Smithfield

Doctr. Purdie.	his father I know. he is a good man. but they are tories.
Wilson Davies.	he was collector of the direct tax, which is sufficient evidence he is a tory. he is recommended too by John Parker appd by our predecessors, ergo a tory.
Dr. Southall.	his father was an excellent man & whig. his brother is said to be a very bad man. of himself I know nothing. Colo. Davies's favor makes his politics suspicious.
Cuningham.	recommendd by T. Newton junr. but not on his own knolege. a republican of 75. he does not live at the place & would be to remove.
John Easson.	strongly recommended by Colo. Newton the father, from an intimate knolege of him, as a very honest man, republican, & living on the spot. he was not long since a member of the Senate of Virginia, chosen by a district of several counties, which is good testimony of respectability, and a shield for us in his appointment.

It appears to me that Easson is the preferable candidate. if you think so let the commission issue. such a paper as this you would not of course let go into the office bundles, but burn or otherwise dispose of as a private communication, & confidential.

Th:J.

Oct. 28. 1802.

RC (NHi: Gallatin Papers); addressed: "Albert Gallatin Secretary of the Treasury"; endorsed. PrC (DLC). Recorded in SJL with notation "nominns."

WILSON Davis (DAVIES) served as an auxiliary officer for the collection of the Direct Tax in Isle of Wight County. He was evidently recommended by JOHN PARKER, a port inspector under the collector's office at Norfolk. John Adams appointed Federalist Copland Parker, a surveyor at Smithfield, as surveyor and inspector of the revenue at Norfolk in December 1799 (*Letter From the Secretary of the Treasury, Transmitting Two Statements, Relating to the Internal Revenues of the United States* [Washington, D.C., 1803], Table A, Shaw-Shoemaker, No. 5341; ASP, *Miscellaneous*, 1:274; JEP, 1:125-6, 330-1; Syrett, *Hamilton*, 11:393; Prince, *Federalists*, 109-10, 114).

Dr. James Barrett SOUTHALL had recently settled in Isle of Wight County

near Smithfield. HIS FATHER WAS AN EXCELLENT MAN: Turner Southall represented Henrico County in the Virginia General Assembly in 1778, at the same time TJ represented Albemarle County. Southall served in the assembly continuously from 1780 to 1790, first in the House of Delegates and by 1785 in the Senate (VMHB, 45 [1937], 283-7; Leonard, *General Assembly*, 129-30, 138, 142, 146, 150, 154, 158, 162, 166, 170, 177, 181).

On this day, Gallatin wrote TJ inquiring, "Is the name of the gentleman recommended for the Surveyor's office at Smithfield, *Lasson*, or *Easson*?" Gallatin also noted: "I enclose a recommendation" (RC in DLC; partially dated; endorsed by TJ as received from the Treasury Department on 28 Oct. and "Easson. Eddins" and so recorded in SJL). The enclosure has not been found, but TJ's endorsement indicates it was probably a recommendation for Samuel Eddins (see TJ to Gallatin, 3 Aug.).

From Charles Willson Peale

DEAR SIR   Museum Octr 28th. 1802.

A Gentleman from Virginia lately viewing the Skeleton of the mammoth, told me that 9 miles from the sweet Springs in Green bryer County, a few months past, was found in a Salt petre cave some large Bones, which they supposed, from the hole in one of Vertebræ's, measuring 9 Inches in circumference, was of a larger species of the Mammoth than my Skeleton, and that a bone of one of the claws measured 9 inches in length. He also informed me that the person who was diging out the bones, intended them for me, but he could not recollect his name, but advised me to write to John Lewes Esqr. a magestrate who had given him this information, and whom he said was of a generous & liberal mind. He also said that the Salt Petre cave, is very long, and in it were found, some of the *finest fur*.

This is the same species of Animal as those bones you presented to the Philosophical Society, and not the Mammoth as those Persons have supposed—The Vertebræ may be one in the front of the Animal, the holes of which is commonly larger than those in the middle or hinder parts of the back. Some of the back bones belonging to my Skeleton has larger holes for the spinal marrow than a circumference of 9 Inches.

The obtaining bones of other nondescript Animals of our Country is now a favorite object with me, and I would have willingly made a visit to the spot, but the situation of my family does not permit it at present.

Doubtless you have seen some paragraphs in the news Papers on the half of the head of the mammoth being found in the barrens of Kentucky—it was dug up in sinking a pit to get salt water, 50 feet below the surface of the Earth—in what the people of that Country, call a sink—Doctr Hunter of this City being in Kentucky, I wrote to him my desire to obtain this relick, that I would not reguard some expence to obtain it, as being Very important to complete our knowledge of the form of the head of my Skeleton. He informs me that Dr. Samuel Brown has undertaken to procure it for me, and that he would send it to Orleans, to be conveyed to Philada. by Water. Dr. Hunter is expected in Philada. in about 2 Weeks, and probably will give me more particulars.

I have just received Letters from my Sons in London—They had obtained a Room for their exhibition of the Skeleton, in the building formerly used for the royal Academy in Pall Mall for which they are to pay 666 Dollrs. for it intill the 25 of March next. Rembrandt has been much favoured by the Officers of the Customs, by means of Letters which Mr. Bond was so obliging as to give him. And the board of Commissioners had ordered that the Valuation of the Skeleton should not exceed 50 £, and after all, the duty amounts to about 130 Dollars.

Rembrandt had gone through a great deal of trouble, with much anxiety, and he says, he could not think of writing to me before he had better Prospects—He was prepairing to get up the Skeleton & he says his next letters will be more interesting to me.

I am fully satisfied that both of my sons will make useful observations on all interresting works of Art &c. They have done well thus far.

My progress of improvements of the Museum is considerable during the absence of the Citizens.

No labour or expence shall be spared to render it conspicuously usefull to my Country.

I am Dr. Sir with much respect your friend   C W Peale

RC (DLC); at foot of text: "His Excelly. Thos. Jefferson Esqr."; endorsed by TJ as received 31 Oct. and so recorded in SJL. Dft (Lb in PPAmP: Peale-Sellers Papers).

JOHN LEWES ESQR.: John Lewis belonged to a prominent family that owned and developed land around the mineral spring at Sweet Springs (Oren F. Morton, *A History of Monroe County, West Virginia* [Staunton, Va., 1916], 201-6, 370-1).

BONES YOU PRESENTED TO THE PHILOSOPHICAL SOCIETY: the megalonyx (Vol. 29:291-304).

Beginning in Staunton, Virginia, early in September, various newspapers reprinted an extract of a letter from Logan County, KENTUCKY, that noted the recovery of a "half skull bone very remarkable for size." The specimen weighed, according to the report, 246 pounds, but the cranial cavity could have been no more than one quart in volume. The opening for the eye was reputedly "so large that a common sized man can creep through it." Peale learned from George HUNTER, a Philadelphia chemist, druggist, and surgeon, that the entire story was "a fabrication." The false report, Peale wrote to his sons, was "a riddle which I must unriddle. I cannot conceive any accasion for the publication of such a story" (Richmond *Virginia Argus*, 8 Sep.; *Washington Federalist*, 13 Sep.; Norwich *Connecticut Centinel*, 21 Sep.;

Peale, *Papers*, v. 2, pt. 1:465-6n, 472; John Francis McDermott, "The Western Journals of George Hunter, 1796-1805," APS, *Proceedings*, 103 [1959], 770-1; Peale to TJ, 12 Dec.).

Rubens and REMBRANDT Peale had written to their father from London early in September. Phineas BOND, resident at Philadelphia, was Great Britain's consul general for the middle and southern states. The British customs office charged duties on "Subjects of Natural history," Rubens Peale reported, at the rate of 33 percent of the item's value. Regarding the customs VALUATION of the mastodon skeleton, Peale wondered in a letter to his sons: "if you have to pay 130 Dolls. when the Skeleton was valued at only £50. what would have been the duty had it been at its true value?" (Peale, *Papers*, v. 2, pt. 1:463, 466, 467; Vol. 29:228n; Vol. 35:410).

ABSENCE OF THE CITIZENS: in Philadelphia during the previous weeks, yellow fever had caused the suspension of some business, delays in opening schools and academies, the postponement of a booksellers' fair, and the temporary removal of the customs office away from the waterfront to the former U.S. Senate chamber at 6th and Chestnut Streets. On 3 Nov., Peale wrote to his sons that the illness had abated following a frost, "and the Citizens are returning again to their Homes" (Peale, *Papers*, v. 2, pt. 1:466; *Philadelphia Gazette*, 30 Sep., 1, 2, 4, 14, 21, 23 Oct.).

From Albert Gallatin, with Jefferson's Opinion

DEAR SIR   Oct. 29th 1802

I saw Mr Munroe to day & stated to him that we were ready to pay to the State of Maryland whatever sum might appear to be payable out of the Treasury under the 6th Section of the Act of the 1st May last. But what is the sum thus payable must be previously ascertained & settled by the accounting officers of the Treasury, and certified by them to me to be due. Mr Munroe said that he would lodge the accounts to morrow morning, but I hardly believe that they can be examined & settled by Monday 1st Nover.—I think also, though it is not within my province to decide, that the only amount which the Treasury can legally pay under that section is the difference between the sum due and the *proceeds*[1] of the sale of lots, which will fall two or three thousand dollars short of the sum wanted together with what the Superintendent has in hand, to pay the claim of Maryland; in as much as the Superintendent has not in hand the whole proceeds of the sale. This arises from an evident defect in drawing the law which should have read thus vizt. Sect. 6—line 12th "and the monies arising thereupon *after deducting the sums necessary to discharge the debts payable by virtue of the 4th Sect. of this law* shall be applied &a." Thus the word "deficiency" in the proviso of the same section, should have applied to the difference between the sum due to Maryland & the balance in the hands of the Superintendent, instead of applying to the difference between the sum due & the proceeds of the lots. The accounting officers will, however, decide as they may think proper, and I will pay the sum they shall certify to me.

With respect Your obedt. Servt.   ALBERT GALLATIN

[*Opinion by TJ:*]

by the act of Congress 1802. c. 41. §. 4. the debts Commrs. are to be paid out of *any* monies recd from the city funds.

§.5. the lots *pledged* for 200. M̶. D. to be sold, unless unwarrantable sacrifice. deficiency pd from treasury

§ 6. lots liable to *resale*, shall be resold. monies arising therefrom to pay the 50. M. D. if sufficiency not *produced*, deficiency to be paid out of treasy.

§ 7. these advances to be reimbursed with intt. by paying into treasy. all monies arisg. from city funds.

the qu. is whether the 4th. § does not first make a lien for the debts of the Commrs. on the whole funds, so as to make them a debt of the first dignity; the residue only can then be the subject of §. 6. every act must be so construed as to give meaning to all it's parts, & that no one may stand in contradiction to another.

RC (DLC); two words written by TJ in margin (see note 1 below); opinion written by TJ on address sheet below endorsement; addressed: "The President of the United States"; endorsed by TJ as received from the Treasury Department on 29 Oct. and "Debt to Maryland" and so recorded in SJL.

SHOULD HAVE READ: Gallatin supplied the words in italics within the quote. The passage in the act reads: "and the monies arising thereupon shall be applied, on or before the first day of November next." Section 4 called for the superintendent to pay all debts previously contracted by the commissioners "which are not herein after specially provided for, out of any monies received by him arising out of the city funds." According to the PROVISO in Section 6, if a sufficient sum to meet the payments "shall not be produced by the sale of the whole of the lots aforesaid, then so much money as may be necessary to provide for the deficiency is hereby appropriated, and shall be paid" from the U.S. Treasury (U.S. Statutes at Large, 2:176).

[1] TJ here wrote in the margin: "money *produced.*"

From Levi Lincoln

SIR   Worcester Octo 29th 1802

The Letter from Mr. Callender inclosed to me by Morton as also Mr Morton's I do myself the honor to forward; I mean to follow them, in eight or ten days, if the situation of my family will permit. They are[1] getting better exerpt my youngest whose situation appears to be critical. It not being probable, that any new commissioners of bankruptcy will be appointed in Boston immediately I shall not trouble you with my observations on Mr Callender's character.

We are looking forward with impatience to next Monday. It is difficult to form any conjectures with respect to some of the districts, both parties appear to be confident. Great exertions are made. with the federalist it is violent; But in reference to the great object, it is the struggle of desperation. As usual, every species of falshood & abuse has been put in a state of requisition, and made to circulate. And falshood has the advantage of truth, in respect of the number of papers directed to it, and other facilities, to give it circulation. Nothing can exceed the virulence of some individuals on the occasion—The clergy are, apparently more cautious, but some of them insideously at work to continue the delusion, & excite to action. I think we have altered in some degree for the better—and shall still progress—The circuit Court proceeding to business, has mortified the violent of the party very much—It is said that Judge Cushing told Parsons, if the court were not competent to do the business, They had been incompetent to a great part of the business, that they had heretofore done—I never had any doubts of the courts sitting & doing the business assinged them, by the last law—

I take the liberty of forwarding a letter from a Mr Cross—He appears to feel very sensably his situation. It is mortifying, what can be done for him, I don't know—I am myself convinced that the Government must be supported by the republicans—From persons of opposite politicks it will never be countenanced, but the reverse—Every measure of theirs furnishes proof, that republicans must depend solely on themselves—

I have the honor to be with perfect respect your most obt Sert

LEVI LINCOLN

RC (DLC); at head of text: "The President of the United States"; endorsed by TJ as received 10 Nov. and so recorded in SJL. Enclosures: (1) John Callender to TJ, 20 Sep. (2) Perez Morton to Lincoln, Dorchester, Massachusetts, 4 Oct., enclosing Callender's "Application" to TJ; Morton often declines writing recommendations for people seeking office, but due to his acquaintance with Callender he will state "what I consider to be the grounds of his pretensions"; Morton has always heard that Callender acted with "Integrity and capacity" in his previous position as bankruptcy commissioner; in politics, Callender "has undoubtedly been attached" to the previous presidential administration, but he is "decent and respectful" toward the present government; Callender told Morton that receiving an appointment from TJ would *"make a deep and lasting impression of Gratitude"* on Callender's mind; if there are to be any further appointments of bankruptcy commissioners, Morton suggests giving "serious consideration" to Callender's application (RC in DNA: RG 59, LAR; endorsed by a clerk). (3) Stephen Cross to Lincoln, Newburyport, 20 Sep., saying that he does not know Lincoln or anyone else near the president but feels he must write, "feeling myself deeply wounded to find myself abandoned by President Jefferson and those with whom he advises after what services I did thro' our Revolution and suffering in such a manner since from those whose Political sentiments I differ"; he was a Massachusetts collector of impost and excise until he be-

came the first U.S. customs collector of Newburyport; the Essex Junto, finding him a "Stubborn Republican," plotted to obtain his ouster, and Alexander Hamilton never told him the reason he was removed; the Junto has undermined Republicans' efforts to elect him to office, including a seat in Congress; thus he has been "Crushed" by his "Political enemies" and left with "no support from any friends who have it in their Power" to fill positions; it was widely expected that Cross would be "restored" as collector following TJ's election; no one thought "that I should have been neglected and my Brother appointed both a Commissioner on the Bankrupt Act, and also Collector of this Port"; Cross would like to see Lincoln in Boston but does not know when Lincoln will be there or how to arrange an interview (RC in same; endorsed by TJ: "Cross Stephen Newbury port to mr Lincoln. for emploiment").

MONDAY, 1 Nov., was election day in Massachusetts (Boston *Republican Gazetteer*, 20 Oct.).

On 20 Oct., the United States CIRCUIT COURT for Massachusetts opened its session in Boston. The members of the court were William CUSHING of the U.S. Supreme Court and John Davis, the federal district judge for Massachusetts (Boston *Independent Chronicle*, 21 Oct.).

PARSONS: the Federalist attorney Theophilus Parsons (ANB; Vol. 33:15, 16, 671, 674).

[1] MS: "a."

From Anna McKnight

SIR   darkesville Berkel County october 29 1802

Permit & Pardon a female Now in humble Life & one that was Bred up & for Many years has Lived in Eas & affluance tho Now at the Ege of 73 is in a fair way to be Reduced to Extream want. to Lay her distress Before her Beloved Presadant My husband Mr Robat McKnight was true a harted demoCrat as the Call him as Ever lived & as honest a Man & by his Policks has been thrown out of all Business & by his good Nature in being sacurity for a friend has Put our Little Movable Property in the Power of the shariff which Consists of 2 slaves & some furniture My slaves are as My Children & if I Could ProCure 5 hundred Dollers I Can seCure all I have sir 2 houses & Lots in this place which is 3 Miles from the sulferspring one of which I would Morgage or indeed give a Clear Feed of for the Money it Rents 1190 Dollars if I Can ProCure this sum by the first of desember it will be a great Blessing to Me No one on Earth Knows of My Writing if My Persumtion is too great distress alone & the Exalted oppinion I have of your Exelancy Must Plead for & you sir Can throw it in the fire if I am honnord with any Notice Mr Wm sumervill Post Master in this County will send it me safe My Husband is a very MeCaniCle Charracter having Been Breed a Mill Write in his youth if your work & where sir would have oCation for such a Person to superintend an honister & more faithfull Man I am sure you sir Could Not imploy PerMitt me once more to implore your Pardon & to have the honnor to subscribe My self your sinCear tho humble friend & servt   ANNA McKNIGHT

RC (DLC); at foot of text: "To the first & best of Men"; endorsed by TJ as received 8 Nov. and so recorded in SJL.

THIS COUNTY: Berkeley County, Virginia.

From James Ogilvie

SIR,   Stevensburg Octr. 29. 1802

I take the liberty of requesting your attention to an Address to the Inhabitants of the City of Washington & its Vicinity, which I have transmitted for insertion in the next Intelligencer.—Whilst I disclaim every intention of soliciting any thing at your hands, that requires the preface of an apology & have not the smallest right to expect from you any exertion of the nature of private favour, or personal friendship, I could not but regard it, as a pleasing evidence of the utility of my existence & exertions & an auspicious earnest of future success, if, after perusing the Address, you should deem the design it announces worthy of your approbation & countenance, nor, could I fail to consider any aid you may have it in your power and think proper to afford me, in the accomplishment of my design, under a conviction of its probable public utility, as an additional proof of the sincerity &

ardour of your wishes, to promote the happiness & improvement of the nation, which has so emphatically manifested its affiance in your integrity & veneration for your talents.—I remain, with lively respect & esteem,

Sir, your affectionate fellow Citizen   JAMES OGILVIE

RC (DLC); endorsed by TJ as received 4 Nov. and so recorded in SJL.

In his ADDRESS "To the Inhabitants of Washington and Its Vicinity," Ogilvie, who had been an instructor at Stevensburg Academy, proposed to move to Washington by the beginning of 1803 "for the permanent establishment of a Seminary" for young men. His design of a four-year plan of juvenile education consisted of a rudimentary curriculum followed by a sequence including philosophy, geometry, history, and logic. Lectures, discussions, exercises in elocution and composition, as well as public examinations supplemented his instructional methods. For this new venture, he required a pledged enrollment of at least 30 pupils with a tuition of $30 for boys 15 and younger and $40 for older students (*National Intelligencer*, 8 Nov. 1802).

From Joseph Priestley

DEAR SIR,   Northumberland Oct 29. 1802

As there are some particulars in a letter I have lately received from Mr Stone at Paris which I think it will give you pleasure to know, and Mr Cooper has been so obliging as to transcribe them for me, I take the liberty to send them, along with a copy of my *Dedication*, with the correction that you suggested, and a *Note* from the letter with which you favoured me concerning what you did with respect to the *constitution*, and which is really more, than I had ascribed to you. For almost everything of importance to political liberty in that instrument was, as it appears to me, suggested by you; and as this was unknown to myself, and I believe is so to the world in general, I was unwilling to omit this opportunity of noticing it.

I shall be glad if you will be so good as to engage any person sufficiently qualified to draw up such an account of the *constitutional form* of this country as my friend says will be agreable to the emperor, and I will transmit it to Mr Stone

Not knowing any certain method of sending a letter to France and presuming that you do I take the liberty to inclose my letter to Mr Stone. It is, however, so written, that no danger can arise to him from it, into whatever hands it may fall.

The state of my health, tho, I thank God, much improved, will not permit me to avail myself of your kind invitation to pay you a visit. Where ever I am, you may depend upon my warmest attachment and best wishes   JOSEPH PRIESTLEY.

P.S. I send a copy of the *Preface* as well as of the *Dedication*, that you may form some idea of the work you are pleased to patronize.

RC (DLC); endorsed by TJ as received 6 Nov. and so recorded in SJL. Enclosures: (1) Priestley to John Hurford Stone, not found. (2) For dedication and preface, see below.

For the DEDICATION of the second part of Priestley's *General History*, see Vol. 37:592-5. TJ's suggested CORRECTION, mentioned in his letter to Priestley of 19 June, was incorporated into the final dedication of July 1802 and appeared in print as an asterisked NOTE about TJ's involvement in the plan and establishment of the CONSTITUTION: "When the constitution was formed Mr. Jefferson was absent on the service of his country in Europe, but on receiving a copy of it he wrote strongly to Mr. Madison, urging the want of provision for the freedom of religion, the freedom of the press, the trial by jury, the habeas corpus, the substitution of a militia for a standing army, and an express reservation to the states of all the rights not specifically granted to the union. Mr. Madison accordingly moved in the first session of congress for these amendments, and they were agreed to, and ratified, by the states as they now stand" (Priestley, *General History of the Christian Church, from the Fall of the Western Empire to the Present Time*, 4 vols. [Northumberland, Pa., 1802-03], 1:iv).

In his PREFACE of 3 July 1802 to the *General History*, Priestley explained his decision to resume his history and carry it forward in time. He also presented his methodology with a focus on events rather than centuries, a reliance on general ecclesiastical histories rather than original writers, and an opinion about biases in recorded events. He expressed a hope that the history would be useful for the instruction of youth (same, 1:ix-xxxii). Priestley also sent a copy of the preface to his friend Theophilus Lindsey, to whom he related that it was the longest he had ever written and that "it consists chiefly of reflections on the middle and dark ages" (Thomas Belsham, *Memoirs of the Late Reverend Theophilus Lindsey, M.A.* [London, 1812], 438).

ENCLOSURE

Extract from a Letter of John Hurford Stone to Joseph Priestley

Extract of a letter from the emperor Alexander   to M. de la Harpe, a Swiss, the primary mover of the revolution in Switzerland, one of their Directory, afterwards retired to his Chateau 2 leagues from Paris. he had been chosen by the late Empress Catharine to educate the present Emperor & Constantine his brother, & was chosen not only as a man of talents, but, still more extraordinary, as a Republican. Alexander has therefore recieved a thoroughly republican education, & is by disposition & character virtuous & exemplary. he corresponded with Le Harpe (in Switzerld) during his banishmt by Paul. the letters of the prince are homilies of republican principles, not extravagant & chimerical projects of reformation, but wise & well weighed plans of government. in a late one of 8. pages to Le Harpe he says 'to you my dear friend I owe every thing that I possess. it is from you alone that I have imbibed those principles which shall be the regulators of my conduct; whilst I fill the arduous post which Providence has assigned me, it is impossible for me ever to repay you the immense obligations which I owe. the only recompence I can ever hope to make you will be[1] by reducing to practice the lessons you have taught, & by becoming an instrument of the happiness & liberty of this hitherto ill instructed and ill governed people. if I durst exact any thing more from you, it is to come hither, if your avocations will permit you to finish the education which you have begun. I know the snares by which I am surrrounded. I know also my own weakness but I shall be strong in your strength.' La Harpe returned to Petersburgh. Alexander had already begun his reformation by publishing his Ukases for the liberty of the press & abolition of slavery.

La Harpe while residing near Paris, was intimate with mr Stone the English patriot now a refugee in France & corresponding with Dr. Priestly, in a letter to whom he communicates the above & many other particulars in the same style.

Tr (DLC: TJ Papers, 146:25396); entirely in TJ's hand; endorsed by TJ: "Alexander Emperor of Russia."

EXTRACT OF A LETTER: the "particulars" of a letter from John Hurford Stone that Priestley enclosed to TJ on 29 Oct. have not been found, but they may survive in the form of this copy by TJ. Writing to Priestley on 29 Nov., TJ thanked his friend for "the extract of mr Stone's letter on the subject of Alexander."

Frédéric César de La Harpe was a member of the DIRECTORY of the Helvetic Republic from 1798 to 1800 (Jean Charles Biaudet and Françoise Nicod, eds., *Correspondance de Frédéric-César de*

La Harpe et Alexandre Ier, 3 vols. [Neuchâtel, 1978], 1:19-20).

LATE ONE OF 8. PAGES: the quoted passage is a representation of the contents of a letter that Alexander wrote to La Harpe in French in May 1801 (same, 1:21, 240-1).

LIBERTY OF THE PRESS: Alexander loosened restrictions on dissent and publication (Derek Offord, *Nineteenth-Century Russia: Opposition to Autocracy* [Harlow, Eng., 1999], 13; Sergei Pushkarev, *The Emergence of Modern Russia, 1801-1917*, trans. Robert H. McNeal and Tova Yedlin [Edmonton, Alberta, 1985], 54.

[1] Word supplied by Editors.

From Martha Jefferson Randolph

DEAR PAPA   October 29. [1802]

We recieved your letter and are preparing with all speed to obey its summons, by next friday I hope we shall be able to fix a day, and probably the shortest time in which the horses can be sent after recieving our letter will determine it. tho as yet it is not entirely certain that we can get off so soon. will you be so good as to send orders to the milliner Mde Pick I believe her name is, thro Mrs Madison who very obligingly offered to execute any little commission for us, to send to Philadelphia for 2 wigs of the colour of the hair enclosed and of the most fashionable shapes, that they may be at Washington when we arrive they are universally worn and will relieve us as to the necessity of dressing our own hair a business in which neither of us are adepts I believe Mde. Pick is in the habit of doing those things when desired and they can be procured in a short time from Philadelphia where she corresponds much handsomer and cheaper than elsewhere. adieu Dearest Father Maria is with in good health and Spirits believe me with tender affection

    yours   M. RANDOLPH

RC (ViU: Edgehill-Randolph Papers); partially dated; endorsed by TJ as received 31 Oct. 1802 and so recorded in SJL.

On 20 Nov., TJ recorded sending Dolley Madison $38 for the purchase of 2 WIGS from Marie Ann Pic, a Washington milliner (MB, 2:1086).

From Thomas Mann Randolph

DEAR SIR,   Edgehill October 29th. [1802]

I thank you most sincerely for the trouble you have taken in writing to So. Carolina for the information I wanted. I did not doubt that it might be obtained at Washington: upon learning that my scheme of obtaining leave to pass through that state with Slaves was practicable I could have made the application and arrangment myself: I have at present great hope of escaping the circuitous rout as I have learnt lately there is great relaxation of the rigor observed last year. Many companies of slaves have been marched through very lately with out molestation. By the 1st. Jan: the latest day of my departure I am sanguine I may obtain assurance of the safety of my property from that danger. I feel the warmest gratitude for your offers to aid my views in this journey: there cannot I hope arise a necessity for that beyond what you have done allready by making me acquainted with Mr. Milledge. If I should make a purchase of Land on installments I can give Virginia lands of value along with the Slaves I settle as a pledge. Mr. M.s information and goodness will, I have confidence, keep me from difficulties and errors.   The expression respecting Marthas health meant her recovery from a very smart relapse into the pectoral complaint she had while at Monticello: she is now as well as usual; but I shall be subject in future to alarms about her upon that account which I have not felt heretofore.   The last passage of your letter which seems to embrace me within the narrow circle of your family affects my heart deeply, but there is a mixture of pain with the emotion; something like shame accompanying it and checking the swell of tenderness, from consciousness that I am so essentially & widely different from all within it, as to look like something extraneous, fallen in by accident and destroying the homogeneity. I cannot like the proverbially silly bird feel at my ease in the company of the Swans. Yet I can, alone, or surrounded with any number nearly on the same social & intellectual level with myself be as happy and as benevolent as any being alive. The sentiment of my mind when it contemplates yourself alone is one, of the most lofty elevation and most unmixed delight. The rapture of my fancy when it takes in view your extraordinary powers and considers the manner in which they have been, with unceasing and unvarying force for so many years employed and directed, is too strong for a man of less enthusiasm to feel. The feelings of my heart, the gratitude and affection it overflows with when I attempt to estimate the value to the whole human race, as an example; the precious worth to all who live under it, as the benignant sky which covers them; of the incredibly, inconcievably excellent political system which you have with much more hindrance [...] opposition than aid, created, developed, [...] matured, and at last I think permanently established: will no doubt yet render absolutely eternal by some additional arrangements which will make it, like the work of the Allmighty, go, by laws enacted at its completion, as long as the people which form it shall endure: the feelings of my heart when I make these reflexions are such as a disposition of weak benevolence could never generate.   I find I am writing a Rhapsody but I was kindled and I have not now time to write again or alter.

With sincere & ardent affection   TH: M. RANDOLPH

RC (MHi); partially dated; torn at seal; addressed: "Thomas Jefferson President of the U.S. Washington"; endorsed by TJ as received 31 Oct. and so recorded in SJL.

YOUR LETTER: TJ to Randolph, 22 Oct.

From a "Citizen free Born"

SIR,   October 30th. 1802

The Times Are much Altered Since your Administration, Thousands are released from hard Taxes, And the Union at large are eased of many thousands of Dollars, by your Justice, may you long live to Administer Justice to all your fellow Citizens—

But there is one thing more in Justice you Ought To Do, humanity Calls loudly on you & the rest of the Rulers to do (And that is the FREEDOM of the Negroes) The Basses of Our goverment stands on FREEDOM,—how is it that we hold to freedom & many of the states are filled with so many miserable Creatures that are Weltering under so hard a yoke as the poor blacks do: It is certainly time to ease the Creatures from their Servile State, and make them happy also.

Sir, if you could only be among the Vulgar Sort of Overseers, And be an eye & an ear Witness to the Cruelties of those Barbarous Wretches, And hear the Groans and Cries of the Poor Creatures, I think your huminity Would melt into Tears (in pity to the poor Creatures) Your own Domestic Slaves[1] that are immediately under your Notice, are Chastized with a rod for their Crimes But those that are Under hard Task masters (to use the Scripture language, with Scorpions) large sticks, and Poles, And at Best a Cow Skin; And that for Small Crimes, Perhaps an hours Sleep; a Small Omission in duty (or the Like) I have Known many tied & stript And a hundred hard Lashes laid on the Naked Backs I know that it is hard for you to Emancipate them And you'l find many of those Barbarous Wretches that Will Oppose you, But fear not, you have Justice on your Side & thousand of Friends to Support you in so laudable An Undertaking; Safety to these states Calls you to do it (for while we ruleing them with a rod of Iron and they themselves Uneasy, should some Dareing, bold Massanello, or Some Great BOANAPARTE, stand at their heads) What miserable Destruction would be made, Amongst our Wives, our Sons & our Daughters—Remember FREEDOM is the Birth Right of All mankind And sooner or Later they Will enjoy it, the history of the Hebrews furnish's us with a great deal of matter they did obtain their FREEDOM, but it was at the expence of the Flower of Egypt, Let us not harden our hearts, But let the people go in mercy.

Some Say it would Ruin many families to free the Negroes; Well I will admit it. But I would purpose a gradial liberation, which would not very sencibly be felt; in the first place Let all that are 40. years old Be Set free and upwards—then Four years After that all that are 28 years old be set free and upwards—then Four years after that all that are 21 and upwards be set free—& four years after that the Whole Race—   One thing more that appears to hurt the minds of the People they say it will never do to set them free & let them stay amongst us Send them clear off & I should be glad they were gone But for my Part I am not of that way of thinking they would greatly Contribute to the Union But I would have them Set on Some Large plat of Land (As we have in the United States such a vast Quantity of Unlocked Lands, And Claimed by Different Indians tribes that never do these states any Service, but are very hurtful to them in holding the Lands) Let a spot on the Missippi be Laid out; And as the Creatures are Liberated, let them immegrate themselves thither within one year after they are set free, And there Let them have 50 Acres laid off to each male so made free, And after his settling it Two or more years let him be Subject to a rent of two Dollars Annually forever—And by this means the people will be happy And the revenue greatly increased, I do Suppose on a moderate computation not less than 200000 Dollars.—And also I would Advise that all free Negroes, Mustezeoes & Mulattoes Should be sent thither on the same terms / But with Liberty to purchase more Lands if they are able, as you in your Justice & Wisdom Shall think fit, And as a National guard has be come necessary to us let a Part of those guards be sent to this new Settlement in order to keep the negroes in subjection, And in some few years they will add greatly to the Strength, as well as the Revenue of these States, Sir do not think that I am Laying down positive rules, I only mean hints that you may see how to do in your Wisdom, And I hope For Our own Sakes you'l not neglect the Salvation of these Poor Blacks any Longer: then you'l see the blessing of heaven poured Down on your peaceful head These things I want you to consider, for thousands of these poor wretches are neither Cloathed and fed as Well as our Brute Beasts are—

Many of them I know are not fed as they ought to be, And Report Says that near Charleston they Are allowanced on half Rations & for a supply for the rest they have Cotton Seed to live on—Cruel indeed / Well might the poet say

half naked hungry & cold ⎱
and if we beg we meet a Scold. ⎰

———

And again these Creatures are by some Cruel masters kept up Late & are beaten if they are Found only taking what Nature Calls for, and hot or cold wet or Dry they are Driven out before it is day, Which made the same poet say

We work all day & half the night
And Rise again with the morning light
And after all the Tedious round
at night we are stretched upon the ground. &c

O Friend of mankind Pity the Creatures, your Just Administration to the rest of your fellow Citizens emboldens me to hope your humanity will do Something for these Poor Creatures

I am a Citizen free Born of the United States of America

RC (DLC); endorsed by TJ as received from "Anon. probably S. Carola." on 20 Nov. and "Slaves" and so recorded in SJL.

MASSANELLO: that is, Masaniello, a Neapolitan fisherman who in 1647 briefly assumed leadership over a popular revolt in Naples before being assassinated and who became a mythic subject for many European commentators and artists. The reference may have derived from Thomas Paine's *Common Sense* (Rosario Villari, *The Revolt of Naples*, trans. James Newell [Cambridge, 1993], 153-70; Thomas Paine, *Common Sense and Other Writings*, ed. Gordon Wood [New York, 2003], 32).

The lines of the POET came from the anonymously written "The Negro's Prayer," the earliest known publication of which was in an 1801 issue of the *Baltimore Weekly Magazine* (James G. Basker, ed., *Amazing Grace: An Anthology of Poems about Slavery, 1660-1810* [New Haven, 2002], 553-4).

[1] MS: "Salves."

From Gideon Granger

DR: SIR.   Trenton. Saturday. Oct: 30th 1802

I am so far on my Journey to Washington after an absence of ten days from my family—In the Course of next week I shall reach the Seat of Govermt. my tardy progress arises from a severe cough & pain in my breast occasioned by a cold some weeks past. The Legislature of this State is exactly ballanced—They cannot agree on a Governor & will not unless the Tories yield. The Republicans have the President of the Senate who will officiate as Governor if no Choice takes place—he can and will (if necessary) appoint a Senator in the room of Ogden. Nothing is to be feared—I am more pleased with our friends in Jersey than ever—They have strength & will succeed, tho they have been out witted much to their own Mortification. In great haste

Yours Affectionately   GIDN GRANGER

RC (DLC); at foot of text: "The President." Recorded in SJL as received 3 Nov.

EXACTLY BALLANCED: when the New Jersey legislature convened on 26 Oct., Federalists controlled the 39-member House of Assembly by one vote and elected William Coxe speaker. The Republicans controlled by one vote the second chamber, the Legislative Council, which consisted of one member from each county, 13 in all. They reelected Republican John Lambert vice president. On 28 Oct., the two chambers held a joint meeting to appoint the state's governor and a U.S. senator. Voting along strict party lines, incumbent governor Joseph Bloomfield and Federalist candidate Richard Stockton each received 26 votes. The vote for a senator had the same outcome. Republican John Condit received 26 votes as did the incumbent Federalist senator Aaron Ogden. The impasse remaining unresolved, Lambert was given the power to OFFICIATE AS GOVERNOR on 15 Nov. He appointed Condit to the U.S. Senate in the summer of 1803. Condit took his seat when the Eighth Congress convened on 17 Oct. (*Journal of the Proceedings of the Legislative Council of the State of New-Jersey, Convened, in General-Assembly, at Trenton, on Tuesday the Twenty-Sixth Day of October, One Thousand Eight Hundred and Two* [Trenton, 1803], 150-4; *Minutes and Proceedings of the Joint Meeting . . . October 28, 1802* [Trenton, 1803; Shaw-Shoemaker, No. 4747]; Trenton *True American*, 1 Nov. 1802; 29 Aug., 24 Oct. 1803; Philadelphia *Aurora*,

1 Sep. 1803; js, 3:295-6; Vol. 37:491n). Republicans regained control of the state legislature in the fall of 1803 (Walter R. Fee, *The Transition from Aristocracy to Democracy in New Jersey, 1789-1829* [Somerville, N.J., 1933], 136-7). For partisan politics in New Jersey during the early years of TJ's presidency, see same, 128-37, and Carl E. Prince, *New Jersey's Jeffersonian Republicans: The Genesis of an Early Party Machine, 1789-1817* (Chapel Hill, 1967), 98-107.

From Mary Ingraham

RESPECTED SIR,   Bristol Octo 30 1802

After You have heard the Petition presented for an unhappy Man, will you not Sir lend a favorable ear to mine? It is a Wife petitioning for the liberty—for the life of her husband, for will not his health—his life be the sacrifice of an imprisonment embittered by the painful reflection of a suffering Wife and five lovely children consign'd to poverty and distress.

We Sir have no Parent to reach forth the fostering hand,—or shelter us beneath the paternal roof through the approaching inclement season.   A widowed Mother alone[1] survives to mourn the disappointment of her hopes. Of seven Sons (by a life of prudence and economy reared to manhood) two only survives the rest have been swallowed up by the devouring seas.   From my Husband she looked for comfort and support in her decline of life.

Oh Sir, will You not pity her?   Will You not have compassion on us all? We offer no excuse—We attempt no palliation! It is your Clemency Great Sir we entreat—

Speak but the word, and my Husband will be released—restored to his usefulness—and rendered to happiness Pardon respected Sir this tale of woe This intrusion on your time, reflect on the importance of the subject to a Wife to a Mother, and that it is natural to affliction to complain.—You Sir who are a son, and probably a Father, will you not bring our case home to your own feelings?

Your known charactar for humanity and tenderness makes me hope that you will—and that I shall not plead in vain; in that hope (Oh may it not prove illusive)

I subscribe myself Great Sir Your most Obedient Humble Servant

MARY INGRAHAM

RC (DLC); at head of text: "To the President of the United State"; endorsed by TJ as received 8 May 1803 and so recorded in SJL.

For THE PETITION of the mariner Nathaniel Ingraham, see Vol. 37:199-200.

[1] Word interlined.

From Thomas Sumter, Sr.

DEAR SIR   Stateburgh 31st. Octr. 1802

I have the Honour, just now, to receive your favour of the 22d. Int. Which has been delayed by the failure of a Trip of the Mail—I hasten to Answer to the first part—the other requires Circumspection. it shall be duely attended to—

inregard of the Law of this State, which prohibits the introduction of Slaves into it, Certainly extends its penalties to every case. Still I am persuaded, very little risque will be run in the attempting to pass through in the Manner Suggested, rather none, provided Mr. Randolph will be at the Trouble to use a Little precaution—

The Legislature of this State will be in Session from the 22d. of the next, untill the same time in the month following i.e. Decemr—The Govonor will also be at the Seat of Government i.e. Columbia, which is but a small distance off the most frequented route from the interior of Virginia, to that of Georgia. therefore, when at Danville or even Sailsbury, if a person were Dispatched Either to the Executive, or the Legislature, asking Protection through the State, it would beyond a Doubt be attaind, without delay, & in time for the person Transacting the business to meet, his party, at Charlotte in Norther Carolina, or on the Verge of this State—I will confer, with some of our Members on Cases of this sort. Should any occur they will be prepaired and write a line in General Terms to the Governor—I have myself, allways Considered the Law, both unjust & impolitick.

I am Dear Sir with the highest respect your Most Obedt. Servt

THOS. SUMTER

RC (DLC); endorsed by TJ as received 16 Nov. and so recorded in SJL.

Note on Value of District of Columbia Loans

[before 1 Nov. 1802]

200,000.	D. from Maryld on guar. of Congr. in stock yielded	169.873.41
100,000.	lent by Congr.	
50,000.	stock lent by Maryld. payable Nov. 1. 1802 yielded	42,738.36
		212,611.77

MS (DLC: TJ Papers, 192:34074); undated; entirely in TJ's hand.

STOCK YIELDED: the Maryland loans to the District of Columbia commissioners consisted of U.S six percent stock at par value, which the commissioners sold for specie at the market price. LENT BY CONGR.: the act of 18 Apr. 1798 authorized the president to lend $100,000 to the commissioners (ASP, *Miscellaneous*, 1:258; Vol. 33:481n; Vol. 35:99n).

To William Bache

DEAR DOCTR: Washington Nov. 1. 1802.

I recieved yesterday yours of the 26th. mentioning that you would set out the next day for Richmond, where of course you would arrive on the 28th. three days before I recieved your letter. as I had lodged money in mr Jefferson's hands, he might possibly pay you the 143. D 33 c on sight of the letter I wrote you. but I now write to him to do it, and I inclose you an order on him accordingly for that sum, which however you cannot recieve till the 3d.

Be so good as to present my most friendly respects to mrs Bache and with my wishes for a pleasant voyage and safe arrival at your destination, accept assurances of my constant & affectionate esteem.

TH: JEFFERSON

RC (Mrs. W. F. Magie, Princeton, New Jersey, 1945); addressed: "Doctr. William Bache who will call for it at the Post office of Richmond"; franked and postmarked. Enclosure not found, but see below.

YOURS OF THE 26TH.: a letter from Bache, written at Edgehill on 26 Oct., is recorded in SJL but has not been found. ON SIGHT OF THE LETTER: TJ to Bache, 11 Oct. The ORDER was on Gibson & Jefferson for $143.33, of which $33.33 was for Polly Carr (MB, 2:1085). I NOW WRITE TO HIM: TJ to George Jefferson, 1 Nov.

From John Barnes

[ca. 1 Nov. 1802]

Sketch of Octr: & Novr: a/c. The President US: wth J Barnes.

1802
Octr. 1. To Amt. of Balance favr J.B. ℔ a/. rend.   2019.
to
Oct 27. To Amt. of Cash & Orders paid. Ee.   2853.67.
To store a/c, £49.2.8½ equal to   131. 3.   2984.70   5003.70
Cr By this sum WSt. wth: G & J—2d. Augt. }
subject to your Crdt. since pd. WS.   }   198

Oct 11. By Treasury Warrt: on a/c   2000   2198
   27th.   in favr of JB $2805.70
      NB. real balance due last Mo.   1821.
                  Oct. increase   984.70   2805.70.

for the Mo of Novr: on Supposition
                       Octr. Balance as above   2805.70
Memod: Nov. paymt. as ℔ Presidents list...say 1391.60.
             from whence deduct already pd.
       viz ⎧ Cap Lewis Compn.   150.
in List. Oct a/c ⎨ T. Claxton (waggon)   50.
          ⎩ Oldhams suit.   100.   300 —
                              1091.60.
Nov.   expenditures Allowed to be   900 —   1991.60. 4797.30
Nov. 4th. say, the 8th By Warrt. Compensation a/- to be recd   2000 —
               appr. Balance still due JB. $2797.30
exclusive of any Extra paymts not Noticed in Novr. list:

even this Balance of $2805.70 will not, deter me from avoiding
the insuing Mo. that dreaded Alternative—the Bank.—on a Variety
of Accts.—Allowing for a short time the Assistance it Affords—on a
singular Occasion—should it become a more general one, permit me
Sir, to point out the eventfull consequences, that might possibly
insue—payments wth. a full Bank, (thus circumstanced) are more
readily made—but, with held—and more sparingly dealt Out, when
Otherwise—yet sufficiently prompt to insure satisfaction, to the
Creditor. The too frequent Use of the Bank, from unexpected, unavoidable demands—may induce—If not Constrain—the drawer and
indorser, to renew their Notes, in Order, to meet the one becoming
due. this forced expedient (on a false Credit) serves, but to increase
the growing evil, creates suspicion—numberless inconveniencys—
and at length bring on—if not timely everted,—a *demur*, at least, discredit, on Both—is the fatal rock, that many, very many, good Men
have thus unguardedly experienced—even for my *self* I would not for
a Moeity of the Usual sum—sustain the shock of a demur, and I do—
with the same sincerity add, that of *yours.*—for the whole Amot: do
than I pray you Sir—forgo these risques—your constant Compensations will, I fondly hope, Answer all your purposes, without the
Application—it is, only to protract, such paymts.—you can best designate, for a time—so—as to inable me, to fulfill your engagemts.
with as much punctuality—as the Case will admit.—My determined
resolution of declining business here: under so many disadvantages
in point of extra expences &c. &c. &c. of course no general purchases

Necessary—as was last fall: is, the principal reason, I have been so well prepared to meet your extra demands, without recuring to other means. to the remnant of my shatterd Capital than—insted of investing it, in some Public stock—you are most Assuredly Welcome to the Use of the insuing Winter—by the Spring, I trust and Hope, your engagemts. may be so regulated, as to guard against every Appt. embarrismt.—in making these Observations—I have taken a liberty—perhaps—unbecoming my station—but, as they flow from the dictates of a sincere disposition—to preserve—from the slightest reproach, (of those whose sole business & wish—is to degrade—if possible)—a Character—so eminently usefull & Virtuous—I flatter myself you will have the goodness to Excuse—whatever at first View may appear improper—permit me than Sir, to refer you, to your former View—lists of demands expenditures & Compensations on supposition from 31st. May—4th. Octr. By this estimate your a/cs}. were brought nearly to a Close, only $41.46 in my favr—but, by these unavoidable—unforeseen demands (which will ever Await these uncertain Estimates)—you may perceive, how widely they differ from the reality—as in the present instance—when compared with your View of the 12th. Instant stated to be abt. $1700—was by my private, Abstracted Accts: $1817.60 and by the present annexed a/- 27 Inst. $2805.70—while your Nov. a/c—on supposition are, as stated & annexed (without any extra unexpected demands being added—) $2797.30.—it is from these very interesting Circumstances—I draw my conclusions—and fearing the least disagreable consequences, Compel me—with great reluctance be Assured—(but as in duty bound.) to submit them to your Attentive Consideration—

with the greatest—Esteem & respect, I am Sir, your mst Obedt: & very H St   JOHN BARNES

RC (ViU: Edgehill-Randolph Papers); partially dated; at foot of text: "The President of the UStates"; endorsed by TJ. Recorded in SJL as received 1 Nov.

OLDHAMS SUIT: see Barnes to TJ, 28 Sep. 1802.

YOUR VIEW OF THE 12TH. INSTANT: a letter from TJ to Barnes dated 12 Oct. has not been found and is not recorded in SJL. Barnes may be referring to TJ's letter to him of 15 Oct. (see Barnes to TJ, 15 Oct.).

From Joseph Bartlett

SIR,   Cambridge 1. Novr. 1802.

Delicacy in most instances ought to prevent personal application— Man is too fond to appreciate his own abilities.—Letters of recommendation have become too much the custom of the Day, friends are partial, & they usually write as they feel—seldom as they beleive— There are times when a Man should do justice to himself—those are seasons when imperious, stern necessity should influence his con- duct—the command of Nature, is, to love thyself & he who will not obey is little intitled to the patronage of Others.—I am not insensible that in your elevated situation, having in your power so many favors to distribute, that you are deluged with petitions, memorials and re- monstrances—& that you must depend frequently on report, without having personal knowledge of the applicants—My sensibility is awak- ened, & I shrink from the task—when I find it necessary, to introduce the writer to your notice, "as a stranger bid him welcome"—as the question will arise, who are you? & what are your pretensions? it be- comes necessary to say—that I received my early education at Cam- bridge university—that I was admited to the honors of that society 1782—that I read law in Boston under the direction of the Honorable Benjamin Hichborn Esquire & that I have been in the profession ever since the year 1788—I have been a member of our State Legislature, untill my republican tenets, caused the united exertions of the Uni- versity & a contemptable Aristocracy in this place to prevent my re- election last May—that the tide of opposition & oppression has Come hard against me—mainly on the score of politicks my property has been reduced—my professional buissiness injured—they have not only extended it to me but to my innocent unoffending Family—I have ever been attached to a republican Government. that legacy I inher- ited from my Ancestors, who were some of the first Pilgrims of Plym- outh, & whose posterity were early, & strenuous advocates in our revolutionay war—I have ever been a firm & decided supporter of your administration—that I have been, because I considered the measures persued were calculated to promote the happiness & Inter- est of our common Country—to evidence, that my naked assertions are not without good & the best support—I can refer for the truth of the above statement—to the Honorable Elbridge Gerry Esquire, with whom I have the Honor to be on Terms of friendship—Mr. Gerry in a line to me of the 19th. Octr. says, "Nothing could give me more pleasure, than to see you triumphant over your implacable Enemies &c &c"—I can obtain his Letter—also from Genl. Hull, Mr. Hich- born, Col. Varnum &c &c—if necessary—but I wish to rely on myself & to be indebted to your goodness for all I may possess—Will you for- give a private undignified Citizen, if *with confidence* & *in confidence*, he states in truth & sincerity the following facts—(vizt)—that most of the Offices within the gift of Government are in *this quarter*, filled with Men who are enemies to the present Administration—& are warm in opposite measures, which they falsly stile federal—these Men, have so many dependants under them, that they have a very great influence on our state elections, especially in our Capitals—& should Mr. Adams this day be elected in Boston instead of Dr. Eustiss, I verily beleive it would arise from that cause—need I mention the Collectors of the Ports of Plymouth and Marblehead—the Marshalls of Boston & Portland—the District Attorney in the District of Maine—some of the Commissioners of the Board of Bankruptcy in Boston and its vicinity—with a variety of others—pardon the sugestion—it was dictated from the best of principles—not being willing that those People who eat your Bread (if we can judge from the villianous, unjustifiable, unequalled abuse publickly & privatly in circulation) should be allowed to mix poison in your Cup—Let me now Sir, say one Word for myself—if either of the above places should be vacated—or any new appointments be Made in the Board of Commissioners—let me be remembered—or if either of the Marshalls of Boston or Portland should be vacant—I should be filld with gratitude for the designation—if it should be thought expedient, I will visit Washington on this occasion—Will you Sir, think of a Man, who has done ev'ry thing for the cause of a free elective Government—who has been in a great measure sacrificd, by the intemporate Malevolence of a disappointed expiring faction—altho you Sir, are deservedly situated at the Head, of a Brave, a great & a free People I am well assured, you will attend to the decent request of any Citizen—however humble his station in society—beleive me I do not wish to take from Men— more deserving & who have merited more than myself—may the answer I receive be consoling to my feelings—such a One as will save me from those who rise up against me—one that will gratify me & give pleasure to all real republicans in this quarter—God Almighty grant, that you may ever receive the united suffrages of an enlightned People—of this I am well assured that you will ever have the support of all those who love their God—their Country—or themselves—

I am Sir, with the most perfect respect—your most obedient & very Humble Sert.   JOSEPH BARTLETT

RC (DNA: RG 59, LAR); at foot of text: "His Excellency President Jefferson"; endorsed by TJ as received 10 Nov. and "for emploiment" and so recorded in SJL.

Joseph Bartlett (1762-1827) was a lawyer, legislator, and writer from Massachusetts. A graduate of Harvard College, Bartlett's acknowledged brilliance was undermined by his cantankerous and eccentric personality, which frequently left him at odds with his fellow citizens and in financial distress. He served in the Massachusetts House of Representatives from 1799 to 1802 and in the state senate from 1804 to 1805. Several of his poems, orations, and essays appeared in print, including his collection of *Aphorisms on Man, Manners, Principles & Things*, a copy of which he sent to TJ in 1824. The following year, Bartlett sought TJ's support for a proposed autobiography of his "Adventurous and Chequered Life," but the former president declined the request (ANB; Bartlett to TJ, 7 Jan. 1824, 4 Mch. 1825; TJ to Bartlett, 9 Feb. 1824, 16 Mch. 1825, all in DLC). On 21 Oct. 1802, Bartlett sent a similarly worded letter seeking an appointment to James Madison (DNA: RG 59, LAR, endorsed by TJ: "for employment").

AS A STRANGER BID HIM WELCOME: a slight variation from Shakespeare, *Hamlet*, 1.5.

In the 1 Nov. statewide elections for Congress in Massachusetts, Federalist candidate John Quincy ADAMS narrowly lost his bid to unseat incumbent Republican William Eustis (EUSTISS) as the representative from Suffolk District. Adams's slight edge in Boston was offset by Eustis's majorities in Charlestown, Malden, and Hull (Keene *New-Hampshire Sentinel*, 6 Nov. 1802; New York *Morning Chronicle*, 8 Nov. 1802).

COLLECTORS OF THE PORTS OF PLYMOUTH AND MARBLEHEAD: William Wat-son, an active Federalist, was removed as collector for Plymouth by TJ in March 1803. Samuel R. Gerry had been dismissed from the Marblehead collectorship for delinquency in August 1802 and was replaced by Joseph Wilson (Prince, *Federalists*, 25-6, 41-2; Vol. 35:223n; TJ to Elbridge Gerry, 28 Aug. 1802; Memorandum from the State Department, [on or before 18 Oct. 1802]).

MARSHALLS OF BOSTON & PORTLAND: Samuel Bradford was the U.S. marshal for Massachusetts and Isaac Parker held the same office for the district of Maine. Although both men were Federalists, each was permitted to complete his term of office. TJ replaced Bradford with Tompson J. Skinner in December 1804, while Parker was replaced with Thomas G. Thornton in December 1803 (JEP, 1:460, 476; Vol. 33:219; Vol. 34:130, 131n).

In July 1801, TJ named Silas Lee, a moderate Federalist, the U.S. ATTORNEY for the DISTRICT OF MAINE. The appointment eventually paid political dividends for TJ and his party. In February 1808, Levi Lincoln reported that Lee had become an active Republican (Paul Goodman, *The Democratic-Republicans of Massachusetts: Politics in a Young Republic* [Cambridge, Mass, 1964], 146-7; Vol. 33:219, 677; Vol. 35:195; Lincoln to TJ, 26 Feb. 1808).

From Albert Gallatin

DEAR SIR   1st Nover. 1802

My absence and the sickness of a clerk having suspended the transmission of the weekly list of Warrants, I now enclose a summary statement of all the Warrants issued during the quarter ending the 30th Septer. 1802; and also a similar statement for October. To commence from this week, you shall here after be furnished with the usual weekly return

With sincere respect Your obedt. Servt.

ALBERT GALLATIN

The return for Octer. is delayed till to morrow.

RC (DLC); at foot of text: "The President"; endorsed by TJ as received from the Treasury Department on 1 Nov. and so recorded in SJL with notation "Warrts. of 3d. quarter. 2,253,100.71";

also endorsed by TJ: "Warrants Qr." Enclosure not found.

SICKNESS OF A CLERK: Daniel Sheldon (see Gallatin to TJ, 16 Oct.).

From Albert Gallatin

DEAR SIR   Nover. 1st 1802

We will send to Mr Steele for his signature all the Warrants bearing date before the 5th of August the day when his absence commenced, and also all the reports on settlements of accounts posterior to that date which may, at any future time, become a subject of controversy, in suits instituted by the United States. It so happens that *all* those papers, to be sent to him, may, in case of accident, be replaced in the Treasury without any application to officers or persons out of it.

For a variety of other papers, principally Warrants issued after that date & which are receipted by the parties on the Warrants themselves, it is more eligible that another person should be appointed by you to sign. That appointment must of course take place before Mr Steele's resignation is accepted; if sent to morrow, Mr Rawn may in the course of that & the ensuing day sign all the papers, and on Thursday Mr S.'s resignation may be accepted. I enclose the rough draught of an authorization to be signed by you, drawn on the model of one heretofore given by Mr Adams; the words between crotchets are the only alterations; whether they are proper you must judge.

With respect Your obedt. Servt.   ALBERT GALLATIN

RC (DLC): addressed: "The President of the United States"; endorsed by TJ as received from the Treasury Department on 1 Nov. and "David Rawn to perform duties Comptroll." and so recorded in SJL. Enclosure not found.

MODEL OF ONE HERETOFORE GIVEN: see enclosure described at John Steele to TJ, 30 Sep. 1802.

To George Jefferson

DEAR SIR   Washington Nov. 1. 1802.

Mr. Brown and mr Wells, for whom 419.16 D of the money sent you on the 5th. & 6th. of Oct. were destined, have chosen to recieve their money in bank bills in Albemarle, which are accordingly sent them from hence. this sum being free therefore, be pleased to pay one hundred and forty three dollars thirty three cents of it to Dr. William Bache, who will be in Richmond before you recieve this. I shall about the end of the week make you a further remittance for the purpose of answering some draughts which will be made. Accept assurances of my affectionate esteem.   TH: JEFFERSON

PrC (MHi); at foot of text: "Mr. George Jefferson"; endorsed by TJ in ink on verso. Recorded in SJL with notation "Bache 143.33."

A letter from Benjamin BROWN to TJ

of 29 Oct., recorded in SJL as received 31 Oct., has not been found. A response from TJ, recorded in SJL on 2 Nov., has also not been found. On 9 Nov., the president recorded in his financial memoranda sending $319.16 to Brown (MB, 2:1085).

From Lafayette

[ca. 1 Nov. 1802]

[...] [...]ngston Has [...] My frien[...] [...] you and the philosophical Society With two Copies of a Work [Which], [not]wistanding the Actual turn of the public Spirit, Has Attracted Much Notice in France, and Will I am Sure Appear to You a Very Distinguished performance—An other Friend of Mine, Cen Tracy, My Colleague in the Constituent Assembly, My Son's Father in Law, Now a Senator as Well as Cabanis, and on the Same political Side, Has Desired me to Have presented to You and to the philosophical Society Copies of a Book of His Which Accompagny this Letter—He Also Begs Leave to Offer You two Copies of His Observations Respecting public Studies—I am Happy to Have Been Choosen By Both to introduce, through the American Minister, this tribute of their Respect to You, My Dear Sir, and to the Society of Which Cen Cabanis Has the Honor to be a Member—I am With the Most Affectionate Regard Yours   LAFAYETTE

RC (DLC: TJ Papers, 235:42133); torn; date supplied (see the next document).

TWO COPIES OF A WORK: the *Rapports du physique et du moral de l'homme* of Pierre Jean Georges Cabanis; see Cabanis to TJ, [20 Oct.].

Antoine Louis Claude Destutt de TRACY sent TJ an inscribed copy of his *Projet d'éléments d'idéologie á l'usage des écoles centrales de la République Française*, published in Paris in 1801. It became the

first part of the author's *Éléments d'idéologie*. TJ did not receive the book until late 1803 or January 1804. The American Philosophical Society formally received its copy at a meeting of 1 Nov. 1805 and elected Destutt de Tracy to membership the following January. Lafayette's son had married Destutt de Tracy's daughter in June 1802 (APS, *Proceedings*, 22, pt. 3 [1884], 379, 382; Sowerby, No. 1239; Vol. 36:481n; TJ to Lafayette, 31 Jan. 1804).

OBSERVATIONS RESPECTING PUBLIC

STUDIES: another work by Destutt de Tracy, *Observations sur le systême actuel d'instruction publique* (Paris, 1801).

HAS THE HONOR: Pierre Jean Georges Cabanis became a member of the APS in 1786 (APS, *Proceedings*, 22, pt. 3 [1884], 144).

From Lafayette

MY DEAR SIR   Paris 10th Brumaire [i.e. 1 Nov.] 1802

On My Coming for a few Days to Paris I find two Opportunities to write to You and Am Happy to Repeat the Expression of My old Constant Affectionate Regard—Mr Levingston's Official Correspondance and that of Mr King, Now in this place Will Let You know All the politics of Europe—The Interior politics of France I Have No pleasure to Expatiate Upon, Nor Can You fail Anticipating My Sentiments on the Occasion—they are the Same Which Having Uniformly Actuated me in All and Every One of the Circumstances of the American and French Revolutions Did Accompagny me into the Royal and imperial Dungeons—With me they Now Are Retired into the State of Rural Life Where I am fixed Among the Comforts of An United Loving family—it Has Been, Encreased, as I Did in time inform You, By the Happy Acquisition of an Amiable Daughter in Law whose Father Tracy, and our Common friend Cabanis, Have Taken the liberty to present You with Copies of their Latest Works—I Have Had the Good Fortune to find Within Me a Warm farming inclination, the Display of which Has been Retarded By the Avocations of public Afairs, But Which Affords me Actual pleasure, Altho' I Have not Yet Been Able to Set Up for Myself, and promises me inexpressible Delight, should I Ever Be in, a Situation to indulge My Agricultural Ardor—in the Mean While there Would be in the pure Affectation to Seem Unconscious of the kind personal Dispositions You Have Been pleased to Express to our friend Dupont—No Letter from You Has, Since a long time, Reached My Hands—Nor a Line from Madison to Whom I shall write as Soon as I Reach La Grange—present My Most Affectionate Compliments to Him—My Best Respects to Your Daughters—I am Requested by My Wife and Family and By Mde de Tessé to Remember them to You and the Ladies—Adieu, My Good Friend, Accept the Best Wishes and Respectfull Affection of

Your old Sincere friend   LAFAYETTE

RC (DLC); English date supplied; endorsed by TJ as received 18 Mch. 1803 and so recorded in SJL.

NO LETTER FROM YOU: TJ had last written to Lafayette in March 1801 (Vol. 33:270). Lafayette wrote to MADISON on

1 Dec. and referred to himself as "the old friend Who Has Not for Many, Many Years Received one Line from You" (Madison, *Papers, Sec. of State Ser.,* 4:166).

From William Moultrie

SIR New York Novemr. 1st. 1802

I have the honor to address you by the hands of Mr Berry, and my grandson William A. Moultrie who are travelling to South Carolina; I have directed them to call upon you, and to present to you, my most respectfull compliments: I have long wished for the opportunity of paying my respects to you in person; and I hope at the close of this month to have that honor; particular business will detain me here 'till then; in the mean.

I have the honor to be with the greatest regard & the highest respect Your most Obt. & very humble Servant

WILLM: MOULTRIE

RC (DLC); at foot of text: "The President of the United States"; endorsed by TJ as received 14 Nov. and so recorded in SJL with notation "by Moultrie & Berry."

William Moultrie (1730-1805) was one of South Carolina's most distinguished heroes of the American Revolution, most notable for orchestrating the successful defense of Charleston in 1776. His public service to the state also included two terms as governor and multiple terms in the legislature. As governor in 1793, Moultrie enthusiastically welcomed the arrival of French minister Edmond Charles Genet at Charleston. Retiring from public life in 1794, Moultrie concen-

trated on his sizable planting endeavors. TJ appointed him a commissioner of bankruptcy for South Carolina in June 1802 (ANB; Stanley Elkins and Eric McKitrick, *The Age of Federalism: The Early American Republic, 1788-1800* [New York, 1993], 335-6; Vol. 37:513n).

Moultrie's PARTICULAR BUSINESS probably related to the publication of his wartime reminiscences, *Memoirs of the American Revolution,* which was printed in New York in 1802 by David Longworth. TJ received a special presentation copy of the work, which included an inlaid calf label written in gilt: "Thomas Jefferson/President of the U.S./from the Author" (New York *Morning Chronicle,* 28 Oct. 1802; Sowerby, No. 494).

From Robert Patterson

SIR Philadelphia Novr. 1st. 1802

It was not till the day before yesterday that, upon coming to the city, I received your favour of the 16th. ulto; and this must be my apology for not replying sooner. The usual course with the Phil. Socy. is to refer every communication to a committee, who report their opinion to the socy, merely on the propriety of publishing the communication in their Transactions: but neither the Socy, nor any committee thereof, ever give their opinion on the *merits* of any paper laid before them, either to the author, or the public—In compliance, therefore, with your desire, I shall, as an *individual*, give my opinion of the communication from Capt. Groves.

A telescope proper, for observing the eclipses of Jupiter's satellites must have a considerable magnifying power; consequently its field of view can be but small; probably not exceeding 20 or 30 minutes of a degree: Any angular motion, therefore, of the instrument, amounting only to this small quantity, must throw the object out of the field of the telescope. Nor will the contrivance, proposed by the Captain, of bringing the image of the object down to the horizon, by two previous reflections, in the least degree, obviate this difficulty: for as every vertical motion of the instrument must vary the angle of incidence, and consequently that of reflection, both at the first and second speculum, the last reflected ray will thus be thrown above or below the axis, or intirely out of the field of the telescope. Besides the loss of light from these two additional reflections would be so great as perhaps to render any telescope whatever inadequate to the purpose of making such observations. But of what advantage, it may be asked, would such an improvement be to navigation? supposing it possible to be effected, which I am sure it is not—Certainly of none at all—for it has been clearly proved, by Mr. Ellicott, and other able astronomers, that the mean of a set of good observations of the lunar distance, will give the longitude with as much accuracy as a single observation of the immersion or emersion of one of Jupiter's satellites; and as the former observations may be repeated at pleasure as well on sea as on land, the method of finding the longitude by lunar observation has, of consequence, a decided advantage over that by the eclipses of Jupiter's satellites.

I am, Sir, with the greatest respect & esteem Your most obedient servant   R. PATTERSON

RC (DLC); endorsed by TJ. Enclosed in TJ to Matthew C. Groves, 7 Nov. FC (PPAmP); in Patterson's hand, on a sheet endorsed for the American Philosophical Society as a wrapper for Groves's "proposed method of ascertaining the Longitude," received by the society on 5 Nov., and for TJ's letter to Patterson of 16 Oct. conveying the essay to the APS; with some variant wording. Recorded in SJL as received 4 Nov.

CLEARLY PROVED, BY MR. ELLICOTT: early in 1802, Patterson and Benjamin Latrobe had reviewed, for the American Philosophical Society, Andrew Ellicott's theories and data on the use of LUNAR observations to find longitude (Vol. 36:229-30).

From Henry Dearborn

War Department

2nd. November 1802

The Secretary of War has the honor to solicit permission from the President of the United States to appoint Joseph Gilbert Totton, a Cadet in the Corps of Engineers.

FC (Lb in DNA: RG 107, LSP).

A nephew and ward of Jared Mansfield, Joseph Gilbert Totten (TOTTON) enjoyed a distinguished career as a mili-

tary engineer following his graduation from West Point in 1805. In 1838, he was appointed head of the Corps of Engineers and retained the post until his death in 1864 (ANB).

To Benjamin H. Latrobe

DEAR SIR   Washington Nov. 2. 1802.

The placing of a navy in a state of perfect preservation, so that at the beginning of a subsequent war it shall be as sound as at the end of the preceding one when laid up, and the lessening the expence of repairs, perpetually necessary while they lie in the water, are objects of the first importance to a nation which to a certain degree must be maritime. the dry docks of Europe, being below the level of tide water, are very expensive in their construction, & in the manner of keeping them clear of water, and are only practicable at all where they have high tides: insomuch that no nation has ever proposed to lay up their whole navy in dry docks. but if the dry dock were above the level of the tide water, and there be any means of raising the vessels up into them, and of covering the dock with a roof, thus withdrawn from the wet and sun, they would last as long as the interior timbers, doors & floors of a house. the vast command of running water, at this place, at different heights from 30. to 200 feet above the tide water, enables us to effect this desireable object by forming a lower bason, into which the tide water shall float the vessel & then have it's gates closed, and adjoining to this, but 24 feet higher, an upper bason 175 feet wide, & 800 f. long (sufficient to contain 12. frigates) into which running water can be introduced from above, so that filling both basons (as in a lock) the vessel shall be raised up & floated into the upper one, & the water then being discharged leave her dry. over a bason, not wider than 175. feet, a roof can be thrown, in the manner of that of the Halle au blé at Paris, which needing no underworks to support it, will permit the bason to be entirely open &

free for the movement of the vessels. I mean to propose the construction of one of these to the National legislature, convinced it will be a work of no great cost, that it will save us great annual expence, & be an encouragement to prepare in peace the vessels we shall need in war, when we find they can be kept in a state of perfect preservation & without expence.

The first thing to be done is to chuse from which of the streams we will derive our water for the lock. these are the Eastern branch, Tyber, Rock-creek, & the Potomak itself. then to trace the canal, draw plans of that and of the two basons, and calculate the expence of the whole, that we may lead the legislature to no expence in the execution of which they shall not be apprised in the beginning. for this I ask your aid, which will require your coming here. some surveys and levellings[1] have been already made by mr N. King, a very accurate man in that line, and who will assist in any thing you desire, and execute on the ground any tracings you may so direct, unless you prefer doing them yourself. it is very material too that this should be done immediately, as we have little more than 4. weeks to the meeting of the legislature, and there will then be but 3. weeks for them to consider and decide before the day arrives (Jan. 1.) at which alone any number of labourers can be hired here. should that pass, either the work must be over for a year, or be executed by day labourers at double expence. I propose that such a force shall be provided as to compleat the work in one year. if this succeeds, as it will recieve all our present ships, the next work will be a second one, to build and lay up additional ships. on the subject of your superintending the execution of the work it would be premature to say any thing till the legislature shall have declared their will. be so good as to let me hear from you immediately, if you cannot come as soon as you can write. Accept my best wishes and respects. Th: Jefferson

PrC (DLC); at foot of first page: "Mr. Latrobe."

HALLE AU BLÉ: as designed by Nicolas Le Camus de Mézières, the Paris grain market, the Halle aux Bleds, was a circular building surrounding a courtyard that stood open to the sky. Several years after the completion of the building in 1767, architects Jacques Guillaume Legrand and Jacques Molinos, using methods developed by the Renaissance builder Philibert Delorme, constructed a great dome of wooden ribs and tall windows to turn the courtyard into a vast interior rotunda, protected from the elements but filled with light. After the dome was finished in 1782, municipal authorities used the Halle aux Bleds as the site of significant public ceremonies, and the building was an attraction for visitors to Paris intrigued by the rotunda's design and carpentry. In 1786, TJ, seeking ideas for the design of a public market for Richmond, decided to visit "the noble dome of the Halle aux bleds," which he called a "wonderful piece of architecture." As memorialized in his famous "Head and Heart" letter, it was on an excursion to see the great dome with John Trumbull that TJ first met Maria Cosway. The dome burned and collapsed in 1802 and was rebuilt beginning in 1809 using iron ribs rather than wooden joinery (Harold C. Rice, Jr., *Thomas Jefferson's Paris* [Princeton, 1976], 6, 18-21; Vol. 10:xxix, facing 434, 444-5).

For the SURVEYS by Nicholas KING, see Enclosure No. 2 described at Robert Smith to TJ, 23 Oct.

OVER FOR A YEAR: slaves hired out by their masters on an annual basis made up a large proportion of the labor force on big construction projects in and around Washington (Robert J. Kapsch, *The Potomac Canal: George Washington and the Waterway West* [Morgantown, W.Va., 2007], 82, 106, 213; Letitia W. Brown, "Residence Patterns of Negroes in the District of Columbia, 1800-1860," RCHS, 69-70 [1969-70], 68; Cora Bacon-Foster, "Early Chapters in the Development of the Potomac Route to the West," same, 15 [1912], 159, 193; Bob Arnebeck, *Through a Fiery Trial: Building Washington, 1790-1800* [Lanham, Md., 1991], 205-6).

[1] Preceding two words interlined.

To Craven Peyton

DEAR SIR   Washington Nov. 2. 1802.

I recieved by last post your favor of Oct. 27. informing me of the purchase of the lands of Bennet Hill Henderson, Eliza Henderson, Frances Henderson, Lucy Henderson & Nancy Henderson for 650. £ and the widow's dower for £250. certainly I am very glad to get them secured, but the paiment of £650. by the 10th. instant is utterly out of my power. from this time to February I have to pay for [some] parcels of lands adjoining Monticello bought of mr Overton & mr Brown & mr Wells, for the hire of 10. negroes, for 450. barrels of corn, & for work done by workmen this last summer [...][1] it was in contemplation of this that I had wished you to put off the paiment for Henderson's land, if purchased, till some time next year. I am therefore in great pain lest in endeavoring to serve me you should be incommoded yourself. in order to see the earliest time at which I could possibly raise the money, I have taken a rigorous view of all my engagements and probable current expences, & of my resources, and I find that I could pay 1000. D. in the 1st. week of February, 1000. D. in the 1st. week in March, and the remaining 1000. D. in the summer, say by July. should you not be able to make this answer your purpose, I know not what else to propose, having really nothing better in my power. I shall therefore be very anxious to hear from you by return of post or as soon as you can write. accept my friendly respects & best wishes.

TH: JEFFERSON

PrC (ViU); blurred; at foot of text: "Mr. Craven Peyton"; endorsed by TJ in ink on verso.

In his account statement with Craven Peyton "for Henderson's lands," extending from 4 July 1801 to 7 Jan. 1809, TJ recorded the PURCHASE OF THE LANDS, "except the warehouse," from the Henderson heirs for £650 or $2,166.67 in November 1802. He also entered the purchase of the WIDOW'S DOWER, "except warehouse," at that date, for £250 or $833.33. TJ recorded a third sum in November 1802 for £140 or $466.67 for "John Henderson's 102. acres + 6¼ as = 108¼ acres." TJ allowed £64 or $213.33 for interest on these three sums (MS in MHi). For TJ's wishes to acquire the land inherited by John Henderson, see TJ to Peyton, 3 Dec. 1801.

HIRE OF 10 NEGROES: in his analysis of expenditures from 4 Mch. 1802 to 4 Mch. 1803, TJ indicated in his financial memoranda under the category "Buildings," the sum of $200 for "negro hire." He listed $466.67 under the category "negros" in a column with the heading "Plantation" and indicated "negro hire= maintenance." On 8 Feb. 1803, TJ recorded payment to George Jefferson of $400 for Christopher Smith for "negro hire" (MB, 2:1092, 1098).

TJ sent Gabriel Lilly $150 on 7 Dec. in partial payment for CORN bought of the Lewises and sent George Jefferson an additional $600 on 8 Feb. 1803 (same, 2:1087, 1092).

Recent WORK DONE BY WORKMEN at Monticello included framing over TJ's bed; installation of Venetian blinds; completion of dependencies, necessaries, and rooms off the southeast arcade; foundations for the Mulberry Row nailery and the southwest offices; and instructions for the icehouse (Jack McLaughlin, *Jefferson and Monticello: The Biography of a Builder* [New York, 1988], 296; Malone, *Jefferson*, 4:168; Vol. 37:653, 654-5).

INCOMMODED YOURSELF: for Peyton's own financial pressures at this time from the collapsing family business interests of his father-in-law, Charles L. Lewis, see Boynton Merrill, Jr., *Jefferson's Nephews: A Frontier Tragedy* [Princeton, 1976], 50-3, 65.

TJ expressed concern over his CURRENT EXPENCES and RESOURCES in his letter to William Short, printed at 9 Oct. According to his financial memoranda of 23 Feb. 1803, TJ gave Craven Peyton an order on Gibson & Jefferson for $1000 for "part paimt. land." He enclosed the same amount, on 4 Mch. 1803, to Gibson & Jefferson "to answer the order in favr. of Craven Peyton ante Feb. 23" (MB, 2:1093).

¹ Seven or eight illegible words interlined.

To Martha Jefferson Randolph

MY DEAR MARTHA   Washington Nov. 2. 1802.

Your letter of the 29th. has relieved me from the great anxiety I had felt on your previous entire silence about your journey. there was no hair inclosed in your letter: but I sent the letter to mrs Madison who has had the order given as you desired, for colours from her own judgment, perhaps those of your own hair. if this should not please, send hair in your Friday's letter, and within a fortnight from that time others suitable can be here from Philadelphia. remember to tell me in your next whether I am to send a carriage, or whether you prefer coming on in your own. it makes no odds here whether horses are sent with or without a carriage.—I spoke to you soon after the arrival of my sister Marks about getting necessaries for her from Higginbotham's. it escaped me to repeat it when I came away. I hope however it has been done, or that she may be still with you & it can yet be done.—pray enable yourself to direct us here how to make muffins in Peter's method. my cook here cannot succeed at all in them, and they are a great luxury to me. deliver to my dear Maria my love, & my rebukes that she should not once have written to me. kiss the little ones, and be assured yourself of my unceasing affections.   TH: JEFFERSON

RC (NNPM); at foot of text: "Mrs. Randolph." PrC (MHi); endorsed by TJ in ink on verso.

To Thomas Mann Randolph

DEAR SIR   Washington November 2. 1802.

Your's of Oct. 29. has been recieved. the day after my last letter to you, say Oct. 23. I enquired of Doctr. Tucker as to the difficulty of getting your negroes across the state of S.C. he could give me no information but he wrote the next day to Govr. Drayton, & I think his answer & General Sumpter's will be here about the time of your own arrival here.

The favorable expressions in your letter, as to myself, I recieve as proofs of an affection which I value in the highest degree: but the shade into which you throw yourself neither your happiness nor mine will admit that you remain in. this can be made perfect only by a mutual consciousness of mutual esteem. while my own feelings and desires have always made me look towards you as a part of myself, they have never permitted me to doubt a return of the same affection. certainly there could not have been an alliance on earth more pleasing to me from the beginning or rendered more dear to me in the sequel of it's continuance. if any circumstance has given me more pain than all other things, it has been the old embarrasments hanging on me & preventing my being as useful to you as my heart made me wish to be. in matters of interest I know no difference between yours & mine. I hope therefore you will feel a conviction that I hold the virtues of your heart and the powers of your understanding in a far more exalted view than you place them in; and that this conviction will place your mind in the same security and ease in which mine has always been. altho' I trust it could never be doubted, yet I am happy in having an occasion of making these declarations to you: and of assuring you that it is not from form, but from the sincere feelings of my heart that I always tender you assurances of my affectionate attachment and great respect.   TH: JEFFERSON

RC (DLC); at foot of text: "T M Randolph"; endorsed by Randolph. PrC (MHi); endorsed by TJ in ink on verso.

For the response of John DRAYTON to Thomas Tudor Tucker, see TJ to Randolph, 25 Nov.

From George Vanleer

SIR   New Jersey Woodbury Novemr. 2nd 1802

As a Citizen of the State of New Jersey I take the Liberty to inform you that the Election in this State has terminated very Contrary to our Expectations and in favor of the Federal Interest. It appears by the Result of the late Election that we have a Majority in the Council and the Federalists a Majority in the Assembly which last Year we had in both. For my part I know not what has produced this unexpected Change, unless it be by a Repeal of the Excise on Loaf Sugar and Carriages which is a very unpopular thing[1] in this State and by Retaining the Imposts on Brown Sugar and Bohea Tea which is also another very unpopular thing. For my part if I were to give my Opinion upon this Subject that as Supposing there was no refined Sugar in this Country us'd there would not be so much Brown Sugar imported to this Country which enhances the price at a foreign Market of the Brown Sugar and which falls upon the poor people which would not be the Case if there was to be no Sugars refined in this Country; as undoubtetly there is so much wasted in the refining, more than would be us'd, takeing the Refined and unrefined together, than without the refined, therefore as the Rich are the Cause of the high price of Sugars for there certainly would not be so much Sugars Exported, and of course the price would not be so high, and they use so little of the Brown Sugars I think it reasonable they ought to pay an Excise on the Refined Sugars, for there never would be an equal Impost and Excise Law without it unless they made it up in some other Article of foreign or Domestic produce, there can be but one thing urg'd in favor of no [...] Sugars and that is that it encourages our own Manufactures. As for the[2] Bohea Tea and Carriage Tax, if any Class of Citizens was to be Screen'd it ought to be the poor from Taxation. All which mentiond things the Federalists get a handle of to make Dupes to their party. there is one thing in my Opinion which I think ought to be Amended that is the Naturalization Law for five Years seems to be most an age to serve for a foreigner to serve, for he might make a useful Citizen within that period: we should not like it ourselves were we in their Case, for it is certain the more favor's we shew'd them, would induce them to become more Worthy Citizens.

It is my Opinion that one, two or three years at farthest would be Long enough to make them Citizens For my part I shall follow you and your Administration so long as you do Right, & no farther, & then for a Reformation

I am with Respect

G. VANLEER

RC (MoSHi: Jefferson Papers); torn; addressed: "To Thomas Jefferson Esqr. President of the United States City of Washington"; franked and postmarked; endorsed by TJ as received 6 Nov. from "Vanlee" and so recorded in SJL.

George Vanleer (c. 1734-1807) married Elizabeth Roberts at Gloria Dei Church in Philadelphia in 1756 and by her had 11 children. As a member of the New Jersey committee of observation, he helped select his state's representatives to the First Continental Congress in 1774-1775. He resided in Woolwich Township, Gloucester County, New Jersey, and remained active in the Swedesboro Church throughout his life (*Bulletin of the Gloucester County Historical Society*, 7 [1959], 8; *Trenton Federalist*, 18 Feb. 1805).

In the successful effort by Republicans to repeal all internal taxes by the act of 6 Apr. 1802, the EXCISE taxes on refined or LOAF SUGAR AND CARRIAGES were eliminated. The Federalists argued that instead of getting rid of the taxes on such luxuries, the import duties on necessities, including brown sugar, salt, tea, and coffee, should be lowered or abolished. In his speech before Congress on 16 Mch. 1802, New Jersey Republican Ebenezer Elmer argued that more than half of the carriages in his state were necessities used as market wagons rather than for pleasurable purposes. He also asserted that tea and coffee were not necessities (*Annals*, 11:1015-24, 1027; U.S. Statutes at Large, 2:148-50; Newark, N.J., *Centinel of Freedom*, 3 Aug. 1802).

[1] MS: "thing thing."
[2] Canceled: "Brown Sugar and."

From William Barton

SIR,   Lancaster, November 3d. 1802.

Observing by the public prints, that Mr. Steele has signified his intention of soon resigning the Comptrollership of the Treasury, I pray that I may be honoured with your attention to my name, when the appointment of a sucessor to that office is contemplated.—

The motives which actuate me on this occasion, are such as I took the liberty of stating to You, in some of my former letters: But not wishing, Sir, to trouble You with the *details* of those motives, which I presume will justify an application of this kind, I communicated them fully to Mr. Gallatin, in a letter which I did myself the honor of addressing to him on the 3d. of July last. Not having received an answer from that gentleman, and my letter having (as I believe) arrived at Washington during his absence from that city,—I am uncertain whether it reached his hands. Should he, however, have received it, he has doubtless, Sir, apprized You of its contents,—agreeably to my request.—My friend Mr. Saml. H. Smith has also been informed, some time since, of the reasons which impel me to desire a change of my present official situation.—

I will only crave the indulgence of now adding, that, after a recurrence to the Testimonials in Your hands, I trust my wishes on the subject of this letter will not be deemed presumptuous; And that, if those wishes should be gratified, my conduct would prove an ample justification of the favorable opinion of me, which my friends have been pleased to entertain.—

With the highest Respect and sincerest personal Attachmt. I have the Honor to be, Sir, Your most obedt. servt.   W BARTON

RC (DNA: RG 59, LAR); at foot of text: "The President of the United States"; endorsed by TJ as received 9 Nov. and "to be Comptroller" and so recorded in SJL.

SOME OF MY FORMER LETTERS: early in TJ's presidency Barton had asked TJ to keep him in mind for any future federal appointments. In a letter of 3 July 1802 to Albert GALLATIN, Barton worried that the president might have gained the incorrect impression that his appointment as prothonotary of the Lancaster County Court had proven lucrative, when it actually was insufficient to support his large family. He requested that Gallatin communicate this information to the president (Gallatin, *Papers*, 7:295-6; Vol. 34:182-3).

To Michael Bowyer

DEAR SIR   Washington Nov. 3. 1802.

I have been just informed that about 9. miles from the Sweet springs in Greenbriar county, a few months past, was found in a saltpetre cave, some large bones, one of which, a claw, measured 9. inches in length: and that the person who was digging out the bones, intended them for mr Peale. if this has been done, or shall be done, it is all that is desired. but if this destination of them has not been pursued, then the favor I have to ask of you is to endeavor to get them, to have them packed in a box securely against breaking, and forwarded *by water* to Richmond to the care of Messrs. Gibson & Jefferson merchts. there, who will be instructed to pay all expence attending them, & forward them to mr Peale in Philadelphia. I understand that my friend Genl. John Bowyer lives not far from the head navigation of James river, and am sure he will do me the favor to see them safely forwarded. I presume these bones are of the same species of animal with some formerly sent me by Colo. Stewart of Green briar, and which till then had been utterly unknown, being entirely different from the big bones on the Ohio. it is interesting therefore to procure all the remains of it we can, in order to ascertain what it was, & to learn if it still exists in any part of the Continent. the favor I am asking of you on this occasion is asked with the less reluctance as it gives me an opportunity of recalling myself to your recollection, and of tendering you assurances of my constant esteem and most friendly wishes for your happiness.   TH: JEFFERSON

PrC (DLC); at foot of text: "Michael Bowyer esq."

Michael Bowyer (d. 1808) owned the Sulphur Springs, later known as White Sulphur Springs, in Greenbrier County. In the late 1760s and early 1770s, he was a deputy sheriff of Augusta County and employed TJ as his attorney in lawsuits. Bowyer was a member of the Virginia House of Delegates in the mid-1780s. He did not receive the letter printed above until mid-May 1803, and replied on 28 June (Thomas A. Chambers, *Drinking the Waters: Creating an American Leisure Class at Nineteenth-Century Mineral Springs* [Washington, D.C., 2002], 8; John W. Jengo, " 'Mineral Productions of Every Kind': Geological Observations in the Lewis and Clark Journals and the Role of Thomas Jefferson and the American Philosophical Society in the Geological Mentoring of Meriwether Lewis,"

APS, *Transactions*, new ser., 94 [2004], 184-5; Leonard, *General Assembly*, 153, 156; MB, 1:14n, 15, 48, 56, 62, 98, 105, 109, 165, 170, 183, 224, 231, 274, 303).

JUST INFORMED: see Charles Willson Peale to TJ, 28 Oct.

Bowyer's brother, JOHN BOWYER, and TJ had been acquainted since 1769 or earlier. John Bowyer, who was a brigadier general of the Virginia militia, represented Rockbridge County for a number of terms in the House of Delegates. In 1796, he arranged for the exchange of saltpeter from a cave owned by TJ for blasting powder manufactured in western Virginia (DVB, 2:163-4; WMQ, 1st ser., 5 [1896], 109; MB, 1:90; Vol. 29:44).

SENT ME BY COLO. STEWART: in 1796, John Stuart sent TJ the bones that became the source for TJ's Memoir on the Megalonyx (Vol. 29:64-5, 152-3).

From Henry Dearborn

War Department
3d. November 1802

The Secretary of War has the honor of proposing to the President of the United States, that Doctor   Maupire of Virginia, be appointed a Surgeon's Mate, in the Army of the United States.

FC (Lb in DNA: RG 107, LSP).

George Washington Maupin (MAUPIRE) was commissioned a surgeon's mate on 5 Nov. 1802 (Heitman, *Dictionary*, 1:697).

To Handsome Lake

BROTHER HANDSOME LAKE   Washington Nov. 3. 1802.

I have recieved the message in writing which you sent me through Captain[1] Irvine, our confidential agent, placed near you for the purpose of communicating, and transacting, between us, whatever may be useful for both nations. I am[2] happy to learn you have been so far favored by the divine spirit as to be made sensible of those things which are for your good & that of your people, & of those which[3] are hurtful to you: & particularly that you & they see the ruinous effects which the abuse of spirituous liquors have produced upon them. it has weakened their bodies, enervated their minds, exposed them to hunger, cold, nakedness, & poverty, kept them in perpetual broils, & reduced their population. I do not wonder then, brother, at your censures, not only on your own people, who have voluntarily gone into these fatal habits, but on all the nations of white people who have[4] supplied their calls for this article. but these nations have done to you[5] only what they do among themselves. they have sold what individuals wish to buy; leaving to every one to be the guardian of his own health and happiness. Spirituous liquors are not in themselves bad. they are often found to be an excellent medecine for the sick. it is the improper & intemperate use of them, by those in health, which makes them injurious. but as you find that your people cannot refrain from an ill use of them, I greatly applaud your resolution not to use them at all. we have too affectionate a concern for your happiness to place the paultry gain on the sale of these articles in competition with the injury they do you. and as it is the desire of your nation that no spirits should be sent among them, & I am authorised by the great council of the US. to prohibit them, I will sincerely cooperate with your wise men[6] in any proper measures for this purpose which shall be agreeable to them.

You remind me, brother, of what I said to you, when you visited me the last winter; that the lands you then held would remain yours, & should never go from you but when you should be disposed to sell. this I now repeat, & will ever abide by. we indeed are always ready to buy land; but we will never ask but when you wish to sell: and[7] our laws, in order to protect you against imposition, have forbidden[8] individuals to purchase lands from you: and have rendered it necessary, when you desire[9] to sell, even to a state, that an Agent from the US. should attend the sale, see that your consent is freely given,[10] a satisfactory price paid, and report to us what has been done, for our approbation. this was done in the late case of which you complain. the deputies of your nation came forward, in all the forms which we have been used to consider as evidence of the will of your nation. they proposed to sell to the state of New York certain parcels of land, of small extent, and detached from the body of your other lands. the state of New York was desirous[11] to buy. I sent an Agent, in whom we could trust, to see that your consent was free, & the sale fair. all was reported to be free & fair. the lands were your property. the right to sell is one of the rights of property. to forbid you the exercise of that right would be a wrong to your nation. Nor do I think, brother, that the sale of lands is, under all circumstances, injurious to your people. while they depended on hunting, the more extensive the forests[12] around them, the more game they would yield. but, going[13] into a state of agriculture, it may be as advantageous to a society, as it is to an individual, who has more land than he can improve, to sell a part, and lay out the money in stocks & implements of agriculture, for the better improvement of the residue. a little land, well stocked & improved, will yield more than a great deal without stock or improvement. I hope therefore[14] that, on further reflection, you will see this transaction in a more favorable light, both as it concerns the interest of your nation, & the exercise of that superintending care which I am sincerely anxious to employ for their subsistence and happiness. Go on then brother in the great reformation you have undertaken. persuade our red brethren[15] to be sober, and to cultivate their lands; and their women to spin & weave for their families. you will soon see your women & children well fed & clothed, your men living happily in peace & plenty, and your numbers increasing from year to year. it will be a great glory to you[16] to have been the instrument of so happy a change, & your children's children, from generation to generation, will repeat your name with love and[17] gratitude for ever. in all your enterprises for the good of your people, you may count with confidence on the aid and protection of the United States, and[18] on the sincerity & zeal with which I am myself animated in the furthering of this humane work. you are our brethren of the same land: we wish your prosperity as brethren should do. Farewell.

TH: JEFFERSON

RC (NNFoM). PrC (DLC). Dft (PHi, 1944, sold 1965); endorsed by Dearborn: "The President's answer to the handsome Lake." Enclosed in Dearborn to Callender Irvine, 5 Nov.: "Enclosed I have the pleasure of forwarding you the reply of the President of the United States to the speech lately addressed to him by the handsome Lake. This reply written by the hand of the Chief Magistrate of the United States, and breathing throughout a spirit of harmony and affection for his red brethren, cannot fail to excite in them corresponding sentiments, and insure the continuance of that friendly intercourse which now happily prevails between the

Citizens of the United States, and the Indian Tribes. You will please to communicate the reply of the President to the Handsome Lake in the manner which shall be most agreeable to him" (FC in Lb in DNA: RG 75, LSIA).

The MESSAGE from Handsome Lake has not been found and is not recorded in SJL. Callender IRVINE sent it from Presque Isle on 7 Oct. Irvine wrote Dearborn on 26 Nov. to acknowledge the receipt of "the Presidents talk to the Handsome Lake" (DNA: RG 107, RLRMS). Dearborn and TJ may have thought at first that a reply to the Seneca leader by the secretary of war would be sufficient. Dearborn wrote to Irvine briefly on 23 Oct. enclosing "an answer to the talk of Handsome Lake, which you will be pleased to deliver him." In that response, Dearborn addressed Handsome Lake as "Brother" and said that he was replying on behalf of the president, "your father," who was "highly pleased with the exertions you have made" to encourage Indians "to quit drinking strong liquors, and for changing their habits in such a manner as to introduce a more happy state of society. It is to be hoped," Dearborn wrote, "that the Great Spirit will continue to enable you to set such an example of sobriety, honesty and Brotherly love among your red brethren as will have a good effect on the white people." Any sale of the Senecas' lands "must at all times depend on the will of your Chiefs," who would not part with land "unless they were satisfied that the sale would meet the approbation of the majority of the nation." Dearborn assured Handsome Lake that "your father the President of the United States will at all times be happy in hearing of your wellfare and of the improvements and means of happiness you may introduce amonge your Brethren." Dearborn hoped "that the Great Spirit will hold you by the hand and support you in every good work in which your red Brethren may be engaged" (DNA: RG 75, LSIA).

AUTHORISED BY THE GREAT COUNCIL OF THE US: an act of 30 Mch. 1802 allowed the president "to prevent or restrain" the sale or distribution of spiritous

liquor to Indians (U.S. Statutes at Large, 1:146; Vol. 36:279, 443n).

Handsome Lake and a delegation of Senecas had VISITED Washington in March (Vol. 37:29-43).

FORBIDDEN INDIVIDUALS TO PURCHASE LANDS: the act of 30 Mch., like previous congressional acts governing "trade and intercourse" with Native Americans, stated that "no purchase, grant, lease, or other conveyance of lands, or of any title or claim thereto, from any Indian, or nation, or tribe of Indians" was valid unless the transaction was "by treaty or convention, entered into pursuant to the constitution." The law made it a misdemeanor for anyone "not employed under the authority of the United States" to negotiate land transactions with Indians, allowing an exception only for an agent of a state, who could attend treaty negotiations and, in the presence of federal commissioners, "propose to, and adjust with the Indians, the compensation to be made" for lands that fell within the agent's state (U.S. Statutes at Large, 1:472, 746; 2:143).

LATE CASE: the sale of the Black Rock tract along the Niagara River; see Dearborn to TJ, 3 Sep. SENT AN AGENT: John Tayler.

GO ON THEN BROTHER: writing near the end of the twentieth century, Anthony F. C. Wallace noted that "the framed text" of TJ's letter to Handsome Lake "hangs today on the walls of the council houses where the rituals and the recitations of the code of the Old Way of Handsome Lake are still performed." The Seneca visionary's followers "treasured" the letter, Wallace observed, as an affirmation by the president of the United States of the program of revitalization that was fundamental to the Code of Handsome Lake and the Longhouse religion (Anthony F. C. Wallace, *Jefferson and the Indians: The Tragic Fate of the First Americans* [Cambridge, Mass., 1999], 292; Anthony F. C. Wallace, *The Death and Rebirth of the Seneca* [New York, 1969], 272; Vol. 37:30).

[1] Rank interlined in Dft in place of "mr."

[2] Here in Dft TJ canceled "very."

3 Here in Dft TJ canceled "will be."

4 Here in Dft TJ canceled "administered" and "sold them."

5 Here in Dft TJ canceled "brother."

6 Preceding two words interlined in Dft in place of "people."

7 TJ interlined the preceding passage, beginning "we indeed," in Dft.

8 Word interlined in Dft in place of "made it unlawful for any."

9 Word interlined in Dft in place of "are willing."

10 Here in Dft TJ canceled "and a fair price."

11 Word interlined in Dft in place of "willing."

12 Word interlined in Dft in place of "deserts."

13 Here in Dft TJ canceled "as you are."

14 Here in Dft TJ canceled "brother."

15 Word interlined in Dft in place of "brothers," here and at two places in the letter's concluding passages.

16 Here in Dft TJ canceled "brother."

17 Preceding two words interlined in Dft.

18 Here in Dft TJ canceled "be assured that nobody, with more sincerity or with more zeal than myself, will."

From John Hollins

SIR   Baltimore 3d. Novem: 1802

Permitt me to call to your recollection, that about three years past, you obliged me exceedingly by a letter you wrote to the Havanna, upon the subject of a very large sum of money attached there, my own property; Your letter I have good reason to believe had at the time its due effect, & about 12 or 14 months thereafter a Judgement was obtained to my satisfaction, but my opponents (the Trustees of Louis Beltran Gonet) appealed therefrom, & altho' it has repeatedly been stated to me from thence, that ano. judgement equal to the former one might *soon* be expected, I am as yet deprived of that pleasure, & when to look for it is not in my power to say; The sum at risque ought to exceed Two hundred thousand Dollars, & as it, or the greatest proporn., ought & must ultimately come to me, I fear every possible delay on the part of my Opponents; it is therefore my present intention to depart for Spain next year, to endeavour to obtain Justice, or loose more in the attempt; even in that Country I may be compelled to remain longer than I coud wish, & the time of Course will hang heavy on my hands; having for the last 25 Years been much engaged in Commercial pursuits; therefore reflecting upon this subject, it has occured to me, that if no more deserving or proper Characters offer to be sent as Commissrs. to Spain, it might not be an objection to your Excellency to grant me such an appointment, which woud be very gratifying, & agreeable to my feelings—Shd. it however appear to you, that any other Person or Persons, have a prior claim, or better qualifications, I have such an exalted opinion of your Excellency's uprightness & Conduct in every stage of life, that no pain or mortification, shall for one moment be fel't by me

Who have the Honor to be Your Excellency's Obdt & very hble Servt.   JNO. HOLLINS

RC (DNA: RG 59, LAR); endorsed by TJ as received 4 Nov. and "to be Commr. under convention with Spain" and so recorded in SJL.

John Hollins (1760-1827) worked as a banker in Liverpool before immigrating to Baltimore, where he married Jane Smith, a sister of Samuel and Robert Smith, and became a highly successful merchant. He established the auction house of John Hollins & Co., and his mercantile firm of Hollins and McBlair was one of the most prominent trading houses in Baltimore, outfitting numerous ships and commanding substantial amounts of domestic and overseas credit. Longtime president of the Maryland Insurance Company, he also held a range of civic offices. Hollins had known TJ at least since 1800, probably through Wilson Cary Nicholas (*Maryland Journal and Baltimore Advertiser*, 6 Jan. 1786, 30 May 1790; Jerome R. Garitee, *The Republic's Private Navy: The American Privateering Business as Practiced by Baltimore during the War of 1812* [Middletown, Conn., 1977], 20, 22, 39, 68-9,

234-5, 267; RS, 2:197-8n; Vol. 32:17-18n; TJ to Peter Carr, 6 July 1802).

There is no evidence that TJ ever wrote a LETTER on Hollins's behalf to Havana. Hollins may have been referring to a letter from then secretary of state John Marshall to the acting American consul in Havana, requesting permission for Hollins to travel there. Permission was granted in the spring of 1801 (Marshall, *Papers*, 6:512; Madison, *Papers, Sec. of State Ser.*, 1:107-8). Hollins claimed property that was embargoed in Havana pending final settlement of a lawsuit between him and Cuban merchant Luís Beltrán GONET, with whom he had been a trading partner (Barbara H. Stein and Stanley J. Stein, *Edge of Crisis: War and Trade in the Spanish Atlantic, 1789-1808* [Baltimore, 2009], 252; Madison, *Papers, Sec. of State Ser.*, 6:64-5n, 144; 8:334).

For the convention of 11 Aug. 1802 between the United States and Spain that would have empowered COMMISSRS. to negotiate American claims resulting from Spanish shipping spoliations, see Joseph Yznardi, Sr. to TJ, 12 Aug.

From James Monroe

DEAR SIR   Richmond Novr. 3. 1802

I have endeavour'd to find suitable persons out of whom you might select one to fill the vacancy in the comn. of bankruptcy at Norfolk, but so little am I acquainted there that it is really a difficult task. Mr. Tazewell could give a name, but I did not wish to write him on the subject. Of those whom I have heard spoken of, Jas. Bennett mercht. and Jas. Nimmo an attorney are the fitest among the republicans. The first of these I have some acquaintance with; he is a man in good business, a captn of the artilery compy of militia in Norfolk, and according to my information, a worthy man. But I cannot say whether he has precisely that standing in the place to justify an attention of the kind from you: whether the appointment of him wod. tend to elevate the repubn. party there and do service, or by lessening the character of the Ex: do injury. When appointments are conferr'd on republicans of real merit, and respectable standing in society, it accomplishes at one stroke two objects, the elevation of sound men and principles, and the depression of those of opposit character. There is much of what is called fashionable society in Norfolk, in which you find a vast number of federalists, merchants &c, and a few republicans or rather very few. Tazewell & young Newton* were those, of a decided cast, whom I saw in that circle of the latter description. The older Newton is an honest respectable citizen, republican in his principles, but too mild by nature, & still more so by age, to be a marked character in the party. There are others of his stamp with infr. pretentions from fortune, publick service, & influence, in the community, among whom may be named Vaughan the present Mayor. In the other circle, or rather the republican circle, the two gentn. already named and a Mr. McIntosh from Scotland a mercht. of respectability, married & a citizen, were those of whom I heard & saw most. These latter seemed to have little or no intercourse with the society above referr'd to: I cannot say how far it wod. be practicable to make the well meaning among the federalists sensible of their errors, and diffuse republican principles thro' the town of Norfolk, by committing trust to persons of this description only. It is much to be fear'd that it never would be done by commiting them to those of the opposit party, I mean by original appointments; wh. is in a genl. wish an act very distinguishable in its nature and effect from a tolerance of those already in place. I have thus far endeavour'd to explain the reason why in complying with yr. request & giving you names, I have not done it with confidence. You will perceive that in exercising the power of nomination, with a view to promote sound principles, & bring the people together in the same republican track, Norfolk presents one of the most difficult subjects on wh. you have to act. It is a little world in itself, growing in importance, at present wealthy but rapidly accumulating more wealth. It wod. be fortunate if it could be brought by an union of parties into a positive & active support of the present admn. and the republican cause, nor do I think it impracticable: but it requires more knowledge in the detail to suggest a plan to accomplish it than I possess. Mr. Tazewell is perhaps the most able to give useful hints on the subject of any one in that quarter. I am sincerely yr: friend   JAS. MONROE

* R. E. Lee and family are of this circle but mingle little in it.

RC (DNA: RG 59, LAR); endorsed by TJ as received 7 Nov. and so recorded in SJL; also endorsed by TJ: "Nimmo James. to be commr. bkrptcy."

TJ appointed James NIMMO a bankruptcy commissioner for Norfolk in place of Littleton W. Tazewell, who declined the appointment. Nimmo would likewise resign the office the following year (Vol. 37:710; TJ to Madison, 2 Dec. 1802; Thomas Newton, Jr., to TJ, 19 June 1803).

William VAUGHAN was elected mayor of Norfolk in June 1802 (Baltimore *Federal Gazette*, 1 July 1802). During the city's insurrection panic of April 1802, merchant George MCINTOSH ardently maintained the innocence of the slave Jerry (Jeremiah), who was later executed for his alleged role in the conspiracy (Bertram Wyatt-Brown, *Southern Honor: Ethics and Behavior in the Old South* [New York, 1982], 427-31; Vol. 37:336n).

From Thomas Paine

DEAR SIR   Baltimore [on or before 3] Novr. 1802

I arrived here on Saturday from Havre after a passage of 60 days. I have several Cases of Models of Bridges, wheels &c and as soon as I can get them from the Vessel and put on board the packet for George town I shall sit off to pay my respects to you

Your much obliged fellow Citizen   THOMAS PAINE

P.S. I have a letter for you from Mr. Du blois respecting the Consulship of Havre.

RC (DLC); partially dated; endorsed by TJ as received 3 Nov. and so recorded in SJL.

SATURDAY: 30 Oct.

Paine hoped to earn money from his de-

signs of iron BRIDGES and wooden carriage WHEELS (Vol. 32:189-90, 192-3n; Vol. 34:284-5).

MR. DU BLOIS: see William Deblois to TJ, 29 Aug.

To Charles Willson Peale

DEAR SIR   Washington Nov. 3. 1802.

Immediately on the reciept of your favor of Oct. 28. I wrote to a friend of mine, mr Michael Bowyer who owns & resides at the Sweet springs, on the subject of the bones you mention as lately found in a cave of Greenbriar county, and which are probably of the Megalonyx. I observed to him that I had learned that the finder was preparing to send them to you; that if that was done, it was all that was desired. but if not done, I begged he would procure & pack them securely in a box, and forward them by water, to wit, down James river to messrs.

Gibson & Jefferson merchants at Richmond, whom I would instruct to pay all expences and forward the box on to you in Philadelphia. this I am in hopes will secure them to you, and I am happy in every occasion wherein I can render you a service.   the newly found half head of the Mammoth being under the view of Doctr. Samuel Brown, cannot be placed in a better channel.

I am happy to hear of your son's safe arrival in London. the first moments are always the most difficult: but I have no doubt the first information you shall recieve after the exhibition shall be opened, will be as favorable as you can expect. in the mean time let us omit no opportunity of compleating the skeleton you possess. perhaps it would not be amiss to publish a list of the bones you already have, and of those wanting as far as may be presumed of an animal whose structure we do not yet actually & fully know. Accept assurances of my great esteem & best wishes.   TH: JEFFERSON

RC (TxU); at foot of text: "Mr. C. W. Peale." PrC (DLC).

Michael Bowyer lived at Sulphur Springs rather than SWEET SPRINGS, but according to his reply to TJ's letter of 3 Nov., his residence was within about 15 miles of the cave in which the bones had been found. He was able to provide TJ with some information about the find (Bowyer to TJ, 28 June 1803).

From David Stone

                                        Bertie County 3d Novr 1802
It is here said [it is] probable Mr West the present Marshall [for] this District will decline acting again in that capacity—should Mr West (against whom it is not understood there is any cause of complaint) decline, or it be thought a[dvis]able to appoint another to his place I take the liberty to mention Mr. John Lockhart of Northampton County as very capable to discharge the duties of that Office. Mr. Lockhart has acted a considerable time as Sheriff of the County in which he lives and latterly as a deputy to Mr. West and as far as I can learn has the United Testimony of the Bench and Bar in favor of his skilful, impartial, diligent and punctual discharge of his duty in both capacities

I have the honor to be with the highest Respect & Esteem &c
                                        DAVID STONE

RC (DNA: RG 59, LAR); torn; endorsed by TJ as received 7 Dec. and "Lockhart John to be Marshal N.C. v. West" and so recorded in SJL.

TJ nominated John Spence WEST for reappointment as marshal for North Carolina on 17 Dec. The Senate consented to the nomination three days later (TJ to the Senate, 17 Dec. 1802; JEP, 1:426).

JOHN LOCKHART had forwarded to James Madison letters of recommendation from Nathaniel Macon and Henry Potter (Macon to Madison, 4 Sep. 1802, in DNA: RG 59, LAR, endorsed by TJ: "John Lockhart to be Marshal N.C."; Potter to Madison, 7 Sep. 1802, same; Lockhart to Madison, 8 Oct. 1802, same; Madison, *Papers, Sec. of State Ser.*, 3:547-8, 556-7; 4:4). TJ appointed Lockhart to the North Carolina marshalcy in December 1806 (JEP, 2:45).

From Caesar A. Rodney

[before 4 Nov. 1802]

HONORED & DEAR SIR, Cool Spring (near Wilmington)

I returned to this place (where I have taken shelter from the prevailing fever, & which I am about improving) from Dover, on yesterday. Whilst in Kent I had the pleasure of seeing old Mr. Killen who is much pleased with the letter you were kind eneough to send him.

I congratulate you most sincerely on the bright prospects in Penna. & altho' New-jersey may throw a shade over them in some degree I trust it will not materially effect the progress of honest principles. May it not be accounted for in the different policies of the two Executives? Mr. McKean whom I consider as my "second father" adopted a firm decisive conduct; Mr Bloomfield the reverse. Here we see a fair experiment made, & the result furnishes an useful lesson. It is remarkable that Mr. McKean is in every District almost, the highest man in the polls.

I consider it my duty to communicate to you every thing which may be improvd so as to advance the general cause. You have witnessed the event of the Kent election which has deprived us of a Senator. I feel little hesitation in saying that had the advice from this state been attended to, we should have succeeded there & that the loss is to be attributed to this circumstance principally. I could enclose you letters from our most active, influential & intelligent men there, to me, declaring that they would not exert themselves unless their memorial was attended to. Every effort to breathe into them that zeal so essential to secure victory proved fruitless, & for myself I was confined to my bed the moment I arrived in that County. Who their senators will be seems uncertain, tho' I still think it must be Bayard. The "Federal Ark" of this state announces that Bayard is to be kept up to run against me in 1804. & that he declines being a senator for that purpose. I have not the least objection to this. White they say is to be continued.

I believe there is now an opening to the measure which has been so strongly sollicited, & that the way is paved to a step without which this County so remarkable for its old & unshaken patriotism will also be paralized.

On my way up I saw Col: MClane at the *Cross roads.* He stated to me that he had written on to Mr. Gallatin, that if the Supporters of administration here wished his removal, that he did not desire to embarrass the President by a continuance in office, but yet he wished to leave it in that way which would secure to him the commissions on the money bonded for whilst in office, (as in the case of Mr. Latimore I suppose.) He stated to me that this indemnification was necessary in order to start his farm &c. To this I readily assented & told him if Government communicated with me on the subject such should be my advice to them. in which case he said he should make no publication on the business, as otherwise he might be disposed to do.

I communicate the above *in confidence*, earnestly requesting that due advantage may be taken of it, as it appears to me essential to the Republican cause in this State. A great deal depends on the manner in which we are enabled to effect any measure, as well as on the measure itself to be accomplished. In the present instance the retiring from the post will satisfy the Republicans & yet it will be done in such a way that the present officer will acquiesce in it.

Our success in defeating Bayard has mortified our *Feds* beyond expression. In the lower counties many of their partizans declare that as they could not carry him they have no longer any hopes. Nothing could exceed their malignity. Every tye of private life all the bonds of relationship or friendship which bound them down to some decency were broken asunder, & without restraint they vomited their calumnies & abuse. They levelled their base artillery principally at you & attacked with the most gross wanton & shameful falsehood's your private character hitherto deemed & yet known to be unexceptionable & irreproachable. Then they proclaimed me your supporter or to use their own expression *devotee.* They stated in the address of the Federal Committee on the authority I presume of Senator White that you were anxious for my election & this alone ought to be sufficient for my rejection. How different their story a few years ago! Capt: White was about publishing a conversation which took place when he introduced Dr. McCreery to you, but Dr. McCreery differed from him on the *whole point* of it & he desisted. I shall take care to preserve every thing necessary on this subject, should they ever have the timerity which I believe they will not, to come forward with it, These idle tales, this mere sound *vox et nihil praeterea* can have no effect on any mind of common firmness. I am confident they all pass you by as "the idle wind which you regard not." I can assure you, they have not the weight of a feather with me. It is a source however of some consolation, that during so severe a campaign & when their papers were litterally big with abuse tho' I have been seven years in our House of Representatives there was not a single act of my public conduct impeached, nor did they question either my integrity or morality. A few silly tales thro' the medium of their papers, appeared to be the burthen of their [song?] in public, whilst in print they circulated old *tory lies* about my father's conduct in the revolution for which he has been so much persecuted, tho' so many of them are indebted to him for their lives.

That I am a Supporter of you & your administration, because you are the supporter of the good old principles of 1776. is my pride & my boast; That *you* were anxious for my election I consider my greatest honor. Of your letter which was flattering to me they are utterly ignorant & so they shall remain, but Capt: White's story of your anxiety was the ground work of the stories on this subject. As I have succeeded in turning out a man, more violent on every question than any other on the floor of Congress & particularly as it relates to yourself I most sincerely rejoice that I opposed him, especially as from their papers the Federalists thought the Union appear to have been affected by the result. They seem to have attached more importance to him than I had conceived. But for your solicitations I should not however have stood a poll, tho' my venerable father had come up to Wilmington himself on purpose to persuade me so to do. I do not suppose that it is in contemplation for the eighth Congress to sit before December twelvemonth. If it be I should wish to be informed of it, that I may arrange my business so as to suit the same. With great personal & political esteem & respect I remain Dr. Sir

Yours most Sincerely   C. A. RODNEY

P.S. I rejoice to find that Thomas Paine is coming over to this country in whose cause he laboured so faithfully, to use his own expression "in those times which tried men's souls." I disapprove of his writings on religion but his pen will be a pillar of support to an honest administration. His style is calculated for the plain understanding of every good citizen He will be a masterly hand at detecting and exposing federal misrepresentations. I forgot to mention that Capt: Mendenhall did all he could to injure my election.   C. A. R.

RC (DLC); one illegible word; endorsed by TJ as received 4 Nov. and so recorded in SJL.

PREVAILING FEVER: on and after 23 Oct., Philadelphia newspapers reported an "alarming increase" in cases of yellow fever in Wilmington, Delaware, which caused the *Mirror of the Times* to suspend publication. The next issue appeared on 6 Nov. (Wilmington *Mirror of the Times*, 23 Oct., 6 Nov.; *Philadelphia Gazette & Daily Advertiser*, 23 Oct.; *Poulson's American Daily Advertiser*, 25 Oct. 1802).

TJ wrote William KILLEN on 14 Oct. POLICIES OF THE TWO EXECUTIVES: Thomas McKean dismissed a number of Federalists and appointed Republicans to office shortly after his inauguration; he was noted for rewarding his family and friends and chastising his political foes. Governor Bloomfield, in contrast, was criticized by Republicans for appointing Federalist lawyers to state posts and for remaining in close contact with his Federalist friends (Rowe, *McKean*, 319-21; Carl E. Prince, *New Jersey's Jeffersonian Republicans: The Genesis of an Early Party Machine, 1789-1817* [Chapel Hill, 1967], 103-4). See also Elijah Griffiths to TJ, 8 June 1803.

For the MEMORIAL calling for the removal of Allen McLane, see Delaware Democratic Republicans to TJ, 5 June.

On 3 Nov., McLane wrote Albert GALLATIN that the "clammer" for his office as collector at Wilmington had revived. He noted that he would be greatly injured financially if he were dismissed before the bonds taken during the last summer at his great risk were collected. He would be more financially secure if the president allowed him to stay in office until the end of the first quarter of 1803. By that time, McLane remarked, "the commissn. that I shall be entitled to, for the Services rendered this season will enable me to stock, a small farm that I have under a tennant, whose time will then expire, and the least injury will be done me, by a removal." He was submitting his case to the president and would continue to attend to his "prominent duties" (Gallatin, *Papers*, 7:714). CASE OF MR. LATIMORE: that is George Latimer (Gallatin to TJ, [7 July 1802], second letter).

CAPT. WHITE: for Senator Samuel White's service in the provisional army, see Vol. 35:207-8n. INTRODUCED DR. MCCREERY TO YOU: when Joseph McCreery visited Washington in April, he also brought letters of introduction from Caesar A. Rodney and James Tilton (Vol. 37:247-8, 249).

VOX ET NIHIL PRAETEREA: that is, an empty threat.

THE IDLE WIND WHICH YOU REGARD NOT: in act 4, scene 3, of William Shakespeare's *Julius Caesar*, Brutus responds, "There is no terror, Cassius, in your threats; For I am armed so strong in honesty That they pass by me as the idle wind, Which I respect not."

To Gabriel Duvall

DEAR SIR   Washington Nov. 5. 1802.

The place of Comptroller of the US. is vacant by the resignation of mr Steele. it is in it's nature partly Executive, and partly judiciary, as the Comptroller decides in the first instance all questions of law arising in matters of account between the US. and individuals. the office hours are from 9. A.M. to [3]. P.M. during which it furnishes pretty steady daily occupation. the Salary is 3500. D. I shall be very happy if it shall appear acceptable to you, and shall think I have well performed my duty if I can get the office placed in hands who enjoys and who has so much merited the public confidence. as soon as you can satisfactorily to yourself decide on this proposition I will thank you for an answer, & only observe that the sooner it is obtained the more convenient it will be to the department, which suffers while wanting so important an officer in it's organisation. I pray you to accept assurances of my sincere esteem & high consideration.   TH: JEFFERSON

RC (privately owned, 2011); with one numeral overwritten by TJ; at foot of text: "The honble Gabriel Duval." PrC (DLC).

From Mary Jefferson Eppes

November 5th

Mr. Randolph has been summon'd to Richmond My Dear Papa about the time we were to set off, which will prevent his going, with us & obliges us to request Mr Lewis to meet us at Strodes on Tuesday week. Mr Eppes will go that far with us but says he cannot possibly go farther. I Lament sincerely that it has not been possible for us to go sooner, as the visit will be scarcely worth making for so short a time & should prefer waiting till the spring & returning there with you as we could then remain with you some time but my sister will not agree to[1] put it off any longer on Tuesday week then if Mr Lewis can meet us at Strodes we shall be there Adieu dearest Papa. I am afraid the post will be gone & must conclude this scrawl, excuse it & believe me with the tenderest love yours   M EPPES

P.S. I send the lock of hair which is to be the colour of the wigs

RC (ViU: Edgehill-Randolph Papers); endorsed by TJ as received 10 Nov. and so recorded in SJL.

[1] Preceding two words interlined.

From Peter Kuhn, Jr.

SIR   Philad 5 Novr. 1802

Since my Arrival in Philadelphia I have determined on returning to Gibraltar earlier than I contemplated, when I had the honour of Seeing you, and expect to Sail in about ten days;—it will give me Much pleasure, in taking charge of any commands, that you may be pleased to commit to my Care for that quarter—

I am Sir With Much respect Your Most Obt Hle Svt

PETER KUHN JUNR

RC (DLC); at head of text: "His Excellency Thomas Jefferson President of the United States of America"; endorsed by TJ as received 9 Nov. and so recorded in SJL.

Peter Kuhn, Jr., son of a Philadelphia merchant, operated a commercial house in Gibraltar. In 1803, he expanded his business to Genoa and formed the partnership Kuhn, Green & Co., which on a few occasions filled TJ's orders for items such as wine and macaroni. The president named Kuhn the American consul in Genoa in 1804, a post he retained until being arrested and exiled by the French in 1807 under suspicion of spying for the British. After returning to the U.S., he advertised for publication by subscription his treatise *A System of Exchange Operations between the Principal Places of Eu-*rope, which advised American merchants on how best to negotiate currency exchange rates in Europe (*Poulson's American Daily Advertiser*, 27 July 1808; JEP, 1:476-7; MB, 2:1117, 1238; Peter Kuhn, Sr., to TJ, 6 Dec. 1803; Kuhn, Green & Co. to TJ, 24 Dec. 1803; Anna Kuhn to TJ, 2 Oct. 1807; John Armstrong to TJ, 28 Oct. 1807).

HAD THE HONOUR: Kuhn met with the president in Washington on 26 Oct. when he delivered five letters, which TJ recorded in SJL and connected by a brace with the notation "Kuhn P. junr. to be Consul at Gibraltar." The letters were from Caspar Wistar, 15 Oct.; J. P. G. Muhlenberg, 18 Oct. (not found); Michael Leib, 19 Oct.; William Barton, 22 Oct.; and Thomas McKean, 22 Oct. (not found).

To Edward Thornton

Th: Jefferson asks the favor of Mr. E. Thornton's company to dinner and chess on Monday next, the 8th. Inst., at half after three. Friday Novr. 5th. 1802.

The favor of an answer is requested.

RC (Stanley F. Horn, Nashville, Tennessee, 1958); in Meriwether Lewis's hand.

To Henry Dearborn

TH:J. TO THE SECRETARY AT WAR.

In the case of Crutchelow & John Williams, two of the murderers of the Indians who have fled, had the case happened in any of the states which proceed according to the forms of the English law, an indictment would be preferred to a grand jury, the witnesses called to appear, and on it's being found a true bill, a capias issues, which being returned non est inventus, an Exigent goes out, on the return of which the party stands outlawed, convicted & attainted, his blood corrupted; & all his lands and goods forfeited. I presume the Indiana territory has made analogous provisions by it's laws. if so, would it not be well to suggest to the Governor or district attorney of the territory, to set that proceeding on foot, and on the indictment being found by the grand jury, authorize them to offer a reward of   Dollars for each of the offenders on their safe delivery to any prison in any part of the US.? this reward may be operating while the process of outlawry is going on.

Nov. 6. 1802.

PrC (DLC). Recorded in SJL as a letter to the War Department with notation "Crutchelow & Williams."

CASE OF CRUTCHELOW & JOHN WILLIAMS: in his correspondence with Dearborn, Governor William Henry Harrison had forwarded complaints from Indian leaders about several unpunished murders committed by whites against Indians in the western territories. In a 22 Dec. 1801 reply, Dearborn wrote that in cases where a murderer was still at large, the president requested that Harrison "issue proclamations offering a handsome reward for the apprehension of the offender, and use every means in your power for apprehending and bringing him to justice, and particularly that you will not lose sight of the case of Williams." This case involved the 1797 murder of a Delaware Indian hunting party, consisting of two men and one woman, by brothers John and Martin Williams and John Crutchelow. Learning that the three men were now residing in Kentucky, in February 1802 Harrison sent a territorial representative to secure their extradition. Only John Williams was apprehended and carried to Indiana, where he was placed in the Knox County jail. On 4 May, however, Williams escaped and Harrison subsequently issued a proclamation offering a $300 reward for his recapture, as well as $100 for information regarding any accomplices in the jailbreak. Writing Harrison in June and July 1802, Dearborn reemphasized the president's "earnest wish" that Harrison "exert every means" in his power to apprehend the guilty parties, and also assured the governor that "all reasonable expences" incurred in bringing the offenders to justice would be paid by the United States. Martin Williams voluntarily surrendered to U.S.

district judge Harry Innes at Frankfort on 12 July and was released on bail to appear at the November term of the court. Neither John Williams nor Crutchelow surrendered, however, and on 23 Aug. Innes issued warrants against both men and subpoenas for witnesses. John Williams was arrested and held briefly in the Breckinridge County court house, but a mob led by prominent local resident William Hardin freed him and he eluded subsequent efforts by a federal posse to recapture him. The U.S. district court discharged Martin Williams in March 1803 and none of the three accused were ever brought to trial (Owens, *Jefferson's Hammer*, 61-2; Esarey, *William Henry Harrison*, 1:25-6, 48-9; *Terr. Papers*, 7:37, 55; Mary K. Bonsteel Tachau, *Federal Courts in the Early Republic: Kentucky, 1789-1816* [Princeton, 1978], 129-33; Harry Innes to Dearborn, 14 Oct. 1802, in DLC: Harry Innes Papers; Dearborn to Harrison, 17 June, 3 July 1802, in DNA: RG 75, LSIA).

SUGGEST TO THE GOVERNOR: Writing to Harrison on 11 Nov., Dearborn stated that although the apprehension of Williams and Crutchelow appeared doubtful, justice and "good policy" required that the government undertake "every reasonable exertion" to secure their capture. "I am directed by the President of the U. States," Dearborn continued, to suggest that Harrison call proper witnesses before a grand jury. If an indictment is thereafter issued, then Harrison should undertake the "usual proceedings" that would bring the fugitives to trial or declare them outlawed. Dearborn suggested that a reward of $500 be offered for each and that, once apprehended, they be committed to a public jail or delivered to the nearest military post in the territory. "I presume the common

Law of England as adopted by many of the States has been adopted in the Territory," Dearborn concluded, "the foregoing proceeding can only be had under that Law unless a statute Law of some State to that effect has been adopted" (DNA: RG 75, LSIA).

To Matthew C. Groves

SIR   Washington Nov. 7. 1802.

The inclosed letter from mr Patterson being just recieved[1] I now forward it according to promise. I should certainly have been more gratified if his opinion of the utility of your proposed method of observing the eclipses of Jupiter's Satellites had been more favorable. having had no experience myself in the business of making observations at sea, I am not at all competent to decide on the merit of the method you propose. Accept my best wishes & respects.

TH: JEFFERSON

PrC (DLC); at foot of text: "Capt Matthew C. Groves"; endorsed by TJ in ink on verso. Enclosure: Robert Patterson to TJ, 1 Nov. 1802.

[1] MS: "recieve."

From Nathaniel Macon

SIR   Warrenton 7 Novr 1802

I have received yours of the 18 ult. and regret most sincerely that proper recommendations have not been made for the Commissioners of Bankruptcy. This is in a great measure owing to the death of our much esteemed friend Mr. Johnson, who promised to name to you proper persons for the appointments

Since receipt of yours, I have fortunately met with a friend from Newbern, in whom dependence may be placed, and have obtained from him the enclosed names as the most fit for the appointment in that place, the two first on the list are lawyers; Mr. Harriss was the Judge who held the last federal court under the old system; Mr. Webber is a merchant and Mr. Gerock has been one, is going into business again, The three first live in Newbern; the other some times in the town, but mostly at a seat he has within two or three miles of it

I have written to Mr. Bloodworth for Wilmington, and Mr. Stone will give those for Edenton, perhaps not till the meeting of Congress, as I have not written to him

I am Sir with the utmost respect yr. most obt. sert.

NATHL MACON

RC (DNA: RG 59, LAR, 12:0177-8); endorsed by TJ as received 13 Nov. and "Commrs. bkrptcy." Enclosure: untitled list with four names appearing in the following order: Edward Harris ("Harriss"), William Blackledge, Thomas Webber, and Samuel Gerock (MS in same, 12:0176; undated; in an unidentified hand).

Congressman Charles JOHNSON died at his plantation near Edenton, North Carolina, in July 1802 (New York *Spectator*, 25 Aug.; Vol. 37:343n).

TWO FIRST ON THE LIST: that is, Harris and Blackledge. THE OTHER: Gerock, who became postmaster at New Bern in December 1803 (*New-York Herald*, 22 Feb. 1804; Stets, *Postmasters*, 199). All four on the list were appointed bankruptcy commissioners for the District of North Carolina, with commissions dated 24 Nov. (list of commissions in Lb in DNA: RG 59, MPTPC). On 14 Dec., Webber wrote the secretary of state that he could not accept the appointment because he expected "to be absent from the State a great part of the ensuing year" (RC in DNA: RG 59, RD; endorsed by TJ as a letter from Webber "of Newbern" to Madison and "declines commn bkrptcy"). See Timothy BLOODWORTH to TJ, 30 Nov. 1802, and David STONE and others to TJ, 19 Oct. 1803, for other recommendations for North Carolina.

From Benjamin Dearborn

SIR,   Washington Nov. 8th 1802

As the application of some natural principle, to the construction of a Standard of Measures, has been considered a Desideratum in Philosophic Research, the importance of the subject has induced me to spend some time in forming a Theory, applicable in practice, for obtaining a lineal standard, as nearly invariable as the case might require, or reason expect, in a state of being, where Nothing is Stationary—

Fully aware that Pleasing Theories are often Impracticable, I ever rely on them with a Diffidence, which is proportionate to the Difficulty of bringing them within the sphere of Mathematical Demonstration, and the Laws which regulate the Mechanical Powers: But, as the theory above referred to, appears to me in all its parts, to be subjected to such Demonstration, and to those Immutable Laws,—and, as pursuits of this kind, through a series of years, have given me an opportunity of knowing Pretty Accurately, how to estimate my own Theories, I feel a degree of Assurance in speaking of this.—

It consists of a Simple Time-Piece, with that part of the work which is termed the Scapement, so constructed, as to give Equal Impulse to the alternate vibrations of the Pendulum, and to perform what is commonly called the Dead Beat; that is, a progressive motion by seconds, without a recession, or what is termed by artists the Recoil. The Rod of the Pendulum will be so attached to the time-piece, as to be Easily taken out, and exchanged, and its Length as easily ascertained. The Bob of the pendulum will be divided into two equal parts of weight, either by a straight line, or by the Arc of a Circle, the centre of which is the Point of Oscillation; at this line the Rod (which will be made of Wood) may be cut off, or mark'd as most expedient, to a Degree of Exactness as great, as can be ascertained by the Eye, with or without the assistance of Glasses. The weight of the bob will act Independently of the weight of the rod, which is a necessary principle in constructing a Time-Piece for this purpose;—otherwise a Lighter rod would depress the Centre of Gravity, and a Heavier would raise it.

These few particulars are sufficient to give a general idea of the instrument—Should it ever be thought worthy of Public Attention, I would construct one on These Conditions, viz. That if it should answer the Designed Purpose, I should meet a stipulated Reward, if not, that I should loose my Labor;—the decision to be made by a Committee Previously appointed, whose Candour and Information should give them the Power of Deciding Justly—

I have the Honor to be Sr yr most obt and very hble Servt

BENJAMIN DEARBORN.

RC (DLC); addressed: "Thomas Jefferson Esqure President of the United States"; endorsed by TJ as received 8 Nov. and so recorded in SJL.

Dearborn, who had been settled in Boston for many years and would return there, may have been staying in WASH-INGTON with an eye toward becoming head of the U.S. Patent Office, a position about which he asked James Madison a week later (Madison, *Papers, Sec. of State Ser.*, 4:123; Vol. 37:541).

From Thomas Worthington

SIR   Chilicothe Novr 8th 1802

I have the honour to enclose to you herewith the Sioto Gazette from which you will find our convention has commenced its sitting— you will also see a communication made by Governor St Clair to the convention which is expressive of his wishes & opinions in this business—Haveing taken a very active part in obtaining the passage of the law of Congress for our admission I have felt very deeply interested in the event of our elections for members to the Convention—My gratification has in some measure equalled my anxiety. The republican ticket has succeed beyond my most sanguine expectations. 26 decided republicans have been elected 7 federalists & 2 doubtful in all 35 the number given us by the law—I feel the greatest pleasure Sir in giveing you this information as our republican friends in Congress have exhibited the strongest proof of their friendship towards in enabling us to form for ourselves a constitution and state government congenial to the feelings of free men without respect to any difference in political opinion—I have good reason to believe there will not be two federalists in our first Legislature—It will therefore follow that our Senators to Congress will also be republican—I have the honour to enclose a communication made to the people soon after my return to this country from which you will observe sir that my small might has not been wanting in support of what I believed right—I beg you will accept of my most sincere and grateful thanks for the kind and polite attentions I received from you (during my troubles for such I called them) last winter in the city and accept of my most sincere wishes for your health & happiness. I have the honour to be with the highest respect Sir

Your Obt St   T. WORTHINGTON

RC (DLC); addressed: "Thomas Jefferson Esquire President of the United States"; endorsed by TJ as received 19 Nov. and so recorded in SJL. Enclosures: (1) *Scioto Gazette*, 6 Nov. 1802, which includes journal extracts from the first four days of the Ohio constitutional convention at Chillicothe, and a 3 Nov. address to the convention by Arthur St. Clair, defending his actions as governor and denying Congress the power to authorize the convention; "That the people of the Territory should form a convention and a constitution, needed no act of congress," argues St. Clair, and "To pretend to authorise it was, on their part, an interference with the internal affairs of the country, which they had neither the power nor the right to make"; St. Clair deems the Enabling Act a "nullity, and could it be brought before that tribunal where acts of congress can be tried, would be declared a nullity"; the internal affairs of the territory were the province of its own legislature, which was no more bound by an act of Congress "than we would be bound by an edict of the first consul of France"; St. Clair denounces terms in the Enabling Act that limits the new state to one representative until the next census and excludes Wayne County from the state's boundaries; he calls on representatives to demand admission of the entire territory to statehood, and if refused by Congress, to govern itself under its new constitution; "We have the means in our hands to bring congress to reason, if we should be forced to use them," St. Clair concludes, "If we submit to the degradation, we shall be trodden upon, and what is worse, we shall deserve to be trodden on" (Alfred Byron Sears, *Thomas Worthington: Father of Ohio Statehood* [Columbus, 1998], 95-7). (2) Thomas Worthington, *Communication, to Those Citizens of the North-Western Territory, Opposed to an*

Alteration of the Boundaries of the States, as Established by Congress, and Who Are Favourable to the Formation of a Constitution and State Government within the Eastern State, as Originally Established, dated 5 July 1802, congratulating the inhabitants of the Northwest Territory on the defeat in Congress of efforts to redivide the territory and thereby postpone statehood for the eastern division; enactment of the redivision scheme would have delayed the territory's emancipation from "an obnoxious government" and been "destructive to their rights and liberties," and Worthington hopes this past experience "may make you watchful and guarded in future"; Worthington also congratulates his fellow citizens on the passage of the Enabling Act, which provides a detailed explanation of its terms and conditions, and also attaches a copy of the act; he points out that every Federalist present in Congress voted against the act, while the Republicans "uniformly declared it was their intention to do us that justice they believed we merited"; Worthington strongly approves of the act and leaves his fellow citizens to determine whether it will be advantageous to accede to its propositions (Sowerby, No. 3337).

OUR CONVENTION: as authorized by the Enabling Act passed by Congress on 30 Apr. 1802, the Ohio constitutional convention convened at Chillicothe on 1 Nov. and adjourned on 29 Nov., after ratifying a state constitution and approving an address to the president and Congress. Worthington was a member of the Ross County delegation (U.S. Statutes at Large, 2:173-5; Sears, *Thomas Worthington*, 94, 107; Worthington to TJ, 22 Dec. 1802).

From Nicolas Gouin Dufief

MONSIEUR,   à Philadelphie, ce 9 de Novembre, 1802

Il y a près de deux ans que j'eus l'honneur de vous entretenir de mon travail sur la vraie & unique methode d'enseigner les langues, que je crois avoir découverte—Je vous priais de vouloir bien être mon juge, touchant la maniere dont J'ai traité un sujet, toujours digne de l'attention du Philosophe, par l'influence qu'ont les *Langues* sur notre faculté de Penser, laquelle pour parler le langage de *Condillac* & d'*Euler*, n'existe que par elles—

Encouragé par l'idée que vous ne me refusiez pas cette faveur inestimable, J'ai redoublé d'attention et d'efforts, & J'ai amené mon ouvrage au point d'être entierement terminé, à l'exception, cependant, de quelques pages qui me restent encore à ecrire pour la seconde Section, la plus importante dans l'ordre des choses, mais heureusement la moins difficile à manier—

Afin de vous mettre en état de prononcer sur le plan de l'ouvrage, j'ai pensé que je devais vous envoyer mon *discours Préliminaire*, où il est developpé et analysé dans le plus grand détail. Vous connaîtrez ma manière d'écrire par le premier Chapitre que j'y ai joint—Il est intitulé *Conversation*, ainsi que les suivans, pour de petites raisons de Nouveauté & d'intérêt. Vous vous formerez aussi une idée des

Vocabulaires de la seconde Section, par celui que je vous envoye; c'est un des plus Importans, puis qu'il a rapport aux mots servant *de Lieu & de complément de sens entre les autres parties du Discours*—

J'aurais bien désiré vous envoyer plusieurs autres de mes *conversations*, mais il aurait fallu pour cela vous faire passer tout l'ouvrage, qui sera encore entre les mains du Copiste, pendant un mois—

Je m'abstiendrai, comme il convient, de faire aucune reflexion sur ma méthode; je me bornerai à observer qu'elle ne saurait être adoptée sans faire une revolution complète dans l'Education qui ne consiste presque uniquement qu'à aprendre des Langues *mortes* ou *Vivantes*. Il me faudrait avant qu'elle ait le moindre succès, soutenir une longue lutte avec tous les Pédans des Collèges & des Ecoles, qui par leurs clameurs pourraient réussir à prévenir le Public contre l'ouvrage & peut-être contre l'auteur lui même en l'accusant, par exemple, de *matérialisme*, à cause du titre qu'il a choisi—

Cette Reflexion m'a Suggeré l'idée de faire Imprimer ma methode, *par souscription.* J'ai adopté, sauf un meilleur, le plan suivant Que je prends la liberté de vous Communiquer.

Afin de mettre les Souscripteurs en état de la juger par eux-mêmes, Je me propose de publier conjointement avec le *Prospectus*, Le *dis. Prel* & d'y Joindre un échantillon de ma maniere de traiter ce qu'il y a de plus abstrait en Grammaire, Comme l'origine des *Genres*, des *adjectives*, des *noms Abstraits*; le tout formera une brochure d'environ 45. Pages, 8vo. Je la ferai porter chez les Citoyens de Philadelphie & des autres villes des Etats-Unis, qui sont le plus en possession de l'estime publique. Quelques Jours après on les priera de la remettre, (conformément à l'avis qui sera en tête,) à celui qui sera chargé de recueillir la souscription de ceux que l'ouvrage aura intéressés; elle sera de deux dollars & demie par Exemplaire, d'environ 5 à 600 Pages in 8vo. imprimé correctement sur Beau papier.

Rien ne serait plus propre à me concilier les suffrages du Public que votre approbation, en cas que vous en jugiez l'ouvrage digne. Si J'avais l'avantage de l'obtenir Je ne ferais rien Imprimer de la Brochure (excepté ce que vous en auriez lu) sans vous le Communiquer auparavant—

Le moment que je regarde comme le plus propice pour ouvrir la Souscription, est le Commencement de decembre, époque ou se rendront à Philadelphie les Libraires des Etats-Unis, mes Confrères pour assister à la Foire littéraire. Je vous serais donc bien obligé de me renvoyer le Dis. Pre. &ca dès que vous aurez eu la bonté de le Parcourir—

Le Libraire de Paris que j'ai chargé de remplir ma demande de livres, oû les vôtres étaient compris & particulièrement recommandés, a reçu mon Catalogue, & comme j'ai apris de Mr. *Tarascon*, Negociant de cette ville, qu'il avait touché le montant de la lettre de Change que je lui avais fait passer en payment à cet effet je me plais à croire qu'ils vont bientôt arriver—

Mr *Duane*, m'a témoigné quelque désir d'acheter environ 2000. Volumes qui me restent de la Bibliotheque du Dr. Franklin; il se trouve parmi ces livres plusieurs manuscripts, & quelques ouvrages apostillés de la propre main du Dr. Si ce Monsieur ne faisait pas cette acquisition que Je lui faciliterai en les evaluant au plus bas prix possible, & que vous desiriez parcourir le Nouveau Catalogue que je viens de dresser, je vous l'enverrai dès que vous me l'ordonnerez—

Il me serait, peut-être utile de lire un Ouvrage dont *Garat*, fait mention dans un Mercure de France; il est intitulé *Essai Synthétique sur l'origine & la formation des Langues.*

S'il était dans votre belle & nombreuse Bibliothèque, & qu'il fût possible de le faire venir à *Washington*; en me l'envoyant de là à Philadelphie, oû Je ne le Garderais que quelques Jours, vous me rendriez un service pour lequel J'aurais une reconnaissance eternelle—

Recevez avec votre bonté accoutumée, les assurances de ma profonde Estime & de mon respectueux devouëment

N. G. DUFIEF

EDITORS' TRANSLATION

SIR,   Philadelphia, 9 Nov. 1802

Almost two years ago, I had the honor of talking to you about the true and unique method of language teaching that I believe I have discovered. I asked you to be kind enough to judge how I treat a subject that has always merited philosophers' attention, given the influence of language on our capacity to think, since, to borrow the terminology of Condillac and Euler, thought does not exist without language.

Encouraged by the knowledge that you did not refuse this inestimable favor, I redoubled my focus and efforts, and have now completed the work, except for a few pages in the second section, which is the most important one but, fortunately, the least difficult to deal with.

As background for judging the work as a whole, I felt I should send you the "Preliminary Discourse," where it is outlined and analyzed in the greatest detail. I am also enclosing the first chapter, which will give you a sense of my style. It is entitled "Conversation," as are subsequent ones, for minor reasons of novelty and interest. This chapter will give you an idea of the language of the second section. It is one of the most important since it concerns the words *where other parts of speech come together and acquire meaning.*

I would have liked to send you several other of my "conversations," but that would have meant sending the entire work, which will be in the hands of the copyist for another month.

I will refrain, as is fitting, from offering any commentary on my method, and limit myself to observing that this method could not be adopted without a complete revolution in education, which consists almost entirely in learning dead or living languages. Before my method can achieve the slightest success, I would have to undertake a long battle with all the pedants in primary and secondary schools whose protests could warn the public against the work and perhaps against the author himself, by accusing him, for example, of *materialism*, because of the title he chose.

This prospect prompts me to adopt the subscription method of publishing my work. Barring a better plan, I have adopted the following one, which I take the liberty of communicating to you.

To allow subscribers to form their own opinions, I propose to publish a brochure of approximately 45 pages, octavo, containing the prospectus, the preliminary discourse, and a sample of my method for treating the most abstract aspects of grammar, such as the origin of genders, adjectives, and abstract nouns. I will take the brochure to the most respected citizens of Philadelphia and other cities in the United States. A few days later, they will be invited to return the brochure (according to the notice printed on its cover) to the person charged with soliciting subscriptions. Subscription will be two dollars and fifty cents for a volume of 500-600 pages, octavo, fittingly printed on fine paper.

Nothing would be more valuable for gaining public support than your approval, if you judge the work worthy. Should I have the good fortune of deserving your approval, I would not publish anything in the brochure without first sending it to you (except for what you have already read).

Early December seems to me the most propitious time to launch subscriptions, since this is the season when my fellow booksellers gather in Philadelphia for the book fair. I would thus be very grateful if you could return the "Preliminary Discourse" and the rest as soon as you have been kind enough to read them.

The Paris bookseller from whom I ordered books, including and with special emphasis on your order, has received my catalogue. Mr. Tarascon, a merchant there, informs me that the bookseller received my payment by bill of exchange, so I am confident the books will arrive soon.

Mr. Duane expressed a desire to purchase the approximately 2000 remaining volumes from Dr. Franklin's library that I still possess. Among them are several manuscripts and some works annotated in the Doctor's hand. I will facilitate the purchase by evaluating them at the lowest possible price, but if Mr. Duane does not acquire them, and if you wish to consult my new catalogue, I will send it to you immediately upon request.

It might be useful for me to read a work that Garat mentions in the *Mercure de France*, entitled *Synthetic Essay on the Origin and Formation of Languages*. If this book figures in your large, beautiful library, I would be eternally grateful if you could send it to Washington and from there to Philadelphia, where I would keep it only a few days.

Receive, with your customary goodness, the assurance of my high esteem and respectful devotion.   N. G. Dufief

RC (DLC); at foot of first page: "Thomas Jefferson, Président des Etats-Unis"; endorsed by TJ as received 12 Nov. and so recorded in SJL. Enclosures not found, but see below.

MON OUVRAGE: the first edition of Dufief's work, *Nature Displayed, in her Mode of Teaching Language to Man*, a text for speakers of English learning the French language, appeared in Philadelphia in 1804. The introduction, titled "Preliminary Discourse" (DISCOURS PRÉLIMINAIRE), recounted that after his arrival in the United States, Dufief had taught himself English by first learning phrases before moving on to systematic study of grammar. Citing philosophers of the mind and language, particularly John Locke and Étienne Bonnot de Condillac—Dufief dedicated his book to them—he argued that his method was based on natural principles. It was, according to one of his book's subtitles, a system "deduced from the analysis of the human mind." The first volume contained short chapters consisting of lists of CONVERSATION phrases in English and French that were intended to build vocabulary. The first chapter of the published version, for example, included sentences that used nouns relating to food, beginning with "Buy me a three pound loaf." The second volume discussed the philosophy of language, explained conjugations of French verbs, and discussed syntax. Dufief regularly offered courses in the French language based on "an Analytical Plan" (*Philadelphia Gazette*, 16 Sep. 1801, 26 Oct. 1802; Dufief, *Nature Displayed, in her Mode of Teaching Language to Man*, 2 vols. [Philadelphia, 1804], 1:ix-xl; Sowerby, No. 4819).

PAR SOUSCRIPTION: in the fall of 1803, Dufief issued his proposal for publishing his work by subscription (*Washington Federalist*, 28 Oct. 1803).

FOIRE LITTÉRAIRE: the booksellers and publishers who attended the book fair organized by Mathew Carey in New York in June 1802 resolved to gather twice a year on a regular basis, in New York in the spring and Philadelphia in the fall. The first Philadelphia literary fair, scheduled for October 1802, was postponed until December due to yellow fever (*Philadelphia Gazette*, 10 July, 21 Sep., 26 Oct.; New York *Commercial Advertiser*, 8 Dec.; Vol. 37:687).

Dufief had sold books from the library of Benjamin FRANKLIN to TJ and the American Philosophical Society (Vol. 35:482-4, 542, 699).

ESSAI SYNTHÉTIQUE: TJ probably did not own a copy of the *Essai synthétique sur l'origine et la formation des langues* (Paris, 1774), a book on the origins of language by the Abbé Copineau (*Dictionnaire*, 9:557).

To Gibson & Jefferson

DEAR SIR   Washington Nov. 9. 1802.

To keep you in bank I inclose you one hundred and fifty dollars to be entered to my credit.

I have this day drawn on you in favor of John Rogers of Albemarle for 43. D 91 c and in favor of Joseph Morin of Columbia for two hundred dollars, which please to honor when presented. Accept assurances of my friendly attachment & best wishes.

TH: JEFFERSON

PrC (MHi); at foot of text: "Messrs. Gibson & Jefferson"; endorsed by TJ in ink on verso. Recorded in SJL with notation "150. D."

The draft on behalf of JOSEPH MORIN (Moran) was a portion of the $848 TJ owed for stone work done on the nailery and offices at Monticello. Starting with an initial payment of $100 in October, the president was to pay Moran in monthly installments of $200. A letter of this day from TJ to Moran has not been found but was recorded in SJL with the notation "200. D." (MB, 2:1080, 1086).

From Benjamin H. Latrobe

DEAR SIR,   Philadelphia Novr. 9th. 1802

In the haste in which I was under the necessity of answering your letter of the 2d inst. I fear I could not do justice to my sense of the obligation I owe to your kindness. If any thing I have written should have borne the slightest appearance of false pride, or of a mercenary disposition, I have done the greatest injustice to my sentiments of respectful attachment to you, as a public, and as a private character. I cannot better convince you of my sincerity than by candidly stating to you the exact situation in which I am now placed.

During the 3 first Years of my residence in Philadelphia, I have expended in erecting the Bank of Pensylvania and in supplying the city with Water, near 500.000 Dollars. Both works are completed, and their adequacy to the purposes for which they were designed, and the oeconomy & integrity with which they have been conducted, is not disputed even by those who have used the public prints as the vehicle of their calumnies against me. And yet my emoluments have been disputed with me inch by inch, and I have the prospect before me, of a lawsuit with the city, for a considerable part of my compensation, which has been awarded to me by two references, by a joint Committee of both councils, by the Select council,—but which the common council has neglected or refused to vote to me.

I will not take up your time by stating many other instances in which I have devoted time, talents, & have incurred expence without any return. The labor of the mind, is not *here* supposed to be a *merchantable article.*

The result of all this has been that my private fortune, and the slow and hardly earned proceeds of my professional employ have barely supported me & my family in the enjoyment of those indulgences, and of that society in which I have been educated, and in which all my habits have been formed; and having for the last twelve month been wholly without professional employment, I have turned my attention to business of more permanent & independent emolument.

The Gentleman who erected the Steam engines of the Waterworks contracted for the use of all the power which they should possess, beyond that used in the daily supply of the city with water,—and in order to increase this power, the size of the Engine on Schuylkill was doubled. As the funds of this Gentleman failed, some of my friends were induced, by their confidence in my statements, to join with him in attaching rolling & slitting works to the Engine; and I also placed the whole of my own capital in those works. Their expence has been very great,—and they have as yet produced nothing. My honor with my friends, my reputation with the public, & my own fortunes are at risk in their Success.—Within these few weeks we have begun to manufacture Iron, and our most sangine wishes begin to be accomplished.—But the daily support of my family depends upon an allowance, in advance of future profits, paid to me in the manner of a Salary by my partners, who themselves have received nothing. This allowance is at the rate of 2.500 Dollars ℀ Annum, and is absolutely my only resource. It depends on my personal attendance, & is suspended during occasional absence.

Since I last had the honor to see you, I have married the daughter of Mr. Isaac Hazlehurst of this city, who is I believe known to you. I have also two Children. Were I single I should have waited upon you before this letter could arrive, & should not have incurred the possibility of a doubt of my confidence in You. The noble plan suggested by your letter, is sufficient to excite the ambition of a man much less an enthusiast in his profession than I am. But independently of ambition, & the fair prospect of future emolument, I should have required no motive but to have been called upon by You.

I have now only to beg that you will think as favorably of my disposition, as you have done me the honor to conceive of my talents. In the mean time, I am preparing to leave Philadelphia in a few days. I hope to hear again from You, and am with the highest respect

Your obliged hble Servant   B H LATROBE.

RC (DLC); endorsed by TJ as received 12 Nov. and so recorded in SJL.

ANSWERING YOUR LETTER: a letter from Latrobe of 8 Nov., which TJ received on the 11th and referred to Robert Smith, is recorded in SJL but has not been found. In the letter, Latrobe brought up the matter of compensation for the design of a dry dock (TJ to Latrobe, 13 Nov.).

In 1805, the COMMON COUNCIL of Philadelphia approved a payment to Latrobe beyond what had been specified in the contract for the city's waterworks (Latrobe, *Correspondence*, 1:226n).

Nicholas J. Roosevelt, who engaged in several ventures that involved steam power and metals processing, built the STEAM ENGINES for the Philadelphia waterworks and the rolling and slitting mill that was also powered by the engines (same, 143n, 145, 146n, 226n, 560-1n; Vol. 31:548).

Latrobe MARRIED Mary Elizabeth Hazlehurst, the daughter of a Philadelphia merchant with whom TJ was acquainted, in May 1800. It was Latrobe's

second marriage. He had TWO CHIL-
DREN, a daughter named Lydia and a
son, Henry, with his first wife, who was
also named Lydia and who died in 1793
(Latrobe, *Correspondence*, 1:84n, 177n;
Vol. 27:586).

PREPARING TO LEAVE PHILADELPHIA:
later in November, Latrobe traveled to
Washington to begin planning for the
proposed dry dock project (Latrobe, *Correspondence*, 1:231n).

From Thomas Munroe

Superintendants Office
SIR, Washington 9th November 1802

The proper Officer has rendered, in behalf of the State of Maryland, the enclosed Account of a quarters Interest due the 1st. Octo.
last on the two Loans of $100,000 each by the said State for the use
of the City of Washington—I have no monies in my hands wherewith
I can pay the same, nor do I believe a sum sufficient for the purpose
can at present be raised by a sale of the Lots in the City which are
pledged for the repayment of the said Loans & Interest, without an
unwarrantable sacrafice of said Lots—

I have the Honor to be with the most respectful consideration Sir
Yr mo Obt Servt THOMAS MUNROE SUPT

RC (DLC); at foot of text: "President
of the United States"; endorsed by TJ as
received 10 Nov. and "Maryland debt"
and so recorded in SJL. Enclosure not
found, but see below.

PROPER OFFICER: in a 16 Nov. letter to
Thomas Harwood, treasurer of the western shore of Maryland, Munroe enclosed

a Treasury draft for $3,000 for the inter-
est due 1 Oct. on the $200,000 loaned to
the city of Washington. Munroe also
noted that the account received from Harwood "some days ago" had been filed in
the Treasury Department "with a certificate & direction of the President to the
Secretary subjoined thereto" authorizing
payment (Dft in DNA: RG 42, LR).

From Thomas Munroe

Superintendant's office
SIR Washington 9th November 1802

I have perused and considered the inclosed representation of
James M. Lingan, the original proprietor of the Ground within an
open space in front of Square No. 78 in the City of Washington
bounded by Pennsylvania Avenue, 20th. Street west and I. Street
north, as also the enclosed three Letters from a Committee of the Citizens and House holders in that part of the City which lies west of the
President's house; in which representation and Letters the original

proprietor aforesaid, as well as all the said Citizens and Householders two, who are absent excepted, by their Committee, solicit that the said open space may be appropriated or permitted to be used as a site for a Market house intended to be erected by private Contributions and established after the 1st December next, agreeably to an act of the City Corporation—under all the Circumstances attending the subject I think it would be right and proper to appropriate the said Space as solicited, and should appropriate the same accordingly, if I considered myself authorised so to do, but as I believe the President alone is authorised to grant the prayer of the applicants I have taken the liberty to submit it to his Consideration.

I have the Honor to be with the most respectful consideration Yr. mo. obt. Servt.   THOMAS MUNROE

RC (DLC); at foot of text: "President of the US"; endorsed by TJ as received 10 Nov. and "Western market house." and so recorded in SJL. Dft (DNA: RG 42, LR). Enclosures: (1) James M. Lingan to Munroe, 28 Oct. 1802, stating that he consents to and joins in the solicitation of the president to appropriate an open space west of the President's House, bound by Pennsylvania Avenue, 20th Street West, and I Street North, for the purpose of erecting a market house; Lingan is the original proprietor of the space and holds lots and houses nearby. (2) Joseph Hodgson, Timothy Caldwell, Joseph Brumley, James C. King, and Benjamin Perkins to Munroe, 27 Oct. 1802, responding to Munroe's "verbal request" to know whether the market scheme would meet the approbation of property owners and residents contiguous to the proposed site; the authors give their consent to the plan, excepting "Mr. Gilchrist who resides in Philada. and Mr. Key who is now absent." (3) Joseph Hodgson to Munroe, 8 Nov. 1802, noting the approach of winter and the anxiety of

the subscribers to the proposed western market, and again soliciting "the necessary appropriations of the Ground heretofore applied for"; the committee appointed to erect the market house consider it improper to proceed until the site is secured, and Hodgson will call on Munroe in the afternoon in the hope that the business can be settled today (all in same). Other enclosure not found.

ACT OF THE CITY CORPORATION: as part of an act to establish and regulate markets passed 6 Oct. 1802, the Washington city council authorized a majority of householders residing west of the President's House to petition the mayor after 1 Dec. for the establishment of a market, provided that the market house was built at private expense. Mayor Robert Brent proclaimed the opening of the West Market on 3 Dec. 1802 (*Acts of the Corporation of the City of Washington, Passed by the First Council* [Washington, D.C., 1803], 20; *National Intelligencer*, 6 Dec. 1802).

From Martha Jefferson Randolph

DEAR PAPA   November 9th

It will be more convenient to us to leave this on wednesday than monday it will occasion a delay of 2 days only, as this is a flying visit only to shew that we are in earnest with regard to Washington I have determined to leave the children all but Jefferson considering the lateness of the season and the bad weather we may reasonably expect in december. The short time [we] shall have to spend with you it is better to part with them for a time than risk such a journey with a carriage full of small children. next spring I hope I shall have it in my power to return with you and carry them all. Maria thinks it would be better to send a carriage with the horses as Mr. Eppes' in which we shall go is much out of repair and ours absolutely not in a travelling condition. adieu Dearest Father yours most truly affectionate

M R

RC (MHi); torn at seal; addressed: "Thomas Jefferson President of the U.S. Washington"; franked; postmarked Milton, Virginia; endorsed by TJ as received 13 Nov.

WEDNESDAY: that is, 17 Nov.

From John Smith

SIR   Chillicothe Nov 9th 1802

Although I have not the honour of being made known to you, I am impelled as a member of the convention now in session and as a real friend of your administration of the general governmt. to enclose you a paper containing the Governors speech, by which you will discover the temper and disposition of his mind; as well respecting the policy of the national Legislature towards the United States generally, as to our Territory in particular—

I consider the law of Congress well adapted to the impressions, the wishes and the interests of the people of this Territory. They were tired of the Colonial Yoke—They now hope for a change and I trust they will not be disappointed. I think our body is composed of 24 Republican members out of thirty five. We are progressing in the business of framing a constitution—We have concluded to call the new State (Ohio) and are determined to put an end to this Territorial government as soon as possible in order that we may form an additional link to the Republican chain—

Governor St Clair left this for Cincinnati with a few of his friends yesterday and I have no doubt with some chagrin & disappointment. He took the pains to ride to this place unsolicited under the pretext of organizing the Convention—On the day of our meeting he entered our chamber appointed his Secretary and requested the members to hand in to him the certificates of their election & the Secretary would have them Registered—The measure was not acceeded to[*] & we proceeded to the choice of a president & Secretary & to our own organization—The second day following his Freinds from Marietti took their seats & he again appeared & beged leave not as a public officer, but, as a private Citizen to make a few observations—under this impression leave was granted—The moment he sat down it was determined to take no notice of it—And resolution passed declaring our intention to terminate this government & that he should be requested to prorouge the Assembly—After which he withdrew & issued his proclamation & ordered the printer to publish his speech—I hope Sir you will pardon me for troubling you with this lengthy detail—The confidence I have in the Interest which you feel for the welfare of every description of american Citizens is the only apoligy that can be offered by

 Sir your most obedient Sevnt.   JOHN SMITH

[*] Col. Thomas Worthington with a manly intrepidity & with his usual firmness in support of political Justice succesfully interfered.

RC (DLC); addressed: "Thomas Jefferson Esquire President of the United States of America"; endorsed by TJ as received 19 Nov. and so recorded in SJL. Enclosure: see Enclosure No. 1 described at Thomas Worthington to TJ, 8 Nov.

A native of Virginia and a former Baptist minister, John Smith (ca. 1735-1824) migrated to the Cincinnati area around 1790, where he became a successful merchant and land speculator. Elected to the Northwest Territory legislature in 1798, he emerged as a leading opponent of Arthur St. Clair's administration and a strong supporter of statehood. He was a delegate to the Ohio constitutional convention in November 1802, and was subsequently chosen to be one of the new state's first two United States senators. He later became enmeshed in the Aaron Burr conspiracy and narrowly avoided expulsion from the Senate in April 1808. Resigning his seat shortly thereafter, Smith relocated to Louisiana in 1810, where he died in poverty (ANB).

LAW OF CONGRESS: the Enabling Act of 1802.

Immediately following Arthur St. Clair's speech to the Chillicothe convention on 3 Nov., delegates passed a RESOLUTION by a vote of 32 to 1 declaring it expedient to form a constitution and state government at the present time. Two days later, on 5 Nov., another resolution requested that St. Clair dissolve or prorogue the territorial legislature. The governor complied and issued a PROCLAMATION the same day proroguing the legislature (*Journal of the Convention, of the Territory of the United States Northwest of the Ohio* [Chillicothe, 1802], 9, 11-12; *Scioto Gazette*, 6 Nov. 1802).

From Jean Pierre Paulin Hector Daure

Au Cap, le 19 Brumaire an 11 de la

MONSIEUR LE PRÉSIDENT.   république. 10 Novembre 1802.

Je profite du passage du Citoyen Perrin Capitaine, aide de camp du Général en chef Leclerc, Pour vous annoncer que nous avons perdu ce respectable chef dans la nuit du 10 au 11 Brumaire.

Le Général Rochambeau est appelé par le gouvernement français, au Commandement de cette armée, je l'attends d'un moment à l'autre, il était au port-au-prince.

J'espére, monsieur le président que la mort du Général en chef Leclerc, ne diminuera point, votre bienveillance pour la Colonie de Saint Domingue.

nos derniers Succès ont été complets Sur les insurgés.

Je vous prie, Monsieur le président, d'agréer mes Salutations respectueuses.   J. DAURE

EDITORS' TRANSLATION

At Cap-Français, 19 Brumaire, Year 11 of

MISTER PRESIDENT.   the Republic 10 Nov. 1802

I am taking advantage of the passage of Citizen Perrin, captain and aide-de-camp to commander Leclerc, to inform you that we lost this esteemed leader during the night of 10-11 Brumaire.

The French government has called General Rochambeau to command the army. I expect him any minute. He was in Port-au-Prince.

I hope, Mister President, that the death of commander Leclerc will not diminish your good will toward the colony of Saint-Domingue.

Our most recent victories over the insurgents have been complete.

Please accept, Mister President, my respectful greetings.   J. DAURE

RC (DLC); on Daure's printed letter-head stationery as colonial prefect for the western part of the colony of Saint-Domingue; letterhead includes the slogan "Liberté, Égalité" and partial dateline, with blank for day and month filled by Daure; English date added by Daure; at head of text: "Capitaine Général, (Par intérim)" and "À Monsieur Jefferson, Président des états unis"; endorsed by TJ as received 8 Jan. 1803 and so recorded in SJL.

Jean Pierre Paulin Hector Daure

(1774-1846) accompanied the French expeditionary force to Saint-Domingue in the fall of 1801 as the chief pay commissioner of Victoire Emmanuel Leclerc's army. Daure had formerly held a similar position with French armies in Egypt and Italy. After Pierre Bénézech, the colonial prefect at Cap-Français, died of yellow fever in the spring of 1802, Leclerc gave Bénézech's duties to Daure and the home government formally appointed him the colonial prefect for Saint-Domingue. Daure later served as a minister in the government of the kingdom of Naples, where he reputedly had an affair with the queen, Bonaparte's sister Caroline, and entered into an unsuccessful intrigue against the king, Caroline's husband Joachim Murat. Daure was the chief paymaster of Napoleon's army during the invasion of Russia, and later became master of petitions (*maître des requêtes*) of the *Conseil d'État*. Daure identified himself as Hector Daure on the stationery he used for the letter printed above (Thierry Lentz and others, eds., *Napoléon Bonaparte: Correspondance Général*, 6 vols. to date [Paris, 2004-], 3:248, 829, 1334; Tulard, *Dictionnaire Napoléon*, 374, 571;

Paul Roussier, ed., *Lettres du Général Leclerc, commandant en chef de l'armée de Saint-Domingue en 1802* [Paris, 1937], 172, 245, 248; Vol. 35:535, 539n).

NOUS AVONS PERDU CE RESPECTABLE CHEF: Leclerc died of complications of yellow fever during the night of 1-2 Nov. On 31 Oct., he dictated orders from his deathbed that gave the Vicomte de ROCHAMBEAU command of the army in Saint-Domingue (Henri Mézière, *Le général Leclerc (1772-1802) et l'expédition de Saint-Domingue* [Paris, 1990], 237-8; Vol. 35:539n).

Proclamation on Land for Market

To all whom it may concern. Greeting.

Whereas a Committee appointed by and in behalf of the Citizens and House holders in that part of the City of Washington which lies west of the Presidents house have solicited that the open space of Ground between Squares numbered seventy eight and one hundred and one, bounded by Pennsylvania Avenue, I Street north, and twentieth street West may be appropriated as a site for a Market in which solicitation the original proprietor of the Ground within said space has joined and united with said Committee, and the said Committee having certified that all the owners of property and Inhabitants contiguous to the said Space two, who are absent, excepted anxiously wish that the same space may be appropriated as aforesaid.

I do therefore declare and make known that the said open space be, and the same hereby is appropriated and granted as a site for a Market during the pleasure of the proper Authority and subject to the rules and regulations such Authority may have ordained and established, or shall hereafter ordain and establish.

Given under my Hand at the City of Washington—aforesaid this tenth day of November in the Year one thousand eight hundred and two.   TH: JEFFERSON

MS (DLC: District of Columbia Papers); in a clerk's hand, signed by TJ; at head of text: "Thomas Jefferson President of the United States." Dft (DNA: RG 42, LR); in Thomas Munroe's hand; lacks signature.

For the COMMITTEE representing residents of the area in question, see Thomas Munroe to TJ, 9 Nov. (second letter).

From Samuel Ward

Salem Massachusetts November 10th. 1802
The Petition of the Subscriber respectfully sheweth.

That being reduced by repeated misfortunes from a State of affluence to a very low ebb as to Wealth or means of support, He is desirous of obtaining some Office under Goverment that will enable him to support a large (and he thinks) promising Family, And as his Republican Friends anticipate a further removal of Public Officers, He is induced by their advice to request, that shou'd the person who is now Surveyor & Inspector for this port be removed, he may succeed him in those Offices—

Your Petitioner is fully sencible that whatever are his political principals, Integrity and abilities are necessary requisites to recommend any candidate for Office, and feels conscious that on enquiry Your Excellency will be satisfied in that regard—

Your Petitioner is now sixty two years old, and has a Wife, and ten children under his immediate care from seven years old and upwards, and whom with his utmost industry and economy he is unable to support in a decent manner. He has also two sons married who are unable to afford him any assistance—

He therefore submits the foregoing to your consideration, and is with due respect & regard

Your Excellency's most obedient servant   SAMUEL WARD

RC (DNA: RG 59, LAR); at head of text: "To His Excellency Thomas Jefferson Esquire President of the United States of America"; endorsed by TJ as received 30 Nov. and "to be Surveyor of Salem" and so recorded in SJL.

Samuel Ward (1739-1812), a Salem magistrate and military officer, had served in the Massachusetts legislature from 1778 to 1781 and in 1792 before suffering commercial setbacks. In 1797, he was involved in a land title dispute with other proprietors of the Salem Market. A former excise collector for Essex County, he ran unsuccessfully in a March 1801 election for county register of deeds against incumbent John Pickering. Ward had been a clerk in the register's office for four years and believed "his great and repeated misfortunes ought to entitle him to the vote of every friend of humanity." He informed Gideon Granger on 11 Nov. 1802 that he had previously "held many offices of Honour & some of profit," had petitioned the president, and solicited an appointment as postmaster. In May 1803, when TJ removed the Federalist naval officer of Salem and Joseph Story declined to succeed him, TJ appointed Ward, who served for the district of Salem and Beverly until his death (Madison, *Papers, Sec. of State Ser.*, 4:503-4; Charles S. Osgood and H. M. Batchelder, *Historical Sketch of Salem, 1626-1879* [Salem, Mass., 1879], 208; Prince, *Federalists*, 208; Joseph B. Felt, *Annals of Salem*, 2 vols. [Salem, 1845-49], 2:565; Salem *Impartial Register*, 5 Mch. 1801; *Salem Gazette*, 6 Feb. 1783, 27 Sep. 1785, 1 Dec. 1797, 6, 10 Mch. 1801; *Newburyport Herald*, 7 Aug. 1812; Ward to Granger, 16 May 1803 in DNA: RG 59, LAR; Vol. 33:673, Vol. 36:120n).

PERSON WHO IS NOW SURVEYOR & IN-SPECTOR: Bartholomew Putnam, the surveyor of Salem from 1789 to 1809, was a ship's officer and ship's master during the Revolution and a relation through marriage to Timothy Pickering (Osgood and Batchelder, *Historical Sketch of Salem*, 207; Prince, *Federalists*, 33).

From Henry Warren

SIR   Plymouth, Mass: Novr. 10. 1802.

I had the honor some months since to address a letter of thanks to you for the intended honor of an appointment as Collector for the Port of Marblehd.

I recieved from General Dearborn an intimation of this your intention, & was highly flattered with your notice & consideration. It was with extreme reluctance that I could bring my mind to decline any appointment conferred by you, under an administration conducted on principles which I have imbibed from infancy, & which are confirmed by experience & reflection: but various circumstances of an imperious nature combined to prevent my acceptance of the proposed office. I will not trouble you, Sir, with the detail as I presume General Dearborn must have communicated to you my letter to him on that subject, which I flatter myself must have assured you that my reasons were such as *ought* to have operated on my mind, & would exonerate me from the smallest possible suspicion of slighting your favours, or retiring from your service: So far from that, Sir, I still solicit your notice & patronage. I will not have the presumption to lay claim to them, although should any one assume that privilege, perhaps none could do it with more propriety. But I must take the liberty to make some suggestions to which I am the more emboldened by your consideration, & some late circumstances which have taken place in this district.—

The republican character, sentiments, & conduct of my family— the uniform adherence to the whig principles of the revolution has exposed us a long time to peculiar markes of obloquy & abuse: we were neglected by one administration & abused by another. My father is an aged veteran of the cause who was long wounded by the prostration of those sentiments in support of which he devoted the best period of his life, & is now only rejoicing like old Simeon at their revivification. I have one brother, who is a poor pensioner with but one leg, having left another in fighting the battles of his country. I had another immolated on the plains of the Miami. I alone am left in health to prop the remnants of the family, and our enemies are determined that this shall fail.

I have long been the object of persecution of an inveterate junto in this County, which would long since have been extinct but for the influence of federal officers here. The collector & his under officers—the deputy marshal—the post office so create an influence here which it is impossible to counteract: they are all open & undisguised in their hostility to the present administration & their measures. The late election of Member of Congress was altogether affected by this untoward influence. Every effort on the part of the republicans has been made to check the progress of these people in their opposition to government, but it seems at present without effect. And while I solicit a change in my own favor, I combine the support of the republican principles which actuate your conduct & which have always had strong operation on mine, with the personal, interested views of succeeding to some of the advantages resulting from a revolution which has hitherto in its effects operated to a constant depression of every individual of my family, while every one of it has had resolution & fortitude to maintain the principle while suffering from its exercise.—

Sir, I declare to you, & accept not my declaration alone but suffer me to refer you to the representative of this district, I declare to you that the Collector of this Port is incompetent—unfaithful & in principles & ability wholly unqualified for his office.—

I also; Sir avow myself to you as the candidate to succeed *him*, or the Marshal of Massachusetts, both of which it has been wonderful should be retained. The latter alone ought to have the decency to keep deputies who should not openly revile & calumniate to the President of the United States with every epithet that violence and baseness can suggest.

With great deference I would ask & you will pardon the questions If Mr. Tyng should be displaced for hostility to Republican principles, why not the Collector of Plymouth? If Mr Hillot should be displaced for being in league with the Essex junto why not the Collector of Plymouth? If Mr: Tuck should be removed for violent opposition to government, why not the Collector of Plymouth? all will apply with equal force to him. how far they were watchful as officers I know not, but he is notoriously negligent; & it is a common suggestion that such great & numerous frauds & dilapidations would not be committed on the revenue unless by the connivance of the officer.   I perhaps press this point with more zeal than delicacy; but you must pardon it when I confess I feel indignant at the constant triumph of these people, who are enjoying all the benefits that could accrue from a life of virtuous conduct, instead of abandoned principle; & when I am confident that nothing would more gratify the republicans of this

County, or more mortify their enemies than my appointment as the Collector of this Port.—

Accept, Sir, the assurances of my profound respect for your person & character & that I am

Your obed. hum: Servt.   HENRY WARREN

RC (DNA: RG 59, LAR); at foot of text: "The President of the U.S."; endorsed by TJ as received 3 Dec. and "for office" and so recorded in SJL.

LETTER OF THANKS: Warren to TJ, 29 Aug. 1802.

MY FATHER: James Warren, Sr. (Vol. 33:167-8).

Warren's BROTHER, James Jr., enlisted in the American navy and had his leg amputated as a result of a cannonball injury suffered while serving aboard the ship *Alliance* in 1781. His brother Winslow, a second lieutenant with the Second Regiment of the U.S. Army who served under Arthur St. Clair on the western frontier, was killed in an Indian attack on his encampment in 1791 (Rosemarie Zagarri, *A Woman's Dilemma: Mercy Otis Warren and the American Revolution* [Wheeling, Ill., 1995], 108-9, 127).

COLLECTOR & HIS UNDER OFFICERS: William Watson, the collector at Plymouth since 1789, whose conduct had been under investigation by the Treasury Department, had filled the subordinate customs offices with members of the town elite and local Federalist party activists such as the gauger of customs, Ephraim Spooner, and the inspector of customs, Thomas Matthews (Prince, *Federalists*, 26, 41-2; Vol. 37:555-6n).

THE POST OFFICE SO CREATE AN INFLUENCE HERE WHICH IT IS IMPOSSIBLE TO COUNTERACT: William Goodwin, the son of an original Plymouth family, was post officer, selectman, bank cashier, and collector of the internal revenue, as well as the owner of extensive property. He replaced William Watson as the town's postmaster in May 1798 and was succeeded in this office by James Warren, Jr., in February 1803 (Prince, *Federalists*, 41; Stets, *Postmasters*, 149; William T. Davis, *History of the Town of Plymouth* [Philadelphia, 1885], 102, 170, 172).

CANDIDATE TO SUCCEED HIM: Henry Warren replaced William Watson as customs collector for Plymouth in March 1803 (JEP, 1:453, 455; Vol. 37:555-6).

MR. HILLOT: that is, Joseph Hiller.

From Jacob Lewis

                                  Barney's Hotel George Town
SIR/   Thursday. 2 ock PM [11 Nov. 1802]

The repeated disopointments which I meet with, In my Consular appointments, has brought upon me a series of Expenses, & thereby greatly disminished my fortune—having a perfect Confidence In the Justice & loyalty of the President of the U.S., I came hither for the purpose of once more soliciting your Patronage—you have assurd me that I still hold my rank In the mind of the President—this Circumstance Is highly gratifying, and alone flatters me to hope, that his good will toward me will be evinced by that readiness which he has at all times shown to repare the sufferings of all those who reliy on his Justice,—I am perfectly Aware of the many applications which are now before you for Consulur offices,—I trust (notwithstanding) that among the whole number of applicants few, *if any*, will be found, whose claims stand anteceedant to my own, and I will venture to add, that, None, be them whom they may, have sacrificed more or have been more ready In supporting republicans and the administration of Mr. Jefferson, than myself—Mr. Granger the Postmaster General, Is perfectly well acquainted with my politicul creed & carracter. & *Knows well*, In what manner I have been persecuted by Federal wrath—

I have the Honor to be with the highest Consideration & Respt your very Obt. Servt   J LEWIS

RC (DNA: RG 59, LAR); partially dated; endorsed by TJ as a letter of 12 Nov. received the same day and "to be consul" and so recorded in SJL.

For Lewis's previous CONSULAR APPOINTMENTS to Île de France and Calcutta, see Vol. 33:378-9 and Vol. 34:656-7. Lewis arrived in New York from London on the *Jupiter* about 20 Oct. and proceeded to Washington. George W. Erving entrusted Lewis with a letter to the secretary of state, dated 1 and 3 Sep., in which he characterized Rufus King's "ministry" at London. In the same letter,

Erving described Lewis as "a man of very good sense, full of spirit & activity, of a very firm & Energetic character, & a sound republican." While he assumed Lewis would solicit another consular appointment, Erving thought he would be "a valuable acquisition" at the Navy Department, being fit "Either for the command of a frigate or the direction of a navy yard" (Madison, *Papers, Sec. of State Ser.*, 3:531-6; *New-York Evening Post*, 21 Oct. 1802). Lewis evidently applied to Madison for a consulship, but declined the positions offered to him (Lewis to TJ, 13 Mch. 1803).

From John F. Mercer

DEAR SIR   Annapolis Nov. 11. 1802.

I cannot permit my friend Mr. DuVall to leave this without offering you my sincere congratulations on the pleasing prospect our political horizon now affords.—things progress in this State beyond my expectations & if the severe draft's you make on the talents, & merit of the State do not paralize our efforts I shoud think the Republican character of Maryland confirm'd—it is granted that this species of consumption carries with it a reproductive principle—when preferment is confered on distinguishd & acknowledgd worth, it fertilizes the fields of talent & virtue—they produce stronger[1] & better growth.—

I must now beg to present to your view, one of my earliest frends in this State—whose Republican principles withstood the first & ardent shocks of the [...] British Spirit.—Capt. Kilty was distiguishd in our Revolution, & by the uninterrupted confidence of the Legislature until Genl. Washington promoted him altho' avowedly hostile to the principles pursued under his Administration,—he has a wife & 6 young children, much unprovided for, & has been a sufferer as you know by the suppression of his Office.—I consider his talents of the highest grade among us,—his mind is strong, & altho' rather harsh & forbidden in his manner more benevolent [virtue] I believe does not inhabit an American Bosom—excuse the inacuracy of this hasty scraul as the Judge has sent for my Letter & believe me when I assure you of my entire respect & attachment   JOHN F: MERCER

RC (DNA: RG 59, LAR); several illegible words; endorsed by TJ as received 12 Nov. and so recorded in SJL; also endorsed by TJ: "Kilty to be employed."

For the Treasury secretary's consideration of John KILTY for the office of comptroller of the Treasury, see Gallatin to TJ, 19 Oct.

[1] MS: "strugr."

Opinions on the Common Law: The Case of William Hardin

I. OBSERVATIONS ON THE COMMON LAW AND HARDIN'S CASE, 11 NOV. 1802

II. ALBERT GALLATIN'S OPINION ON THE COMMON LAW AND HARDIN'S CASE, [CA. 11 NOV. 1802]

III. ROBERT SMITH'S OPINION ON THE COMMON LAW AND HARDIN'S CASE, [CA. 11 NOV. 1802]

EDITORIAL NOTE

The case of William Hardin evolved as an adjunct to the ongoing efforts by the Jefferson administration to bring accused Indian murderers John Williams, Martin Williams, and John Crutchelow to justice. Since committing their alleged crime several years earlier in what became the Indiana Territory, the three suspects had taken up residence in Kentucky, where they evaded repeated efforts by federal and state officials to apprehend them. Their success was in large part due to a sympathetic local population in the western states and territories, which was reluctant to submit an Indian killer to justice. John Williams had already escaped from the Knox County, Indiana, jail in May 1802 with the help, Governor William Henry Harrison believed, of local sympathizers. Subsequent efforts by federal and state officers were likewise thwarted by local residents, who tipped off the fugitives before they could be apprehended. The most flagrant episode of local citizens abetting the fugitives took place in Breckinridge County, Kentucky, where John Williams had been taken into custody and held at the county court house. A mob led by William Hardin gathered, overpowered the guards, and allowed Williams to escape (Mary K. Bonsteel Tachau, *Federal Courts in the Early Republic: Kentucky, 1789-1816* [Princeton, 1978], 128-33; *Terr. Papers*, 7:37, 55; Harry Innes to Henry Dearborn, 14 Oct. 1802, in DLC: Innes Papers; TJ to Dearborn, 6 Nov. 1802).

News of Hardin's actions apparently reached Jefferson and his cabinet sometime late in the spring of 1802. On 17 June, Henry Dearborn wrote the U.S. attorney in Kentucky, Joseph Hamilton Daveiss, and forwarded papers detailing the conduct of Hardin and his accomplices. Dearborn also enclosed an opinion by Attorney General Levi Lincoln on the "propriety of commencing a prosecution against Hardin and his associates," and closed his letter by informing Daveiss that "it is the wish of the President of the U. States that you should take all due measures for bringing said Hardin to justice" (FC in Lb in DNA: RG 75, LSIA). Although Lincoln's opinion is not extant, it apparently recommended that Daveiss pursue a prosecution of Hardin under the common law. Daveiss, a Federalist, replied by reminding Dearborn of "the public heat" that Republicans had raised when Federalists claimed the existence of a federal common law to justify prosecutions under the Sedition Act. He therefore requested further instructions before proceeding against Hardin, who was scheduled to appear before the November 1802 term of the U.S. district court in Kentucky (Tachau, *Federal Courts*, 130-132; DHSC, 3:321-2). A letter from Daveiss to Dearborn dated 16 Oct. 1802 relating to the case is recorded in War Department registers as having been received 11 Nov., but has not been found (DNA: RG 107, RLRMS).

At the height of the controversy over the Sedition Act during the late 1790s, Jefferson had been an ardent critic of Federalist claims for the existence of a federal common law of crimes. Writing to Edmund Randolph in 1799, Jefferson damned the novel doctrine as an "audacious, barefaced and sweeping pretension to a system of law for the US. without the adoption of their legislature and so infinitely beyond their power to adopt" (Vol. 31:169). As such, Jefferson viewed a common law prosecution against William Hardin with understandable caution, desiring neither to embarrass his attorney general nor leave himself open to accusations of hypocrisy from his political opponents. Jefferson's observations on the common law and Hardin's case printed below (Document I) first appeared in H. A. Washington's 1854 edition of Jefferson's writings, under the date 11 Nov. 1812. The current Editors have redated it from 1812 to 1802, since Hardin's case went before the U.S. district court in November of the latter year. It was reprinted by Andrew Lipscomb and Albert Bergh in 1903, but was not included in any other published collection of Jefferson's writings until this volume. The original manuscript has not been found (HAW, 9:485-9; L & B, 17:410-17).

In his observations (Document I), Jefferson begins by defining the common law of England and discussing how the system was adopted by the future states during the colonial era. He emphasizes the fact that every colony except Connecticut adopted the system at a different time, so that no two colonies possessed an identical version of the common law. Jefferson presumably made this point to undermine claims of a uniform federal common law. Under the Constitution, Jefferson notes, federal courts only possess cognizance of certain specified cases. Quoting from the Judiciary Act of 1789, he proceeds to explain that, except when provided for in the Constitution, treaties, or federal statutes, federal courts operating in the individual states shall have adopted the laws of that state, including the portions of the common law adopted by the state. Jefferson is careful to make explicit, however, that any common law claims by federal courts are made "not by any innate authority of its own, but by the adoption or enacting of it by the State authority." Opinions expressed to the contrary by certain federal and state judges remained "heretical" to Jefferson and his fellow Republicans. Any case presented to a federal court must therefore meet the specific criteria set forth carefully by Jefferson if it was to properly claim cognizance of the case.

When applying this standard to Hardin's case, however, Jefferson appears to equivocate. Citing an 1802 federal statute that made the murder of an Indian within a United States territory a capital offense, Jefferson asserts that the case is within the jurisdiction of Congress. Since Congress possessed power over the territories and could thus make laws necessary to carry their powers into execution, Jefferson holds that Congress could therefore make it a crime to protect such a murderer in any of the states. He appears less certain, however, as to whether the circumstances surrounding Hardin's actions justify federal cognizance of the case. Rather than committing himself to a definite opinion on the question, Jefferson instead calls for further examination of federal criminal statutes, the common and statute law of Kentucky as adopted by the federal courts, and any additional circumstances that might render state laws inapplicable to Hardin's offense. Thus, Jefferson lays out specific criteria for determining if the U.S. district court in Kentucky could rightfully claim cognizance, but leaves it for others to decide whether or not the criteria have been met.

The opinions of Albert Gallatin and Robert Smith on the case (Documents II and III) imply that the president circulated his observations among at least two or more of his cabinet secretaries, although opinions by James Madison or Henry Dearborn, if requested by the president, have not been found. Gallatin and Smith's comments also indicate that Jefferson and his colleagues had only partial information regarding the case, lacking both Lincoln's opinion and knowledge as to whether Hardin and his confederates attacked a federal or a state officer. Regardless, both Gallatin and Smith adamantly deny any federal cognizance of the case under the common law, with Gallatin taking the opportunity, like Jefferson, to refute Federalist arguments for the existence of a federal common law. The secretaries put forth nearly identical opinions regarding Hardin's actions. If he attacked a state officer, the case should be tried in the state courts. If the attack was against a federal officer, then Hardin could be tried in federal court under sections 22 or 23 of the 1790 act of Congress for punishing certain crimes against the United States. Jefferson likewise cited the 1790 statute toward the end of his opinion, but doubted whether the law covered the particular characteristics of Hardin's offense. Neither Gallatin nor Smith held such doubts, with each firmly believing that the federal district court had cognizance of Hardin's case under the 1790 act (U.S. Statutes at Large, 1:112-19).

At the close of his opinion, however, Gallatin offered perhaps the soundest advice on Hardin's case. "The subject is so complex and delicate," he observed, "that it seems to me better not to send to Kentucky the opinion which has been prepared nor any other on the subject generally." Better to let an occasional offender go unpunished, Gallatin suggested, "than to open that new field of jurisdiction to our courts; a field in which they shall be unrestrained by any legislative controul." This appears to have been the decision Jefferson arrived at as well. When Hardin was brought before the November 1802 term of the U.S. district court in Kentucky, his attorney moved that he be discharged, "the offense presented being only a misdemeanor at common law and not cognizable by this court." Daveiss, the U.S. attorney, likewise expressed his opinion that the federal court lacked jurisdiction in the case. Presiding judge Harry Innes agreed and Hardin was discharged. Shortly thereafter, Daveiss received a letter from Dearborn instructing the U.S. attorney not to proceed with the indictment (Tachau, *Federal Courts*, 131-2).

I. Observations on the Common Law and Hardin's Case

Observations on the force and obligation of the common law in the United States, on the occasion of Hardin's case, in Kentucky. November 11th, 1812 [i.e. 1802].

The *common law of England* is that system of law which was established in that country anterior to the Magna Charta, 9 H. 3, before which period no statutes are extant of record. It is used in contradistinction to the term *statute law*, which comprehends all the laws passed by their Parliament from the Magna Charta down to this day.

The term *common law* is used also in contradistinction to the *chancery*, as when we speak of the doctrines or courts of the common law, the doctrines or courts of chancery, and then include the *statute law* also. In which sense the term is used, must always depend on the subject matter.

On the settlement of the colonies now composing the United States, and the establishment of a legislature in each of them, that legislature, in some cases, finding that the enacting a complete code of laws, which should reach every transaction needing legislative regulation, would be far beyond their time and abilities, adopted, by an express act of their own, the laws of England as they stood at that date, comprehending the common law, statutes to that period, and the chancery law. In other cases, instead of adopting them by an express statute of their own, they considered themselves as having brought with them, and been, even on their passage, under the constant obligation of the laws of the mother country, and on their arrival they continued to practice them without any act of adoption, which practice or usage is evidence that there was an adoption by general consent. In the case of Connecticut, they did not adopt the common law of England at all as their basis, but declared by an act of their own, that the law of God, as it stood revealed in the Old and New Testament, should be the basis of their laws, to be subject to such alterations as they should make. In all the cases where the common law, or laws of England, were adopted either expressly or tacitly, the legislatures held of course, and exercised the power of making additions and alterations.

As the different States were settled at very different periods, and the adoption for each State was the laws of England as they stood at the moment of the adoption by the State, it is evident that the system as adopted in 1607 by Virginia, was one thing, as by Pennsylvania was another thing, as by Georgia, in 1759, was still a different one. And when to this is added the very diversified modifications of the adoptive code, produced by the subsequent laws passed by the legislatures of the different States, the system of common law in force in any one State on the 24th of September, 1789, when Congress assumed the jurisdiction given them by the Constitution, was very different from the systems in force at the same moment in the several other States: that in all of these the common law was in force by virtue of the adoption of the State, express or tacit, and that it was not in force in Connecticut, because they had never adopted it.

Having settled, by way of preliminary, to what extent, and by what authority, the common law of England is the law of each of the States, we will proceed to consider how far, and by what authority, it is the law of the United States as a national government.

By the Constitution, the General Government has jurisdiction in all cases arising under the Constitution, under the (constitutional) laws of the United States, and under treaties; in all cases, too, of ambassadors, of admiralty jurisdiction, where the United States is a party, between a State or its citizens, or another State or its citizens, or a foreign State or its citizens.

The General Government, then, had a right to take under their cognizance all these cases, and no others. This might have been done by Congress, by passing a complete code, assuming the whole field of their jurisdiction, and applying uniformly to every State, without any respect to the laws of that State. But, like the State legislatures, who had been placed before in a similar situation, they felt that it was a work of too much time and difficulty to be undertaken. Observing, therefore, that (except cases of piracy and murder on the high seas) all the cases within their jurisdiction must arise in some of the States, they declared by the act Sept. 24, 1789, c. 20, § 34, "That the laws of the several States, except where the Constitution, treaties, or statutes of the United States shall otherwise provide, shall be regarded as rules of decision in trials at *common law* in the courts of the United States in cases where they apply."

Here, then, Congress adopt for each State the laws of that State; and among the laws so adopted were portions of the common law, greater or less in different States, and in force, not by any innate authority of its own, but by the adoption or enacting of it by the State authority.

Now what was the opinion to which this was opposed? Several judges of the General Government declared that "the common law of England is the unwritten law of the United States in their national and federal capacity." A State judge, in a printed work, lays it down as "certainly wrong to say that the judiciary power of the nation can exercise no authority but what depends for its principle on acts of the national legislature." And then quoting the preamble to the Constitution of the United States, which says that its object is "to insure domestic tranquillity, promote the general welfare," &c., he adds, that "what is here expressed is the *common law* of the whole country," and that "whatever is in opposition to it, whether treason, insurrection, sedition, murder, riot, assults, batteries, thefts or robberies, may be punished as crimes, independent of any act of Congress." And opinions equivalent to this were declared by one party on the floor of Congress. This is the doctrine which the republicans declared heretical. They deny that Congress can pass any law not authorized by the Constitution, and that the judges can act on any law not authorized by Congress, or by the Constitution in very direct terms.

If the true doctrine then be, that certain portions of the common and statute law of England be in force in the different States by virtue of the adoption of that State, and in the federal courts of the same State by virtue of the adoption by Congress of the laws of that State within its limits, then whenever a case is presented to a federal court, they are to ask themselves the following questions:

1. Is this case within any of the definitions of jurisdiction given by the Constitution to the General Government? If it be decided that it is, then

2. Has Congress by any positive statute assumed cognizance of this case as permitted them by the Constitution? To determine this question, the judge must first look into the statutes of Congress generally; if he finds it not there, he must look into the laws of the State, as well as that portion of the English code which the State may have adopted, as the acts passed specially by the legislature. If the case be actually found provided for in these laws, another question still remains, viz.:

3. Is the law of the State applicable to the analogous case of the General Government? for it may happen that a law of the State, adapted perfectly to its own organization and local circumstances, may not tally with the different organization or circumstances of the federal government. If the difference be such as to defeat the application, it must be considered as a case unprovided for by Congress, and not cognizable in their courts. Just so parts of the common or statute law of England are found by the State judges inapplicable to their State from a difference of circumstance. These differences of circumstance will be shaded off from nothing to direct inconsistence, and it will be only by many decisions on a great variety of cases that the line will at length be drawn.

Let us apply these questions to Hardin's case, which is simply this: Congress, by an express statute, 1802, c. 13, § 6, have made the murder of an Indian within the territory of the United States punishable by death. A murder is committed on an Indian in that territory. The murderers fly to Kentucky. They are demanded by the Governor of Indiana of the Governor of Kentucky; under whose authority our officer attempting to take them, they are protected by Hardin and others in arms.

1. Is this case within the jurisdiction of Congress? *Answer.* Congress having a right "to make all rules and regulations respecting the territory of the United States," have declared this to be a case of murder. As they can "make all laws necessary and proper for carrying their powers into execution," they can make the protecting a murderer criminal in any part of the United States.

2. Has Congress assumed cognizance of the offence of Hardin? We must first examine whether the act of Congress, 1790, c. 9, § 22, takes in this offence. Then whether the laws of Kentucky, common, statute, or State law, as adopted by Congress, comprehend this offence.

3. Whether any difference of organization or other circumstance renders the law of Kentucky inapplicable to this offence, can be decided by those only who are particularly acquainted with that law.

Printed in HAW, 9:485-9.

SEVERAL JUDGES OF THE GENERAL GOVERNMENT: TJ here cites St. George Tucker's pamphlet, *Examination of the Question, "How Far the Common Law of England is the Law of the Federal Government of the United States?"* published in Richmond in 1800. In it, Tucker refers to the address by Chief Justice Oliver Ellsworth in the 1799 trial of Isaac Williams in Connecticut, in which Ellsworth stated his belief that "the common law of England is the unwritten law of the United States, in their national or federal capacity." Tucker added that Justice Bushrod Washington reportedly voiced "a similar opinion, upon another occasion." Newspaper accounts of Ellsworth's statement, however, quote the chief justice as stating "the common law of this country remains the same as it was before the revolution" (Tucker, *Examination of the Question*, 3; DHSC, 3:321-3; Hartford *Connecticut Courant*, 30 Sep. 1799). TJ also observed that Justice James Iredell endorsed the doctrine (DHSC, 2:467-9; Vol. 31:171n, 227).

A STATE JUDGE: James Sullivan. TJ quotes from Sullivan's printed work entitled *The History of Land Titles in Massachusetts* (Boston, 1801; Sowerby, No. 2155), 344-5.

ACT OF CONGRESS, 1790: Congress passed "An Act for the Punishment of Certain Crimes Against the United States" on 30 Apr. 1790. Under Section 22, persons guilty of obstructing or as-

saulting officers of the United States carrying out federal court orders were subject to up to 12 months imprisonment and $300 in fines. Section 23 of the act made it a federal crime to rescue persons convicted of treason, murder, or other capital crimes, with convicted offenders subject to the death penalty themselves. In addition, persons guilty of rescuing a prisoner accused of a capital offense before conviction, or persons convicted of any other offense against the United States, were subject to fines of up to $500 and imprisonment for up to one year (U.S. Statutes at Large, 1:112, 117).

II. Albert Gallatin's Opinion on the Common Law and Hardin's Case

[ca. 11 Nov. 1802]

William Hardin rescued or prevented the arrest of certain persons charged with the murder of some Indians.

Either the officer, who arrested or had a writ against the supposed murderers, was an officer of the United States acting under the authority of the United States, or he was an officer of the State of Kentucky acting under the state authority.

If he was an officer of the United States, Hardin's offence is cognizable under the 22d or 23d section of the Act for the punishment of crimes against the United States; and he may, therefore, be indicted, not at common law, but under the statute.

If the officer was a state officer acting under state authority, it is not perceivable how the rescue or resistance on Hardin's part can be considered as an offence against the United States, how it could be made punishable as such by any statute, or how it could as such be punishable at common law, supposing even that misdemeanors agt. the U. States not provided against by Statute, can be punished by the mere effect of the common law. But it was most certainly an offence against the State and as such may be punished in the State-courts.

What was the Attorney general's opinion is not known; only that he considered the offence as indictable, but whether under the Statute of the United States, or at common law as an offence agt. the U.

States, or at common law as an offence against the State, does not appear.

But, supposing Hardin's offence to be an offence or misdemeanor against the United States if the common law of Kentucky shall be considered as the law of the U. States for offences committed in that State, will it follow that the Courts of the United States can punish it although no mention made of it in the statute?

The judiciary power of the U. States extends to certain specific[1] cases defined in the Constitution and to all cases arising under the Constitution, laws, or treaties of the U. States.

Hence it has been maintained that no criminal prosecution could be instituted in the courts of the United except in some of the particularly specified cases, or for some offence defined by a statute law of the United States.

The partisans of constructive power have, on the contrary insisted that the federal[2] Courts could take congnizance of any offence against the United States, which, if committed against the State, would by the common law in force in such State, be indictable and punishable.

In support of this doctrine they have used two arguments; 1st. that the common law being acknowledged by several parts of the Constitution and by our laws as the law of the[3] United States, that description of offence called "offences at common law" were, if committed agt. the U. States, properly punishable by the judiciary as cases arising under the laws of the U. States—

2d. that every offence against the Govt. of the United States, being an offence against a legitimate authority derived from the Constitution was a case arising under the constitution & therefore punishable by the federal judiciary.

In answer to the first position, it has been insisted[4] that those parts of the Constitution which imply the existence of the common law, and particularly such of our laws as relate to the subject, do only recognize or adopt that law as a proper rule of decision in all such cases or trials as were within the jurisdiction of the judiciary of the United States, but do not bring within that jurisdiction any new cases,[5] by virtue of that recognition—

In answer to the second position, (which was recurred to in last resort) it was only said that the words "cases under the consititution" implied nothing more than Such as depended on a disputed construction of the constitution & were never intended to give a vague undefined extent of jurisdiction.

The question is shortly this

Shall[6] the judiciary take cognizance of supposed misdemeanors not defined or embraced by any statute, because they are of the description of offences called "offences at common law?"[7] Is it not better that now & then some misdemeanors which Congress has neglected to notice shall remain unpunished, than to open that new field of jurisdiction to our courts; a field in which they shall be unrestrained by any legislative controul.

The subject is so complex and delicate that it seems to me better not to send to Kentucky the opinion which has been prepared nor any other on the subject generally; but, taking the substance of what is contained in the first page of those observations, to write to the Attorney that if the act of rescue or resistance was against the State authority, it is in the State courts that Hardin ought to be indicted—that if the act was against the officers of the United States, he is indictable under the Statute & not at common law.

Respectfully submitted by   A. G.

MS (DLC: TJ Papers, 236:42311-12); undated; endorsed by Gallatin: "Common law. Kentucky case."

[1] Word interlined.
[2] Word interlined.
[3] Canceled: "land."
[4] Interlined in place of "stated."

[5] Gallatin first wrote "any cases, which" before altering the phrase to read as above.
[6] Canceled: "offences which if committed."
[7] Closing quotation mark supplied by Editors.

III. Robert Smith's Opinion on the Common Law and Hardin's Case

Mem.   [ca. 11 Nov. 1802]

If in a Case of Criminal jurisdiction there be not a Statute of Congress, *defining* the offence and *prescribing* the punishment, the prosecution cannot be sustained in any Court of the United States. If the federal judge does not find such an act of Congress, he cannot resort to the common or Statute law of the State. An action, which Congress may constitutionally declare to be an Offence, punishable in the Courts of the United States, is nevertheless not an Offence cognizable in those Courts, unless it has been so declared by Congress. A criminal prosecution cannot be founded but upon a positive Statute of Congress *defining* the offence and also *ascertaining* the punishment.

The Constitution does not say that certain acts are offences punishable in a Course of judicial proceeding. It only says that Congress shall have *power* to *define* and *punish* certain Offences. Until then Congress shall conceive it expedient to assume and exercise the power thus delegated to them of *defining* an Offence and of *ascertaining* the punishment, the jurisdiction of the federal Courts, with respect to such Offence, is the same as if no such power had been granted to Congress. It is to be considered merely as a power given, but not exercised. It is a special grant of powers *entrusted* to one department of the government and that department not deeming it necessary to exercise it, it is not to be assumed by another.

The act of Congress of 1789 did not adopt the Criminal Code or any part of the Criminal Code of the several States. It only adopted the rules of *practice* obtaining in the several States in *Trials* at Common Law. It was not a substantive grant of jurisdiction to the Courts. It was only an authority given to them to adopt in the trial of causes the rules of decision Obtaining in the respective States as a means of prosecuting to final judgments and Executions the cases submitted by the Statutes of Congress[1] to their Cognizance.

The case of Harden & others is not cognizable in any of the Courts of the United States. It is an Offence against the laws of Kentucky and as such cognizable in the Courts of that State. It is true that Congress had the power of *defining* and *punishing* this Offence and of giving the Courts of the United States cognizance of it. But not having *exercised* the power, these Courts cannot assume a jurisdiction over the Offence as a Crime recognised by the federal code. These Observations respecting the Case of Harden and others are made under the impression that the resistance had been to a State Officer. If it had been to an Officer acting under process for a Court or Judge of the United States, the federal Courts can take Cognizance of the case under the Act of Congress of 1790.

These murderers might have been apprehended in Kentucky under process from the federal Judge of Kentucky, and might also have been removed for Trial by the Marshall under a Warrant from such judge to the District wherein the Murder had been committed.

Rt Smith

MS (DLC: TJ Papers, 235:42174-6); undated; endorsed by TJ: "Common Law. official opinions."

[1] Preceding five words interlined.

To John Barnes

DEAR SIR   Washington Nov. 12. 1802

Martin Wanscher writes to me for 40. Dollars. there will then remain due to him about 90. or 100. D. which he will be drawing for from time to time. the demand of his balance having been expected to have laid over till the spring, will be an addition to my last estimate. I am to inclose the money to him in Alexandria, so that I suppose it should be in bills of that bank or the Washington. I do not know if those of the Columbia bank pass there. health and esteem.

                                              TH: JEFFERSON

RC (ViU: Edgehill-Randolph Papers); at foot of text in Barnes's hand: "NB. said $40. not charged—12 Nov. ℔ JB. in his Novr a/c—& not noticed by him untill after the Presidts Novr a/c had been closed—shall therefore charge it in his decr. a/c."; endorsed by Barnes: "$40–B, of Columbia"; endorsed by TJ in ink on verso: "Wanscher Martin. 40. D."

For TJ's account with Marten WANSCHER for plaster work done at Monticello, see Vol. 35:96n. TJ received $40 from Barnes on 13 Nov. and sent that amount to Wanscher the same day (MB, 2:1086). The president had made several payments to Wanscher recently. On 6 July, at Wanscher's request, TJ ordered Barnes to pay $16 to Alexander Wilson on Wanscher's account (MS in MHi; in TJ's hand and signed by him; written on note from Wanscher to TJ, dated 3 July, requesting payment to Wilson, in James Dinsmore's hand and attested by him, signed by Wanscher; signed by Wilson acknowledging payment). The plasterer also received payments of $14 and $10 on 7 and 29 Sep., respectively (MB, 2:1077, 1080, 1081). On 2 Nov., TJ ordered Barnes to pay Wanscher an additional $30 (MS in MHi; in TJ's hand and signed by him; signed by Wanscher acknowledging payment; see MB, 2:1085).

MY LAST ESTIMATE: see Barnes to TJ, [ca. 1 Nov. 1802].

To David Gelston

SIR   Washington Nov. 12. 1802.

The motives which induce the writer of a letter to withold his name are generally suspicious, but not however always blameable. I consider anonymous letters as sufficient foundation for enquiry into the facts they communicate. as the person who is the subject of the inclosed letter is I presume within your department, I inclose it to you merely that you may do in the case exactly what you would have done had it been addressed to you instead of me. men of worth do sometimes languish in an obscurity from which they would be raised were their worth known. whether that is the present case your enquiries may decide; and if it be so, I have no doubt you would keep him in your eye as a person to be taken care of. Accept assurances of my esteem & respect.

                                              TH: JEFFERSON

PrC (DLC); at foot of text: "David Gelston esq." Enclosure: Anonymous to TJ, 6 Nov., recorded in SJL as received from New York on 11 Nov. with notation "Colo. Walter Blicker," but not found.

A merchant, who was born in Suffolk County, Long Island, David Gelston (1744-1828) was an early supporter of the colonial cause, signing the articles of association in 1775. He served in the New York provincial congress from 1775 to 1777, was a member of the New York state constitutional convention in 1777, and held other positions in state government, including speaker of the assembly in 1784 and 1785. He moved to New York City in 1786 and three years later became a member of the last Confederation Congress. He represented the Southern District in the state senate for several terms between 1791 and 1802. An Anti-Federalist who became an ardent Republican, Gelston succeeded James Nicholson as president of the Democratic Society of the City of New-York in 1794. Gelston was among the political associates whom Burr recommended for office in March 1801. TJ appointed him collector of New York in early July of that year, a position he held until 1820 (*Biog. Dir. Cong.*; Philip S. Foner, ed., *The Democratic-Republican Societies, 1790-1800* [Westport, Conn., 1976], 171, 183-4; Kline, *Burr*, 1:225-6; Nancy Isenberg, *Fallen Founder: The Life*

of Aaron Burr [New York, 2007], 103, 105, 126, 140, 226; RS, 1:282n; Vol. 33:11-12, 330-2; Vol. 34:513, 515n; Vol. 35:274-5n; Vol. 36:85).

SUBJECT OF THE INCLOSED LETTER: probably Walter Bicker, one of the weighers in charge of the public scales in the surveyor's office at the New York custom house. Bicker received almost $1,400 in commissions and fees in 1800 (New York *Daily Advertiser*, 5 Aug. 1800; ASP, *Miscellaneous*, 1:270; *Longworth's American Almanac, New-York Register, and City-Directory, for the Twenty Seventh Year of American Independence* [New York, 1802], 147). For Bicker's military service, see Washington, *Papers, Rev. War Ser.*, 16:187n and same, *Pres. Ser.*, 2:449-50.

On 22 Nov., Gelston responded from New York that he had received TJ's letter of the 12th with its enclosure. He continued: "Many of the circumstances related in the anonymous communication are within my knowlege—the Gentleman therein mentioned I am acquainted with, and tho' I feel disposed to render him all the assistance in my power, I do not think it would be prudent in me to appoint him to a more important office.—I am, Sir, very respectfully, your most obedient Servt." (RC in MHi; at foot of text: "Thomas Jefferson Esquire"; endorsed by TJ as received 25 Nov. and so recorded in SJL).

From James Monroe

DEAR SIR   Richmond Novr. 12. 1802

The inclosed was lately sent me by Col: Newton to be forwarded to you.   Since my last R. Evers Lee has been here and a suitable occasion presenting itself, I confered with him on the subject of the comr of bankruptcy at Norfolk, in which he informed me that William Bennett a merchant the brother of the person mentioned in my last was the most suitable of the two. He lamented that there was no one of the republicans who held that standing in the town, since Mr. Tazewell's resignation whose appointment wod. be impressive in the views which are desirable. He spoke well of Nimmo, a lawyer, as being now more especially, sound in his principles well informed diligent & moral, and approaching nearer that station than any other, and Wm. B. as standing next to him: but that he was much inclined to think the appointment of a Mr. Wheeler, provided he would serve of wh. he was ignorant, as one of them, would on the whole produce a good effect in the place. Either he, Col: Newton or Mr. Tazewell might sound him on the subject. He represents Wheeler to be a moderate respectable & intelligent federalist. I have no doubt, where the theatre is well understood and it appears evident that the appointment of a federalist of the above character, especially to a subaltern office in a comn. a majority of whom are republicans, will produce a conciliary effect, that it is sound policy to do so. His refusal to serve puts others on their guard & indisposes them also. I shod. have requested Mr Lee to sound him but thought it might be improper. I am

very sincerely yr. friend & servt   JAS. MONROE

RC (DNA: RG 59, LAR); endorsed by TJ as received 17 Nov. and "Nimmo to be Commr. bkrptcy. Norfolk" and so recorded in SJL. Enclosure: probably Thomas Newton to TJ, 25 Oct. 1802, which TJ also received on 17 Nov.

MR. WHEELER: probably merchant Luke Wheeler, a director of the Bank of the United States branch in Norfolk and a future mayor of the city (*Simmons' Norfolk Directory* [Norfolk, 1801], 32, 88; Spencer Tucker, *Stephen Decatur: A Life Most Bold and Daring* [Annapolis, 2005], 81).

Appendix I

Jefferson kept an ongoing list of appointments and removals, which extended throughout his two terms as president, with entries extending from 5 Mch. 1801 to 23 Feb. 1809. For the first two installments of this list, see Vol. 33, Appendix I, List 4 and Vol. 37, Appendix I. This third installment continues at 1 July 1802 and includes the entries for the period covered by this volume. This was a working list, which Jefferson updated, often partially canceling a name and adding "decld." to the entry when he learned an appointee had declined the office. Jefferson usually entered the names on his list as he signed the commissions sent to him by the State Department. This explains why the date on the commission is often a day or two before the entry date on Jefferson's list. Bankruptcy commissions for Connecticut and Delaware, dated 1 July, are entered below at 2 July. On 6 July, the president listed his choices for bankruptcy commissioners for Norfolk, Virginia; New Jersey; Boston and Newburyport, Massachusetts; and Portland, Maine. The State Department issued commissions for them all the same day. Jefferson added them to his list below at 7 and 9 July. While at Monticello, Jefferson did not always know exactly when commissions were issued. After his return to Washington in early October, the president apparently requested that the State Department send him a list of the commissions issued while he was away. That State Department communication provides the information for the entries between 28 July and 11 Oct. in the list below (for one discrepancy, that of Joseph Wood, see Memorandum from the State Department, printed at 18 Oct.). The commission for William Carey as collector at Yorktown, Virginia, dated 20 Sep., was canceled on the State Department list and does not appear on the list below because it was already known that Carey had declined the appointment; Thomas Archer was appointed in his place with a commission dated 11 Oct.

Jefferson added a numeral in pencil in the left margin by several entries, evidence that he used this ongoing list to compile another list of appointments and removals in 1803 (see Vol. 33, Appendix I, List 3). TJ penciled the numeral "1" by the entries for J. P. G. Muhlenberg, Tench Coxe, William R. Lee, and George Wentworth. Their names, along with that of Abraham Bloodgood, appear on Jefferson's 1803 list under the first category of appointments "in place of those resigned, declined, promoted or dead." He penciled "6" alongside the entries for John Gibaut, Ralph Cross, and John Shore. In the 1803 list, they appear in seventh category, being "removals on the principle of giving some participation in office to republicans," and to disarm those who were using "their official influence to oppose the order of things established." A "7" is penciled by Joseph Farley and an "8" by Robert Anderson New, who appear under categories eight and nine, respectively. The eighth included those appointed in place of removals "on mixed grounds including delinquency or misconduct" and the ninth for "Misconduct or delinquency" only. For Jefferson's compilation of the 1803 list, see also Noble E. Cunningham, *The Jeffersonian Republicans in Power: Party Operations, 1801-1809* (Chapel Hill, 1963), 61-3.

List of Appointments

July. 1. John P. Vanness   ⎫ Majors of militia Columbia.
       William Lee   ⎭

    2. George Tucker. Commr. bkrpt Virga vice Hay.

       Hezekiah Huntington ⎫
       *<Jonat>*han Bull.   ⎬ Hartford.
       Joseph Hart
       <John> Dodd   ⎭

       Henry Waggaman Edwards ⎫
       Elihu Munson   ⎬ N. Haven   ⎬ Commrs. bkrpt
       Jehosaphat Starr   for Connecticut.
       *<John N>*ichols   ⎭

       Elisha Hyde decld. ⎫
       Jonathan Frisbie   ⎬ New London
       Nichol Fosdick
       Jacob DeWitt   ⎭

       French Mc.Mullin. Newcastle
       James Brobson.   ⎫ Commrs.
       John Warner.   ⎬ Wilmington   ⎬ bkrpt
       Isaac H. Starr.   ⎭   ⎭ Delaware.

       Francis Peyton Colo. Commdt. 2d legion ⎫ militia of
       Henry Rose Major   ⎭ Columbia.
       John Mc.kinney Majr.

    6. James Clarke of N.Ca. Surveyor & Inspector of the port of
       Tombstone N.C.[1] see Nov. 20. & qu? new
       William White of Virga Survr. & Inspectr. of the port of
       East river Virga. new
       Griffin Grene of N.W. territy. Collector for district of Mari-
       etta. & Inspector of same. new

    7. Silas Crane of N. J. Collector & Inspector of district of Lit-
       tle Egg harbour. see May 14.
       Francis Armistead. Virga. Collector of East river. new
       *<Lyttle>*ton W. Tazewell. decld. ⎫
       Richd Evers Lee   ⎬ Norfolk. Commrs.
       <Moses> Myers decld.   bkrptcy for Virga.
       Thomas Blanchard   ⎭

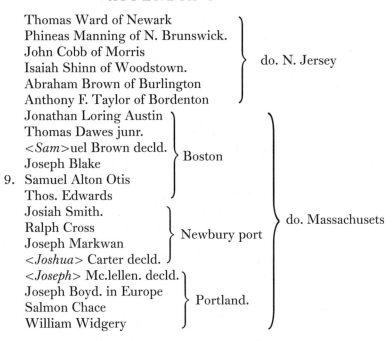

Thomas Ward of Newark
Phineas Manning of N. Brunswick.
John Cobb of Morris
Isaiah Shinn of Woodstown.
Abraham Brown of Burlington
Anthony F. Taylor of Bordenton
} do. N. Jersey

Jonathan Loring Austin
Thomas Dawes junr.
<*Sam*>uel Brown decld.
Joseph Blake
9. Samuel Alton Otis
Thos. Edwards
} Boston

Josiah Smith.
Ralph Cross
Joseph Markwan
<*Joshua*> Carter decld.
} Newbury port

<*Joseph*> Mc.lellen. decld.
Joseph Boyd. in Europe
Salmon Chace
William Widgery
} Portland.

} do. Massachusets

1802.
July 8. Thomas Stuart Atty of the US. in Tennissee. v. Wm. P. Anderson resigned.

<*Jacob*> Crowninshield. Salem decld.
<*Nathan*> Danna. Beverley decld.
Isaac Story. M.[2] Supersedd.
Wm <*Burley*>. Beverley decld.
} Commrs. bkrptcy Mass.

John Swartwout Marshal for N. York
John Smith. do. Pensylva.
Joseph Scott. do. Virginia.
Henry Tooley N.C. Surveyor & Inspector of the port of Slade's creek N.C. new

Aug. 1. Joseph Wood. Register of the land office at Marietta. vice Peregrine Foster resigned.

27. William Cleveland
Killam
} of Salem, Commrs. bkrptcy Mass.

Sep. 10.[3] Joseph Storey of   to be Commr. bkrptcy Mass.

July 28 Peter Muhlenberg. Collector of customs for district of Pensva. v. George Latimer resigned.

Tench Coxe Supervisor of the revenue for district of Pensva v. P. Muhlenberg. promoted[4]

31. Wm R. Lee Collector for Salem & Beverley vice Joseph Hiller <*removed*> resigned.

Aug. 1. John Selman commissioner on Symes's land claims. v. Wm. Goforth resigned[5]

Aug. 11. Danl. Bissell Collector for Massac. & Inspector of revenue. vice   Chribbs removed for infamy

25. Joseph Farley. Mass.[6] Collector & Inspector for the district of Waldoborough in Mass. vice Joshua Head removd. delinquent

John Gibaut, Mass Collector for Gloucester. vice William Tuck removed

George Wentworth Inspector & Surveyor of the revenue for Mass.[7] Portsmouth vice Saml Adams decd.

Joseph Wilson Mass Collector & Inspector for distr. of Marblehead. vice Saml. R. Gerry removd for delinquency.

Ralph Cross Collector Mass for Newbury port. vice Dudley A. Tyng removed.

28. Abraham Bloodgood N.Y.[8] Surveyor & inspector for Port of Albany. vice Henry J. Bogart resigned

Sep. 6. John Shore Collector for Petersbg vice William Heath. removed.

Oct. 11. Thos. Archer Collector & inspector for Yorktown vice William Reynolds dead.

Robert Anderson New Collector & Inspector of the revenue for the district of Louisville. vice James Mc.Connel re-movd. delinquent

18. Wm. Richardson Davie. Commr. to hold a treaty between the Tuscarora Indians & Agents of N. Carolina.

20. Robert Elliott Cochran. Marshal S.C. vice Charles B. Cochran resigned.

Nov. 2. David Ker. third judge of the Missipi territory vice Daniel Tilton resigned.

John Easson Surveyor & Inspector of the port of Smithfield Virga vice   Blow resigned.

MS (DLC: TJ Papers, 186:33096-7); entirely in TJs hand, including cancellations and emendations made at later sittings; being the continuation of a list that extends from 5 Mch. 1801 to 23 Feb. 1809; for the preceding sections of the list, see Vol. 33:674-9 and Vol. 37:697-700; TJ also added, while compiling a later list, numbers in pencil in the left margin, which have not been reproduced here (see Editorial Note above).

SEE NOV. 20: at that date TJ recorded Jehu Nichols's appointment as surveyor and inspector at Tombstone, North Carolina, in place of "James Clarke resigned." In fact, James West Clark declined the post at the newly established port of delivery and the commissions were returned (same; Vol. 37:394-5; Gallatin to TJ, [23 Oct. 1802]).

At 14 May 1802, TJ entered the appointment of SILAS CRANE as collector at Little Egg Harbor, New Jersey. TJ sent Crane's nomination to the Senate on 27 Apr. and he was confirmed on the 29th. At that time, however, he was not nominated as inspector of the port. This oversight was rectified in January 1803, when TJ submitted the nomination of Crane "who is Collector" to be "Inspector of the revenue for the same" (Vol. 33:679; Vol. 37:325, 348; TJ to the Senate, 11 Jan. 1803, second letter).

[1] Remainder of entry added later by TJ. At the same time he also added "new" here and at other entries below.

[2] That is, Marblehead (Vol. 37:708).

[3] TJ probably added this date at a later sitting. The State Department dated this "13" Sep. (see Memorandum at 18 Oct.).

[4] Entry interlined.

[5] Entry interlined, including date.

[6] Here and in the next four entries TJ interlined "Mass."

[7] Interlined in place of "Portsmouth," which TJ had written twice.

[8] TJ interlined "N.Y."

Appendix II

Letters Not Printed in Full

EDITORIAL NOTE

In keeping with the editorial method established for this edition, the chronological series includes "in one form or another every available letter known to have been written by or to Thomas Jefferson" (Vol. 1:xv). Most letters are printed in full. In some cases, the letter is not printed but a detailed summary appears at the document's date (for an example, see Benjamin H. Latrobe to TJ, 24 Oct. 1802). Other letters have been described in annotation, which, for the period covered by this volume, are listed in this appendix. Arranged in chronological order, this list includes for each letter the correspondent, date, and location in the volumes where it is described. Among the letters included here are brief letters of transmittal, multiple testimonials recommending a particular candidate for office, repetitive letters from a candidate seeking a post, and official correspondence that the president saw in only a cursory way. In other instances, documents are described in annotation due to the near illegibility of the surviving text. Using the list in this appendix, the table of contents, and Appendix III (correspondence not found but recorded in Jefferson's Summary Journal of Letters), readers will be able to reconstruct Jefferson's chronological epistolary record from 1 July to 12 Nov. 1802.

From Mitchell & Buel, 2 July. Noted at TJ to Mitchell & Buel, 22 June 1802.

From Henry Dearborn, 8 July. Noted at Dearborn to TJ, 8 July 1802.

From George Deneale, 10 July. Noted at William Kilty and James M. Marshall to TJ, 10 July 1802.

From Daniel Carroll Brent, 11 July. Noted at William Kilty and James M. Marshall to TJ, 10 July 1802.

From Fulwar Skipwith, 30 July. Noted at John Jones Waldo to TJ, 21 Sep. 1802.

From Joseph Scott, 9 Aug. Noted at TJ to Joseph Scott, 1 Aug. 1802.

To Henry Dearborn, 16 Aug. Noted at TJ to Craven Peyton, 16 Aug. 1802.

From Archibald McElroy, Jr., 2 Sep. Noted at William Duane to TJ, 10 June 1801.

From James McCrea, 13 Sep. Noted at David Thomas to TJ, 3 Mch. 1803.

To Robert Patterson, 16 Oct. Noted at TJ to Patterson, 16 Oct. 1802.

From Albert Gallatin, 26 Oct. Noted at Gallatin to TJ, 25 Oct. 1802.

From Albert Gallatin, 28 Oct. Noted at TJ to Gallatin, 28 Oct. 1802.

From William Judd, 28 Oct. Noted at Connecticut Republicans to TJ, 27 Oct. 1802.

From Christopher Gore, 3 Nov. Noted at Gore to TJ, 10 Oct. 1802.

Appendix III

Letters Not Found

E D I T O R I A L   N O T E

This appendix lists chronologically letters written by and to Jefferson during the period covered by this volume for which no text is known to survive. Jefferson's Summary Journal of Letters provides a record of the missing documents. For incoming letters, Jefferson typically recorded in SJL the date that the letter was sent and the date on which he received it. He sometimes included the location from which it was dispatched and an abbreviated notation indicating the government department to which it pertained: "N" for Navy, "S" for State, "T" for Treasury, and "W" for War.

From Ninian McGruder, 1 July; received 2 July from Georgetown.

From Samuel J. Potter and others, 1 July; received 29 July from Newport, R.I.; notation: "Wm. Nicholls collector v. Ellery."

From Charles Bulfinch, 3 July; received 10 July from Boston; notation: "for office."

From Gibson & Jefferson, 3 July; received 8 July from Richmond.

From Watson & Higginbotham, 4 July; received 7 July from North Milton.

From Benjamin Brown, 5 July; received 11 July; connected by a brace with the following entry.

From Thomas Wells, Jr., 5 July; received 11 July; connected by a brace with the preceding entry.

To William Maddox, 6 July.

From Caleb Strong, 6 July; received 12 July from Boston.

From John Wayles Eppes, 8 July; received 13 July from Bermuda Hundred.

From Gabriel Lilly, 8 July; received 11 July from Monticello.

From Samuel Thurber, Jr., 9 July; received 22 Nov. from Providence.

From John Bird, 10 July; received 14 July from New Castle, Del.; notation: "to be Collector vice Mc.lane."

From DeWitt Clinton, 10 July; received 15 July from Newtown; connected by a brace with entries for letters received the same day from Thomas Jenkins of 7 July and Samuel Osgood of 10 July, with notation: "Isaac Dayton to be collector of Hudson vice Tenbroeck."

From Samuel Osgood, 10 July; received 15 July from New York; for notation, see preceding entry.

From Robert Rives, 10 July; received 25 July from Warminster.

From James Dinsmore, 12 July; received 19 July from Monticello.

From James Monroe, 12 July; received 16 July from Richmond; notation: "Chas. Jouett Indn. affairs."

From Joseph Stanton, Jr., 12 July; received 20 July from Charlestown, R.I.

To Anne Cary Randolph, 13 July.

From John Perry, 14 July; received 19 July from Monticello.

From William Geddy, 16 July; received 29 July from Richmond.

From William Wardlaw, 16 July; received 19 July from Charlottesville.

From John Wayles Eppes, 18 July; received 25 July.

From Burgess Griffin, 19 July; received 5 Aug. from Poplar Forest.

From Charles McKnight, 19 July; received 20 July from Alexandria; connected by a brace with entries for letters received the same day from George Wise of 19 July and Alexander Kerr of 20 July, with notation: "resigng. commns. W."

From Josiah Smith, 19 July; received 12 Aug. from Pembroke, Mass.

From John Stewart, 19 July; received 25 July from Alexandria; notation: "Lieutt."; connected by a brace with entries for letters received the same day from Josiah Faxon of 20 July and John Johnston of 21 July, with notation "resign Commns. W."

From George Wise, 19 July; received 20 July from Alexandria; for notation, see from Charles McKnight, 19 July, above.

From Josiah Faxon, 20 July; received 25 July from Alexandria; notation: "Captn.," and see from John Stewart, 19 July, above.

From Alexander Kerr, 20 July; received 20 July from Washington; for notation, see from Charles McKnight, 19 July, above.

From Ferdinand Marsteller, 20 July; received 31 July from Alexandria; notations: "2d Lt. militia" and "resigns. W."

To John F. Mercer, 20 July.

From John Johnston, 21 July; received 25 July from Alexandria; notation: "Lieutt.," and see from John Stewart, 19 July, above.

From Joseph Stanton, Jr., 24 July; received 5 Aug. from Charlestown, R.I.

From John Minor, 25 July; received 29 July from Fredericksburg.

To Henry Sheaff, 26 July; notation: "6. dozen Sauterne."

From Isaac Darneille, 27 July; received 29 Aug. from Cahokia.

From William Short, 28 July; received 5 Aug. from Norfolk.

From Joel Barlow, 29 July; received 5 Oct. from Paris; notation: "Waldo."

From Thomas G. Addison, 30 July; received 5 Aug.; notation: "resigns Captcy. W."

From Benjamin Dame, 30 July; received 12 Aug. from Newington; notation: "W."

From Robert Stewart, 30 July; received 5 Aug. from Alexandria; notation: "resigns Lieutcy."

From John Gibson; received 31 July from Clarke Co., Indiana Territory; notation: "W."

To Anna Scott Marks, 31 July.

From George Balfour, 1 Aug.; received 26 Aug.

From Isaac Mansfield, 2 Aug.; received 16 Aug. from Marblehead; notation: "N."

To William Geddy, 3 Aug.

From Archibald Alexander, 4 Aug.; received 16 Aug. from New Castle, Del.

To William Short, 5 Aug.

To Burgess Griffin, 6 Aug.

From William Short, 6 Aug.; received 10 Aug. from Richmond.

From William Henry Harrison, 8 Aug.; received 29 Aug. from Vincennes.

To John Thomson Mason, 8 Aug.

From Benjamin Stoddert, 8 Aug.; received 8 Aug. from Georgetown.

From House & Saltonstall, 9 Aug.; received 25 Aug. from New London.

From Joel Barlow, 12 Aug.; received 8 Nov. from Paris; notation: "J. Lyle."

From James Lovell, 12 Aug.; received 22 Aug. from Boston.

To   Bradman, 13 Aug.

From Randolph Jefferson, 13 Aug.; received 14 Aug.

To Randolph Jefferson, 14 Aug.

From Thomas Newton, 14 Aug.; received 26 Aug. from Norfolk: notation: "Balfour Superintt. Marine hosp."

To Kemp Catlett, 15 Aug.

To Richard Anderson, 16 Aug.; notation: "Postmaster Milton."

From Craven Peyton, 16 Aug.; received 16 Aug.

From William Short, 17 Aug.; received 19 Aug. from Washington.

From Foster Swift, 18 Aug.; received 26 Aug. from Taunton, Mass.; notation: "W."

From William Short, 19 Aug.; received 26 Aug. from Georgetown.

From Richard Anderson, 22 Aug.; received 22 Aug. from Milton.

From John F. Mercer, 22 Aug.; received 2 Nov. from Annapolis; notation: "Lemar to be Consul Madeira."

From Caleb Strong, 23 Aug.; received 2 Sep. from Boston; notation: "W."

From John Harris, 24 Aug.; received 29 Aug. from Baltimore; notation: "N."

To Craven Peyton, 24 Aug.

From Craven Peyton, 25 Aug.; received 25 Aug.

From Samuel Sheild, 25 Aug.; received 2 Sep. from York Co., Va.; notation: "Wm. Carey to be Collectr. York."

From William Carey, 26 Aug.; received 2 Sep. from York, Va.; notation: "to be Collector York."

From Craven Peyton, 27 Aug.; received 28 Aug.

From Inhabitants of Cahokia; received 29 Aug.; notation: "petition."

From Inhabitants of Louisiana; received 29 Aug.; notation: "petition."

To Henry Dearborn, 31 Aug.; notation: "Storer's commn bkrptcy."

From Burgess Griffin, 1 Sep.; received 11 Sep. from Poplar Forest.

To Randolph Jefferson, 2 Sep.

From Randolph Jefferson, 2 Sep.; received 2 Sep.

To Richard Overton, 2 Sep.

To John Barnes, 3 Sep.

From Samuel Nobbs, 4 Sep.; received 6 Oct. from Charleston; notation: "T."

To Burgess Griffin, 5 Sep.; notation: "by Nace."

To Burgess Griffin, 5 Sep.; notation: "by post."

From Samuel J. Potter, 6 Sep.; received 19 Sep. from South Kingston, R.I.; notation: "Nichols Collectr. Newp."

To John Barnes, 7 Sep.

To Randolph Jefferson, 7 Sep.

From John Bird, 8 Sep.; received 16 Sep. from New Castle, Del.

From William Thornton, 8 Sep.; received 9 Sep. from Orange.

To John Barnes, 9 Sep.

From Benjamin Brown, received 11 Sep.

From Meriwether Lewis, 12 Sep.; received 12 Sep.

To William Meriwether, 12 Sep.

To Burgess Griffin, 16 Sep.

To John Barnes, 17 Sep.

From Burgess Griffin, 20 Sep.; received 24 Sep. from Lynchburg.

To Thomas Carr, 22 Sep.; notation: "Colo Bell's acct. £29-4."

From Nehemiah Knight, 23 Sep.; received 5 Oct. from Cranston, R.I.

From Samuel J. Potter; received 23 Sep. from South Kingston, R.I.; notation: "Wm. Nichols to be Collector Newport."

To John Barnes, 24 Sep.

From Burgess Griffin, 29 Sep.; received 5 Oct. from Lynchburg.

From William Wardlaw, 29 Sep.; received 29 Sep.

From François de Navoni, 30 Sep.; received 16 Feb. 1803 from Cagliari, Sardinia.

To Michael Hope, 1 Oct.

From Brown, Rives & Co., 4 Oct.; received 7 Oct. from Richmond.

From George Jefferson, 4 Oct.; received 6 Oct. from Richmond.

To Benjamin Brown, 5 Oct.; notation: "285.83."

From James Mitchell, 5 Oct.; received 6 Oct. from Alexandria; notation: "N."

From William Short, 5 Oct.; received 8 Oct. from Richmond.

To Thomas Wells, Jr., 5 Oct.; notation: "133.33."

To Martin Dawson, 7 Oct.; notation: "1000."

From Samuel Dyer, 7 Oct.; received 13 Oct. from Albemarle.

To Gabriel Lilly, 7 Oct.

To William Stewart, 7 Oct.

From George Purdie, 8 Oct.; received 13 Oct. from Smithfield.

From John Hyndman Purdie, 8 Oct.; received 13 Oct. from Smithfield; notation: "to be Surveyor Smithfield vice Thos. Blow resigned."

From Thomas Wells, Jr., 8 Oct.; received 10 Oct.

From Martin Dawson, 10 Oct.; received 13 Oct. from Milton.

From William Short, 12 Oct.; received 15 Oct. from Richmond.

From Charles Willing Byrd, 14 Oct.; received 4 Nov. from Cincinnati; notation: "S."

From John Perry, 14 Oct.; received 21 Oct. from Columbia.

To John Barnes, 15 Oct.

To Samuel Dyer, 15 Oct.

To Gabriel Lilly, 15 Oct.

From Samuel Thurber, Jr., 15 Oct.; received 22 Nov. from Providence; notation: "for office."

From John Hog, 16 Oct.; received 17 Oct. from Fredericksburg.

To Joseph Anderson, 18 Oct.; connected by a brace with entries for letters sent the same day to Abraham Baldwin, William Cocke, William Dickson, James Jackson, Nathaniel Macon, and John Milledge with notation: "Commrs. bkrptcy."

To Abraham Baldwin, 18 Oct.; for notation, see the preceding entry.

To William Cocke, 18 Oct.; for notation, see to Joseph Anderson, 18 Oct., above.

To William Dickson, 18 Oct.; for notation, see to Joseph Anderson, 18 Oct., above.

From David Higginbotham, 18 Oct.; received 20 Oct. from Milton.

To James Jackson, 18 Oct.; for notation, see to Joseph Anderson, 18 Oct., above.

To John Milledge, 18 Oct.; for notation, see to Joseph Anderson, 18 Oct., above.

From J. P. G. Muhlenberg, 18 Oct.; received 26 Oct. from Philadelphia; connected by a brace with entries for letters received the same day from Caspar Wistar of 15 Oct., Michael Leib of 19 Oct., William Barton of 22 Oct., and Thomas McKean of 22 Oct., with notation: "Kuhn P. junr. to be Consul at Gibraltar."

From Henry Sheaff, 18 Oct.; received 20 Oct. from Philadelphia.

From James Monroe, 19 Oct.; received 31 Oct. from Richmond.

From William Short, 19 Oct.; received 19 Oct. from Georgetown.

From Lilburne Lewis, 20 Oct.; received 24 Oct. from Mont Gallatin.

From Gabriel Lilly, 20 Oct.; received 24 Oct. from Monticello.

From Thomas Newton, 21 Oct.; received 26 Oct. from Norfolk.

From Thomas Newton, 21 Oct.; received 27 Oct. from Norfolk; notation: "John Easson Surveyor Smithfield."

From Anonymous; received 22 Oct.; notation: "Euriskotes."

From Thomas McKean, 22 Oct.; received 26 Oct. from Lancaster; for notation, see from J. P. G. Muhlenberg, 18 Oct., above.

To John Perry, 22 Oct.

To Richard Price, 22 Oct.

To Lilburne Lewis, 25 Oct.

From William Short, 25 Oct.; received 25 Oct.

From William Bache, 26 Oct.; received 31 Oct. from Edgehill.

From Stephen Sayre, 27 Oct.; received 29 Oct. from Philadelphia.

From Christopher Clark, 28 Oct.; received 7 Nov. from Mt. Prospect.

From Benjamin Brown, 29 Oct.; received 31 Oct. from Charlottesville.

From Francis Eppes, 30 Oct.; received 7 Nov. from Eppington.

To John Barnes, 31 Oct.

From James [i.e. Jared?] Mansfield, October; received 31 Oct. from West Point.

To Benjamin Brown, 2 Nov.

From Lilburne Lewis, 4 Nov.; received 10 Nov. from Mont Gallatin.

From Anonymous, 6 Nov.; received 11 Nov. from New York; notation: "Colo. Walter Blicker."

From Benjamin H. Latrobe, 8 Nov.; received 11 Nov. from Phila.

From Louis Landais, 8 Nov.; received 20 Nov. from Fort Moultrie; notation: "W."

To Gabriel Lilly, 9 Nov.; notation: "685. D. Price, Peyton, Allen, Perry, Brown."

To David Higginbotham, 9 Nov.

To Joseph Moran, 9 Nov.; notation: "200. D."

From William Stewart, 9 Nov.; received 14 Dec. from Monticello.

From William Stewart, 10 Nov.; received 14 Dec. from Monticello.

Appendix IV

Financial Documents

E D I T O R I A L   N O T E

This appendix briefly describes, in chronological order, the orders and invoices pertaining to Jefferson's finances during the period covered by this volume that are not printed in full or accounted for elsewhere in this volume. The orders for payments to Étienne Lemaire and Joseph Dougherty pertain, for the most part, to expenses associated with running the President's House. The *Memorandum Books* are cited when they are relevant to a specific document and provide additional information.

Order on John Barnes for payment of $243.17 to Étienne Lemaire, Washington, 5 July (MS in University Archives, Autographs and Historical Documents, Westport, Connecticut, 1994; in TJ's hand and signed by him; signed by Lemaire acknowledging payment). TJ recorded this transaction as payment of Lemaire's accounts from June 27 to July 3 for provisions, stores, wood, wine, contingencies, and servants' wages (MB, 2:1076).

Order on John Barnes for payment of $7.08 to Joseph Dougherty, Washington, 12 July (MS in MHi; in TJ's hand and signed by him; signed by Dougherty acknowledging payment; endorsed by Barnes as paid on 12 July). TJ recorded this transaction as payment for saddlery, boot straps, hat repair, and portage (MB, 2:1077).

Order on John Barnes for payment of $74.21 to Étienne Lemaire, Washington, 12 July (MS in Christie's, New York City, 1996; in TJ's hand and signed by him; signed by Lemaire acknowledging payment). TJ recorded this transaction as payment of Lemaire's accounts from July 4 to 11 for provisions and servants (MB, 2:1077).

Order on John Barnes for payment of $20 to Joseph Dougherty, Washington, 13 July (MS in MHi; in TJ's hand and signed by him; signed by Dougherty acknowledging payment; endorsed by Barnes as paid on 13 July). TJ recorded this transaction as payment "for the man who is to carry P. Carr's carriage & Ursula" (MB, 2:1077).

Invoice submitted by John Winter, "Late Printer, of Frederick Town," to TJ for £1.2.6 for an 18 month subscription to his newspaper, Rights of Man, at $2.00 per year, 11 Sep. (MS in MHi; endorsed by TJ: "Newspapers. Rights of man. pd Nov. 24. 04"). See MB, 2:1140.

Order on John Barnes for payment of $6.50 to J. B. Anderson, 5 Oct. (MS in MHi; in TJ's hand and signed by him; written on invoice from Anderson to TJ dated Washington, 6 June, for making three print frames; signed by Isaac Cooper for Anderson acknowledging payment).

Invoice submitted by Henry Ingle to TJ for $5.25 for cast and German steel plane irons and for sandpaper, Washington, 6 Oct. (MS in MHi; endorsed by TJ).

Order on John Barnes for payment of $17.62 to Joseph Dougherty, Washington, 12 Oct. (MS in MHi; in TJ's hand and signed by him; endorsed by

Barnes as paid on 14 Oct.). TJ recorded this transaction as payment for forage, farrier work, contingencies, and a payment of $3.50 to George Blagden for two marble plinths (MB, 2:1084).

Order on John Barnes for payment of $14.68 to Thomas Munroe, Washington, 14 Oct. (MS in ViU: Edgehill-Randolph Papers; in TJ's hand and signed by him; endorsed by TJ: "Lewis Meriwether"; signed on verso by Thomas Turner acknowledging payment; endorsed by Barnes as paid on 15 Oct.). TJ recorded this transaction as an order in favor of Munroe for Meriwether Lewis (MB, 2:1084).

Order on John Barnes for payment of $75 to the Reverend Stephen B. Balch, Washington, 20 Oct. (MS in CtY; in TJ's hand and signed by him; signed by Balch acknowledging payment; endorsed by Barnes as paid on 1 Nov.). TJ recorded this transaction as charity (MB, 2:1084).

Order on John Barnes for payment of $10 to Matthew C. Groves, Washington, 22 Oct. (MS in MHi; in TJ's hand and signed by him; signed by Groves acknowledging payment; endorsed by Barnes as paid on 22 Oct.). TJ recorded this transaction as charity (MB, 2:1084).

Order on John Barnes for payment of $13 to Joseph Dougherty, 8 Nov. (MS in CSmH; in TJ's hand and signed by him; written on invoice from Jd. Donoghou to Dougherty for purchase of 1,200 pounds of hay on 25 Oct. at $12 and horse shoeing on 27 Oct. at $1; signed by Dougherty acknowledging payment). See MB, 2:1085.

INDEX

abolition, 563n, 602-5

Abrégé chronologique de l'histoire ancienne des empires et des républiques (Jacques Lacombe), 76

Abrégé chronologique de l'histoire d'Angleterre (Thomas Salmon), 78

Abrégé chronologique de l'histoire de Pologne (Friedrich August von Schmidt), 76

Abrégé chronologique de l'histoire des Juifs (François Nicolas Charbuy), 76

Abrégé chronologique de l'histoire d'Espagne et de Portugal (Charles Jean François Henault), 76

Abrégé chronologique de l'histoire du Nord: ou des etats de Dannemarck, de Russie, de Suède, de Pologne, de Prusse, de Courlande, &c (Jacques Lacombe), 76

Abrégé chronologique de l'histoire universelle depuis les premiers empires du monde (Johannes Sleidanus, trans. Antoine Hornot), 76

Abridgment des plusieurs cases et resolutions del common ley (Henry Rolle), 78

accountants, 103n

Ackermann, Suardy, & Co., 62n

Adams, Abijah, 249n. *See also* Adams & Rhoades

Adams, John: late-term appointments, 60n, 254n, 420n; criticism of, 90, 92, 126n, 187, 352, 421, 451; popularity of, 124; and Sweden, 190n; and France, 227, 228; makes appointments, 243-4n, 254n, 255n, 257n, 590, 591n; removals by, 243n, 425; correspondence of, published, 249-50; and Indian affairs, 316n; and Saint-Domingue, 324n; and Sedition Act, 452; TJ recommends books to, 525n

Adams, John Quincy, 124, 190n, 420n, 612, 613n

Adams, Samuel, 249-50

Adams, Samuel (N.H.), 243n, 682

Adams, Thomas, 188n, 249n

Adams, Fort, 172n, 217, 254, 255n

Adams (U.S. frigate): in the Mediterranean, 175, 177, 189, 193, 530; Simpson awaits arrival of, 191n, 266n, 290, 319n, 334, 395; money sent with, 232

Adams & Rhoades: letter from, 249-50; sends pamphlet to TJ, 249-50. *See also* Adams, Abijah; Rhoades, Ebenezer

Addison, Alexander: letter from, 456-8; persecution of Republicans by, 44; complains about postal service, 456-8; identified, 457n; letter from cited, 458n

Addison, Thomas: letter from cited, 151n, 686

Address, to the People of the United States, on the Subject of the Report of a Committee of the House of Representatives (Oliver Wolcott, Jr.), 394

Address to the People Called Quakers (Samuel Stephens), 106n

Adelaide (ship), 565

Adgate, Matthew: letter from, 39-40; sends religious writings to TJ, 39-40; *Digest, or, Plain facts stated: in which the Gospel and Law are compared,* 40n; *Northern Light; or New Index to the Bible,* 40n

Africa: maps of, xlviii; removal of condemned slaves to, 54-7, 326, 474-6

African Association, xlviii

agriculture: cultivating machines, 67n; "animated oats," 197-8, 309; merino sheep, 200n. *See also* cotton; Indians: Economy; Jefferson, Thomas: Agriculture; tobacco

Ainsworth, Robert: *Latin and English Dictionary Abridged,* 79

Albany Register, 92

Albemarle Co., Va.: Dunlora estate, 5; measles in, 10, 13, 50, 60-1, 80-1; Music Hall estate, 137n; Castle Hill plantation, 259n; militia, 359n; courts, 372n, 397, 580n; Montalto, 372n; sheriffs, 398n; roads, 401n; Henderson lands in, 578-80

Alberti de Villaneuve, François d': *Nuovo Dizionario Italiano-Francese,* 77

alcoholism: removals from office due to, viii, 12, 243n, 446, 459, 462, 464; among Indians, x-xi, 342n, 628-30

Alembert, Jean Le Rond d': *Encyclopédie,* 77

Alexander I, Emperor of Russia: influence of La Harpe on, xlix-l, 553-4n, 561n, 599-600; admiration for TJ, l; portrait of, l, 314 (illus.); compared with TJ, 552, 554-6; relations with

INDEX

Arbuthnot, John: *Tables of Ancient Coins, Weights and Measures,* 79

Arcambal, Louis, 311, 312n, 400n

Arcana Parliamentaria: or Precedents Concerning Elections, Proceedings, Privileges, and Punishments in Parliament, 79

Archer, Thomas, 446, 447n, 462, 519, 679, 682

architects, 4, 461n, 481n. *See also* Hadfield, George; Latrobe, Benjamin Henry

architecture: of jails, xi, 164-5; of hospitals, 460-2; Halle aux Bleds, 619, 620-1n; plinths, 691. *See also* Jefferson, Thomas: Architecture

Argou, Gabriel: *Institution au droit françois,* 77

Argus (U.S. brig), 63n

Ariosto, Ludovico, 558

Aristotle, 483

Armistead, Francis, 680

Army, U.S. *See* War, U.S. Department of

art: illustration of medical works, 20; miniature portraits, 96; sculpture, 377n; study of European, 592

Ashash, Abd al-Rahman, 176n, 190n, 266n, 319n, 360, 395

Ashby, Matthew: *Ashby and White,* 79

Ashby and White: or, the great question, whether an action lies at common law for an elector (Matthew Ashby and William White), 79

Asnet (child), 244-5

assault and battery, 43

astronomy: astronomical instruments, 14, 134, 153, 154n, 504, 618; TJ's interest in, 14; calculation of longitude, 44, 45n, 153-4, 485, 504-5, 618

Athenæ Oxonienses: An Exact History of all the Writers and Bishops who have had Their Education in the Most Ancient and Famous University of Oxford (Anthony à Wood), 78

Atlas portatif à l'usage des colleges (L'Abbé Grenet and Rigobert Bonne), 77

attorneys: mentioned, 32n, 93, 99-101, 143, 151, 241, 304n, 333n; education of, 101, 262-3, 611; as Federalists, 513. *See also* law

Atwater, Reuben, 388, 515

Aubrée, Mr., 59

Augusta Co., Va., 74, 75n

Augustus, Emperor, 557

Aurora (Philadelphia), 294, 422n, 498, 499n. *See also* Duane, William

Austin, Benjamin, Jr., 124, 126n

Austin, Jonathan L., 28, 681

Austria, 558, 562n

Authentic Information Relative to the Conduct of the Present & Last Administrations of the United States (Caesar A. Rodney), 497, 498n

Avaux, Claude de Mesmes and Bougeant, G.-H.: *Histoire du traité de Westphalie,* 77

Azara, José Nicolás de, 383, 584, 588n

Bache, Benjamin Franklin, 513

Bache, Catharine Wistar, 3, 30, 66, 480, 608

Bache, Richard, Jr., 513

Bache, William: letters to, 3-4, 480-1, 608; letter from, 29-30; appointed physician to New Orleans marine hospital, 3-4, 6, 65-6, 214, 217, 254; removal to Miss. Terr., 5, 29-30, 404, 480-1, 608; postal address, 11; attends Randolph children, 50; payments to, 608, 615; letter from cited, 608n, 689

Backus, Mathew, 7n

Bacon, Matthew: *New Abridgment of the Law,* 78

Bacon, Nathaniel: *Historicall Discourse of the Uniformity of the Government of England,* 79

Bailey, Theodorus, 241, 242n, 243n, 498n, 571

Bainbridge, William, 195n, 223

Baker, John Martin, 263-4

Baker, Dr. William (Md.), 108n

Baker, William (N.Y.), 239

Balance (Hudson, N.Y.), 521n

Balch, Stephen Bloomer, 691

Baldwin, Abraham: letter to cited, 515n, 688

Baldwin, Luther, 90

Balfour, George: letter from cited, 686; seeks appointment, 687

Baltimore, Charles Calvert, fifth Lord, 325, 336, 338n

Baltimore, Md.: surveyors, 67; accountants, 103n; physicians, 103n; justices of the peace, 429n; merchants, 429n, 632n; banks, 459-60; booksellers, 498; Society of Friends in, 498; rivalry with Philadelphia, 545-6; and Chesapeake and Delaware canal,

INDEX

Baltimore, Md. (*cont.*)
545-8; yellow fever, 565; insurance companies, 632n
Baltimore Weekly Magazine, 605n
Baltimore, Bank of, 459-60, 464
Bangs, Edward, 37n, 125, 126n
Bank of the United States: employees, 111n; and the Mint, 233; branches, 253n, 297n, 449, 460n, 464, 475n, 678n; criticism of, 294; relationship with federal government, 294, 459-60, 464; bills of, 449, 453-4, 511, 676; foreign investment in, 459, 460n, 569-70
bankruptcy: of merchants, 247, 420n
bankruptcy commissioners: TJ seeks recommendations for, viii, 25-6, 32-3, 68, 216, 224, 298, 302, 303, 346, 358, 387-8, 389n, 508-9, 514-15, 632-3, 643-4, 677-8; in Pa., 25-6, 93-5, 99-101, 103, 115, 117, 119-20, 122, 123n, 143, 151, 156, 293-5; in Va., 27, 28n, 32-3, 68, 145n, 221n, 233, 508-9, 529-30, 632-4, 677-8, 679, 680; in N.J., 28, 679, 681; in Mass., 28-9, 37n, 38n, 51n, 125, 136, 145, 160, 161-2, 199, 200n, 216, 220, 221-2, 253, 254n, 266-7, 272, 273n, 300, 302, 361-2, 369-70, 378, 380, 408-9, 424, 519, 595, 596n, 612, 679, 681; in Me., 28-9, 222, 679, 681; decline, resign appointments, 29n, 144, 145n, 173, 174n, 199, 224, 515n, 634n, 644n, 679-81; TJ on qualifications for, 32, 161-2, 298, 303, 514; in Conn., 173-4, 189, 220, 224, 225n, 391, 392n, 679, 680; commission serves as proof of appointment, 189, 220, 221n, 391; locations for, 221-2, 233, 241, 242n, 259, 298-9, 303, 388, 514; in N.Y., 241, 242n, 259; in Vt., 298-9, 302, 303, 387-9, 515; in Tenn., 469-70; in N.C., 514-15, 643-4; in S.C., 617n; in Del., 679, 680
Bankrupt Law of America, Compared with the Bankrupt Law of England (Thomas Cooper), 483, 484n
Banks, Sir Joseph, 562n
banks: specie preferred over bank bills, 517; currency exchange, 641n. *See also* Baltimore, Bank of; Columbia, Bank of (Georgetown); Pennsylvania, Bank of
Baptists, 121n, 333n, 657n
Barbary states: special U.S. agent to,

proposed, vii, 222-3. *See also* Algiers; Morocco; Tripoli; Tunis
Barbeyrac, Jean: *Recueil de discours sur diverses matieres importantes,* 76
Barcelona, Spain, 18n, 206, 207, 497n
Barde, Robert G., 40
Baring, Alexander, 460n
Barlow, James, 579
Barlow, Joel: asked to write history of U.S., 407n; as reference, 419; letters from cited, 419n, 686; and J. H. Stone, 556; translates Volney's *Ruines,* 560n
Barnes, John: letters to, 107, 140-1, 164, 511, 519, 544, 676; letters from, 141-2, 154-5, 196-7, 225-6, 257-8, 323-5, 361, 392-3, 415-16, 422-3, 427, 494, 499-500, 500, 608-10; handles financial transactions, xi, 73n, 107, 108n, 112n, 128n, 130-1, 140-1, 142n, 154-5, 210, 226, 258, 361, 392-3, 423-4, 450, 459n, 485n, 494, 549n, 676, 690-1; and W. Short's affairs, 105, 114, 140-1, 155, 161, 164, 196-7, 205, 225-6, 257-8, 323, 361, 415, 427, 454, 465, 469, 608; and Kosciuszko, 140, 154; obtains items, handles shipments, 141, 155, 164, 196; sends political news to TJ, 141-2; TJ's account with, 155, 258, 323, 361, 392-3, 494, 608-10, 676n; and Lemaire, 172-3, 226, 258; and published criticism of TJ, 323-5; letters to cited, 361n, 393n, 416n, 427n, 494n, 500n, 687, 688; reports on slave conspiracy in Georgetown, 422-3; and Oldham's suit, 427, 609; plans to return to Philadelphia, 479, 499-500; recommended to Muhlenberg, 479, 493, 499-500; TJ's opinion of, 479; TJ requests bank bills from, 511, 519, 544; declines new business, 609-10
Barnet, Isaac Cox: letters from, 58-60, 377-8; seeks appointment, 58-60; thanks TJ, 377-8
Barnwell, William, 65
barracks, 15
Barron, James, 236, 248-9, 306, 327-8, 334
Barron, Samuel, 62-3, 533
Barry, William (marine): letters from, 444-5, 520; seeks discharge of W. W. Burrows, 444-5, 520, 533; identified, 445n; letter from cited, 445n

Burr, Aaron (*cont.*)
reference, 123n; advises on appointments, 264n, 677n; reported visit to Boston, 294; and Le Guen, 340n; and N.J. elections, 357; family of, 530n; western conspiracy of, 657n

Burrows, William Ward, 444-5, 520

Burrus, Bartholomew, 209n

Burt, Joel, 89n

Büsching, Anton Friedrich: *New System of Geography,* 79

Busnach, Naphtali, 510n

Busti, Paul, 342, 343-4n, 358

Butler, Dr., 14-15

Butler, Pierce, 121n, 241, 243-4n

Bynkershoek, Cornelius van: *Observationum Juris Romani,* 78

Byrd, Charles Willing: letter from, 494-6; and St. Clair, 494-6; letter from cited, 688

Cabanis, Pierre Jean Georges: letter from, 524-5; *Rapports du physique et du moral de l'homme,* 524-5, 615, 616; sends writings to TJ, 524-5, 586, 615, 616; identified, 525n

Cabo de Hornos (Spanish brig), 206, 207, 311, 312n

Cadbury, Henry, 496n

Cadiz, Spain, 261, 296n

Cahokia: calls for troops from, 314, 342n; letter from cited, 315n, 687

Cahoone, John, 491n

Calais, France, 437n

Calcutta, 664n

Caldwell, Timothy, 655

Calepino, Ambrogio: *Dictionarium Undecim Linguarum,* 77

Calhoun, John C., 113n

Callender, James Thomson: receives financial assistance from TJ, xii, 36-8, 72-4, 90, 92-3, 131; reports on TJ's relationship with Sally Hemings, xii, 37n, 323-5n; feud with Meriwether Jones, 37-8n; editor of the *Recorder,* 37n, 456; *Prospect Before Us,* 37n, 68, 74n, 90, 92; sedition trial, 68, 69n, 74n, 89-90, 92; *History of the United States for 1796,* 72, 73n; *Political Progress of Britain,* 72, 73n; *Sketches of the History of America,* 73n; and Leiper, 319; and Duane, 324n, 513; remission of fine, 448-9, 452; TJ's opinion of, 477

Callender, John: letter from, 408-9;

seeks appointment, 408-9, 595, 596n; identified, 409n

Callières, François de: *De la Manière de negocier avec les souverains,* 76

Calvinists, 560, 564n

Calvinus, Johannes: *Lexicon Iuridicum,* 79

Campbell, Hugh G., 189

Canada, 22-3, 88

canals, 280-2, 438, 544-8. *See also* Chesapeake and Delaware Canal Company; James River Company; Potomac Canal Company

Cap-Français, Saint-Domingue, 279n, 398, 399n, 658n

capital punishment. *See* law

Capitol, U.S., 4n, 16n, 62n, 568-9, 575-6

Caracas, 462

Caractacus, A Dramatic Poem: Written on the Model of the Ancient Greek Tragedy (William Mason), 559, 563n

Carey, Mathew: letter from, 99-100; advises on appointments, 99-100; criticism of, 119n; works published by, 284n; and J. T. Callender, 324n; literary fair organized by, 651n

Carey, William: and Yorktown collectorship, 349, 374n, 390, 392, 400, 446, 462, 519, 679, 687; letter from cited, 349n, 687

Carlos (Charles) IV, King of Spain: letter to, 496-7; letters from, 17-18, 370; family of, 17-18, 370, 496-7, 588n; identified, 17-18n; letter to cited, 370n; and cession of Louisiana to France, 480n

Carlota Joaquina, Princess of Brazil, 572

Carmichael, John F., 255n

Carnes, Thomas P., 113, 114n

Carpenter, Thomas: account with TJ, 107-8

Carr, Dabney (TJ's nephew), 5, 160, 369

Carr, Eleanor (Nelly, Mrs. Samuel Carr), 5

Carr, Elizabeth Carr, 5

Carr, Hester Smith Stevenson (Hettie, Mrs. Peter Carr), 5, 19

Carr, John (b. 1753), 372, 397

Carr, Martha Jefferson (Mrs. Dabney Carr, TJ's sister), 5

Carr, Mary (Polly, TJ's niece), 480, 608

Carr, Peter (TJ's nephew): letter to, 18-19; to visit Washington, 5; carriage of, 18-19, 690

Cooper, Thomas (*cont.*)
552n; transcribes letter for Priestley, 561n, 598
Copineau, Abbé: *Essai synthétique,* 649, 650, 651n
Coppinger, Joseph: letter to, 535; letter from, 507-8; seeks patent, 507-8, 535; *American Practical Brewer and Tanner,* 508n; identified, 508n
Coppinger, William, 508n
Cordell, George E.: letter from, 465-6; reports on Md. politics, 465-6; identified, 466n
corn, xi, 621, 622n
Cornplanter (Seneca Indian), 273, 275n
Corps universel diplomatique du droit des gens (Jean Dumont), 77
Corpus juris civilis Romani (Denys Godefroy), 79
Correct Statement of the Various Sources from which The History of the Administration of John Adams was Compiled (John Wood), 179, 180n
Cosway, Maria Hadfield, 621n
cotton: waterproof cotton, 62; regulation of trade in, 171, 172n, 487n, 491; plantations, 505-6, 532-3
Couasnon, Jean Louis, 377n
Country Builder's Assistant (Asher Benjamin), 461n

COURTS, U.S.

Circuit
District of Columbia, 43, 46-7, 237n, 268; clerks, 47n, 346; and capital punishment, 237n, 268; oppose repeal of Judiciary Act, 453n; in Mass., 595, 596n

District
Va., 68, 69n; and common law, 642n; Ky., 642n, 666, 668

Public Opinion
dominated by Federalists, 32; calls to reduce judicial tenure, 81n; dual officeholding by judges, 81n; little work to be done by, 318, 346; duties of justice of the peace, 548; competence of, 595; and common law, 665-75

Supreme Court
constitutionality of repeal of Judiciary Act, 453n; and common law, 670, 671-2n

cowpox. *See* smallpox
Coxe, Daniel W., 487n
Coxe, John Redman: letter to, 67-8; letters from, 19-20, 142; *Practical Observations on Vaccination,* 19-20, 142; and smallpox vaccination, 19-20, 67-8, 142
Coxe, Tench: letter from, 100-1; appointed supervisor, 31, 32n, 88, 104, 109, 110, 122, 518, 519, 679, 681; advises on appointments, 100-1; appointed purveyor of public supplies, 122, 123n, 156; asked to stand for Congress, 122; reports on France and Louisiana, 242; and Pa. politics, 408, 512-13
Coxe, William, Jr., 605n
Coyer, Gabriel François, 76
Craig, James, 578n, 580n
Cranch, William, 420n, 471-2, 478, 590
Crane, Silas, 680, 683n
Creek Indians. *See* Indians: Creeks (Muskogees, Muscogees)
Cromwell, Oliver, 321n
Cross, Ralph: appointed commissioner of bankruptcy, 28, 681; recommended, appointed collector, 51-2, 53, 178, 179, 199, 218, 372, 518, 596n, 679, 682
Cross, Stephen, 595-6
Crowninshield, Jacob: advises on appointments, 12n, 145, 178-9, 180n, 199, 210, 216, 218, 242, 272, 372-3, 501; appointed, declines bankruptcy commission, 28-9n, 199, 216, 681
Crozier, John, 469-70
Crutchelow, John, 641-3, 665
Cullen, William, 239
Cumberland, Richard: *Treatise of the Laws of Nature,* 78
Cumpston, Thomas, 94n, 293-5
Cunningham, Mr., 590
Cunningham, Timothy: *New and Complete Law-Dictionary,* 78, 473
Cushing, Isaac, 42
Cushing, Thomas H., 209n, 452n
Cushing, William, 595, 596n
Custis, Edmund: letter from, 203; seeks appointment, 203
Cutler, Samuel, 169n
Cutter, Daniel, 564
Cuvier, Georges, 97n, 377n
Cyrus the Great, 564n

INDEX

Daily Advertiser (New York), 142n, 487n

Dale, Richard, 163-4n, 195n, 306n, 360, 531n

Dallas, Alexander J.: and Latimer's resignation, 31-2n; recommended, appointed commissioner of bankruptcy, 94n; advises on appointments, 120n, 133n, 293-4; as reference, 123n; opinions on politics, 124; criticism of, 294; opposes repeal of Judiciary Act of 1801, 294, 295n, 512, 513n; and Pa. politics, 408, 421, 512-13

Dallas, Arabella Maria Smith, 294

Dallas, Sophia Burrell, 294

Dalton, Tristram: letter from, 253-4; appointed, declines Newburyport collectorship, 31n, 32n, 41, 51, 53, 88, 254n; forwards letter to TJ, 253-4; identified, 253-4n; appointed commissioner of bankruptcy, 254n

Damascenus, Johannes: *Vita di san Giosafat convertito da Barlaam,* 483

Dame, Benjamin: seeks son's discharge, 208-9; letter from cited, 208-9n, 686

Dame, John, 209n

Danbury, battle of, 299n

Dandridge, Bartholomew, Jr., 203

Dandridge, William, 243n

Dane, Nathan, 28-9n, 145, 199, 216, 267, 681

Dangerfield, William Allen, 8

Darneille, Isaac: petitions for troops at Peoria, 314, 343n; letter from cited, 315n, 686

Dartmouth College, 333n

Dashkova, Princess Ekaterina Romanovna, 149n

Daure, Jean Pierre Paulin Hector: letter from, 658-9; reports death of Leclerc, 658-9; identified, 658-9n

Daveiss, Joseph Hamilton, 666, 668

David, Jacques Louis, 377n

Davidson, William (mariner), 589n

Davie, William R., 682

Davies, William, 178, 180n, 482, 488, 590

Davis, Augustine, 280n

Davis, George (Philadelphia): letter from, 101-2; seeks appointment, 101-2; identified, 101-2n; *Bibliotheca Legum Angliae,* 101n

Davis, John, 220, 596n

Davis, Thomas (Boston), 344, 345n

Davis, Thomas T., 447n

Davis, Wilson, 590, 591n

Dawes, Thomas, Jr., 28, 125, 681

Dawson, John, 143n, 221n

Dawson, Martin: payment to, 454; letter from cited, 454n, 688; letter to cited, 454n, 688

Day, Benjamin, 221n

Dayton, Isaac: letter from, 520-1; seeks appointment, 33-4, 520-1, 685; identified, 521n

Dayton, Jonathan, 294

Dayton, Susan W., 294

Deaderick, George M., 251n, 469-70

Dearborn, Benjamin: letter from, 644-5; develops lineal standard of measurement, 644-5

Dearborn, Henry: letters to, 150-1, 160-1, 165, 175-6, 208-9, 209-10, 216, 226, 258-9, 299-300, 314-16, 340-1, 358, 389-90, 402, 423, 641-3; letters from, 9, 38-9, 40, 51-2, 138-40, 145, 145-7, 169-70, 199-200, 222-3, 272-5, 341-4, 364, 409, 452, 458, 463, 486, 619, 627; advises on Barbary affairs, vii, 175-6, 222-3, 258-9, 278; and Morocco, vii-viii, 175-6, 222-3, 389-90, 402, 409, 423; advises on appointments, viii, 12, 28n, 51-2, 178-9, 199-200, 200n, 216, 218, 241, 259, 261, 272, 277, 300, 313, 361, 486, 661; and Indian policy, x-xi, 138-9, 150, 209-10; and Indian land cessions, xi, 139-40, 169-70, 209-10, 342-4, 358, 572-3; recommends commissions, promotions, 9, 39n, 40, 458, 463, 619, 627; and Massac collectorship, 21; and books and equipment for West Point, 38-9; letter from cited, 39n, 684; visits Norfolk, 52, 53, 118, 178, 180n; and waterproof paper, 62; and Mass. claim on the U.S., 63-4, 340-1, 350; and Mentges's claim, 71; and Indian boundaries, 112-14, 226, 272-3, 299, 300n, 389; and Indian agents, 139n, 273, 274-5n, 629-30; and I. Story's appointment, 145, 160-1, 216, 342, 361; armory, arsenal in S.C., 145-7, 160, 165; and militia resignations, 150-1, 175, 208, 296, 297n; health of, 160-1, 199, 272, 286, 302; and minors in the army, 208-9, 452, 489; and certificate for John Peyton, 234-5n; letters to cited, 234-5n, 362n, 452n, 684, 687; operates newly designed boat, 272n;

[705]

INDEX

Dictionnaire raisonné de diplomatique
(François Jean de Vaines), 76
*Dictionnaire universel des sciences
morale, économique, politique et diplo-
matique* (Jean Baptiste René Robi-
net), 77
Diderot, Denis: *Encyclopédie,* 77; men-
tioned, 321n
Dieppe, France, 589n
*Digest, or, Plain facts stated: in which the
Gospel and Law are compared*
(Matthew Adgate), 40n
Digest of the Laws of England (Sir John
Comyns), 78
Dillion, Thomas, 379
Dinmore, Richard, 480n
Dinsmore, James: letters to, 108-9, 497;
receives building instructions from
TJ, vii, 108-9, 497; letter from cited,
109n, 685; management of nailery,
136-7; and Wanscher, 676n
Diogene Laërce, de la Vie des Philosophes
(Diogenes Laertius), 483-4
Direct Tax (1798), 447-8, 482-3, 590,
591n
Discours sur l'art de negocier (Antoine
Pecquet), 76
Discours sur l'histoire universelle
(Jacques Benigne Bossuet), 78
*Dissertation on the Numbers of Mankind
in Antient and Modern Times* (Robert
Wallace), 79
distilleries, 502n
District of Columbia: Md. loans to, xi,
30, 35-6, 85, 175n, 405, 576-7, 593-5,
607-8, 654; sale of lots in, xi, 35-6,
174-5, 196, 211-12, 381-2, 384, 404-5,
411, 594, 654; alterations to plan of,
15; dissolution of board of commissioners, 15, 254n, 405n; superintendent of, 16n; U.S. circuit court, 43,
46-7, 237n, 268; militia, 150-1, 175,
296-7, 680; jails, 155-6, 164-5; surveyors, 211-12, 234, 287-8, 327; justices
of the peace, 548-9. *See also* Alexandria, D.C.; Georgetown, D.C.; Washington, D.C.
Divers, George: letter from, 410; recommends F. Mitchell, 410, 533
Dobell, Peter, 59, 60n, 295, 309, 310n
Dobson, Thomas: *Encyclopaedia,* 134
Dodd, John, 173, 174n, 224, 680
Dodsley (Margaret Page), 284n
Dolphin (schooner), 53, 197
Donaldson, William T., 421

Donelson, Samuel, 469-70
Donoghou, Jd., 691
Doolittle, Amos, l-li
Dougherty, Joseph: carries papers to,
from TJ, 107n, 544n; stable accounts,
361, 690-1
Downey's ford (Rapidan River), 74
D'Oyley, Daniel: letter to, 224; letter
from, 120-1; forwards Furman's sermon, 120-1, 224; identified, 121n;
opinions on S.C. politics, 452-3, 463-
4; criticism of, 463-4, 486, 534
Drayton, John: letters from, 316-17,
384-6, 526-7; and black exiles from
Guadeloupe, x, 384-6, 526-7; forwards copy of Cherokee talk, 316-17,
389; criticism of, 452n; and T. M.
Randolph's slaves, 623, 624n
dredging, 91, 548-9
*Droit public de l'Europe, fondé sur les
traités* (Gabriel Bonnot de Mably), 76
dry docks: proposed by TJ, at Washington, 90-1, 92n, 126-8, 506, 542-3,
619-21, 653, 654n
Duane, William: letters to, 75-6, 472;
letter from, 511-14; supplies books for
Library of Congress, ix, 75-6, 77, 80,
82, 86, 105, 241, 244n, 472, 473, 511;
and M. Leib, 119n; bookselling, stationery business of, 135n; and Leiper's
appointment, 293; and J. T. Callender, 324n, 513; and Rising Sun tavern
meeting, 421, 422n; reports on Pa.
politics, 511-14; evaluates political
sympathies of government clerks,
542n; wishes to purchase Franklin's
library, 649, 650, 651n. *See also Aurora* (Philadelphia)
Duane, William J., 293
Dublin, 106n
Du Commerce de l'Ame et du Corps
(Emanuel Swedenborg), 483, 484n
Dufief, Nicolas Gouin: letter from, 647-
51; method for learning languages,
647-51; offers books from Franklin's
library, 649, 650, 651n; *Nature Displayed,* 651n
Dumont, Jean, Baron de Carlscroon:
*Corps universel diplomatique du droit
des gens,* 77
Dunkirk, France, 38n
Dunmore, John Murray, fourth Earl of,
454
Dunn, Christian, 239
Dunn, James, Jr., 239

FRANCE (*cont.*)

Politics and Government
decline of republicanism in, 65, 556-7;
Council of Five Hundred, 525n;
coup of 18 Brumaire, 525n; *idéologistes,* 525n; *Sénat,* 525n, 615;
newspaper restrictions, 551, 552-3n,
557, 561-2n; prospects for republicanism, 551-2, 557-8; Huguenots,
553n; Fructidor, 558. *See also* Bonaparte, Napoleon

Science and Learning
medicine, 525n

Society
restoration of Catholic Church in, 215,
560, 564n; status of Protestant
churches in, 559-60, 564n

U.S. Relations with
French consuls in U.S., 70-1, 147-8;
and naval prizes, 144n, 583n; complaints about McNeill, 204n; and
debt payments, 204n, 589n; export
duties, 204n; and slave trade, 204n;
and support of Saint-Domingue
rebels, 204n, 442, 444; French investment in U.S. stocks, 227, 228,
569-70; French opinion of the U.S.,
227, 228; appointment of U.S. commercial agents in France, 252n; im-
migrants to U.S., 321n; and Florida,
383n, 391, 441, 443, 585; French as
U.S. consuls, 419; hostility toward
U.S., 476-7; French role in American Revolution, 589n. *See also* Convention of 1800; Guadeloupe, W.I.;
Louisiana

Francesco, Principe Ereditario of the
Two Sicilies, 17, 18n, 496
Franklin, Benjamin: and torpedo fish,
116n; descendants of, 214; minister to
France, 524, 525; library of, 649, 650,
651n
Franklin (armed schooner), 248n
Franklin (brig): captured by Tripolitan
corsairs, xlviii, 206, 207, 208n, 282,
283n, 290, 291n, 509-10
*Frederician Code: or, a Body of Law for
the Dominions of the King of Prussia,*
79
Frederick II, King of Prussia (Frederick
the Great), 324n
Fredericksburg, Va., 215n, 221n, 233,
418-19n

Frederick William III, King of Prussia,
562n
Freeman, John, 108
Freemasons, 238n, 426n
French language, 263n, 279n, 373n,
651n
French Revolution: TJ's opinion on, 65;
Reign of Terror, 321n, 481n, 525n;
declining influence of, 556-7
Fresnoy, Nicolas Lenglet du: *Tablettes
chronologiques,* 76
"Friend" (pseudonym): letter from, 537-
41; and McGurk's case, 537-41
Friends, Society of, 33n, 106n, 498, 513
"Friend to Truth" (pseudonym), 279-
80n
Frisbie, Jonathan, 680
Furman, Richard: *America's Deliverance
and Duty,* 120-1, 224

Gaines, Edmund P., 40

GALLATIN, ALBERT: letters to, 11-12,
41, 42, 52-3, 82-3, 109-10, 135, 156-8,
176-7, 210, 216-18, 218-19, 259-60,
277-8, 300-1, 317-18, 365, 390-1, 403,
410-11, 424-5, 452-3, 459-60, 461-2,
466, 486-8, 569, 590-1; letters from,
6-7, 12, 20-1, 22-3, 30, 31-2, 87-9,
121-3, 170-2, 177, 178-80, 229-33,
241-4, 254-5, 256-7, 261-2, 286, 301,
372-4, 374, 416-18, 445-6, 446-7, 447-
8, 448-9, 453, 460-1, 463-5, 467, 482,
482-3, 488, 488-9, 490-1, 491-2, 501,
521-3, 541-2, 564, 569-71, 593-5, 613-
14, 614, 672-4; letters from cited,
564n, 591n, 684

Personal Affairs
absent from Washington, 41n, 53n,
144, 178, 286, 301, 302, 317, 372,
416, 424-5; health of, 88, 110, 122,
157, 278, 286, 301, 302, 317, 372,
417; family, 372, 416

Politics
and Beaumont, 44, 45n; and Pa. politics, 122, 179, 408; reports on N.Y.
politics, 179, 417, 418n; criticism of,
294, 295n, 311n; comments on J. T.
Callender's fine, 448-9, 452-3; and
D'Oyley, 452-3, 463-4, 486

Secretary of the Treasury
and Morocco, vii-viii, 176-7, 229-33,
261-2, 270n, 290; advises on appointments, viii-ix, 6-7, 11, 12, 20-1,

INDEX

INDEX

Presbyterians in, 333n; Black Rock, 342, 343n, 344n, 358; lighthouses, 490-1; Long Island Sound, 490-1; Hudson surveyorship, 501-2, 520-1; postmasters, 502n; Supreme Court, 502n; marshal, 681. *See also* Federalists; Republicans

New York City: black exiles from Guadeloupe at, x, 302, 311-12, 364, 376-7, 384-6, 389, 391-2, 400-1, 526-7; mayor, 122, 123n; physicians, 240n; postal service, 300; navy yard at, 322; American Revolution in, 336n; merchants, 336n, 419; elections in, 357; quarantine station at, 364; hospitals in, 550n; naval officer at, 571; book fairs, 651n; custom house, 676-7; Democratic Society, 677n

New York (U.S. frigate): ordered to the Mediterranean, 222-3, 230-2, 235-6, 265-6, 276, 278, 283, 290n, 373, 530; officers and crew for, 235-6, 306; departure of, 304, 305n, 327-8, 334, 359, 360, 413, 506

New-York Evening Post, 19n, 195n

New-York Gazette & General Advertiser, 218n

New-York Magazine; or Literary Repository, 284n

New York Theistical Society, 333n

Niagara River, 22, 23n, 342, 343n, 344n

Nicholas, John, 436n

Nicholas, John, Jr. (clerk of Albemarle Co. Court), 578n, 580n

Nicholas, Margaret Smith, 19

Nicholas, Philip Norborne, 69n

Nicholas, Wilson Cary, 19, 293, 632n

Nichols, Jehu, 541-2, 682n

Nichols, Walter, 685, 687, 688

Nicholson, James, 677n

Nicholson, Joseph H., 53n

Nicholson, Peter, 526-7n

Nicholson, William: *Introduction to Natural Philosophy,* 134

Nicoll (Nichols), John, 173, 174n, 224, 680

Niles, Elizabeth Marston Watson, 412

Niles, Hezekiah, 498-9

Niles, Nathaniel: letter from, 411-12; recommends W. Watson, 411-12

Nimmo, James, 632, 634n, 677-8

Nine Letters on the Subject of Aaron Burr's Political Defection (James Cheetham), 418n

Nobbs, Samuel: letter from cited, 687

Nones, Benjamin: letter from, 95; seeks appointment, 95

Norfolk, Va.: bankruptcy commissioners, 27, 28n, 32, 33n, 68, 145n, 508-9, 529-30, 632-4, 677-8, 679, 680; H. Dearborn visits, 52, 53, 118, 178, 180n; fortifications at, 52n; trade of, 118; Monroe visits, 131; yellow fever in, 131, 215n; marine hospital, 178, 180n, 488, 687; measles in, 215n; navy yard at, 327-8, 506; Anglican property in, 454-5, 568; militia, 632; merchants, 632-4; society, 632-4; descriptions of, 633; slave conspiracy in, 634n; banks, 678n; mayors, 678n

Norman, James, 194, 195n

Norris, Nicholas: letter to, 493-4; letter from, 428-9; forwards letter to TJ, 428-9; identified, 429n; thanked by TJ, 493-4

Norris, Opie, 360n

North Carolina: Edenton collectorship, 6; Slade's Creek surveyorship, 6, 11-12, 88, 110, 178, 180n, 219, 681; Tombstone surveyorship, 6, 11, 541-2, 680, 682-3n; Windsor surveyorship, 6, 7n, 11; Winton surveyorship, 6; Cape Hatteras, 8, 446, 447n; shipwrecks, 8; Salmon Creek, 11n; Beacon Island, 12, 21; boundary of, 325, 326n, 337; and black exiles from Guadeloupe, 385; Shell Castle Island lighthouse, 446, 447n; elections in, 477; Edenton, 514, 644; New Bern, 514, 643-4; Wilmington, 514, 643; bankruptcy commissioners, 514-15, 643-4; Bertie Co., 542n; legislature, 542n; Northampton Co., 635; marshal, 635-6; merchants, 643; postmasters, 644n; and Indian affairs, 682. *See also* Federalists; Republicans

Northern Light; or New Index to the Bible (Matthew Adgate), 40n

Northwest Territory: registers of land offices in, 109, 241, 244n, 259, 519, 571n, 681; Symmes purchase, 109, 110n, 122, 150, 156, 519, 682; receivers of public monies, 110n; postal service in, 280n; legislature, 495, 657; redivision of, 646-7n. *See also* Federalists; Ohio; Republicans; St. Clair, Arthur

Norvell, William: letter from, 440-1; and TJ's letter to B. Griffin, 440-1; identified, 440-1n

INDEX

INDEX

Treasury, U.S. Department of the (*cont.*)
122, 123n, 156; salaries and compensation, 133n, 183-7, 188n, 246-7, 307, 482n, 493, 637, 639, 677n; commissioners of loans, 159-60; surveyor general, 174n, 224, 279; lighthouses, 177, 210, 446-7, 462; revenue cutters, 241, 243n, 244n, 301, 373, 403, 425, 445-6; clerks, 242, 286, 288n, 302, 435n, 501, 541, 542n, 613, 614n; and quarantine laws, 390n; statement on duties and drawbacks, 391n; examination of public accounts, 394n; lax oversight of, under Federalists, 394n; resignation of revenue supervisors, 420, 447-8, 482-3; comptroller, 434-5, 521-2, 541, 542n, 570-1, 614, 625-6, 639-40, 665n; and remission of fines, 448-9; printing contracts, 451; and Bank of the U.S., 459-60, 464; statement on revenues from duties on imports, 571; building for, 575n; warrants drawn on, 613-14; appointment of naval officers, 660n; weighers, 677n. *See also* Gallatin, Albert; Nourse, Joseph; Steele, John (comptroller of Treasury); United States: Public Finance
Treatise of Captures in War (Richard Lee), 78
Treatise of the Laws of Nature (Richard Cumberland), 78
Treatise of the Pleas of the Crown (William Hawkins), 78
Treatise on the Maritime Laws of Rhodes (Alexander Crowcher Schomberg), 78
Tredwell, Samuel, 542n
Tredwell, William, 264n
Trieste, 194
Trigg, William, 423
Trinidad, 585, 588n
Tripoli: wheat for, vii, xlvii, 118n, 175-7, 189-91, 193, 194, 195n, 219, 262n, 266n, 269-70, 275, 510n; captures U.S. vessels, xlviii, 206, 207, 208n, 282, 283n, 290, 291n, 509-10; war against U.S., 162-4, 189, 193, 235-6, 268-9, 359, 360, 395, 410, 413, 484; war against Sweden, 190n, 208n, 291n; warships at Gibraltar, 194, 195n; estimate of marine force of, 208n; peace negotiations with, 222-3, 230-1, 275-7, 285, 305n, 322, 334, 347n, 350, 365, 390, 530; blockade of, 230-1, 235, 262n. *See also* Qaramanli, Yusuf, Pasha and Bey of Tripoli

Trist, Hore Browse, 5
Truitt, George, 482-3
Trumbull, John: letter to, 65; seeks reappointment of S. Cabot, 65; and Maria Cosway, 621n
Tryal (schooner), 197
Tuck, William: removal of, 179, 180n, 199, 218, 261, 272, 372, 662, 682
Tucker, George, 508, 680
Tucker, St. George: and Page, 284n; *Examination of the Question,* 670, 671-2n
Tucker, Thomas Tudor, 242, 277, 487-8n, 532, 623, 624n
Tuley, Henry, 178, 180n, 219, 681
Tunis: and wheat for Tripoli, vii, 176n, 190n; map of, xlviii, 314 (illus.); alleged U.S. engagement with ships of, xlix, 194, 195n, 220, 229-32, 235, 261, 276, 277n, 290, 305n; and capture of the *Franklin,* 208n; uncertain state of relations with, 223, 236, 261, 359, 360, 395; peaceful relations with, 285, 365, 390, 410, 413, 484, 506; and Sweden, 347n; demands made on Eaton, 366-8. *See also* Hammuda Bey (of Tunis)
Turkey Foot (Potawatomi Indian), 315n
Turnbull, John, 340
Turner, Joseph, 446, 447n, 462, 464
Turner, Thomas, 691
Tyng, Dudley Atkins: removal of, 31, 32n, 41, 51, 104, 178-9, 199, 218, 662, 682; opposition to removal of, 168-9, 242, 244n, 260

Ugulayacabe (Chickasaw chief), 315-16, 318, 319n
Underwood, Thomas, Jr.: letter from, 129; reports misconduct by commissioner of loans, 129, 156-7, 241, 243n; identified, 129n
Unitarians, 106n, 563n

UNITED STATES

Economy
trade with Canada, 22-3, 88; imprisonment for debt, 46-7, 67n, 184, 480, 484-5; impact of peace on, 105; trade with W. Indies, 145n; regulation of the Mississippi trade, 170-2, 178, 216-18; trade with Spain, 171, 172n, 220, 221n, 233, 332, 531; trade in the Mediter-

[750]

INDEX

A comprehensive index of Volumes 1-20 of the
First Series has been issued as Volume 21.
Each subsequent volume has its own index,
as does each volume or set of volumes
in the Second Series.

THE PAPERS OF THOMAS JEFFERSON are composed in Monticello, a font based on the "Pica No. 1" created in the early 1800s by Binny & Ronaldson, the first successful typefounding company in America. The face is considered historically appropriate for The Papers of Thomas Jefferson because it was used extensively in American printing during the last quarter-century of Jefferson's life, and because Jefferson himself expressed cordial approval of Binny & Ronaldson types. It was revived and rechristened Monticello in the late 1940s by the Mergenthaler Linotype Company, under the direction of C. H. Griffith and in close consultation with P. J. Conkwright, specifically for the publication of the Jefferson Papers. The font suffered some losses in its first translation to digital format in the 1980s to accommodate computerized typesetting. Matthew Carter's reinterpretation in 2002 restores the spirit and style of Binny & Ronaldson's original design of two centuries earlier.

✧

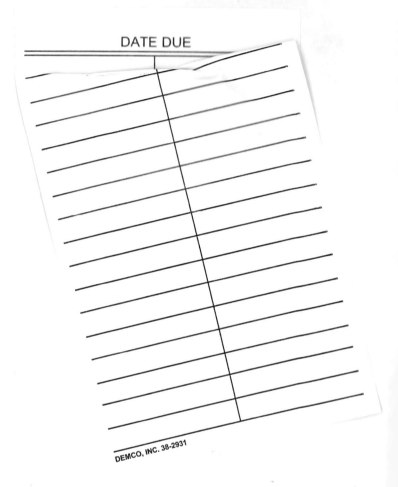

DATE DUE

DEMCO, INC. 38-2931